ELEVENTH EDITION

Current Issues and Enduring Questions

A Guide to Critical Thinking and Argument, with Readings

SYLVAN BARNET
Professor of English, Late of Tufts University

HUGO BEDAU
Professor of Philosophy, Late of Tufts University

JOHN O'HARA
*Associate Professor of Critical Thinking,
Reading, and Writing, Stockton University*

bedford/st.martin's
Macmillan Learning

Boston | New York

For Bedford/St. Martin's
Vice President, Editorial, Macmillan Learning Humanities: Edwin Hill
Editorial Director, English: Karen S. Henry
Senior Publisher for Composition, Business and Technical Writing, Developmental Writing: Leasa Burton
Executive Editor: John E. Sullivan III
Developmental Editor: Alicia Young
Senior Production Editor: Jessica Gould
Media Producers: Allison Hart and Rand Thomas
Production Supervisor: Victoria Anzalone
Marketing Manager: Joy Fisher Williams
Copy Editor: Alice Vigliani
Photo Editor: Martha Friedman
Photo Researcher: Jen Simmons
Permissions Editor: Elaine Kosta
Senior Art Director: Anna Palchik
Text Design: Laura Shaw Feit
Cover Design: John Callahan
Cover Photo: Martin Hardman/Getty Images
Composition: Jouve
Printing and Binding: LSC Communications

Manufactured in the United States of America.

1   0   9   8   7   6
f   e   d   c   b   a

For information, write: Bedford/St. Martin's, 75 Arlington Street, Boston, MA 02116
(617-399-4000)

ISBN 978-1-319-03547-1

Acknowledgments
Text acknowledgments and copyrights appear at the back of the book on page 758, which constitutes an extension of the copyright page. Art acknowledgments and copyrights appear on the same page as the art selections they cover.

Preface

This book is a text — a book about reading other people's arguments and writing your own arguments — and it is also an anthology — a collection of more than a hundred selections, ranging from Plato to the present, with a strong emphasis on contemporary arguments and, in this edition, the first in full color, new modes of argument. Before we describe these selections further, we'd like to describe our chief assumptions about the aims of a course that might use *Current Issues and Enduring Questions: A Guide to Critical Thinking and Argument, with Readings.*

Probably most students and instructors would agree that, as *critical readers*, students should be able to

- summarize accurately an argument they have read;
- locate the thesis (the claim) of an argument;
- locate the assumptions, stated and unstated, of an argument;
- analyze and evaluate the strength of the evidence and the soundness of the reasoning offered in support of the thesis; and
- analyze, evaluate, and account for discrepancies among various readings on a topic (for example, explain why certain facts are used, why probable consequences of a proposed action are examined or are ignored, or why two sources might interpret the same facts differently).

Probably, too, students and instructors would agree that, as *thoughtful writers*, students should be able to

- imagine an audience and write effectively for it (for instance, by using the appropriate tone and providing the appropriate amount of detail);
- present information in an orderly and coherent way;
- be aware of their own assumptions;

- locate sources and incorporate them into their own writing, not simply by quoting extensively or by paraphrasing but also by having digested material so that they can present it in their own words;

- properly document all borrowings — not merely quotations and paraphrases but also borrowed ideas; and

- do all these things in the course of developing a thoughtful argument of their own.

In the first edition of this book we quoted Edmund Burke and John Stuart Mill. Burke said,

> He that wrestles with us strengthens our nerves, and sharpens our skill.
> Our antagonist is our helper.

Mill said,

> He who knows only his own side of the cause knows little.

These two quotations continue to reflect the view of argument that underlies this text: In writing an essay one is engaging in a serious effort to know what one's own ideas are and, having found them, to contribute to a multisided conversation. One is not setting out to trounce an opponent, and that is partly why such expressions as "marshaling evidence," "attacking an opponent," and "defending a thesis" are misleading. True, on television talk shows we see right-wingers and left-wingers who have made up their minds and who are concerned only with pushing their own views and brushing aside all others. But in an academic community, and indeed in our daily lives, we learn by listening to others and also by listening to ourselves.

We draft a response to something we have read, and in the very act of drafting we may find — if we think critically about the words we are putting down on paper — we are changing (perhaps slightly, perhaps radically) our own position. In short, one reason that we write is so that we can improve our ideas. And even if we do not drastically change our views, we and our readers at least come to a better understanding of why we hold the views we do.

Features

THE TEXT

Part One: Critical Thinking and Reading (Chapters 1–4) and Part Two: Critical Writing (Chapters 5–7) together offer a short course in methods of thinking about and writing arguments. By "thinking," we mean serious analytic thought, including analysis of one's own assumptions (Chapter 1); by "writing" we mean the use of effective, respectable techniques, not gimmicks (such as the notorious note a politician scribbled in the margin of the text of his speech: "Argument weak; shout here"). For a delightfully wry account of the use of gimmicks, we recommend that you consult "The Art of Controversy" in *The Will to Live* by the nineteenth-century German philosopher Arthur Schopenhauer. Schopenhauer reminds readers that a Greek or Latin quotation (however irrelevant) can be impressive to the uninformed and that one can knock down almost any proposition by loftily saying, "That's all very well in theory, but it won't do in practice."

We offer lots of advice about how to set forth an argument, but we do not offer instruction in one-upmanship. Rather, we discuss responsible ways of arguing persuasively. We know, however, that before one can write a persuasive argument, one must clarify one's own ideas — a process that includes arguing with oneself — to find out what one really thinks about a problem. Therefore, we devote Chapter 1 to critical thinking; Chapters 2, 3, and 4 to critical reading (Chapter 4 is about reading images); and Chapters 5, 6, and 7 to critical writing.

Parts One and Two together contain thirty readings (seven are student papers) for analysis and discussion. Some of these essays originated as op-ed newspaper pieces, and we reprint some of the letters to the editor that they generated, so students can easily see several sides to a given issue. In this way students can, in their own responses, join the conversation, so to speak. (We have found, by the way, that using the format of a letter helps students to frame their ideas, and therefore in later chapters we occasionally suggest writing assignments in the form of a letter to the editor.)

All of the essays in the book are accompanied by a list of Topics for Critical Thinking and Writing.[1] This is not surprising, given the emphasis we place on asking questions in order to come up with ideas for writing. Among the chief questions that writers should ask, we suggest, are "What is X?" and "What is the value of X?" (pp. 226–27). By asking such questions — for instance (to look only at these two types of questions), "Is the fetus a person?" or "Is Arthur Miller a better playwright than Tennessee Williams?" — a writer probably will find ideas coming, at least after a few moments of head scratching. The device of developing an argument by identifying issues is, of course, nothing new. Indeed, it goes back to an ancient method of argument used by classical rhetoricians, who identified a stasis (an issue) and then asked questions about it: Did X do such and such? If so, was the action bad? If bad, how bad? (Finding an issue or stasis — a position where one stands — by asking questions is discussed in Chapter 6.)

In keeping with our emphasis on writing as well as reading, we raise issues not only of what can roughly be called the "content" of the essays but also of what can (equally roughly) be called the "style" — that is, the *ways* in which the arguments are set forth. Content and style, of course, cannot finally be kept apart. As Cardinal Newman said, "Thought and meaning are inseparable from each other. . . . *Style is thinking out into language.*" In our Topics for Critical Thinking and Writing, we sometimes ask the student

---

1 The paragraphs in the essays are, for ease of reference, numbered in increments of five (5, 10, 15, and so on).

- to evaluate the effectiveness of an essay's opening paragraph,

- to explain a shift in tone from one paragraph to the next, or

- to characterize the persona of the author as revealed in the whole essay.

In short, the book is not designed as an introduction to some powerful ideas (though in fact it is that, too); it is designed as an aid to *writing* thoughtful, effective arguments on important political, social, scientific, ethical, legal, and religious issues.

The essays reprinted in this book also illustrate different styles of argument that arise, at least in part, from the different disciplinary backgrounds of the various authors. Essays by journalists, lawyers, judges, social scientists, policy analysts, philosophers, critics, activists, and other writers — including first-year undergraduates — will be found in these pages. The authors develop and present their views in arguments that have distinctive features reflecting their special training and concerns. The differences in argumentative styles found in these essays foreshadow the differences students will encounter in the readings assigned in many of their other courses.

Parts One and Two, then, offer a preliminary (but we hope substantial) discussion of such topics as

- identifying assumptions;

- getting ideas by means of invention strategies;

- finding, evaluating, and citing printed and electronic sources;

- interpreting visual sources;

- evaluating kinds of evidence; and

- organizing material as well as an introduction to some ways of thinking.

Part Three: Further Views on Argument consists of Chapters 8 through 12.

- Chapter 8, A Philosopher's View: The Toulmin Model, is a summary of the philosopher Stephen Toulmin's method for analyzing arguments, covering claims, grounds, warrants, backing, modal qualifiers, and rebuttals. This summary will assist those who wish to apply Toulmin's methods to the readings in our book.

- Chapter 9, A Logician's View: Deduction, Induction, Fallacies, offers a more rigorous analysis of these topics than is usually found in composition courses and reexamines from a logician's point of view material already treated briefly in Chapter 3.

- Chapter 10, A Psychologist's View: Rogerian Argument, with an essay by psycho-therapist Carl R. Rogers and an essay by a student, complements the discussion of audience, organization, and tone in Chapter 6.

- Chapter 11, A Literary Critic's View: Arguing about Literature, should help students to see the things literary critics argue about and *how* they argue. Students can apply what they learn not only to the literary readings that appear in the chapter (poems by Robert Frost and Andrew Marvell and a story by Kate Chopin) but also to the readings that appear in Part Six, Enduring Questions: Essays, a Story, Poems, and a Play. Finally, Part Three concludes with

- Chapter 12, A Debater's View: Individual Oral Presentations and Debate, which introduces students to standard presentation strategies and debate format.

THE ANTHOLOGY

Part Four: Current Issues: Occasions for Debate (Chapters 13–18) begins with some comments on binary, or pro-con, thinking. It then gives a Checklist for Analyzing a Debate and reprints five pairs of arguments — on student loan debt (should it be forgiven?), using technology in the classroom (is it a boon or a distraction?), the local food movement (is it a better way to eat?), childhood and parenting (what's best for kids?), genetic modification of human beings, and mandatory military service (should it be required?). Here, as elsewhere in the book, many of the selections (drawn from popular journals and newspapers) are short — scarcely longer than the 500-word essays that students are often asked to write. Thus, students can easily study the *methods* the writers use, as well as the issues themselves.

Part Five: Current Issues: Casebooks (Chapters 19–25) presents seven chapters on issues discussed by several writers. For example, the first casebook concerns the nature and purpose of a college education: Should students focus their studies in STEM fields in the hopes of securing a more stable future and contributing to the economy, or should college be a place where students learn empathy, citizenship, and critical thinking — attributes often instilled by the humanities?

Part Six: Enduring Questions: Essays, a Story, Poems, and a Play (Chapters 26–28) extends the arguments to three topics: Chapter 26, What Is the Ideal Society? (the voices here range from Thomas More, Thomas Jefferson, and Martin Luther King Jr. to literary figures W. H. Auden, Walt Whitman, and Ursula K. Le Guin); Chapter 27, How Free Is the Will of the Individual within Society? (authors in this chapter include Plato, Susan Glaspell, and George Orwell); and Chapter 28, What Is Happiness? (among the nine selections in this chapter are writings by Epictetus, C. S. Lewis, and the Dalai Lama).

What's New in the Eleventh Edition

This eleventh edition brings highly significant changes. The authors of the previous ten editions established a firm foundation for the book: Hugo Bedau, professor of philosophy, brought analytical rigor to the instruction in argumentation. and Sylvan Barnet, professor of English, contributed expertise in writing instruction. They have now turned the project over to John O'Hara, professor of critical thinking, to contribute a third dimension, augmenting and enriching the material on critical thinking throughout, especially in the early chapters. Other changes have been made to ensure practical instruction and current topics.

Fresh and timely new readings. Thirty-seven of the essays (about one-third of the total) are new, as are topics such as genetically engineered foods, protection of religious rights in prison, marijuana regulation, technology's place in classrooms, social media's effect on "real life," over- and under-parenting, American exceptionalism, police violence against minorities, and the widespread jailing of U.S. citizens.

New debates and casebook topics. New debates include Technology in the Classroom: Useful or Distracting?, The Current State of Childhood: Is "Helicopter Parenting" or "Free-Range Childhood" Better for Kids?, and Mandatory Military Service: Should It Be Required? New casebooks — which were developed based on feedback from users of the text — include Race and Police Violence: How Do We Solve the Problem?, Online Versus IRL: How Has Social Networking Changed How We Relate to One Another?, The Carceral State: Why Are So Many Americans in Jail?, and American Exceptionalism: How Should the United States Teach about Its Past?

A vibrant new design. A new full-color layout makes the book more engaging and easier for students to navigate, and an expanded trim size allows more space for students to annotate and take notes. Over fifty new visuals, including ads, cartoons, photographs, and Web pages, provide occasions for critical inquiry.

Expanded coverage of critical thinking in Part One. Part One has been heavily revised to help better show students how effective reading, analysis, and writing all begin with critical thinking. Enhancements include an expanded vocabulary for critical thinking, instruction on writing critical summaries, guidance on confronting unfamiliar issues in reading and writing, new strategies for generating essay topics, and extended critical reading approaches.

New "Thinking Critically" activities. Throughout the text, new interactive exercises test students' ability to apply critical thinking, reading, and writing concepts. Students can also complete these exercises online in LaunchPad.

Expanded discussion of developing thesis statements in Chapter 6. This updated section helps better illustrate for students what the difference is between taking a truly critical position versus resting on their laurels in argumentative essays.

Updated coverage of visual rhetoric in Chapter 4. The "Visual Rhetoric" chapter has been expanded to include discussion of how to analyze images rhetorically, including how to recognize and resist the meanings of images, how to identify visual emotional appeals, and what the difference is exactly between *seeing* passively and truly *looking* critically.

LaunchPad for *Current Issues and Enduring Questions*. This edition of *Current Issues* includes access to LaunchPad — an interactive platform that brings together the resources students need to prepare for class, working with the textbook. Features include interactive questions and exercises and quizzes on all of the readings and instructional content, allowing instructors to quickly get a sense of what students understand and what they need help with. You and your students can access LaunchPad at **macmillanhighered.com/barnetbedauohara**. Students receive access automatically with the purchase of a new book. Students can purchase standalone access at **macmillanhighered.com/barnetbedauohara**. To get instructor access, register as an instructor at this site.

Acknowledgments

Finally, the authors would like to thank those who have strengthened this book by their comments and advice on the eleventh edition: Heidi Ajrami, Victoria College; Rick Alley, Tidewater Community College; Kristen Bennett, Wentworth Institute of Technology; David Bordelon, Ocean County College; Linda Borla, Cypress College; Chris Brincefield, Forsyth Technical Community College; Erin Carroll, Ocean County College; Tamy Chapman, Saddleback College; Donald Carreira Ching, Leeward Community College; Jeanne Cosmos, Mass Bay Community College; Marlene Cousens, Yakima Community College; Christie Diep, Cypress College; Sarah Fedirka, University of Findlay; Mary Ellen Gleason, Paul D. Camp Community College; Michael Guista, Allan Hancock College; Anthony Halderman, Allan Hancock College; Tony Howard, Collin College; Tariq Jawhar, Tidewater Community College; Patrick Johnson, Northwest Iowa Community College; Amy Jurrens, Northwest Iowa Community College; Fay Lee, Lone Star College CyFair; James McFadden, Buena Vista University; Patricia Mensch, Bellevue College; Cornelia Moore, Victor Valley College; Sylvia Newman, Weber State University; Robert Piluso, Chaffey College; Jenni Runte, Metropolitan State University; Anne Spollen, Ocean County College; Rosanna Walker, College of the Desert; Ronald Tulley, University of Findlay; Steve Yarborough, Bellevue College; and our anonymous reviewers from San Joaquin Delta College, University of South Alabama, and Worcester State University. We would also like to thank Kalina Ingham, Elaine Kosta, Martha Friedman, Angela Boehler, and Jen Simmons, who adeptly managed art research and text permissions.

We are also deeply indebted to the people at Bedford/St. Martin's, especially to our editor, Alicia Young, who is wise, patient, supportive, and unfailingly helpful. Steve Scipione, Maura Shea, John Sullivan, and Adam Whitehurst, our editors for all of the preceding editions, have left a lasting impression on us and on the book; without their work on the first ten editions, there probably would not be an eleventh. Others at Bedford/St. Martin's to whom we are deeply indebted include Edwin Hill, Leasa Burton, Karen Henry, Joy Fisher Williams, Jennifer Prince, Elise Kaiser, and Jessica Gould, all of whom have offered countless valuable (and invaluable) suggestions. Intelligent, informed, firm yet courteous, persuasive — all of these folks know how to think and how to argue.

Get the Most Out of Your Course with
Current Issues and Enduring Questions

Bedford/St. Martin's offers resources and format choices that help you and your students get even more out of your book and course. To learn more about or to order any of the following products, contact your Macmillan sales representative, e-mail sales support (**sales_support@ bfwpub.com**), or visit the Web site at **macmillanhighered.com/currentissues11e/catalog**.

LAUNCHPAD FOR *CURRENT ISSUES AND ENDURING QUESTIONS*: WHERE STUDENTS LEARN

LaunchPad provides engaging content and new ways to get the most out of your book. Get an **interactive e-book** combined with **useful, highly relevant materials** in a fully customizable course space; then assign and mix our resources with yours.

- Auto-graded **reading quizzes**, **comprehension quizzes on argument topics**, and **interactive writing templates** help students to engage actively with the material you assign.

- **Pre-built units** — including readings, videos, quizzes, discussion groups, and more — are **easy to adapt and assign** by adding your own materials and mixing them with our high-quality multimedia content and ready-made assessment options, such as **LearningCurve** adaptive quizzing. LearningCurve now includes argument modules focusing on topic, purpose, and audience, arguable claims, reasoning and logical fallacies, and persuasive appeals (*logos, pathos,* and *ethos*).

- LaunchPad also provides access to a **Gradebook** that provides a clear window on the performance of your whole class, individual students, and even results of individual assignments.

- A **streamlined interface** helps students focus on what's due, and social commenting tools let them **engage**, make connections, and learn from each other. Use LaunchPad on its own or integrate it with your school's learning management system so that your class is always on the same page.

To get the most out of your book, order LaunchPad for *Current Issues and Enduring Questions* packaged with the print book. (LaunchPad for *Current Issues and Enduring Questions* can also be purchased on its own.) An activation code is required. To order LaunchPad for *Current Issues and Enduring Questions* with the print book, use ISBN 978-1-319-05917-0.

CHOOSE FROM ALTERNATIVE FORMATS OF *CURRENT ISSUES AND ENDURING QUESTIONS*

Current Issues and Enduring Questions is available in a variety of e-book formats. For details about our e-book partners, visit **macmillanlearning.com/ebooks**.

SELECT VALUE PACKAGES

Add value to your text by packaging one of the following resources with *Current Issues and Enduring Questions*. To learn more about package options for any of the following products, contact your Bedford/St. Martin's sales representative or visit **macmillanhighered.com /currentissues11e/catalog**.

Writer's Help 2.0 is a powerful online writing resource that helps students find answers whether they are searching for writing advice on their own or as part of an assignment.

- **Smart search:** Built on research with more than 1,600 student writers, the smart search in Writer's Help 2.0 provides reliable results even when students use novice terms, such as *flow* and *unstuck*.

- **Trusted content from our best-selling handbooks:** Choose *Writer's Help 2.0, Hacker Version* or *Writer's Help 2.0, Lunsford Version* and ensure that students have clear advice and examples for all of their writing questions.

- **Adaptive exercises that engage students:** Writer's Help 2.0 includes *LearningCurve*, game-like online quizzing that adapts to what students already know and helps them focus on what they need to learn.

Student access is packaged with *Current Issues and Enduring Questions* at a significant discount. Order ISBN 978-1-319-10225-8 for *Writer's Help 2.0, Hacker Version* or ISBN 978-1-319-10224-1 for *Writer's Help 2.0, Lunsford Version* to ensure your students have easy access to online writing support. Students who rent a book or buy a used book can purchase access to Writer's Help 2.0 at **macmillanhighered.com/writershelp2**.

Instructors may request free access by registering as an instructor at **macmillanhighered .com/writershelp2**.

For technical support, visit **macmillanhighered.com/getsupport**.

Portfolio Keeping, **Third Edition, by Nedra Reynolds and Elizabeth Davis**, provides all the information students need to use the portfolio method successfully in a writing course. *Portfolio Teaching*, a companion guide for instructors, provides the practical information instructors and writing program administrators need to use the portfolio method successfully in a writing course. To order *Portfolio Keeping* packaged with this text, contact your sale representative for a package ISBN.

INSTRUCTOR RESOURCES

macmillanhighered.com/currentissues11e/catalog

You have a lot to do in your course. Bedford/St. Martin's wants to make it easy for you to find the support you need — and to get it quickly.

Resources for Teaching Current Issues and Enduring Questions is available as a PDF that can be downloaded from the Bedford/St. Martin's online catalog at the URL above. In addition to chapter overviews and teaching tips, the instructor's manual includes a sample syllabus and suggested classroom activities.

Join Our Community! The Macmillan English Community is now Bedford/St. Martin's home for professional resources, featuring Bedford *Bits*, our popular blog site offering new ideas for the composition classroom and composition teachers. Connect and converse with a growing team of Bedford authors and top scholars who blog on *Bits*: Andrea Lunsford, Nancy

Sommers, Steve Bernhardt, Traci Gardner, Barclay Barrios, Jack Solomon, Susan Bernstein, Elizabeth Wardle, Doug Downs, Liz Losh, Jonathan Alexander, and Donna Winchell.

In addition, you'll find an expanding collection of additional resources that support your teaching:

- Sign up for webinars.

- Download resources from our professional resource series that support your teaching.

- Start a discussion.

- Ask a question.

- Follow your favorite members.

- Review projects in the pipeline.

Visit **community.macmillan.com** to join the conversation with your fellow teachers.

Brief Contents

Contents

28 WHAT IS HAPPINESS?   729

Thoughts about Happiness, Ancient and Modern   729

PART ONE

Critical Thinking and Reading

1

Critical Thinking

What is the hardest task in the world? To think.   — RALPH WALDO EMERSON

In all affairs it's a healthy thing now and then to hang a question mark on the things you have long taken for granted.   — BERTRAND RUSSELL

Although Emerson said the hardest task in the world is simply "to think," he was using the word *think* in the sense of *critical thinking*. By itself, *thinking* can mean almost any sort of cognitive activity, from idle daydreaming ("I'd like to go camping") to simple reasoning ("but if I go this week, I won't be able to study for my chemistry exam"). Thinking by itself may include forms of deliberation and decision-making that occur so automatically they hardly register in our consciousness ("What if I do go camping? I won't be likely to pass the exam. Then what? I better stay home and study").

When we add the adjective *critical* to the noun *thinking,* we begin to examine this thinking process consciously. When we do this, we see that even our simplest decisions involve a fairly elaborate series of calculations. Just in choosing to study and not to go camping, for instance, we weighed the relative importance of each activity (both are important in different ways); considered our goals, obligations, and commitments (to ourselves, our parents, peers, and professors); posed questions and predicted outcomes (using experience and observation as evidence); and resolved to take the most prudent course of action.

Many people associate being critical with fault-finding and nit-picking. The word *critic* might conjure an image of a sneering art or food critic eager to gripe about everything that's wrong with a particular work of art or menu item. People's low estimation of the stereotypical critic comes to light humorously in Samuel Beckett's play *Waiting for Godot*, when the two vagabond heroes, Vladimir and Estragon, engage in a name-calling contest to see who can hurl the worst insult at the other. Estragon wins hands-down when he fires the ultimate invective:

V: Moron!
E: Vermin!
V: Abortion!

E: Morpion!
V: Sewer-rat!
E: Curate!
V: Cretin!
E: (*with finality*) Crritic!
V: Oh! (*He wilts, vanquished, and turns away*)

However, being a good *critical* thinker isn't the same as being a "critic" in the derogatory sense. Quite the reverse: Because critical thinkers approach difficult questions and seek intelligent answers, they must be open-minded and self-aware, and they must interrogate *their own* thinking as rigorously as they interrogate others'. They must be alert to *their own* limitations and biases, the quality of evidence and forms of logic *they themselves* tentatively offer. In college, we may not aspire to become critics, but we all should aspire to become better critical thinkers.

Becoming more aware of our thought processes is a first step in practicing critical thinking. The word *critical* comes from the Greek word *krinein*, meaning "to separate, to choose"; above all, it implies *conscious* inquiry. It suggests that by breaking apart, or examining, our reasoning we can understand better the basis of our judgments and decisions — ultimately, so that we can make better ones.

Thinking through an Issue: Gay Marriage Licenses

By way of illustration, let's examine a case from Kentucky that was reported widely in the news in 2015. After the U.S. Supreme Court's landmark decision making gay marriage legal in all fifty states, a Rowan County clerk, Kim Davis, refused to begin issuing marriage licenses to same-sex couples. Citing religious freedom as her reason, Davis contended that the First Amendment of the Constitution protects her from being forced to act against her religious convictions and conscience. As a follower of Apostolic Christianity, she believes gay marriage is not marriage at all. To act against her belief, she said, "I would be asked to violate a central teaching of Scripture and of Jesus Himself regarding marriage. . . . It is not a light issue for me. It's a Heaven or Hell decision."

Let's think critically about this — and let's do it in a way that's fair to all parties and not just a snap judgment. Critical thinking means questioning not only the beliefs and assumptions of others, but also *one's own* beliefs and assumptions. We'll discuss this point at some length later, but for now we'll say only that when writing an argument you ought to be *thinking* — identifying important problems, exploring relevant issues, and evaluating available evidence — not merely collecting information to support a pre-established conclusion.

In 2015, Kim Davis was an elected county official. She couldn't be fired from her job for not performing her duties because she had been placed in that position by the vote of her constituency. And as her lawyers pointed out, "You don't lose your conscience rights, or your religious freedom rights, or your constitutional rights just because you accept public employment." However, once the Supreme Court established the legality of same-sex marriage,

Ty Wright/Getty Images

Davis's right to exercise her religious freedom impinged upon others' abilities to exercise their equal right to marriage (now guaranteed to them by the federal government). And so there was a problem: Whose rights have precedence?

We may begin to identify important problems and explore relevant issues by using a process called *clustering*. (We illustrate clustering again on p. 13.) Clustering is a method of brainstorming, a way of getting ideas on paper to see what develops, what conflicts and issues exist, and what tentative conclusions you can draw as you begin developing an argument. To start clustering, take a sheet of paper, and in the center jot down the most basic issue you can think of related to the problem at hand. In our example, we wrote a sentence that we think gets at the heart of the matter. It's important to note that we conducted this demonstration in "real time" — just a few minutes — so if our thoughts seem incomplete or off-the-cuff, that's fine. The point of clustering is to get ideas on paper. Don't be afraid to write down whatever you think, because you can always go back, cross out, rethink. This process of working through an issue can be messy. In a sense, it involves conducting an argument with yourself.

At the top of our page we wrote, "The law overrides individual religious freedom." (Alternatively, we could have written from the perspective of Davis and her supporters, saying "Individual religious freedom supersedes the law," and seen where that might have taken us.) Once we have a central idea, we let our minds work and allow one thought to lead to another. We've added numbers to our thoughts so you can follow the progression of our thinking.

1. The law overrides individual religious freedom.

2. Not always. The law can't tell people what to believe or how to practice religion.

4. What are the limits of individual religious freedom? When *can* the law compel or prohibit behavior?

3. What about drugs or animal sacrifice? What is *not* allowed under religious exemption? Murder? Jail? Polygamy? **Not really the issue. Real issue is Kim Davis.**

5. The law can limit some things, but it cannot force a person to act against his or her religion (how to speak, think, dress, etc.).

6. But Davis is not just any citizen. She is a government representative sworn to act according to law, not her religion.

7. Maybe she should resign or be fired?

10. Impeachment? Complicated, not a long-term solution.

8. Why should she resign? Should one's religion prevent one from public employment?

9. She can't be fired. She was elected to the county office by vote.

11. Davis as crusader, civil disobedience, the American individualist tradition?

12. Davis isn't signing religious licenses to marry. She is signing civil licenses. The legal terms of marriage are secular.

13. Any workarounds? Someone else in the office could sign the licenses? Or maybe same-sex couples could simply go to a different county clerk? But how far should they have to go and why? And what if the next county had another clerk like Kim Davis?

14. Why is the county clerkship an elected position, after all? If it were an appointed position, it would be clear. Davis could be removed from office for not upholding her oath to execute the law.

Notice that from our first idea about the law being more important than individual religious freedom, we immediately challenged our initial thinking. The law, in fact, protects religious freedom (2), and in some cases allows individuals to "break the law" if their religious rituals require it. We learned this when we wrote down a number of illegal activities sometimes associated with religion, and quickly looked up whether or not there was a legal precedent protecting these activities. We found the Supreme Court has allowed for the use of illegal drugs in some ceremonies (*Gonzalez v. O Centro Espirita*), and for the ritual sacrifice of animals in another (*Church of Lakumi Bablu Aye v. Hialeah*). Still, religions cannot do *anything they want* in the name of religious freedom. Religions cannot levy taxes, or incarcerate or kill people, for example. We then realized that what religions do as part of their ceremonies is not really the issue at all. The questions we are asking have to do with Kim Davis, her individual religious freedom, and what the law might force her to do (4).

Individuals cannot simply break the law and claim religious exemption. But the government cannot force people to act against their religious beliefs (5). Then (6) it occurred to us that Davis isn't just any citizen but a government employee whose job is to issue marriage licenses under the law. She may be free to believe what she wants and exercise her rights accordingly, but she cannot use her authority legally as a government official to deny people the rights they've been afforded by law.

We then posed several questions to ourselves in trying to determine the right way to think. We considered whether Davis should resign or be fired (7), which we then realized isn't possible (8, 9), and we wondered how else a person may be removed from office (10). We considered her as a figure of civil disobedience, defying the law in defense of religious liberties (11), trying to see the situation from her perspective. But we returned again to the idea that she isn't just a regular citizen but an agent of the law whose oath compels her to uphold the law (6). She shouldn't be able to use her authority to deprive others of exercising their rights. We also considered that the government doesn't take particular interest in the religious basis of marriage (12), so why should Davis be permitted to impose her religious beliefs on a lawful act of marriage?

By the time we got to (13), we thought, "Isn't there some workaround? Can't *deputy clerks* continue to sign the licenses as long as the state accepts them?" This way, Davis wouldn't have to violate the deeply held beliefs that she is free to hold, and yet those seeking to exercise their rights to marriage would still be satisfied. Later, on page 374, we discuss a facet of compromise solutions to difficult problems when we explore Rogerian argument (named for Carl Rogers, a psychologist), a way of arguing that promotes finding common ground and solutions in which both sides win by conceding some elements to the opposition. We also thought in (13) that maybe same-sex couples could just get their licenses from a different place, one where Davis doesn't work.

At this point, it may be useful to mention another facet of critical thinking and argument that we'll also explore in more detail later: considering the implications of the decisions to which our thinking leads. What happens when our judgments on matters are settled and we draw a reasonable conclusion? If we were to settle on a compromise in the Davis case, it might work for the moment, but what would happen if other clerks in the state held the same beliefs as Davis (13)? In (13), we also considered the implications if same-sex couples were simply asked to go to a different office. How far should a same-sex couple have to go to find someone willing to issue the license if all clerks can decide based on their religious convictions what kinds of marriage they will authorize? Additionally, and maybe even more important, why should same-sex couples be hindered in any way in acquiring their license or be treated as a different class of citizens?

Again, if you think with pencil and paper in hand and let your mind make associations by clustering, you'll find (perhaps to your surprise) that you have plenty of interesting ideas and that some can lead to satisfying conclusions. Doubtless you'll also have some ideas that represent gut reactions or poorly thought-out conclusions, but that's okay. When clustering, allow your thoughts to take shape without restriction; you can look them over again and organize them later. Originally, we wrote in our cluster (7) that Davis could be fired for not performing her job according to its requirements. We then realized that this wouldn't involve a simple process. Because she's an elected official, there would have to be a state legislative action to impeach her (9). This made us think, "The state of Kentucky could impeach Davis" (10). But then we also considered the consequences and decided this would not be a long-term solution. What if the next election cycle brought someone else who shares Davis's beliefs into the same position? In fact, what if citizens in Kentucky continued to elect county clerks in Rowan County — or any county — who refused to issue marriage licenses based on religious convictions? Would the state have to impeach clerks over and over again? We then thought, "Why is the county clerkship an elected position" (14)? Could it become an appointed position instead, such that governors could emplace county clerks, whose primary job is to administer legislative policy? Perhaps this is the argument we'll want to make. (Of course, it might open up new questions and issues that we would have to explore: What else does the clerk do? Is the autonomy of an elected position necessary? Do all states elect county clerks? And so on.)

> **A RULE FOR WRITERS**
> One good way to start writing an essay is to generate ideas by clustering — and at this point not to worry that some ideas may be off-the-cuff or even nonsense. Just get ideas down on paper. You can evaluate them later.

At the time of this writing, Kim Davis had continued to refuse signing marriage licenses for same-sex couples. When ordered by a judge to do so or face contempt of court, she held firm to her position and spent six days in jail as a result. Her supporters cheered her act of civil disobedience (defined as breaking a law based on moral or religious conscience) and even compared her to Rosa Parks, Martin Luther King Jr., and other civil rights leaders who fought against unjust laws on the basis of religious principles. Davis returned to her position as Rowan County clerk and authorized her deputy clerks to issue marriage licenses to same-sex couples, but without her signature. Time will tell how the case plays out.

Topics for Critical Thinking and Writing

1. As noted, some of Kim Davis's supporters have compared her to celebrated figures from American history like Rosa Parks who practiced civil disobedience by breaking laws they believed were immoral, unfair, or unjust. What are the similarities and differences in the case

of Rosa Parks, who violated the law in Montgomery, Alabama, in 1955 by refusing to move to the "black" section of a public bus, and that of Kim Davis, who has refused to abide by laws established by the U.S. Supreme Court regarding gay marriage? How do the similarities and differences justify or not justify Davis's actions?

2. On a Facebook page dedicated to Davis's case, one commenter wrote, "Davis is a hero for all of us Christians who feel this country is abandoning our God." Think critically about this statement by writing about the assumptions it reveals.

3. In denying Davis's appeal to a federal court to not be forced to authorize same-sex marriage licenses, Judge David Bunning wrote that individuals "cannot choose what orders they follow" and that religious conscience "is not a viable defense" for not adhering to the law. At the same time, the free exercise clause of the First Amendment of the U.S. Constitution says that Congress shall make no law prohibiting the free exercise of religion. What do you think about Kim Davis's exercise of religion? Is it fair that in order to keep her job after the Court's decision about the legality of gay marriage, she has to regularly violate one of her religion's central beliefs about marriage? Explain your response.

On Flying Spaghetti Monsters: Analyzing and Evaluating from Multiple Perspectives

Let's think critically about another issue related to religious freedom, equality, and the law — one that we hope brings some humor to the activity but also inspires careful thinking and debate.

In 2005, in response to pressure from some religious groups, the Kansas Board of Education gave preliminary approval for teaching alternatives to evolution in public school science classes. New policies would require science teachers to present "intelligent design" — the idea that the universe was created by an intentional, conscious force such as God — as an equally plausible explanation for natural selection and human development.

In a quixotic challenge to the legislation, twenty-four-year-old physics graduate Bobby Henderson wrote an open letter that quickly became popular on the Internet and then was published in the *New York Times*. Henderson appealed for recognition of another theory that he said was equally valid: that an all-powerful deity called the Flying Spaghetti Monster created the world. While clearly writing satirically on behalf of science, Henderson nevertheless kept a straight face and argued that if creationism were to be taught as a theory in science classes, then "Pastafarianism" must also be taught as another legitimate possibility. "I think we can all look forward to the time," he wrote, "when these three theories are given equal time in our science classes. . . . One third time for Intelligent Design; one third time for Flying Spaghetti Monsterism (Pastafarianism); and one third time for logical conjecture based on overwhelming observable evidence."

Since that time, the Church of the Flying Spaghetti Monster has become a creative venue where secularists and atheists construct elaborate mythologies, religious texts, and rituals, most of which involve cartoonish pirates and various noodle-and-sauce images. ("R'amen," they say at the end of their prayers.) However, although tongue-in-cheek, many followers have also used the organization seriously as a means to champion the First Amendment's establishment clause, which prohibits government institutions from *establishing*, or preferring, any one religion over another. Pastafarians have challenged policies and laws in various states that appear to discriminate among religions or to provide exceptions or exemptions based on religion. In Tennessee, Virginia, and Wisconsin, church members have successfully petitioned for permission to display statues or signs of the Flying Spaghetti Monster in places where other religious icons are permitted, such as on state government properties. One petition in Oklahoma argued that because the state allows a marble and granite Ten Commandments monument on the state courthouse lawn, then a statue of the Flying Spaghetti Monster must also be permitted; this effort ultimately forced the state to remove the Ten Commandments monument in 2015. In the past three years, individuals in California, Georgia, Florida, Texas, California, and Utah have asserted their right to wear religious head coverings in their driver's license photos—a religious exemption afforded to Muslims in those states—and have had their pictures taken with colanders on their heads.

Let's stop for a moment. Take stock of your initial reactions to the Church of the Flying Spaghetti Monster. Some responses might be quite uncritical, quite unthinking: "That's outrageous!" or "What a funny idea!" Others might be the type of snap judgment we discussed earlier: "These people are making fun of real religions!" or "They're just causing trouble." Think about it: If your hometown approved placing a Christmas tree on the town square during the holiday season, and the Church of the Flying Spaghetti Monster argued that it too should be allowed to set up its holiday symbol as a matter of religious equality—perhaps a statue like the one pictured above—should it be afforded equal space? Why, or why not?

Be careful here, and exercise critical thinking. Can one simply say, "No, that belief is ridiculous," in response to a religious claim? What if members of a different religious group were asking for equal space? Should a menorah (a Jewish holiday symbol) be allowed? A mural celebrating Kwanzaa? A Native American symbol? Can some religious expressions be included in public spaces and not others? If so, why? If not, why not?

In thinking critically about a topic, we must try to see it from all sides before reaching a conclusion. We conduct an argument with ourselves, advancing and then questioning different opinions:

- What can be said *for* the proposition?
- What can be said *against* it?

Critical thinking requires us to support our position and also see the other side. The heart of critical thinking is a *willingness to face objections to one's own beliefs,* to adopt a skeptical attitude not only toward views opposed to our own but also toward our own common sense — that is, toward views that seem to us as obviously right. If we assume we have a monopoly on the truth and dismiss those who disagree with us as misguided fools, or if we say that our opponents are acting out of self-interest (or a desire to harass the community) and we don't analyze their views, we're being critical but we aren't engaging in critical thinking.

When thinking critically, it's important to ask key questions about any position, decision, or action we take and any regulation, policy, or law we support. We must ask:

- Is it fair?
- What is its purpose?
- Is it likely to accomplish its purpose?
- What will its effects be? Might it unintentionally cause some harm?
- If it might cause harm, to whom? What kind of harm? Can we weigh the potential harm against the potential good?
- Who gains something and who loses something as a result?
- Are there any compromises that might satisfy different parties?

What do you think? If you were on your hometown's city council, how would you answer the above questions in relation to a petition from the Church of the Flying Spaghetti Monster to permit a Spaghetti Monster display alongside the traditional Christmas tree on the town square? How would you vote, and why? What other questions and issues might arise from your engagement with this issue? (*Hint:* Try clustering. Place the central question in the middle of a sheet of a paper, and brainstorm the issues that flower from it.)

CALL-OUT: OBSTACLES TO CRITICAL THINKING   Because critical thinking requires engaging seriously with potentially difficult topics, topics about which you may already have strong opinions, and topics that elicit powerful emotional responses, it's important to recognize the ways in which your thinking may be compromised or clouded. Write down or discuss how each of the following attitudes might impede or otherwise negatively affect your critical thinking in real life. How might each one be detrimental in making conclusions?

1. The topic is too controversial and will never be resolved.
2. The topic hits "too close to home" (i.e., "I've had direct experience with this").

3. The topic disgusts me.

4. The topic angers me.

5. Everyone I know thinks roughly the same thing I do about this topic.

6. Others may judge me if I verbalize what I think.

7. My opinion on this topic is *X* because it benefits me, my family, or my kind the most.

8. My parents raised me to think *X* about this topic.

9. One of my favorite celebrities believes *X* about this topic, so I do too.

10. I know what I think, but my solutions are probably unrealistic. It's impossible to change the system.

Think of some more obstacles to critical thinking, and provide examples of how they might lead to unsound conclusions or poor solutions.

> **A RULE FOR WRITERS**
> Early in the process of jotting down your ideas on a topic, stop to ask yourself, "What might someone reasonably offer as an *objection* to my view?"

In short, as we will say several times (because the point is key), *argument is an instrument of learning* as well as of persuasion. In order to formulate a reasoned position and make a vote, you'll have to gather some information, find out what experts say, and examine the points on which they agree and disagree. You'll likely want to gather opinions from religious leaders, community members, and legal experts (after all, you wouldn't want the town to be sued for discrimination). You'll want to think beyond a knee-jerk value judgment like, "No, a Spaghetti Monster statue would be ugly."

Seeing the issue from multiple perspectives will require familiarizing yourself with current debates — perhaps about religious equality, free speech, or the separation of church and state — and considering the responsibility of public institutions to accommodate different viewpoints and various constituencies. Remember, the Church of the Flying Spaghetti Monster didn't gain so much traction by being easy to dismiss. Thus, you must do the following:

Survey, considering as many perspectives as possible.

Analyze, identifying and then separating out the parts of the problem, trying to see how its pieces fit together.

Evaluate, judging the merit of various ideas and claims and the weight of the evidence in their favor or against them.

If you survey, analyze, and evaluate comprehensively, you'll have better and more informed ideas; you'll generate a wide variety of ideas, each triggered by your own responses and the ideas your research brings to light. As you form an opinion and prepare to vote, you'll be constructing an argument to yourself at first, but also one you may have to present to the community, so you should be as thorough as possible and sensitive to the ideas and rights of many different people.

We have already seen an example of clustering on page 6, which illustrates the prewriting process of thinking through an issue and generating ideas by imagining responses — counterthoughts — to our initial thoughts. Here's another example, this time showing an actual student's thoughts about an issue related to the Church of the Flying Spaghetti Monster. The student, Alexa Cabrera, was assigned to write approximately 500 words about a specific legal challenge made by a member of the Church of the Flying Spaghetti Monster. She selected the case of Stephen Cavanaugh, a prisoner who made a complaint against the Nebraska State Penitentiary after being denied the right to practice Pastafarianism while incarcerated there. Because the Department of Corrections denied him those privileges, Cavanaugh filed suit citing civil rights violations and asked for his rights to be accommodated. Notice that in the essay — the product of several revised drafts — the student introduced points she had *not* thought of while clustering. The cluster, in short, was a *first* step, not a road map of the final essay.

6. Who can say Pastafarianism isn't a "real" religion just because it's newer than Christianity, Judaism, etc.?

5. He should *not* be allowed, because Pastafarianism isn't a "real" religion.

7. The state can't decide what counts as a legitimate religious belief.

4. Stephen Cavanaugh, a "Pastafarian," was denied the right to practice in a Nebraska prison.

8. Nebraska prisoners are protected under the Religious Land Use and Institutionalized Persons Act (RLUIPA).

1. Prisoners should be allowed to practice religion.

2. But prisoners are being punished. Why should their religious beliefs be accommodated?

3. Religious rights can't be denied — First Amendment guarantees protection.

Stirred and Strained: Pastafarians Should Be Allowed to Practice in Prison

Stephen Cavanaugh is a member of the Church of the Flying Spaghetti Monster, a mostly Web-based religious group that has earned notoriety for its members' demands that they be treated under the First Amendment like any other religion. The group strives to show that if Christians can place Nativity scenes on public grounds, or if Muslims can wear head coverings in state driver's license photographs, then by god (or pasta, as the case may be), they can too. Cavanaugh is in the Nebraska State Penitentiary, where inmates are permitted under the Religious Land Use and Institutionalized Persons Act (RLUIPA) to exercise religious freedoms guaranteed by the First Amendment. He wants the same rights and privileges given to incarcerated Christians, Muslims, Jews, and Buddhists—namely, to be able to wear religious clothing, to eat specially prepared meals, and to be given resources, space, and time to conduct worship with his fellow "believers." For Cavanaugh, this means being able to dress up as a pirate, eat pasta on selected holidays, order satirical holy books, and lead a weekly "prayer" group. Many people consider these requests absurd, but Cavanaugh should be permitted under the First Amendment and the RLUIPA to practice his faith.

Some arguments against Cavanaugh are easier to dismiss than others. One of these simply casts aside the spiritual needs and concerns of prisoners: They are being punished, after all, so why should they receive any religious accommodations? This position is both immoral and unconstitutional. Religion is an important sustaining force for prisoners who might otherwise struggle to find meaning and purpose in life, and it is protected by the First Amendment *because* it helps prisoners find purpose and become rehabilitated—the fundamental goal of correctional facilities (even for those serving life without parole). Another argument sees religion as important as long as it conforms to Judeo-Christian belief structures, which has for a long time been the only spiritual path available in American prisons. But today, in our diverse society, the RLUIPA *requires* prisons to provide religious accommodations for all faiths equally unless an undue administrative, financial, or security burden can be proven. Obviously, many religious observances cannot be accommodated. Prisons cannot permit inmates to carry crosses and staves, construct temples and sweat lodges, or make required religious pilgrimages. However, as long as some religious accommodations can be and are made—such as Catholics being offered fish on Fridays, or Jewish and Muslim prisoners receiving kosher and halal meals—all religious groups must be similarly accommodated.

The more challenging question about the Church of the Flying Spaghetti Monster is whether it is a religion at all, whether it deserves equal treatment among more established religions. When Cavanaugh was first denied his request, the prison claimed that FSM was not a religion but a "parody" of religion. The Nebraska State Penitentiary suggested it could not grant privileges to anyone who presents his whimsical desires as part of a religious philosophy. In dealing with a humorous and politically motivated "religion" without a strong tradition and whose founder may write a new gospel at any time, should the prison have to keep up with the possibility of constantly changing prisoner demands? Can anyone just make up a religion and then expect to be accommodated?

For better or worse, the answer is yes — as long as the accommodations represent valid forms of observance, are reasonable, and do not pose a substantial burden to the institution. Many religions have councils that at times alter the tenets of their faith. The state does not have the authority to determine what is or is not a "real" religion or religious practice. It does have an obligation under the RLUIPA to accommodate not just some but all forms of faith for incarcerated persons. As long as individuals sincerely hold certain beliefs, and as long as the accommodations requested meet the standards of reasonability and equity, state prisons, like all other government agencies and institutions, cannot discriminate. Some might argue that Cavanaugh's faith is not sincere — that he does not *really* believe that the Earth was literally created by a ball of pasta with meatball-shaped eyes. But this is not the point. The government cannot apply a religious test to measure the degree of one's sincerity or faith. Like others in the Flying Spaghetti Monster movement — secularists, atheists, and professed believers — Cavanaugh should not be treated as an exploiter of religious freedom. In fact, in a pluralistic society with laws to ensure religious freedom and equality, his challenge helps protect all faiths.

THE ESSAY ANALYZED

The title, in its words *stirred* and *strained*, engages readers' attention by playing with words related to pasta, prison, and the frustration likely to be encountered by an individual who is denied religious freedom. The subtitle states the thesis. This introductory material — a paper begins with its title, not with its first paragraph — makes readers curious and lets them know where the essay will take them.

Paragraph 1 sets the stage. The first sentence clarifies what the Church is and uses a nifty turn of phrase, "by god (or by pasta)," to encourage engagement and make the author's voice, like the FSM, playful but dead serious. The second, third, and fourth sentences provide the basis for Cavanaugh's claims. The last sentence presents a clear thesis.

Paragraph 2 draws on the student's preliminary map. It sets forth objections to making religious accommodations for prisoners and disputes them, providing a citation of the law that guarantees religious freedom in prison, a definition of its limits, and a few examples of these limits. The last sentence sustains the thesis by arguing that accommodations must be equal among religions. However, it also anticipates that readers are likely to agree on this point but still not consider the FSM as a religion.

Paragraph 3 addresses the potential counterargument set up by paragraph 2 and highlights the most common criticism of the FSM: that it isn't *really* a religion at all. The writer raises the problematic question that if prisons must accommodate Cavanaugh, then where would the protest end? What new accommodations might he ask for in the future? Paragraph 3 in effect suggests the *implications* of granting Cavanaugh his request, inviting the reader to imagine a potentially slippery argumentative slope.

Paragraph 4 halts readers' imaginings, reminding them that the writer is still in the realm of talking about *reasonable* and *fair* treatment among inmates, not an "anything goes" proposition. It reminds readers that the state cannot determine a "real" or "unreal" religion, just as it cannot judge the depth, rigor, or literalness of an inmate's belief (Christian, Pastafarian, or otherwise). The fact is that our society has laws to ensure religious freedom and equality for all citizens. In this way, the writer makes a shrewd rhetorical move, presenting Cavanaugh's complaint not just as antagonistic but also as something essential to protecting prisoners of all faiths. Such an appeal to democratic insistence on fairness is normally effective, although in this instance a reader may wonder if the writer has demonstrated convincingly that fairness requires prisons to accommodate Pastafarians. Are you convinced that it would be *unfair* to deny Cavanaugh and other Pastafarian inmates their demands? Why, or why not?

Generating Ideas: Writing as a Way of Thinking

We have already seen, in the clusters that students have generated, concise examples of how the act of writing helps thinkers to think better. "To learn to write," Robert Frost said, "is to learn to have ideas." But how does one "learn to have ideas"? Often we discover ideas while talking with others. A friend says *X* about some issue, and we — who have never really thought much about the matter — say,

- "Well, yes, I see what you're saying, but come to think of it, I'm not of your opinion. I see it differently — *not as* X *but as* Y."

Or maybe we say,

- *"Yes, X, sure, and also a bit of* Y, *too."*

Mere chance — a friend's comment — has led us to an idea that we didn't know we had. This sort of discovery may seem like the one we make when reaching under the couch to retrieve the dog's ball and finding a ten-dollar bill instead: "How it got there, I'll never know, but I'm sure glad I found it."

In fact, learning to have ideas is not largely a matter of chance. Or if chance *is* involved, well, as Louis Pasteur put it, "Chance favors the prepared mind." This means that lurking in the mind are bits of information or hints or hunches that in the unexpected circumstance — when talking, when listening to a lecture or a classroom discussion, or especially when reading — are triggered and lead to useful thoughts. This is a sort of seat-of-the-pants knowledge that, when brought to the surface in the right circumstances, produces good results.

Consider the famous example of Archimedes, the ancient Greek mathematician who discovered a method to determine the volume of an irregularly shaped object. The problem: A king gave a goldsmith a specific weight of gold with which to make a crown in the shape of laurel leaves. When the job was finished, the king weighed the crown and found that it matched the weight of the gold he had provided, but he nevertheless suspected that the goldsmith might have substituted some silver for some of the gold. How could the king find out (without melting or otherwise damaging the crown) if the crown was pure gold? For Archimedes, meditating on this problem produced no ideas, but when he entered a bathtub he noticed that the water level rose as he immersed his body. He suddenly realized that he could thus determine the volume of the crown — by measuring the amount of displaced water. Since silver is less dense than gold, it takes a greater volume of silver to equal a given weight of gold. That is, a given weight of gold will displace less water than the same weight of silver. Archimedes then immersed the given weight of gold, measured the water it displaced, and found that indeed the crown displaced more water than the gold did. In his excitement at confirming his idea, Archimedes is said to have leaped out of the tub and run naked through the street, shouting "Eureka!" (Greek for "I have found [it]!").

Why do we tell this story? Partly because we like it, but chiefly because the word *eureka* comes from the same Greek word that has given our language the word **heuristic** (pronounced hyoo-RIS-tik), which refers to a method or process of discovering ideas — in short, of thinking. In this method, one thought triggers another. (*Note:* In computer science, *heuristic* has a more specialized meaning.) Of course, one of the best ways of generating ideas is to hear what's going on around you — and that is talk, both in and out of the classroom, as well as in the world of books. You'll find, as we said early in this discussion, that your response may be, "Well, yes, I see what you're saying, but come to think of it, I don't see it quite that way. I see it differently — not as *X* but as *Y*." As we've said, argument is an instrument of learning as well as of persuasion. For instance:

> *Yes*, solar power is a way of conserving energy, *but* do we need to despoil the Mojave Desert and endanger desert life with — literally — fifty thousand solar mirrors so that folks in Los Angeles can heat their pools? Doesn't it make sense to reduce our use of energy, rather than develop sources of renewable energy that violate the environment? Some sites should be off-limits.

Maybe your response to the proposal (now at least fifteen years old) that wind turbines be placed in the waters off Cape Cod, Massachusetts, would go like this:

> *Given our need* for wind power, *how can a reasonable person object* to the proposal that we put 130 wind turbines in the waters off Cape Cod, Massachusetts? *Yes*, the view will be changed, *but* in fact the turbines are quite attractive. No one thinks that windmills in Holland spoil the landscape. So the view will be changed, but not spoiled; *and furthermore*, the verdict is still out on whether or not wind turbines pose a significant risk to birds or aquatic life.

When you're asked to write about something you've read in this book, if your first response is that you have no ideas, remember the responses that we have mentioned — "No, I don't see it that way" or "Yes, but" or "Yes, and moreover" — and see if one of them helps you respond to the work — helps you, in short, to develop ideas.

CONFRONTING UNFAMILIAR ISSUES

Generating ideas can be a challenge when you, as a student, are asked to read about and respond to an unfamiliar issue. Sometimes, students wonder why they have to engage in particular topics and generate ideas about them. "I want to be a speech pathologist," you might say, "so why do I need to read essays and formulate ideas about capital punishment?"

One answer is that a college curriculum should spur students to think about pressing issues facing our society, so learning about capital punishment is important to all students. But this isn't the only answer. One could never study "all" the important social problems we face (anyway, many of them change very rapidly). Instead, colleges seek to equip students with tools, methods, and habits of mind that enable them to confront arguments about *any* potential issue or problem (including those within the field of speech pathology!). The primary goal of a college education (and of this book) is to help students develop an *intellectual apparatus* — a toolkit that can be applied to any subject matter, any issue.

The techniques presented in this book offer a practical framework for approaching issues, thinking about them carefully, asking good questions, identifying problems, and offering reasonable solutions — not necessarily because we want you to form opinions about the issues we have selected (though we hope you do), but because we want you to practice critical thinking, reading, and writing in ways that transfer to other aspects of your education as well as to your personal, professional, and civic life.

The playwright Edward Albee once said, "Good writers define reality; bad ones merely restate it." Rather than thinking that you must "agree or disagree" with the authors whose works you'll read in this book, imagine that you'll be practicing how to discover your unique point of view by finding pathways into debates, negotiating different positions, and generating new ideas. So when you confront an unfamiliar issue in this book (or elsewhere), consider the strategies discussed below as practical methods for generating new ideas. That is what critical thinking (and writing) is all about.

TOPICS

One way of generating ideas, practiced by the ancient Greeks and Romans and still regarded as among the best ways, is to consider what the ancients called **topics** — from the Greek *topos*, meaning "place," as in our word *topography* (a description or representation of a place). For the ancients, certain topics, when formulated as questions, were places where they went to find ideas. Among the classical topics were *definition, comparison, relationship,* and *testimony.* By prompting oneself with questions about these topics, one moves toward answers.

If you're at a loss for ideas when confronted with an issue (and an assignment to write about it), you might discover ideas by turning to the relevant classical topics and jotting down your responses. (In classical terminology, this means engaging in the process of invention, from the Latin *invenire,* "to come upon, to find.") Seeing your ideas on paper — even in the briefest form — will help bring other ideas to mind and will also help you evaluate them. For instance, after jotting down ideas as they come and your responses to them, you might do the following:

1. First, organize them into two lists, pro and con.

2. Next, delete ideas that, upon consideration, seem wrong or irrelevant.

3. Finally, develop the ideas that strike you as pretty good.

You probably won't know where you stand until you've gone through such a process. It would be nice to be able to make a quick decision, immediately justify it with three excellent reasons, and then give three further reasons showing why the opposing view is inadequate. In fact, however, people almost never can reach a reasoned decision without a good deal of preliminary thinking.

Consider the following brief essay about the Food and Drug Administration's approval, in 2015, of a genetically engineered salmon. Although GMO (genetically modified organisms) foods and medicines are common in the United States, this salmon will soon be the first genetically modified animal approved for food consumption in the United States. After you read the essay, refer to Thinking Critically: Generating Topics, which asks you to begin jotting down ideas on a sheet of paper along the lines of the classical topics. As an example of how to respond to the questions, we've included columns related to the Kim Davis and Stephen Cavanaugh cases. As you attempt to formulate ideas related to the essay about genetically engineered salmon, answer the questions related to the classical topics. There's no need to limit yourself to one answer per item as we did.

NINA FEDOROFF

Nina Fedoroff (b. 1942) is the Evan Pugh professor emerita at Penn State University. She served as science and technology adviser to the U.S. secretary of state from 2007 to 2010. The following essay originally appeared in the New York Times *in December 2015.*

The Genetically Engineered Salmon Is a Boon for Consumers and Sustainability

This is great news for consumers and the environment. Wild salmon populations have long been in deep trouble because of overfishing, and open-water cage farming of salmon pollutes coastal waters, propagates fish diseases, and sacrifices a lot of wild-caught fish to be consumed as salmon feed.

The fish is virtually identical to wild salmon, but it is a more sustainable food source, growing faster to maturity.

But just imagine, you'll soon be able to eat salmon guilt-free. AquaBounty has spent more than 20 years developing and testing this faster-growing salmon that will require less feed to bring it to a marketable size. It can be farmed economically in closed, on-land facilities that recirculate water and don't dump waste into the sea. Since the fish live in clean, managed water, they don't get diseases that are spread among caged fish in the sea. And the growing facilities could be closer to markets, cutting shipping costs.

All of these elements take pressure off wild salmon and make salmon farming more sustainable.

Much of the concern about AquaBounty's 5 salmon centers around several bits of added DNA, taken from another fish, that let the salmon grow continuously, not just seasonally. That does not make them "unnatural" or dangerous, it just makes them grow to market size on less feed.

We've been tinkering with our plants and animals to serve our food needs for somewhere between 10 and 20 thousand years. We created corn, for example. The seed-bearing structure of the original "wild" version, called teosinte, looked very different from the modern-day ear, packed with hundreds of soft, starch-and-protein-filled kernels. And it's people who developed the tomatoes we eat today. Mother Nature's are tiny: A pioneering breeder described them in an 1893 grower's guide as "small, hollow, tough, watery" fruits.

But there's money (and fame) in being anti-G.M.O. The organic food marketers want to sell their food, which is over-priced because organic farming is inefficient — not because the food's better — so they tell scare stories about the dangers of G.M.O.s.

There is also no reason to fear that these genetically engineered salmon will escape and destroy wild populations. Only sterile females will be grown for food. And since the fish will be grown in contained facilities on land, escapees can't survive either.

AquaBounty's salmon is salmon, plain and simple. I, for one, can't wait to taste it.

THINKING CRITICALLY *Generating Topics*

Provide the relevant information for the topic of genetically engineered salmon.

TOPICS	QUESTIONS	DAVIS	CAVANAUGH	GENETICALLY ENGINEERED SALMON
Definition *Categories* *Descriptions* *Definitions* *Explanations*	*What is it?*	"The Kim Davis case involves one woman's dissent against the Supreme Court decision of 2015 legalizing gay marriage. The law says X, but Davis draws upon Y. "	"The RLUIPA requires state prisons to provide religious accommodations under the First Amendment, which says X. Cavanaugh asserted his 'right' to ..."	

Comparison	What is it like or unlike?	"Other cases in which individuals defied the law because of conscience include X, Y, and Z. The Davis case is similar/different because . . ."	"This case is like other challenges made by the FSM Church; however, since he is a prisoner asking for XYZ, Cavanaugh's case is different because . . ."	
Similarities Differences Analogies Applications				
Relationship	What caused it, and what will it cause?	"The issue of gay marriage had been a state's rights issue but was unevenly applied across states. When the Court legalized it at the federal level, it required all public officials including judges and clerks to abide by the law, yet the result is . . ."	"Prisoners deserve to exercise their religious freedom, but for most of U.S. history Christianity was the only available option, which violated the establishment clause . . ."	
Antecedents Precedents Consequences Outcomes				
Testimony	What is known or said about it, especially by experts?	"Supreme Court Justice Kennedy asserted in his opinion that the Constitution guarantees X, though Justice Scalia in his dissent said . . ."	"In American prisons, there are over X number of recognized religious groups, including Satanists and Wiccans. If they can have their rights, then . . ."	
Statistics Maxims Laws Quotations				

LaunchPad   To complete this activity online, go to **macmillanhighered.com/barnetbedauohara**

Here's an inner dialogue that you might engage in as you think critically about the question of genetically engineered salmon:

> The purpose of genetically engineered salmon is to protect against the ecological effects of overfishing — that seems to be a good thing.
>
> Another purpose is to protect consumers by ensuring that the price of salmon, one of the most commonly eaten fish, will not become so high that few people could afford it.
>
> But other issues are apparent. Should we turn to altering the genes of animals to protect the environment or consumer prices? Are there other solutions, like eating less salmon or regulating overfishing?
>
> Who gains and who loses, and what do they stand to gain or lose, by this FDA approval of genetically modified salmon?
>
> The author says no one should worry about "several bits of DNA added"; but come to think of it, is this modification unethical or dangerous in any way? Is it okay to create a new type of animal by altering genes?
>
> The author attacks anti-GMO activists, saying they're just after money (and fame — why fame?). Isn't money (and fame?) also the goal of AquaBounty and other GMO food producers?

Notice how part of the job is *analytic,* recognizing the elements or complexities of the whole, and part is *evaluative,* judging the adequacy of all the ideas, one by one. Both tasks require critical thinking in the form of analyzing and evaluating, and those processes themselves require a disciplined *imagination.*

So far we have jotted down a few thoughts and then immediately given some second thoughts contrary to the first. Be aware that your own counterthoughts might not come to mind right away. For instance, they might not occur until you reread your notes or try to explain the issue to a friend, or until you begin drafting an essay aimed at supporting or undermining the new FDA rules. Most likely, in fact, some good ideas won't occur until a second or third or fourth draft.

Here are some further thoughts on the genetically modified salmon. We list them more or less as they occurred to us and as we typed them into a computer — not sorted neatly into two groups, pro and con, or evaluated as you should do in further critical thinking of your own. Of course, a later step would be to organize the material into a useful pattern. As you read, try writing your responses in the margin.

> According to one article, the FDA is not requiring companies to label the salmon as genetically engineered. Should this information at least be made available to consumers? Maybe their religious, ethical, or personal preferences would be not to eat modified fish species. If the fish were properly labeled and people knew of any risks associated with eating it, they could avoid it if they wished.
>
> Are there any animal rights issues at stake here? Is it okay to breed "only sterile females"? Critics say that scientists shouldn't create new kinds of animals. Is this even what AquaBounty is doing?

The author says we shouldn't worry about these fish breeding with other salmon, but is she understating the risks? I hadn't thought of the possibility, but clearly someone has. Is there an actual risk of threatening the natural species? If there was really zero risk, why are they bothering to breed only *sterile* females?

Maybe the FDA shouldn't have approved genetically modified salmon for food. If we start with the salmon, where will it end? What other foods are being reviewed for similar kinds of farming? Is this really the same as the development of corn and other vegetables, as the author suggests — or is animal life something different?

Doubtless there is much that we haven't asked or thought about, but we hope you'll agree that the issue deserves careful thought, given that the availability of genetically modified food animals has serious implications for the environment and the future of food production.

If you worked for the FDA and were part of this decision, you would *have* to think about these questions and issues. As a thought experiment, imagine you had to contribute to the decision about approving these fish. Try to put your tentative views into writing.

Note that you would want to get answers to questions such as the following:

- What sort of evidence exists about the safety of genetically engineered salmon? Who has studied it?

- What do biologists and bioethicists say about the genetically engineered salmon?

- What kind of people and organizations oppose the approval of this genetically engineered salmon, and what are their primary critiques?

Some of these questions require you to do **research** on the topic. Some raise issues of fact, and relevant evidence probably is available. In order to reach a conclusion in which you have confidence, you'll have to do some research to find out what the facts — the objective data — are. Merely explaining your position without giving the evidence will not be convincing.

Even without doing any research, however, you might want to look over the pros and cons, perhaps adding some new thoughts or modifying or even rejecting (for reasons that you can specify) some of those already given. If you do

> ## A CHECKLIST FOR CRITICAL THINKING
>
> Attitudes:
>
> ☐ Does my thinking show imaginative open-mindedness and intellectual curiosity?
>
> ☐ Am I willing to examine my assumptions?
>
> ☐ Am I willing to entertain new ideas — both those that I encounter while reading and those that come to mind while writing?
>
> ☐ Am I willing to exert myself — for instance, to do research — to acquire information and to evaluate evidence?
>
> Skills:
>
> ☐ Can I summarize an argument accurately?
>
> ☐ Can I evaluate assumptions, evidence, and inferences?
>
> ☐ Can I present my ideas effectively — for instance, by organizing and by writing in a manner appropriate to my imagined audience?

think further about this issue (and we hope that you will), notice an interesting point about *your own* thinking: It probably isn't *linear* (moving in a straight line from *A* to *B* to *C*) but *recursive,* moving from *A* to *C* and back to *B* or starting over at *C* and then back to *A* and *B.* By zigging and zagging almost despite yourself, you'll reach a conclusion that may finally seem correct. In retrospect, it might seem obvious; *now* you can chart a nice line from *A* to *B* to *C* — but that probably wasn't at all evident at the start.

A Short Essay Calling for Critical Thinking

When reading an essay, we expect the writer to have thought carefully about the topic. We don't want to read every false start, every fuzzy thought, every ill-organized paragraph that the writer knocked off. Yes, writers make false starts, put down fuzzy thoughts, write ill-organized paragraphs; but then they revise and revise yet again, ultimately producing a readable essay that seems effortlessly written. Still — and this is our main point — writers of argumentative essays need to show readers that they have made some effort; they need to show *how* they got to their final (for the moment) views. It isn't enough for the writer to say, "I believe *X*"; rather, he or she must in effect say, "I believe *X* — and I hope you'll believe it also — because *Y* and *Z,* though attractive, just don't stand up to inquiry as well as *X* does. *Y* is superficially plausible, but . . . , and *Z,* which is an attractive alternative to *Y,* nevertheless fails because. . . ."

Notice in the following short essay — on employers using biometric devices to monitor employees' performance — that the author, Lynn Stuart Parramore, positions herself against these workplace technologies in a compelling way. As you read, think critically about how she presents her position, how she encourages readers to sympathize with her views. Ask questions about what she includes and excludes, whether she presents other perspectives amply or fairly, and what additional positions might be valid on these recent developments in the rapidly growing field of biometrics in business.

LYNN STUART PARRAMORE

Lynn Stuart Parramore is a contributing editor of AlterNet, *a frequent contributor to* Al-Jazeera America, Reuters, *and the* Huffington Post, *and a member of the editorial board of* Lapham's Quarterly. *Reprinted here is an essay published by* Al-Jazeera America *on September 18, 2015.*

Fitbits for Bosses

Imagine you've just arrived at your job with the Anywhere Bank call center. You switch on your computer and adjust the height of your chair. Then, you slide on the headset, positioning the mic in front of your lips. All that's left to do is to activate your behavior-monitoring device — the gadget hanging from your neck that tracks your tone of voice, your heart rate, and your physical movements throughout the day, sending real-time reports to your supervisor.

A scene from a dystopian movie? Nope. It's already happening in America. Welcome to the brave new world of workplace biosurveillance.

It's obvious that wearable tracking technology has gone mainstream: Just look at the explosion of smart watches and activity monitors that allow people to count steps and check their calorie intake. But this technology has simultaneously been creeping into workplaces: The military uses sensors that scan for injuries, monitor heart rate, and check hydration. More and more, professional athletes are strapping on devices that track every conceivable dimension of performance. Smart ice skates that measure a skater's jump. Clothes that measure an athlete's breathing and collect muscle data. At this year's tryouts in Indianapolis, some NFL hopefuls wore the "Adidas miCoach," a device that sends data on speed and acceleration straight to trainers' iPads. Over the objection of many athletes, coaches and team owners are keen to track off-the-field activity, too, such as sleep patterns and diet. With million-dollar players at stake, big money seems poised to trump privacy.

Now employers from industries that don't even require much physical labor are getting in on the game.

Finance is adopting sophisticated analytics to ensure business performance from high-dollar employees. Cambridge neuroscientist and former Goldman Sachs trader John Coates works with companies to figure out how monitoring biological signals can lead to trading success; his research focuses on measuring hormones that increase confidence and other desirable states as well as those that produce negative, stressful states. In a report for Bloomberg, Coates explained that he is working with "three or four hedge funds" to apply an "early-warning system" that would alert supervisors when traders are getting into the hormonal danger zone. He calls this process "human optimization."

People who do the most basic, underpaid work in our society are increasingly subject to physical monitoring, too — and it extends far beyond the ubiquitous urine test. Bank of America has started using smart badges that monitor the voice and behavior patterns of call-center workers, partnering with the creepily named Humanyze, a company specializing in "people analytics." Humanyze is the brainchild of the MIT Media Lab, the fancy research institute at the Massachusetts Institute of Technology dedicated to the "betterment of humanity," which, incidentally, receives a quarter of its funding from taxpayers. Humanyze concocted a computer dashboard complete with graphs and pie charts that can display the location of employees (Were you hanging out in the lounge today?) and their "social context" (Do you spend a lot of time alone?).

Humanyze founder Ben Waber points out that companies already spend enormous resources collecting analytics on their customers. Why not their employees?

A growing number of workers are being monitored by GPS, often installed on their smartphones. In the U.S. the Supreme Court ruled that law enforcement officials need a warrant to use GPS devices to track a suspect. But employers don't worry over such formalities in keeping tabs on employees, especially those who are mobile, such as truck drivers. A *Washington Post* report on GPS surveillance noted a 2012 study by the research firm Aberdeen Group, which showed that 62 percent of "field employees" — those who regularly perform duties away from the office — are tracked this way. In May, a California woman filed a lawsuit against her former employer, Intermex Wire Transfer, for forcing her to install a tracking app on her phone, which she was required to keep on 24/7. She described feeling like a prisoner wearing an ankle bracelet. After removing the app, the woman was fired.

Sensitive to Big Brother accusations, the biosurveillance industry is trying to keep testing and tool evaluations under the radar. Proponents of the technology point to its potential to improve health conditions in the workplace and enhance public safety. Wouldn't it be better, they argue, if nuclear power plant operators, airline pilots, and oil rig operatives had their physical state closely monitored on the job?

Young Americans nurtured in a digital world where their behavior is relentlessly collected and monitored by advertisers may shrug at an employer's demands for a biosurveillance badge. In a world of insecure employment, what choice do they have, anyway? Despite the revelations of alarming National Security Agency spying and increased government and corporate surveillance since 9/11, the young haven't had much experience yet with what's at stake for them personally. What could possibly go wrong?

A lot: Surveillance has a way of dehumanizing workers. It prevents us from experimenting and exercising our creativity on the job because it tends to uphold the status quo and hold back change. Surveillance makes everyone seem suspicious, creating perceptions and expectations of dishonesty. It makes us feel manipulated. Some researchers have found that increased monitoring actually decreases productivity.

Philosopher and social theorist Michel Foucault observed that the relationship between the watcher and the watched is mostly about power. The power of the observer is enhanced, while the person observed feels more powerless. When an employer or manager interprets our personal data, she gets to make categorical judgments about us and determine how to predict our behavior.

What if she uses the information to discriminate? Coerce? Selectively apply the rules?

The data she uses to make her judgments may not even be telling the truth: Researchers have warned that big data can produce big errors. People looking at numbers tend to use them to confirm their own biases, cherry-picking the information that supports their beliefs and ditching the rest. And since algorithms are constructed by human beings, they are not immune to human biases, either. A consumer might be labeled "unlikely to pay a credit card bill" because of an ethnic name, thus promulgating a harmful stereotype.

As Americans, we like to tell ourselves that we value freedom and undue interference from authority. But when we are subjected to surveillance, we feel disempowered and disrespected. We may be more inclined to accept the government getting involved because of fears about terrorism — but when it comes to surveillance on the job, our tendency to object may be chilled by weakened worker protections and increased employment insecurity.

Instead of producing an efficient and productive workplace, biosurveillance may instead deliver troops of distracted, apathetic employees who feel loss of control and decreased job satisfaction. Instead of feeling like part of a team, surveilled workers may develop an us-versus-them mentality and look for opportunities to thwart the monitoring schemes of Big Boss.

Perhaps what we really need is biosurveillance from the bottom up — members of Congress and CEOs could don devices that could, say, detect when they are lying or how their hormones are behaving. Colorful PowerPoints could display the results of data collection on public billboards for the masses to pore over. In the name of safety and efficiency, maybe we ought to ensure that those whose behavior can do society the most harm do not escape the panopticon.

OVERALL VIEW OF THE ESSAY

Before we comment in detail on Parramore's essay, we need to say that in terms of the length of some of its paragraphs, it isn't necessarily a model for you to imitate. Material in print or online news sources is typically presented in very short paragraphs (notice Parramore's one-sentence-long paragraph 4). This is partly because people read it while eating breakfast or commuting to work, and in the case of print newspapers partly because the columns are narrow (a paragraph of only two or three sentences may still be an inch or two deep).

The title, "Fitbits for Bosses," is provocative, captures readers' attention, and leaves them with a sense of where Parramore's argument is heading.

Paragraph 1 compels readers by asking them to imagine an ordinary day at work, presenting the routine activities of getting work under way — turning on the computer, adjusting the chair — before throwing in the "behavior-monitoring device" almost as an afterthought, as if to shock us with the possibility that such devices could become routine.

Paragraph 2 presses the idea of invasion of privacy, almost aggressively, by using words like *dystopian* and a reference to a science fiction novel ("brave new world") whose title has become a shorthand for technological intrusions into individuals' lives.

Paragraph 3 presents as "obvious" the fact that self-monitoring technology has gone mainstream. (One of the authors of this book just purchased a new mobile device that came preinstalled with an application that records the number of steps and miles the user walks in a day. Going deeper into the menu, it includes functions for recording everything from nutrient intake to sexual activity.) The writer is clearly drawing on readers' familiarity with these technologies. Then she presents the portent of these devices "creeping" into the workplace, first by showing how such technologies have already been used in military applications and in businesses like professional sports. "So what?" we might think, but Parramore is about tell us.

Paragraph 4 is a single-sentence paragraph, turning the essay's focus from two specialized fields to the everyday jobs that millions of people hold. Notice how the language ("getting in on the game") reveals Parramore's position that this trend signals something new and troubling.

Paragraph 5 turns to the finance industry to show how some industries are beginning to monitor not just employee health but hormonal flows that have been correlated to emotional and psychological states. The dystopian theme is extended here as these technologies are presented as reaching into new realms where independent action and decision-making occur. Phrases like "human optimization" and references to an "early warning system" that would "alert supervisors" hint at potential limitations on human independence and deeper control of employees by managers.

Paragraph 6 focuses on Bank of America's partnership with Humanyze and shows more ways in which biosurveillance technologies could be used to monitor employees. Parramore is enhancing her argument through careful language use. In fact, her position is arguably coming most strongly through tone. What language cues indicate her position on these technologies? What specific words and phrases does she use ironically or sardonically?

Paragraph 7 quotes Humanyze's founder, Ben Waber, who rationally states that companies spend enormous amounts of money tracking consumers, so why not track employees too?

But Parramore presents this statement as anything but appealing; instead, it comes across as a kind of dangerous rationality.

Paragraph 8 starts out by noting that the government doesn't permit law enforcement to do what employers regularly do in various industries. It cites a study showing how widespread the use of these devices is, and a case in which a woman lost her job by refusing to be monitored.

Paragraph 9 provides the defense offered by the industries that create these technologies, pointing out that some highly sensitive jobs such as power plant operator and airline pilot require the closest scrutiny of individuals' physical conditions.

Paragraph 10 mentions "Young Americans," raised in a digital world, who may just "shrug" at the latest developments in surveillance technology without realizing the implications to them personally. "What could go wrong?" Parramore asks.

Paragraph 11 answers that question, first with the word *dehumanizing*, then by claiming that surveillance dampens creativity and change, encourages suspicion, presumes dishonesty, and hurts productivity.

Paragraph 12 brings into the mix a philosopher, Michel Foucault — one of the twentieth century's most recognized theorists of power. Foucault leads Parramore to wonder about what kinds of power may be exercised by using the information gained from surveillance technology.

Paragraph 13 considers hypothetical scenarios in which a manager might be able to discriminate or coerce an employee by using collected data. Parramore seems to be asking how employees are protected from such strict oversight.

Paragraph 14 reminds readers that measurements are just measurements, prone to error and to biases that could lead to unfair or discriminatory uses of data.

Paragraph 15 presents a summary of the potentially harmful outcomes of widespread implementation of biometric surveillance of employees, pointing especially to decreased job satisfaction and an "us-versus-them" mentality among employees and employers.

Paragraph 16 drives home the author's point by offering a reversal of the expected order of surveillance arrangements. What if, Parramore suggests, the public demanded surveillance of those in power, especially since those in important managerial positions are presumably the ones whose behaviors and actions might impact the most people? The essay finishes with a suggestion that it is those in power who most need to be watched "in the name of safety and efficiency" — ostensibly the terms used to justify the practice as applied to workers.

Topics for Critical Thinking and Writing

1. Do you think biometric measurement by employers is ever justified, or do the privacy and security of one's own body always trump the concerns of employers? Why, or why not?

2. If your teachers or parents could monitor the time you spent, and how you felt, while doing homework and studying, what benefits and drawbacks might result? What types of personal

monitoring are already in place (or possible) in schools and homes, and are these different from biometric surveillance?

3. Do you think Lynn Parramore fairly portrays the founder of Humanyze and others who see potential in the possibilities for biometric monitoring? Why, or why not? In what other ways might biometric measurements help employees and employers?

4. List some examples of Parramore's use of language, word choice, and phrasing that would influence readers to be suspicious of biometric monitoring. How does this language make the essay more or less effective or convincing?

5. In what way does Parramore's recommendation in the final paragraph support or contradict her argument about individuals' basic rights to privacy?

Examining Assumptions

In Chapter 3, we will discuss **assumptions** in some detail, but here we introduce the topic by emphasizing the importance of *identifying* and *examining* assumptions—those you'll encounter in the writings of others and those you'll rely on in your own essays.

With this in mind, let's again consider some of the assumptions suggested in this chapter's earlier readings. The student who wrote about Stephen Cavanaugh's case pointed out that Nebraska prison officials simply did not see the Church of the Flying Spaghetti Monster as a real religion. Their assumption was that some religions can be more or less "real" than others or can make more sense than others. Assumptions may be *explicit* or *implicit*, stated or unstated. In this case, the prison officials were forthright about their assumptions in their stated claim about the Church, perhaps believing their point was obvious to anyone who thought seriously about the idea of a Flying Spaghetti Monster. It didn't occur to them to consider that even major and mainstream religions honor stories, claims, and rituals that seem absurd to others.

An implicit assumption is one that is not stated but, rather, is taken for granted. It works like an underlying belief that structures an argument. In Lynn Stuart Parramore's essay on workplace biometric devices, the unstated assumption is that these sorts of technology in the workplace represent a kind of evil "big brother" intent on subduing and exploiting employees with newer and newer forms of invasion of privacy. Parramore's assumption, while not stated directly, is evident in her choice of language, as we've pointed out above. Another way to discern her assumption is by looking at the scenarios and selections of examples she chooses. For example, in imagining a company that would seek to know how much time an employee spends in the lounge area or alone, Parramore sees only obsessive monitoring of employees for the purposes of regulating their time. But what if these technologies could enable a company to discover that productivity or worker satisfaction increases in proportion to the amount of time employees spend collaborating in the lounge? Maybe workplace conditions would improve instead of deteriorating (a bigger lounge, more comfortable chairs), and maybe more efforts would be made for team-building and improving interpersonal employee relations.

Consider now two of the assumptions involved in the Kim Davis case. Thanks to the clustering exercise (p. 6), these and other assumptions are already on display. Perhaps the most important and fundamental assumption Davis and her supporters made is this:

> Where private religious beliefs conflict with duly enacted laws, the former should prevail.

This assumption is widely held in our society; it is by no means unique to Davis and her supporters. Opponents, however, probably assumed a very different but equally fundamental proposition:

> Private religious practices and beliefs must yield to the demands of laws guaranteeing citizens equal rights.

Obviously, these two assumptions are opposed to each other, and neither side can prevail so long as the key assumption of the other side is ignored.

Assumptions can be powerful sources of ideas and opinions, and understanding our own and others' assumptions is a major part of critical thinking. Assumptions about race, class, disability, sex, and gender are among the most powerful sources of social inequality. The following essay arguing that women should be permitted to serve in combat roles in the military was published in 2012, well before the Department of Defense lifted the ban on women in combat roles in the armed forces in 2013. More recently, Defense Secretary Ashton Carter further lifted exclusions pertaining to women by granting them access to serve in all capacities in combat, including in elite special forces units. Following that development, General Lori J. Robinson made history as the first female combatant commander when she was appointed leader of the North American Aerospace Defense Command and U.S. Northern Command in Colorado in May 2016. Still, we reprint McGregor's essay because it compels readers to consider some of their assumptions about women (and men). Topics for discussion appear after the essay.

JENA McGREGOR

Jena McGregor, a graduate of the University of Georgia, is a freelance writer and a daily columnist for the Washington Post. *This article was published on May 25, 2012.*

Military Women in Combat: Why Making It Official Matters

It's been a big couple of weeks for women in the military.

Last week, female soldiers began formally moving into jobs in previously all-male battalions, a program that will later go Army-wide. The move is a result of rule changes following a February report that opened some 14,000 new positions to women in critical jobs much closer to the front lines. However, some 250,000 combat jobs still remain officially closed to them.

The same week, Rep. Loretta Sanchez (D, Calif.) and Sen. Kirsten Gillibrand (D, N.Y.) introduced legislation in both houses of Congress that would encourage the "repeal of the Ground Combat Exclusion policy" for women in the armed forces. Then this Wednesday, two female U.S. Army reservists filed a lawsuit that seeks to overturn the remaining restrictions on women in combat, saying they limit "their current and future earnings, their potential for promotion and advancement, and their future retirement benefits." (A Pentagon spokesperson told Bloomberg News that Defense Secretary Leon Panetta "is strongly committed to examining the expansion of roles for women in the U.S. military, as evidenced by the recent step of opening up thousands of more assignments to women.")

One of the arguments behind both the lawsuit and the new legislation is that the remaining restrictions hurt women's opportunities for advancement. Advocates for women in the military say that even if women like

Gen. Ann Dunwoody have reached four-star general status, she and women like her without official frontline combat experience apparently haven't been considered for the military's very highest posts. "If women remain restricted to combat service and combat service support specialties, we will not see a woman as Commandant of the Marine Corps, or CENTCOM commander, or Chairman of the Joint Chiefs of Staff," writes Greg Jacob, policy director for the Service Women's Action Network. "Thus women in the military are being held back simply because they are women. Such an idea is not only completely at odds with military ethics, but is distinctly un-American."

Women have been temporarily "attached" to battalions for the last decade; still, allowing women to formally serve in combat operations could help to break down the so-called brass ceiling.

Another way to break down the ceiling would be to consider talented women for top military leadership positions, whether or not they've officially held certain combat posts. Presidents have chosen less-senior officers for Joint Chiefs roles, which are technically staff jobs, wrote Laura Conley and Lawrence Korb, a former assistant defense secretary in the Reagan administration and a senior fellow at the Center for American Progress, in the *Armed Forces Journal* last year. They argue that putting a woman on the Joint Chiefs would help the military grapple with rising sexual harassment issues, bring nontraditional expertise (which women have developed because of some of their role exclusions) at a time when that's increasingly critical, and send the signal that the military is not only open to women, but puts no barriers in their way.

Yes, putting women in combat roles beyond those that have been recently formalized would require many adjustments, both logistical and psychological, for the military and for its male troops. There are plenty of women who may not be interested in these jobs, or who do not meet the physical demands required of them. And gradual change may be prudent. The recent openings are a start; Army Chief of Staff Ray Odierno's acknowledgment last week that if women are allowed into infantry, they will at some point probably go through Ranger School, is encouraging.

But at a time when experience like the infantry is reportedly crucial for getting top posts, it's easy to see how official and sizable policy changes are needed in order to create a system that lets talented women advance to the military's highest echelons. In any field where there are real or perceived limitations for women's advancement, it's that much harder to attract the best and brightest. Indeed, the Military Leadership Diversity Commission recommended last March that the services end combat exclusion policies for women, along with other "barriers and inconsistencies, to create a level playing field for all qualified service members." As the commission chairman, Retired Air Force Gen. Lester L. Lyles, told the American Forces Press Service at the time, "we know that [the exclusion] hinders women from promotion."

For the military to achieve the diverse workforce it seeks, interested and capable women should either not face exclusions, or the culture of the armed forces needs to change so that women without that particular experience can still reach the very top. Both changes may be difficult, but the latter is extraordinarily so. Ending the restrictions is the shortest route to giving the military the best pool of talent possible and the most diverse viewpoints for leading it.

Topics for Critical Thinking and Writing

1. How would you characterize Jena McGregor's tone (her manner)? Is it thoughtful? Pushy? Identify passages that support your view.

2. Explain the term *brass ceiling* (para. 5).

3. One argument *against* sending women onto an actual battlefield, as infantry or as members of a tank crew, is that if they're captured they might be gang-raped. In your view, how significant is this argument? Explain your response.

4. Here is a second argument against sending women into direct combat: Speaking generally, women do not have the upper-body strength that men have, and a female soldier (again, speaking generally, not about a particular individual) would thus be less able to pull a wounded companion out of a burning tank or off a battlefield. To put the matter differently: Male soldiers might feel that they couldn't count on their female comrades in a time of need. What is your reply?

5. In her final paragraph, McGregor suggests that if the armed forces were to change their policy and not require battlefield experience for the very highest jobs, the military would

achieve diversity at the top and women would have an opportunity for top pay. What are your thoughts? For instance, is the idea that the top officers should have experienced hand-to-hand combat out of date, romantic, hopelessly macho, or irrelevant to modern warfare? Explain.

6. What do you make of the following question? Since women are now permitted to serve in all military combat positions, should all women, like all men, have to register for Selective Service and be subject to the military draft, if one were needed? Construct an argument to defend your position on this question.

Four Exercises in Critical Thinking

As you draft essays for one or more of the assignments, consider typing your notes in a Google document or in Microsoft OneNote, or using another collaborative application or service (perhaps offered free by your school), so that you can easily share your thoughts and writing on the topic. As always, submit and complete assignments in the way that your instructor directs. However, remember that services such as Google and OneNote can be good places to maintain copies of your notes and essays for later consultation.

1. Think further about the issues of privacy and surveillance raised by Lynn Parramore's essay. Consider several different kinds of work, types of employers, and the various types of employee monitoring that do or may occur. Jot down pros and cons, and then write a balanced dialogue between two imagined speakers who hold opposing views on the issue. You'll doubtless have to revise your dialogue several times, and in revising your drafts you'll likely come up with further ideas. Present *both* sides as strongly as possible. (You may want to give the two speakers distinct characters; for instance, one may be an employer seeking to introduce a new technology, and the other may be an employee intent on protecting his privacy and freedom. Alternatively, one could be an employee looking forward to a new "healthy workplace" initiative using biometrics, and the other could be a colleague suspicious of the new program.)

2. Choose one of the following topics, and write down all the pro and con arguments you can think of in, say, ten minutes. Then, at least an hour or two later, return to your notes and see whether you can add to them. Finally, as in Exercise 1, write a balanced dialogue, presenting each idea as strongly as possible. (If none of these topics interests you, ask your instructor about the possibility of choosing a topic of your own.) Suggested topics:
   a. Colleges with large athletic programs should pay student athletes a salary or stipend.
   b. Bicyclists and motorcyclists should be required by law to wear helmets.
   c. High school teachers should have the right to carry concealed firearms in schools.
   d. Smoking should be prohibited on all college campuses, including in all buildings *and* outdoors.
   e. College students should have the right to request alternative assignments from their professors if class material is offensive or traumatic.

    f.   Students should have the right to drop out of school at any age.

    g. Sororities and fraternities should be coeducational (allowing both males and females).

    h. The government should tax sugary foods and drinks in order to reduce obesity.

3. In April 2012, Williams College in Williamstown, Massachusetts, hosted a lecture and film screening of work by Jiz Lee, described in campus advertisements as a "genderqueer porn star." After inviting the adult entertainer to campus, the college came under fire by some students and members of the public (especially after the story was reported by national media). Opponents questioned the appropriateness and academic value of the event, which was brought to campus by the Mike Dively Committee, an endowment established to help "develop understanding of human sexuality and sexual orientation and their impact on culture." Proponents argued that (1) pornography is a subject that deserves critical analysis and commentary; (2) the Dively series is intended to create conversations about sexuality and sexual orientation in society and culture; and (3) treating any potential subject in an academic setting under the circumstances of the program is appropriate. What are your views? Should adult film stars ever be invited to college campuses? Should pornography constitute a subject of analysis on campus? Why, or why not?

Imagine you're a student member of the campus programming board, and the Gender and Sexuality Program comes to your committee seeking funds to invite a female former adult film star to campus to lecture on "The Reality of Pornography." Faculty and student sponsors have assured your committee that the visit by the actress in question is part of an effort to educate students and the public about the adult film industry and its impact on popular culture. Images and short film clips may be shown. Pose as many questions as you can about the potential benefits and risks of approving this invitation. How would you vote, and why? (If you can find a peer who has an opposing view, construct a debate on the issue.)

4. In 1985, the U.S. Congress passed the National Minimum Drinking Age Act, mandating that all states implement and enforce raising the minimum drinking age from eighteen to twenty-one years. Through this legislation, the United States became one of a handful of developed countries to have such a high drinking age. In 2009, John McCardell, president of Middlebury College in Vermont, wrote a declaration signed by 135 college presidents supporting returning the drinking age to eighteen. McCardell's organization, Choose Responsibly, says that people age eighteen to twenty should be treated as the adults they are — for example, in terms of voting, serving on juries and in the military, or buying legal weapons. The organization encourages educational programs and awareness efforts that would introduce alcohol-related issues to young college students and demystify and discourage problem drinking. Such a move is opposed by Mothers Against Drunk Drivers (MADD), whose members argue that raising the drinking age to twenty-one has curbed traffic accidents and fatalities caused by drunk driving. Opponents to lowering the drinking age also claim that it would introduce alcohol to even younger people, as many eighteen-year-olds would inevitably interact in social situations with underage peers.

Critical Reading: Getting Started

Some books are to be tasted, others to be swallowed, and some few to be chewed and digested.
— FRANCIS BACON

Active Reading

In the passage that we quote above, Bacon makes two good points. One is that books are of varying worth; the second is that a taste of some books may be enough.

But even a book (or an essay) that you will chew and digest is one that you first may want to taste. How can you get a taste — that is, how can you get some sense of a piece of writing — *before* you sit down to read it carefully?

PREVIEWING

Even before reading a work, you may have some ideas about it, perhaps because you already know something about the **author**. You know, for example, that a work by Martin Luther King Jr. will probably deal with civil rights. You know, too, that it will be serious and eloquent. In contrast, if you pick up an essay by Stephen King, you'll probably expect it to be about fear, the craft of writing, or his experiences as a horror novelist. It may be about something else, but it's probable the essay will follow your expectations. For one thing, you know that King writes for a broad audience, so his essay won't be terribly difficult to understand.

In short, a reader who has knowledge of the author probably has some idea of what the subject will be and what the writing will be like, so the reader approaches it in a certain light. But even if you don't know the author, you can often discern important information about him or her by looking at biographical information provided in the text or by doing a quick Internet search. You can use this information to predict not only the essay's subject and style but also the author's approach to the topic, which helps when trying to diagnose assumptions and biases, among other things.

The **place of publication** may also reveal something about the essay in terms of its subject, style, and approach. For instance, the *National Review* is a conservative journal. If you notice that an essay on affirmative action was published in the *National Review,* you're probably safe in tentatively assuming that the essay will not endorse affirmative action. In contrast, *Ms.* magazine is a liberal publication, and an essay on affirmative action published there will probably be an endorsement. You often can learn a good deal about a journal or magazine simply by flipping through it and noticing the kinds of articles and advertisements in it.

The **title** of an essay, too, may give an idea of what to expect. Of course, a title may announce only the subject and not the author's thesis or point of view ("On Gun Control"; "Should Drugs Be Legal?"), but fairly often it will indicate the thesis too (as in "Give Children the Vote" or "We Need Campaign Finance Reform Now"). By knowing more or less what to expect, you can probably take in some of the major points even on a quick reading.

When engaging with an essay, you can also consider the role of **context** — the situational conditions in which it was written. Context can refer to the time period, geographical location, cultural climate, political environment, or any other setting for a piece of writing. Recognizing the context of any piece of writing can reveal a lot about how an author treats a subject. For example, an essay written before September 11, 2001, about how to contain global terrorism might have a less urgent approach and advocate more lenient measures than one written today. An article about transgender identity or police brutality might convey different assumptions about those topics depending on whether it was written before or after Bruce Jenner publicly became Caitlyn Jenner, for instance, or before or after the events of Ferguson, Missouri, brought the issue of race and police violence into the public's consciousness in new ways.

Anything you read exists in at least two broad contexts: the context of its *production* (where and when it was written or published) and the context of its *consumption* (where and when it is encountered and read). One thing all good critical thinkers do when considering the validity of claims and arguments is to take *both* types of context into account. This means asking questions not only about the approach, assumptions, and beliefs that were in place when an essay was written, but also about how current events and understandings generate new issues and challenges within the subject of the essay. The state of affairs in the time and place in which that argument is made *and received* shapes the questions you might ask, the evidence you might consider, and the responses you might produce.

Notice that you can apply these previewing techniques before reading a single word of the essay. And once you have a good sense of the what, who, where, and when of an essay, you should keep them in mind while reading.

Your first reading might involve another previewing technique, **skimming**. Sometimes, you can find the **thesis** (the main point or major claim) of an essay by looking at the first paragraph. Other times, especially if the paragraphs are short, you can locate the thesis within the first several paragraphs. Depending on what you discover while skimming, you can speed up or slow down your reading as needed while you locate the thesis and get a sense of how the argument for it is structured. If the essay has sections, pay attention to *headings* and *subheadings.* Look for key expressions that indicate an author's conclusive statements, such as "Finally, then, it is time that we . . ." or "Given this evidence, it is clear that. . . ." These kinds of sentences frequently appear at the beginnings or endings of paragraphs and sections. Final paragraphs are particularly important because they often summarize the argument and restate the thesis.

By previewing and skimming effectively, you can quickly ascertain quite a bit of information about an article or essay. You can detect the author's claims and methods, see the evidence he or she uses (experience, statistics, quotations, etc.), ascertain the tone and difficulty level, and determine whether the piece of writing offers useful ideas for you. This strategy works well if you're researching a topic and need to review many essays — you can read efficiently to find those that are most important or relevant to you, or those that offer different perspectives. Of course, if you do find an essay to be compelling during previewing, you can begin "chewing and digesting," as Francis Bacon put it — reading more closely and carefully (or else putting it aside for later when you can give it more time).

CALL OUT: CRITICAL READING TIP   Instead of imagining previewing and close reading as two separate stages to be completed consecutively, think of previewing as an activity that might at any time develop into close reading.

A SHORT ESSAY FOR PREVIEWING PRACTICE

Before skimming the following essay, apply the previewing techniques discussed above, and complete the Thinking Critically: Previewing activity on page 41.

SANJAY GUPTA

Dr. Sanjay Gupta (b. 1969) is a neurosurgeon and multiple Emmy award–winning television personality. As a leading public health expert, he has appeared widely on television, including the Oprah Winfrey Show, *the* Late Show with David Letterman, *the* Jon Stewart Show, *and* 60 Minutes. *He is most well known as CNN's chief medical correspondent. In 2011,* Forbes *magazine named him one of the ten most influential celebrities in America. The essay reprinted below originally appeared on CNN.com in August 2013.*

Why I Changed My Mind on Weed

Over the last year, I have been working on a new documentary called "Weed." The title "Weed" may sound cavalier, but the content is not.

I traveled around the world to interview medical leaders, experts, growers and patients. I spoke candidly to them, asking tough questions. What I found was stunning.

Long before I began this project, I had steadily reviewed the scientific literature on medical marijuana from the United States and thought it was fairly unimpressive. Reading these papers five years ago, it was hard to make a case for medicinal marijuana. I even wrote about this in a *Time* magazine article, back in 2009, titled "Why I Would Vote No on Pot."

Well, I am here to apologize.

I apologize because I didn't look hard 5 enough, until now. I didn't look far enough. I didn't review papers from smaller labs in other countries doing some remarkable research, and I was too dismissive of the loud chorus of legitimate patients whose symptoms improved on cannabis.

Instead, I lumped them with the high-visibility malingerers, just looking to get high. I mistakenly believed the Drug Enforcement Agency listed marijuana as a Schedule 1 substance because of sound scientific proof. Surely, they must have quality reasoning as to why marijuana is in the category of the most dangerous drugs that have "no accepted medicinal use and a high potential for abuse."

They didn't have the science to support that claim, and I now know that when it comes to marijuana neither of those things are true. It doesn't have a high potential for abuse, and there are very legitimate medical applications. In fact, sometimes marijuana is the only thing that works. Take the case of Charlotte Figi, whom I met in Colorado. She started having seizures soon after birth. By age 3, she was having 300 a week, despite being on 7 different medications. Medical marijuana has calmed her brain, limiting her seizures to 2 or 3 per month.

I have seen more patients like Charlotte first hand, spent time with them and come to the realization that it is irresponsible not to provide the best care we can as a medical community, care that could involve marijuana.

We have been terribly and systematically misled for nearly 70 years in the United States, and I apologize for my own role in that.

I hope this article and upcoming documentary will help set the record straight. [10]

On August 14, 1970, the Assistant Secretary of Health, Dr. Roger O. Egeberg, wrote a letter recommending the plant, marijuana, be classified as a Schedule 1 substance, and it has remained that way for nearly 45 years. My research started with a careful reading of that decades-old letter. What I found was unsettling. Egeberg had carefully chosen his words:

"Since there is still a considerable void in our knowledge of the plant and effects of the active drug contained in it, our recommendation is that marijuana be retained within Schedule 1 at least until the completion of certain studies now under way to resolve the issue."

Not because of sound science, but because of its absence, marijuana was classified as a Schedule 1 substance. Again, the year was 1970. Egeberg mentions studies that are under way, but many were never completed. As my investigation continued, however, I realized Egeberg did in fact have important research already available to him, some of it from more than 25 years earlier.

HIGH RISK OF ABUSE

In 1944, New York mayor Fiorello LaGuardia commissioned research to be performed by the New York Academy of Science. Among their conclusions: they found marijuana did not lead to significant addiction in the medical sense of the word. They also did not find any evidence marijuana led to morphine, heroin or cocaine addiction.

We now know that while estimates vary, [15] marijuana leads to dependence in around 9 to 10% of its adult users. By comparison, cocaine, a Schedule 2 substance "with less abuse potential than Schedule 1 drugs," hooks 20% of those who use it. Around 25% of heroin users become addicted.

The worst is tobacco, where the number is closer to 30% of smokers, many of whom go on to die because of their addiction.

There is clear evidence that in some people marijuana use can lead to withdrawal symptoms, including insomnia, anxiety and nausea. Even considering this, it is hard to make a case that it has a high potential for abuse. The physical symptoms of marijuana addiction are nothing like those of the other drugs I've mentioned. I have seen the withdrawal from alcohol, and it can be life threatening.

I do want to mention a concern that I think about as a father. Young, developing brains are likely more susceptible to harm from marijuana than adult brains. Some recent studies suggest that regular use in teenage years leads to a permanent decrease in IQ. Other research hints at a possible heightened risk of developing psychosis.

Much in the same way I wouldn't let my own children drink alcohol, I wouldn't permit marijuana until they are adults. If they are adamant about trying marijuana, I will urge them to wait until they're in their mid-20s, when their brains are fully developed.

MEDICAL BENEFIT

While investigating, I realized something else quite important. Medical marijuana is not new, and the medical community has been writing about it for a long time. There were in fact hundreds of journal articles, mostly documenting the benefits. Most of those papers, however, were written between the years 1840 and 1930. The papers described the use of medical marijuana to treat "neuralgia, convulsive disorders, emaciation," among other things.

A search through the U.S. National Library of Medicine this past year pulled up nearly 20,000 more recent papers. But the majority were research into the harm of marijuana, such as "Bad trip due to anticholinergic effect of cannabis," or "Cannabis induced pancreatitis" and "Marijuana use and risk of lung cancer."

In my quick running of the numbers, I calculated about 6% of the current U.S. marijuana studies investigate the benefits of medical marijuana. The rest are designed to investigate harm. That imbalance paints a highly distorted picture.

THE CHALLENGES OF MARIJUANA RESEARCH

To do studies on marijuana in the United States today, you need two important things.

First of all, you need marijuana. And marijuana is illegal. You see the problem. Scientists can get research marijuana from a special farm in Mississippi, which is astonishingly located in the middle of the Ole Miss campus, but it is challenging. When I visited this year, there was no marijuana being grown.

The second thing you need is approval, and the scientists I interviewed kept reminding me how tedious that can be. While a cancer study may first be evaluated by the National Cancer Institute, or a pain study may go through the National Institute for Neurological Disorders, there is one more approval required for marijuana: NIDA, the National Institute on Drug Abuse. It is an organization that has a core mission of studying drug abuse, as opposed to benefit.

Stuck in the middle are the legitimate patients who depend on marijuana as a medicine, oftentimes as their only good option.

Keep in mind that up until 1943, marijuana was part of the United States drug pharmacopeia. One of the conditions for which it was prescribed was neuropathic pain. It is a miserable pain that's tough to treat. My own patients have described it as "lancinating, burning and a barrage of pins and needles."

While marijuana has long been documented to be effective for this awful pain, the most common medications prescribed today come from the poppy plant, including morphine, oxycodone and dilaudid.

Here is the problem. Most of these medications don't work very well for this kind of pain, and tolerance is a real problem.

Most frightening to me is that someone dies in the United States every 19 minutes from a prescription drug overdose, mostly accidental. Every 19 minutes. It is a horrifying statistic. As much as I searched, I could not find a documented case of death from marijuana overdose.

It is perhaps no surprise then that 76% of physicians recently surveyed said they would approve the use of marijuana to help ease a woman's pain from breast cancer.

When marijuana became a Schedule 1 substance, there was a request to fill a "void in our knowledge." In the United States, that has been challenging because of the infrastructure surrounding the study of an illegal substance, with a drug abuse organization at the heart of the approval process. And yet, despite the hurdles, we have made considerable progress that continues today.

Looking forward, I am especially intrigued by studies like those in Spain and Israel looking at the anti-cancer effects of marijuana and its components. I'm intrigued by the neuroprotective study by Lev Meschoulam in Israel, and research in Israel and the United States on whether the drug might help alleviate symptoms of PTSD. I promise to do my part to help, genuinely and honestly, fill the remaining void in our knowledge.

Citizens in 20 states and the District of Columbia have now voted to approve marijuana for medical applications, and more states will be making that choice soon. As for Dr. Roger Egeberg, who wrote that letter in 1970, he passed away 16 years ago.

I wonder what he would think if he were alive today.

THE "FIRST AND LAST" RULE   As noted above, authors often place main points of emphasis at the beginnings and endings of *essays*. They also place important material at the beginnings and endings of *paragraphs* and *sentences*.

When writing, you can emphasize main points by using the first and last rule. Don't bury your most important material in the middle of sentences, paragraphs, or entire papers. Make it stand out.

Consider the following observations. Select two that you find to be most important.

1. Gupta is one of the most respected voices in public health.

2. Gupta argues for the legalization of medical marijuana.

3. Gupta's article was written for CNN News in 2011.

4. Gupta rejects his previous position on medical marijuana and apologizes for his oversight.

5. The article was important because it represented a shift in approach by a leading doctor.

THINKING CRITICALLY *Previewing*

Provide the missing information for Sanjay Gupta and his essay "Why I Changed My Mind on Weed."

PREVIEWING STRATEGIES	TYPES OF QUESTIONS	ANSWERS
Author	Who is he? What expertise does he have? What credibility does he have? How difficult is the writing likely to be?	
Title	What does the title reveal about the essay's content? Does it give any clues about how the argument will take shape?	
Place of Publication	How does the place of publication help you understand the argument? What type of audiences will it be likely to target?	
Context	By placing the article in the context of its time — given trends in the conversations about or popular understandings of the subject — what can you expect about the author's position?	
Skimming	As you skim over the first several paragraphs, where do you first realize the purpose of the essay? What is Gupta's argument? What major forms of evidence does he offer?	

LaunchPad To complete this activity online, go to **macmillanhighered.com/barnetbedauohara**

Now arrange these statements in a short paragraph, using the first and last rule to emphasize the two that you selected as most important. Compare your paragraph to your classmates' paragraphs. How do they compare?

READING WITH A CAREFUL EYE: UNDERLINING, HIGHLIGHTING, ANNOTATING

Once you have a general idea of the work — not only an idea of its topic and thesis but also a sense of the way in which the thesis is argued — you can go back and start reading it carefully.

As you read, **underline** or **highlight** key passages, and make **annotations** in the margins. Because you're reading actively, or interacting with the text, you won't simply let your eye rove across the page.

- Highlight what seem to be the chief points, so that later when reviewing the essay you can easily locate the main passages.

- But don't overdo a good thing. If you find yourself highlighting most of a page, you're probably not thinking carefully enough about what the key points are.

- Similarly, your marginal annotations should be brief and selective. They will probably consist of hints or clues, comments like "doesn't follow," "good," "compare with Jones," "check this," and "really?"

- In short, in a paragraph you might highlight a key definition, and in the margin you might write "good," or "in contrast," or "?" if you think the definition is unclear or incorrect.

- With many electronic formats, you can use tools to highlight or annotate. Also consider copying and pasting passages that you would normally highlight in a Google document. Include a link to the piece, and create an RSS feed to the journal's Web site. Having your notes in an electronic format makes it easy to access and use them later.

In all these ways, you interact with the text and lay the groundwork for eventually writing your own essay on what you have read.

What you annotate will depend largely on your **purpose**. If you're reading an essay in order to see how the writer organizes an argument, you'll annotate one sort of thing. If you're reading in order to challenge the thesis, you'll annotate other things. Here is a passage from an essay entitled "On Racist Speech," with a student's rather skeptical, even aggressive, annotations. But notice that the student apparently made at least one of the annotations — "Definition of 'fighting words'" — chiefly in order to remind herself to locate where the definition of an important term appears in the essay. The essay, printed in full on page 71, is by Charles R. Lawrence III, a professor of law at Georgetown University. It originally appeared in the *Chronicle of Higher Education* (October 25, 1989), a publication read chiefly by college and university faculty members and administrators.

Example of such a policy? University officials who have formulated <u>policies</u> to respond to incidents of racial harassment have been characterized in the press as "thought police," but such policies generally do nothing more than *?* impose (sanctions) against intentional face-to-face insults. When <u>racist</u> *Example?* <u>speech</u> takes the form of <u>face-to-face insults</u>, catcalls, or other assaul- *What about sexist speech?* tive speech aimed at an individual or small group of persons, it falls directly within the "<u>fighting words</u>" exception to First Amendment *Definition of "fighting words"* protection. The Supreme Court has held that <u>words "which 'by their</u> <u>very utterance inflict</u> injury or tend to incite an immediate breach of the peace'" are not protected by the First Amendment.

If the purpose of the First Amendment is to foster the greatest amount of speech, racial insults disserve that purpose. Assaultive *Really? Probably depends on the individual.* racist speech functions as a preemptive strike. The invective is experienced as a blow, not as a <u>proffered idea,</u> and once the blow is struck, it is unlikely that a dialogue will follow. Racial insults are particu- *Why must speech always seek "to discover truth"?* larly undeserving of First Amendment protection because the perpetrator's <u>intention is not to discover truth</u> or initiate dialogue but *How does he know?* to injure the victim. <u>In most situations,</u> members of minority groups realize that they are likely to lose if they respond to epithets by fighting and are forced to remain silent and submissive.

"THIS; THEREFORE, THAT"

To arrive at a coherent thought or series of thoughts that will lead to a reasonable conclusion, a writer has to go through a good deal of preliminary effort. When we discussed heuristics in Chapter 1 (p. 17), we talked about patterns of thought that stimulate initial ideas. The path to sound conclusions involves similar thought patterns that carry forward the arguments presented in the essay:

- While these arguments are convincing, they fail to consider . . .
- While these arguments are convincing, they must also consider . . .
- These arguments, rather than being convincing, instead prove . . .
- While these authors agree, in my opinion . . .
- Although it is often true that . . .
- Consider also . . .
- What sort of audience would agree with such an argument?
- What sort of audience would be opposed?
- What are the differences in values between these two kinds of audiences?

All of these patterns can serve as heuristics or prompts — that is, they can stimulate the creation of ideas.

Moreover, for the writer to convince the reader that the conclusion is sound, the reasoning behind the conclusion must be set forth in detail, with a good deal of "This; therefore, that"; "If this, then that"; and "Others might object at this point that. . . ." The arguments in this book require more comment than President Calvin Coolidge supposedly provided when his wife, who hadn't been able to attend church one Sunday, asked him what the preacher talked about in his sermon. "Sin," Coolidge said. His wife persisted: "What did the preacher say about it?" Coolidge's response: "He was against it."

But, again, when we say that most of the arguments in this book are presented at length and require careful reading, we don't mean that they are obscure; we mean, rather, that you have to approach the sentences thoughtfully, one by one. In this vein, recall an episode from Lewis Carroll's *Through the Looking-Glass*:

"Can you do Addition?" the White Queen asked. "What's one and one and one and one and one and one and one and one and one and one?"

"I don't know," said Alice. "I lost count."

"She can't do Addition," the Red Queen said.

Alice with the Red Queen and the White Queen

It's easy enough to add one and one and one and so on, and of course Alice can do addition — but not at the pace that the White Queen sets. Fortunately, you can set your own pace in reading the cumulative thinking set forth in the essays we reprint in this book. Skimming won't work, but slow reading — and thinking about what you're reading — will.

When you first pick up an essay, you may indeed want to skim it, for some of the reasons mentioned on page 36, but sooner or later you have to settle down to read it and think about it. The effort will be worthwhile. Consider what John Locke, a seventeenth-century English philosopher, said:

> *Reading* furnishes the mind with materials of knowledge; it is *thinking* [that] makes what we read ours. We are of the ruminating kind, and it is not enough to cram ourselves with a great load of collections; unless we chew them over again they will not give us strength and nourishment.

Often students read an essay just once, supposing that to reread would be repetitious. But much can be gleaned from a second reading, as new details will likely emerge and new ideas will be generated. Roland Barthes, a twentieth-century philosopher, warned against accepting a first reading as final. Far from being repetitive, "[r]e-reading," he wrote, "*saves* the text from repetition, multiplies it in its variety and plurality." What may actually be repetitious is reading something only once and, thinking you have it pinned down, repeating it (in your writing) and thereby sticking to your first and only impression.

DEFINING TERMS AND CONCEPTS

Suppose you're reading an argument about whether a certain set of images is pornography or art. For the present purpose, let's use a famous example from 1992, when American photographer Sally Mann published *Immediate Family*, a controversial book featuring numerous images of her three children (then ages 12, 10, and 7) in various states of nakedness during their childhood on a rural Kentucky farm. Mann is considered a great photographer and artist ("America's Best Photographer," according to *Time* magazine in 2001), and *Immediate Family* is very well regarded in the art community ("one of the great photograph books of our time," according to the *New Republic*). But some critics couldn't separate the images of Mann's own naked children from the label "child pornography."

When reading, attend carefully to how terms and concepts are used for the purposes of advancing an argument. In this case, you might begin by asking, "What is *pornography*? What is *art*?" If writers and readers cannot agree on basic definitions of the terms and concepts that structure the debate, then argument is futile. And if an author doesn't share *your* definition of a term or concept, then you might challenge the premise of his or her argument. If someone were to define pornography to include *any* images of nude children, that definition would include photographs taken for any reason — medical, sociological, anthropological, scientific — and would include even the innocent photographs taken by proud parents of their children swimming, bathing, and so on. It would also apply to some of the world's great art. Most people do not seriously think the mere image of the naked body, adult or child, is pornography.

Pornography is often defined according to its intended effect on the viewer ("genital commotion," Father Harold Gardiner, S.J., called it in *Catholic Viewpoint on Censorship*). In this definition, if images are eroticized (i.e., made erotic through style or symbolism), if they invite a sexual gaze, they are pornographic. This seems to be the definition that novelist Mary Gordon applied in a 1996 critique of Sally Mann:

> Unless we believe it is ethically permissible for adults to have sex with children, we must question the ethics of an art which allows the adult who has the most power over these children — a parent, in this case a mother — to place them in a situation where they become the imagined sexual partner of adults. . . . It is inevitable that Sally Mann's photographs arouse the sexual imaginations of strangers.

But is it enough to say something is pornographic if it "arouses the sexual imagination"? No, you might contend, because there is no way to predict what will arouse people's sexual imaginations. Many kinds of images might arouse the sexual imaginations of different people. You might say in rebutting Gordon, "These are just pictures of children. Sure, they're naked in some of them, but children have been symbols of purity and innocence in art since the dawn of civilization. If some people see these images as sexual, that's their problem, not Mann's."

Writers often attempt to provide a provisional definition of important terms and concepts in their arguments. They may write, for example, "For the purposes of this argument, let's define terrorism as *X*" (a broad definition) or "According to federal law, the term 'international terrorism' means *A*, *B*, and *C*" (a technical definition). If you do this and a reader wants to challenge your ideas, he must argue on your terms or else offer a different definition.

So that we are consistent with our own recommendations, allow us to define the difference between a "term" and a "concept." A rule of thumb is that a *term* is more concrete and fixed than a *concept*. You may be able to find an authoritative source (like a federal law or an official policy) to help define a *term*. A *concept* is more open-ended and

> **A RULE FOR WRITERS**
> Be alert to how terms and concepts are defined both in your source material and in your own writing. Are your terms broadly, narrowly, or technically construed?

THINKING CRITICALLY *Defining Terms and Concepts*

Examine each claim, and note the terms and concepts used. Provide a terminological (strict, codified by an authoritative source) or a conceptual (loose, self-generated) definition for each. What sources did you use? Compare your answers to those of your peers to see if they are similar or different.

STATEMENT	DEFINITION	TYPE OF DEFINITION
Video games are **addictive.**		
Poor people will suffer most from the new law.		
The **epidemic of obesity** needs to be solved.		
We must send troops to protect **the national interest**.		
The Internet has ushered in a new age of **progress**.		

🔲 LaunchPad   To complete this activity online, go to **macmillanhighered.com/barnetbedauohara**

may have a generally agreed-upon definition, but rarely a strict or unchanging one. Concepts can be abstract but can also function powerfully in argumentation; love, justice, morality, psyche, health, freedom, bravery, obscenity, masculinity — these are all concepts. You may look up such words in the dictionary for general definitions, but the source won't say much about how to apply the concepts.

Since you cannot assume that everyone has a shared understanding of concepts you may be using, it's prudent for the purposes of effective writing to define them. You may find a useful definition of a concept given by an authoritative person, such as an expert in a field, as in "Stephen Hawking defines time as. . . ." You might cite a respected authority, as in "Mahatma Gandhi defines love as. . . ." Alternatively, you can combine several views and insert your own provisional definition. See "Thinking Critically: Defining Terms and Concepts" for an exercise.

Summarizing and Paraphrasing

After a first reading, perhaps the best approach to a fairly difficult essay is to reread it and simultaneously take notes on a sheet of paper, summarizing each paragraph in a sentence or two. Writing a summary will help you to:

- understand the contents and
- see the strengths and weaknesses of the piece.

Don't confuse a summary with a paraphrase. A paraphrase is a word-by-word or phrase-by-phrase rewording of a text, a sort of translation of the author's language into your own. A paraphrase is therefore as long as the original or even longer; a summary is much shorter. An entire essay, even a whole book, may be summarized in a page, in a paragraph, even in a sentence. Obviously, the summary will leave out most details, but it will accurately state the essential thesis or claim of the original.

Why would anyone summarize, and why would anyone paraphrase? Because, as we've already said, these two activities — in different ways — offer a way to introduce other authors' ideas into your arguments in a way that readers can follow. You may do this for a number of reasons. Summaries and paraphrases can accomplish the following:

- **validate** the basis of your argument by providing an instance in which someone else wrote about the same topic
- **clarify** in short order the complex ideas contained in another author's work
- **support** your argument by showing readers where someone else "got it right" (corroborating your ideas) or "got it wrong" (countering your ideas, but giving you a chance to refute that position in favor of your own)
- **lend authority** to your voice by showing readers that you have considered the topic carefully by consulting other sources
- **help you build new ideas** from existing ideas on the topic, enabling you to insert your voice into an ongoing debate made evident by the summary or paraphrase

When you summarize, you're standing back, saying briefly what the whole adds up to; you're seeing the forest, as the saying goes, not the individual trees. **When you paraphrase**, you're inching through the forest, scrutinizing each tree—finding a synonym for almost every word in the original in an effort to ensure you know exactly what the original is saying. (*Caution:* Do not incorporate a summary or a paraphrase into your own essay without acknowledging the source and stating that you are summarizing or paraphrasing.)

Let's examine the distinction between summary and paraphrase in connection with the first two paragraphs of Paul Goodman's essay "A Proposal to Abolish Grading," excerpted from Goodman's book *Compulsory Miseducation and the Community of Scholars* (1966).

> Let half a dozen of the prestigious universities—Chicago, Stanford, the Ivy League— abolish grading, and use testing only and entirely for pedagogic purposes as teachers see fit.
>
> Anyone who knows the frantic temper of the present schools will understand the transvaluation of values that would be effected by this modest innovation. For most of the students, the competitive grade has come to be the essence. The naive teacher points to the beauty of the subject and the ingenuity of the research; the shrewd student asks if he is responsible for that on the final exam.

A **summary** of these two paragraphs might read like this:

> If some top universities used tests only to help students to learn and not for grades, students would stop worrying about whether they got an A, B or C and might begin to share the teacher's interest in the beauty of the subject.

Notice that the summary doesn't convey Goodman's style or voice (e.g., the wry tone in his pointed contrast between "the naive teacher" and "the shrewd student"). That is not the purpose of summary.

Now for a **paraphrase**. Suppose you're not sure what Goodman is getting at, maybe because you're uncertain about the meanings of some words (e.g., *pedagogic* and *transvaluation*), or else you just want to make sure you understand the point. In such a case, you may want to move slowly through the sentences, restating them in your own words. You might turn Goodman's "pedagogic purposes" into "goals in teaching," "attempts to help students to learn," or something else. Here is a paraphrase—not a summary, but a rewording—of Goodman's paragraphs:

> Suppose some of the top universities—such as Chicago, Stanford, Harvard, Yale, and others in the Ivy League—stopped using grades and instead used tests only in order to help students to learn.
>
> Everyone who is aware of the rat race in schools today will understand the enormous shift in values about learning that would come about by this small change. At present, idealistic instructors talk about how beautiful their subjects are, but smart students know that grades are what count. They only want to know if it will be on the exam.

In short, you may decide to paraphrase an important text if you want the reader to see the passage itself but you know that the full passage will be puzzling. In this situation, you offer help, *paraphrasing* before making your own point about the author's claim.

A second good reason to offer a paraphrase is if there is substantial disagreement about what the text says. The Second Amendment to the U.S. Constitution is a good example of this sort of text:

> A well regulated Militia being necessary to the security of a free State, the right of the people to keep and bear Arms shall not be infringed.

Exactly what, one might ask, is a "Militia"? What does it mean for a militia to be "well regulated"? And does "the people" mean each individual or the citizenry as a unified group? After all, elsewhere in the document, where the Constitution speaks of individuals, it speaks of a "man" or a "person," not "the people." To speak of "the people" is to use a term (some argue) that sounds like a reference to a unified group — perhaps the citizens of each of the thirteen states — rather than a reference to individuals. However, if Congress did mean a unified group rather than individuals, why didn't it say, "Congress shall not prohibit the states from organizing militias"?

Gun control supporters marching in 2013 at the Washington Monument in Washington, D.C.

Bill Clark/Getty Images

In fact, thousands of pages have been written about this sentence, and if you're going to talk about it, you certainly have to let readers know exactly how you interpret each word. In short, you almost surely will paraphrase the sentence, going word by word, giving readers your own sense of what each word or phrase means. Here is one possible paraphrase:

> Because an independent society needs the protection of an armed force if it is to remain free, the government may not limit the right of the individuals (who may someday form the militia needed to keep the society free) to possess weapons.

In this interpretation, the Constitution grants individuals the right to possess weapons, and that is that.

Other students of the Constitution, however, offer very different paraphrases, usually along these lines:

> Because each state that is now part of the United States may need to protect its freedom (from the new national government), the national government may not infringe on the right of each state to form its own disciplined militia.

This paraphrase says that the federal government may not prevent each state from having a militia; it says nothing about every individual person having a right to possess weapons.

The first paraphrase might be offered by the National Rifle Association or any other group that interprets the Constitution as guaranteeing individuals the right to own guns. The second paraphrase might be offered by groups that seek to limit the ownership of guns.

Why paraphrase? Here are two reasons why you might paraphrase a passage:

- To help yourself to understand it. In this case, the paraphrase does not appear in your essay.

- To help your reader to understand a passage that is especially important but that is not immediately clear. In this case, you paraphrase to let the reader know exactly what the passage means. This paraphrase does appear in your essay.

Paraphrase, Patchwriting, and Plagiarism

We have indicated that only rarely will you have reason to introduce a paraphrase into your essays. But in your preliminary work, when taking notes, you might sometimes do one or more of the following: copy word for word, paraphrase (usually to establish an author's idea clearly in your mind), summarize, and / or produce a medley of borrowed words and original words. The latter strategy is known as *patchwriting*, and it can be dangerous: If you submit such a medley in your final essay, you risk the charge of **plagiarism** *even if you have rearranged the phrases and clauses, and even if you have cited your source.*

Here's an example. First, we give the source: a paragraph from Jena McGregor's essay on whether women serving in the armed forces should be allowed to participate directly in combat. (The entire essay is printed on pp. 31–32.)

> Last week, female soldiers began formally moving into jobs in previously all-male battalions, a program that will later go Army-wide. The move is a result of rule changes following a February report that opened some 14,000 new positions to women in critical jobs much closer to the front lines. However, some 250,000 combat jobs still remain officially closed to them.

Here is a student's patchwriting version:

> Women in the army recently began to formally move into jobs in battalions that previously were all-male. This program later will go throughout the Army. According to author Jena McGregor,

the move comes from changes in the rules following a February report that opened about 14,000 new jobs to women in critical jobs that are much closer to the front lines. About 250,000 jobs, however — as McGregor points out — continue to be officially closed to women.

As you can see, the student writer has followed the source almost phrase by phrase — certainly, sentence by sentence — making small verbal changes, such as substituting *Women in the army recently* for McGregor's *Last week, female soldiers* and substituting *the move comes from changes in the rules* for McGregor's *The move is a result of rule changes. . . .*

What the student should have done is either (1) *quote the passage exactly,* setting it off to indicate that it's a quotation and indicating the source, or (2) *summarize it briefly* and credit the source — maybe in a sentence such as this:

Jena McGregor points out that although a recent change in army rules has resulted in new jobs being opened for women in the military, some 250,000 jobs "continue to be officially closed."

As opposed to the above example of a sentence that frankly summarizes a source, patchwriting is *not* the student's writing but, rather, the source material thinly disguised. In a given paragraph of patchwriting, usually some of the words are copied from the source, and all or most of the rest consists of synonyms substituted for the source's words, with minor rearrangement of phrases and clauses. That is, the sequence of ideas and their arrangement, as well as most of the language, are entirely or almost entirely derived from the source, even if some of the words are different.

The fact that you may cite a source is not enough to protect you from the charge of plagiarism. Citing a source tells the reader that some fact or idea — or some groups of words enclosed within quotation marks or set off by indentation — comes from the named source; it does *not* tell the reader that almost everything in the paragraph is, in effect, someone else's writing with a few words changed, a few words added, and a few phrases moved.

The best way to avoid introducing patchwriting into your final essay is to make certain that when taking notes you indicate, *in the notes themselves,* what sorts of notes they are. For example:

- When quoting word for word, put the passage within quotation marks, and cite the page number(s) of the source.

- When paraphrasing — perhaps to ensure that you understand the writer's idea, or because your readers won't understand the source's highly technical language unless you put it into simpler language — use some sign, perhaps *(par),* to remind yourself later that this passage is a paraphrase and thus is not really *your* writing.

- When summarizing, use a different key, such as *(sum),* and cite the page(s) of the source.

Make certain that your notes indicate the degree of indebtedness to your source, and again, do *not* think that if you name a source in a paraphrase you're not plagiarizing. The reader assumes that the name indicates the source of a fact or an idea — not that the paragraph is a rewriting of the original with an occasional phrase of your own inserted here and there.

If you have taken notes properly, with indications of the sort we've mentioned, when writing your paper you can say things like the following:

X's first reason is simple. He says, ". . ." (here you quote *X*'s words, putting them within quotation marks).

X's point can be summarized thus . . . (here you cite the page).

X, writing for lawyers, uses some technical language, but we can paraphrase her conclusion in this way: . . . (here you give the citation).

In short:

- Avoid patchwriting; it is *not* acceptable.
- Enclose direct quotations within quotation marks, or, if the quotations are long, set them off as a block quotation. (Consult your specific style guide for instructions on how to set off block quotations.)
- If you offer a paraphrase, tell readers that you are paraphrasing and explain *why* you are doing so rather than quoting directly or summarizing.

For additional information about plagiarism, see pages 275–278.

A CHECKLIST FOR A PARAPHRASE

☐ Do I have a good reason for offering a paraphrase rather than a summary?

☐ Is the paraphrase entirely in my own words — a word-by-word "translation" — rather than a patchwork of the source's words and my own, with some of my own rearrangement of phrases and clauses?

☐ Do I not only cite the source but also explicitly say that the entire passage is a paraphrase?

STRATEGIES FOR SUMMARIZING

As with paraphrases, summaries can be useful for helping you to establish your understanding of an essay or article. Summarizing each paragraph or each group of closely related paragraphs will enable you to follow the threads of the argument and will ultimately provide a useful map of the essay. Then, when rereading the essay, you may want to underline passages that you now realize are the author's key ideas — for instance, definitions, generalizations, summaries. You may also want to jot notes in the margins, questioning the logic, expressing your uncertainty, or calling attention to other writers who see the matter differently.

Summaries are also useful for your readers, for the reasons noted on page 47. How long should your summaries be? They can be as short as a single sentence or as long as an entire paragraph. Here's a one-sentence summary of Martin Luther King Jr.'s famous essay "Letter from Birmingham Jail." King wrote this essay after his arrest for marching against racial segregation and injustice in Birmingham, Alabama.

In his letter, King argues that the time is ripe for nonviolent protest throughout the segregated South, dismissing claims by local clergymen who opposed him, and arguing that unjust laws need to be challenged by black people who have been patient and silent for too long.

A RULE FOR WRITERS
Your essay is *likely to include brief summaries* of points of view with which you agree or disagree, but it will *rarely include a paraphrase* unless the original is obscure and you feel compelled to present a passage at length in words that are clearer than those of the original. If you do paraphrase, explicitly identify the material as a paraphrase. Never submit patchwriting.

King's essay, however, is quite long. Obviously, our one-sentence summary cannot convey substantial portions of King's eloquent arguments, sacrificing almost all the nuance of his rationale, but it serves as an efficient summation and allows the writer to move on to his own analysis promptly.

A longer summary might try to capture more nuance, especially if, for the purposes of your essay, you need to capture more. How much you summarize depends largely on the *purpose* of your summary (see again our list of reasons to summarize on p. 47). Here is a longer summary of King's letter:

In his letter, King argues that the time is ripe for nonviolent protest in the segregated South despite the criticism he and his fellow civil rights activists received from various authorities, especially the eight local clergymen who wrote a public statement against him. King addresses their criticism point by point, first claiming his essential right to be in Birmingham with his famous statement, "injustice anywhere is a threat to justice everywhere," and then saying that those who see the timing of his group's nonviolent direct action as inconvenient must recognize at least two things: one, that his "legitimate and unavoidable impatience" resulted from undelivered promises by authorities in the past; and two, that African Americans had long been told over and over again to wait for change with no change forthcoming. "This 'wait' has almost always meant 'never,'" King writes. For those who criticized his leadership, which encouraged people to break laws prohibiting their march, King says that breaking *unjust* laws may actually be construed as a *just* act. For those who called him an extremist, he revels in the definition ("was not Jesus an extremist in love?" he asks) and reminds them of the more extremist groups who call for violence in the face of blatant discrimination and brutality (and who will surely rise, King suggests, if no redress is forthcoming for the peaceful southern protestors he leads). Finally, King rails against "silence," saying that to hold one's tongue in the face of segregation is tantamount to supporting it—a blow to "white moderates" who believe in change but do nothing to help bring it about.

This summary, obviously much longer than the first, raises numerous points from King's argument and preserves through quotation some of King's original tone and substance. It sacrifices much, of course, but seeks to provide a thorough account of a long and complex document containing many primary and secondary claims.

If your instructor asks for a summary of an essay, most often he or she won't want you to include your own thoughts about the content. Of course, you'll be using your own words, but try to "put yourself in the original author's shoes" and provide a summary that reflects the approach taken by the source. It should *not* contain ideas that the original piece doesn't express. If you use exact words and phrases drawn from the source, enclose them in quotation marks.

Summaries may be written for exercises in reading comprehension, but the point of summarizing when writing an essay is to assist your own argument. A faithful summary — one without your own ideas interjected — can be effective when using a source as an example or showing another writer's concordance with your argument. Consider the following paragraph written by a student who was arguing that if a person today purchases goods manufactured in sweatshops or under other inadequate labor conditions, then he or she is just as responsible for the abuses of labor as the companies who operate them. Notice how the student provides a summary (underlined) along the way and how it assists her argument.

> Americans today are so disconnected from the source and origins of the products they buy that it is entirely possible for them one day to march against global warming and the next to collect a dividend in their 401k from companies that are the worst offenders. It is possible to weep over a news report on child labor in China and then post an emotional plea for justice on Facebook using a mobile device made by Chinese child laborers. In 1849, Henry David Thoreau wrote in "Resistance to Civil Government" how ironic it was to see his fellow citizens in Boston opposed to slavery in the South, yet who read the daily news and commodity prices and "fall asleep over them both," not recognizing their own investments in, or patronage of, the very thing that offends their consciences. To Thoreau, such "gross inconsistency" makes even well-intentioned people "agents of injustice." Similarly, today we do not see the connections between our consumer habits and the various kinds of oppression that underlie our purchases — forms of oppression we would never support directly and outright.

The embedded short summary addresses only one point of Thoreau's original essay, but it shows how summaries may serve in an integrative way — as analogy, example, or illustration — to support an argument even without adding the writer's own commentary or analysis.

CRITICAL SUMMARY

When writing a longer summary that you intend to integrate into your argument, you may interject your own ideas; the appropriate term for this is **critical summary**. It signifies that you're offering more than a thorough and accurate account of an original source, because you're adding your evaluation of it as well. Think of this as weaving together your neutral summary with your own argument so that the summary meshes seamlessly with your overall writing goal. Along the way, during the summary, you may appraise the original author's ideas, commenting on them as you go — even while being faithful to the original.

How can you faithfully account for an author's argument while commenting on its merits or shortcomings? One way is to offer examples from the original. In addition, you might assess the quality of those examples or present others that the author didn't consider. Remember, being critical doesn't necessarily mean refuting the author. Your summary can refute, support, or be more balanced, simply recognizing where the original author succeeds and fails.

A STRATEGY FOR WRITING A CRITICAL SUMMARY   Follow these five steps when writing a critical summary:

1. **Introduce** the summary. You don't have to provide all these elements, but consider offering the *author's name* and *expertise*, the *title* of the source, the *place* of publication, the *year* of publication, or any other relevant information. You may also start to explain the author's main point that you are summarizing:

> Pioneering feminist Betty Friedan, in her landmark book *The Feminine Mystique* (1963), argued that . . .

> In an essay on the state of higher education today, University of Illinois English professor Cary Nelson complains about . . .

2. **Explain** the major point the source makes. Here you have a chance to tell your readers what the original author is saying, so be faithful to the original but also highlight the point you're summarizing:

> Pioneering feminist Betty Friedan, in her landmark book *The Feminine Mystique* (1963), argued that women of the early 1960s were falling victim to a media-created image of ideal femininity that pressured them to prioritize homemaking, beauty, and maternity above almost all other concerns.

Here you can control the readers' understanding through simple adjectives such as *pioneering* and *landmark*. (Compare how "*stalwart* feminist Betty Friedan, in her *provocative* book" might dispose the reader to interpret your material differently.)

> In a *blunt critique* of the state of higher education today, University of Illinois professor Cary Nelson complains that universities are underpaying and overworking part-time, adjunct teachers.

3. **Exemplify** by offering one or more representative examples or evidence on which the original author draws. Feel free to quote if needed, though it is not required in a summary.

> Friedan examines post–World War II trends that included the lowering of the marriage age, the rise of the mass media, and what she calls "the problem that has no name" — that of feminine un-fulfillment, or what we might today call "depression."

4. **Problematize** by placing your assessment, analysis, or question into the summary.

> While the word *depression* never comes up in Friedan's work, one could assume that terms like *malaise*, *suffering*, and *housewives' fatigue* signal an emerging

understanding of the relationship between stereotypical media representations of social identity and mental health.

If you're working toward a balanced critique or rebuttal, here is a good place to insert your ideas or those of someone with a slightly different view.

Nelson is right to say that schools should model themselves on the ideals being taught in classrooms, but having a flexible workforce is perfectly logical for a large organization (something probably also taught in many business classes).

5. **Extend** by tying the summary to your argument, helping transition out of the critical summary and back into your own analysis.

Friedan's work should raise questions about how women are portrayed in the media today, and about what mental health consequences are attributable to the ubiquitous and consistent messages given to women about their bodies, occupations, and social roles.

The biggest problem with using too many contingent faculty is with preserving the quality of undergraduate education and the basic principles of academic freedom. Paying contingent faculty more money while increasing the number of tenure-track positions is not just a question of principles but a hallmark of the investment a university makes in its students.

It is possible to use this method—**Introduce**, **Explain**, **Exemplify**, **Problematize**, and **Extend**—in many ways, but essentially it is a way of providing a critical summary, any element of which can be enhanced or built upon as needed.

> **A RULE FOR WRITERS**
> Remember that when writing a summary you are putting yourself into the author's shoes.

Having insisted earlier that you should read the essays in this book slowly because the writers build one reason on another, we will now seem to contradict ourselves by presenting an essay that you can almost skim. Susan Jacoby's piece originally appeared in the *New York Times*, a thoroughly respectable newspaper but not one that requires readers to linger over every sentence. Still, compared with most news accounts, Jacoby's essay requires close reading. Notice that it zigs and zags, not because Jacoby is careless but because in building a strong case to support her point of view, she must consider some widely held views that she does *not* accept; she must set these forth and then give her reasons for rejecting them.

SUSAN JACOBY

Susan Jacoby (b. 1946), a journalist since the age of seventeen, is well known for her feminist writings. "A First Amendment Junkie" (our title) appeared in the Hers column in the New York Times *in 1978.*

A First Amendment Junkie

It is no news that many women are defecting from the ranks of civil libertarians on the issue of obscenity. The conviction of Larry Flynt, publisher of *Hustler* magazine—before his metamorphosis into a born-again Christian—was greeted with unabashed feminist approval. Harry Reems, the unknown actor who was convicted by a Memphis jury for conspiring to distribute the movie *Deep Throat*, has carried on his legal battles with almost no support from women who ordinarily regard themselves as supporters of the First Amendment. Feminist writers and scholars have even discussed the possibility of making common cause against pornography with adversaries of the women's movement—including opponents of the Equal Rights Amendment and "right-to-life" forces.

All of this is deeply disturbing to a woman writer who believes, as I always have and still do, in an absolute interpretation of the First Amendment. Nothing in Larry Flynt's garbage convinces me that the late Justice Hugo L. Black was wrong in his opinion that "the Federal Government is without any power whatsoever under the Constitution to put any type of burden on free speech and expression of ideas of any kind (as distinguished from conduct)." Many women I like and respect tell me I am wrong; I cannot remember having become involved in so many heated discussions of a public issue since the end of the Vietnam War. A feminist writer described my views as those of a "First Amendment junkie."

Many feminist arguments for controls on pornography carry the implicit conviction that porn books, magazines, and movies pose a greater threat to women than similarly repulsive exercises of free speech pose to other offended groups. This conviction has, of course, been shared by everyone—regardless of race, creed, or sex—who has ever argued in favor of abridging the First Amendment. It is the argument used by some Jews who have withdrawn their support from the American Civil Liberties Union because it has defended the right of American Nazis to march through a community inhabited by survivors of Hitler's concentration camps.

If feminists want to argue that the protection of the Constitution should not be extended to *any* particularly odious or threatening form of speech, they have a reasonable argument (although I don't agree with it). But it is ridiculous to suggest that the porn shops on 42nd Street are more disgusting to women than a march of neo-Nazis is to survivors of the extermination camps.

The arguments over pornography also blur 5 the vital distinction between expression of ideas and conduct. When I say I believe unreservedly in the First Amendment, someone always comes back at me with the issue of "kiddie porn." But kiddie porn is not a First Amendment issue. It is an issue of the abuse of power—the power adults have over children—and not of obscenity. Parents and promoters have no more right to use their children to make porn movies than they do to send them to work in coal mines. The responsible adults should be prosecuted, just as adults who use children for back-breaking farm labor should be prosecuted.

Susan Brownmiller, in *Against Our Will: Men, Women, and Rape,* has described pornography as "the undiluted essence of antifemale propaganda." I think this is a fair description of some types of pornography, especially of the brutish subspecies that equates sex with death and portrays women primarily as objects of violence.

The equation of sex and violence, personified by some glossy rock record album covers as well as by *Hustler,* has fed the illusion that censorship of pornography can be conducted on a more rational basis than other types of censorship. Are all pictures of naked women obscene? Clearly not, says a friend. A Renoir nude is art, she says, and *Hustler* is trash. "Any reasonable person" knows that.

But what about something between art and trash — something, say, along the lines of *Playboy* or *Penthouse* magazines? I asked five women for their reactions to one picture in *Penthouse* and got responses that ranged from "lovely" and "sensuous" to "revolting" and "demeaning." Feminists, like everyone else, seldom have rational reasons for their preferences in erotica. Like members of juries, they tend to disagree when confronted with something that falls short of 100 percent vulgarity.

In any case, feminists will not be the arbiters of good taste if it becomes easier to harass, prosecute, and convict people on obscenity charges. Most of the people who want to censor girlie magazines are equally opposed to open discussion of issues that are of vital concern to women: rape, abortion, menstruation, contraception, lesbianism — in fact, the entire range of sexual experience from a woman's viewpoint.

Feminist writers and editors and filmmakers 10 have limited financial resources: Confronted by a determined prosecutor, Hugh Hefner[1] will fare better than Susan Brownmiller. Would the Memphis jurors who convicted Harry Reems for his role in *Deep Throat* be inclined to take a more positive view of paintings of the female genitalia done by sensitive feminist artists? *Ms.* magazine has printed color reproductions of some of those art works; *Ms.* is already

banned from a number of high school libraries because someone considers it threatening and/or obscene.

Feminists who want to censor what they regard as harmful pornography have essentially the same motivation as other would-be censors: They want to use the power of the state to accomplish what they have been unable to achieve in the marketplace of ideas and images. The impulse to censor places no faith in the possibilities of democratic persuasion.

It isn't easy to persuade certain men that they have better uses for $1.95 each month than to spend it on a copy of *Hustler*. Well, then, give the men no choice in the matter.

I believe there is also a connection between the impulse toward censorship on the part of people who used to consider themselves civil libertarians and a more general desire to shift responsibility from individuals to institutions. When I saw the movie *Looking for Mr. Goodbar,* I was stunned by its series of visual images equating sex and violence, coupled with what seems to me the mindless message (a distortion of the fine Judith Rossner novel) that casual sex equals death. When I came out of the movie, I was even more shocked to see parents standing in line with children between the ages of ten and fourteen.

I simply don't know why a parent would take a child to see such a movie, any more than I understand why people feel they can't turn off a television set their child is watching. Whenever I say that, my friends tell me I don't know how it is because I don't have children. True, but I do have parents. When I was a child, they did turn off the TV. They didn't expect the Federal Communications Commission to do their job for them.

I am a First Amendment junkie. You can't 15 OD on the First Amendment, because free speech is its own best antidote.

[1] **Hugh Hefner** Founder and longtime publisher of *Playboy* magazine.

SUMMARIZING JACOBY

Suppose we want to make a *rough summary*, more or less paragraph by paragraph, of Jacoby's essay. Our summary might look like this:

Paragraph 1. Although feminists usually support the First Amendment, when it comes to pornography many feminists take pretty much the position of those who oppose the Equal Rights Amendment and abortion and other causes of the women's movement.

Paragraph 2. Larry Flynt produces garbage, but I think his conviction represents an unconstitutional limitation of freedom of speech.

Paragraphs 3, 4. Feminists who want to control (censor) pornography argue that it poses a greater threat to women than similar repulsive speech poses to other groups. If feminists want to say that all offensive speech should be restricted, they can make a case, but it is absurd to say that pornography is a "greater threat" to women "than a march of neo-Nazis is to survivors of the extermination camps."

Paragraph 5. Trust in the First Amendment is not refuted by kiddie porn; kiddie porn is not a First Amendment issue but an issue of child abuse.

Paragraphs 6, 7, 8. Some feminists think censorship of pornography can be more "rational" than other kinds of censorship, but a picture of a nude woman strikes some women as base and others as "lovely." There is no unanimity.

Paragraphs 9, 10. If feminists censor girlie magazines, they will find that they are unwittingly helping opponents of the women's movement to censor discussions of rape, abortion, and so on. Some of the art in the feminist magazine *Ms.* would doubtless be censored.

Paragraphs 11, 12. Like other would-be censors, feminists want to use the power of the state to achieve what they have not achieved in "the marketplace of ideas." They display a lack of faith in "democratic persuasion."

Paragraphs 13, 14. This attempt at censorship reveals a "desire to shift responsibility from individuals to institutions." The responsibility—for instance, to keep young people from equating sex with violence—is properly the parents'.

Paragraph 15. We can't have too much of the First Amendment.

Jacoby's **thesis** (i.e., major claim or chief proposition)—that any form of censorship of pornography is wrong—is clear enough, even as early as the end of paragraph 1, but it gains force from the **reasons** she offers throughout the essay. If we want to reduce our summary further, we might say that she supports her thesis by arguing several subsidiary points. Here we'll merely assert them briefly, but Jacoby **argues** them—that is, she gives reasons:

- Pornography can scarcely be thought of as more offensive than Nazism.
- Women disagree about which pictures are pornographic.
- Feminists who want to censor pornography will find that they help antifeminists to censor discussions of issues advocated by the women's movement.

- Feminists who favor censorship are in effect turning to the government to achieve what they haven't achieved in the free marketplace.
- One sees this abdication of responsibility in the fact that parents allow their children to watch unsuitable movies and television programs.

If we want to present a *brief summary* in the form of one coherent paragraph — perhaps as part of an essay arguing for or against — we might write something like the one shown in the paragraph below. (Of course, we would **introduce** it with a lead-in along these lines: "Susan Jacoby, writing in the *New York Times,* offers a forceful argument against censorship of pornography. Jacoby's view, briefly, is. . . .")

> When it comes to censorship of pornography, some feminists take a position shared by opponents of the feminist movement. They argue that pornography poses a greater threat to women than other forms of offensive speech offer to other groups, but this interpretation is simply a mistake. Pointing to kiddie porn is also a mistake, for kiddie porn is an issue involving not the First Amendment but child abuse. Feminists who support censorship of pornography will inadvertently aid those who wish to censor discussions of abortion and rape or censor art that is published in magazines such as *Ms.* The solution is not for individuals to turn to institutions (i.e., for the government to limit the First Amendment) but for individuals to accept the responsibility for teaching young people not to equate sex with violence.

In contrast, a *critical summary* of Jacoby — an evaluative summary in which we introduce our own ideas and examples — might look like this:

> Susan Jacoby, writing for the *New York Times* in 1978, offers a forceful argument against censorship of pornography, but one that does not have foresight of the Internet age and the new availability of extreme and exploitative forms of pornography. While she dismisses claims by feminists that pornography should be censored because it constitutes violence against women, what would Jacoby think of such things as "revenge porn" and "voyeuristic porn" today, or the array of elaborate sadistic fantasies readily available to anyone with access to a search engine? Jacoby says that censoring pornography is a step toward censoring art, and she proudly wears the tag "First Amendment junkie," ostensibly to protect what she finds artistic (such as images of female genitalia in *Ms.* Magazine). However, her argument does not help us account for these new forms of exploitation and violence disguised as art or "free speech." Perhaps she would see revenge porn and voyeur porn in the same the way she sees kiddie porn — not so much as an issue of free speech but as an issue of other crimes. Perhaps she would hold her position that we can avoid pornography by just "turning off the TV," but the new Internet pornography is intrusive, entering our lives and the lives of our children whether we like it or not. Education is part of the solution, Jacoby would agree, but we could also consider. . . .

The example above not only summarizes and applies the other techniques presented in this chapter (e.g., accounting for context and questioning definitions of terms and concepts) but also weaves them together with a central argument that offers a new response and a practicable solution.

Topics for Critical Thinking and Writing

1. What does Susan Jacoby mean by saying she is a "First Amendment junkie" (para. 15)?

2. The essay is primarily an argument against the desire of some feminists to censor the sort of pornography that appealed to some heterosexual adult males in 1978. How does the context of the article's publication reflect events and perspectives of that period? How are conditions different now, and how do these new contexts offer ways to support or challenge Jacoby's argument?

3. Evaluate the final paragraph as a conclusion. (Effective final paragraphs are not all of one sort. Some round off the essay by echoing one or more points from the opening; others suggest that the reader, having now seen the problem, should think further about it or act on it. No matter what form it takes, a good final paragraph should make the reader feel that the essay has come to a satisfactory conclusion, not a sudden breaking-off of the argument.)

4. This essay originally appeared in the *New York Times*. If you're unfamiliar with this newspaper, consult an issue or two in your school library. Next, in a paragraph, try to characterize the paper's readers — that is, Jacoby's audience.

5. Jacoby claims in paragraph 2 that she "believes . . . in an absolute interpretation of the First Amendment." What does such an interpretation involve? Would it permit shouting "Fire!" in a crowded theater even when there is no fire? Posting racist insults on the Internet? Spreading untruths about someone's past? (*Does* the First Amendment, as actually interpreted by the Supreme Court today, permit any or all of these claims? Consult your reference librarian for help in answering this question.)

6. Jacoby implies that permitting prosecution of persons on obscenity charges will lead eventually to censorship of "open discussion" of important issues such as "rape, abortion, menstruation, contraception, lesbianism" (para. 9). Do you find her fears convincing? Does she give evidence to support her claim? Explain your responses.

A CHECKLIST FOR GETTING STARTED

- ❏ Have I adequately previewed the work?

- ❏ Can I state the thesis?

- ❏ If I have written a summary, is it accurate?

- ❏ Does my summary mention all the chief points?

- ❏ If there are inconsistencies, are they in the summary or the original selection?

- ❏ Will my summary be clear and helpful?

- ❏ Have I considered the audience for whom the author is writing?

Essays for Analysis

ZACHARY SHEMTOB AND DAVID LAT

Zachary Shemtob teaches criminal justice at Central Connecticut State University; David Lat is a former federal prosecutor. Their essay originally appeared in the New York Times *in 2011.*

Executions Should Be Televised

Earlier this month, Georgia conducted its third execution this year. This would have passed relatively unnoticed if not for a controversy surrounding its videotaping. Lawyers for the condemned inmate, Andrew Grant DeYoung, had persuaded a judge to allow the recording of his last moments as part of an effort to obtain evidence on whether lethal injection caused unnecessary suffering.

Though he argued for videotaping, one of Mr. DeYoung's defense lawyers, Brian Kammer, spoke out against releasing the footage to the public. "It's a horrible thing that Andrew DeYoung had to go through," Mr. Kammer said, "and it's not for the public to see that."

We respectfully disagree. Executions in the United States ought to be made public.

Right now, executions are generally open only to the press and a few select witnesses. For the rest of us, the vague contours are provided in the morning paper. Yet a functioning democracy demands maximum accountability and transparency. As long as executions remain behind closed doors, those are impossible. The people should have the right to see what is being done in their name and with their tax dollars.

This is particularly relevant given the current debate on whether specific methods of lethal injection constitute cruel and unusual punishment and therefore violate the Constitution.

There is a dramatic difference between reading or hearing of such an event and observing it through image and sound. (This is obvious to those who saw the footage of Saddam Hussein's hanging in 2006 or the death of Neda Agha-Soltan during the protests in Iran in 2009.) We are not calling for opening executions completely to the public — conducting them before a live crowd — but rather for broadcasting them live or recording them for future release, on the Web or TV.

When another Georgia inmate, Roy Blankenship, was executed in June, the prisoner jerked his head, grimaced, gasped, and lurched, according to a medical expert's affidavit. The *Atlanta Journal-Constitution* reported that Mr. DeYoung, executed in the same manner, "showed no violent signs in death." Voters should not have to rely on media accounts to understand what takes place when a man is put to death.

Cameras record legislative sessions and presidential debates, and courtrooms are allowing greater television access. When he was an Illinois state senator, President Obama successfully pressed for the videotaping of homicide interrogations and confessions. The most serious penalty of all surely demands equal if not greater scrutiny.

Opponents of our proposal offer many objections. State lawyers argued that making Mr. DeYoung's execution public raised safety concerns. While rioting and pickpocketing occasionally marred executions in the public square in the eighteenth and nineteenth centuries, modern security and technology obviate this concern. Little would change in the death chamber; the faces of witnesses and executioners could be edited out, for privacy reasons, before a video was released.

Of greater concern is the possibility that 10 broadcasting executions could have a numbing effect. Douglas A. Berman, a law professor, fears that people might come to equate human executions with putting pets to sleep. Yet this seems overstated. While public indifference might result over time, the initial broadcasts would undoubtedly get attention and stir debate.

Still others say that broadcasting an execution would offer an unbalanced picture — making the condemned seem helpless and sympathetic, while keeping the victims of the crime out of the picture. But this is beside the point: the defendant is being executed precisely because a jury found that his crimes were so heinous that he deserved to die.

Ultimately the main opposition to our idea seems to flow from an unthinking disgust — a sense that public executions are archaic, noxious, even barbarous. Albert Camus related in his essay "Reflections on the Guillotine" that viewing executions turned him against capital punishment. The legal scholar John D. Bessler suggests that public executions might have the same effect on the public today; Sister Helen Prejean, the death penalty abolitionist, has urged just such a strategy.

That is not our view. We leave open the possibility that making executions public could strengthen support for them; undecided viewers might find them less disturbing than anticipated.

Like many of our fellow citizens, we are deeply conflicted about the death penalty and how it has been administered. Our focus is on accountability and openness. As Justice John Paul Stevens wrote in *Baze v. Rees*, a 2008 case involving a challenge to lethal injection, capital punishment is too often "the product of habit and inattention rather than an acceptable deliberative process that weighs the costs and risks of administering that penalty against its identifiable benefits."

A democracy demands a citizenry as 15 informed as possible about the costs and benefits of society's ultimate punishment.

Topics for Critical Thinking and Writing

1. In paragraphs 9–13, the authors discuss objections to their position. Are you satisfied with their responses to the objections, or do you think they do not satisfactorily dispose of one or more of the objections? Explain.

2. In paragraph 4, the authors say that "[t]he people should have the right to see what is being done in their name and with their tax dollars." But in terms of *rights*, should the person being executed have a right to die in privacy? Articulate a position that weighs the public's right to see what is being done with its tax dollars against death row prisoners' rights to privacy.

3. In the concluding paragraph, the authors imply that their proposal, if enacted, will help to inform citizens "about the costs and benefits of society's ultimate punishment." Do you agree? Why, or why not? What reasons do the authors offer to support their proposal?

4. In your view, what is the strongest argument the authors give on behalf of their proposal? What is the weakest? Explain why you made these choices.

GWEN WILDE

This essay was written for a composition course at Tufts University.

Why the Pledge of Allegiance Should Be Revised (Student Essay)

All Americans are familiar with the Pledge of Allegiance, even if they cannot always recite it perfectly, but probably relatively few know that the *original* Pledge did *not* include the words "under God." The original Pledge of Allegiance, published in the September 8, 1892, issue of the *Youth's Companion,* ran thus:

> I pledge allegiance to my flag, and to the Republic for which it stands: one Nation indivisible, with Liberty and justice for all (Djupe 329).

In 1923, at the first National Flag Conference in Washington, D.C., it was argued that immigrants might be confused by the words "my Flag," and it was proposed that the words be changed to "the Flag of the United States." The following year it was changed again, to "the Flag of the United States of America," and this wording became the official — or, rather, unofficial — wording, unofficial because no wording had ever been nationally adopted (Djupe 329).

In 1942, the United States Congress included the Pledge in the United States Flag Code (4 USC 4, 2006), thus for the first time officially sanctioning the Pledge. In 1954, President Dwight D. Eisenhower approved adding the words "under God." Thus, since 1954 the Pledge reads:

> I pledge allegiance to the flag of the United States of America, and to the Republic for which it stands: one nation under God, indivisible, with Liberty and Justice for all. (Djupe 329)

In my view, the addition of the words "under God" is inappropriate, and they are needlessly divisive — an odd addition indeed to a nation that is said to be "indivisible."

Very simply put, the Pledge in its latest form requires all Americans to say something that some Americans do not believe. I say "requires" because although the courts have ruled that students may not be compelled to recite the Pledge, in effect peer pressure does compel all but the bravest to join in the recitation. When President Eisenhower authorized the change, he said, "In this way we are reaffirming the transcendence of religious faith in America's heritage and future; in this way we shall constantly strengthen those spiritual weapons which forever will be our country's most powerful resource in peace and war" (Sterner).

Exactly what did Eisenhower mean when he spoke of "the transcendence of religious faith in America's heritage" and when he spoke of "spiritual weapons"? I am not sure what "the transcendence of religious faith in America's heritage" means. Of course, many Americans have been and are deeply religious — no one doubts it — but the phrase certainly goes far beyond saying that many Americans have been devout. In any case, many Americans have *not* been devout, and many Americans have *not* believed in "spiritual weapons," but they have nevertheless been patriotic Americans. Some of them have fought and died to keep America free.

In short, the words "under God" cannot be uttered in good faith by many Americans. True, something like 70 or even 80% of Americans say they are affiliated with some form of Christianity, and approximately another 3% say they are Jewish. I don't have the figures for persons of other faiths, but in any case we can surely all agree that although a majority of Americans say they have a religious affiliation, nevertheless several million Americans do *not* believe in God.

If one remains silent while others are reciting the Pledge, or even if one remains silent only while others are speaking the words "under God," one is open to the charge that one is unpatriotic, is "unwilling to recite the Pledge of Allegiance." In the Pledge, patriotism is connected with religious belief, and it is this connection that makes it divisive and (to be blunt) un-American. Admittedly, the belief is not very specific: one is not required to say that one believes in the divinity of Jesus, or in the power of Jehovah, but the fact remains, one is required to express belief in a divine power, and if one doesn't express this belief one is — according to the Pledge — somehow not fully an American, maybe even un-American.

Please notice that I am not arguing that the Pledge is unconstitutional. I understand that the First Amendment to the Constitution says that "Congress shall make no law respecting an establishment of religion, or prohibiting the free exercise thereof." I am not arguing that the words "under God" in the Pledge add up to the "establishment of religion," but they certainly do assert a religious doctrine. Like the words "In God we trust," found on all American money, the words "under God" express an idea that many Americans do not hold, and there is no reason why these Americans — loyal people who may be called upon to defend the country with their lives — should be required to say that America is a nation "under God."

It has been argued, even by members of the Supreme Court, that the words "under God" are not to be taken terribly seriously, not to be taken to say what they seem to say. For instance, Chief Justice Rehnquist wrote:

> To give the parent of such a child a sort of "heckler's veto" over a patriotic ceremony willingly participated in by other students, simply because the Pledge of Allegiance contains the descriptive phrase "under God," is an unwarranted extension of the establishment clause, an extension which would have the unfortunate effect of prohibiting a commendable patriotic observance. (qtd. in Stephens et al. 104)

Chief Justice Rehnquist here calls "under God" a "descriptive phrase," but descriptive of *what*? If a phrase is a "descriptive phrase," it describes something, real or imagined. For many Americans, this phrase does *not* describe a reality. These Americans may perhaps be mistaken — if so, they may learn of their error at Judgment Day — but the fact is, millions of intelligent Americans do not believe in God.

Notice, too, that Chief Justice Rehnquist goes on to say that reciting the Pledge is "a commendable patriotic observance." Exactly. That is my point. It is a *patriotic* observance, and it should not be connected with religion. When we announce that we respect the flag — that we are loyal Americans — we should not also have to announce that we hold a particular religious belief, in this case a belief in monotheism, a belief that there is a God and that God rules.

One other argument defending the words "under God" is often heard: The words "In God We Trust" appear on our money. It is claimed that these words on American money are analogous to the words "under God" in the Pledge. But the situation really is very different. When we hand some coins over, or some paper money, we are concentrating on the business transaction, and we are not making any affirmation about God or our country. But when we recite the Pledge — even if we remain silent at the point when we are supposed to say "under God" — we are very conscious that we are supposed to make this affirmation, an affirmation that many Americans cannot in good faith make, even though they certainly can unthinkingly hand over (or accept) money with the words "In God We Trust."

Because I believe that *reciting* the Pledge is to be taken seriously, with a full awareness of the words that is quite different from when we hand over some money, I cannot understand the recent comment of Supreme Court Justice Souter, who in a case said that the phrase "under God" is "so tepid, so diluted, so far from compulsory prayer, that it should, in effect, be beneath the constitutional radar" (qtd. in "Guide"). I don't follow his reasoning that the phrase should be "beneath the constitutional radar," but in any case I am willing to put aside the issue of constitutionality. I am willing to grant that this phrase does not in any significant sense signify the "establishment of religion" (prohibited by the First Amendment) in the United States. I insist, nevertheless, that the phrase is neither "tepid" nor "diluted." It means what it says — it *must* and *should* mean what it says, to everyone who utters it — and, since millions of loyal Americans cannot say it, it should not be included in a statement in which Americans affirm their loyalty to our great country.

15   In short, the Pledge, which ought to unite all of us, is divisive; it includes a phrase that many patriotic Americans cannot bring themselves to utter. Yes, they can remain silent when others recite these two words, but, again, why should they have to remain silent? The Pledge of Allegiance should be something that *everyone* can say, say out loud, and say with pride. We hear much talk of returning to the ideas of the Founding Fathers. The Founding Fathers did not create the Pledge of Allegiance, but we do know that they never mentioned God in the Constitution. Indeed, the only reference to religion, in the so-called establishment clause of the First Amendment, says, again, that "Congress shall make no law respecting an establishment of religion, or prohibiting the free exercise thereof." Those who wish to exercise religion are indeed free to do so, but the place to do so is not in a pledge that is required of all schoolchildren and of all new citizens.

WORKS CITED

Djupe, Paul A. "Pledge of Allegiance." *Encyclopedia of American Religion and Politics*. Edited by Paul A. Djupe and Laura R. Olson, Facts on File, 2003.

"Guide to Covering 'Under God' Pledge Decision." *ReligionLink*, 17 Sept. 2005, religionlink.com/database/ guide-to-covering-under-god/.

Stephens, Otis H., et al., editors. *American Constitutional Law*. 6th ed., vol. 1, Cengage Learning, 2014.

Sterner, Doug. "The Pledge of Allegiance." *Home of Heroes*, homeofheroes.com/ hallofheroes/1st_floor/flag/ 1bfc_pledge_print.html. Accessed 13 Apr. 2016.

Topics for Critical Thinking and Writing

1. Summarize the essay in a paragraph.

2. What terms and concepts are defined in this essay? Explain how one term or concept is defined.

3. Does the writer, Gwen Wilde, give enough weight to the fact that no one is compelled to recite the Pledge? Explain your answer.

4. What arguments does Wilde offer in support of her position?

5. Does Wilde show an adequate awareness of counterarguments? Identify one place where she raises and refutes a counterargument.

6. What is Wilde's strongest argument? Are any of her arguments notably weak? If so, how could they be strengthened?

7. What assumptions — tacit or explicit — does Wilde make? Do you agree or disagree with them? Explain your response.

8. What do you take the words "under God" to mean? Do they mean "under God's special protection"? Or "acting in accordance with God's rules"? Or "accountable to God"? Or something else? Explain.

9. Chief Justice Rehnquist wrote that the words "under God" are a "descriptive phrase." What do you think he meant by this?

10. What is the purpose of the Pledge of Allegiance? Does the phrase "under God" promote or defeat that purpose? Explain your answer.

11. What do you think about substituting "with religious freedom" for "under God"? Set forth your response, supported by reasons, in about 250 words.

12. Wilde makes a distinction between the reference to God on U.S. money and the reference to God in the Pledge. Do you agree with her that the two cases are not analogous? Explain.

13. What readers might *not* agree with Wilde's arguments? What values do they hold? How might you try to persuade an audience who disagrees with Wilde to consider her proposal?

14. Putting aside your own views on the issue, what grade would you give this essay as a work of argumentative writing? Support your evaluation with reasons.

A CASEBOOK FOR CRITICAL READING:
Should Some Kinds of Speech Be Censored?

Now we present a series of essays that are somewhat more difficult than Jacoby's, Shemtob and Lat's, and Wilde's but that address in more detail some of the free speech issues raised by the earlier essays. We suggest you read each one through to get its gist and then read it a second time, writing down after each paragraph a sentence or two summarizing the paragraph. Keep in mind the First Amendment to the Constitution, which reads, in its entirety, as follows:

> Congress shall make no law respecting an establishment of religion, or prohibiting the free exercise thereof; or abridging the freedom of speech, or of the press; or the right of the people peaceably to assemble, and to petition the government for a redress of grievances.

SUSAN BROWNMILLER

Susan Brownmiller (b. 1935), a graduate of Cornell University, is the founder of Women against Pornography and the author of several books, including Against Our Will: Men, Women, and Rape *(1975). The essay reprinted here is from* Take Back the Night *(1980), a collection of essays edited by Laura Lederer. The book has been called "the manifesto of antipornography feminism."*

Let's Put Pornography Back in the Closet

Free speech is one of the great foundations on which our democracy rests. I am old enough to remember the Hollywood Ten, the screenwriters who went to jail in the late 1940s because they refused to testify before a congressional committee about their political affiliations. They tried to use the First Amendment as a defense, but they went to jail because in those days there were few civil liberties lawyers around who cared to champion the First Amendment right to free speech, when the speech concerned the Communist Party.

The Hollywood Ten were correct in claiming the First Amendment. Its high purpose is the protection of unpopular ideas and political dissent. In the dark, cold days of the 1950s, few civil libertarians were willing to declare themselves First Amendment absolutists. But in the brighter, though frantic, days of the 1960s, the principle of protecting unpopular political speech was gradually strengthened.

It is fair to say now that the battle has largely been won. Even the American Nazi Party has found itself the beneficiary of the dedicated, tireless work of the American Civil Liberties Union. But — and please notice the quotation marks coming up — "To equate the free and robust exchange of ideas and political debate with commercial exploitation of obscene material demeans the grand conception of the First Amendment and its high purposes in the historic struggle for freedom. It is a misuse of the great guarantees of free speech and free press."

I didn't say that, although I wish I had, for I think the words are thrilling. Chief Justice Warren Burger said it in 1973, in the United States Supreme Court's majority opinion in *Miller v. California.* During the same decades that the right to political free speech was being strengthened in the courts, the nation's obscenity laws also were undergoing extensive revision.

It's amazing to recall that in 1934 the question of whether James Joyce's *Ulysses* should be banned as pornographic actually went before the Court. The battle to protect *Ulysses* as a work of literature with redeeming social value was won. In later decades, Henry Miller's *Tropic* books, *Lady Chatterley's Lover,* and the *Memoirs of Fanny Hill* also were adjudged not obscene. These decisions have been important to me. As the author of *Against Our Will,* a study of the history of rape that does contain explicit sexual material, I shudder to think how my book would have fared if James Joyce, D. H. Lawrence, and Henry Miller hadn't gone before me.

I am not a fan of *Chatterley* or the *Tropic* books, I should quickly mention. They are not to my literary taste, nor do I think they represent female sexuality with any degree of accuracy. But I would hardly suggest that we ban them. Such a suggestion wouldn't get very far anyway. The battle to protect these books is ancient history. Time does march on, quite methodically. What, then, is unlawfully obscene, and what does the First Amendment have to do with it?

In the *Miller* case of 1973 (not Henry Miller, by the way, but a porn distributor who sent unsolicited stuff through the mails), the Court came up with new guidelines that it hoped would strengthen obscenity laws by giving more power to the states. What it did in actuality was throw everything into confusion. It set up a three-part test by which materials can be adjudged obscene. The materials are obscene if they depict patently offensive, hard-core sexual conduct; lack serious scientific, literary, artistic, or political value; and appeal to the prurient interest of an average person — as measured by contemporary community standards.

"Patently offensive," "prurient interest," and "hard-core" are indeed words to conjure with. "Contemporary community standards" are what we're trying to redefine. The feminist objection to pornography is not based on prurience, which the dictionary defines as lustful,

itching desire. We are not opposed to sex and desire, with or without the itch, and we certainly believe that explicit sexual material has its place in literature, art, science, and education. Here we part company rather swiftly with old-line conservatives who don't want sex education in the high schools, for example.

No, the feminist objection to pornography is based on our belief that pornography represents hatred of women, that pornography's intent is to humiliate, degrade, and dehumanize the female body for the purpose of erotic stimulation and pleasure. We are unalterably opposed to the presentation of the female body being stripped, bound, raped, tortured, mutilated, and murdered in the name of commercial entertainment and free speech.

These images, which are standard pornographic fare, have nothing to do with the hallowed right of political dissent. They have everything to do with the creation of a cultural climate in which a rapist feels he is merely giving in to a normal urge and a woman is encouraged to believe that sexual masochism is healthy, liberated fun. Justice Potter Stewart once said about hard-core pornography, "You know it when you see it," and that certainly used to be true. In the good old days, pornography looked awful. It was cheap and sleazy, and there was no mistaking it for art. 10

Nowadays, since the porn industry has become a multimillion dollar business, visual technology has been employed in its service. Pornographic movies are skillfully filmed and edited, pornographic still shots using the newest tenets of good design artfully grace the covers of *Hustler, Penthouse,* and *Playboy,* and the public — and the courts — are sadly confused.

The Supreme Court neglected to define "hard-core" in the *Miller* decision. This was a mistake. If "hard-core" refers only to explicit sexual intercourse, then that isn't good enough.

When women or children or men—no matter how artfully—are shown tortured or terrorized in the service of sex, that's obscene. And "patently offensive," I would hope, to our "contemporary community standards."

Justice William O. Douglas wrote in his dissent to the *Miller* case that no one is "compelled to look." This is hardly true. To buy a paper at the corner newsstand is to subject oneself to a forcible immersion in pornography, to be demeaned by an array of dehumanized, chopped-up parts of the female anatomy, packaged like cuts of meat at the supermarket. I happen to like my body and I work hard at the gym to keep it in good shape, but I am embarrassed for my body and for the bodies of all women when I see the fragmented parts of us so frivolously, and so flagrantly, displayed.

Some constitutional theorists (Justice Douglas was one) have maintained that any obscenity law is a serious abridgement of free speech. Others (and Justice Earl Warren was one) have maintained that the First Amendment was never intended to protect obscenity. We live quite compatibly with a host of free-speech abridgements. There are restraints against false and misleading advertising or statements—shouting "fire" without cause in a crowded movie theater, etc.—that do not threaten, but strengthen, our societal values. Restrictions on the public display of pornography belong in this category.

The distinction between permission to publish and permission to display publicly is an essential one and one which I think consonant with First Amendment principles. Justice Burger's words which I quoted above support this without question. We are not saying "Smash the presses" or "Ban the bad ones," but simply "Get the stuff out of our sight." Let the legislatures decide—using realistic and humane contemporary community standards—what can be displayed and what cannot. The courts, after all, will be the final arbiters.

Topics for Critical Thinking and Writing

1. Objecting to Justice Douglas's remark that no one is "'compelled to look'" (para. 13), Brownmiller says, "This is hardly true. To buy a paper at the corner newsstand is to subject oneself to a forcible immersion in pornography, to be demeaned by an array of dehumanized, chopped-up parts of the female anatomy, packaged like cuts of meat at the supermarket." How does the ubiquity (high visibility) of pornography in the Internet age trouble Douglas's argument and assist Brownmiller's? How does the advent of the Internet hurt Brownmiller's call for restrictions on what can be shown?

2. Who is Brownmiller's intended audience? Do you think she holds their attention? Why, or why not?

3. When Brownmiller attempts to restate the "three-part test" for obscenity established by the Supreme Court in *Miller v. California,* she writes (para. 7): "The materials are obscene if they depict . . ." and so on. She should have written: "The materials are obscene if and only if they depict . . ." and so on. Explain what is wrong here with her "if," and why "if and only if" is needed.

4. When Brownmiller accuses "the public—and the courts" of being "sadly confused" (para. 11), what does she think is making them confused? The definition of *pornography* or

obscenity? The effects of such literature on men and women? Something else? Explain your response.

5. In paragraph 14, Brownmiller reminds us that we already live quite "compatibly" with some "free-speech abridgements." Her examples are that we may not make false statements such as shouting "fire" in a crowded theater and may not issue misleading advertisements. Do you think that these widely accepted restrictions are valid evidence in arguing on behalf of limiting the display of what Brownmiller considers pornography? Why, or why not?

6. Brownmiller insists that defenders of the First Amendment, who will surely oppose laws that interfere with the freedom to publish, need not condemn laws that regulate the freedom to publicly display pornographic publications. Do you agree? Why, or why not? Suppose a publisher insists that he cannot sell his product at a profit unless he is permitted to display it to advantage and that restriction on the latter amounts to interference with his freedom to publish. How might Brownmiller reply?

7. In her last paragraph, Brownmiller says that "contemporary community standards" should be decisive. Can it be argued that because standards vary from one community to another and from time to time even in the same place, her recommendation subjects the rights of a minority to the whims of a majority? Why, or why not? (The Bill of Rights, after all, was supposed to safeguard the constitutional rights of the minority from the possible tyranny of the majority.) How is "contemporary community standards" defined in the essay? How do you define the phrase?

CHARLES R. LAWRENCE III

Charles R. Lawrence III (b. 1943), author of numerous articles in law journals and coauthor of We Won't Go Back: Making the Case for Affirmative Action *(1997), teaches law at Georgetown University. This essay originally appeared in the* Chronicle of Higher Education *(October 25, 1989), a publication read chiefly by faculty and administrators at colleges and universities. An amplified version of the essay appeared in the* Duke Law Journal *(February 1990).*

On Racist Speech

I have spent the better part of my life as a dissenter. As a high school student, I was threatened with suspension for my refusal to participate in a civil defense drill, and I have been a conspicuous consumer of my First Amendment liberties ever since. There are very strong reasons for protecting even racist speech. Perhaps the most important of these is that such protection reinforces our society's commitment to tolerance as a value, and that by protecting bad speech from government regulation, we will be forced to combat it as a community.

But I also have a deeply felt apprehension about the resurgence of racial violence and the corresponding rise in the incidence of verbal and symbolic assault and harassment to which blacks and other traditionally subjugated and excluded groups are subjected. I am troubled by the way the debate has been framed in response to the recent surge of racist incidents on college and university campuses and in response to some universities' attempts to regulate harassing speech. The problem has been framed as one in which the liberty of free speech is in conflict with the elimination of racism. I believe this has placed the bigot on the moral high ground and fanned the rising flames of racism.

Above all, I am troubled that we have not listened to the real victims, that we have shown so little understanding of their injury, and that we have abandoned those whose race, gender, or sexual preference continues to make them second-class citizens. It seems to me a very sad irony that the first instinct of civil libertarians has been to challenge even the smallest, most narrowly framed efforts by universities to provide black and other minority students with the protection the Constitution guarantees them.

The landmark case of *Brown v. Board of Education* is not a case that we normally think of as a case about speech. But *Brown* can be broadly read as articulating the principle of equal citizenship. *Brown* held that segregated schools were inherently unequal because of the *message* that segregation conveyed — that black children were an untouchable caste, unfit to go to school with white children. If we understand the necessity of eliminating the system of signs and symbols that signal the inferiority of blacks, then we should hesitate before proclaiming that all racist speech that stops short of physical violence must be defended.

University officials who have formulated 5 policies to respond to incidents of racial harassment have been characterized in the press as "thought police," but such policies generally do nothing more than impose sanctions against intentional face-to-face insults. When racist speech takes the form of face-to-face insults, catcalls, or other assaultive speech aimed at an individual or small group of persons, it falls directly within the "fighting words" exception to First Amendment protection. The Supreme Court has held that words which "by their very utterance inflict injury or tend to incite an immediate breach of the peace" are not protected by the First Amendment.

If the purpose of the First Amendment is to foster the greatest amount of speech, racial insults disserve that purpose. Assaultive racist speech functions as a preemptive strike. The invective is experienced as a blow, not as a proffered idea, and once the blow is struck, it is unlikely that a dialogue will follow. Racial insults are particularly undeserving of First Amendment protection because the perpetrator's intention is not to discover truth or initiate dialogue but to injure the victim. In most situations, members of minority groups realize that they are likely to lose if they respond to epithets by fighting and are forced to remain silent and submissive.

Courts have held that offensive speech may not be regulated in public forums such as streets where the listener may avoid the speech by moving on, but the regulation of otherwise protected speech has been permitted when the speech invades the privacy of the unwilling listener's home or when the unwilling listener cannot avoid the speech. Racist posters, fliers, and graffiti in dormitories, bathrooms, and other common living spaces would seem to clearly fall within the reasoning of these cases. Minority students should not be required to remain in their rooms in order to avoid racial assault. Minimally, they should find a safe haven in their dorms and in all other common rooms that are a part of their daily routine.

I would also argue that the university's responsibility for ensuring that these students receive an equal educational opportunity provides a compelling justification for regulations that ensure them safe passage in all common areas. A minority student should not have to risk becoming the target of racially assaulting speech every time he or she chooses to walk across campus. Regulating vilifying speech that cannot be anticipated or avoided would not preclude announced speeches and rallies — situations that would give minority-group members and their allies the chance to organize counterdemonstrations or avoid the speech altogether.

The most commonly advanced argument against the regulation of racist speech proceeds something like this: We recognize that minority groups suffer pain and injury as the result of racist speech, but we must allow this hate mongering for the benefit of society as a whole. Freedom of speech is the lifeblood of our democratic system. It is especially important for minorities because often it is their only vehicle for rallying support for the redress of their grievances. It will be impossible to formulate a prohibition so precise that it will prevent the racist speech you want to suppress without catching in the same net all kinds of speech that it would be unconscionable for a democratic society to suppress.

Whenever we make such arguments, we [10] are striking a balance on the one hand between our concern for the continued free flow of ideas and the democratic process dependent on that flow, and, on the other, our desire to further the cause of equality. There can be no meaningful discussion of how we should reconcile our commitment to equality and our commitment to free speech until it is acknowledged that there is real harm inflicted by racist speech and that this harm is far from trivial.

To engage in a debate about the First Amendment and racist speech without a full understanding of the nature and extent of that harm is to risk making the First Amendment an instrument of domination rather than a vehicle of liberation. We have not all known the experience of victimization by racist, misogynist, and homophobic speech, nor do we equally share the burden of the societal harm it inflicts. We are often quick to say that we have heard the cry of the victims when we have not.

The *Brown* case is again instructive because it speaks directly to the psychic injury inflicted by racist speech by noting that the symbolic message of segregation affected "the hearts and minds" of Negro children "in a way unlikely ever to be undone." Racial epithets and harassment often cause deep emotional scarring and feelings of anxiety and fear that pervade every aspect of a victim's life.

Brown also recognized that black children did not have an equal opportunity to learn and participate in the school community if they bore the additional burden of being subjected to the humiliation and psychic assault contained in the message of segregation. University students bear an analogous burden when they are forced to live and work in an environment where at any moment they may be subjected to denigrating verbal harassment and assault. The same injury was addressed by the Supreme Court when it held that sexual harassment that creates a hostile or abusive work environment violates the ban on sex discrimination in employment of Title VII of the Civil Rights Act of 1964.

Carefully drafted university regulations would bar the use of words as assault weapons and leave unregulated even the most heinous of ideas when those ideas are presented at times and places and in manners that provide an opportunity for reasoned rebuttal or escape from immediate injury. The history of the development of the right to free speech has been one of carefully evaluating the importance of free expression and its effects on other important societal interests. We have drawn the line between protected and unprotected speech before without dire results. (Courts have, for example, exempted from the protection of the First Amendment obscene speech and speech that disseminates official secrets, that defames or libels another person, or that is used to form a conspiracy or monopoly.)

Blacks and other people of color are skepti- 15 cal about the argument that even the most injurious speech must remain unregulated because, in an unregulated marketplace of ideas, the best ones will rise to the top and gain acceptance. Our experience tells us quite the opposite. We have seen too many good liberal politicians shy away from the issues that might brand them as being too closely allied with us.

Whenever we decide that racist speech must be tolerated because of the importance of maintaining societal tolerance for all unpopular speech, we are asking blacks and other subordinated groups to bear the burden for the good of all. We must be careful that the ease with which we strike the balance against the regulation of racist speech is in no way influenced by the fact that the cost will be borne by others. We must be certain that those who will pay that price are fairly represented in our deliberations and that they are heard.

At the core of the argument that we should resist all government regulation of speech is the ideal that the best cure for bad speech is good, that ideas that affirm equality and the worth of all individuals will ultimately prevail. This is an empty ideal unless those of us who would fight racism are vigilant and unequivocal in that fight. We must look for ways to offer assistance and support to students whose speech and political participation are chilled in a climate of racial harassment.

Civil rights lawyers might consider suing on behalf of blacks whose right to an equal education is denied by a university's failure to ensure a nondiscriminatory educational climate or conditions of employment. We must embark upon the development of a First Amendment jurisprudence grounded in the reality of our history and our contemporary experience. We must think hard about how best to launch legal attacks against the most indefensible forms of hate speech. Good lawyers can create exceptions and narrow interpretations that limit the harm of hate speech without opening the floodgates of censorship.

Everyone concerned with these issues must find ways to engage actively in actions that resist and counter the racist ideas that we would have the First Amendment protect. If we fail in this, the victims of hate speech must rightly assume that we are on the oppressors' side.

Topics for Critical Thinking and Writing

1. Summarize Charles Lawrence's essay in a paragraph. (You may find it useful first to summarize each paragraph in a sentence and then to revise these summary sentences into a paragraph.)

2. In one sentence, state Lawrence's thesis (his main point).

3. Why do you suppose Lawrence included his first paragraph? What does it contribute to his argument?

4. In paragraph 8, Lawrence speaks of "racially assaulting speech" and of "vilifying speech." It's easy to think of words that fit these descriptions, but what about other words? Is *Uncle Tom*, used by an African American about another African American who is eager to please whites, an example of "racially assaulting speech"? Or consider the word *gay*. Surely this word is acceptable because it's widely used by homosexuals, but what about *queer* (used by some homosexuals but usually derogatory when used by heterosexuals)? What might make these words seem "assaulting" or "vilifying"?

5. Think about the provisions in the Code of Conduct of Shippensburg University in Pennsylvania. The code says that each student has a "primary" right to be free from harassment, intimidation, physical harm, and emotional abuse and has a "secondary" right to express personal beliefs in a manner that does not "provoke, harass, demean, intimidate, or harm" another. The code prohibits conduct that "annoys, threatens, or alarms a person or group," such as sexual harassment, "innuendo," "comments, insults," "propositions," "humor / jokes about sex or gender-specific traits," and "suggestive or insulting sounds, leering, whistling, [and] obscene gestures." The university's president has said (according to the *New York Times*, April 24, 2003, p. A23) that the university encourages free speech as a means to examine ideas and that the university is "committed to the principle that this discussion be conducted appropriately. We do have expectations that our students will conduct themselves in a civil manner that allows them to express their opinions without interfering with the rights of others." Use this material to generate your own thoughts about speech on college campuses.

6. Find out if your college or university has a code — perhaps online — governing hate speech. If it does, evaluate it. If your college has no such code, make a case for why such a policy should be readily available to students and faculty. Compose a blog entry evaluating your current code, or draft your own code.

DEREK BOK

Derek Bok was born in 1930 in Bryn Mawr, Pennsylvania, and educated at Stanford University and Harvard University, where he received a law degree. From 1971 to 1991 he served as president of Harvard University. The following essay, first published in the Boston Globe *in 1991, was prompted by the display of Confederate flags hung from a window of a Harvard dormitory.*

Protecting Freedom of Expression on the Campus

For several years, universities have been struggling with the problem of trying to reconcile the rights of free speech with the desire to avoid racial tension. In recent weeks, such a controversy has sprung up at Harvard. Two students hung Confederate flags in public view, upsetting students who equate the Confederacy with slavery. A third student tried to protest the flags by displaying a swastika.

These incidents have provoked much discussion and disagreement. Some students have urged that Harvard require the removal of symbols that offend many members of the community. Others reply that such symbols are a form of free speech and should be protected.

Different universities have resolved similar conflicts in different ways. Some have enacted codes to protect their communities from forms of speech that are deemed to be insensitive to the feelings of other groups. Some have refused to impose such restrictions.

It is important to distinguish between the appropriateness of such communications and their status under the First Amendment. The fact that speech is protected by the First Amendment does not necessarily mean that it is right, proper, or civil. I am sure that the vast majority of Harvard students believe that hanging a Confederate flag in public view — or displaying a swastika in response — is insensitive and unwise because any satisfaction it gives to the students who display these symbols is far outweighed by the discomfort it causes to many others.

I share this view and regret that the stu- 5 dents involved saw fit to behave in this fashion. Whether or not they merely wished to manifest their pride in the South — or to demonstrate the insensitivity of hanging Confederate flags, by mounting another offensive symbol in return — they must have known that they would upset many fellow students and ignore the decent regard for the feelings of others so essential to building and preserving a strong and harmonious community.

To disapprove of a particular form of communication, however, is not enough to justify prohibiting it. We are faced with a clear example of the conflict between our commitment to free speech and our desire to foster a community founded on mutual respect. Our society has wrestled with this problem for many years. Interpreting the First Amendment, the Supreme Court has clearly struck the balance in favor of free speech.

While communities do have the right to regulate speech in order to uphold aesthetic standards (avoiding defacement of buildings) or to protect the public from disturbing noise, rules of this kind must be applied across the board and cannot be enforced selectively to prohibit certain kinds of messages but not others.

Under the Supreme Court's rulings, as I read them, the display of swastikas or Confederate flags clearly falls within the protection of the free-speech clause of the First Amendment and cannot be forbidden simply because it offends the feelings of many members of the community. These rulings apply to all agencies of government, including public universities.

Although it is unclear to what extent the First Amendment is enforceable against private institutions, I have difficulty understanding why a university such as Harvard should have less free speech than the surrounding society — or than a public university.

One reason why the power of censorship 10 is so dangerous is that it is extremely difficult to decide when a particular communication is offensive enough to warrant prohibition or to weigh the degree of offensiveness against the potential value of the communication. If we begin to forbid flags, it is only a short step to prohibiting offensive speakers.

I suspect that no community will become humane and caring by restricting what its members can say. The worst offenders will simply find other ways to irritate and insult.

In addition, once we start to declare certain things "offensive," with all the excitement and attention that will follow, I fear that much ingenuity will be exerted trying to test the limits, much time will be expended trying to draw tenuous distinctions, and the resulting publicity will eventually attract more attention to the offensive material than would ever have occurred otherwise.

Rather than prohibit such communications, with all the resulting risks, it would be better to ignore them, since students would then have little reason to create such displays and would soon abandon them. If this response is not possible—and one can understand why—the wisest course is to speak with those who perform insensitive acts and try to help them understand the effects of their actions on others.

Appropriate officials and faculty members should take the lead, as the Harvard House Masters have already done in this case. In talking with students, they should seek to educate and persuade, rather than resort to ridicule or intimidation, recognizing that only persuasion is likely to produce a lasting, beneficial effect. Through such efforts, I believe that we act in the manner most consistent with our ideals as an educational institution and most calculated to help us create a truly understanding, supportive community.

Topics for Critical Thinking and Writing

1. Derek Bok sketches the following argument (paras. 8 and 9): The First Amendment protects free speech in public universities and colleges; Harvard is not a public university; therefore, Harvard does not enjoy the protection of the First Amendment. Bok finds this argument invalid. He clearly rejects the conclusion. "I have difficulty understanding why . . . Harvard should have less free speech . . . than a public university." What would need to be revised in the premises to make the argument valid? Do you think Bok would accept or reject such a revision? Why, or why not?

2. Bok objects to censorship that simply prevents students from being "offended." He would not object to the campus police preventing students from being harmed. In an essay of 100 words, explain the difference between conduct that is *harmful* and conduct that is *offensive*. (If you think that such a distinction cannot be made, explain why.)

3. Bok advises campus officials (and students) to "ignore" offensive words, flags, and so forth (para. 13). Do you agree with this advice? Or do you favor a different kind of response? Write a 250-word essay on the theme "How We Ought to Respond to the Offensive Misconduct of Others."

THINKING FURTHER: FREEDOM OF EXPRESSION AND SOCIAL MEDIA

On February 8, 2009, the *New York Times* reported that a high school senior, Katherine Evans, believed that her English teacher, Sarah Phelps, behaved offensively in two ways: Evans said that the teacher ignored her requests for help with assignments and, further, that Phelps brusquely reproached her when Evans missed a class because she had attended a blood drive. Evans, an honor student, logged into Facebook and wrote about her teacher:

> To those select students who have had the displeasure of having Ms. Sarah Phelps, or simply knowing her and her insane antics: Here is the place to express your feelings of hatred.

The posting drew several responses, including some that criticized the student and supported the teacher. Here is one, written by a former student of Ms. Phelps, quoted by the *Times*:

Whatever your reasons for hating her are, they're probably very immature.

Ms. Evans removed the posting a few days later, but subsequently she was nevertheless reprimanded by the principal and received a three-day suspension for "cyberbullying." Ms. Evans sued the principal of the high school. She was not asking for money other than legal fees. Moreover, she wanted the suspension removed from her record. (She eventually settled the suit, and the suspension was wiped from her record.)

The issue to consider: Was the suspension an attack on Ms. Evans's right to free speech? Or did her comment and her invitation to "express feelings of hatred" constitute a verbal assault that crossed the line of freedom of expression? Howard Simon, executive director of the American Civil Liberties Union of Florida, takes the first position. The *Times* quotes him as saying, "Since when did criticism of a teacher morph into assault? If Katie Evans said what she said over burgers with her friends at the mall, there is no question it would be protected by free speech."

Three-Part Exercise in Definition

1. Construct a definition (three to five sentences) of *cyberbullying*. If you use sources, cite them.

2. Find a technical definition of cyberbullying as defined by a law, rule, or code, and compare it to your definition in #1 above. What limits and restrictions are included? (Be sure to cite your source.)

3. Given the admittedly scanty information that we have on the Evans case, do you think a suspension was reasonable, in light of the definitions of cyberbullying above? If you think it was reasonable, explain why. If you think it was unreasonable, explain why. Indicate also whether you think a different punishment might have been appropriate. Your essay should be about 250 to 300 words in length.

Exercise: Letter to the Editor

Your college newspaper has published a letter that links a hateful attribute to a group and that clearly displays hatred for the entire group. (For instance, the letter charges that interracial marriages should be made illegal because "African Americans carry a criminal gene" or that "Jews should not be elected to office because their loyalty is to Israel, not the United States" or that "Muslims should not be allowed to enter the country because they are intent on destroying America.") The letter generates many letters of response; some, supporting the editor's decision to publish the letter, make these points:

- The writer of the offending letter is a student in the college, and she has a right to express her views.

- The point of view expressed is probably held only by a few persons, but conceivably it expresses a view held by a significant number of students.

- Editors should not act as censors.

- The First Amendment guarantees freedom of speech.

- Freedom of expression is healthy — that is, society gains.

In contrast, among the letters opposing the editor's decision to publish, some make points along these lines:

- Not every view of every nutty student can be printed; editors must make responsible choices.

- The First Amendment, which prohibits the government from controlling the press, has nothing to do with a college newspaper.

- Letters of this sort do not foster healthy discussion; they merely heat things up.

Write a 250- to 500-word letter to the editor expressing your view of the decision to publish the first letter. (If you wish, you can assume that the letter addressed one of the topics we specify in the second sentence of this exercise. In any case, address the general issue of the editor's decision, not just the specific issue of the charge or charges made in the first letter.)

3

Critical Reading: Getting Deeper into Arguments

He that wrestles with us strengthens our nerves, and sharpens our skill.
Our antagonist is our helper.

— EDMUND BURKE

Persuasion, Argument, Dispute

When we think seriously about an argument, not only do we encounter ideas that may be unfamiliar but also we are forced to examine our own cherished opinions — and perhaps for the first time really see the strengths and weaknesses of what we believe. As John Stuart Mill put it, "He who knows only his own side of the case knows little."

It is useful to distinguish between **persuasion** and **argument**. Persuasion has the broader meaning. To **persuade** is to convince someone else to accept or adopt your position, which can be accomplished in a number of ways, including

- by giving reasons (i.e., by argument, by logic),
- by appealing to the emotions, or
- by using torture.

Argument, we mean to say, represents only one form of persuasion, one that relies on the cognitive or intellectual capacity for reason. Rhetoricians often use the Greek word *logos*, which means "word" or "reason," to denote this aspect of persuasive writing. An appeal to reason may by conducted by using such things as

- physical evidence,
- the testimony of experts,
- common sense, and
- probability.

We can put it this way: The goal of *argument* is to convince by demonstrating the truth (or probable truth) of an assertion, whereas the goal of *persuasion* is simply to convince by one means or another. *Logos*, the root word of *logic*, means appealing to the intellect to make rational claims and reasoned judgments.

The appeal to the emotions is known as **pathos**. Strictly speaking, *pathos* is Greek for "feeling." It covers all sorts of emotional appeals — for instance, appeals that elicit pity or sympathy (derived from the Greek for "feeling with"), or one's sense of duty or patriotism.

Notice that an argument doesn't require two speakers or writers with opposing positions. In practice, of course, they may, but it is not a requirement that arguments advance claims in opposition to another position. **Dispute** is a special kind of argument in which two or more people express views that are at odds. But the Declaration of Independence is also an argument, setting forth the colonists' reasons for declaring their independence. An essay showing indecisiveness to be Hamlet's tragic flaw would present an argument. Even when writing only for oneself, trying to clarify one's thinking by setting forth reasons and justifications for an idea, the result is an argument.

Most of this book is about argument in the sense of presenting reasonable support of claims, but reason is not the whole story. If an argument is to be effective, it must be presented persuasively. For instance, the writer's **tone** (presentation of self, topic, and audience) must be appropriate if the discourse is to persuade the reader. The careful presentation of the self is not something disreputable, nor is it something that publicity agents or advertising agencies invented. Aristotle (384–322 B.C.E.) emphasized the importance of impressing on the audience that the speaker is a person of good sense and high moral character. (He called this aspect of persuasion **ethos**, the Greek word for "character," a basis of persuasion different from *logos*, which involves persuasion by appealing to reason, and *pathos*, which persuades by appealing to emotion.)

Writers convey their *ethos*, their good character or trustworthiness, by doing the following:

- using language appropriate to the setting, avoiding vulgar language, slang, and colloquialism;
- showing an awareness of the issue's complexity (e.g., by offering other points of view in goodwill and by recognizing that contrary points of view may have some merit); and
- showing attention to detail (e.g., by citing relevant statistics).

In short, writers who are concerned with *ethos* — and all writers should be — employ devices that persuade readers that the writers are reliable, fair-minded, intelligent persons in whom their readers can have confidence.

We talk at length about tone, along with other matters such as the organization of an argument, in Chapter 5, Writing an Analysis of an Argument, but here we deal with some of the chief devices used in reasoning, and we glance at emotional appeals.

We should note at once, however, that an argument presupposes a fixed **topic**. Suppose we're arguing about Thomas Jefferson's assertion, in the Declaration of Independence, that "all men are created equal." Jones subscribes to this statement, but Smith says it's nonsense and argues that some people are obviously brighter than others, or healthier, or better coordinated, and so on. Jones and Smith, if they intend to argue the point, will do well to examine what Jefferson actually wrote:

> We hold these truths to be self-evident, that all men are created equal: that they are endowed by their Creator with certain unalienable rights; and that among these are life, liberty, and the pursuit of happiness.

There is room for debate over what Jefferson really meant and whether he is right, but clearly he was talking about *equality of rights*. If Smith and Jones wish to argue about Jefferson's view of equality — that is, if they wish to offer their reasons for accepting, rejecting, or modifying it — they must first agree on what Jefferson said or probably meant to say. Jones and Smith

THINKING CRITICALLY *Establishing Trustworthiness and Credibility*

For each method listed, provide your own example of a sentence that helps to establish trustworthiness and credibility. (Pick a topic that interests you. If you need ideas, look at the topics addressed by the authors presented in this chapter.) Be sure to use a tone and language that are appropriate and respectful of your audience.

METHOD	EXAMPLE	YOUR TURN
Acknowledge weaknesses, exceptions, and complexities.	"Although the unemployment rate continues to decline, further investigation into underemployment and the loss of jobless benefits is necessary in order to truly understand the unemployment crisis in the United States."	
Use personal experience when appropriate.	"As a student who works and attends school full-time, I can speak firsthand about the importance of increased availability of financial aid."	
Mention the qualifications of any sources as a way to boost your own credibility.	"According to Deborah Tannen, author and noted professor of linguistics at Georgetown University, . . ."	

📙 LaunchPad   To complete this activity online, go to **macmillanhighered.com/barnetbedauohara**

may still hold different views; they may continue to disagree on whether Jefferson was right and proceed to offer arguments and counterarguments to settle the point. But only if they can agree on *what* they disagree about will their dispute get somewhere.

Reason versus Rationalization

Reason may not be the only way of finding the truth, but it is a way on which we often rely. "The subway ran yesterday at 6:00 A.M. and the day before at 6:00 A.M. and the day before that, so I infer from this evidence that it will also run today at 6:00 A.M." (a form of reasoning known as **induction**). "Bus drivers require would-be passengers to present the exact change; I don't have the exact change; therefore, I infer I cannot ride on the bus" (**deduction**). (The terms *deduction* and *induction* are discussed in more detail on pp. 91 and 95.)

We also know that if we set our minds to a problem, we can often find reasons (not always necessarily sound ones) for almost anything we want to justify. Here's an entertaining example from Benjamin Franklin's *Autobiography:*

> I believe I have omitted mentioning that in my first voyage from Boston, being becalmed off Block Island, our people set about catching cod and hauled up a great many. Hitherto I had stuck to my resolution of not eating animal food, and on this occasion, I considered with my master Tryon the taking of every fish as a kind of unprovoked murder, since none of them had or ever could do us any injury that might justify the slaughter. All this seemed very reasonable. But I had formerly been a great lover of fish, and when this came hot out of the frying pan, it smelt admirably well. I balanced some time between principle and inclination, till I recollected that when the fish were opened I saw smaller fish taken out of their stomachs. Then thought I, if you eat one another, I don't see why we mayn't eat you. So I dined upon cod very heartily and continued to eat with other people, returning only now and then occasionally to a vegetable diet. So convenient a thing it is to be a *reasonable creature,* since it enables one to find or make a reason for everything one has a mind to do.

Franklin is being playful; he is *not* engaging in critical thinking. He tells us that he loved fish and that this fish "smelt admirably well," so we're prepared for him to find a reason (here one as weak as "Fish eat fish, therefore people may eat fish") to abandon his vegetarianism. (But think: Fish also eat their own young. May we therefore eat ours?)

Still, Franklin touches on a truth: If necessary, we can find reasons to justify whatever we want. That is, instead of reasoning, we may *rationalize* (devise a self-serving but dishonest reason), like the fox in Aesop's fables who, finding the grapes he desired were out of reach, consoled himself with the thought that they were probably sour.

Perhaps we can never be certain that we aren't rationalizing, except when being playful like Franklin. But we can seek to think critically about our own beliefs, scrutinizing our assumptions, looking for counterevidence, and wondering if it's reasonably possible to draw different conclusions.

Some Procedures in Argument

DEFINITION

Definition, we mentioned in Chapter 1, is one of the classical topics, a "place" to which one goes with questions; in answering the questions, one finds ideas. When we define, we're answering the question "What is it?" In answering this question as precisely as we can, we will find, clarify, and develop ideas.

We have already glanced at an argument over the proposition that "all men are created equal," and we saw that the words needed clarification. *Equal* meant, in the context, not physically or mentally equal but something like "equal in rights," equal politically and legally. (And, of course, *men* meant "white men and women.") Words don't always mean exactly what they seem to mean: There's no lead in a lead pencil, and a standard 2-by-4 is currently 1⅝ inches in thickness and 3⅜ inches in width.

DEFINITION BY SYNONYM Let's return for a moment to *pornography,* a word that is not easy to define. One way to define a word is to offer a **synonym**. Thus, pornography can be defined, at least roughly, as "obscenity" (something indecent). But definition by synonym is usually only a start because then we have to define the synonym; besides, very few words have exact synonyms. (In fact, *pornography* and *obscenity* are not exact synonyms.)

DEFINITION BY EXAMPLE A second way to define a word is to point to an example (this is often called **ostensive definition**, from the Latin *ostendere,* "to show"). This method can be very helpful, ensuring that both writer and reader are talking about the same thing, but

Tom Cheney, The New Yorker Collection / The Cartoon Bank

"It all depends on how you define 'chop.'"

it also has limitations. A few decades ago, many people pointed to James Joyce's *Ulysses* and D. H. Lawrence's *Lady Chatterley's Lover* as examples of obscene novels, but today these books are regarded as literary masterpieces. It's possible that they can be obscene and also be literary masterpieces. (Joyce's wife is reported to have said of her husband, "He may have been a great writer, but . . . he had a very dirty mind.")

One of the difficulties of using an example, however, is that the example is richer and more complex than the term it's being used to define, and this richness and complexity get in the way of achieving a clear definition. Thus, if one cites *Lady Chatterley's Lover* as an example of pornography, a reader may erroneously think that pornography has something to do with British novels (because Lawrence was British) or with heterosexual relationships outside of marriage. Yet neither of these ideas relates to the concept of pornography.

We are not trying here to formulate a satisfactory definition of *pornography*. Our object is to make the following points clear:

- An argument will be most fruitful if the participants first agree on what they are talking about.

- One way to secure such agreement is to define the topic ostensively.

- Choosing the right example, one that has all the central or typical characteristics, can make a topic not only clear but also vivid.

DEFINITION BY STIPULATION   Arguments frequently involve matters of definition. In a discussion of gun control, for instance, you probably will hear one side speak of *assault weapons* and the other side speak instead of *so-called assault weapons*. In arguing, you can hope to get agreement — at least on what the topic of argument is — by offering a **stipulative definition** (from a Latin verb meaning "to bargain"). For instance, you and a representative of the other side can agree on a definition of *assault weapon* based on the meaning of the term in the ban approved by Congress in 1994, which expired in 2004, and which President Obama in 2013 asked Congress to renew. Although the renewal of the ban was unsuccessful, the definition was this: a semiautomatic firearm (the spent cartridge case is automatically extracted, and a new round is automatically reloaded into the chamber but isn't fired until the trigger is pulled again) with a detachable magazine *and at least two of the following five characteristics*:

- collapsible or folding stock
- pistol grip (thus allowing the weapon to be fired from the hip)
- bayonet mount
- grenade launcher
- flash suppressor (to keep the shooter from being blinded by muzzle flashes)

Again, this was the agreed-upon definition for the purposes of the legislation. Congress put *fully* automatic weapons into an entirely different category, and the legislatures of California and of New York each agreed on a stipulation different from that of Congress: In these two states, an assault weapon is defined as a semiautomatic firearm with a detachable magazine and with any *one* (not two) of the five bulleted items. The point is that for an argument to proceed rationally, and especially in the legal context, the key terms need to be precisely defined and agreed upon by all parties.

Let's now look at stipulative definitions in other contexts. Who is a *Native American*? In discussing this issue, you might stipulate that *Native American* means any person with any Native American blood; or you might say, "For the purpose of the present discussion, I mean that a *Native American* is any person who has at least one grandparent of pure Native American blood." A stipulative definition is appropriate in the following cases:

- when no fixed or standard definition is available, and
- when an arbitrary specification is necessary to fix the meaning of a key term in the argument.

Not everyone may accept your stipulative definition, and there will likely be defensible alternatives. In any case, when you stipulate a definition, your audience knows what *you* mean by the term.

It would *not* be reasonable to stipulate that by *Native American* you mean anyone with a deep interest in North American aborigines. That's too idiosyncratic to be useful. Similarly, an essay on Jews in America will have to rely on a definition of the key idea. Perhaps the writer will stipulate the definition used in Israel: A Jew is a person who has a Jewish mother or, if not born of a Jewish mother, a person who has formally adopted the Jewish faith. Perhaps the writer will stipulate another meaning: Jews are people who consider themselves to be Jews. Some sort of reasonable definition must be offered.

To stipulate, however, that *Jews* means "persons who believe that the area formerly called Palestine rightfully belongs to the Jews" would hopelessly confuse matters. Remember the old riddle: If you call a dog's tail a leg, how many legs does a dog have? The answer is four. Calling a tail a leg doesn't make it a leg.

Later in this chapter you will see, in an essay titled "When 'Identity Politics' Is Rational," that the author, Stanley Fish, begins by stipulating a definition. His first paragraph begins thus:

> If there's anything everyone is against in these election times, it's "identity politics," a phrase that covers a multitude of sins. Let me start with a definition. (It may not be yours, but it will at least allow the discussion to be framed.) You're practicing identity politics when you vote for or against someone because of his or her skin color, ethnicity, religion, gender, sexual orientation, or any other marker that leads you to say yes or no independently of a candidates' ideas or policies.

Fish will argue in later paragraphs that sometimes identity politics makes very good sense, that it is *not* irrational, is *not* logically indefensible; but here we simply want to make two points — one about how a definition helps the writer, and one about how it helps the reader:

- A definition is a good way to get started when drafting an essay, a useful stimulus (idea prompt, pattern, template, heuristic) that will help *you* to think about the issue, a device that will stimulate your further thinking.
- A definition lets readers be certain that they understand what the author means by a crucial word.

Readers may disagree with Fish, but at least they know what he means when he speaks of identity politics.

A stipulation may be helpful and legitimate. Here's the opening paragraph of a 1975 essay by Richard B. Brandt titled "The Morality and Rationality of Suicide." Notice that the author does two things:

- He first stipulates a definition.
- Then, aware that the definition may strike some readers as too broad and therefore unreasonable or odd, he offers a reason on behalf of his definition.

"Suicide" is conveniently defined, for our purposes, as doing something which results in one's death, either from the intention of ending one's life or the intention to bring about some other state of affairs (such as relief from pain) which one thinks it certain or highly probable can be achieved only by means of death or will produce death. It may seem odd to classify an act of heroic self-sacrifice on the part of a soldier as suicide. It is simpler, however, not to try to define "suicide" so that an act of suicide is always irrational or immoral in some way; if we adopt a neutral definition like the above we can still proceed to ask when an act of suicide in that sense is rational, morally justifiable, and so on, so that all evaluations anyone might wish to make can still be made. (61)

Sometimes, a definition that at first seems extremely odd can be made acceptable by offering strong reasons in its support. Sometimes, in fact, an odd definition marks a great intellectual step forward. For instance, in 1990 the U.S. Supreme Court recognized that *speech* includes symbolic nonverbal expression such as protesting against a war by wearing armbands or by flying the American flag upside down. Such actions, because they express ideas or emotions, are now protected by the First Amendment. Few people today would disagree that *speech* should include symbolic gestures. (We include an example of controversy over this issue in Derek Bok's essay "Protecting Freedom of Expression on the Campus" in Chapter 2.)

A definition that seems notably eccentric to many readers and thus far has not gained much support is from Peter Singer's *Practical Ethics*, in which the author suggests that a non-human being can be a *person*. He admits that "it sounds odd to call an animal a person" but says that it seems so only because of our habit of sharply separating ourselves from other species. For Singer, *persons* are "rational and self-conscious beings, aware of themselves as distinct entities with a past and a future." Thus, although a newborn infant is a human being, it isn't a person; however, an adult chimpanzee isn't a human being but probably is a person. You don't have to agree with Singer to know exactly what he means and where he stands. Moreover, if you read his essay, you may even find that his reasons are plausible and that by means of his unusual definition he has broadened your thinking.

THE IMPORTANCE OF DEFINITIONS   Trying to decide on the best way to define a key idea or a central concept is often difficult as well as controversial. *Death*, for example, has been redefined in recent years. Traditionally, a person was considered dead when there was no longer any heartbeat. But with advancing medical technology, the medical profession has persuaded legislatures to redefine death as cessation of cerebral and cortical functions — so-called brain death.

Some scholars have hoped to bring clarity into the abortion debate by redefining *life*. Traditionally, human life has been seen as beginning at birth or perhaps at viability (the capacity of a fetus to live independently of the uterine environment). However, others have proposed a *brain birth* definition in the hope of resolving the abortion controversy. Some thinkers want abortion to be prohibited by law at the point where "integrated brain functioning begins to emerge," allegedly about seventy days after conception. Whatever the merits of such a redefinition may be, the debate is convincing evidence of just how important the definition of certain terms can be.

LAST WORDS ABOUT DEFINITION Since Plato's time in the fourth century B.C.E, it has often been argued that the best way to give a definition is to state the *essence* of the thing being defined. Thus, the classic example defines *man* as "a rational animal." (Today, to avoid sexist implications, instead of *man* we would say *human being* or *person*.) That is, the property of *rational animality* is considered to be the essence of every human creature, so it must be mentioned in the definition of *man*. This statement guarantees that the definition is neither too broad nor too narrow. But philosophers have long criticized this alleged ideal type of definition on several grounds, one of which is that no one can propose such definitions without assuming that the thing being defined has an essence in the first place — an assumption that is not necessary. Thus, we may want to define *causality,* or *explanation,* or even *definition* itself, but it's doubtful whether it is sound to assume that any of these concepts has an essence.

A much better way to provide a definition is to offer a set of **sufficient and necessary conditions**. Suppose we want to define the word *circle* and are conscious of the need to keep circles distinct from other geometric figures such as rectangles and spheres. We might express our definition by citing sufficient and necessary conditions as follows: "Anything is a circle *if and only if* it is a closed plane figure and all points on the circumference are equidistant from the center." Using the connective "if and only if" (called the *biconditional*) between the definition and the term being defined helps to make the definition neither too exclusive (too narrow) nor too inclusive (too broad). Of course, for most ordinary purposes we don't require such a formally precise definition. Nevertheless, perhaps the best criterion to keep in mind when assessing a proposed definition is whether it can be stated in the "if and only if" form, and whether, if so stated, it is true; that is, if it truly specifies *all and only* the things covered by the word being defined. The Thinking Critically exercise that follows provides examples.

We aren't saying that the four sentences in the table below are incontestable. In fact, they are definitely arguable. We offer them merely to show ways of defining, and the act of defining is one way of helping to get your own thoughts going. Notice, too, that the fourth example, a "statement of necessary and sufficient conditions" (indicated by *if and only if*), is a bit stiff for ordinary writing. An informal prompt along this line might begin, "Essentially, something can be called *pornography* if it presents. . . ."

THINKING CRITICALLY *Giving Definitions*

In the spaces provided, define one of the "new terms" provided according to the definition type stipulated.

DEFINITION TYPE	EXAMPLE	NEW TERM	YOUR DEFINITION
Synonym	"*Pornography*, simply stated, is obscenity."	Police brutality Helicopter parenting Alternative music Organic foods	
Example	"*Pornography* can be seen, for example, in D. H. Lawrence's *Lady Chatterley's Lover*, in the scene where . . ."	Police brutality Helicopter parenting Alternative music Organic foods	
Stipulation	"For the purposes of this essay, *pornography* means any type of media that . . ."	Police brutality Helicopter parenting Alternative music Organic foods	
Statement of necessary and sufficient conditions	"Something can be called *pornography* if and only if it presents sexually stimulating material without offering anything of redeeming social value."	Police brutality Helicopter parenting Alternative music Organic foods	

LaunchPad To complete this activity online, go to **macmillanhighered.com/barnetbedauohara**

ASSUMPTIONS

In Chapter 1, we discussed the **assumptions** made by the authors of two essays on religious freedoms. But we have more to say about assumptions. We've already said that in the form of discourse known as argument, certain statements are offered as reasons for other statements. But even the longest and most complex chain of reasoning or proof is fastened to assumptions — one or more *unexamined beliefs*. (Even if writer and reader share such a belief, it is no less an assumption.) Benjamin Franklin argued against paying salaries to the holders of executive offices in the federal government on the grounds that men are moved by ambition (love of power) and by avarice (love of money) and that powerful positions conferring wealth incite men to do their worst. These assumptions he stated, although he felt no need to argue them at length because he assumed that his readers shared them.

An assumption may be unstated. A writer, painstakingly arguing specific points, may choose to keep one or more of the argument's assumptions tacit. Or the writer may be completely unaware of an underlying assumption. For example, Franklin didn't even bother to state another assumption. He must have assumed that persons of wealth who accept an unpaying job (after all, only persons of wealth could afford to hold unpaid government jobs) will have at heart the interests of all classes of people, not only the interests of their own class. Probably Franklin didn't state this assumption because he thought it was perfectly obvious, but if you think critically about it, you may find reasons to doubt it. Surely one reason we pay our legislators is to ensure that the legislature does not consist only of people whose incomes may give them an inadequate view of the needs of others.

As another example, here are two assumptions in the argument for permitting abortion:

1. Ours is a pluralistic society, in which we believe that the religious beliefs of one group should not be imposed on others.

2. Personal privacy is a right, and a woman's body is hers, not to be violated by laws that forbid her from doing certain things to her body.

But these (and other) arguments *assume* that a fetus is not — or not yet — a person and therefore is not entitled to the same protection against assaults that we are. Virtually all of us assume that it is usually wrong to kill a human being. Granted, there may be instances in which we believe it's acceptable to take a human life, such as self-defense against a would-be murderer. But even here we find a shared assumption that persons are ordinarily entitled not to be killed.

The argument about abortion, then, usually depends on opposed assumptions. For one group, the fetus is a human being and a potential person — and this potentiality is decisive. For the other group, it is not. Persons arguing one side or the other of the abortion issue ought to be aware that opponents may not share their assumptions.

PREMISES AND SYLLOGISMS

Premises are stated assumptions that are used as reasons in an argument. (The word comes from a Latin word meaning "to send before" or "to set in front.") A premise thus is a statement set down — assumed — before the argument begins. The joining of two premises — two statements taken to be true — to produce a conclusion, a third statement, is a **syllogism** (from the Greek for "a reckoning together"). The classic example is this:

Major premise:	All human beings are mortal.
Minor premise:	Socrates is a human being.
Conclusion:	Socrates is mortal.

DEDUCTION

The mental process of moving from one statement ("All human beings are mortal") through another ("Socrates is a human being") to yet a further statement ("Socrates is mortal") is **deduction**, from the Latin for "lead down from." In this sense, deductive reasoning doesn't give us any new knowledge, although it's easy to construct examples that have so many premises, or premises that are so complex, that the conclusion really does come as news to most who examine the argument. Thus, the great fictional detective Sherlock Holmes was credited by his admiring colleague, Dr. Watson, with having unusual powers of deduction. Watson meant in part that Holmes could see the logical consequences of apparently disconnected reasons, the number and complexity of which left others at a loss. What is common in all cases of deduction is that the reasons or premises offered are supposed to contain within themselves, so to speak, the conclusion extracted from them.

Often a syllogism is abbreviated. Martin Luther King Jr., defending a protest march, wrote in "Letter from Birmingham Jail":

> You assert that our actions, even though peaceful, must be condemned because they precipitate violence.

Fully expressed, the argument that King attributes to his critics would be stated thus:

> Society must condemn actions (even if peaceful) that precipitate violence.
>
> This action (though peaceful) will precipitate violence.
>
> Therefore, society must condemn this action.

An incomplete or abbreviated syllogism in which one of the premises is left unstated, of the sort found in King's original quotation, is an **enthymeme** (from the Greek for "in the mind").

Here is another, more whimsical example of an enthymeme, in which both a premise and the conclusion are left implicit. Henry David Thoreau remarked that "circumstantial evidence can be very strong, as when you find a trout in the milk." The joke, perhaps intelligible only to people born before 1930 or so, depends on the fact that milk used to be sold "in bulk" — that is, ladled out of a big can directly to the customer by the farmer or grocer. This practice was prohibited in the 1930s because for centuries the sellers, seeking to increase their profit, were diluting the milk with water. Thoreau's enthymeme can be fully expressed thus:

> Trout live only in water.
>
> This milk has a trout in it.
>
> Therefore, this milk has water in it.

These enthymemes have three important properties: Their premises are *true*, the form of their argument is *valid*, and they leave *implicit* either the conclusion or one of the premises.

NOT AN ENTRANCE

NOT AN EXIT

DEPT OF LOGIC

SOUND ARGUMENTS

The purpose of a syllogism is to present reasons that establish its conclusion. This is done by making sure that the argument satisfies both of two independent criteria:

- First, all of the premises must be *true.*
- Second, the syllogism must be *valid.*

Once these criteria are satisfied, the conclusion of the syllogism is guaranteed. Any such argument is said to establish or to prove its conclusion — to use another term, it is said to be **sound**. Here's an example of a sound argument, a syllogism that proves its conclusion:

Extracting oil from the Arctic Wildlife Refuge would adversely affect the local ecology.

Adversely affecting the local ecology is undesirable, unless there is no better alternative fuel source.

Therefore, extracting oil from the Arctic Wildlife Refuge is undesirable, unless there is no better alternative fuel source.

Each premise is **true**, and the syllogism is **valid**, so it establishes its conclusion.

But how do we tell in any given case that an argument is sound? We perform two different tests, one for the truth of each of the premises and another for the validity of the argument.

The basic test for the **truth** of a premise is to determine whether what it asserts corresponds with reality; if it does, then it is true, and if it doesn't, then it is false. Everything depends on the premise's content — what it asserts — and the evidence for it. (In the preceding syllogism, it's possible to test the truth of the premises by checking the views of experts and interested parties, such as policymakers, environmental groups, and experts on energy.)

The test for **validity** is quite different. We define a valid argument as one in which the conclusion follows from the premises, so that if all the premises are true, then the conclusion *must* be true, too. The general test for validity, then, is this: If one grants the premises, one must also grant the conclusion. In other words, if one grants the premises but denies the conclusion, is one caught in a self-contradiction? If so, the argument is valid; if not, the argument is invalid.

The preceding syllogism passes this test. If you grant the information given in the premises but deny the conclusion, you contradict yourself. Even if the information were in error, the conclusion in this syllogism would still follow from the premises — the hallmark of a valid argument! The conclusion follows because the validity of an argument is a purely formal matter concerning the *relation* between premises and conclusion based on what they mean.

It's possible to see this relationship more clearly by examining an argument that is valid but that, because one or both of the premises are false, does *not* establish its conclusion. Here's an example of such a syllogism:

> The whale is a large fish.
> All large fish have scales.
> Therefore, whales have scales.

We know that the premises and the conclusion are false: Whales are mammals, not fish, and not all large fish have scales (sharks have no scales, for instance). But in determining the argument's validity, the truth of the premises and the conclusion is beside the point. Just a little reflection assures us that *if* both premises were true, then the conclusion would have to be true as well. That is, anyone who grants the premises of this syllogism yet denies the conclusion contradicts herself. So the validity of an argument does not in any way depend on the truth of the premises or the conclusion.

A sound argument, as we said, is one that passes both the test of true premises and the test of valid inference. To put it another way, a sound argument does the following:

- It passes the test of content (the premises are true, as a matter of fact).
- It passes the test of form (its premises and conclusion, by virtue of their very meanings, are so related that it is impossible for the premises to be true and the conclusion false).

Accordingly, an unsound argument, one that fails to prove its conclusion, suffers from one or both of two defects:

- Not all the premises are true.
- The argument is invalid.

Usually, we have in mind one or both defects when objecting to someone's argument as "illogical." In evaluating a deductive argument, therefore, you must always ask: Is it vulnerable to criticism on the grounds that one (or more) of its premises is false? Or is the inference itself vulnerable because even if all the premises are true, the conclusion still wouldn't follow?

A deductive argument proves its conclusion if and only if *two conditions* are satisfied: (1) All the premises are true, and (2) it would be inconsistent to assert the premises and deny the conclusions.

A WORD ABOUT FALSE PREMISES   Suppose that one or more of a syllogism's premises are false but the syllogism itself is valid. What does that indicate about the truth of the conclusion? Consider this example:

> All Americans prefer vanilla ice cream to other flavors.
>
> Jimmy Fallon is an American.
>
> Therefore, Jimmy Fallon prefers vanilla ice cream to other flavors.

The first (or major) premise in this syllogism is false. Yet the argument passes our formal test for validity; if one grants both premises, then one must accept the conclusion. So we can say that the conclusion *follows from* its premises, even though the premises *do not prove* the conclusion. This is not as paradoxical as it may sound. For all we know, the argument's conclusion may in fact be true; Jimmy Fallon may indeed prefer vanilla ice cream, and the odds are that he does because consumption statistics show that a majority of Americans prefer vanilla. Nevertheless, if the conclusion in this syllogism is true, it's not because this argument proved it.

A WORD ABOUT INVALID SYLLOGISMS   Usually, one can detect a false premise in an argument, especially when the suspect premise appears in someone else's argument. A trickier business is the invalid syllogism. Consider this argument:

> All terrorists seek publicity for their violent acts.
>
> John Doe seeks publicity for his violent acts.
>
> Therefore, John Doe is a terrorist.

In this syllogism, let's grant that the first (major) premise is true. Let's also grant that the conclusion may well be true. Finally, the person mentioned in the second (minor) premise could indeed be a terrorist. But it's also possible that the conclusion is false; terrorists aren't the only ones who seek publicity for their violent acts — consider, for example, the violence committed against doctors, clinic workers, and patients at clinics where abortions are performed. In short, the truth of the two premises is no guarantee that the conclusion is also true. It's possible to assert both premises and deny the conclusion without being self-contradictory.

How do we tell, in general and in particular cases, whether a syllogism is valid? Chemists use litmus paper to determine instantly whether the liquid in a test tube is an acid or a base. Unfortunately, logic has no litmus test to tell us instantly whether an argument is valid or invalid. Logicians beginning with Aristotle have developed techniques to test any given argument, no matter how complex or subtle, to determine its validity. But the results of their labors cannot be expressed in a paragraph or even a few pages; this is why entire semester-long courses are devoted to teaching formal deductive logic. Apart from advising you to consult Chapter 9, A Logician's View: Deduction, Induction, Fallacies, all we can do here is repeat two basic points.

First, the validity of deductive arguments is a matter of their *form* or *structure*. Even syllogisms like the one on the Arctic Wildlife Refuge on page 92 come in a large variety of forms (256 forms, to be precise), and only some of these forms are valid. Second, all valid deductive arguments (and only such arguments) pass this test: If one accepts all the premises, then one must accept the conclusion as well. Hence, if it's possible to accept the premises but reject the conclusion (without self-contradiction, of course), then the argument is invalid.

Let's exit from further discussion of this important but difficult subject on a lighter note. Many illogical arguments masquerade as logical. Consider this example: If it takes a horse and carriage four hours to go from Pinsk to Chelm, does it follow that a carriage with two horses will get there in two hours?

Note: In Chapter 9, we discuss at some length other kinds of deductive arguments, as well as **fallacies**, which are kinds of invalid reasoning.

INDUCTION

Whereas deduction takes beliefs and assumptions and extracts their hidden consequences, **induction** uses information about observed cases to reach a conclusion about unobserved cases. (The word comes from the Latin *in ducere,* "to lead into" or "to lead up to.") If we observe that the bite of a certain snake is poisonous, we may conclude on the basis of this evidence that the bite of another snake of the same general type is also poisonous. Our inference might be even broader: If we observe that snake after snake of a certain type has a poisonous bite and that these snakes are all rattlesnakes, then we're tempted to **generalize** that all rattlesnakes are poisonous.

By far the most common way to test the adequacy of a generalization is to consider one or more **counterexamples**. If the counterexamples are genuine and reliable, then the generalization must be false. For example, Ronald Takaki's essay on the "myth" of Asian racial superiority (p. 124) is full of examples that contradict the alleged superiority of Asians; they are counterexamples to that thesis, and they help to expose it as a "myth." What is true of Takaki's reasoning is true generally in argumentative writing: We constantly test our generalizations by considering them against actual or possible counterexamples, or by doing research on the issue.

Unlike deduction, induction yields conclusions that go beyond the information contained in the premises used in their support. It's not surprising that the conclusions of inductive reasoning are not always true, even when all the premises are true. On page 83, we gave as an example our observation that on previous days a subway has run at 6:00 A.M. and that therefore we conclude that it runs at 6:00 A.M. every day. Suppose, following this reasoning, we arrive at the subway platform just before 6:00 A.M. on a given day and wait for an hour without seeing a single train. What inference should we draw to explain this? Possibly today is Sunday, and the subway doesn't run before 7:00 A.M. Or possibly there was a breakdown earlier this morning. Whatever the explanation might be, we relied on a sample that wasn't large enough (a larger sample might have included some early morning breakdowns) or representative enough (a more representative sample would have included the later starts on Sundays and holidays).

A WORD ABOUT SAMPLES   When we reason inductively, much depends on the size and the quality of the sample (we say "sample" because a writer probably cannot examine every instance). If, for example, we're offering an argument concerning the politics of members of sororities and fraternities, we probably cannot interview *every* member. Rather, we select a sample. But is the sample a fair one? Is it representative of the larger group? We may interview five members of Alpha Tau Omega and find that all five are Republicans, yet we cannot legitimately conclude that all members of ATO are Republicans. The problem doesn't always involve failing to interview an adequately large sample group. For example, a poll of ten thousand college students tells us very little about "college students" if all ten thousand are white males at the University of Texas. Because such a sample leaves out women and minority males, it isn't sufficiently *representative* of "college students" as a group. Further, though not all students at the University of Texas are from Texas or even from the Southwest, it's quite likely that the student body is not fully representative (e.g., in race and in income) of American college students. If this conjecture is correct, even a truly representative sample of University of Texas students wouldn't enable us to draw firm conclusions about American college students.

In short: An argument that uses samples ought to tell the reader how the samples were chosen. If it doesn't provide this information, the reader should treat the argument with suspicion.

EVIDENCE: EXPERIMENTATION, EXAMPLES, AUTHORITATIVE TESTIMONY, STATISTICS

Different disciplines use different kinds of evidence:

- In literary studies, the texts are usually the chief evidence.
- In the social sciences, field research (interviews, surveys) usually provides evidence.
- In the sciences, reports of experiments are the usual evidence; if an assertion cannot be tested — if one cannot show it to be false — it is a *belief,* an *opinion,* not a scientific hypothesis.

EXPERIMENTATION   Induction is obviously useful in arguing. If, for example, one is arguing that handguns should be controlled, one will point to specific cases in which handguns caused accidents or were used to commit crimes. In arguing that abortion has a traumatic effect on women, one will point to women who testify to that effect. Each instance constitutes **evidence** for the relevant generalization.

In a courtroom, evidence bearing on the guilt of the accused is introduced by the prosecution, and evidence to the contrary is introduced by the defense. Not all evidence is admissible (e.g., hearsay is not, even if it's true), and the law of evidence is a highly developed subject in jurisprudence. In the forum of daily life, the sources of evidence are less disciplined. Daily experience, a particularly memorable observation, an unusual event — any or all of these may serve as evidence for (or against) some belief, theory, hypothesis, or explanation. Science involves the systematic study of what experience can yield, and one of the most distinctive features of the evidence that scientists can marshal on behalf of their claims is that it is the result of **experimentation**. Experiments are deliberately contrived situations, often complex in their technology, that are designed to yield particular observations. What the ordinary person does with unaided eye and ear, the scientist does, much more carefully and thoroughly, with the help of laboratory instruments.

The variety, extent, and reliability of the evidence obtained in daily life are quite different from those obtained in the laboratory. It's no surprise that society attaches much more weight to the "findings" of scientists than to the corroborative (much less the contrary) experiences of ordinary people. No one today would seriously argue that the sun really does go around the earth just because it looks that way; nor would we argue that because viruses are invisible to the naked eye they cannot cause symptoms such as swellings and fevers, which are plainly evident.

EXAMPLES One form of evidence is the **example**. Suppose we argue that a candidate is untrustworthy and shouldn't be elected to public office. We point to episodes in his career — his misuse of funds in 2008 and the false charges he made against an opponent in 2016 — as examples of his untrustworthiness. Or if we're arguing that President Truman ordered the atom bomb dropped to save American (and, for that matter, Japanese) lives that otherwise would have been lost in a hard-fought invasion of Japan, we point to the stubbornness of the Japanese defenders in battles on the islands of Saipan, Iwo Jima, and Okinawa, where Japanese soldiers fought to the death rather than surrender.

These examples, we say, indicate that the Japanese defenders of the main islands would have fought to their deaths without surrendering, even though they knew defeat was certain. Or if we argue that the war was nearly won when Truman dropped the bomb, we can cite secret peace feelers as examples of the Japanese willingness to end the war.

An *example* is a *sample*. These two words come from the same Old French word, *essample,* from the Latin *exemplum,* which means "something taken out" — that is, a selection from the group. A Yiddish proverb shrewdly says, "'For example' is no proof," but the evidence of well-chosen examples can go a long way toward helping a writer to convince an audience.

In arguments, three sorts of examples are especially common:

- real events
- invented instances (artificial or hypothetical cases)
- analogies

We will treat each of these briefly.

Real Events In referring to Truman's decision to drop the atom bomb, we've already touched on examples drawn from real events — the battles at Saipan and elsewhere. And we've also seen Ben Franklin pointing to an allegedly real happening, a fish that had consumed a smaller fish. The advantage of an example drawn from real life, whether a great historical event or a local incident, is that its reality gives it weight. It cannot simply be brushed off.

Yet an example drawn from reality may not be as clear-cut as we would like. Suppose, for instance, that someone cites the Japanese army's behavior on Saipan and on Iwo Jima as evidence that the Japanese later would have fought to the death in an American invasion of Japan and would therefore have inflicted terrible losses on themselves and on the Americans. This example is open to the response that in June and July 1945 certain Japanese diplomats sent out secret peace feelers, so that in August 1945, when Truman authorized dropping the bomb, the situation was very different.

Similarly, in support of the argument that nations will no longer resort to using atomic weapons, some people have offered as evidence the fact that since World War I the great powers have not used poison gas. But the argument needs more support than this fact provides. Poison gas wasn't decisive or even highly effective in World War I. Moreover, the invention of gas masks made its use obsolete.

In short, any *real* event is so entangled in historical circumstances that it might not be adequate or relevant evidence in the case being argued. In using a real event as an example (a perfectly valid strategy), the writer must demonstrate that the event can be taken out of its historical context for use in the new context of argument. Thus, in an argument against using atomic weapons in warfare, the many deaths and horrible injuries inflicted on the Japanese at Hiroshima and Nagasaki can be cited as effects of nuclear weapons that would invariably occur and did not depend on any special circumstances of their use in Japan in 1945.

Invented Instances **Artificial** or **hypothetical cases — invented instances** — have the great advantage of being protected from objections of the sort we have just given. Recall Thoreau's trout in the milk; that was a colorful hypothetical case that illustrated his point well. An invented instance ("Let's assume that a burglar promises not to shoot a householder if the householder swears not to identify him. Is the householder bound by the oath?") is something like a drawing of a flower in a botany textbook or a diagram of the folds of a mountain in a geology textbook. It is admittedly false, but by virtue of its simplifications it sets forth the relevant details very clearly. Thus, in a discussion of rights, the philosopher Charles Frankel says:

> Strictly speaking, when we assert a right for *X,* we assert that *Y* has a duty. Strictly speaking, that *Y* has such a duty presupposes that *Y* has the capacity to perform this duty. It would be nonsense to say, for example, that a nonswimmer has a moral duty to swim to the help of a drowning man.

This invented example is admirably clear, and it is immune to charges that might muddy the issue if Frankel, instead of referring to a wholly abstract person, *Y,* talked about some real person, Jones, who did not rescue a drowning man. For then Frankel would get bogged down over arguing about whether Jones *really* couldn't swim well enough to help, and so on.

Yet invented examples have drawbacks. First and foremost, they cannot serve as evidence. A purely hypothetical example can illustrate a point or provoke reconsideration of a generalization, but it cannot substitute for actual events as evidence supporting an inductive inference. Sometimes, such examples are so fanciful that they fail to convince the reader. Thus, the philosopher Judith Jarvis Thomson, in the course of an argument entitled "A Defense of Abortion," asks the reader to imagine waking up one day and finding that against her will a celebrated violinist whose body is not adequately functioning has been hooked up into her body for life support. Does she have the right to unplug the violinist? As you read the essays we present in this textbook, you'll have to decide for yourself whether the invented cases proposed by various authors are helpful or whether they are so remote that they hinder thought. Readers will have to decide, too, about when they can use invented cases to advance their own arguments.

But we add one point: Even a highly fanciful invented case can have the valuable effect of forcing us to see where we stand. A person may say that she is, in all circumstances, against vivisection — the practice of performing operations on live animals for the purpose of research. But what would she say if she thought that an experiment on one mouse would save the life of someone she loves? Conversely, if she approves of vivisection, would she also approve of sacrificing the last giant panda to save the life of a senile stranger, a person who in any case probably wouldn't live longer than another year? Artificial cases of this sort can help us to see that we didn't really mean to say such-and-such when we said so-and-so.

Analogies   The third sort of example, **analogy**, is a kind of comparison. An analogy asserts that things that are alike in some ways are alike in yet another way as well. Here's an example:

> Before the Roman Empire declined as a world power, it exhibited a decline in morals and in physical stamina; our society today shows a decline in both morals (consider the high divorce rate and the crime rate) and physical culture (consider obesity in children). America, like Rome, will decline as a world power.

Strictly speaking, an analogy is an extended comparison in which different things are shown to be similar in several ways. Thus, if one wants to argue that a head of state should have extraordinary power during wartime, one can argue that the state at such a time is like a ship in a storm: The crew is needed to lend its help, but the decisions are best left to the captain. (Notice that an analogy compares things that are relatively *un*like. Comparing the plight of one ship to another or of one government to another isn't an analogy; it's an inductive inference from one case of the same sort to another such case.)

Let's consider another analogy. We have already glanced at Judith Thomson's hypothetical case in which the reader wakes up to find

"*Do you mind if I use yet another sports analogy?*"

herself hooked up to a violinist in need of life support. Thomson uses this situation as an analogy in an argument about abortion. The reader stands for the mother; the violinist, for the unwanted fetus. You may want to think about whether this analogy is close enough to pregnancy to help illuminate your own thinking about abortion.

The problem with argument by analogy is this: Two admittedly different things are agreed to be similar in several ways, and the arguer goes on to assert or imply that they are also similar in another way — the point being argued. (That's why Thomson argues that if something is true of the reader-hooked-up-to-a-violinist, it is also true of the pregnant-mother-hooked-up-to-a-fetus.) But the two things that are said to be analogous and that are indeed similar in characteristics *A, B,* and *C* are also different — let's say in characteristics *D* and *E*. As Bishop Butler is said to have remarked in the early eighteenth century, "Everything is what it is, and not another thing."

Analogies can be convincing, especially because they can make complex issues seem simple. "Don't change horses in midstream" isn't a statement about riding horses across a river but, rather, about choosing new leaders in critical times. Still, in the end, analogies don't necessarily prove anything. What may be true about riding horses across a stream may not be true about choosing new leaders in troubled times. Riding horses across a stream and choosing new leaders are fundamentally different things, and however much they may be said to resemble each other, they remain different. What is true for one need not be true for the other.

Analogies can be helpful in developing our thoughts and in helping listeners or readers to understand a point we're trying to make. It is sometimes argued, for instance — on the analogy of the doctor–patient, the lawyer–client, or the priest–penitent relationship — that newspaper and television reporters should not be required to reveal their confidential sources. That is worth thinking about: Do the similarities run deep enough, or are there fundamental differences? Consider another example: Some writers who support abortion argue that the fetus is not a person any more than the acorn is an oak. That is also worth thinking about. But one should also think about this response: A fetus is not a person, just as an acorn is not an oak; but an acorn is a potential oak, and a fetus is a potential person, a potential adult human being. Children, even newborn infants, have rights, and one way to explain this claim is to call attention to their potentiality to become mature adults. Thus, some people argue that the fetus, by analogy, has the rights of an infant, for the fetus, like the infant, is a potential adult.

Three analogies for consideration: First, let's examine a brief comparison made by Jill Knight, a member of the British Parliament, speaking about abortion:

> Babies are not like bad teeth, to be jerked out because they cause suffering.

Her point is effectively put; it remains for the reader to decide whether fetuses are *babies* and if a fetus is not a baby, *why* it can or cannot be treated like a bad tooth.

Now a second bit of analogical reasoning, again about abortion: Thomas Sowell, an economist at the Hoover Institute, grants that women have a legal right to abortion, but he objects to a requirement that the government pay for abortions:

> Because the courts have ruled that women have a legal right to an abortion, some
> people have jumped to the conclusion that the government has to pay for it. You have

a constitutional right to privacy, but the government has no obligation to pay for your window shades. (*Pink and Brown People*, 1981, p. 57)

We leave it to you to decide whether the analogy is compelling — that is, if the points of resemblance are sufficiently significant to allow you to conclude that what's true of people wanting window shades should be true of people wanting abortions.

And one more: A common argument on behalf of legalizing gay marriage drew an analogy between gay marriage and interracial marriage, a practice that was banned in sixteen states until 1967, when the Supreme Court declared miscegenation statutes unconstitutional. The gist of the analogy was this: Racism and discrimination against gay and lesbian people are the same. If marriage is a fundamental right — as the Supreme Court held in its 1967 decision striking down bans on miscegenation — then it is a fundamental right for gay and lesbian people as well as heterosexual people.

AUTHORITATIVE TESTIMONY   Another form of evidence is **testimony**, the citation or quotation of authorities. In daily life, we rely heavily on authorities of all sorts: We get a doctor's opinion about our health, we read a book because an intelligent friend recommends it, we see a movie because a critic gave it a good review, and we pay at least a little attention to the weather forecaster.

In setting forth an argument, one often tries to show that one's view is supported by notable figures — perhaps Jefferson, Lincoln, Martin Luther King Jr., or scientists who won the Nobel Prize. You may recall that in Chapter 2, in talking about medical marijuana legalization, we presented an essay by Sanjay Gupta. To make certain that you were impressed by his ideas, we described him as CNN's chief medical correspondent and a leading public health expert. In our Chapter 2 discussion of Sally Mann, we qualified our description of her controversial photographs by noting that *Time* magazine called her "America's Best Photographer" and the *New Republic* called her book "one of the great photograph books of our time." But heed some words of caution:

- Be sure that the authority, however notable, is *an authority on the topic in question.* (A well-known biologist might be an authority on vitamins but not on the justice of war.)

- Be sure that the authority is *unbiased.* (A chemist employed by the tobacco industry isn't likely to admit that smoking may be harmful, and a producer of violent video games isn't likely to admit that playing those games stimulates violence.)

- Beware of *nameless* authorities: "a thousand doctors," "leading educators," "researchers at a major medical school." (If possible, offer at least one specific name.)

- Be careful when using authorities who indeed were great authorities in their day but *who now may be out of date.* (Examples would include Adam Smith on economics, Julius Caesar on the art of war, Louis Pasteur on medicine).

- Cite authorities *whose opinions your readers will value.* (William F. Buckley Jr.'s conservative/libertarian opinions mean a good deal to readers of the magazine that he founded, the *National Review*, but probably not to most liberal thinkers. Gloria Steinem's liberal/feminist opinions carry weight with readers of the magazines that she cofounded, *New York* and *Ms.* magazine, but probably not with most conservative thinkers.) When writing for the general reader — your usual audience — cite authorities whom the general reader is likely to accept.

One other point: *You* may be an authority. You probably aren't nationally known, but on some topics you might have the authority of personal experience. You may have been injured on a motorcycle while riding without wearing a helmet, or you may have escaped injury because you wore a helmet. You may have dropped out of school and then returned. You may have tutored a student whose native language isn't English, you may be such a student who has received tutoring, or you may have attended a school with a bilingual education program. In short, your personal testimony on topics relating to these issues may be invaluable, and a reader will probably consider it seriously.

STATISTICS   The last sort of evidence we discuss here is quantitative, or statistical. The maxim "More is better" captures a basic idea of quantitative evidence: Because we know that 90 percent is greater than 75 percent, we're usually ready to grant that any claim supported by experience in 90 percent of cases is more likely to be true than an alternative claim supported by experience in only 75 percent of cases. The greater the difference, the greater our confidence. Consider an example. Honors at graduation from college are often computed on the basis of a student's cumulative grade-point average (GPA). The undisputed assumption is that the nearer a student's GPA is to a perfect record (4.0), the better scholar he or she is and therefore the more deserving of highest honors. Consequently, a student with a GPA of 3.9 at the end of her senior year is a stronger candidate for graduating summa cum laude than another student with a GPA of 3.6. When faculty members on the honors committee argue over the relative academic merits of graduating seniors, we know that these quantitative, statistical differences in student GPAs will be the basic (if not the only) kind of evidence under discussion.

Graphs, Tables, Numbers   Statistical information can be presented in many forms, but it tends to fall into two main types: the graphic and the numerical. Graphs, tables, and pie charts are familiar ways of presenting quantitative data in an eye-catching manner. (See pp. 165–70.) To prepare the graphics, however, one first has to decide how best to organize and interpret the numbers, and for some purposes it may be more appropriate to directly present the numbers themselves.

But is it better to present the numbers in percentages or in fractions? Should a report say that the federal budget (1) underwent a twofold increase over the decade; (2) increased by 100 percent; (3) doubled; or (4) at the beginning of the decade was one-half what it was at the end? These are equivalent ways of saying the same thing. Making a choice among them, therefore, will likely rest on whether one's aim is to dramatize the increase (a 100 percent increase looks larger than a doubling) or to play down its size.

Thinking about Statistical Evidence   Statistics often get a bad name because it's so easy to misuse them (unintentionally or not) and so difficult to be sure that they were gathered correctly in the first place. (One old saying goes, "There are lies, damned lies, and statistics.") Every branch of social science and natural science needs statistical information, and countless decisions in public and private life are based on quantitative data in statistical form. It's important, therefore, to be sensitive to the sources and reliability of the statistics and to develop a healthy skepticism when you confront statistics whose parentage is not fully explained.

Consider statistics that pop up in conversations about wealth distribution in the United States. In 2014, the Census Bureau calculated that the **median** household income in the United States was $53,657, meaning that half of households earned less than this amount and half earned above it. However, the **average** — technically, the **mean** — household income in the same year was $72,641, about $19,000 (or 39 percent) higher. Which number more accurately represents the typical household income? Both are "correct," but both are calculated with different measures, median and mean. If a politician wanted to argue that the United States has a strong middle class, he might use the average (mean) income as evidence, a number calculated by dividing the total income of all households by the total number of households. If another politician wished to make a rebuttal, she could point out that the average income paints a rosy picture because the wealthiest households skew the average higher. The median income (representing the number above and below which two halves of all households fall) should be the measure we use, the rebutting politician could argue, because it helps reduce the effect of the limitless ceiling of higher incomes and the finite floor of lower incomes at zero.

Consider the following statistics: Suppose in a given city in 2014, 1 percent of the victims in fatal automobile accidents were bicyclists. In the same city in 2015, the percentage of bicyclists killed in automobile accidents was 2 percent. Was the increase 1 percent (not an alarming figure), or was it 100 percent (a staggering figure)? The answer is both, depending on whether we're comparing (1) bicycle deaths in automobile accidents *with all deaths in automobile accidents* (that's an increase of 1 percent), or (2) bicycle deaths in automobile accidents *only with other bicycle deaths in automobile accidents* (an increase of 100 percent). An honest statement would say that bicycle deaths due to automobile accidents doubled in 2015, increasing from 1 to 2 percent. But here's another point: Although every such death is lamentable, if there was one such death in 2014 and two in 2015, the increase from one death to two (an increase of 100 percent!) hardly suggests a growing problem that needs attention. No one would be surprised to learn that in the next year there were no deaths at all, or only one or two.

If it's sometimes difficult to interpret statistics, it's often at least equally difficult to establish accurate statistics. Consider this example:

> Advertisements are the most prevalent and toxic of the mental pollutants. From the moment your radio alarm sounds in the morning to the wee hours of late-night TV, microjolts of commercial pollution flood into your brain at the rate of about three thousand marketing messages per day. (Kalle Lasn, *Culture Jam* [1999], 18–19)

Lasn's book includes endnotes as documentation, so, being curious about the statistics, we turn to the appropriate page and find this information concerning the source of his data:

> "three thousand marketing messages per day." Mark Landler, Walecia Konrad, Zachary Schiller, and Lois Therrien, "What Happened to Advertising?" *Business Week,* September 23, 1991, page 66. Leslie Savan in *The Sponsored Life* (Temple University Press, 1994), page 1, estimated that "16,000 ads flicker across an individual's consciousness daily." I did an informal survey in March 1995 and found the number to be closer to 1,500 (this included all marketing messages, corporate images, logos, ads, brand names, on TV, radio, billboards, buildings, signs, clothing, appliances, in cyberspace, etc., over a typical twenty-four hour period in my life). (219)

Well, this endnote is odd. In the earlier passage, the author asserted that about "three thousand marketing messages per day" flood into a person's brain. In the documentation, he cites a source for that statistic from *Business Week*—though we haven't the faintest idea how the authors of the *Business Week* article came up with that figure. Oddly, he goes on to offer a very different figure (16,000 ads) and then, to our confusion, offers yet a third figure, 1,500, based on his own "informal survey."

Probably the one thing we can safely say about all three figures is that none of them means very much. Even if the compilers of the statistics explained exactly how they counted—let's say that among countless other criteria they assumed that the average person reads one magazine per day and that the average magazine contains 124 advertisements—it would be hard to take them seriously. After all, in leafing through a magazine, some people may read many ads and some may read none. Some people may read some ads carefully—but perhaps just to enjoy their absurdity. Our point: Although the author in his text said, without implying any uncertainty, that "about three thousand marketing messages per day" reach an individual, it's evident (by checking the endnote) that even he is confused about the figure he gives.

Unreliable Statistics   We'd like to make a final point about the unreliability of some statistical information—data that looks impressive but that is, in fact, insubstantial. For instance, Marilyn Jager Adams studied the number of hours that families read to their children in the five or so years before the children start attending school. In her book *Beginning to Read: Thinking and Learning about Print* (1994), she pointed out that in all those preschool years, poor families read to their children only 25 hours, whereas in the same period middle-income families read 1,000 to 1,700 hours. The figures were much quoted in newspapers and by children's advocacy groups. Adams could not, of course, interview every family in these two groups; she had to rely on samples. What were her samples? For poor families, she selected 24 children in 20 families, all in Southern California. Ask yourself: Can families from only one geographic area provide an adequate sample for a topic such as this? Moreover, let's think about Adams's sample of middle-class families. How many families constituted that sample? Exactly one—her own. We leave it to you to judge the validity of her findings.

Quiz

What is wrong with the following statistical proof that children do not have time for school?

> One-third of the time they are sleeping (about 122 days).
>
> One-eighth of the time they are eating (three hours a day, totaling 45 days).
>
> One-fourth of the time they are on summer and other vacations (91 days).
>
> Two-sevenths of the year is weekends (104 days).
>
> Total: 362 days — so how can a kid have time for school?

Nonrational Appeals

SATIRE, IRONY, SARCASM, HUMOR

In talking about definition, deduction, and evidence, we've been talking about means of rational persuasion. However, as mentioned earlier, there are also other means of persuasion. Force is an example. If *X* kicks *Y*, threatens to destroy *Y*'s means of livelihood, or threatens *Y*'s life, *X* may persuade *Y* to cooperate. But writers, of course, cannot use such kinds of force on their readers. Instead, one form of irrational but sometimes highly effective persuasion is **satire** — that is, witty ridicule. A cartoonist may persuade viewers that a politician's views are unsound by caricaturing (thus ridiculing) her appearance or by presenting a grotesquely distorted (funny, but unfair) picture of the issue she supports.

Satiric artists often use caricature; satiric writers, also seeking to persuade by means of ridicule, often use **verbal irony**. This sort of irony contrasts what is said and what is meant. For instance, words of praise may actually imply blame (when Shakespeare's Cassius says, "Brutus is an honorable man," he wants his hearers to think that Brutus is dishonorable), and words of modesty may actually imply superiority ("Of course, I'm too dumb to understand this problem"). Such language, when heavy-handed, is **sarcasm** ("You're a great guy," said to someone who won't lend the speaker ten dollars). If it's witty and clever, we call it irony rather than sarcasm.

Although ridicule isn't a form of argument (because it isn't a form of reasoning), passages of ridicule, especially verbal irony, sometimes appear in argument essays. These passages, like reasons or like appeals to the emotions, are efforts to persuade the reader to accept the writer's point of view. The key to using humor in an argument is, on the one hand, to avoid wisecracking like a smart aleck, and on the other hand, to avoid mere clownishness. Later in this chapter (p. 110), we print an essay by George F. Will that is (or seeks to be) humorous in places. You be the judge.

EMOTIONAL APPEALS

It is sometimes said that good argumentative writing appeals only to reason, never to emotion, and that any emotional appeal is illegitimate and irrelevant. "Tears are not arguments," the Brazilian writer Machado de Assis said. Logic textbooks may even stigmatize with Latin labels the various sorts of emotional appeal — for instance, *argumentum ad populam* (appeal to the prejudices of the mob, as in "Come on, we all know that schools don't teach anything anymore") and *argumentum ad misericordiam* (appeal to pity, as in "No one ought to blame this poor kid for stabbing a classmate because his mother was often institutionalized for alcoholism and his father beat him").

True, appeals to emotion may distract from the facts of the case; they may blind the audience by, in effect, throwing dust in its eyes or by provoking tears.

LEARNING FROM SHAKESPEARE A classic example is in Shakespeare's *Julius Caesar,* when Marc Antony addresses the Roman populace after Brutus, Cassius, and others have assassinated Caesar. The real issue is whether Caesar was becoming tyrannical (as the assassins claim) and would have curtailed the freedom of the Roman people. Antony turns from the evidence and stirs the mob against the assassins by appealing to its emotions. In the ancient Roman biographical writing that Shakespeare drew on, Sir Thomas North's translation of Plutarch's *Lives of the Noble Grecians and Romans,* Plutarch says this about Antony:

> perceiving that his words moved the common people to compassion, . . . [he] framed his eloquence to make their hearts yearn [i.e., grieve] the more, and, taking Caesar's gown all bloody in his hand, he laid it open to the sight of them all, showing what a number of cuts and holes it had upon it. Therewithal the people fell presently into such a rage and mutiny that there was no more order kept.

Here are a few extracts from Antony's speeches in Shakespeare's play. Antony begins by asserting that he will speak only briefly:

> Friends, Romans, countrymen, lend me your ears;
> I come to bury Caesar, not to praise him.

After briefly offering insubstantial evidence that Caesar gave no signs of behaving tyrannically (e.g., "When that the poor have cried, Caesar hath wept"), Antony begins to play directly on his hearers' emotions. Descending from the platform so that he may be in closer contact with his audience (like a modern politician, he wants to work the crowd), he calls attention to Caesar's bloody toga:

> If you have tears, prepare to shed them now.
> You all do know this mantle; I remember
> The first time ever Caesar put it on:
> 'Twas on a summer's evening, in his tent,
> That day he overcame the Nervii.
> Look, in this place ran Cassius' dagger through;
> See what a rent the envious Casca made;
> Through this, the well-belovèd Brutus stabbed. . . .

In these few lines, Antony accomplishes the following:

- He prepares the audience by suggesting to them how they should respond ("If you have tears, prepare to shed them now").

- He flatters them by implying that they, like Antony, were intimates of Caesar (he credits them with being familiar with Caesar's garment).

- He then evokes a personal memory of a specific time ("a summer's evening") — not just any specific time, but a very important one, the day that Caesar won a battle against the Nervii (a particularly fierce tribe in what is now France).

In fact, Antony was not at the battle, and he did not join Caesar until three years later.

Antony doesn't mind being free with the facts; his point here is not to set the record straight but to stir the mob against the assassins. He goes on, daringly but successfully, to identify one particular slit in the garment with Cassius's dagger, another with Casca's, and a third with Brutus's. Antony cannot know which dagger made which slit, but his rhetorical trick works.

Notice, too, that Antony arranges the three assassins in climactic order, since Brutus (Antony claims) was especially beloved by Caesar:

> Judge, O you gods, how dearly Caesar loved him!
> This was the most unkindest cut of all;
> For when the noble Caesar saw him stab,
> Ingratitude, more strong than traitor's arms,
> Quite vanquished him. Then burst his mighty heart. . . .

Nice. According to Antony, the noble-minded Caesar — Antony's words have erased all thought of the tyrannical Caesar — died not from wounds inflicted by daggers but from the heartbreaking perception of Brutus's ingratitude. Doubtless there wasn't a dry eye in the house. Let's all hope that if we are ever put on trial, we'll have a lawyer as skilled in evoking sympathy as Antony.

ARE EMOTIONAL APPEALS FALLACIOUS? Antony's oration was obviously successful in the play and apparently was successful in real life, but it is the sort of speech that prompts logicians to write disapprovingly of attempts to stir feeling in an audience. (As mentioned earlier, the evocation of emotion in an audience is *pathos,* from the Greek word for "emotion" or "suffering.") There is nothing inherently wrong in stimulating an audience's emotions when attempting to establish a claim, but when an emotional appeal confuses the issue being argued or shifts attention away from the facts, we can reasonably speak of the fallacy of emotional appeal.

No fallacy is involved, however, when an emotional appeal heightens the facts, bringing them home to the audience rather than masking them. In talking about legislation that would govern police actions, for example, it's legitimate to show a photograph of the battered, bloodied face of an alleged victim of police brutality. True, such a photograph cannot tell the whole truth; it cannot tell if the subject threatened the officer with a gun or repeatedly resisted an order to surrender. But it can demonstrate that the victim was severely beaten and (like a comparable description in words) evoke emotions that may properly affect the audience's decision about the permissible use of police evidence. Similarly, an animal rights activist who argues that calves are cruelly confined might reasonably talk about the inhumanely small size of their pens, in which they cannot turn around or even lie down. Others may argue that calves don't care about turning around or have no right to turn around, but the evocative verbal description of their pens, which makes an emotional appeal, cannot be called fallacious or irrelevant.

In appealing to emotions, then, important strategies are as follows:

- Do not falsify (especially by oversimplifying) the issue.
- Do not distract attention from the facts of the case.
- Do think ethically about how emotional appeals may affect the audience.

You should focus on the facts and offer reasons (essentially, statements linked with "because"), but you may also legitimately bring the facts home to your readers by seeking to provoke appropriate emotions. Your words will be fallacious only if you stimulate emotions that aren't connected with the facts of the case.

Does All Writing Contain Arguments?

Our answer to the question above is no — however, *most* writing probably *does* contain an argument of sorts. The writer wants to persuade the reader to see things the way the writer sees them — at least until the end of the essay. After all, even a recipe for a cherry pie in a food magazine — a piece of writing that's primarily expository (how to do it) rather than argumentative (how a reasonable person ought to think about this topic) — probably starts out with a hint of an argument, such as "*Because* [a sign that a *reason* will be offered] this pie can be made quickly and with ingredients (canned cherries) that are always available, give it a try. It will surely become one of your favorites." Clearly, such a statement cannot stand as a formal argument — a discussion that addresses counter-arguments, relies chiefly on logic and little if any emotional appeal, and draws a conclusion that seems irrefutable.

Still, the statement is an argument on behalf of making a pie with canned cherries. In this case, we can identify a claim (the pie will become a favorite) and two *reasons* in support of the claim:

- It can be made quickly.
- The chief ingredient — because it is canned — can always be at hand.

There are two underlying *assumptions*:

- Readers don't have a great deal of time to waste in the kitchen.
- Canned cherries are just as tasty as fresh cherries — and even if they aren't, no one who eats the pie will know the difference.

A CHECKLIST FOR ANALYZING AN ARGUMENT

What is the writer's claim or thesis? Ask yourself:

❏ What claim is asserted?

❏ What evidence is imagined?

❏ What assumptions are being made — and are they acceptable?

❏ Are important terms satisfactorily defined?

What support (evidence) is offered on behalf of the claim? Ask yourself:

❏ Are the examples relevant and convincing?

❏ Are the statistics (if any) relevant, accurate, and complete? Do they allow only the interpretation that is offered in the argument?

❏ If authorities are cited, are they indeed authorities on this topic, and can they be considered impartial?

❏ Is the logic — deductive and inductive — valid?

❏ If there is an appeal to emotion (e.g., if satire is used to ridicule the opposing view), is this appeal acceptable?

Does the writer seem to be fair? Ask yourself:

❏   Are counterarguments adequately considered?

❏   Is there any evidence of dishonesty or of a discreditable attempt to manipulate the reader?

❏   How does the writer establish the image of himself or herself that readers sense in the essay? What is the writer's tone, and is it appropriate?

When we read a lead-in to a recipe, then, we won't find a formal argument, but we'll probably see a few words that seek to persuade us to keep reading. And most writing does contain such material — sentences that engage our interest and give us a reason to keep reading. If the recipe is difficult and time consuming, the lead-in may say:

> Although this recipe for a cherry pie, using fresh cherries that you will have to pit, is a bit more time consuming than the usual recipes that call for canned cherries, once you have tasted it you will never go back to canned cherries.

Again, although the logic is scarcely compelling, the persuasive element is evident. The assumption is that readers have a discriminating palate; once they've tasted a pie made with fresh cherries, they'll never again enjoy the canned stuff. The writer isn't making a formal argument with abundant evidence and detailed refutation of counterarguments, but we know where he stands and how he wishes us to respond.

In short, almost all writers are trying to persuade readers to see things *their* way.

An Example: An Argument and a Look at the Writer's Strategies

This essay concerns President George W. Bush's proposal to allow drilling in part of the Arctic National Wildlife Refuge (ANWR, pronounced "An-war"). The ANWR section where drilling is proposed is called the 1002 area, as defined by Section 1002 of the Alaska National Interest Lands Conservation Act of 1980. In March 2003, the Senate rejected the Bush proposal, but the issue remains alive.

We follow George F. Will's essay with some comments about the ways in which he constructs his argument.

GEORGE F. WILL

George F. Will (b. 1941), a syndicated columnist whose writing appears in 460 newspapers, was born in Champaign, Illinois, and educated at Trinity College (in Hartford), Oxford University, and Princeton University. Will has served as the Washington, D.C., editor of the National

Review and now writes a regular column for Newsweek. *His essays have been collected in several books.*

This essay was originally published in 2002, so it is in some respects dated—for instance, in its reference to the price of gasoline—but it still serves as an excellent model of certain ways to argue.

Being Green at Ben and Jerry's

Some Environmental Policies Are Feel-Good Indulgences for an Era of Energy Abundance

If you have an average-size dinner table, four feet by six feet, put a dime on the edge of it. Think of the surface of the table as the Arctic National Wildlife Refuge in Alaska. The dime is larger than the piece of the coastal plain that would have been opened to drilling for oil and natural gas. The House of Representatives voted for drilling, but the Senate voted against access to what Sen. John Kerry, Massachusetts Democrat and presidential aspirant, calls "a few drops of oil." ANWR could produce, for twenty-five years, at least as much oil as America currently imports from Saudi Arabia.

Six weeks of desultory Senate debate about the energy bill reached an almost comic culmination in . . . yet another agriculture subsidy. The subsidy is a requirement that will triple the amount of ethanol, which is made from corn, that must be put in gasoline, ostensibly to clean America's air, actually to buy farmers' votes.

Over the last three decades, energy use has risen about 30 percent. But so has population, which means per capita energy use is unchanged. And per capita GDP has risen substantially, so we are using 40 percent less energy per dollar output. Which is one reason there is no energy crisis, at least none as most Americans understand such things—a shortage of, and therefore high prices of, gasoline for cars, heating oil for furnaces and electricity for air conditioners.

In the absence of a crisis to concentrate the attention of the inattentive American majority, an intense faction—full-time environmentalists—goes to work. Spencer Abraham, the secretary of Energy, says "the previous administration . . . simply drew up a list of fuels it *didn't* like—nuclear energy, coal, hydropower, and oil—which together account for 73 percent of America's energy supply." Well, there are always windmills.

Sometimes lofty environmentalism is a 5 cover for crude politics. The United States has the world's largest proven reserves of coal. But Mike Oliver, a retired physicist and engineer, and John Hospers, professor emeritus of philosophy at USC, note that in 1996 President Clinton put 68 billion tons of America's cleanest-burning coal, located in Utah, off-limits for mining, ostensibly for environmental reasons. If every existing U.S. electric power plant burned coal, the 68 billion tons could fuel them for forty-five years at the current rate of consumption. Now power companies must import clean-burning coal, some from mines owned by Indonesia's Lippo Group, the heavy contributor to Clinton, whose decision about Utah's coal vastly increased the value of Lippo's coal.

The United States has just 2.14 percent of the world's proven reserves of oil, so some people say it is pointless to drill in places like ANWR because "energy independence" is a chimera.[1] Indeed it is. But domestic supplies can provide important insurance against uncertain foreign supplies. And domestic supplies can mean exporting hundreds of billions of dollars less to oil-producing nations, such as Iraq.

Besides, when considering proven reserves, note the adjective. In 1930 the United States had proven reserves of 13 billion barrels. We then fought the Second World War and fueled the most fabulous economic expansion in human history, including the electricity-driven "New Economy." (Manufacturing and running computers consume 15 percent of U.S. electricity. Internet use alone accounts for half of the growth in demand for electricity.) So by 1990 proven reserves were . . . 17 billion barrels, not counting any in Alaska or Hawaii.

In 1975 proven reserves in the Persian Gulf were 74 billion barrels. In 1993 they were 663 billion, a ninefold increase. At the current rate of consumption, today's proven reserves would last 150 years. New discoveries will be made, some by vastly improved techniques of deep-water drilling. But environmental policies will define opportunities. The government estimates that beneath the U.S. outer continental shelf, which the government owns, there are at least 46 billion barrels of oil. But only 2 percent of the shelf has been leased for energy development.

Opponents of increased energy production usually argue for decreased consumption. But they flinch from conservation measures. A new $1 gasoline tax would dampen demand for gasoline, but it would stimulate demands for the heads of the tax increasers. After all, Americans get irritable when impersonal market forces add 25 cents to the cost of a gallon. Tougher fuel-efficiency requirements for vehicles would save a lot of energy. But who would save the legislators who passed those requirements? Beware the wrath of Americans who like to drive, and autoworkers who like to make cars that are large, heavy, and safer than the gasoline-sippers that environmentalists prefer.

Some environmentalism is a feel-good 10 indulgence for an era of energy abundance, which means an era of avoided choices. Or ignored choices — ignored because if acknowledged, they would not make the choosers feel good. Karl Zinsmeister, editor in chief of the *American Enterprise* magazine, imagines an oh-so-green environmentalist enjoying the most politically correct product on the planet — Ben & Jerry's ice cream. Made in a factory that depends on electricity-guzzling refrigeration, a gallon of ice cream requires four gallons of milk. While making that much milk, a cow produces eight gallons of manure, and flatulence with another eight gallons of methane, a potent "greenhouse" gas. And the cow consumes lots of water plus three pounds of grain and hay, which is produced with tractor fuel, chemical fertilizers, herbicides and insecticides, and is transported with truck or train fuel:

"So every time he digs into his Cherry Garcia, the conscientious environmentalist should visualize (in addition to world peace) a pile of grain, water, farm chemicals, and energy inputs much bigger than his ice cream bowl on one side of the table, and, on the other side of the table, a mound of manure eight times the size of his bowl, plus a balloon of methane that would barely fit under the dining room table."

Cherry Garcia. It's a choice. *Bon appétit.*

---

[1] **chimera** Something that is hoped or wished for but is impossible to actually achieve. [Editors' note.]

GEORGE F. WILL'S STRATEGIES

Now let's look at Will's essay to see what techniques he uses to engage readers' interest and perhaps enable him to convince them — or at least make them think — that he is on to something. If you think some or all of his strategies are effective, consider adapting them for use in your own essays.

The title, "Being Green at Ben and Jerry's," does not at all prepare readers for an argument about drilling in the National Arctic Wildlife Refuge. But if you have read any of Will's other columns in *Newsweek*, you probably know that he is conservative and can guess that in this essay he'll poke some fun at the green folk — the environmentalists. Will can get away with using a title that isn't focused because he has a body of loyal readers who will read his pieces no matter what the topic is, but the rest of us have to give our readers some idea of our topic. In short, let your readers know early, perhaps in the title, where you'll be taking them.

The subtitle, "Some Environmental Policies Are Feel-Good Indulgences for an Era of Energy Abundance," perhaps added by the magazine's editor, suggests that the piece will concern energy. Moreover, the words "feel-good indulgences" signal to readers that Will believes the environmentalists are indulging themselves.

Paragraph 1 offers a striking comparison. Will wants his readers to believe that the area proposed for drilling is tiny, so he says that if they imagine the entire Arctic National Wildlife Refuge as a dinner table, the area proposed for drilling is the size of a dime. We think you'll agree that this opening seizes a reader's attention. Although some opponents to drilling in the ANWR have contested Will's analogy (saying the area would be much larger, perhaps comparable to the size of a dinner plate, or even a dinner plate broken in pieces, with roads and pipelines crossing between the fragments), the image is still highly effective. A dime is so small! And worth so little!

Another point about paragraph 1: Will's casual voice sounds like one you might hear in your own living room: "If you have an average-size dinner table," "The dime is larger," "at least as much oil." Your own essays need not adopt a highly formal style. Readers should think of you as serious but not solemn.

Will goes on to say that Senator John Kerry, an opponent of drilling and therefore on the side that Will opposes, dismisses the oil in the refuge as "a few drops." Will replies that it "could produce, for twenty-five years, at least as much oil as America currently imports from Saudi Arabia." Kerry's "a few drops" isn't literal, of course; he means that the oil is a drop in the bucket. But when one looks into the issue, one finds that estimates by responsible sources vary considerably — from 3.2 billion barrels to 11.5 billion barrels.

Paragraph 2 dismisses the Senate's debate ("almost comic . . . actually to buy farmers' votes").

Paragraph 3 offers statistics to make the point that "there is no energy crisis." Here, as in paragraph 1 (where he showed his awareness of Kerry's view), Will indicates that he's familiar with views other than his own. In arguing a case, it's important for a writer to let readers know that indeed there are other views — which the writer then shows are less substantial than the writer's own. Will is correct in saying that "per capita energy use is unchanged," but opponents might say, "Yes, per capita consumption hasn't increased; but given the population increase, the annual amount has vastly increased, which means that resources are being depleted and that pollution is increasing."

Paragraph 4 asserts again that there is no energy crisis, pokes fun at "full-time environmentalists" (perhaps even implying that such people ought to get respectable jobs), and ends with a bit of whimsy: These folks probably think we should go back to using windmills.

Paragraph 5, in support of the assertion that "Sometimes lofty environmentalism is a cover for crude politics," cites an authority (often an effective technique). Since readers aren't likely to recognize the name, Will also identifies him ("professor emeritus of philosophy at USC") and then offers further statistics. The paragraph begins by talking about "crude politics" and ends with this assertion: "Now power companies must import clean-burning coal, some from mines owned by Indonesia's Lippo Group, the heavy contributor to Clinton." In short, Will makes several strategic moves to suggest that at least some environmentalists' views are rooted in money and politics.

Paragraph 6 offers another statistic ("The United States has just 2.14 percent of the world's proven reserves of oil") and turns it against those who argue that therefore it's pointless to drill in Alaska. In effect, Will is replying to people like Senator Kerry who say that the Arctic refuge provides only "a few drops of oil." The point, Will suggests, is not that it's impossible for the nation to achieve independence; rather, the point is that "domestic supplies can provide important insurance against uncertain foreign supplies."

Paragraph 7 begins smoothly with a transition, "Besides," and then offers additional statistics concerning the large amount of oil that the United States has held in proven reserves. For instance, by the end of World War II these reserves were enough to fuel "the most fabulous economic expansion in human history."

Paragraph 8 offers additional statistics, first about "proven reserves in the Persian Gulf" and then about an estimate — but only an estimate — of oil "beneath the U.S. outer continental shelf." We are not certain of Will's point here, but in any case the statistics suggest that he has done some homework.

Paragraph 9 summarizes the chief position (as Will sees it) of those on the other side of this issue: They "usually argue for decreased consumption," but they're afraid to argue for the sort of gasoline tax that might indeed decrease consumption because they know that many Americans want to drive large, heavy cars. Further, the larger, heavier cars that the environmentalists object to are in fact "safer than the gasoline-sippers that environmentalists prefer."

Paragraph 10 uses the term "feel-good indulgence," which also appears in the essay's subtitle; and now in the paragraph's third sentence we hear again of Ben and Jerry, whose names we haven't seen since reading the essay's title, "Being Green at Ben and Jerry's." Perhaps we've been wondering all this time why the title mentions Ben and Jerry. Surely most readers know that Ben and Jerry are associated with ice cream and therefore with cows and meadows, and probably many readers know that Ben and Jerry support environmentalism and other liberal causes. Drawing on an article by Karl Zinsmeister, editor of the *American Enterprise*, Will writes an extremely amusing paragraph in which he points out that the process of making ice cream "depends on electricity-guzzling refrigeration" and that the cows are essentially supported by fuel that transports fertilizers, herbicides, and insecticides. Further, in the course of producing the four gallons of milk required for one gallon of ice cream, the cows themselves — those darlings of the environmentalists — contribute "eight gallons of manure, and flatulence with another eight gallons of methane, a potent 'greenhouse' gas." As we'll soon see in Will's next paragraph, the present paragraph is largely a lead-in for the quotation he gives in the next paragraph. He knows it isn't enough to give a quotation; a writer has to make use of it — by leading in to it, by commenting on it after inserting it, or both.

Paragraph 11 is entirely devoted to quoting Zinsmeister, who imagines an environmentalist digging into a dish of one of Ben and Jerry's most popular flavors, Cherry Garcia. We're invited to see the bowl of ice cream on one side of the table — here Will effectively evokes the table of paragraph 1 — and a pile of manure on the other side, "plus a balloon of methane that would barely fit under the dining room table." This statement is vulgar, no doubt, but it's funny too. Will knows that humor as well as logic (and statistics and other evidence) can be among the key tools a writer uses in getting an audience to consider or accept an argument.

Paragraph 12 consists of three short sentences, adding up to less than a single line of type: "Cherry Garcia. It's a choice. *Bon appétit.*" None of the sentences mentions oil or the Arctic Refuge or statistics; therefore, this ending might seem irrelevant to the topic, but Will is very effectively saying, "Sure, you have a choice about drilling in the Arctic Refuge; any sensible person will choose the ice cream (drilling) rather than the manure and the gas (not drilling)."

Topics for Critical Thinking and Writing

1. What, if anything, makes George Will's essay interesting to you? What, if anything, makes it highly persuasive? How might it be made more persuasive?

2. In paragraph 10, Will clowns about the gas that cows emit, but apparently this gas, which contributes to global warming, is no laughing matter. The government of New Zealand, in an effort to reduce livestock emissions of methane and nitrous oxide, proposed a tax that would subsidize future research on the emissions. The tax would cost the average farmer $300 a year. Imagine that you're a New Zealand farmer. Write a letter to your representative, arguing for or against the tax.

3. Senator Barbara Boxer, campaigning against the proposal to drill in ANWR, spoke of the refuge as "God's gift to us" (*New York Times*, March 20, 2002). How strong an argument is this? Some opponents of the proposal have said that drilling in ANWR is as unthinkable as drilling in Yosemite or the Grand Canyon. Again, how strong is this argument? Can you imagine circumstances in which you would support drilling in these places? Why, or why not? Do we have a moral duty to preserve certain unspoiled areas? Explain your response.

4. The Inupiat (Eskimo) who live in and near ANWR by a large majority favor drilling, seeing it as a source of jobs and a source of funding for schools, hospitals, and police. But the Ketchikan Indians, who speak of themselves as the "Caribou People," see drilling as a threat to the herds on which they depend for food and hides. How is it possible to balance the conflicting needs of these two groups?

5. Opponents of drilling in ANWR argue that over its lifetime of fifty years, the area would produce less than 1 percent of the fuel we need during the period and that therefore we

shouldn't risk disturbing the area. Further, they argue that drilling in ANWR is an attempt at a quick fix to U.S. energy needs, whereas what the nation really needs are sustainable solutions, such as the development of renewable energy sources (e.g., wind and sun) and fuel-efficient automobiles. How convincing do you find these arguments? Explain your response.

6. Proponents of drilling include a large majority — something like 75 percent — of the people of Alaska, including its governor and its two senators. How much attention do their voices deserve?

7. Analyze the essay in terms of its use of *ethos, pathos,* and *logos.*

8. What sort of audience do you think Will is addressing? What values do his readers probably share? What makes you think so?

Arguments for Analysis

STANLEY FISH

Stanley Fish (b. 1938) established his reputation as a scholar of English literature — he has taught literature at the University of California–Berkeley, Johns Hopkins University, and Duke University — but he has also published on legal issues. He now teaches at Florida International University's College of Law. This essay was published in 2008, when Hillary Clinton and Barack Obama were candidates for the Democratic Party's nomination for president. Inevitably, there was much talk about the candidacy of a woman and an African American.

When "Identity Politics" Is Rational

If there's anything everyone is against in these election times, it's "identity politics," a phrase that covers a multitude of sins. Let me start with a definition. (It may not be yours, but it will at least allow the discussion to be framed.) You're practicing identity politics when you vote for or against someone because of his or her skin color, ethnicity, religion, gender, sexual orientation, or any other marker that leads you to say yes or no independently of a candidate's ideas or policies. In essence identity politics is an affirmation of the tribe against the claims of ideology, and by ideology I do not mean something bad (a mistake frequently made), but any agenda informed by a vision of what the world should be like.

An identity politics voter says, in effect, I don't care what views he holds, or even what bad things he may have done, or what lack of ability he may display; he's my brother, or he's my kinsman, or he's my landsman, or he comes from the neighborhood, or he's a Southerner, or (and here the tribe is really big) my country right or wrong. "My country right or wrong" is particularly useful in making clear how identity politics differs from politics as many Americans would prefer to see it practiced. Rather than saying she's right on immigration or he's wrong on the war, the identity-politics voter says he looks like me or she and I belong to the same church.

Identity politics is illiberal. That is, it is particularist whereas liberalism is universalist. The history of liberalism is a history of extending the franchise to those who were once excluded from it by their race, gender, or national origin. Although these marks of identification were retained (by the census and other forms of governmental classification) and could still be celebrated in private associations like the church and the social club, they were not supposed to be the basis of decisions one might make "as a citizen," decisions about who might best lead the country or what laws should be enacted or voted down. Deciding as a citizen means deciding not as a man or a woman or a Jew or an African American or a Caucasian or a heterosexual, but as a human being.

Stanley Crouch believes that the project of liberal universalizing is now pretty much complete and that "elements of distinction" — his phrase for the thinking that was fashionable in "the era of 'identity politics'" — "have become secondary to the power of human qualities with which anyone can identify or reject" (*Daily News*, Feb. 11). But his judgment is belied by almost everything that is going on in this campaign. As I write this I am watching the returns from the "Potomac Primary" and the news is being presented entirely in racial, ethnic, and gender terms. Every newspaper or magazine article I read does the same thing. The Obama and Clinton campaigns accuse each other of playing the race card or the gender card. An Hispanic superdelegate warns that by replacing her Latino campaign manager with a black one, Senator Clinton risks losing his vote and the vote of other Hispanic delegates he is in the process of contacting.

Christopher Hitchens looks at the scene 5 and is disgusted by behavior that, in his view, "keeps us anchored in the past" (*Wall Street Journal*, Jan. 18). He will not, he tells us, vote for Clinton just so that we can have the "'first woman president'" (I don't remember that one from the past); and he won't vote for Obama who, he says, "wants us to transcend something at the same time he implicitly asks us to give that same something as a reason to vote for him." It would seem that we are far from realizing Ken Connor's dream that we might judge "all of the presidential hopefuls on the basis of the content of their character and their qualifications to serve" (Townhall.com, Jan. 20).

But is it as bad as all that? Is it so irrational and retrograde to base one's vote on the gender or race or religion or ethnicity of a candidate? Not necessarily. If the vote is given (or withheld) only because the candidate looks like you or has the same religion, it does seem a shallow and meretricious act, for it is an act unsupported by reasons. "Because she is a woman as I am" is of course a reason, but it is not a reason of the relevant kind, a reason that cites goals and programs, and argues for them. But suppose what was said was something like this: "As a woman I find government sponsored research skewed in the direction of diseases that afflict men and inattentive to the medical problems faced by women, and it is my belief that a woman president will devote resources to the solution of those problems." That's an identity politics argument which is thick, not thin; the she's-like-me point is not invoked as sufficient unto itself, but as it relates to a matter of policy. The calculation may or may not pan out (successful candidates both disappoint and surprise), but it is a calculation of the right kind.

One objection to identity politics (Crouch makes it in the same column) is that groups and populations are not monolithic, but display a diversity of attitudes and positions. Yes they do, but members of a group who might disagree with each other on any number of things could nevertheless come together on a matter of shared concern. American Jews, for example, have widely varying views on many important issues — tax cuts, tort reform, gay marriage, the Iraq war. Still, the vast majority believes that it is important to defend the security of Israel. This is a belief shared even by those American Jews who are strongly critical of Israel's treatment of the Palestinians. They may deplore Israel's actions and agree with Jimmy Carter when he likens them to apartheid, but if the choice is between a politician who pledges to support Israel and a politician who would withdraw support and leave the Jewish state to fend for itself, most of them would vote for the first candidate every time.

African Americans are no less heterogeneous in their views than Jewish Americans. Yet every African American — conservative or liberal, rich or poor, barely educated or highly educated — meets with obstacles to his or her success and mobility that are all the more frustrating because they are structural (built into the culture's ways of perceiving) rather than official. To the non–African American these obstacles will be more or less invisible, especially in a country where access to opportunity is guaranteed by law. It makes sense, therefore, that an African American voter could come to the conclusion that an African American candidate would be likely to fight for changes that could remove barriers a white candidate might not even see. A vote given for that reason would be a vote based on identity, but it would be more than a mere affirmation of fellowship (he's one of mine and I have to support him); it would be a considered political judgment as to which candidate will move the country in a preferred direction. Identity might be the trigger of the vote, but it would not be the whole of its content.

We should distinguish, I think, between two forms of identity politics. The first I have already named "tribal"; it is the politics based on who a candidate is rather than on what he or she believes or argues for. And that, I agree, is usually a bad idea. (I say "usually" because it is possible to argue that the election of a black or female president, no matter what his or her positions happen to be, will be more than a symbolic correction of the errors that have marred the country's history, and an important international statement as well.) The second form of identity politics is what I call "interest" identity politics. It is based on the assumption (itself resting on history and observation) that because of his or her race or ethnicity or gender a candidate might pursue an agenda that would advance the interests a voter is committed to. Not only is there nothing wrong with such a calculation — it is both rational and considered — I don't see that there is an alternative to voting on the basis of interest.

The alternative usually put forward is Crouch's: Vote "for human qualities" rather than sectarian qualities. That is, vote on the basis of reasons everyone, no matter what his or her identity, will acknowledge as worthy. But there are no such reasons and no such human qualities. To be sure, there are words often attached to this chimera — integrity, dedication, honesty, intellect, to name a few. But these qualities, even when they are found, will always be in the service of some set of policies you either favor or reject. It is those policies, not the probity[1] of their proposer, that you will be voting for. (If your candidate is also a good person, that's a nice bonus, but it isn't the essential thing.) You will be voting, in short, for interests, and those who do not have an investment in those interests will be voting for someone else.

What this means is that the ritual deprecation of "special interests" makes no sense. All interests are special interests — they proceed from some contestable point of view — and none is "generally human." And that is why identity interests, as long as they are ideological and not merely tribal, constitute a perfectly respectable reason for awarding your vote.

---

[1] **probity** Integrity or morality; goodness. [Editors' note.]

Topics for Critical Thinking and Writing

1. Stanley Fish begins his essay with a formal and explicit definition of "identity politics." What do you think of that definition? Is it too broad? Too narrow? Too vague? Can you think of any ways to improve it? Explain your responses.

2. What is the origin of the epigram "My country right or wrong"? Does Fish endorse it? Do you? Why, or why not? Why does Fish offer it as an example of identity politics? Explain your views.

3. Suppose someone says that it's naïve to advocate deciding issues of public concern by appealing to one's status as "a human being" (para. 3). How would you reply? Do so in an essay of 300 words.

4. Fish speaks of two different practices under the rubric of "identity politics." What are they? Which one, if either, does Fish prefer, and why? Is either of these practices related to what Fish's essay title refers to as "rational" politics? Explain.

5. Is the appeal of Fish's essay entirely to *logos* and *ethos*, or do you also find some humor and some *pathos*? If so, cite passages.

GLORIA JIMÉNEZ

Gloria Jiménez married immediately after she graduated from high school, worked briefly, had two children, and then, after her younger child started school, continued her own formal education. This essay, written for a composition course at Tufts University in 2003, was her first publication.

Against the Odds, and against the Common Good (Student Essay)

State-run lotteries are now so common — thirty-nine states and Washington, D.C., operate lotteries — that the states probably will never get out of the lottery business. Still, when all is said and done about lotteries bringing a bit of excitement into the lives of many people and bringing a vast amount of money into the lives of a few, the states should not be in the business of urging people to gamble.

And they *do* urge people. Consider a slogan used in Maryland, "Play Today. Cash Tomorrow." If the statement were, "Get a job today and you will have cash tomorrow," it would be true; it would make sense, however small the earnings might be. But "Play Today. Cash Tomorrow" falsely suggests that the way to have money tomorrow is to buy a ticket today. In fact, buying a ticket is an almost sure-fire way of getting nothing for something.

Maryland is not the only state that uses a clever slogan to get its citizens to part with hard-earned money. New York's ads say, "You Can't Win If You Don't Play," and Oregon's ads say, "There Is No Such Thing as a Losing

Ticket." This last slogan — which at first glance seems to say that every ticket will benefit the purchaser — is built on the idea that the state's share of the money goes to a worthy cause, usually education or some social service. But no matter how you look at it, this slogan, like the others, urges people to buy a product — a jackpot — that they have almost no chance of receiving.

The chief arguments *in favor* of state-run lotteries seem to be these: (1) people freely choose to participate; (2) funds are used for education or for other important services; (3) if this source of funding disappears, the states will have to compensate by imposing taxes of one sort or another; (4) operation by the government ensures that the lotteries are run honestly; and (5) lotteries create jobs. We can respond briefly to the last two points, and then concentrate on the first three.

It probably is true that the lotteries are run 5 honestly (though I seem to recall reading in the newspaper about one state in which corruption was found in administering the lottery), but that is not the point. If it is wrong to encourage people to gamble, it is hardly relevant to say that the game is run honestly. The other point that can be dismissed briefly is that lotteries create jobs. This argument is usually advanced in connection with the creation of casinos, which surely do create jobs, not only in the casinos but also in nearby restaurants, parking lots, movie theaters, and so forth. But lottery tickets are sold in places where the clerks are already employed. Presumably the only new jobs created by the lottery are the relatively few jobs of the people who dream up the slogans or who are in charge of collecting and processing the receipts.

The three other claims require more attention. The first, that people freely choose to participate, probably is largely true. Although some buyers are compulsive gamblers, people who are addicted and therefore cannot really be said to choose freely, I grant that most people do have a free choice — although, as I have already said, I think that some of the slogans that states use are deceptive, and if this is the case, purchasers who are misled by the ads are not entirely free. Consider a slogan that Illinois used on billboards, especially in poor neighborhoods: "This Could Be Your Ticket Out." Yes, a person might hit the jackpot and get out of poverty, but the chances are one in several million, and to imply that the lottery is a reasonable option to get out of present poverty is to be deceptive. Further, the message is essentially unwholesome. It implies that the way out is luck, rather than education and hard work. Of course, luck plays a part in life, but 99.99 percent of the people who rely on the ticket as the "ticket out" of poverty are going to be terribly disappointed. But again, we can grant that except for gambling addicts, people who buy lottery tickets are freely doing so.

Probably the strongest claim is that the funds are used for important purposes, usually education. This claim apparently is true: the legislators are smart enough to package the lottery bills this way. And the revenue gained seems enormous — $20 billion in 2002, according to the *New York Times* (May 18, 2003, sec. 4, p. 1). On the other hand, this amount is only about 4 percent of the total revenue of the states. That is, this amount *could* be raised by other means, specifically by taxation, but legislators understandably do not want to be associated with increasing taxes. And so, again, advocates of state lotteries emphasize the voluntary nature of the lottery: by buying lottery tickets, they say, people are in effect volunteering to give money to the states, in exchange for the chance (however remote) of getting a ticket out. Buying a ticket, in this view, is paying an optional tax; if you don't want to pay the tax, don't buy the ticket.

I now get to the point in my argument where I may sound condescending, where I may offend decent people. The point is this: studies show that most of the tickets are bought by people who don't have much money, people who are near the bottom of the economic scale. According to one study, adults whose income was under $10,000 spent nearly three times as much buying lottery tickets as did adults who earned $50,000 or more.[1] I say that this argument is delicate because anyone who advances it is liable to be accused of being snobbish and paternalistic, of saying, in effect, "Poor people don't know how to manage their money, so we ought to remove temptation from their eyes." But such a reply does not get to the central issues: the central issues are (1) that the state should not tempt people, rich or poor, with dreams of an easy buck and (2) that education and social services are immensely important to the whole of society, so they should not be disproportionately financed by the poor and the addicted.

Let me end a bit indirectly. Surely everyone will grant that tobacco is a harmful product.

_____
[1] Verna V. Gehring, "The American State Lottery: Sale or Swindle?" *Report from the Institute for Philosophy and Public Policy* 20 (Winter/Spring 2000): 15.

Yes, it is legal, but everyone knows it is harmful. The state puts very heavy taxes on it, presumably not to raise revenue but to discourage the use of tobacco. We agree, surely, that it would be almost criminal if, in an effort to increase its revenues, the state *enticed* people to smoke — for example, by posting billboards showing attractive people smoking or cartoon characters that appealed to children. Would we say, "Oh, well, we need the revenue (from the taxes) to provide services, so let's make smoking as attractive as we can to get people to buy cigarettes"? No, we would say, "People should not smoke, but if they will, well, let's use the revenue from the taxes for two chief purposes: *to dissuade* people from smoking and *to treat* people who have become ill from smoking."

State legislators who genuinely have the interests of their constituents at heart will not pass bills that put the state into the lottery business and that cause the state to engage in an activity that is close to pickpocketing. Rather, they will recognize that, however unpopular taxes are, taxes may have to be raised to support education and social services that the people rightly expect the state to provide. It's against the odds to expect politicians to act this way, but let's hope that some politicians will do the right thing and will vote for the common good.

Topics for Critical Thinking and Writing

1. Gloria Jiménez omits at least one important argument that advocates of state-run lotteries sometimes offer: If our state doesn't run a lottery, residents will simply go to nearby states to buy tickets, so we will just be losing revenue that other states pick up; poor people will still be spending money that they can't afford, and our state will in no way benefit. What do you suppose Jiménez might say in reply? And what is your own view of this argument?

2. A bit of humor appears at the end of paragraph 2. Is it appropriate? Or is the essay too solemn, too preachy? If you think it's too preachy, cite some sentences, and then revise them to make them more acceptable.

3. What are the strengths and weaknesses of this essay? What grade would you give it, and why? If you were the instructor in a first-year composition course, what comment (three or four sentences) would you write at the end of the essay?

4. Jiménez wrote the essay in a composition course. If you were the editor of your college's newspaper, might you run it as an op-ed piece? Why, or why not?

ANNA LISA RAYA

Daughter of a second-generation Mexican American father and a Puerto Rican mother, Anna Lisa Raya grew up in Los Angeles. In 1994, while she was an undergraduate at Columbia University in New York, she wrote and published this essay on identity.

It's Hard Enough Being Me (Student Essay)

When I entered college, I *discovered* I was Latina. Until then, I had never questioned who I was or where I was from: My father is a second-generation Mexican American, born and raised in Los Angeles, and my mother was born in Puerto Rico and raised in Compton, California. My home is El Sereno, a predominantly Mexican neighborhood in L.A. Every close friend I have back home is Mexican. So I was always just Mexican. Though sometimes I was just Puerto Rican — like when we would visit Mamo (my grandma) or hang out with my Aunt Titi.

Upon arriving in New York as a first-year student, 3,000 miles from home, I not only experienced extreme culture shock, but for the first time I had to define myself according to the broad term "Latina." Although culture shock and identity crisis are common for the newly minted collegian who goes away to school, my experience as a newly minted Latina was, and still is, even more complicating. In El Sereno, I felt like I was part of a majority, whereas at the College I am a minority.

I've discovered that many Latinos like myself have undergone similar experiences. We face discrimination for being a minority in this country while also facing criticism for being "whitewashed" or "sellouts" in the countries of our heritage. But as an ethnic group in college, we are forced to define ourselves according to some vague, generalized Latino experience. This requires us to know our history, our language, our music, and our religion. I can't even be a content "Puerto Mexican" because I have to be a politically-and-socially-aware-Latina-with-a-chip-on-my-shoulder-because-of-how-repressed-I-am-in-this-country.

I am none of the above. I am the quintessential imperfect Latina. I can't dance salsa to save my life, I learned about Montezuma and the Aztecs in sixth grade, and I haven't prayed to the *Virgen de Guadalupe* in years.

Apparently I don't even look Latina. I 5 can't count how many times people have just assumed that I'm white or asked me if I'm Asian. True, my friends back home call me *güera* ("whitey") because I have green eyes and pale skin, but that was as bad as it got. I never thought I would wish my skin were a darker shade or my hair a curlier texture, but since I've been in college, I have — many times.

Another thing: My Spanish is terrible. Every time I call home, I berate my mama for not teaching me Spanish when I was a child. In fact, not knowing how to speak the language of my home countries is the biggest problem that I have encountered, as have many Latinos. In Mexico there is a term, *pocha*, which is used by native Mexicans to ridicule Mexican Americans. It expresses a deep-rooted antagonism and dislike for those of us who were raised on the other side of the border. Our failed attempts to speak pure, Mexican Spanish are largely responsible for the dislike. Other Latin American natives have this same attitude. No matter how well a Latino speaks Spanish, it can never be good enough.

Yet Latinos can't even speak Spanish in the U.S. without running the risk of being called "spic" or "wetback." That is precisely why my mother refused to teach me Spanish when I was a child. The fact that she spoke Spanish was constantly used against her: It prevented her from getting good jobs, and it would have placed me in bilingual education — a construct of the Los Angeles public school system that has proved to be more of a hindrance to intellectual development than a help.

To be fully Latina in college, however, I *must* know Spanish. I must satisfy the equation: Latina [equals] Spanish-speaking.

So I'm stuck in this black hole of an identity crisis, and college isn't making my life any easier, as I thought it would. In high school, I was being prepared for an adulthood in which I would be an individual, in which I wouldn't have to wear a Catholic school uniform anymore. But though I led an anonymous adolescence, I knew who I was. I knew I was different from white, black, or Asian people. I knew there was a language other than English that I could call my own if I only knew how to speak it better. I knew there were historical reasons why I was in this country, distinct reasons that make my existence here easier or more difficult than other people's existence. Ultimately, I was content.

Now I feel pushed into a corner, always 10 defining, defending, and proving myself to classmates, professors, or employers. Trying to understand who and why I am, while understanding Plato or Homer, is a lot to ask of myself.

A month ago, I heard three Nuyorican (Puerto Ricans born and raised in New York) writers discuss how New York City has influenced their writing. One problem I have faced as a young writer is finding a voice that is true to my community. I was surprised and reassured to discover that as Latinos, these writers had faced similar pressures and conflicts as myself; some weren't even taught Spanish in childhood. I will never forget the advice that one of them gave me that evening: She said that I need to be true to myself. "Because people will always complain about what you are doing — you're a 'gringa' or a 'spic' no matter what," she explained. "So you might as well do things for yourself and not for them."

I don't know why it has taken 20 years to hear this advice, but I'm going to give it a try. *Soy yo* and no one else. *Punto.*[1]

---

[1] **Soy yo . . . Punto.** I'm me . . . Period (Spanish). [Editors' note.]

Topics for Critical Thinking and Writing

1. When Anna Lisa Raya says she "*discovered*" she was Latina (para. 1), to what kind of event is she referring? Was she coerced or persuaded to declare herself as Latina, or did it come about in some other way? Explain.

2. Is Raya glad or sorry that she didn't learn Spanish as a child? What evidence in her essay indicates one way or the other?

3. What is an "identity crisis" (para. 9)? Does everyone go through such a crisis upon entering college? Did you? Or is this an experience that only racial minorities in predominantly white American colleges undergo? Explain your responses.

RONALD TAKAKI

Ronald Takaki (1939–2009), the grandson of agricultural laborers who immigrated from Japan, was a professor of ethnic studies at the University of California–Berkeley. He edited From Different Shores: Perspectives on Race and Ethnicity in America *(1987) and wrote (among other works)* Strangers from a Different Shore: A History of Asian-Americans *(1989). The essay reprinted here appeared originally in the* New York Times *on June 16, 1990.*

The Harmful Myth of Asian Superiority

Asian Americans have increasingly come to be viewed as a "model minority." But are they as successful as claimed? And for whom are they supposed to be a model?

Asian Americans have been described in the media as "excessively, even provocatively" successful in gaining admission to universities. Asian American shopkeepers have been congratulated, as well as criticized, for their ubiquity and entrepreneurial effectiveness.

If Asian Americans can make it, many politicians and pundits ask, why can't African Americans? Such comparisons pit minorities against each other and generate African American resentment toward Asian Americans. The victims are blamed for their plight, rather than racism and an economy that has made many young African American workers superfluous.

The celebration of Asian Americans has obscured reality. For example, figures on the high earnings of Asian Americans relative to Caucasians are misleading. Most Asian Americans live in California, Hawaii, and New York — states with higher incomes and higher costs of living than the national average.

Even Japanese Americans, often touted for 5 their upward mobility, have not reached equality. While Japanese American men in California earned an average income comparable to Caucasian men in 1980, they did so only by acquiring more education and working more hours.

Comparing family incomes is even more deceptive. Some Asian American groups do have higher family incomes than Caucasians. But they have more workers per family.

The "model minority" image homogenizes Asian Americans and hides their differences. For example, while thousands of Vietnamese American young people attend universities, others are on the streets. They live in motels and hang out in pool halls in places like East Los Angeles; some join gangs.

Twenty-five percent of the people in New York City's Chinatown lived below the poverty level in 1980, compared with

17 percent of the city's population. Some 60 percent of the workers in the Chinatowns of Los Angeles and San Francisco are crowded into low-paying jobs in garment factories and restaurants.

"Most immigrants coming into Chinatown with a language barrier cannot go outside this confined area into the mainstream of American industry," a Chinese immigrant said. "Before, I was a painter in Hong Kong, but I can't do it here. I got no license, no education. I want a living; so it's dishwasher, janitor, or cook."

Hmong and Mien refugees from Laos 10 have unemployment rates that reach as high as 80 percent. A 1987 California study showed that three out of ten Southeast Asian refugee families had been on welfare for four to ten years.

Although college-educated Asian Americans are entering the professions and earning good salaries, many hit the "glass ceiling" — the barrier through which high management positions can be seen but not reached. In 1988, only 8 percent of Asian Americans were "officials" and "managers," compared with 12 percent for all groups.

Finally, the triumph of Korean immigrants has been exaggerated. In 1988, Koreans in the New York metropolitan area earned only 68 percent of the median income of non-Asians. More than three-quarters of Korean greengrocers, those so-called paragons of bootstrap entrepreneurialism, came to America with a college education. Engineers, teachers, or administrators while in Korea, they became shopkeepers after their arrival. For many of them, the greengrocery represents dashed dreams, a step downward in status.

For all their hard work and long hours, most Korean shopkeepers do not actually earn very much: $17,000 to $35,000 a year, usually representing the income from the labor of an entire family.

But most Korean immigrants do not become shopkeepers. Instead, many find themselves trapped as clerks in grocery stores, service workers in restaurants, seamstresses in garment factories, and janitors in hotels.

Most Asian Americans know their "suc- 15 cess" is largely a myth. They also see how the celebration of Asian Americans as a "model minority" perpetuates their inequality and exacerbates relations between them and African Americans.

Topics for Critical Thinking and Writing

1. What is the thesis of Ronald Takaki's essay? What evidence does he offer for its truth? Do you find his argument convincing? Explain your answers to these questions in an essay of 500 words. Alternatively, write a 500-word blog post that responds to the essay.

2. Takaki several times uses statistics to make a point. What effect do the statistics have on the reader? Do some of the statistics seem more convincing than others? Explain your responses.

3. Consider the title of Takaki's essay. To what group(s) is the myth of Asian superiority harmful?

4. Suppose you believed that Asian Americans are economically more successful in America today, relative to white Americans, than African Americans are. Does Takaki agree

or disagree with you? Why, or why not? What evidence, if any, does he cite to support or reject the belief?

5. Takaki attacks the "myth" of Asian American success and thus rejects the idea that Asian Americans are a "model minority" (recall the opening and closing paragraphs). What do you think a genuine model minority would be like? Can you think of any racial or ethnic minority in the United States that can serve as a model? Explain why or why not in an essay of 500 words.

JAMES Q. WILSON

James Q. Wilson (1931–2012) was Collins Professor of Management and Public Policy at the University of California–Los Angeles. Among his books are Thinking about Crime *(1975),* Bureaucracy *(1989),* The Moral Sense *(1993), and* Moral Judgment *(1997). The essay reprinted here appeared originally in the* New York Times Magazine *on March 20, 1994.*

Just Take Away Their Guns

The president wants still tougher gun control legislation and thinks it will work. The public supports more gun control laws but suspects they won't work. The public is right.

Legal restraints on the lawful purchase of guns will have little effect on the illegal use of guns. There are some 200 million guns in private ownership, about one-third of them handguns. Only about 2 percent of the latter are employed to commit crimes. It would take a Draconian,[1] and politically impossible, confiscation of legally purchased guns to make much of a difference in the number used by criminals. Moreover, only about one-sixth of the handguns used by serious criminals are purchased from a gun shop or pawnshop. Most of these handguns are stolen, borrowed, or obtained through private purchases that wouldn't be affected by gun laws.

What is worse, any successful effort to shrink the stock of legally purchased guns (or of ammunition) would reduce the capacity of law-abiding people to defend themselves. Gun control advocates scoff at the importance of self-defense, but they are wrong to do so. Based on a household survey, Gary Kleck, a criminologist at Florida State University, has estimated that every year, guns are used — that is, displayed or fired — for defensive purposes more than a million times, not counting their use by the police. If his estimate is correct, this means that the number of people who defend themselves with a gun exceeds the number of arrests for violent crimes and burglaries.

Our goal should not be the disarming of law-abiding citizens. It should be to reduce the number of people who carry guns unlawfully, especially in places — on streets, in taverns — where the mere presence of a gun can increase the hazards we all face. The most effective way to reduce illegal gun-carrying is to encourage the police to take guns away from people who carry them without a permit. This means encouraging the police to make street frisks.

The Fourth Amendment to the Constitution bans "unreasonable searches and

---

[1] **Draconian** Harsh or severe, often excessively so. [Editors' note.]

seizures." In 1968 the Supreme Court decided (*Terry v. Ohio*) that a frisk — patting down a person's outer clothing — is proper if the officer has a "reasonable suspicion" that the person is armed and dangerous. If a pat-down reveals an object that might be a gun, the officer can enter the suspect's pocket to remove it. If the gun is being carried illegally, the suspect can be arrested.

The reasonable-suspicion test is much less stringent than the probable-cause standard the police must meet in order to make an arrest. A reasonable suspicion, however, is more than just a hunch; it must be supported by specific facts. The courts have held, not always consistently, that these facts include someone acting in a way that leads an experienced officer to conclude criminal activity may be afoot; someone fleeing at the approach of an officer; a person who fits a drug courier profile; a motorist stopped for a traffic violation who has a suspicious bulge in his pocket; a suspect identified by a reliable informant as carrying a gun. The Supreme Court has also upheld frisking people on probation or parole.

Some police departments frisk a lot of people, but usually the police frisk rather few, at least for the purpose of detecting illegal guns. In 1992 the police arrested about 240,000 people for illegally possessing or carrying a weapon. This is only about one-fourth as many as were arrested for public drunkenness. The average police officer will make *no* weapons arrests and confiscate *no* guns during any given year. Mark Moore, a professor of public policy at Harvard University, found that most weapons arrests were made because a citizen complained, not because the police were out looking for guns.

It is easy to see why. Many cities suffer from a shortage of officers, and even those with ample law-enforcement personnel worry about having their cases thrown out for constitutional reasons

or being accused of police harassment. But the risk of violating the Constitution or engaging in actual, as opposed to perceived, harassment can be substantially reduced.

Each patrol officer can be given a list of people on probation or parole who live on that officer's beat and be rewarded for making frequent stops to insure that they are not carrying guns. Officers can be trained to recognize the kinds of actions that the Court will accept as providing the "reasonable suspicion" necessary for a stop and frisk. Membership in a gang known for assaults and drug dealing could be made the basis, by statute or Court precedent, for gun frisks.

The available evidence supports the claim [10] that self-defense is a legitimate form of deterrence. People who report to the National Crime Survey that they defended themselves with a weapon were less likely to lose property in a robbery or be injured in an assault than those who did not defend themselves. Statistics have shown that would-be burglars are threatened by gun-wielding victims about as many times a year as they are arrested (and much more often than they are sent to prison) and that the chances of a burglar being shot are about the same as his chances of going to jail. Criminals know these facts even if gun control advocates do not and so are less likely to burgle occupied homes in America than occupied ones in Europe, where the residents rarely have guns.

Some gun control advocates may concede these points but rejoin that the cost of self-defense is self-injury: Handgun owners are more likely to shoot themselves or their loved ones than a criminal. Not quite. Most gun accidents involve rifles and shotguns, not handguns. Moreover, the rate of fatal gun accidents has been declining while the level of gun ownership has been rising. There are fatal gun accidents just as there are fatal car accidents, but in fewer than 2 percent of the gun fatalities was the victim someone mistaken for an intruder.

Those who urge us to forbid or severely restrict the sale of guns ignore these facts. Worse, they adopt a position that is politically absurd. In effect, they say, "Your government, having failed to protect your person and your property from criminal assault, now intends to deprive you of the opportunity to protect yourself."

Opponents of gun control make a different mistake. The National Rifle Association and its allies tell us that "guns don't kill, people kill" and urge the Government to punish more severely people who use guns to commit crimes. Locking up criminals does protect society from future crimes, and the prospect of being locked up may deter criminals. But our experience with meting out tougher sentences is mixed. The tougher the prospective sentence the less likely it is to be imposed, or at least to be imposed swiftly. If the Legislature adds on time for crimes committed with a gun, prosecutors often bargain away the add-ons; even when they do not, the judges in many states are reluctant to impose add-ons.

Worse, the presence of a gun can contribute to the magnitude of the crime even on the part of those who worry about serving a long prison sentence. Many criminals carry guns not to rob stores but to protect themselves from other armed criminals. Gang violence has become more threatening to bystanders as gang members have begun to arm themselves. People may commit crimes, but guns make some crimes worse. Guns often convert spontaneous outbursts of anger into fatal encounters. When some people carry them on the streets, others will want to carry them to protect themselves, and an urban arms race will be under way.

And modern science can be enlisted to help. 15 Metal detectors at airports have reduced the number of airplane bombings and skyjackings to nearly zero. But these detectors only work at very close range. What is needed is a device that will enable the police to detect the presence of a large lump of metal in someone's pocket from a distance of ten or fifteen feet. Receiving such a signal could supply the officer with reasonable grounds for a pat-down. Underemployed nuclear physicists and electronics engineers in the post-cold-war era surely have the talents for designing a better gun detector.

Even if we do all these things, there will still be complaints. Innocent people will be stopped. Young black and Hispanic men will probably be stopped more often than older white Anglo males or women of any race. But if we are serious about reducing drive-by shootings, fatal gang wars and lethal quarrels in public places, we must get illegal guns off the street. We cannot do this by multiplying the forms one fills out at gun shops or by pretending that guns are not a problem until a criminal uses one.

Topics for Critical Thinking and Writing

1. If you had to single out one sentence in James Wilson's essay that best states his thesis, what sentence would that be? Why do you think it states, better than any other sentence, the essay's thesis?

2. In paragraph 3, Wilson reviews research by a criminologist purporting to show that guns are important for self-defense in American households. Does the research as reported show that displaying or firing guns in self-defense actually prevented crimes? Or wounded

aggressors? Suppose you were also told that in households where guns may be used defensively, thousands of innocent people are injured and hundreds are killed — for instance, children who find a loaded gun and play with it. Would you regard these injuries and deaths as a fair trade-off? Explain. What does the research presented by Wilson really show?

3. In an essay of no more than 100 words, explain the difference between the "reasonable-suspicion" test (para. 5) and the "probable-cause standard" (para. 6) that the courts use in deciding whether a street frisk is lawful. (You may want to organize your essay into two paragraphs, one on each topic, or perhaps into three if you include a brief introductory paragraph.)

4. Wilson reports in paragraph 7 that the police arrest four times as many drunks on the streets as they do people carrying unlicensed firearms. Does this strike you as absurd, reasonable, or mysterious? Does Wilson explain it to your satisfaction? Why, or why not?

5. In paragraph 12, Wilson says that people who want to severely restrict the ownership of guns are in effect saying, "'Your government, having failed to protect your person and your property from criminal assault, now intends to deprive you of the opportunity to protect yourself.'" What reply might an advocate of severe restrictions make? (Even if you strongly believe Wilson's summary is accurate, put yourself in the shoes of an advocate of gun control, and come up with the best reply that you can.)

6. In his final paragraph, Wilson grants that his proposal entails a difficulty: "Innocent people will be stopped. Young black and Hispanic men will probably be stopped more often than older white Anglo males or women of any race." Assuming that his predictions are accurate, is his proposal therefore fatally flawed and worth no further thought, or (taking the other extreme view) will innocent people who fall into certain classifications just have to put up with frisking for the public good? Explain your response.

7. Wilson criticizes both gun control advocates and the National Rifle Association for their ill-advised views. In an essay of 500 words, state his criticisms of each side, and explain whether and to what extent you agree.

KAYLA WEBLEY

Kayla Webley, education correspondent for Time *magazine, did her undergraduate work at the University of Washington, concentrating on journalism and political science, and her graduate work at Northwestern University, specializing in new media. The essay reprinted here originally appeared in* Time *magazine on April 20, 2012.*

Is Forgiving Student Loan Debt a Good Idea?

Every few weeks now a petition pops up in my Facebook newsfeed urging the government to forgive all student debt. The comment from the person posting the petition usually goes something like this, "Guessing this will never happen, but can't hurt to sign on!"

The petition now has nearly 670,000 signatures. Scrolling through the stories posted on the petition (and similar stories told on the related Occupy Student Debt site) can be a heart-wrenching experience. Former students tell stories of unemployment, worthless majors, low-paying jobs and resulting six-figure debt, insurmountable interest, forbearance, and default. From a human standpoint, it's easy to see why forgiving student debt holds some appeal. But many have questioned not only the enormous and economically unfeasible cost, but the purported benefits and fairness of a one-time student loan bailout.

Feeling shackled by an estimated $88,000 in student loan debt, Robert Applebaum started the petition in 2009 and has seen its popularity skyrocket since last fall as some members of the Occupy Wall Street movement adopted the battle cry. His proposal is simple: Provide a one-time bailout of student loan debt — currently valued at $1 trillion — as a way to stimulate the still-limping economy. After all, college graduates are the type of people society needs to do things like start businesses, buy homes and cars, invent things, and make babies — and people burdened with debt are less likely to make those kinds of decisions. Unburden them and the housing market might improve, along with the overall economy. "With the stroke of the President's pen, millions of Americans would suddenly have hundreds, or in some cases, thousands of extra dollars in their pockets each and every month with which to spend on ailing sectors of the economy," Applebaum writes in the petition.

That sounds like a very expensive proposition, of course. But so were the bank and auto bailouts — and, the thinking goes, if "fat cat" bankers and auto makers got a bailout, why not college graduates?

Well, as Justin Wolfers writes on the Freakonomics blog, one reason why not is that such a scheme wouldn't be a particularly efficient fiscal stimulus. Someone who has $50,000 in debt forgiven isn't likely to pump all those dollars back into the economy in a short amount of time. A much more effective stimulus, Wolfers says, would be to give fifty poor people $1,000 each because that money would almost immediately be spent.

Another problem with such a plan is that most borrowers actually can afford to pay off their student loan debt. There are some borrowers who desperately need relief, but there are many others who would just rather not have to fork over a certain percentage of their income each month to pay for the education they received years ago. But if forgiveness was offered, who wouldn't take the handout?

As it turns out, the six-figure debts that we keep hearing about in the media are actually pretty unusual. By most estimates, only a tiny minority of student loan borrowers — as little as 1 percent — graduate with more than $100,000 in debt. Mark Kantrowitz of FinAid.org and FastWeb.com says that only a few thousand students out of the several million who finish college each year graduate with that much debt. The average debt total at graduation is a much more reasonable — yet still significant — $27,500.

What's more, even borrowers who can't afford the standard repayment plan have existing alternatives if the loan is from the government. There are already programs in place that offer forgiveness, not to mention the government's effective and underutilized Income Based Repayment program. What might be a more politically viable approach to student debt — although it would provide less fiscal stimulus — would be for the government and loan providers to have a better way of distinguishing between those borrowers who really need help and those who don't. But of course that's no easy task.

Many of the concerns surrounding Applebaum's plan involve the idea of fairness. Why should current debt holders be forgiven when for years people have paid their debts? Why should taxpayers — especially those who never attended college in the first place — foot the bill for the borrowers' education? What about future generations? Will they just take out loads of money in college and cross their fingers for a bailout? There are no easy answers to these questions other than to say, life isn't fair.

But perhaps the biggest roadblock to Applebaum's plan is that a one-time bailout is a temporary fix to an ongoing problem. What's really needed is a long look at how higher education in the United States is financed. Many would argue the current model is fundamentally broken.

Virtually everyone who applies is approved for almost unlimited student loans, regardless of how likely they are to be able to pay them back. But lenders aren't really concerned about that because student loans cannot be discharged in bankruptcy. They know they'll get their money back one way or another.

As a result, lenders have no incentive to work with students toward a reasonable repayment plan. And further, colleges have no incentive to keep tuition low — tuition is increasing at a rate double that of inflation — because whether they can afford it or not, students will find a way to pay the bill.

10 Applebaum's proposal offers a radical and wildly unfeasible solution, both politically and economically, but it's an idea nonetheless. "I'm not saying my solution to the student debt crisis is the very best," he says. "If you disagree with me, what's your solution?"

Topics for Critical Thinking and Writing

1. Why do you suppose Kayla Webley prefaces her argument by telling readers in paragraph 2 that some of the stories on the Occupy Student Debt site are "heart-wrenching"?

2. What do you think of Webley's final paragraph as a way of concluding her essay? Is it effective? Why, or why not?

3. Do you have any ideas about forgiving student debt that Webley's essay doesn't address? If so, what are they? How would you work them into the essay?

Ron Bailey / Getty Images

ALFRED EDMOND JR.

Alfred Edmond Jr. (b. 1960) is senior vice president/multimedia editor-at-large of Black Enterprise, a media organization that publishes Black Enterprise *magazine. He appears often on television and on nationally syndicated radio programs. The following essay was originally published in* Black Enterprise *in 2012.*

Why Asking for a Job Applicant's Facebook Password Is Fair Game

"Should business owners be allowed to ask job applicants for their Facebook passwords?" Many people who watched me on MSNBC's *Your Business* on Sunday were surprised to hear that my answer is "Yes," including the show's host, J. J. Ramberg. This question became a hot news topic last week, especially in business and social media circles, when Congress failed to pass legislation that would have banned the practice of employers asking employees to reveal their Facebook passwords.

Now, if I was asked the same question as a guest on a show called *Your Career*, I would have been hard-pressed to think of a situation where I would share my Facebook password with a potential employer. For me to consider it, I would have to want the job pretty badly, with the amount and type of compensation (including benefits, perks, and even an equity stake in the company) being major considerations. But before doing so, I would see if there were other ways I could address the potential employer's concerns without revealing my password, such as changing my privacy settings to give them the ability to view all of my Facebook content. If they persisted with their request for my password, I would try to negotiate terms to strictly limit both their use of the password and the length of time the potential employer would have access to it before I could change it. I might even consider getting an employment attorney to negotiate an agreement, including terms of confidentiality, to be signed by both me and the potential employer before sharing my password.

Of course, for the vast majority of positions, neither I nor a company looking to hire would deem it worth the time and expense to jump through all of these hoops. Most companies would not care to have password access to an applicant's social media accounts. (For what it's worth, Facebook's terms of rights and responsibilities forbids users from sharing their passwords.) In probably 99 percent of such cases, if a potential employer made such a request, my answer would be, "No, I will not share my password. Are there alternatives you are willing to consider to satisfy your concerns?" I'd accept that I'd risk not being hired as a result. On the other hand, if that was all it took for me not to be hired, I'd question how badly they really wanted me in the first place, as well as whether that was the kind of place I would have been happy working for. But for certain companies and positions, especially if I wanted the job badly enough, I'd consider a request for my Facebook password at least up for negotiation.

That said, my response on *Your Business* was from the perspective of the business owner. And if I'm the owner of certain types of businesses, or trying to fill certain types of positions, I believe I should be able to ask job applicants for access to their Facebook accounts. The applicant may choose not to answer, but I should be able to ask. Depending on the position, knowing everything I possibly can about an applicant is critical to not only making the best hire, but to protecting the interests of my current employees, customers, and partners as well as the financial interests of the company.

On *Your Business*, I pointed to an example 5 where I believe a request for a Facebook password as part of the hiring process is entirely reasonable: the child care industry. If I am running a school or a day care center, the time to find out that a teacher or other worker has a record of inappropriate social media communication with minors, or worse, a history of or predilection for sexual relationships with students, is during the hiring process — as New York City is finding out the hard way, with an epidemic of public school employees being revealed to have had such relationships with students. To me, such a request falls into the same category of checking the backgrounds of potential employees as the common (also still debated) practice of asking job applicants to agree to a credit check, especially for jobs that will require them to handle money, keep the books, or carry out other fiscal duties on behalf of a company. In these and other cases, safety and security issues, and the legal liability that they create for business owners if they are not adequately addressed during the hiring process, outweigh the job applicant's expectation of privacy when it comes to their social media activities.

Speaking of which, I can still hear people screaming (actually tweeting and retweeting) that an employer asking for your Facebook password is a horrible invasion of privacy. Well, for those of you who still believe in Santa Claus, I strongly recommend that you read *The Filter Bubble: What the Internet Is Hiding from You* by Eli Pariser (Penguin Press). Or you can just take my advice and let go of the illusion of privacy on social media. The courts are conflicted, at best, on whether we as social media users have a right to an expectation of privacy, with many cases being decided against such expectations. The last place you want to share anything that is truly private is on your Facebook page or any other social media platform. Better to think of social media as the ultimate

"Front Street." No matter what Facebook's privacy policies are (which they can change at will without your permission) and what privacy tools and settings they offer (which they also change whenever it suits their business models), always assume that posting on Facebook is just the ticking time bomb version of you shouting your private business from the middle of Times Square — on steroids.

To paraphrase a quote shared in *The Filter Bubble*, if you're getting something for free, you're not the customer, you're the product. Social media is designed for the information shared on it to be searched and shared — and mined for profit. The business model is the very antithesis of the expectation of privacy. To ignore that reality is to have blind faith in Facebook, Google, Twitter, etc., operating in your best interests above all else, at all times. (I don't.)

Whether you agree with me or not about whether a potential employer asking you for your Facebook password is fair game, I hope you'll take my advice: When considering what to share via social media, don't think business vs. personal. Think public vs. private. And if something is truly private, do not share it on social media out of a misplaced faith in the expectation of privacy.

This debate is far from over, and efforts to update existing, but woefully outdated, privacy laws — not to mention the hiring practices of companies — to catch up with the realities of social media will definitely continue. I'd like to know where you stand, both as entrepreneurs and business owners, as well as potential job applicants. And I'd especially like to hear from human resources and recruiting experts. How far is too far when it comes to a potential employer investigating the social media activity of a job applicant?

Topics for Critical Thinking and Writing

1. Employers *do* (at least at the time we're writing this textbook) have the right to require drug tests and personality tests. Do you think they should also legally be allowed to ask for a password to Facebook, or should Congress pass legislation outlawing the practice? If employers are legally allowed to ask, would you provide your password? Why, or why not?

2. Would Alfred Edmond Jr.'s case be strengthened if he gave one or two additional examples — beyond the "child care industry" that he mentions in paragraph 5 — of jobs that, a reader might agree, require a thorough background check? What examples can you suggest? Would you say that applicants for these jobs should be willing to reveal their Facebook password to a potential employer? Why, or why not?

3. In paragraph 7, Edmond paraphrases: "if you're getting something for free, you're not the customer, you're the product." Paraphrase this passage yourself (on paraphrase, see p. 48) so that it would be clear to a reader who finds it puzzling.

Jeff Parker / Cagle Cartoons

SHERRY TURKLE

Sherry Turkle, born in Brooklyn, New York, in 1948, is Professor of the Social Studies of Science and Technology at the Massachusetts Institute of Technology. The author of numerous books, including Alone Together *(2011), Turkle often appears on television as a commentator on media. Here we reprint an essay that originally appeared in the* New York Times *on April 22, 2012.*

The Flight from Conversation

We live in a technological universe in which we are always communicating. And yet we have sacrificed conversation for mere connection.

At home, families sit together, texting and reading e-mail. At work, executives text during board meetings. We text (and shop and go on Facebook) during classes and when we're on dates. My students tell me about an important new skill: It involves maintaining eye contact with someone while you text someone else; it's hard, but it can be done.

Over the past fifteen years, I've studied technologies of mobile connection and talked to hundreds of people of all ages and circumstances about their plugged-in lives. I've learned that the little devices most of us carry around are so powerful that they change not only what we do, but also who we are.

We've become accustomed to a new way of being "alone together." Technology-enabled, we are able to be with one another, and also elsewhere, connected to wherever we want to be. We want to customize our lives. We want to move in and out of where we are because the thing we value most is control over where we focus our attention. We have gotten used to the idea of being in a tribe of one, loyal to our own party.

Our colleagues want to go to that board meeting but pay attention only to what interests them. To some this seems like a good idea, but we can end up hiding from one another, even as we are constantly connected to one another.

A businessman laments that he no longer has colleagues at work. He doesn't stop by to talk; he doesn't call. He says that he doesn't want to interrupt them. He says they're "too busy on their e-mail." But then he pauses and corrects himself. "I'm not telling the truth. I'm the one who doesn't want to be interrupted. I think I should. But I'd rather just do things on my BlackBerry."

A sixteen-year-old boy who relies on texting for almost everything says almost wistfully, "Someday, someday, but certainly not now, I'd like to learn how to have a conversation."

In today's workplace, young people who have grown up fearing conversation show up on the job wearing earphones. Walking through a college library or the campus of a high-tech start-up, one sees the same thing: We are together, but each of us is in our own bubble, furiously connected to keyboards and tiny touch screens. A senior partner at a Boston law firm describes a scene in his office. Young associates lay out their suite of technologies: laptops, iPods, and multiple phones. And then they put their earphones on. "Big ones. Like pilots. They turn their desks into cockpits." With the young lawyers in their cockpits, the office is quiet, a quiet that does not ask to be broken.

In the silence of connection, people are comforted by being in touch with a lot of people — carefully kept at bay. We can't get enough of one another if we can use technology to keep one another at distances we can control: not too close, not too far, just right. I think of it as a Goldilocks effect.

Texting and e-mail and posting let us [10] present the self we want to be. This means we can edit. And if we wish to, we can delete. Or retouch: the voice, the flesh, the face, the body. Not too much, not too little — just right.

Human relationships are rich; they're messy and demanding. We have learned the habit of cleaning them up with technology. And the move from conversation to connection is part of this. But it's a process in which we shortchange ourselves. Worse, it seems that over time we stop caring, we forget that there is a difference.

We are tempted to think that our little "sips" of online connection add up to a big gulp of real conversation. But they don't. E-mail, Twitter, Facebook, all of these have their places — in politics, commerce, romance, and friendship. But no matter how valuable, they do not substitute for conversation.

Connecting in sips may work for gathering discrete bits of information or for saying, "I am thinking about you." Or even for saying, "I love you." But connecting in sips doesn't work as well when it comes to understanding and knowing one another. In conversation we tend to one another. (The word itself is kinetic; it's derived from words that mean to move, together.) We can attend to tone and nuance. In conversation, we are called upon to see things from another's point of view.

Face-to-face conversation unfolds slowly. It teaches patience. When we communicate on our digital devices, we learn different habits. As we ramp up the volume and velocity of online connections, we start to expect faster answers. To get

these, we ask one another simpler questions; we dumb down our communications, even on the most important matters. It is as though we have all put ourselves on cable news. Shakespeare might have said, "We are consum'd with that which we were nourish'd by."

And we use conversation with others to [15] learn to converse with ourselves. So our flight from conversation can mean diminished chances to learn skills of self-reflection. These days, social media continually asks us what's "on our mind," but we have little motivation to say something truly self-reflective. Self-reflection in conversation requires trust. It's hard to do anything with 3,000 Facebook friends except connect.

As we get used to being shortchanged on conversation and to getting by with less, we seem almost willing to dispense with people altogether. Serious people muse about the future of computer programs as psychiatrists. A high school sophomore confides to me that he wishes he could talk to an artificial intelligence program instead of his dad about dating; he says the A.I. would have so much more in its database. Indeed, many people tell me they hope that as Siri, the digital assistant on Apple's iPhone, becomes more advanced, "she" will be more and more like a best friend — one who will listen when others won't.

During the years I have spent researching people and their relationships with technology, I have often heard the sentiment "No one is listening to me." I believe this feeling helps explain why it is so appealing to have a Facebook page or a Twitter feed — each provides so many automatic listeners. And it helps explain why — against all reason — so many of us are willing to talk to machines that seem to care about us. Researchers around the world are busy inventing sociable robots, designed to be companions to the elderly, to children, to all of us.

One of the most haunting experiences during my research came when I brought one of these robots, designed in the shape of a baby seal, to an elder-care facility, and an older woman began to talk to it about the loss of her child. The robot seemed to be looking into her eyes. It seemed to be following the conversation. The woman was comforted.

And so many people found this amazing. Like the sophomore who wants advice about dating from artificial intelligence and those who look forward to computer psychiatry, this enthusiasm speaks to how much we have confused conversation with connection and collectively seem to have embraced a new kind of delusion that accepts the simulation of compassion as sufficient unto the day. And why would we want to talk about love and loss with a machine that has no experience of the arc of human life? Have we so lost confidence that we will be there for one another?

We expect more from technology and less from one another and seem increasingly drawn to technologies that provide the illusion of companionship without the demands of relationship. Always-on/always-on-you devices provide three powerful fantasies: that we will always be heard; that we can put our attention wherever we want it to be; and that we never have to be alone. Indeed our new devices have turned being alone into a problem that can be solved.

When people are alone, even for a few moments, they fidget and reach for a device. Here connection works like a symptom, not a cure, and our constant, reflexive impulse to connect shapes a new way of being.

Think of it as "I share, therefore I am." We use technology to define ourselves by sharing our thoughts and feelings as we're having them. We used to think, "I have a feeling; I want to make a call." Now our impulse is, "I want to have a feeling; I need to send a text."

So, in order to feel more, and to feel more like ourselves, we connect. But in our rush to connect, we flee from solitude, our ability to be separate and gather ourselves. Lacking the capacity for solitude, we turn to other people but don't experience them as they are. It is as though we use them, need them as spare parts to support our increasingly fragile selves.

We think constant connection will make us feel less lonely. The opposite is true. If we are unable to be alone, we are far more likely to be lonely. If we don't teach our children to be alone, they will know only how to be lonely.

I am a partisan for conversation. To make room for it, I see some first, deliberate steps. At home, we can create sacred spaces: the kitchen, the dining room. We can make our cars "device-free zones." We can demonstrate the value of conversation to our children. And we can do the same thing at work. There we are so busy communicating that we often don't have time to talk to one another about what really matters. Employees asked for casual Fridays; perhaps managers should introduce conversational Thursdays. Most of all, we need to remember — in between texts and e-mails and Facebook posts — to listen to one another, even to the boring bits, because it is often in unedited moments, moments in which we hesitate and stutter and go silent, that we reveal ourselves to one another.

I spend the summers at a cottage on Cape Cod, and for decades I walked the same dunes that Thoreau once walked. Not too long ago, people walked with their heads up, looking at the water, the sky, the sand, and at one another, talking. Now they often walk with their heads down, typing. Even when they are with friends, partners, children, everyone is on their own devices.

So I say, look up, look at one another, and let's start the conversation.

Topics for Critical Thinking and Writing

1. Imagine a period when the book — or even the handwritten manuscript — was not yet invented. Now look at Sherry Turkle's first paragraph. Think of someone saying what Turkle says, but saying it about the invention of writing, and of the manuscript or book. Write a brief (250–500 words) expression of concern about the perils of the "new" inventions of writing and books.

2. In paragraph 3, Turkle says that the little devices that we carry "change not only what we do, but also who we are." We might reply that yes, of course, almost everything that touches us changes what we are. The invention of the movie theater changed us: Instead of conversing with family or friends and generating our own entertainment, we sat isolated in the dark for several hours. The possession of an automobile changes us, the move to a new address brings us into contact with new people who may change us (we may even marry one of them), and certainly the engendering of children changes us (or it ought to). But do you agree with Turkle that today's electronic devices produce changes of an unexpected sort? Why, or why not?

3. In paragraph 14, Turkle suggests that when we communicate electronically, as opposed to when communicating face-to-face or with pen and paper, "we dumb down our communications, even on the most important matters." Is she describing your behavior? Explain.

4. In paragraph 23, Turkle says, "we flee from solitude, our ability to be separate and gather ourselves." Is this passage true for you? Explain. Might a case be made that far from being lonely, people who use Facebook and comparable sites are often stimulated to participate in civic and political activities? Does your own experience offer evidence one way or the other? Explain.

5. Do you think Turkle's final two paragraphs make an effective ending? Why, or why not?

Visual Rhetoric: Thinking about Images as Arguments

A picture is worth a thousand words.

— PROVERB

*"What is the use of a book," thought Alice, "without pictures
or conversations?"*

— LEWIS CARROLL

Uses of Visual Images

Most visual materials that accompany written arguments serve one of several functions. One of the most common is to appeal to the reader's emotions (e.g., a photograph of a sad-eyed calf in a narrow pen can assist an argument against eating meat by inspiring sympathy for the animal). Pictures can also serve as visual evidence, offering proof that something occurred or appeared in a certain way at a certain moment. Pictures can help clarify numerical data (e.g., a graph showing five decades of law school enrollment by males and females). They can also add humor or satire to an essay. In this chapter, we concentrate on thinking critically about visual images. This means reading images in the same way we read print (or electronic) texts: by looking closely at them and discerning not only *what* they show but also *how* and *why* they convey a particular message, or argument.

When we discussed the **appeal to emotion** in Chapter 3 (p. 106), we quoted from Marc Antony's speech to the Roman populace in Shakespeare's play *Julius Caesar.* You'll recall that Antony stirred the mob by displaying Caesar's blood-stained mantle. He wasn't holding up a picture, but in a similar way he supplemented his words with visual material:

> Look, in this place ran Cassius' dagger through;
> See what a rent the envious Casca made;
> Through this, the well-belovèd Brutus stabbed. . . .

In courtrooms today, trial lawyers and prosecutors accomplish the same thing when doing the following:

- exhibiting photos of a bloody corpse, or
- holding up a murder weapon for jurors to see, or
- introducing victims as witnesses who sob while describing their ordeal.

Lawyers know that such visuals help make good arguments. Whether presented sincerely or gratuitously, visuals can have a significantly persuasive effect. Such appeals to emotion work on feelings, not logic. Think about the suit and tie that lawyers advise their male clients to wear: The attire helps make an argument to the jury about the defendant's character or credibility, even if he is actually lacking these qualities. Images, too, may be rationally connected to an argument (e.g., a gruesome image of a diseased lung in an anti-smoking ad makes a reasonable claim), but their immediate impact is more on the viewer's heart than the mind.

Like any kind of evidence, images make statements and support arguments. When Congress debated over whether to allow drilling in the Arctic National Wildlife Refuge (ANWR), both opponents and supporters made use of images:

- *Opponents* of drilling showed beautiful pictures of polar bears frolicking, wildflowers in bloom, and caribou on the move.
- *Proponents* of drilling showed bleak pictures of what they called "barren land" and "a frozen wasteland."

Both sides knew very well that images are powerfully persuasive, and they didn't hesitate to use them as supplements to words.

We invite you to think about the appropriateness of using such images in arguments. Was either side manipulating the "reality" of the ANWR? Or do images such as those described provide reasonable support for the ideas under consideration? Should argument be entirely a matter of reason, of logic (*logos*), without appeals to the emotions (*pathos*)? A statement that "the Arctic National Wildlife Refuge is a home for abundant wildlife, notably polar bears, caribou, and wildflowers" may not mean much until it is reinforced with breathtakingly beautiful images. Similarly, a statement that "most of the ANWR land is barren" may not mean much until it is corroborated by images of the vast bleakness. Each side selected a particular kind of image for a specific purpose — to support its position on drilling in the ANWR. Neither side was being dishonest, but both were appealing to emotions.

TYPES OF EMOTIONAL APPEALS

We began the preceding chapter by distinguishing between *argument,* which relies on reason (*logos*), and *persuasion,* which is a broad term that can include appeals to the emotions (*pathos*) — for example, an **appeal to pity**, such as an image of a sad-eyed calf. You might say, "Well, eating meat implies confining and killing animals," and regard the image as both reasonable and emotionally powerful. Or you might say, "Although it's emotionally powerful, this appeal to pity doesn't describe the condition of every meat animal. Some are treated humanely, slaughtered humanely, and eaten ethically." You might write a counterargument and include an image of free-range cattle on a farm (although in doing this, you too would be appealing to emotions).

The point is that images can be persuasive even if they don't make good arguments, in the same way threats of violence can be persuasive but do not make good arguments. The gangster Al Capone famously said, "You can get a lot more done with a kind word and a gun than with a kind word alone." Threats of violence appeal exclusively to the emotions — specifically, fear.

Advertisers commonly use the **appeal to fear** as a persuasive technique. While it is not a threat of violence, the appeal to fear is a threat of sorts. Showing a burglary, a car crash, embarrassing age spots, or a cockroach infestation can successfully convince consumers to buy a product — a home security system, a new car insurance policy, an age-defying skin cream, or a pesticide. Such images generate fear and anxiety at the same time that they offer the solution for it.

Appeal to self-interest is another persuasive tactic that writers can use. Consider these remarks, which use the word *interest* in the sense of "self-interest":

Would you persuade, speak of Interest, not Reason. — BENJAMIN FRANKLIN

There are two levers for moving men — interest and fear. — NAPOLEON BONAPARTE

Appeals to self-interest may be quite persuasive because they speak directly to what benefits you the most, not necessarily what benefits others in the community, society, or world. Such appeals are also common in advertising. "You can save bundles by shopping at Maxi-Mart," a commercial might claim, without making reference to sweatshop labor conditions, the negative impact of global commerce, or other troublesome aspects of what you see only as a great savings for yourself. You may be familiar with other types of emotional appeals in advertising that speak to the senses more than to the rational mind. Again, these kinds of appeals don't necessarily make good arguments for the products in question, but each can be highly persuasive — sometimes affecting us subconsciously. (The same applies to appeals in written arguments. This is why thinking critically about both words and images is so important.)

Here is a list of some additional kinds of appeals to emotion:

Sexual appeals (Example: showing a bikini-clad model standing near a product)

Bandwagon appeals (Example: showing crowds of people rushing to a sale)

Humor appeals (Example: showing a cartoon animal drinking *X* brand of beverage)

Celebrity appeals (Example: showing a famous person driving *X* brand of car)

Testimonial appeals (Example: showing a doctor giving *X* brand of vitamins to her kids)

Identity appeals (Example: showing a "good family" going to *X* restaurant)

Prejudice appeals (Example: showing a "loser" drinking *X* brand of beer)

Lifestyle appeals (Example: showing a jar of X brand of mustard on a silver platter)

Stereotype appeals (Example: showing a Latino person enjoying *X* brand of salsa)

Patriotic appeals (Example: showing *X* brand of mattress alongside an American flag)

Exercise

Watch the commercials that air during a television show, or examine the print advertisements in a popular magazine. Identify as many examples as possible of the types of appeals mentioned on the preceding pages. Is there a rational basis for any of the appeals you see? Are any appeals irrational even if they are effective? Why, or why not?

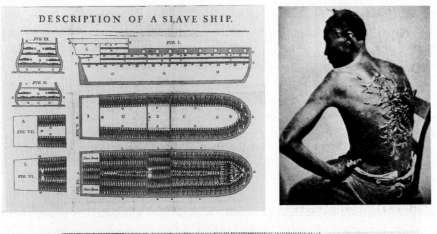

Images played an important role in the antislavery movement in the nineteenth century. On the top left is a diagram showing how human cargo was packed into a slave ship; it was distributed with Thomas Clarkson's *Essay on the Slavery and Commerce of the Human Species* (1804). On the top right is Frederick W. Mercer's photograph (April 2, 1863) of Gordon, a "badly lacerated" runaway slave. Images such as the slave ship and the runaway slave worked against slave owners' claims that slavery was a humane institution — claims that also were supported by illustrations, such as the woodcut at the bottom, titled *Attention Paid to a Poor Sick Negro*, from *Josiah Priest's In Defense of Slavery* (1843).

Seeing versus Looking: Reading Advertisements

Advertising is one of the most common forms of visual persuasion we encounter in everyday life. The influence of advertising in our culture is pervasive and subtle. Part of its power comes from our habit of internalizing the intended messages of words and images without thinking deeply about them. Once we begin decoding the ways in which advertisements are constructed — once we view them critically — we can understand how (or if) they work as arguments. We may then make better decisions about whether to buy particular products and what factors convinced us or failed to convince us.

To read an advertisement — or any image — critically, it helps to consider some basic rules from the field of **semiotics**, the study of signs and symbols. Fundamental to semiotic analysis is the idea that visual signs have shared meanings in a culture. If you approach a sink and see a red faucet and a blue faucet, you can be pretty sure which one will produce hot water and which one will produce cold. In a similar way, we almost subconsciously recognize the meanings of images in advertisements. Thus, one of the first strategies we can use in reading advertisements critically is **deconstructing** them, taking them apart to see what makes them work. It's helpful to remember that advertisements are enormously expensive to produce and disseminate, so nothing is left to chance. Teams of people typically scrutinize every part of an advertisement to ensure it communicates the intended message — although this doesn't imply that viewers must accept those messages. In fact, taking advertisements apart is the first step in being critical about them.

Taking apart an advertisement means examining each visual element. Consider this advertisement for Nike shoes featuring basketball star LeBron James. Already, you should see the celebrity appeal — an implicit claim that Nike shoes help make James a star player. The ad creates an association between the shoes and the sports champion. James's uniform number, 23, assists

Nike, Inc.

in this association by referencing another basketball legend (and Nike spokesperson), Michael Jordan. James is, in a way, presented as the progeny of Michael Jordan, as a new incarnation of a sports "god." WE ARE ALL WITNESSES, the text reads, drawing on language commonly used in religious settings to describe the second coming of Christ. James's arms are outstretched, Christ-like, and seem to be illuminated by divine light from above. The uniform also references James's famous return to the Cleveland Cavaliers, his hometown team, after leaving the team abruptly to play four seasons with the Miami Heat. His "return" to Cleveland — his own second coming — the son of a sports god — and with the resonance of forgiveness, redemption, and salvation for Cleveland sports fans: All these associations work together to elevate James, Jordan, and Nike to exalted status. Of course, our description here is tongue-in-cheek. We're not gullible enough to believe this literally, and the ad's producers don't expect us to be; but they do hope that such an impression will be powerful enough to make us think of Nike the next time we shop for athletic shoes. If sports gods wear Nike, why shouldn't we?

This kind of analysis is possible when we recognize a difference between *seeing* and *looking*. **Seeing** is a physiological process involving light, the eye, and the brain. **Looking**, however, is a social process involving the mind. It suggests apprehending an image in terms of symbolic, metaphorical, and other social and cultural meanings. To do this, we must think beyond the *literal* meaning of an image or image element and consider its *figurative* meanings. If you look up *apple* in the dictionary, you'll find its literal, **denotative** meaning — a round fruit with thin red or green skin and a crisp flesh. But an apple also communicates figurative, **connotative** meanings. Connotative meanings are the cultural or emotional associations that an image suggests.

The long-running ABC television series *Desperate Housewives*, which dramatized the furtive sex lives and exploits of suburban women, featured apples prominently in its advertisements.

CHAPTER 4 | VISUAL RHETORIC: THINKING ABOUT IMAGES AS ARGUMENTS

How does the DKNY advertisement use the symbolic, connotative meanings of the apple? In what ways does the advertisement for Bulova watches attempt to make an argument about the product?

The connotative meaning of an apple in Western culture dates back to the biblical story of the Garden of Eden, where Eve, tempted by a serpent, eats the fruit from the forbidden tree of knowledge and brings about the end of paradise on earth. Throughout Western culture, apples have come to represent knowledge and the pursuit of knowledge. Think of the ubiquitous Apple logo gracing so many mobile phones, tablets, and laptops: With its prominent bite, it symbolizes the way technology opens up new worlds of knowing. Sometimes, apples represent forbidden knowledge, temptation, or seduction — and biting into one suggests giving in to desires for new understandings and experiences. The story of Snow White offers just one example of an apple used as a symbol of temptation.

Let's look at two additional advertisements (pictured on p. 146), each of which relies almost entirely on images rather than words. The first, an ad for a TV comedy that made its debut in 2009, boldly displays the show's title and highlights the network name by setting it apart, but the most interesting words are in much smaller print:

Funny. On so many levels.

These words flatter the ad's readers, thus making them susceptible to the implicit message: "Look at this program." Why do we say the words are flattering? For three reasons:

- The small type size implies that the reader isn't someone whose attention can be caught only by headlines.

- The pun on "levels" (physical levels, and levels of humor) is a witty way of saying that the show offers not only the low comedy of physical actions but also the high comedy of witty talk — talk that, for instance, may involve puns.

- The two terse, incomplete sentences assume that the sophisticated reader doesn't need to have things explained at length.

The picture itself is attractive, showing what seems to be a wide variety of people (though not any faces or body types that in real life might cause viewers any uneasiness) posed in the style of a family portrait. Indeed, these wholesome figures, standing in affectionate poses, are all dressed in white (no real-life ketchup stains here) and are neatly framed — except for the patriarch, at the extreme right — by a pair of seated youngsters whose legs dangle down from the levels. The modern family, we're told, is large and varied (this one includes a gay son and his partner, and their adopted Vietnamese baby), smart and warm. Best of all, it is "Funny. On so many levels."

The second ad features just a single line of text: "No In-App Purchases." These words are set below the image of a shopping cart with a plus sign, which has come to be an almost universally recognized symbol for an electronic shopping cart. Both the text and the icon are textured and look a little rough at the edges, suggesting that they are made out of the very item they are advertising. After all, Play-Doh has been around since the 1930s; though the way children play has changed dramatically since then (most kids born now will grow

ABC/Modern Family

up knowing what an "in-app purchase" is), by fashioning the electronic icon and text out of a nearly century-old product, the ad implies that just because a toy—or anything else—is new and high-tech, that does not make it inherently better than old-fashioned things. After all, the product being advertised has been around for nearly a century; how long will an app on a smartphone or tablet last until it is replaced with a newer version?

A CHECKLIST FOR ANALYZING IMAGES (ESPECIALLY ADVERTISEMENTS)

☐ What is the overall effect of the design? Colorful and busy (suggesting activity)? Quiet and understated (e.g., chiefly white and grays, with lots of empty space)? Old-fashioned or cutting edge?

☐ What single aspect of the image immediately captures your attention? Its size? Its position on the page? The beauty of the image? The grotesqueness of the image? Its humor?

☐ Who is the audience for the image? Affluent young men? Housewives? Retired persons?

☐ What is the argument?

☐ Does the text make a rational appeal (*logos*)? ("Tests at a leading university prove that . . ."; "If you believe *X*, you should vote 'No' on this referendum" appeal to our sense of reason.)

☐ Does the image appeal to the emotions or to dearly held values (*pathos*)? (Images of starving children or maltreated animals appeal to our sense of pity; images of military valor may appeal to our patriotism; images of luxury may appeal to our envy; images of sexually attractive people may appeal to our desire to be like them; images of violence or of extraordinary ugliness — as in ads showing a human fetus being destroyed — may seek to shock us.)

☐ Does the image make an ethical appeal — that is, does it appeal to our character as a good human being (*ethos*)? (Ads by charitable organizations often appeal to our sense of decency, fairness, and pity; but ads that appeal to our sense of prudence — such as ads for insurance companies or investment houses — also make an ethical appeal).

☐ What is the relation of print to image? Does the image do most of the work, or does it serve to attract us and lead us on to read the text?

Topics for Critical Thinking and Writing

1. Imagine that you work for a business — for instance, a vacation resort, a clothing manufacturer, or an automaker — that advertises in a publication such as *Time* or *Newsweek*. Design an advertisement for the business: Describe the picture and write the text, and then, in an essay of 500 words, identify your target audience (college students? young couples about to

buy their first home? retired persons?) and explain your purpose in choosing certain types of appeals (e.g., to reason, to the emotions, to the audience's sense of humor).

2. It is often said that colleges, like businesses, are selling a product. Examine a brochure or catalog that is sent to prospective college applicants, or locate your own college's view book, and analyze the kinds of appeals that some of the images make.

Other Aspects of Visual Appeals

As we saw with the uses of images relating to the Arctic National Wildlife Refuge, photographs can serve as evidence but have a peculiar relationship to the truth. We must never forget that images are constructed, selected, and used for specific purposes. When advertisers use images, they're trying to convince consumers to purchase a product or service. But when images serve as documentary evidence, we often assume they're showing the "truth" of the matter at hand. Our skepticism may be lower when we see an image in the newspaper or a magazine, assuming it captures a particular event or moment in time *as it really happened*. But historical images, images of events, news photographs, and other forms of visual evidence are not free from the potential for conscious or unconscious bias. Consider how liberal and conservative media sources portray the nation's president in images: One source may show him proud and smiling in bright light with the American flag behind him, while another might show him scowling in a darkened image suggestive of evil intent. Both are "real" images, but the framing, tinting, setting, and background can inspire significantly different responses in viewers.

As we saw with the image of LeBron James, certain postures, facial expressions, and settings can contribute to a photograph's interpretation. Martin Luther King Jr.'s great speech of

Bettmann/Getty Images

Martin Luther King Jr. delivering his "I Have a Dream" speech on August 28, 1963, from the steps of the Lincoln Memorial.

August 28, 1963, "I Have a Dream," still reads very well on the page, but part of its immense appeal derives from its setting: King spoke to some 200,000 people in Washington, D.C., as he stood on the steps of the Lincoln Memorial. That setting, rich with associations of slavery and freedom, strongly assists King's argument. In fact, images of King delivering his speech are nearly inseparable from the very argument he was making. The visual aspects — the setting (the Lincoln Memorial with the Washington Monument and the Capitol in the distance) and King's gestures — are part of the speech's persuasive rhetoric.

Derrick Alridge, a historian, examined dozens of accounts of Martin Luther King Jr. in history books, and he found that images of King present him overwhelmingly as a messianic figure — standing before crowds, leading them, addressing them in postures reminiscent of a prophet. While King is an admirable figure, Alridge asserts, history books err by presenting him as more than human. Doing so ignores his personal struggles and failures and makes a myth out of the real man. This myth suggests he was the epicenter of the civil rights movement, an effort that was actually conducted in different ways via different

Martin Luther King Jr. on "Chicken Bone Beach" in Atlantic City.

strategies on the part of many other figures whom King eclipsed. We may even get the idea that the entire civil rights movement began and ended with King alone. When he's presented as a holy prophet, it becomes easier to focus on his abstract messages about love, equality, and justice, and not on the specific policies and politics he advocated — his avowed socialist stances, for instance. While photographs of King seek to help us remember, they may actually portray him in a way that causes us to forget other things — for example, the fact that his approval rating among whites at the time of his death was lower than 30 percent, and among blacks lower than 50 percent.

LEVELS OF IMAGES

One helpful way of discerning the meanings of images by *looking* at them (see p. 143) is to utilize *seeing* first as a way to define what is plainly or literally present in them. You can begin by *seeing* — identifying the elements that are indisputably "there" in an image (the denotative level). Then you move on to *looking* — interpreting the meanings suggested by the elements that are present (the connotative level).

Semioticians distinguish between images' surface levels and deeper levels. The surface level is the **syntagmatic level**, and the deeper level is the **paradigmatic level**. The words *syntagmatic* and *paradigmatic* are related to the words *syntax* and *paradigm*.

Arguably, when we *see*, we pay attention only to the syntagmatic level. We notice the various elements included in an image. We *see* denotatively — that is, we observe just the explicit elements of the image. We aren't concerned with the meaning of the image's elements, but just with the fact that they're present.

When we *look*, we move to the paradigmatic level. That is, we speculate on the elements' deeper meanings — what they suggest figuratively, symbolically, or metaphorically in our cultural system. We may also consider the relationship of different elements to one another. When we do this, we look connotatively.

Syntagmatic analysis	Paradigmatic analysis
Seeing	Looking
Denotation	Connotation
Literal	Figurative
What is present	What it means
Understanding / Textual	Interpreting / Subtextual / Contextual

Exercise

Examine the images on this page and the next. As you examine each one, do the following:

1. *See* the image. Perform a syntagmatic analysis thoroughly describing the image elements you observe. Write down as many elements as possible that you see.

2. *Look* at the image. Perform a paradigmatic analysis in which you take the elements you have observed and relate what they suggest by considering their figurative meanings, their meanings in relation to one another, and their meanings in the context of the images' production and consumption.

Margaret Bourke-White/Time & Life Pictures/Getty Images

Residents of Louisville, Kentucky, waiting in a bread line in 1937. A massive flood from January to February that year left nearly four hundred people dead and roughly one million people homeless across five states.

Adam Bettcher/Getty Images

Protestors rallying outside the office of Dr. Walter Palmer, a dentist from Bloomington, Minnesota. In July 2015, Palmer was accused of poaching a 13-year-old lion named Cecil that was living at Hwange National Park in Zimbabwe. Palmer reportedly paid $50,000 for the hunt and lured Cecil out of the sanctuary to shoot him.

The point here is that photographs promise a clear window into a past reality but are not unassailable guarantors of truth. In the digital age, it's remarkably easy to alter photographs, and we have become more suspicious of photographs as direct evidence of reality. Yet we still tend to trust certain sources more than others. To counteract this tendency, we can be more critical about images by asking three overarching questions about the contexts in which they are created, disseminated, and received. Within each question, other questions arise.

1. Who produced the image? Who was the photographer? Under what circumstances was the picture taken? How is the subject of the image framed? What other visual information is included in the frame? What is emphasized and de-emphasized? What do you think is the image's intended effect?

2. Who distributed the image? How widely has the image been distributed? Where has it been published (magazine, newspaper, blog, social media page)? What is the intended audience of the publication where the image appears? What purpose does the image serve? How does the image support the accompanying text? What alternative images exist?

3. Who consumed the image? What type of audience is the likeliest viewer of the image? Are they likely to see it as negative or positive? Does the image inspire an emotional response? If so, what kind? What elements in the photograph are likely to generate certain kinds of responses?

> **A RULE FOR WRITERS**
> If you think that pictures will help you to make the point you are arguing, include them with captions explaining their sources and relevance.

Accommodating, Resisting, and Negotiating the Meaning of Images

Most images are produced, selected, and published in order to have a specific effect on readers and viewers. This dominant meaning of an image supposes that the audience will react in a predictable way, usually based on the widespread **cultural codes** that operate within a society. Images of elegant women in designer dresses, rugged men driving pickup trucks, stodgy teachers, cutthroat CEOs, hipster computer programmers, and so on speak to generally accepted notions of what certain types of people are like. An image of a suburban couple in an automobile advertisement washing their new car subconsciously confirms and perpetuates a certain ideal of middle-class suburban life (a heterosexual couple, a well-trimmed lawn, a neatly painted house and picket fence — and a brand-new midsize sedan). An image of a teary-eyed young woman accepting a diamond ring from a handsome man will likely touch the viewer in a particular way, in part because of our society's cultural codes about the rituals of romantic love and marriage, gender roles, and the diamond ring as a sign of love and commitment.

These examples demonstrate that images can be constructed according to dominant connotations of gender, class, and racial, sexual, and political identity. When analyzing an image, ask yourself what cultural codes it endorses, what ideals it establishes as natural, what social norms or modes of everyday life it idealizes or assumes.

As image consumers, we often *accommodate* (i.e., passively accept) the cultural codes promoted in the media. For example, in the hypothetical advertisement featuring a wedding proposal, you might accept the producer's communicated ideals that men should propose to women, that women are emotional beings, and that diamond rings are the appropriate objects to represent love and commitment. When you **accommodate** cultural codes without understanding them critically, you allow the media that perpetuate these codes to interpret the world for you. That is, you accept their interpretations without questioning the social and cultural values implicit in their assumptions, many of which may actually run counter to your own or others' social and cultural values.

If you *resist* the cultural codes of an image, you actively criticize its message and meaning. Suppose you (1) question how the ad presents gender roles and marriage, (2) claim that it idealizes heterosexual marriage, and (3) point out that it confirms and extends traditional gender roles in which men are active and bold and women are passive and emotional. Moreover, you (4) argue that the diamond ring represents a misguided commodification of love because diamonds are kept deliberately scarce by large companies and, as such, are overvalued and overpriced; meanwhile, the ad prompts young couples to spend precious money at a time when their joint assets might be better saved, and because many diamonds come from third-world countries under essentially slave labor conditions, the diamond is more a symbol of oppression than of love. If your analysis follows such paths, you **resist** the dominant message of the image in question. Sometimes, this is called an *oppositional reading*.

Negotiation, or a *negotiated reading*, the most useful mode of reading and viewing, involves a middle path — a process of revision that seeks to recognize and change the conditions that give rise to certain negative aspects of cultural codes. Negotiation implies a practical intervention into common viewing processes that help construct and maintain social conditions and relations. This intervention can be important when inequalities or stereotypes are perpetuated by cultural codes. A negotiated reading enables you to emphasize the ways in which individuals, social groups, and others relate to images and their dominant meanings, and how different personal and cultural perspectives can challenge those meanings. Without intervention there can be no revision, no positive social or cultural change. You **negotiate** cultural codes when:

- you understand the underlying messages of images and accept the general cultural implications of these codes, *but*
- you acknowledge that in some circumstances the general codes do not apply.

Using this scheme will help you analyze diverse kinds of images as well as develop more nuanced arguments about the messages those images convey.

Exercise

Examine the image above, which is an advertisement for Lego building blocks. Provide brief examples of how a viewer could accommodate, resist, or negotiate the images in the ad.

Are Some Images Not Fit to Be Shown?

Images of suffering — either human or animal — can be immensely persuasive. In the nineteenth century, for instance, the antislavery movement made extremely effective use of images in its campaign. We reproduce two antislavery images earlier in this chapter, as well as a counterimage that sought to assure viewers that slavery is a beneficent system (p. 142). But are there some images not fit to print?

Until recently, many newspapers did not print pictures of lynched African Americans, hanged and burned and maimed. The reasons for not printing such images probably differed between South and North: Southern papers may have considered the images to be discreditable to whites, while northern papers may have deemed the images too revolting. Even today, when it's commonplace for newspapers and television news to show pictures of dead victims of war, famine, or traffic accidents, one rarely sees bodies that are horribly maimed. (For traffic accidents, the body is usually covered, and we see only the smashed car.) The U.S. government has refused to release photographs showing the bodies of American soldiers killed in the war in Iraq, and it has been most reluctant to show pictures of dead Iraqi soldiers and civilians. Only after many Iraqis refused to believe that former Iraqi president Saddam Hussein's two sons had been killed did the U.S. government reluctantly release pictures showing the two men's blood-spattered faces — and some American newspapers and television programs refused to use the images.

There have been notable exceptions to this practice, such as Huynh Cong (Nick) Ut's 1972 photograph of children fleeing a napalm attack in Vietnam (below), which was widely reproduced in the United States and won the photographer a Pulitzer Prize in 1973. It's impossible to measure the influence of this particular photograph, but many people believe that it played a substantial role in increasing public pressure to end the Vietnam War. Another widely reproduced picture of horrifying violence is Eddie Adams's 1968 picture (p. 155) of a South Vietnamese chief of police firing a pistol into the head of a Viet Cong prisoner.

Huynh Cong (Nick) Ut, *The Terror of War: Children on Route 1 near Trang Bang,* 1972

Eddie Adams, *Execution of Viet Cong Prisoner, Saigon*, 1968

The issue remains: Are some images unacceptable? For instance, although capital punishment — by methods including lethal injection, hanging, shooting, and electrocution — is legal in parts of the United States, every state in the Union prohibits the publication of pictures showing a criminal being executed.[1]

The most famous recent example of an image widely thought to be unprintable showed the murder of Daniel Pearl, a reporter for the *Wall Street Journal*. Pearl was captured and murdered in June 2002 by Islamic terrorists in Pakistan. His killers videotaped Pearl reading a statement denouncing American policy and then being decapitated. The video also shows a man's arm holding Pearl's head. The video ends with the killers making demands (such as the release of Muslim prisoners being held by the United States in Guantánamo Bay, Cuba) and asserting, "if our demands are not met, this scene will be repeated again and again."

The chief arguments against newspapers reproducing material from this video were as follows:

- The video and still images from it are unbearably gruesome.
- Showing the video would traumatize the Pearl family.
- The video is enemy propaganda.

---

[1]For more on this topic, see Wendy Lesser, *Pictures at an Execution* (1993).

Alexander Gardner, *Home of a Rebel Sharpshooter*, 1863. This photo illustrates the devastation wrought by the Battle of Gettysburg through focusing on a single dead soldier splayed out in a "sharpshooter's den."

Those who favored broadcasting the video on television and printing still images from it in newspapers offered these arguments:

- The photos would show the world what sort of enemy the United States is fighting.

- Newspapers have published pictures of other terrifying sights (notably, people leaping out of windows of the World Trade Center's Twin Towers on 9/11 and the space shuttle *Challenger* exploding in 1986).

- No one was worried about protecting the families of 9/11 or *Challenger* victims from seeing those traumatic images.

But is the comparison of the Daniel Pearl video to the photos of the Twin Towers and the *Challenger* valid? You may respond that individuals in the Twin Towers pictures aren't specifically identifiable and that the *Challenger* images, although horrifying, aren't as visually revolting as the picture of a severed head held up for view.

The *Boston Phoenix*, a weekly newspaper, published some images from the Pearl video and also put a link to the video (with a warning that the footage is "extremely graphic") on its Web site. The weekly's editor justified publication on the three grounds we list above. Pearl's wife, Mariane Pearl, was quoted in various newspapers as condemning the "heartless decision to air this despicable video." And a spokeswoman for the Pearl family, when asked for comment, referred reporters to a statement issued earlier, which said that broadcasters who show the video

fall without shame into the terrorists' plan. . . . Danny believed that journalism was a tool to report the truth and foster understanding — not perpetuate propaganda and sensationalize tragedy. We had hoped that no part of this tape would ever see the light of day. . . . We urge all networks and news outlets to exercise responsibility and not aid the terrorists in spreading their message of hate and murder.[2]

Although some journalists expressed regret that Pearl's family was distressed, they insisted that journalists have a right to reproduce such material and that the images can serve the valuable purpose of shocking viewers into awareness.

POLITICS AND PICTURES

Consider, too, the controversy that erupted in 1991, during the Persian Gulf War, when the U.S. government decided that news media would not be allowed to photograph coffins returning with the bodies of military personnel killed during the war. In later years the policy was sometimes ignored, but in 2003 the George W. Bush administration decreed that there would be "no arrival ceremony for, or media coverage of, deceased military personnel return-ing [from Iraq or Afghanistan] . . . to the Dover (Delaware) base." The government enforced the policy strictly.

Members of the news media strongly protested, as did many others, chiefly on the basis of these arguments:

- The administration was trying to sanitize the war; that is, the government was depriving the public of important information — images — that showed the war's real cost.

- Grief for the deaths of military personnel is not a matter only for the families of the deceased. The sacrifices were made on behalf of the nation, and the nation should be allowed to grieve. Canada and Britain have no such ban; when military coffins are transported there, the public lines the streets to honor the fallen warriors. In fact, in Canada a portion of the highway near the Canadian base has been renamed "Highway of Heroes."

- The coffins at Dover Air Force base are not identified by name, so there is no issue about intruding on the privacy of grieving families.

The chief arguments in defense of the ban were as follows:

- Photographs violate the families' privacy.

- If the arrival of the coffins at Dover is publicized, some grieving families will think they should travel to Dover to be present when the bodies arrive. This may cause a financial hardship on the families.

- If the families give their consent, the press is *not* barred from individual graveside ceremonies at hometown burials. The ban extends only to the coffins' arrival at Dover Air Force Base.

---

[2]Quoted in the *Hartford Courant*, June 5, 2002, and reproduced on the Internet by the Freedom of Information Center, under the heading "Boston Paper Creates Controversy."

The Washington Post/Getty Images

In February 2009, President Obama changed the policy and permitted coverage of the transfer of bodily remains. In his Address to the Joint Session of Congress on February 24, 2009, he said, "For seven years we have been a nation at war. No longer will we hide its price." On February 27, Defense Secretary Robert M. Gates announced that the government ban was lifted and that families will decide whether to allow photographs and videos of the "dignified transfer process at Dover."

Exercise

In an argumentative essay of about 250 words — perhaps two or three paragraphs — give your view of the issue of permitting photos of military coffins. In an opening paragraph, you may want to both explain the issue and summarize the arguments that you reject. The second paragraph of a two-paragraph essay may present your reasons for rejecting those arguments. Additionally, you might devote a third paragraph to a more general reflection.

Topics for Critical Thinking and Writing

1. Marvin Kalb, a distinguished journalist, was quoted as saying that the public has a right to see the tape of Daniel Pearl's murder but that "common sense, decency, [and] humanity would encourage editors . . . to say 'no, it is not necessary to put this out.' There is no urgent demand on the part of the American people to see Daniel Pearl's death." What is your view?

2. In June 2006, two American soldiers were captured in Iraq. Later their bodies were found, dismembered and beheaded. Should newspapers have shown photographs of the mutilated bodies? Why, or why not? (In July 2006, insurgents in Iraq posted images on the Internet showing a soldier's severed head beside his body.)

Another issue concerning the appropriateness of showing certain images arose early in 2006. In September 2005, a Danish newspaper, accused of being afraid to show political cartoons that were hostile to Muslim terrorists, responded by publishing twelve cartoons. One cartoon showed the prophet Muhammad wearing a turban that looked like a bomb. The images at first didn't arouse much attention, but when they were reprinted in Norway in January 2006, they attracted worldwide attention and outraged Muslims, most of whom regard any depiction of Muhammad as blasphemous. Some Muslims in various Islamic nations burned Danish embassies and engaged in other acts of violence. Most non-Muslims agreed that the images were in bad taste; and apparently in deference to Islamic sensibilities (but possibly also out of fear of reprisals), very few Western newspapers reprinted the cartoons when they covered the news events. Most newspapers (including the *New York Times*) merely described the images. The editors of these papers believed that readers should be told the news, but that because the drawings were so offensive to some persons, they should be described rather than reprinted. A controversy then arose: Do readers of a newspaper deserve to *see* the evidence for themselves, or can a newspaper adequately fulfill its mission by offering only a verbal description? These questions arose again after the 2007 bombing of the French satirical newspaper *Charlie Hebdo*, and then after another mass shooting at the same newspaper in 2015 that claimed the lives of twelve editors and staff members.

Persons who argued that the images should be reproduced in the media generally made these points:

- Newspapers should yield neither to the delicate sensibilities of some readers nor to threats of violence.

- Jews for the most part do not believe that God should be depicted (the prohibition against "graven images" appears in Exodus 20.3), but they raise no objections to such Christian images as Michelangelo's painting of God awakening Adam, depicted on the ceiling of the Sistine Chapel. Further, when Andres Serrano (a Christian) in 1989 exhibited a photograph of a small plastic crucifix submerged in urine, it outraged a wider public (several U.S. senators condemned it because the artist had received federal funds), but virtually all newspapers showed the image, and many even printed its title, *Piss Christ*. The subject was judged to be newsworthy, and the fact that some viewers would regard the image as blasphemous was not considered highly relevant.

- Our society values freedom of speech, and newspapers should not be intimidated. When certain pictures are a matter of news, readers should be able to see them.

In contrast, opposing voices made these points:

- Newspapers must recognize deep-seated religious beliefs. They should indeed report the news, but there is no reason to *show* images that some people regard as blasphemous. The images can be adequately *described* in words.

- The Jewish response to Christian images of God, and even the tolerant Christians' response to Serrano's image of the crucifix immersed in urine, are irrelevant to the issue of whether a Western newspaper should represent images of the prophet Muhammad. Virtually all Muslims regard depictions of Muhammad as blasphemous, and that's what counts.

- Despite all the Western talk about freedom of the press, the press does *not* reproduce all images that become matters of news. For instance, news items about the sale of child pornography do not include images of the pornographic photos.

Exercises: Thinking about Images

1. Does the display of the Muhammad cartoons constitute an argument? If so, what is the conclusion, and what are the premises? If not, then what sort of statement, if any, does publishing these cartoons constitute?

2. Hugh Hewitt, an Evangelical Christian, offered a comparison to the cartoon of Muhammad wearing a bomblike turban. Suppose, he asked, an abortion clinic were bombed by someone claiming to be an Evangelical Christian. Would newspapers publish "a cartoon of Christ's crown of thorns transformed into sticks of TNT"? Do you think they would? If you were the editor of a newspaper, would you? Why, or why not?

3. One American newspaper, the *Boston Phoenix*, didn't publish any of the cartoons "out of fear of retaliation from the international brotherhood of radical and bloodthirsty Islamists who seek to impose their will on those who do not believe as they do. . . . We could not in good conscience place the men and women who work at the *Phoenix* and its related companies in physical jeopardy." Evaluate this position.

4. A week after the 2015 attack on *Charlie Hebdo*, and in response to media hesitancy to re-publish the offending images of Muhammad, the Index on Censorship and several other journalistic organizations called for all newspapers to publish them simultaneously and globally on January 8, 2015. "This unspeakable act of violence has challenged and assailed the entire press," said Lucie Morillon of Reporters Without Borders. "Journalism as a whole is in mourning. In the name of all those who have fallen in the defence of these fundamental values, we must continue *Charlie Hebdo*'s fight for the right to freedom of information." Evaluate this position.

Writing about a Political Cartoon

Most editorial pages print political cartoons as well as editorials. Like the writers of editorials, cartoonists seek to persuade, but they rarely use words to *argue* a point. True, they may use a few words in speech balloons or in captions, but generally the drawing does most of the work. Because their aim usually is to convince the viewer that some person's action or proposal is ridiculous, cartoonists almost always **caricature** their subjects:

- They exaggerate the subject's distinctive features to the point at which . . .
- . . . the subject becomes grotesque and ridiculous — absurd, laughable, contemptible.

We agree that it's unfair to suggest that because, say, the politician who proposes such-and-such is short, fat, and bald, his proposal is ridiculous; but that's the way cartoonists work. Further, cartoonists are concerned with producing a striking image, not with exploring an issue, so they almost always oversimplify, implying that there really is no other sane view.

In the course of saying that (1) the figures in a cartoon are ridiculous and *therefore* their ideas are contemptible, and (2) there is only one side to the issue, cartoonists often use **symbolism**. Here's a list of common symbols:

- symbolic figures (e.g., the U.S. government as Uncle Sam)
- animals (e.g., the Democratic Party as donkey and the Republican Party as elephant)
- buildings (e.g., the White House as representing the nation's president)
- things (e.g., a bag with a dollar sign on it as representing a bribe)

For anyone brought up in U.S. culture, these symbols (like the human figures they represent) are obvious, and cartoonists assume that viewers will instantly recognize the symbols and figures, will get the joke, and will see the absurdity of whatever issue the cartoonist is seeking to demolish.

In writing about the argument presented in a cartoon, normally you will discuss the ways in which the cartoon makes its point. Caricature usually implies, "This is ridiculous, as you can plainly see by the absurdity of the figures depicted" or "What *X*'s proposal adds up to, despite its apparent complexity, is nothing more than. . . ." As we have said, this sort of persuasion, chiefly by ridicule, probably is unfair: An unattractive person certainly can offer a thoughtful political proposal, and almost always the issue is more complicated than the cartoonist indicates. But cartoons work largely by ridicule and the omission of counterarguments, and we shouldn't reject the possibility that the cartoonist has indeed highlighted the absurdity of the issue.

Walt Handelsman

Your essay will likely include an *evaluation* of the cartoon. Indeed, the *thesis* underlying your analytic/argumentative essay may be that the cartoon is effective (persuasive) for such-and-such reasons but unfair for such-and-such other reasons.

In analyzing the cartoon — in determining the cartoonist's attitude — consider the following elements:

- the relative size of the figures in the image
- the quality of the lines (e.g., thin and spidery, or thick and seemingly aggressive)
- the amount of empty space in comparison with the amount of heavily inked space (a drawing with lots of inky areas conveys a more oppressive tone than a drawing that's largely open)
- the degree to which text is important, as well as its content and tone (is it witty, heavy-handed, or something else?)

Caution: If your instructor lets you choose a cartoon, be sure to select one with sufficient complexity to make the exercise worthwhile. (See also Thinking Critically: Analysis of a Political Cartoon.)

Let's look at an example. Jackson Smith wrote this essay in a composition course at Tufts University.

THINKING CRITICALLY *Analysis of a Political Cartoon*

Look at the cartoon on page 161. For each Type of Analysis section in the chart below, provide your own answer based on the cartoon. (Sample answers appear in the third column.)

TYPE OF ANALYSIS	QUESTIONS TO ASK	SAMPLE ANSWER	YOUR ANSWER
Context	*Who is the artist? Where and when was the cartoon published?*	"This cartoon by Walt Handelsman was originally published in *Newsday* on September 12, 2009. Handelsman, a Pulitzer Prize–winning cartoonist, drew this cartoon in response to recent breaches of political decorum."	
Description	*What does the cartoon look like?*	"It depicts a group of Washington, D.C., tourists being driven past what the guide calls 'The Museum of Modern American Political Discourse,' a building in the shape of a giant toilet."	
Analysis	*How does the cartoon make its point? Is it effective?*	"The toilet as a symbol of the level of political discussion dominates the cartoon, effectively driving home the point that Americans are watching our leaders sink to new lows as they debate the future of our nation. By drawing the toilet on a scale similar to that of familiar monuments in Washington, Handelsman may be pointing out that today's politicians, rather than being remembered for great achievements like those of George Washington or Abraham Lincoln, will instead be remembered for their rudeness and aggression."	

📷 **LaunchPad**   To complete this activity online, go to **macmillanhighered.com/barnetbedauohara**

JACKSON SMITH

Pledging Nothing? (Student Essay)

Gary Markstein's cartoon about the Pledge of Allegiance is one of dozens that can be retrieved by a search engine. It happens that every one of the cartoons that I retrieved mocked the courts for ruling that schools cannot require students to recite the Pledge of Allegiance in its present form, which includes the words "under God." I personally object to these words, so the cartoons certainly do not speak for me, but I'll try as impartially as possible to analyze the strength of Markstein's cartoon.

Markstein shows us, in the cartoon, four schoolchildren reciting the Pledge. Coming out of all four mouths is a speech balloon with the words, "One nation under nothing in particular." The children are facing a furled American flag, and to the right of the flag is a middle-aged female teacher, whose speech balloon is in the form of a cloud, indicating that she is *thinking* rather than saying the words, "God help us."

Certainly the image grabs us: little kids lined up reciting the Pledge of Allegiance, an American flag, a maternal-looking teacher, and, in fact, if one examines the cartoon closely, one sees an apple on the teacher's desk. It's almost a Norman Rockwell scene, except, of course, it is a cartoon, so the figures are all a bit grotesque — but, still, they are nice folks. What is *not* nice, Markstein says, is what these kids must recite, "One nation under nothing in particular." In fact, the cartoon is far from telling the truth. Children who recite the Pledge without the words "under God" will still be saying that they are pledging allegiance to something quite specific — the United States:

> I pledge allegiance to the flag of the United States of America, and to the Republic for which it stands: one nation indivisible, with Liberty and Justice for all.

That's really quite a lot, very far from Markstein's "under nothing in particular." But no one, I suppose, expects fairness in a political cartoon — and of course this cartoon *is* political, because the issue of the Pledge has become a political football, with liberals on the whole wanting the words "under God" removed and conservatives on the whole wanting the words retained.

Let's now look at some of the subtleties of the cartoon. First, although, as I have said, cartoons present grotesque caricatures, the figures here are all affectionately presented. None of these figures is menacing. The teacher, with her spectacles and her rather dumpy figure, is clearly a benevolent figure, someone who in the eyes of the cartoonist rightly is disturbed

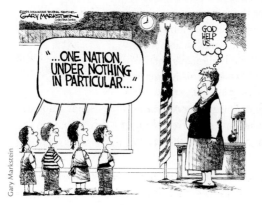

Gary Markstein

about the fate of these little kids who are not allowed to say the words "under God." (Nothing, of course, prevents the children from speaking about God when they are not in the classroom. Those who believe in God can say grace at mealtime, can go to Sunday School, can go to church regularly, can pray before they go to bed, etc.) Markstein suggests that the absence of these words makes the entire Pledge meaningless ("under nothing in particular"), and in a master stroke he has conveyed this idea of impoverishment by showing a tightly furled flag, a flag that is presented as minimally as possible. After all, the flag could have been shown more fully, perhaps hanging from a pole that extended from a wall into the classroom, or the flag could have been displayed extended against a wall. Instead we get the narrowest of flags, something that is not much more than a furled umbrella, identifiable as the American flag by its stripes and a few stars in the upper third. Markstein thus cleverly suggests that with the loss of the words "under God," the flag itself is reduced to almost nothing.

Fair? No. Effective? Yes, and that's the job of a cartoonist. Readers probably give cartoons no more than three or four seconds, and Markstein has made the most of those few seconds. The reader gets his point, and if the reader already holds this view, he or she probably says, "Hey, here's a great cartoon." I don't hold that view, but I am willing to grant that it is a pretty good cartoon, effectively making a point that I think is wrong-headed.

Visuals as Aids to Clarity: Maps, Graphs, and Pie Charts

Maps were part of the argument in the debate over drilling in the Arctic National Wildlife Refuge.

- Advocates of drilling argued that it would take place only in a tiny area. Their map showed Alaska, with an indication (in gray) of the much smaller part of Alaska that was the Refuge, and a further indication (cross-hatched) of what the advocates emphasized was a minuscule part of the Refuge.

- Opponents showed maps indicating the path of migrating caribou and the roads that would have to be constructed across the Refuge to get to the area where the drilling would take place.

Graphs, tables, and pie charts usually present quantitative data in visual form, helping writers to clarify dry statistical assertions. For instance, a line graph may illustrate how many immigrants came to the United States in each decade of the last century.

A bar graph (with bars running either horizontally or vertically) offers similar information. In the Coming to America graph, we can see at a glance that, say, the second bar on the lower left is almost double the length of the first, indicating that the number of immigrants almost doubled between 1850 and 1860.

A pie chart is a circle divided into wedges so that we can see, literally, how a whole comprises its parts. We can see, for instance, on page 166, that of an entire pie representing the regions of foreign-born U.S. immigrants, 36 percent were born in Central America and Mexico, 26 percent in Asia, 14 percent in Europe, and so on.

COMING TO AMERICA...

Both the percentage and number of foreign-born people in the United States dropped during much of the twentieth century, but after 1970, the tide was turning again.

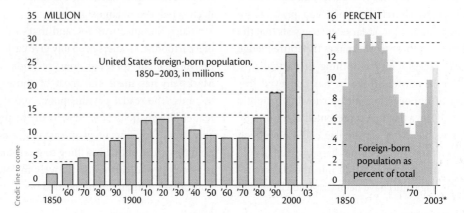

... FROM NEAR AND FAR

Central America, Mexico, and Asia contribute most to the foreign-born population.

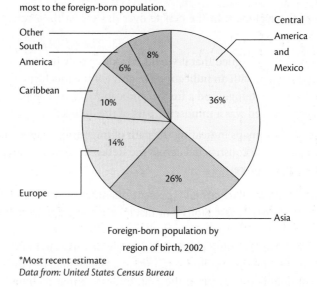

Foreign-born population by
region of birth, 2002

*Most recent estimate
Data from: United States Census Bureau

Because maps, charts, and graphs offer empirical data to support arguments, they communicate a high degree of reliability and tend to be convincing. "Numbers don't lie," it is sometimes said, and to some extent this is true. It's difficult to spin a fact like 1 + 1 = 2. However, as Charles Seife (whose essay on video games we reprint in Chapter 22) notes in his book,

Proofiness, numbers are cold facts, but the measurements that numbers actually chart aren't always so clear or free from bias and manipulation. Consider two examples of advertising claims that Seife cites — one for a L'Oréal mascara offering "twelve times more impact," and another for a new and improved Vaseline product that "delivers 70% more moisture in every drop." Such measurements *sound* good but remain relatively meaningless. (How was eyelash "impact" measured? What is a percentage value of moisture?)

Another way in which data can be relatively meaningless is by addressing only part of the question at stake. In 2013, a Mayo Clinic study found that drinking coffee regularly lowered participants' risk of the liver disease known as primary sclerosing cholangitis (PSC). But PSC is already listed as a "rare disease" by the Centers for Disease Control and Prevention, affecting fewer than 1 in 2,000 people. So even if drinking coffee lowered the risk of PSC by 25 percent, a person's chances would improve only slightly from .0005 percent chance to .0004 percent chance — hardly a change at all, and hardly a rationale for drinking more coffee. Yet, statistical information showing a 25 percent reduction in PSC sounds significant, even more so when provided under a headline proclaiming "Drinking coffee helps prevent liver disease."

Consider other uses of numbers that Seife shows in his book to constitute "proofiness" (his title and word to describe the misuse of numbers as evidence):

- In 2006, George W. Bush declared No Child Left Behind a success in his State of the Union Address: "[B]ecause we acted," he said, "students are performing better in reading and math." (True, fourth to eighth graders showed improved scores, but other grade levels declined. In addition, fourth- to eighth-grade reading and math scores had been improving at an unchanged rate both before and after the NCLB legislation.)

- In 2000, the *New York Times* reported "Researchers Link Bad Debt to Bad Health" (the "dark side of the economic boom"). The researchers claimed that debt causes more illness, but in doing so they committed the correlation-causation fallacy: Just because two phenomena are correlated does not mean they are causally related. (Example: More people wear shorts in the summer and more people eat ice cream in the summer than during other seasons, but wearing shorts does not *cause* higher ice cream consumption.)

Finally, consider the following graph showing that eating Quaker Oats decreases cholesterol levels after just four weeks of daily servings. The bar graph suggests that cholesterol levels will plummet. But a careful look at the graph reveals that the vertical axis doesn't begin at zero. In this case, a relatively small change has been (mis)represented as much bigger than it actually is.

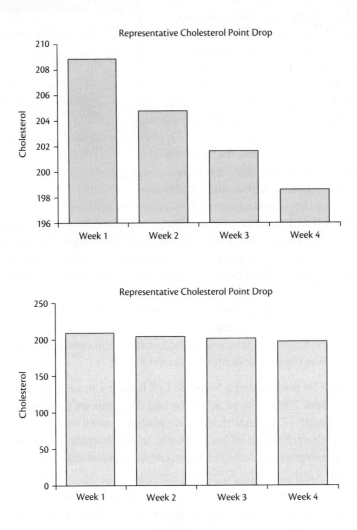

A more accurate representation of cholesterol levels after four weeks of eating Quaker Oats, using a graph that starts at zero, would look more like the second graph — showing essentially unchanged levels.

Here is another example showing unemployment rates during the Obama presidency. Note that here, too, the vertical axis doesn't start at zero, making the "rise" appear more dramatic than it actually was in reality.

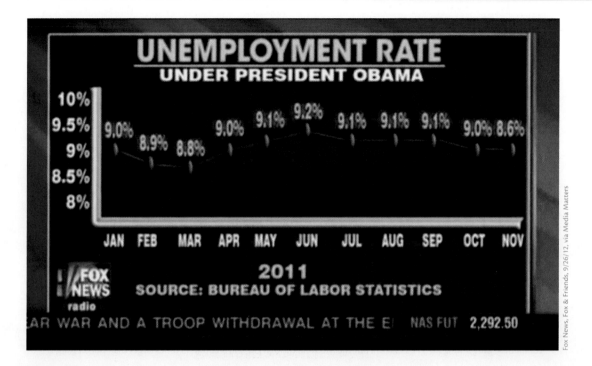

UNEMPLOYMENT RATE
UNDER PRESIDENT OBAMA

10%
9.5%   9.0%   9.0%   9.1%   9.2%   9.1%   9.1%   9.1%   9.0% 8.6%
9%   8.9%   8.8%
8.5%
8%

JAN   FEB   MAR   APR   MAY   JUN   JUL   AUG   SEP   OCT   NOV

FOX
NEWS   2011
radio   SOURCE: BUREAU OF LABOR STATISTICS

AR WAR AND A TROOP WITHDRAWAL AT THE E   NAS FUT 2,292.50

Fox News, Fox & Friends, 9/26/12, via Media Matters

Using Visuals in Your Own Paper

Every paper uses some degree of visual persuasion, merely in its appearance. Consider these elements of a paper's "look": title page; margins (ample, but not so wide that they indicate the writer's inability to produce a paper of the assigned length); double-spacing for the reader's convenience; headings and subheadings that indicate the progression of the argument; paragraphing; and so on. But you may also want to use visuals such as pictures, graphs, or pie charts. Keep a few guidelines in mind as you work with visuals, "writing" them into your own argument with as much care as you would read them in others' arguments:

- Consider your audience's needs and attitudes, and select the type of visuals — graphs, drawings, photographs — likely to be most persuasive to that audience.

- Consider the effect of color, composition, and placement within your document. Because images are most effective when they appear near the text that they supplement, do not group all images at the end of the paper.

Remember especially that images are almost never self-supporting or self-explanatory. They may be evidence for your argument (e.g., Ut's photograph of napalm victims is *very* compelling evidence of suffering), but they aren't arguments themselves.

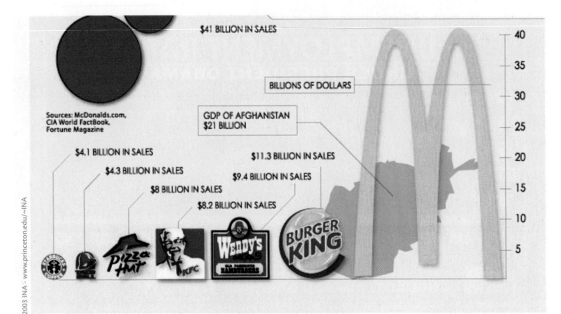

In this graph, McDonald's $41 billion in sales are shown to be about 3.5 times higher than the revenues of its next closest competitor, Burger King (at $11.3 billion), but the McDonald's logo graphic is about 13 times larger than Burger King's.

- Be sure to explain each visual that you use, integrating it into the verbal text that provides the logic and principal support behind your thesis.
- Be sure to cite the source of any visual that you paste into your argument.

Be alert to common ways in which graphs can be misleading:

- Vertical axis doesn't start at zero or skips numbers.
- Scale is given in very small units to make changes look big.
- Pie charts don't accurately divide on scale with percentages shown.
- Oversized graphics don't match the numbers they represent.

Additional Images for Analysis

In 1936, photographer Dorothea Lange (1895–1965) took a series of pictures, including the two below, of a migrant mother and her children. Widely reprinted in the nation's newspapers, these photographs helped to dramatize for the American public the poverty of displaced workers during the Great Depression.

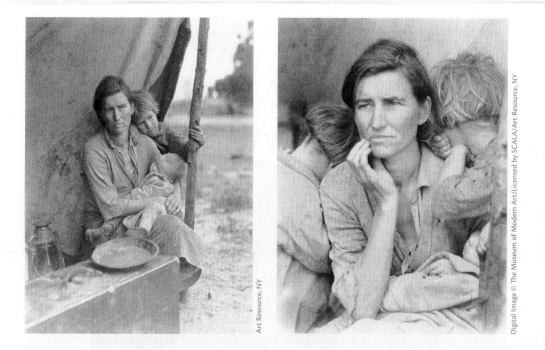

Art Resource, NY

Digital Image © The Museum of Modern Art/Licensed by SCALA/Art Resource, NY

Topics for Critical Thinking and Writing

1. Dorothea Lange drew increasingly near to her subject as she took a series of pictures. Make a list of details gained and lost by framing the mother and children more closely. The final shot in the series (above) became the most famous and most widely reprinted. Do you find it more effective than the other? Why, or why not?

2. Note the expression on the mother's face, the position of her body, and the way she interacts with her children. What sorts of relationships are implied? Why is it significant that she doesn't look at her children or at the camera? How do the photographs' effects change according to how much you can see of the children's faces?

3. These photographs constitute a sort of persuasive "speech." Of what, exactly, might the photographer be trying to persuade her viewers? Try to state the purpose of Lange's photographs by completing this sentence: "Lange would like the viewers of her photographs to. . . ." Write a brief essay (250 words) making the same case. Compare your written argument to Lange's visual one. Which form of persuasion do you find more effective? Why?

4. Whom do you think Lange had in mind as her original audience? What assumptions does she make about that audience? What sorts of evidence does she use to reach them?

During World War II, the U.S. government produced a series of recruitment posters bearing the legend "This is the enemy." These posters depicted racially stereotyped images of both German and Japanese soldiers, typically engaged in acts of savage violence or clandestine surveillance.

National Archives and Records Administration

Topics for Critical Thinking and Writing

1. It has been claimed that one role of propaganda is to dehumanize the enemy so that (1) soldiers will feel less remorse about killing opposing soldiers and (2) civilians will continue to support the war effort. What specific features of this poster contribute to this propaganda function?

2. Some would claim that such a racially provocative image of a Japanese soldier should never have been used because of the potential harm to all Asians, including patriotic Asian Americans. (Did you know that that the 442nd Regimental Combat Team, consisting solely of Japanese American volunteers, was by war's end the most decorated unit in U.S. military

history for its size and length of service?) Others believe that the ordinary rules do not apply in times of national crisis and that, as an old saying has it, "All's fair in love and war." In an essay of about 500 words, argue for one or the other of these propositions. Refer to this poster as one piece of your evidence.

Additional Topics for Critical Thinking and Writing

Gather some of the graphic materials used to promote and reflect your college or university — including a screen shot of its Web site, the college catalog, and the brochures and other materials sent to prospective students.

1. What is the dominant image that your college or university administration seems to be promoting? Are there different, even competing, images of your school at work? How accurate is the story that these materials tell about your campus? Write an essay (250 words) in which you explain to prospective students the ways in which the promotional materials capture, or fail to capture, the true spirit of your campus.

2. Compare the Web site of your institution to one or two from very different institutions — perhaps a community college, a large state university, or an elite private college. How do you account for the similarities and differences among the sites?

NORA EPHRON

Nora Ephron (1941–2012) attended Wellesley College and then worked as a reporter for the New York Post *and as a columnist and senior editor for* Esquire. *Ephron wrote screenplays and directed films, including* Sleepless in Seattle *(1993), and continued to write essays on a wide variety of topics. "The Boston Photographs" is from her collection* Scribble, Scribble: Notes on the Media *(1978).*

The Boston Photographs

"I made all kinds of pictures because I thought it would be a good rescue shot over the ladder . . . never dreamed it would be anything else. . . . I kept having to move around because of the light set. The sky was bright and they were in deep shadow. I was making pictures with a motor drive and he, the fire fighter, was reaching up and, I don't know, everything started falling. I followed the girl down taking pictures. . . . I made three or four frames. I realized what was going on and I completely turned around, because I didn't want to see her hit."

You probably saw the photographs. In most newspapers, there were three of them. The first showed some people on a fire escape — a fireman, a woman, and a child. The fireman had a nice strong jaw and looked very brave. The woman was holding the child. Smoke was pouring from the building behind them. A rescue ladder was approaching, just a few feet away, and the fireman had one arm around the woman and one arm reaching out toward the ladder. The second picture showed the fire escape slipping off the building. The child had fallen on the escape and seemed about to slide off the edge. The woman was grasping desperately at the legs of the fireman, who had managed to grab the ladder. The third picture showed the woman and child in midair, falling to the ground. Their arms and legs were outstretched, horribly distended. A potted plant was falling too. The caption said that the woman, Diana Bryant, nineteen, died in the fall. The child landed on the woman's body and lived.

The pictures were taken by Stanley Forman, thirty, of the *Boston Herald American*. He used a motor-driven Nikon F set at 1/250, f5.6-S. Because of the motor, the camera can click off three frames a second. More than four hundred newspapers in the United States alone carried the photographs: The tear sheets from overseas are still coming in. The *New York Times* ran them on the first page of its second section; a paper in south Georgia gave them nineteen columns; the *Chicago Tribune*, the *Washington Post*, and the *Washington Star* filled almost half their front pages, the *Star* under a somewhat redundant headline that read: SENSATIONAL PHOTOS OF RESCUE ATTEMPT THAT FAILED.

The photographs are indeed sensational. They are pictures of death in action, of that split second when luck runs out, and it is impossible to look at them without feeling their extraordinary impact and remembering, in an almost subconscious way, the morbid fantasy of falling, falling off a building, falling to one's death. Beyond that, the pictures are classics, old-fashioned but perfect examples

Stanley Forman

Stanley Forman

Stanley Forman

Stanley Forman

of photojournalism at its most spectacular. They're throwbacks, really, fire pictures, 1930s tabloid shots; at the same time they're technically superb and thoroughly modern — the sequence could not have been taken at all until the development of the motor-driven camera some sixteen years ago.

Most newspaper editors anticipate some 5 reader reaction to photographs like Forman's; even so, the response around the country was enormous, and almost all of it was negative. I have read hundreds of the letters that were printed in letters-to-the-editor sections, and they repeat the same points. "Invading the privacy of death." "Cheap sensationalism." "I thought I was reading the *National Enquirer.*" "Assigning the agony of a human being in terror of imminent death to the status of a side-show act." "A tawdry way to sell newspapers." The *Seattle Times* received sixty letters and calls; its managing editor even got a couple of them at home. A reader wrote the *Philadelphia Inquirer:* "*Jaws* and *Towering Inferno* are playing downtown; don't take business away from people who pay good money to advertise in your own paper." Another reader wrote the *Chicago Sun-Times:* "I shall try to hide my disappointment that Miss Bryant wasn't wearing a skirt when she fell to her death. You could have had some award-winning photographs of her underpants as her skirt billowed over her head, you voyeurs." Several newspaper editors wrote columns defending the pictures: Thomas Keevil of the *Costa Mesa* (California) *Daily Pilot* printed a ballot for readers to vote on whether they would have printed the pictures; Marshall L. Stone of Maine's *Bangor Daily News,* which refused to print the famous assassination picture of the Vietcong prisoner in Saigon, claimed that the Boston pictures showed the dangers of fire escapes and raised questions about slumlords. (The

burning building was a five-story brick apartment house on Marlborough Street in the Back Bay section of Boston.)

For the last five years, the *Washington Post* has employed various journalists as ombudsmen, whose job is to monitor the paper on behalf of the public. The *Post*'s current ombudsman is Charles Seib, former managing editor of the *Washington Star;* the day the Boston photographs appeared, the paper received over seventy calls in protest. As Seib later wrote in a column about the pictures, it was "the largest reaction to a published item that I have experienced in eight months as the *Post*'s ombudsman. . . .

"In the *Post*'s newsroom, on the other hand, I found no doubts, no second thoughts . . . the question was not whether they should be printed but how they should be displayed. When I talked to editors . . . they used words like 'interesting' and 'riveting' and 'gripping' to describe them. The pictures told of something about life in the ghetto, they said (although the neighborhood where the tragedy occurred is not a ghetto, I am told). They dramatized the need to check on the safety of fire escapes. They dramatically conveyed something that had happened, and that is the business we're in. They were news. . . .

"Was publication of that [third] picture a bow to the same taste for the morbidly sensational that makes gold mines of disaster movies? Most papers will not print the picture of a dead body except in the most unusual circumstances. Does the fact that the final picture was taken a millisecond before the young woman died make a difference? Most papers will not print a picture of a bare female breast. Is that a more inappropriate subject for display than the picture of a human being's last agonized instant of life?" Seib offered no answers to the questions he raised, but he went on to say that although as an editor he would probably have run the pictures, as a reader he was revolted by them.

In conclusion, Seib wrote: "Any editor who decided to print those pictures without giving at least a moment's thought to what purpose they served and what their effect was likely to be on the reader should ask another question: Have I become so preoccupied with manufacturing a product according to professional traditions and standards that I have forgotten about the consumer, the reader?"

It should be clear that the phone calls and letters and Seib's own reaction were occasioned by one factor alone: the death of the woman. Obviously, had she survived the fall, no one would have protested; the pictures would have had a completely different impact. Equally obviously, had the child died as well — or instead — Seib would undoubtedly have received ten times the phone calls he did. In each case, the pictures would have been exactly the same — only the captions, and thus the responses, would have been different.

But the questions Seib raises are worth discussing — though not exactly for the reasons he mentions. For it may be that the real lesson of the Boston photographs is not the danger that editors will be forgetful of reader reaction, but that they will continue to censor pictures of death precisely because of that reaction. The protests Seib fielded were really a variation on an old theme — and we saw plenty of it during the Nixon-Agnew years — the "Why doesn't the press print the good news?" argument. In this case, of course, the objections were all dressed up and cleverly disguised as righteous indignation about the privacy of death. This is a form of puritanism that is often justifiable; just as often it is merely puritanical.

Seib takes it for granted that the widespread though fairly recent newspaper policy against printing pictures of dead bodies is a sound one; I don't know that it makes any sense at all. I recognize that printing pictures of corpses raises all sorts of problems about taste and titillation and sensationalism; the fact is, however, that people die. Death happens to be one of life's main events. And it is irresponsible — and more than that, inaccurate — for newspapers to fail to show it, or to show it only when an astonishing set of photos comes in over the Associated Press wire. Most papers covering fatal automobile accidents will print pictures of mangled cars. But the significance of fatal automobile accidents is not that a great deal of steel is twisted but that people die. Why not show it? That's what accidents are about. Throughout the Vietnam War, editors were reluctant to print atrocity pictures. Why *not* print them? That's what that was about. Murder victims are almost never photographed; they are granted their privacy. But their relatives are relentlessly pictured on their way in and out of hospitals and morgues and funerals.

I'm not advocating that newspapers print these things in order to teach their readers a lesson. The *Post* editors justified their printing of the Boston pictures with several arguments in that direction; every one of them is irrelevant. The pictures don't show anything about slum life; the incident could have happened anywhere, and it did. It is extremely unlikely that anyone who saw them rushed out and had his fire escape strengthened. And the pictures were not news — at least they were not national news. It is not news in Washington, or New York, or Los Angeles that a woman was killed in a Boston fire. The only newsworthy thing about the pictures is that they were taken. They deserve to be printed because they are great pictures, breathtaking pictures of something that happened. That they disturb readers is exactly as it should be: that's why photojournalism is often more powerful than written journalism.

Topics for Critical Thinking and Writing

1. In paragraph 5, Nora Ephron refers to "the famous assassination picture of the Vietcong prisoner in Saigon" (see p. 155). The photo shows the face of a prisoner who is about to be shot in the head at close range. Jot down the reasons why you would or would not approve of printing this photo in a newspaper. Think, too, about this: If the photo on page 154 weren't about a war — if it didn't include the soldiers and the burning village in the rear but, instead, showed children fleeing from an abusive parent or an abusive sibling — would you approve of printing it in a newspaper?

2. In paragraph 9, Ephron quotes a newspaperman as saying that before printing Forman's pictures of the woman and the child falling from the fire escape, editors should have asked themselves "what purpose they served and what their effect was likely to be on the reader." If you were an editor, what would your answers be? By the way, the pictures were *not* taken in a poor neighborhood, and they did *not* expose slum conditions.

3. In 50 words or so, write a precise description of what you see in the third of the Boston photographs. Do you think readers of your description would be "revolted" by the picture (para. 8), as were many viewers, the *Washington Post*'s ombudsman among them? Why, or why not?

4. Ephron thinks it would be good for newspapers to publish more photographs of death and dying (paras. 11–13). In an essay of approximately 500 words, state her reasons and your evaluation of them.

PART TWO

Critical Writing

5

Writing an Analysis of an Argument

This is what we can all do to nourish and strengthen one another: listen to one another very hard, ask questions, too, send one another away to work again, and laugh in all the right places.

— NANCY MAIRS

I don't wait for moods. You accomplish nothing if you do that. Your mind must know it has got to get down to work.

— PEARL S. BUCK

Fear not those who argue but those who dodge.

— MARIE VON EBNER-ESCHENBACH

Analyzing an Argument

EXAMINING THE AUTHOR'S THESIS

Most of your writing in other courses will require you to write an analysis of someone else's writing. In a course in political science you may have to analyze, say, an essay first published in *Foreign Affairs,* perhaps reprinted in your textbook, that argues against raising tariff barriers to foreign trade. Or a course in sociology may require you to analyze a report on the correlation between fatal accidents and drunk drivers under the age of twenty-one. Much of your writing, in short, will set forth reasoned responses to your reading as preparation for making an argument of your own.

Obviously, you must understand an essay before you can analyze it thoughtfully. You must read it several times — not just skim it — and (the hard part) you must think critically about it. Again, you'll find that your thinking is stimulated if you take notes and if you ask yourself questions about the material. Are there any Web sites or organizations dedicated to the material you are analyzing? If there are, visit some to see what others are saying about the material you are reviewing. Notes will help you to keep track of the writer's thoughts and also of your own responses to the writer's thesis. The writer probably *does* have a thesis, a claim, a point, and if so, you must try to locate it. Perhaps the thesis is explicitly stated in the title or in a sentence or two near the beginning of the essay or in a concluding paragraph, but perhaps you will have to infer it from the essay as a whole.

Notice that we said the writer *probably* has a thesis. Much of what you read will indeed be primarily an argument; the writer explicitly or implicitly is trying to support some thesis and to convince readers to agree with it. But some of what you read will be relatively neutral, with the argument just faintly discernible — or even with no argument at all. A work may, for instance, chiefly be a report: Here are the data, or here is what *X*, *Y*, and *Z* said; make of it what you will. A report might simply state how various ethnic groups voted in an election. In a report of this sort, of course, the writer hopes to persuade readers that the facts are correct, but no thesis is advanced — at least not explicitly or perhaps even consciously; the writer is not evidently arguing a point and trying to change readers' minds. Such a document differs greatly from an essay by a political analyst who presents similar findings to persuade a candidate to sacrifice the votes of one particular ethnic bloc and thereby get more votes from other blocs.

EXAMINING THE AUTHOR'S PURPOSE

While reading an argument, try to form a clear idea of the author's **purpose**. Judging from the essay or the book, was the purpose to persuade, or was it to report? An analysis of a pure report (a work apparently without a thesis or argumentative angle) on ethnic voting will deal chiefly with the accuracy of the report. It will, for example, consider whether the sample poll was representative.

Much material that poses as a report really has a thesis built into it, consciously or unconsciously. The best evidence that the prose you are reading is argumentative is the presence of two kinds of key terms: transitions that imply the drawing of a conclusion (such as *therefore, because, for the reason that,* and *consequently*) and verbs that imply proof (such as *confirms, verifies, accounts for, implies, proves, disproves, is [in]consistent with, refutes,* and *it follows that*). Keep your eye out for such terms, and scrutinize their precise role whenever they appear. If the essay does not advance a thesis, think of one that it might support or some conventional belief that it might undermine. (See also Thinking Critically: Drawing Conclusions and Implying Proof on page 190.)

EXAMINING THE AUTHOR'S METHODS

If the essay advances a thesis, you will want to analyze the strategies or methods of argument that allegedly support the thesis.

- Does the writer quote authorities? Are these authorities competent in this field? Does the writer consider equally competent authorities who take a different view?

- Does the writer use statistics? If so, who compiled them, and are they appropriate to the point being argued? Can they be interpreted differently?

- Does the writer build the argument by using examples or analogies? Are they satisfactory?

- Are the writer's assumptions acceptable?

- Does the writer consider all relevant factors? Has he or she omitted some points that you think should be discussed? For instance, should the author recognize certain opposing positions and perhaps concede something to them?

- Does the writer seek to persuade by means of ridicule? If so, is the ridicule fair? Is it supported also by rational argument?

- Is the argument aimed at a particular audience?

In writing your analysis, you will want to tell readers something about the author's purpose and something about the author's **methods**. It is usually a good idea at the start of your analysis — if not in the first paragraph, then in the second or third — to let the reader know the purpose (and thesis, if there is one) of the work you are analyzing and then to summarize the work briefly.

Next, you will probably find it useful (readers will certainly find it helpful) to write out *your* thesis (your evaluation or judgment). You might say, for instance, that the essay is impressive but not conclusive, or is undermined by convincing contrary evidence, or relies too much on unsupported generalizations, or is wholly admirable. Remember, because your paper is itself an argument, it needs its own thesis.

And then, of course, comes the job of setting forth your analysis and the support for your thesis. There is no one way of going about this work. If, say, the author whose work you're analyzing gives four arguments (e.g., an appeal to common sense, the testimony of authorities, the evidence of comparisons, and an appeal to self-interest), you might want to do one of the following:

- Take up these four arguments in sequence.

- Discuss the simplest of the four, and then go on to the more difficult ones.

- Discuss the author's two arguments that you think are sound, and then turn to the two that you think are not sound (or perhaps the reverse).

- Apply one of these approaches, and then clinch your case by constructing a fifth argument that is absent from the work under scrutiny but is, in your view, highly important.

In short, the organization of your analysis may or may not follow the organization of the work you are analyzing.

EXAMINING THE AUTHOR'S PERSONA

You will probably also want to analyze something a bit more elusive than the author's explicit arguments: the author's self-presentation. Does the author seek to persuade readers partly by presenting himself or herself as conscientious, friendly, self-effacing, authoritative, tentative, or in some other light? Most writers do two things:

- They present evidence.

- They present themselves (or, more precisely, they present the image of themselves that they wish us to behold).

In some persuasive writing this **persona** or **voice** or presentation of the self may be no less important than the presentation of evidence. In other cases, the persona may not much matter, but our point is that you should spend a little time looking at the author's self-presentation to consider if it's significant.

In establishing a persona, writers adopt various rhetorical strategies, ranging from the use of characteristic words to the use of a particular form of organization. For instance:

- The writer who speaks of an opponent's "gimmicks" instead of "strategy" probably is trying to downgrade the opponent and also to convey the self-image of a streetwise person.

- On a larger scale, consider the way in which evidence is presented and the kind of evidence that's offered. One writer may first bombard the reader with facts and then spend relatively little time drawing conclusions. Another may rely chiefly on generalizations, waiting until the end of the essay to bring the thesis home with a few details. Another may begin with a few facts and spend most of the space reflecting on these. One writer may seem professorial or pedantic, offering examples of an academic sort; another, whose examples are drawn from ordinary life, may seem like a regular guy.

All such devices deserve comment in your analysis.

The writer's persona, then, may color the thesis and help it develop in a distinctive way. If we accept the thesis, it is partly because the writer has won our goodwill by persuading us of his or her good character (*ethos,* in Aristotle's terms). Later we talk more about the appeal to the speaker's character — the so-called *ethical appeal,* but here we may say that good writers present themselves not as wise-guys, bullies, or pompous asses but as decent people whom the reader would like to invite to dinner.

The author of an essay may, for example, seem fair-minded and open-minded, treating the opposition with great courtesy and expressing interest in hearing other views. Such a tactic is itself a persuasive device. Another author may appear to rely on hard evidence such as statistics. This reliance on seemingly objective truths is itself a way of seeking to persuade — a rational way, to be sure, but a mode of persuasion nonetheless.

Especially in analyzing a work in which the author's persona and ideas are blended, you will want to spend some time commenting on the persona. Whether you discuss it near the beginning of your analysis or near the end will depend on how you want to construct your essay, and this decision will partly depend on the work you are analyzing. For example, if the author's persona is kept in the background and is thus relatively invisible, you may want to make that point fairly early to get it out of the way and then concentrate on more interesting matters. If, however, the persona is interesting — and perhaps seductive, whether because it seems so scrupulously objective or so engagingly subjective — you may want to hint at this quality early in your essay and then develop the point while you consider the arguments.

In short, the author's self-presentation usually matters. Recognize its effect, whether positive or negative.

A key element in understanding an argument lies in thinking about the intended audience — how the author perceives the audience and what strategies the author uses to connect to it. We have already said something about the creation of the author's persona. An author with a loyal following is, almost by definition, someone who in earlier writings has presented an engaging persona, a persona with a trustworthy *ethos*. A trusted author can sometimes cut corners and can perhaps adopt a colloquial tone that would be unacceptable in the writing of an unknown author.

Authors who want to win the assent of their audiences need to think about how they present information and how they present *themselves*. Consider how you prefer people to talk to you. What sorts of language do you find engaging? Much of course depends on the circumstances, notably the topic, the audience, and the place. A joke may be useful in an argument about whether the government should regulate junk food, but almost surely a joke will be inappropriate — will backfire, will alienate the audience — in an argument about abortion. The *way* an author addresses the reader (through an invented persona) can have a significant impact on the reader's perception of the author, which is to say perception of the author's *views*, the author's *argument*. A slip in tone or an error of fact, however small, may be enough for the audience to dismiss the author's argument. Understanding audience means thinking about all of the possible audiences who may come into contact with your writing or your message, and thinking about the consequences of what you write and where it is published.

Lebron James, considering his audience while he was with the Miami Heat.

You may recall a tweet by Lebron James, who formerly played basketball for the Cleveland Cavaliers but left to play for the Miami Heat. After James left the Cavaliers (and his home state of Ohio), the Los Angeles Lakers beat the Cavaliers by fifty-five points, and James tweeted: "Crazy. Karma is a b****. Gets you every time. It's not good to wish bad on anybody. God sees everything!" Cleveland fans not surprisingly perceived his tweet as a slap in the face. The broader audience, too, outside of Cleveland, perceived it as inappropriate. Though he has since returned to Cleveland and been largely forgiven by fans, Lebron James clearly did not think about his audience(s). To put it in rhetorical terms, Lebron James vastly diminished his *ethos*. Doubtless he wishes he could retract the tweet, but as the ancient Roman poet Horace said, *"Nescit vox missa reverti"* ("The word once spoken can never be recalled"), or, in plain proverbial English, "Think twice before you speak."

Consider Facebook status updates. Have you ever posted a status update and wished you could take it back only to find out it was too late? People you did not want to see it saw it before you could remove it. Have you ever tweeted or even texted something you wished you hadn't? When reading and writing more formal essays, it is equally important to think about who wrote what you are reading, and who will read what you are writing.

SUMMARY

In the last few pages we have tried to persuade you that, in writing an analysis of a reading, you must do the following:

- Read and reread thoughtfully. Composing and keeping notes will help you to think about what you are reading.

- Be aware of the purpose of the material to which you are responding.

We have also tried to point out these facts:

- Most of the nonliterary material that you will read is designed to argue, to report, or to do both.

- Most of this material also presents the writer's personality, or voice, and this voice usually merits attention in an analysis. An essay on, say, nuclear war, in a journal devoted to political science, may include a voice that moves from an objective tone to a mildly ironic tone to a hortatory tone, and this voice is worth commenting on.

Possibly all this explanation is obvious. There is yet another point, equally obvious but often neglected by students who begin by writing an analysis and end up by writing only a summary, a shortened version of the work they have read: Although your essay is an analysis of someone else's writing, and you may have to include a summary of the work you are writing about, your essay is *your* essay, your analysis, not a mere summary. The thesis, the organization, and the tone are yours.

- Your thesis, for example, may be that although the author is convinced she has presented a strong case, her case is far from proved because . . .

- Your organization may be deeply indebted to the work you are analyzing, but it need not be. The author may have begun with specific examples and then gone on to make generalizations and to draw conclusions, but you may begin with the conclusions.

- Your tone, similarly, may resemble your subject's (let's say the voice is courteous academic), but it will nevertheless have its own ring, its own tone of, say, urgency, caution, or coolness.

Most of the essays that we have included thus far are more or less in an academic style, and indeed several are by students and by professors. But argumentative writing is not limited to academicians — if it were, your college would not be requiring you to take a course in the subject. The following essay, in a breezy style, comes from a columnist who writes for the *New York Times*.

A CHECKLIST FOR ANALYZING A TEXT

Have I considered all of the following matters?

☐ Who is the author? What stake might he or she have in writing this piece?

☐ Is the piece aimed at a particular audience? A neutral audience? Persons who are already sympathetic to the author's point of view? A hostile audience? What evidence enables me to identify the target audience?

☐ What is the author's thesis (argument, main point, claim)?

☐ What assumptions does the author make? Do I share them? If not, why not?

☐ Does the author ever confuse facts with beliefs or opinions?

☐ What appeals does the author make? To reason (*logos*), for instance, with statistics, the testimony of authorities, and personal experience? To the emotions (*pathos*), for instance, by an appeal to "our better nature" or to widely shared values? To our sense that the speaker is trustworthy (*ethos*)?

☐ How convincing is the evidence? Why do I think so?

☐ Are significant objections and counterevidence adequately discussed?

(continues on next page)

An Argument, Its Elements, and a Student's Analysis of the Argument

NICHOLAS D. KRISTOF

Nicholas D. Kristof (b. 1959), a two-time Pulitzer Prize winner, grew up on a farm in Oregon. After graduating from Harvard, he was awarded a Rhodes scholarship to Oxford, where he studied law. In 1984 he joined the New York Times *as a correspondent, and since 2001 he has written as a columnist. The editorial that follows first appeared in the* New York Times *in 2005.*

For Environmental Balance, Pick Up a Rifle

Here's a quick quiz: Which large American mammal kills the most humans each year?

It's not the bear, which kills about two people a year in North America. Nor is it the wolf, which in modern times hasn't killed anyone in this country. It's not the cougar, which kills one person every year or two.

Rather, it's the deer. Unchecked by predators, deer populations are exploding in a way that is profoundly unnatural and that is destroying the ecosystem in many parts of the country. In a wilderness, there might be ten deer per square mile; in parts of New Jersey, there are up to 200 per square mile.

One result is ticks and Lyme disease, but deer also kill people more directly. A study for the insurance industry estimated that deer kill about 150 people a year in car crashes nationwide and cause $1 billion in damage. Granted, deer aren't stalking us, and they come out worse in these collisions — but it's still true that in a typical year, an American is less likely to be killed by Osama bin Laden than by Bambi.

If the symbol of the environment's being 5 out of whack in the 1960s was the Cuyahoga River in Cleveland catching fire, one symbol today is deer congregating around what they think of as salad bars and what we think of as suburbs.

So what do we do? Let's bring back hunting.

Now, you've probably just spilled your coffee. These days, among the university-educated crowd in the cities, hunting is viewed as barbaric.

The upshot is that towns in New York and New Jersey are talking about using birth control to keep deer populations down. (Liberals presumably support free condoms, while conservatives back abstinence education.) Deer contraception hasn't been very successful, though.

Meanwhile, the same population bomb has spread to bears. A bear hunt has been scheduled for this week in New Jersey — prompting outrage from some animal rights groups (there's also talk of bear contraception: make love, not cubs).

As for deer, partly because hunting is per- 10 ceived as brutal and vaguely psychopathic, towns are taking out contracts on deer through discreet private companies. Greenwich, Connecticut, budgeted $47,000 this year to pay a company to shoot eighty deer from raised platforms over four nights — as well as $8,000 for deer birth control.

Look, this is ridiculous.

We have an environmental imbalance caused in part by the decline of hunting. Humans first wiped out certain predators — like wolves and cougars — but then expanded their own role as predators to sustain a rough ecological balance. These days, though, hunters are on the decline.

According to "Families Afield: An Initiative for the Future of Hunting," a report by an alliance of shooting organizations, for every hundred hunters who die or stop hunting, only sixty-nine hunters take their place.

I was raised on *Bambi* — but also, as an Oregon farm boy, on venison and elk meat.

But deer are not pets, and dead deer are as natural as live deer. To wring one's hands over them, perhaps after polishing off a hamburger, is soggy sentimentality.

What's the alternative to hunting? Is it 15 preferable that deer die of disease and hunger? Or, as the editor of *Adirondack Explorer* magazine suggested, do we introduce wolves into the burbs?

To their credit, many environmentalists agree that hunting can be green. The New Jersey Audubon Society this year advocated deer hunting as an ecological necessity.

There's another reason to encourage hunting: it connects people with the outdoors and creates a broader constituency for wilderness preservation. At a time when America's wilderness is being gobbled away for logging, mining, or oil drilling, that's a huge boon.

Granted, hunting isn't advisable in suburban backyards, and I don't expect many soccer moms to install gun racks in their minivans. But it's an abdication of environmental responsibility to eliminate other predators and then refuse to assume the job ourselves. In that case, the collisions with humans will simply get worse.

In October, for example, Wayne Goldsberry was sitting in a home in northwestern Arkansas when he heard glass breaking in the next room. It was a home invasion — by a buck.

Mr. Goldsberry, who is six feet one inch 20 and weighs two hundred pounds, wrestled with the intruder for forty minutes. Blood spattered the walls before he managed to break the buck's neck.

So it's time to reestablish a balance in the natural world — by accepting the idea that hunting is as natural as bird-watching.

Topics for Critical Thinking and Writing

1. What is Nicholas Kristof's chief thesis? (State it in one sentence.)

2. Does Kristof make any assumptions — tacit or explicit — with which you disagree? With which you agree? Write them down.

3. Is the slightly humorous tone of Kristof's essay inappropriate for a discussion of deliberately killing wild animals? Why, or why not?

4. If you are familiar with *Bambi*, does the story make any *argument* against killing deer, or does the story appeal only to our emotions?

5. Do you agree that "hunting is as natural as bird-watching" (para. 21)? In any case, do you think that an appeal to what is "natural" is a good argument for expanding the use of hunting?

6. To whom is Kristof talking? How do you know?

THINKING CRITICALLY *Drawing Conclusions and Implying Proof*

Look at Nicholas D. Kristof's essay on page 188. Provide two examples of sentences from Kristof's essay that use each type of conclusion or proof.

INDICATOR OF CONCLUSION OR PROOF	EXAMPLES	TWO EXAMPLES FROM KRISTOF'S ESSAY
Transitions that imply the drawing of a conclusion	*therefore, because, for the reason that, consequently*	
Verbs that imply proof	*confirms, verifies, accounts for, implies, proves, disproves, is (in)consistent with, refutes, it follows that*	

LaunchPad To complete this activity online, go to **macmillanhighered.com/barnetbedauohara**

THE ESSAY ANALYZED

OK, time's up. Let's examine Kristof's essay with an eye to identifying those elements we mentioned earlier in this chapter (pp. 181–88) that deserve notice when examining *any* argument: the author's *thesis, purpose, methods, persona,* and *audience*. And while we're at it, let's also notice some other features of Kristof's essay that will help us appreciate its effects and evaluate it. We will thus be in a good position to write an evaluation or an argument that confirms, extends, or even rebuts Kristof's argument.

But first, a caution: Kristof's essay appeared in a newspaper where paragraphs are customarily very short, partly to allow for easy reading and partly because the columns are narrow and even short paragraphs may extend for an inch or two. If his essay were to appear in a book, doubtless the author would run many of the paragraphs together, making longer units. In analyzing a work, think about where it originally appeared. A blog, a print journal, an online magazine? Does the format in some measure influence the piece?

Title   By combining "Environmental Balance" with "Rifle" — terms that don't seem to go together — Kristof starts off with a bang. He gives a hint of his *topic* (something about the environment) and of his thesis (some sort of way of introducing ecological balance). He also conveys something of his persona by introducing a rifle into the environment. He is, the title suggests, a no-nonsense, hard-hitting guy.

Opening Paragraphs   Kristof immediately grabs hold of us ("Here's a quick quiz") and asks a simple question, but one that we probably have not thought much about: "Which large American mammal kills the most humans each year?" In paragraph 2 he tells us it is *not* the bear — the answer most readers probably come up with — nor is it the cougar. Not until paragraph 3 does Kristof give us the answer, the deer. But remember, Kristof is writing in a newspaper, where paragraphs customarily are very short. It takes us only a few seconds to get to the third paragraph and the answer.

Thesis   What is the basic thesis Kristof is arguing? Somewhat unusually, Kristof does *not* announce it in its full form until paragraph 6 ("Let's bring back hunting"), but, again, his paragraphs are very short, and if the essay were published in a book, Kristof's first two paragraphs probably would be combined, as would the third and fourth.

Purpose   Kristof's purpose is clear: He wants to *persuade* readers to adopt his view. This amounts to trying to persuade us that his thesis (stated above) is *true*. Kristof, however, does not show that his essay is argumentative or persuasive by using many of the key terms that normally mark argumentative prose. He doesn't call anything his *conclusion*, none of his statements is labeled *my premises*, and he doesn't connect clauses or sentences with *therefore* or *because*. Almost the only traces of the language of argument are "Granted" (para. 18) and "So" (i.e., *therefore*) in his final paragraph.

Despite the lack of argumentative language, the argumentative nature of his essay is clear. He has a thesis — one that will strike many readers as highly unusual — and he wants readers to accept it, so he must go on to *support* it; accordingly, after his introductory paragraphs, in which he calls attention to a problem and offers a solution (his thesis), he must offer evidence. And that is what much of the rest of the essay seeks to do.

Methods   Although Kristof will have to offer evidence, he begins by recognizing the folks on the other side, "the university-educated crowd in the cities, [for whom] hunting is viewed as barbaric" (para. 7). He goes on to spoof this "crowd" when, speaking of methods of keeping the deer population down, he says in paragraph 8, "Liberals presumably support free condoms, while conservatives back abstinence education." Ordinarily, it is a bad idea to make fun of persons who hold views other than your own — after all, they just may be on to something, they just might know something you don't know, and, in any case, impartial readers rarely want to align themselves with someone who mocks others. In the essay we are looking at, however, Kristof gets away with this smart-guy tone because he not only has loyal readers but also has written the entire essay in a highly informal or playful manner. Think again about paragraph 1, which begins "Here's a quick quiz." The informality is not only in the contraction (*Here's* versus *Here is*), but in the very idea of beginning by grabbing the readers and thrusting a quiz at them. The playfulness is evident throughout: For instance, immediately after Kristof announces his thesis, "Let's bring back hunting," he begins a new paragraph (7) with "Now, you've probably just spilled your coffee."

Kristof's methods of presenting evidence include providing **statistics** (paras. 3, 4, 10, and 13), giving **examples** (paras. 10, 19–20), and citing **authorities** (paras. 13 and 16).

Persona   Kristof presents himself as a confident, no-nonsense fellow, a persona that not many writers can get away with, but that probably is acceptable in a journalist who regularly writes a newspaper column. His readers know what to expect, and they read him with pleasure. But it would be inadvisable for an unknown writer to adopt this persona, unless perhaps he or she were writing for an audience that could be counted on to be friendly (in this instance, an audience of hunters). If this essay appeared in a hunting magazine, doubtless it would please and entertain its audience. It would not convert anybody, but conversion would not be its point if it appeared in a magazine read by hunters. In the *New York Times*, where the essay originally appeared, Kristof could count on a moderately sympathetic audience because he has a large number of faithful readers, but one can guess that many of these readers — chiefly city dwellers — read him for entertainment rather than for information about how they should actually behave.

By the way, when we speak of "faithful readers" we are in effect saying that the author has established good *ethos*, has convinced those readers that he or she is *worth* reading.

Closing Paragraphs   The first two of the last three paragraphs report an episode (the home invasion by a buck) that Kristof presumably thinks is pretty conclusive evidence. The final paragraph begins with "So," strongly implying a logical conclusion to the essay.

Let's now turn to a student's analysis of Kristof's essay and then to our own analysis of the student's analysis. (We should say that the analysis of Kristof's essay that you have just read is partly indebted to the student's essay that you are about to read.)

Swinton 1

Betsy Swinton
Professor Knowles
English 101B
March 12, 2016

Tracking Kristof

Nicholas D. Kristof's "For Environmental Balance, Pick Up a Rifle" is an engaging piece of writing, but whether it is convincing is something I am not sure about. And I am not sure about it for two reasons: (1) I don't know much about the deer problem, and that's my fault; (2) I don't know much about the deer problem, and that's Kristof's fault. The first point needs no explanation, but let me explain the second.

Kristof is making an argument, offering a thesis: Deer are causing destruction, and the best way to reduce the destruction is to hunt deer. For all that I know, he may be correct both in his comment about what deer are doing and also in his comment about what must be done about deer. My ignorance of the situation is regrettable, but I don't think that I am the only reader from Chicago who doesn't know much about the deer problems in New Jersey, Connecticut, and Arkansas, the states that Kristof specifically mentions in connection with the deer problem. He announces his thesis early enough, in his sixth paragraph, and he is entertaining throughout his essay, but does he make a convincing case? To ask "Does he make a convincing case?" is to ask "Does he offer adequate evidence?" and "Does he show that his solution is better than other possible solutions?"

To take the first question: In a short essay Kristof can hardly give overwhelming evidence, but he does convince me that there is a problem. The most convincing evidence he gives appears in paragraph 16, where he says that the New Jersey Audubon Society "advocated deer hunting as an ecological necessity." I don't really know anything about the New Jersey Audubon Society, but I suppose that they are people with a deep interest in nature and in conservation, and if even such a group advocates deer hunting, there must be something to this solution.

I am even willing to accept his argument that, in this nation of meat-eaters, "to wring one's hands over them [dead deer], perhaps after polishing off a hamburger, is soggy sentimentality" (para. 14). According to Kristof, the present alternative to hunting deer is that we leave the deer to "die of disease and hunger" (para. 15). But what I am not convinced of is that there is no way to reduce the deer population other than by hunting. I don't think Kristof adequately explains why some sort of birth control is inadequate. In his eighth paragraph he makes a joke about controlling the birth of deer ("Liberals presumably support free condoms, while conservatives back abstinence education"), and the joke is funny, but it isn't an argument, it's just a joke. Why can't food containing some sort of sterilizing medicine be put out for the starving deer, food that will nourish them and yet make them unreproductive? In short, I don't think he has fairly informed his readers of alternatives to his own positions, and because he fails to look at counterproposals, he weakens his own proposal.

Although Kristof occasionally uses a word or phrase that suggests argument, such as "Granted" (para. 18), "So" (final paragraph), and "There's another reason" (para. 17), he relies chiefly on forceful writing rather than on reasoning. And the second of his two reasons for hunting seems utterly unconvincing to me. His first, as we have seen, is that the deer population (and apparently the bear population) is out of control. His second (para. 17) is that hunting "connects people with the outdoors and creates a broader constituency for wilderness preservation." I am not a hunter and I have never been one. Perhaps that's my misfortune, but I don't think I am missing anything. And when I hear Kristof say, in his final sentence—the climactic place in his essay—that "hunting is as natural as bird-watching," I rub my eyes in disbelief. If he had me at least half-convinced by his statistics and his citation of the Audubon Society, he now loses me when he argues that hunting is "natural." One might as well say that war is natural, rape is natural, bribery is natural—all these terrible things occur, but we ought to deplore them and we ought to make every effort to see that they disappear.

In short, I think that Kristof has written an engaging essay, and he may well have an important idea, but I think that in his glib final paragraph, where he tells us that "hunting is as natural as bird-watching," he utterly loses the reader's confidence.

AN ANALYSIS OF THE STUDENT'S ANALYSIS

Swinton's essay seems to us to be excellent, doubtless the product of a good deal of thoughtful revision. She does not cover every possible aspect of Kristof's essay — she concentrates on his reasoning and says very little about his style — but we think that given the limits of space (about 500 words), she does a good job. What makes this student's essay effective?

- The essay has a title ("Tracking Kristof") that is of at least a little interest; it picks up Kristof's point about hunting, and it gives a hint of what is to come.

- The author promptly identifies her subject (she names the writer and the title of his essay) early.

- Early in the essay she gives us a hint of where she will be going (in her first paragraph she tells us that Kristof's essay is "engaging . . . *but . . .*").

A CHECKLIST FOR WRITING AN ANALYSIS OF AN ARGUMENT

Have I asked myself the following questions?

- ☐ Early in my essay have I accurately stated the writer's thesis (claim) and summarized his or her supporting reasons? Have I explained to my reader any disagreement about definitions of important terms?

- ☐ Have I, again fairly early in my essay, indicated where I will be taking my reader (i.e., have I indicated my general response to the essay I am analyzing)?

- ☐ Have I called attention to the strengths, if any, and the weaknesses, if any, of the essay?

- ☐ Have I commented not only on the *logos* (logic, reasoning) but also on the *ethos* (character of the writer, as presented in the essay)? For instance, has the author convinced me that he or she is well informed and is a person of goodwill? Or, in contrast, does the writer seem to be chiefly concerned with ridiculing those who hold a different view?

- ☐ If there is an appeal to *pathos* (emotion, originally meaning "pity for suffering," but now interpreted more broadly to include appeals to patriotism, humor, or loyalty to family, for example), is it acceptable? If not, why not?

- ☐ Have I used occasional brief quotations to let my reader hear the author's tone and to ensure fairness and accuracy?

- ☐ Is my analysis effectively organized?

- ☐ Have I taken account of the author's audience(s)?

- ☐ Does my essay, perhaps in the concluding paragraphs, indicate my agreement or disagreement with the writer but also my view of the essay as a piece of argumentative writing?

- ☐ Is my tone appropriate?

- She recognizes Kristof's audience at the start, and she suggests that he may not have given thought to this matter of the audience.

- She uses a few brief quotations, to give us a feel for Kristof's essay and to let us hear the evidence for itself, but she does not pad her essay with long quotations.

- She takes up all of Kristof's main points.

- She gives her essay a reasonable organization, letting us hear Kristof's thesis, letting us know the degree to which she accepts it, and finally letting us know her specific reservations about the essay.

- She concludes without the formality of "in conclusion"; "in short" nicely does the trick.

- Notice, finally, that she sticks closely to Kristof's essay. She does not go off on a tangent about the virtues of vegetarianism or the dreadful politics of the *New York Times*, the newspaper that published Kristof's essay. She was asked to analyze the essay, and she has done so.

Exercise

Take one of the essays not yet discussed in class or an essay assigned now by your instructor, and in an essay of 500 words analyze and evaluate it, guided by the checklists and examples we have provided.

Arguments for Analysis

JEFF JACOBY

Jeff Jacoby (b. 1959) is a columnist for the Boston Globe*, where this essay was originally published on the op-ed page on February 20, 1997.*

Bring Back Flogging

Boston's Puritan forefathers did not indulge miscreants lightly.

For selling arms and gunpowder to Indians in 1632, Richard Hopkins was sentenced to be "whipt, & branded with a hott iron on one of his cheekes." Joseph Gatchell, convicted of blasphemy in 1684, was ordered "to stand in pillory, have his head and hand put in & have his toung drawne forth out of his mouth, & peirct through with a hott iron." When Hannah Newell pleaded guilty to adultery in 1694, the court ordered "fifteen stripes Severally to be laid on upon her naked back at the Common Whipping post." Her consort, the aptly named Lambert Despair, fared worse: He was sentenced to twenty-five lashes "and that on the next Thursday Immediately after Lecture he stand upon the Pillory for . . . a full hower with Adultery in Capitall letters written upon his brest."

Corporal punishment for criminals did not vanish with the Puritans — Delaware didn't get around to repealing it until 1972 — but for all relevant purposes, it has been out of fashion for at least 150 years. The day is long past when the stocks had an honored place on the Boston Common, or when offenders were publicly flogged. Now we practice a more enlightened, more humane way of disciplining wrongdoers: We lock them up in cages.

Imprisonment has become our penalty of choice for almost every offense in the criminal code. Commit murder; go to prison. Sell cocaine; go to prison. Kite checks; go to prison. It is an all-purpose punishment, suitable — or so it would seem — for crimes violent and nonviolent, motivated by hate or by greed, plotted coldly or committed in a fit of passion. If anything, our preference for incarceration is deepening — behold the slew of mandatory minimum sentences for drug crimes and "three-strikes-you're-out" life terms for recidivists. Some 1.6 million Americans are behind bars today. That represents a 250 percent increase since 1980, and the number is climbing.

We cage criminals at a rate unsurpassed in the free world, yet few of us believe that the criminal justice system is a success. Crime is out of control, despite the deluded happy talk by some politicians about how "safe" cities have become. For most wrongdoers, the odds of being arrested, prosecuted, convicted, and incarcerated are reassuringly long. Fifty-eight percent of all murders do *not* result in a prison term. Likewise 98 percent of all burglaries.

Many states have gone on prison-building sprees, yet the penal system is choked to bursting. To ease the pressure, nearly all convicted felons are released early — or not locked up at all. "About three of every four convicted criminals," says John DiIulio, a noted Princeton criminologist, "are on the streets without meaningful probation or parole supervision." And while everyone knows that amateur thugs should be deterred before they become career criminals, it is almost unheard of for judges to send first- or second-time offenders to prison.

Meanwhile, the price of keeping criminals in cages is appalling — a common estimate is $30,000 per inmate per year. (To be sure, the cost to society of turning many inmates loose would be even higher.) For tens of thousands of convicts, prison is a graduate school of criminal studies: They emerge more ruthless and savvy than when they entered. And for many offenders, there is even a certain cachet to doing time — a stint in prison becomes a sign of manhood, a status symbol.

But there would be no cachet in chaining a criminal to an outdoor post and flogging him. If young punks were horsewhipped in public after their first conviction, fewer of them would harden into lifelong felons. A humiliating and painful paddling can be applied to the rear end of a crook for a lot less than $30,000 — and prove a lot more educational than ten years' worth of prison meals and lockdowns.

Are we quite certain the Puritans have nothing to teach us about dealing with criminals?

Of course, their crimes are not our crimes: We do not arrest blasphemers or adulterers, and only gun control fanatics would criminalize the sale of weapons to Indians. (They would criminalize the sale of weapons to anybody.) Nor would the ordeal suffered by poor Joseph Gatchell — the tongue "peirct through" with a hot poker — be regarded today as anything less than torture.

But what is the objection to corporal punishment that doesn't maim or mutilate? Instead of a prison term, why not sentence at least some criminals — say, thieves and drunk drivers — to a public whipping?

"Too degrading," some will say. "Too brutal." But where is it written that being whipped is more degrading than being caged? Why is it more brutal to flog a wrongdoer than to throw him in prison — where the risk of being beaten, raped, or murdered is terrifyingly high?

The *Globe* reported in 1994 that more than two hundred thousand prison inmates are raped each year, usually to the indifference of the guards. "The horrors experienced by many young inmates, particularly those who . . . are convicted of nonviolent offenses," former Supreme Court Justice Harry Blackmun has written, "border on the unimaginable." Are those horrors preferable to the short, sharp shame of corporal punishment?

Perhaps the Puritans were more enlightened than we think, at least on the subject of punishment. Their sanctions were humiliating and painful, but quick and cheap. Maybe we should readopt a few.

Topics for Critical Thinking and Writing

1. When Jeff Jacoby says (para. 3) that today we are more "enlightened" than our Puritan forefathers because where they used flogging, "We lock them up in cages," is he being ironic? Explain.

2. Suppose you agree with Jacoby. Explain precisely (1) what you mean by *flogging* (does Jacoby explain what he means?) and (2) how much flogging is appropriate for the crimes of house-breaking, rape, robbery, and murder.

3. In an essay of 250 words, explain why you think that flogging would be more (or less) degrading and brutal than imprisonment.

4. At the end of his essay Jacoby draws to our attention the terrible risk of being raped in prison as an argument in favor of replacing imprisonment with flogging. Do you think he mentions this point at the end because he believes it is the strongest or most persuasive of all those he mentions? Why, or why not?

5. It is often said that corporal punishment does not have any effect or, if it does, that the effect is the negative one of telling the recipient that violence is an acceptable form of behavior. But suppose it were demonstrated that the infliction of physical pain reduced at least certain kinds of crimes, perhaps shoplifting or unarmed robbery. Should we adopt the practice? Why, or why not?

6. Jacoby draws the line (para. 11) at punishment that would "maim or mutilate." Why draw the line here? Some societies punish thieves by amputating a hand. Suppose we knew that this practice really did seriously reduce theft. Should we adopt it? How about adopting castration (surgical or chemical) for rapists? For child molesters? Explain your response.

GERARD JONES

Gerard Jones (b. 1957), author of several works of fiction and nonfiction, has written many comic books for Marvel Comics and other publishers. This essay was published in Mother Jones *magazine in 2000.*

Violent Media Is Good for Kids

At thirteen I was alone and afraid. Taught by my well-meaning, progressive, English-teacher parents that violence was wrong, that rage was something to be overcome and cooperation was always better than conflict, I suffocated my deepest fears and desires under a nice-boy persona. Placed in a small, experimental school that was wrong for me, afraid to join my peers in their bumptious rush into adolescent boyhood, I withdrew into passivity and loneliness. My parents, not trusting the violent world of the late 1960s, built a wall between me and the crudest elements of American pop culture.

Then the Incredible Hulk smashed through it.

One of my mother's students convinced her that Marvel Comics, despite their apparent juvenility and violence, were in fact devoted to lofty messages of pacifism and tolerance. My mother borrowed some, thinking they'd be good for me. And so they were. But not because they preached lofty messages of benevolence. They were good for me because they were juvenile. And violent.

The character who caught me, and freed me, was the Hulk: overgendered and undersocialized, half-naked and half-witted, raging against a frightened world that misunderstood and persecuted him. Suddenly I had a fantasy self to carry my stifled rage and buried desire for power. I had a fantasy self who was a self: unafraid of his desires and the world's disapproval, unhesitating and effective in action.

"Puny boy follow Hulk!" roared my fantasy self, and I followed.

I followed him to new friends — other sensitive geeks chasing their own inner brutes — and I followed him to the arrogant, self-exposing, self-assertive, superheroic decision to become a writer. Eventually, I left him behind, followed more sophisticated heroes, and finally my own lead along a twisting path to a career and an identity. In my thirties, I found myself writing action movies and comic books. I wrote some Hulk stories, and met the geek-geniuses who created him. I saw my own creations turned into action figures, cartoons, and computer games. I talked to the kids who read my stories. Across generations, genders, and ethnicities I kept seeing the same story: people pulling themselves out of emotional traps by immersing themselves in violent stories. People integrating the scariest, most fervently denied fragments of their psyches into fuller senses of selfhood through fantasies of superhuman combat and destruction.

I have watched my son living the same story — transforming himself into a blood-thirsty dinosaur to embolden himself for the plunge into preschool, a Power Ranger to muscle through a social competition in kindergarten. In the first grade, his friends started climbing a tree at school. But he was afraid: of falling, of the centipedes crawling on the trunk, of sharp branches, of his friends' derision. I took my cue from his own fantasies and read him old Tarzan comics, rich in combat

A scene from Gerard Jones and Gene Ha's comic book "Oktane"

and bright with flashing knives. For two weeks he lived in them. Then he put them aside. And he climbed the tree.

But all the while, especially in the wake of the recent burst of school shootings, I heard pop psychologists insisting that violent stories are harmful to kids, heard teachers begging parents to keep their kids away from "junk culture," heard a guilt-stricken friend with a son who loved Pokémon lament, "I've turned into the bad mom who lets her kid eat sugary cereal and watch cartoons!"

That's when I started the research.

"Fear, greed, power-hunger, rage: these are aspects of our selves that we try not to

experience in our lives but often want, even need, to experience vicariously through stories of others," writes Melanie Moore, Ph.D., a psychologist who works with urban teens. "Children need violent entertainment in order to explore the inescapable feelings that they've been taught to deny, and to reintegrate those feelings into a more whole, more complex, more resilient selfhood."

Moore consults to public schools and local 10 governments, and is also raising a daughter. For the past three years she and I have been studying the ways in which children use violent stories to meet their emotional and developmental needs—and the ways in which adults can help them use those stories healthily. With her help I developed Power Play, a program for helping young people improve their self-knowledge and sense of potency through heroic, combative storytelling.

We've found that every aspect of even the trashiest pop-culture story can have its own developmental function. Pretending to have superhuman powers helps children conquer the feelings of powerlessness that inevitably come with being so young and small. The dual-identity concept at the heart of many superhero stories helps kids negotiate the conflicts between the inner self and the public self as they work through the early stages of socialization. Identification with a rebellious, even destructive, hero helps children learn to push back against a modern culture that cultivates fear and teaches dependency.

At its most fundamental level, what we call "creative violence"—head-bonking cartoons, bloody videogames, playground karate, toy guns—gives children a tool to master their rage. Children will feel rage. Even the sweetest and most civilized of them, even those whose parents read the better class of literary magazines, will feel rage. The world is uncontrollable and incomprehensible; mastering it is a terrifying, enraging task. Rage can be an energizing emotion, a shot of courage to push us to resist greater threats, take more control, than we ever thought we could. But rage is also the emotion our culture distrusts the most. Most of us are taught early on to fear our own. Through immersion in imaginary combat and identification with a violent protagonist, children engage the rage they've stifled, come to fear it less, and become more capable of utilizing it against life's challenges.

I knew one little girl who went around exploding with fantasies so violent that other moms would draw her mother aside to whisper, "I think you should know something about Emily. . . ." Her parents were separating, and she was small, an only child, a tomboy at an age when her classmates were dividing sharply along gender lines. On the playground she acted out *Sailor Moon* fights, and in the classroom she wrote stories about people being stabbed with knives. The more adults tried to control her stories, the more she acted out the roles of her angry heroes: breaking rules, testing limits, roaring threats.

Then her mother and I started helping her tell her stories. She wrote them, performed them, drew them like comics: sometimes

The title character of "Oktane" gets nasty.

bloody, sometimes tender, always blending the images of pop culture with her own most private fantasies. She came out of it just as fiery and strong, but more self-controlled and socially competent: a leader among her peers, the one student in her class who could truly pull boys and girls together.

I worked with an older girl, a middle-class "nice girl," who held herself together through a chaotic family situation and a tumultuous adolescence with gangsta rap. In the mythologized street violence of Ice T, the rage and strutting of his music and lyrics, she found a theater of the mind in which she could be powerful, ruthless, invulnerable. She avoided the heavy drug use that sank many of her peers, and flowered in college as a writer and political activist.

I'm not going to argue that violent entertainment is harmless. I think it has helped inspire some people to real-life violence. I am going to argue that it's helped hundreds of people for every one it's hurt, and that it can help far more if we learn to use it well. I am going to argue that our fear of "youth violence" isn't well-founded on reality, and that the fear can do more harm than the reality. We act as though our highest priority is to prevent our children from growing up into murderous thugs — but modern kids are far more likely to grow up too passive, too distrustful of themselves, too easily manipulated.

We send the message to our children in a hundred ways that their craving for imaginary gun battles and symbolic killings is wrong, or at least dangerous. Even when we don't call for censorship or forbid *Mortal Kombat*, we moan to other parents within our kids' earshot about the "awful violence" in the entertainment they love. We tell our kids that it isn't nice to play-fight, or we steer them from some monstrous

15

action figure to a prosocial doll. Even in the most progressive households, where we make such a point of letting children feel what they feel, we rush to substitute an enlightened discussion for the raw material of rageful fantasy. In the process, we risk confusing them about their natural aggression in the same way the Victorians confused their children about their sexuality. When we try to protect our children from their own feelings and fantasies, we shelter them not against violence but against power and selfhood.

Topics for Critical Thinking and Writing

1. In his final paragraph, Gerard Jones mentions the Victorian treatment of sexuality. Why does he bring this in? Does his use of this point make for an effective ending? Explain.

2. In an essay of 300 words, explain whether you think Jones has made the case for violence in an effective and persuasive way. If so, what is it about his article that makes it effective and persuasive? If it is not, where do the problems lie?

3. What kinds of violence does Jones advocate?

4. Does violence play as large a part in the life of teenage girls as it does in the life of teenage boys? Why, or why not?

5. How would you characterize the audience Jones is addressing? What is your evidence?

JUSTIN CRONIN

Justin Cronin (b. 1962) is an award-winning novelist who teaches at Rice University in Houston, Texas. The following selection was published in the New York Times.

Confessions of a Liberal Gun Owner

I am a New England liberal, born and bred. I have lived most of my life in the Northeast — Boston, New York, and Philadelphia — and my politics are devoutly Democratic. In three decades, I have voted for a Republican exactly once, holding my nose, in a mayoral election in which the Democratic candidate seemed mentally unbalanced.

I am also a Texas resident and a gun owner. I have half a dozen pistols in my safe, all semi-automatics, the largest capable of holding twenty rounds. I go to the range at least once a week, have applied for a concealed carry license, and am planning to take a tactical training course in the spring. I'm currently shopping for a shotgun, either a Remington 870 Express Tactical or a Mossberg 500 Flex with a pistol grip and adjustable stock.

Except for shotguns (firing one feels like being punched by a prizefighter), I enjoy shooting. At the range where I practice, most of the staff knows me by sight if not by name. I'm the guy in the metrosexual eyeglasses and Ralph Lauren polo, and I ask a lot of questions: What's the best way to maintain my sight picture with both eyes open? How do I clear a stove-piped round?

There is pleasure to be had in exercising one's rights, learning something new in mid-life, and mastering the operation of a complex tool, which is one thing a gun is. But I won't deny the seductive psychological power that firearms possess. I grew up playing shooting games, pretending to be Starsky or Hutch or one of the patrolmen on *Adam-12*, the two most boring TV cops in history.

A prevailing theory holds that boys are simultaneously aware of their own physical powerlessness and society's mandate that they serve as protectors of the innocent. Pretending to shoot a bad guy assuages this anxiety, which never goes away completely. This explanation makes sense to me. Another word for it is catharsis, and you could say that, as a novelist, I've made my living from it.

There are a lot of reasons that a gun feels right in my hand, but I also own firearms to protect my family. I hope I never have to use one for this purpose, and I doubt I ever will. But I am my family's last line of defense. I have chosen to meet this responsibility, in part, by being armed. It wasn't a choice I made lightly. I am aware that, statistically speaking, a gun in the home represents a far greater danger to its inhabitants than to an intruder. But not every choice we make is data-driven. A lot comes from the gut.

Apart from the ones in policemen's holsters, I don't think I saw a working firearm until the year after college, when a friend's girlfriend, after four cosmopolitans, decided to show off the .38 revolver she kept in her purse. (Half the party guests dived for cover, including me.)

It wasn't until my mid-forties that my education in guns began, in the course of writing a novel in which pistols, shotguns, and rifles, but also heavy weaponry like the AR-15 and its military analogue, the M-16, were widely used. I suspected that much of the gunplay I'd witnessed in movies and television was completely wrong (it is) and hired an instructor for a daylong private lesson "to shoot everything in the store." The gentleman who met me at the range was someone whom I would have called "a gun nut." A former New Yorker, he had relocated to Texas because of its lax gun laws and claimed to keep a pistol within arm's reach even when he showered. He was perfect, in other words, for my purpose.

My relationship to firearms might have ended there, if not for a coincidence of weather. Everybody remembers Hurricane Katrina; fewer recall Hurricane Rita, an even more intense storm that headed straight for Houston less than a month later. My wife and I arranged to stay at a friend's house in Austin, packed up the kids and dog, and headed out of town — or tried to. As many as 3.7 million people had the same idea, making Rita one of the largest evacuations in history, with predictable results.

By two in the morning, after six hours on the road, we had made it all of fifty miles. The scene was like a snapshot from the Apocalypse: crowds milling restlessly, gas stations and mini-marts picked clean and heaped with trash, families sleeping by the side of the road. The situation had the hopped-up feel of barely bottled chaos. After Katrina, nobody had any illusions that help was on its way. It also occurred to me that there were probably a lot of guns out there — this was Texas, after all. Here I was with two tiny children, a couple of thousand dollars in cash, a late-model S.U.V. with half a tank of gas and not so much as a heavy book to throw. When my wife wouldn't let me get out of the car so the dog could do his business, that was it for me. We jumped the median, turned around, and were home in under an hour.

As it happened, Rita made a last-minute turn away from Houston. But what if it hadn't? I believe people are basically good, but not all of them and not all the time. Like most citizens of our modern, technological world, I am wholly reliant upon a fragile web of services to meet my most basic needs. What would happen if those services collapsed? Chaos, that's what.

It didn't happen overnight, but before too long my Northeastern liberal sensibilities, while intact on other issues, had shifted on the question of gun ownership. For my first pistol I selected a little Walther .380. I shot it enough to decide it was junk, upgraded to a full-size Springfield 9-millimeter, liked it but wanted something with a thumb safety, found a nice Smith & Wesson subcompact that fit the bill, but along the way got a little bit of a gun-crush on the Beretta M-9 — and so on.

Lots of people on both sides of the aisle own firearms, or don't, for reasons that supersede their broader political and cultural affiliations. Let me be clear: my personal armory notwithstanding. I think guns are woefully under-regulated. It's far too easy to buy a gun — I once bought one in a parking lot — and I loathe the National Rifle Association. Some of the Obama administration's proposals strike me as more symbolic than effective, with some 300 million firearms on the loose. But the White House's recommendations seem like a good starting point and nothing that would prevent me from protecting my family in a crisis. The AR-15 is a fascinating weapon, and, frankly, a gas to shoot. So is a tank, and I don't need to own a tank.

Alas, the days of à la carte politics like mine seem over, if they ever even existed. The bigger culprit is the far right and the lunatic pronouncements of those like Rush Limbaugh. But in the weeks since Newtown, I've watched my Facebook feed, which is dominated by my coastal friends, fill up with antigun dispatches that seemed divorced from reality. I agree it would be nice if the world had exactly zero guns in it. But I don't see that happening, and calling gun owners "a bunch of inbred rednecks" doesn't do much to advance rational discussion.

Thus, my secret life — though I guess it's 15 not such a secret anymore. My wife is afraid of my guns (though she also says she's glad I have them). My sixteen-year-old daughter is a different story. The week before her fall semester exams, we allowed her to skip school for a day, a tradition in our house. The rule is, she gets to do whatever she wants. This time, she asked to take a pistol lesson. She's an NPR listener like me, but she's also grown up in Texas, and the fact that one in five American women is a victim of sexual assault is not lost on her. In the windowless classroom off the range, the instructor ran her through the basics, demonstrating with a Glock 9-millimeter: how to hold it, load it, pull back the slide.

"You'll probably have trouble with that part," he said. "A lot of the women do."

"Oh really?" my daughter replied, and with a cagey smile proceeded to rack her weapon with such authority you could have heard it in the parking lot.

A proud-papa moment? I confess it was.

Topics for Critical Thinking and Writing

1. This essay could with equal accuracy be called "Confessions of a Texas Gun Owner." Why do you suppose Justin Cronin chose the title he did, rather than our imagined title? That is, why is his title better — better for his purposes — than our invented title?

2. Why does Cronin devote so many sentences to autobiographical matters, since, in fact, none of the autobiography actually involves using a gun to protect himself or his family against an intruder?

3. How would you characterize Cronin's persona as he presents it in this essay? Does he try to speak with authority, connect with his audience on a personal level, or employ another strategy to gain his reader's trust? Do you feel that his persona effectively connects with you as a reader? Why, or why not?

4. What *arguments* does Cronin offer on behalf of gun ownership? Do you think his case — his thesis, his point, his Big Idea — might have been strengthened if he had cited statistics or authorities, or do you think that such evidence probably would have been inappropriate in what is essentially a highly personal essay? Explain your response.

5. In paragraph 12, Cronin writes, "It didn't happen overnight, but before too long my North-eastern liberal sensibilities . . . had shifted on the question of gun ownership." Suppose a reader said to you, "I don't really understand exactly why his attitude shifted. What *happened* that made him shift? I don't get it." What would you say to this questioner?

6. In paragraph 13, Cronin says that he believes "guns are woefully under-regulated" and that he "loathe[s] the National Rifle Association," but he doesn't go into any detail about what sorts of regulations he favors. Do you think his essay might have been more convincing if he had given us details along these lines? Explain.

7. Each of Cronin's last three paragraphs is very short. We have discussed how, in general, a short paragraph is usually an underdeveloped paragraph. Do you think these paragraphs are underdeveloped — or do you think Cronin knows exactly what he is doing? Explain.

PETER SINGER

Peter Singer (b. 1946) is the Ira W. DeCamp Professor of Bioethics at Princeton University. A native of Australia, he is a graduate of the University of Melbourne and Oxford University and the author or editor of more than two dozen books, including Animal Liberation *(1975),* Practical Ethics *(1979),* Rethinking Life and Death *(1995), and* One World: The Ethics of Globalization *(2002). He has written on a variety of ethical issues, but he is especially known for caring about the welfare of animals.*

This essay originally appeared in the New York Review of Books *(April 5, 1973), as a review of* Animals, Men and Morals, *edited by Stanley and Roslind Godlovitch and John Harris.*

Animal Liberation

I

We are familiar with Black Liberation, Gay Liberation, and a variety of other movements. With Women's Liberation some thought we had come to the end of the road. Discrimination on the basis of sex, it has been said, is the last form of discrimination that is universally accepted and practiced without pretense, even in those liberal circles which have long prided themselves on their freedom from racial discrimination. But one should always be wary of talking of "the last remaining form of discrimination." If we have learned anything from the liberation movements, we should have learned how difficult it is to be aware of the ways in which we discriminate until they are forcefully pointed out to us. A liberation movement demands an expansion of our moral horizons, so that practices that were previously regarded as natural and inevitable are now seen as intolerable.

Animals, Men and Morals is a manifesto for an Animal Liberation movement. The contributors to the book may not all see the issue this way. They are a varied group. Philosophers, ranging from professors to graduate students, make up the largest contingent. There are five of them, including the three editors, and there is also an extract from the unjustly neglected German philosopher with an English name, Leonard Nelson, who died in 1927. There are essays by two novelist/critics, Brigid Brophy and Maureen Duffy, and another by Muriel the Lady Dowding, widow of Dowding of Battle of Britain fame and the founder of "Beauty without Cruelty," a movement that campaigns against the use of animals for furs and cosmetics. The other pieces are by a psychologist, a botanist, a sociologist, and Ruth Harrison, who is probably best described as a professional campaigner for animal welfare.

Whether or not these people, as individuals, would all agree that they are launching a liberation movement for animals, the book as a whole amounts to no less. It is a demand for a complete change in our attitudes to nonhumans. It is a demand that we cease to regard the exploitation of other species as natural and inevitable, and that, instead, we see it as a continuing moral outrage. Patrick Corbett, Professor of Philosophy at Sussex University, captures the spirit of the book in his closing words:

> We require now to extend the great principles of liberty, equality, and fraternity over the lives of animals. Let animal slavery join human slavery in the graveyard of the past.

The reader is likely to be skeptical. "Animal Liberation" sounds more like a parody of liberation movements than a serious objective. The reader may think: We support the claims of blacks and women for equality because blacks and women really are equal to whites and males — equal in intelligence and in abilities, capacity for leadership, rationality, and so on. Humans and nonhumans obviously are not equal in these respects. Since justice demands only that we treat equals equally, unequal treatment of humans and nonhumans cannot be an injustice.

This is a tempting reply, but a dangerous 5 one. It commits the nonracist and nonsexist to a dogmatic belief that blacks and women really are just as intelligent, able, etc., as whites and males — and no more. Quite possibly this happens to be the case. Certainly attempts to prove that racial or sexual differences in these respects have a genetic origin have not been conclusive. But do we really want to stake our demand for equality on the assumption that there are no genetic differences of this kind between the different races or sexes? Surely the appropriate response to those who claim to have found evidence for such genetic differences is not to stick to the belief that there are no differences, whatever the evidence to the contrary; rather one should be clear that the claim to equality does not depend on IQ. Moral equality is distinct from factual equality. Otherwise it would be nonsense to talk to the equality of human beings, since humans, as individuals, obviously differ in intelligence and almost any ability one cares to name. If possessing greater intelligence does not entitle one human to exploit another, why should it entitle humans to exploit nonhumans?

Jeremy Bentham expressed the essential basis of equality in his famous formula: "Each to count for one and none for more than one." In other words, the interests of every being that has interests are to be taken into account and treated equally with the like interests of any other being. Other moral philosophers, before and after Bentham, have made the same point in different ways. Our concern for others must not depend on whether they possess certain characteristics, though just what that concern involves may, of course, vary according to such characteristics.

Bentham, incidentally, was well aware that the logic of the demand for racial equality did not stop at the equality of humans. He wrote:

> The day *may* come when the rest of the animal creation may acquire those rights which never could have been withholden from them but by the hand of tyranny. The French have already discovered that the blackness of the skin is no reason why a human being should be abandoned without redress to the caprice of a tormentor. It may one day come to be recognized that the number of the legs, the villosity of the skin, or the termination of the *os sacrum*, are reasons equally insufficient for abandoning a sensitive being to the same fate. What else is it that should trace the insuperable line? Is it the faculty of reason, or perhaps the faculty of discourse? But a full-grown horse or dog is beyond comparison a more rational, as well as a more conversable animal, than an infant of a day, or a week, or even a month, old. But suppose they were otherwise, what would it avail? The question is not, Can they *reason*? nor Can they *talk*? but, Can they *suffer*?[1]

Surely Bentham was right. If a being suffers, there can be no moral justification for refusing to take that suffering into consideration, and, indeed, to count it equally with the like suffering (if rough comparisons can be made) of any other being.

So the only question is: Do animals other than man suffer? Most people agree unhesitatingly that animals like cats and dogs can and do suffer, and this seems also to be assumed by those laws that prohibit wanton cruelty to such animals. Personally, I have no doubt at all about this and find it hard to take seriously the doubts that a few people apparently do have. The editors and contributors of *Animals, Men and Morals* seem to feel the same way, for although the question is raised more than once, doubts are quickly dismissed each time. Nevertheless, because this is such a fundamental point, it is worth asking what grounds we have for attributing suffering to other animals.

It is best to begin by asking what grounds any individual human has for supposing that other humans feel pain. Since pain is a state of consciousness, a "mental event," it can never be directly observed. No observations, whether behavioral signs such as writhing or screaming or physiological or neurological recordings, are observations of pain itself. Pain is something one feels, and one can only infer that others are feeling it from various external indications. The fact that only philosophers are ever skeptical about whether other humans feel pain shows that we regard such inference as justifiable in the case of humans.

---

[1] *The Principles of Morals and Legislation*, ch. XVII, sec. 1, footnote to paragraph 4. [All notes are the author's unless otherwise specified.]

Is there any reason why the same infer- [10] ence should be unjustifiable for other animals? Nearly all the external signs which lead us to infer pain in other humans can be seen in other species, especially "higher" animals such as mammals and birds. Behavioral signs—writhing, yelping, or other forms of calling, attempts to avoid the source of pain, and many others—are present. We know, too, that these animals are biologically similar in the relevant respects, having nervous systems like ours which can be observed to function as ours do.

So the grounds for inferring that these animals can feel pain are nearly as good as the grounds for inferring other humans do. Only nearly, for there is one behavioral sign that humans have but nonhumans, with the exception of one or two specially raised chimpanzees, do not have. This, of course, is a developed language. As the quotation from Bentham indicates, this has long been regarded as an important distinction between man and other animals. Other animals may communicate with each other, but not in the way we do. Following Chomsky,[2] many people now mark this distinction by saying that only humans communicate in a form that is governed by rules of syntax. (For the purposes of this argument, linguists allow those chimpanzees who have learned a syntactic sign language to rank as honorary humans.) Nevertheless, as Bentham pointed out, this distinction is not relevant to the question of how animals ought to be treated, unless it can be linked to the issue of whether animals suffer.

This link may be attempted in two ways. First, there is a hazy line of philosophical thought, stemming perhaps from some doctrines associated with Wittgenstein, which maintains that we cannot meaningfully attribute states of consciousness to beings without language. I have not seen this argument made explicit in print, though I have come across it in conversation. This position seems to me very implausible, and I doubt that it would be held at all if it were not thought to be a consequence of a broader view of the significance of language. It may be that the use of a public, rule-governed language is a precondition of conceptual thought. It may even be, although personally I doubt it, that we cannot meaningfully speak of a creature having an intention unless that creature can use a language. But states like pain, surely, are more primitive than either of these, and seem to have nothing to do with language.

Indeed, as Jane Goodall points out in her study of chimpanzees, when it comes to the expression of feelings and emotions, humans tend to fall back on nonlinguistic modes of communication which are often found among apes, such as a cheering pat on the back, an exuberant embrace, a clasp of hands, and so on.[3] Michael Peters makes a similar point in his contribution to *Animals, Men and Morals* when he notes that the basic signals we use to convey pain, fear, sexual arousal, and so on are not specific to our species. So there seems to be no reason at all to believe that a creature without language cannot suffer.

The second, and more easily appreciated way of linking language and the existence of pain is to say that the best evidence that we can have that another creature is in pain is when he tells us that he is. This is a distinct line of argument, for it is not being denied that a nonlanguage-user conceivably could suffer, but

---

[2]**Chomsky** Noam Chomsky (b. 1928), a professor of linguistics and the author of (among other books) *Language and Mind* (1972). [Editors' note.]

[3]Jane van Lawick-Goodall, *In the Shadow of Man* (Houghton Mifflin, 1971), p. 225.

only that we could know that he is suffering. Still, this line of argument seems to me to fail, and for reasons similar to those just given. "I am in pain" is not the best possible evidence that the speaker is in pain (he might be lying) and it is certainly not the only possible evidence. Behavioral signs and knowledge of the animal's biological similarity to ourselves together provide adequate evidence that animals do suffer. After all, we would not accept linguistic evidence if it contradicted the rest of the evidence. If a man was severely burned, and behaved as if he were in pain, writhing, groaning, being very careful not to let his burned skin touch anything, and so on, but later said he had not been in pain at all, we would be more likely to conclude that he was lying or suffering from amnesia than that he had not been in pain.

Even if there were stronger grounds for refusing to attribute pain to those who do not have a language, the consequences of this refusal might lead us to examine these grounds unusually critically. Human infants, as well as some adults, are unable to use language. Are we to deny that a year-old infant can suffer? If not, how can language be crucial? Of course, most parents can understand the responses of even very young infants better than they understand the responses of other animals, and sometimes infant responses can be understood in the light of later development.

This, however, is just a fact about the relative knowledge we have of our own species and other species, and most of this knowledge is simply derived from closer contact. Those who have studied the behavior of other animals soon learn to understand their responses at least as well as we understand those of an infant. (I am not referring to Jane Goodall's and other well-known studies of apes. Consider, for example, the degree of understanding achieved by

Tinbergen from watching herring gulls.[4]) Just as we can understand infant human behavior in the light of adult human behavior, so we can understand the behavior of other species in the light of our own behavior (and sometimes we can understand our own behavior better in the light of the behavior of other species).

The grounds we have for believing that other mammals and birds suffer are, then, closely analogous to the grounds we have for believing that other humans suffer. It remains to consider how far down the evolutionary scale this analogy holds. Obviously it becomes poorer when we get further away from man. To be more precise would require a detailed examination of all that we know about other forms of life. With fish, reptiles, and other vertebrates the analogy still seems strong, with molluscs like oysters it is much weaker. Insects are more difficult, and it may be that in our present state of knowledge we must be agnostic about whether they are capable of suffering.

If there is no moral justification for ignoring suffering when it occurs, and it does occur in other species, what are we to say of our attitudes toward these other species? Richard Ryder, one of the contributors to *Animals, Men and Morals*, uses the term "speciesism" to describe the belief that we are entitled to treat members of other species in a way in which it would be wrong to treat members of our own species. The term is not euphonious, but it neatly makes the analogy with racism. The nonracist would do well to bear the analogy in mind when he is inclined to defend human behavior toward nonhumans. "Shouldn't we worry about improving the lot of our own species before we concern ourselves with other species?" he may ask. If we substitute "race" for

---

[4]N. Tinbergen, *The Herring Gull's World* (Basic Books, 1961).

"species" we shall see that the question is better not asked. "Is a vegetarian diet nutritionally adequate?" resembles the slaveowner's claim that he and the whole economy of the South would be ruined without slave labor. There is even a parallel with skeptical doubts about whether animals suffer, for some defenders of slavery professed to doubt whether blacks really suffer in the way whites do.

I do not want to give the impression, however, that the case for Animal Liberation is based on the analogy with racism and no more. On the contrary, *Animals, Men and Morals* describes the various ways in which humans exploit nonhumans, and several contributors consider the defenses that have been offered, including the defense of meat-eating mentioned in the last paragraph. Sometimes the rebuttals are scornfully dismissive, rather than carefully designed to convince the detached critic. This may be a fault, but it is a fault that is inevitable, given the kind of book this is. The issue is not one on which one can remain detached. As the editors state in their Introduction:

> Once the full force of moral assessment has been made explicit there can be no rational excuse left for killing animals, be they killed for food, science, or sheer personal indulgence. We have not assembled this book to provide the reader with yet another manual on how to make brutalities less brutal. Compromise, in the traditional sense of the term, is simple unthinking weakness when one considers the actual reasons for our crude relationships with the other animals.

The point is that on this issue there are few critics who are genuinely detached. People who eat pieces of slaughtered nonhumans every day find it hard to believe that they are doing wrong; and they also find it hard to imagine what else they could eat. So for those who do not place nonhumans beyond the pale of morality, there comes a stage when further argument seems pointless, a stage at which one can only accuse one's opponent of hypocrisy and reach for the sort of sociological account of our practices and the way we defend them that is attempted by David Wood in his contribution to his book. On the other hand, to those unconvinced by the arguments, and unable to accept that they are merely rationalizing their dietary preferences and their fear of being thought peculiar, such sociological explanations can only seem insultingly arrogant.

II

The logic of speciesism is most apparent in the practice of experimenting on nonhumans in order to benefit humans. This is because the issue is rarely obscured by allegations that nonhumans are so different from humans that we cannot know anything about whether they suffer. The defender of vivisection cannot use this argument because he needs to stress the similarities between man and other animals in order to justify the usefulness to the former of experiments on the latter. The researcher who makes rats choose between starvation and electric shocks to see if they develop ulcers (they do) does so because he knows that the rat has a nervous system very similar to man's, and presumably feels an electric shock in a similar way.

Richard Ryder's restrained account of experiments on animals made me angrier with my fellow men than anything else in this book. Ryder, a clinical psychologist by profession, himself experimented on animals before he came to hold the view he puts forward in his essay. Experimenting on animals is now a large industry, both academic and commercial. In 1969, more than 5 million experiments were performed in Britain, the vast majority without anesthetic (though how many of these involved pain is not known). There are no accurate U.S. figures, since there is no federal law on the subject, and in many cases no state law either. Estimates vary from 20 million to 200 million. Ryder suggests that 80 million may be the best guess. We tend to think that this is all for vital medical research, but of course it is not. Huge numbers of animals are used in university departments from Forestry to Psychology, and even more are used for commercial purposes, to test whether cosmetics can cause skin damage, or shampoos eye damage, or to test food additives or laxatives or sleeping pills or anything else.

A standard test for foodstuffs is the "LD50." The object of this test is to find the dosage level at which 50 percent of the test animals will die. This means that nearly all of them will become very sick before finally succumbing or surviving. When the substance is a harmless one, it may be necessary to force huge doses down the animals, until in some cases sheer volume or concentration causes death.

Ryder gives a selection of experiments, taken from recent scientific journals. I will quote two, not for the sake of indulging in gory details, but in order to give an idea of what normal researchers think they may legitimately do to other species. The point is not that the individual researchers are cruel men, but that they are behaving in a way that is allowed by our speciesist attitudes. As Ryder points out, even if only 1 percent of the experiments involve severe pain, that is 50,000 experiments in Britain each year, or nearly 150 every day

(and about fifteen times as many in the United States, if Ryder's guess is right). Here then are two experiments:

O. S. Ray and R. J. Barrett of Pittsburgh gave electric shocks to the feet of 1,042 mice. They then caused convulsions by giving more intense shocks through cup-shaped electrodes applied to the animals' eyes or through pressure spring clips attached to their ears. Unfortunately some of the mice who "successfully completed Day One training were found sick or dead prior to testing on Day Two." [*Journal of Comparative and Physiological Psychology,* 1969, vol. 67, pp. 110–116]

At the National Institute for Medical Research, Mill Hill, London, W. Feldberg and S. L. Sherwood injected chemicals into the brains of cats — "with a number of widely different substances, recurrent patterns of reaction were obtained. Retching, vomiting, defecation, increased salivation and greatly accelerated respiration leading to panting were common features." . . .

The injection into the brain of a large dose of Tubocuraine caused the cat to jump "from the table to the floor and then straight into its cage, where it started calling more and more noisily whilst moving about restlessly and jerkily . . . finally the cat fell with legs and neck flexed, jerking in rapid clonic movements, the condition being that of a major [epileptic] convulsion . . . within a few seconds the cat got up, ran for a few yards at high speed, and fell in another fit. The whole process was repeated several times within the next ten minutes, during which the cat lost faeces and foamed at the mouth."

This animal finally died thirty-five minutes after the brain injection. [*Journal of Physiology,* 1954, vol. 123, pp. 148–167]

There is nothing secret about these experiments. One has only to open any recent volume of a learned journal, such as the *Journal of Comparative and Physiological Psychology,* to find full descriptions of experiments of this sort, together with the results obtained — results that are frequently trivial and obvious. The experiments are often supported by public funds. 25

It is a significant indication of the level of acceptability of these practices that, although these experiments are taking place at this moment on university campuses throughout the country, there has, so far as I know, not been the slightest protest from the student movement. Students have been rightly concerned that their universities should not discriminate on grounds of race or sex, and that they should not serve the purposes of the military or big business. Speciesism continues undisturbed, and many students participate in it. There may be a few qualms at first, but since everyone regards it as normal, and it may even be a required part of a course, the student soon becomes hardened and, dismissing his earlier feelings as "mere sentiment," comes to regard animals as statistics rather than sentient beings with interests that warrant consideration.

Argument about vivisection has often missed the point because it has been put in absolutist terms: Would the abolitionist be prepared to let thousands die if they could be saved by experimenting on a single animal? The way to reply to this purely hypothetical question is to pose another: Would the experimenter be prepared to experiment on a human orphan under six months old, if it were the only way to save many lives? (I say "orphan" to avoid the complication of parental feelings, although in doing so I am being overfair to the experimenter, since the nonhuman subjects of experiments are not orphans.) A negative answer to this question indicates that the experimenter's readiness to use nonhumans is simple discrimination, for adult apes, cats, mice, and other mammals are more conscious of what is happening to them, more self-directing, and, so far as we can tell, just as sensitive to pain as a human infant. There is no characteristic that human infants possess that adult mammals do not have to the same or a higher degree.

(It might be possible to hold that what makes it wrong to experiment on a human infant is that the infant will in time develop into more than the nonhuman, but one would then, to be consistent, have to oppose abortion, and perhaps contraception, too, for the fetus and the egg and sperm have the same potential as the infant. Moreover, one would still have no reason for experimenting on a nonhuman rather than a human with brain damage severe enough to make it impossible for him to rise above infant level.)

The experimenter, then, shows a bias for his own species whenever he carries out an experiment on a nonhuman for a purpose that

Pigs at sausage-processing factory in Spain

he would not think justified him in using a human being at an equal or lower level of sentience, awareness, ability to be self-directing, etc. No one familiar with the kind of results yielded by these experiments can have the slightest doubt that if this bias were eliminated the number of experiments performed would be zero or very close to it.

III

If it is vivisection that shows the logic of speciesism most clearly, it is the use of other species for food that is at the heart of our attitudes toward them. Most of *Animals, Men and Morals* is an attack on meat eating — an attack which is based solely on concern for nonhumans, without reference to arguments derived from consideration of ecology, macrobiotics, health, or religion.

The idea that nonhumans are utilities, means to our ends, pervades our thought. Even conservationists who are concerned about the slaughter of wildfowl but not about the vastly greater slaughter of chickens for our tables are thinking in this way — they are worried about what we would lose if there were less wildlife. Stanley Godlovitch, pursuing the Marxist idea that our thinking is formed by the activities we undertake in satisfying our needs, suggests that man's first classification of his environment was into Edibles and Inedibles. Most animals came into the first category, and there they have remained.

Man may always have killed other species for food, but he has never exploited them so ruthlessly as he does today. Farming has succumbed to business methods, the objective being to get the highest possible ratio of output (meat, eggs, milk) to input (fodder, labor costs, etc.). Ruth Harrison's essay "On Factory Farming" gives an account of some aspects of modern methods, and of the unsuccessful British campaigns for effective controls, a campaign which was sparked off by her *Animal Machines* (London: Stuart, 1964).

Her article is in no way a substitute for her earlier book. This is a pity since, as she says, "Farm produce is still associated with mental pictures of animals browsing in the fields . . . of hens having a last forage before going to roost. . . ." Yet neither in her article nor elsewhere in *Animals, Men and Morals* is this false image replaced by a clear idea of the nature and extent of factory farming. We learn of this only indirectly, when we hear of the code of reform proposed by an advisory committee set up by the British government.

Among the proposals, which the government refused to implement on the grounds that they were too idealistic, were: "*Any animal should at least have room to turn around freely.*"

Factory farm animals need liberation in the most literal sense. Veal calves are kept in stalls 5 feet by 2 feet. They are usually slaughtered when about four months old, and have been too big to turn in their stalls for at least a month. Intensive beef herds, kept in stalls only proportionally larger for much longer periods, account for a growing percentage of beef production. Sows are often similarly confined when pregnant, which, because of artificial methods of increasing fertility, can be most of the time. Animals confined in this way do not waste food by exercising, nor do they develop unpalatable muscle.

"*A dry bedded area should be provided for all stock.*" Intensively kept animals usually have to stand and sleep in slatted floors without straw, because this makes cleaning easier.

"*Palatable roughage must be readily available to all calves after one week of age.*" In order to produce the pale veal housewives are said to prefer, calves are fed on an all-liquid diet until slaughter, even though they are long past the age at which they would normally eat grass. They develop a craving for roughage, evidenced by attempts to gnaw wood from their stalls. (For the same reason, their diet is deficient in iron.)

"*Battery cages for poultry should be large enough for a bird to be able to stretch one wing at a time.*" Under current British practice, a cage for four or five laying hens has a floor area of 20 inches by 18 inches, scarcely larger than a double page of the *New York Review of Books*. In this space, on a sloping wire floor (sloping so the eggs roll down, wire so the dung drips through) the birds live for a year or eighteen months while artificial lighting and temperature conditions combine with drugs in their food to squeeze the maximum number of eggs out of them. Table birds are also sometimes kept in cages. More often they are reared in sheds, no less crowded. Under these conditions all the birds' natural activities are frustrated, and they develop "vices" such as pecking each other to death. To prevent this, beaks are often cut off, and the sheds kept dark.

How many of those who support factory farming by buying its produce know anything about the way it is produced? How many have heard something about it, but are reluctant to check up for fear that it will make them uncomfortable? To nonspeciesists, the typical consumer's mixture of ignorance, reluctance to find out the truth, and vague belief that nothing really bad could be allowed seems analogous to the attitudes of "decent Germans" to the death camps.

There are, of course, some defenders of factory farming. Their arguments are considered, though again rather sketchily, by John Harris. Among the most common: "Since they have never known anything else, they don't suffer." This argument will not be put by anyone who knows anything about animal behavior, since he will know that not all behavior has to be learned. Chickens attempt to stretch wings, walk around, scratch, and even dustbathe or build a nest, even though they have never lived under conditions that allowed these activities. Calves can suffer from maternal deprivation no matter at what age they were taken from their mothers. "We need these intensive methods to provide protein for a growing population." As ecologists and famine relief organizations know, we can produce far more protein per acre if we grow the right vegetable crop, soy beans for instance, than if we use the land to grow crops to be converted into protein by animals who use nearly 90 percent of the protein themselves, even when unable to exercise.

There will be many readers of this book who will agree that factory farming involves an unjustifiable degree of exploitation of sentient creatures, and yet will want to say that there is nothing wrong with rearing animals for food, provided it is done "humanely." These people are saying, in effect, that although we should not cause animals to suffer, there is nothing wrong with killing them.

There are two possible replies to this view. One is to attempt to show that this combination of attitudes is absurd. Roslind Godlovitch takes this course in her essay, which is an examination of some common attitudes to animals. She argues that from the combination of "animal suffering is to be avoided" and "there is nothing wrong with killing animals" it follows that all animal life ought to be exterminated (since all sentient creatures will suffer to some degree at some point in their lives). Euthanasia is a contentious issue only because we place some value on living. If we did not, the least amount of suffering would justify it. Accordingly, if we deny that we have a duty to exterminate all animal life, we must concede that we are placing some value on animal life.

This argument seems to me valid, although one could still reply that the value of animal life is to be derived from the pleasures that life can have for them, so that, provided their lives have a balance of pleasure over pain, we are justified in rearing them. But this would imply that we ought to produce animals and let them live as pleasantly as possible, without suffering.

At this point, one can make the second of the two possible replies to the view that rearing and killing animals for food is all right so long as it is done humanely. This second reply is that so long as we think that a nonhuman may be killed simply so that a human can satisfy his taste for meat, we are still thinking of nonhumans as means rather than as ends in themselves. The factory farm is nothing more than the application of technology to this concept. Even traditional methods involve castration, the separation of mothers and their young, the breaking up of herds, branding or earpunching, and of course transportation to the abattoirs and the final moments of terror when the animal smells blood and senses danger. If we were to try rearing animals so that they lived and died without suffering, we should find that to do so on anything like the scale of today's meat industry would be a sheer impossibility. Meat would become the prerogative of the rich.

I have been able to discuss only some of the contributions to this book, saying nothing about, for instance, the essays on killing for furs and for sport. Nor have I considered all the detailed questions that need to be asked once we start thinking about other species in the radically different way presented by this book. What, for instance, are we to do about genuine conflicts of interest like rats biting slum children? I am not sure of the answer, but the essential point is just that we *do* see this as a conflict of interests, that we recognize that rats have interests too. Then we may begin to think about other ways of resolving the conflict—perhaps by leaving out rat baits that sterilize the rats instead of killing them.

I have not discussed such problems because they are side issues compared with the exploitation of other species for food and for experimental purposes. On these central matters, I hope that I have said enough to show that this book, despite its flaws, is a challenge to every human to recognize his attitudes to nonhumans as a form of prejudice no less objectionable than racism or sexism. It is a challenge that demands not just a change of attitudes, but a change in our way of life, for it requires us to become vegetarians.

Can a purely moral demand of this kind succeed? The odds are certainly against it. The book holds out no inducements. It does not tell us that we will become healthier, or enjoy life more, if we cease exploiting animals. Animal Liberation will require greater altruism on the part of mankind than any other liberation movement, since animals are incapable of demanding it for themselves, or of protesting against their exploitation by votes, demonstrations, or bombs. Is man capable of such genuine altruism? Who knows? If this book does have a significant effect, however, it will be a vindication of all those who have believed that man has within himself the potential for more than cruelty and selfishness.

Topics for Critical Thinking and Writing

1. In paragraph 4, Peter Singer formulates an argument on behalf of the skeptical reader. Examine that argument closely, restate it in your own words, and evaluate it. Which of its premises is most vulnerable to criticism? Why?

2. Singer quotes with approval (para. 7) Bentham's comment, "The question is not, Can they *reason*? nor Can they *talk*? but, Can they *suffer*?" Do you find this argument persuasive? Can you think of any effective challenge to it?

3. Singer allows that although developed linguistic capacity is not necessary for a creature to have pain, perhaps such a capacity is necessary for "having an intention" (para. 12). Do you think this concession is correct? Have you ever seen animal behavior that you would be willing to describe or explain as evidence that the animal has an intention to do something, despite knowing that the animal cannot talk? Explain your response.

4. Singer thinks that the readiness to experiment on animals argues against believing that animals don't suffer pain (see para. 21). Do you agree with this reasoning? Why, or why not?

5. Singer confesses (para. 22) to being made especially angry "with my fellow men" after reading the accounts of animal experimentation. What is it that aroused his anger? Do such feelings, and the acknowledgment that one has them, have any place in a sober discussion about the merits of animal experimentation? Why, or why not?

6. What is "factory farming" (paras. 32–40)? Why is Singer opposed to it?

7. To the claim that there is nothing wrong with "rearing animals for food," provided it is done "humanely" (para. 41), Singer offers two replies (paras. 42–44). In an essay of 250 words, summarize them briefly and then indicate whether either persuades you and why or why not.

8. Suppose someone were to say to Singer: "You claim that capacity to suffer is the relevant factor in deciding whether a creature deserves to be treated as my moral equal. But you're wrong. The relevant factor is whether the creature is *alive*. Being alive is what matters, not being capable of feeling pain." In one or two paragraphs declare what you think would be Singer's reply.

9. Do you think it is worse to kill an animal for its fur than to kill, cook, and eat an animal? Is it worse to kill an animal for sport than to kill it for medical experimentation? What is Singer's view? Explain your view, making use of Singer's if you wish, in an essay of 500 words.

10. Are there any arguments, in your opinion, that show the immorality of eating human flesh (cannibalism) but that do not show a similar objection to eating animal flesh? Write a 500-word essay in which you discuss the issue.

JONATHAN SAFRAN FOER

Jonathan Safran Foer (b. 1977) is an American author best known for his novels, Everything Is Illuminated *(2002) and* Extremely Loud and Incredibly Close *(2005). In addition to writing two more recent novels, Safran Foer also wrote a nonfiction work expressing his views on vegetarianism,* Eating Animals *(2009). The following piece is from the* Wall Street Journal *around the time* Eating Animals *was published.*

Let Them Eat Dog: A Modest Proposal for Tossing Fido in the Oven

Despite the fact that it's perfectly legal in 44 states, eating "man's best friend" is as taboo as a man eating his best friend. Even the most enthusiastic carnivores won't eat dogs. TV guy and sometimes cooker Gordon Ramsay can get pretty macho with lambs and piglets when doing publicity for something he's selling, but you'll never see a puppy peeking out of one of his pots. And though he once said he'd electrocute his children if they became vegetarian, one can't help but wonder what his response would be if they poached the family pooch.

Dogs are wonderful, and in many ways unique. But they are remarkably unremarkable in their intellectual and experiential capacities. Pigs are every bit as intelligent and feeling, by any sensible definition of the words. They can't hop into the back of a Volvo, but they can fetch, run and play, be mischievous and reciprocate affection. So why don't they get to curl up by the fire? Why can't they at least be spared being tossed on the fire? Our taboo against dog eating says something about dogs and a great deal about us.

The French, who love their dogs, sometimes eat their horses.

The Spanish, who love their horses, sometimes eat their cows.

The Indians, who love their cows, some-⁵ times eat their dogs.

While written in a much different context, George Orwell's words (from *Animal Farm*) apply here: "All animals are equal, but some animals are more equal than others."

So who's right? What might be the reasons to exclude canine from the menu? The selective carnivore suggests:

Don't eat companion animals. But dogs aren't kept as companions in all of the places they are eaten. And what about our petless neighbors? Would we have any right to object if they had dog for dinner?

OK, then: Don't eat animals with significant mental capacities. If by "significant mental capacities" we mean what a dog has, then good for the dog. But such a definition would also include the pig, cow and chicken. And it would exclude severely impaired humans.

Then: It's for good reason that the eternal ¹⁰ taboos — don't fiddle with your crap, kiss your sister, or eat your companions — are taboo. Evolutionarily speaking, those things are bad for us. But dog eating isn't a taboo in many places, and it isn't in any way bad for us. Properly cooked, dog meat poses no greater health risks than any other meat.

Dog meat has been described as "gamey," "complex," "buttery" and "floral." And there is a proud pedigree of eating it. Fourth-century tombs contain depictions of dogs being slaughtered along with other food animals. It was a fundamental enough habit to have informed language itself: the Sino-Korean character for "fair and proper" (yeon) literally translates into "as cooked dog meat is delicious." Hippocrates praised dog meat as a source of strength. Dakota Indians enjoyed dog liver, and not so long ago Hawaiians ate dog brains and blood. Captain Cook ate dog. Roald Amundsen famously ate his sled dogs. (Granted, he was really hungry.) And dogs are still eaten to overcome bad luck in the Philippines; as medicine in China and Korea; to enhance libido in Nigeria and in numerous places, on every continent, because they taste good. For centuries, the Chinese have raised special breeds of dogs, like the black-tongued chow, for chow, and many European countries still have laws on the books regarding postmortem examination of dogs intended for human consumption.

Of course, something having been done just about everywhere is no kind of justification for doing it now. But unlike all farmed meat, which requires the creation and maintenance of animals, dogs are practically begging to be eaten. Three to four million dogs and cats are euthanized annually. The simple disposal of these euthanized dogs is an enormous ecological and economic problem. But eating those strays, those runaways, those not-quite-cute-enough-to-take and not-quite-well-behaved-enough-to-keep dogs would be killing a flock of birds with one stone and eating it, too.

In a sense it's what we're doing already. Rendering — the conversion of animal protein unfit for human consumption into food for livestock and pets — allows processing plants to transform useless dead dogs into productive members of the food chain. In America, millions of dogs and cats euthanized in animal shelters every year become the food for our food. So let's just eliminate this inefficient and bizarre middle step.

This need not challenge our civility. We won't make them suffer any more than necessary. While it's widely believed that adrenaline makes dog meat taste better — hence the traditional methods of slaughter: hanging, boiling alive, beating to death — we can all agree that if we're going to eat them, we should kill them quickly and painlessly, right? For example, the traditional Hawaiian means of holding the dog's nose shut — in order to conserve blood — must be regarded (socially if not legally) as a no-no. Perhaps we could include dogs under the Humane Methods of Slaughter Act. That doesn't say anything about how they're treated during their lives, and isn't subject to any meaningful oversight or enforcement, but surely we can rely on the industry to "self-regulate," as we do with other eaten animals.

Few people sufficiently appreciate the [15] colossal task of feeding a world of billions of omnivores who demand meat with their potatoes. The inefficient use of dogs — conveniently already in areas of high human population (take note, local-food advocates) — should make any good ecologist blush. One could argue that various "humane" groups are the worst hypocrites, spending enormous amounts of money and energy in a futile attempt to reduce the number of unwanted dogs while at the very same time propagating the irresponsible no-dog-for-dinner taboo. If we let dogs be dogs, and breed without interference, we would create a sustainable, local meat supply with low energy inputs that would put even the most efficient grass-based farming to shame. For the ecologically-minded it's time to admit that dog is realistic food for realistic environmentalists.

For those already convinced, here's a classic Filipino recipe I recently came across. I haven't tried it myself, but sometimes you can read a recipe and just know.

STEWED DOG, WEDDING STYLE

First, kill a medium-sized dog, then burn off the fur over a hot fire. Carefully remove the skin while still warm and set aside for later (may be used in other recipes). Cut meat into 1" cubes. Marinate meat in mixture of vinegar, peppercorn, salt, and garlic for 2 hours. Fry meat in oil using a large wok over an open fire, then add onions and chopped pineapple and saute until tender. Pour in tomato sauce and boiling water, add green pepper, bay leaf, and Tabasco. Cover and simmer over warm coals until meat is tender. Blend in puree of dog's liver and cook for additional 5–7 minutes.

There is an overabundance of rational reasons to say no to factory-farmed meat: It is the No. 1 cause of global warming, it systematically forces tens of billions of animals to suffer in ways that would be illegal if they were dogs, it is a decisive factor in the development of swine and avian flus, and so on. And yet even most people who know these things still aren't inspired to order something else on the menu. Why?

Food is not rational. Food is culture, habit, craving and identity. Responding to factory farming calls for a capacity to care that dwells beyond information. We know what we see on undercover videos of factory farms and slaughterhouses is wrong. (There are those who will defend a system that allows for occasional animal cruelty, but no one defends the cruelty, itself.) And despite it being entirely reasonable, the case for eating dogs is likely repulsive to just about every reader of this paper. The instinct comes before our reason, and is more important.

Topics for Critical Thinking and Writing

1. What is the author's persona in this essay? Is his presentation effective?

2. In the headnote for this piece, you are told Jonathan Safran Foer is an outspoken vegetarian, yet the title reveals what he will be arguing. How would you characterize the author's "modest proposal" and the actual goal of his argument?

3. In paragraph 7, Safran Foer begins to address arguments against eating dog meat by "selective carnivores" who apparently do not hesitate to eat other kinds of animals. Is Safran Foer's suggestion that their arguments are not valid convincing? Why, or why not?

4. What other arguments does Safran Foer make to convince readers of the potential benefits of eating dogs? What do you think is his actual position on eating dogs? On factory farming? On using dogs as an efficient solution to factory farming? How do you know he is not serious?

5. What do you think is the purpose for providing the recipe for "Stewed Dog?"

6. Safran Foer is writing his own take on the famous satirical essay by Jonathan Swift. Swift's original "Modest Proposal" (1729) criticized cruel attitudes toward the poor by arguing that the impoverished Irish could sell their children as food to the rich ("A young healthy child well nursed, is, at one year old, a most delicious nourishing and wholesome food . . ."). Write your own "modest proposal," ironically suggesting an absurd solution to a problem. Possible topics: health care, illegal immigrants, overcrowded jails, children who have committed a serious crime, homeless people. The modern version of the problem to which the proposal should be addressed is called "population policy." How would you describe our nation's current population policy? Do we have an adequate population policy, in fact? If not, what would you propose? If we do have one, what changes could you propose?

6

Developing an Argument of Your Own

The difficult part in an argument is not to defend one's opinion but to know what it is.

— ANDRÉ MAUROIS

Imagine that you enter a parlor. You come late. When you arrive, others have long preceded you, and they are engaged in a heated discussion, a discussion too heated for them to pause and tell you exactly what it is about. In fact, the discussion had already begun long before any of them got there, so that no one present is qualified to retrace for you all the steps that had gone before. You listen for a while, until you decide that you have caught the tenor of the argument; then you put in your oar. Someone answers; you answer him; another comes to your defense; another aligns himself against you, to either the embarrassment or gratification of your opponent, depending upon the quality of your ally's assistance. However, the discussion is interminable. The hour grows late, you must depart. And you do depart, with the discussion still vigorously in progress. — KENNETH BURKE

No greater misfortune could happen to anyone than that of developing a dislike for argument.

— PLATO

Planning, Drafting, and Revising an Argument

First, hear the wisdom of Mark Twain: "When the Lord finished the world, He pronounced it good. That is what I said about my first work, too. But Time, I tell you, Time takes the confidence out of these incautious early opinions."

All of us, teachers and students, have our moments of confidence, but for the most part we know that it takes considerable effort to write clear, thoughtful, seemingly effortless prose. In a conversation we can cover ourselves with such expressions as "Well, I don't know, but I sort of think . . ." and we can always revise our position ("Oh, well, I didn't mean it that way"), but once we have handed in the final version of our writing, we are helpless. We are (putting it strongly) naked to our enemies.

GETTING IDEAS: ARGUMENT AS AN INSTRUMENT OF INQUIRY

In Chapter 1 we quoted Robert Frost, "To learn to write is to learn to have ideas," and we offered suggestions about generating ideas, a process traditionally called **invention**. A moment ago we said that we often improve our ideas when explaining them to someone else. Partly, of course, we're responding to questions or objections raised by our companion in the conversation. But partly we're responding to ourselves: Almost as soon as we hear what we have to say, we may find that it won't do, and if we're lucky, we may find a better idea surfacing. One of the best ways of getting ideas is to talk things over.

The process of talking things over usually begins with the text that you're reading: Your notes, your summary, and your annotations are a kind of dialogue between you and the author. You are also having a dialogue when you talk with friends about your topic. You are trying out and developing ideas. You're arguing, but not chiefly to persuade; rather, you're using argument in order to find the truth. Finally, after reading, taking notes, and talking, you may feel that you have some clear ideas and need only put them into writing. So you take up a sheet of blank paper, but then a paralyzing thought suddenly strikes: "I have ideas but just can't put them into words." The blank white page (or screen) stares back at you and you just can't seem to begin.

All writers, even professional ones, are familiar with this experience. Good writers know that waiting for inspiration is usually not the best strategy. You may be waiting a long time. The best thing to do is begin. Recall some of what we said in Chapter 1: *Writing is a way of thinking*. It's a way of *getting and developing ideas*. *Argument* is an instrument of inquiry as well as persuasion. It is an important part of *critical thinking*. It helps us clarify what we think. One reason we have trouble writing is our fear of putting ourselves on record, but another reason is our fear that we have no ideas worth putting down. However, by writing notes — or even free associations — and by writing a draft, no matter how weak, we can begin to think our way toward good ideas.

THREE BRAINSTORMING STRATEGIES: FREEWRITING, LISTING, AND DIAGRAMMING

If you are facing an issue, debate, or topic and don't know what to write, this is likely because you don't yet know what you think. If, after talking about the topic with yourself (via your reading notes) and others, you are still unclear on what you think, try one of these three strategies:

FREEWRITING   Write for five or six minutes, nonstop, without censoring what you produce. You may use what you write to improve your thinking. You may even dim your computer screen so you won't be tempted to look up and fiddle too soon with what you've just written. Once you have spent the time writing out your ideas, you can use what you've written to look further into the subject at hand.

Freewriting should be totally free. If you have some initial ideas, a good freewrite might look like this. (As a topic, let's imagine the writer below is thinking about how children's toys are constructed for different genders. The student is reflecting on the release of the Nerf Rebelle, a type of toy gun made specifically for girls.)

FREEWRITING: This year Nerf released a new toy made for girls, the Nerf Rebelle gun, an attempt the company made to offer toys for girls traditionally made for boys. This seems good — showing an effort toward equality between the sexes. Or is Nerf just trying to broaden its market and sell more toys (after all, boys are only half the population)? Or is it both? That could be my central question. But it is not like the gun makes no distinction between boys and girls. It is pink and purple and has feminine-looking designs on it. And with its "elle" ending the gun sounds small, cute, and girly. Does this toy represent true equality between the sexes, or does it just offer more in the way of feminine stereotypes? It shoots foam arrows, unlike the boys' version of the gun, which shoots bullets. This suggests Cupid, maybe — that is, the figure whose arrows inspire love — a stereotype that girls aren't saving the world but seeking love and marriage. Maybe it's also related to Katniss Everdeen from the *Hunger Games* movie. She carries a bow and arrow, too. Like a lot of female superheroes, Katniss is presented as both strong and sexy, powerful and vulnerable, masculine and feminine at the same time. What kind of messages does this send to young girls? Is it the same message suggested by the gun? Why do powerful women have to project traditional or stereotypical femininity at the same time? How does this work in other areas of life, like business and politics?

Notice that the writer here is jumping around, generating and exploring ideas while writing. Later she can return to the freewriting and begin organizing her ideas and observations. Notice that right in the middle of the freewriting she made a connection between the toy and the *Hunger Games* movie, and by extension to the larger culture in which forms of contemporary femininity can be found. This connection seems significant, and it may help the student to broaden her argument from a critique of the company's motives early on, to a more evidence-based piece about assumptions underlying certain trends in consumer and media culture. The point is that freewriting in this case led to new paths of inquiry and may have inspired further research into different kinds of toys and media.

LISTING   Writing down keywords, just as you do when making a shopping list, is another way of generating ideas. When you make a shopping list, you write *ketchup*, and the act of writing it reminds you that you also need hamburger rolls — and *that* in turn reminds you that you also need tuna fish. Similarly, when preparing a list of ideas for a paper, just writing down one item will often generate another. Of course, when you look over the list, you'll probably drop some of these ideas — the dinner menu will change — but you'll be making progress. If you have a smartphone or tablet, use it to write down your thoughts. You can even e-mail these notes to yourself so you can access them later.

Here's an example of a student listing questions and making associations that could help him focus on a specific argument within a larger debate. The subject here is whether prostitution should be legalized.

LIST: Prostitutes — Law — How has the law traditionally policed sex? — What types of prostitutes exist? — What is prostitution? — Where is it already legal? — How does it work in places where it is legal? — Individual rights vs. public good? — Why shouldn't people be allowed to sell sex? — What are the "bad" effects of prostitution socially? — How many prostitutes are arrested every year? — Could prostitution be taxed? — Who suffers most from enforcement? — Who would suffer most if it were legal? — If it were legal, could its negative effects be better controlled? — Aren't "escort services" really prostitution rings for people with more money? — How is that dealt with? — Who goes into the "oldest business" and why?

Notice that the student doesn't really know the answers yet but is asking questions by free-associating and seeing what turns up as a productive line of analysis. The questions range from the definition of prostitution to its effects, and they might inspire the student to do some basic Internet research or even deeper research. Once you make a list, see if you can observe patterns or similarities among the items you listed, or if you invented a question worthy of its own thesis statement (e.g., "The enforcement of prostitution laws hurts *X* group unequally, and it uses a lot of public money that could better be used in other areas or toward regulating the trade rather than jailing people").

DIAGRAMMING   Sketching a visual representation of an essay is a kind of listing. Three methods of diagramming are especially common.

- **Clustering**   As we discuss on page 6, you can make an effective cluster by writing, in the middle of a sheet of paper, a word or phrase summarizing your topic (e.g., *fracking;* see diagram below), circling it, and then writing down and circling a related word (e.g., *energy independence*). Perhaps this leads you to write *lower gas prices* and *clean energy.* You then circle these phrases and continue making connections. The next thing you think of is *environmental impact,* so you draw a line to *clean energy.* Then you think of *water pollution,* write it down and circle it, and draw another line to *environmental impact.* The next thing that occurs to you is *job creation,* so you write this down and circle it. You won't connect this to *clean energy,* but you might connect it to *lower gas prices* because both are generally positive economic effects. (If you can think of negative economic impacts on other industries or workers, write them down and circle them.) Keep going, jotting down ideas and making connections where possible, indicating relationships. Notice that you appear to be detailing and weighing the economic and environmental impacts of fracking. Whether you realized it or not, an argument is taking shape.

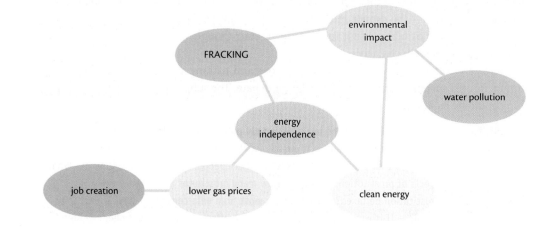

- *Branching*   Some writers find it useful to draw a tree, moving from the central topic to the main branches (chief ideas) and then to the twigs (aspects of the chief ideas).

- *Comparing in columns*   Draw a line down the middle of the page, and then set up two columns showing oppositions. For instance, if you are concerned with the environmental and economic impacts of fracking, you might head one column ENVIRONMENTAL and the other ECONOMIC. In the first column, you might write *water pollution, chemicals used,* and *other hazards?* In the second column, you might write *clean air, employment,* and *independence from unstable oil-producing countries.* You might go on to write, in the first column, *gas leaks* and *toxic waste,* and in the second, *cheaper fuel* and *cheaper electricity* — or whatever else relevant comes to mind.

All these methods can, of course, be executed with pen and paper, but you may also be able to use them on your computer depending on the capabilities of your software.

Whether you're using a computer or a pen, you put down some words and almost immediately see that they need improvement, not simply a little polishing but a substantial overhaul. You write, "Race should be counted in college admissions for two reasons," and as soon as you write those words, a third reason comes to mind. Or perhaps one of those "two reasons" no longer seems very good. As E. M. Forster said, "How can I know what I think till I see what I say?" We have to see what we say — we have to get something down on paper — before we realize that we need to make it better.

Writing, then, is really **rewriting** — that is, **revising** — and a revision is a *re-vision*, a second look. The essay that you submit — whether as hard copy or as a .doc file — should be clear and may appear to be effortlessly composed, but in all likelihood the clarity and apparent ease are the result of a struggle with yourself during which you refined your first thoughts. You begin by putting down ideas, perhaps in random order, but sooner or later comes the job of looking at them critically, developing what's useful in them and removing what isn't. If you follow this procedure you will be in the company of Picasso, who said that he "advanced by means of destruction." Any passages that you cut or destroy can be kept in another file in case you want to revisit those deletions later. Sometimes, you end up restoring them and developing what you discarded into a new essay with a new direction.

Whether you advance bit by bit (writing a sentence, revising it, writing the next, etc.) or whether you write an entire first draft and then revise it and revise it again and again is chiefly a matter of temperament. Probably most people combine both approaches, backing up occasionally but trying to get to the end fairly soon so that they can see rather quickly what they know, or think they know, and can then start the real work of thinking, of converting their initial ideas into something substantial.

FURTHER INVENTION STRATEGIES: ASKING GOOD QUESTIONS

ASKING QUESTIONS   Generating ideas, we said when talking about **topics** and **invention** strategies in Chapter 1 (p. 18) is mostly a matter of asking (and then thinking about) questions. In this book we include questions at the end of each argumentative essay, not to torment you but to help you think about the arguments — for instance, to turn your attention to especially important matters. If your instructor asks you to write an answer to one of these questions, you are lucky: Examining the question will stimulate your mind to work in a specific direction.

If your instructor doesn't assign a topic for an argumentative essay, you'll find that some ideas (possibly poor ones initially, but that doesn't matter because you'll soon revise) come to mind if you ask yourself questions. Begin determining where you stand on an issue (**stasis**) by asking the following five basic questions:

1. What is *X*?
2. What is the value of *X*?
3. What are the causes (or the consequences) of *X*?
4. What should (or ought or must) we do about *X*?
5. What is the evidence for my claims about *X*?

Let's spend a moment looking at each of these questions.

1. *What is X?* We can hardly argue about the number of people sentenced to death in the United States in 2000 — a glance at the appropriate government report will give the answer — but we can argue about whether capital punishment as administered in the United States is discriminatory. Does the evidence support the view that in the United States the death penalty is unfair? Similarly, we can ask whether a human fetus is a human being (in saying what something is, must we take account of its potentiality?), and even if we agree that a fetus is a human being, we can further ask whether it is a person. In *Roe v. Wade* the U.S. Supreme Court ruled that even the "viable" unborn human fetus is not a "person" as that term is used in the Fifth and Fourteenth Amendments. Here the question is this: Is the essential fact about the fetus that it is a person?

An argument of this sort makes a claim — that is, it takes a stand; but notice that it does not also have to argue for an action. Thus, it may argue that the death penalty is administered unfairly — that's a big enough issue — but it need not go on to argue that the death penalty should be abolished. After all, another possibility is that the death penalty should be administered fairly. The writer of the essay may be doing enough if he or she establishes the truth of the claim and leaves to others the possible responses.

2. *What is the value of X?* College courses often call for literary judgments. No one can argue if you say you prefer the plays of Tennessee Williams to those of Arthur Miller. But academic papers are not mere declarations of preferences. As soon as you say that Williams is a better playwright than Miller, you have based your preference on implicit standards, and you must support your preference by giving evidence about the relative skill, insight, and accomplishments of both Williams and Miller. Your argument is an evaluation. The question now at issue is the merits of the two authors and the standards appropriate for making such an appraisal.

In short, an essay offering an evaluation normally has two purposes:

- to set forth an assessment
- to convince the reader that the assessment is reasonable

In writing an evaluation, you have to rely on criteria, and these will vary depending on your topic. For instance, in comparing the artistic merit of plays by Williams and by Miller, you may want to talk about the quality of the characterization, the importance of the theme, and so on. But if the topic is "Which playwright is more suitable to be taught in high school?" other criteria may be appropriate, such as these:

- the difficulty of the author's language
- the sexual content of some scenes
- the presence of obscene words

Alternatively, consider a nonliterary issue: On balance, are college fraternities and sororities good or bad? If good, how good? If bad, how bad? What criteria serve best in making our evaluation? Probably some or all of the following:

- testimony of authorities (e.g., persons who can offer firsthand testimony about the good or bad effects)
- inductive evidence (examples of good or bad effects)
- appeals to logic ("it follows, therefore, that . . .")
- appeals to emotion (e.g., an appeal to our sense of fairness)

3. What are the causes (or the consequences) of X?   Why did the rate of auto theft increase during a specific period? If the death penalty is abolished, will that cause the rate of murder to increase? Problems such as these may be complex. The phenomena that people usually argue about — such as inflation, war, suicide, crime — have many causes, and it can be a mistake to speak of *the* cause of X. A writer in *Time* mentioned that the life expectancy of an average American male is about sixty-seven years, a figure that compares unfavorably with the life expectancy of males in Japan and Israel. The *Time* writer suggested that an important cause of the American male's relatively short life span is "the pressure to perform well in business." Perhaps. But the life expectancy of plumbers is no greater than that of managers and executives. Nutrition authority Jean Mayer, in an article in *Life,* attributed the relatively poor longevity of American males to a diet that is "rich in fat and poor in nutrients." Doubtless other authorities propose other causes, and in all likelihood no one cause entirely accounts for the phenomenon.

Consider a second example of discussions of causality, this one concerning the academic performance of girls in single-sex elementary schools, middle schools, and high schools. It is pretty much agreed (based on statistical evidence) that the graduates of these schools do better, as a group, than girls who graduate from coeducational schools. *Why* do girls in single-sex schools tend, as a group, to do better? What is the *cause*? The administrators of girls' schools usually attribute the success to the fact (we're putting the matter bluntly here) that young women flourish better in an atmosphere free from male intimidation: They allegedly gain confidence and become more expressive when they aren't threatened by the presence of males. This may be the answer, but skeptics have attributed the graduates' success to two other causes:

- Most single-sex schools require parents to pay tuition, and it is a documented fact that the children of well-to-do parents do better, academically, than the children of poor parents.

- Most single-sex schools are private schools, and they select students from a pool of candidates. Admissions officers select those candidates who seem to be academically promising — that is, students who have *already done well academically.*

In short, the girls who graduate from single-sex schools may owe their later academic success not to the schools' single-sex environment but to the fact that even at admission the students were academically stronger (again, we're speaking of a cohort, not of individuals) than the girls who attend coeducational schools.

The lesson? Be cautious in attributing a cause. There may be several causes.

The kinds of support that usually accompany claims of cause include the following:

- factual data, especially statistics
- analogies ("The Roman Empire declined because of X and Y"; "Our society exhibits X and Y; therefore . . .")
- inductive evidence

4. ***What should (or ought or must) we do about*** **X?** Must we always obey the law? Should the law allow eighteen-year-olds to drink alcohol? Should eighteen-year-olds be drafted to do one year of social service? Should pornography be censored? Should steroid use by athletes be banned? Ought there to be Good Samaritan laws, making it a legal duty for a stranger to intervene to save a person from death or great bodily harm, when one might do so with little or no risk to oneself? These questions involve conduct and policy; how we answer them will reveal our values and principles.

An essay answering questions of this sort usually has the following characteristics:

- It begins by explaining what the issue (the problem) is.
- Then it states why the reader should care about the issue.
- Next, it offers the proposed solution.
- Then it considers alternative solutions.
- Finally, it reaffirms the merit of the proposed solution, especially in light of the audience's interests and needs.

You'll recall that throughout this book we have spoken about devices that help a writer to generate ideas. If in drafting an essay concerned with policy you begin by writing down your thoughts on the five bulleted items listed above, you'll almost surely uncover ideas that you didn't know you had.

Support for claims of policy usually include the following:

- statistics
- appeals to common sense and to the reader's moral sense
- testimony of authorities

5. What is the evidence for my claims about X?   In commenting on the four previous topics, we have talked about the kinds of support that writers commonly offer. However, a few additional points are important.

Critical reading, writing, and thinking depend on identifying and evaluating the evidence for and against the claims one makes and encounters in the writings of others. It isn't enough to have an *opinion* or belief one way or the other; you need to be able to support your opinions — the bare fact of your sincere belief in what you say or write is not itself any *evidence* that what you believe is true.

What constitutes good reasons for opinions and adequate evidence for beliefs? The answer depends on the type of belief or opinion, assertion or hypothesis, claim or principle you want to assert. For example, there is good evidence that President John F. Kennedy was assassinated on November 22, 1963, because this is the date for his death reported in standard almanacs. You could further substantiate the date by checking the back issues of the *New York Times*. But a different kind of evidence is needed to support the proposition that the chemical composition of water is H_2O. And you would need still other kinds of evidence to support your beliefs about the likelihood of rain tomorrow, the probability that the Red Sox will win the pennant this year, the twelfth digit in the decimal expansion of pi, the average cumulative grades of graduating seniors over the past three years in your college, the relative merits of *Hamlet* and *Death of a Salesman,* and the moral dimensions of sexual harassment. None of these issues is merely a matter of opinion; yet about some of them, educated and informed people may disagree over the reasons, the evidence, and what they show. Sometimes, equally qualified experts examine the same evidence and draw different conclusions. Your job as a critical thinker is to be alert to the relevant reasons and evidence, as well as the basis of various conclusions, and to make the most of them as you present your views.

Again, an argument may answer two or more of our five basic questions. Someone who argues that pornography should (or should not) be censored will have to do the following:

- Mark out the territory of the discussion by defining pornography (our first question: What is *X*?).

- Examine the consequences of adopting the preferred policy (our third question).

- Perhaps argue about the value of that policy (our second question). Some people maintain that pornography produces crime, but others maintain that it provides a harmless outlet for impulses that otherwise might vent themselves in criminal behavior.

- Address the possible objection that censorship, however desirable on account of some of its consequences, may be unconstitutional and that even if censorship were constitutional, it would (or might) have undesirable side effects, such as repressing freedom of political opinion.

- Keep in mind our fifth question: What is the evidence for my claims?

Thinking about one or more of these questions may get you going. For instance, thinking about What is *X*? will require you to produce a definition; and as you do this, new ideas might arise. If a question seems relevant, it's a good idea to start writing — even just a fragmentary sentence. You'll probably find that one word leads to another and that ideas begin to appear. Even if these ideas seem weak as you write them, don't be discouraged; you will have put something on paper, and returning to these words, perhaps in five minutes or the next day, you'll probably find that some aren't at all bad and that others will stimulate you to better ones.

It may be useful to record your ideas in a special notebook or in a private digital notebook or document reserved for the purpose. Such a **journal** can be a valuable resource when it comes time to write your paper. Many students find it easier to focus their thoughts on writing if during the gestation period they've been jotting down relevant ideas on something more substantial than slips of paper or loose sheets. The very act of designating a traditional or digital notebook or document file as your journal for a course can be the first step in focusing your attention on the eventual need to write a paper.

Take advantage of the free tools at your disposal. Use the Internet and free Web tools, including RSS feeds, Google (Drive, sites, and others), Yahoo!, blogs, and wikis to organize your initial ideas and to solicit feedback. Talking with others can help, but sometimes there isn't time to chat. By using an RSS feed on a Web site that you think will provide good information on your topic (or a topic you're considering), you can receive notifications if the site has uploaded new material such as news links or op-eds. Posting a blog entry in a public space about your topic can also foster conversations about the topic and help you discover other opinions. Using the Internet to uncover and refine a topic is common practice, especially early in the research process.

If what we have just said doesn't sound convincing, and if you know from experience that you have trouble getting started with writing, don't despair. First aid is at hand in a sure-fire method that we will explain next.

THE THESIS OR MAIN POINT

Let's assume that you are writing an argumentative essay — perhaps an evaluation of an argument in this book — and you have what seems to be a pretty good draft or at least a collection of notes that are the result of hard thinking. You really do have ideas now, and you want to present them effectively. How will you organize your essay? No one formula works best for every essayist and for every essay, but it is usually advisable to formulate a basic **thesis** (a claim, a central point, a chief position) and to state it early. Every essay that is any good, even a book-length one, has a thesis (a main point), which can be stated briefly — usually, in a sentence. Remember Coolidge's remark on the preacher's sermon on sin: "He was against it." Don't confuse the **topic** (sin) with the thesis (sin is bad). The thesis is the argumentative theme, the author's primary claim or contention, the proposition that the rest of the essay will explain and defend. Of course, the thesis may sound commonplace, but the book or essay or sermon ought to develop it in an interesting and convincing way.

RAISING THE STAKES OF YOUR THESIS   Imagine walking across campus and coming upon a person ready to perform on a tightrope suspended between two buildings. He is wearing a glittering leotard and is eyeing up his challenge very seriously. Here's the thing, though: His tightrope is only *one foot off the ground*. Would you stop and watch him walk across it? Maybe, maybe not. Most people are likely to take a look and move on. If you did spend a few minutes watching, you wouldn't be very worried about the performer falling. If he lost his balance momentarily, you wouldn't gasp in horror. And if he walked across the tightrope masterfully, you might be somewhat impressed but not enraptured.

Now imagine the rope being a hundred feet off the ground. You and many others would almost certainly stop and witness the feat. The audience would likely be captivated, nervous about the performer potentially falling, "oohing" if he momentarily lost his balance, and cheering if he crossed the rope successfully.

Consider the tightrope as your thesis statement, the performer as writer, and the act of crossing as the argument. What we call "low-stakes" thesis statements are comparable to low tightropes: A low-stakes thesis statement itself may be interesting, but not much about it is vital to any particular audience. Low-stakes thesis statements lack a sense of importance or relevance. They may restate what is already widely known and accepted, or they may make a good point but not discuss any consequences. Some examples:

Good nutrition and exercise can lead to a healthy life.

Our education system focuses too much on standardized tests.

Children's beauty pageants are exploitative.

Students can write well-organized, clear, and direct papers on these topics, but if the thesis is "low stakes" like these, then the performance would be similar to that of an expert walking across a tightrope *one foot off the ground*. The argument may be well executed, but few in the audience will be inspired by it.

However, if you raise the stakes by "raising the tightrope," you can compel readers to *want* to read and keep reading. There are several ways to raise the tightrope. First, *think about what is socially, culturally, or politically important* about your thesis statement and argument. Some

Pornchai Kittiwongsakul/Getty Images

Kay Nietfeld/AFP/Getty Images

Tightropes, like these, can be raised to many different levels.

writing instructors tell students to ask themselves "so what?" about the thesis, but this can be a vague directive. Here are some better questions: Why is your thesis important? What is the impact of your thesis on a particular group or demographic? What are the consequences of what you claim? What could happen if your position were *not* recognized? How can your argument benefit readers or compel them to action (by doing something or adopting a new belief)? What will readers *gain* by accepting your argument as convincing?

In formulating your thesis, keep in mind these points:

Different thesis statements may speak to different target audiences. An argument about changes in estate tax laws may not thrill all audiences, but for a defined group — accountants, lawyers, or the elderly, for instance — this may be quite controversial and highly relevant.

> ### A CHECKLIST FOR A THESIS STATEMENT
>
> Consider the following questions:
>
> ☐ Does the statement make an arguable assertion rather than (1) merely assert an unarguable fact, (2) merely announce a topic, or (3) declare an unarguable opinion or belief?
>
> ☐ Is the statement broad enough to cover the entire argument that I will be presenting, and is it narrow enough for me to cover the topic in the space allotted?

Not all audiences are equal — or equally interested in your thesis or argument. In this book, we generally select topics of broad importance. However, in a literature course, a film history course, or a political science course, you'll calibrate your thesis statements and arguments to an audience who is invested in those fields. In writing about the steep decline in bee populations, your argument might look quite different if you're speaking to ecologists as opposed to gardeners. (We will discuss audience in greater detail in the following section.)

Be wary of compare-and-contrast arguments. One of the most basic approaches to writing is to compare and contrast, a maneuver that produces a low-tightrope thesis. It normally looks like this: "X *and Y are similar in some ways and different in others.*" But if you think about it, *anything* can be compared and contrasted in this way, and doing so doesn't necessarily *tell* anything important. So, if you're writing a compare-and-contrast paper, make sure to include the reasons why it is important to compare and contrast these things. What benefit does the comparison yield? What significance does it have to some audience, some area of knowledge, some field of study?

IMAGINING AN AUDIENCE

Raising the tightrope of your thesis will also require you to imagine the *audience* you're addressing. The questions that you ask yourself in generating thoughts on a topic will primarily relate to the topic, but additional questions that consider the audience are always relevant:

- Who are my readers?
- What do they believe?
- What common ground do we share?

- What do I want my readers to believe?
- What do they need to know?
- Why should they care?

Let's think about these questions. The literal answer to the first probably is "my teacher," but (unless you receive instructions to the contrary) you should not write specifically for your teacher. Instead, you should write for an audience that is, generally speaking, like your classmates. In short, your imagined audience is literate, intelligent, and moderately well informed, but its members don't know everything that you know, and they don't know your response to the problem being addressed. Your audience needs more information along those lines to make an intelligent decision about the issue.

For example, in writing about how children's toys shape the minds of young boys and girls differently, it may not be enough to simply say, "Toys are part of the gender socialization process." ("Sure they are," the audience might already agree.) However, if you raise the stakes, you have an opportunity to frame the questions that result from this observation: You frame the questions, lay out the issues, identify the problems, and note the complications that arise because of your basic thesis. You could point out that toys have a significant impact on the interests, identities, skills, and capabilities that children develop and carry into adulthood.

Because toys are so significant, is it important to ask questions about whether they perpetuate gender-based stereotypes? Do toys help perpetuate social inequalities between the sexes? Most children think toys are "just fun," but they may be teaching kids to conform unthinkingly to the social expectations of their sex, to accept designated sex-based social roles, and to cultivate talents differently based on sex. Is this a good or a bad thing? Do toys facilitate growth, or do they have any limiting effects?

What audiences should be concerned with your topic? Maybe you're addressing the general public who buys toys for children at least some of the time. Maybe you're addressing parents who are raising young children. Maybe you're addressing consumer advocates, encouraging them to pressure toy manufacturers and retailers to produce more gender-neutral offerings. The point is that your essay should contain (and sustain) an assessment of the impact of your high-stakes thesis, and it should set out a clear course of action for a particular audience.

That said, if you know your audience well, you can argue for different courses of action that are most likely to be persuasive. You may not be very convincing if you argue to parents in general that they should never buy princess toys for their girls and avoid all Disney-themed toys. Perhaps you should argue simply that parents should be conscious of the gender messages that toys convey, offer their kids diverse toys, and talk to their children while playing with them about alternatives to the stereotypical messages that the toys convey. However, if you're writing for a magazine called *Radical Parenting* and your essay is titled "Buying Toys the Gender-Neutral Way," your audience and its expectations — therefore, your thesis and argument — may look far different. The bottom line is not just to know your audience but to define it.

The essays in this book are from many different sources with many different audiences. An essay from the *New York Times* addresses educated general readers; an essay from *Ms.* magazine targets readers sympathetic to feminism. An essay from *Commonweal,* a Roman Catholic publication for nonspecialists, is likely to differ in point of view or tone from one in *Time,* even though both articles may advance approximately the same position. The *Commonweal* article may, for example, effectively cite church fathers and distinguished Roman Catholic writers as authorities, whereas the *Time* article would probably cite few or none of these figures because a non-Catholic audience might be unfamiliar with them or, even if familiar, might be unimpressed by their views.

The tone as well as the gist of the argument is in some degree shaped by the audience. For instance, popular journals, such as *National Review* and *Ms.* Magazine, are more likely to use ridicule than are journals chiefly addressed to, say, an academic audience.

THE AUDIENCE AS COLLABORATOR

If you imagine a particular audience and ask yourself what it does and doesn't need to be told, you will find that material comes to mind, just as when a friend asks you what a film you saw was about, who was in it, and how you liked it.

Your readers don't have to be told that Thomas Jefferson was an American statesman in the early years of this country's history, but they do have to be told that Elizabeth Cady Stanton was a late-nineteenth-century American feminist. Why? Because it's your hunch that your classmates never heard of her, or even if they have heard the name, they can't quite identify it. But what if your class has been assigned an essay by Stanton? In that case your imagined readers know Stanton's name and at least a little about her, so you don't have to identify her as an American of the nineteenth century. But you do still have to remind readers about relevant aspects of her essay, and you have to tell them about your responses to those aspects.

After all, even if the instructor has assigned an essay by Stanton, you cannot assume that your classmates know the essay inside out. You can't say, "Stanton's third reason is also unconvincing," without reminding the reader, by means of a brief summary, of her third reason. Again:

- Think of your classmates — people like you — as your imagined readers.
- Be sure that your essay does not make unreasonable demands.

If you ask yourself,

- "What do my readers need to know?" and
- "What do I want them to believe?"

you will find some answers arising, and you will start writing.

We've said that you should imagine your audience as your classmates. But this isn't the whole truth. In a sense, your argument is addressed not simply to your classmates but to the world interested in ideas. Even if you can reasonably assume that your classmates have read only one work by Stanton, you can't begin your essay by writing, "Stanton's essay is deceptively easy." You have to name the work because it's possible that a reader is familiar with some other work by Stanton. And by precisely identifying your subject, you ease the reader into your essay.

Similarly, you won't open with a statement like this:

The majority opinion in *Walker v. City of Birmingham* held that . . .

Rather, you'll write something like this:

In *Walker v. City of Birmingham*, the U.S. Supreme Court ruled in 1966 that city authorities acted lawfully when they jailed Martin Luther King Jr. and other clergymen in 1963 for marching in Birmingham without a permit. Justice Potter Stewart delivered the majority opinion, which held that . . .

By the way, if you suffer from a writing block, the mere act of writing out such readily available facts will help you to get started. You'll find that writing a few words, perhaps merely copying the essay's title or an interesting quotation from the essay, will stimulate other thoughts that you didn't know you had.

Here, again, are the questions about audience. If you write on a computer, consider putting these questions into a file. For each assignment, copy the questions into the file you're working on, and then, as a way of generating ideas, *enter your responses, indented, under each question.*

1. Who are my readers?
2. What do they believe?
3. What common ground do we share?

4. What do I want my readers to believe?

5. What do they need to know?

6. Why should they care?

Thinking about your audience can help you get started; even more important, it can help you generate ideas. Our second and third questions about the audience ("What do they believe?" and "How much common ground do we share?") will usually help you get ideas flowing.

- Presumably, your imagined audience does not share your views, or at least does not fully share them. But why?

- How can these readers hold a position that to you seems unreasonable?

By putting yourself into your readers' shoes — and your essay will almost surely summarize the views that you're going to speak against — and by thinking about what your audience knows or thinks it knows, you will generate ideas. Spend time online reviewing Web sites dedicated to your topic. What do they have to say, and why do the authors hold these views?

Let's assume that you don't believe that people should be allowed to smoke in enclosed public places, but you know that some people hold a different view. Why do they hold it? Try to state their view *in a way that would be satisfactory to them*. Having done so, you may perceive that your conclusions and theirs differ because they're based on different premises — perhaps different ideas about human rights. Examine the opposition's premises carefully, and explain, first to yourself and ultimately to your readers, why you find some of those premises to be unacceptable.

Perhaps some facts are in dispute, such as whether exposure to tobacco is harmful to non-smokers. The thing to do, then, is to check the facts. If you find that harm to nonsmokers has not been proved but you nevertheless believe that smoking should be prohibited in enclosed public places, of course you can't premise your argument on the wrongfulness of harming the innocent (in this case, the nonsmokers). You'll have to develop arguments that take account of the facts.

Among the relevant facts there surely are some that your audience or your opponent will not dispute. The same is true of the values relevant to the discussion; both sides very likely believe in some of the same values (such as the principle mentioned above, that it is wrong to harm the innocent). These areas of shared agreement are crucial to effective persuasion in argument.

There are two good reasons for identifying and isolating the areas of agreement:

- There is no point in disputing facts or values on which you and your readers already agree.

- It usually helps to establish goodwill between yourself and your opponent when you can point to shared beliefs, assumptions, facts, and values.

> **A RULE FOR WRITERS**
> If you wish to persuade, you have to begin by finding premises that you can share with your audience.

In a few moments we will return to the need to share some of the opposition's ideas.

Recall that in composing college papers it's usually best to write for a general audience, an audience rather like your classmates but without the specific knowledge that they all share as students enrolled in one course. If the topic is smoking in public places, the audience presumably consists of smokers and nonsmokers. Thinking about our fifth question on page 236 — "What do [readers] need to know?" — may prompt you to give statistics about the harmful effects of smoking. Or if you're arguing on behalf of smokers, it may prompt you to cite studies claiming that no evidence conclusively demonstrates that cigarette smoking is harmful to nonsmokers. If indeed you are writing for a general audience and you are not advancing a highly unfamiliar view, our second question ("What does the audience believe?") is less important here; but if the audience is specialized, such as an antismoking group, a group of restaurant owners who fear that antismoking regulations will interfere with their business, or a group of civil libertarians, an effective essay will have to address their special beliefs.

In addressing their beliefs (let's assume that you don't share them — at least, not fully), you must try to establish some common ground. If you advocate requiring restaurants to provide nonsmoking areas, you should recognize the possibility that this arrangement will result in inconvenience for the proprietor. But perhaps (the good news) the restaurant will regain some lost customers or attract some new customers. This thought should prompt you to think of other kinds of evidence — perhaps testimony or statistics.

When you formulate a thesis and ask questions about it — such as who the readers are, what they believe, what they know, and what they need to know — you begin to get ideas about how to organize the material (or, at least, you realize that you'll have to work out some sort of organization). The thesis may be clear and simple, but the reasons (the argument) may take many pages. The thesis is the point; the argument sets forth the evidence that supports the thesis.

> ## A CHECKLIST FOR IMAGINING AN AUDIENCE
>
> Have I asked myself the following questions?
>
> ☐ Who are my readers? How do I know?
>
> ☐ How much about the topic do they already know?
>
> ☐ Have I provided necessary background (including definitions of special terms) if the imagined readers probably are not especially familiar with the topic?
>
> ☐ Are these imagined readers likely to be neutral? Sympathetic? Hostile? Have I done enough online research to offer something useful to a hostile audience?
>
> ☐ If they're neutral, have I offered good reasons to persuade them? If they're sympathetic, have I done more than merely reaffirm their present beliefs? That is, have I perhaps enriched their views or encouraged them to act? If they're hostile, have I taken account of their positions, recognized their strengths but also called attention to their limitations, and offered a position that might persuade these hostile readers to modify their position?

THE TITLE

It's a good idea to announce the thesis in your essay's **title**. If you scan the table of contents of this book, you'll notice that a fair number of essayists use the title to let readers know, at least in a general way, what position they will advocate. Here are a few examples of titles that take a position:

Forgive Student Loans? Worst Idea Ever

Millennials Are Selfish and Entitled, and Helicopter Parents Are to Blame

The Draft Would Compel Us to Share the Sacrifice

True, these titles are not especially engaging, but the reader welcomes them because they give some information about the writer's thesis.

Some titles don't announce the thesis, but they do announce the topic:

Are We Slaves to Our Online Selves?

On Racist Speech

Should Governments Tax Unhealthy Foods and Drinks?

Although not clever or witty, the above titles are informative.

Some titles seek to attract attention or to stimulate the imagination:

A First Amendment Junkie

Why I Don't Spare "Spare Change"

Building Baby from the Genes Up

All of these are effective, but a word of caution is appropriate here. In seeking to engage your readers' attention, be careful not to sound like a wise guy. You want to engage the readers, not turn them off.

Finally, be prepared to rethink your title *after* completing the last draft of your paper. A title somewhat different from your working title may be an improvement because the finished paper may emphasize something entirely different from what you expected when you first gave it a title.

THE OPENING PARAGRAPHS

Opening paragraphs are difficult to write, so don't worry about writing an effective opening when you're drafting. Just get some words down on paper and keep going. But when you revise your first draft, you should begin to think seriously about the effect of your opening.

A good introduction arouses readers' interest and prepares them for the rest of the paper. How? Opening paragraphs usually do at least one (and often all) of the following:

- attract readers' interest (often with a bold thesis statement or an interesting relevant statistic, quotation, or anecdote)
- prepare readers by giving some idea of the topic and often of the thesis

- give readers an idea of how the essay is organized
- define a key term

You may not wish to announce your thesis in the title, but if you don't announce it there, you should set it forth early in the argument, in the introductory paragraph or paragraphs. In an essay titled "Human Rights and Foreign Policy" (1982), U.S. ambassador to the United Nations Jeanne J. Kirkpatrick merely announces her topic (subject) as opposed to her thesis (point), but she hints at the thesis in her first paragraph, by deprecating President Jimmy Carter's policy:

> In this paper I deal with three broad subjects: first, the content and consequences of the Carter administration's human rights policy; second, the prerequisites of a more adequate theory of human rights; and third, some characteristics of a more successful human rights policy.

Alternatively, consider this opening paragraph from Peter Singer's "Animal Liberation" (p. 205):

> We are familiar with Black Liberation, Gay Liberation, and a variety of other movements. With Women's Liberation some thought we had come to the end of the road. Discrimination on the basis of sex, it has been said, is the last form of discrimination that is universally accepted and practiced without pretense, even in those liberal circles which have long prided themselves on their freedom from racial discrimination. But one should always be wary of talking of "the last remaining form of discrimination." If we have learned anything from the liberation movements, we should have learned how difficult it is to be aware of the ways in which we discriminate until they are forcefully pointed out to us. A liberation movement demands an expansion of our moral horizons, so that practices that were previously regarded as natural and inevitable are now seen as intolerable.

Although Singer's introductory paragraph nowhere mentions animal liberation, in conjunction with the essay's title it gives a good idea of what Singer is up to and where he is going. He knows that his audience will be skeptical, so he reminds them that in previous years many people were skeptical of reforms that are now taken for granted. He adopts a strategy used fairly often by writers who advance unconventional theses: Rather than beginning with a bold announcement of a thesis that may turn off some readers because it sounds offensive or absurd, Singer warms up his audience, gaining their interest by cautioning them politely that although they may at first be skeptical of animal liberation, if they stay with his essay they may come to feel that they have expanded their horizons.

Notice, too, that Singer begins by establishing common ground with his readers; he assumes, probably correctly, that they share his view that other forms of discrimination (now seen to be unjust) were once widely practiced and were assumed to be acceptable and natural. In this paragraph, then, Singer is not only showing himself to be fair-minded but is also letting readers know that he will advance a daring idea. His opening wins their attention and goodwill. A writer can hardly hope to do more. (Soon we'll talk a little more about winning the audience.)

Keep in mind the following points when writing introductory paragraphs:

- You may have to give background information that readers should keep in mind if they are to follow your essay.

- You may wish to define some terms that are unfamiliar or that you use in an unusual sense.

- If you're writing for an online publication (where your instructor or audience will encounter your argument on the Web), you might establish a context for your argument by linking to a news video that outlines the topic, or you might offer your thesis and then link to a news story that supports your claim. (Remember that using any videos, images, or links also requires a citation of some kind.) The beauty of publishing the piece in an online environment is that you can link directly to sources and use them more easily than if you were submitting a hard copy.

After announcing the topic, giving the necessary background, and stating your position (and perhaps the opposition's) in as engaging a manner as possible, you will do well to give the reader an idea of *how* you will proceed — that is, what the organization will be. In other words, use the introduction to set up the organization of your essay. Your instructors may assign four- to six-page mini-research papers or ten- to fifteen-page research papers; if they assign an online venue, ask them about the approximate word count. No matter what the length, every paper needs to have a clear organization. The introduction is where you can accomplish three key things:

- hook your reader

- reveal your thesis and topic

- explain how you will organize your discussion of the topic — what you'll do first, second, third, and so on.

Look at Kirkpatrick's opening paragraph (p. 239) for an illustration. She tells her readers that she will address three subjects, and she names them. Her approach in the paragraph is concise, obvious, and effective.

A RULE FOR WRITERS
In writing or revising introductory paragraphs, keep in mind this question: What do my readers need to know? Remember, your aim throughout is to write *reader-friendly* prose. Keeping the needs and interests of your audience constantly in mind will help you achieve this goal.

Similarly, you may want to announce fairly early that there are, say, four common objections to your thesis and that you will take them up one by one, beginning with the weakest (or most widely held) and moving to the strongest (or least familiar), after which you will advance your own view in greater detail. Not every argument begins with refuting the other side, though many arguments do. The point to remember is that you usually ought to tell readers where you will be taking them and by what route. In effect, you give them an outline.

ORGANIZING AND REVISING THE BODY OF THE ESSAY

We begin with a wise remark by a newspaper columnist, Robert Cromier: "The beautiful part of writing is that you don't have to get it right the first time — unlike, say, a brain surgeon."

In drafting an essay, you will of course begin with an organization that seems appropriate, but you may find, in rereading the draft, that some other organization is better. Here, for a start, is an organization that is common in argumentative essays:

1. Statement of the problem or issue
2. Statement of the structure of the essay (its organization)
3. Statement of alternative (but less adequate) solutions
4. Arguments in support of the proposed solution
5. Arguments answering possible objections
6. A summary, resolution, or conclusion

Let's look at each of these six steps.

1. Statement of the problem or issue   Whether the problem is stated briefly or at length depends on the nature of the problem and the writer's audience. If you haven't already defined unfamiliar terms or terms you use in a special way, now is the time to do so. In any case, it is advisable here to state the problem objectively (thereby gaining the reader's trust) and to indicate why the reader should care about the issue.

2. Statement of the structure of the essay   After stating the problem at the appropriate length, the writer often briefly indicates the structure of the rest of the essay. The structure used most frequently is suggested below, in points 3 and 4.

3. Statement of alternative (but less adequate) solutions   In addition to stating the alternatives fairly (letting readers know that you've done your homework), the writer conveys a willingness to recognize not only the integrity of opposing proposals but also the (partial) merit of at least some of the alternative solutions.

Our point in the previous sentence is important and worth amplifying. Because it is important to convey your goodwill — your sense of fairness — to the reader, it's advisable to show that you're familiar with the opposition and that you recognize the integrity of those who hold that view. You accomplish this by granting its merits as far as you can. (For more about this approach, see the essay by Carl R. Rogers on p. 375.)

The next stage, which constitutes most of the body of the essay, usually is this:

4. Arguments in support of the proposed solution   The evidence offered will depend on the nature of the problem. Relevant statistics, authorities, examples, or analogies may come to mind or be available. This is usually the longest part of the essay.

5. Arguments answering possible objections   These arguments may suggest the following:

a. The proposal won't work (perhaps it is alleged to be too expensive, to make unrealistic demands on human nature, or to fail to reach the heart of the problem).

b. The proposed solution will create problems greater than the problem under discussion. (A good example of a proposal that produced dreadful unexpected results is the law mandating a prison term for anyone over age eighteen in possession of an illegal drug. Heroin dealers then began to use children as runners, and cocaine importers followed the practice.)

6. A summary, resolution, or conclusion Here the writer may seek to accommodate the opposition's views as far as possible but clearly suggest that the writer's own position makes good sense. A conclusion—the word comes from the Latin *claudere*, "to shut"—ought to provide a sense of closure, but it can be much more than a restatement of the writer's thesis. It can, for instance, make a quiet emotional appeal by suggesting that the issue is important and that the ball is now in the reader's court.

Of course, not every essay will follow this six-step pattern. But let's assume that in the introductory paragraphs you have sketched the topic (and have shown, or implied, that the reader doubtless is interested in it) and have fairly and courteously set forth the opposition's view, recognizing its merits ("I grant that," "admittedly," "it is true that") and indicating the degree to which you can share part of that view. You now want to set forth arguments explaining why you differ on some essentials.

In presenting your own position, you can begin with either your strongest or your weakest reasons. Each method of organization has advantages and disadvantages.

- If you begin with your strongest reason, the essay may seem to peter out.
- If you begin with your weakest reason, you build to a climax; but readers may not still be with you because they may have felt at the start that the essay was frivolous.

The solution to the latter possibility is to ensure that even your weakest argument demonstrates strength. You can, moreover, assure your readers that stronger points will soon follow and you offer this point first in order to show that you are aware of it and that, slight though it is, it deserves some attention. The body of the essay, then, is devoted to arguing a position, which means offering not only supporting reasons but also refutations of possible objections to these reasons.

Doubtless you'll sometimes be uncertain, while drafting an essay, whether to present a given point before or after another point. When you write, and certainly when you revise, try to put yourself into the reader's shoes: Which point do you think the reader needs to know first? Which point *leads to* which further point? Your argument should not be a mere list of points; rather, it should clearly integrate one point with another in order to develop an idea. However, in all likelihood you won't have a strong sense of the best organization until you have written a draft and have reread it.

CHAPTER 6 | DEVELOPING AN ARGUMENT OF YOUR OWN

CHECKING PARAGRAPHS   When you revise a draft, watch out for short paragraphs. Although a paragraph of only two or three sentences (like some in this chapter) may occasionally be helpful as a transition between complicated points, most short paragraphs are undeveloped paragraphs. Newspaper editors favor very short paragraphs because they can be read rapidly when printed in the narrow columns typical of newspapers. Many of the essays reprinted in this book originally were published in newspapers and, thus, consist of very short paragraphs, but they should *not* be regarded as models for your own writing.

A second note about paragraphs: Writers for online venues often "chunk" (i.e., they provide extra space for paragraph breaks) rather than write a continuous flow. These writers chunk their text for several reasons, but chiefly because breaking up paragraphs and adding space between them makes some types of writing "scannable": The screen is easier to navigate because it isn't packed with text in a 12-point font. The breaks in paragraphs also allow the reader to see a complete paragraph without having to scroll.

CHECKING TRANSITIONS   Make sure, in revising, that the reader can move easily from the beginning of a paragraph to the end and from one paragraph to the next. Transitions help to signal the connections between units of the argument. For example ("For example" is a transition, indicating that an illustration will follow), they may illustrate, establish a sequence, connect logically, amplify, compare, contrast, summarize, or concede (see Thinking Critically: Using Transitions in Argument). Transitions serve as guideposts that enable the reader to move easily through your essay.

When writers revise an early draft, they chiefly do these tasks:

- They **unify** the essay by eliminating irrelevancies.
- They **organize** the essay by keeping in mind the imagined audience.
- They **clarify** the essay by fleshing out thin paragraphs, by ensuring that the transitions are adequate, and by making certain that generalizations are adequately supported by concrete details and examples.

We are not talking here about polish or elegance; we are talking about fundamental matters. Be especially careful not to abuse the logical connectives (*thus, as a result,* and so on). If you write several sentences followed by *therefore* or a similar word or phrase, be sure that what you write after the *therefore* really *does follow* from what has gone before. Logical connectives are not mere transitional devices that link disconnected bits of prose. They are supposed to mark a real movement of thought, which is the essence of an argument.

THE ENDING

What about concluding paragraphs, in which you summarize the main points and reaffirm your position?

If you can look back over your essay and add something that both enriches it and wraps it up, fine; but don't feel compelled to say, "Thus, in conclusion, I have argued *X, Y,* and *Z,* and I have refuted Jones." After all, *conclusion* can have two meanings: (1) ending, or finish, as the ending of a joke or a novel; or (2) judgment or decision reached after deliberation. Your essay should finish effectively (the first sense), but it need not announce a judgment (the second).

If the essay is fairly short, so that a reader can keep its general gist in mind, you may not need to restate your view. Just make sure that you have covered the ground and that your last sentence is a good one. Notice that the student essay printed later in this chapter (p. 258) doesn't end with a formal conclusion, although it ends conclusively, with a note of finality.

THINKING CRITICALLY *Using Transitions in Argument*

Fill in examples of the types of transitions listed below, using topics of your choice. The first one has been done as an example.

TYPE OF TRANSITION	TYPE OF LANGUAGE USED	EXAMPLE OF TRANSITION
Illustrate	*for example, for instance, consider this case*	"Many television crime dramas contain scenes of graphic violence. For example, in the episode of *Law and Order* titled . . ."
Establish a sequence	*a more important objection, a stronger example, the best reason*	
Connect logically	*thus, as a result, therefore, so, it follows*	
Amplify	*further, in addition to, moreover*	
Compare	*similarly, in a like manner, just as, analogously*	
Contrast	*on the one hand . . . on the other hand, in contrast, however, but*	
Summarize	*in short, briefly*	
Concede	*admittedly, granted, to be sure*	

 LaunchPad To complete this activity online, go to **macmillanhighered.com/barnetbedauohara**

By "a note of finality" we do *not* mean a triumphant crowing. It's far better to end with the suggestion that you hope you have by now indicated why those who hold a different view may want to modify it and accept yours.

If you study the essays in this book or the editorials and op-ed pieces in a newspaper, you will notice that writers often provide a sense of closure by using one of the following devices:

- a return to something stated in the introduction
- a glance at the wider implications of the issue (e.g., if smoking is restricted, other liberties are threatened)
- a hint toward unasked or answered questions that the audience might consider in light of the writer's argument
- a suggestion that the reader can take some specific action or do some further research (i.e., the ball is now in the reader's court)
- an anecdote that illustrates the thesis in an engaging way
- a brief summary (*Note:* This sort of ending may seem unnecessary and tedious if the paper is short and the summary merely repeats what the writer has already said.)

> **A RULE FOR WRITERS**
> Emulate John Kenneth Galbraith, a distinguished writer on economics. Galbraith said that in his fifth drafts he regularly introduced the note of spontaneity for which his writing was famous.

TWO USES OF AN OUTLINE

THE OUTLINE AS A PRELIMINARY GUIDE Some writers sketch an **outline** as soon as they think they know what they want to say, even before writing a first draft. This procedure can be helpful in planning a tentative organization, but remember that in revising a draft you'll likely generate some new ideas and have to modify the outline accordingly. A preliminary outline is chiefly useful as a means of getting going, not as a guide to the final essay.

THE OUTLINE AS A WAY OF CHECKING A DRAFT Whether or not you use a preliminary outline, we strongly suggest that after writing what you hope is your last draft, you make an outline of it; there is no better way of finding out whether the essay is well organized.

Go through the draft, and write down the chief points in the order in which you make them. That is, prepare a table of contents — perhaps a phrase for each paragraph. Next, examine your notes to see what kind of sequence they reveal in your paper:

- Is the sequence reasonable? Can it be improved?
- Are any passages irrelevant?
- Does something important seem to be missing?

If no coherent structure or reasonable sequence clearly appears in the outline, then the full prose version of your argument probably doesn't have any either. Therefore, produce another draft by moving things around, adding or subtracting paragraphs — cutting and pasting them into a new sequence, with transitions as needed — and then make another outline to see if the sequence now is satisfactory.

You're probably familiar with the structure known as a **formal outline**. Major points are indicated by I, II, III; points within major points are indicated by A, B, C; divisions within A, B, C are indicated by 1, 2, 3; and so on. Thus:

I. Arguments for opening all Olympic sports to professionals

   A. Fairness

      1. Some Olympic sports are already open to professionals.

      2. Some athletes who really are not professionals are classified as professionals.

   B. Quality (achievements would be higher)

You may want to outline your draft according to this principle, or you might simply write a phrase for each paragraph and indent the subdivisions. But keep these points in mind:

- It is not enough for the parts to be ordered reasonably.
- The order must be made clear to the reader, usually by means of transitions such as *for instance, on the one hand . . . on the other hand, we can now turn to an opposing view,* and so on.

Here is another way of thinking about an outline. For each paragraph, write:

- what the paragraph *says*, and
- what the paragraph *does*.

An opening paragraph might be outlined thus:

- What the paragraph *says* is that the words "under God" in the Pledge of Allegiance should be omitted.
- What the paragraph *does* is, first, inform the reader of the thesis, and second, *provide some necessary background* — for instance, that the words were not in the original wording of the Pledge.

A dual outline of this sort will help you to see whether you have a final draft or a draft that needs refinement.

A LAST WORD ABOUT OUTLINES

Outlines may seem rigid to many writers, especially to those who compose online, where we're accustomed to cutting, copying, moving, and deleting as we draft. However, as mentioned earlier, an outline — whether you write it before drafting a single word or use it to evaluate the organization of something you've already written — is meant to be a guide rather than a straitjacket. Many writers who compose electronically find that the ability to keep banging out words — typing is so much easier than pushing a pen or pencil — and to cut and paste without actually reaching for scissors makes it easy to produce an essay that readers may find difficult to follow. (There is much truth in the proverb "Easy writing makes hard reading.") If you compose electronically, and especially if you continually add, delete, and move text around without a clear organizational goal in mind, be sure to read and outline your draft, and *then* examine the outline to see if indeed there is a reasonable organization.

Outlines are especially helpful for long essays, but even short ones benefit from a bit of advanced planning, a list of a few topics (drawn from notes already taken) that keep the writer moving in an orderly way. A longer work such as an honors or a master's thesis typically requires careful planning. An outline will be a great help in ensuring that you produce something that a reader can easily follow — but, of course, you may find as you write that the outline needs to be altered.

When readers reach the end of a piece of writing, they should feel that the writer has brought them to a decisive point and is not simply stopping abruptly and unexpectedly.

TONE AND THE WRITER'S PERSONA

Although this book is chiefly about argument in the sense of rational discourse — the presentation of reasons in support of a thesis or conclusion — the appeal to reason is only one form of persuasion. Another form is the appeal to emotion — to pity, for example. Aristotle saw, in addition to appeals to reason and to emotion, a third form of persuasion — the appeal to the speaker's character. He called it the **ethical appeal** (the Greek word for this kind of appeal is **ethos,** meaning "character"). The idea is that effective speakers convey the suggestion that they are

- informed,
- intelligent,
- fair minded (persons of goodwill), and
- honest.

Because they are perceived as trustworthy, their words inspire confidence in their listeners. It is a fact that when reading an argument we're often aware of the *person* or *voice* behind the words, and our assent

> **A CHECKLIST FOR ORGANIZING AN ARGUMENT**
>
> ❑ Does the introduction let the readers know where the author is taking them?
>
> ❑ Does the introduction state the problem or issue?
>
>   ❑ Does it state the claim (the thesis)?
>
>   ❑ Does it suggest the organization of the essay, thereby helping the reader to follow the argument?
>
> ❑ Do subsequent paragraphs support the claim?
>
>   ❑ Do they offer evidence?
>
>   ❑ Do they face objections to the claim and offer reasonable responses?
>
>   ❑ Do they indicate why the author's claim is preferable?
>
>   ❑ Do transitions (signposts such as *Furthermore, In contrast,* and *Consider as an example*) guide the reader through the argument?
>
> ❑ Does the essay end effectively, with a paragraph (at most, two paragraphs) bringing a note of closure — for instance, by indicating that the proposed solution is relatively simple? By admitting that although the proposed solution will be difficult to implement, it is certainly feasible? By reminding the reader of the urgency of the problem?

to the argument depends partly on the extent to which we can share the speaker's assumptions and see the matter from his or her point of view — in short, the extent to which we can *identify* with the speaker.

How can a writer inspire the confidence that lets readers identify with him or her? First, the writer should possess the virtues Aristotle specified: intelligence or good sense, honesty, and benevolence or goodwill. As a Roman proverb puts it, "No one gives what he does not have." Still, possession of these qualities is not a guarantee that you will convey them in your writing. Like all other writers, you'll have to revise your drafts so that these qualities become apparent; stated more moderately, you'll have to revise so that nothing in the essay causes a reader to doubt your intelligence, honesty, and goodwill. A blunder in logic, a misleading quotation, a snide remark, even an error in spelling — all such slips can cause readers to withdraw their sympathy from the writer.

Of course, all good argumentative essays do not sound exactly alike; they do not all reveal the same speaker. Each writer develops his or her own voice, or (as literary critics and instructors call it) **persona**. In fact, one writer may have several voices or personae, depending on the topic and the audience. The president of the United States delivering an address on the State of the Union has one persona; when chatting with a reporter at his summer home, he has another. This change is not a matter of hypocrisy. Different circumstances call for different language. As a French writer put it, there is a time to speak of "Paris" and a time to speak of "the capital of the nation." When Abraham Lincoln spoke at Gettysburg,

he didn't say "Eighty-seven years ago"; instead, he intoned "Four score and seven years ago." We might say that just as some occasions required him to be the folksy Honest Abe, the occasion of the dedication of hallowed ground at Gettysburg, where so many Civil War soldiers lost their lives, required him to be formal and solemn — thus, as president of the United States he appropriately used biblical language. Lincoln's election campaigns called for one persona, and the dedication of a military cemetery (an entirely different rhetorical situation) called for a different persona. For examples on how to vary tone, see Thinking Critically: Varying Tone.

When we talk about a writer's persona, we mean the way in which the writer presents his or her attitudes

- toward *the self,*
- toward *the audience,* and
- toward *the subject.*

Thus, if a writer says:

I have thought long and hard about this subject, and I can say with assurance that . . .

we may feel that he is a self-satisfied egotist who probably is mouthing other people's opinions. Certainly he's mouthing clichés: "long and hard," "say with assurance."

THINKING CRITICALLY *Varying Tone*

See the example of Abraham Lincoln's tone below. In the spaces provided, rewrite Lincoln's statement in wording that reflects qualities of other tones as indicated in the middle column..

TONE	QUALITIES OF THE TONE	EXAMPLE
Abraham Lincoln	Invokes biblical rhetoric in an appeal to national unity	*Four score and seven years ago our fathers brought forth on this continent a new nation, conceived in liberty, and dedicated to the proposition that all men are created equal.*
More academic tone	Incorporates specific factual information and connects to overarching ideas	
More informal tone	Is accurate but simplified, forgoing much detail	
Too informal for most academic writing	Mischaracterizes or oversimplifies the thought process	

LaunchPad   To complete this activity online, go to **macmillanhighered.com/barnetbedauohara**

Let's look at a subtler example of an utterance that reveals certain attitudes:

President Nixon was hounded out of office by journalists.

The statement above conveys a respectful attitude toward Nixon ("President Nixon") and a hostile attitude toward the press (they are beasts, curs who "hounded" our elected leader). If the writer's attitudes were reversed, she might have said something like this:

The press turned the searchlight on Tricky Dick's criminal shenanigans.

"Tricky Dick" and "criminal" are obvious enough, but notice that "shenanigans" also implies the writer's contempt for Nixon, and "turned the searchlight" suggests that the press is a source of illumination, a source of truth. The original version and the opposite version both say that the press was responsible for Nixon's resignation, but the original version ("President

Nixon was hounded") conveys indignation toward journalists, whereas the revision conveys contempt for Nixon.

These two versions suggest two speakers who differ not only in their view of Nixon but also in their manner, including the seriousness with which they take themselves. Although the passage is very short, it seems to us that the first speaker conveys righteous indignation ("hounded"), whereas the second conveys amused contempt ("shenanigans"). To our ears the tone, as well as the point, differs in the two versions.

We are talking now about **loaded words**, which convey the writer's attitude and, through their connotations, seek to win the reader to the writer's side. Compare the words in the left-hand column with those in the right:

freedom fighter	terrorist
pro-choice	pro-abortion
pro-life	antichoice
economic refugee	illegal alien
terrorist surveillance	domestic spying

The words in the left-hand column sound like good things; speakers who use them seek to establish themselves as virtuous people supporting worthy causes. The **connotations** (associations, overtones) of these pairs of words differ, even though the **denotations** (explicit meanings, dictionary definitions) are the same—just as the connotations of *mother* and *female parent* differ, although the denotations are the same. Similarly, although Lincoln's "four score and seven" and "eighty-seven" both denote "thirteen less than one hundred," they differ in connotation.

Tone is not only a matter of connotation (*hounded out of office* versus, let's say, *compelled to resign,* or *pro-choice* versus *pro-abortion*); it is also a matter of such things as the selection and type of examples. A writer who offers many examples, especially ones drawn from ordinary life, conveys a persona different from that of a writer who offers no examples or only an occasional invented instance. The first writer seems friendlier, more honest, more down-to-earth.

LAST WORDS ON TONE   On the whole, when writing an argument, it's advisable to be courteous and respectful of your topic, your audience, and people who hold views opposite to yours. It is rarely good for one's own intellectual development to regard as villains or fools persons who hold views different from one's own, especially if some of them are in the audience. Keep in mind the story of two strangers on a train who, striking up a conversation, found that both were clergymen, though of different faiths. Then one said to the other, "Well, why shouldn't we be friends? After all, we both serve God, you in your way and I in His."

Complacency is all right when telling a joke, but not when offering an argument:

- Recognize opposing views.
- Assume they are held in good faith.

- State them fairly. If you don't, you do a disservice not only to the opposition but also to your own position because the perceptive reader won't take you seriously.

- Be temperate in arguing your own position: "If I understand their view correctly . . ."; "It seems reasonable to conclude that . . ."; "Perhaps, then, we can agree that. . . ."

- Write calmly. If you become overly emotional, readers may interpret you as biased or unreasonable, and they may lose their confidence in you.

One way to practice thinking about tone and persona is to think about your professional e-mails. As a student, you probably send many e-mails to classmates and to your instructors or other offices on campus (e.g., the financial aid office, your academic advisor). As teachers, we are often surprised at how flippant and inattentive students are when e-mailing. How do you present yourself in your professional e-mails?

WE, ONE, OR I?

The use of *we* in the last sentence brings us to another point: Is it correct to use the first-person pronouns *I* and *we*? In this book, because three of us are writing, we often use *we* to mean the three authors. And we sometimes use *we* to mean the authors and the readers. This shifting use of one word can be troublesome, but we hope (clearly, the *we* here refers only to the authors) that we have avoided ambiguity. But can, or should, or must an individual use *we* instead of *I*? The short answer is no.

If you're simply speaking for yourself, use *I*. Attempts to avoid the first-person singular by saying things like "This writer thinks . . ." and "It is thought that . . ." and "One thinks that . . ." are far more irritating (and wordy) than the use of *I*. The so-called editorial *we* sounds as odd in a student's argument as the royal *we* does. (Mark Twain said that the only ones who can appropriately say *we* are kings, editors, and people with a tapeworm.) It's advisable to use *we* only when you are sure you're writing or speaking directly to an audience who holds membership in the same group, as in "We *students of* X *university* should . . ." or "We *the members of Theta Chi fraternity* need to. . . ." If the *we* you refer to has a referent, simply refer to what it means: Say "Americans are" rather than "We are," or "College students should" rather than "We should," or "Republicans need to" rather than "We need to."

Many students assume that using *one* will solve the problem of pronouns. But because one *one* leads to another, the sentence may end up sounding, as James Thurber once said, "like a trombone solo." It's best to admit that you are the author, and to use *I*. However, there is no need to preface every sentence with "I think." The reader knows that the essay is yours and that the opinions are yours; so use *I* when you must, but not needlessly. Do not write, "I think X movie is terrible"; simply say, "X movie is terrible." And do not add extra words that say more obvious things, like "*It is my idea that* the company needs a new mission statement." Just write, "*The company needs a new mission statement.*"

Often you'll see *I* in journalistic writing and autobiographical writing—and in some argumentative writing, too—but in most argumentative writing it's best to state the facts and (when drawing reasonable conclusions from them) to keep yourself in the background. Why? The more you use *I* in an essay, the more your readers will attach *you* directly to the argument and may regard your position as personal rather than as relevant to themselves.

THINKING CRITICALLY *Eliminating* We, One, *And* I

Rewrite the following sentences to eliminate unnecessary uses of *I, we, one,* and other gratuitous statements of opinion.

ORIGINAL SENTENCE	REWRITTEN SENTENCE
I think fracking is the best way to achieve energy independence and to create jobs.	Fracking is the best way to achieve energy independence and to create jobs.
In our country, we believe in equality and freedom.	
One should consider one's manners at formal dinner parties.	
In my opinion, the government should not regulate the sizes of sodas we can order.	
It is clearly the case that the new policy treats employees unfairly.	

📚 **LaunchPad**   To complete this activity online, go to **macmillanhighered.com/barnetbedauohara**

A CHECKLIST FOR ATTENDING TO THE NEEDS OF THE AUDIENCE

❐   Do I have a sense of what the audience probably knows about the issue?

❐   Do I have a sense of what the audience probably thinks about the issue?

❐   Have I stated the thesis clearly and sufficiently early in the essay?

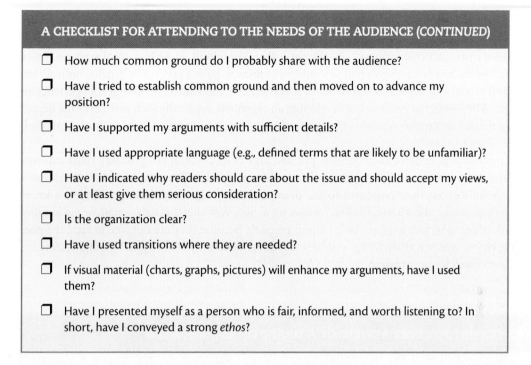

☐ How much common ground do I probably share with the audience?

☐ Have I tried to establish common ground and then moved on to advance my position?

☐ Have I supported my arguments with sufficient details?

☐ Have I used appropriate language (e.g., defined terms that are likely to be unfamiliar)?

☐ Have I indicated why readers should care about the issue and should accept my views, or at least give them serious consideration?

☐ Is the organization clear?

☐ Have I used transitions where they are needed?

☐ If visual material (charts, graphs, pictures) will enhance my arguments, have I used them?

☐ Have I presented myself as a person who is fair, informed, and worth listening to? In short, have I conveyed a strong *ethos*?

AVOIDING SEXIST LANGUAGE

Courtesy as well as common sense requires that you respect your readers' feelings. Many people today find offensive the implicit sexism in the use of male pronouns to denote not only men but also women ("As the reader follows the argument, he will find . . ."). And sometimes the use of the male pronoun to denote all people is ridiculous ("An individual, no matter what his sex, . . .").

In most contexts there is no need to use gender-specific nouns or pronouns. One way to avoid using *he* when you mean any person is to use *he or she* (or *she or he*), but the result is sometimes cumbersome — although superior to the overly conspicuous *he/she* and *s/he*.

Here are two simple ways to solve the problem:

- *Use the plural* ("As readers follow the argument, they will find . . .").
- *Recast the sentence* so that no pronoun is required ("Readers following the argument will find . . .").

Because *man* and *mankind* strike many readers as sexist when used in such expressions as "Man is a rational animal" and "Mankind has not yet solved this problem," consider using such words as *human being, person, people, humanity,* and *we.* (*Examples:* "Human beings are rational animals"; "We have not yet solved this problem.")

Peer Review

Your instructor may suggest — or require — that you submit an early draft of your essay to a fellow student or small group of students for comment. Such a procedure benefits both author and readers: You get the responses of a reader, and the student-reader gets experience in thinking about the problems of developing an argument, especially such matters as the degree of detail that a writer needs to offer to a reader and the importance of keeping the organization evident to a reader.

Oral peer reviews allow for the give and take of discussion, but probably most students and most instructors find written peer reviews more helpful because reviewers think more carefully about their responses to the draft, and they help essayists to get beyond a knee-jerk response to criticism. Online reviews on a class Web site, through e-mail, or via another file-sharing service are especially helpful precisely because they are not face to face; the peer reviewer gets practice *writing*, and the essayist is not directly challenged. Sharing documents works well for peer review.

A CHECKLIST FOR PEER REVIEW OF A DRAFT OF AN ARGUMENT

Read through the draft quickly. Then read it again, with the following questions in mind. Remember: You are reading a draft, a work in progress. You're expected to offer suggestions, and you're expected to offer them courteously.

In a sentence, indicate the degree to which the draft shows promise of fulfilling the assignment.

- ☐ Is the writer's tone appropriate? Who is the audience?

- ☐ Looking at the essay as a whole, what thesis (main idea) is advanced?

- ☐ Are the needs of the audience kept in mind? For instance, do some words need to be defined? Is the evidence (e.g., the examples and the testimony of authorities) clear and effective?

- ☐ Can I accept the assumptions? If not, why not?

- ☐ Is any obvious evidence (or counterevidence) overlooked?

- ☐ Is the writer proposing a solution? If so,

  - ☐ Are other equally attractive solutions adequately examined?

  - ☐ Has the writer overlooked some unattractive effects of the proposed solution?

- ☐ Looking at each paragraph separately,

  - ☐ What is the basic point?

  - ☐ How does each paragraph relate to the essay's main idea or to the previous paragraph?

A Student's Essay, from Rough Notes to Final Version

While we were revising this textbook, we asked the students in one of our classes to write a short essay (500–750 words) on some ethical problem that concerned them. Because this assignment was the first writing assignment in the course, we explained that a good way to generate ideas is to ask oneself some questions, write down responses, question those responses, and write freely for ten minutes or so, not worrying about contradictions. We invited our students to hand in their initial notes along with the finished essay, so that we could get a sense of how they proceeded as writers. Not all of them chose to hand in their notes, but we were greatly encouraged by those who did. What encouraged us was the confirmation of an old belief — we call it a fact — that students will hand in a thoughtful essay if before preparing a final version they ask themselves *why* they think this or that, write down their responses, and are not afraid to change their minds as they proceed.

Here are the first notes of a student, Emily Andrews, who elected to write about whether to give money to street beggars. She simply put down ideas, one after the other.

Help the poor? Why do I (sometimes) do it?

I feel guilty, and think I should help them: poor, cold, hungry (but also some of them are thirsty for liquor, and will spend the money on liquor, not on food).

I also feel annoyed by them — most of them.

Where does the expression "the deserving poor" come from?

And "poor but honest"? Actually, that sounds odd. Wouldn't "rich but honest" make more sense?

Why don't they work? Fellow with red beard, always by bus stop in front of florist's shop, always wants a handout. He is a regular, there all day every day, so I guess he is in a way "reliable," so why doesn't he put the same time in on a job?

Or why don't they get help? Don't they know they need it? They *must* know they need it.

Maybe that guy with the beard is just a con artist. Maybe he makes more money by panhandling than he would by working, and it's a lot easier!

Kinds of poor — how to classify??

> drunks, druggies, etc.
> mentally ill (maybe drunks belong here, too)
> decent people who have had terrible luck

Why private charity?

Doesn't it make sense to say we (fortunate individuals) should give something — an occasional handout — to people who have had terrible luck? (I suppose some people might say there's no need for any of us to give anything — the government takes care of the truly needy — but I *do* believe in giving charity. A month ago a friend of the family passed away, and the woman's children suggested that people might want to make a donation in her name to a shelter for battered women. I know my parents made a donation.)

BUT how can I tell who is who, which are which? Which of these people asking for "spare change" really need (deserve???) help, and which are phonies? Impossible to tell.

Possibilities:

> Give to no one.
> Give to no one but make an annual donation, maybe to United Way.
> Give a dollar to each person who asks. This would probably not cost me even a dollar a day.
> Occasionally do without something — maybe a CD or a meal in a restaurant — and give the money I save to people who seem worthy.

WORTHY? What am I saying? How can I, or anyone, tell? The neat-looking guy who says he just lost his job may be a phony, and the dirty bum — probably a drunk — may desperately need food. (OK, so what if he spends the money on liquor instead of food? At least he'll get a little pleasure in life. No! It's not all right if he spends it on drink.)

Other possibilities:

> Do some volunteer work?
> To tell the truth, I don't want to put in the time. I don't feel *that* guilty.

So what's the problem?

Is it, How I can help the very poor (handouts, or through an organization)? or

How I can feel less guilty about being lucky enough to be able to go to college and to have a supportive family?

I can't quite bring myself to believe I should help every beggar who approaches, but I also can't bring myself to believe that I should do nothing, on the grounds that:

a. it's probably their fault

b. if they are deserving, they can get gov't help. No, I just can't believe that. Maybe some are too proud to look for government help, or don't know that they're entitled to it.

What to do?

On balance, it seems best to:

a. give to United Way

b. maybe also give to an occasional individual, if I happen to be moved, without worrying about whether he or she is "deserving" (since it's probably impossible to know)

A day after making these notes Emily reviewed them, added a few points, and then made a very brief selection from them to serve as an outline for her first draft:

Opening para.: "poor but honest"? Deserve "spare change"?

Charity: private or through organizations?

　　　pros and cons

　　　guy at bus

　　　it wouldn't cost me much, but . . . better to give through organizations

Concluding para.: still feel guilty?

　　　　maybe mention guy at bus again?

After writing and revising a draft, Emily submitted her essay to a fellow student for peer review. She then revised her work in light of the peer's suggestions and her own further thinking.

On the next page we give the final essay. If after reading the final version you reread Emily's early notes, you'll notice that some of her notes never made it into the final version. But without the notes, the essay probably wouldn't have been as interesting as it is. When Emily made the notes, she wasn't so much putting down her ideas as *finding* ideas through the process of writing.

Emily Andrews
Professor Barnet
English 102
January 15, 2016

Why I Don't Spare "Spare Change"

"Poor but honest." "The deserving poor." I don't know the origin of these quotations, but they always come to mind when I think of "the poor." But I also think of people who, perhaps through alcohol or drugs, have ruined not only their own lives but also the lives of others in order to indulge in their own pleasure. Perhaps alcoholism and drug addiction really are "diseases," as many people say, but my own feeling — based, of course, not on any serious study — is that most alcoholics and drug addicts can be classified with the "undeserving poor." And that is largely why I don't distribute spare change to panhandlers.

But surely among the street people there are also some who can rightly be called "deserving." Deserving of what? My spare change? Or simply the government's assistance? It happens that I have been brought up to believe that it is appropriate to make contributions to charity — let's say a shelter for battered women — but if I give some change to a panhandler, am I making a contribution to charity and thereby helping someone, or, on the contrary, am I perhaps simply encouraging someone not to get help? Or maybe even worse, am I supporting a con artist?

If one believes in the value of private charity, one can give either to needy individuals or to charitable organizations. In giving to a panhandler one may indeed be helping a person who badly needs help, but one cannot be certain that one is giving to a needy individual. In giving to an organization such as the United Way, in contrast, one can feel that one's money is likely to be used wisely. True, confronted by a beggar one may feel that *this* particular unfortunate individual needs help at *this* moment — a cup of coffee or a sandwich — and the need will not be met unless I put my hand in my pocket right now. But I have come to think that the beggars whom I encounter can get along without my spare change, and indeed perhaps they are actually better off for not having money to buy liquor or drugs.

It happens that in my neighborhood I encounter few panhandlers. There is one fellow who is always by the bus stop where I catch the bus to the college, and I never give him anything precisely because he is always there. He is such a regular that, I think, he ought to be able to hold a regular job. Putting him aside, I probably don't encounter more than three or four beggars in a week. (I'm not counting street musicians. These people seem quite able to work for a living. If they see their "work" as playing or singing, let persons who enjoy their performances pay them. I do not consider myself among their audience.) The truth of the matter is that since I meet so few beggars, I could give each one a dollar and hardly feel the loss. At most, I might go without seeing a movie some week. But I know nothing about these people, and it's my impression — admittedly based on almost no evidence — that they simply prefer begging to working. I am not generalizing about street people, and certainly I am not talking about street people in the big urban centers. I am talking only about the people whom I actually encounter.

That's why I usually do not give "spare change," and I don't think I will in the future. These people will get along without me. Someone else will come up with money for their coffee or their liquor, or, at worst, they will just have to do without. I will continue to contribute occasionally to a charitable organization, not simply (I hope) to salve my conscience but because I believe that these organizations actually do good work. But I will not attempt to be a mini-charitable organization, distributing (probably to the unworthy) spare change.

Finally, here are a few comments about the essay.

The title is informative, alerting the reader to the topic and the author's position. (By the way, the student told us that in her next-to-last draft, the title was "Is It Right to Spare 'Spare Change'?" This title, unlike the revision, introduces the topic but not the author's position.)

The opening paragraph holds a reader's interest, partly by alluding to the familiar phrase "the deserving poor" and partly by introducing the *un*familiar phrase "the *un*deserving poor." Notice, too, that this opening paragraph ends by clearly asserting the author's thesis. Writers need not always announce their thesis early, but it is usually advisable to do so.

Paragraph 2 begins by voicing what probably is the reader's somewhat uneasy — perhaps even negative — response to the first paragraph. That is, *the writer has a sense of her audience;* she knows how her reader feels, and she takes account of the feeling.

Paragraph 3 clearly sets forth the alternatives. A reader may disagree with the writer's attitude, but the alternatives seem to be stated fairly.

Paragraphs 4 and 5 are more personal than the earlier paragraphs. The writer, more or less having stated what she takes to be the facts, now is entitled to offer a highly personal response to them.

The final paragraph nicely wraps things up by means of the words "spare change," which go back to the title and to the end of the first paragraph. The reader thus experiences a sensation of completeness. The essayist, of course, hasn't solved the problem for all of us for all time, but she presents a thoughtful argument and ends the essay effectively.

Exercise

In a brief essay, state a claim and support it with evidence. Choose an issue in which you are genuinely interested and about which you already know something. You may want to interview a few experts and do some reading, but don't try to write a highly researched paper. Sample topics:

1. Students in laboratory courses should not be required to participate in the dissection of animals.

2. Washington, D.C., should be granted statehood.

3. In wartime, women should be subject to the military draft.

4. The annual Miss America contest is an insult to women.

5. The government should not offer financial support to the arts.

6. The chief fault of the curriculum in high school was . . .

7. No specific courses should be required in colleges or universities.

7

Using Sources

Research is formalized curiosity. It is poking and prying with a purpose.
— ZORA NEALE HURSTON

There is no way of exchanging information that does not involve an act of judgment.
— JACOB BRONOWSKI

For God's sake, stop researching for a while and begin to think. — WALTER HAMILTON MOBERLY

A problem adequately stated is a problem on its way to being solved.
— R. BUCKMINSTER FULLER

I have yet to see any problem, however complicated, which, when you looked at it in the right way, did not become still more complicated. — POUL ANDERSON

Why Use Sources?

We have pointed out that one gets ideas by writing. In the exercise of writing a draft, ideas begin to form, and these ideas stimulate further ideas, especially when one questions—when one *thinks about*—what one has written. But of course in writing about complex, serious questions, nobody is expected to invent all the answers. On the contrary, a writer is expected to be familiar with the chief answers already produced by others and to make use of them through selective incorporation and criticism. In short, writers are not expected to reinvent the wheel; rather, they are expected to make good use of it and perhaps round it off a bit or replace a defective spoke. In order to think out your own views in writing, you are expected to do some preliminary research into the views of others.

When you are trying to understand an issue, high-quality sources will inform you of the various approaches others have taken and will help you establish what the facts are. Once you are informed enough to take a position, the sources you present to your readers will inform and persuade them, just as expert witnesses are sometimes brought in to inform and persuade a jury.

Research isn't limited to the world of professors and scientists. In one way or another, everyone does research at some point. If you want to persuade your city council to increase the number of bicycle lanes on city streets, you could bolster your argument with statistics on how much money the city could save if more people rode their bikes to work. If you decide to open your own business, you would do plenty of market research to persuade the bank that you could repay a loan. Sources (whether published information or data you gather yourself through interviews, surveys, or observation) are not only useful for background information; well-chosen and carefully analyzed sources are evidence for your readers that you know what you're talking about and that your interpretation is sound.

In Chapters 5 and 6 we discussed *ethos* as an appeal that establishes credibility with readers. When you do competent research and thereby let your audience see that you have done your homework, it increases your *ethos*; your audience will trust you because they see that you are well informed, offering them not just your opinions but also an awareness of other opinions and of the relevant facts. Conducting thorough research not only helps you to develop your argument, but it also shows respect for your audience.

Research is often misconstrued as the practice of transcribing information. In fact, it's a process of asking questions and gathering information that helps you come to conclusions about an issue. By using the information you find as evidence, you can develop an effective argument. But don't spend too much time searching and then waiting until the last minute to start writing. As you begin your search, write down observations and questions. When you find a useful source, take notes on what you think it means in your own words. This way, you won't find yourself with a pile of printouts and books and no idea what to say about them. What you have to say will flow naturally out of the prewriting you've already done — and that prewriting will help guide your search.

The process of research isn't always straightforward and neat. It involves scanning what other people have said about a topic and seeing what kinds of questions have been raised. As you poke and pry, you will learn more about the issue, and that, in turn, will help you develop a question to focus your efforts. Once you have a central idea — a thesis — you can sharpen your search to seek out the evidence that will make your readers sit up and take notice.

Consider arguments about whether athletes should be permitted to take anabolic steroids, drugs that supposedly build up muscle, restore energy, and enhance aggressiveness. A thoughtful argument on this subject will have to take account of information that the writer can gather only by doing some research.

- Do steroids really have the effects commonly attributed to them?
- Are they dangerous?
- If they are dangerous, how dangerous are they?

After all, competitive sports are inherently dangerous, some of them highly so. Many boxers, mixed martial arts fighters, jockeys, and football players have suffered severe injury, even death, from competing. Does anyone believe that anabolic steroids are more dangerous than the contests themselves? Obviously, again, a respectable argument about steroids will have to show awareness of what is known about them.

Or consider this question:

Why did President Truman order that atomic bombs be dropped on Hiroshima and Nagasaki?

The most obvious answer is to end the war, but some historians believe he had a very different purpose. In their view, Japan's defeat was ensured before the bombs were dropped, and the Japanese were ready to surrender; the bombs were dropped not to save American (or Japanese) lives but to show Russia that the United States would not be pushed around. Scholars who hold this view, such as Gar Alperovitz in *Atomic Diplomacy* (1965), argue that Japanese civilians in Hiroshima and Nagasaki were incinerated not to save the lives of American soldiers who otherwise would have died in an invasion of Japan but to teach Stalin a lesson. Dropping the bombs, it is argued, marked not the end of the Pacific War but the beginning of the cold war.

One must ask: What evidence supports this argument or claim or thesis, which assumes that Truman could not have thought the bomb was needed to defeat the Japanese because the Japanese knew they were defeated and would soon surrender without a hard-fought defense that would cost hundreds of thousands of lives? What about the momentum that had built up to use the bomb? After all, years of effort and $2 billion had been expended to produce a weapon with the intention of using it to end the war against Germany. But Germany had been defeated without the use of the bomb. Meanwhile, the war in the Pacific continued unabated. If the argument we are considering is correct, all this background counted for little or nothing in Truman's decision, a decision purely diplomatic and coolly indifferent to human life. The task for the writer is to evaluate the evidence available and then to argue for or against the view that Truman's purpose in dropping the bomb was to impress the Soviet government.

A student writing on the topic will certainly want to consult the chief books on the subject (Alperovitz's, cited above, Martin Sherwin's *A World Destroyed* [1975], and John Toland's *The Rising Sun* [1970]) and perhaps reviews of them, especially the reviews in journals devoted to political science. (Reading a searching review of a serious scholarly book is a good way to identify quickly some of the book's main contributions and controversial claims.) Truman's letters and statements, and books and articles about Truman, are also clearly relevant, and doubtless important articles are to be found in recent issues of scholarly journals and electronic sources. In fact, even an essay on such a topic as whether Truman was morally justified in using the atomic bomb for *any* purpose will be a stronger essay if it is well informed about such matters as the estimated loss of life that an invasion would have cost, the international rules governing weapons, and Truman's own statements about the issue.

How does one go about finding the material needed to write a well-informed argument? We will provide help, but first we want to offer a few words about choosing a topic.

Choosing A Topic

We will be brief. If a topic is not assigned, choose one that

- interests you, and
- can be researched with reasonable thoroughness in the allotted time.

Topics such as censorship, the environment, and sexual harassment obviously impinge on our lives, and it may well be that one such topic is of especial interest to you. But the scope of these topics makes researching them potentially overwhelming. Type the word *censorship* into an **Internet** search engine, and you will be referred to millions of information sources.

This brings us to our second point — a manageable topic. Any of the previous topics would need to be narrowed substantially before you could begin searching in earnest. Similarly, a topic such as the causes of World War II can hardly be mastered in a few weeks or argued in a ten-page paper. It is simply too big.

You can, however, write a solid paper analyzing, evaluating, and arguing for or against General Eisenhower's views on atomic warfare. What were they, and when did he hold them? (In his books written in 1948 and 1963 Eisenhower says that he opposed the use of the bomb before Hiroshima and that he argued with Secretary of War Henry Stimson against dropping it, but what evidence supports these claims? Was Eisenhower attempting to rewrite history in his books?) Eisenhower's own writings and books and other information sources on Eisenhower will, of course, be the major sources for a paper on this topic, but you will also want to look at books and articles about Stimson and at publications that contain information about the views of other generals, so that, for instance, you can compare Eisenhower's view with Marshall's or MacArthur's.

Spend a little time exploring a topic to see if it will be interesting and manageable by taking one or more of these approaches:

- **Do a Web search on the topic.** Though you may not use any of the sites that turn up, you can quickly put your finger on the pulse of popular approaches to the issue by scanning the first page or two of results to see what issues are getting the most attention.

- **Plug the topic into one of the library's article databases.** Again, just by scanning titles you can get a sense of what questions are being raised.

- **Browse the library shelves where books on the topic are kept.** A quick check of the tables of contents of recently published books may give you ideas of how to narrow the topic.

- **Ask a librarian to show you where specialized reference books on your topic are found.** Instead of general encyclopedias, try sources like these:

CQ Researcher

Encyclopedia of Applied Ethics

Encyclopedia of Bioethics

Encyclopedia of Crime and Justice

Encyclopedia of Science, Technology, and Ethics

- **Talk to an expert.** Members of the faculty who specialize in the area of your topic might be able to spell out some of the most significant controversies around a topic and may point you toward key sources.

Finding Material

What strategy you use for finding good sources will depend on your topic. Researching a current issue in politics or popular culture may involve reading recent newspaper articles, scanning information on government Web sites, and locating current statistics. Other topics may be best tackled by seeking out books and scholarly journal articles that are less timely but more in-depth and analytical. You may want to supplement library and Web sources with your own fieldwork by conducting surveys or interviews.

Critical thinking is crucial to every step of the research process. Whatever strategy you use, remember that you will want to find material that is authoritative, represents a balanced approach to the issues, and is persuasive. As you choose your sources, bear in mind they will be serving as your "expert witnesses" as you make a case to your audience. Their quality and credibility are crucial to your argument.

If you find what seems to be an excellent source, look at some of the sources that this author repeatedly cites.

FINDING QUALITY INFORMATION ONLINE

The Web is a valuable source of information for many topics and less helpful for others. In general, if you're looking for information on public policy, popular culture, current events, legal affairs, or any subject of interest to agencies of the federal or state government, the Web is likely to have useful material. If you're looking for literary criticism or scholarly analysis of historical or social issues, you will be better off using library databases, described later in this chapter.

To make good use of the Web, try these strategies:

- Use the most specific terms possible when using a general search engine; put phrases in quotes.
- Use the advanced search option to limit a search to a domain (e.g., *.gov* for government sites) or by date (such as Web sites updated in the past week or month).
- If you're not sure which sites might be good ones for research, try starting with one of the selective directories listed below instead of a general search engine.

- Consider which government agencies and organizations might be interested in your topic, and go directly to their Web sites.

- Follow "about" links to see who is behind a Web site and why they put the information on the Web. If there is no "about" link, delete everything after the first slash in the URL to go to the parent site to see if it provides information.

- Use clues in URLs to see where sites originate. For example, URLs containing *.k12* are hosted at elementary and secondary schools, so they may be intended for a young audience; those ending in *.gov* are government agencies, so they tend to provide official information.

- Always bear in mind that the sources you choose must be persuasive to your audience. Avoid sites that may be dismissed as unreliable or biased.

Some useful Web sites include the following:

Selective Web Site Directories
   ipl2 www.ipl.org
   Open Directory Project www.dmoz.org

Current News Sources
   Google News news.google.com
   Reuters www.reuters.com
   WikiNews en.wikinews.org/wiki/Main_Page
   World Newspapers www.world-newspapers.com
   World Press www.worldpress.org

Digital Primary Sources
   American Memory memory.loc.gov
   American Rhetoric www.americanrhetoric.com
   Avalon Project avalon.law.yale.edu/default.asp
   National Archives www.archives.gov
   Smithsonian Source www.smithsoniansource.org

Government Information
   GPO Access www.gpoaccess.gov
   Thomas (federal legislation) thomas.loc.gov
   U.S. Department of Labor www.dol.gov

Scholarly or Scientific Information
   CiteSeer citeseerx.ist.psu.edu/index
   Google Scholar scholar.google.com
   Microsoft Academic academic.microsoft.com/
   Taylor and Francis Open Access Journals www.tandfonline.com/page/openaccess

Statistical Information
   American FactFinder factfinder2.census.gov
   Fedstats www.fedstats.gov

Pew Global Attitudes Project pewglobal.org

U.S. Census Bureau www.census.gov

U.S. Data and Statistics www.usa.gov/statistics

United Nations Statistics Division unstats.un.org

U.S. Bureau of Labor Statistics Guide to U.S. and World Statistical Information
   http://www.bls.gov/bls/other.htm

A WORD ABOUT WIKIPEDIA   Links to Wikipedia (http://www.wikipedia.org) often rise to the top of Web search results. This vast and decentralized site provides over a million articles on a wide variety of topics. However, anyone can contribute to the online encyclopedia, so the accuracy of articles varies, and in some cases, the coverage of a controversial issue is one-sided or disputed. Even when the articles are accurate, they provide only basic information. Wikipedia's founder, Jimmy Wales, cautions students against using it as a source, except for obtaining general background knowledge: "You're in college; don't cite the encyclopedia."[1] Still, Wikipedia often provides valuable bibliographies that will help you to get going.

FINDING ARTICLES USING LIBRARY DATABASES

Your library has a wide range of general and specialized databases available through its Web site. Some databases provide references to articles (and perhaps abstracts or summaries) or may provide direct links to the entire text of articles. General and interdisciplinary databases include Academic Search Premier (produced by the EBSCOhost company) and Expanded Academic Index (from InfoTrac).

More specialized databases include PsycINFO (for psychology research) and ERIC (focused on topics in education). Others, such as JSTOR, are full-text digital archives of scholarly journals. You will likely have access to newspaper articles through LexisNexis or Proquest Newsstand, particularly useful for articles that are not available for free on the Web. Look at your library's Web site to see what your options are, or stop by the reference desk for a quick personalized tutorial.

When using databases, first think through your topic using the listing and diagramming techniques described on pages 223–25. List synonyms for your key search terms. As you search, look at words used in titles and descriptors for alternative ideas and make use of the "advanced search" option so that you can easily combine multiple terms. Rarely will you find exactly what you're looking for right away. Try different search terms and different ways to narrow your topic.

Most databases have an advanced search option that offers forms for combining multiple terms. In Figure 7.1, a search on "anabolic steroids" retrieved far too many articles. In this advanced search, three concepts are being combined in a search: anabolic steroids, legal aspects

---

[1]"Wikipedia Founder Discourages Academic Use of His Creation." *Chronicle of Higher Education: The Wired Campus,* 12 June 2006. chronicle.com/wiredcampus/article/1328/wikipedia-founder-discourages-academic-use-of-his-creation

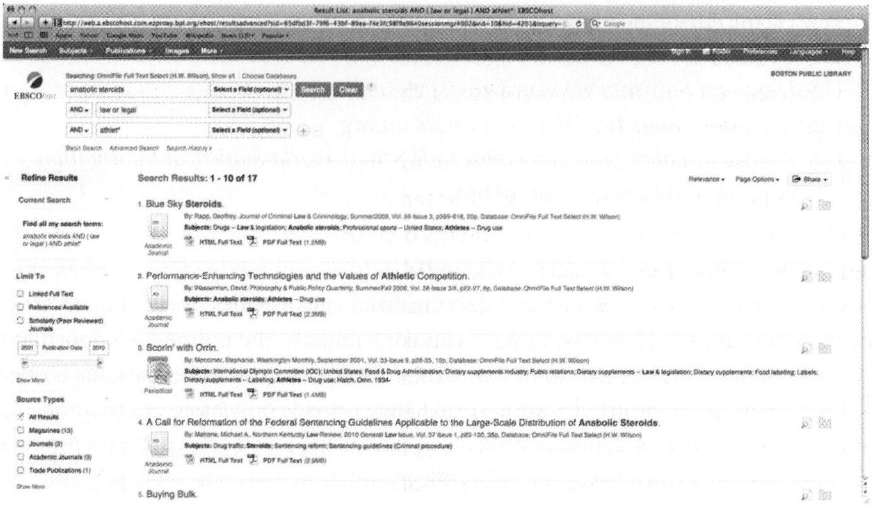

Figure 7.1   An Advanced Web Search

of their use, and use of them by athletes. Related terms are combined with the word "or": *law* or *legal*. The last letters of a word have been replaced with an asterisk so that any ending will be included in the search. *Athlet** will search for *athlete, athletes,* or *athletics.* Options on both sides of the list of articles retrieved offer opportunities to refine a search by date of publication or to restrict the results to only academic journals, magazines, or newspapers.

As with a Web search, you'll need to make critical choices about which articles are worth pursuing. In this example, the first article may not be useful because it concerns German law. The second and third look fairly current and potentially useful. Only the third has a full text link, but the others may be available in another database. Many libraries have a program that will check other databases for you at the push of a button; in this case it's indicated by the "Find full text" button.

As you choose sources, keep track of them by selecting them. Then you can print off, save, or e-mail yourself the references you have selected. You may also have an option to export references to a citation management program such as RefWorks or EndNote. These programs allow you to create your own personal database of sources in which you can store your references and take notes. Later, when you're ready to create a bibliography, these programs will automatically format your references in MLA, APA, or another style. Ask a librarian if one of these programs is available to students on your campus.

LOCATING BOOKS

The books that your library owns can be found through its online catalog. Typically, you can search by author or title or, if you don't have a specific book in mind, by keyword or subject. As with databases, think about different search terms to use, keeping an eye out for subject headings used for books that appear relevant. Take advantage of an "advanced search" option. You may, for example, be able to limit a search to books on a particular topic in English published within recent years. In addition to books, the catalog will also list DVDs, audio and video recordings, and other formats.

Unlike articles, books tend to cover broad topics, so be prepared to broaden your search terms. It may be that a book has a chapter or ten pages that are precisely what you need, but the catalog typically doesn't index the contents of books in detail. Think instead of what kind of book might contain the information you need.

Once you've found some promising books in the catalog, note down the call numbers, find them on the shelves, and then browse. Since books on the same topic are shelved together, you can quickly see what additional books are available by scanning the shelves. As you browse, be sure to look for books that have been published recently enough for your purposes. You do not have to read a book cover-to-cover to use it in your research. Instead, skim the introduction to see if it will be useful, then use its table of contents and index to pinpoint the sections of the book that are the most relevant.

If you are searching for a very specific name or phrase, you might try typing it into Google Book Search (books.google.com), which searches the contents of over seven million scanned books. Though it tends to retrieve too many results for most topics, and you may only be able to see a snippet of content, it can help you locate a particular quote or identify which books might include an unusual name or phrase. There is a "find in a library" link that will help you determine whether the books are available in your library.

Interviewing Peers and Local Authorities

You ought to try to consult experts—for instance, members of the faculty or other local authorities on art, business, law, and so forth. You can also consult interested laypersons. Remember, however, that experts have their biases and that "ordinary" people may have knowledge that experts lack. When interviewing experts, keep in mind Picasso's comment: "You mustn't always believe what I say. Questions tempt you to tell lies, particularly when there is no answer."

If you are interviewing your peers, you will probably want to make an effort to get a representative sample. Of course, even within a group not all members share a single view — many African Americans favor affirmative action, but not all do; some lawmakers support capital punishment, but again, many do not. Make an effort to talk to a range of people who might offer varied opinions. You may learn some unexpected things.

Here we will concentrate, however, on interviews with experts.

1. Finding subjects for interviews   If you are looking for expert opinions, you may want to start with a faculty member on your campus. You may already know the instructor, or you may have to scan the catalog to see who teaches courses relevant to your topic. Department secretaries and college Web sites are good sources of information about the special interests of the faculty and also about lecturers who will be visiting the campus.

2. *Doing preliminary homework* (a) In requesting the interview, make evident your interest in the topic and in the person. (If you know something about the person, you'll be able to indicate why you are asking.) (b) Request the interview, preferably in writing, a week in advance, and ask for ample time — probably half an hour to an hour. Indicate whether the material will be confidential, and (if you want to use a recorder) ask if you may record the interview. (c) If the person accepts the invitation, ask if he or she recommends any preliminary reading, and establish a time and a suitable place, preferably not the cafeteria during lunchtime.

3. *Preparing thoroughly* (a) If your interviewee recommended any reading or has written on the topic, read the material. (b) Tentatively formulate some questions, keeping in mind that (unless you are simply gathering material for a survey of opinions) you want more than yes or no answers. Questions beginning with *Why* and *How* will usually require the interviewee to go beyond yes and no.

Even if your subject has consented to let you bring a recorder, be prepared to take notes on points that strike you as especially significant; without written notes, you will have nothing if the recorder has malfunctioned. Further, by taking occasional notes you will give the interviewee some time to think and perhaps to rephrase or to amplify a remark.

4. *Conducting the interview* (a) Begin by engaging in brief conversation, without taking notes. If the interviewee has agreed to let you use a recorder, settle on the place where you will put it. (b) Come prepared with an opening question or two, but as the interview proceeds, don't hesitate to ask questions that you hadn't anticipated asking. (c) Near the end (you and your subject have probably agreed on the length of the interview) ask the subject if he or she wishes to add anything, perhaps by way of clarifying some earlier comment. (d) Conclude by thanking the interviewee and by offering to provide a copy of the final version of your paper.

5. *Writing up the interview* (a) As soon as possible — certainly, within twenty-four hours after the interview — review your notes and clarify them. At this stage, you can still remember the meaning of your abbreviated notes and shorthand devices (maybe you've been using *n* to stand for *nurses* in clinics where abortions are performed), but if you wait even a whole day you may be puzzled by your own notes. If you have recorded the interview, you may want to transcribe all of it — the laboriousness of this task is one good reason why many interviewers don't use recorders — and you may then want to scan the whole and mark the parts that now strike you as especially significant. If you have taken notes by hand, type them up, along with your own observations (e.g., "Jones was very tentative on this matter, but she said she was inclined to believe that . . ."). (b) Be especially careful to indicate which words are direct quotations. If in doubt, check with the interviewee.

Evaluating Your Sources

Each step of the way, you will be making choices about your sources. As your research proceeds, from selecting promising items in a database search to browsing the book collection, you will want to use the techniques for previewing and skimming detailed on pages 35–37 in order to make your first selection. Ask yourself some basic questions:

- Is this source relevant?

- Is it current enough?

- Does the title and/or abstract suggest it will address an important aspect of my topic?

- Am I choosing sources that represent a range of ideas, not simply ones that support my opinion?

- Do I have a reason to believe that these sources are trustworthy?

Once you have collected a number of likely sources, you will want to do further filtering. Examine each one with these questions in mind:

- *Is this source credible? Does it include information about the author and his or her credentials that can help me decide whether to rely on it?* In the case of books, you might check a database for book reviews for a second opinion. In the case of Web sites, find out where the site came from and why it has been posted online. Don't use a Web source if you can't determine its authorship or purpose.

- *Will my audience find this source credible and persuasive?* Some publishers are more selective about which books they publish than others. University presses, for instance, have several experts read and comment on manuscripts before they decide which to publish. A story about U.S. politics from the *Washington Post*, whose writers conduct firsthand reporting in the nation's capital, carries more clout than a story from a small-circulation newspaper that is drawing its information from a wire service. A scholarly source may be more impressive than a magazine article.

- *Am I using the best evidence available?* Quoting directly from a government report may be more effective than quoting a news story that summarizes the report. Finding evidence that supports your claims in a president's speeches or letters is more persuasive than drawing your conclusions from a page or two of a history textbook.

- *Am I being fair to all sides?* Make sure you are prepared to address alternate perspectives, even if you ultimately take a position. Avoid sources that clearly promote an agenda in favor of ones that your audience will consider balanced and reliable.

- *Can I corroborate my key claims in more than one source?* Compare your sources to ensure that you aren't relying on facts that can't be confirmed. If you're having trouble confirming a source, check with a librarian.

- *Do I really need this source?* It's tempting to use all the books and articles you have found, but if two sources say essentially the same thing, choose the one that is likely to carry the most weight with your audience.

The information you will look for as you evaluate a Web source is often the same as what you need to record in a citation. You can streamline the process of creating a list of works cited by identifying these elements as you evaluate a source.

In Figure 7.2, the URL includes the ending *.gov* — meaning it is a government Web site, an official document that has been vetted. There is an "about" link that will explain the government agency's mission. The date is found above the title of the page: "Revised March 2016." This appears to be a high-quality source of basic information on the issue.

The information you need to cite this report is also on the page; make sure you keep track of where you found the source and when, since Web sites can change. One way to do this is by creating an account at a social bookmarking site such as Delicious (delicious.com) or Diigo (diigo.com) where you can store and annotate Web sites.

Figure 7.2 A Page from a Government Web Site

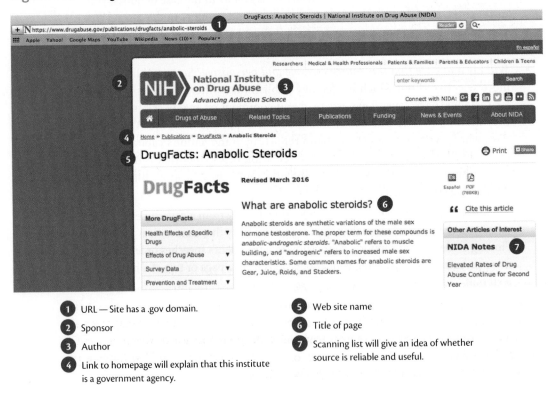

1. URL — Site has a .gov domain.
2. Sponsor
3. Author
4. Link to homepage will explain that this institute is a government agency.
5. Web site name
6. Title of page
7. Scanning list will give an idea of whether source is reliable and useful.

Figure 7.3 A Page from a Commercial Web Site

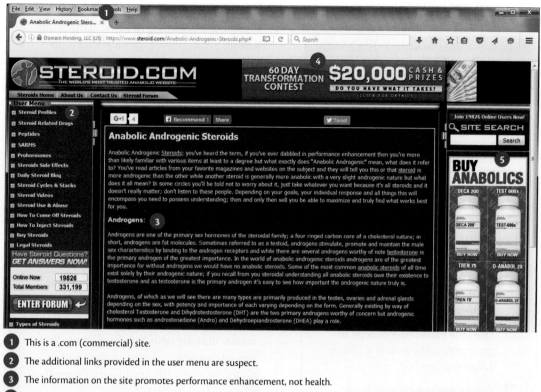

1. This is a .com (commercial) site.
2. The additional links provided in the user menu are suspect.
3. The information on the site promotes performance enhancement, not health.
4. Ads promote steroid use for cash prizes.
5. Steroids are for sale through the site.

Figure 7.3 shows how the information on a Web page might lead you to reject it as a source. Clearly, though this site purports to provide educational information, its primary purpose is to sell products. The graphics and text on the page emphasize the supposed benefits of these performance-enhancing drugs, promoting their use. The focus on performance enhancement and marketing rather than health sends up a red flag.

Taking Notes

When it comes to taking notes, all researchers have their own habits that they swear by, and they can't imagine any other way of working. We still prefer to take notes on four-by-six-inch index cards, while others use a notebook or a computer for note taking. If you use a citation management program, such as RefWorks or EndNote, you can store your personal notes and commentary with the citations you have saved. Using the program's search function, you can easily pull together related notes and citations, or you can create project folders for your references so that you can easily review what you've collected.

Whatever method you use, the following techniques should help you maintain consistency and keep organized during the research process:

A CHECKLIST FOR EVALUATING PRINT SOURCES

For Books:

☐ Is the book recent? If not, is the information I will be using from it likely or unlikely to change over time?

☐ What are the author's credentials?

☐ Is the book titled toward entertainment, or is it in-depth and even-handed?

☐ Is the book broad enough in its focus and written in a style I can understand?

☐ Does the book relate directly to my tentative thesis, or is it of only tangential interest?

☐ Do the arguments in the book seem sound, based on what I have learned about skillful critical reading and writing?

For Articles from Periodicals:

☐ Is the periodical recent?

☐ Is the author's name given? Does he or she seem a credible source?

☐ Does the article treat the topic superficially or in-depth? Does it take sides, or does it offer enough context so that I can make up my own mind?

☐ How directly does the article speak to my topic and tentative thesis?

☐ If the article is from a scholarly journal, am I sure I understand it?

1. If you use a notebook or cards, write in ink (pencil gets smudgy), and write on only one side of the card or paper. (Notes on the backs of cards tend to get lost, and writing on the back of paper will prevent you from later cutting up and rearranging your notes.) Consider using an online tool to keep up with your notes and ideas, for instance, a Google Doc, private blog, or wiki.

2. Summarize, for the most part, rather than quote at length.

3. Quote only passages in which the writing is especially effective or passages that are in some way crucial. These will be easy to access and use if kept in an online venue.

4. Make sure that all quotations are exact. Enclose quoted words within quotation marks, indicate omissions by ellipses (three spaced periods: . . .), and enclose within square brackets ([]) any insertions or other additions you make.

5. *Never* copy a passage, changing an occasional word. *Either* copy it word for word, with punctuation intact, and enclose it within quotation marks, *or* summarize it drastically. If you copy a passage but change a word here and there, you may later make the mistake of using your note verbatim in your essay, and you will be guilty of plagiarism.

6. Give the page number of your source, whether you summarize or quote. If a quotation you have copied runs in the original from the bottom of page 210 to the top of page 211, in your notes put a diagonal line (/) after the last word on page 210, so that later, if in your paper you quote only the material from page 210, you will know that you must cite 210 and not 210–11.

7. Indicate the source. The author's last name is enough if you have consulted only one work by the author; but if you consult more than one work by an author, you need further identification, such as both the author's name and a short title.

8. Add your own comments about the substance of what you are recording. Such comments as "but contrast with Sherwin" or "seems illogical" or "evidence?" will ensure that you are thinking as well as writing and will be of value when you come to transform your notes into a draft. Be sure, however, to enclose such notes within double diagonals (//), or to mark them in some other way, so that later you will know they are yours and not your source's. If you use a computer for note taking, you may wish to write your comments in italics or in a different font.

9. In a separate computer file or notebook page or on separate index cards, write a bibliographic entry for each source. The information in each entry will vary, depending on whether the source is a book, a periodical, an electronic document, and so forth. The kind of information (e.g., author and title) needed for each type of source can be found in the sections on MLA Format: The List of Works Cited (p. 293) or APA Format: The List of References (p. 304).

A Note on Plagiarizing, Paraphrasing, and Using Common Knowledge

Plagiarism is the unacknowledged use of someone else's work. The word comes from a Latin word for "kidnapping," and plagiarism is indeed the stealing of something engendered by someone else. We won't deliver a sermon on the dishonesty (and folly) of

A CHECKLIST FOR EVALUATING ELECTRONIC SOURCES

An enormous amount of valuable material is available online — but so is an enormous amount of junk. True, there is also plenty of junk in books and journals, but most printed material has been subjected to a review process: Book publishers and editors of journals send manuscripts to specialized readers who evaluate them and recommend whether the material should or should not be published. Publishing online is quite different. Anyone can publish online with no review process: All that is needed is sufficient access to the Internet. Ask yourself:

❒ What person or organization produced the site (a commercial entity, a nonprofit entity, a student, an expert)? Check the electronic address to get a clue about the authorship. If there is a link to the author's homepage, check it out to learn about the author. Does the author have an affiliation with a respectable institution?

❒ What is the site's purpose? Is the site in effect an infomercial, or is it an attempt to contribute to a thoughtful discussion?

❒ Are the sources of information indicated and verifiable? If possible, check the sources.

❒ Is the site authoritative enough to use? (If it seems to contain review materials or class handouts, you probably don't want to take it too seriously.)

❒ When was the page made available? Is it out of date?

plagiarism; we intend only to help you understand exactly what plagiarism is. The first thing to say is that plagiarism is not limited to the unacknowledged quotation of words.

A *paraphrase* is a sort of word-by-word or phrase-by-phrase translation of the author's language into your own language. Unlike a summary, then, a paraphrase is approximately as long as the original. Why would anyone paraphrase something? There are two good reasons:

- You may, as a reader, want to paraphrase a passage in order to make certain that you are thinking carefully about each word in the original.
- You may, as a writer, want to paraphrase a difficult passage in order to help your reader.

Paraphrase thus has its uses, but writers often use it unnecessarily, and students who overuse it may find themselves crossing the border into plagiarism. True, if you paraphrase you are using your own words, but

- you are also using someone else's ideas, and, equally important,
- you are using this other person's sequence of thoughts.

Even if you change every third word in your source, you are plagiarizing.

Here is an example of this sort of plagiarism, based on the previous sentence:

Even if you alter every second or third word that your source gives, you still are plagiarizing.

Further, even if the writer of this paraphrase had cited a source after the paraphrase, he or she would still have been guilty of plagiarism. How, you may ask, can a writer who cites a source be guilty of plagiarism? Easy. Readers assume that only the gist of the idea is the source's and that the development of the idea — the way it is set forth — is the present writer's work. A paraphrase that runs to several sentences is in no significant way the writer's work: The writer is borrowing not only the idea but the shape of the presentation, the sentence structure. What the writer needs to do is to write something like this:

Changing an occasional word does not free the writer from the obligation to cite a source.

And the source would still need to be cited, if the central idea were not a commonplace one.

We cannot overemphasize the point that even if you cite a source for your paraphrase you are nevertheless plagiarizing — unless you clearly indicate that the entire passage is a paraphrase of the source.

You are plagiarizing if, without giving credit, you use someone else's ideas — even if you put these ideas entirely into your own words. When you use another's ideas, you must indicate your indebtedness by saying something like "Alperovitz points out that . . ." or "Secretary of War Stimson, as Martin Sherwin notes, never expressed himself on this point." Alperovitz and Sherwin pointed out something that you had not thought of, and so you must give them credit if you want to use their findings.

Again, even if after a paraphrase you cite your source, you are plagiarizing. A reader assumes that the citation refers to information or an opinion, *not* to the presentation or development of the idea; and of course, in a paraphrase you are not presenting or developing the material in your own way.

Now consider this question: *Why* paraphrase? Often there is no good answer. Since a paraphrase is as long as the original, you may as well quote the original, if you think that a passage of that length is worth quoting. Probably it is *not* worth quoting in full; probably you should *not* paraphrase but rather should drastically *summarize* most of it, and perhaps quote a particularly effective phrase or two. As we explained on pages 47–52, the chief reason to paraphrase a passage is to clarify it — that is, to ensure that you and your readers understand a passage that — perhaps because it is badly written — is obscure.

Generally, what you should do is

- Take the idea and put it entirely into your own words, perhaps reducing a paragraph of a hundred words to a sentence of ten words, but you must still give credit for the idea.

- If you believe that the original hundred words are so perfectly put that they cannot be transformed without great loss, you'll have to quote them in full and cite your source. You may in this case want to tell the reader *why* you are quoting at such great length.

In short, chiefly you will quote or you will summarize, and only rarely will you paraphrase, but in all cases you will cite your source. There is no point in paraphrasing an author's hundred words into a hundred of your own. Either quote or summarize, but cite the source.

Keep in mind, too, that almost all generalizations about human nature, no matter how common and familiar (e.g., "males are innately more aggressive than females") are not indisputable facts; they are at best hypotheses on which people differ and therefore should either not

A CHECKLIST FOR AVOIDING PLAGIARISM

❑ In my notes did I *always* put quoted material within quotation marks?

❑ In my notes did I summarize *in my own words* and give credit to the source for the idea?

❑ In my notes did I avoid paraphrasing, that is, did I avoid copying, keeping the structure of the source's sentences but using some of my own words? (Paraphrases of this sort, even with a footnote citing the source, are *not* acceptable, since the reader incorrectly assumes that the writing is essentially yours.)

❑ If in my paper I set forth a borrowed idea, do I give credit, even though the words and the structure of the sentences are entirely my own?

❑ If in my paper I quote directly, do I put the words within quotation marks and cite the source?

❑ Do I *not* cite material that can be considered common knowledge (material that can be found in numerous reference works, such as the date of a public figure's birth or the population of San Francisco or the fact that *Hamlet* is regarded as a great tragedy)?

❑ If I have the slightest doubt about whether I should or should not cite a source, have I taken the safe course and cited the source?

be asserted at all or should be supported by some cited source or authority. Similarly, because nearly all statistics (whether on the intelligence of criminals or the accuracy of lie detectors) are the result of some particular research and may well have been superseded or challenged by other investigators, it is advisable to cite a source for any statistics you use unless you are convinced they are indisputable, such as the number of registered voters in Memphis in 1988.

In contrast, there is something called **common knowledge,** and the sources for such information need not be cited. The term does not, however, mean exactly what it seems to. It is common knowledge, of course, that Ronald Reagan was an American president (so you don't cite a source when you make that statement), and under the conventional interpretation of this doctrine, it is also common knowledge that he was born in 1911. In fact, of course, few people other than Reagan's relatives know this date. Still, information that can be found in many places and that is indisputable belongs to all of us; therefore, a writer need not cite her source when she says that Reagan was born in 1911. Probably she checked a dictionary or an encyclopedia for the date, but the source doesn't matter. Dozens of sources will give exactly the same information, and in fact, no reader wants to be bothered with a citation on such a point.

Some students have a little trouble developing a sense of what is and what is not common knowledge. Although, as we have just said, readers don't want to hear about the sources for information that is indisputable and can be documented in many places, if you are in doubt about whether to cite a source, cite it. Better risk boring the reader a bit than risk being accused of plagiarism.

Your college or your class instructor probably has issued a statement concerning plagiarism. If there is such a statement, be sure to read it carefully.

Compiling an Annotated Bibliography

When several sources have been identified and gathered, many researchers prepare an annotated bibliography. This is a list providing all relevant bibliographic information (just as it will appear in your Works Cited list or References list) as well as a brief descriptive and evaluative summary of each source — perhaps one to three sentences. Your instructor may ask you to provide an annotated bibliography for your research project.

An annotated bibliography serves four main purposes:

- First, constructing such a document helps you to master the material contained in any given source. To find the heart of the argument presented in an article or book, to phrase it briefly, and to comment on it, you must understand it fully.

- Second, creating an annotated bibliography helps you to think about how each portion of your research fits into the whole of your project, how you will use it, and how it relates to your topic and thesis.

- Third, an annotated bibliography helps your readers: They can quickly see which items may be especially helpful in their own research.

- Fourth, in constructing an annotated bibliography at this early stage, you will get some hands-on practice at bibliographic format, thereby easing the job of creating your final bibliography (the Works Cited list or References list for your paper).

Following are two examples of entries for an annotated bibliography in MLA (Modern Language Association) format for a project on the effect of violence in the media. The first is for a book, the second for an article from a periodical. Notice that each entry does two things:

- It begins with a bibliographic entry — author (last name first), title, and so forth.

- Then it provides information about the content of the work under consideration, suggesting how each may be of use to the final research paper.

Clover, Carol J. *Men, Women, and Chain Saws: Gender in the Modern Horror Film*. Princeton UP, 1992. The author focuses on Hollywood horror movies of the 1970s and 1980s. She studies representations of women and girls in these movies and the responses of male viewers to female characters, suggesting that this relationship is more complex and less exploitative than the common wisdom claims.

Winerip, Michael. "Looking for an Eleven O'Clock Fix." *New York Times Magazine*, 11 Jan. 1998, pp. 30–40. The article focuses on the rising levels of violence on local television news and highlights a station in Orlando, Florida, that tried to reduce its depictions of violence and lost viewers as a result. Winerip suggests that people only claim to be against media violence, while their actions prove otherwise.

As you construct your annotated bibliography, consider posting your Word document in Google Drive for easy access and sharing.

CITATION GENERATORS   There are many citation generators available online. These generators allow you to enter the information about your source, and, with a click, they will create Works Cited entries in APA or MLA format. But just as you cannot trust spell- and grammar-checkers in Microsoft Word, you cannot trust these generators. You can use them to cite works, but if you do, be sure to double-check what they produce before submitting your essay. Always remember that responsible writers take care to cite their sources properly and that failure to do so puts you at risk for accusations of plagiarism.

Writing the Paper

ORGANIZING YOUR NOTES

If you have read thoughtfully, taken careful (and, again, thoughtful) notes on your reading, and then (yet again) thought about these notes, you are well on the way to writing a good paper. You have, in fact, already written some of it in your notes. By now you should clearly have in mind the thesis you intend to argue. But you still have to organize the material, and, doubtless, even as you set about organizing it, you will find points that will require you to do some additional research and much additional thinking.

Divide your notes into clusters, each devoted to one theme or point (e.g., one cluster on the extent of use of steroids, another on evidence that steroids are harmful, yet another on arguments that even if harmful they should be permitted). If your notes are in a computer file, rearrange them into appropriate clusters. If you use index cards, simply sort them into packets. If you take notes in a notebook, either mark each note with a number or name indicating the cluster to which it belongs, or cut the notes apart and arrange them as you would cards. Put aside all notes that — however interesting — you now see are irrelevant to your paper.

Next, arrange the clusters or packets into a tentative sequence. In effect, you are preparing a **working outline.** At its simplest, say, you will give three arguments on behalf of *X* and then three counterarguments. (Or you might decide that it's better to alternate material from the two sets of three clusters each, following each argument with an objection. At this stage, you can't be sure of the organization you will finally use, but you can make a tentative decision.)

THE FIRST DRAFT

Draft the essay, without worrying much about an elegant opening paragraph. Just write some sort of adequate opening that states the topic and your thesis. When you revise the whole later, you can put some effort into developing an effective opening. (Most experienced writers find that the opening paragraph in the final version is almost the last thing they write.)

If your notes are on cards or notebook paper, carefully copy into the draft all quotations that you plan to use. If your notes are in a computer, you may simply cut and paste them from one file to another. Do keep in mind, however, that rewriting or retyping quotations will make you think carefully about them and may result in a more focused and thoughtful paper. (In the next section of this chapter we will talk briefly about leading into quotations and about the form of quotations.) Be sure to include citations in your drafts so that if you must check a reference later it will be easy to do so.

LATER DRAFTS

Give the draft, and yourself, a rest — perhaps for a day or two — and then go back to it. Read it over, make necessary revisions, and then **outline** it. That is, on a sheet of paper chart the organization and development, perhaps by jotting down a sentence summarizing each paragraph or each group of closely related paragraphs. Your outline or map may now show you that the paper obviously suffers from poor organization. For instance, it may reveal that you neglected to respond to one argument or that you needlessly treated one point in two places. It may also help you to see that if you gave three arguments and then three counterarguments, you probably should instead have followed each argument with its rebuttal. However, if you alternated arguments and objections, it may now seem better to use two main groups — all the arguments and then all the criticisms.

No one formula is always right. Much will depend on the complexity of the material. If the arguments are highly complex, it is better to respond to them one by one than to expect a reader to hold three complex arguments in mind before you get around to responding. If, however, the arguments can be stated briefly and clearly, it is effective to state all three and then to go on to the responses. If you write on a computer, you will find it easy, even fun, to move passages of text around. Even so, you will probably want to print out a hard copy from time to time to review the structure of your paper. Allow enough time to produce several drafts.

A FEW MORE WORDS ABOUT ORGANIZATION

There is a difference between

- a paper that *has* an organization, and
- a paper that helpfully lets the reader know what the organization is.

You should write papers of the second sort, but (there is always a "but") take care not to belabor the obvious. Inexperienced writers sometimes either hide the organization so thoroughly that a reader cannot find it or they so ploddingly lay out the structure ("Eighth, I will show . . .") that the reader becomes impatient. Yet it is better to be overly explicit than to be obscure.

The ideal, of course, is the middle route. Make the overall strategy of your organization evident by occasional explicit signs at the beginning of a paragraph ("We have seen . . . ," "It is time to consider the objections . . . ," "By far the most important . . ."); elsewhere make certain that the implicit structure is evident to the reader. When rereading your draft, if you try to imagine that you are one of your classmates, you will probably be able to sense exactly where explicit signs are needed and where they are not needed. Better still, exchange drafts with a classmate in order to exchange (tactful) advice.

Another strategy for organizing an essay is to determine early on whether your approach uses **classification** or **division**. These two terms refer to the development of essays and to the function of individual paragraphs, so they may be used profitably together. **Classification** normally suggests surveying many items or aspects of an issue. You might be examining the various roles played by celebrities in international relations, or looking at many types of GMOs, or analyzing a range of characters in a novel. Classification suggests a collection of numerous things within the purview of your thesis. **Division**, in contrast, suggests looking at one thing very closely, and dividing it into parts — perhaps as a key example of your broader thesis. If you are using division, you might be examining the role of one celebrity in international relations (e.g., Bono), or looking at one particular GMO, or analyzing the role of one character within a novel. We can illustrate the difference in a hypothetical essay about the dangers of steroid use. If you're using classification, you might be looking at many different types of drugs and their uses in various sports by various athletes. You might be further pointing out the many effects of these substances and the controversies that surround each to support an overall thesis about the issue. If you're using division, you might be emphasizing a key drug, a key athlete, or a key case study to understand thoroughly its specific effects as representative of the whole.

Classification may be thought of as utilizing many *parts* to understand a *whole*. Division may be thought of as using a *whole* to understand many *parts*.

CHOOSING A TENTATIVE TITLE

By now a couple of tentative titles for your essay should have crossed your mind. If possible, choose a title that is both interesting and informative. Consider these three titles:

> Are Steroids Harmful?
>
> The Fuss over Steroids
>
> Steroids: A Dangerous Game

"Are Steroids Harmful?" is faintly interesting and lets the reader know the gist of the subject, but it gives no clue about the writer's thesis, the writer's contention or argument. "The Fuss over Steroids" is somewhat better, for it gives information about the writer's position. "Steroids: A Dangerous Game" is still better; it announces the subject ("steroids") and the thesis ("dangerous"), and it also displays a touch of wit because "game" glances at the world of athletics.

Don't try too hard, however; better a simple, direct, informative title than a strained, puzzling, or overly cute one. And remember to make sure that everything in your essay is relevant to your title. In fact, your title should help you to organize the essay and to delete irrelevant material.

THE FINAL DRAFT

When at last you have a draft that is for the most part satisfactory, check to make sure that **transitions** from sentence to sentence and from paragraph to paragraph are clear ("Further evidence," "In contrast," "A weakness, however, is apparent"), and then worry about your opening and closing paragraphs. Your **opening paragraph** should be clear, interesting, and focused; if neither the title nor the first paragraph announces your thesis, the second paragraph probably should do so.

The **final paragraph** need not say, "In conclusion, I have shown that. . . ." It should effectively end the essay, but it need not summarize your conclusions. We have already offered a few words about final paragraphs (p. 243–45), but the best way to learn how to write such paragraphs is to study the endings of some of the essays in this book and to adopt the strategies that appeal to you.

Be sure that all indebtedness is properly acknowledged. We have talked about plagiarism; now we will turn to the business of introducing quotations effectively.

Quoting from Sources

INCORPORATING YOUR READING INTO YOUR THINKING: THE ART AND SCIENCE OF SYNTHESIS

At the beginning of Chapter 6 we quoted a passage by Kenneth Burke (1887–1993), a college dropout who became one of America's most important twentieth-century students of rhetoric. It is worth repeating:

> Imagine that you enter a parlor. You come late. When you arrive, others have long preceded you, and they are engaged in a heated discussion, a discussion too heated for them to pause and tell you exactly what it is about. In fact, the discussion had already begun long before any of them got there, so that no one present is qualified to retrace for you all the steps that had gone before. You listen for a while, until you decide that you have caught the tenor of the argument; then you put in your oar. Someone answers; you answer him; another comes to your defense; another aligns himself against you, to either the embarrassment or gratification of your opponent, depending upon the quality of your ally's assistance. However, the discussion is interminable. The hour grows late, you must depart. And you do depart, with the discussion still vigorously in progress.
>
> — *The Philosophy of Literary Form* (Baton Rouge: Louisiana State University Press, 1941), 110–11.

Why do we quote this passage? Because it is your turn to join the unending conversation.

During the process of reading, and afterward, you will want to listen, think, say to yourself something like this:

- "No, no, I see things very differently; it seems to me that . . ." or

- "Yes, of course, but on one large issue I think I differ," or

- "Yes, sure, I agree, but I would go further and add . . ." or

- "Yes, I agree with your conclusion, but I hold this conclusion for reasons very different from the ones that you offer."

During your composition courses at least (and we think during your entire life), you will be reading or listening and will sometimes want to put in your oar — you will sometimes want to respond in writing, for example in the form of a Letter to the Editor or in a memo at your place of employment. In the course of your response you almost surely will have to summarize the idea or ideas you are responding to, so that your readers will understand the context of your remarks. These ideas may not come from a single source; you may be responding to several sources. For instance, you may be responding to a report and also to some comments that the report evoked. In any case, you will state these ideas briefly and fairly and will then set forth your thoughtful responses, thereby giving the reader a statement that you hope represents an advance in the argument, even if only a tiny one. That is, you will **synthesize** sources, combining existing material into something new, drawing nourishment from what has already been said (giving credit, of course), and converting it into something new — a view that you think is worth considering.

Let's pause for a moment and consider this word *synthesis*. You probably are familiar with *photosynthesis*, the chemical process in green plants that produces carbohydrates from carbon dioxide and hydrogen. Synthesis, again, combines pre-existing elements and produces something new. In our use of the word *synthesis*, even a view that you utterly reject becomes a part of your new creation *because it helped to stimulate you to formulate your view*; without the idea that you reject, you might not have developed the view that you now hold. Consider the words of Francis Bacon, Shakespeare's contemporary:

> Some books are to be tasted, others to be swallowed, and some few to be chewed and digested.

Your instructor will expect you to digest your sources — this doesn't mean you need to accept them but only that you need to read them thoughtfully — and that, so to speak, you make them your own thoughts by refining them. Your readers will expect you to tell them *what you make out of your sources*, which means that you will go beyond writing a summary and will synthesize the material into your own contribution. *Your* view is what is wanted, and readers expect this view to be thoughtful — not mere summary and not mere tweeting.

> **A RULE FOR WRITERS**
> In your final draft *you must give credit to all of your sources.* Let the reader know whether you are quoting (in this case, you will use quotation marks around all material directly quoted), or whether you are summarizing (you will explicitly say so), or whether you are paraphrasing (again, you will explicitly say so).

THE USE AND ABUSE OF QUOTATIONS

When is it necessary, or appropriate, to quote? Sometimes, the reader must see the exact words of your source; the gist won't do. If you are arguing that *Z*'s definition of *rights* is too inclusive, your readers have to know exactly how *Z* defined *rights*. Your brief summary of the definition may be unfair to *Z*; in fact, you want to convince your readers that you're being fair, and so you quote *Z*'s definition, word for word. Moreover, if the passage is only a sentence or two long, or even if it runs to a paragraph, it may be so compactly stated that it defies summary. And to attempt to paraphrase it — substituting *natural* for *inalienable*, and so forth — saves no space and only introduces imprecision. There is nothing to do but to quote it, word for word.

Second, you may want to quote a passage that could be summarized but that is so effectively stated that you want the readers to have the pleasure of reading the original. Of course, readers won't give you credit for writing these words, but they will appreciate your taste and your effort to make especially pleasant the business of reading your paper.

In short, use (but don't overuse) quotations. Speaking roughly, quotations

- should occupy no more than 10 to 15 percent of your paper, and
- they may occupy much less.

Most of your paper should set forth your ideas, not other people's ideas.

HOW TO QUOTE

Long and Short Quotations   **Long quotations** (more than four lines of typed prose or three or more lines of poetry) are set off from the text. To set off material, start on a new line, indent one-half inch from the left margin, and type the quotation double-spaced. Do not enclose quotations within quotation marks if you are setting them off.

Short quotations are treated differently. They are embedded within the text; they are enclosed within quotation marks, but otherwise they do not stand out.

All quotations, whether set off or embedded, must be exact. If you omit any words, you must indicate the ellipsis by substituting three spaced periods for the omission; if you insert any words or punctuation, you must indicate the addition by enclosing it within square brackets, not to be confused with parentheses.

Original	The Montgomery bus boycott not only brought national attention to the discriminatory practices of the South, but elevated a twenty-six-year-old preacher to exalted status in the civil rights movement.
Quotation in student paper	"The Montgomery bus boycott . . . elevated [King] to exalted status in the civil rights movement."

Leading into a Quotation   Now for a less mechanical matter: the way in which a quotation is introduced. To say that it is "introduced" implies that one leads into it, though on rare occasions a quotation appears without an introduction, perhaps immediately after the title. Normally one leads into a quotation by giving any one or more of the following (*warning*: using them all at once can get unwieldy and produce awkward sentences):

- the *name of the author* and (no less important) the author's expertise or authority

- an indication of *the source of the quotation, by title and/or year*

- *clues signaling the content of the quotation and the purpose* it serves in the present essay

For example:

William James provides a clear answer to Huxley when he says that ". . ."

Psychologist William James provides a clear answer to Huxley when he says that ". . ."

In *The Will to Believe* (1897), psychologist William James *provides a clear answer* to Huxley when he says that ". . ."

Any of these work, especially because William James is quite well known. When you're quoting from a lesser-known author, it becomes more important to identify his or her expertise and perhaps the source, as in "Biographer Theodora Bosanquet, author of *Henry James at Work* (1982), subtly criticized Huxley's vague ideas on religion by writing '. . .'"

Note that in all of the above samples, the writer uses the lead-in to signal to readers the general tone of the quotation to follow. The writer uses "a clear answer" to signal that what's coming is, in fact, clear. The writer uses "subtly criticized" and "vague" to indicate that the following words by Bosanquet will be critical and will point out a shortcoming in Huxley's ideas. In this way, the writer anticipates and controls the meaning of the quotation for the reader. If the writer believed otherwise, the lead-ins might have run thus:

> William James attempts to answer Huxley, but his response does not really meet the difficulty Huxley calls attention to. James writes, ". . ."

or thus:

> Biographer Theodora Bosanquet, author of *Henry James at Work* (1982), unjustly criticized Huxley's complex notion of religion by writing ". . ."

In this last example, clearly the words "unjustly criticized" imply that the essayist wants the reader to interpret the quotation as an unjust criticism. Similarly, Huxley's idea is presented as "complex," not vague.

Signal Phrases   Think of your writing as a conversation between you and your sources. As in conversation, you want to be able to move smoothly between different, sometimes contrary, points of view. You also want to be able to set your thoughts apart from those of your sources. Signal phrases make it easy for readers to know where your information came from and why it's trustworthy by pointing to key facts about the source:

> *According to* psychologist Stephen Ceci . . .

> A report published by the U.S. Bureau of Justice Statistics *concludes* . . .

> Feminist philosopher Sandra Harding *argues* . . .

To avoid repetitiveness, vary your sentence structure:

> . . . *claims* Stephen Ceci.

> . . . *according to* a report published by the U.S. Bureau of Statistics.

Some useful verbs to introduce sources include the following:

acknowledges	disputes
argues	observes
believes	points out
claims	recommends
contends	reports
denies	suggests

Note that papers written using MLA style refer to sources in the present tense (*acknowledge, argue, believe*). Papers written in APA style use the past tense (*acknowledged, argued, believed*).

THINKING CRITICALLY *Using Signal Phrases*

In the space provided, rewrite each signal phrase using a different structure. The first has been done as an example. Use different verbs to introduce each source.

ORIGINAL SIGNAL PHRASE	REVISED SIGNAL PHRASE
According to political economist Robert Reich . . .	. . . claims Robert Reich.
The National Health Council reports . . .	
The *Harvard Law Review* claims . . .	
As science essayist Jennifer Ackerman suggests . . .	

 LaunchPad   To complete this activity online, go to **macmillanhighered.com/barnetbedauohara**

Leading Out of a Quotation   You might think of providing quotations as a three-stage process that includes the **lead-in**, the **quotation** itself, and the **lead-out**. The lead-out gives you a chance to interpret the quoted material, further controlling the intended meaning, telling the reader what is most important. In the lead-out, you have a chance to reflect upon the quotation and to shift back toward your own ideas and analysis. Consider this three-stage process applied in the following two ways:

> In his first book, *A World Restored* (1954), future Secretary of Defense Henry Kissinger wrote the famous axiom "History is the memory of states." It is the collective story of an entire people, displayed in public museums and libraries, taught in schools, and passed on from generation to generation.

> In his first book, *A World Restored* (1954), Nixon's former Secretary of Defense Henry Kissinger wrote glibly, "History is the memory of states." By asserting that history is largely the product of self-interested propaganda, Kissinger's words suggest that the past is maintained and controlled by whatever groups happen to hold power.

Note the three-step process, and note especially how the two examples convey different meanings of Kissinger's famous phrase. In the lead-in to the first sample, Kissinger's "future" role suggests hope. It signals a figure whose influence is growing. By using *famous* and *axiom*, the author presents the quotation as "true" or even timeless. In the lead-out, the role of the state in preserving history is optimistic and idealistic.

In the second sample, "former" is used in the lead-in, suggesting Kissinger's later association with the ousted president. Readers are told that Kissinger "wrote glibly" even before they are told what he wrote, so readers may tend to read the quoted words that way. In the lead-out, the state becomes a more nefarious source of history-keeping, one not interested in accommodating marginal voices or alternative perspectives, or remembering events inconvenient to its authority or righteousness.

> **A RULE FOR WRITERS**
> In introducing a quotation, it is usually advisable to signal the reader *why* you are using the quotation by means of a lead-in consisting of a verb or a verb and adverb, such as *claims*, or *convincingly shows*, or *admits*.

Again, we hope you can see in these examples how the three-step process facilitates a writer's control over the meanings of quotations. Returning to our earlier example, if after reading something by Huxley the writer had merely stated that "William James says . . . ," readers wouldn't know whether they were getting confirmation, refutation, or something else. The essayist would have put a needless burden on the readers. Generally speaking, the more difficult the quotation, the more important is the introductory or explanatory lead-in, but even the simplest quotation profits from some sort of brief lead-in, such as "James reaffirms this point when he says. . . ."

Documentation

In the course of your essay, you will probably quote or summarize material derived from a source. You must give credit, and although there is no one form of documentation to which all scholarly fields subscribe, you will probably be asked to use one of two. One, established by the Modern Language Association (MLA), is used chiefly in the humanities; the other, established by the American Psychological Association (APA), is used chiefly in the social sciences.

We include two papers that use sources. "An Argument for Corporate Responsibility" (p. 309) uses the MLA format. "The Role of Spirituality and Religion in Mental Health" (p. 316) follows the APA format. (You may notice that various styles are illustrated in other selections we have included.)

In some online venues you can link directly to your sources. If your assignment is to write a blog or some other online text, linking helps the reader to look at a note or citation or the direct source quickly and easily. For example, in describing or referencing a scene in a movie, you can link to reviews of the movie, or to a YouTube of the trailer, or to the exact scene that you're discussing. These kinds of links can help your audience get a clearer sense of your point. When formatting such a link in your text, make sure the link opens in a new window so that readers won't lose their place in your original text. In a blog, linking to sources usually is easy and helpful.

A NOTE ON FOOTNOTES (AND ENDNOTES)

Before we discuss these two formats, a few words about footnotes are in order. Before the MLA and the APA developed their rules of style, citations commonly appeared in footnotes. Although today footnotes are not so frequently used to give citations, they still may be useful for another purpose. (The MLA suggests endnotes rather than footnotes, but most readers seem to think that, in fact, footnotes are preferable to endnotes. After all, who wants to keep shifting from a page of text to a page of notes at the rear?) If you want to include some material that may seem intrusive in the body of the paper, you may relegate it to a footnote: for example, you might translate a quotation given in a foreign language, or you might demote from text to footnote a paragraph explaining why you aren't taking account of such-and-such a point. By putting the matter in a footnote you signal to the reader that it is dispensable; it's relevant but not essential, something extra that you are, so to speak, tossing in. Don't make a habit of writing this sort of note, but there are times when it is appropriate to do so.

MLA FORMAT: CITATIONS WITHIN THE TEXT

Brief citations within the body of the essay give credit, in a highly abbreviated way, to the sources for material you quote, summarize, or make use of in any other way. These *in-text citations* are made clear by a list of sources, titled Works Cited, appended to the essay. Thus, in your essay you may say something like this:

> Commenting on the relative costs of capital punishment and life imprisonment, Ernest van den Haag says that he doubts "that capital punishment really is more expensive" (33).

The **citation,** the number 33 in parentheses, means that the quoted words come from page 33 of a source (listed in the Works Cited) written by van den Haag. Without a Works Cited, a reader would have no way of knowing that you are quoting from page 33 of an article that appeared in the February 8, 1985, issue of the *National Review.*

Usually, the parenthetic citation appears at the end of a sentence, as in the example just given, but it can appear elsewhere; its position will depend chiefly on your ear, your eye, and the context. You might, for example, write the sentence thus:

> Ernest van den Haag doubts that "capital punishment really is more expensive" than life imprisonment (33), but other writers have presented figures that contradict him.

Five points must be made about these examples:

1. Quotation marks   The closing quotation mark appears after the last word of the quotation, *not* after the parenthetic citation. Since the citation is not part of the quotation, the citation is not included within the quotation marks.

2. Omission of words (ellipsis)   If you are quoting a complete sentence or only a phrase, as in the examples given, you do not need to indicate (by three spaced periods) that you are omitting material before or after the quotation. But if for some reason you want to omit an interior part of the quotation, you must indicate the omission by inserting an *ellipsis,* the three spaced dots. To take a simple example, if you omit the word "really" from van den Haag's phrase, you must alert the reader to the omission:

> Ernest van den Haag doubts that "capital punishment . . . is more expensive" than life imprisonment (33).

Suppose you're quoting a sentence but wish to omit material from the end of the sentence. Suppose, also, that the quotation forms the end of your sentence. Write a lead-in phrase, quote what you need from the source, then type the ellipses for the omission, close the quotation, give the parenthetic citation, and finally type a fourth period to indicate the end of your sentence.

Here's an example. Suppose you want to quote the first part of a sentence that runs, "We could insist that the cost of capital punishment be reduced so as to diminish the differences." Your sentence would incorporate the desired extract as follows:

> Van den Haag says, "We could insist that the cost of capital punishment be reduced . . ." (33).

3. *Punctuation with parenthetic citations* In the preceding examples, the punctuation (a period or a comma in the examples) *follows* the citation. If, however, the quotation ends with a question mark, include the question mark *within* the quotation, since it is part of the quotation, and put a period *after* the citation:

> Van den Haag asks, "Isn't it better — more just and more useful — that criminals, if they do not have the certainty of punishment, at least run the risk of suffering it?" (33).

But if the question mark is your own and not in the source, put it after the citation, thus:

> What answer can be given to van den Haag's doubt that "capital punishment really is more expensive" (33)?

4. *Two or more works by an author* If your list of Works Cited includes two or more works by an author, you cannot, in your essay, simply cite a page number because the reader will not know which of the works you are referring to. You must give additional information. You can give it in your lead-in, thus:

> In "New Arguments against Capital Punishment," van den Haag expresses doubt that "capital punishment really is more expensive" than life imprisonment (33).

Or you can give the title, in a shortened form, within the citation:

> Van den Haag expresses doubt that "capital punishment really is more expensive" than life imprisonment ("New Arguments" 33).

5. *Citing even when you do not quote* Even if you don't quote a source directly, but use its point in a paraphrase or a summary, you will give a citation:

> Van den Haag thinks that life imprisonment costs more than capital punishment (33).

Note that in all of the previous examples, the author's name is given in the text (rather than within the parenthetic citation). But there are several other ways of giving the citation, and we shall look at them now. (We've already seen, in the example given under paragraph 4, that the title and the page number can appear within the citation.)

AUTHOR AND PAGE NUMBER IN PARENTHESES

> It has been argued that life imprisonment is more costly than capital punishment (van den Haag 33).

AUTHOR, TITLE, AND PAGE NUMBER IN PARENTHESES

We have seen that if the Works Cited list includes two or more works by an author, you will have to give the title of the work on which you are drawing, either in your lead-in phrase or within the parenthetic citation. Similarly, if you're citing someone who is listed more than once in the Works Cited, and for some reason you don't mention the name of the author or the work in your lead-in, you must add the information in the citation:

> Doubt has been expressed that capital punishment is as costly as life imprisonment (van den Haag, "New Arguments" 33).

A GOVERNMENT DOCUMENT OR A WORK OF CORPORATE AUTHORSHIP

Treat the issuing body as the author. Thus, you will write something like this:

> The Commission on Food Control, in *Food Resources Today*, concludes that there is no danger (37-38).

A WORK BY TWO AUTHORS

If a work is by *two authors,* give the names of both authors, either in the parenthetic citation (the first example below) or in a lead-in (the second example below):

> There is not a single example of the phenomenon (Christakis and Fowler 293).

> Christakis and Fowler insist there is not a single example of the phenomenon (293).

A WORK BY MORE THAN TWO AUTHORS

If there are *more than two authors,* give the last name of the first author, followed by *et al.* (an abbreviation for *et alii,* Latin for "and others"), thus:

> Gittleman et al. argue (43) that . . .

or

> On average, the cost is even higher (Gittleman et al. 43).

PARENTHETIC CITATION OF AN INDIRECT SOURCE (CITATION OF MATERIAL THAT ITSELF WAS QUOTED OR SUMMARIZED IN YOUR SOURCE)

Suppose you're reading a book by Jones in which she quotes Smith and you wish to use Smith's material. Your citation must refer the reader to Jones — the source you're using — but of course, you cannot attribute the words to Jones. You will have to make it clear that you are quoting Smith, and so after a lead-in phrase like "Smith says," followed by the quotation, you will give a parenthetic citation along these lines:

> (qtd. in Jones 324-25).

PARENTHETIC CITATION OF TWO OR MORE WORKS

> The costs are simply too high (Smith 301; Jones 28).

Notice that a semicolon, followed by a space, separates the two sources.

A WORK IN MORE THAN ONE VOLUME

This is a bit tricky. If you have used only one volume, in the Works Cited you will specify the volume, and so in the parenthetic in-text citation you won't need to specify the volume. All you need to include in the citation is a page number, as illustrated by most of the examples that we have given.

If you have used more than one volume, the parenthetic citation will have to specify the volume as well as the page, thus:

> Jackson points out that fewer than 150 people fit this description (2: 351).

The reference is to page 351 in volume 2 of a work by Jackson.

If, however, you are citing not a page but an entire volume — let's say volume 2 — your parenthetic citation will look like this:

> Jackson exhaustively studies this problem (vol. 2).

or

> Jackson (vol. 2) exhaustively studies this problem.

Notice the following points:

- In citing a volume and page, the volume number, like the page number, is given in arabic (not roman) numerals, even if the original used roman numerals to indicate the volume number.
- The volume number is followed by a colon, then a space, then the page number.
- If you cite a volume number without a page number, as in the last example quoted, the abbreviation is *vol.* Otherwise, do *not* use such abbreviations as *vol.* and *p.* and *pg.*

AN ANONYMOUS WORK

For an anonymous work, give the title in your lead-in, or give it in a shortened form in your parenthetic citation:

> *A Prisoner's View of Killing* includes a poll taken of the inmates on death row (32).

or

> A poll is available (*Prisoner's View* 32).

AN INTERVIEW

Probably you won't need a parenthetic citation because you'll say something like

> Vivian Berger, in an interview, said . . .

or

> According to Vivian Berger, in an interview . . .

and when your reader turns to the Works Cited, he or she will see that Berger is listed, along with the date of the interview. But if you don't mention the source's name in the lead-in, you'll have to give it in the parentheses, thus:

> Contrary to popular belief, the death penalty is not reserved for serial killers and depraved murderers (Berger).

AN ELECTRONIC SOURCE

Electronic sources, such as Web sites, are generally not divided into pages. Therefore, the in-text citation for such sources cites only the author's name (or, if a work is anonymous, the title):

> According to the Web site for the American Civil Liberties Union . . .

If the source does use pages or breaks down further into paragraphs or screens, insert the appropriate identifier or abbreviation (*p.* or *pp.* for page or pages; *par.* or *pars.* for paragraph or paragraphs; *screen* or *screens*) before the relevant number:

> The growth of day care has been called "a crime against posterity" by a spokesman for the Institute for the American Family (Terwilliger, screens 1-2).

MLA FORMAT: THE LIST OF WORKS CITED

As the previous pages explain, parenthetic documentation consists of references that become clear when the reader consults the list titled Works Cited at the end of an essay.

The list of Works Cited begins on its own page and continues the pagination of the essay: If the last page of text is 10, then the Works Cited begins on page 11. Type the page number in the upper right corner, a half inch from the top of the sheet and flush with the right margin. Next, type the heading Works Cited (*not* enclosed within quotation marks and not italic), centered, one inch from the top, and then double-space and type the first entry.

Here are some general guidelines.

FORM ON THE PAGE

- Begin each entry flush with the left margin, but if an entry runs to more than one line, indent a half inch for each succeeding line of the entry. This is known as a hanging indent, and most word processing programs can achieve this effect easily.

- Double-space each entry, and double-space between entries.

- Italicize titles of works published independently (which the MLA also calls *containers*; see page 294), such as books, pamphlets, and journals. Enclose within quotation marks a work not published independently — for instance, an article in a journal or a short story.

- If you are citing a book that includes the title of another book, italicize the main title, but do *not* italicize the title mentioned. Example:

  A Study of Mill's On Liberty

- In the sample entries below, pay attention to the use of commas, colons, and the space after punctuation.

ALPHABETICAL ORDER

- Arrange the list alphabetically by author, with the author's last name first.
- For information about anonymous works, works with more than one author, and two or more works by one author, see below.

Here is more detailed advice.

THE AUTHOR'S NAME

Notice that the last name is given first, but otherwise the name is given as on the title page. Do not substitute initials for names written out on the title page.

If your list includes two or more works by an author, do not repeat the author's name for the second title; instead represent it by three hyphens followed by a period. The sequence of the works is determined by the alphabetical order of the titles. Thus, Smith's book titled *Poverty* would be listed ahead of her book *Welfare*. See the example on page 295, listing two works by Roger Brown.

Anonymous works are listed under the first word of the title or the second word if the first is *A, An,* or *The* or a foreign equivalent. We discuss books by more than one author, government documents, and works of corporate authorship on pages 295–96.

CONTAINERS AND PUBLICATION INFORMATION

When a source being documented comes from a larger source, the larger source is considered a *container*, because it contains the smaller source you are citing. For example, a container might be an anthology, a periodical, a Web site, a television program, a database, or an online archive. The context of a source will help you determine what counts as a container.

In Works Cited lists, the title of a container is listed after the period following the author's name. The container title is generally italicized and followed by a comma, since the information that follows describes the container. (More on this below.) Disregard any unusual typography, such as the use of all capital letters or the use of an ampersand (&) for *and*. Italicize the container title (and subtitle, if applicable; separate them by a colon), but do not italicize the period that concludes this part of the entry.

- Capitalize the first word and the last word of the title.
- Capitalize all nouns, pronouns, verbs, adjectives, adverbs, and subordinating conjunctions (e.g., *although, if, because*).
- Do not capitalize (unless it's the first or last word of the title or the first word of the subtitle) articles (e.g., *a, an, the*), prepositions (e.g., *in, on, toward, under*), coordinating conjunctions (e.g., *and, but, or, for*), or the *to* in infinitives.

When citing a source within a container, the title of the source should be the first element following the author's name. The source title should be set within quotation marks with a period inside the closing quotation mark. The title of the container is then listed, followed by a comma, with additional information—including publication information, dates, and page ranges—about the container set off by commas.

> Boyle, T. C. "Achates McNeil." *After the Plague: Stories*, Viking Penguin, 2001, pp. 82-101.

This example cites a story, "Achates McNeil," from an anthology—or container—called *After the Plague: Stories*. The anthology was published by Viking Penguin in 2001, and the story appears on pages 82 through 101.

Note that the full name of the publisher is listed. Always include the full names of publishers, except for terms such as "Inc." and "Company." Retain terms such as "Books" and "Publisher." The only exception is university presses, which are abbreviated thus: *Yale UP, U of Chicago P, State U of New York P.*

Sample Entries   Here are some examples illustrating the points we have covered thus far:

> Brown, Roger. *Social Psychology*. Free Press, 1965.
>
> - - - . *Words and Things*. Free Press, 1958.
>
> Haidt, Jonathan. "The Uses of Adversity." *The Happiness Hypothesis: Finding Modern Truth in Ancient Wisdom*, Basic Books, 2006, pp. 135-154.
>
> Hartman, Chester. *The Transformation of San Francisco*. Rowman and Littlefield Publishers, 1984.
>
> Kellerman, Barbara. *The Political Presidency: Practice of Leadership from Kennedy through Reagan*. Oxford UP, 1984.

These examples provide general guidelines for the kind of information you need to include in your Works Cited list. On the following pages, you will find more specific information for listing different kinds of sources.

A BOOK BY MORE THAN ONE AUTHOR

The book is alphabetized under the last name of the first author named on the title page. If there are *two authors,* the name of the second author is given in the normal order, *first name first, after the first author's name.*

> Gilbert, Sandra M., and Susan Gubar. *The Madwoman in the Attic: The Woman Writer and the Nineteenth-Century Literary Imagination*. Yale UP, 1979.

Notice, again, that although the first author's name is given *last name first*, the second author's name is given in the normal order, first name first. Notice, too, that a comma is added after the first name of the first author, separating the authors.

If there are *more than two authors,* give the name only of the first, followed by a comma, and then add *et al.* (Latin for "and others").

> Zumeta, William, et al. *Financing American Higher Education in the Era of Globalization*. Harvard Education Press, 2012.

GOVERNMENT DOCUMENTS

If the writer is not known, treat the government and the agency as the author. Most federal documents are issued by the Government Printing Office (abbreviated to *GPO*) in Washington, D.C.

> United States, Office of Technology Assessment. *Computerized Manufacturing Automation: Employment, Education, and the Workplace.* GPO, 1984.

WORKS OF CORPORATE AUTHORSHIP

Begin the citation with the corporate author, even if the same body is also the publisher, as in the first example:

> American Psychiatric Association. *Psychiatric Glossary.* American Psychiatric Association, 1984.

> Human Rights Watch. *World Report of 2015: Events of 2014.* Seven Stories Press, 2015.

A REPRINT (E.G., A PAPERBACK VERSION OF AN OLDER CLOTHBOUND BOOK)

After the title, give the date of original publication (it can usually be found on the reverse of the title page of the reprint you are using), then a period, and then the publisher and date of the edition you are using. The example indicates that de Mille's book was originally published in 1951 and that the student is using the 2015 reprint with an introduction by Joan Acocella.

> de Mille, Agnes. *Dance to the Piper.* 1951. Introduction by Joan Acocella, New York Review Books, 2015.

A BOOK IN SEVERAL VOLUMES

If you have used more than one volume, in a citation within your essay you will (as explained on p. 292) indicate a reference to, say, page 250 of volume 3 thus: (3: 250).

If, however, you have used only one volume of the set — let's say volume 3 — in your entry in the Works Cited, specify which volume you used, as in the next example:

> Friedel, Frank. *Franklin D. Roosevelt.* Vol. 3, Little Brown, 1973. 4 vols.

With such an entry in the Works Cited, the parenthetic citation within your essay would be to the page only, not to the volume and page, because a reader who consults the Works Cited will understand that you used only volume 3. In the Works Cited, you may specify volume 3 and not give the total number of volumes, or you may add the total number of volumes, as in the preceding example.

BOOK WITH MORE THAN ONE PUBLISHER

If a book is listed as having been published by two or more publishers, separate the publishers with a slash, and include a space before and after the slash.

> Hornby, Nick. *About a Boy.* Riverhead / Penguin Putnam, 1998.

A BOOK WITH AN AUTHOR AND AN EDITOR

Kant, Immanuel. *The Philosophy of Kant: Immanuel Kant's Moral and Political Writings*. Edited by Carl J. Friedrich, Modern Library, 1949.

If you are making use of the editor's introduction or other editorial material rather than the author's work, list the book under the name of the editor rather than of the author, as shown below under An Introduction, Foreword, or Afterword.

A REVISED EDITION OF A BOOK

Arendt, Hannah. *Eichmann in Jerusalem*. Revised and enlarged ed., Viking, 1965.

Honour, Hugh, and John Fleming. *The Visual Arts: A History*. 7th ed., Laurence King Publishing, 2013.

A TRANSLATED BOOK

Ullmann, Regina. *The Country Road: Stories*. Translated by Kurt Beals, New Directions Publishing, 2015.

AN INTRODUCTION, FOREWORD, OR AFTERWORD

Dunham, Lena. Foreword. *The Liars' Club*, by Mary Karr, Penguin Classics, 2015, pp. xi-xiii.

Usually, an introduction or comparable material is listed under the name of the author of the book (here Karr) rather than under the name of the writer of the foreword (here Dunham), but if you are referring to the apparatus rather than to the book itself, use the form just given. The words *Introduction, Preface, Foreword,* and *Afterword* are neither enclosed within quotation marks nor italicized.

A BOOK WITH AN EDITOR BUT NO AUTHOR

Let's assume that you have used a book of essays written by various people but collected by an editor (or editors), whose name(s) appears on the collection.

Horner, Avril, and Anne Rowe, editors. *Living on Paper: Letters from Iris Murdoch*. Princeton UP, 2016.

A WORK WITHIN A VOLUME OF WORKS BY ONE AUTHOR

The following entry indicates that a short work by Susan Sontag, an essay called "The Aesthetics of Silence," appears in a book by Sontag titled *Styles of Radical Will*. Notice that the inclusive page numbers of the short work are cited, not merely page numbers that you may happen to refer to but the page numbers of the entire piece.

Sontag, Susan. "The Aesthetics of Silence." *Styles of Radical Will*, Farrar, Straus, and Giroux, 1969, pp. 3-34.

A BOOK REVIEW

Here is an example, citing Walton's review of Mitchell's book. Walton's review was published in a journal: *The New York Review of Books*.

> Walton, James. "Noble, Embattled Souls." Review of *The Bone Clocks and Slade House*, by David Mitchell. *The New York Review of Books*, 3 Dec. 2015, pp. 55-58.

In this case, Walton's review has a title ("Noble, Embattled Souls") that appears between the period following the reviewer's name and *Review*.

If a review is anonymous, list it under the first word of the title, or under the second word if the first is *A, An,* or *The*. If an anonymous review has no title, begin the entry with *Review of*, and then give the title of the work reviewed; alphabetize the entry under the title of the work reviewed.

AN ARTICLE OR ESSAY IN A COLLECTION

A book may consist of a collection (edited by one or more persons) of new essays by several authors. Here is a reference to one essay in such a book. (The essay by Sayrafiezadeh occupies pages 3 to 29 in a collection edited by Marcus.)

> Sayrafiezadeh, Saïd. "Paranoia." *New American Stories*, edited by Ben Marcus, Vintage Books, 2015, pp. 3-29.

MULTIPLE WORKS FROM THE SAME COLLECTION

You may find that you need to cite multiple sources from within a single container, such as several essays from the same edited anthology. In these cases, provide an entry for the entire anthology (the entry for Marcus below) and a shortened entry for each selection. Alphabetize the entries by authors' or editors' last names.

> Eisenberg, Deborah. "Some Other, Better Otto." Marcus, pp. 94-136.

> Marcus, Ben, editor. *New American Stories*. Vintage Books, 2015.

> Sayrafiezadeh, Saïd. "Paranoia." Marcus, pp. 3-29.

BOOK WITH A TITLE IN ITS TITLE

If the book title contains a title that is normally italicized, do not italicize the title within the book title. If the book title contains a title normally placed in quotation marks, retain the quotation marks and italicize the entire title.

> Masur, Louis P. *Runaway Dream:* Born to Run *and Bruce Springsteen's American Vision*. Bloomsbury, 2009.

> Lethem, Jonathan. *"Lucky Alan" and Other Stories*. Doubleday, 2015.

BOOK IN A SERIES

After the publication information, list the series name as it appears on the title page.

Denham, A. E., editor. *Plato on Art and Beauty*. Palgrave Macmillan, 2012. Philosophers in Depth.

AN ARTICLE IN A REFERENCE WORK (INCLUDING A WIKI)

For a *signed* article, begin with the author's last name. (If the article is signed with initials, check elsewhere in the volume for a list of abbreviations, which will inform you who the initials stand for, and use the following form.) Provide the name of the article, the publication title, edition number (if applicable), the publisher, and the copyright year.

Robinson, Lisa Clayton. "Harlem Writers Guild." *Africana: The Encyclopedia of the African and African American Experience*. 2nd ed., Oxford UP, 2005.

For an unsigned article, begin with the title of the article:

"Ball's in Your Court, The." *The American Heritage Dictionary of Idioms*. 2nd ed., Houghton Mifflin Harcourt, 2013.

For an online reference work, such as a wiki, include the author name and article name followed by the name of the Web site, the date of publication or the most recent update, and the URL (without *http://* before it).

Durante, Amy M. "Finn Mac Cumhail." *Encyclopedia Mythica*, 17 Apr. 2011, www.pantheon .org/articles/f/finn_mac_cumhail.html.

"House Music." *Wikipedia*, 16 Nov. 2015, en.wikipedia.org/wiki/House_music.

A TELEVISION OR RADIO PROGRAM

Be sure to include the title of the episode or segment (in quotation marks), the title of the show (italicized), the producer or director of the show, the network, and the date of the airing. Other information, such as performers, narrator, and so forth, may be included if pertinent.

"Fast Times at West Philly High." *Frontline*, produced by Debbie Morton, PBS, 17 July 2012.

"Federal Role in Support of Autism." *Washington Journal*, narrated by Robb Harleston, C-SPAN, 1 Dec. 2012.

AN ARTICLE IN A SCHOLARLY JOURNAL

The title of the article is enclosed within quotation marks, and the title of the journal is italicized.

Some journals are paginated consecutively; the pagination of the second issue begins where the first issue leaves off. Other journals begin each issue with page 1.

Matchie, Thomas. "Law versus Love in The Round House." *Midwest Quarterly*, vol. 56, no. 4, Summer 2015, pp. 353-64.

Matchie's article occupies pages 353 to 364 in volume 56, which was published in 2015. When available, give the issue number as well. (If the journal is, for instance, a quarterly, there will be four page *1*'s each year, so the issue number must be given.)

AN ARTICLE IN A WEEKLY, BIWEEKLY, MONTHLY, OR BIMONTHLY PUBLICATION

Do not include volume or issue numbers, even if given.

> Thompson, Mark. "Sending Women to War: The Pentagon Nears a Historic Decision on Equality at the Front Lines." *Time*, 14 Dec. 2015, pp. 53-55.

AN ARTICLE IN A NEWSPAPER

Because a newspaper usually consists of several sections, a section number or a capital letter may precede the page number. The example indicates that an article appears on page 1 of section C.

> Bray, Hiawatha. "As Toys Get Smarter, Privacy Issues Emerge." *The Boston Globe*, 10 Dec. 2015, p. C1.

AN UNSIGNED EDITORIAL

> "The Religious Tyranny Amendment." *New York Times,* 15 Mar. 1998, p. 16. Editorial.

A LETTER TO THE EDITOR

> Lasken, Douglas. *New York Times.* 15 Mar. 1998, p. 16. Letter.

A PUBLISHED OR BROADCAST INTERVIEW

Give the name of the interview subject and the interviewer, followed by the relevant publication or broadcast information, in the following format:

> Weddington, Sarah. "Sarah Weddington: Still Arguing for *Roe*." Interview by Michele Kort, *Ms.*, Winter 2013, pp. 32-35.

> Tempkin, Ann, and Anne Umland. Interview by Charlie Rose. *Charlie Rose: The Week*, PBS, 9 Oct. 2015.

AN INTERVIEW YOU CONDUCT

> Akufo, Dautey. Personal interview, 11 Apr. 2016.

A PERSONAL OR PROFESSIONAL WEB SITE

Include the following elements, separated by periods: the name of the person who created the site (omit if not given, as in Figure 7.4), site title (italicized), name of any sponsoring institution or organization; date of electronic publication or of the latest update (if given; if not, provide the date you accessed the site at the end of the citation); and the URL (without *http://*).

> *Legal Guide for Bloggers.* Electronic Frontier Foundation, www.eff.org/issues/bloggers/legal. Accessed 5 Apr. 2016.

Figure 7.4   Citing a Blog

1. URL
2. Sponsor of Web site
3. No author given; start citation with the title.
4. No date of publication given; include date of access in citation.

AN ARTICLE IN AN ONLINE PERIODICAL

Give the same information as you would for a print article, plus the URL. (See Figure 7.5.)

> Acocella, Joan. "In the Blood: Why Do Vampires Still Thrill?" *New Yorker,* 16 March 2009.
> www.newyorker.com/magazine/2009/03/16/in-the-blood.

A POSTING TO AN ONLINE DISCUSSION LIST

The citation includes the author's name, the subject line of the posting, the name of the forum, the host of the forum, the date the material was posted, and the URL.

> Robin, Griffith. "Write for the Reading Teacher." *Developing Digital Literacies*, NCTE,
> 23 Oct. 2015, ncte.connectedcommunity.org/communities/community-home/digestviewer
> /viewthread?GroupId=1693&MID=24520&tab=digestviewer&CommunityKey=628d2ad6
> -8277-4042-a376-2b370ddceabf.

Figure 7.5   Citing an Online Magazine

1. URL
2. Title of periodical
3. Title of article
4. Subtitle of article
5. Author
6. Publication date. If the article doesn't have a publication date, include the date you accessed it.

A FACEBOOK POST OR COMMENT

Include the name of the Facebook page on which the post appeared, the name of the post (or the post on which the comment appears), the name of the site, the date, and the URL of the post or comment.

> Bedford English. "Stacey Cochran Explores Reflective Writing in the Classroom and as a Writer: http://ow.ly/YkjVB." *Facebook*, 15 Feb. 2016, www.facebook.com/BedfordEnglish /posts/10153415001259607.

AN E-MAIL MESSAGE

Include the name of the sender, the title of the message, the name of the recipient, and the date of the message.

> Thornbrugh, Caitlin. "Coates Lecture." Received by Rita Anderson, 20 Oct. 2015.

A TEXT MESSAGE

Include the name of the sender, the title of the message, the name of the recipient, and the date of the message.

Naqvi, Sahin. Message to the author, 18 Nov. 2015.

TWITTER POST (TWEET)

Include the handle of the poster, the content of the Tweet (enclosed in quotation marks), the name of the site, the date and time of the post, and the URL.

Curiosity Rover. "Can you see me waving? How to spot #Mars in the night sky: https://youtu
.be/hv8hVvJlcJQ." *Twitter*, 5 Nov. 2015, 11:00 a.m., twitter.com/marscuriosity/status
/672859022911889408.

A DATABASE SOURCE

Treat material obtained from a database like other printed material, but at the end of the entry add (if available) the title of the database (italicized), and a permalink or DOI (digital object identifier) if the source has one. If a source does not, then include a URL (without the protocol, such as *http://*).

Coles, Kimberly Anne. "The Matter of Belief in John Donne's Holy Sonnets." *Renaissance Quarterly*,
vol. 68, no. 3, Fall 2015, pp. 899-931. JSTOR, doi:10.1086/683855.

Macari, Anne Marie. "Lyric Impulse in a Time of Extinction." *American Poetry Review*, vol. 44,
no. 4, July/Aug. 2015, pp. 11-14. *General OneFile*, go.galegroup.com/.

Caution: Although we have covered many kinds of sources, it's entirely possible that you will come across a source that doesn't fit any of the categories that we have discussed. For greater explanations of these matters, covering the proper way to cite all sorts of troublesome and unbelievable (but real) sources, see the *MLA Handbook,* Eighth Edition (Modern Language Association of America, 2016).

APA FORMAT: CITATIONS WITHIN THE TEXT

Your paper will conclude with a separate page headed References, on which you list all of your sources. If the last page of your essay is numbered 10, number the first page of the References 11.

The APA style emphasizes the date of publication; the date appears not only in the list of references at the end of the paper but also in the paper itself, when you give a brief parenthetic citation of a source that you have quoted or summarized or in any other way used. Here is an example:

Statistics are readily available (Smith, 1989, p. 20).

The title of Smith's book or article will be given at the end of your paper in the list titled References. We discuss the form of the material listed in the References after we look at some typical citations within the text of a student's essay.

A SUMMARY OF AN ENTIRE WORK

Smith (1988) holds the same view.

or

Similar views are held widely (Smith, 1988; Jones & Metz, 1990).

A REFERENCE TO A PAGE OR TO PAGES

Smith (1988) argues that "the death penalty is a lottery, and blacks usually are the losers" (p. 17).

A REFERENCE TO AN AUTHOR WHO HAS MORE THAN ONE WORK IN THE LIST OF REFERENCES

If in the References you list two or more works that an author published in the same year, the works are listed in alphabetical order, by the first letter of the title. The first work is labeled *a*, the second *b*, and so on. Here is a reference to the second work that Smith published in 1989:

Florida presents "a fair example" of how the death penalty is administered (Smith, 1989b, p. 18).

APA FORMAT: THE LIST OF REFERENCES

Your brief parenthetic citations are made clear when the reader consults the list you give in the References. Type this list on a separate page, continuing the pagination of your essay.

An Overview Here are some general guidelines.

FORM ON THE PAGE

- Begin each entry flush with the left margin, but if an entry runs to more than one line, indent five spaces for each succeeding line of the entry.
- Double-space each entry, and double-space between entries.

ALPHABETICAL ORDER

- Arrange the list alphabetically by author.
- Give the author's last name first and then the initial of the first name and of the middle name (if any).
- If there is more than one author, name all of the authors up to seven, again inverting the name (last name first) and giving only initials for first and middle names. (But do not invert the editor's name when the entry begins with the name of an author who has written an article in an edited book.) When there are two or more authors, use an ampersand (&) before the name of the last author. Example (here, of an article in the tenth volume of a journal called *Developmental Psychology*):

Drabman, R. S., & Thomas, M. H. (1974). Does media violence increase children's tolerance of real-life aggression? *Developmental Psychology, 10,* 418-421.

- For eight or more authors, list the first six followed by three ellipsis dots and then the last author. If you list more than one work by an author, do so in the order of publication, the earliest first. If two works by an author were published in the same year, give them in alphabetical order by the first letter of the title, disregarding *A, An,* or *The,* and their foreign equivalent. Designate the first work as *a,* the second as *b.* Repeat the author's name at the start of each entry.

Donnerstein, E. (1980a). Aggressive erotica and violence against women. *Journal of Personality and Social Psychology, 39,* 269-277.

Donnerstein, E. (1980b). Pornography and violence against women. *Annals of the New York Academy of Sciences, 347,* 227-288.

Donnerstein, E. (1983). Erotica and human aggression. In R. Green & E. Donnerstein (Eds.), *Aggression: Theoretical and empirical reviews* (pp. 87-103). New York, NY: Academic Press.

FORM OF TITLE

- In references to books, capitalize only the first letter of the first word of the title (and of the subtitle, if any) and capitalize proper nouns. Italicize the complete title (but not the period at the end).

- In references to articles in periodicals or in edited books, capitalize only the first letter of the first word of the article's title (and subtitle, if any) and all proper nouns. Do not put the title within quotation marks or italicize it. Type a period after the title of the article. For the title of the journal and the volume and page numbers, see the next instruction.

- In references to periodicals, give the volume number in arabic numerals, and italicize it. Do *not* use *vol.* before the number, and do not use *p.* or *pg.* before the page numbers.

Sample References   Here are some samples to follow.

A BOOK BY ONE AUTHOR

Pavlov, I. P. (1927). *Conditioned reflexes* (G. V. Anrep, Trans.). London, England: Oxford University Press.

A BOOK BY MORE THAN ONE AUTHOR

Belenky, M. F., Clinchy, B. M., Goldberger, N. R., & Torule, J. M. (1986). *Women's ways of knowing: The development of self, voice, and mind.* New York, NY: Basic Books.

A COLLECTION OF ESSAYS

Christ, C. P., & Plaskow, J. (Eds.). (1979). *Woman-spirit rising: A feminist reader in religion.* New York, NY: Harper & Row.

A WORK IN A COLLECTION OF ESSAYS

Fiorenza, E. (1979). Women in the early Christian movement. In C. P. Christ & J. Plaskow (Eds.), *Woman-spirit rising: A feminist reader in religion* (pp. 84-92). New York, NY: Harper & Row.

GOVERNMENT DOCUMENTS

If the writer is not known, treat the government and the agency as the author. Most federal documents are issued by the U.S. Government Printing Office in Washington, D.C. If a document number has been assigned, insert that number in parentheses between the title and the following period.

United States Congress. Office of Technology Assessment. (1984). *Computerized manufacturing automation: Employment, education, and the workplace*. Washington, DC: U.S. Government Printing Office.

AN ARTICLE IN A JOURNAL WITH CONTINUOUS PAGINATION

Tversky, A., & Kahneman, D. (1981). The framing of decisions and the psychology of choice. *Science, 211*, 453-458.

AN ARTICLE IN A JOURNAL THAT PAGINATES EACH ISSUE SEPARATELY

Foot, R. J. (1988-89). Nuclear coercion and the ending of the Korean conflict. *International Security, 13*(4), 92-112.

The reference informs us that the article appeared in issue number 4 of volume 13.

AN ARTICLE FROM A MONTHLY OR WEEKLY MAGAZINE

Greenwald, J. (1989, February 27). Gimme shelter. *Time, 133,* 50-51.

Maran, S. P. (1988, April). In our backyard, a star explodes. *Smithsonian, 19,* 46-57.

AN ARTICLE IN A NEWSPAPER

Connell, R. (1989, February 6). Career concerns at heart of 1980s campus protests. *Los Angeles Times*, pp. 1, 3.

(*Note:* If no author is given, simply begin with the title followed by the date in parentheses.)

A CHECKLIST FOR CRITICAL PAPERS USING SOURCES

Ask yourself the following questions:

☐ Are all borrowed words and ideas credited, including those from Internet sources?

☐ Are all summaries and paraphrases acknowledged as such?

☐ Are quotations and summaries not too long?

☐ Are quotations accurate? Are omissions of words indicated by three spaced periods? Are additions of words enclosed within square brackets?

☐ Are quotations provided with helpful lead-ins?

☐ Is documentation in proper form?

And, of course, you will also ask yourself the questions that you would ask of a paper that did not use sources, such as:

☐ Is the topic sufficiently narrowed?

☐ Is the thesis (to be advanced or refuted) stated early and clearly, perhaps even in the title?

☐ Is the audience kept in mind? Are opposing views stated fairly and as sympathetically as possible? Are controversial terms defined?

☐ Are assumptions likely to be shared by readers? If not, are they argued rather than merely asserted?

☐ Is the focus clear (evaluation, recommendation of policy)?

☐ Is evidence (examples, testimony, statistics) adequate and sound?

☐ Are inferences valid?

☐ Is the organization clear (effective opening, coherent sequence of arguments, unpretentious ending)?

☐ Is all worthy opposition faced?

☐ Is the tone appropriate?

☐ Has the paper been carefully proofread?

☐ Is the title effective?

☐ Is the introduction effective?

☐ Is the structure reader-friendly?

☐ Is the ending effective?

A BOOK REVIEW

> Daniels, N. (1984). Understanding physician power [Review of the book *The social transformation of American medicine*]. *Philosophy and Public Affairs, 13*, 347-356.

Daniels is the reviewer, not the author of the book. The book under review is called *The Social Transformation of American Medicine,* but the review, published in volume 13 of *Philosophy and Public Affairs,* had its own title, "Understanding Physician Power."

If the review does not have a title, retain the square brackets, and use the material within as the title. Proceed as in the example just given.

A WEB SITE

> American Psychological Association. (1995). Lesbian and gay parenting. Retrieved June 12, 2000, from http://www.apa.org/pi/parent.html

AN ARTICLE IN AN ONLINE PERIODICAL

> Carpenter, S. (2000, October). Biology and social environments jointly influence gender development. *Monitor on Psychology 31*(9). Retrieved from http://www.apa.org/monitor/

For a full account of the APA method of dealing with all sorts of unusual citations, see the sixth edition (2010) of the APA manual, *Publication Manual of the American Psychological Association.*

An Annotated Student Research Paper in MLA Format

The following argument makes good use of sources. Early in the semester the students were asked to choose one topic from a list of ten and to write a documented argument of 750 to 1,250 words (three to five pages of double-spaced typing). The completed paper was due two weeks after the topics were distributed. The assignment, a prelude to working on a research paper of 2,500 to 3,000 words, was in part designed to give students practice in finding and in using sources. Citations are given in the MLA form.

Lesley Timmerman
Professor Jennifer Wilson
English 102
15 August 2016

An Argument for Corporate Responsibility

Opponents of corporate social responsibility (CSR) argue that a company's sole duty is to generate profits. According to them, by acting for the public good, corporations are neglecting their primary obligation to make money. However, as people are becoming more and more conscious of corporate impacts on society and the environment, separating profits from company practices and ethics does not make sense. Employees want to work for institutions that share their values, and consumers want to buy products from companies that are making an impact and improving people's lives. Furthermore, businesses exist in an interdependent world where the health of the environment and the well-being of society really do matter. For these reasons, corporations have to take responsibility for their actions, beyond making money for shareholders. For their own benefit as well as the public's, companies must strive to be socially responsible.

In his article "The Case against Corporate Social Responsibility," *Wall Street Journal* writer Aneel Karnani argues that CSR will never be able to solve the world's problems. Thinking it can, Karnani says, is a dangerous illusion. He recommends that instead of expecting corporate managers to act in the public interest, we should rely on philanthropy and government regulation. Karnani maintains that "Managers who sacrifice profit for the common good [. . .] are in effect imposing a tax on their shareholders and arbitrarily deciding how that money should be spent." In other words, according to Karnani, corporations should not be determining what constitutes socially responsible behavior; individual donors and the government should. Certainly, individuals should continue to make charitable gifts, and governments should maintain laws and regulations to protect the public interest. However, Karnani's reasoning for why corporations should be exempt from social responsibility is flawed. With very few exceptions, corporations' socially responsible actions are not arbitrary and do not sacrifice long-term profits.

Title is focused and announces the thesis.

Double-space between the title and first paragraph—and throughout the essay.

Brief statement of one side of the issue.

Summary of the opposing view.

Lead-in to quotation.

1" margin on each side and at bottom.

Essayist's response to the quotation.

Author concisely
states her
position.

In fact, corporations have already proven that they can contribute profitably and meaningfully to solving significant global problems by integrating CSR into their standard practices and long-term visions. Rather than focusing on shareholders' short-term profits, many companies have begun measuring their success by "profit, planet and people" — what is known as the "triple bottom line." Businesses operating under this principle consider their environmental and social impacts, as well as their financial impacts, and make responsible and compassionate decisions. For example,

Transitions ("For
example," "also")
alert readers to
where the writer
is taking them.

such businesses use resources efficiently, create healthy products, choose suppliers who share their ethics, and improve economic opportunities for people in the communities they serve. By doing so, companies often save money. They also contribute to the sustainability of life on earth and ensure the sustainability of their own businesses. In their book *The Triple Bottom Line: How Today's Best-Run Companies Are Achieving Economic, Social, and Environmental Success*, coauthors Savitz and Weber demonstrate that corporations need to become sustainable, in all ways. They argue that "the only way to succeed in today's interdependent world is to embrace sustainability" (xi). The authors go on to show that, for the vast majority of companies, a broad commitment to sustainability enhances profitability (Savitz and Weber 39).

For example, PepsiCo has been able to meet the financial expectations of its shareholders while demonstrating its commitment to the triple bottom line. In addition to donating over $16 million to help victims of natural disasters, Pepsi has woven concerns for people and for the planet into its company practices and culture (Bejou 4). For instance, because of a recent water shortage in an area of India where Pepsi runs a plant, the company began a project to build community wells (Savitz and Weber 160). Though Pepsi did not cause the water shortage nor was its manufacturing threatened by it, "Pepsi realizes that the well-being of the community is part of the company's responsibility" (Savitz and Weber 161). Ultimately, Pepsi chose to look beyond the goal of maximizing short-term profits. By doing so, the company improved its relationship with this Indian community, improved people's daily lives and opportunities, and improved its own reputation. In other words, Pepsi embraced CSR and ensured a more sustainable future for everyone involved.

Another example of a wide-reaching company that is working toward greater sustainability on all fronts is Walmart. The corporation has issued a CSR policy that includes three ambitious goals: "to be fully supplied by renewable energy, to create zero waste and to sell products that sustain people and the environment" ("From Fringe to Mainstream"). As Dr. Doug Guthrie, dean of George Washington University's School of Business, noted in a recent lecture, if a company as powerful as Walmart were to succeed in these goals, the impact would be huge. To illustrate Walmart's potential influence, Dr. Guthrie pointed out that the corporation's exports from China to the United States are equal to Mexico's total exports to the United States. In committing to CSR, the company's leaders are acknowledging how much their power depends on the earth's natural resources, as well as the communities who produce, distribute, sell, and purchase Walmart's products. The company is also well aware that achieving its goals will "ultimately save the company a great deal of money" ("From Fringe to Mainstream"). For good reason, Walmart, like other companies around the world, is choosing to act in *everyone's* best interest.

Recent research on employees' and consumers' social consciousness offers companies further reason to take corporate responsibility seriously. For example, studies show that workers care about making a difference (Meister). In many cases, workers would even take a pay cut to work for a more responsible, sustainable company. In fact, 45% of workers said they would take a 15% reduction in pay "for a job that makes a social or environmental impact" (Meister). Even more said they would take a 15% cut in pay to work for a company with values that match their own (Meister). The numbers are most significant among Millennials (those born between, approximately, 1980 and the early 2000s). Fully 80% of Millennials said they "wanted to work for a company that cares about how it impacts and contributes to society," and over half said they would not work for an "irresponsible company" (Meister). Given this more socially conscious generation, companies are going to find it harder and harder to ignore CSR.

Author now introduces statistical evidence that, if introduced earlier, might have turned the reader off.

To recruit and retain employees, employers will need to earn the admiration, respect, and loyalty of their workers by becoming "good corporate citizen[s]" (qtd. in "From Fringe to Mainstream").

Similarly, studies clearly show that CSR matters to today's consumers. According to an independent report, 80% of Americans say they would switch brands to support a social cause (Cone Communications 6). Fully 88% say they approve of companies' using social or environmental issues in their marketing (Cone Communications 5). And 83% say they "wish more of the products, services and retailers would support causes" (Cone Communications 5). Other independent surveys corroborate these results, confirming that today's customers, especially Millennials, care about more than just price ("From Fringe to Mainstream"). Furthermore, plenty of companies have seen what happens when they assume that consumers do not care about CSR. For example, in 1997, when Nike customers discovered that their shoes were manufactured by child laborers in Indonesia, the company took a huge financial hit (Guthrie). Today, Information Age customers are even more likely to educate themselves about companies' labor practices and environmental records. Smart corporations will listen to consumer preferences, provide transparency, and commit to integrating CSR into their long-term business plans.

> **Author argues that it is in the *companies'* interest to be socially responsible.**

In this increasingly interdependent world, the case against CSR is becoming more and more difficult to defend. Exempting corporations and relying on government to be the world's conscience does not make good social, environmental, or economic sense. Contributors to a recent article in the online journal *Knowledge@Wharton,* published by the Wharton School of Business, agree. Professor Eric Orts maintains that "it is an outmoded view to say that one must rely only on the government and regulation to police business responsibilities. What we need is re-conception of what the purpose of business is" (qtd. in "From Fringe to Mainstream"). The question is, what should the purpose of a business be in today's world? Professor of Business Administration David Bejou of Elizabeth City State University has a thoughtful and sensible answer to that question. He writes,

> **Author's lead-in to the quotation guides the reader's response to the quotation.**

. . . it is clear that the sole purpose of a business is not merely that of generating profits for its owners. Instead, because compassion provides the necessary equilibrium between a company's purpose and the needs of its communities, it should be the new philosophy of business. (Bejou 1)

As Bejou implies, the days of allowing corporations to act in their own financial self-interest with little or no regard for their effects on others are over. None of us can afford such a narrow view of business. The world is far too interconnected. A seemingly small corporate decision — to buy coffee beans directly from local growers or to install solar panels — can affect the lives and livelihoods of many people and determine the environmental health of whole regions. A business, just like a government or an individual, therefore has an ethical responsibility to act with compassion for the public good.

Fortunately, corporations have many incentives to act responsibly. Customer loyalty, employee satisfaction, overall cost-saving, and long-term viability are just some of the advantages businesses can expect to gain by embracing comprehensive CSR policies. Meanwhile, companies have very little to lose by embracing a socially conscious view. These days, compassion is profitable. Corporations would be wise to recognize the enormous power, opportunity, and responsibility they have to effect positive change.

Upbeat ending.

Works Cited

Bejou, David. "Compassion as the New Philosophy of Business." *Journal of Relationship Marketing*, vol. 10, no. 1, Apr. 2011, pp. 1-6. *Taylor and Francis*, doi:10.1080/15332667.2011.550098.

Cone Communications. 2010 *Cone Cause Evolution Study*. Cone, 2010, www.conecomm.com/research-blog/2010-cause-evolution-study.

"From Fringe to Mainstream: Companies Integrate CSR Initiatives into Everyday Business." *Knowledge@Wharton*, 23 May 2012, knowledge .wharton.upenn.edu/article/from-fringe-to-mainstream-companies -integrate-csr-initiatives-into-everyday-business/.

Guthrie, Doug. "Corporate Social Responsibility: A State Department Approach." *Promoting a Comprehensive Approach to Corporate Social Responsibility (CSR)*, George P. Shultz National Foreign Affairs Train-ing Center, 22 May 2012. *YouTube*, 23 Aug. 2013, www.youtube.com /watch?v=99cJMe6wERc.

Karnani, Aneel. "The Case against Corporate Social Responsibility." *Wall Street Journal*, 14 June 2012, www.wsj.com/articles /SB10001424052748703338004575230112664504890.

Meister, Jeanne. "Corporate Social Responsibility: A Lever for Employee Attraction & Engagement." *Forbes*, 7 June 2012, www.forbes.com /sites/jeannemeister/2012/06/07/corporate-social-responsibility -a-lever-for-employee-attraction-engagement/#6125425a7511.

Savitz, Andrew W., with Karl Weber. *The Triple Bottom Line: How Today's Best-Run Companies Are Achieving Economic, Social, and Environmental Success*, Jossey-Bass, 2006.

Alphabetical by author's last name.

Hanging indent ½".

An article on a blog without a known author.

A clip from YouTube.

An Annotated Student Research Paper in APA Format

The following paper is an example of a student paper that uses APA format.

The APA-style cover page gives title, author, and course information.

The Role of Spirituality and Religion
in Mental Health
Laura DeVeau
English 102
Professor Gardner
April 12, 2016

Short form of title and page number as running head.

The Role of Spirituality and Religion
in Mental Health

It has been called "a vestige of the childhood of mankind,"
"the feeling of something true, total and absolute," "an otherworldly
answer as regards the meaning of life" (Jones, 1991, p. 1; Amaro, 1998;
Kristeva, 1987, p. 27). It has been compared to medicine, described as a
psychological cure for mental illness, and also referred to as the cause of
a dangerous fanaticism. With so many differing opinions on the impact
of religion in people's lives, where would one begin a search for the
truth? Who has the answer: Christians, humanists, objectivists, atheists,
psychoanalysts, Buddhists, philosophers, cults? This was my dilemma at the
advent of my research into how religion and spirituality affect the mental
health of society as a whole.

Citation of multiple works from references.

In this paper, I explore the claims, widely accepted by professionals
in the field of psychology, that religious and spiritual practices have a
negative impact on mental health. In addition, though, I cannot help but
reflect on how this exploration has changed my beliefs as well. Religion is
such a personal experience that one cannot be dispassionate in reporting it.
One can, however, subject the evidence provided by those who have studied
the issue to critical scrutiny. Having done so, I find myself in disagreement
with those who claim religious feelings are incompatible with sound mental
health. There is a nearly limitless number of beliefs regarding spirituality.
Some are organized and involve rituals like mass or worship. Many are
centered around the existence of a higher being, while others focus on the
self. I have attempted to uncover the perfect set of values that lead to a
better lifestyle, but my research has pointed me in an entirely different
direction, where no single belief seems to be adequate but where spiritual
belief in general should be valued more highly than it is currently in mental
health circles.

Acknowledgment of opposing viewpoints.

Thesis explicitly introduced.

I grew up in a moderately devout Catholic family. Like many
young people raised in a household where one religion is practiced by
both parents, it never occurred to me to question those beliefs. I went
through a spiritual cycle, which I believe much of Western society also

experiences. I attended religious services because I had to. I possessed a blind, unquestioning acceptance of what I was being taught because the adults I trusted said it was so. Like many adolescents and young adults, though, I stopped going to church when I was old enough to decide because I thought I had better things to do. At this stage, we reach a point when we begin searching for a meaning to our existence. For some, this search is brought on by a major crisis or a feeling of emptiness in their daily lives, while for others it is simply a part of growing up. This is where we begin to make personal choices, but with the barrage of options, where do we turn?

Beginning with the holistic health movement in the eighties, there has been a mass shift from traditional religions to less structured spiritual practices such as meditation, yoga, the Cabala, and mysticism (Beyerman, 1989). They venture beyond the realm of conventional dogmatism and into the new wave of spirituality. Many of these practices are based on the notion that health of the mind and spirit equals health of the body. Associated with this movement is a proliferation of retreats offering a chance to get in touch with the beauty and silence of nature and seminars where we can take "a break from our everyday environment where our brains are bustling and our bodies are exhausting themselves" ("Psychological benefits," 1999). A major concept of the spiritual new wave is that it focuses inward toward the individual psyche, rather than outward toward another being like a god. Practitioners do not deny the existence of this being, but they believe that to fully love another, we must first understand ourselves. Many find this a preferable alternative to religions where the individual is seen as a walking dispenser of sin who is very fortunate to have a forgiving creator. It is also a relief from the scare tactics like damnation used by traditional religions to make people behave. Many, therefore, praise the potential psychological benefits of such spirituality.

While I believe strongly in the benefits of the new wave, I am not willing to do away with structured religion, for I find that it also has its benefits. Without the existence of churches and temples, it would be harder

---

Author and date cited for summary or paraphrase.

Anonymous source cited by title and date.

Clear transition refers to previous paragraph.

to expose the public to values beneficial to mental stability. It is much more difficult to hand a child a copy of the Cabala and say "Read this, and then get back to me on it" than it is to bring a child to a service where the ideas are represented with concrete examples. My religious upbringing presented me with a set of useful morals and values, and it does the same for millions of others who are brought up in this manner. Many people, including some followers of the new wave, are bitter toward Christianity because of events in history like the Crusades, the Inquisition, the Salem witch trials, and countless other horrific acts supposedly committed in the name of God. But these events were based not on biblical teachings but on pure human greed and lust for power. We should not reject the benevolent possibilities of organized religion on the basis of historical atrocities any more than we should abandon public education because a few teachers are known to mistreat children.

   Another factor contributing to the reluctance concerning religion is the existence of cults that seduce people into following their extreme teachings. The victims are often at vulnerable times in their lives, and the leaders are usually very charming, charismatic, and sometimes also psychotic or otherwise mentally unstable. Many argue that if we acknowledge these groups as dangerous cults, then we must do the same for traditional religions such as Christianity and Islam, which are likewise founded on the teachings of charismatic leaders. Again, though, critics are too quick to conflate all religious and spiritual practice; we must distinguish between those who pray and attend services and those who commit group suicide because they think that aliens are coming to take over the world. Cults have provided many psychologists, who are eager to discount religion as a factor in improving mental health, with an easy target. Ellis (1993), the founder of rational-emotive therapy, cites many extreme examples of religious commitment, such as cults and antiabortion killings, to show that commitment is hazardous to one's sanity. Anomalies like these should not be used to speak of religion as a whole, though. Religion is clearly the least of these people's mental problems.

> When the author's name appears in text, only the date is cited in parentheses.

Besides Ellis, there are many others in the field of psychology who do not recognize religion as a potential aid for improving the condition of the psyche. Actually, fewer than 45% of the members of the American Psychiatric Association even believe in God. The general American public has more than twice that percentage of religious devotees (Larson, 1998). Going back to the days of Freud, many psychologists have held atheist views. The father of psychoanalysis himself called religion a "universal obsessional neurosis." Psychologists have long rejected research that demonstrates the benefits of spirituality by saying that this research is biased. They claim that such studies are out to prove that religion helps because the researchers are religious people who need to justify their beliefs.

While this may be true in some instances, there is also some quite empirical research available to support the claims of those who promote religion and spirituality. The *Journal for the Scientific Study of Religion* has conducted many studies examining the effects of religion on individuals and groups. In one example, the relationship between religious coping methods and positive recovery after major stressful events was observed. The results indicated not only that spirituality was not harmful to the mind but that "the positive religious coping pattern was tied to benevolent outcomes, including fewer symptoms of psychological distress, [and] reports of psychological and spiritual growth as a result of the stressor" (Pargament, Smith, Koening, and Perez, 1998, p. 721). Clearly, the benefits of piety can, in fact, be examined empirically, and in some cases the results point to a positive correlation between religion and mental health.

But let us get away from statistics and studies. If religion is both useless and dangerous, as so many psychologists claim, we must ask why has it remained so vital a part of humanity for so long. Even if it can be reduced to a mere coping method that humans use to justify their existence and explain incomprehensible events, is it futile? I would suggest that this alone represents a clear benefit to society. Should religion, if it cannot be proven as "true," be eliminated and life be based on scientific fact alone?

Bracketed word in quotation not in original source.

Author, date, and page number are cited for a direct quotation.

Surely many would find this a pointless existence. With all the conflicting knowledge I have gained about spirituality during my personal journey and my research, one idea is clear. It is not the depth of devotion, the time of life when one turns to religion, or even the particular combination of beliefs one chooses to adopt that will improve the quality of life. There is no right or wrong answer when it comes to self-fulfillment. It is whatever works for the individual, even if that means holding no religious or spiritual beliefs at all. But clearly there *are* benefits to be gained, at least for some individuals, and mental health professionals need to begin acknowledging this fact in their daily practice.

Conclusion restates and strengthens thesis.

References begin on a new page. ➡   References

Amaro, J. (1998). Psychology, psychoanalysis and religious faith. *Nielsen's*

    psychology of religion pages. Retrieved March 17, 2016, from http://

An online source. ➡   www.psywww.com/psyrelig/amaro.html

Beyerman A. K. (1989). *The holistic health movement*. Tuscaloosa, AL:

A book. ➡   Alabama University Press.

Ellis, A. (1993). Dogmatic devotion doesn't help, it hurts. In B. Slife (Ed.),

    Taking sides: Clashing views on controversial psychological issues

An article or a chapter in a book. ➡   (pp. 297-301). New York, NY: Scribner.

Jones, J. W. (1991). *Contemporary psychoanalysis and religion: Transference*

    and transcendence. New Haven, CT: Yale University Press.

Kristeva, J. (1987). *In the beginning was love: Psychoanalysis and faith*. New

    York, NY: Columbia University Press.

Larson, D. (1998). Does religious commitment improve mental health?

    In B. Slife (Ed.), *Taking sides: Clashing views on controversial*

    psychological issues (pp. 292-296). New York, NY: Scribner.

Pargament, K. I., Smith, B. W., Koening, H. G., & Perez, L. (1998). Patterns

An article in a journal. ➡   of positive and negative religious coping with major life stressors.

    Journal for the Scientific Study of Religion, 37, 710-724.

Anonymous source alphabetized by title. ➡ "Psychological benefits." (1999). *Walking the labyrinth*. Retrieved April 3,

    2016, from http://www.labyrinthway.com/html/benefits.html

PART THREE

Further Views on Argument

A Philosopher's View:
The Toulmin Model

All my ideas hold together, but I cannot elaborate them all at once. — JEAN-JACQUES ROUSSEAU

*Clarity has been said to be not enough. But perhaps it will be time
to go into that when we are within measurable distance of achieving clarity
on some matter.* — J. L. AUSTIN

[Philosophy is] a peculiarly stubborn effort to think clearly. — WILLIAM JAMES

*Philosophy is like trying to open a safe with a combination lock:
Each little adjustment of the dials seems to achieve nothing, only
when everything is in place does the door open.* — LUDWIG WITTGENSTEIN

In Chapter 3, we explained the contrast between making *deductive* and *inductive* arguments, the two main methods people use to reason. Either:

- we make explicit something concealed in what we already accept (**deduction**), or
- we use what we have observed as a basis for asserting or proposing something new (**induction**).

These two types of reasoning share some structural features, as we also noticed. Both deductive and inductive reasoning seek to establish a **thesis** (or conclusion) by offering **reasons** for accepting the conclusion. Thus, every argument contains both a thesis and one or more supportive reasons.

After a little scrutiny, we can in fact point to several features shared by all arguments, whether deductive or inductive, good or bad. We use the vocabulary popularized by Stephen Toulmin, Richard Rieke, and Allan Janik in their book *An Introduction to Reasoning* (1979; second edition 1984) to explore the various elements of argument. Once these elements are understood, it is possible to analyze an argument using their approach and their vocabulary in what has come to be known as "The Toulmin Method."

The Claim

Every argument has a purpose, goal, or aim — namely, to establish a **claim** (*conclusion* or *thesis*). Suppose you are arguing in favor of equal rights for women. You might state your thesis or claim as follows:

Men and women ought to have equal rights.

A more precise formulation of the claim might be this:

Men and women ought to have equal legal rights.

A still more precise formulation might be this:

Equal legal rights for men and women ought to be protected by our Constitution.

The third version of this claim states what the controversy in the 1970s over the Equal Rights Amendment was all about. (Both houses of Congress passed it in 1972, but the number of state legislatures that needed to ratify it before the Amendment could be added to the Constitution failed to do so before Congress's mandated deadline of June 30, 1982.)

In other words, the *claim* being made in an argument is the whole point of making the argument in the first place. Consequently, when you read or analyze someone else's argument, the first questions you should ask are these:

- What is the argument intended to prove or establish?
- *What claim is it making?*
- Has this claim been clearly and precisely formulated, so that it unambiguously asserts what its advocate wants it to assert?

Grounds

Once we have the argument's purpose or point clearly in mind and thus know what the arguer is aiming to establish, then we can look for the evidence, reasons, support — in short, for the **grounds** — on which that claim is based. In a *deductive* argument, these grounds are the premises from which the claim is deduced; in an *inductive* argument, the grounds are the evidence — which could be based on a sample, an observation, or an experiment — that makes the claim plausible or probable.

Not every kind of claim can be supported by every kind of ground, and, conversely, not every kind of ground gives equally good support for every kind of claim. Suppose, for instance, that I claim half the students in the classroom are women. I can establish the *grounds* for this claim in any of several ways. For example:

1. I can count all the women and all the men. Suppose the total equals fifty. If the number of women is twenty-five and the number of men is twenty-five, I have vindicated my claim.

2. I can count a sample of ten students — perhaps the first ten to walk into the classroom — and find that in the sample five of the students are women. I thus have inductive — plausible but not conclusive — grounds for my claim.

3. I can point out that the students in the college divide equally into men and women and then claim that this class is a representative sample of the whole college.

Clearly, ground 1 is stronger than ground 2, and 2 is much stronger than 3.

Up to this point, we have merely restated points about premises and conclusions that were covered in Chapter 3. We want now to consider four additional features of arguments.

Warrants

Once we have the claim or the point of an argument fixed in mind and have isolated the evidence or reasons offered in its support, the next question to ask is this:

Exactly how do the reasons offered in support of the conclusion work? In other words, what kind of guarantee — **warrant** — is provided to demonstrate that the reasons proffered actually do support the claim or lead to the conclusion? (A *warrant* in this context is like the *warranty* you get when you buy something.)

In ordinary and straightforward *deductive* arguments, warrants take different forms. In the simplest cases, we can point to the way in which the *meanings* of the key terms are really equivalent. Thus, if John is taller than Bill, then Bill must be shorter than John. We know this because we know what "is shorter than" and "is taller than" mean. If A is taller than B, it must be the case that B is shorter than A; those are the meanings of the phrases being used here. Of course, everyone involved does have to know the language well enough to understand the relationship between "is taller than" and "is shorter than." The *warrant* in this case is the common understanding of what those two phrases mean.

In other cases, we may need to be more resourceful. A reliable tactic is to think up a simple *parallel argument*, an argument exactly parallel in form and structure to the argument we are trying to defend. If the two arguments really do have the same form and structure, and we are ready to accept the simpler one, then we can point out that the more complex argument must be accepted — because the two arguments have exactly the same structure. For example, if we want to argue that it is reasonable for FedEx to charge more for its delivery services than the U.S. Postal Service (USPS) does, we could point out that since it seems entirely reasonable to pay higher costs for special services from the USPS such as overnight delivery promised by a certain time (depending on factors such as location), then it is reasonable to pay even higher fees for similar overnight delivery by FedEx because that service includes sending someone to pick up what you want delivered.

In simple *inductive* arguments, we are likely to point to the way in which observations or sets of data constitute a *representative sample* of a whole population, even if not every member of the sample is strictly in evidence. For instance, when scattered information is plotted on a graph, the trend line does not have to touch each (or even any) of the data points as long as they are scattered above and below the line in roughly equal numbers in pairs that are roughly equidistant from the trend line. We can defend this projection on the grounds that it takes all of the points into account in the least complicated way. In such a case, the warrant is this combination of *inclusiveness* and *simplicity.*

Establishing the warrants for our reasoning — that is, explaining why our grounds really do support our claims — can quickly become a highly technical and exacting procedure that goes far beyond the aims of this book. Even so, developing a "feel" for why reasons or grounds are or are not relevant to what they are alleged to support is important. "That's just my view" is *not* a convincing warrant for any argument. Even without formal training, however, one can sense that something is wrong with many bad arguments. Here is one example: British professor C. E. M. Joad found himself standing on a station platform, annoyed because he had just missed his train. Then another train, making an unscheduled stop, pulled up to the platform in front of him. Joad decided to jump aboard, only to hear the conductor say, "I'm afraid you'll have to get off, Sir. This train doesn't stop here." "In that case," replied the professor, "don't worry. I'm not on it."

Backing

A really solid argument may need even further support, especially if what we're arguing is complicated. *Warrants*, remember, explain the way our *grounds* support our *claims.* The next task, however, is to be able to show that we can back up what we have claimed by showing that the reasons we have given for a claim are good reasons. To establish that kind of further support for an argument is to provide **backing.**

What is appropriate backing for one kind of argument might be quite inappropriate for another kind of argument. For example, the kinds of reasons relevant to support an amendment to the Constitution are completely different from the kinds appropriate to settle the question of what caused the defeat of Napoleon's invasion of Russia in 1812. Arguments for the amendment might be rooted in an appeal to fairness, whereas arguments about the military defeat might be rooted in letters and other documents in French and Russian archives. The *canons* (established conventions) of good argument in two such dramatically different cases have to do with the means that scholarly communities in law and history, respectively, have developed over the years to support, defend, challenge, and undermine a given kind of argument.

Another way of stating this point is to recognize that once you have given reasons for a claim, you are then likely to be challenged to explain why your reasons are good reasons — why, that is, anyone should believe your reasons rather than regard them skeptically. They have to be the right kinds of reasons, given the field you are arguing about. Why (to give a simple example) should we accept the testimony of Dr. *X* when Dr. *Y*, equally renowned, supports the opposite side? What more do we need to know before "expert testimony" is appropriately invoked? For a different kind of case: When and why is it safe to rest a prediction on a small though admittedly carefully selected sample? And still another: Why is it legitimate to argue that (1) if I dream I am the king of France, then I must exist, whereas it is illegitimate to argue that (2) if I dream I am the king of France, then the king of France must exist?

To answer challenges of these sorts is to back up one's reasons, to give them legitimate *backing.* No argument is any better than its backing.

Modal Qualifiers

As we have seen, all arguments are made up of assertions or propositions that can be sorted into four categories:

- the *claim* (conclusion, thesis to be established)
- the *grounds* (explicit reasons advanced)
- the *warrant* (guarantee, evidence, or principle that legitimates the ground by connecting it to the claim)
- the *backing* (relevant support, implicit assumptions)

All of the kinds of propositions that emerge when we assert something in an argument have what philosophers call a **modality**. This means that propositions generally indicate — explicitly or tacitly — the *character* and *scope* of what is believed to be their likely truth.

Character has to do with the nature of the claim being made, the extent of an argument's presumed reach. Both making and evaluating arguments require being clear about whether they are *necessary, probable, plausible,* or *possible.* Consider, for example, a claim that it is to the advantage of a college to have a racially diverse student body. Is that *necessarily* or only *probably* true? What about an argument that a runner who easily wins a 100-meter race should also be able to win at 200 meters? Is this *plausible* — or only *possible*? Indicating the *character* with which an assertion is advanced is crucial to any argument for or against it. Furthermore, if there is more than one reason for making a claim, and all of those reasons are *good,* it is still possible that one of those good reasons may be *better* than the others. If so, the better reason should be stressed.

Indicating the *scope* of an assertion is equally crucial to how an argument plays out. *Scope* entails such considerations as whether the proposition is thought to be true *always* or just *sometimes.* Further, is the claim being made supposed to apply in *all* instances or just in *some*? Assertions are usually clearer, as well as more likely to be true, if they are explicitly *quantified* and *qualified.* Suppose, for example, that you are arguing against smoking, and the ground for your claim is this:

Heavy smokers cut short their life span.

In this case, there are three obvious alternative quantifications to choose among: *All* smokers cut short their life span, *most* do, or only *some* do. Until the assertion is quantified in one of these ways, we really don't know what is being asserted — and so we don't know what degree and kind of evidence or counterevidence is relevant. Other quantifiers include *few, rarely, often, sometimes, perhaps, usually, more or less, regularly, occasionally.*

Scope also has to do with the fact that empirical generalizations are typically *contingent* on various factors. Indicating such contingencies clearly is an important way to protect a generalization against obvious counterexamples. Thus, consider this empirical generalization:

Students do best on final examinations if they study hard for them.

Are we really to believe that students who cram ("study hard" in that concentrated sense) for an exam will do better than those who do the work diligently throughout the whole course ("study hard" in that broader sense) and therefore do not need to cram for the final? Probably not; what is really meant is that *all other things being equal* (in Latin, *ceteris paribus*), concentrated study just before an exam will yield good results. Alluding in this way to the contingencies — the things that might derail the argument — shows that the writer is aware of possible exceptions and is conceding them from the start.

In sum, sensitivity to both character and (especially) scope — paying attention to the role played by quantifiers, qualifiers, and contingencies and making sure you use appropriate ones for each of your assertions — will strengthen your arguments enormously. Not least of the benefits is that you will reduce the peculiar vulnerabilities of an argument that is undermined by exaggeration and other misguided generalizations.

Rebuttals

Very few arguments of any interest are beyond dispute, conclusively knockdown affairs. Only very rarely is the claim of an argument so rigidly tied to its grounds, warrants, and backing — and with its quantifiers and qualifiers argued in so precise a manner — that it proves its conclusion beyond any possibility of doubt. On the contrary, most arguments have many counterarguments, and sometimes one of these counterarguments is more convincing than the original argument.

Suppose someone has taken a sample that appears to be random: An interviewer on your campus accosts the first ten students she encounters, and seven of them are fraternity or sorority members. She is now ready to argue that seven-tenths of enrolled students belong to Greek organizations.

You believe, however, that the Greeks are in the minority; you point out that she happens to have conducted her interview around the corner from the Panhellenic Society's office just off Sorority Row. Her random sample is anything but random. The ball is now back in her court as you await her response to your rebuttal.

As this example illustrates, it is safe to say that we do not understand our own arguments very well until we have tried to get a grip on the places in which they are vulnerable to criticism, counterattack, or refutation. We have already, in Chapter 3, quoted Edmund Burke — but the passage is worth repeating: "He that wrestles with us strengthens our nerves, and sharpens our skill. Our antagonist is our helper."

To be sure, in everyday conversation we may not enjoy being in the company of people who interrupt to ask what are our grounds, warrants, backing, and so forth. The poet T. S. Eliot amusingly characterized himself as such a person:

How Unpleasant to Meet Mr. Eliot!

How unpleasant to meet Mr. Eliot!
With his features of clerical cut.
And his brow so grim

And his mouth so prim
And his conversation, so nicely
Restricted to What Precisely
And If and Perhaps and But . . .
How unpleasant to meet Mr. Eliot!
(Whether his mouth be open or shut.)

Still, if we wish to make serious progress in thinking and arguing about significant issues, cultivating alertness to possible weak spots in arguments—our own arguments as well as those of others—and incorporating thoughtful responses to anticipated criticisms will always be helpful.

Would you want to argue with Mr. Eliot?

THINKING CRITICALLY Constructing a Toulmin Argument

Choose a topic or issue that interests you. In the spaces provided, supply a sentence or two for each step of a Toulmin argument about your topic.

STEP OF TOULMIN ARGUMENT	QUESTION THIS STEP ADDRESSES	YOUR SENTENCE(S)
Claim	*What is your argument?*	
Grounds	*What is your evidence?*	
Warrant	*What reasoning connects your evidence to your argument?*	
Backing	*Why should the reader agree with your grounds?*	
Rebuttal	*What are the objections to this argument?*	
Qualifier	*What are the limits of your argument?*	

LaunchPad To complete this activity online, go to **macmillanhighered.com/barnetbedauohara**

PUTTING THE TOULMIN METHOD TO WORK:

Responding to an Argument

Let's take a look at another argument — it happens to be on why buying directly from farmers near you won't save the planet — and see how the Toulmin method can be applied. The checklist on page 333 can help you focus your thoughts as you read.

JAMES E. McWILLIAMS

James E. McWilliams (b. 1968), the author of Just Food, is an associate professor of history at Texas State University. This piece first appeared in Forbes Magazine on August 3, 2009.

The Locavore Myth: Why Buying from Nearby Farmers Won't Save the Planet

Buy local, shrink the distance food travels, save the planet. The locavore movement has captured a lot of fans. To their credit, they are highlighting the problems with industrialized food. But a lot of them are making a big mistake. By focusing on transportation, they overlook other energy-hogging factors in food production.

Take lamb. A 2006 academic study (funded by the New Zealand government) discovered that it made more environmental sense for a Londoner to buy lamb shipped from New Zealand than to buy lamb raised in the U.K. This finding is counterintuitive — if you're only counting food miles. But New Zealand lamb is raised on pastures with a small carbon footprint, whereas most English lamb is produced under intensive factory-like conditions with a big carbon footprint. This disparity overwhelms domestic lamb's advantage in transportation energy.

New Zealand lamb is not exceptional. Take a close look at water usage, fertilizer types, processing methods, and packaging techniques and you discover that factors other than shipping far outweigh the energy it takes to transport food. One analysis, by Rich Pirog of the Leopold Center for Sustainable Agriculture, showed that transportation accounts for only 11 percent of food's carbon footprint. A fourth of the energy required to produce food is expended in the consumer's kitchen. Still more energy is consumed per meal in a restaurant, since restaurants throw away most of their leftovers.

Locavores argue that buying local food supports an area's farmers and, in turn, strengthens the community. Fair enough. Left unacknowledged, however, is the fact that it also hurts farmers in other parts of the world. The U.K. buys most of its green beans from Kenya. While it's true that the beans almost always arrive in airplanes — the form of transportation that consumes the most energy — it's also true that a campaign to shame English consumers with small airplane stickers affixed to flown-in produce threatens the livelihood of 1.5 million sub-Saharan farmers.

Another chink in the locavores' armor 5 involves the way food miles are calculated. To choose a locally grown apple over an apple trucked in from across the country might seem easy. But this decision ignores economies of scale. To take an extreme example, a shipper sending a truck with 2,000 apples over 2,000 miles would consume the same amount of fuel per apple as a local farmer who takes a pickup 50 miles to sell 50 apples at his stall at the green market. The critical measure here is not food miles but apples per gallon.

The one big problem with thinking beyond food miles is that it's hard to get the information you need. Ethically concerned consumers know very little about processing practices, water availability, packaging waste, and fertilizer application. This is an opportunity for watchdog groups. They should make life-cycle carbon counts available to shoppers.

Until our food system becomes more transparent, there is one thing you can do to shrink the carbon footprint of your dinner: Take the meat off your plate. No matter how you slice it, it takes more energy to bring meat, as opposed to plants, to the table. It takes 6 pounds of grain to make a pound of chicken and 10 to 16 pounds to make a pound of beef. That difference translates into big differences in inputs. It requires 2,400 liters of water to make a burger and only 13 liters to grow a tomato. A majority of the water in

the American West goes toward the production of pigs, chickens, and cattle.

The average American eats 273 pounds of meat a year. Give up red meat once a week and you'll save as much energy as if the only food miles in your diet were the distance to the nearest truck farmer.

If you want to make a statement, ride your bike to the farmer's market. If you want to reduce greenhouse gases, become a vegetarian.

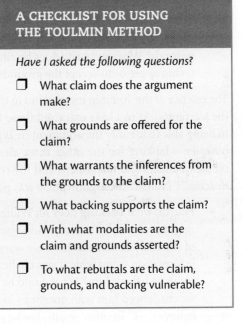

A CHECKLIST FOR USING THE TOULMIN METHOD

Have I asked the following questions?

- ☐ What claim does the argument make?
- ☐ What grounds are offered for the claim?
- ☐ What warrants the inferences from the grounds to the claim?
- ☐ What backing supports the claim?
- ☐ With what modalities are the claim and grounds asserted?
- ☐ To what rebuttals are the claim, grounds, and backing vulnerable?

Thinking with Toulmin's Method

Remember to make use of the checklist above as you work to find the claim(s), grounds, and warrant(s) that McWilliams puts forward in this short essay.

- First and foremost, what **claim** is the author making? Is it in his title? The opening sentence? Or is it buried in the first paragraph?

McWilliams really gives away his game in his title, even though he opens the essay itself in a way that might make the reader think he is about to launch into a defense of the locavore movement. He even goes out of his way to praise its members ("To their credit . . ."). The signal that his claim really appears already in the title and that he is *not* going to defend the locavore movement is the way he begins the fourth sentence. Notice that although you may have been told that starting a sentence with *But* isn't the best way to write, McWilliams here does so to good effect. Not only does he dramatically counter what he said just prior to that; he also sets up the final sentence of the paragraph, which turns out to be crucial. In this way, he draws sharp attention to his *claim*. How would you state his claim?

- Second, what are the **grounds,** the evidence or reasons, that the author advances in support of his claim?

As it turns out, McWilliams spells out only one example as evidence for his claim. What is it? Is it convincing? Should he have provided more evidence or reasons at this point? It turns out that he does have other grounds to offer—but he mentions them only later. What are those other pieces of evidence?

- Third, what **warrants** does McWilliams offer to show why we should accept his grounds? What authority does he cite? How effective and convincing is this way of trying to get us to accept the grounds he offered in support of his claim?

The essence of the Toulmin method lies in these three elements: the claim(s), the grounds, and the warrant(s). If you have extracted these from McWilliams's essay, you are well on the way to being able to identify the argument he is putting forward. So far, so good. Further probing, however—looking for the other three elements of the Toulmin method (the backing, the modal qualifiers and quantifiers, and the rebuttal)—is essential before you are in a position to actually evaluate the argument. So let's go on.

- Fourth, what **backing** does McWilliams provide? What reasons does he give that might persuade us to accept his argument? Look for what he claimed came out of the analysis that was his basic warrant. He certainly seems to be using factual information—but what if you challenged him? Has he provided adequate reasons for us to believe him? What could he (or would he have to) be able to tell us if we challenged him with questions like "How do you know . . . ?" or "Why do you believe . . . ?" In other words, has he provided adequate backing? Or does he want us to just accept his statement of the facts?

- Fifth, does McWilliams use **modal qualifiers**? Can you find phrases like "in most cases" or "generally it is true that . . . "? Or does he write so boldly—with little in the way of qualifiers or quantifiers—that readers are left uncertain about whether to accept his position? Where might he have effectively used qualifiers?

- Finally, does McWilliams use **rebuttals,** the reasons given in anticipation of someone rejecting the author's claim, or conceding the claim but rejecting the grounds? Does McWilliams anticipate rejections and prepare rebuttals? Does he offer anything to forestall criticisms? If so, what is it that he does? If not, what could or should he have done?

Just how good an argument has McWilliams made? Is he convincing? If you identified weak points in his argument, what are they? Can you help strengthen the argument? If so, how?

9

A Logician's View: Deduction, Induction, Fallacies

Logic is the anatomy of thought.

— JOHN LOCKE

Logic takes care of itself; all we have to do is to look and see how it does it. — LUDWIG WITTGENSTEIN

In Chapter 3 we introduced the terms *deduction*, *induction*, and *fallacy*. Here we discuss them in greater detail.

Deduction

The basic aim of deductive reasoning is to start with some assumption or premise and extract from it a conclusion — a logical consequence — that is concealed but implicit in it. Thus, taking the simplest case, if I assert as a premise

1a. Nuclear power poses more risks of harm to the environment than fossil fuels.

then it is a matter of simple deduction to infer the conclusion that

1b. Fossil fuels pose fewer risks of harm to the environment than nuclear power.

Anyone who understands English would grant that 1b follows 1a — or equivalently, that 1b can be validly deduced from 1a — because whatever two objects, *A* and *B*, you choose, if *A* does *more things than B*, then *B* must do *fewer things than A*.

Thus, in this and all other cases of valid deductive reasoning, we can say not only that we are entitled to *infer* the conclusion from the premise — in this case, infer 1b from 1a — but that the premise *implies* the conclusion. Remember, too, the conclusion (1b) that fossil fuels pose fewer risks than nuclear power — inferred or deduced from the statement (1a) that nuclear power poses more risks — does not depend on the truth of the statement that nuclear power poses more risks. If the speaker (falsely) asserts that nuclear power poses more risks, then the hearer validly (i.e., logically) concludes that fossil fuels pose fewer risks. Thus, 1b follows from 1a whether or not 1a is true; consequently, if 1a is true, then so is 1b; but if 1a is false, then 1b must be false also.

Let's take another example — more interesting but comparably simple:

2a. President Truman was underrated by his critics.

Given 2a, a claim amply verified by events of the 1950s, one is entitled to infer that

2b. His critics underrated President Truman.

On what basis can we argue that 2a implies 2b? The two propositions are equivalent because a rule of English grammar assures us that we can convert the position of subject and predicate phrases in a sentence by shifting from the passive to the active voice (or vice versa) without any change in the conditions that make the proposition true (or false).

Both pairs of examples illustrate that in deductive reasoning, our aim is to transform, reformulate, or restate in our conclusion some (or, as in the two examples above, all) of the information contained in our premises.

Remember, even though a proposition or statement follows from a previous proposition or statement, the statements need not be true. We can see why if we consider another example. Suppose someone asserts or claims that

3a. The Gettysburg Address is longer than the Declaration of Independence.

As every student of American history knows, 3a is false. But false or not, we can validly deduce from it that

3b. The Declaration of Independence is shorter than the Gettysburg Address.

This inference is valid (even though the conclusion is untrue) because the conclusion follows logically (more precisely, deductively) from 3a: In English, as we know, the meaning of "*A* is shorter than *B*," which appears in 3b, is simply the converse of "*B* is longer than *A*," which appears in 3a.

The deductive relation between 3a and 3b reminds us again that the idea of validity, which is so crucial to deduction, is not the same as the idea of truth. False propositions have implications — logical consequences — too, just as true propositions do.

In the three pairs of examples so far, what can we point to as the warrant for our claims? Well, look at the reasoning in each case; the arguments rely on rules of ordinary English, on the accepted meanings of words like *on*, *under*, and *underrated*.

In many cases, of course, the deductive inference or pattern of reasoning is much more complex than that which we have seen in the examples so far. When we introduced the idea of deduction in Chapter 3, we gave as our primary example the *syllogism*. Here is another example:

4. Texas is larger than California; California is larger than Arizona; therefore, Texas is larger than Arizona.

The conclusion in this syllogism can be derived from the two premises; that is, anyone who asserts the two premises is committed to accepting the conclusion as well, whether or not one thinks of it.

Notice again that the *truth* of the conclusion is not established merely by validity of the inference. The conclusion in this syllogism happens to be true. And the premises of this syllogism imply the conclusion. But the argument establishes the conclusion only because both of the premises on which the conclusion depends are true. Even a Californian admits that Texas is larger than California, which in turn is larger than Arizona. In other words, argument 4 is a *sound* argument because (as we explained in Chapter 3) it is valid and all its premises are true. All — and only — arguments that *prove* their conclusions have these two traits.

How might we present the warrant for the argument in 4? Short of a crash course in formal logic, either of two strategies might suffice. One is to argue from the fact that the validity of the inference depends on the meaning of a key concept, *being larger than*. This concept has the property of *transitivity*, a property that many concepts share (e.g., *is equal to, is to the right of, is smarter than* — all are transitive concepts). Consequently, whatever A, B, and C are, if A is larger than B, and B is larger than C, then A will be larger than C. The final step is to substitute "Texas," "California," and "Arizona" for A, B, and C, respectively.

A second strategy, less abstract and more graphic, is to think of representing Texas, California, and Arizona by nested circles. Thus, the first premise in argument 4 would look like this:

The second premise would look like this:

The conclusion would look like this:

We can see that this conclusion follows from the premises because it amounts to nothing more than what one gets by superimposing the two premises on each other. Thus, the whole argument can be represented like this:

The so-called middle term in the argument—California—disappears from the conclusion; its role is confined to be the link between the other two terms, Texas and Arizona, in the premises. (This is an adaptation of the technique used in elementary formal logic known as Venn diagrams.) In this manner one can give graphic display to the important fact that the conclusion follows from the premises because one can literally *see* the conclusion represented by nothing more than a representation of the premises.

Both of these strategies bring out the fact that validity of deductive inference is a purely *formal* property of argument. Each strategy abstracts the form from the content of the propositions involved to show how the concepts in the premises are related to the concepts in the conclusion.

For the sake of illustration, here is another syllogistic argument with the same logical features as argument 4. (A nice exercise is to restate argument 5 using diagrams in the manner of argument 4.)

5. African American slaves were treated worse than white indentured servants. Indentured white servants were treated worse than free white labor. Therefore, African American slaves were treated worse than free white labor.

Not all deductive reasoning occurs in syllogisms, however, or at least not in syllogisms like the ones in 4 and 5. (The term *syllogism* is sometimes used to refer to any deductive argument of any form, provided only that it has two premises.) In fact, syllogisms such as 4 are not the commonest form of our deductive reasoning at all. Nor are they the simplest (and, of course, not the most complex). For an argument that is even simpler, consider this:

6. If a youth is an African American slave, he is probably treated worse than a youth in indentured service. This youth is an African American slave. Therefore, he is probably treated worse than if he had been an indentured servant.

Here the pattern of reasoning has the form: If *A*, then *B*; *A*; therefore, *B*. Notice that the content of the assertions represented by *A* and *B* don't matter; any set of expressions having the same form or structure will do equally well, including assertions built out of meaningless terms, as in this example:

7. If the slithy toves, then the gyres gimble. The slithy toves. Therefore, the gyres gimble.

Argument 7 has the form: If *A*, then *B*; *A*; therefore *B*. As a piece of deductive inference it is every bit as good as argument 6. Unlike 6, however, 7 is of no interest to us because none of its assertions make any sense (unless you're a reader of Lewis Carroll's "Jabberwocky," and even then the sense of 7 is doubtful). You cannot, in short, use a valid deductive argument to prove anything unless the premises and the conclusion are *true*, but they can't be true unless they *mean* something in the first place.

This parallel between arguments 6 and 7 shows once again that deductive validity in an argument rests on the *form* or structure of the argument, and not on its content or meaning. If all one can say about an argument is that it is valid—that is, its conclusion follows from the premises — one has not given a sufficient reason for accepting the argument's conclusion. It has been said that the devil can quote scripture; similarly, an argument can be deductively valid and of no further interest or value whatever because valid (but false) conclusions can be drawn from false or even meaningless assumptions. For example:

8. New York's Metropolitan Museum of Art has the finest collection of abstract impressionist paintings in the world. The finest collection of abstract impressionist paintings includes dozens of canvases by Winslow Homer. Therefore, the Metropolitan Museum of Art has dozens of paintings by Winslow Homer.

Here the conclusion follows validly from the premises, even though all three propositions are false. Nevertheless, although validity by itself is not enough, it is a necessary condition of any deductive argument that purports to establish its conclusion.

Now let's consider another argument with the same form as 8, only more interesting:

9. If President Truman knew the Japanese were about to surrender, then it was immoral of him to order that atom bombs be dropped on Hiroshima and Nagasaki. Truman knew the Japanese were about to surrender. Therefore, it was immoral of him to order dropping those bombs.

As in the two previous examples, anyone who assents to the premises in argument 9 must assent to the conclusion; the form of arguments 8 and 9 is identical. But do the premises of argument 9 *prove* the conclusion? That depends on whether both premises are true. Well, are they? This turns on a number of considerations, and it is worthwhile pausing to examine this argument closely to illustrate the kinds of things that are involved in answering this question.

Let's begin by examining the second (minor) premise. Its truth is controversial even to this day. Autobiography, memoranda, other documentary evidence — all are needed to assemble the evidence to back up the grounds for the thesis or claim made in the conclusion of this valid argument. Evaluating this material effectively will probably involve not only further deductions but inductive reasoning as well.

Now consider the first (major) premise in argument 9. Its truth doesn't depend on what history shows but on the moral principles one accepts. The major premise has the form of a hypothetical proposition ("if . . . then . . .") and asserts a connection between two very different kinds of things. The antecedent of the hypothetical (the clause following "if") mentions facts about Truman's *knowledge,* and the consequent of the hypothetical (the clause following "then") mentions facts about the *morality* of his conduct in light of such knowledge. The major premise as a whole can thus be seen as expressing *a principle of moral responsibility.*

Such principles can, of course, be controversial. In this case, for instance, is the principle peculiarly relevant to the knowledge and conduct of a president of the United States? Probably not; it is far more likely that this principle is merely a special case of a more general proposition about anyone's moral responsibility. (After all, we know a great deal more about the conditions of our own moral responsibility than we do about those of high government officials.) We might express this more general principle in this way: If we have knowledge that would make our violent conduct unnecessary, then we are immoral if we deliberately act violently anyway. Thus, accepting this general principle can serve as a basis for defending the major premise of argument 9.

We have examined this argument in some detail because it illustrates the kinds of considerations needed to test not only whether a given argument is valid but also whether its premises are true — that is, whether its premises really prove the conclusion.

The great value of the form of argument known as hypothetical syllogism, exemplified by arguments 6 and 7, is that the structure of the argument is so simple and so universally applicable in reasoning that it is often both easy and worthwhile to formulate one's claims so that they can be grounded by an argument of this sort.

Before leaving the subject of deductive inference, let's consider three other forms of argument, each of which can be found in actual use elsewhere in the readings in this volume. The simplest of these is **disjunctive syllogism,** so called because its major premise is a **disjunction.** For example:

10. Either censorship of television shows is overdue, or our society is indifferent to the education of its youth. Our society is not indifferent to the education of its youth. Therefore, censorship of television is overdue.

Notice, by the way, that the validity of an argument, as in this case, does not turn on pedantic repetition of every word or phrase as the argument moves along; nonessential elements can be dropped, or equivalent expressions substituted for variety without adverse effect on the reasoning. Thus, in conversation or in writing, the argument in 10 might actually be presented like this:

11. Either censorship of television is overdue, or our society is indifferent to the education of its youth. But, of course, we aren't indifferent; it's censorship that's overdue.

The key feature of disjunctive syllogism, as example 11 suggests, is that the conclusion is whichever of the disjuncts is left over after the others have been negated in the minor premise. Thus, we could easily have a very complex disjunctive syllogism, with a dozen disjuncts in the major premise, and seven of them denied in the minor premise, leaving a conclusion of the remaining five. Usually, however, a disjunctive argument is formulated in this manner: Assert a disjunction with two or more disjuncts in the major premise; then *deny all but one* in the minor premise; and infer validly the remaining disjunct as the conclusion. That was the form of argument 11.

Another type of argument, especially favored by orators and rhetoricians, is the **dilemma.** Ordinarily, we use the term *dilemma* in the sense of an awkward predicament, as when we say, "His dilemma was that he didn't have enough money to pay the waiter." But when logicians refer to a dilemma, they mean a forced choice between two or more equally unattractive alternatives. For example, the predicament faced by the U.S. government in 2014 in deciding how to deal with the growth of the Islamic State in Syria can be posed as a dilemma. Two major choices emerged. The United States could ally itself with the Syrian government, or it could support rebel groups inside Syria who fight against ISIS. The dilemma is that the Syrian government, a dictatorship under Bashar al-Assad, has attempted to crush political reform movements in Syria, and it actively supports groups the United

States deems terrorist organizations, such as Hamas and Hezbollah. Also, some important U.S. allies such as Saudi Arabia oppose the al-Assad regime. On the other hand, if the United States were to support resistance groups within Syria, it would open itself up to charges that it was funding and arming groups hostile to the al-Assad regime, making them vulnerable to attack from the Syrian government and angering Syrian allies such as Russia, which may well be called upon to support strikes against the United States. The dilemma might be phrased as such:

12. If the United States supports the Syrian government, it would also be supporting a dictatorship that has been linked to terrorism and crimes against humanity, and that furthermore is an enemy of some of our closest Middle Eastern allies. If the United States supports rebel groups within Syria, it may be subject to attack by the al-Assad regime, extending the Syrian civil war and inviting potentially dangerous conflict with Russia. Either the United States supports a dictatorship, or it supports internal resistance groups. In either case, unattractive consequences follow.

Notice first the structure of the argument: two conditional propositions asserted as premises, followed by another premise that states a **necessary truth**. (The premise, "Either we support the Libyan dictatorship, or we support the Libyan rebels," is a disjunction; since its two alternatives are exhaustive, one of the two alternatives must be true. Such a statement is often called analytically true, or a *tautology*.) No doubt the conclusion of this dilemma follows from its premises.

But does the argument prove, as it purports to do, that whatever the U.S. government does, it will suffer "unattractive consequences"? It is customary to speak of "the horns of the dilemma," as though the challenge posed by the dilemma were like a bull ready to gore us no matter which direction we turn. But if the two conditional premises failed to exhaust the possibilities, then we can escape from the dilemma by going "between the horns," that is, by finding a third alternative. If (as in this case) that isn't possible, we can still ask whether both of the main premises are true. (In this argument, it should be clear that neither of the main premises spells out all or even most of the consequences that could be foreseen.) Even so, in cases where both of these conditional premises are true, it may be that the consequences of one alternative are nowhere nearly so bad as those of the other. If that is true, but our reasoning stops before evaluating that fact, we may be guilty of failing to distinguish between the greater and the lesser of two admitted evils. The logic of the dilemma itself cannot decide this choice for us. Instead, we must bring to bear empirical inquiry and imagination to the evaluation of the grounds of the dilemma itself.

Writers commonly use the term *dilemma* without explicitly formulating the dilemma to which they refer, leaving it for the readers to do. And sometimes, what is called a dilemma really isn't one. (Remember the dog's tail? Calling it a leg doesn't make it a leg.) As an example, consider the plight of Sophie in William Styron's novel, *Sophie's Choice*. The scene is Birkenau, the main Nazi extermination camp during World War II. Among the thousands arriving at the prison gates are Sophie and her two children, Jan and Eva. On the train platform a Nazi SS medical officer confronts them. He will decide which are the lucky ones; they will live to work in the camp. The rest will go to their death in the gas chambers. When Sophie insists she is Polish but not Jewish, the officer says she may choose one of her children to be saved. Which of the two should she save? On what basis ought Sophie resolve her dilemma? It looks as if she has only two alternatives, each of which presents an agonizing outcome. Or is there a third way out?

Finally, one of the most powerful and dramatic forms of argument is **reductio ad absurdum** (from the Latin, meaning "reduction to absurdity"). The idea of a reductio argument is to disprove a proposition by showing the absurdity of its inevitable conclusion. It is used, of course, to refute your opponent's position and prove your own. For example, in Plato's *Republic*, Socrates asks an old gentleman, Cephalus, to define right conduct. Cephalus says that it consists of paying your debts and keeping your word. Socrates rejects this answer by showing that it leads to a contradiction. He argues that Cephalus cannot have given the correct answer because if we believe that he did, we will quickly encounter contradictions; in some cases, when you keep your word you will nonetheless be doing the wrong thing. For suppose, says Socrates, that you borrowed a weapon from a man, promising to return it when he asks for it. One day he comes to your door, demanding his weapon and swearing angrily that he intends to murder a neighbor. Keeping your word under those circumstances would be absurd, Socrates implies, and the reader of the dialogue is left to infer that Cephalus's definition, which led to this result, has been refuted.

Let's take a closer look at another example. Suppose you are opposed to any form of gun control, whereas I am in favor of gun control. I might try to refute your position by attacking it with a reductio argument. To do that, I start out by assuming the very opposite of what I believe or favor; instead, I try to establish a contradiction that results from following out the consequences of this initial assumption. My argument might look like this:

13. Let's assume your position — namely, that there ought to be no legal restrictions of any kind on the sale and ownership of guns. That means that you'd permit having every neighborhood hardware store sell pistols and rifles to whoever walks in the door. But that's not all. You apparently also would permit selling machine guns to children, antitank weapons to lunatics, small-bore cannons to the nearsighted, as well as guns and ammunition to anyone with a criminal record. But this is utterly preposterous. No one could favor such a dangerous policy. So the only question worth debating is what kind of gun control is necessary.

Now in this example, my reductio of your position on gun control is not based on claiming to show that you have strictly contradicted yourself, for there is no purely logical contradiction in opposing all forms of gun control. Instead, what I have tried to do is to show that there is a contradiction between what you profess — no gun controls at all — and what you probably really believe, if only you'll stop to think about it — which is that no lunatic should be allowed to buy a loaded machine gun.

My refutation of your position rests on whether I succeed in establishing an inconsistency among your own beliefs. If it turns out that you really believe lunatics should be free to purchase guns and ammunition, then my attempted refutation fails.

In explaining reductio ad absurdum, we have had to rely on another idea fundamental to logic, that of **contradiction,** or inconsistency. (We used this idea, remember, to define validity in Chapter 3. A deductive argument is valid if and only if the process of affirming the premises and denying the conclusion results in a contradiction.) The opposite of contradiction is **consistency,** a notion of hardly less importance to good reasoning than validity. These concepts deserve a few words of further explanation and illustration. Consider this pair of assertions:

14. Abortion is homicide.
15. Racism is unfair.

No one would plausibly claim that we can infer or deduce 15 from 14, or, for that matter, 14 from 15. This almost goes without saying because there is no evident connection between these two assertions. They are unrelated assertions; logically speaking, they are *independent* of each other. In such cases the two assertions are mutually *consistent;* that is, both could be true — or both could be false. But now consider another proposition:

16. Euthanasia is not murder.

Could a person assert 14 (*Abortion is homicide*) and also assert 16 (*Euthanasia is not murder*) and be consistent? This question is equivalent to asking whether one could assert the **conjunction** of these two propositions — namely:

17. Abortion is homicide, and euthanasia is not murder.

It's not so easy to say whether 17 is consistent or inconsistent. The kinds of moral scruples that might lead a person to assert one of these conjuncts (i.e., one of the two initial propositions, *Abortion is homicide* and *Euthanasia is not murder*) might lead to the belief that the other one must be false and thus to the conclusion that 17 is inconsistent. (Notice that if 14 were the assertion that *Abortion is murder,* instead of *Abortion is homicide,* the problem of asserting consistently both 14 and 16 would be more acute.) Yet if we think again, we might imagine someone being convinced that there is no inconsistency in asserting that *Abortion is homicide,* say, and that *Euthanasia is not murder,* or even the reverse. (For instance, suppose you believed that the unborn deserve a chance to live and that putting terminally ill persons to death in a painless manner and with their consent confers a benefit on them.)

Let us generalize: We can say of any set of propositions that they are *consistent* if and only if *all could be true together.* (Notice that it follows from this definition that propositions mutually imply each other, as do *Seabiscuit was America's fastest racehorse* and *America's fastest racehorse was Seabiscuit.*) Remember that, once again, the truth of the assertions in question doesn't matter. Two propositions can be consistent or not, quite apart from whether they are true. Not so with falsehood: It follows from our definition of consistency that an *inconsistent* proposition must be *false.* (We have relied on this idea in explaining how a reductio ad absurdum argument works.)

Assertions or claims that are not consistent can take either of two forms. Suppose you assert proposition 14, that abortion is homicide, early in an essay you are writing, but later you assert that

18. Abortion is harmless.

You have now asserted a position on abortion that is strictly contrary to the one with which you began — contrary in the sense that both assertions 14 and 18 cannot be true. It is simply not true that if an abortion involves killing a human being (which is what *homicide* strictly means), then it causes no one any harm (killing a person always causes harm — even if it is excusable, justifiable, not wrong, the best thing to do in the circumstances, and so on). Notice that although 14 and 18 cannot both be true, they *can* both be false. In fact, many people who are perplexed about the morality of abortion believe precisely this. They concede that abortion does harm the fetus, so 18 must be false; but they also believe that abortion doesn't kill a person, so 14 must also be false.

Let's consider another, simpler case. If you describe the glass as half empty and I describe it as half full, both of us can be right; the two assertions are consistent, even though they sound vaguely incompatible. (This is the reason that disputing over whether the glass is half full or half empty has become the popular paradigm of a futile, purely *verbal disagreement*.) But if I describe the glass as half empty whereas you insist that it is two-thirds empty, then we have a real disagreement; your description and mine are strictly contrary, in that both cannot be true — although both *can* be false. (Both are false if the glass is only one-quarter full.)

This, by the way, enables us to define the difference between a pair of **contradictory** propositions and a pair of **contrary** propositions. Two propositions are contrary if and only if both cannot be true (though both can be false); two propositions are contradictory if and only if they are such that if one is true the other must be false, and vice versa. Thus, if Jack says that Alice Walker's *The Color Purple* is a better novel than Mark Twain's *Huckleberry Finn*, and Jill says, "No, *Huckleberry Finn* is better than *The Color Purple*," she is contradicting Jack. If what either one of them says is true, then what the other says must be false.

A more subtle case of contradiction arises when two or more of one's own beliefs implicitly contradict each other. We may find ourselves saying "Travel is broadening," and saying an hour later "People don't really change." Just beneath the surface of these two beliefs lies a self-contradiction: How can travel broaden us unless it influences — and changes — our beliefs, values, and outlook? But if we can't really change ourselves, then traveling to new places won't change us, either. (Indeed, there is a Roman saying to the effect that travelers change the skies above them, not their hearts.) "Travel is broadening" and "People don't change" collide with each other; something has to give.

Our point, of course, is not that you must never say today something that contradicts something you said yesterday. Far from it; if you think you were mistaken yesterday, of course you will take a different position today. But what you want to avoid is what George Orwell called *doublethink* in his novel *1984*: "*Doublethink* means the power of holding two contradictory beliefs in one's mind simultaneously, and accepting them both."

Genuine contradiction, and not merely contrary assertion, is the situation we should expect to find in some disputes. Someone advances a thesis — such as the assertion in 14, *Abortion is homicide* — and someone else flatly contradicts it by the simple expedient of negating it, thus:

19. Abortion is not homicide.

If we can trust public opinion polls, many of us are not sure whether to agree with 14 or with 19. But we should agree that whichever is true, *both* cannot be true, and *both* cannot be false. The two assertions, between them, exclude all other possibilities; they pose a forced choice for our belief. (Again, we have met this idea, too, in a reductio ad absurdum.)

Now it is one thing for Jack and Jill in a dispute or argument to contradict each other. It is quite another matter for Jack to contradict himself. One wants (or should want) to avoid self-contradiction because of the embarrassing position that results: Once I have contradicted myself, what are others to believe I really believe? What, indeed, *do* I believe, for that matter?

It may be, as Emerson observed, that a "foolish consistency is the hobgoblin of little minds" — that is, it may be shortsighted to purchase a consistency in one's beliefs at the expense of flying in the face of common sense. But making an effort to avoid a foolish inconsistency is the hallmark of serious thinking.

While we're speaking of inconsistency, let's spend a moment on **paradox.** The word refers to two different things:

- an assertion that is essentially self-contradictory and therefore cannot be true
- a seemingly contradictory assertion that nevertheless may be true

An example of the first might be "Evaluations concerning quality in literature are all a matter of personal judgment, but Shakespeare is the world's greatest writer." It is hard to make any sense out of this assertion. Contrast it with a paradox of the second sort, a *seeming* contradiction that may make sense, such as "The longest way around is the shortest way home," or "Work is more fun than fun," or "The best way to find happiness is not to look for it." Here we have assertions that are striking because as soon as we hear them we realize that although they seem inconsistent and self-defeating, they contain (or may contain) profound truths. Paradoxes of this second sort are especially common in religious texts, where they may imply a mysterious reality concealed by a world of contradictory appearances. Examples are "Some who are last shall be first, and some who are first shall be last" (Jesus, quoted in Luke 13:30), and "Death, thou shalt die" (the poet John Donne, alluding to the idea that the person who has faith in Jesus dies to this world but lives eternally). If you use the word *paradox* in your own writing — for instance, to characterize an argument that you're reading — be sure that the reader will understand in which sense you're using the word. (And, of course, you won't want to write paradoxes of the first, self-contradictory sort.)

Induction

Deduction involves logical thinking that applies to absolutely any assertion or claim — because every possible statement, true or false, has deductive logical consequences. Induction is relevant to one kind of assertion only; namely, to **empirical** or *factual* claims. Other kinds of assertions (such as definitions, mathematical equations, and moral or legal norms) simply are not the product of inductive reasoning and cannot serve as a basis for further inductive thinking.

And so, in studying the methods of induction, we are exploring tactics and strategies useful in gathering and then using **evidence** — empirical, observational, experimental — in support of a belief as its ground. Modern scientific knowledge is the product of these methods, and they differ somewhat from one science to another because they depend on the theories and technology appropriate to each of the sciences. Here all we can do is discuss generally the more abstract features common to inductive inquiry generally. For fuller details, you must eventually consult a physicist, chemist, geologist, or their colleagues and counterparts in other scientific fields.

OBSERVATION AND INFERENCE

Let's begin with a simple example. Suppose we have evidence (actually we don't, but that won't matter for our purposes) in support of the claim that

1. In a sample of 500 smokers, 230 persons observed have cardiovascular disease.

The basis for asserting 1 — the evidence or ground — would be, presumably, straightforward physical examination of the 500 persons in the sample, one by one.

With this claim in hand, we can think of the purpose and methods of induction as pointing in two opposite directions: toward establishing the basis or ground of the very empirical proposition with which we start (in this example, the observation stated in 1) or toward understanding what that observation indicates or suggests as a more general, inclusive, or fundamental fact of nature.

In each case, we start from something we *do* know (or take for granted and treat as a sound starting point) — some fact of nature, perhaps a striking or commonplace event that we have observed and recorded — and then go on to something we do *not* fully know and perhaps cannot directly observe. In example 1, only the second of these two orientations is of any interest, so let's concentrate exclusively on it. Let's also generously treat as a *method* of induction any regular pattern or style of nondeductive reasoning that we could use to support a claim such as that in 1.

Anyone truly interested in the observed fact that *230 of 500 smokers have cardiovascular disease* is likely to start speculating about, and thus be interested in finding out, whether any or all of several other propositions are also true. For example, one might wonder whether

2. *All* smokers have cardiovascular disease or will develop it during their lifetimes.

This claim is a straightforward generalization of the original observation as reported in claim 1. When we think inductively about the linkage between 1 and 2, we are reasoning from an observed sample (some smokers — i.e., 230 of the 500 *observed*) to the entire membership of a more inclusive class (*all* smokers, whether observed or not). The fundamental question raised by reasoning from the narrower claim 1 to the broader claim 2 is whether we have any ground for believing that what is true of *some* members of a class is true of them *all*. So the difference between 1 and 2 is that of *quantity* or scope.

We can also think inductively about the *relation* between the factors mentioned in 1. Having observed data as reported in 1, we may be tempted to assert a different and more profound kind of claim:

3. Smoking *causes* cardiovascular disease.

Here our interest is not merely in generalizing from a sample to a whole class; it is the far more important one of *explaining* the observation with which we began in claim 1. Certainly, the preferred, even if not the only, mode of explanation for a natural phenomenon is a *causal* explanation. In proposition 3, we propose to explain the presence of one phenomenon (cardiovascular disease) by the prior occurrence of an independent phenomenon (smoking). The observation reported in 1 is now serving as evidence or support for this new conjecture stated in 3.

Our original claim in 1 asserted no causal relation between anything and anything else; whatever the cause of cardiovascular disease may be, that cause is not observed, mentioned, or assumed in assertion 1. Similarly, the observation asserted in claim 1 is consistent with many explanations. For example, the explanation of 1 might not be 3, but some other, undetected, carcinogenic factor unrelated to smoking — for instance, exposure to high levels of radon. The question one now faces is what can be added to 1, or teased out of it, to produce an adequate ground for claiming 3. (We shall return to this example for closer scrutiny.)

But there is a third way to go beyond 1. Instead of a straightforward generalization, as we had in 2, or a pronouncement on the cause of a phenomenon, as in 3, we might have a more complex and cautious further claim in mind, such as this:

4. Smoking is a factor in the causation of cardiovascular disease in some persons.

This proposition, like 3, advances a claim about causation. But 4 is obviously a weaker claim than 3. That is, other observations, theories, or evidence that would require us to reject 3 might be consistent with 4; evidence that would support 4 could easily fail to be enough to support 3. Consequently, it is even possible that 4 is true although 3 is false, because 4 allows for other (unmentioned) factors in the causation of cardiovascular disease (e.g., genetic or dietary factors) that may not be found in all smokers.

Propositions 2, 3, and 4 differ from proposition 1 in an important respect. We began by assuming that 1 states an empirical fact based on direct observation, whereas these others do not. Instead, they state empirical *hypotheses* or conjectures — tentative generalizations not fully confirmed — each of which goes beyond the observed facts asserted in 1. Each of 2, 3, and 4 can be regarded as an *inductive inference* from 1. We can also say that 2, 3, and 4 are hypotheses relative to 1, even if they are not relative to some other starting point (such as all the information that scientists today really have about smoking and cardiovascular disease).

PROBABILITY

Another way of formulating the last point is to say that whereas proposition 1, a statement of observed fact (*230 out of 500 smokers have cardiovascular disease*), has a **probability** of 1.0 — that is, it is absolutely certain — the probability of each of the hypotheses stated in 2, 3, and 4, *relative* to 1, is smaller than 1.0. (We need not worry here about how much smaller than 1.0 the probabilities are, nor about how to calculate these probabilities precisely.) Relative to some starting point other than 1, however, the probability of the same three hypotheses might be quite different. Of course, it still wouldn't be 1.0, absolute certainty. But it takes only a moment's reflection to realize that no matter what the probability of 2 or 3 or 4 may be relative to 1, those probabilities in each case will be quite different relative to different information, such as this:

5. Ten persons observed in a sample of 500 smokers have cardiovascular disease.

The idea that a *given proposition can have different probabilities* relative to different bases is fundamental to all inductive reasoning. The following example makes a convincing illustration. Suppose we want to consider the probability of this proposition being true:

6. Susanne Smith will live to be eighty.

Taken as an abstract question of fact, we cannot even guess what the probability is with any assurance. But we can do better than guess; we can in fact even calculate the answer, if we get some further information. Thus, suppose we are told that

7. Susanne Smith is seventy-nine.

Our original question then becomes one of determining the probability that 6 is true given 7; that is, relative to the evidence contained in proposition 7. No doubt, if Susanne Smith really is seventy-nine, then the probability that she will live to be eighty is greater than if we know only that

8. Susanne Smith is more than nine years old.

Obviously, a lot can happen to Susanne in the seventy years between nine and seventy-nine that isn't very likely to happen in the one year between seventy-nine and eighty. And so, proposition 6 is more probable relative to proposition 7 than it is relative to proposition 8.

Let's suppose for the sake of the argument that the following is true:

9. Ninety percent of women alive at age seventy-nine live to be eighty.

Given this additional information, and the information that Susanne is seventy-nine, we now have a basis for answering our original question about proposition 6 with some precision. But suppose, in addition to 8, we are also told that

10. Susanne Smith is suffering from inoperable cancer.

and also that

11. The survival rate for women suffering from inoperable cancer is 0.6 years (i.e., the average life span for women after a diagnosis of inoperable cancer is about seven months).

With this new information, the probability that 6 will be true drops significantly, all because we can now estimate the probability in relation to a new body of evidence.

The probability of an event, thus, is not a fixed number but one that varies because it is always relative to some evidence — and given different evidence, one and the same event can have different probabilities. In other words, the probability of any event is always relative to how much is known (assumed, believed), and because different persons may know different things about a given event, or the same person may know different things at different times, one and the same event can have two or more probabilities. This conclusion is not a paradox but a logical consequence of the concept of what it is for an event to have (i.e., to be assigned) a probability.

If we shift to the *calculation* of probabilities, we find that generally there are two ways to calculate them. One way to proceed is by the method of **a priori** or **equal probabilities** — that is, by reference to the relevant possibilities taken abstractly and apart from any other information. Thus, in an election contest with only two candidates, Smith and Jones, each of the candidates has a fifty-fifty chance of winning (whereas in a three-candidate race, each candidate would have one chance in three of winning). Therefore, the probability that Smith will win is 0.5, and the probability that Jones will win is also 0.5. (The sum of the probabilities of all possible independent outcomes must always equal 1.0, which is obvious enough if you think about it.)

But in politics the probabilities are not reasonably calculated so abstractly. We know that many empirical factors affect the outcome of an election and that a calculation of probabilities in ignorance of those factors is likely to be drastically misleading. In our example of the two-candidate election, suppose Smith has strong party support and is the incumbent, whereas Jones represents a party long out of power and is further handicapped by being relatively unknown. No one who knows anything about electoral politics would give Jones the same chance of winning as Smith. The two events are not equiprobable in relation to all the information available.

Moreover, a given event can have more than one probability. This happens whenever we calculate a probability by relying on different bodies of data that report how often the event in question has been observed to happen. Probabilities calculated in this way are **relative frequencies.** Our earlier hypothetical example of Susanne Smith provides an illustration. If she is a smoker and we have observed that 100 out of a random set of 500 smokers have cardiovascular disease, we have a basis for claiming that she has a probability of 100 in 500, or 0.2 (one-fifth), of having this disease. However, if other data have shown that 250 out of 500 women smokers ages eighty or older have cardiovascular disease, we have a basis for believing that there is a probability of 250 in 500, or 0.5 (one-half), that she has this disease. Notice that in both calculations we assume that Susanne Smith is not among the persons we have examined. In both cases we infer the probability of her having this disease from observing its frequency in populations that exclude her.

Both methods of calculating probabilities are legitimate; in each case the calculation is relative to observed circumstances. But as the examples show, it is most reasonable to have recourse to the method of equiprobabilities only when few or no other factors affecting possible outcomes are known.

MILL'S METHODS

Now let's return to our earlier discussion of smoking and cardiovascular disease and consider in greater detail the question of a causal connection between the two phenomena. We began thus:

1. In a sample of 500 smokers, 230 persons observed have cardiovascular disease.

We regarded 1 as an observed fact, though in truth, of course, it is mere supposition. Our question now is how we might augment this information so as to strengthen our confidence that

3. Smoking *causes* cardiovascular disease.

or at least that

4. Smoking is a factor in the causation of cardiovascular disease in some persons.

Suppose further examination showed that

12. In the sample of 230 smokers with cardiovascular disease, no other suspected factor (such as genetic predisposition, lack of physical exercise, age over fifty) was also observed.

Such an observation would encourage us to believe that 3 or 4 is true. Why? Because we're inclined to believe also that no matter what the cause of a phenomenon is, it must *always* be present when its effect is present. Thus, the inference from 1 to 3 or 4 is supported by 12, using **Mill's Method of Agreement,** named after the British philosopher, John Stuart Mill (1806–1873), who first formulated it. It's called a method of agreement because of the way in which the inference relies on *agreement* among the observed phenomena where a presumed cause is thought to be *present*.

Let's now suppose that in our search for evidence to support 3 or 4 we conduct additional research and discover that

13. In a sample of 500 nonsmokers, selected to be representative of both sexes, different ages, dietary habits, exercise patterns, and so on, none is observed to have cardiovascular disease.

This observation would further encourage us to believe that we had obtained significant additional confirmation of 3 or 4. Why? Because we now know that factors present (such as male sex, lack of exercise, family history of cardiovascular disease) in cases where the effect is absent (no cardiovascular disease observed) cannot be the cause. This is an example of **Mill's Method of Difference,** so called because the cause or causal factor of an effect must be *different* from whatever factors are present when the effect is *absent*.

Suppose now that, increasingly confident we've found the cause of cardiovascular disease, we study our first sample of 230 smokers ill with the disease, and we discover this:

14. Those who smoke two or more packs of cigarettes daily for ten or more years have cardiovascular disease either much younger or much more severely than those who smoke less.

This is an application of **Mill's Method of Concomitant Variation,** perhaps the most convincing of the three methods. Here we deal not merely with the presence of the conjectured cause (smoking) or the absence of the effect we are studying (cardiovascular disease), as we were previously, but with the more interesting and subtler matter of the *degree and regularity of the correlation* of the supposed cause and effect. According to the observations reported in 14, it strongly appears that the more we have of the "cause" (smoking), the sooner or the more intense the onset of the "effect" (cardiovascular disease).

Notice, however, what happens to our confirmation of 3 and 4 if, instead of the observation reported in 14, we had discovered that

15. In a representative sample of 500 nonsmokers, cardiovascular disease was observed in 34 cases.

(We won't pause here to explain what makes a sample more or less representative of a population, although the representativeness of samples is vital to all statistical reasoning.) Such an observation would lead us almost immediately to suspect some other or additional causal factor: Smoking might indeed be *a* factor in causing cardiovascular disease, but it can hardly be *the* cause because (using Mill's Method of Difference) we cannot have the effect, as we do in the observed sample reported in 15, unless we also have the cause.

An observation such as the one in 15, however, is likely to lead us to think our hypothesis that *smoking causes cardiovascular disease* has been disconfirmed. But we have a fallback position ready — we can still defend a weaker hypothesis; namely, 4: *Smoking is a factor in the causation of cardiovascular disease in some persons.* Even if 3 stumbles over the evidence in 15, 4 does not. It is still quite possible that smoking is a factor in causing this disease, even if it isn't the *only* factor — and if it is, then 4 is true.

CONFIRMATION, MECHANISM, AND THEORY

Notice that in the discussion so far, we have spoken of the *confirmation* of a hypothesis, such as our causal claim in 4, but not of its *verification*. (Similarly, we have imagined very different evidence, such as that stated in 15, leading us to speak of the *disconfirmation* of 3, though not of its *falsification*.) Confirmation (getting some evidence for) is weaker than verification (getting sufficient evidence to regard as true), and our (imaginary) evidence so far in favor of 4 falls well short of conclusive support. Further research — the study of more representative or much larger samples, for example — might yield very different observations. It might lead us to conclude that although initial research had confirmed our hypothesis about smoking as the cause of cardiovascular disease, the additional information obtained subsequently disconfirmed the hypothesis. For most interesting hypotheses, both in detective stories and in modern science, there is both confirming and disconfirming evidence simultaneously. The challenge is to evaluate the hypothesis by considering such conflicting evidence.

As long as we confine our observations to *correlations* of the sort reported in our several (imaginary) observations, such as proposition 1, *230 smokers in a group of 500 have cardiovascular disease,* or 12, *230 smokers with the disease share no other suspected factors,* such as lack of exercise, any defense of a *causal* hypothesis such as claim 3, *Smoking causes cardiovascular disease,* or claim 4, *Smoking is a factor in causing the disease,* is not likely to convince the skeptic or lead those with beliefs alternative to 3 and 4 to abandon them and agree with us. Why is that? It is because a causal hypothesis without any account of the *underlying mechanism* by means of which the (alleged) cause produces the effect will seem superficial. Only when we can specify in detail *how* the (alleged) cause produces the effect will the causal hypothesis be convincing.

In other cases, in which no mechanism can be found, we seek instead to embed the causal hypothesis in a larger *theory,* one that rules out as incompatible any causal hypothesis except the favored one. (That is, we appeal to the test of consistency and thereby bring deductive reasoning to bear on our problem.) Thus, perhaps we cannot specify any mechanism — any underlying structure that generates a regular sequence of events, one of which is the effect we are studying — to explain why, for example, the gravitational mass of a body causes it to attract other bodies. But we can embed this claim in a larger context of physical theory that rules out as inconsistent any alternative causal explanation. To do that convincingly in regard to any given causal hypothesis, as this example suggests, requires detailed knowledge of the current state of the relevant body of scientific theory — something far beyond our need to consider in further detail here.

Fallacies

The straight road on which sound reasoning proceeds gives little latitude for cruising about. Irrationality, carelessness, passionate attachment to one's unexamined beliefs, and the sheer complexity of some issues occasionally spoil the reasoning of even the best of us. Although in this book we reprint many varied voices and arguments, we hope we've reprinted no readings that exhibit the most flagrant errors or commit the graver abuses against the canons of good reasoning. Nevertheless, an inventory of those abuses and their close examination can be an instructive (as well as an amusing) exercise — instructive because the diagnosis and repair of error help to fix more clearly the principles of sound reasoning on which such remedial labors depend; amusing because we are so constituted that our perception of the nonsense of others can stimulate our minds, warm our hearts, and give us comforting feelings of superiority.

The discussion that follows, then, is a quick tour through the twisting lanes, mudflats, forests, and quicksands of the faults that one sometimes encounters in reading arguments that stray from the highway of clear thinking.

FALLACIES OF AMBIGUITY

Ambiguity   Near the center of the town of Concord, Massachusetts, is an empty field with a sign reading "Old Calf Pasture." Hmm. A pasture in former times in which calves grazed? A pasture now in use for old calves? An erstwhile pasture for old calves? These alternative readings arise because of **ambiguity;** brevity in the sign has produced a group of words that give rise to more than one possible interpretation, confusing the reader and (presumably) frustrating the sign writer's intentions.

Consider a more complex example. Suppose someone asserts *People have equal rights* and also *Everyone has a right to property.* Many people believe both these claims, but their combination involves an ambiguity. According to one interpretation, the two claims entail that everyone has an *equal right* to property. (That is, you and I each have an equal right to whatever property we have.) But the two claims can also be interpreted to mean that everyone has a *right to equal property.* (That is, whatever property you have a right to, I have a right to the same, or at least equivalent, property.) The latter interpretation is revolutionary, whereas the former is not. Arguments over equal rights often involve this ambiguity.

Division   In the Bible, we read that the apostles of Jesus were twelve and that Matthew was an apostle. Does it follow that Matthew was twelve years old? No. To argue in this way from a property of a group to a property of a member of that group is to commit the **fallacy of division.** The example of the apostles may not be a very tempting instance of this error; here is a classic version that is a bit more interesting: If it is true that the average American family has 1.8 children, does it follow that your brother and sister-in-law are likely to have 1.8 children? If you think it does, you have committed the fallacy of division.

Composition   Could an all-star team of professional basketball players beat the Boston Celtics in their heyday — say, the team of 1985–1986? Perhaps in one game or two, but probably not in seven out of a dozen games in a row. As students of the game know, teamwork is an indispensable part of outstanding performance, and the 1985–1986 Celtics were famous for their self-sacrificing style of play.

The **fallacy of composition** can be convincingly illustrated, therefore, in this argument: *A team of five NBA all-stars is the best team in basketball if each of the five players is the best* *at his position.* The fallacy is called composition because the reasoning commits the error of arguing from the true premise that each member of a group has a certain property to the not necessarily true conclusion that the group (the composition) itself has the property. (That is, because *A* is the best player at forward, *B* is the best center, and so on, therefore, the team of *A, B, . . .* is the best team.)

Equivocation   In a delightful passage in Lewis Carroll's *Through the Looking-Glass*, the king asks his messenger, "Who did you pass on the road?" and the messenger replies, "Nobody." This prompts the king to observe, "Of course, Nobody walks slower than you," provoking the messenger's sullen response: "I do my best. I'm sure nobody walks much faster than I do." At this the king remarks with surprise, "He can't do that or else he'd have been here first!" (This, by the way, is the classic predecessor of the famous comic dialogue "Who's on First?" between the comedians Bud Abbott and Lou Costello.) The king and the messenger are equivocating on the term *nobody.* The messenger uses it in the normal way as an indefinite pronoun equivalent to "not anyone." But the king uses the word as though it were a proper noun, *Nobody,* the rather odd name of some person. No wonder the king and the messenger talk right past each other.

Equivocation (from the Latin for "equal voice" — i.e., giving utterance to two meanings at the same time in one word or phrase) can ruin otherwise good reasoning, as in this example: *Euthanasia is a good death; one dies a good death when one dies peacefully in old age; therefore, euthanasia is dying peacefully in old age.* The etymology of *euthanasia* is literally "a good death," so the first premise is true. And the second premise is certainly plausible. But the conclusion of this syllogism is false. Euthanasia cannot be defined as a peaceful death in one's old age, for two reasons. First, euthanasia requires the intervention of another person who kills someone (or lets the person die); second, even a very young person can be euthanized. The problem arises because "a good death" works in the second premise in a manner that does not apply to euthanasia. Both meanings of "a good death" are legitimate, but when used together, they constitute an equivocation that spoils the argument.

The fallacy of equivocation takes us from the discussion of confusions in individual claims or grounds to the more troublesome fallacies that infect the linkages between the claims we make and the grounds (or reasons) for them. These are the fallacies that occur in statements that, following the vocabulary of the Toulmin method, are called the *warrant* of reasoning. Each fallacy is an example of reasoning that involves a **non sequitur** (Latin for "It does not follow"). That is, the *claim* (the conclusion) does not follow from the *grounds* (the premises).

For a start, here is an obvious non sequitur: "He went to the movies on three consecutive nights, so he must love movies." Why doesn't the claim ("He must love movies") follow from the grounds ("He went to the movies on three consecutive nights")? Perhaps the person was just fulfilling an assignment in a film course (maybe he even hated movies so much that he had postponed three assignments to see films and now had to see them all in quick succession), or maybe he went with a girlfriend who was a movie buff, or maybe . . . — well, there are any number of other possible reasons.

FALLACIES OF PRESUMPTION

Distorting the Facts   Facts can be distorted either intentionally (to deceive or mislead) or unintentionally, and in either case usually (but not invariably) to the benefit of whoever is doing the distortion. Consider this not entirely hypothetical case. A pharmaceutical company spends millions of dollars to develop a new drug that will help pregnant women avoid spontaneous abortion. The company reports its findings, but it doesn't also report that its researchers have learned of a serious downside for this drug in many cases, resulting in deformed limbs in the neonate. Had the company informed the public of this fact, the drug would not have been certified for use.

Here is another case. Half a century ago the surgeon general reported that smoking cigarettes increased the likelihood that smokers would eventually suffer from lung cancer. The cigarette manufacturers vigorously protested that the surgeon general relied on inconclusive research and was badly misleading the public about the health risks of smoking. It later turned out that the tobacco companies knew that smoking increased the risk of lung cancer — a fact established by the company's own laboratories but concealed from the public. Today, thanks to public access to all the facts, it is commonplace knowledge that inhaled smoke — including secondhand smoke — is a risk factor for many illnesses.

Post Hoc, Ergo Propter Hoc   One of the most tempting errors in reasoning is to ground a claim about causation on an observed temporal sequence; that is, to argue "after this, therefore because of this" (which is what the phrase ***post hoc, ergo propter hoc*** means in Latin). Nearly forty years ago, when the medical community first announced that smoking tobacco caused lung cancer, advocates for the tobacco industry replied that doctors were guilty of this fallacy.

These industry advocates argued that medical researchers had merely noticed that in some people, lung cancer developed *after* considerable smoking, indeed, years after; but (they insisted) this correlation was not at all the same as a causal relation between smoking and lung cancer. True enough. The claim that *A causes B* is not the same as the claim that *B comes after A*. After all, it was possible that smokers as a group had some other common trait and that this factor was the true cause of their cancer.

As the long controversy over the truth about the causation of lung cancer shows, to avoid the appearance of fallacious *post hoc* reasoning one needs to find some way to link the observed phenomena (the correlation between smoking and the onset of lung cancer). This step requires some further theory and preferably some experimental evidence for the exact sequence or physical mechanism, in full detail, of how ingestion of tobacco smoke is a crucial factor — and is not merely an accidental or happenstance prior event — in the subsequent development of the cancer.

Many Questions   The old saw, "When did you stop beating your wife?" illustrates the **fallacy of many questions**. This question, as one can readily see, is unanswerable unless all three of its implicit presuppositions are true. The questioner presupposes that (1) the addressee has or had a wife, (2) he has beaten her, and (3) he has stopped beating her. If any of these presuppositions is false, then the question is pointless; it cannot be answered strictly and simply with a date or time.

Hasty Generalization   From a logical point of view, **hasty generalization** is the precipitous move from true assertions about *one* or a *few* instances to dubious or even false assertions about *all*. For example, while it may be true that the only native Hungarians you personally know do not speak English very well, that is no basis for asserting that all Hungarians do not speak English very well. Or if the clothes you recently ordered online turn out not to fit very well, it doesn't follow that *all* online clothes turn out to be too large or too small. A hasty generalization usually lies behind a **stereotype** — that is, a person or event treated as typical of a whole class. Thus, in 1914, after the German invasion of Belgium, during which the invaders committed numerous atrocities, the German troops were quickly stereotyped by the Allies as brutal savages who skewered helpless babies on their bayonets.

The Slippery Slope   One of the most familiar arguments against any type of government regulation is that if it is allowed, then it will be just the first step down the path that leads to ruinous interference, overregulation, and totalitarian control. Fairly often we encounter this mode of argument in the public debates over handgun control, the censorship of pornography, and physician-assisted suicide. The argument is called the **slippery slope argument** (or the **wedge argument,** from the way people use the thin end of a wedge to split solid things apart; it is also called, rather colorfully, "letting the camel's nose under the tent"). The fallacy here is in implying that the first step necessarily leads to the second, and so on down the slope to disaster, when in fact there is no necessary slide from the first step to the second. (Would handgun registration lead to a police state? Well, it hasn't in Switzerland.) Sometimes, the argument takes the form of claiming that a seemingly innocent or even attractive principle that is being applied in a given case (censorship of pornography, to avoid promoting sexual violence) requires one for the sake of consistency to apply the same principle in other cases, only with absurd and catastrophic results (censorship of everything in print, to avoid hurting anyone's feelings).

Here's an extreme example of this fallacy in action:

> Automobiles cause more deaths than handguns do. If you oppose handguns on the ground that doing so would save lives of the innocent, you'll soon find yourself wanting to outlaw the automobile.

Does opposition to handguns have this consequence? Not necessarily. Most people accept without dispute the right of society to regulate the operation of motor vehicles by requiring drivers to have a license, a greater restriction than many states impose on gun ownership. Besides, a gun is a lethal weapon designed to kill, whereas an automobile or truck is a vehicle designed for transportation. Private ownership and use in both cases entail risks of death to the innocent. But there is no inconsistency in a society's refusal to tolerate this risk in the case of guns and its willingness to do so in the case of automobiles.

Closely related to the slippery slope is what lawyers call a **parade of horrors,** an array of examples of terrible consequences that will or might follow if we travel down a certain path. A good example appears in Justice William Brennan's opinion for the Supreme Court in *Texas v. Johnson* (1989), regarding a Texas law against burning the American flag in political protest. If this law is allowed to stand, Brennan suggests, we may next find laws against burning the presidential seal, state flags, and the Constitution.

False Analogy   Argument by analogy, as we point out in Chapter 3 and as many of the selections in this book show, is a familiar and even indispensable mode of argument. But it can be treacherous because it runs the risk of the **fallacy of false analogy.** Unfortunately, we have no simple or foolproof way of distinguishing between the useful, legitimate analogies and the others. The key question to ask yourself is this: Do the two things put into analogy differ in any essential and relevant respect, or are they different only in unimportant and irrelevant aspects?

In a famous example from his discussion in support of suicide, philosopher David Hume rhetorically asked: "It would be no crime in me to divert the Nile or Danube from its course, were I able to effect such purposes. Where then is the crime of turning a few ounces of blood from their natural channel?" This is a striking analogy, except that it rests on a false assumption. No one has the right to divert the Nile or the Danube or any other major international watercourse; it would be a catastrophic crime to do so without the full consent of people living in the region, their government, and so forth. Therefore, arguing by analogy, one might well say that no one has the right to take his or her own life, either. Thus, Hume's own analogy can be used to argue against his thesis that suicide is no crime. But let's ignore the way in which his example can be turned against him. The analogy is a terrible one in any case. Isn't it obvious that the Nile, regardless of its exact course, would continue to nourish Egypt and the Sudan, whereas the blood flowing out of someone's veins will soon leave that person dead? The fact that the blood is the same blood, whether in a person's body or in a pool on the floor (just as the water of the Nile is the same body of water no matter what path it follows to the sea) is, of course, irrelevant to the question of whether one has the right to commit suicide.

Let's look at a more complex example. During the 1960s, when the United States was convulsed over the purpose and scope of its military involvement in Southeast Asia, advocates of more vigorous U.S. military participation appealed to the so-called domino effect, supposedly inspired by a passing remark from President Eisenhower in the 1950s. The analogy refers to the way in which a row of standing dominoes will collapse, one after the other, if the first one is pushed. If Vietnam turns Communist, according to this analogy, so too will its neighbors, Laos and Cambodia, followed by Thailand and then Burma, until the whole region is as communist as China to the north. The domino analogy (or metaphor) provided, no doubt, a vivid illustration and effectively portrayed the worry of many anti-Communists. But did it really shed any light on the likely pattern of political and military developments in the region? The history of events there during the 1970s and 1980s did not bear out the domino analogy.

Straw Man   It is often tempting to reframe or report your opponent's thesis to make it easier to attack and perhaps refute it. If you do this in the course of an argument, you are creating a straw man, a thing of no substance that's easily blown away. The straw man you've constructed is usually a radically conservative or extremely liberal thesis, which few if any would want to defend. That's why it is easier to refute than the view your opponent actually holds. "So you defend the death penalty — and all the horrible things done in its name. No one in his right mind would hold such a view." It's highly unlikely that your opponent supports *everything* that has been done in the name of capital punishment — crucifixion and beheading, for example, or execution of the children of the guilty offender.

Special Pleading   We all have our favorites — relatives, friends, and neighbors — and we're all too likely to show that favoritism in unacceptable ways. How about this: "Yes, I know Billy hit Sally first, but he's my son. He's a good boy, and I know he must have had a good reason." Or this: "True, she's late for work again — the third time this week! — but her uncle's my friend, and it will be embarrassing to me if she's fired, so we'll just ignore it." Special pleading inevitably leads to unmerited advantages.

Begging the Question   The argument over whether the death penalty is a deterrent illustrates another fallacy. From the fact that you live in a death-penalty state and were not murdered yesterday, we cannot infer that the death penalty was a deterrent. Yet it is tempting to make this inference, perhaps because — all unaware — we are relying on the **fallacy of begging the question.** If someone tacitly assumes from the start that the death penalty is an effective deterrent, then the fact that you weren't murdered yesterday certainly looks like evidence for the truth of that assumption. But it isn't, so long as there are competing but unexamined alternative explanations, as in this case. (The fallacy is called "begging the question," *petitio principii* in Latin, because the conclusion of the argument is hidden among its assumptions — and so the conclusion, not surprisingly, follows from the premises.)

Of course, the fact that you weren't murdered is *consistent* with the claim that the death penalty is an effective deterrent, just as someone else's being murdered is also consistent with that claim (because an effective deterrent need not be a *perfect* deterrent). In general, from the fact that two propositions are consistent with each other, we cannot infer that either is evidence for the other.

Note: The term "begging the question" is often wrongly used to mean "raises the question," as in "His action of burning the flag begs the question, What drove him to do such a thing?"

False Dichotomy   Sometimes, oversimplification takes a more complex form, in which contrary possibilities are wrongly presented as though they were exhaustive and exclusive. "Either we get tough with drug users, or we must surrender and legalize all drugs." Really? What about doing neither and instead offering education and counseling, detoxification programs, and incentives to "Say no"? A favorite of debaters, **either/or reasoning** always runs the risk of ignoring a third (or fourth) possibility. Some disjunctions are indeed exhaustive: "Either we get tough with drug users, or we do not." This proposition, though vague (what does "get tough" really mean?), is a tautology; it cannot be false, and there is no third alternative. But most disjunctions do not express a pair of *contradictory* alternatives: They offer only a pair of *contrary* alternatives, and mere contraries do not exhaust the possibilities (recall our discussion of contraries versus contradictories on pp. 342–45).

An example of **false dichotomy** appears in the essay by Jeff Jacoby on flogging (pp. 196–98). His entire discussion is built on the relative superiority of whipping over imprisonment, as though there was no alternative punishment worth considering. But of course, there is — notably, community service (especially for white-collar offenders, juveniles, and many first offenders).

Oversimplification   "Poverty causes crime," "Taxation is unfair," "Truth is stranger than fiction" — these are examples of generalizations that exaggerate and therefore oversimplify the truth. Poverty as such can't be the sole cause of crime because many poor people do not break the law. Some taxes may be unfairly high, others unfairly low — but there is no reason to believe that *every* tax is unfair to all those who have to pay it. Some true stories do amaze us as much or more than some fictional stories, but the reverse is true, too. (In the language of the Toulmin method, **oversimplification** is the result of a failure to use suitable modal qualifiers in formulating one's claims or grounds or backing.)

Red Herring   The fallacy of **red herring,** less colorfully named irrelevant thesis, occurs when one tries to distract one's audience by invoking a consideration that is irrelevant to the topic under discussion. (This fallacy probably gets its name from the fact that a rotten herring, or a cured herring, which is reddish, will throw pursuing hounds off the right track.) Consider this case: Some critics, seeking to defend our government's refusal to sign the Kyoto accords to reduce global warming, argue that signing is supported mainly by left-leaning scientists. This argument supposedly shows that global warming — if there is such a thing — is not a serious, urgent issue. But claiming that the supporters of these accords are left-inclined is a red herring, an irrelevant thesis. By raising doubts about the political views of the advocates of signing, critics distract attention from the scientific question (Is there global warming?) and also from the separate political question (Ought the U.S. government sign the accords?). The refusal of a government to sign the accords doesn't show there is no such thing as global warming. And even if all the advocates of signing were left-leaning (they aren't), this fact (if it were a fact, but it isn't) would not show that worries about global warming are exaggerated.

FALLACIES OF RELEVANCE

Tu Quoque   The Romans had a word for it: *Tu quoque* means "you, too." Consider this: "You're a fine one, trying to persuade me to give up smoking when you indulge yourself with a pipe and a cigar from time to time. Maybe I should quit, but then so should you. As things stand now, however, it's hypocritical of you to complain about my smoking when you persist in the same habit." The fallacy is this: The merit of a person's argument has nothing to do with the person's character or behavior. Here the assertion that smoking is bad for one's health is *not* weakened by the fact that a smoker offers the argument.

The Genetic Fallacy   A member of the family of fallacies that includes poisoning the well and ad hominem (see below) is the **genetic fallacy.** Here the error takes the form of arguing against a claim by pointing out that its origin (genesis) is tainted or that it was invented by someone deserving our contempt. Thus, one might attack the ideas of the Declaration of Independence by pointing out that its principal author, Thomas Jefferson, was a slaveholder. Assuming that it is not anachronistic and inappropriate to criticize a public figure of two centuries ago for practicing slavery, and conceding that slavery is morally outrageous, it is nonetheless fallacious to attack the ideas or even the sincerity of the Declaration by attempting to impeach the credentials of its author. Jefferson's moral faults do not by themselves falsify, make improbable, or constitute counterevidence to the truth or other merits of the claims made in his writings. At most, one's faults cast doubt on one's integrity or sincerity if one makes claims at odds with one's practice.

The genetic fallacy can take other forms less closely allied to ad hominem argument. For example, an opponent of the death penalty might argue this:

> Capital punishment arose in barbarous times; but we claim to be civilized; therefore, we should discard this relic of the past.

Such reasoning shouldn't be persuasive because the question of the death penalty for our society must be decided by the degree to which it serves our purposes — justice and defense against crime, presumably — to which its historic origins are irrelevant. The practices of beer- and wine-making are as old as human civilization, but their origin in antiquity is no reason to outlaw them in our time. The curious circumstances in which something originates usually play no role in its validity. Anyone who would argue that nothing good could possibly come from molds and fungi is refuted by Sir Alexander Fleming's discovery of penicillin in 1928.

Poisoning the Well   During the 1970s some critics of the Equal Rights Amendment (ERA) argued against it by pointing out that Marx and Engels, in their *Communist Manifesto,* favored equality of women and men — and therefore the ERA was immoral, undesirable, and perhaps even a Communist plot. This kind of reasoning is an attempt to **poison the well;** that is, an attempt to shift attention from the merits of the argument — the validity of the reasoning, the truth of the claims — to the source or origin of the argument. Such criticism deflects attention from the real issue; namely, whether the view in question is true and what the quality of evidence is in its support. The mere fact that Marx (or Hitler, for that matter) believed something does not show that the belief is false or immoral; just because some scoundrel believes the world is round, that is no reason for you to believe it is flat.

Appeal to Ignorance   In the controversy over the death penalty, the issues of deterrence and executing the innocent are bound to be raised. Because no one knows how many innocent persons have been convicted for murder and wrongfully executed, it is tempting for abolitionists to argue that the death penalty is too risky. It is equally tempting for proponents of the death penalty to argue that since no one knows how many people have been deterred from murder by the threat of execution, we abolish it at society's peril.

Each of these arguments suffers from the same flaw: the **fallacy of appeal to ignorance.** Each argument invites the audience to draw an inference from a premise that is unquestionably true — but what is that premise? It asserts that there is something "we don't know." But what we *don't* know cannot be *evidence* for (or against) anything. Our ignorance is no reason for believing anything, except perhaps that we ought to undertake an appropriate investigation in order to replace our ignorance with reliable information.

Ad Hominem   Closely allied to poisoning the well is another fallacy, **ad hominem** argument (from the Latin for "against the person"). A critic can easily yield to the temptation to attack an argument or theory by trying to impeach or undercut the credentials of its advocates.

Example: Jones is arguing that prayer should not be permitted in public schools, and Smith responds by pointing out that Jones has twice been convicted of assaulting members of the clergy. Jones's behavior doubtless is reprehensible, but the issue is not Jones, it is prayer in school, and what must be scrutinized is Jones's argument, not his police record or his character.

Appeal to Authority   The example of Jefferson that we gave to illustrate the genetic fallacy can be turned around to illustrate another fallacy. One might easily imagine someone from the South in 1860 defending the slave-owning society of that day by appealing to the fact that no less a person than Jefferson — a brilliant public figure, thinker, and leader by any measure — owned slaves. Or today one might defend capital punishment on the ground that Abraham Lincoln, surely one of the nation's greatest presidents, signed many death warrants during the Civil War, authorizing the execution of Union soldiers. No doubt the esteem in which such figures as Jefferson and Lincoln are deservedly held amounts to impressive endorsement for whatever acts and practices, policies, and institutions, they supported. But the **authority** of these figures in itself is not evidence for the truth of their views, so their authority cannot be a reason for anyone to agree with them. Obviously, Jefferson and Lincoln themselves could not support their beliefs by pointing to the fact that they held them. Because their own authority is no reason for them to believe what they believe, it is no reason for anyone else, either.

Sometimes, the appeal to authority is fallacious because the authoritative person is not an expert on the issue in dispute. The fact that a high-energy physicist has won the Nobel Prize is no reason for attaching any special weight to her views on the causes of cancer, the reduction of traffic accidents, or the legalization of marijuana. However, one would be well advised to attend to her views on the advisability of ballistic missile-defense systems, for there may be a connection between the kind of research for which she received the prize and the defense research projects.

All of us depend heavily on the knowledge of various experts and authorities, so we tend to respect their views. Conversely, we should resist the temptation to accord their views on diverse subjects the same respect that we grant them in the area of their expertise.

Appeal to Fear   The Romans called this fallacy *ad baculum*, "resorting to violence" (*baculum* means "stick" or "club"). Trying to persuade people to agree with you by threatening them with painful consequences is obviously an appeal that no rational person would contemplate. The violence need not be physical; if you threaten someone with the loss of a job, for instance, you are still using a stick. Violence or the threat of harmful consequences in the course of an argument is beyond reason and always shows the haste or impatience of those who appeal to it. It is also an indication that the argument on its merits would be unpersuasive, inconclusive, or worse. President Teddy Roosevelt's epigrammatic doctrine for the kind of foreign policy he favored — "Speak softly but carry a big stick" — illustrates an attempt to have it both ways; an appeal to reason for starters but a recourse to coercion, or the threat of coercion, as a backup if needed.

Finally, we add two fallacies, not easily embraced by Engels's three categories that have served us well thus far (ambiguity, erroneous presumption, and irrelevance): death by a thousand qualifications and protecting the hypothesis.

Death by a Thousand Qualifications   In a letter of recommendation sent in support of an applicant for a job on your newspaper, you find this sentence: "Young Smith was the best student I've ever taught in an English course." Pretty strong endorsement, you think, except that you don't know, because you haven't been told, that the letter writer is a very junior faculty member, has been teaching for only two years, is an instructor in the history department, taught a section of freshman English as a courtesy for a sick colleague, and had only eight students enrolled in the course. Thanks to these implicit qualifications, the letter writer did not lie or exaggerate in his praise; but the effect of his sentence on you, the unwitting reader, is quite misleading. The explicit claim in the letter, and its impact on you, is quite different from the tacitly qualified claim in the mind of the writer.

Death by a thousand qualifications gets its name from the ancient torture of death by a thousand small cuts. Thus, a bold assertion can be virtually killed, its true content reduced to nothing, bit by bit, as all the appropriate or necessary qualifications are added to it. Consider another example. Suppose you hear a politician describing another country (let's call it Ruritania so as not to offend anyone) as a "democracy" — except it turns out that Ruritania doesn't have regular elections, lacks a written constitution, has no independent judiciary, prohibits religious worship except of the state-designated deity, and so forth. So what remains of the original claim that Ruritania is a democracy is little or nothing. The qualifications have taken all the content out of the original description.

Protecting the Hypothesis   In Chapter 3, we contrasted *reasoning* and *rationalization* (or the finding of bad reasons for what one intends to believe anyway). Rationalization can take subtle forms, as the following example indicates. Suppose you're standing with a friend on the shore or on a pier, and you watch as a ship heads out to sea. As it reaches the horizon, it slowly disappears — first the hull, then the upper decks, and finally the tip of the mast. Because the ship (you both assume) isn't sinking, it occurs to you that this sequence of observations provices evidence that the earth's surface is curved. Nonsense, says your companion. Light waves sag, or bend down, over distances of a few miles, and so a flat surface (such as the ocean) can intercept them. Hence, the ship, which appears to be going "over" the horizon, really isn't: It's just moving steadily farther and farther away in a straight line. Your friend, you discover to your amazement, is a card-carrying member of the Flat Earth Society (yes, there really is such an organization). Now most of us would regard the idea that light rays bend down in the manner required by the Flat Earther's argument as a rationalization whose sole purpose is to protect the flat-earth doctrine against counterevidence. We would be convinced it was a rationalization, and not a very good one at that, if the Flat Earther held to it despite a patient and thorough explanation from a physicist that showed modern optical theory to be quite incompatible with the view that light waves sag.

This example illustrates two important points about the *backing* of arguments. First, it is always possible to protect a hypothesis by abandoning adjacent or connected hypotheses;

this is the tactic our Flat Earth friend has used. This maneuver is possible, however, only because — and this is the second point — whenever we test a hypothesis, we do so by taking for granted (usually, quite unconsciously) many other hypotheses as well. So the evidence for the hypothesis we think we are confirming is impossible to separate entirely from the adequacy of the connected hypotheses. As long as we have no reason to doubt that light rays travel in straight lines (at least over distances of a few miles), our Flat Earth friend's argument is unconvincing. But once that hypothesis is itself put in doubt, the idea that seemed at first to be a pathetic rationalization takes on an even more troublesome character.

There are, then, not one but two fallacies exposed by this example. The first and perhaps graver one is in rigging your hypothesis so that *no matter what* observations are brought against it, you will count nothing as falsifying it. The second and subtler one is in thinking that as you test one hypothesis, all of your other background beliefs are left safely to one side, immaculate and uninvolved. On the contrary, our beliefs form a corporate structure, intertwined and connected to one another with great complexity, and no one of them can ever be singled out for unique and isolated application, confirmation, or disconfirmation to the world around us.

A CHECKLIST FOR EVALUATING AN ARGUMENT FROM A LOGICAL POINT OF VIEW

☐ Is the argument purely deductive, purely inductive, or a mixture of the two?

☐ If it is deductive, is it valid?

☐ If it is valid, are all its premises and assumptions true?

☐ If it is not valid, what fallacy does it commit?

☐ If it is not valid, are the claims at least consistent with each other?

☐ If it is not valid, can you think of additional plausible assumptions that would make it valid?

☐ If the argument is inductive, on what observations is it based?

☐ If the argument is deductive, how probable are its premises and its conclusion?

☐ In any case, can you think of evidence that would further confirm the conclusion? Disconfirm the conclusion?

Exercise: Fallacies — or Not?

Here, for diversion and practice, are some fallacies in action. Some of these statements, however, are not fallacies. Can you tell which is which? Can you detect *what* has gone wrong in the cases where something has gone wrong? Please explain your reasoning.

1. Abortion is murder — and it doesn't matter whether we're talking about killing a human embryo or a human fetus.

2. Euthanasia is not a good thing, it's murder — and it doesn't matter how painful one's dying may be.

3. Never loan a tool to a friend. I did once and never got it back.

4. If the neighbors don't like our loud music, that's just too bad. After all, we have a right to listen to the music we like when and where we want to play it.

5. The Good Samaritan in the Bible was pretty foolish; he was taking grave risks with no benefits for him in sight.

6. "Shoot first and ask questions afterward" is a good epigram for the kind of foreign policy we need.

7. "You can fool some of the people all of the time, and you can fool all the people some of the time, but you can't fool all the people all of the time." That's what Abraham Lincoln said, and he was right.

8. It doesn't matter whether Shakespeare wrote the plays attributed to him. What matters is whether the plays are any good.

9. The Golden Gate Bridge in San Francisco ought to be closed down. After all, just look at all the suicides that have occurred there.

10. Reparations for African Americans are way overdue; it's just another version of the reparations eventually paid to the Japanese Americans who were wrongly interned in 1942 during World War II.

11. Animals don't have rights any more than do trees or stones. They don't have desires, either. What they have are feelings and needs.

12. The average American family is said to have 2.1 children. This is absurd — did you ever meet 2.1 children?

13. My marriage was a failure, which just proves my point: Don't ever get married in the first place.

14. The Red Queen in *Alice in Wonderland* was right: Verdict first, evidence later.

15. Not until astronauts sailed through space around the moon and could see its back side for themselves did we have adequate reason to believe that the moon even had a back side.

16. If you start out with a bottle of beer a day and then go on to a glass or two of wine on the weekends, you're well on your way to becoming a hopeless drunk.

17. Two Indians are sitting on a fence. The small Indian is the son of the big Indian, but the big Indian is not the small Indian's father. How is that possible?

18. If you toss a coin five times and each time it comes up heads, is it more likely than not that on the sixth throw you'll come up heads again — or is it more likely that you'll come up tails? Or is neither more likely?

19. Going to church on a regular basis is bad for your health. Instead of sitting in a pew for an hour each Sunday, you'd be better off taking an hour's brisk walk.

20. You can't trust anything he says. When he was young, he was an avid Communist.

21. Since 9/11 we've tried and convicted few terrorists, so our defense systems must be working.

22. We can trust the White House in its press releases because it's a reliable source of information.

23. Intelligent design must be true because the theory of evolution can't explain how life began.

24. Andreas Serrano's notorious photograph called *Piss Christ* (1989), showing a small plastic crucifix submerged in a glass of urine, never should have been put on public display, let alone financed by public funds.

25. Doubting Thomas was right — you need more than somebody's say-so to support a claim of resurrection.

26. You are a professional baseball player and you have a good-luck charm. When you wear it, the team wins. When you don't wear it, the team loses. What do you infer?

27. Resolve the following dilemma: When it rains, you can't fix the hole in the roof. When it's not raining, there is no need to mend the roof. Conclusion: Leave the roof as it is.

28. You are at the beach, and you watch a ship steaming toward the horizon. Bit by bit it disappears from view — first the masts, then the upper deck, then the main deck, then the stern, and then it's gone. Why would it be wrong to infer that the ship is sinking?

29. How can it be true that "it's the exception that proves the rule"? If anything, isn't it the exception that *disproves* the rule?

30. How come herbivores don't eat herbs?

31. In the 1930s it was commonplace to see ads announcing "More Doctors Smoke Camels." What do you make of such an ad?

32. Suppose the only way you could save five innocent people was by killing one of them. Would you do it? Suppose the only way you could save one innocent person was by killing five others. Would you do it?

MAX SHULMAN

Having read about proper and improper arguments, you are now well equipped to read a short story on the topic.

Max Shulman (1919–1988) began his career as a writer when he was a journalism student at the University of Minnesota. Later he wrote humorous novels, stories, and plays. One of his novels, Barefoot Boy with Cheek *(1943), was made into a musical, and another,* Rally Round the Flag, Boys! *(1957), was made into a film starring Paul Newman and Joanne Woodward.* The Tender Trap *(1954), a play he wrote with Robert Paul Smith, still retains its popularity with theater groups.*

"Love Is a Fallacy" was first published in 1951, when demeaning stereotypes about women and minorities were widely accepted in the marketplace as well as the home. Thus, jokes about domineering mothers-in-law or about dumb blondes routinely met with no objection.

Love Is a Fallacy

Cool was I and logical. Keen, calculating, perspicacious, acute, and astute — I was all of these. My brain was as powerful as a dynamo, as precise as a chemist's scales, as penetrating as a scalpel. And — think of it! — I was only eighteen.

It is not often that one so young has such a giant intellect. Take, for example, Petey Bellows, my roommate at the university. Same age, same background, but dumb as an ox. A nice enough fellow, you understand, but nothing upstairs. Emotional type. Unstable.

Impressionable. Worst of all, a faddist. Fads, I submit, are the very negation of reason. To be swept up in every new craze that comes along, to surrender yourself to idiocy just because everybody else is doing it — this, to me, is the acme of mindlessness. Not, however, to Petey.

One afternoon I found Petey lying on his bed with an expression of such distress on his face that I immediately diagnosed appendicitis. "Don't move," I said. "Don't take a laxative. I'll call a doctor."

"Raccoon," he mumbled thickly.

"Raccoon?" I said, pausing in my flight. 5

"I want a raccoon coat," he wailed.

I perceived that his trouble was not physical, but mental. "Why do you want a raccoon coat?"

"I should have known it," he cried, pounding his temples. "I should have known they'd come back when the Charleston came back. Like a fool I spent all my money for textbooks, and now I can't get a raccoon coat."

"Can you mean," I said incredulously, "that people are actually wearing raccoon coats again?"

"All the Big Men on Campus are wearing 10 them. Where've you been?"

"In the library," I said, naming a place not frequented by Big Men on Campus.

He leaped from the bed and paced the room. "I've got to have a raccoon coat," he said passionately. "I've got to!"

"Petey, why? Look at it rationally. Raccoon coats are unsanitary. They shed. They smell bad. They weigh too much. They're unsightly. They ——"

"You don't understand," he interrupted impatiently. "It's the thing to do. Don't you want to be in the swim?"

"No," I said truthfully. 15

"Well, I do," he declared. "I'd give anything for a raccoon coat. Anything!"

My brain, that precision instrument, slipped into high gear. "Anything?" I asked, looking at him narrowly.

"Anything," he affirmed in ringing tones.

I stroked my chin thoughtfully. It so happened that I knew where to get my hands on a raccoon coat. My father had had one in his undergraduate days; it lay now in a trunk in the attic back home. It also happened that Petey had something I wanted. He didn't *have* it exactly, but at least he had first rights on it. I refer to his girl, Polly Espy.

I had long coveted Polly Espy. Let me 20 emphasize that my desire for this young woman was not emotional in nature. She was, to be sure, a girl who excited the emotions, but I was not one to let my heart rule my head. I wanted Polly for a shrewdly calculated, entirely cerebral reason.

I was a freshman in law school. In a few years I would be out in practice. I was well aware of the importance of the right kind of wife in furthering a lawyer's career. The successful lawyers I had observed were, almost without exception, married to beautiful, gracious, intelligent women. With one omission, Polly fitted these specifications perfectly.

Beautiful she was. She was not yet of pin-up proportions, but I felt sure that time would supply the lack. She already had the makings.

Gracious she was. By gracious I mean full of graces. She had an erectness of carriage, an ease of bearing, a poise that clearly indicated the best of breeding. At table her manners were exquisite. I had seen her at the Kozy Kampus Korner eating the specialty of the house — a sandwich that contained scraps of pot roast, gravy, chopped nuts, and a dipper of sauerkraut — without even getting her fingers moist.

Intelligent she was not. In fact, she veered in the opposite direction. But I believed that under my guidance she would smarten up. At any rate, it was worth a try. It is, after all, easier to make a beautiful dumb girl smart than to make an ugly smart girl beautiful.

"Petey," I said, "are you in love with Polly Espy?"

"I think she's a keen kid," he replied, "but I don't know if you'd call it love. Why?"

"Do you," I asked, "have any kind of formal arrangement with her? I mean are you going steady or anything like that?"

"No. We see each other quite a bit, but we both have other dates. Why?"

"Is there," I asked, "any other man for whom she has a particular fondness?"

"Not that I know of. Why?"

I nodded with satisfaction. "In other words, if you were out of the picture, the field would be open. Is that right?"

"I guess so. What are you getting at?"

"Nothing, nothing," I said innocently, and took my suitcase out of the closet.

"Where you going?" asked Petey.

"Home for the weekend." I threw a few things into the bag.

"Listen," he said, clutching my arm eagerly, "while you're home, you couldn't get some money from your old man, could you, and lend it to me so I can buy a raccoon coat?"

"I may do better than that," I said with a mysterious wink and closed my bag and left.

"Look," I said to Petey when I got back Monday morning. I threw open the suitcase and revealed the huge, hairy, gamy object that my father had worn in his Stutz Bearcat in 1925.

"Holy Toledo!" said Petey reverently. He plunged his hands into the raccoon coat and then his face. "Holy Toledo!" he repeated fifteen or twenty times.

"Would you like it?" I asked.

"Oh yes!" he cried, clutching the greasy pelt to him. Then a canny look came into his eyes. "What do you want for it?"

"Your girl," I said, mincing no words.

"Polly?" he said in a horrified whisper. "You want Polly?"

"That's right."

He flung the coat from him. "Never," he said stoutly.

I shrugged. "Okay. If you don't want to be in the swim, I guess it's your business."

I sat down in a chair and pretended to read a book, but out of the corner of my eye I kept watching Petey. He was a torn man. First he looked at the coat with the expression of a waif at a bakery window. Then he turned away and set his jaw resolutely. Then he looked back at the coat, with even more longing in his face. Then he turned away, but with not so much resolution this time. Back and forth his head swiveled, desire waxing, resolution waning. Finally he didn't turn away at all; he just stood and stared with mad lust at the coat.

"It isn't as though I was in love with Polly," he said thickly. "Or going steady or anything like that."

"That's right," I murmured.

"What's Polly to me, or me to Polly?"

"Not a thing," said I.

"It's just been a casual kick — just a few laughs, that's all."

"Try on the coat," said I.

He complied. The coat bunched high over his ears and dropped all the way down to his shoe tops. He looked like a mound of dead raccoons. "Fits fine," he said happily.

I rose from my chair. "Is it a deal?" I asked, extending my hand.

He swallowed. "It's a deal," he said and shook my hand.

I had my first date with Polly the following evening. This was in the nature of a survey; I wanted to find out just how much work I had to do to get her mind up to the standard I required. I took her first to dinner. "Gee, that was a delish dinner," she said as we left the restaurant. Then I took her to a movie. "Gee, that was a marvy movie," she said as we left the theater. And then I took her home. "Gee, I had a sensaysh time," she said as she bade me good night.

I went back to my room with a heavy heart. I had gravely underestimated the size of my task. This girl's lack of information was terrifying. Nor would it be enough merely to supply her with information. First she had to be taught to *think*. This loomed as a project of no small dimensions, and at first I was tempted to give her back to Petey. But then I got to thinking about her abundant physical charms and about the way she entered a room and the way she handled a knife and fork, and I decided to make an effort.

I went about it, as in all things, systematically. I gave her a course in logic. It happened that I, as a law student, was taking a course in logic myself, so I had all the facts at my fingertips. "Polly," I said to her when I picked her up on our next date, "tonight we are going over to the Knoll and talk."

"Oo, terrif," she replied. One thing I will say 60 for this girl: You would go far to find another so agreeable.

We went to the Knoll, the campus trysting place, and we sat down under an old oak, and she looked at me expectantly: "What are we going to talk about?" she asked.

"Logic."

She thought this over for a minute and decided she liked it. "Magnif," she said.

"Logic," I said, clearing my throat, "is the science of thinking. Before we can think correctly, we must first learn to recognize the common fallacies of logic. These we will take up tonight."

"Wow-dow!" she cried, clapping her hands 65 delightedly.

I winced, but went bravely on. "First let us examine the fallacy called Dicto Simpliciter."

"By all means," she urged, batting her lashes eagerly.

"Dicto Simpliciter means an argument based on an unqualified generalization. For example: Exercise is good. Therefore everybody should exercise."

"I agree," said Polly earnestly. "I mean exercise is wonderful. I mean it builds the body and everything."

"Polly," I said gently, "the argument is a fal- 70 lacy. *Exercise is good* is an unqualified generalization. For instance, if you have heart disease, exercise is bad, not good. Many people are ordered by their doctors *not* to exercise. You must *qualify* the generalization. You must say exercise is *usually* good, or exercise is good *for most people*. Otherwise you have committed a Dicto Simpliciter. Do you see?"

"No," she confessed. "But this is marvy. Do more! Do more!"

"It will be better if you stop tugging at my sleeve," I told her, and when she desisted, I continued. "Next we take up a fallacy called Hasty Generalization. Listen carefully: You can't speak French. I can't speak French. Petey Bellows can't speak French. I must therefore conclude that nobody at the University of Minnesota can speak French."

"Really?" said Polly, amazed. "*Nobody?*"

I hid my exasperation. "Polly, it's a fallacy. The generalization is reached too hastily. There are too few instances to support such a conclusion."

"Know any more fallacies?" she asked 75 breathlessly. "This is more fun than dancing even."

I fought off a wave of despair. I was getting nowhere with this girl, absolutely nowhere. Still, I am nothing if not persistent. I continued. "Next comes Post Hoc. Listen to this: Let's not take Bill on our picnic. Every time we take him out with us, it rains."

"I know somebody just like that," she exclaimed. "A girl back home — Eula Becker, her name is. It never fails. Every single time we take her on a picnic ——"

"Polly," I said sharply, "it's a fallacy. Eula Becker doesn't *cause* the rain. She has no connection with the rain. You are guilty of Post Hoc if you blame Eula Becker."

"I'll never do it again," she promised contritely. "Are you mad at me?"

I sighed. "No, Polly, I'm not mad." 80

"Then tell me some more fallacies."

"All right. Let's try Contradictory Premises."

"Yes, let's," she chirped, blinking her eyes happily.

I frowned, but plunged ahead. "Here's an example of Contradictory Premises: If God can do anything, can He make a stone so heavy that He won't be able to lift it?"

"Of course," she replied promptly. 85

"But if He can do anything, He can lift the stone," I pointed out.

"Yeah," she said thoughtfully. "Well, then I guess He can't make the stone."

"But He can do anything," I reminded her.

She scratched her pretty, empty head. "I'm all confused," she admitted.

"Of course you are. Because when the 90 premises of an argument contradict each other, there can be no argument. If there is an irresistible force, there can be no immovable object. If there is an immovable object, there can be no irresistible force. Get it?"

"Tell me some more of this keen stuff," she said eagerly.

I consulted my watch. "I think we'd better call it a night. I'll take you home now, and you go over all the things you've learned. We'll have another session tomorrow night."

I deposited her at the girls' dormitory, where she assured me that she had had a perfectly terrif evening, and I went glumly home to my room. Petey lay snoring in his bed, the raccoon coat huddled like a great hairy beast at his feet. For a moment I considered waking him and telling him that he could have his girl back. It seemed clear that my project was doomed to failure. The girl simply had a logic-proof head.

But then I reconsidered. I had wasted one evening; I might as well waste another. Who knew? Maybe somewhere in the extinct crater of her mind a few embers still smoldered. Maybe somehow I could fan them into flame. Admittedly it was not a prospect fraught with hope, but I decided to give it one more try.

Seated under the oak the next evening 95 I said, "Our first fallacy tonight is called Ad Misericordiam."

She quivered with delight.

"Listen closely," I said. "A man applies for a job. When the boss asks him what his qualifications are, he replies that he has a wife and six children at home, the wife is a helpless cripple, the children have nothing to eat, no clothes to wear, no shoes on their feet, there are no beds in the house, no coal in the cellar, and winter is coming."

A tear rolled down each of Polly's pink cheeks. "Oh, this is awful, awful," she sobbed.

"Yes, it's awful," I agreed, "but it's no argument. The man never answered the boss's question about his qualifications. Instead he appealed to the boss's sympathy. He committed the fallacy of Ad Misericordiam. Do you understand?"

"Have you got a handkerchief?" she 100 blubbered.

I handed her a handkerchief and tried to keep from screaming while she wiped her eyes. "Next," I said in a carefully controlled tone, "we will discuss False Analogy. Here is an example: Students should be allowed to look at their textbooks during examinations. After all, surgeons have X rays to guide them during an operation, lawyers have briefs to guide them during a trial, carpenters have blueprints to guide them when they are building a house. Why, then, shouldn't students be allowed to look at their textbooks during an examination?"

"There now," she said enthusiastically, "is the most marvy idea I've heard in years."

"Polly," I said testily, "the argument is all wrong. Doctors, lawyers, and carpenters aren't taking a test to see how much they have learned, but students are. The situations are altogether different, and you can't make an analogy between them."

"I still think it's a good idea," said Polly.

"Nuts," I muttered. Doggedly I pressed on. "Next we'll try Hypothesis Contrary to Fact."

"Sounds yummy," was Polly's reaction.

"Listen: If Madame Curie had not happened to leave a photographic plate in a drawer with a chunk of pitchblende, the world today would not know about radium."

"True, true," said Polly, nodding her head. "Did you see the movie? Oh, it just knocked me out. That Walter Pidgeon is so dreamy. I mean he fractures me."

"If you can forget Mr. Pidgeon for a moment," I said coldly, "I would like to point out that the statement is a fallacy. Maybe Madame Curie would have discovered radium at some later date. Maybe somebody else would have discovered it. Maybe any number of things would have happened. You can't start with a hypothesis that is not true and then draw any supportable conclusions from it."

"They ought to put Walter Pidgeon in more pictures," said Polly. "I hardly ever see him any more."

One more chance, I decided. But just one more. There is a limit to what flesh and blood can bear. "The next fallacy is called Poisoning the Well."

"How cute!" she gurgled.

"Two men are having a debate. The first one gets up and says, 'My opponent is a notorious liar. You can't believe a word that he is going to say.' . . . Now, Polly, think. Think hard. What's wrong?"

I watched her closely as she knit her creamy brow in concentration. Suddenly a glimmer of intelligence — the first I had seen — came into her eyes. "It's not fair," she said with indignation. "It's not a bit fair. What chance has the second man got if the first man calls him a liar before he even begins talking?"

"Right!" I cried exultantly. "One hundred percent right. It's not fair. The first man has *poisoned the well* before anybody could drink from it. He has hamstrung his opponent before he could even start. . . . Polly, I'm proud of you."

"Pshaw," she murmured, blushing with pleasure.

"You see, my dear, these things aren't so hard. All you have to do is concentrate. Think — examine — evaluate. Come now, let's review everything we have learned."

"Fire away," she said with an airy wave of her hand.

Heartened by the knowledge that Polly was not altogether a cretin, I began a long, patient review of all I had told her. Over and over and over again I cited instances, pointed out flaws, kept hammering away without letup. It was like digging a tunnel. At first everything was work, sweat, and darkness. I had no idea when I would reach the light, or even *if* I would. But I persisted. I pounded and clawed and scraped, and finally I was rewarded. I saw a chink of light. And then the chink got bigger and the sun came pouring in and all was bright.

Five grueling nights this took, but it was worth it. I had made a logician out of Polly; I had taught her to think. My job was done. She was worthy of me at last. She was a fit wife for me, a proper hostess for my many mansions, a suitable mother for my well-heeled children.

It must not be thought that I was without love for this girl. Quite the contrary. Just as Pygmalion loved the perfect woman he had fashioned, so I loved mine. I decided to acquaint her with my feelings at our very next meeting. The time had come to change our relationship from academic to romantic.

"Polly," I said when next we sat beneath our oak, "tonight we will not discuss fallacies."

"Aw, gee," she said, disappointed.

"My dear," I said, favoring her with a smile, "we have now spent five evenings together. We have gotten along splendidly. It is clear that we are well matched."

"Hasty Generalization," said Polly brightly. 125

"I beg your pardon," said I.

"Hasty Generalization," she repeated. "How can you say that we are well matched on the basis of only five dates?"

I chuckled with amusement. The dear child had learned her lessons well. "My dear," I said, patting her hand in a tolerant manner, "five dates is plenty. After all, you don't have to eat a whole cake to know that it's good."

"False Analogy," said Polly promptly. "I'm not a cake. I'm a girl."

I chuckled with somewhat less amuse- 130 ment. The dear child had learned her lesson perhaps too well. I decided to change tactics. Obviously the best approach was a simple, strong, direct declaration of love. I paused for a moment while my massive brain chose the proper words. Then I began:

"Polly, I love you. You are the whole world to me, and the moon and the stars and the constellations of outer space. Please, my darling, say that you will go steady with me, for if you will not, life will be meaningless. I will languish. I will refuse my meals. I will wander the face of the earth, a shambling, hollow-eyed hulk."

There, I thought, folding my arms, that ought to do it.

"Ad Misericordiam," said Polly.

I ground my teeth. I was not Pygmalion; I was Frankenstein, and my monster had me by the throat. Frantically I fought back the tide of panic surging through me. At all costs I had to keep cool.

"Well, Polly," I said, forcing a smile, "you 135 certainly have learned your fallacies."

"You're darn right," she said with a vigorous nod.

"And who taught them to you, Polly?"

"You did."

"That's right. So you do owe me something, don't you, my dear? If I hadn't come along you never would have learned about fallacies."

"Hypothesis Contrary to Fact," she said 140 instantly.

I dashed perspiration from my brow. "Polly," I croaked, "you mustn't take all these things so literally. I mean this is just classroom stuff. You know that the things you learn in school don't have anything to do with life."

"Dicto Simpliciter," she said, wagging her finger at me playfully.

That did it. I leaped to my feet, bellowing like a bull. "Will you or will you not go steady with me?"

"I will not," she replied.

"Why not?" I demanded. 145

"Because this afternoon I promised Petey Bellows that I would go steady with him."

I reeled back, overcome with the infamy of it. After he promised, after he made a deal, after he shook my hand! "That rat!" I shrieked, kicking up great chunks of turf. "You can't go with him, Polly. He's a liar. He's a cheat. He's a rat."

"Poisoning the Well," said Polly, "and stop shouting. I think shouting must be a fallacy too."

With an immense effort of will, I modulated my voice. "All right," I said. "You're a logician. Let's look at this thing logically. How could you choose Petey Bellows over me? Look at me — a brilliant student, a tremendous intellectual, a man with an assured future. Look at Petey — a knothead, a jitterbug, a guy who'll never know where his next meal is coming from. Can you give me one logical reason why you should go steady with Petey Bellows?"

"I certainly can," declared Polly. "He's got a raccoon coat." 150

Topic for Critical Thinking and Writing

After you have finished reading "Love Is a Fallacy," you may want to write an argumentative essay of 500 to 750 words on one of the following topics: (1) the story, rightly understood, is not antiwoman; (2) if the story is antiwoman, it is equally antiman; (3) the story is antiwoman but nevertheless belongs in this book; or (4) the story is antiwoman and does not belong in the book.

10

A Psychologist's View: Rogerian Argument

Real communication occurs ... when we listen with understanding. —CARL ROGERS

The first duty of a wise advocate is to convince his opponents that he understands their arguments, and sympathizes with their just feelings. —SAMUEL TAYLOR COLERIDGE

Rogerian Argument: An Introduction

Carl R. Rogers (1902–1987), perhaps best known for his book entitled *On Becoming a Person* (1961), was a psychotherapist, not a teacher of writing. This short essay by Rogers (on pp. 375–80) has, however, exerted much influence on instructors who teach argument. Written in the 1950s, this essay reflects the political climate of the cold war between the United States and the Soviet Union, which dominated headlines for more than forty years (1947–1989). Several of Rogers's examples of bias and frustrated communication allude to the tensions of that era.

On the surface, many arguments seem to show *A* arguing with *B*, presumably seeking to change *B*'s mind; but *A*'s argument is really directed not to *B* but to *C*. This attempt to persuade a non-participant is evident in the courtroom, where neither the prosecutor (*A*) nor the defense lawyer (*B*) is really trying to convince the opponent. Rather, both are trying to convince a third party, the jury (*C*). Prosecutors don't care whether they convince defense lawyers; they don't even mind infuriating defense lawyers because

Carl R. Rogers leading a panel discussion in 1966.

their only real goal is to convince the jury. Similarly, the writer of a letter to a newspaper, taking issue with an editorial, doesn't expect to change the paper's policy. Rather, the writer hopes to convince a third party, the reader of the newspaper.

But suppose *A* really does want to bring *B* around to *A*'s point of view. Suppose Mary really wants to persuade the teacher to allow her little lamb to stay in the classroom. Rogers points out that when we engage in an argument, if we feel our integrity or our identity is threatened, we will stiffen our position. (The teacher may feel that his or her dignity is compromised by the presence of the lamb and will scarcely attend to Mary's argument.) The sense of threat may be so great that we are unable to consider the alternative views being offered, and we therefore remain unpersuaded. Threatened, we may defend ourselves rather than our argument, and little communication will take place. Of course, a third party might say that we or our opponent presented the more convincing case, but we, and perhaps the opponent, have scarcely listened to each other, and so the two of us remain apart.

Rogers suggests, therefore, that a writer who wishes to communicate with someone (as opposed to convincing a third party) needs to reduce the threat. In a sense, the participants in the argument need to become partners rather than adversaries. Rogers writes, "Mutual communication tends to be pointed toward solving a problem rather than toward attacking a person or group." Thus, in an essay on whether schools should test students for use of drugs, the writer need not—and probably should not—see the issue as black or white, as *either/or*. Such an essay might indicate that testing is undesirable because it may have bad effects, *but in some circumstances* it may be acceptable. This qualification does not mean that one must compromise. Thus, the essayist might argue that the potential danger to liberty is so great that no circumstances justify testing students for drugs. But even such an essayist should recognize the merit (however limited) of the opposition and should grant that the position being advanced itself entails great difficulties and dangers.

A writer who wishes to reduce the psychological threat to the opposition and thus facilitate partnership in the study of some issue can do several things:

- show sympathetic understanding of the opposing argument
- recognize what is valid in it
- recognize and demonstrate that those who take the other side are nonetheless persons of goodwill

Advocates of Rogerian argument are likely to contrast it with Aristotelian argument, saying that the style of argument associated with Aristotle (384–322 B.C., Greek philosopher and rhetorician) has these two characteristics:

- It is adversarial, seeking to refute other views.
- It sees the listener as wrong, as someone who now must be overwhelmed by evidence.

In contrast to the confrontational Aristotelian style, which allegedly seeks to present an airtight case that compels belief, Rogerian argument (it is said) has the following characteristics:

- It is nonconfrontational, collegial, and friendly.

- It respects other views and allows for multiple truths.

- It seeks to achieve some degree of assent rather than convince utterly.

Thus, in the first part of an argumentative essay, a writer who takes Rogers seriously will usually

1. state the problem,

2. give the opponent's position, and

3. grant whatever validity the writer finds in that position — for instance, will recognize the circumstances in which the position would indeed be acceptable.

Next, the writer will, if possible,

4. attempt to show how the opposing position will be improved if the writer's own position is accepted.

Sometimes, of course, the differing positions may be so far apart that no reconciliation can be proposed, in which case the writer will probably seek to show how the problem can best be solved by adopting the writer's own position. We have discussed these matters in Chapter 6, but not from the point of view of a psychotherapist, and so we reprint Rogers's essay here. (This essay was orginally presented on October 11, 1951, at Northwestern University's Centennial Conference on Communications.)

CARL R. ROGERS

Communication: Its Blocking and Its Facilitation

It may seem curious that a person whose whole professional effort is devoted to psychotherapy should be interested in problems of communication. What relationship is there between providing therapeutic help to individuals with emotional maladjustments and the concern of this conference with obstacles to communication? Actually the relationship is very close indeed. The whole task of psychotherapy is the task of dealing with a failure in communication. The emotionally maladjusted person, the "neurotic," is in difficulty first because communication within himself has broken down, and second because as a result of this his communication with others has been damaged. If this sounds somewhat strange, then let me put it in other terms. In the "neurotic" individual, parts of himself which have been termed unconscious, or repressed, or denied to awareness, become blocked off so that they no longer communicate themselves to the conscious or managing part of himself. As long as this is true, there are distortions in the way he communicates himself to others, and so he suffers both within himself, and in his interpersonal relations. The task of psychotherapy is to help the person achieve, through a special relationship with a therapist, good communication within himself. Once this is achieved he can communicate more freely and more effectively with others. We may say then that psychotherapy is good communication, within and between men. We may also turn that statement around and it will still be true. Good communication, free communication, within or between men, is always therapeutic.

It is, then, from a background of experience with communication in counseling and psychotherapy that I want to present here two ideas. I wish to state what I believe is one of the major factors in blocking or impeding communication, and then I wish to present what in our experience has proven to be a very important way to improving or facilitating communication.

I would like to propose, as an hypothesis for consideration, that the major barrier to mutual interpersonal communication is our very natural tendency to judge, to evaluate, to approve or disapprove, the statement of the person, or the other group. Let me illustrate my meaning with some very simple examples. As you leave the meeting tonight, one of the statements you are likely to hear is, "I didn't like that man's talk." Now what do you respond? Almost invariably your reply will be either approval or disapproval of the attitude expressed. Either you respond, "I didn't either. I thought it was terrible," or else you tend to reply, "Oh, I thought it was really good." In other words, your primary reaction is to evaluate what has just been said to you, to evaluate it from *your* point of view, your own frame of reference.

Or take another example. Suppose I say with some feeling, "I think the Republicans are behaving in ways that show a lot of good sound sense these days," what is the response that arises in your mind as you listen? The overwhelming likelihood is that it will be evaluative.

You will find yourself agreeing, or disagreeing, or making some judgment about me such as "He must be a conservative," or "He seems solid in his thinking." Or let us take an illustration from the international scene. Russia says vehemently, "The treaty with Japan is a war plot on the part of the United States." We rise as one person to say "That's a lie!"

This last illustration brings in another 5 element connected with my hypothesis. Although the tendency to make evaluations is common in almost all interchange of language, it is very much heightened in those situations where feelings and emotions are deeply involved. So the stronger our feelings, the more likely it is that there will be no mutual element in the communication. There will be just two ideas, two feelings, two judgments, missing each other in psychological space. I'm sure you recognize this from your own experience. When you have not been emotionally involved yourself, and have listened to a heated discussion, you often go away thinking, "Well, they actually weren't talking about the same thing." And they were not. Each was making a judgment, an evaluation, from his own frame of reference. There was really nothing which could be called communication in any genuine sense. This tendency to react to any emotionally meaningful statement by forming an evaluation of it from our own point of view, is, I repeat, the major barrier to interpersonal communication.

But is there any way of solving this problem, of avoiding this barrier? I feel that we are making exciting progress toward this goal and I would like to present it as simply as I can. Real communication occurs, and this evaluative tendency is avoided, when we listen with understanding. What does that mean? It means *to see the expressed idea and attitude from the other person's point of view, to sense how it feels to him, to achieve his frame of reference in regard to the thing he is talking about.*

Stated so briefly, this may sound absurdly simple, but it is not. It is an approach which we have found extremely potent in the field of psychotherapy. It is the most effective agent we know for altering the basic personality structure of an individual, and improving his relationships and his communications with others. If I can listen to what he can tell me, if I can understand how it seems to him, if I can see its personal meaning for him, if I can sense the emotional flavor which it has for him, then I will be releasing potent forces of change in him. If I can really understand how he hates his father, or hates the university, or hates communists — if I can catch the flavor of his fear of insanity, or his fear of atom bombs, or of Russia — it will be of the greatest help to him in altering those very hatreds and fears, and in establishing realistic and harmonious relationships with the very people and situations toward which he has felt hatred and fear. We know from our research that such empathic understanding — understanding *with* a person, not *about* him — is such an effective approach that it can bring about major changes in personality.

Some of you may be feeling that you listen well to people, and that you have never seen such results. The chances are very great indeed that your listening has not been of the type I have described. Fortunately I can suggest a little laboratory experiment which you can try to test the quality of your understanding. The next time you get into an argument with your wife, or your friend, or with a small group of friends, just stop the discussion for a moment and for an experiment, institute this rule. "Each person can speak up for himself only *after* he has first restated the ideas and feelings of the previous speaker accurately, and to that speaker's satisfaction." You see what this would

mean. It would simply mean that before presenting your own point of view, it would be necessary for you to really achieve the other speaker's frame of reference — to understand his thoughts and feelings so well that you could summarize them for him. Sounds simple, doesn't it? But if you try it you will discover it one of the most difficult things you have ever tried to do. However, once you have been able to see the other's point of view, your own comments will have to be drastically revised. You will also find the emotion going out of the discussion, the differences being reduced, and those differences which remain being of a rational and understandable sort.

Can you imagine what this kind of an approach would mean if it were projected into larger areas? What would happen to a labor-management dispute if it was conducted in such a way that labor, without necessarily agreeing, could accurately state management's point of view in a way that management could accept; and management, without approving labor's stand, could state labor's case in a way that labor agreed was accurate? It would mean that real communication was established, and one could practically guarantee that some reasonable solution would be reached.

If then this way of approach is an effective ¹⁰ avenue to good communication and good relationships, as I am quite sure you will agree if you try the experiment I have mentioned, why is it not more widely tried and used? I will try to list the difficulties which keep it from being utilized.

In the first place it takes courage, a quality which is not too widespread. I am indebted to Dr. S. I. Hayakawa, the semanticist, for pointing out that to carry on psychotherapy in this fashion is to take a very real risk, and that courage is required. If you really understand another person in this way, if you are willing to enter his private world and see the way life appears to him, without any attempt to make evaluative judgments, you run the risk of being changed yourself. You might see it his way, you might find yourself influenced in your attitudes or your personality. This risk of being changed is one of the most frightening prospects most of us can face. If I enter, as fully as I am able, into the private world of a neurotic or psychotic individual, isn't there a risk that I might become lost in that world? Most of us are afraid to take that risk. Or if we had a Russian communist speaker here tonight, or Senator Joe McCarthy, how many of us would dare to try to see the world from each of these points of view? The great majority of us could not *listen*; we would find ourselves compelled to *evaluate*, because listening would seem too dangerous. So the first requirement is courage, and we do not always have it.

But there is a second obstacle. It is just when emotions are strongest that it is most difficult to achieve the frame of reference of the other person or group. Yet it is the time the attitude is most needed, if communication is to be established. We have not found this to be an insuperable obstacle in our experience in psychotherapy. A third party, who is able to lay aside his own feelings and evaluations, can assist greatly by listening with understanding to each person or group and clarifying the views and attitudes each holds. We have found this very effective in small groups in which contradictory or antagonistic attitudes exist. When the parties to a dispute realize that they are being understood, that someone sees how the situation seems to them, the statements grow less exaggerated and less defensive, and it is no longer necessary to maintain the attitude, "I am 100 percent right and you are 100 percent wrong." The influence of such an understanding catalyst in the group permits the members to come closer and closer to the objective truth involved in the relationship. In this way mutual communication is established and some type of agreement becomes much more possible. So we may say that though heightened emotions make it much more difficult to understand *with* an opponent, our experience makes it clear that a neutral, understanding, catalyst type of leader or therapist can overcome this obstacle in a small group.

This last phrase, however, suggests another obstacle to utilizing the approach I have described. Thus far all our experience has been with small face-to-face groups — groups exhibiting industrial tensions, religious tensions, racial tensions, and therapy groups in which many personal tensions are present. In these small groups our experience, confirmed by a limited amount of research, shows that this basic approach leads to improved communication, to greater acceptance of others and by others, and to attitudes which are more positive and more problem-solving in nature. There is a decrease in defensiveness, in exaggerated statements, in evaluative and critical behavior. But these findings are from small groups. What about trying to achieve understanding between larger groups that are geographically remote? Or between face-to-face groups who are not speaking for themselves, but simply as representatives of others, like the delegates at Kaesong?[1] Frankly we do not know the answers to these questions. I believe the situation might be put this way. As social scientists we have a tentative test-tube solution of the problem of breakdown in communication. But to confirm the validity of this test-tube solution, and to adapt it to the enormous problems of communication

---

[1] **the delegates at Kaesong** Representatives of North and South Korea met at the border town of Kaesong to arrange terms for an armistice to hostilities during the Korean War (1950–1953). [All notes are the editors'.]

breakdown between classes, groups, and nations, would involve additional funds, much more research, and creative thinking of a high order.

Even with our present limited knowledge we can see some steps which might be taken, even in large groups, to increase the amount of listening *with,* and to decrease the amount of evaluation *about.* To be imaginative for a moment, let us suppose that a therapeutically oriented international group went to the Russian leaders and said, "We want to achieve a genuine understanding of your views and even more important, of your attitudes and feelings, toward the United States. We will summarize and resummarize the views and feelings if necessary, until you agree that our description represents the situation as it seems to you." Then suppose they did the same thing with the leaders in our own country. If they then gave the widest possible distribution to these two views, with the feelings clearly described but not expressed in name-calling, might not the effect be very great? It would not guarantee the type of understanding I have been describing, but it would make it much more possible. We can understand the feelings of a person who hates us much more readily when his attitudes are accurately described to us by a neutral third party, than we can when he is shaking his fist at us.

But even to describe such a first step is to 15 suggest another obstacle to this approach of understanding. Our civilization does not yet have enough faith in the social sciences to utilize their findings. The opposite is true of the physical sciences. During the war[2] when a test-tube solution was found to the problem of synthetic rubber, millions of dollars and an army of talent was turned loose on the problem of using that finding. If synthetic rubber could

be made in milligrams, it could and would be made in the thousands of tons. And it was. But in the social science realm, if a way is found of facilitating communication and mutual understanding in small groups, there is no guarantee that the finding will be utilized. It may be a generation or more before the money and the brains will be turned loose to exploit that finding.

In closing, I would like to summarize this small-scale solution to the problem of barriers in communication, and to point out certain of its characteristics.

I have said that our research and experience to date would make it appear that breakdowns in communication, and the evaluative tendency which is the major barrier to communication, can be avoided. The solution is provided by creating a situation in which each of the different parties come to understand the other from the *other's* point of view. This has been achieved, in practice, even when feelings run high, by the influence of a person who is willing to understand each point of view empathically, and who thus acts as a catalyst to precipitate further understanding.

This procedure has important characteristics. It can be initiated by one party, without waiting for the other to be ready. It can even be initiated by a neutral third person, providing he can gain a minimum of cooperation from one of the parties.

This procedure can deal with the insincerities, the defensive exaggerations, the lies, the "false fronts" which characterize almost every failure in communication. These defensive distortions drop away with astonishing speed as people find that the only intent is to understand, not judge.

This approach leads steadily and rapidly 20 toward the discovery of the truth, toward a realistic appraisal of the objective barriers

---
[2] **the war** World War II.

to communication. The dropping of some defensiveness by one party leads to further dropping of defensiveness by the other party, and truth is thus approached.

This procedure gradually achieves mutual communication. Mutual communication tends to be pointed toward solving a problem rather than toward attacking a person or group. It leads to a situation in which I see how the problem appears to you, as well as to me, and you see how it appears to me, as well as to you. Thus accurately and realistically defined, the problem is almost certain to yield to intelligent attack, or if it is in part insoluble, it will be comfortably accepted as such.

This then appears to be a test-tube solution to the breakdown of communication as it occurs in small groups. Can we take this small-scale answer, investigate it further, refine it; develop it and apply it to the tragic and well-nigh fatal failures of communication which threaten the very existence of our modern world? It seems to me that this is a possibility and a challenge which we should explore.

A CHECKLIST FOR ANALYZING ROGERIAN ARGUMENT

- ☐ Have I stated the problem and indicated that a dialogue is possible?

- ☐ Have I stated at least one other point of view in a way that would satisfy its proponents?

- ☐ Have I been courteous to those who hold views other than mine?

- ☐ Have I enlarged my own understanding to the extent that I can grant validity, at least in some circumstances, to at least some aspects of other positions?

- ☐ Have I stated my position and indicated the contexts in which I believe it is valid?

- ☐ Have I pointed out the ground that we share?

- ☐ Have I shown how other positions will be strengthened by accepting some aspects of my position?

EDWARD O. WILSON

Edward O. Wilson, born in Birmingham, Alabama, in 1929, is an emeritus professor of evolutionary biology at Harvard University. A distinguished writer as well as a researcher and teacher, Wilson has twice won the Pulitzer Prize for General Non-Fiction. We reprint a piece first published in 2006 in Wilson's book The Creation: An Appeal to Save Life on Earth.

Letter to a Southern Baptist Minister

Dear Pastor:

We have not met, yet I feel I know you well enough to call you friend. First of all, we grew up in the same faith. As a boy I too answered the altar call; I went under the water.

Although I no longer belong to that faith, I am confident that if we met and spoke privately of our deepest beliefs, it would be in a spirit of mutual respect and good will. I know we share many precepts of moral behavior. Perhaps it also matters that we are both Americans and, insofar as it might still affect civility and good manners, we are both Southerners.

I write to you now for your counsel and help. Of course, in doing so, I see no way to avoid the fundamental differences in our respective worldviews. You are a literalist interpreter of Christian Holy Scripture. You reject the conclusion of science that mankind evolved from lower forms. You believe that each person's soul is immortal, making this planet a way station to a second, eternal life. Salvation is assured those who are redeemed in Christ.

I am a secular humanist. I think existence is what we make of it as individuals. There is no guarantee of life after death, and heaven and hell are what we create for ourselves, on this planet. There is no other home. Humanity originated here by evolution from lower forms over millions of years. And yes, I will speak plain, our ancestors were apelike animals. The human species has adapted physically and mentally to life on Earth and no place else. Ethics is the code of behavior we share on the basis of reason, law, honor, and an inborn sense of decency, even as some ascribe it to God's will.

For you, the glory of an unseen divinity; for me, the glory of the universe revealed at last. For you, the belief in God made flesh to save mankind; for me, the belief in Promethean[1] fire seized to set men free. You have found your final truth; I am still searching. I may be wrong, you may be wrong. We may both be partly right.

Does this difference in worldview separate us in all things? It does not. You and I and every other human being strive for the same

imperatives of security, freedom of choice, personal dignity, and a cause to believe in that is larger than ourselves.

Let us see, then, if we can, and you are willing, to meet on the near side of metaphysics in order to deal with the real world we share. I put it this way because you have the power to help solve a great problem about which I care deeply. I hope you have the same concern. I suggest that we set aside our differences in order to save the Creation. The defense of living Nature is a universal value. It doesn't rise from, nor does it promote, any religious or ideological dogma. Rather, it serves without discrimination the interests of all humanity.

Pastor, we need your help. The Creation—living Nature—is in deep trouble. Scientists estimate that if habitat conversion and other destructive human activities continue at their present rates, half the species of plants and animals on Earth could be either gone or at least fated for early extinction by the end of the century. A full quarter will drop to this level during the next half century as a result of climate change alone. The ongoing extinction rate is calculated in the most conservative estimates to be about a hundred times above that prevailing before humans appeared on Earth, and it is expected to rise to at least a thousand times greater or more in the next few decades. If this rise continues unabated, the cost to humanity, in wealth, environmental security, and quality of life, will be catastrophic.

Surely we can agree that each species, however inconspicuous and humble it may seem to us at this moment, is a masterpiece of biology, and well worth saving. Each species possesses a unique combination of genetic traits that fits it more or less precisely to a particular part of the environment. Prudence alone dictates that we act quickly to prevent the extinction of

---

[1]**Promethean** In Greek mythology, Prometheus was a Titan who looked after mankind, going so far as to steal fire from Mount Olympus to give it to humans. [Editors' note.]

species and, with it, the pauperization of Earth's ecosystems — hence of the Creation.

You may well ask at this point, Why me? Because religion and science are the two most powerful forces in the world today, including especially the United States. If religion and science could be united on the common ground of biological conservation, the problem would soon be solved. If there is any moral precept shared by people of all beliefs, it is that we owe ourselves and future generations a beautiful, rich, and healthful environment.

I am puzzled that so many religious leaders, who spiritually represent a large majority of people around the world, have hesitated to make protection of the Creation an important part of their magisterium.[2] Do they believe that human-centered ethics and preparation for the afterlife are the only things that matter? Even more perplexing is the widespread conviction among Christians that the Second Coming is imminent, and that therefore the condition of the planet is of little consequence. Sixty percent of Americans, according to a 2004 poll, believe that the prophecies of the book of Revelation are accurate. Many of these, numbering in the millions, think the End of Time will occur within the life span of those now living. Jesus will return to Earth, and those redeemed by Christian faith will be transported bodily to heaven, while those left behind will struggle through severe hard times and, when they die, suffer eternal damnation. The condemned will remain in hell, like those already consigned in the generations before them, for a trillion trillion years, enough for the universe to expand to its own, entropic death, time enough for countless universes like it afterward to be born, expand, and likewise die away. And that is just

10 the beginning of how long condemned souls will suffer in hell — all for a mistake they made in choice of religion during the infinitesimally small time they inhabited Earth.

For those who believe this form of Christianity, the fate of 10 million other life forms indeed does not matter. This and other similar doctrines are not gospels of hope and compassion. They are gospels of cruelty and despair. They were not born of the heart of Christianity. Pastor, tell me I am wrong!

However you will respond, let me here venture an alternative ethic. The great challenge of the twenty-first century is to raise people everywhere to a decent standard of living while preserving as much of the rest of life as possible. Science has provided this part of the argument for the ethic: the more we learn about the biosphere, the more complex and beautiful it turns out to be. Knowledge of it is a magic well: the more you draw from it, the more there is to draw. Earth, and especially the razor-thin film of life enveloping it, is our home, our wellspring, our physical and much of our spiritual sustenance.

I know that science and environmentalism are linked in the minds of many with evolution, Darwin, and secularism. Let me postpone disentangling all this (I will come back to it later) and stress again: to protect the beauty of Earth and of its prodigious variety of life forms should be a common goal, regardless of differences in our metaphysical beliefs.

To make the point in good Gospel manner, let me tell the story of a young man, newly trained for the ministry, and so fixed in his Christian faith that he referred all questions of morality to readings from the Bible. When he visited the cathedral-like Atlantic rainforest of Brazil, he saw the manifest hand of God and in his notebook wrote, "It is not possible to give an adequate idea of the higher feelings of

---

[2]**magisterium** The official teaching of the Roman Catholic Church. [Editors' note.]

wonder, admiration, and devotion which fill and elevate the mind."

That was Charles Darwin in 1832, early 15 into the voyage of HMS *Beagle*, before he had given any thought to evolution.

And here is Darwin, concluding *On the Origin of Species* in 1859, having first abandoned Christian dogma and then, with his newfound intellectual freedom, formulated the theory of evolution by natural selection: "There is grandeur in this view of life, with its several powers, having been originally breathed into a few forms or into one; and that, whilst this planet has gone cycling on according to the fixed law of gravity, from so simple a beginning endless forms most beautiful and most wonderful have been, and are being, evolved."

Darwin's reverence for life remained the same as he crossed the seismic divide that divided his spiritual life. And so it can be for the divide that today separates scientific humanism from mainstream religion. And separates you and me.

You are well prepared to present the theological and moral arguments for saving the Creation. I am heartened by the movement growing within Christian denominations to support global conservation. The stream of thought has arisen from many sources, from evangelical to unitarian. Today it is but a rivulet. Tomorrow it will be a flood.

I already know much of the religious argument on behalf of the Creation, and would like to learn more. I will now lay before you and others who may wish to hear it the scientific argument. You will not agree with all that I say about the origins of life — science and religion do not easily mix in such matters — but I like to think that in this one life-and-death issue we have a common purpose.

Topics for Critical Thinking and Writing

1. Wilson claims to be a "secular humanist" (para. 3). How would you define that term? Are you a secular humanist? Why, or why not?

2. What does Wilson mean by "metaphysics" (para. 6)? Which if any of his views qualify as metaphysical?

3. Wilson obviously seeks to present his views in a fashion that makes them as palatable as possible. Do you think he succeeds in this endeavor? Write an essay of 500 words arguing for or against his achievement in this regard.

11

A Literary Critic's View: Arguing about Literature

Literary criticism [is] a reasoned account of the feeling produced upon the critic by the book he is reading.
— D. H. LAWRENCE

A writer is someone for whom writing is more difficult than it is for other people.
— THOMAS MANN

You can never draw the line between aesthetic criticism and social criticism. . . . You start with literary criticism, and however rigorous an aesthete you may be, you are over the frontier into something else sooner or later. The best you can do is to accept these conditions and know what you are doing when you are doing it.
— T. S. ELIOT

Nothing is as easy as it looks.
— MURPHY'S LAW #23

Everything is what it is and not another thing.
— BISHOP JOSEPH BUTLER

You might think that literature — fiction, poetry (including songs), drama — is meant only to be enjoyed, not to be argued about. Yet literature is constantly the subject of argumentative writing — not all of it by teachers of English. For instance, if you glance at the current issue of *Time* or *The New Yorker*, you probably will find a review of a play suggesting that the play is worth seeing or is not worth seeing. Or in the same magazine you may find an article reporting that a senator or member of Congress argued that the National Endowment for the Humanities wasted its grant money by funding research on such-and-such an author or that the National Endowment for the Arts insulted taxpayers by making an award to a writer who defamed the American family.

Probably most writing about literature, whether done by college students, their professors, journalists, members of Congress, or whomever, is devoted to interpreting, judging (evaluating), and theorizing. Let's look at each of these, drawing our examples chiefly from comments about Shakespeare's *Macbeth*.

Interpreting

Interpreting is a matter of setting forth the *meaning* or the meanings of a work. For some readers, a work has *a* meaning, the one intended by the writer, which we may or may not perceive. For most critics today, however, a work has *many* meanings — for instance, the meaning it had for the writer, the meanings it has accumulated over time, and the meanings it has for each of today's readers. Take *Macbeth*, a play about a Scottish king, written soon after a Scot — James VI of Scotland — had been installed as James I, King of England. The play must have meant something special to the king — we know that it was presented at court — and something a little different to the ordinary English citizen. And surely it means something different to us. For instance, few if any people today believe in the divine right of kings, although James I certainly did; and few if any people today believe in malevolent witches, although witches play an important role in the tragedy. What *we* see in the play must be rather different from what Shakespeare's audience saw in it.

Many interpretations of *Macbeth* have been offered. Let's take two fairly simple and clearly opposed views:

1. Macbeth is a villain who, by murdering his lawful king, offends God's rule, so he is overthrown by God's earthly instruments, Malcolm and Macduff. Macbeth is justly punished; the reader or spectator rejoices in his defeat.

One can offer a good deal of evidence — and if one is taking this position in an essay, of course one must *argue* it — by giving supporting reasons rather than merely asserting the position.

2. Macbeth is a hero-villain, a man who commits terrible crimes but who never completely loses the reader's sympathy; although he is justly punished, the reader believes that with the death of Macbeth the world has become a smaller place.

Again, one *must* offer evidence in an essay that presents this thesis or indeed presents any interpretation. For instance, one might offer as evidence the fact that the survivors, especially Macduff and Malcolm, have not interested us nearly as much as Macbeth has. One might argue, too, that although Macbeth's villainy is undeniable, his conscience never deserts him — here one would point to specific passages and would offer some brief quotations. Macbeth's pained awareness of what he has done, one can argue, enables the reader to sympathize with him continually.

Or consider an interpretation of Lady Macbeth. Is she simply evil through and through, or are there mitigating reasons for her actions? Might one argue, perhaps in a feminist interpretation, that despite her intelligence and courage she had no outlet for expression except through her husband? To make this argument, the writer might want to go beyond the text of the play, offering as evidence Elizabethan comments about the proper role of women.

Judging (or Evaluating)

Literary criticism is also concerned with such questions as these: Is *Macbeth* a great tragedy? Is *Macbeth* a greater tragedy than *Romeo and Juliet*? The writer offers an opinion about the worth of the literary work, but the opinion must be supported by an argument, expressed in sentences that offer supporting evidence.

Let's pause for a moment to think about evaluation in general. When we say "This is a great play," are we in effect saying only "I like this play"? That is, are we merely *expressing* our taste rather than *asserting* something independent of our tastes and feelings? (The next few paragraphs won't answer this question, but they may start you thinking about your own answer.) Consider these three sentences:

1. It's raining outside.

2. I like vanilla.

3. This is a really good book.

If you are indoors and you say that it is raining outside, a hearer may ask for verification. Why do you say what you say? "Because," you reply, "I'm looking out the window." Or "Because Jane just came in, and she is drenched." Or "Because I just heard a weather report." If, however, you say that you like vanilla, it's almost unthinkable that anyone would ask you why. No one expects you to justify — to support, to give a reason for — an expression of taste.

Now consider the third statement, "This is a really good book." It is entirely reasonable, we think, for someone to ask you *why* you say that. And you reply, "Well, the characters are realistic, and the plot held my interest," or "It really gave me an insight into what life among the rich [or the poor] must be like," or some such thing.

That is, statement 3 at least seems to be stating a fact, and it seems to be something we can discuss, even argue about, in a way that we cannot argue about a personal preference for vanilla. Almost everyone would agree that when offering an aesthetic judgment we ought to be able to give reasons for it. At the very least, we might say, we hope to show *why* we evaluate the work as we do and to suggest that if readers try to see it from our point of view they may then accept our evaluation.

Evaluations are always based on assumptions, although these assumptions may be unstated, and in fact the writer may even be unaware of them. Some of these assumptions play the role of criteria; they control the sort of evidence the writer believes is relevant to the evaluation. What sorts of assumptions may underlie value judgments? We will mention a few, merely as examples. Other assumptions are possible, and all of these assumptions can themselves become topics of dispute:

1. A good work of art, although fictional, says something about real life.

2. A good work of art is complex yet unified.

3. A good work of art sets forth a wholesome view of life.

4. A good work of art is original.

5. A good work of art deals with an important subject.

Let's look briefly at these views, one by one.

1. A good work of art, although fictional, says something about real life. If you hold the view that literature is connected to life and believe that human beings behave in fairly consistent ways — that is, that each of us has an enduring "character" — you probably will judge as inferior a work in which the figures behave inconsistently or seem to be inadequately motivated. (We must point out, however, that different literary forms or genres are governed by different rules. For instance, consistency of character is usually expected in tragedy but not in melodrama or in comedy, where last-minute reformations may be welcome and greeted with applause. The novelist Henry James said, "You will not write a good novel unless you possess the sense of reality." He's probably right — but does his view hold for the writer of farces?) In the case of *Macbeth* you might well find that the characters are consistent: Although the play begins by showing Macbeth as a loyal defender of King Duncan, Macbeth's later treachery is understandable, given the temptation and the pressure. Similarly, Lady Macbeth's descent into madness, although it may come as a surprise, may strike you as entirely plausible: At the beginning of the play she is confident that she can become an accomplice to a murder, but she has overestimated herself (or, we might say, she has underestimated her own humanity, the power of her guilty conscience, which drives her to insanity).

2. A good work of art is complex yet unified. If Macbeth is only a "tyrant" (Macduff's word) or a "butcher" (Malcolm's word), he is a unified character, but he may be too simple and too uninteresting a character to be the subject of a great play. But, one argument holds, Macbeth in fact is a complex character, not simply a villain but a hero-villain, and the play as a whole is complex. *Macbeth* is a good work of art, one might argue, partly because it shows us so many aspects of life (courage, fear, loyalty, treachery, for a start) through richly varied language (the diction ranges from a grand passage in which Macbeth says that his bloody hands will "incarnadine," or make red, "the multitudinous seas" to colloquial passages such as the drunken porter's "Knock, knock"). The play shows the heroic Macbeth tragically destroying his own life, and it shows the comic porter making coarse jokes about deceit and damnation, jokes that (although the porter doesn't know it) connect with Macbeth's crimes.

3. A good work of art sets forth a wholesome view of life. The general public widely believes that a work should be judged partly or largely on the moral view that it sets forth. (Esteemed philosophers, notably Plato, have felt the same way.) Thus, a story that demeans women — perhaps one that takes a casual view of rape — would receive a low rating, as would a play that treats a mass murderer as a hero.

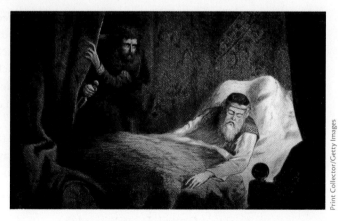

A seventeenth-century artist's interpretation of Macbeth's murder of King Duncan.

Implicit in this approach is what is called an *instrumentalist* view — the idea that a work of art is an instrument, a means, to some higher value. Thus, many people hold that reading great works of literature makes us better — or at least does not make us worse. In this view, a work that is pornographic or in some other way considered immoral will receive a low value. At the time we are writing this chapter, a law requires the National Endowment for the Arts to take into account standards of decency when making awards.

Moral judgments, it should be noted, do not come only from the conservative right; the liberal left has been quick to detect political incorrectness. In fact, except for those people who subscribe to the now unfashionable view that a work of art is an independent aesthetic object with little or no connection to the real world — something like a pretty floral arrangement or a wordless melody — most people judge works of literature largely by their content, by what the works seem to say about life.

- Marxist critics, for instance, have customarily held that literature should make the reader aware of the political realities of life.
- Feminist critics are likely to hold that literature should make us aware of gender relationships — for example, aware of patriarchal power and of women's accomplishments.

4. A good work of art is original. This assumption puts special value on new techniques and new subject matter. Thus, the *first* playwright who introduces a new subject (say, AIDS) gets extra credit, so to speak. Or to return to Shakespeare, one sign of his genius, it is held, is that he was so highly varied; none of his tragedies seems merely to duplicate another, each is a world of its own, a new kind of achievement. Compare, for instance, *Romeo and Juliet*, with its two youthful and innocent heroes, with *Macbeth*, with its deeply guilty hero. Both plays are tragedies, but we can hardly imagine two more different plays — even if a reader perversely argues that the young lovers are guilty of impetuosity and of disobeying appropriate authorities.

5. A good work of art deals with an important subject. Here we are concerned with theme: Great works, in this view, must deal with great themes. Love, death, patriotism, and God, say, are great themes; a work that deals with these may achieve a height, an excellence, that, say, a work describing a dog scratching for fleas may not achieve. (Of course, if the reader feels that the dog is a symbol of humanity plagued by invisible enemies, then the poem about the dog may reach the heights; but then, too, it is *not* a poem about a dog and fleas: It is really a poem about humanity and the invisible.)

The point: In writing an evaluation you must let the reader know *why* you value the work as you do. Obviously, it is not enough just to keep saying that *this* work is great whereas *that* work is not so great; the reader wants to know *why* you offer the judgments that you do, which means that you

- must set forth your criteria, and then
- offer evidence that is in accord with them.

Theorizing

Some literary criticism is concerned with such theoretical questions as these:

What is tragedy? Can the hero be a villain? How does tragedy differ from melodrama?

Why do tragedies — works showing good or at least interesting people destroyed — give us pleasure?

Does a work of art — a play or a novel, say, a made-up world with imagined characters — offer anything that can be called "truth"? Does our experience of a work of art affect our character?

Does a work of art have meaning in itself, or is the meaning simply whatever anyone wishes to say it is? Does *Macbeth* tell us anything about life, or is it just an invented story?

And, yet again, one hopes that anyone asserting a thesis concerned with any of these topics will offer evidence — will, indeed, *argue* rather than merely assert.

A CHECKLIST FOR AN ARGUMENT ABOUT LITERATURE

☐ Is my imagined reader like a typical classmate of mine, someone who is not a specialist in literature but who is open-minded and interested in hearing my point of view about a work?

☐ Is the essay supported with evidence, usually from the text itself but conceivably from other sources (such as a statement by the author, a statement by a person regarded as an authority, or perhaps the evidence of comparable works)?

☐ Is the essay inclusive? Does it take into account all relevant details (which is not to say that it includes everything the writer knows about the work — for instance, that it was made into a film or that the author died poor)?

☐ Is the essay focused? Does the thesis stay steadily before the reader?

☐ Does the essay use quotations, but as evidence, not as padding? Whenever possible, does it abridge or summarize long quotations?

☐ Are all sources fully acknowledged? (For the form of documentation, see Chapter 7.)

Examples:
Two Students Interpret Robert Frost's "Mending Wall"

Let's consider two competing interpretations of a poem, Robert Frost's "Mending Wall." We say "competing" because these interpretations clash head-on. Differing interpretations need not be incompatible, of course. For instance, a historical interpretation of *Macbeth*, arguing that an understanding of the context of English–Scottish politics around 1605 helps us to appreciate the play, need not be incompatible with a psychoanalytic interpretation that tells us that Macbeth's murder of King Duncan is rooted in an Oedipus complex, the king being a father figure. Different approaches thus can illuminate different aspects of the work, just as they can emphasize or subordinate different elements in the plot or characters portrayed. But, again, in the next few pages we will deal with mutually incompatible interpretations of the meaning of Frost's poem.

After reading the poem and the two interpretations written by students, spend a few minutes thinking about the questions that we raise after the second interpretation.

ROBERT FROST

Robert Frost (1874–1963) studied for part of one term at Dartmouth College in New Hampshire, then did odd jobs (including teaching), and from 1897 to 1899 was enrolled as a special student at Harvard. He then farmed in New Hampshire, published a few poems in newspapers, did some more teaching, and in 1912 left for England, where he hoped to achieve success as a writer. By 1915 he was known in England, and he returned to the United States. By the time of his death he was the nation's unofficial poet laureate. "Mending Wall" was first published in 1914.

Mending Wall

Something there is that doesn't love a wall,
That sends the frozen-ground-swell under it,
And spills the upper boulders in the sun;
And makes gaps even two can pass abreast.
The work of hunters is another thing: 5
I have come after them and made repair
Where they have left not one stone on a stone,
But they would have the rabbit out of hiding,
To please the yelping dogs. The gaps I mean,
No one has seen them made or heard them
        made,   10
But at spring mending-time we find them there.
I let my neighbor know beyond the hill;
And on a day we meet to walk the line
And set the wall between us once again.
We keep the wall between us as we go.   15
To each the boulders that have fallen to each.
And some are loaves and some so nearly balls
We have to use a spell to make them balance:
"Stay where you are until our backs are turned!"
We wear our fingers rough with handling them.   20
Oh, just another kind of outdoor game,
One on a side. It comes to little more:
There where it is we do not need the wall:

He is all pine and I am apple orchard.
My apple trees will never get across   25
And eat the cones under his pines, I tell him.
He only says, "Good fences make good
        neighbors."
Spring is the mischief in me, and I wonder
If I could put a notion in his head:
"*Why* do they make good neighbors? Isn't it   30
Where there are cows? But here there are no cows.
Before I built a wall I'd ask to know
What I was walling in or walling out,
And to whom I was like to give offense.
Something there is that doesn't love a wall,   35
That wants it down." I could say "Elves" to him,
But it's not elves exactly, and I'd rather
He said it for himself. I see him there
Bringing a stone grasped firmly by the top
In each hand, like an old-stone savage armed.   40
He moves in darkness as it seems to me,
Not of woods only and the shade of trees.
He will not go behind his father's saying,
And he likes having thought of it so well
He says again, "Good fences make good
        neighbors."   45

Jonathan Deutsch
Professor Walton
English 102
5 March 2016

The Deluded Speaker in Frost's "Mending Wall"

Our discussions of "Mending Wall" in high school showed that most people think Frost is saying that walls between people are a bad thing and that we should not try to separate ourselves from each other unnecessarily. Perhaps the wall, in this view, is a symbol for race prejudice or religious differences, and Frost is suggesting that these differences are minor and that they should not keep us apart. In this common view, the neighbor's words, "Good fences make good neighbors" (lines 27 and 45), show that the neighbor is shortsighted. I disagree with this view, but first I want to present the evidence that might be offered for it, so that we can then see whether it really is substantial.

First of all, someone might claim that in lines 23 to 26 Frost offers a good argument against walls:

> There where it is we do not need the wall:
> He is all pine and I am apple orchard.
> My apple trees will never get across
> And eat the cones under his pines, I tell him.

The neighbor does not offer a valid reply to this argument; in fact, he doesn't offer any argument at all but simply says, "Good fences make good neighbors."

Another piece of evidence supposedly showing that the neighbor is wrong, it is said, is found in Frost's description of him as "an old-stone savage" and someone who "moves in darkness" (40, 41). And a third piece of evidence is said to be that the neighbor "will not go behind his father's saying" (43), but he merely repeats the saying.

There is, however, another way of looking at the poem. As I see it, the speaker is a very snide and condescending person. He is confident that he knows it all and that his neighbor is an ignorant savage; he is even willing to tease his supposedly ignorant neighbor. For instance, the speaker admits to "the mischief in me" (28), and he is confident that he could tell the truth to the neighbor but arrogantly thinks that it would be a more effective form of teaching if the neighbor "said it for himself" (38).

The speaker is not only unpleasantly mischievous and condescending toward his neighbor, but he is also shallow, for he does not see the great wisdom that there is in proverbs. The *American Heritage Dictionary of the English Language*, Third Edition, defines a proverb as "A short, pithy saying in frequent and widespread use that expresses a basic truth." Frost, or at least the man who speaks this poem, does not seem to realize that proverbs express truths. He just dismisses them, and he thinks the neighbor is wrong not to "go behind his father's saying" (43). But there is a great deal of wisdom in the sayings of our fathers. For instance, in the Bible (in the Old Testament) there is a whole book of proverbs, filled with wise sayings such as "Reprove not a scorner, lest he hate thee: rebuke a wise man, and he will love thee" (9:8); "He that trusteth in his riches shall fall" (11:28); "The way of a fool is right in his own eyes" (12:15; this might be said of the speaker of "Mending Wall"); "A soft answer turneth away wrath" (15:1); and (to cut short what could be a list many pages long), "Whoso diggeth a pit shall fall therein" (26:27).

The speaker is confident that walls are unnecessary and probably bad, but he doesn't realize that even where there are no cattle, walls serve the valuable purpose of clearly marking out our territory. They help us to preserve our independence and our individuality. Walls — man-made structures — are a sign of civilization. A wall more or less says, "*This* is mine, but I respect *that* as yours." Frost's speaker is so confident of his shallow view that he makes fun of his neighbor for repeating that "Good fences make good neighbors" (27, 45). But he himself repeats his own saying, "Something there is that doesn't love a wall" (1, 35). And at least the neighbor has age-old tradition on his side, since the proverb is the saying of his father. In contrast, the speaker has only his own opinion, and he can't even say what the "something" is.

It may be that Frost meant for us to laugh at the neighbor and to take the side of the speaker, but I think it is much more likely that he meant for us to see that the speaker is mean-spirited (or at least given to unpleasant teasing), too self-confident, foolishly dismissing the wisdom of the old times, and entirely unaware that he has these unpleasant characteristics.

Felicia Alonso

Professor Walton

English 102

5 March 2016

The Debate in Robert Frost's "Mending Wall"

I think the first thing to say about Frost's "Mending Wall" is this: The poem is not about a debate over whether good fences do or do not make good neighbors. It is about two debaters: one of the debaters is on the side of vitality, and the other is on the side of an unchanging, fixed — dead, we might say — tradition.

How can we characterize the speaker? For one thing, he is neighborly. Interestingly, it is *he*, and not the neighbor, who initiates the repairing of the wall: "I let my neighbor know beyond the hill" (line 12). This seems strange, since the speaker doesn't see any point in this wall, whereas the neighbor is all in favor of walls. Can we explain this apparent contradiction? Yes; the speaker is a good neighbor, willing to do his share of the work and willing (perhaps in order not to upset his neighbor) to maintain an old tradition even though he doesn't see its importance. It may not be important, he thinks, but it is really rather pleasant, "another kind of outdoor game" (21). In fact, sometimes he even repairs fences on his own, after hunters have destroyed them.

Second, we can say that the speaker is on the side of nature. "Something there is that doesn't love a wall," he says (1, 35), and of course, the "something" is nature itself. Nature "sends the frozen-ground-swell" under the wall and "spills the upper boulders in the sun; / And makes gaps even two can pass abreast" (2–4). Notice that nature itself makes the gaps and that "two can pass abreast" — that is, people can walk together in a companionable way. It is hard to imagine the neighbor walking side by side with anyone.

Third, we can say that the speaker has a sense of humor. When he thinks of trying to get his neighbor interested in the issue, he admits that "the mischief" is in him (28), and he amusingly attributes his playfulness to a natural force, the spring. He playfully toys with the obviously preposterous idea of suggesting to his neighbor that elves caused the stones to fall, but he stops short of making this amusing suggestion to his very serious neighbor. Still, the mere thought assures us that he has a playful, genial nature, and the idea also again implies that not only the speaker but also some sort of mysterious natural force dislikes walls.

Finally, though, of course, he thinks he is right and that his neighbor is mistaken, he at least is cautious in his view. He does not call his neighbor "an old-stone savage" (40); rather, he uses a simile ("like") and then adds that this is only his opinion, so the opinion is softened quite a bit. Here is the description of the neighbor, with italics added to clarify my point. The neighbor is . . .

> *like* an old-stone savage armed.
> He moves in darkness *as it seems to me* . . . (40–41)

Of course, the only things we know about the neighbor are those things that the speaker chooses to tell us, so it is not surprising that the speaker comes out ahead. He comes out ahead not because he is right about walls (real or symbolic) and his neighbor is wrong — that's an issue that is not settled in the poem. He comes out ahead because he is a more interesting figure, someone who is neighborly, thoughtful, playful. Yes, maybe he seems to us to feel superior to his neighbor, but we can be certain that he doesn't cause his neighbor any embarrassment. Take the very end of the poem. The speaker tells us that the neighbor

> . . . will not go behind his father's saying,
> And he likes having thought of it so well
> He says again, "Good fences make good neighbors."

The speaker is telling *us* that the neighbor is utterly unoriginal and that the neighbor confuses *remembering* something with *thinking*. But the speaker doesn't get into an argument; he doesn't rudely challenge his neighbor and demand reasons, which might force the neighbor to see that he can't think for himself. And in fact we probably like the neighbor just as he is, and we don't want him to change his mind. The words that ring in our ears are not the speaker's but the neighbor's: "Good fences make good neighbors." The speaker of the poem is a good neighbor. After all, one can hardly be more neighborly than to let the neighbor have the last word.

Topics for Critical Thinking and Writing

1. State the thesis of each essay. Do you believe the theses are sufficiently clear and appear sufficiently early in the essays? Why, or why not?

2. Consider the evidence that each essay offers by way of supporting its thesis. Do you find some of the evidence unconvincing? Explain.

3. Putting aside the question of which interpretation you prefer, comment on the organization of each essay. Is the organization clear? Do you want to propose some other pattern that you think might be more effective? Explain your responses.

4. Consult the Checklist for Peer Review on pages 254–55, and offer comments on one of the two essays. Or: If you were the instructor in the course in which these two essays were submitted, what might be your final comments on each of them? Or: Write an analysis (250–500 words) of the strengths and weaknesses of either essay.

EXERCISES: READING A POEM AND A STORY

ANDREW MARVELL

Andrew Marvell (1621–1678), born in Hull, England, and educated at Trinity College, Cambridge, was traveling in Europe when the civil war between the Royalists and the Puritans broke out in England in 1642. The Puritans were victorious and established the Commonwealth (the monarchy was restored later, in 1660), and Marvell became a tutor to the daughter of the victorious Lord-General. In 1657 he became an assistant to the blind poet John Milton, who held the title of Latin Secretary (Latin was the language of international diplomacy). In 1659 Marvell was elected to represent Hull in Parliament. As a man of letters, during his lifetime he was known chiefly for some satiric prose and poetry; most of the writings for which he is now esteemed were published posthumously. The following poem was first published in 1681.

To His Coy Mistress°

Had we but world enough, and time,
This coyness,° Lady, were no crime.
We would sit down, and think which way
To walk, and pass our long love's day.
Thou by the Indian Ganges' side   5
Shouldst rubies find; I by the tide
Of Humber° would complain. I would
Love you ten years before the Flood,
And you should, if you please, refuse

Till the Conversion of the Jews.°   10
My vegetable° love should grow
Vaster than empires and more slow;
An hundred years should go to praise
Thine eyes, and on thy forehead gaze;
Two hundred to adore each breast,   15
But thirty thousand to the rest;
An age at least to every part,
And the last age should show your heart.

Mistress Beloved woman.
2 coyness Reluctance.
7 Humber An estuary at Hull, Marvell's birthplace.

10 Conversion of the Jews Something that would take place in the remote future, at the end of history.
11 vegetable Vegetative or growing.

For, Lady, you deserve this state,°   Sits on thy skin like morning dew,
Nor would I love at lower rate.   20   And while thy willing soul transpires   35
   But at my back I always hear   At every pore with instant fires,
Time's wingèd chariot hurrying near;   Now let us sport us while we may,
And yonder all before us lie   And now, like amorous birds of prey,
Deserts of vast eternity.   Rather at once our time devour
Thy beauty shall no more be found,   25   Than languish in his slow-chapt° power.   40
Nor, in thy marble vault, shall sound   Let us roll all our strength and all
My echoing song; then worms shall try°   Our sweetness up into one ball,
That long-preserved virginity,   And tear our pleasures with rough strife
And your quaint° honour turn to dust,   Thorough° the iron gates of life:
And into ashes all my lust: 30   Thus, though we cannot make our sun   45
The grave's a fine and private place,   Stand still,° yet we will make him run.
But none, I think, do there embrace.
   Now therefore, while the youthful hue

---

19 **state** Ceremonious treatment.
27 **try** Test.
29 **quaint** Fastidious or finicky, with a pun on a coarse word defined in an Elizabethan dictionary as "a woman's privities."

40 **slow-chapt** Slow-jawed.
44 **Thorough** Through.
46 **make our sun stand still** An allusion to Joshua, the ancient Hebrew who, according to the Book of Joshua (10.12–13), made the sun stand still.

Topics for Critical Thinking and Writing

1. The motif that life is short and that we should seize the day (Latin: *Vita brevis carpe diem*) is old. Marvell's poem, in fact, probably has its ultimate source in a classical text called *The Greek Anthology*, a collection of about six thousand short Greek poems composed between the first century B.C. and the tenth century A.D. One poem goes thus, in a fairly literal translation:

   > You spare your maidenhead, and to what profit? For when you come to Hades
   > you will not find your lover, girl. Among the living are the delights of Venus, but,
   > maiden, we shall lie in the underworld mere bones and dust.

   If you find Marvell's poem more impressive, offer reasons for your belief.

2. A student, working from the translation just given, produced this rhyming version:

   > You keep your virginity, but to what end?
   > Below, in Hades, you won't find your friend.
   > On earth we enjoy Venus' sighs and moans;
   > Buried below, we are senseless bones.

   What do you think of this version? Why? Prepare your own version — your instructor may divide the class into groups of four, and each group can come up with a collaborative version — and then compare it with other versions, giving reasons for your preferences.

3. Marvell's poem takes the form of a syllogism (see pp. 90–95). It can be divided into three parts:

   a. "Had we" (i.e., "If we had") (line 1), a supposition, or suppositional premise;
   b. "But at my back" (line 21), a refutation;
   c. "Now therefore" (line 33), a deduction.

Look closely at the poem and develop the argument using these three parts, devoting a few sentences to each part.

4. A student wrote of this poem:

> As a Christian I can't accept the lover's statement that "yonder all before us lie / Deserts of vast eternity" (lines 23–24). The poem may contain beautiful lines, and it may offer clever reasoning, but the reasoning is based on what my religion tells me is wrong. I not only cannot accept the idea of the poem, but I also cannot enjoy the poem, since it presents a false view of reality.

What assumptions is this student making about a reader's response to a work of literature? Do you agree or disagree? Why?

5. Here are three additional comments by students. For each, list the writer's assumptions, and then evaluate each comment. You may agree or disagree, in whole or in part, with any comment, but give your reasons.

a. The poem is definitely clever, and that is part of what is wrong with it. It is a blatant attempt at seduction. The man seems to think he is smarter than the woman he is speaking to, and he "proves" that she should go to bed with him. Since we don't hear her side of the argument, Marvell implies that she has nothing to say and that his argument is sound. What the poet doesn't seem to understand is that there is such a thing as virtue, and a woman need not sacrifice virtue just because death is inevitable.

b. On the surface, "To His Coy Mistress" is an attempt to persuade a woman to go to bed with the speaker, but the poem is really less about sex than it is about the terrifying shortness of life.

c. This is not a love poem. The speaker admits that his impulse is "lust" (line 30), and he makes fun of the girl's conception of honor and virginity. If we enjoy this poem at all, our enjoyment must be in the hope that this would-be date-rapist is unsuccessful.

6. Read the poem several times slowly, perhaps even aloud. Do certain lines seem especially moving, especially memorable? If so, which ones? Give reasons for your belief.

7. In *On Deconstruction* (1982), a study of contemporary literary theory, Jonathan Culler remarks that feminist criticism has often stressed "reading as a woman." This concept, Culler says, affirms the "continuity between women's experience of social and familial structures and their experiences as readers." Do you agree with his suggestion that men and women often interpret literary works differently? Consider Marvell's poem in particular: Identify and discuss phrases and images in it to which men and women readers might (or might not) respond very differently.

8. A small point, but perhaps one of some interest. In the original text, line 34 ends with *glew*, not with *dew*. Most editors assume that the printer made an error, and — looking for a word to rhyme with *hue* — they replace *glew* with *dew*. Another possible emendation is *lew*, an archaic word meaning "warmth." But the original reading has been defended, as a variant of the word *glow*. Your preference? Your reasons?

KATE CHOPIN

Kate Chopin (1851–1904) was born in St. Louis and named Katherine O'Flaherty. At the age of nineteen she married a cotton broker in New Orleans, Oscar Chopin (the name is pronounced something like "show pan"), who was descended from the early French settlers in Louisiana. After her husband's death in 1883, Kate Chopin turned to writing fiction. The following story was first published in 1894.

The Story of an Hour

Knowing that Mrs. Mallard was afflicted with a heart trouble, great care was taken to break to her as gently as possible the news of her husband's death.

It was her sister Josephine who told her, in broken sentences, veiled hints that revealed in half concealing. Her husband's friend Richards was there, too, near her. It was he who had been in the newspaper office when intelligence of the railroad disaster was received, with Brently Mallard's name leading the list of "killed." He had only taken the time to assure himself of its truth by a second telegram, and had hastened to forestall any less careful, less tender friend in bearing the sad message.

She did not hear the story as many women have heard the same, with a paralyzed inability to accept its significance. She wept at once, with sudden, wild abandonment, in her sister's arms. When the storm of grief had spent itself she went away to her room alone. She would have no one follow her.

There stood, facing the open window, a comfortable, roomy armchair. Into this she sank, pressed down by a physical exhaustion that haunted her body and seemed to reach into her soul.

She could see in the open square before 5 her house the tops of trees that were all aquiver with the new spring life. The delicious breath of rain was in the air. In the street below a peddler was crying his wares. The notes of a distant song which some one was singing reached her faintly, and countless sparrows were twittering in the eaves.

There were patches of blue sky showing here and there through the clouds that had met and piled one above the other in the west facing her window.

She sat with her head thrown back upon the cushion of the chair, quite motionless, except when a sob came up into her throat and shook her, as a child who has cried itself to sleep continues to sob in its dreams.

She was young, with a fair, calm face, whose lines bespoke repression and even a certain strength. But now there was a dull stare in her eyes, whose gaze was fixed away off yonder on one of those patches of blue sky. It was not a glance of reflection, but rather indicated a suspension of intelligent thought.

There was something coming to her and she was waiting for it, fearfully. What was it? She did not know; it was too subtle and elusive to name. But she felt it, creeping out of the sky, reaching toward her through the sounds, the scents, the color that filled the air.

Now her bosom rose and fell tumultuously. 10 She was beginning to recognize this thing that was approaching to possess her, and she was striving to beat it back with her will — as powerless as her two white slender hands would have been.

When she abandoned herself a little whispered word escaped her slightly parted lips. She said it over and over under her breath: "Free, free, free!" The vacant stare and the look of terror that had followed it went from her eyes. They stayed keen and bright. Her pulses beat fast, and the coursing blood warmed and relaxed every inch of her body.

She did not stop to ask if it were not a monstrous joy that held her. A clear and exalted perception enabled her to dismiss the suggestion as trivial.

She knew that she would weep again when she saw the kind, tender hands folded in death; the face that had never looked save with love upon her, fixed and gray and dead. But she saw beyond that bitter moment a long procession of years to come that would belong to her absolutely. And she opened and spread her arms out to them in welcome.

There would be no one to live for her during those coming years; she would live for herself. There would be no powerful will bending her in that blind persistence with which men and women believe they have a right to impose a private will upon a fellow creature. A kind intention or a cruel intention made the act seem no less a crime as she looked upon it in that brief moment of illumination.

And yet she had loved him — sometimes. [15] Often she had not. What did it matter! What could love, the unsolved mystery, count for in face of this possession of self-assertion which she suddenly recognized as the strongest impulse of her being.

"Free! Body and soul free!" she kept whispering.

Josephine was kneeling before the closed door with her lips to the keyhole, imploring for admission. "Louise, open the door! I beg; open the door — you will make yourself ill. What are you doing, Louise? For heaven's sake open the door."

"Go away. I am not making myself ill." No; she was drinking in a very elixir of life through that open window.

Her fancy was running riot along those days ahead of her. Spring days, and summer days, and all sorts of days that would be her own. She breathed a quick prayer that life might be long. It was only yesterday she had thought with a shudder that life might be long.

She arose at length and opened the door [20] to her sister's importunities. There was a feverish triumph in her eyes, and she carried herself unwittingly like a goddess of Victory. She clasped her sister's waist, and together they descended the stairs. Richards stood waiting for them at the bottom.

Some one was opening the front door with a latchkey. It was Brently Mallard who entered, a little travel-stained, composedly carrying his gripsack and umbrella. He had been far from the scene of accident, and did not even know there had been one. He stood amazed at Josephine's piercing cry; at Richards' quick motion to screen him from the view of his wife.

But Richards was too late.

When the doctors came they said she had died of heart disease — of joy that kills.

Topics for Critical Thinking and Writing

Read the following assertions, and consider whether you agree or disagree, and why. For each assertion, draft a paragraph with your arguments.

1. The railroad accident is a symbol of the destructiveness of the industrial revolution.

2. The story claims that women rejoice in the deaths of their husbands.

3. Mrs. Mallard's death at the end is a just punishment for the joy she takes in her husband's death.

4. The story is rich in irony. Some examples: (1) The other characters think she is grieving, but she is rejoicing; (2) she prays for a long life, but she dies almost immediately; (3) the doctors say she died of "the joy that kills," but they think her joy was seeing her husband alive.

5. The story is excellent because it has a surprise ending.

Thinking about the Effects of Literature

Works of art are artifacts — things constructed, made up, fashioned, just like chairs and houses and automobiles. In analyzing works of literature it is therefore customary to keep one's eye on the complex, constructed object and not simply tell the reader how one feels about it. Instead of reporting their feelings, critics usually analyze the relationships between the parts and the relationship of the parts to the whole.

For instance, in talking about literature we can examine the relationship of plot to character, of one character to another, or of one stanza in a poem to the next. Still, although we may try to engage in this sort of analysis as dispassionately as possible, we all know that inevitably

- we are not only examining something out there,
- but also examining our own responses.

Why? Because literature has an effect on us. Indeed, it probably has several kinds of effects, ranging from short-range emotional responses ("I really enjoyed this," "I burst out laughing," "It revolted me") to long-range effects ("I have always tried to live up to a line in *Hamlet*, 'This above all, to thine own self be true'"). Let's first look, very briefly, at immediate emotional responses.

Analysis usually begins with a response: "This is marvelous," or "What a bore," and we then go on to try to account for our response. A friend mentions a book or a film to us, and we say, "I couldn't stay with it for five minutes." The friend expresses surprise, and we then go on to explain, giving reasons (to the friend and also to ourselves) why we couldn't stay with it. Perhaps the book seemed too remote from life or perhaps it seemed to be nothing more than a transcript of the boring talk that we can overhear on a bus or in an elevator.

In such discussions, when we draw on our responses, as we must, the work may disappear; we find ourselves talking about ourselves. Let's take two extreme examples: "I can't abide *Huckleberry Finn*. How am I expected to enjoy a so-called masterpiece that has a character in it called 'Nigger Jim?'" Or: "T. S. Eliot's anti-Semitism is too much for me to take. Don't talk to me about Eliot's skill with meter, when he has such lines as 'Rachel, *née* Rabinovitch / Tears at the grapes with murderous paws.'"

Although everyone agrees that literature can evoke this sort of strong emotional response, not everyone agrees on how much value we should put on our personal experience. Several of the Topics for Critical Thinking and Writing below invite you to reflect on this issue.

What about the *consequences of the effects* of literature? Does literature shape our character and therefore influence our behavior? It is generally believed that it does have an effect. One hears, for example, that literature (like travel) is broadening, that it makes us aware of, and tolerant of, kinds of behavior that differ from our own and from what we see around us. One of the chief arguments against pornography, for instance, is that it desensitizes us, makes us too tolerant of abusive relationships, relationships in which people (usually men) use other people (usually women) as mere things or instruments for pleasure. (A contrary view: Some people argue that pornography provides a relatively harmless outlet for fantasies that otherwise might be given release in the real world. In this view, pornography acts as a sort of safety valve.)

Discussions of the effects of literature that get into the popular press almost always involve pornography, but other topics are also the subjects of controversy. For instance, in recent decades parents and educators have been much concerned with fairy tales. Does the violence in some fairy tales ("Little Red Riding Hood," "The Three Little Pigs") have a bad effect on children? Do some of the stories teach the wrong lessons, implying that women should be passive, men active ("Sleeping Beauty," for instance, in which the sleeping woman is brought to life by the action of the handsome prince)? The Greek philosopher Plato (427–347 B.C.) strongly believed that the literature we hear or read shapes our later behavior, and since most of the ancient Greek traditional stories (notably Homer's *Odyssey* and *Iliad*) celebrate acts of love and war rather than of justice, he prohibited the reading of such material in his ideal society. (We reprint a relevant passage from Plato on page 404.)

Topics for Critical Thinking and Writing

1. If you have responded strongly (favorably or unfavorably) to some aspect of the social content of a literary work — for instance, its depiction of women or of a particular minority group — in an essay of 250 to 500 words analyze the response, and try to determine whether you are talking chiefly about yourself or the work. (Two works widely regarded as literary masterpieces but nonetheless often banned from classrooms are Shakespeare's *The Merchant of Venice* and Mark Twain's *Huckleberry Finn*. If you have read either of these, you may want to write about it and your response.) Can we really see literary value — *really* see it — in a work that deeply offends us?

2. Most people believe that literature influences life — that in some mysterious way it helps to shape character. Certainly, anyone who believes that some works should be censored, or at least should be made unavailable to minors, assumes that they can have a bad influence, so why not assume that other works can have a good influence?

   Read the following brief claims about literature; then choose one and write a 250-word essay offering support or taking issue with it.

   The pen is mightier than the sword.   — EDWARD BULWER LYTTON

   The writer isn't made in a vacuum. Writers are witnesses. The reason we need writers is because we need witnesses to this terrifying century.   — E. L. DOCTOROW

When we read of human beings behaving in certain ways, with the approval of the author, who gives his benedictions to this behavior by his attitude towards the result of the behavior arranged by himself, we can be influenced towards behaving in the same way.   — T. S. ELIOT

Poetry makes nothing happen.   — W. H. AUDEN

Literature is *without proofs*. By which it must be understood that it cannot prove, not only *what* it says, but even that it is worth the trouble of saying it.   — ROLAND BARTHES

Of course the illusion of art is to make one believe that great literature is very close to life, but exactly the opposite is true. Life is amorphous, literature is formal.   — FRANÇOISE SAGAN

3. At least since the time of Plato (see the piece directly following), some thoughtful people have wanted to ban certain works of literature because they allegedly stimulate the wrong sorts of pleasure or cause us to take pleasure in the wrong sorts of things. Consider, by way of comparison, bullfighting and cockfighting. Of course, they cause pain to the animals, but branding animals also causes pain and is not banned. Bullfighting and cockfighting probably are banned in the United States largely because most of us believe that people should not take pleasure in these activities. Now to return to literature: Should some kinds of writing be prohibited because they offer the wrong sorts of pleasure?

PLATO

Plato (427–347 B.C.), an Athenian aristocrat by birth, was the student of one great philosopher (Socrates) and the teacher of another (Aristotle). His legacy of more than two dozen dialogues — imaginary discussions between Socrates and one or more other speakers, usually young Athenians — has been of such influence that the whole of Western philosophy can be characterized, A. N. Whitehead wrote, as "a series of footnotes to Plato." Plato's interests encompassed the full range of topics in philosophy: ethics, politics, logic, metaphysics, epistemology, aesthetics, psychology, and education.

This selection from Plato's Republic, *one of his best-known and longest dialogues, is about the education suitable for the rulers of an ideal society. The* Republic *begins, typically, with an investigation into the nature of justice. Socrates (who speaks for Plato) convincingly explains to Glaucon that we cannot reasonably expect to achieve a just society unless we devote careful attention to the moral education of the young men who are scheduled in later life to become the rulers. (Here as elsewhere, Plato's elitism and aristocratic bias shows itself; as readers of* The Republic *soon learn, Plato is no admirer of democracy or of a classless society.) Plato cares as much about what the educational curriculum should exclude as what it should include. His special target was the common practice in his day of using for pedagogy the Homeric tales and other stories about the gods. He readily embraces the principle of censorship, as the excerpt explains, because he thinks it is a necessary means to achieve the ideal society.*

"The Greater Part of the Stories Current Today We Shall Have to Reject"

"What kind of education shall we give them then? We shall find it difficult to improve on the time-honored distinction between the physical training we give to the body and the education we give to the mind and character."

"True."

"And we shall begin by educating mind and character, shall we not?"

"Of course."

"In this education you would include stories, 5 would you not?"

"Yes."

"These are of two kinds, true stories and fiction.[1] Our education must use both, and start with fiction."

"I don't know what you mean."

"But you know that we begin by telling children stories. These are, in general, fiction, though they contain some truth. And we tell children stories before we start them on physical training."

"That is so." 10

"That is what I meant by saying that we must start to educate the mind before training the body."

"You are right," he said.

"And the first step, as you know, is always what matters most, particularly when we are dealing with those who are young and tender. That is the time when they are easily molded and when any impression we choose to make leaves a permanent mark."

"That is certainly true."

"Shall we therefore readily allow our 15 children to listen to any stories made up by anyone, and to form opinions that are for the most part the opposite of those we think they should have when they grow up?"

"We certainly shall not."

"Then it seems that our first business is to supervise the production of stories, and choose only those we think suitable, and reject the rest. We shall persuade mothers and nurses to tell our chosen stories to their children, and by means of them to mold their minds and characters which are more important than their bodies. The greater part of the stories current today we shall have to reject."

"Which are you thinking of?"

"We can take some of the major legends as typical. For all, whether major or minor, should be cast in the same mold and have the same effect. Do you agree?"

"Yes: but I'm not sure which you refer to 20 as major."

"The stories in Homer and Hesiod and the poets. For it is the poets who have always made up fictions and stories to tell to men."

"What sort of stories do you mean and what fault do you find in them?"

"The worst fault possible," I replied, "especially if the fiction is an ugly one."

"And what is that?"

"Misrepresenting the nature of gods and 25 heroes, like a portrait painter whose portraits bear no resemblance to their originals."

"That is a fault which certainly deserves censure. But give me more details."

"Well, on the most important of subjects, there is first and foremost the foul story about Ouranos[2] and the things Hesiod says he did,

---

[1] The Greek word *pseudos* and its corresponding verb meant not only "fiction" — stories, tales — but also "what is not true" and so, in suitable contexts, "lies": and this ambiguity should be borne in mind. [Editors' note: All footnotes are by the translator, but some have been omitted.]

[2] **Ouranos** The sky, the original supreme god. Ouranos was castrated by his son Cronos to separate him from Gaia (mother earth). Cronos was in turn deposed by Zeus in a struggle in which Zeus was helped by the Titans.

and the revenge Cronos took on him. While the story of what Cronos did, and what he suffered at the hands of his son, is not fit as it is to be lightly repeated to the young and foolish, even if it were true; it would be best to say nothing about it, or if it must be told, tell it to a select few under oath of secrecy, at a rite which required, to restrict it still further, the sacrifice not of a mere pig but of something large and difficult to get."

"These certainly are awkward stories."

"And they shall not be repeated in our state, Adeimantus," I said. "Nor shall any young audience be told that anyone who commits horrible crimes, or punishes his father unmercifully, is doing nothing out of the ordinary but merely what the first and greatest of the gods have done before."

"I entirely agree," said Adeimantus, "that 30 these stories are unsuitable."

"Nor can we permit stories of wars and plots and battles among the gods; they are quite untrue, and if we want our prospective guardians to believe that quarrelsomeness is one of the worst of evils, we must certainly not let them be told the story of the Battle of the Giants or embroider it on robes, or tell them other tales about many and various quarrels between gods and heroes and their friends and relations. On the contrary, if we are to persuade them that no citizen has ever quarreled with any other, because it is sinful, our old men and women must tell children stories with this end in view from the first, and we must compel our poets to tell them similar stories when they grow up. But we can admit to our state no stories about Hera being tied up by her son, or Hephaestus being flung out of Heaven by his father for trying to help his mother when she was getting a beating, nor any of Homer's Battles of the Gods, whether their intention is allegorical or not. Children cannot distinguish between what is allegory and what isn't, and opinions formed at that age are usually difficult to eradicate or change; we should therefore surely regard it as of the utmost importance that the first stories they hear shall aim at encouraging the highest excellence of character."

"Your case is a good one," he agreed, "but if someone wanted details, and asked what stories we were thinking of, what should we say?"

To which I replied, "My dear Adeimantus, you and I are not engaged on writing stories but on founding a state. And the founders of a state, though they must know the type of story the poet must produce, and reject any that do not conform to that type, need not write them themselves."

"True: but what are the lines on which our poets must work when they deal with the gods?"

"Roughly as follows," I said. "God must 35 surely always be represented as he really is, whether the poet is writing epic, lyric, or tragedy."

"He must."

"And in reality of course god is good, and he must be so described."

"Certainly."

"But nothing good is harmful, is it?"[3]

"I think not." 40

"Then can anything that is not harmful do harm?"

"No."

"And can what does no harm do evil?"

"No again."

"And can what does no evil be the cause of 45 any evil?"

"How could it?"

"Well then; is the good beneficial?"

---

[3]The reader of the following passage should bear the following ambiguities in mind: (1) the Greek word for good (*agathos*) can mean (a) morally good, (b) beneficial or advantageous; (2) the Greek word for evil (*kakos*) can also mean harm or injury; (3) the adverb of *agathos* (*eu* — the well) can imply either morally right or prosperous. The word translated "cause of" could equally well be rendered "responsible for."

"Yes."

"So it must be the cause of well-being."

"Yes."

"So the good is not the cause of everything, but only of states of well-being and not of evil."

"Most certainly," he agreed.

"Then god, being good, cannot be responsible for everything, as is commonly said, but only for a small part of human life, for the greater part of which he has no responsibility. For we have a far smaller share of good than of evil, and while god must be held to be the sole cause of good, we must look for some factors other than god as cause of the evil."

"I think that's very true," he said.

"So we cannot allow Homer or any other poet to make such a stupid mistake about the gods, as when he says that

> Zeus has two jars standing on the floor of his palace, full of fates, good in one and evil in the other

and that the man to whom Zeus allots a mixture of both has 'varying fortunes sometimes good and sometimes bad,' while the man to whom he allots unmixed evil is 'chased by ravening despair over the face of the earth.'[4] Nor can we allow references to Zeus as 'dispenser of good and evil.' And we cannot approve if it is said that Athene and Zeus prompted the breach of solemn treaty and oath by Pandarus,

---

[4] Quotations from Homer are generally taken from the translations by Dr. Rieu in the Penguin series. At times (as here) the version quoted by Plato differs slightly from the accepted text.

or that the strife and contentions of the gods were due to Themis and Zeus. Nor again can we let our children hear from Aeschylus that

> God implants a fault in man, when he wishes to destroy a house utterly.

No: We must forbid anyone who writes a play about the sufferings of Niobe (the subject of the play from which these last lines are quoted), or the house of Pelops, or the Trojan war, or any similar topic, to say they are acts of god; or if he does he must produce the sort of interpretation we are now demanding, and say that god's acts were good and just, and that the sufferers were benefited by being punished. What the poet must not be allowed to say is that those who were punished were made wretched through god's action. He may refer to the wicked as wretched because they needed punishment, provided he makes it clear that in punishing them god did them good. But if a state is to be run on the right lines, every possible step must be taken to prevent anyone, young or old, either saying or being told, whether in poetry or prose, that god, being good, can cause harm or evil to any man. To say so would be sinful, inexpedient, and inconsistent."

"I should approve of a law for this purpose and you have my vote for it," he said.

"Then of our laws laying down the principles which those who write or speak about the gods must follow, one would be this: *God is the cause, not of all things, but only of good.*"

"I am quite content with that," he said.

Topics for Critical Thinking and Writing

1. In the beginning of the dialogue Plato says that adults recite fictions to very young children and that these fictions help to mold character. Think of some stories that you heard or read when young, such as "Snow White and the Seven Dwarfs" or "Ali Baba and the Forty Thieves." Try to think of a story that, in the final analysis, is not in accord with what you consider to be proper morality, such as a story in which a person triumphs through trickery

or a story in which evil actions — perhaps murders — are set forth without unfavorable comment. (Was it naughty of Jack to kill the giant?) On reflection, do you think children should not be told such stories? Why, or why not? Or think of the early film westerns, in which, on the whole, the Indians (except for an occasional Uncle Tonto) are depicted as bad guys and the whites (except for an occasional coward or rustler) are depicted as good guys. Many people who now have gray hair enjoyed such films in their childhood. Are you prepared to say that such films are not damaging? Or, in contrast, are you prepared to say they are damaging and should be prohibited?

2. It is often objected that censorship of reading matter and of television programs available to children underrates their ability to think for themselves and to discount the dangerous, obscene, and tawdry. Do you agree with this objection? Does Plato? Explain your response.

3. Plato says that allowing poets to say what they please about the gods in his ideal state would be "inconsistent." Explain what he means by this criticism, and then explain why you agree or disagree with it.

4. Do you believe that parents should censor the "fiction" their children encounter (literature, films, pictures, music) but that the community should not censor the "fiction" of adults? Write an essay of 500 words on one of these topics: "Censorship and Rock Lyrics"; "X-Rated Films"; "Ethnic Jokes." (These topics are broadly worded; you can narrow one and offer any thesis you wish.)

5. Were you taught that any of the founding fathers ever acted disreputably or that any American hero had any serious moral flaw? Or that America ever acted immorally in its dealings with other nations? Do you think it appropriate for children to hear such things? Explain your responses.

Thinking about Government Funding for the Arts

Our government supports the arts, including writers, by giving grants to numerous institutions. However, the amount that the government contributes is extremely small when compared to the amounts given to the arts by most European governments. Consider the following questions.

1. Should taxpayers' dollars be used to support the arts? Why, or why not?

2. What possible public benefit can come from supporting the arts? Can one argue that we should support the arts for the same reasons that we support public schools, that is, to have a civilized society? Explain your response.

3. If dollars are given to the arts, should the political content of the works be taken into account, or only the aesthetic merit? Can we separate content from aesthetic merit? (The best way to approach this issue probably is to begin by thinking of a strongly political work.)

4. Is it censorship not to award public funds to writers whose work is not approved of, or is it simply a matter of refusing to reward them with taxpayers' dollars?

5. Should decisions about grants to writers be made chiefly by government officials or chiefly by experts in the field? Why?

12

A Debater's View: Individual Oral Presentations and Debate

He who knows only his own side of the case knows little of that. — JOHN STUART MILL

A philosopher who is not taking part in discussions is like a boxer who never goes into the ring. — LUDWIG WITTGENSTEIN

Freedom is hammered out on the anvil of dissension, dissent, and debate. — HUBERT HUMPHREY

Individual Oral Presentations

Forensic comes from the Latin word *foris,* meaning "out of doors," which also produced the word *forum,* an open space in front of a public building. In the language of rhetoricians, the place where one delivers a speech to an audience is the forum — whether it is a classroom, a court of law, or the steps of the Lincoln Memorial.

Your instructor may ask you to make an oral presentation (in this case, the forum is the classroom), and if he or she doesn't make such a demand, later life almost certainly will: You'll find that at a job interview you will be expected to talk persuasively about what good qualities or experience you can bring to the place of employment. When you have a job, you'll sometimes have to summarize a report orally or orally argue a case — for instance, that your colleagues should do something they may be hesitant to do.

The goal of your classroom talk is to persuade the audience to share your view, or, if you can't get them to agree completely, to get them to see that at least there is something to be said for this view — that it is a position a reasonable person can hold.

Elsewhere in this book we have said that the subjects of persuasive writing are usually

- matters of fact (e.g., statistics show that the death penalty does — or does not — deter crime), or

- matters of value (abortion is — or is not — immoral), or

TWO RULES FOR SPEAKERS:

• *In preparing your oral presentation, keep your thesis in mind.* You may be giving counter-arguments, examples, definitions, and so forth, but make sure that your thesis is always evident to the audience.

• *Keep your audience in mind.* Inevitably, you will have to make assumptions about what the audience does and does not know about your topic. Do not overestimate their knowledge, and do not underestimate their intelligence.

■ matters of policy (government should — or should not — give money to faith-based institutions).

No matter what your subject is, when you draft and revise your talk, make certain that a thesis statement underlies the whole (e.g., "Proposition 2 is a bad idea because . . ."").

The text of an oral presentation ought not to be identical with the text of a written presentation. Both must have a clear **organization,** but oral presentations usually require making the organization a bit more obvious, with abundant **signposts** such as "Before I talk about *X*," "When I discussed *Y*, I didn't mention such-and-such because I wanted to concentrate on a single instance, but now is the time to consider *Y*," and so on. You will also have to repeat a bit more than you would in a written presentation. After all, a reader can turn back to check a sentence or a statistic, but a listener cannot; so rather than saying (as one might in a printed text), "When we think further about Smith's comment, we realize. . . ," you'll repeat what Smith said before you go on to analyze the statement.

You will want to think carefully about the organization of your talk. We've already stressed the need to develop essays with clear thesis statements and logical supporting points. Oral presentations are no different, but remember that when you are speaking in public, a clear organization will always help alleviate anxiety and reassure you. Thus, you can deliver a powerful message without getting tripped up yourself. We suggest you try the following:

■ Outline your draft in advance in order to make sure that it has clear organization.

■ Inform the audience at the start what the organization of your presentation will be. Early in the talk you probably should say something along these lines, though not in so abbreviated a form:

> "In talking about *A*, I'll have to define a few terms, *B* and *C*, and I will also have to talk about two positions that differ from mine, *D* and *E*. I'll then try to show why *A* is the best policy to pursue, clearly better than *D* and *E*."

■ So that the listeners can easily follow you, be sure to use transitions such as "Furthermore," "Therefore," "Although it is often said," and "It may be objected that," so that the listeners can easily follow your train of thought. Sometimes, you may even remind the listeners what the previous stages were, with such a comment as "We have now seen three approaches to the problem of. . ."

METHODS OF DELIVERY

After thinking about helping the audience to follow your speech, consider how much help you'll need delivering it. Depending on your comfort level with the topic and your argument, you might decide to

- deliver a memorized talk without notes,
- read the talk from a text, or
- speak from an outline, perhaps with quotations and statistics written down.

Each of these methods has strengths and weaknesses. A memorized talk allows for plenty of eye contact with the audience but unless you are a superb actor it is almost surely going to seem a bit mechanical. A talk that you read from a text will indeed let you say to an audience exactly what you intend (with the best possible wording), but reading a text inevitably establishes some distance between you and the audience, even if you occasionally glance up from your pages. If you talk from a mere outline, almost surely some of your sentences will turn out to be a bit awkward — though a little awkwardness may help to convey sincerity and therefore be a plus.

No matter what form of delivery you choose, try to convey the impression that you're conversing with the audience, not talking down to them — even though if you're standing on a platform you will be literally talking down.

You may want to use **audiovisual aids** in your presentation. These can range from such low-tech materials as handouts, blackboards, and whiteboards to high-tech PowerPoint presentations. Each has advantages and disadvantages. For instance, if you distribute handouts when the talk begins, the audience may start thumbing through them during your opening comments. And although PowerPoint can be a highly useful aid, some speakers make too much use of it simply because it's available. It happens that the day before writing this discussion the author witnessed a PowerPoint presentation that began with the speaker projecting on the screen the date, the speaker's name, and the name of the university at which the talk was being delivered. Well, most of us knew the date, and we all knew the speaker's name and the name of the university. It seemed like overkill. The truth is, the talk simply didn't need any images at all, and we ended up wondering why the speaker bothered with PowerPoint.

For a delightful parody of this sort of talk, consider "The Gettysburg Powerpoint Presentation" (http://norvig.com/Gettysburg/). It begins thus:

> **And now please welcome President Abraham Lincoln.**
> Good morning. Just a second while I get this connection to work. Do I press this button here? Function-F7? No, that's not right. Hmmm. Maybe I'll have to reboot. Hold on a minute. Um, my name is Abe Lincoln and I'm your president. While we're waiting, I want to thank Judge David Wills, chairman of the committee supervising the dedication of the Gettysburg cemetery. It's great to be here, Dave, and you and the committee are doing a great job. Gee, sometimes this new **technology** does have glitches, but **we couldn't live without it, could we?** Oh — is it ready? OK, here we go.

The lesson? Yes, use audiovisual material if it will help you to present your material, but don't use it if it adds nothing or if you haven't mastered the technology.

One final point: If you do use visual material, *make certain that any words on the images are large enough to be legible to the audience:* A graph with tiny words won't impress your audience, even if you read the words aloud.

The Audience

It is not merely because topics are complicated that we cannot agree that one side is reasonable and right and the other side irrational and wrong. The truth is, we are swayed not only by reason (*logos*) but also by appeals to the emotions (*pathos*) and by the speaker's character (*ethos*). We can combine these last two factors, and put it this way: Sometimes we are inclined to agree with X rather than with Y because X strikes us as a more appealing person (perhaps more open-minded, more intelligent, better informed, more humane, and less cold). X is the sort of person we want to have as a friend. We disagree with Y—or at least we're unwilling to associate ourselves with Y—because Y is, well, Y just isn't the sort of person we want to agree with. Y's statistics don't sound right, or Y seems like a bully; for some reason, we just don't have confidence in Y. Confidence is easily lost: Alas, even a mispronunciation will diminish the audience's confidence in Y. As Peter de Vries said, "You can't be happy with someone who pronounces both *d*'s in Wednesday."

Earlier in the book we talked about the importance of **tone** and of the writer's **persona**. And we have made the point that the writer's tone will depend partly on the audience. A person writing for a conservative journal whose readership is almost entirely conservatives can adopt a highly satiric manner in talking about liberals and will win much approval. But if this conservative writer is writing in a liberal journal and hopes to get a sympathetic hearing, he or she will have to avoid satire and wisecracks and, instead, present himself or herself as a person of goodwill who is open-minded and eager to address the issue seriously.

The **language** that you use — the degree to which it is formal as opposed to colloquial, and the degree to which it is technical as opposed to general — will also depend on the audience. Speaking broadly, in oral argument you should speak politely but not formally. You do *not* want to be one of those people who "talk like a book." But you also don't want to be overly colloquial. Choose a middle course, probably a notch below the style you would use in a written paper. For instance, in an oral presentation you might say, "We'll consider this point in a minute or two," whereas in a written paper you probably would write, "We will consider this point shortly."

Technical language is entirely appropriate *if* your audience is familiar with it. If you are arguing before members of Amnesty International about the use of torture, you can assume certain kinds of specialized knowledge. You can, for ins tance, breezily speak of the DRC and of KPCS, and your listeners will know what you're talking about because Amnesty International has been active with issues concerning the Democratic Republic of Congo and the Kimberley Process Certification Scheme. In contrast, if you are arguing the same case before a general public, you'll have to explain these abbreviations, and you may even have to explain what Amnesty International is.

If you are arguing before an audience of classmates, you probably have a good idea of what they know and don't know.

Delivery

Your audience will in some measure determine not only your tone but also the way you appear when giving the speech. Part of the delivery is the speaker's **appearance.** The medium is part of the message. The president can appear in jeans when he chats about his reelection plans, but he wears a suit and a tie when he delivers the State of the Union address. Just as we wear one kind of **clothing** when playing tennis, another when attending classes, and yet another when going for a job interview, an effective speaker dresses appropriately. A lawyer arguing before the Supreme Court wears a dark suit or dress, and if the lawyer is male he wears a necktie. The same lawyer, arguing at a local meeting, speaking as a community resident who objects to a proposal to allow a porno store to open near a school, may well dress informally — maybe in jeans — to show that he is not at all stuffy but still feels that a porno store goes too far.

Your appearance when you speak is not merely a matter of clothing; it includes your **facial expressions,** your **posture,** your **gestures,** your general demeanor. All that we can say here is that you should avoid those bodily motions — swaying, thumping the table, putting on and taking off eyeglasses, craning your neck, smirking — that are so distracting that they cause the audience to concentrate on the distraction rather than on the argument. ("That's the third time he straightened his necktie. I wonder how many more times he will — oops, that's the fourth!") Most of us are unaware of our annoying habits; if you're lucky, a friend, when urged, will tell you about them. You may lose a friend, but you will gain some good advice.

You probably can't do much about your **voice** — it may be high-pitched, or it may be gravelly — but you can make sure you speak loudly enough for the audience members to hear you, slowly enough for them to understand you, and clearly enough for them to understand you.

We have some advice about **quotations.** First, if possible, use an effective quotation or two, partly because — we'll be frank here — the quotations probably are more impressively worded than anything you come up with on your own. A quotation may be the chief thing that your audience comes away with: "Hey, yes, I liked that: 'War is too important to be left to the generals'" or "When it comes down to it, I agree with that Frenchman who said 'If we are to abolish the death penalty, I should like to see the first step taken by the murderers'" or "You know, I think it was all summed up in that line by Margaret Mead, something like, 'No one would remember the Good Samaritan if he'd had only good intentions. He had money as well.' Yes, that's pretty convincing. Morality isn't enough. You need money." You didn't invent the words that you quote, but you did bring them to your listeners' attention, and they will be grateful to you.

A second bit of advice about quotations: When quoting, do *not* begin by saying "quote," and do not end by saying "end quote" (or as we once heard a speaker endlessly say, quotation after quotation, "unquote"), and do not hook the air with your fingers. How do you make it clear that you are quoting and that you have finished quoting? Begin with a clear lead-in ("In *Major Barbara* George Bernard Shaw touches on this issue, when Barbara says, . . ."), slightly pause, and then slightly change (e.g., elevate) your voice. When you have finished quoting — again, a slight pause and a return to your normal voice — be sure to use words that clearly indicate the quotation is finished, such as "Shaw here says what everyone thinks," or "Shaw's comment is witty but short-sighted," or "Barbara's point, then, is. . . ."

Our third and last piece of advice concerning quotations is this: If the quotation is only a phrase or a brief sentence, you can memorize it and be confident that you'll remember it, but if it's longer than a sentence, write it on a sheet in your notes or on a four-by-six-inch card in print large enough for you to read easily. You have chosen these words because they are effectively put, so you don't want to misquote them or hesitate in delivering them.

The Talk

As for the talk itself, well, we have been touching on it in our discussion of such matters as the speaker's relation to the audience, the need to provide signposts, and the use of quotations. All of our comments in earlier chapters about developing a written argument are relevant also to oral arguments, but here we should merely emphasize that because the talk is oral and the audience cannot look back to an earlier page to remind itself of some point, the speaker may have to repeat and summarize a bit more than is usual in a written essay.

Remember, too, that a reader can *see* when the essay ends — there is blank space at the end of the page — but a listener depends on aural cues. Nothing is more embarrassing — and less effective as argument — than a speaker who seems (to the audience) to suddenly stop and sit down. In short, give your hearers ample clues that you are ending (post such signs as "Finally" or "Last" or "Let me end by saying"), and be sure to end with a strong sentence. It probably won't be as good as the end of the Gettysburg address ("government of the people, by the people, for the people, shall not perish from the earth"), nor will it be as good as the end of Martin Luther King Jr.'s "I Have a Dream" speech ("Free at last! Free at last! Thank God Almighty, we are free at last!"), but those are the models to emulate.

Formal Debates

It would be nice if all arguments ended with everyone, participants and spectators, agreeing that the facts are clear, that one presentation is more reasonable than the other, and therefore that one side is right and the other side is wrong. But in life, most issues are complicated. High school students may earnestly debate — this is a real topic in a national debate —

Resolved: That education has failed its mission in the United States,

but it takes only a moment of reflection to see that neither the affirmative nor the negative can be true. Yes, education has failed its mission in many ways, but, No, it has succeeded in many ways. Its job now is (in the words of Samuel Beckett) to try again: "Fail. Fail again. Fail better."

Debates of this sort, conducted before a judge and guided by strict rules concerning "Constructive Speeches," "Rebuttal Speeches," and "Cross-Examinations" are not attempts to get at the truth; like lawsuits, they are attempts to win a case. Each speaker seeks not to persuade the opponent but only to convince the judge. Although most of this section is devoted not to forensics in the strictest sense but more generally to the presentation of oral arguments, we begin with the standard format.

STANDARD DEBATE FORMAT

Formal debates occur within a structure that governs the number of speeches, their order, and the maximum time for each one. The format may vary from place to place, but there is always a structure. In most debates, a formal resolution states the reason for the debate ("Resolved: That capital punishment be abolished in juvenile cases"). The affirmative team supports the resolution; the negative team denies its legitimacy. The basic structure has three parts:

- *The constructive phase,* in which the debaters construct their cases and develop their arguments (usually for ten minutes).

- *The rebuttal,* in which debaters present their responses and also present their final summary (usually for five minutes).

- *The preparation,* in which the debater prepares for presenting the next speech. (During the preparation — a sort of time-out — the debater is not addressing the opponent or audience. The total time allotted to a team is usually six or eight minutes, which the individual debaters divide as they wish.)

We give, very briefly, the usual structure of each part, though we should mention that another common format calls for a cross-examination of the First Affirmative Construction

U.S. Democratic presidential candidates Hillary Clinton and Bernie Sanders during a debate at the University of New Hampshire in Durham on February 4, 2016. A successful debate can help change the tide of a candidate's campaign.

by the Second Negative, a cross-examination of the First Negative Construction by the First Affirmative, a cross-examination of the Second Affirmative by the First Negative, and a cross-examination of the Second Negative by the Second Affirmative:

First Affirmative Constructive Speech: Serves as introduction, giving summary overview, definitions, criteria for resolution, major claims and evidence, statement, and intention to support the resolution.

First Negative Constructive Speech: Responds by introducing the basic position, challenges the definitions and criteria, suggests the line of attack, emphasizes that the burden of proof lies with the affirmative, rejects the resolution as unnecessary or dangerous, and supports the status quo.

Second Affirmative Constructive: Rebuilds the affirmative case; refutes chief attacks, especially concerning definitions, criteria, and rationale (philosophic framework); and further develops the affirmative case.

Second Negative Constructive: Completes the negative case, if possible advances it by rebuilding portions of the first negative construction, and contrasts the entire negative case with the entire affirmative case.

First Negative Rebuttal: Attacks the opponents' arguments and defends the negative constructive arguments (but a rebuttal may *not* introduce new constructive arguments).

First Affirmative Rebuttal: Usually responds first to the second negative construction and then to the first negative rebuttal.

Second Negative Rebuttal: Constitutes final speech for the negative, summarizing the case and explaining to the judge why the negative should be declared the winner.

Second Affirmative Rebuttal: Summarizes the debate, responds to issues pressed by the second negative rebuttal, and suggests to the judge that the affirmative team should win.

A CHECKLIST FOR PREPARING FOR A DEBATE

- ❏ Have I done adequate preparation in my research?
- ❏ Are my notes legible, with accurate quotations and credible sources?
- ❏ Am I prepared to take good notes during the debate?
- ❏ Is my proposition clearly stated?
- ❏ Do I have adequate evidence to support the thesis (main point)?
- ❏ Do I have backup points in mind?
- ❏ Have I given thought to issues my opponents might raise?
- ❏ Does the opening properly address the instructor, the audience, the opponents? (Remember, you are addressing an audience, not merely the opponents.)
- ❏ Are my visual aids focused on major points?
- ❏ Is my demeanor professional, and is my dress appropriate?

PART FOUR

Current Issues:
Occasions for Debate

Debates As an Aid to Thinking

Throughout this book we emphasize critical thinking, which — to put the matter briefly — means thinking analytically not only about the ideas of others but also about one's *own* ideas. As we often say in these pages, *you* are your first reader, and you should be a demanding one. You have ideas, but you want to think further about them, to improve them — partly so that you can share them with others, but also so that they can help you build a thoughtful, useful, satisfying life.

This means, as we say elsewhere in the book, that you have (or at least try to have) an open mind, one that welcomes comments on your own ideas. You are, we hope, ready to grant that someone with differing views may indeed have something to teach you. When you hear other views, of course you won't always embrace them; but at times you may find merit in some aspects of them, and you will to some degree reshape your own views. (We discuss the importance of trying to find shared ground and moving onward and upward from there in Chapter 10, A Psychologist's View: Rogerian Argument.)

Much of the difficulty in improving our ideas lies in our tendency to think in an either/or pattern. To put the point in academic terms, we incline toward *binary* (Latin, "two by two") or *dichotomous* (Greek, "divided into two") thinking. We often think in terms of contrasts: life and death, good and evil, right and left, up and down, on and off, white and black, boys and girls, men and women (men are from Mars; women from Venus), yes and no, freedom and tyranny. We understand what something is partly by thinking of what it is not: "He is liberal; she is conservative." In Gilbert and Sullivan's *Iolanthe*, one of the characters sees things this way:

> I am an intellectual chap,
> And think of things that would astonish you.
> I often think it is comical
> How nature always does contrive
> That every boy and every gal,
> That's born into the world alive,
> Is either a little Liberal,
> Or else a little Conservative.

We have our liberals and conservatives too, our Democrats and Republicans, and we talk about fate and free will, day and night, and so on. But we also know that there are imperceptible gradations. We know that there are conservative Democrats and liberal Republicans, and that although day differs from night, we cannot say at any given moment, "We have just now gone from day to night." True, there are times when gradations are irrelevant: In the polling booth, when voting for a political candidate or a particular bill, we must decide between X and Y. At that stage it is either/or, not both/and or "Well, let's think further about this." But in much of life we are finding our way, acting provisionally — decisively at the moment, yes, but later we may modify our ideas in the light of further thinking, which often is stimulated by the spoken or written thoughts of someone who holds a different view. Elsewhere we quote Virginia Woolf on the topic of writing about complex issues, but the comment is worth repeating:

> When a subject is highly controversial . . . one cannot hope to tell the truth. One can only show how one came to hold whatever opinion one does hold. One can only give one's audience the chance of drawing their own conclusions as they observe the limitations, the prejudices, the idiosyncrasies of the speaker.

What we're getting at is this: The debates in the next five chapters present sharply opposed views, usually of an either/or, day/night sort. Each essay sets forth a point of view, often with the implication that on this particular issue there are only two points of view — the writer's view and the wrong view. Some of the writers in these debates, convinced that only one view makes sense, evidently are not interested in hearing other opinions; they are out to convince — indeed, to conquer.

The very word *debate* (from Latin *battere*, "to fight," "to battle") implies a combative atmosphere, a contest in which there will be a winner and a loser. And, indeed, the language used to describe a debate is often militant. Debaters *aim* their arguments, *destroy* the arguments of their *opponents* by *rebutting* (from Old French, *boter*, "to butt") and *refuting* (from Latin *futare*, "to beat") them.

We urge you, however, to read these arguments not in order to decide who is right and who is wrong but in order to think about the issues. In short, although the debates may be reductive, stating only two sides and supporting only one, you should think critically about both sides of any given argument, and allow the essays to enrich your own ideas about the topics. Above all, use the cut and thrust of debate as a device to explore the controversy, not as a weapon to force the other side into submission.

See, too, what you can learn about *writing* from these essays — about ways of organizing thoughts, about ways of presenting evidence, and especially about ways of establishing a voice, a *tone* that the reader takes as a representation of the sort of person you are. Remember, as E. B. White said, "No author long remains incognito." Authors reveal their personalities — belligerent, witty, thoughtful, courteous, whatever. If an author here turns you off, let's say by using heavy sarcasm or by being unwilling to face contrary evidence, well, there is a lesson for you as a writer.

In reading essays debating a given issue, keep in mind the questions given on pages 109–10, "A Checklist for Analyzing an Argument." We list them again below, with a few additional points of special relevance to debates.

A CHECKLIST FOR ANALYZING A DEBATE

Have I asked myself the following questions?

- ❑ What is the writer's thesis?
  - ❑ What claim is asserted?
  - ❑ What assumptions are made?
  - ❑ Are key terms defined satisfactorily?
- ❑ What support is offered on behalf of the claim?
  - ❑ Are examples relevant and convincing?
  - ❑ Are statistics relevant, accurate, and convincing?
  - ❑ Are the authorities appropriate?
  - ❑ Is the logic — deductive and inductive — valid?
  - ❑ If there is an appeal to emotion, is this appeal acceptable?
- ❑ Does the writer seem fair?
  - ❑ Are counterarguments considered?
  - ❑ Is there any evidence of dishonesty?

Have I asked myself the following additional questions?

- ❑ Do the disputants differ in
  - ❑ assumptions?
  - ❑ interpretations of relevant facts?
  - ❑ selection of and emphasis on these facts?
  - ❑ definitions of key terms?
  - ❑ values and norms?
  - ❑ goals?
- ❑ What common ground do the disputants share?
- ❑ Which disputant seems to me to have the better overall argument? Why?

13

Student Loans: Should Some Indebtedness Be Forgiven?

ROBERT APPLEBAUM

Congressman Hansen Clarke (D-MI) in 2012 introduced (with seventeen cosponsors) the Student Loan Forgiveness Act of 2012 (HR 4170). This proposal included the 10/10 Loan Repayment Plan, which (a) would for ten years automatically withdraw 10 percent of the debtor's income and then (b) would forgive loan debt up to $45,000. Robert Applebaum (b. 1952), a graduate of Fordham University School of Law, initiated a petition — now signed by well over a million people — supporting Congressman Clarke's proposal. The petition claimed that forgiving debt would stimulate the economy by in effect giving the former students more money to spend. In the petition Applebaum wrote:

> Student loan debt has become the latest financial crisis in America and, if we do absolutely nothing, the entire economy will eventually come crashing down again, just as it did when the housing bubble popped. . . . [T]hose buried under the weight of their student loan debt are not buying homes or cars, not starting businesses or families, and they're not investing, inventing, innovating, or otherwise engaged in any of the economically stimulative activities that we need all Americans to be engaged in if we're ever to dig ourselves out of the giant hole created by the greed of those at the very top.

We reprint here a short essay Applebaum later published, in 2012, in the Hill, *a Washington, D.C., publication.*

Debate on Student Loan Debt Doesn't Go Far Enough

As Congress debates the extremely narrow issue of whether to extend the current 3.4 percent interest rate on Federal Student Loans, or to let that rate expire and, thus, double to its previous level of 6.8 percent, both sides of the aisle are missing an opportunity to do something unique, decisive, and bold: adopt legislation that forgives excessive student loan debt after a reasonable repayment period.

Representative Hansen Clarke (D-MI) introduced an unprecedented piece of legislation in March — HR 4170, The Student Loan Forgiveness Act of 2012, in response to over 660,000 people who signed a petition I started in favor of student loan forgiveness. Yet, despite the public outcry, only one member initially stepped up to put his name and reputation on the line in order to draw attention to the ever-growing crisis of student loan debt. Rep. Clarke has taken on the role of Champion for the educated poor — the 36 million Americans who are drowning under the weight of their student loan debts. A new petition I started in favor of HR 4170 currently has over 939,000 signatures.

The Student Loan Forgiveness Act of 2012 is not a free ride, nor is it a bailout. It's a recognition that millions of Americans have grossly overpaid for their educations, due in part to governmental interference in the marketplace. With the availability of so much seemingly "free money" available to anyone with a pulse who wants to take out a student loan, colleges and universities have had no incentive to keep costs down — and they haven't. The outrageous costs of obtaining a college education or beyond today have very little to do with the inherent value of the degrees sought; rather, it has much more to do with brand new stadiums and six-figure administrative salaries. After all, if the degrees obtained today were worth the increased cost to obtain them, compared with thirty to forty years ago, then shouldn't those degrees also yield greater salaries upon graduation?

Tuition rates continue to soar and students are required to go further and further into debt each year, merely to obtain an education. Every other country in the industrialized world has figured out how to pay for higher education for its citizens, but here in America, we continue to treat education as a commodity that benefits only the individual obtaining the education, rather than what it truly is: a public good and an investment in our collective future as a country.

Education should be a right, not a commodity reserved only for the rich or those willing to hock their futures for the chance (not a guarantee) to get a job. Gone are the days when tuition rates had any kind of rational connection to the salaries one could expect upon graduating. With each passing year, students are left with no choice but to borrow more and more through both Federal and private student loans to finance their educations, as if the degrees obtained today are worth any more than they were a generation or two ago. In fact, they're worth far, far less than in years past, precisely because of the high cost of tuition combined with the decimated job market where middle-class wages have gone down, not up, over the last decade.

We've long ago passed the point where we have become what my friend, Aaron Calafato, writer, director, and star of the play *For Profit*, would call a "borrow to work" society. Far worse than "pay to play," borrow to work is a modern form of indentured servitude, where millions of Americans are told since birth that in order to get ahead, they must obtain a higher education.

What they aren't being told, however, is that in order to obtain that education, students must necessarily mortgage their futures and spend the rest of their lives paying back the loans that gave them the "privilege" of working at jobs they hate for salaries that simply do not allow them to make ends meet.

How do we ever expect the housing market to improve when the very people we rely upon to purchase homes — college grads and professionals — are graduating with mortgage-sized debts that they can neither live in, nor use as intended in today's job market?

Are we content to live in a society where only the privileged few are able to obtain an education without sacrificing their future? Do we really want to price the middle and working classes out of public service? And who's going to be buying cars, starting businesses, and making investments in our future if not the middle class? We're not yet an oligarchy, but we're fast on our way toward becoming one if we knowingly fail to address this ever-growing crisis, before it's too late.

Unfortunately, the $1 trillion in student 10 loan debt outstanding in America is not a ceiling, merely a disturbing milestone along the national path to poverty. If Congress does nothing, it'll only get worse.

Topics for Critical Thinking and Writing

1. In paragraph 1, Robert Applebaum speaks of "excessive" student debt. Whom does he blame for this debt — students, colleges, lenders, or someone else? And in this context, is he committing the fallacy of begging the question (on this fallacy, see page 358)? Why, or why not?

2. In paragraph 5, Applebaum says that education — meaning higher education — should be a right. In the United States, education through high school is of course free — it is a right — though one can argue that there really is no such thing as "free" education (or "free" medical care, etc.); somebody pays for it. Should all citizens have a right to (presumably *free*) post–high school education? Does this include programs in vocational training? Explain.

3. By the end of paragraph 6, if not earlier, it is evident that Applebaum is furious with the present system. Do you think his essay would be more persuasive if he were less obviously angry? Explain.

Analyzing a Visual: Student Loan Debt

Anadolu Agency/Getty Images

Topic for Critical Thinking and Writing

Briefly, what arguments are on display in the photo on page 424? What particular aspects of college education are these protesters critical of? Do you agree or disagree with them? Why?

JUSTIN WOLFERS

Justin Wolfers (b. 1972), an economist at the Wharton School, University of Pennsylvania, was invited by Freakonomics *to comment on Robert Applebaum's idea in his petition* Signon.org *that forgiving student loan indebtedness would stimulate the nation's economy: Freed from debt, Applebaum argued, consumers would spend thousands of additional dollars, which would then encourage businesses to hire more workers to meet the increased demand for goods. (The argument that forgiveness of loans will stimulate job growth is offered also in Congressman Clarke's Student Loan Forgiveness Act of 2012 [HR 4170].)*

We reprint Wolfers's contribution to Freakonomics, *September 19, 2011. When he wrote this short piece in 2011, Applebaum's petition had 300,000 signatures. It now has well over a million signatures.*

Forgive Student Loans? Worst Idea Ever

Let's look at this through five separate lenses:

Distribution: If we are going to give money away, why on earth would we give it to college grads? This is the one group who we know typically have high incomes, and who have enjoyed income growth over the past four decades. The group who has been hurt over the past few decades is high school dropouts.

Macroeconomics: This is the worst macro policy I've ever heard of. If you want stimulus, you get more bang-for-your-buck if you give extra dollars to folks who are most likely to spend each dollar. Imagine what would happen if you forgave $50,000 in debt. How much of that would get spent in the next month or year? Probably just a couple of grand (if that). Much of it would go into the bank. But give $1,000 to each of fifty poor people, and nearly all of it will

get spent, yielding a larger stimulus. Moreover, it's not likely that college grads are the ones who are liquidity-costrained. Most of 'em could spend more if they wanted to; after all, they are the folks who could get a credit card or a car loan fairly easily. It's the hand-to-mouth consumers — those who can't get easy access to credit — who are most likely to raise their spending if they get the extra dollars.

Education Policy: Perhaps folks think that forgiving educational loans will lead more people to get an education. No, it won't. This is a proposal to forgive the debt of folks who already have an education. Want to increase access to education? Make loans more widely available, or subsidize those who are yet to choose whether to go to school. But this proposal is just a lump-sum transfer that won't increase education attainment. So why transfer to these folks?

Political Economy: This is a bunch of kids who don't want to pay their loans back. And worse: Do this once, and what will happen in the next recession? More lobbying for free money, rather than doing something socially constructive. Moreover, if these guys succeed, others will try, too. And we'll just get more spending in the least socially productive part of our economy—the lobbying industry.

Politics: Notice the political rhetoric? Give free money to us, rather than "corporations, millionaires, and billionaires." Opportunity cost is one of the key principles of economics. And that principle says to compare your choice with the next best alternative. Instead, they're comparing it with the worst alternative. So my question for the proponents: Why give money to college grads rather than the 15 percent of the population in poverty?

Conclusion: Worst. Idea. Ever.

And I bet that the proponents can't find a single economist to support this idiotic idea.

Topics for Critical Thinking and Writing

1. What do you think of Justin Wolfers's suggestion that if we want individuals to put money into circulation, it makes more sense to give $1,000 to each of fifty poor people than to forgive $50,000 of a college graduate's debt?

2. Would Wolfers's essay be more effective if he omitted his final paragraph? Or if he reversed the sequence of the last two paragraphs? Explain.

3. Imagine that you are Applebaum. Write a response to Wolfers.

14

Technology in the Classroom: Useful or Distracting?

SIG BEHRENS

Sig Behrens is currently the general manager of Global Education at Stratasys, and he is the past president of global sales for Blackboard, Inc., one of the leading services seeking to improve student performance through the use of technology. In this article, which first appeared in U.S. News and World Report *on March 1, 2013, he argues that in the past technological advances failed to change the fundamental dynamics of classroom instruction, but today's new technology, taking advantage of social media and mobile applications, will create real change.*

The Education-Technology Revolution Is Coming

Higher education is the next bubble. Facebook will replace classroom instruction. Textbooks will go away, and some colleges will, too.

In other words, everything is going to change. Or, at least, that's the talk we in education and technology regularly hear these days. It sounds exciting — and, to some, scary.

But it also sounds like what I heard during the dot-com boom of the 1990s when a lot of companies — including Blackboard — began using technology to "disrupt" the education status quo. Since then we've made some important progress, but in many ways the classroom still looks the same as it did 100 years ago. So what's different this time? Is all the talk just hype? Or are we really starting to see the beginnings of major change?

I believe we are.

There are a lot of reasons, but one of the 5 biggest is the way that technology has given rise to a new kind of education consumer — the active learner — who is using technology to drive change in ways that we haven't seen before. In the past, change was usually a top-down process, led by campus administrators, district leaders, and other officials. It was often slow in coming, if at all. Look at technology: Mainframe computing gave way to client/server computing and later intranet computing. These shifts were slow and phased — an orderly rollout from the administration with little urgency or room for consumer choice.

And why would there be? Typically students had few choices of any kind, particularly before new options, globalization, and competition began to put cracks in the traditional model of education delivery. But technology has finally tipped the balance. Today the power to drive real change lies with the learner, not the institution.

In the publishing industry, Borders had difficulty meeting changing customer preferences in the digital era. While they struggled to adapt, Amazon established an open platform that gave users more control, letting readers buy and share and discover on their own terms. It let them go mobile with the Kindle and Kindle apps.

Education institutions are now grappling with the same challenge Borders faced: how to connect with savvier and more discerning consumers who have more options today than they did even a few years ago. These consumers — these active learners — have different expectations for their education experience. Administrators must be aware that active learners are willing to go elsewhere if they don't feel their expectations are being met.

Active learners spend more time using mobile apps than they do surfing the Web. They have instant access to information I used to spend countless hours hunting for in the local library. They spend 4.6 hours a week on social media — more time than they spend reading or writing e-mails. But they are often forced to "power down" when they enter the classroom. Instead of leveraging the mobile and social Web to fuel exploration and discovery, education is often still an analog, one-way activity: The instructor delivers information, students have to learn it.

If we're really going to engage active learners, I believe that education needs to become much more open, mobile, social, and analytical.

Instead of relying only on a teacher and a textbook, students should be learning from each other and from countless sources online. In fact, they already are. Therefore, both educators and education companies should engage learners online and off, through desktops and mobile devices, at night and on weekends. We should harness the learning activity data that is growing every day to give more insight to instructors — and students and parents — to help them improve.

So far, the overall impact of technology in education has been modest compared to its impact in other fields. According to Pew research, 60 percent of students say their technology expectations are still not being met. But it is clear that today's students have more options than ever, with virtual schools, open education initiatives and massive open online courses, and online classes and programs.

Of course, technology is no silver bullet. And it's no replacement for good teaching. But no doubt education is becoming more of a marketplace. With budgets tight and revenue sources less predictable, institutions will need to compete and innovate in order to stay relevant.

Increasingly, education will be a choice made by learners who are looking for something different. And it's increasingly easy for them to differentiate between options that are serious about the future and those that aren't.

Active learners move fast. To remain (or become) successful, institutions must keep up with them, or risk being left behind.

Topics for Critical Thinking and Writing

1. Sig Behrens begins the article with the suggestion that for years, companies have tried to use technology to change education, but that education has remained largely unchanged. What does he mean by that? Do you agree or disagree with his assessment? Why, or why not? Cite, for examples, ways that you have seen technology being used in the education environment.

2. In paragraph 5, Behrens introduces the term "active learner," and he uses the term frequently throughout the rest of the article, but without specifically defining it. What do you think he means by that term, and how is an active learner connected to the use of technology?

3. Behrens uses the term "education delivery" in paragraph 6, and in paragraph 9 he says that traditional education is characterized thus: "The instructor delivers information, students have to learn it." What does this reveal about assumptions regarding the nature of education in the classroom, the various roles played by instructors and students? What alternative learning model, if any, does Behrens propose?

4. In paragraph 7, Behrens refers to the struggles of Borders bookstores to adapt to changing technologies in the publishing world. He doesn't mention that Borders eventually filed for bankruptcy and closed operations in 2011. Research the specifics of Borders's struggles. What does this example tell us about the advance of technology? Is the example relevant to the world of education? Why, or why not?

5. In paragraph 13, Behrens makes the comment that technology is "no replacement for good teaching." How can this statement be resolved with his earlier statements about the role of technology in the classroom?

Analyzing a Visual: Technology in Classrooms

SCHOOL RESUMES TODAY AROUND THE COUNTRY.
TEACHERS TRANSITION CHILDREN SLOWLY.

Topics for Critical Thinking and Writing

1. Does the cartoon on page 429 simply humorously reflect the familiar adjustments students must make in any new classroom using technology, or does it critique the use of technology in the classroom? Explain your answer by drawing on components of the image.

2. What assumptions are present in the image?

RUTH STARKMAN

Ruth Starkman teaches ethics at the University of San Francisco and bioethics at Stanford University. She writes frequently about ethics, medicine, political theory, and higher education. In this article, which initially appeared in the online newspaper Huffington Post, *she writes about her experience with the struggle to use technology in the classroom while avoiding "cyberslacking"—that is, using technology in ways that are unrelated to what is happening in the classroom.*

Cyberslacking in Shanghai: What My Students Taught Me

Teaching a writing and "Great Books" course to 21 middle school students at an international school in Shanghai this summer, I found myself amidst an intense debate about using electronic devices in the classroom. The anti-device faction, which included parents and students, worried about one particular problem: Cyberslacking, which usually refers to surfing the Internet and shirking one's duties at work.

Cyberslacking is also a problem in education settings, which is why so many institutions and teachers ban personal devices in the classroom. Several important statistical studies corroborate claims about the seemingly inevitable temptation of cyberslacking in classroom environments, showing that factors such as consumerism, escapism, lack of attention, distraction by others' "misuse" of technology, boredom, and apathy towards course material may all contribute to cyberslacking.

I should say up front, when I teach college in the US I have students bring their own devices, and I also struggle with their distraction. But I continue to allow devices for numerous reasons: Conscious of college costs, trying to conserve paper, and teaching older texts, I use exclusively pdfs and links. I deploy a lot of social media and Google docs in class. Most importantly, my students, especially the international ones, benefit from the ability to search words in the texts and compare with translations in their own language. I know many of my colleagues who appreciate technology nevertheless adopt a different tack.

For example, Joshua Landy, Professor in French Language, Literature and Civilization at Stanford University, finds "a laptop-free zone conducive to more engaged teaching experiences." Likewise, Dan Edelstein, Professor of French and, by courtesy, of History at Stanford University, has "moved away from distributing readings as PDF's, or links when available (particularly older primary sources):"

> Not only do students seem to read them less carefully on a screen, but they tend to bury themselves in their devices during class, rather than face the other students and myself. So even if the students are still technically "on task," the device can act as a barrier for discussion.

Not disagreeing with Landy and Edelstein, but anticipating language and knowledge differences in Shanghai, especially with middle schoolers aged 11–13, I opted to include devices.

When I teach I walk around the class. All too often I can feel students quickly switching screens back to the course material as I approach. Rather than chide an individual student, I announce to the class as a whole: "You don't really want to surf the Internet or text in class, do you? Unless you are prepared, or your family is, to pay $300 an hour for you to zone out."

Cyberslacking is so prevalent I even use it as an example when explaining the Greek concept of *Akrasia*, or weakness of the will, to my college philosophy students. In Shanghai, I also found ample opportunity to introduce the concept of *Akrasia* to middle schoolers: "What do you do in the classroom that you know is bad for you and others, you're not supposed to do, but do it anyway?" The students quickly responded: *Surf the web. Check email. Text. Shop. Game.*

Considering banning devices, I consulted my colleagues at *Hybrid Pedagogy*, an academic journal of teaching and technology. Sean-Michael Morris, Senior Editor of Research and Education at Instructure, and co-director of *Hybrid Pedagogy*, asserts that technology itself is no panacea, and prefers to ask instead "how does learning happen now that human experience relies on, is mediated by, and engages constantly with digital technology?" For him shutting down the laptops isolates students from this reality:

> When instructors' policies keep laptops closed, tablets and phones turned off, we are closing the door on what is real and relevant in student lives.

In a piece called "Trust, Agency, and Connected Learning," Jesse Stommel, Assistant Professor at UW–Madison, founder and director of *Hybrid Pedagogy*, describes his use of technology in the classroom as "more about encouraging agency" than deploying and policing technology for its own sake. Does he have to monitor students' usage? Sometimes. Is it as big a problem as others might suggest?

> There are times I might step in as an "authority," but the situation has to rise well above the clicking of a keyboard or a distracted glance at a Facebook wall.

For Stommel technology is less the problem than traditional classroom dynamics. "Start by abolishing fixed-seat, face-forward lecture halls where feigned attention is valorized," he asserts. "Then, let's talk learning and distraction."

In trying to apply such advice to my classroom in Shanghai — middle schoolers! distraction! six-hour class! five days a week!! — it was also helpful to remember Howard Rheingold's measured view of technology: "It is possible to think critically about technology without running off to the woods."

Following Rheingold's advice of a "mindful" usage of technology, using it sometimes where appropriate, and also turning it off, I decided to teach some classes with devices, some without, and asked students to respond in writing with their opinions. Empirically the experience presented some interesting differences.

During days without devices the students were unable to easily look up new vocabulary or concepts and relied on me to give them definitions. Their group work became less independent because I provided the sole authority for any information they sought. (I encounter this problem in college as well when the Internet goes down in my classrooms.)

At break time without devices, however, these middle school students ran outside to play sports and socialize. On rainy days they played a lively game of indoor tag that included all genders and ages. Students shrieked happily, tearing around their school hallways and upsetting various administrators, who were keen for me to return technology to the classroom, if only to silence the noise!

I also sorely missed the Internet, even in its censored state behind the Great Fire Wall of China and the school's own filters.

But technology in the classroom presented problems as well. On days when I permitted devices I also noticed that students felt less inclined to physical activity and social interaction during breaks. Even when I tried to shoo them out of the classroom for a break, they engaged entirely in sedentary gendered segregation: the boys played *Age of Empires* on their laptops and the girls watched movies and TV together.

Worst of all, I found that technology invited a new kind of tension in the classroom. Not only were there students and parents peering in from other classes checking for potential cyberslacking, some students in the class felt the need to police each other, and the slackers responded by trying to shame those students — "why are you such a snitch!" growled one boy, who had been busted for texting under the table by the girl near him.

Even some of our collaborative teacher/student designed projects foundered if they went on too long. Using *Minecraft* for a thought experiment, students worked well for about 20 minutes with lots of productive discussion in each group. And then, gaming addiction mode took over. Forsaking their break time, the students couldn't stop building their projects, and began competing with, spying on, and sabotaging each other in polarized gendered groups. The quality of discussion and educational rewards rapidly diminished after 30 minutes. When we finished the project, some of the best designs were simple sketches on paper.

My students, who are all proponents of using the Internet and electronic devices in class, acknowledge the difficulties. The one who got shamed for "snitching" and had her *Minecraft* design attacked by some of the boys argued that it was as much the student responsibility to resist cyberslacking as the teacher's duty to monitor.

Other students affirmed this measured view of using personal devices in class, but argued that such usage trained them in important research skills and even helped them formulate better questions. One student remarked:

> Sometimes I missed something in the discussion, and I didn't want to disrupt the class or get in trouble for whispering to a friend, so I looked it up on my phone and then sometimes the answers I found helped me ask my question in a better way that helped me more and the other students too.

Another student offered this argument:

> It's awesome when you ask the teacher a question that brings up new material and during class discussion she can send us all a document or link to a related article in class and we can compare readings and different arguments.

Still another student wrote with this suggestion:

> I think it's great practice having phones and laptops in the classroom. If we can practice using them responsibly in class then we might also be better at using them at home in our free time. Right now, we're just trying to use our devices all the time, but if we got used to using them at set times and in the right way we would be more rational using them.

The students also drew up some guidelines, which we discussed:

1. Teachers and students together must set the norms for device usage and ensure their consistent adoption.

2. Technology can be successfully employed in the classroom if the task segment period is short — a single activity longer than 20–30 minutes can deteriorate into surfing, gaming, etc. I believe this time limit is as true for college students as it is for middle schoolers.

3. Course material requires both non-technological as well as tech presentations.

4. Teachers must work to promote gender integration with their technology usage.

Very impressed with the students' arguments for developing habits of excellence with their devices, I nevertheless worry about the power of *Akrasia*. Electronic devices are tempting. Especially if one uses one all the time to fill any pause: Waiting for teachers to return one's work, standing in line in the cafeteria or at grocery store, or anywhere.

In the end, our social contract for rules 20 of usage in the classroom worked often, but imperfectly. Most importantly for me, however, was this discussion itself. It seems to me that if the teacher can find some collectively positive method of maintaining the classroom social contract, monitoring technology usage while using the Internet and student devices to disseminate new materials and expand discussion, class time will become both more enjoyable and valuable.

Topics for Critical Thinking and Writing

1. In paragraph 1, Ruth Starkman defines "cyberslacking" as "surfing the Internet and shirking one's duties at work." She then states that it happens in educational environments as well. Based on your own experience, do you agree that cyberslacking is a problem at school? Why, or why not?

2. In paragraph 4, Starkman points out Edelstein's observation that students do not read as attentively when reading on a screen. Why might that be? What are the differences between reading something on a screen and reading something printed on paper? How might that have an impact on comprehension, analysis, and critical thinking?

3. The experiences Starkman relates in this article come largely from a course she taught in Shanghai. She also regularly teaches at two private universities, Stanford and the University of San Francisco. Thus, her admonition to her students in paragraph 5 that they're wasting a considerable amount of their parents' money makes sense. However, in other schools and colleges, the costs are considerably lower, and such an appeal might not work. What sort of admonition might be more appropriate in less costly classrooms? Consider what beyond money is being wasted by these students.

4. The article discusses two approaches: having a device-free classroom, or encouraging use of the devices. Therefore, Starkman created an experiment: some days with no devices, other days with them. What were the results? Was there anything in particular that surprised or concerned you? Why, or why not?

5. Based on your own experiences, have you found that the use of devices such as laptops and cell phones has led to a more productive classroom, or has it led to more distractions and cyberslacking? What would be your own proposal governing the use of such devices in the classroom? Explain your responses.

The Local Food Movement:
Is It a Better Way to Eat?

STEPHEN BUDIANSKY

Stephen Budiansky (b. 1957), a former editor of U.S. News & World Report *and of* Nature *and the recipient of a Guggenheim Award, writes chiefly about history and science. We reprint a piece that was originally published in the* New York Times *in 2010, and we follow it with a response.*

Math Lessons for Locavores

It's forty-two steps from *my* back door to the garden that keeps my family supplied nine months of the year with a modest cornucopia of lettuce, beets, spinach, beans, tomatoes, basil, corn, squash, brussels sprouts, the occasional celeriac and, once when I was feeling particularly energetic, a couple of small but undeniable artichokes. You'll get no argument from me about the pleasures and advantages to the palate and the spirit of eating what's local, fresh and in season.

But the local food movement now threatens to devolve into another one of those self-indulgent — and self-defeating — do-gooder dogmas. Arbitrary rules, without any real scientific basis, are repeated as gospel by "locavores," celebrity chefs, and mainstream environmental organizations. Words like "sustainability" and "food-miles" are thrown around without any clear understanding of the larger picture of energy and land use.

The result has been all kinds of absurdities. For instance, it is sinful in New York City to buy a tomato grown in a California field because of the energy spent to truck it across the country; it is virtuous to buy one grown in a lavishly heated greenhouse in, say, the Hudson Valley.

The statistics brandished by local-food advocates to support such doctrinaire assertions are always selective, usually misleading, and often bogus. This is particularly the case with respect to the energy costs of transporting food. One popular and oft-repeated statistic is that it takes thirty-six (sometimes it's ninety-seven) calories of fossil fuel energy to bring one calorie of iceberg lettuce from California to the East Coast. That's an apples and oranges (or maybe apples and rocks) comparison to begin with, because you can't eat petroleum or burn iceberg lettuce.

It is also an almost complete misrepresen- 5 tation of reality, as those numbers reflect the entire energy cost of producing lettuce from seed to dinner table, not just transportation. Studies have shown that whether it's grown in California or Maine, or whether it's organic or conventional, about 5,000 calories of energy go into one pound of lettuce. Given how efficient trains and tractor-trailers are, shipping a head of lettuce across the country actually adds next to nothing to the total energy bill.

It takes about a tablespoon of diesel fuel to move one pound of freight 3,000 miles by rail; that works out to about 100 calories of energy. If it goes by truck, it's about 300 calories, still a negligible amount in the overall picture. (For those checking the calculations at home, these are "large calories," or kilocalories, the units used for food value.) Overall, transportation accounts for about 14 percent of the total energy consumed by the American food system.

Other favorite targets of sustainability advocates include the fertilizers and chemicals used in modern farming. But their share of the food system's energy use is even lower, about 8 percent.

The real energy hog, it turns out, is not industrial agriculture at all, but you and me. Home preparation and storage account for 32 percent of all energy use in our food system, the largest component by far.

A single ten-mile round trip by car to the grocery store or the farmers' market will easily eat up about 14,000 calories of fossil fuel energy. Just running your refrigerator for a week consumes 9,000 calories of energy. That assumes it's one of the latest high-efficiency models; otherwise, you can double that figure.

Cooking and running dishwashers, freezers, and second or third refrigerators (more than 25 percent of American households have more than one) all add major hits. Indeed, households make up for 22 percent of all the energy expenditures in the United States.

Agriculture, on the other hand, accounts 10 for just 2 percent of our nation's energy usage; that energy is mainly devoted to running farm machinery and manufacturing fertilizer. In return for that quite modest energy investment, we have fed hundreds of millions of people, liberated tens of millions from backbreaking manual labor, and spared hundreds of millions of acres for nature preserves, forests, and parks that otherwise would have come under the plow.

Don't forget the astonishing fact that the total land area of American farms remains almost unchanged from a century ago, at a little under a billion acres, even though those farms now feed three times as many Americans and export more than ten times as much as they did in 1910.

The best way to make the most of these truly precious resources of land, favorable climates, and human labor is to grow lettuce, oranges, wheat, peppers, bananas, whatever, in the places where they grow best and with the most efficient technologies — and then pay the relatively tiny energy cost to get them to market, as we do with every other commodity in the economy. Sometimes that means growing vegetables in your backyard. Sometimes that means buying vegetables grown in California or Costa Rica.

Eating locally grown produce is a fine thing in many ways. But it is not an end in itself, nor is it a virtue in itself. The relative pittance of our energy budget that we spend on modern farming is one of the wisest energy investments we can make, when we honestly look at what it returns to our land, our economy, our environment, and our well-being.

Topics for Critical Thinking and Writing

1. What does Stephen Budiansky's opening paragraph do, in terms of building his argument?

2. Budiansky's second paragraph begins "But." Did this word come as a surprise, or did you sense, even in reading the first paragraph, that he was soon going to sing a different song?

3. How would you characterize the overall tone of this essay? Genial? No-nonsense? Aggressive? If tomorrow you came across another example of Budiansky's writing, would you pick it up eagerly, or would you pass it by? Why?

Analyzing a Visual: Local Farming

George Rose/Getty Images

Topics for Critical Thinking and Writing

1. Why should a consumer care whether a farm is "locally owned" and whether food is "locally grown"?

2. How would you define *local*? A common definition is "within 100 miles, or, if further, still within the state where the product is sold." Does this make sense to you? Why, or why not?

3. Why do you suppose the farmer chose to put the message on the side of a horse-drawn wagon rather than on a pickup truck or a billboard?

Kerry Trueman is a cofounder of EatingLiberally.org, a netroots Web site that, in her words, "advocates sustainable agriculture, progressive politics, and a less consumption-driven way of life." We reprint her response, published in the Huffington Post, *to the preceding essay. In her final paragraph, Trueman refers to "the Old Grey Lady," an allusion to the* New York Times, *which had published the essay she is commenting on.*

The Myth of the Rabid Locavore

Stephen Budiansky, self-proclaimed "liberal curmudgeon," has stuffed together another flimsy, flammable straw man out of boilerplate antilocavore rhetoric on the *New York Times* op-ed page, with the patronizing title "Math Lessons for Locavores."

It's a familiar formula: start by establishing yourself as the voice of reason by professing your own deep appreciation of the merits of locally grown food as evidenced by the bounty of your own backyard. Then, launch into a diatribe against a mythical army of dour, sour food nazis, including "celebrity chefs and mainstream environmental organizations," whose support for local farmers is based on wildly misguided and naïve notions about curbing one's carbon "foodprint."

Throw in a bunch of dubious and/or irrelevant statistics that appear to be truly locally sourced — i.e., pulled out of your own behind. Add a few disingenuous claims about the environmental benefits of industrial agriculture. Wrap things up with a statement so ludicrous that you have to publish it on your own Web site because hey, the *New York Times* is only willing to go so far:

> . . . eating food from a long way off is often the single best thing you can do for the environment, as counterintuitive as that sounds.

Budiansky's argument tars all eat-local proponents with the same broad brush, warning us that we're turning into a bunch of joyless, sanctimonious schmucks who are flimflamming an unsuspecting public:

> For instance, it is sinful in New York City to buy a tomato grown in a California field because of the energy spent to truck it across the country; it is virtuous to buy one grown in a lavishly heated greenhouse in, say, the Hudson Valley.

Sinful according to whom? As I wrote on 5 page 27 of Rodale's *Whole Green Catalog*:

> Bear in mind that buying local is often the most low-impact choice — but not always: an out-of-season local tomato grown in a fossil fuel-heated greenhouse could consume more energy than one that's been field grown and shipped from Mexico.

But hey, what do I know? I'm just one of those local-food advocates who brandishes statistics that are "always selective, usually misleading and often bogus" to back up our "doctrinaire assertions."

That describes Budiansky's own modus operandi in a nutshell. His op-ed focuses almost exclusively on the question of how much fossil fuel is used to grow and ship food, and concludes that the amount of energy used is negligible in the grand scheme of things.

Sure, and because eggs weigh less than the grain it costs to feed the factory farm hens that produce them, it was presumably quite energy efficient to ship those 380 million factory farmed eggs that have since been recalled for possible salmonella contamination from Iowa to fourteen other states.

But energy efficiency is only one small part of the equation when you add up the reasons to buy local. Other factors include: flavor and nutrition; support for more ecological farming practices; reduction of excess packaging; avoidance of pesticides and other toxins; more humane treatment of livestock and workers; preservation of local farmland; spending one's dollars closer to home; the farmers' market as community center, and so on.

Budiansky totally ignores these issues, 10 except to challenge the assumption that sustainable agriculture is better for the environment than industrial agriculture. After establishing the folly of food miles, he goes on to note:

> Other favorite targets of sustainability advocates include the fertilizers and chemicals used in modern farming. But their share of the food system's energy use is even lower, about 8 percent.

Again with the energy usage! Geez. As if that were our big beef with fertilizers and chemicals. What about soil erosion, pollution, loss of biodiversity, the rise of superweeds and antibiotic-resistant infections, the dead zones in our oceans and rivers, exposure to contaminants, and all the other environmentally disastrous consequences of "conventional" farming?

According to Budiansky, the real culprit, when it comes to squandering energy, is us:

> Home preparation and storage account for 32 percent of all energy use in our food system, the largest component by far.

He cites the miles we drive to do our grocery shopping and the energy it takes to run our fridges, dishwashers, stoves, etc. But what do any of these things have to do with whether you choose to buy food locally? Your fridge uses the same amount of energy regardless of where the food you put in it came from.

If Budiansky sincerely cares to examine what constitutes a truly low-impact diet, why does he ignore one of the biggest sources of food-related wasted energy in the average American household? As *New Scientist* recently noted:

> More energy is wasted in the perfectly edible food discarded by people in the US each year than is extracted annually from the oil and gas reserves off the nation's coastlines.

What's so maddening about sloppy op-eds 15 like this is that they give fodder to folks who hate the very notion that their food choices have any consequences beyond their own waistlines and bank balances. At a time when global warming is surely fueling fires, floods, and drought all over the world, we need to have an honest conversation about how the way we eat contributes to climate change.

What we don't need is dishonest misrepresentations and tiresome stereotypes about the eat local movement. If you actually read what us good food folks have to say about eating ecologically, you'll see that the emphasis is on adopting a predominantly plant-based diet, eating foods when they're in season, limiting your consumption of animal products and processed convenience foods, and avoiding the chemicals and pesticides that are used in conventional farming.

Buying local produce is obviously a part of the equation. But to portray it as the sole consideration of sustainable food advocates is to adopt a lazy contrarian position that is guaranteed to generate controversy, and just as sure to do absolutely nothing to engender a meaningful discussion about these issues.

Budiansky needs to be taken out to the food-shed and pummeled with his own lousy logic.

At the end of his blog post elaborating on his op-ed, he writes: "More seriously: environmentalism ought to be about pragmatism, not dogmatism."

Seriously? Such a deeply unserious piece such as his doesn't deserve to take up valuable real estate like the *Times* op-ed page. Though, like most real estate, it's worth less than it once was. Publishing stuff like this doesn't do much for the Old Grey Lady's property values.

Topics for Critical Thinking and Writing

1. Do you think Kerry Trueman's opening paragraph is effective, or is it too aggressive? Explain.

2. Has Trueman's essay helped you to think about Budiansky's essay and perhaps caused you to seriously modify your earlier view of his essay? Explain.

3. Now that you have read the two essays, do you think that either one may cause you to change your eating habits in any way? Explain.

16

The Current State of Childhood: Is "Helicopter Parenting" or "Free-Range Childhood" Better for Kids?

NICK GILLESPIE

Nick Gillespie (b. 1963) is the editor-in-chief for Reason.com *and* Reason TV, *which are online platforms for the libertarian periodical* Reason. *Gillespie, who holds a doctorate in literature from the State University of New York–Buffalo, is also the co-author of* The Declaration of Independents: How Libertarian Politics Can Fix What's Wrong with America *(2011). This article was originally published in* Time *magazine as an opinion piece on parenting on August 21, 2014.*

Millennials Are Selfish and Entitled, and Helicopter Parents Are to Blame

It's natural to resent younger Americans—*they're younger!*—but we're on the verge of a new generation gap that may make the nasty old fights between baby boomers and *their* "Greatest Generation" parents look like something out of a Norman Rockwell painting.

Seventy-one percent of American adults think of 18-to-29-year-olds — millennials, basically — as "selfish," and 65% of us think of them as "entitled." That's according to the latest Reason-Rupe Poll, a quarterly survey of 1,000 representative adult Americans.

If millennials are self-absorbed little monsters who expect the world to come to them and for their parents to clean up their rooms well into their 20s, we've got no one to blame but ourselves — especially the moms and dads among us.

Indeed, the same poll documents the ridiculous level of kid-coddling that has now become the new normal. More than two-thirds of us think there ought to be a law that kids as old as 9 should be supervised while playing at a public park, which helps explain (though not justify) the arrest of a South Carolina mother who let her phone-enabled daughter play in a busy park while she worked at a nearby McDonald's. We think on average that kids should be 10 years old before they "are allowed to play in the front yard unsupervised." Unless you live on a traffic island or a war zone, that's just nuts.

It gets worse: We think that our precious bundles of joy should be 12 before they can wait alone in a car for five minutes on a cool day or walk to school without an adult, and that they should be 13 before they can be trusted to stay home alone. You'd think that kids raised on *Baby Einstein* DVDs should be a little more advanced than that.

Curiously, this sort of ridiculous hyper-protectiveness is playing out against a backdrop in which children are safer than ever. Students reporting bullying is one-third of what it was 20 years ago, and according to a study in *JAMA Pediatrics*, the past decade has seen massive declines in exposure to violence for kids. Out of 50 trends studied, summarize the authors, "there were 27 significant declines and no significant increases between 2003 and 2011. Declines were particularly large for assault victimization, bullying, and sexual victimization. There were also significant declines in the perpetration of violence and property crime."

There are surely many causes for the mainstreaming of helicopter parenting. Kids cost a hell of a lot to raise. The U.S. Department of Agriculture figures a child born in 2013 will set back middle-income parents about $245,000 up to age 17 (and that's before college bills kick in). We're having fewer children, so we're putting fewer eggs in a smaller basket, so to speak. According to the Reason-Rupe poll, only 27% of adults thought the media were overestimating threats to the day-to-day safety of children, suggesting that 73% of us are suckers for sensationalistic news coverage that distorts reality (62% of us erroneously think that today's youth face greater dangers than previous generations). More kids are in institutional settings — whether preschool or school itself — at earlier ages, so maybe parents just assume someone will always be on call.

But whatever the reasons for our insistence that we childproof the world around us, this way madness lies. From *King Lear* to *Mildred Pierce*, classic literature (and basic common sense) suggests that coddling kids is no way to raise thriving, much less grateful, offspring. Indeed, quite the opposite. And with 58% of millennials calling *themselves* "entitled" and more than 70% saying they are "selfish," older Americans may soon be learning that lesson the hard way.

Topics for Critical Thinking and Writing

1. In paragraphs 4 and 5, Nick Gillespie cites a number of statistics indicating support for restrictions on when and where children can be on their own. He ends paragraph 4 with the statement, "Unless you live on a traffic island or a war zone, that's just nuts." Does the dismissive tone of that statement undercut Gillespie's argument? In your opinion, what would have been a more convincing response to parental concerns about their children's safety?

2. Gillespie states in paragraph 6 that contrary to popular belief, "children are safer than ever." He cites a study that shows the decline in violence against children over the past decade. What does Gillespie suggest are the reasons that popular perceptions of danger toward children have increased? Do you agree with his argument? Why, or why not?

3. Gillespie's final paragraph ends with an implied threat: Children who have been coddled will grow up to be selfish adults who will ignore the needs of their parents when they reach their senior years. Do you agree with Gillespie's assessment? Why, or why not?

Analyzing a Visual: Overparenting

Topics for Critical Thinking and Writing

1. Explain the visual metaphor presented in this image as extensively as you can. What does the image suggest about parents? What does it suggest about children? Is the image effective? How?

2. Provide a reading of the image above that negotiates the meaning of intended message (see Chapter 4, p. 152). To do this, account for some of the ways the image shown overstates the problem or ignores aspects of parenting that are important to children's development.

3. Make a list (on your own or collaboratively) of as many things you can think of that parents "do" for their children's benefit, protection, or well-being. Which items on your list might be considered reasonable, and which might be considered too much parenting? Discuss, or pick one you think is "overparenting" and tell why.

ALFIE KOHN

Alfie Kohn (b. 1957) has made a career of being a critic of conventional wisdom regarding education, parenting, and human behavior. In his many books, Kohn has argued against the use of grades, standardized testing, homework, values education, conventional parenting and discipline practices, and even workplace incentives. This excerpt is from his recent book, The Myth of the Spoiled Child: Challenging the Conventional Wisdom about Children and Parenting *(2014).*

The One-Sided Culture War against Children

Have a look at the unsigned editorials in left-of-center newspapers, or essays by columnists whose politics are mostly progressive. Listen to speeches by liberal public officials. On any of the controversial issues of our day, from tax policy to civil rights, you'll find approximately what you'd expect.

But when it comes to schooling and education, almost all of them take a hard-line position very much like what we hear from conservatives. In education, they endorse a top-down, corporate-style version of school reform that includes prescriptive, one-size-fits-all teaching standards and curriculum mandates; weakened job protection for teachers; frequent standardized testing; and a reliance on rewards and punishments to raise scores on those tests and compel compliance on the part of teachers and students.

Admittedly, there is some disagreement about the proper role of the federal government in all of this — and also about the extent to which public schooling should be privatized — but otherwise, liberal Democrats and conservative Republicans, the *New York Times* and the *Daily Oklahoman*, sound the identical themes of "accountability," "raising the bar" and "global competitiveness" (meaning that education is conceived primarily in economic terms). President Barack Obama didn't just continue George W. Bush's education policies; he intensified them, piling the harsh test-driven mandates of a program called "Race to the Top" on the harsh test-driven mandates of "No Child Left Behind."

Applause for this agenda has come not only from corporate America but also from both sides of the aisle in Congress and every major media outlet in the United States. Indeed, the generic phrase "school reform" has come to be equated with these specific get-tough policies. To object to them is to risk being labeled a defender of the "status quo," even though they have defined the status quo for some time now.

Many of the people who have objected are 5 teachers and other education experts who see firsthand just how damaging this approach has been, particularly to low-income students and the schools that serve them. But a key element of "reform" is to define educators as part of the problem, so their viewpoint has mostly been dismissed.

What's true of attitudes about education is also largely true of the way we think about children in general — what they're like and how they should be raised. Of course, politicians are far less likely to speak (or newspapers to editorialize) about parenting. But columnists do weigh in from time to time and, when they do, those who are generally liberal — like the *New York Times*' Frank Bruni, the *Boston Globe*'s Scot Lehigh and the late William Raspberry of the *Washington Post* — once again do a remarkable imitation of conservatives. Articles about parenting in general-interest periodicals, meanwhile, reflect the same trend. The range of viewpoints on other topics gives way to a stunningly consistent perspective where children are concerned.

That perspective sounds something like this:

- We live in an age of indulgence in which permissive parents refuse to set limits for, or say no to, their children.

- Parents overprotect their kids rather than let them suffer the natural consequences of their own mistakes. Children would benefit from experiencing failure, but their parents are afraid to let that happen.

- Adults are so focused on making kids feel special that we're raising a generation of entitled narcissists. They get trophies even when their team didn't win; they're praised even when they didn't do anything impressive; and they receive A's for whatever they turn in at school. Alas, they'll be in for a rude awakening once they get out into the unforgiving real world.

- What young people need — and lack — is not self-esteem but self-discipline: the ability to defer gratification, control their impulses and persevere at tasks over long periods of time.

These "traditionalist" convictions (for lack of a better word) are heard everywhere and repeated endlessly. Taken together, they have become our society's conventional wisdom about children, to the point that whenever a newspaper or magazine addresses any of these topics, it will almost always be from this direction. If the subject is self-esteem, the thesis will be that children have an oversupply. If the subject is discipline (and limits imposed by parents), the writer will insist that kids today get too little. And perseverance or "grit" is always portrayed positively, never examined skeptically.

This widespread adoption of a traditionalist perspective helps us to make sense of the fact that, on topics related to children, even liberals tend to hold positions whose premises are deeply conservative. Perhaps it works the other way around as well: The fact that people on the left and center find themselves largely in agreement with those on the right explains how the traditionalist viewpoint has become the conventional wisdom. Child rearing might be described as a hidden front in the culture wars, except that no one is fighting on the other side.

Writing a book about the conventional wisdom on childrearing, I've had to track down research studies on the relevant issues so as to be able to distinguish truth from myth. But I've also come across dozens of articles in the popular press, articles with titles like "Spoiled Rotten: Why Do Kids Rule the Roost?" (*New Yorker*, 7/2/12), "How to Land Your Kid in Therapy" (*Atlantic*, 6/7/11), "Just Say No: Why Parents Must Set Limits for Kids Who Want It All" (*Newsweek*, 9/12/04), "Parents and Children: Who's in Charge Here?" (*Time*, 8/6/01), "The Child Trap: The Rise of Overparenting" (*New Yorker* again, 11/17/08), "The Abuse of Overparenting" (*Psychology Today*, 4/2/12), "The Trouble with Self-Esteem," (*New York Times Magazine*, 2/3/12) and "Millennials: The Me Me Me Generation" (*Time* again, 5/9/13), to name just a few.

If you've read one of these articles, you've pretty much read all of them. The same goes for newspaper columns, blog posts and books on the same themes. Pick any one of them at random and the first thing you'll notice is that it treats a diverse assortment of complaints as if they're interchangeable. Parents are criticized for hovering and also for being too lax (with no acknowledgment that these are two very different things). In one sentence, kids are said to have too many toys; in the next, they're accused of being disrespectful. Or unmotivated. Or self-centered.

Anything that happens to annoy the writer may be tossed into the mix. Kids are exposed to too many ads! Involved in too many extra-curricular activities! Distracted by too much technology! They're too materialistic and individualistic and narcissistic — probably because they were raised by parents who are pushy, permissive, progressive. (If the writer is an academic, a single label may be used to organize the indictment — "intensive parenting" or "nurturance overload," for example — but a bewildering variety of phenomena are offered as examples.)

In fact, the generalizations offered in these books and articles sometimes seem not merely varied but contradictory. We're told that parents push their children too hard to excel (by ghostwriting their homework and hiring tutors, and demanding that they triumph over their peers), but also that parents try to protect kids from competition (by giving trophies to everyone), that expectations have declined, that too much attention is paid to making children happy.

Similarly, young adults are described as self-satisfied twits — more pleased with themselves than their accomplishments merit — but also as being so miserable that they're in therapy. Or there's an epidemic of helicopter parenting, even though parents are so focused on their gadgets that they ignore their children. The assumption seems to be that readers will just nod right along, failing to note any inconsistencies, as long as the tone is derogatory and the perspective is traditionalist.

Rarely are any real data cited — either about the prevalence of what's being described or the catastrophic effects being alleged. Instead, writers tend to rely primarily on snarky anecdotes, belaboring them to give the impression that these carefully chosen examples are representative of the general population, along with quotes from authors who accept and restate the writer's thesis about permissive parents and entitled kids who have never experienced failure.

Oddly, though, even as these writers repeat what everyone else is saying, they present themselves as courageous contrarians who are boldly challenging the conventional wisdom.

Perhaps the experience of reading all those articles — sloppy, contradictory or unpersuasive though they may be — wouldn't have been so irritating if it were also possible to find essays that questioned the dominant assumptions, essays that might have been titled "The New Puritanism: Who Really Benefits When Children Are Trained to Put Work before Play?" or "Why Parents Are So Controlling… and How It Harms Their Kids" or "The Invention of 'Helicopter Parenting': Creating a Crisis out of Thin Air." If anything along these lines has appeared in a mainstream publication, I've been unable to locate it.

The numbing uniformity of writings on children and parenting, and the lack of critical inspection on which the consensus rests, is troubling in itself. When countless publications offer exactly the same indictment of spoiled children and entitled Millennials — and accuse their parents of being lax or indulgent — this has a very real impact on the popular consciousness, just as a barrage of attack ads, no matter how misleading, can succeed in defining a political candidate in the minds of voters. But of course what matters more than whether a consensus exists is whether it makes sense, whether there's any merit to the charges.

Consider the accusation that parents involve themselves too closely in their children's lives and don't allow them to fail. It's common to come across — in fact, it's hard to avoid — hyperbolic references in the media to "kids who leave for college without ever having crossed the street by themselves" (*New York Times*, 2/9/09) and "'Lawnmower Parents' [who] have 'mowed down' so many obstacles (including interfering at their children's workplaces,

regarding salaries and promotions) that these kids have actually never faced failure" (*Business Insider*, 8/17/12). Just in the few years before my book went to press in 2013, articles about over-parenting appeared in the *Atlantic* (1/29/13), the *New Yorker* (11/17/08), *Time* (11/30/09), *Psychology Today* (4/2/12), *Boston Magazine* (12/11) and countless newspapers and blogs.

In each case, just as with condemnations [20] of permissiveness, the phenomenon being attacked is simply assumed to be pervasive; there's no need to prove what everyone knows. The spread of overparenting is vigorously condemned by journalists and social critics, but mostly on the basis of anecdotes and quotations from other journalists and social critics. On the relatively rare occasions when a writer invokes research in support of the claim that overparenting is widespread (or damaging), it's instructive to track down the study itself to see what it actually says.

A case in point: In 2013, several prominent American blogs, including those sponsored by the *Atlantic* (1/29/13) and the *New York Times* (1/25/13), reported an Australian study purportedly showing that parents were excessively involved in their children's schooling. But anyone who took the time to actually read the study realized that the authors had just asked a handpicked group of local educators to tell stories about parents whom they personally believed were doing too much for their children. There were no data about what impact, if any, this practice had on the kids, nor was there any way to draw conclusions about how common the practice was — at least beyond this small, presumably unrepresentative sample.

More remarkably, only 27 percent of the educators in the sample report having seen "many" examples of this sort of overinvolved parenting. (This low number somehow did not make it into any of the press coverage.) If anything, the effect of the study was to raise doubts about the assumption that overparenting is a widespread problem. But the study's very existence allowed bloggers to recycle a few anecdotes, giving the appearance that fresh evidence supported what they (and many of their readers) already believed.

Another example: In 2010, Lisa Belkin, a writer for the *New York Times Magazine*, devoted a blog post (7/19/10) to an article in a California law review (*UC Davis Law Review*, 4/12/10) that declared a tilt toward excess "has dominated parenting in the last two decades." But how did the authors of the law review article substantiate this remarkable assertion? They included a footnote that referenced a 2009 *New York Times Magazine* column (5/29/09) written by . . . Lisa Belkin.

It's striking that evidence on this topic is so scarce that academic journals must rely on opinion pieces in the popular press. But in this case, the popular press was actually claiming that the trend had already peaked. That was true not only of Belkin's column ("Could the era of overparenting be over?") but of a *Time* cover story ("The Growing Backlash against Overparenting," 11/20/09) that was cited by an essay in another academic journal. The latter essay began with the sweeping (and rather tautological[1]) statement that an "epidemic" of overparenting was "running rampant" — which is exactly what its sources claimed was no longer true.

So who's right? There are, as far as I can tell, no good data to show that most parents do too much for their children. It's all impressionistic, anecdotal and, like most announcements of trends, partly self-fulfilling.

------

[1]**tautological** Needlessly repetitive. [Editors' note.]

Topics for Critical Thinking and Writing

1. In the opening paragraphs of this excerpt, Alfie Kohn argues that otherwise liberal writers and public officials have taken conservative or "traditionalist" positions when it comes to the subject of raising children. Why does the fact that many liberals and conservatives are in agreement on this issue bother Kohn? What alternatives, if any, does he propose?

2. In paragraph 7, Kohn presents a bullet-point list of common observations that older Americans make about children and young adults today. Do you agree with the statements in the list? Why, or why not?

3. In paragraph 8, Kohn argues that values such as "perseverance or 'grit'" have not been examined skeptically. In what ways might "grit" be bad? Be specific in your response.

4. In paragraph 15, Kohn comments that most of the conclusions about children these days are not based on data but on "snarky anecdotes." What is the problem with anecdotal information? In contrast, what problems could there be with data-based research about attitudes and values? How can the limitations of either approach be solved, if indeed they can?

5. In what ways are the commentators about how today's children are raised contradictory? What can account for the apparent contradictions? In particular, to what does Kohn ascribe these contradictions?

17

Genetic Modification of Human Beings: Is It Acceptable?

RONALD M. GREEN

Ronald M. Green teaches in the Department of Religion at Dartmouth College, where he is the director of the Ethics Institute. He is the author of several books, including Babies by Design: The Ethics of Genetic Choice *(2007). This article was posted online at washingtonpost.com on April 1, 2008.*

Building Baby from the Genes Up

The two British couples no doubt thought that their appeal for medical help in conceiving a child was entirely reasonable. Over several generations, many female members of their families had died of breast cancer. One or both spouses in each couple had probably inherited the genetic mutations for the disease, and they wanted to use in-vitro fertilization and preimplantation genetic diagnosis (PGD) to select only the healthy embryos for implantation. Their goal was to eradicate breast cancer from their family lines once and for all.

In the United States, this combination of reproductive and genetic medicine — what one scientist has dubbed "reprogenetics" — remains largely unregulated, but Britain has a formal agency, the Human Fertilization and Embryology Authority (HFEA), that must approve all requests for PGD. In July 2007, after considerable deliberation, the HFEA approved the procedure for both families. The concern was not about the use of PGD to avoid genetic disease, since embryo screening for serious disorders is commonplace now on both sides of the Atlantic. What troubled the HFEA was the fact that an embryo carrying the cancer mutation could go on to live for forty or fifty years before ever developing cancer, and there was a chance it might never develop. Did this warrant selecting and discarding embryos? To its critics, the HFEA, in approving this request, crossed a bright line separating legitimate medical genetics from the quest for "the perfect baby."

Like it or not, that decision is a sign of things to come — and not necessarily a bad sign. Since the completion of the Human Genome Project in 2003, our understanding of the genetic bases of human disease and non-disease traits has been growing almost exponentially. The National Institutes of Health has initiated a quest for the "$1,000 genome," a ten-year program to develop machines that could identify all the genetic letters in anyone's genome at low cost (it took more than $3 billion to sequence the first human genome). With this technology, which some believe may be just four or five years away, we could not only scan an individual's — or embryo's — genome, we could also rapidly compare thousands of people and pinpoint those DNA sequences or combinations that underlie the variations that contribute to our biological differences.

With knowledge comes power. If we understand the genetic causes of obesity, for example, we can intervene by means of embryo selection to produce a child with a reduced genetic likelihood of getting fat. Eventually, without discarding embryos at all, we could use gene-targeting techniques to tweak fetal DNA sequences. No child would have to face a lifetime of dieting or experience the health and cosmetic problems associated with obesity. The same is true for cognitive problems such as dyslexia. Geneticists have already identified some of the mutations that contribute to this disorder. Why should a child struggle with reading difficulties when we could alter the genes responsible for the problem?

Many people are horrified at the thought of such uses of genetics, seeing echoes of the 1997 science-fiction film *Gattaca*, which depicted a world where parents choose their children's traits. Human weakness has been eliminated through genetic engineering, and the few parents who opt for a "natural" conception run the risk of producing offspring — "invalids" or "degenerates" — who become members of a despised underclass. Gattaca's world is clean and efficient, but its eugenic obsessions have all but extinguished human love and compassion.

These fears aren't limited to fiction. Over the past few years, many bioethicists have spoken out against genetic manipulations. The critics tend to voice at least four major concerns. First, they worry about the effect of genetic selection on parenting. Will our ability to choose our children's biological inheritance lead parents to replace unconditional love with a consumerist mentality that seeks perfection?

Second, they ask whether gene manipulations will diminish our freedom by making us creatures of our genes or our parents' whims. In his book *Enough*, the techno-critic Bill McKibben asks: If I am a world-class runner, but my parents inserted the "Sweatworks2010 GenePack" in my genome, can I really feel pride in my accomplishments? Worse, if I refuse to use my costly genetic endowments, will I face relentless pressure to live up to my parents' expectations?

Third, many critics fear that reproductive genetics will widen our social divisions as the affluent "buy" more competitive abilities for their offspring. Will we eventually see "speciation," the emergence of two or more human populations so different that they no longer even breed with one another? Will we re-create the horrors of eugenics that led, in Europe, Asia, and the United States, to the sterilization of tens of thousands of people declared to be "unfit" and that in Nazi Germany paved the way for the Holocaust?

Finally, some worry about the religious implications of this technology. Does it amount to a forbidden and prideful "playing God"?

To many, the answers to these questions are clear. Not long ago, when I asked a large class at Dartmouth Medical School whether they thought that we should move in the direction of human genetic engineering, more than 80 percent said no. This squares with public opinion polls that show a similar degree of opposition. Nevertheless, "babies by design" are probably in our future—but I think that the critics' concerns may be less troublesome than they first appear.

Will critical scrutiny replace parental love? Not likely. Even today, parents who hope for a healthy child but have one born with disabilities tend to love that child ferociously. The very intensity of parental love is the best protection against its erosion by genetic technologies. Will a child somehow feel less free because parents have helped select his or her traits? The fact is that a child is already remarkably influenced by the genes she inherits. The difference is that we haven't taken control of the process. Yet.

Knowing more about our genes may actually increase our freedom by helping us understand the biological obstacles — and opportunities — we have to work with. Take the case of Tiger Woods. His father, Earl, is said to have handed him a golf club when he was still in the playpen. Earl probably also gave Tiger the genes for some of the traits that help make him a champion golfer. Genes and upbringing worked together to inspire excellence. Does Tiger feel less free because of his inherited abilities? Did he feel pressured by his parents? I doubt it. Of course, his story could have gone the other way, with overbearing parents forcing a child into their mold. But the problem in that case wouldn't be genetics, but bad parenting.

Granted, the social effects of reproductive genetics are worrisome. The risks of producing a "genobility," genetic overlords ruling a vast genetic underclass, are real. But genetics could also become a tool for reducing the class divide. Will we see the day when perhaps all youngsters are genetically vaccinated against dyslexia? And how might this contribute to everyone's social betterment?

As for the question of intruding on God's domain, the answer is less clear than the critics believe. The use of genetic medicine to cure or prevent disease is widely accepted by religious traditions, even those that oppose discarding embryos. Speaking in 1982 at the Pontifical Academy of Sciences, Pope John Paul II observed that modern biological research "can ameliorate the condition of those who are affected by chromosomic diseases," and he lauded this as helping to cure "the smallest and weakest of human beings . . . during their intrauterine life or in the period immediately after birth." For Catholicism and some other traditions, it is one thing to cure disease, but another to create children who are faster runners, longer-lived, or smarter.

But why should we think that the human genome is a once-and-for-all-finished, untamperable product? All of the biblically derived faiths permit human beings to improve on nature using technology, from agriculture to aviation. Why not improve our genome? I have no doubt that most people considering these questions for the first time are certain that human genetic improvement is a bad idea, but I'd like to shake up that certainty.

Genomic science is racing toward a future in which foreseeable improvements include reduced susceptibility to a host of diseases, increased life span, better cognitive functioning, and maybe even cosmetic enhancements such as whiter, straighter teeth. Yes, genetic orthodontics may be in our future. The challenge is to see that we don't also unleash the demons of discrimination and oppression. Although I acknowledge the risks, I believe that we can and will incorporate gene technology into the ongoing human adventure.

Topics for Critical Thinking and Writing

1. By the end of paragraph 2, did you think that the British are probably right to be cautious, to require approval for all requests for PGD? Explain your position.

2. Paragraph 4 talks, by way of example, about avoiding obesity and "cognitive problems." At this stage in your reading of the essay, did you find yourself saying "Great, let's go for it," or were you thinking "Wait a minute"? Why, or why not?

3. Do paragraphs 5 and 6 pretty much set forth your own response? If not, what *is* your response?

4. Does Bill McKibben's view, mentioned in paragraph 7, represent your view? If not, what would you say to McKibben?

5. If you are a believer in any of "the biblically derived faiths," does the comment in paragraph 15 allay whatever doubts you may have had about the acceptability of human genetic improvement? Explain.

6. In his final paragraph, Ronald Green says, "I acknowledge the risks." Are you satisfied that he does acknowledge them adequately? Explain.

Analyzing a Visual: Genetic Modification of Human Beings

Caroline Purser/Getty Images

Topics for Critical Thinking and Writing

1. What does this photograph seem to say about human genetic modification? Why do you think the photographer included a bar code in the image? In a couple of paragraphs, evaluate this photo's effectiveness.

2. Do you agree with the point of view expressed in the photograph? In 250 words, write up a description of a photograph that might work as a rebuttal to this one.

RICHARD HAYES

Born in 1945, Richard Hayes is executive director of the Center for Genetics and Society, an organization that describes itself as "working to encourage responsible uses and effective society governance of the new human genetic and reproductive technologies. . . . The Center supports benign and beneficent medical applications of the new human genetic and reproductive technologies, and opposes those applications that objectify and commodify human life and threaten to divide human society."

This reprinted essay originally appeared in the Washington Post *on April 15, 2008.*

Genetically Modified Humans? No Thanks

In an essay in Sunday's Outlook section, Dartmouth ethics professor Ronald Green asks us to consider a neoeugenic future of "designer babies," with parents assembling their children quite literally from genes selected from a catalogue. Distancing himself from the compulsory, state-sponsored eugenics that darkened the first half of the last century, Green instead celebrates the advent of a libertarian, consumer-driven eugenics motivated by the free play of human desire, technology, and markets. He argues that this vision of the human future is desirable and very likely inevitable.

To put it mildly: I disagree. Granted, new human genetic technologies have real potential to help prevent or cure many terrible diseases, and I support research directed towards that end. But these same technologies also have the potential for real harm. If misapplied, they would exacerbate existing inequalities and reinforce existing modes of discrimination. If

more widely abused, they could undermine the foundations of civil and human rights. In the worst case, they could undermine our experience of being part of a single human community with a common human future.

Once we begin genetically modifying our children, where do we stop? If it's acceptable to modify one gene, why not two, or twenty or two hundred? At what point do children become artifacts designed to someone's specifications rather than members of a family to be nurtured?

Given what we know about human nature, the development and commercial marketing of human genetic modification would likely spark a techno-eugenic rat-race. Even parents opposed to manipulating their children's genes would feel compelled to participate in this race, lest their offspring be left behind.

Green proposes that eugenic technologies 5 could be used to reduce "the class divide." But nowhere in his essay does he suggest how such a proposal might ever be made practicable in the real world.

The danger of genetic misuse is equally threatening at the international level. What happens when some rogue country announces an ambitious program to "improve the genetic stock" of its citizens? In a world still barely able to contain the forces of nationalism, ethnocentrism, and militarism, the last thing we need to worry about is a high-tech eugenic arms race.

In his essay, Green doesn't distinguish clearly between different uses of genetic technology — and the distinctions are critical. It's one thing to enable a couple to avoid passing on a devastating genetic condition, such as Tay-Sachs.[1] But it's a different thing altogether to create children with a host of "enhanced" athletic, cosmetic, and cognitive traits that could be passed to their own children, who in turn could further genetically modify their children, who in turn . . . you get the picture. It's this second use of gene technology (the technical term is "heritable genetic enhancement") that Green most fervently wants us to embrace.

In this position, Green is well outside the growing national and international consensus on the proper use of human genetic science and technology. To his credit, he acknowledges that 80 percent of the medical school students

_____
[1]**Tay-Sachs** A progressive disorder that destroys nerve neurons in the brain and spinal cord. [Editors' note.]

he surveyed said they were against such forms of human genetic engineering, and that public opinion polls show equally dramatic opposition. He could have noted, as well, that nearly forty countries — including Brazil, Canada, France, Germany, India, Japan, and South Africa — have adopted socially responsible policies regulating the new human genetic technologies. They allow genetic research (including stem cell research) for medical applications, but prohibit its use for heritable genetic modification and reproductive human cloning.

In the face of this consensus, Green blithely announces his confidence that humanity "can and will" incorporate heritable genetic enhancement into the "ongoing human adventure."

Well, it's certainly possible. Our desires for good looks, good brains, wealth and long lives, for ourselves and for our children, are strong and enduring. If the gene-tech entrepreneurs are able to convince us that we can satisfy these desires by buying into genetic modification, perhaps we'll bite. Green certainly seems eager to encourage us to do so.

But he would be wise to listen to what medical students, the great majority of Americans, and the international community appear to be saying: We want all these things, yes, and genetic technology might help us attain them, but we don't want to run the huge risks to the human community and the human future that would come with altering the genetic basis of our common human nature.

Topics for Critical Thinking and Writing

1. Do you believe that in his first paragraph, Richard Hayes fairly summarizes Green's essay? If your answer is no, what are your objections?

2. Does the prospect raised in paragraph 6 frighten you? Why, or why not?

3. In his final paragraph, Hayes speaks of "huge risks." What are these risks? Are you willing to take them? Why, or why not?

18

Mandatory Military Service: Should It Be Required?

CHARLES RANGEL

Charles Rangel (b. 1930), from Harlem, New York, is a Korean War veteran who has served in the House of Representatives for over four decades. A Democrat, Rangel has been an outspoken voice for civil rights and social justice. This article, in which he argues in favor of a universal national service requirement, initially appeared in the January/February 2013 issue of the Saturday Evening Post.

The Draft Would Compel Us to Share the Sacrifice

On a freezing night in November of 1950, I found myself and dozens of fellow soldiers marching along the icy banks of the Ch'ongch'on River amid the cracks of mortar fire and the glints of Chinese bayonets. The war in Korea was in full force, and my battalion was retreating because our vehicle column had sustained an attack. After a three-day nightmarish trek through enemy territory, 40 of us escaped. In the battles around Kunu-ri, more than 5,000 American soldiers were killed, wounded, or captured. Ninety percent of my unit was killed.

When we returned home, many of my comrades were haunted by memories of their combat experience. They were consumed with guilt, couldn't sleep or function in their jobs,

and became severely depressed. In short, they developed "shell shock," or what today we call post-traumatic stress disorder or PTSD. Following the lead of generations of soldiers, most of them suffered in silence, did not seek treatment, and never got better.

Today, we have the awareness and the resources to protect our troops from PTSD. We now know that prolonged exposure to combat is a primary cause of this affliction. A 2008 Army Surgeon General's study confirmed that more tours of duty mean a greater risk of PTSD for soldiers. Twelve percent of soldiers on their first deployment suffer mental health problems, compared to 27 percent of those on their third and fourth tours. Moreover, suicide rates among veterans of the Iraq and Afghanistan Wars are approximately three times higher than in the general population. Yet we subject our troops to more cumulative months of combat than ever before, with shorter rest periods in between.

During Vietnam, almost no Americans were required to serve more than a single tour of duty overseas, although some volunteered for more. In Iraq and Afghanistan, however, nearly half of all soldiers are sent on multiple combat tours — sometimes as many as four. These are separated by reprieves that constantly shift in length, but are always too short to allow for substantive mental health treatment.

This is the inevitable result of having less 5 than 1 percent of our population carry the burden of war for the remaining 99 percent. More than 15 million registered for the Selective Service System; only 1.4 million are on active duty. This explains why 300,000 veterans of the Iraq and Afghanistan wars — nearly 20 percent of the returning forces — suffer from PTSD or major depression. It is not fair or morally defensible to saddle the brave Americans who volunteer for the Armed Forces with tours of duty that expand in length and frequency as our conflicts intensify.

As a nation we should ask ourselves how we can protect our troops' mental health while maintaining our national defense. Two years of civil service from all U.S. residents would allow us to meet both of these goals. Our military ranks would swell and there would be no need to demand repeated service from our troops. That is why I continue to call for Universal National Service, which would mandate a two-year service requirement for Americans ages 18 to 25. While my "draft" bill is unlikely to become law, it is important that we open a national conversation about how we can all share in the sacrifice for our country.

Requiring two years of service from everyone would compel us to rethink how and why we send young Americans into harm's way. Too few of the country's leaders have a personal stake in the well-being of the Armed Forces, and the outcome is predictable. Since the end of the draft in 1973, every president, Democrat and Republican alike, has approached warfare with the mind-set of invading, occupying, and expanding our nation's influence. It was this attitude that got us into the unnecessary and costly wars in Iraq and Afghanistan and that threatens to mire us in deadly wars in the future. We make decisions about war without worry over who fights them. Those who do the fighting have no choice; when the flag goes up, they salute and follow orders.

A universal service mandate would do more than deter future military entanglements. As shown in a report by the Congressional Budget Office, most of our volunteer troops come from economically depressed urban and rural areas. We have developed, in effect, a mercenary army. In New York City, an overwhelming majority of volunteers are black or Hispanic, recruited from lower income communities such as the South Bronx, East New York, and Long Island City. These enlistees are enticed by bonuses up to $40,000 and thousands in educational benefits.

Military service is a privilege, and it should not be shouldered only by those for whom the economic benefits justify great personal risk. If young men and women of all races and socioeconomic statuses served together, our citizens would come to share or at least understand one another's values, points of view, and beliefs. Empathy and mutual respect would provide a much-needed antidote to the cynicism that today's youth feel because of the extreme partisanship in Washington.

A universal national service requirement, 10 even if it does not mandate enlistment in the Armed Forces, is the one mechanism we know will truly protect our troops, unify the nation, and bring fairness to our military. Furthermore, it will season our future leaders with the harrowing realities of war, ensuring that they will never commit our troops to the battlefield unless they are willing to send their own children.

Topics for Critical Thinking and Writing

1. What is the effect of Charles Rangel starting his argument about national service with a recounting of a harrowing experience during the Korean War? How does recounting the incident serve as a way to introduce his overall argument?

2. How is the comparison to the experiences of Vietnam veterans appropriate for a discussion of the experiences of veterans of the conflicts in Iraq and Afghanistan? What conclusion does Rangel draw from the difference?

3. In paragraph 6, Rangel proposes that all U.S. residents should be required to give two years of civil service. What points does he use to specifically support such a proposal? Do you agree with his proposal or not? Why, or why not?

4. Consider that in paragraph 6 Rangel concedes that his proposal "is unlikely to become law." Yet he doesn't specifically address the reasons why, or offer rebuttal arguments to those who oppose a draft. What does this say about the strength, or weakness, of Rangel's own arguments? How might you have approached supporting his argument differently?

5. Much of Rangel's argument rests on the idea that the nation needs to share the burden of military service across a broader spectrum of society. He points out in paragraph 5 that less than 1 percent of the population is at any one time serving in the military. What does Rangel argue is the effect of this? Do you agree or disagree? Why?

Analyzing a Visual: Military Recruiting

Topics for Critical Thinking and Writing

1. If you had to guess at the approximate date this poster was created, what year would you guess? What elements in the image helped you estimate? What knowledge of your own did you bring to your guess?

2. To whom is this image speaking (who is the "you" in the context of this image's production)? Who exactly does Uncle Sam want in the U.S. Army (and who does he not want)?

3. Find one or two current images or advertisements that address "you" as the viewer and consider who is included and excluded by the usage of the pronoun "you."

4. Compare an Army recruitment poster or print advertisement from today with the Uncle Sam image. How is it different? What appeals does it make to encourage enlistment?

JAMES LACEY

James Lacey (b. 1958) holds a degree in history from the Citadel and a Ph.D. from Leeds University in military history. He has written extensively about military and financial issues, and is a professor of strategic studies at the Marine Corps University in Quantico, Virginia. This article, in which he argues against a universal national service requirement, initially appeared in the January/February 2013 issue of the Saturday Evening Post.

We Need Trained Soldiers, Not a Horde of Draftees

Thanks to Rep. Charles B. Rangel, the recurring question of whether to reinstate the draft has been thrust to the front of the public-policy debate. Those calling for a renewed draft have a variety of arguments at their disposal. These range from the high cost of payrolls and recruiting to building a common experience in our youth that will bind us together as a nation. Under close examination, none of them holds a lot of water.

The best reason for not calling for a draft is that no member of the combined Joint Chiefs of Staff is asking for one. These are the men responsible for protecting our country and ensuring that our armed forces are fully prepared to meet any potential enemy. It is a trust that these men take very seriously. After 10 years of war they are intimately acquainted with the kind of army the nation needs to meet the uncertainties of the future. All of these senior officers came of age in the wreckage of the post-Vietnam military. They saw first-hand the ruinous effects a large draft force can have when there is no national emergency to justify the call to arms. These men built from the bottom up the professional military that has not lost a single engagement in a generation. If they prefer a highly trained professional force over a large influx of half-trained, short-serving draftees the nation would do well to heed their advice.

If the Joint Chiefs do not want a draft, there had better be a good reason to force one on them. The congressman claims that we need a draft to ensure that the burden of any future conflict is shared by all and does not fall primarily on the poor and on minorities. This is an old canard that he trots out from time to time to make his fellow legislators feel guilty about voting to commit military force. Disproportionate military losses among minorities is a myth that began in the Vietnam era and is a total fabrication. Minorities did not die in Vietnam or in any conflict thereafter in any greater numbers than they are represented in the population. And, with the exception of 1966, the exact opposite has been the case. Blacks made up 12 percent of the deaths in Vietnam, 13.1 percent of the U.S. population, and almost 11 percent of our troops in Vietnam. Whites (including Hispanics) made up 86.4 percent of those who served in Vietnam and 88 percent of those who died there. The highest rate of black deaths in Vietnam was 16.3 percent (in 1966) — and almost all of those killed that year were volunteers for elite units, not reluctant draftees.

That still leaves open the question of whether our military is composed mostly of economic refugees. The evidence says no. Virtually every member of the armed forces has a high-school diploma, in contrast to 79 percent of the comparable youth population. Practically all new recruits place in the top three intellect categories (as measured by the Armed Forces Qualification Test), versus 69 percent of their civilian counterparts. New soldiers also read at a higher level than their civilian counterparts. Overall, the U.S. military closely reflects the makeup of our large middle class.

The real moral danger of a draft is that 5 it will provide so many troops that there might be a temptation to waste them in useless engagements. This is what history has demonstrated over and over again. The bloody charges into massed rifles during the Civil War could not have been sustained without a draft to replace those slaughtered. In World War I, British Prime Minister David Lloyd George actually began holding back reinforcements so that his generals could not waste their lives in another big-push offensive. Finally, does anyone think the useless carnage of Vietnam could have continued year after year if we had a volunteer force?

Furthermore, those who are calling for a draft fail to recognize that war has changed dramatically in the past three decades. A high-technology force conducting incredibly rapid operations requires well-trained professionals, not short-term draftees. An army of draftees would be little more than cannon fodder for any advanced force to chew up. Moreover, in the complex counterinsurgency environments of Afghanistan and Iraq, success depends on sending long-serving professionals repeatedly back into situations in which they are intimately familiar. Sending a new crop of annual draftees into these countries would have translated into skyrocketing casualty lists and failure on the battlefield. The thoroughly trained and professional U.S. military is the most dominant battlefield force in the world, capable of winning a stand-up fight against any opponent. Our national policy makers may

misuse this force from time to time, but why would we ever put our military preeminence at risk in favor of a mass of half-trained grumbling draftees?

Then there is the cost. If we require every able-bodied male to serve 18 months to two years after he turns 18, then we are talking about inducting more than 1.5 million draftees a year. Equipping and training that force to even a reasonable standard would cost in the area of $3 trillion — and another $1 trillion a year to maintain it. Of course, no one is going to bankrupt the nation to build a military 10 times larger than what we currently need. This means that less than one in five of the eligible draftees would be needed or called.

Given that only a proportion of the eligible males would be called, anyone who thinks that the draft will remain a fair cross section of our society is living in a dream world. More likely the military would become even less representative of society as the rich and middle class would do whatever they had to in order to avoid contact with the "undesirable elements" who would be caught up in a draft. At present, recruiters seeking the highest-quality volunteers turn these undesirables away. As a former recruiting commander, I often lamented how many people we had to interview, physically examine, and test just to get one qualified applicant. Throughout my tenure, the ratio never fell below 14-to-1, though some other districts did a bit better. If the services lowered their standards even minimally, they could enlist their yearly goals by March and close their recruiting offices.

Some, including Rangel, make the argument that if the military cannot use all of the draftees, then they should be enlisted into some other form of national service. Has anyone thought about the size of the bureaucracy that would have to be created to mobilize, train, deploy, feed, house, and monitor several million 18 year olds every year? You would need a second army dedicated to doing nothing but keeping track of teenagers. Besides, what rational being believes that the federal government is the best organization for putting our youth to useful work? In no time at all our children will become pawns for whatever is the political flavor of the day.

As Doug Bandow states in his Cato Institute study of the draft, "A return to conscription 10 would yield a less experienced, less stable, and less efficient military. Inducement, not coercion, is the answer to sagging retention. Studies have consistently indicated that the most effective remedy is improved compensation." By taking care of our soldiers, using them only for critical missions, and ensuring that they have the best equipment and training available, we maintain a quality force, capable of defeating any enemies we may face in coming decades.

Topics for Critical Thinking and Writing

1. James Lacey appeals to the authority of the Joint Chiefs of Staff, the highest-level officers of the different military services, when he says that because they don't want a draft, there should be no draft. Lacey states in paragraph 2 that senior officers' experiences showed them "the ruinous effects a large draft force can have when there is no national emergency to justify the call to arms." In what ways does the experience of the Vietnam War argue against the use of the draft? If necessary, research that period of American military history to form your own conclusions.

2. Also in paragraph 2, Lacey uses the term "half-trained" to describe draftees called into service. What is the effect of using that term? How justified is Lacey in referring to draftees as half-trained? If necessary, do research to determine the training and effectiveness of a military built on the draft versus an all-volunteer force.

3. In paragraph 3, Lacey asserts that in 1966, "almost all [of black soldiers] killed that year were volunteers for elite units, not reluctant draftees." Research the truth of this claim. What does that say about the nature of deaths in the Vietnam War in 1966 based on race?

4. In paragraph 5, Lacey argues that having a draft might encourage military leaders to "waste" lives in "useless engagements." He cites evidence from the Civil War and the British use of forces during World War I. In your opinion, is this still a likely scenario? Why, or why not?

5. A prime aspect of Lacey's argument is that the military needs to rely on experienced professionals to fight today's battles, not "half-trained grumbling draftees" as he states in paragraph 6. Given that Charles Rangel argues that rates of PTSD increase as soldiers go on more and more tours, what sort of balance can be struck between the need for experience and the desire not to subject fighting men and women to unbearable wartime stress?

PART FIVE

Current Issues: Casebooks

19

A College Education: What Is Its Purpose?

ANDREW DELBANCO

Andrew Delbanco, born in 1952, teaches at Columbia University, where he is director of American Studies. We reprint an essay that first appeared in Parade, *a magazine-like supplement that is part of the Sunday edition of many newspapers, and then was published in Delbanco's book* College: What It Was, Is, and Should Be *(2012).*

3 Reasons College Still Matters

The American college is going through a period of wrenching change, buffeted by forces — globalization, economic instability, the information technology revolution, the increasingly evident inadequacy of K–12 education, and, perhaps most important, the collapse of consensus about what students should know — that make its task more difficult and contentious than ever before.

For a relatively few students, college remains the sort of place that Anthony Kronman, former dean of Yale Law School, recalls from his days at Williams, where his favorite class took place at the home of a philosophy professor whose two golden retrievers slept on either side of the fireplace "like bookends beside the hearth" while the sunset lit the Berkshire Hills "in scarlet and gold." For many more students, college means the anxious pursuit of marketable skills in overcrowded, underresourced institutions. For still others, it means traveling by night to a fluorescent office building or to a "virtual classroom" that only exists in cyberspace.

It is a pipe dream to imagine that every student can have the sort of experience that our richest colleges, at their best, provide. But it is a nightmare society that affords the chance to learn and grow only to the wealthy, brilliant, or lucky few. Many remarkable teachers in America's community colleges, unsung private colleges, and underfunded public colleges live this truth every day, working to keep the ideal of democratic education alive. And so it is my unabashed aim to articulate in my forthcoming book, *College: What It Was, Is, and Should Be*, what a college — any college — should seek to do for its students.

What, then, are today's prevailing answers to the question, what is college for? The most common answer is an economic one. It's clear that a college degree long ago supplanted the high school diploma as the minimum qualification for entry into the skilled labor market, and there is abundant evidence that people with a college degree earn more money over the course of their lives than people without one. Some estimates put the worth of a bachelor of arts degree at about a million dollars in incremental lifetime earnings.

For such economic reasons alone, it is 5 alarming that for the first time in history, we face the prospect that the coming generation of Americans will be less educated than its elders.

Within this gloomy general picture are some especially disturbing particulars. For one thing, flat or declining college attainment rates (relative to other nations) apply disproportionately to minorities, who are a growing portion of the American population. And financial means have a shockingly large bearing on educational opportunity, which, according to one authority, looks like this in today's America: If you are the child of a family making more than $90,000 per year, your odds of getting a BA by age twenty-four are roughly one in two; if your parents make less than $35,000, your odds are one in seventy.

Moreover, among those who do get to college, high-achieving students from affluent families are four times more likely to attend a selective college than students from poor families with comparable grades and test scores. Since prestigious colleges serve as funnels into leadership positions in business, law, and government, this means that our "best" colleges are doing more to foster than to retard the growth of inequality in our society. Yet colleges are still looked to as engines of social mobility in American life, and it would be shameful if they became, even more than they already are, a system for replicating inherited wealth.

Not surprisingly, as in any discussion of economic matters, one finds dissenters from the predominant view. Some on the right say that pouring more public investment into higher education, in the form of enhanced subsidies for individuals or institutions, is a bad idea. They argue against the goal of universal college education as a fond fantasy and, instead, for a sorting system such as one finds in European countries: vocational training for the low scorers, who will be the semiskilled laborers and functionaries; advanced education for the high scorers, who will be the diplomats and doctors.

Other thinkers, on the left, question whether the aspiration to go to college really makes sense for "low-income students who can least afford to spend money and years" on such a risky venture, given their low graduation rates and high debt. From this point of view, the "education gospel" seems a cruel distraction from "what really provides security to families and children: good jobs at fair wages, robust unions, affordable access to health care and transportation."

One can be on either side of these ques- 10 tions, or somewhere in the middle, and still believe in the goal of achieving universal college education. Consider an analogy from another sphere of public debate: health care. One sometimes hears that eliminating smoking would save untold billions because of the immense cost of caring for patients who develop lung cancer, emphysema, heart disease, or diabetes. It turns out, however, that reducing the incidence of disease by curtailing smoking may actually end up costing us more, since people who don't smoke live longer and eventually require expensive therapies for

expert testemency

example

chronic diseases and the inevitable infirmities of old age.

In other words, measuring the benefit as a social cost or gain does not quite get the point — or at least not the whole point. The best reason to end smoking is that people who don't smoke have a better chance to lead better lives. The best reason to care about college — who goes, and what happens to them when they get there — is not what it does for society in economic terms but what it can do for individuals, in both calculable and incalculable ways.

The second argument for the importance of college is a political one, though one rarely hears it from politicians. This is the argument on behalf of democracy. "The basis of our government," as Thomas Jefferson put the matter near the end of the eighteenth century, is "the opinion of the people." If the new republic was to flourish and endure, it required, above all, an educated citizenry.

This is more true than ever. All of us are bombarded every day with pleadings and persuasions — advertisements, political appeals, punditry of all sorts — designed to capture our loyalty, money, or, more narrowly, our vote. Some say health care reform will bankrupt the country, others that it is an overdue act of justice; some believe that abortion is the work of Satan, others think that to deny a woman the right to terminate an unwanted pregnancy is a form of abuse. The best chance we have to maintain a functioning democracy is a citizenry that can tell the difference between demagoguery and responsible arguments.

Education for democracy also implies something about what kind of education democratic citizens need. A very good case for college in this sense has been made recently by Kronman, the former Yale dean who now teaches in a Great Books program for Yale

undergraduates. In his book *Education's End*, Kronman argues for a course of study that introduces students to the constitutive ideas of Western culture, including, among many others, "the ideals of individual freedom and toleration," "a reliance on markets as a mechanism for the organization of economic life," and "an acceptance of the truths of modern science."

Anyone who earns a BA from a reputable college ought to understand something about the genealogy of these ideas and practices, about the historical processes from which they have emerged, the tragic cost when societies fail to defend them, and about alternative ideas both within the Western tradition and outside it. That's a tall order for anyone to satisfy on his or her own — and one of the marks of an educated person is the recognition that it can never be adequately done and is therefore all the more worth doing.

There is a third case for college, seldom heard, perhaps because it is harder to articulate without sounding platitudinous and vague. I first heard it stated in a plain and passionate way after I had spoken to an alumni group from Columbia, where I teach. The emphasis in my talk was on the Jeffersonian argument — education for citizenship. When I had finished, an elderly alumnus stood up and said more or less the following: "That's all very nice, professor, but you've missed the main point." With some trepidation, I asked him what that point might be. "Columbia," he said, "taught me how to enjoy life."

What he meant was that college had opened his senses as well as his mind to experiences that would otherwise be foreclosed to him. Not only had it enriched his capacity to read demanding works of literature and to grasp fundamental political ideas, it had also heightened and deepened his alertness to color and form, melody and harmony. And now, in the late years of his life, he was grateful. Such an education is a hedge against utilitarian values. It slakes the human craving for contact with works of art that somehow register one's own longings and yet exceed what one has been able to articulate by and for oneself.

If all that seems too pious, I think of a comparably personal comment I once heard my colleague Judith Shapiro, former provost of Bryn Mawr and then president of Barnard, make to a group of young people about what they should expect from college: "You want the inside of your head to be an interesting place to spend the rest of your life."

What both Shapiro and the Columbia alum were talking about is sometimes called "liberal education" — a hazardous term today, since it has nothing necessarily to do with liberal politics in the modern sense of the word. The phrase "liberal education" derives from the classical tradition of *artes liberales*, which was reserved in Greece and Rome — where women were considered inferior and slavery was an accepted feature of civilized society — for "those free men or gentlemen possessed of the requisite leisure for study." The tradition of liberal learning survived and thrived throughout European history but remained largely the possession of ruling elites. The distinctive American contribution has been the attempt to democratize it, to deploy it on behalf of the cardinal American principle that all persons, regardless of origin, have the right to pursue happiness — and that "getting to know," in poet and critic Matthew Arnold's much-quoted phrase, "the best which has been thought and said in the world" is helpful to that pursuit.

This view of what it means to be educated is often caricatured as snobbish and narrow, beholden to the old and wary of the new; but in fact it is neither, as Arnold makes clear by the (seldom quoted) phrase with which he completes his point: "and through this knowledge, turning a stream of fresh and free thought upon our stock notions and habits."

In today's America, at every kind of institution — from underfunded community colleges to the wealthiest Ivies — this kind of education is at risk. Students are pressured and programmed, trained to live from task to task, relentlessly rehearsed and tested until winners are culled from the rest. Too many colleges do too little to save them from the debilitating frenzy that makes liberal education marginal — if it is offered at all.

In this respect, notwithstanding the bigotries and prejudices of earlier generations, we might not be so quick to say that today's colleges mark an advance over those of the past.

Consider a once-popular college novel written a hundred years ago, *Stover at Yale*, in which a young Yalie declares, "I'm going to do the best thing a fellow can do at our age, I'm going to loaf." The character speaks from the immemorial past, and what he says is likely to sound to us today like a sneering boast from the idle rich. But there is a more dignified sense in which "loaf" is the colloquial equivalent of contemplation and has always been part of the promise of American life. "I loaf and invite my soul," says Walt Whitman in that great democratic poem "Song of Myself."

Surely, every American college ought to defend this waning possibility, whatever we call it. And an American college is only true to itself when it opens its doors to all — the rich, the middle, and the poor — who have the capacity to embrace the precious chance to think and reflect before life engulfs them. If we are serious about democracy, that means everyone.

Topics for Critical Thinking and Writing

1. In a sentence or two, state the author's thesis.

2. In your view, does the author offer adequate *support* for the thesis?

3. Do you think the final paragraph makes an effective ending? Why, or why not?

4. In paragraph 3, Delbanco speaks of "a pipe dream" and of "a nightmare." Explain his use of these terms to a student who doesn't quite grasp Delbanco's meaning.

5. In paragraph 6, Delbanco says that "if your parents make less than $35,000, your odds [of getting a BA by age 24] are one in seventy." Does this assertion disturb you? Why, or why not? (Before you respond, read Delbanco's next three paragraphs.)

6. In paragraph 10, Delbanco introduces, as an analogy — though he goes on to reject this comparison — the cost of lung cancer and other life-threatening diseases. Do you think his use of this analogy is effective? Why, or why not?

7. Delbanco gives three reasons that college matters. Why do you think he puts the three in the sequence that he does? If you were advising him, might you have recommended a different sequence? If so, why?

8. What sort of personality does the author convey? If he were teaching at your college, would you consider taking a course with him? Why, or why not?

CARLO ROTELLA

Carlo Rotella (b. 1964), director of the American Studies Program at Boston College, is the author of several books. He also is a regular columnist for the Boston Globe, *which published this essay on December 24, 2011.*

No, It Doesn't Matter What You Majored In

I woke up on Wednesday morning with two routine but pressing jobs to accomplish: I had a column to write, and I had a stack of twenty-page papers to grade. The two duties wouldn't seem to have anything to do with each other. But they do, and what they have in common says something about the value of higher education.

Almost everybody agrees that college costs too much. If a relative handful of relatively rich people want to pay a lot to go to the most exclusive schools, that's up to them; it's a victimless crime. But if a good college education costs too much across the board, that's a major social problem, especially because a college degree has increasingly become a minimum qualification for the kind of job that puts you in the middle class — which is where most Americans, wishfully or not, still imagine themselves to belong. And this all looks worse because the economic crisis has hit many public institutions especially hard.

Some have called this situation a higher-education bubble. Some have begun to investigate what students are really getting out of college for their money. They're asking necessary questions about curriculum and teaching, and about institutions' and students' commitment to academic excellence.

But this vitally important discussion is often hamstrung by a tendency to reduce college to vocational education in the crudest, most unrealistic ways. This kind of reduction often zeroes in on the humanities and parts of the social sciences — together often mislabeled as "the liberal arts" (when, in fact, math and science are also part of the liberal arts) — as the most overvalued, least practical aspect of higher education. If you study engineering you can become an engineer, if you study biology or physics you can be a scientist, and if you're pre-med or pre-law then you can go on to be a doctor or a lawyer. But what kind of job can you get if you study Renaissance art, or Indonesian history, or any kind of literature at all?

It's a fair question, even when asked 5 unfairly. If Deval Patrick,[1] an English major, was available, I'd let him answer. But he's busy being governor, so I'll take a shot at it.

Let's first defenestrate a mistaken assumption that many students and their parents cling to. Prospective employers frequently don't really care what you majored in. They might look at where you went to school and how you did, and they will definitely consider whether you wrote a decent cover letter, but they don't sit there and think, "Anthropology?! We don't need an anthropologist."

They do care that you're a college graduate. What that means, if you worked hard and did your job properly and your teachers did theirs, is that you have spent four years developing a set of skills that will serve you in good stead in the postindustrial job market. You can assimilate and organize large, complex bodies of information; you can analyze that information to create outcomes that have value to others; and you can express your ideas in clear, purposeful language. Whether you honed these skills in the study of foreign policy or Russian novels is secondary, even trivial. What matters is that you pursued training in the craft of mastering complexity, which you can apply in fields from advertising to zoo management.

The papers on my desk are from a course on the city in literature and film. They're about, among other things, 9/11 stories, inner-city documentaries, and the literary tradition of Washington, D.C. Instead of worrying about whether you can get paid to know about these topics, consider this: You can't fake a twenty-page paper. Either you've done the work this semester and know what you're talking about, or you don't. Either you can deliver a sustained reasoned argument, or you can't. It's a craft, like cabinet making.

I make my living building such figurative cabinets — like this column, a miniature one I assembled using skills I learned first in school and then honed doing various jobs in the private and public sectors: policy analyst, teacher, reporter, writer, very small businessman. Whatever else happens at college, higher education is about learning to drive the postindustrial nails straight.

---

[1]**Deval Patrick** was governor of Massachusetts when Rotella's article was published. [Editor's note.]

Topics for Critical Thinking and Writing

1. In a sentence or two, state the author's thesis.

2. In your view, does the author offer adequate *support* for the thesis?

3. Do you think the final paragraph — and in particular the final sentence — makes an effective ending? Why, or why not?

4. What sort of personality does the author convey? If he were teaching at your college, would you consider taking a course with him? Why, or why not?

EDWARD CONARD

Edward Conard (b. 1956), who has an M.B.A. from Harvard, is a visiting scholar at the American Enterprise Institute. He is best known for his controversial book on the American economy, Unintended Consequences: Why Everything You've Been Told about the Economy Is Wrong *(2012), and he has made over one hundred television appearances, debating luminaries such as Paul Krugman and Jon Stewart. In this article, which appeared as part of a Pro/Con debate in the* Washington Post *on July 30, 2013, Conard argues that people with degrees in technical fields are far better at growing the economy than those who get degrees in the humanities.*

We Don't Need More Humanities Majors

It's no secret that innovation grows America's economy. But that growth is constrained in two ways. It is constrained by the amount of properly trained talent, which is needed to produce innovation. And it is constrained by this talent's willingness to take the entrepreneurial risks critical to commercializing innovation. Given those constraints, it is hard to believe humanities degree programs are the best way to train America's most talented students.

According to the Bureau of Labor Statistics (BLS), U.S. employment has grown roughly 45 percent since the early 1980s. Over the same period, Germany's employment grew roughly 20 percent, while France's employment grew less than 20 percent and Japan's only 13 percent. U.S. employment growth put roughly 10 million immigrants to work since the BLS started keeping track in 1996 and it has employed tens of millions of people offshore.

The share of people in the world living on less than $1.25-a-day has fallen from over 50 percent to nearly 20 percent today, according to The World Bank. Name another high-wage economy that has done more than the United States for the employment of the world's poor and middle class during this time period.

Contrary to popular belief, U.S. employment growth isn't outpacing other high-wage economies because of growing employment in small businesses. Europe has plenty of small family-owned businesses. U.S. growth is predominately driven by successful high-tech start-ups, such as Google, Microsoft, and Apple, which have spawned large industries around them.

A Kauffman Institute survey of over 500 engineering and tech companies established between 1995 and 2005 reveals that 55 percent of the U.S.-born founders held degrees in the science, engineering, technology or mathematics, so called STEM-related fields, and over 90 percent held terminal degrees in STEM, business, economics, law and health care. Only 7 percent held terminal degrees in other areas — only 3 percent in the arts, humanities or social sciences. It's true some advanced degree holders may have earned undergraduate degrees in humanities, but they quickly learned humanities degrees alone offered inadequate training, and they returned to school for more technical degrees.

Other studies reach similar conclusions. A ₅ seminal study by Stanford economics professor Charles Jones estimates that 50 percent of the growth since the 1950s comes from increasing the number of scientific researchers relative to the population.

Another recent study from UC–Davis economics professor Giovanni Peri and Colgate economics associate professor Chad Sparber finds the small number of "foreign scientists and engineers brought into this country under the H-1B visa program have contributed to 10%–20% of the yearly productivity growth in the U.S. during the period 1990–2010." Despite the outsized importance of business and technology to America's economic growth, nearly half of all recent bachelor's degrees in the 2010–2011 academic year were awarded in fields outside these areas of study. Critical thinking is valuable in all forms, but it is more valuable when applied directly to the most pressing demands of society.

At the same time, U.S. universities expect to graduate a third of the computer scientists our society demands, according to a study released by Microsoft. The talent gap in the information technology sector has been bridged by non-computer science majors, according to a report by Daniel Costa, the Economic Policy Institute's director of immigration law and policy research. Costa finds that the sector has recruited two-thirds of its talent from other disciplines—predominately workers with other technical degrees. But with the share of U.S. students with top quintile SAT/ACT scores and GPAs earning STEM-related degrees declining sharply over the last two decades, the industry has turned to foreign-born workers and increasingly off-shore workers to fill its talent needs. While American consumers will benefit from discoveries made in other countries, discoveries made and commercialized here have driven and will continue to drive demand for U.S. employment—both skilled and unskilled.

UC–Berkeley economics professor Enrico Moretti estimates each additional high-tech job creates nearly five jobs in the local economy, more than any other industry. Unlike a restaurant, for example, high-tech employment tends to increase demand overall rather than merely shifting employment from one competing establishment to another. If talented workers opt out of valuable training and end up underemployed, not only have they failed to create employment for other less talented workers, they have taken jobs those workers likely could have filled.

Thirty years ago, America could afford to misallocate a large share of its talent and still grow faster than the rest of the world. Not anymore; much of the world has caught up. My analysis of data collected by economics professors Robert Barro of Harvard University and Jong-Wha Lee of Korea University reveals that over the last decade America only supplied 10 percent of the increase in the world's college graduates, much less than the roughly 30 percent it supplied thirty years ago. Fully harnessing America's talent and putting it to work addressing the needs of mankind directly would have a greater impact on raising standards of living in both the United States and the rest of the world than other alternatives available today.

Topics for Critical Thinking and Writing

1. In paragraph 1, Edward Conard makes clear his thesis: "it is hard to believe humanities degree programs are the best way to train America's most talented students." In making this argument, what assumption is Conard making about college degrees and the economy? Do you agree? Why or why not?

2. Conard argues in paragraph 2 that the rate of employment in the United States has outpaced that of other advanced nations. To what does he attribute this growth? How does the U.S. economy in turn provide worldwide prosperity? Research the relationship between first world economies (such as the American economy) and the economies of developing nations. Do you find what Conard says is accurate? Why, or why not?

3. Conard also argues that economic growth is not generated by small businesses, as many people believe, but by start-up companies that become huge, such as Google, Microsoft, and Apple (para. 3). Why is the distinction between large companies and small companies important?

4. The three companies Conard cites in paragraph 3 are all based on technology. Are there other large companies that have started up in recent decades outside of the technological fields that have had a major impact on the economy, including job growth? How does that affect what Conard is arguing? Do research to support your answer.

5. In paragraph 6, Conard points out that the United States is graduating only about one-third of the number of graduates needed in the STEM fields. Why is that? Do research to support your answer.

6. Conard's arguments are driven almost entirely by economic concerns, not issues of personal happiness or career satisfaction. In your opinion, to what extent should those factors play a role in one's choice of a major, versus economic concerns? Defend your answer.

CHRISTIAN MADSBJERG AND MIKKEL B. RASMUSSEN

Christian Madsbjerg and Mikkel B. Rasmussen are senior partners at ReD Associates, a consulting firm that, in the words of its Web site, uses "social science tools to understand how people experience their reality" so that businesses can better reach customers. Together, Madsbjerg and Rasmussen wrote The Moment of Clarity: Using Human Sciences to Solve Your Toughest Business Problems *(2014). In this article, which appeared as part of a Pro/Con debate in the* Washington Post *on July 30, 2013, Madsbjerg and Rasmussen argue that people with degrees in the humanities can be invaluable in solving business problems because of their ability to understand the customer.*

We Need More Humanities Majors

It has become oddly fashionable to look down on the humanities over the last few decades. Today's students are being told that studying the classics of English literature, the history of the twentieth century, or the ethics of privacy are a fun but useless luxury. To best prioritize our scarce education resources, we ought instead to focus on technical subjects such as math and engineering.

This short-term market logic doesn't work across the thirty-or-so-year horizon of a full career. A generation ago, lawyers made more money than investment bankers. Today, we have too many law graduates (though there appears to be data to support it's still worth the money) and the investment banks complain about a lack of talent. It is basically impossible to project that sort of thing into the far future.

We are also told that a degree in the humanities is unlikely to make you successful. Take North Carolina Governor Pat McCrory (R), who, while making the case for subsidizing state community colleges and universities based on how well they do in terms of placing students in the workforce, said this in January:

> " . . . frankly, if you want to take gender
> studies, that's fine. Go to a private
> school and take it, but I don't want to
> subsidize that if that's not going to get
> someone a job. . . . It's the tech jobs that
> we need right now."

But quite a few people with humanities degrees have had successful careers and, in the process, created numerous jobs. According to a report from *Business Insider*, the list includes A.G. Lafley of Procter & Gamble (French and History), former Massachusetts Governor and Republican presidential nominee Mitt Romney (English), George Soros (Philosophy), Michael Eisner of Disney (English and Theater), Peter Thiel of Paypal (Philosophy), Ken Chenault of American Express (History), Carl Icahn (Philosophy), former Secretary of the Treasury Hank Paulson (English), Supreme Court Justice Clarence Thomas (English), Ted Turner of CNN (History), and former IBM CEO Sam Palmisano (History). *Business*

Insider has a list of 30 business heavyweights in total.

One might think that most people starting 5 out or running tech companies in the heart of Silicon Valley would be from the science, technology, engineering and mathematics (STEM) fields. Not so. Vivek Wadhwa, a columnist for *The Washington Post*'s Innovations section and a fellow at the Rock Center for Corporate Governance at Stanford University, found that 47 percent of the 652 technology and engineering company founders surveyed held terminal degrees in the STEM fields, with 37 percent of those degrees being in either engineering or computer technology and 2 percent in mathematics. The rest graduated with a healthy combination of liberal arts, health-care and business degrees.

This leads us to a very important question: What good is a degree in the humanities in the real world of products and customers? Here's the answer: Far more than most people think. It all comes down to this: Is it helpful to know your customers? Deeply understanding their world, seeing what they see and understanding why they do the things they do, is not an easy task. Some people have otherworldly intuitions. But for most of us, getting under the skin of the people we are trying to serve takes hard analytical work.

By analytical work we mean getting and analyzing data that can help us understand the bigger picture of people's lives. The real issue with understanding people, as opposed to bacteria, or numbers, is that we change when we are studied. Birds or geological sediments do not suddenly turn self-conscious, and change their behavior just because someone is looking. Studying a moving target like this requires a completely different approach than the one needed to study nature. If you want to understand the kinds of beings we are, you need to use your own humanity and your own experience.

Such an approach can be found in the humanities. When you study the writings of, say, David Foster Wallace, you learn how to step into and feel empathy for a different world than your own. His world of intricate, neurotic detail and societal critique says more about living as a young man in the 1990s than most market research graphs. But more importantly: The same skills involved in being a subtle reader of a text are involved in deeply understanding Chinese or Argentinian consumers of cars, soap or computers. They are hard skills of understanding other people, their practices and context.

The market is naturally on to this: In a recent study, Debra Humphreys from the Association of American College & Universities concludes that 95 percent of employers say that "a candidate's demonstrated capacity to think critically, communicate clearly, and solve complex problems is more important than their undergraduate major." These all are skills taught at the highest level in the humanities.

Companies — with the most sophisticated 10 ones such as Intel, Microsoft and Johnson & Johnson leading the charge — are starting to launch major initiatives with names such as "customer-centric marketing" and "deep customer understanding." The goal of these programs is to help companies better understand the people they're selling to.

The issue is that engineers and most designers, by and large, create products for people whose tastes resemble their own. They simply don't have the skill set of a humanities major — one that allows a researcher or executive to deeply understand what it is like to be an Indonesian teenager living in Jakarta and getting a new phone, or what kind of infused beverages a Brazilian 25-year-old likes and needs.

The humanities are not in crisis. We need humanities majors more now than before to strengthen competitiveness and improve products and services. We have a veritable goldmine on our hands. But, in order for that to happen, we need the two cultures of business and the humanities to meet. The best place to start is collaboration between companies and universities on a research level — something that ought to be at the top of the minds of both research institutions and R&D departments in the coming decade.

Topics for Critical Thinking and Writing

1. The authors note at the beginning that there has been a significant trend of pushing students to major in the fields of science, technology, engineering, and mathematics (STEM). Why has that trend occurred? What do they say is the problem with doing so? Why?

2. In paragraph 4, the authors list several big-name business people, politicians, and others who have degrees in the humanities. Is this merely cherry-picking examples (i.e., finding the few examples that support your position while ignoring the vast majority that do not), or does this accurately reflect the broader whole? Do research to support your answer.

3. What argument do the authors make about the abilities of humanities majors being superior to the abilities of those who major in technical fields? Do you find the authors' argument credible? Why, or why not?

4. In paragraph 9, the authors use the example of studying literature as a way to better understand human nature. Is this a fair claim? Why, or why not?

5. The authors point out that employers want to see employment candidates who can "think critically, communicate clearly, and solve complex problems" (para. 10). The authors argue that humanities graduates best fit that description. In your opinion, is this true or not? Be specific in your response.

6. In paragraph 12, the authors state, "The issue is that engineers and most designers, by and large, create products for people whose tastes resemble their own." Consider a specific recent product or invention, and argue whether its design is reflective of what a customer wants or what an engineer or designer wants. Why?

7. In their conclusion, the authors argue that the "two cultures of business and the humanities" need to come together (para. 13). What does this assume about the purpose of higher education? What objections can you think of to this? Why?

SCOTT SAMUELSON

Scott Samuelson (b. 1973) is an associate professor of philosophy at Kirkwood Community College in Cedar Rapids, Iowa. He is author of The Deepest Human Life: An Introduction to Philosophy for Everyone *(2014), a book meant, in his own words, to bring philosophy to "wrestlers and chiropractors, preschool music teachers and undertakers, soldiers and moms, chefs and divorcees — you and me, in fact." In this article, which appeared in the April 2014 issue of the* Atlantic, *Samuelson defends the teaching of humanities in general and philosophy in particular, arguing that the liberal arts help us to lead fuller lives.*

Why I Teach Plato to Plumbers

Once, when I told a guy on a plane that I taught philosophy at a community college, he responded, "So you teach Plato to plumbers?" Yes, indeed. But I also teach Plato to nurses' aides, soldiers, ex-cons, preschool music teachers, janitors, Sudanese refugees, prospective wind-turbine technicians, and any number of other students who feel like they need a diploma as an entry ticket to our economic carnival. As a result of my work, I'm in a unique position to reflect on the current discussion about the value of the humanities, one that seems to me to have lost its way.

As usual, there's plenty to be worried about: the steady evaporation of full-time teaching positions, the overuse and abuse of adjunct professors, the slashing of public funding, the shrinkage of course offerings and majors in humanities disciplines, the increase of student debt, the peddling of technologies as magic bullets, the ubiquitous description of students as consumers. Moreover, I fear in my bones that the supremacy of a certain kind of economic-bureaucratic logic — one of "outcomes," "assessment," and "the bottom-line" — is eroding the values that undergird not just our society's commitment to the humanities, but to democracy itself.

The problem facing the humanities, in my view, isn't just about the humanities. It's about the liberal arts generally, including math, science, and economics. These form half of the so-called STEM (science, technology, engineering, math) subjects, but if the goal of an education is simply economic advancement and technological power, those disciplines, just like the humanities, will be—and to some degree already are—subordinated to future employment and technological progress. Why shouldn't educational institutions predominately offer classes like Business Calculus and Algebra for Nurses? Why should anyone but hobbyists and the occasional specialist take courses in astronomy, human evolution, or economic history? So, what good, if any, is the study of the liberal arts, particularly subjects like philosophy? Why, in short, should plumbers study Plato?

My answer is that we should strive to be a society of free people, not simply one of well-compensated managers and employees. Henry David Thoreau is as relevant as ever when he writes, "We seem to have forgotten that the expression 'a liberal education' originally meant among the Romans one worthy of free men; while the learning of trades and professions by which to get your livelihood merely, was considered worthy of slaves only."

Traditionally, the liberal arts have been the ₅ privilege of an upper class. There are three big reasons for this. First, it befits the leisure time of an upper class to explore the higher goods of human life: to play Beethoven, to study botany, to read Aristotle, to go on an imagination-expanding tour of Italy. Second, because their birthright is to occupy leadership positions in politics and the marketplace, members of the aristocratic class require the skills to think for themselves. Whereas those in the lower classes are assessed exclusively on how well they meet various prescribed outcomes, those in the upper class must know how to evaluate outcomes and consider them against a horizon of values. Finally (and this reason generally goes unspoken), the goods of the liberal arts get coded as markers of privilege and prestige, so that the upper class can demarcate themselves clearly from those who must work in order to make their leisure and wealth possible.

We don't intellectually embrace a society where the privileged few get to enjoy the advantages of leisure and wealth while the masses toil on their behalf. Yet that's what a sell-out of the liberal arts entails. For the most part, the wealthy in this country continue to pay increasingly exorbitant tuition to private prep schools, good liberal arts colleges, and elite universities, where their children get strong opportunities to develop their minds, dress themselves in cultural capital, and learn the skills necessary to become influential members of society. Meanwhile, the elite speak of an education's value for the less privileged in terms of preparation for the global economy. Worse yet, they often support learning systems designed to produce "good employees"—i.e., compliant laborers. Then, money for public education is slashed, and tuition soars. Those in the middle class, let alone the poor, have to fight an ever-steepening uphill battle to spend their time and money on the arts appropriate to free people.

As a professor with lots of experience giving Ds and Fs, I know full well that the value of the liberal arts will always be lost on some people, at least at certain points in their lives. (Whenever I return from a conference, I worry that many on whom the value of philosophy is lost have found jobs teaching philosophy!) But I don't think that this group of people is limited to any economic background or form of employment. My experience of having taught at relatively elite schools, like Emory University and Oglethorpe University, as well as at schools like Kennesaw State University and Kirkwood Community College, is that there are among future plumbers as many devotees of Plato as among the future wizards of Silicon Valley, and that there are among nurses' aides and soldiers as many important voices for our democracy as among doctors and business moguls.

I recently got a letter from a former student, a factory worker, thanking me for introducing him to Schopenhauer. I was surprised, because I hadn't assigned the German pessimist. The letter explained that I'd quoted some lines from Schopenhauer in class, and they'd sparked my student's imagination. When he didn't find what I'd quoted after reading all of volumes one and two of *The World as Will and Representation*, he started in on *Parerga and Paralipomena*, where he was eventually successful. Enclosing a short story that he'd recently written on a Schopenhauerian theme, he wrote me a long letter of thanks for inadvertently turning him on to a kindred mind.

Once, during a lecture I gave about the Stoics, who argue that with the proper spiritual discipline one can be truly free and happy even while being tortured, I looked up to see one of the students in tears. I recalled that her sister in Sudan had been recently imprisoned for challenging the local authorities. Through her tears my student was processing that her sister was likely seeking out a hard Stoic freedom as I was lecturing.

I once had a janitor compare his mystical 10 experiences with those of the medieval Sufi al-Ghazali's. I once had a student of redneck parents — his way of describing them — who read both parts of Don Quixote because I used the word "quixotic." A mother who'd authorized for her crippled son a risky surgery that led to his death once asked me with tears in her eyes, "Is Kant right that the consequences of an action play no role in its moral worth?" A wayward veteran I once had in Basic Reasoning fell in love with formal logic and is now finishing law school at Berkeley.

The fire will always be sparked. Are we going to fan it, or try to extinguish it?

Topics for Critical Thinking and Writing

1. In paragraph 2, Scott Samuelson lists some of his worries. To what extent are these worries particular to the humanities, and to what extent do they affect all subjects in higher education? Explain your response.

2. When Samuelson speaks of STEM fields (science, technology, engineering, and math) in paragraph 3, he notes that science and math are part of the liberal arts. What does he mean by this? What are the broader implications of defining them as liberal arts?

3. Samuelson states, "we should strive to be a society of free people" (para. 4). What does he mean by this? How is being free connected with the teaching of the humanities?

4. Samuelson also refers to the original meaning of the term "liberal education" in ancient Rome (para. 4). Significantly, the liberal arts were taught to the elite, while learning a trade was for slaves. To what extent does this sort of division still exist in today's society? Provide examples.

5. What does Samuelson mean when he states, "the goods of the liberal arts get coded as markers of privilege and prestige" (para. 5)? Provide examples.

6. Samuelson relies on references to stereotypical working class jobs (e.g., plumber, nurse's aide, factory worker). How does this serve to support his thesis about the need for the humanities for all students? Do you think this is effective? Why, or why not?

7. A larger issue that plays a role in Samuelson's argument has to do with the purpose of higher education: Is it to create employees for job markets, or to enhance the life people live? Are these two aims compatible or not? If so, how? If not, what are the consequences of privileging one purpose above the other?

MARK SLOUKA

Mark Slouka (b. 1958), a Guggenheim Fellowship winner (2005), has published six books, including War of the Worlds: Cyberspace and the High-Tech Assault on Reality *(1995) and more recently* Brewster: A Novel *(2013). Slouka is also a contributing editor to* Harper's *magazine, where this work was published in September 2009. Taken from a larger essay called* "Dehumanized," *this excerpt argues that the current educational emphasis on teaching math and science is, in fact, antidemocratic and potentially harmful in the long run.*

Mathandscience

> *Nobody was ever sent to prison for espousing the wrong value for the Hubble constant.*
>
> — Dennis Overbye

Nothing speaks more clearly to the relentlessly vocational bent in American education than its long-running affair with math and science. I say "affair" because I am kind; in truth, the relationship is obsessive, exclusionary, altogether unhealthy. Whatever the question, math and science (so often are they spoken of in the same breath, they've begun to feel singular) are, or is, the answer. They make sense; they compute. They're everything we want: a solid return on capital investment, a proven route to "success." Everything else can go fish.

Do we detect a note of bitterness, a hint of jealousy? No doubt. There's something indecent about the way math and science gobble up market share. Not content with being heavily subsidized by both government and private industry and with serving as a revenue-generating gold mine for higher education (which pockets the profits from any patents and passes on research expenses to students through tuition increases — effectively a kind of hidden "science tax"), math and science are now well on the way to becoming the default choice for anyone having trouble deciding where to park his (or the taxpayers') money, anyone trying to burnish his no-nonsense educational bona fides, or, most galling, anyone looking for a way to demonstrate his or her civic pride.

But let me be clear: I write this not to provide tinder to our latter-day inquisitors, ever eager to sacrifice the spirit of scientific inquiry in the name of some new misapprehension. That said, I see no contradiction between my respect for science and my humanist's discomfort with its ever-greater role in American culture, its ever-burgeoning coffers, its often dramatically anti-democratic ways, its symbiotic relationship with government, with industry, with our increasingly corporate institutions of higher learning. Triply protected from criticism by the firewall of their jargon (which immediately excludes the non-specialist and assures a jury of motivated and sympathetic peers), their economic efficacy, and the immunity conferred by conveniently associated terms like "progress" and "advancement," the sciences march, largely untouched, under the banner of the inherently good.[1] And this troubles me.

It troubles me because there are many things "math and science" do well, and some they don't. And one of the things they don't do well is democracy. They have no aptitude for it, no connection to it, really. Which hasn't prevented some in the sciences from arguing precisely the opposite, from assuming even this last, most ill-fitting mantle, by suggesting that science's spirit of questioning will automatically infect the rest of society.

In fact, it's not so. Science, by and large, keeps to its reservation, which explains why scientists tend to get in trouble only when they step outside the lab.[2] That no one has ever been sent to prison for espousing the wrong value for the Hubble constant is precisely to the point. The work of democracy involves espousing those values that in a less democratic society *would* get one sent to prison. To maintain its "sustainable edge," a democracy requires its citizens to actually risk something, to test the limits of the acceptable; the "trajectory of capability-building" they must devote themselves to, above all others, is the one that advances the capability for making trouble. If the value you're espousing is one that could never get anyone, anywhere, sent to prison, then strictly democratically speaking you're useless.

All of this helps explain why, in today's repressive societies, the sciences do not come in for the same treatment as the humanities. Not only are the sciences, with a few notable exceptions, politically neutral; their specialized languages tend to segregate them from the wider population, making ideological contagion difficult. More importantly, their work, quite often, is translatable into "product," which any aspiring dictatorship recognizes as an unambiguous good, whereas the work of the humanities almost never is.

To put it simply, science addresses the outer world; the humanities, the inner one. Science explains how the material world is now for *all* men; the humanities, in their indirect, slippery way, offer the raw materials from which the individual constructs a self — a self *distinct* from others. The sciences, to push the point a bit, produce people who study things, and who can therefore, presumably, make or fix or improve these things. The humanities don't.

One might, then, reasonably expect the two, each invaluable in its own right, to operate on an equal footing in the United States, to receive equal attention and respect. Not so. In fact, not even close. From the Sputnik-inspired emphasis on "science and math" to the pronouncements of our recently retired "Education President" (the jury is still out on Obama), the call is always for more investment in "math and science." And then a little more. The "American Competitiveness Initiative"

---

[1]Despite the "debates" surrounding issues like evolution, climate change, and stem-cell research, science continues to enjoy almost unimaginable fiscal and cultural advantages. [Author's note.]
[2]Andrei Sakharov leaps to mind, though of course the roster of genuinely courageous, politically involved scientists is extensive. [Author's note.]

calls for doubling federal spending on basic research grants in the physical sciences over ten years, at a cost of $50 billion. The federal government is asked to pay the cost of finding 30,000 new math and science teachers. Senator Bill Frist pushes for grants for students majoring in math and science.

Whether the bias trickles down or percolates up, it's systemic. The New York City Department of Education announces housing incentives worth up to $15,000 to lure teachers "in math and science" to the city's schools. Classes in history and art and foreign languages are cut back to make room for their more practical, "rigorous" cousins. The Howard Hughes Medical Institute announces its selection of twenty new professors who will use their million-dollar grants to develop fresh approaches to teaching science. Nothing remotely comparable exists in the humanities.

Popular culture, meanwhile, plays backup, 10 cementing bias into cliché. Mathandscience becomes the all-purpose shorthand for intelligence; it has that all-American aura of money about it. The tax collector, to recall Mayakovsky, runs the show.

Topics for Critical Thinking and Writing

1. Why does Mark Slouka compress math and science into one word: "mathandscience"? What is the effect of doing this as it relates to his broader arguments?

2. In paragraph 1, Slouka calls American education's attraction to math and science an "affair." (He also uses the word "jealousy" in para. 2.) Given that an affair refers to an illicit romantic or sexual relationship, is the use of this metaphor appropriate? Why, or why not?

3. Slouka argues that science is "dramatically anti-democratic" (para. 3). What is the basis for his claim? Do you agree or disagree? Why?

4. In paragraph 5, Slouka writes, "Science, by and large, keeps to its reservation, which explains why scientists tend to get in trouble only when they step outside the lab." What does he mean by this? Is there a sense that science operates behind a veil of secrecy? How does this relate to his argument that science is antidemocratic?

5. Also in paragraph 5, Slouka argues that "[t]he work of democracy involves espousing those values that in a less democratic society *would* get one sent to prison" [italics are the author's]. In your opinion, is this a fair definition of the work of democracy? Provide specific examples to support your position.

6. Slouka argues in paragraph 6 that the sciences are mostly "politically neutral" and contrasts that with the humanities, which can be dangerous to authoritarian regimes. Research examples of artists, musicians, writers, dancers, and academics in the humanities who lived in authoritarian nations, such as the former Soviet Union. How did they represent a threat to the established order? What happened to them?

7. To what extent does the privileging of the sciences in the United States echo the privileging of the sciences in authoritarian nations? Is this ultimately a threat to freedom in the United States? Why, or why not? Support your answer.

8. Slouka speaks about money in much of this excerpt; after all, money that flows into the sciences is money that is not going into the humanities. He mentions federal spending on research grants, money for new math and science teachers, grants for students to major in math and science (paras. 8–9). In your opinion, is this inequitable funding justified? Why, or why not?

9. Underneath much of Slouka's argument is an old idea about the value of the humanities: that the study of the humanities improves people's lives — and by extension, the society that embraces the humanities as well. Or, as Slouka puts it: "science addresses the outer word; the humanities, the inner one" (para. 7). Is this a romantic notion that public education can no longer afford to support, or does it still have validity? Support your answer.

10. In the final paragraph, Slouka refers to popular culture as supporting science, at least in the sense that the scientist is perceived as very intelligent, others less so. Does this correspond with your own experiences and observations with popular culture and its approaches to the sciences and the humanities? Be specific. (You may also wish to read the poem "Talking with the Taxman about Poetry" by Vladimir Mayakovsky, alluded to in the final sentence, to get additional thoughts on the subject.)

DAVID FOSTER WALLACE

David Foster Wallace (1962–2008) was an American writer who was the first Roy E. Disney Professor of Creative Writing and Professor of English at Pomona College in California. His final book, The Pale King *(2011), was unfinished at the time of his death but was published with the help of an editor who worked from Wallace's notes. This speech was given at Kenyon College in 2005 and later turned into a book,* This Is Water *(2009).*

Commencement Address, Kenyon College

(If anybody feels like perspiring [cough], I'd advise you to go ahead, because I'm sure going to. In fact I'm gonna [mumbles while pulling up his gown and taking out a handkerchief from his pocket].) Greetings ["parents"?] and congratulations to Kenyon's graduating class of 2005. There are these two young fish swimming along and they happen to meet an older fish swimming the other way, who nods at them and says, "Morning, boys. How's the water?" And the two young fish swim on for a bit, and then eventually one of them looks over at the other and goes "What the hell is water?"

This is a standard requirement of U.S. commencement speeches, the deployment of didactic little parable-ish stories. The story ["thing"] turns out to be one of the better, less bullshitty conventions of the genre, but if you're worried that I plan to present myself here as the wise, older fish explaining what water is to you younger fish, please don't be. I am not the wise old fish. The point of the fish story is merely that the most obvious, important realities are often the ones that are hardest to see and talk about. Stated as an English sentence, of course, this is just a banal platitude, but the fact is that in the day to day trenches of adult existence, banal platitudes can have a life or death importance, or so I wish to suggest to you on this dry and lovely morning.

Of course the main requirement of speeches like this is that I'm supposed to talk about your liberal arts education's meaning, to try to explain why the degree you are about to receive has actual human value instead of just a material payoff. So let's talk about the single most pervasive cliché in the commencement speech genre, which is that a liberal arts education is not so much about filling you up with knowledge as it is about "teaching you how to think." If you're like me as a student, you've never liked hearing this, and you tend to feel a bit insulted by the claim that you needed anybody to teach you how to think, since the fact that you even got admitted to a college this good seems like proof that you already know how to think. But I'm going to posit to you that the liberal arts cliché turns out not to be insulting at all, because the really significant education in thinking that we're supposed to get in a place like this isn't really about the capacity to think, but rather about the choice of what to think about. If your total freedom of choice regarding what to think about seems too obvious to waste time discussing, I'd ask you to think about fish and water, and to bracket for just a few minutes your scepticism about the value of the totally obvious.

Here's another didactic little story. There are these two guys sitting together in a bar in the remote Alaskan wilderness. One of the guys is religious, the other is an atheist, and the two are arguing about the existence of God with that special intensity that comes after about the fourth beer. And the atheist says: "Look, it's not like I don't have actual reasons for not believing in God. It's not like I haven't ever experimented with the whole God and prayer thing. Just last month I got caught away from the camp in that terrible blizzard, and I was totally lost and I couldn't see a thing, and it was 50 below, and so I tried it: I fell to my knees in the snow and cried out 'Oh, God, if there is a God, I'm lost in this blizzard, and I'm gonna die if you don't help me.'" And now, in the bar, the religious guy looks at the atheist all puzzled. "Well then you must believe now," he says, "After all, here you are, alive." The atheist just rolls his eyes. "No, man, all that was was a couple Eskimos happened to come wandering by and showed me the way back to camp."

It's easy to run this story through kind of a standard liberal arts analysis: the exact same experience can mean two totally different things to two different people, given those people's two different belief templates and two different ways of constructing meaning from experience. Because we prize tolerance and diversity of belief, nowhere in our liberal arts analysis do we want to claim that one guy's interpretation is true and the other guy's is false or bad. Which is fine, except we also never end up talking about just where these individual templates and beliefs come from. Meaning, where they come from INSIDE the two guys. As if a person's most basic orientation toward the world, and the meaning of his experience were somehow just hard-wired, like height or shoe-size; or automatically absorbed from the culture, like language. As if how we construct meaning were not actually a matter of personal, intentional choice. Plus, there's the whole matter of arrogance. The nonreligious guy is so totally certain in his dismissal of the possibility that the passing Eskimos had anything to do with his prayer for help. True, there are plenty of religious people who seem arrogant and certain of their own interpretations, too. They're probably even more repulsive than atheists, at least to most of us. But religious dogmatists' problem is exactly the same as the story's unbeliever: blind certainty, a close-mindedness that amounts to an imprisonment so total that the prisoner doesn't even know he's locked up.

The point here is that I think this is one part of what teaching me how to think is really supposed to mean. To be just a little less arrogant. To have just a little critical awareness about myself and my certainties. Because a huge percentage of the stuff that I tend to be automatically certain of is, it turns out, totally wrong and deluded. I have learned this the hard way, as I predict you graduates will, too.

Here is just one example of the total wrongness of something I tend to be automatically sure of: everything in my own immediate experience supports my deep belief that I am the absolute center of the universe; the realest, most vivid and important person in existence. We rarely think about this sort of natural, basic self-centeredness because it's so socially repulsive. But it's pretty much the same for all of us. It is our default setting, hard-wired into our boards at birth. Think about it: there is no experience you have had that you are not the absolute center of. The world as you experience it is there in front of YOU or behind YOU, to the left or right of YOU, on YOUR TV or YOUR monitor. And so on. Other people's thoughts and feelings have to be communicated to you somehow, but your own are so immediate, urgent, real.

Please don't worry that I'm getting ready to lecture you about compassion or other-directedness or all the so-called virtues. This is not a matter of virtue. It's a matter of my choosing to do the work of somehow altering or getting free of my natural, hard-wired default setting which is to be deeply and literally self-centered and to see and interpret everything through this lens of self. People who can adjust their natural default setting this way are often described as being "well-adjusted," which I suggest to you is not an accidental term.

Given the triumphant academic setting here, an obvious question is how much of this work of adjusting our default setting involves actual knowledge or intellect. This question gets very tricky. Probably the most dangerous thing about an academic education — least in my own case — is that it enables my tendency to over-intellectualize stuff, to get lost in abstract argument inside my head, instead of simply paying attention to what is going on right in front of me, paying attention to what is going on inside me.

As I'm sure you guys know by now, it is [10] extremely difficult to stay alert and attentive, instead of getting hypnotized by the constant monologue inside your own head (may be happening right now). Twenty years after my own graduation, I have come gradually to understand that the liberal arts cliché about teaching you how to think is actually shorthand for a much deeper, more serious idea: learning how to think really means learning how to exercise some control over how and what you think. It means being conscious and aware enough to choose what you pay attention to and to choose how you construct meaning from experience. Because if you cannot exercise this kind of choice in adult life, you will be totally hosed. Think of the old cliché about "the mind being an excellent servant but a terrible master."

This, like many clichés, so lame and unexciting on the surface, actually expresses a great and terrible truth. It is not the least bit coincidental that adults who commit suicide with firearms almost always shoot themselves in: the head. They shoot the terrible master. And the truth is that most of these suicides are actually dead long before they pull the trigger.

And I submit that this is what the real, no bullshit value of your liberal arts education is supposed to be about: how to keep from going through your comfortable, prosperous, respectable adult life dead, unconscious, a slave to your head and to your natural default setting of being uniquely, completely, imperially alone day in and day out. That may sound like hyperbole, or abstract nonsense. Let's get concrete. The plain fact is that you graduating seniors do not yet have any clue what "day in day out" really means. There happen to be whole, large parts of adult American life that nobody talks about in commencement speeches. One such part involves boredom, routine and petty frustration. The parents and older folks here will know all too well what I'm talking about.

By way of example, let's say it's an average adult day, and you get up in the morning, go to your challenging, white-collar, college-graduate job, and you work hard for eight or ten hours, and at the end of the day you're tired and somewhat stressed and all you want is to go home and have a good supper and maybe unwind for an hour, and then hit the sack early because, of course, you have to get up the next day and do it all again. But then you remember there's no food at home. You haven't had time to shop this week because of your challenging job, and so now after work you have to get in your car and drive to the supermarket. It's the end of the work day and the traffic is apt to be: very bad. So getting to the store takes way longer than it should, and when you finally get there, the supermarket is very crowded, because of course it's the time of day when all the other people with jobs also try to squeeze in some grocery shopping. And the store is hideously lit and infused with soul-killing muzak or corporate pop and it's pretty much the last place you want to be but you can't just get in and quickly out; you have to wander all over the huge, over-lit store's confusing aisles to find the stuff you want and you have to maneuver your junky cart through all these other tired, hurried people with carts (et cetera, et cetera, cutting stuff out because this is a long ceremony) and eventually you get all your supper supplies, except now it turns out there aren't enough checkout lanes open even though it's the end-of-the-day rush. So the checkout line is incredibly long, which is stupid and infuriating. But you can't take your frustration out on the frantic lady working the register, who is overworked at a job whose daily tedium and meaninglessness surpasses the imagination of any of us here at a prestigious college.

But anyway, you finally get to the checkout line's front, and you pay for your food, and you get told to "Have a nice day" in a voice that is the absolute voice of death. Then you have to take your creepy, flimsy, plastic bags of groceries in your cart with the one crazy wheel that pulls maddeningly to the left, all the way out through the crowded, bumpy, littery parking lot, and then you have to drive all the way home through slow, heavy, SUV-intensive, rush-hour traffic, et cetera et cetera.

Everyone here has done this, of course. But it hasn't yet been part of you graduates' actual life routine, day after week after month after year.

But it will be. And many more dreary, annoying, seemingly meaningless routines besides. But that is not the point. The point is that petty, frustrating crap like this is exactly where the work of choosing is gonna come in. Because the traffic jams and crowded aisles and long checkout lines give me time to think, and if I don't make a conscious decision about how to think and what to pay attention to, I'm gonna be pissed and miserable every time I have to shop. Because my natural default setting is the certainty that situations like this are really all about me. About MY hungriness and MY fatigue and MY desire to just get home, and it's going to seem for all the world like everybody else is just in my way. And who are all these people in my way? And look at how repulsive most of them are, and how stupid and cow-like and dead-eyed and nonhuman they seem in the checkout line, or at how annoying and rude it is that people are talking loudly on cell phones in the middle of the line. And look at how deeply and personally unfair this is.

Or, of course, if I'm in a more socially conscious liberal arts form of my default setting, I can spend time in the end-of-the-day traffic being disgusted about all the huge, stupid, lane-blocking SUVs and Hummers and V-12 pickup trucks, burning their wasteful, selfish, 40-gallon tanks of gas, and I can dwell on the fact that the patriotic or religious bumper-stickers always seem to be on the biggest, most disgustingly selfish vehicles, driven by the ugliest [responding here to loud applause] (this is an example of how NOT to think, though) most disgustingly selfish vehicles, driven by the ugliest, most inconsiderate and aggressive drivers. And I can think about how our children's children will despise us for wasting all the future's fuel, and probably screwing up the climate, and how spoiled and stupid and selfish and disgusting we all are, and how modern consumer society just sucks, and so forth and so on.

You get the idea.

If I choose to think this way in a store and on the freeway, fine. Lots of us do. Except thinking this way tends to be so easy and automatic that it doesn't have to be a choice. It is my natural default setting. It's the automatic way that I experience the boring, frustrating, crowded parts of adult life when I'm operating on the automatic, unconscious belief that I am the center of the world, and that my immediate needs and feelings are what should determine the world's priorities.

The thing is that, of course, there are totally [20] different ways to think about these kinds of situations. In this traffic, all these vehicles stopped and idling in my way, it's not impossible that some of these people in SUVs have been in horrible auto accidents in the past, and now find driving so terrifying that their therapist has all but ordered them to get a huge, heavy SUV so they can feel safe enough to drive. Or that the Hummer that just cut me off is maybe being driven by a father whose little child is hurt or sick in the seat next to him, and he's trying to get this kid to the hospital, and he's in a bigger, more legitimate hurry than I am: it is actually I who am in HIS way.

Or I can choose to force myself to consider the likelihood that everyone else in the supermarket's checkout line is just as bored and frustrated as I am, and that some of these people probably have harder, more tedious and painful lives than I do.

Again, please don't think that I'm giving you moral advice, or that I'm saying you are supposed to think this way, or that anyone expects you to just automatically do it. Because it's hard. It takes will and effort, and if you are like me, some days you won't be able to do it, or you just flat out won't want to.

But most days, if you're aware enough to give yourself a choice, you can choose to look differently at this fat, dead-eyed, over-made-up lady who just screamed at her kid in the checkout line. Maybe she's not usually like this. Maybe she's been up three straight nights holding the hand of a husband who is dying of bone cancer. Or maybe this very lady is the low-wage clerk at the motor vehicle department, who just yesterday helped your spouse resolve a horrific, infuriating, red-tape problem through some small act of bureaucratic kindness. Of course, none of this is likely, but it's also not impossible. It just depends what you want to consider. If you're automatically sure that you know what reality is, and you are operating on your default setting, then you, like me, probably won't consider possibilities that aren't annoying and miserable. But if you really learn how to pay attention, then you will know there are other options. It will actually be within your power to experience a crowded, hot, slow, consumer-hell type situation as not only meaningful, but sacred, on fire with the same force that made the stars: love, fellowship, the mystical oneness of all things deep down.

Not that that mystical stuff is necessarily true. The only thing that's capital-T True is that you get to decide how you're gonna try to see it.

This, I submit, is the freedom of a real education, of learning how to be well-adjusted. You get to consciously decide what has meaning and what doesn't. You get to decide what to worship.

Because here's something else that's weird but true: in the day-to-day trenches of adult life, there is actually no such thing as atheism. There is no such thing as not worshipping. Everybody worships. The only choice we get is what to worship. And the compelling reason for maybe choosing some sort of god or spiritual-type thing to worship — be it JC or Allah, be it YHWH or the Wiccan Mother Goddess, or the Four Noble Truths, or some inviolable set of ethical principles — is that pretty much anything else you worship will eat you alive. If you worship money and things, if they are where you tap real meaning in life, then you will never have enough, never feel you have enough. It's the truth. Worship your body and beauty and sexual allure and you will always feel ugly. And when time and age

start showing, you will die a million deaths before they finally grieve you. On one level, we all know this stuff already. It's been codified as myths, proverbs, clichés, epigrams, parables; the skeleton of every great story. The whole trick is keeping the truth up front in daily consciousness.

Worship power, you will end up feeling weak and afraid, and you will need ever more power over others to numb you to your own fear. Worship your intellect, being seen as smart, you will end up feeling stupid, a fraud, always on the verge of being found out. But the insidious thing about these forms of worship is not that they're evil or sinful, it's that they're unconscious. They are default settings.

They're the kind of worship you just gradually slip into, day after day, getting more and more selective about what you see and how you measure value without ever being fully aware that that's what you're doing.

And the so-called real world will not discourage you from operating on your default settings, because the so-called real world of men and money and power hums merrily along in a pool of fear and anger and frustration and craving and worship of self. Our own present culture has harnessed these forces in ways that have yielded extraordinary wealth and comfort and personal freedom. The freedom all to be lords of our tiny skull-sized kingdoms, alone at the center of all creation. This kind of freedom has much to recommend it. But of course there are all different kinds of freedom, and the kind that is most precious you will not hear much talk about much in the great outside world of wanting and achieving. . . . The really important kind of freedom involves attention and awareness and discipline, and being able truly to care about other people and to sacrifice for them over and over in myriad petty, unsexy ways every day.

That is real freedom. That is being edu- [30] cated, and understanding how to think. The alternative is unconsciousness, the default setting, the rat race, the constant gnawing sense of having had, and lost, some infinite thing.

I know that this stuff probably doesn't sound fun and breezy or grandly inspirational the way a commencement speech is supposed to sound. What it is, as far as I can see, is the capital-T Truth, with a whole lot of rhetorical niceties stripped away. You are, of course, free to think of it whatever you wish. But please don't just dismiss it as just some finger-wagging Dr. Laura sermon. None of this stuff is really about morality or religion or dogma or big fancy questions of life after death.

The capital-T Truth is about life BEFORE death.

It is about the real value of a real education, which has almost nothing to do with knowledge, and everything to do with simple awareness; awareness of what is so real and essential, so hidden in plain sight all around us, all the time, that we have to keep reminding ourselves over and over:

"This is water."

"This is water." [35]

It is unimaginably hard to do this, to stay conscious and alive in the adult world day in and day out. Which means yet another grand cliché turns out to be true: your education really IS the job of a lifetime. And it commences: now.

I wish you way more than luck.

Topics for Critical Thinking and Writing

1. David Foster Wallace begins his speech with a brief parable about two fish. He then comments that the form of giving a commencement speech often requires "the deployment of didactic little parable-ish stories" (para. 2). Why does Wallace point out to the audience that the form of his text (a commencement speech) dictates the content? How does this serve to advance his point?

2. Wallace continues to address the expectations of a commencement speech in paragraph 3 when he states, "I'm supposed to talk about your liberal arts education's meaning. . . ." He follows that quickly with the statement that college is supposed to teach the students how to think. What is Wallace's response to that statement? How does it serve as a jumping-off point for the rest of his speech?

3. What does Wallace mean when he talks about the "value of the totally obvious" (para. 3)?

4. In paragraph 5, Wallace raises the issue of how we react to the world around, whether it might be, as he says, "somehow just hard-wired" inside of us, or if it is something learned culturally. What is the point of this distinction? How does it relate to his second parable about the two men arguing in a bar?

5. Wallace points out that all experiences are experienced by the individual. He says, "there is no experience you have had that you are not the absolute center of" (para. 7). What are the implications of this that Wallace points out? Are there other implications that he does not mention? Explain.

6. In paragraph 10, Wallace expands on his earlier comment about college teaching students to think. He says, "learning how to think really means learning how to exercise some control over how and what you think." What does he mean by this? Why is it so important?

7. In paragraph 13, Wallace paints the picture of "an average adult day" that seems far from appealing. He begins with a stereotype: the average hard-working white-collar employee having a dull yet difficult day. But Wallace breaks away from that stereotype. How and why? What is the effect of the twists and turns that he gives the story?

8. Wallace frequently uses the metaphor "default setting." Where does that phrase come from? What are the implications of using that metaphor rather than another expression?

9. In paragraph 23, Wallace makes an appeal to his audience to see the world with greater empathy. How does he do this? In your opinion, is this effective or not? Support your answer.

10. Wallace argues in paragraph 26 that everyone worships something, but it's our choice as to what we worship. Analyze his argument about worship. Which choices of worship lead to positive results, and which to negative ones? Why?

11. In his conclusion, Wallace states that the job for the graduates is "to stay conscious and alive in the adult world day in and day out." What does he mean by this? Why is this so hard to do?

20

Race and Police Violence: How Do We Solve the Problem?

GENE DEMBY

Gene Demby is a founding member of National Public Radio's Code Switch, and he also started PostBourgie, a blog that is self-described as a "running, semi-orderly conversation about race and gender and class and politics and media and whatever else we can think of." Demby previously worked for both the Huffington Post *and the* New York Times. *In this article, which appeared in* Politico.com *on December 31, 2014, Demby examines how the civil rights activism of millennials is different from the traditional, establishment civil rights movement, and how tensions have risen between the two camps.*

The Birth of a New Civil Rights Movement

The shattering events of 2014, beginning with Michael Brown's death in Ferguson, Missouri, in August, did more than touch off a national debate about police behavior, criminal justice and widening inequality in America. They also gave a new birth of passion and energy to a civil rights movement that had almost faded into history, and which had been in the throes of a slow comeback since the killing of Trayvon Martin in 2012. That the nation became riveted to the meta-story of Ferguson—and later the videotaped killing of Eric Garner in New York—was due in large part to the work of a loose but increasingly coordinated network of millennial activists who had been beating the drum for the past few years. In 2014, the new

social justice movement became a force that the political mainstream had to reckon with.

This re-energized millennial movement, which will make itself felt all the more in 2015, differs from its half-century-old civil rights-era forebear in a number of important ways. One, it is driven far more by social media and hashtags than marches and open-air rallies. Indeed, if you wanted a megaphone for a movement spearheaded by young people of color, you'd be hard-pressed to find a better one than Twitter, whose users skew younger and browner than the general public, which often has the effect of magnifying that group's broad priorities and fascinations. It's not a coincidence that the Twitterverse helped surface and magnify the stories of Trayvon Martin and Eric Garner and Michael Brown.

Two, the new social-justice grass roots reflects a broader agenda that includes LGBTQ (lesbian-gay-bisexual-transgender-questioning) issues and immigration reform. The young grass-roots activists I've spoken to have a broad suite of concerns: the school-to-prison pipeline, educational inequality, the over-policing of black and Latino communities. In essence, they're trying to take on deeply entrenched discrimination that is fueled less by showy bigotry than systemic, implicit biases.

Three, the movement's renewal has exposed a serious generational rift. It is largely a bottom-up movement being led by young unknowns who have rejected, in some cases angrily, the presumption of leadership thrust on them by veteran celebrities like Al Sharpton. While both the younger and older activists both trace their lineage to the civil rights movement, they seem to align themselves with different parts of that family tree. And in several ways, these contemporary tensions are updates of the disagreements that marked the earlier movement.

Sarah Jackson, a professor at Northeastern University whose research focuses on social movements, said the civil rights establishment embraces the "Martin Luther King-Al Sharpton model" — which emphasizes mobilizing people for rallies and speeches and tends to be centered around a charismatic male leader. But the younger activists are instead inclined to what Jackson called the "Fannie Lou Hamer-Ella Baker model" — an approach that embraces a grass roots and in which agency is widely diffused. Indeed, many of the activists name-checked Baker, a lesser-known but enormously influential strategist of the civil rights era. She helped found Martin Luther King's Southern Christian Leadership Conference but became deeply skeptical of the cult of personality that she felt had formed around him. And she vocally disagreed with the notion that power in the movement should be concentrated among a few leaders, who tended to be men with bases of power that lay in the church. "My theory is, strong people don't need strong leaders," she said.

Baker's theories on participatory democracy were adopted by later social movements, like Occupy Wall Street, which notably resisted naming leaders or spokespeople. But James Hayes, an organizer with the Ohio Student Association, said that he didn't think of this new social justice movement as "leaderless" in the Occupy style. "I think of it as leader-ful," he said.

By December, some of these same uncelebrated community organizers who spent the year leading "die-ins," voting drives and the thousands-deep rallies around the country would meet privately with President Barack Obama in the Oval Office. ("We got a chance to really lay it out — we kept it real," Hayes told me about the meeting. "We were respectful, but we didn't pull any punches.") A few days after that White House meeting, Hillary Clinton, widely assumed to be eyeing another bid for the presidency in 2016, nodded to them when she dropped one of the mantras of the demonstrators — "black lives matter" — into a speech at a posh awards ceremony in New York City.

All this new energy comes, ironically, as the country's appetite for fighting racial inequality — never all that robust in the best of times — appears to be ebbing. The tentpole policy victories of the civil rights movement are even now in retrenchment: 60 years after *Brown v. Board of Education,* American schools — especially in the South — are rapidly resegregating; the Voting Rights Act, which turns 50 in 2015, has been effectively gutted; and, despite the passage of the Fair Housing Act, our neighborhoods are as segregated as ever. Once-narrowing racial gaps in life outcomes have again become gaping chasms.

At the same time, the new movement's emergence has caused friction with the traditional civil rights establishment that identifies with those earlier, historic victories. At a recent march put together by Sharpton's National Action Network in Washington, D.C. — meant to protest the recent decisions not to indict the officers in several high-profile police-involved killings and push for changes in the protocol from prosecutors — younger activists from St. Louis County were upset at what they saw as a lineup of older speakers on the podium who were not on the ground marching in Ferguson. So they climbed onto the stage and took the mic. "It should be nothing but young people up here!" a woman named Johnetta Elzie yelled into the microphone. "We started this!" Some people cheered them. Others called for them to get off the stage. After a few minutes, the organizers cut off their mics. (In the crowd, someone held up a neon-green sign making their discontent with the march's organizers plain: "WE, THE YOUTH, DID NOT ELECT AL SHARPTON OUR SPOKESPERSON. HAVE A SEAT.")

A few days later, Elzie downplayed the 10 incident and told me that the disagreement was simply about "someone who doesn't want to give up the reins and who has a huge platform."

Other activists were more pointed. Tory Russell, a St. Louis-area native and a founder of a group called Hands Up United, wasn't at the Washington march — "I don't have to travel that far to go to a circus," he told me — but he bristled at the idea that Sharpton was headlining it. "It was people like me who came out

[to march in Ferguson]," he said. "I didn't see no suits, I didn't see no NAACP or National Action Network. It was people like me — poor black people — out there."

Why is this movement's moment coming right now? It's hard to say whether there are more cases like those of Mike Brown or Eric Garner, since there's no comprehensive database on police use of force or accurate tallies of how many people are killed in encounters with the police each year, or if it seems like there are more because more people are paying attention. But one factor might be the growing disconnect in the way different generations of Americans think about crime and violence. While violent crime has plummeted to record lows over the last 15 years, our posture toward it hasn't kept pace. Florida's stand-your-ground self-defense law was the first of its kind in the nation when it passed in 2005; nearly two dozen other states have passed similar statutes since. And for many police departments, the broken windows theory of policing — which holds that cracking down on petty offenses prevents more serious crimes from happening — is still an organizing principle. Americans continue to gird themselves for an outbreak that has long since waned.

Millennials who have come of age in this much less violent country don't necessarily nurture those same animating neuroses toward punishing violent criminals. But young people — and especially young people of color — often find themselves on the business end of those anxieties.

A quick scan of the names that have become hashtags or been invoked in chants at the past year's many protests reveals a grim litany of non-crime and misdemeanors. Trayvon Martin was killed in a confrontation with a local who wrongly assumed him to be planning a burglary. Ramarley Graham was shot at point-blank range in his bathroom by a police officer who thought he was carrying a gun; Graham was apparently flushing weed down the toilet. Police confronted Eric Garner and put him in a chokehold over suspicion that he was selling loose, untaxed cigarettes on the street. John Crawford was shot and killed by the police at a Wal-Mart while absent-mindedly chatting on the phone and holding an air rifle sold in the store. Akai Gurley was walking up the stairwell of the housing project where he lived; the officer who shot him was patrolling that same dark stairwell with his gun drawn. Twelve-year-old Tamir Rice was sitting in a playground with a toy gun when he, too, was shot by the police. Tanisha Anderson, a schizophrenic, died after a police officer slammed her to the pavement; her family had called 911 to have officers take her to a psychiatric hospital for evaluation. And, depending on which version of events you believe, the precipitating event of Michael Brown's fatal encounter with a police officer in Ferguson was either his alleged theft of cigarillos from a convenience store or his alleged jaywalking.

Had any of them lived long enough to be arrested, it's unlikely that any of the people on this list would have faced jail time. As it stands, none of the people who killed them will have to, either.

What we've been seeing over the past year might be best understood as the collision of some fundamentally opposed generational orthodoxies: one set of people see the police as a necessary bulwark against random violence; another, younger group sees them as the proximate causes of it. And if you're a young person from one of the many minority communities in our country where contact with the police is a given, it's harder to see these stories as mere abstractions.

As it goes with all histories, the catalyzing moment in this social-justice revolution is hard to pin down. One academic I spoke with pegged it to the death of 19-year-old Oscar Grant in Oakland, California, early on New Year's Day in 2009. And you can see a now-familiar trajectory in how that story played out: Grant was shot in the back by a transit police officer as he lay face down and hand-cuffed on a train platform, and the footage of Grant's shooting was captured on witnesses' cell phones. Demonstrations and civil unrest broke out in Oakland in the days that followed, and the story became national news.

Elzie, the young activist from Ferguson who grabbed the mic at the Sharpton event, told me that her personal moment came during the lead-up to the execution of Troy Davis, a black Georgia man who was eventually put to death in 2011 for killing a police officer despite the fact that several of the eyewitnesses in his murder trial later recanted their testimony. (That story, too, took root on social media before it became national news.) "That hurt me," Elzie said. "That was the first time I'd ever been hurt by something happening to a stranger."

But for many, the tipping point came in February 2012, when George Zimmerman shot and killed Trayvon Martin in Sanford, Florida. That case, too, churned on Twitter for weeks. When it finally bubbled into the mainstream, it exploded. There were rallies in cities and campuses across the country. In solidarity, people shared photos of themselves in hoodies like the one Martin was wearing when he was killed. The longer Zimmerman went uncharged, the louder the protests became. Obama eventually waded into the conversation, saying at a news conference that if he had a son, he would look like Trayvon. The president's comments summed up the anxieties that many black parents felt. It also made the story unavoidable, and it effectively polarized the case along party lines.

"I think that Trayvon really woke a lot [20] of people up, and a lot of people came of age politically," said James Hayes. Hayes, who had been active in the Occupy movement, had helped start a grass-roots group called the Ohio Students Association just weeks before the shooting. His new group had its cause.

In the six weeks that passed between the shooting and when Zimmerman was charged, new grass-roots organizations, like Million Hoodies and the Dream Defenders, started sprouting up around the country. They called for a federal investigation into the handling of the case and protested the stand-your-ground self-defense laws that had become part of the conversation around it.

Zimmerman's acquittal in the summer of 2013 was another seminal moment—a devastating emotional setback for many new activists that nonetheless spurred a new round of direct action and organizing. The Dream Defenders staged a monthlong sit-in in the Florida Capitol building to press Gov. Rick Scott to call a special session on the state's stand-your-ground law. (Scott agreed to meet with them but didn't budge.) New groups, like Black Lives Matter and The Black Youth Project 100, who would later play a large role in the organizing that followed the Michael Brown shooting, came into being in direct response to the Zimmerman verdict.

By 2014, the new social-justice grass-roots groups had grown more assured and more coordinated, and their activism reflected millennial sensibilities in both substance and execution. Many of the organizations pointedly centered LGBTQ issues and experiences on their agenda—Black Lives Matter, notably, was founded by queer women—and while

they didn't have the resources of the legacy outfits, they could be more nimble. In July, dozens of young activists of color from different organizations launched a collective called Freedom Side, inspired by the 50th anniversary of the Freedom Summer and the young activists who participated in it. The Freedom Side groups lent each other organizational support and boosted the signals for each other's causes, like ending mass deportations, reining in college costs and protecting voting rights.

"We've all been trying to build a network of young-people-of-color organizations," Hayes said. "The groundwork was already in place."

And then Michael Brown was shot, and [25] the Twitterverse exploded again. Protesters and news outlets headed to Ferguson. Jackson, the professor from Northeastern, worked with other researchers to map the routes that the hashtags for those stories took on Twitter, via retweets and favorites, to reach the broader public. "What we saw was the first people who hashtagged Mike Brown's name were young people who lived in Ferguson and who saw his body laying in the street," Jackson said. "The people driving the Michael Brown story and Ferguson — and this is also true of the Trayvon Martin case — were young and had some connection to the victim. It was young folks from those communities who don't necessarily tweet about political things or even have many followers."

The hashtags in those stories were picked up by an ever-widening spiral of Twitter users: friends of the hashtag originators, friends of their friends, then local grass-roots groups who are plugged into the community begin tweeting about it. Eventually — but always last, Jackson said — those conversations land on the radars of national civil rights groups and elite media.

But the researchers noted an important change in the way that happened this summer after the Brown shooting: that timeline is becoming more and more condensed. "It's happening way faster," Jackson said. The Trayvon Martin shooting churned on social media for weeks before it was getting national coverage. By the time of the Ferguson incident, Jackson said the lag time was "hours, at most."

Another reason Ferguson became such a huge story, then, might be explained by the worlds of activism and media, both new and legacy, becoming so much better at mobilizing around cases like these. And, of course, the size of the universe of these thematically similar calamities has provided them with plenty of opportunities to practice.

The microphone incident at the National Action Network in December offered a good example of how influence has remained concentrated among the legacy civil rights groups. Later, Sharpton's group released a letter from Emerald Snipes-Garner, Eric Garner's daughter, that chided Elzie and some of the younger marchers. The letter also noted that after Garner's death, the Garner family reached out to Sharpton and his people. Because when these things happen, Sharpton is who the traumatized families call.

While Sharpton wasn't present for the kerfuffle on the stage, he dismissed the criticism in an interview with the *Root*. "I have spent an inordinate amount of time trying to make sure that we can continue this movement and National Action Network for the next 30 to 40 years when I am gone," he said. "Leadership cannot be willed. I can't pass the torch. I can only keep the flame lit."

But the ambivalence many younger activists feel toward Sharpton — and the civil rights establishment more broadly — isn't just some intergenerational beef between old-heads and young bucks. Some of it is tactical. Tory Russell of Hands Up United thought that Sharpton's proximity to the families of Michael Brown and Eric Garner was, in part, a way to shield himself from criticism. "When Al Sharpton comes to St. Louis, he don't come out unless he's with the parents," Russell said. "It's a cloak. He can say 'you're attacking the family!'"

But Hayes said that there was a financial and socioeconomic divide, too. "Organizers, a lot of times, have advanced degrees and worry about things like proper email etiquette," he said with some sarcasm in his voice. "The nonprofitization of social movements has led to their professionalization."

He said that the existence of a professional civil rights class has made it harder for people with less education or money to participate, and those older, more established groups often soak up resources and donations that the newer organizers need. "If the only way we can get [financial] help is to be a 501(c)(3)" — the tax designation for nonprofits — then something's wrong," Russell said.

There is also a struggle for the ear of the powerful. Sharpton, for instance, is known to be confidant of Obama. But Ashley Yates of Millennial Activists United, one of the organizers who met with Obama in the White House in December, said the president seemed open about who to listen to. "He didn't come from a place of the highest authority in the land," she said. "He came from a place of — 'let's have a conversation about it.'" Their meeting with the president ran long.

I asked Yates about the seeming contradiction of being a grass-roots activist who also is listened to by the White House. She said she didn't think of those positions as necessarily in tension. "You have to [have an] inside game and you have to [have] an outside game," she said. She and other organizers met with other White

House officials while they were there. (Sharpton was also present for part of those sessions, Yates said. "He spoke about the importance of young people on the ground [protesting], but he didn't know any of our names.")

She said the officials touted some of the administration's post-Ferguson initiatives, like funding body cameras for police departments, and asked the young activists if the initiatives addressed their demands. "They seemed like they were trying to quell the streets," Yates said.

The White House officials also pointed to new guidelines for the 1033 program, the federal plan that allows local police departments to procure military equipment from the Defense Department for ostensible use in cracking down on drug trafficking and terrorism. The obscure program became closely scrutinized during the unrest in Ferguson in August, after the city's startlingly well-armed police used equipment from that program — like armored personnel carriers and smoke bombs — to crack down on protesters.

Yates and other organizers had wanted for the program to be scuttled completely, but she said that federal oversight was a start.

"The idealists in us hoped that they'd wake up and said, 'you know, this program isn't working. Let's get rid of it!'" she said. "But the realists in us knew that it wasn't how it works. It's a step — I definitely wouldn't call it a win, but it's definitely a result of this movement."

She put the meeting with the president in 40 historical perspective. "The day we met with the president was Dec. 1 — it was the 59th anniversary of Rosa Parks not getting up from her seat," she pointed out. The die-ins and demonstrations of the past year were part of a long tradition of intentionally polarizing civil disobedience, she said. "We definitely realize that we're standing on the shoulders of the people who came before us."

Topics for Critical Thinking and Writing

1. In paragraph 1, Gene Demby remarks that before the death of Michael Brown in Ferguson, Missouri, the civil rights movement appeared to have "almost faded into history." Do you agree with his assessment? Why, or why not?

2. Demby states that this new movement is "driven far more by social media and hashtags than marches and open-air rallies" (para. 2). What are the ramifications of these differences on the movement and its ability to get a message out to the general public?

3. Demby cites Sarah Jackson in paragraph 5 as arguing that in the past, the civil rights movement had been led by a "charismatic male leader." This would include leaders such as Martin Luther King, Jesse Jackson, and Al Sharpton — all of whom were (or are) ordained ministers, too. How does the new movement by the millennial generation differ from this traditional organizational model? What advantages do you see in shifting to a movement less focused on a strong leader? What are the disadvantages?

4. In paragraph 8, Demby argues that civil rights advances are being overturned and that America is getting "as segregated as ever." Based on your experiences and observations, do you agree with him or not? Support your answer.

5. Demby argues that one of the possible motivations behind the generational differences toward the police's use of force is "the growing disconnect in the way different generations of Americans think about crime and violence" (para. 12). Violent crime across America has dropped to record lows, so the argument goes, but the older generation still continues "to gird themselves for an outbreak [of crime] that has long since waned." If rates of violent crime have gone done, does that argue that the get-tough-on-crime approach has worked and should continue, or that it is no longer needed? Support your answer.

6. The list of names of unarmed blacks, usually men, who have been killed in encounters with police is long and continues to grow longer: Trayvon Martin, Ramarley Graham, Eric Garner, John Crawford, Tamir Rice, Tanisha Anderson, and Michael Brown (para. 14). Research other killings of unarmed blacks by police. What is the significance of these killings? Is protesting these killings creating a new frontier of civil rights, or will these be seen as isolated problems, not systemic ones? Why, or why not?

7. Demby states that the new generation of civil rights activists also embraces LGBTQ (lesbian, gay, bisexual, transgender, and questioning) rights issues. How is this different from the traditional civil rights movement, and why is that difference important?

8. As noted in paragraph 27, one advantage of social media is that news can be transmitted across a broad spectrum very quickly. Thus, what might remain strictly a local story for weeks can be national in a matter of hours. What are the consequences of this? What drawbacks can result from such quick exposure?

9. A central figure in the article is the Rev. Al Sharpton, president of the National Action Network. What is it about Sharpton that so infuriates the millennial civil rights activists? To what extent is this not simply a generational difference, but also a class difference? Why is that significant?

10. In the final paragraph, Ashley Yates of Millennial Activists United speaks of her meeting with President Barack Obama as occurring on the fifty-ninth anniversary of the day that Rosa Parks refused to give up her seat in the front of a bus. What is the relevance of the comparison between past protests (as represented by Parks) and current methods? What are their similarities? What are their differences?

HEATHER Mac DONALD

Heather Mac Donald (b. 1956), educated at Stanford, Yale, and Cambridge, is an American conservative columnist and Thomas W. Smith fellow at the Manhattan Institute. She is co-author of Immigration Solution: A Better Plan than Today's *(2007), along with Victor Davis Hanson and Steven Malanga, as well as being the author of* Are Cops Racist? *(2003). In this commentary, which appeared in the* Wall Street Journal *on May 29, 2015, Mac Donald argues that the nation is experiencing an increase in violent crime that is directly related to police reaction to criticisms about their actions in deadly encounters with young black men.*

The New Nationwide Crime Wave

The nation's two-decades-long crime decline may be over. Gun violence in particular is spiraling upward in cities across America. In Baltimore, the most pressing question every morning is how many people were shot the previous night. Gun violence is up more than 60% compared with this time last year, according to Baltimore police, with 32 shootings over Memorial Day weekend. May has been the most violent month the city has seen in 15 years.

In Milwaukee, homicides were up 180% by May 17 over the same period the previous year. Through April, shootings in St. Louis were up 39%, robberies 43%, and homicides 25%. "Crime is the worst I've ever seen it," said St. Louis Alderman Joe Vacarro at a May 7 City Hall hearing.

Murders in Atlanta were up 32% as of mid-May. Shootings in Chicago had increased 24% and homicides 17%. Shootings and other violent felonies in Los Angeles had spiked by 25%; in New York, murder was up nearly 13%, and gun violence 7%.

Those citywide statistics from law-enforcement officials mask even more startling neighborhood-level increases. Shooting incidents are up 500% in an East Harlem precinct compared with last year; in a South Central Los Angeles police division, shooting victims are up 100%.

By contrast, the first six months of 2014 5 continued a 20-year pattern of growing public safety. Violent crime in the first half of last year dropped 4.6% nationally and property crime was down 7.5%. Though comparable national figures for the first half of 2015 won't be available for another year, the January through June 2014 crime decline is unlikely to be repeated.

The most plausible explanation of the current surge in lawlessness is the intense agitation against American police departments over the past nine months.

Since last summer, the airwaves have been dominated by suggestions that the police are the biggest threat facing young black males today. A handful of highly publicized deaths of unarmed black men, often following a resisted arrest — including Eric Garner in Staten Island, N.Y., in July 2014, Michael Brown in Ferguson, Mo., in August 2014 and Freddie Gray in Baltimore last month — have led to riots, violent protests and attacks on the police. Murders of officers jumped 89% in 2014, to 51 from 27.

President Obama and Attorney General Eric Holder, before he stepped down last month, embraced the conceit that law enforcement in black communities is infected by bias. The news media pump out a seemingly constant stream of stories about alleged police mistreatment of blacks, with the reports often buttressed by cellphone videos that rarely capture the behavior that caused an officer to use force.

Almost any police shooting of a black person, no matter how threatening the behavior that provoked the shooting, now provokes angry protests, like those that followed the death of Vonderrit Myers in St. Louis last October. The 18-year-old Myers, awaiting trial on gun and resisting-arrest charges, had fired three shots at an officer at close range. Arrests in black communities are even more fraught than usual, with hostile, jeering crowds pressing in on officers and spreading lies about the encounter.

Acquittals of police officers for the use of 10 deadly force against black suspects are now automatically presented as a miscarriage of justice. Proposals aimed at producing more cop convictions abound, but New York state seems especially enthusiastic about the idea.

The state's attorney general, Eric Schneiderman, wants to create a special state prosecutor dedicated solely to prosecuting cops who use lethal force. New York Gov. Andrew Cuomo would appoint an independent monitor whenever a grand jury fails to indict an officer for homicide and there are "doubts" about the fairness of the proceeding (read: in every instance of a non-indictment); the governor could then turn over the case to a special prosecutor for a second grand jury proceeding.

This incessant drumbeat against the police has resulted in what St. Louis police chief Sam Dotson last November called the "Ferguson effect." Cops are disengaging from discretionary enforcement activity and the "criminal element is feeling empowered," Mr. Dotson reported. Arrests in St. Louis city and county by that point had dropped a third since the shooting of Michael Brown in August. Not surprisingly, homicides in the city surged 47% by early November and robberies in the county were up 82%.

Similar "Ferguson effects" are happening across the country as officers scale back on proactive policing under the onslaught of anti-cop rhetoric. Arrests in Baltimore were down 56% in May compared with 2014.

"Any cop who uses his gun now has to worry about being indicted and losing his job and family," a New York City officer tells me. "Everything has the potential to be recorded. A lot of cops feel that the climate for the next couple of years is going to be nonstop protests."

Police officers now second-guess themselves about the use of force. "Officers are trying to invent techniques on the spot for taking down resistant suspects that don't look as bad as the techniques taught in the academy," says Jim Dudley, who recently retired as deputy police chief in San Francisco. Officers complain that civilians don't understand how hard it is to control someone resisting arrest.

A New York City cop tells me that he was amazed to hear people scoffing that Ferguson police officer Darren Wilson, who killed Michael Brown, only looked a "little red" after Brown assaulted him and tried to grab his weapon: "Does an officer need to be unconscious before he can use force? If someone is willing to fight you, he's also willing to take your gun and shoot you. You can't lose a fight with a guy who has already put his hands on you because if you do, you will likely end up dead."

Milwaukee Police Chief Edward A. Flynn, discussing hostility toward the police, told me in an interview on Friday: "I've never seen anything like it. I'm guessing it will take five years to recover."

Even if officer morale were to miraculously rebound, policies are being put into place that will make it harder to keep crime down in the future. Those initiatives reflect the belief that any criminal-justice action that has a disparate impact on blacks is racially motivated.

In New York, pedestrian stops — when the police question and sometimes frisk individuals engaged in suspicious behavior — have dropped nearly 95% from their 2011 high, thanks to litigation charging that the NYPD's stop, question and frisk practices were racially biased. A judge agreed, and New York Mayor Bill de Blasio, upon taking office last year, did too, embracing the resulting judicial monitoring of the police department. It is no surprise that shootings are up in the city.

Politicians and activists in New York and 20 other cities have now taken aim at "broken windows" policing. This police strategy has shown remarkable success over the past two decades by targeting low-level public-order offenses, reducing the air of lawlessness in rough neighborhoods and getting criminals off the streets before they commit bigger crimes. Opponents of broken-windows policing somehow fail to notice that law-abiding residents of poor communities are among the strongest advocates for enforcing laws against public drinking, trespassing, drug sales and drug use, among other public-order laws.

As attorney general, Eric Holder pressed the cause of ending "mass incarceration" on racial grounds; elected officials across the political spectrum have jumped on board. A 2014 California voter initiative has retroactively downgraded a range of property and drug felonies to misdemeanors, including forcible theft of guns, purses and laptops. More than 3,000 felons have already been released from California prisons, according to the Association of Deputy District Attorneys in Los Angeles County. Burglary, larceny and car theft have surged in the county, the association reports.

"There are no real consequences for committing property crimes anymore," Los Angeles Police Lt. Armando Munoz told *Downtown News* earlier this month, "and the criminals know this." The Milwaukee district attorney, John Chisholm, is diverting many property and drug criminals to rehabilitation programs to reduce the number of blacks in Wisconsin prisons; critics see the rise in Milwaukee crime as one result.

If these decriminalization and deincarceration policies backfire, the people most harmed will be their supposed beneficiaries: blacks, since they are disproportionately victimized by crime. The black death-by-homicide rate is six times higher than that of whites and Hispanics combined. The killers of those black homicide victims are overwhelmingly other black civilians, not the police. The police could end all use of lethal force tomorrow and it would have at most a negligible impact on the black death rate. In any case, the strongest predictor of whether a police officer uses force is whether a suspect resists arrest, not the suspect's race.

Contrary to the claims of the "black lives matter" movement, no government policy in the past quarter century has done more for urban reclamation than proactive policing. Data-driven enforcement, in conjunction with stricter penalties for criminals and "broken windows" policing, has saved thousands of black lives, brought lawful commerce and jobs to once drug-infested neighborhoods and allowed millions to go about their daily lives without fear.

To be sure, police officers need to treat 25 everyone they encounter with courtesy and respect. Any fatal police shooting of an innocent person is a horrifying tragedy that police training must work incessantly to prevent. But unless the demonization of law enforcement ends, the liberating gains in urban safety over the past 20 years will be lost.

Topics for Critical Thinking and Writing

1. The essay begins with a list of statistics from several large American cities showing an increase in violent crime. What is the effect of presenting this information? Were you surprised to learn that violent crime was on the rise? Why, or why not?

2. In paragraph 6, Heather Mac Donald presents her thesis: "The most plausible explanation of the current surge in lawlessness is the intense agitation against American police

departments over the past nine months." What alternative explanations does she examine in this essay, if any? If she does not, does that omission weaken her overall argument? Why, or why not?

3. Mac Donald uses the term "conceit" in paragraph 8. Look up the definition of the word in a dictionary as used in this context. Argue whether her use of the word is appropriate or inappropriate. Support your position.

4. In paragraphs 11 and 12, Mac Donald argues that police are seen as guilty until proven innocent and that even after grand juries refuse to indict an officer, the perception of guilt remains. Why do many people, including government officials, assume the police are guilty? What history or cultural experiences may lie behind these perceptions?

5. What does Mac Donald mean by the "Ferguson effect"? Where does this term come from, and why has it led to less policing?

6. In paragraph 14, a New York City officer states, "Everything has the potential to be recorded." In your opinion, is recording the actions of police officers and the civilians they encounter good for public safety or not? Defend your answer.

7. Mac Donald also cites the chief of police in Milwaukee, Edward A. Flynn, as stating that it may take five years for hostility toward police to die down. Why is there so much hostility toward police, and why do you suspect Flynn argues it will take so long to recover?

8. Mac Donald also refers to "broken windows policing" in paragraph 20, in which police respond to low-level problems as a way of discouraging more serious crimes. Research the success of this strategy. Argue either for or against Mac Donald's position. Support your answer with specific details.

9. In paragraph 23, Mac Donald states, "If these decriminalization and deincarceration policies backfire, the people most harmed will be their supposed beneficiaries: blacks, since they are disproportionately victimized by crime." Research recent trends toward decriminalization and deincarceration, especially for nonviolent drug offenses, and argue whether this trend is more likely to succeed or fail at improving public safety. Support your answer.

10. Mac Donald does not write much about the history of hostility between the police and the black community. Research on your own how the relationship between police and black communities has been destructive and dysfunctional, and what can be done to improve the relationship.

BALTIMORE SUN EDITORIAL BOARD

The Baltimore Sun *is the major newspaper in Baltimore, Maryland, a city that was hit by riots after Freddie Gray, a twenty-five-year-old black man, died while in police custody. He had sustained injuries to his neck and spine despite being healthy at the time of his arrest. This editorial appeared on October 26, 2015, shortly after FBI director James Comey spoke publically about a "YouTube effect" that was inhibiting good police work.*

No "Ferguson Effect"

On Friday, FBI Director James Comey told an audience in Chicago that he believes that the "YouTube effect" — that is, the heightened scrutiny police officers have faced after a series of highly publicized incidents of questionable use of force, including Freddie Gray's arrest in Baltimore — has contributed to the nationwide rise in violent crime. This is not a new theory — it has been voiced here by the head of the police union and by the former police commissioner, who said he believed officers "took a knee" after April's riots. Chicago Mayor Rahm Emanuel recently said he believed officers had gone "fetal" under the scrutiny. But given what Mr. Comey admits is a lack of any real data to support it, the theory is a damaging one to advance, as it only underscores the disconnect between police and the communities they are supposed to serve.

Mr. Comey said he has heard anecdotal evidence that officers are being told by superiors that their political leaders have "no tolerance for a viral video," and that as a consequence, officers are reluctant to get out of their cars and question suspicious people. "Lives are saved when those potential killers are confronted by a police officer, a strong police presence and actual, honest-to-goodness, up-close 'What are you guys doing on this corner at 1 o'clock in the morning' policing," Mr. Comey told an audience at the University of Chicago Law School. "We need to be careful it doesn't drift away from us in the age of viral videos, or there will be profound consequences."

What is so troubling about this line of reasoning is that it suggests officers have no idea about what has brought us to this point. The issue is not officers doing their jobs in an energetic, proactive way. The issue is the use of force when it's not needed, the violation of civil rights

and the general dehumanization of people who live in high crime areas, usually African Americans. The killing of Michael Brown in Ferguson, Mo., which sparked the era of heightened scrutiny for officers, was not captured on video and proved less clear-cut than reports initially suggested. But a series of subsequent cases — the killings of Eric Garner, Tamir Rice, Walter Scott and Sam DuBose, the arrest of Sandra Bland and others — cannot be construed as situations conscientious officers would find themselves in simply by doing their jobs.

The case of Freddie Gray serves well to highlight the distinction between what Mr. Comey and others are talking about and what motivates those now calling for greater scrutiny of police. Given the history of drug dealing and other crime in the area, few would question officers' decision to approach the corner where Gray and another man were hanging out on the morning of April 12. The officers' decision to chase after him when he ran away probably wouldn't have raised many eyebrows either.

But from that point onward, the officers' actions get harder and harder to defend. Did they need to use as much force as they did to restrain him? Was the allegedly illegal knife they found in his pocket really sufficient grounds to arrest him? Was there true justification for ignoring his reported requests for a medic? Was there good reason for not buckling him into a seat belt in the back of a police van? Is there some defensible rationale for placing him face down on the floor of the van with his hands and feet restrained, as prosecutors allege?

Whether or not all that amounts to criminal conduct remains to be seen, but how many officers would defend it as good police work?

Are those who say officers are afraid of scrutiny willing to argue that actions like those are necessary — or even in any way helpful — to the cause of preventing violent crime?

If Mr. Comey and the others making the "YouTube effect" argument want to understand what's really driving the push for heightened scrutiny of officers, they should read the *New York Times* investigation this Sunday into the differences in police conduct based on race. The Times analyzed traffic stop data from Greensboro, N.C., and found racially disparate treatment on virtually every metric. African Americans were stopped at a rate far beyond their share of the population, but more to the point, black motorists were twice as likely to be searched as white ones — even though

drugs and weapons turned up more frequently in cars driven by whites. Blacks were charged with a variety of minor offenses — from possession of small amounts of marijuana to resisting, obstructing or delaying an officer — far more frequently than whites. North Carolina keeps more detailed data on such encounters than other states, but the pattern held in other places where the *Times* was able to conduct a similar analysis. That kind of thing is what is prompting people to pull out video cameras when police approach.

We don't know what has caused the increase in shootings and murders in Baltimore and other cities during the last few months, but we do know the answer is not to exempt the police from public scrutiny.

Topics for Critical Thinking and Writing

1. The editors cite the speech James Comey gave at the University of Chicago Law School on October 23, 2015, as arguing that scrutiny of police actions is actually leading to higher rates of crime because officers are more reluctant to "get out of their cars and question suspicious people" (para. 2). The editors argue that without real data, this just "underscores the disconnect between police and the communities they are supposed to serve" (para. 1). Research the increase in policy scrutiny, including the use of body cameras by officers, and argue whether there is convincing proof of a correlation between greater policy scrutiny and rises in crime.

2. In paragraph 3, the editors write, "What is so troubling about this line of reasoning is that it suggests officers have no idea about what has brought us to this point." Indeed, what has brought us to this point? Research the perspective of law enforcement as well as that of the community. What is revealed about attitudes toward the use of force, including deadly force, even on unarmed suspects? Be specific.

3. The editors list a series of names of victims of police violence, including Freddie Gray, the Baltimore man who died after sustaining injuries while in police custody. Choose one of the examples, and do further research on the incident. Argue whether or not there was police misconduct. Be specific.

4. In paragraph 7, the editors cite a study done by the *New York Times* in which police stops in North Carolina were investigated. The study consistently found high rates of racial bias in who was pulled over and searched, in spite of the fact that white motorists had more drugs and weapons in their vehicles than blacks. Investigate the use of racial profiling in law enforcement, and argue whether its use is justifiable.

5. The overall message of the editorial is stated in its final paragraph: Police cannot be exempt from public scrutiny (para. 8). By itself, that seems like a harmless statement. However, at what point might scrutiny be, as Comey suggests has already occurred, counterproductive? What concrete steps or actions need to be taken to ensure both the safety of the public and that of police officers? Use research to support your answer.

STEVE CHAPMAN

Steve Chapman (b. 1954) is a columnist and editorial writer for the Chicago Tribune. *Chapman has contributed work to numerous other publications as well, including* Slate, *the* Weekly Standard, American Spectator, *and* National Review. *In this article, published on December 5, 2014, Chapman points out that blaming the black community for violent crime by blacks overlooks the realities of much of today's crime.*

Are Blacks to Blame for Cops' Actions?

When a white cop kills an unarmed black man, many blacks see a pattern of prejudice that generates official suspicion, hostility and abuse based on skin color. Many whites, however, say it's the fault of blacks. If they weren't committing so much crime, they wouldn't get so much attention from police.

This is not just a favorite theme of overt bigots and Internet trolls. It's the view of Rudy Giuliani, the former New York mayor and Republican presidential candidate, and many other whites.

Black-on-black crime "is the reason for the heavy police presence in the black community," he asserted on NBC's *Meet the Press*. "So why don't (they) cut it down so so many white police officers don't have to be in black areas?"

In this view, African-Americans have only themselves to blame for the presence and behavior of cops in their neighborhoods. If they would get serious about cleaning up the problems in their own communities, police would not be arresting or killing so many black people.

There's an element of truth to this line of argument. Violent crime rates are far higher among blacks than among whites and other groups. One reason cops have a disproportionate number of interactions with African-American males is that these men commit a disproportionate number of offenses.

Where the argument fails is in its assumption that blacks are complacent about these realities and that whites are blameless. The gist of the message is that blacks created the problem and blacks need to solve it.

But the problem didn't originate recently. In 1958 — a time of lynchings, universal discrimination and legal segregation — *Time* magazine reported that in big cities, the "biggest and most worrisome problem is the crime rate among Negroes" and said Negro leaders and civil rights groups should start "accepting responsibility in an area where they habitually look the other way."

The common impulse of whites, then and now, was to blame blacks for pathologies that whites played a central role in creating.

Criminologist Charles Silberman wrote in 1978 that "it would be hard to imagine an environment better calculated to evoke violence than the one in which black Americans have lived." Pretending black crime is a black-created problem is like pretending New Orleans never got hit by a hurricane.

The Giuliani view omits some vital facts. The epidemic of unarmed blacks being killed by police comes not when black crime is high but when it is low.

Homicides committed by African-Americans 10 declined by half between 1991 and 2008.

Since the early 1990s, arrests of black juveniles have plunged by more than half.

In New York City, where Eric Garner was killed by police, the rate of homicides by blacks is down by 80 percent. In Chicago, where most murders are committed by African-Americans, the number last year was the lowest since 1965 — and this year's could be lower yet.

What is also easy to forget in the denunciation of black crime is that the vast majority of blacks are not criminals. In any given year, less than 5 percent of African-Americans are involved in violent crime as perpetrators or victims. The fact that blacks make up a large share of the violent criminal population gives many whites the impression that violent criminals make up a large share of the black population. They don't.

Why don't more blacks living in bad neighborhoods learn to behave like sober middle-class suburbanites, some people ask? One reason is the shortage of stable families, steady incomes, good schools and safe streets. If you grow up with those advantages, it's relatively easy to do the right thing. If you don't, it's a lot harder.

People trapped in a poor and dangerous 15 slum can't depend on the authorities to keep them safe. They face serious threats every time they leave home. But a young black man who packs or uses a weapon to protect himself against gangs is committing a crime. Even motivated, well-intended kids can wind up in jail.

Crime and poverty create a vicious cycle: A child raised in a chaotic environment is not likely to learn the habits that foster success. Black children afflicted with these disadvantages often take the wrong path as teens or adults. And when they turn out badly, people like Giuliani act as though whites bear no responsibility.

Conservatives are right to say that many of the problems afflicting black communities grow out of lamentable conditions in black communities. Their mistake is thinking that's the end of the discussion. It's only the beginning.

Topics for Critical Thinking and Writing

1. Steve Chapman begins his article by discussing the black / white divide toward the killing of unarmed black men by white police officers. What does this divide illustrate about different attitudes toward the police and crime? What contributes to these different attitudes?

2. In paragraph 4, Chapman writes that many whites have the attitude that "If they [blacks] would get serious about cleaning up the problems in their own communities, police would not be arresting or killing so many black people." He follows that in the next paragraph with this comment: "There's an element of truth to this line of argument." What truth is he referring to? In what ways is the statement true, and in what ways is it not?

3. In paragraph 7, Chapman points out that whites blaming blacks for crime has a long past. He cites a *Time* magazine article blaming blacks for crime in 1958, which was "a time of lynchings, universal discrimination and legal segregation" — conditions that whites themselves created. Can the white community be said to have contributed to crimes by blacks? Defend your answer.

4. Beginning in paragraph 9, Chapman points out that data shows crime has been trending downward across the board, including crimes by blacks. Thus, the "epidemic" of police shooting unarmed black men doesn't appear to be caused by police responding to rampant crime. What, then, might be the cause of the increase in police shootings? Do research to support your answer.

5. In paragraph 14, Chapman argues that blacks living in bad neighborhoods cannot be expected to act like "sober middle-class suburbanites." Do you find his argument convincing? Why, or why not?

6. Chapman states, "Crime and poverty create a vicious cycle" (para. 16). Research whether rates of crime are connected to the presence of poverty or other economic problems. Argue whether poverty is a major cause of crime. Defend your answer.

7. Chapman also argues that whites bear some responsibility for black crime because white actions created many of the bad conditions in which blacks live. Research the history of race relations in this country, and decide whether you agree or disagree with this argument. Defend your answer.

DAVID H. BAYLEY, MICHAEL A. DAVIS, AND RONALD L. DAVIS

David H. Bayley (b. 1933) is a distinguished professor emeritus in the School of Criminal Justice at the State University of New York–Albany. Michael A. Davis is the chief law enforcement officer for Northeastern University in Boston. Ronald L. Davis (b. 1964) was appointed by U.S. attorney general Eric Holder in November 2013 as the director of the Office of Community Oriented Policing Services (COPS Office) of the U.S. Department of Justice (DOJ). Together, they co-authored this report for the Executive Session on Policy and Public Safety at the Harvard Kennedy School, Program in Criminal Justice Policy and Management. The article was published in June 2015.

Race and Policing: An Agenda for Action

American police confront issues of race, daily, in almost everything they do. They confront race in the geographic distribution of criminality and the fear of crime as well as in assumptions about what criminals look like. They confront race in the suspicion and hostility of many young African American men they encounter on the street. They confront race in complaints from ethnic communities about being either over- or under-policed. They confront race in charges of racial profiling and unequal justice. And they confront race in decisions about hiring, promoting and assigning police officers. In short, race remains an "American dilemma," as Gunnar Myrdal famously observed in 1944 (Myrdal, 1944), especially and inescapably for today's police.

The importance of race in policing has been demonstrated in discussions held since 2008 at the Second Executive Session on Policing and Public Safety at Harvard University. At almost every session, race emerged as a troubling preoccupation for police executives. Although many suggestions for dealing with the issue were discussed, the Executive Session did not try to formulate policies to deal with the various issues involving race. Concern about race seemed to become stalled in discussion rather than advancing to action. So, the authors of this article suggested to the Session members that we try to cull an agenda for action from the years of frank, insightful and sometimes passionate conversation. The Session readily agreed. These are the ideas we think are most promising in terms of what police executives might do to alleviate the problems of race in contemporary policing. They reflect what we have learned that might help the most. We alone are responsible for the contents of this agenda.

Readers should also understand that the agenda consists of suggestions, not directions. Although some of these ideas have been tried, few, if any, have been evaluated. Furthermore, many of them are controversial. We include them nonetheless in order to provoke thought, often explicitly acknowledging their shortcomings. We hope that this agenda will move discussions about race from anger and yearning to concrete action by police leaders, and beyond. This is also not a "scholarly" paper that cites and explores all the writing that has been done on the activities suggested. That is beyond our ability. Therefore, before following any of our leads, readers should do their homework. Others, often more experienced than we, have thought about these issues before.

The agenda is organized into two parts — Strategic Voice and Tactical Agency. Strategic Voice argues that problems of race in policing cannot be resolved by the police alone. Other people must help by understanding and ameliorating the social conditions that cause race to be associated with crime and hence become a dilemma for American policing. Rather than accepting these conditions as givens, police leaders with their powerful collective voice should actively call attention to what needs to be changed.

Tactical Agency outlines what the police can do on their own initiative to deal with the operational dilemmas of race — in the communities they serve and in their own organizations.

STRATEGIC VOICE

We believe there are two messages that police leaders must find the voice to deliver: (1) Police need to be supported by policies that address conditions causing criminality and disorder to be concentrated in particular places, especially in communities of color; and (2) police strategies must expand freedom and justice, not just provide safety.

Strategic Voice One

Police officers know, through hard-won experience, that crime is not randomly distributed in society. It is concentrated in particular places. Any good cop can drive immediately to the neighborhoods where crimes rates are the highest and 911 calls are most common. Most of the rest of their jurisdictions are virtually free of reported crime.

The problem is that the highest rates of violent crime are in minority neighborhoods — those where African Americans, Latinos and new immigrants live. This creates the impression that race or ethnicity is implicated in criminality and that serious crime in America is particularly a "black problem" (Braga and Brunson, 2015). However, this reasoning gets the causality backward. Race does not generate criminality but, rather, the circumstances that create compacted disadvantage for minority groups also create criminality. As the police who work in minority communities know, people of color are no more tolerant of crime and disorder than others. It also obscures the fact that minority people are more likely than the majority of white people to be victims of crime.

Police also know that their ability to reduce crime where it matters most, as in disadvantaged neighborhoods, is limited through both reactive law enforcement and proactive crime prevention programs. This is not to say that the police cannot do anything, although it is generally agreed that deterrence alone will not reduce crime for people most at risk from it. Police officers are often frustrated by what little they can achieve as they respond over and over to the same problems among the same people in the same places. They feel that they are only "a band-aid on a cancer."

So, our first recommendation is that police leaders call attention publicly to the conditions of economic and social disadvantage that generate crime and disorder and undermine the ability of communities to protect themselves. They should speak loudly about the connections they see in their own experience between serious crime and conditions of unemployment, poverty, truancy, education attrition, teen pregnancy, housing segregation, inadequate health care, crowded and unsanitary housing, homelessness, underfinanced public services, and a lack of civic amenities such as parks, public transportation and street lighting. They should say publicly, out loud, as one commentator said almost 40 years ago, that police can only "perform a holding operation until other institutions attack such problems with an array of resources" (Robinson, 1975: 278).

Of course, it is one thing to be critical of, even outraged by, persistent, self-perpetuating conditions associated with high crime rates. It is another to frame policies that will successfully remedy them. Doing this will take the finest minds the country has. All we can do is suggest the sorts of policy changes that should be considered:

1. Recognize that race endures as an issue in America, not just because people are prejudiced but also because they fail to support structural changes that equalize opportunity. Law enforcement should not be viewed as a morality play between good guys and bad guys. It is about circumstances that put people on different life courses. Police, black communities and even street gangs are, as David Kennedy (2011) has said:

   all, all of them, in their own ways strong and aspirational and resilient. They are, all of them, dealing as best they can with a world they did not make. They are all doing profoundly destructive things without understanding what they do.

There is, on all sides, malice, craziness, and evil, but not much, it turns out, not much at all. There is, on all sides, a deep reservoir of core human decency. (p. 17)

2. Focus crime prevention programs on communities and neighborhoods, not just on individuals. In particular, improve physical environments, fix the famous "broken windows," and develop the capacity of communities to organize for the advancement of common interests, whether using their own resources or mobilizing wider public and private help.

3. Mobilize and coordinate all government services bearing on public safety rather than assigning responsibility exclusively to the police. If criminality is rooted in social conditions, especially chronic deprivations, then more than police action is required to prevent it. Effective crime prevention requires that all the resources of government — welfare, education, health, sanitation, recreation, public transport — be focused where criminality is concentrated. It requires whole-of-government planning and implementation.

Strategic Voice One may be sensible and righteous, but it poses risks for police. It puts them squarely into politics by challenging the policy shortcomings of the very governments that hired them. Furthermore, these brave words undermine what police chiefs promise and what the public expects from the police — safety represented by effective crime control. They challenge the very raison d'être of police. Although social policies undoubtedly contribute to crime, the police have been created precisely to minimize their effects.

Strategic Voice One is also out of sync with American public opinion about structural inequality, according to an NBC/Wall Street Journal poll in June 2013 (Blow, 2013). Asked to explain poverty in the U.S., most people (24 percent) blamed the individuals themselves, especially citing receipt of welfare that eroded individual initiative. Only 4 percent blamed "lack of government money." They did implicate unemployment (18 percent) and poor schooling (13 percent), although one wonders where they thought the remedies would come from, if not from government. The article concludes that "the stereotypes of poor people in the United States are among the most negative prejudices that we have. . . . It seems like Washington is a place without pity right now" (Blow, 2013). That these uncharitable views may be laced with racism goes without saying.

Scholars, too, have been complicit in fostering doubts about the efficacy of structural interventions. In his 1975 book, *Thinking about Crime*, James Q. Wilson argued that government was ill-equipped to remedy the root causes of crime, even if they could be identified with certainty (Wilson, 1975). He believed that public policy should focus on changing the incentives for crime by increasing the risk to offenders and lowering the relative rewards. Criminology in the following years seemed to follow his lead, focusing more on exploring factors that facilitated criminality (such as "routine activity theory," Cohen and Felson, 1979) or changing criminal trajectories of individuals than on macrosocial correlates

(Sampson, 2012). Advocates for structural reform have been very few (Currie, 2010). Intellectual predispositions, it would seem, may shape scholarship just as ideology does politics.

Asking police leaders to speak with Strategic Voice One is asking a lot. It requires them to articulate a larger vision of the social forces and structural factors linked to crime, even as they direct the everyday efforts of their police officers to address specific incidents of crime. As one member of the Executive Session said, "I feel like if we are going to be the canaries in the coal mine about this issue [race] from a macro level, we are going to really injure our ability to do any good at the micro level."

Strategic Voice Two

The primary purpose for which police have been created is to safeguard life and property. This should continue to be their operational focus because public safety is not only a human right; it is fundamental to any constructive social activity, including the kind of community reconstruction suggested by Strategic Voice One. Implementing this purpose is more complex in the United States, however, because public safety must be created in a particularly demanding way, namely, within a rule of law that protects individuals from unjustified intrusions of governmental power. American policing is not just about crime fighting; it involves enhancing human freedom at the same time. Policing in America has two goals, both equally important (Manning, 2011).

Accordingly, we recommend that police leaders explain, publicly and repeatedly, what is involved in combining effective law enforcement with liberty. It begins with finding the voice to criticize criminal justice policies that produce high rates of black male incarceration, perceptions of racial profiling, unequal enforcement of drug laws, and justice outcomes affected by race and class.

But it goes farther. It requires police, through word and deed, to obtain the public's consent for their actions. Policing with consent is an old theme in the democratic police tradition. Sir Robert Peel, considered the founding father of modern Anglo-American policing (1829), is credited with formulating nine principles of policing, three of which involve policing with communities (CIVITAS, 2014):

- "To recognise always that the power of the police to fulfil their functions and duties is dependent on public approval of their existence, actions and behaviour and on their ability to secure and maintain public respect."

- "To recognise always that to secure and maintain the respect and approval of the public means also the securing of the willing co-operation of the public in the task of securing observance of laws."

- "To maintain at all times a relationship with the public that gives reality to the historic tradition that the police are the public and that the public are the police, the police being only members of the public who are paid to give full[-]time attention to duties which are incumbent on every citizen in the interests of community welfare and existence."

These principles became meaningful at first through the encouragement of the public to contact police directly whenever something is wrong that needs authoritative intervention, such as the commission of crime. Operationally, this became the 911 dispatch system developed during the 20th century. The importance of public input in creating the police agenda was reaffirmed by the First Executive Session on Police and Public Safety, 1986–1992, but with a new wrinkle. Rather than having police work defined by individuals as well as the police themselves, the First Session stressed the importance of police consulting with, as well as mobilizing, communities with common interests. This was called community policing. Two of the recommendations were to create neighborhood advisory boards and for police officers to conduct periodic visits to individual homes and businesses. In effect, community policing introduced a new level of social organization into policing by consent — groups of individuals organized by interest and/or geography.

Together, 911 and community policing [20] empowered the public to shape what police do through individual and neighborhood instigation. Through them, policing by consent became radically democratized. It shifted the authority for determining what police do away from formal government, represented by the police, and directly to the public. As a result, police in the United States and in other democratic countries became more than agents of government. They became the citizens' police (Bayley, 1985). "Consent" in democratic countries means more than acceptance by the public of what the police are doing; it also means the ability to shape that activity directly through personal contact. This represents a radical change in the relation of security institutions to the public — one that has become the distinguishing characteristic of democratic policing. Policing by consent, in this sense, exists in only a handful of countries worldwide.

Policing with consent has another dimension, one more recently discovered: namely, how the police act in their encounters with the public. Beginning in the early 1990s, Professor Tom Tyler showed that when people are treated by the police in ways they regard as respectful and fair, they are less likely to resist and more likely to conform to what the law requires (Tyler, 2006). Robert Peel, in fact, made much the same point in one of his nine principles of policing (CIVITAS, 2014):

> [Police should] seek and preserve public favour, not by pandering to public opinion[,] but by constantly demonstrating absolutely impartial service to law, in complete independence of policy, and without regard to the justice or injustice of the substance of individual laws[;] by ready offering of individual service and friendship to all members of the public without regard to their wealth or social standing[;] by ready exercise of courtesy and friendly good humour; and by ready offering of individual sacrifice in protecting and preserving life.

Tyler's research moved significantly beyond Peel's generalities by showing that police behavior, both in attitude and procedure, could improve law enforcement outcomes even with people who have violated the law. "Procedural justice," as he calls it, undercuts a common belief among police that authority has to be visibly demonstrated to actual and potential lawbreakers and that adhering to technicalities of legal procedure undermines deterrence. Procedural justice challenges the mindset that there are tradeoffs between effectiveness in controlling crime and observance of civil rights guaranteed by the Constitution.

Giving voice to policing by consent is probably less controversial than the social reforms of Strategic Voice One. Priorities in police work and the behavior of officers are ongoing topics of conversation within contemporary police agencies, well within the "police line of work." Moreover, police officers understand from their own experience the importance of having the public "on their side." Exercising "discretion" in applying the law is an accepted part of police professionalism. Police officers know that different folks need different strokes. The crucial question is, which folks?

At the same time, some of the issues embedded in policing with consent are controversial among police, and discussing them in public is not something they may be comfortable doing.

Responding to calls for service in a timely manner, for example, is enormously popular with the public and politicians alike. It is costly, however, and may divert resources that might be more effectively employed in proactive crime prevention. Some of the popular new strategies, such as predictive and hot spots policing, depend on analyses done by headquarters staff, not input from the public. Police may also know better, in some cases, about how to deal with particular forms of crime. Furthermore, police are increasingly expected to address not just crimes that affect individuals (street crime) but also crimes that affect the society as a whole, such as terrorism, drug markets, human trafficking and violent youth gangs. Within this crowded agenda, encouraging and facilitating direct public input may seem a luxury from a bygone age (Bayley and Nixon, 2010).

So, too, with procedural justice. Many police officers believe that respect comes from a display of authority. They believe that they are the best judges of people who are deserving of soft or hard treatment, and they resent having their decisions challenged. The public, too, is ambivalent about procedural justice. Many people believe strongly in being "tough on crime" and not "coddling criminals," and they are willing to excuse intrusive and punitive policing when they fear the crime is close at hand.

Selling procedural justice will be much easier in the abstract than in the particular. In areas experiencing high levels of violence, police and the public may doubt that procedural justice will gain enough consent, especially from troublemakers, to improve safety significantly. Perhaps in those situations, consent is more likely to come from being "tough on crime" rather than from procedural justice (Tankebe, 2009). Issues like these are being explored and tested in a departmentwide training program developed by the Chicago Police Department in 2011. It has already been given to over 3,000 employees (Meares and Neyroud, 2015).

Finally, supporting policing by consent involves taking a stand on another development that is very controversial among police, namely, civilian review. In the U.S., racial minorities have repeatedly criticized the willingness of police agencies to investigate themselves. Their consent to be policed turns, to a considerable degree, on whether they believe police are being held to account. Civilian review is supposed to provide that assurance. Civilian review panels have been used to evaluate both the crime-control effectiveness of the police and the behavior of police in carrying out assigned duties.

The questions for American police are not "whether" to allow civilian review but, instead, "when" and "how." More than 100 American cities have already developed some form of it. All Canadian provinces and all Australian states have; so, too, has Great Britain (Stenning, 2011; Walker, 2010). Civilian review is being advocated by both the United Nations and the U.S. government as fundamental to police reform in countries emerging from civil strife. For many people in democratic countries, civilian review is essential for ensuring that police are practicing procedural justice.

What is often not recognized in debates about civilian review is that it is not uni-dimensional. It varies from place to place in membership, powers and ambit of oversight. Some civilian review boards, for example, only evaluate the rigor with which the police receive, investigate and discipline allegations of misbehavior and then publish the results. Others have the power to oversee particular investigations and provide advice about them. Still others completely remove investigations and the determination of sanctions from police authority. Being either in favor or opposed to civilian review in principle is naive — especially when one considers that, in democratic countries, civilian review already occurs by elected officials, courts and the media. "Civilian review" may be new, but review by civilians is not.

In sum, speaking with Strategic Voice 30 Two is easy to do in normative generalities. It fits America's democratic heritage. The difficulty comes in convincing police officers and the public that policing with consent improves the effectiveness of crime control. Scholars and many police officers believe that it does. Strategic Voice Two requires police leaders to participate in a public discussion about the importance of policing with consent in achieving public safety. In particular,

it challenges them to discuss openly whether small encroachments on civil rights enhance public safety or, at the very least, to explain when exceptions are justified.

TACTICAL AGENCY

Police may do important things to address the dilemmas of race in policing without waiting for outside support in the form of either additional resources or progressive social policies. Indeed, many departments have courageously accepted the need to confront issues of race, instituting new programs and revising customary ways of doing business. We provide references to some active programs (see "References"). However, given the number and variety of American police agencies, the implementation of such actions has been uneven. To encourage and assist in reform, we make the following suggestions, drawing on the growing experience of police themselves and on the research by scholars. Our suggestions are divided into two parts — engaging the community and managing police agencies.

Engaging the Community

1. Reorient the culture of policing from going to war against lawbreakers to engaging with communities to help those at risk and in need. One way to do this is to take the time to educate police officers about the history of the communities to which they are assigned, stressing the fact that their inhabitants, especially the children, have no control over that history.

2. Embrace community policing as the primary strategy for policing. This is not an uncomplicated suggestion. Community policing has been consistently advocated as a philosophy applicable throughout policing (see, e.g., Bayley and Skolnick, 1988). Views differ considerably, however, about its programmatic elements (Maguire et al., 1997). As a result, officers have been confused about what it means for their work, frequently dismissing it with the comment, "community policing, whatever that means." For this reason, many officers have come to the conclusion that it was largely a matter of rhetoric, a flavor-of-the-month whose time had passed. Problem-oriented policing (POP), often associated with community-oriented policing, has enjoyed greater staying power precisely because it has a clear implementation program. POP quickly became identified as a set of activities — scanning, analysis, response and assessment — identified by the acronym SARA.

3. Police officers should develop the habit of explaining what they are doing whenever they act (Fridell et al., 2001). This is particularly important when an encounter has occurred as a result of the initiative of the police officer, especially when African Americans are the target.

4. Patrol supervisors should regularly assess how people contacted by the police feel about the treatment they received. This may be done systematically through surveys or by direct contact with individuals who have solicited help or have been contacted proactively.

5. A simple, user-friendly system for receiving complaints from the public about police behavior should be created. Its receptiveness should be tested periodically by sending civilians or plainclothes police officers to file complaints. For example, the Charlotte-Mecklenburg police in North Carolina have created a website for filing complaints online (http://charmeck.org/city /charlotte/CMPD/Pages /Complaints.aspx).

6. Routinely collect and publish information about allegations of police misbehavior, the results of investigations into them, and their disciplinary outcomes. This kind of transparency is important for reassuring communities that police are serious about investigating and punishing misbehavior. It makes the issue of police discipline discussable publicly.

Managing the Organization

Police organizations are themselves microcosms of the community they serve, where larger societal issues have very real implications for running an effective organization. In order to make progress externally, the police need to improve race relations internally.

1. Officers in supervisory positions must demonstrate, by word and action, that protection of human rights should permeate all aspects of policing. Their performance in this regard should be part of their annual evaluations. In particular, supervisors at all levels must never tolerate attitudes (often revealed in denigrating language) that excuse differential treatment of particular groups, such as "We have to be tough with those people" and "Those people only respect force."

2. Managers must search out and confront racial and ethnic tensions among officers, especially perceptions by minorities that they have not received equitable treatment in assignments or promotions. Frank discussions with organizations representing minority officers can be very helpful.

3. In place of detailed regulations, statements of values should be developed that guide all aspects of policing that involve the public. Having clear statements about standards of behavior is necessary in order to empower supervisors in taking corrective action. As one participant at the Executive Session remarked, "It's easier to act your way to right thinking than to think your way to right acting." Right behavior is ensured when it is required by the immediate supervisors.

   The Madison, Wis., police department pioneered this approach in the early 1980s. The Milwaukee Police Department has a detailed code of conduct specifying the department's mission, values and disciplinary guidelines. (See http://city. milwaukee.gov/police under "About MPD/Code of Conduct & Standard Operating Procedures").

4. Take time to explain the importance of neighborhood histories so that officers understand the people they will be dealing with. This is usually done through "cultural sensitivity" programs featuring presentations by members of racial and ethnic communities.

   A better way is to show recruits what the world looks like from subcultural points of view. This can be done by assigning recruit officers to live among and with minority families for short periods of time or to serve as interns for neighborhood nonprofit organizations.

5. Develop procedures for evaluating whether officers engage effectively with communities, and reward them in recognizable ways.

6. Create early warning systems for detecting patterns of behavior, such as complaints filed against officers, that indicate potential vulnerabilities for the officer and the department. The primary purpose of such systems is not to punish but to provide counseling to officers so as to reduce their level of risk. The creation of such a system was a key recommendation in the 1997 consent decree between the U.S. Department of Justice and the Pittsburgh police department, and many other accords since then.

CONCLUSION

The purpose of this article has been to move the discussion about the dilemmas of race in policing from talk to action. Although we think these actions will help to ease tensions at the intersection of policing and race, race will remain difficult to talk about. However, at some point in the career of every senior officer, the need to do so will almost inevitably arise. It will occur when a white officer shoots a black man, when police of any color arrest distraught minority women amid a jeering crowd, and when crime-control activities in high-crime neighborhoods weigh more heavily on minority people. In situations like these, race becomes "the third rail" in discussions between police leaders and their communities, leading to an angry disconnect. Because of its sensitivity, therefore, police leaders should think carefully about what they should say when race-infused events occur.

The key is for police leaders to remember that they are not trying to change the minds of the people who are either irretrievably bigoted or already open-minded. Some people are attuned to expect prejudice in all dealings with the police, others reflexively defend the police and discount charges of unequal treatment, and still others wave the "bloody flag" of race for their own purposes. The target audience is not these, but the vast majority who know little about either policing or race. For these people, the discussion needs to move away from charge and countercharge to an understanding of what police work requires and what minority status compels with regard to treatment.

If approached with forethought and no small amount of courage, controversial race-implicated events should be seen as opportunities to develop new understandings and not just as inevitable public relations disasters. Police officials should not speak hastily before they have basic facts about what occurred. And they must be willing to "let the chips fall where they may" if mistakes, individual or organizational, have been made. This requires police leaders to do a tricky two-step — reassuring their officers that there will be no rush to judgment while convincing minority communities that justice will be done.

Police officials should use these occasions to point out that confrontations between police and minorities do not arise primarily out of differences in values. Minority individuals, except for a few unredeemable criminals, want safety and order as much as the majority of people. Sadly, however, many minority individuals have been raised within a structure that limits their ability to have stable families, obtain necessary education, and be gainfully employed. Their culture is not at fault, but the circumstances into which they were born are.

On the other hand, most police officers are [50] not prejudiced against minorities, although some are. Most act according to inherited understandings that focus enforcement attention on minority people, especially young males. Police officers are required to prevent crime by acting on suspicion within a society where many people, white as well as black, identify young, black males as likely threats and stereotype them as criminals.

Developing this kind of empathic voice in contemporary policing is a tall order. But words can shape events, creating new and more positive directions as scenarios unfold. In particular, they can diminish the perception that race is the sole or primary issue affecting police-minority relations.

REFERENCES

Bayley, David H. 1985. *Patterns of Policing: A Comparative International Analysis.* New Brunswick, New Jersey: Rutgers University Press.

Bayley, David H., and Christine Nixon. 2010. *The Changing Environment for Policing, 1985–2008.* Cambridge, Massachusetts: Harvard Kennedy School.

Bayley, David H., and Jerome H. Skolnick. 1988. *Community Policing: Issues and Practices Around the World.* Washington, D.C.: U.S. Department of Justice, National Institute of Justice.

Blow, Charles M. "A Town Without Pity," *The New York Times,* Aug. 10, 2013, A19. Report of NBC News/*Wall Street Journal* poll, June 2013.

Braga, Anthony, and Rod K. Brunson. 2015. *The Police and Public Discourse on "Black-on-Black" Violence.* New Perspectives in Policing Bulletin. Washington, D.C.: U.S. Department of Justice. NCJ 248588.

CIVITAS (The Institute for the Study of Civil Society). 2014. *The Nine Principles of Policing.* Based on "General Instructions" to British Metropolitan Police, 1829, by Sir Robert Peel, and republished 1956 as appendix in *A New Study of Police History,* by Charles Reith (London: Oliver and Boyd). www.civitas.org.uk/pubs/policeNine.php.

Cohen, Lawrence E., and Marcus K. Felson. 1979. Social change and crime rate trends: A routine activity approach. *American Sociological Review* 44: 588–608. http://dx.doi.org/10.2307/2094589

Currie, Elliott. 2010. "On Being Right, but Unhappy." *Criminology and Public Policy* 9(1): 1–10. (Vollmer Award Address, American Society of Criminology, 2009.)

Fridell, Laurie, Bob Lunney, Drew Diamond and Bruce Kobe. 2001. *Racial Profiling — A Principled Response.* Washington, D.C.: Police Executive Research Forum.

Kennedy, David. 2011. *Don't Shoot: One Man, a Street Fellowship, and the End of Violence in Inner-City America.* New York: Bloomsbury.

Maguire, Edward R., Joseph B. Kuhns, Craig D. Uchida and Stephen M. Cox. 1997. "Patterns of Community Policing in Nonurban America." *Journal of Research in Crime and Delinquency* 34 (3): 368–394.

Manning, Peter K. 2011. *Democratic Policing in a Changing World.* Boulder, Colorado: Paradigm Publishers.

Meares, Tracey L., with Peter Neyroud. 2015. *Rightful Policing.* New Perspectives in Policing Bulletin. Washington, D.C.: U.S. Department of Justice. National Institute of Justice. NCJ 248411.

Myrdal, Gunnar. 1944. *An American Dilemma: The Negro Problem and Modern Democracy.* New York: Harper & Bros.

Robinson, Cyril D. 1975. "The Mayor and the Police — the Political Role of the Police in Society," in George L. Mosse (ed.), *Police Forces in History,* vol. 2. Beverly Hills, California: Sage Publications.

Sampson, Robert J. 2012. *Great American City: Chicago and the Enduring Neighborhood Effect.* Chicago: University of Chicago Press.

Stenning, Phillip. 2011. "Governance of the Police: Independence, Accountability and Interference." *Flinders Law Journal* 13 (2): 241–267.

Tankebe, P.J. 2009. "Public Cooperation with the Police in Ghana: Does Procedural Fairness Matter?" *Criminology* 47 (4): 1265–1294.

Tyler, Tom R. 2006. *Why People Obey the Law*. Princeton, New Jersey: Princeton University Press.

Walker, Sam. 2010. "Police Accountability and the Central Problem of American Criminal Justice," in Candace McCoy (ed.), *Holding Police Accountable*. Washington, D.C.: The Urban Institute.

Wilson, James Q. 1975. *Thinking About Crime*. New York: Basic Books.

Topics for Critical Thinking and Writing

1. In the opening paragraph, the authors cite Gunnar Myrdal's observation that race is an "American dilemma." What does that mean? Why is this specifically identified as an American problem and not a worldwide problem? Do you agree with this statement? Why, or why not?

2. The authors have a disclaimer in paragraph 3: their work consists only of suggestions, few of their ideas have actually been evaluated, and some of what they say is controversial. Why do you suppose the authors felt it was necessary to include the disclaimer, and in your opinion does it make the authors more or less credible? Explain your response.

3. In paragraph 8, the authors state that because communities with high crime rates are typically in minority neighborhoods, people associate race with crime. However, the authors claim, this erroneous association is backwards: "Race does not generate criminality but, rather, the circumstances that create compacted disadvantage for minority groups also create criminality." What do the authors mean by the expression "compacted disadvantage"? Do you agree with authors' statement about the causes of crime? Why, or why not?

4. The authors' first recommendation is that "police leaders call attention publicly to the conditions of economic and social disadvantage that generate crime and disorder . . ." (para. 10). Why is this recommendation controversial? What are the potential pitfalls for police leaders in following this advice?

5. In paragraph 11, the authors state, "Law enforcement should not be viewed as a morality play between good guys and bad guys." Research to what extent good guy/bad guy thinking pervades law enforcement. Why does that thinking occur? Can it be changed? Should it be changed? Why, or why not?

6. What does the term "structural inequality" mean as used in paragraph 13? How does that affect the way in which people think about crime, race, and law enforcement?

7. In paragraph 17, the authors call on police leaders to criticize their own, saying that they need to find "the voice to criticize criminal justice policies that produce high rates of black male incarceration, perceptions of racial profiling, unequal enforcement of drug laws, and justice outcomes affected by race and class." In your opinion, is this a realistic suggestion? Why, or why not?

8. What do the authors mean by the expression "policing with consent" (para. 18)? What do they advise that is different from standard policing as conducted in the United States? Does this concept weaken or strengthen the public's trust in the police — especially the portion of the public that may experience a large amount of interaction with the police? Explain your response.

9. In the section titled "Tactical Agency" (beginning with para. 31), the authors offer concrete advice, broken into two subsections: "Engaging the Community" and "Managing the Organization." Examine the first subsection, "Engaging the Community." Choose one point in particular to defend or criticize. Be specific.

10. Examine the second subsection of "Tactical Agency," called "Managing the Organization." Choose one point in particular to defend or criticize. Be specific.

11. In the conclusion, the authors state that they want to move "from talk to action" (para. 46). Why is change so hard to effect, especially in the criminal justice system? Support your answer with specific examples and details.

21

Junk Food: Should the Government Regulate Our Intake?

I n the summer of 2012, Mayor Michael R. Bloomberg of New York City made a proposal to severely restrict the sale of certain kinds of drinks. In September 2012, it was approved by the New York City Board of Health and scheduled to go into effect in 2013. Here is the gist of Bloomberg's thinking:

> Sugary drinks — here defined as those with twenty-five or more calories per eight-ounce serving — if consumed in large quantities unquestionably contribute to obesity. It is therefore desirable to discourage the consumption of large amounts of these drinks.
>
> Ban the sale — in delis, fast-food franchises, and street stands — of bottles containing more than sixteen fluid ounces of such drinks.
>
> Larger bottles would be available at grocery stores and convenience stores.
>
> Other kinds of drinks, such as fruit drinks, diet sodas, dairy-based drinks (e.g., milk shakes), and alcoholic beverages, would not be restricted.

In short, this proposal was a ban only on selling large containers of certain kinds of drinks in certain kinds of places. And even in the restricted places, consumers could buy any number of the smaller bottles, so the determined consumer could indeed get more than sixteen ounces if he or she wanted to, though at the cost of some inconvenience.

On March 11, 2013, the day before the law was to go into effect, Justice Milton A. Tingling Jr. of the New York State Supreme Court struck down the ban, saying that it was "arbitrary and capricious." Examples of the alleged arbitrariness were (1) the ban did *not* apply to dairy-based sugary drinks such as milk shakes, and (2) it would be enforced in restaurants, delicatessens, theaters, and food-carts but not in convenience stores and bodegas. Do these examples strike you as "arbitrary"?

This editorial was published on June 1, 2012. We follow it with two letters, both published on June 2, 2012.

A Ban Too Far

Mayor Michael Bloomberg has done a lot to help improve the health of New York City residents. Smoking is outlawed in workplaces, restaurants, and bars. Trans fat is banned in restaurants. Chain restaurants are required to post calorie counts, allowing customers to make informed choices.

Mr. Bloomberg, however, is overreaching with his new plan to ban the sale of sugary drinks larger than sixteen ounces. He argues that prohibiting big drinks at restaurants, movie theaters, stadiums, and other food sellers can help combat obesity. But as he admits, customers can get around the ban by purchasing two drinks.

The administration should be focusing its energies on programs that educate and encourage people to make sound choices. For example, obesity rates have declined slightly among students in elementary and middle schools, with the city's initiatives to make lunches healthier with salad bars, lower-calorie drinks, and water fountains in cafeterias. Requiring students to get more exercise has also helped.

The city should keep up its tough anti-obesity advertising campaigns—one ad shows that it takes walking from Union Square to Brooklyn to burn off the calories from a twenty-ounce soda. The mayor has also started adult exercise programs and expanded the program for more fresh produce vendors around the city.

Promoting healthy lifestyles is impor- 5 tant. In the case of sugary drinks, a regular reminder that a sixty-four-ounce cola has 780 calories should help. But too much nannying with a ban might well cause people to tune out.

Letters of Response by Gary Taustine and Brian Elbel

To the Editor:

Mayor Michael R. Bloomberg's effort to promote healthier lifestyles is commendable, but the government has no right whatsoever to go beyond promotion to enforcement. You can't reduce obesity with smaller cups any more than you can reduce gun violence with smaller bullets.

This proposal sets a very bad, very dangerous precedent. Freedom is rarely taken away in supersize amounts; more typically it is slowly siphoned off drop by drop so people don't even notice until they've lost it entirely.

Mayor Bloomberg has spent his eleven years in office stripping away our freedoms one drop at a time. Minorities are stopped and frisked, Muslims are watched, protesters are silenced, and smokers are taxed and harassed beyond reason.

In their apathy, New Yorkers have given the mayor an inch and he has already taken a mile. If we permit him to regulate portion control without a fight, then we don't deserve the few freedoms we have left.

GARY TAUSTINE
New York, June 1, 2012

To the Editor:

Re "A Ban Too Far" (editorial, June 1):

To focus on education when discussing solutions to obesity misunderstands the scientific evidence about what can alter our staggering statistics and what manifestly cannot.

Mayor Michael R. Bloomberg's proposal to restrict the sale of large sugar-sweetened beverages changes the food environment — the places where foods and beverages are bought. The best science affirms that this is exactly the approach that could curb obesity trends. This same science indicates that education-based approaches, which also have their place, will do much less by comparison.

That sugary beverages contribute to obesity is clear. The science also tells us that changing the default beverage choice to something smaller could induce people to consume just that smaller beverage rather than deal with the cost and hassle of buying and carrying two or more.

Time and further research will tell. But the continued focus on simply informing and educating consumers is doomed to failure and diminishes this important policy and the influence it could have on obesity.

BRIAN ELBEL

New York, June 1, 2012

The writer is an assistant professor of population health and health policy at the New York University School of Medicine.

Topic for Critical Thinking and Writing

Draft a letter to the newspaper expressing your support or disapproval —full or in part — of the position taken in the editorial. In your letter you may, if you wish, include a comment about either or both of the published letters of response.

The Nanny

You only thought *you lived in the land of the free.*

Bye Bye Venti

Nanny Bloomberg has taken his strange obsession with what you eat one step further. He now wants to make it illegal to serve "sugary drinks" bigger than 16 oz. What's next? Limits on the width of a pizza slice, size of a hamburger or amount of cream cheese on your bagel?

New Yorkers need a Mayor, not a Nanny.

© consumerfreedom.com

Find out more at ConsumerFreedom.com

Topics for Critical Thinking and Writing

1. Is the ad on page 521, showing Mayor Bloomberg as a nanny, funny? Why, or why not? Might anyone, apart perhaps from the mayor, find the ad offensive? Why, or why not?

2. Is the ad truthful in saying that the mayor "wants to make it illegal to serve 'sugary drinks' bigger than 16 oz."?

DANIEL E. LIEBERMAN

Daniel E. Lieberman (b. 1964), a professor of human evolutionary biology at Harvard, is the author of The Evolution of the Human Head *(2011). His chief academic interest is why the human body looks the way it does — why, for instance, we have short necks and why we don't have snouts. This op-ed piece was published in the* New York Times *on June 6, 2012.*

Evolution's Sweet Tooth

Of all the indignant responses to Mayor Michael R. Bloomberg's plan to ban the sale of giant servings of soft drinks in New York City, libertarian objections seem the most worthy of serious attention. People have certain rights, this argument goes, including the right to drink lots of soda, to eat junk food, to gain weight, and to avoid exercise. If Mr. Bloomberg can ban the sale of sugar-laden soda of more than sixteen ounces, will he next ban triple scoops of ice cream and large portions of French fries and limit sales of Big Macs to one per order? Why not ban obesity itself?

The obesity epidemic has many dimensions, but at heart it's a biological problem. An evolutionary perspective helps explain why two-thirds of American adults are overweight or obese, and what to do about it. Lessons from evolutionary biology support the mayor's plan: when it comes to limiting sugar in our food, some kinds of coercive action are not only necessary but also consistent with how we used to live.

Obesity's fundamental cause is long-term energy imbalance — ingesting more calories than you spend over weeks, months, and years. Of the many contributors to energy imbalance today, plentiful sugar may be the worst.

Since sugar is a basic form of energy in food, a sweet tooth was adaptive in ancient times, when food was limited. However, excessive sugar in the bloodstream is toxic, so our bodies also evolved to rapidly convert digested sugar in the bloodstream into fat. Our hunter-gatherer ancestors needed plenty of fat — more than other primates — to be active during periods of food scarcity and still pay for large, expensive brains and costly reproductive strategies (hunter-gatherer mothers could pump out babies twice as fast as their chimpanzee cousins).

Simply put, humans evolved to crave sugar, 5 store it, and then use it. For millions of years, our cravings and digestive systems were exquisitely balanced because sugar was rare. Apart from honey, most of the foods our hunter-gatherer ancestors ate were no sweeter than a carrot. The invention of farming made starchy foods more abundant, but it wasn't until very recently that technology made pure sugar bountiful.

The food industry has made a fortune because we retain Stone Age bodies that crave sugar but live in a Space Age world in which sugar is cheap and plentiful. Sip by sip and nibble by nibble, more of us gain weight because we can't control normal, deeply rooted urges for a valuable, tasty, and once limited resource.

What should we do? One option is to do nothing, while hoping that scientists find better cures for obesity-related diseases like heart disease and Type 2 diabetes. I'm not holding my breath for such cures, and the costs of inaction, already staggering, would continue to mushroom.

A more popular option is to enhance public education to help us make better decisions about what to eat and how to be active. This is crucial but has so far yielded only modest improvements.

The final option is to collectively restore our diets to a more natural state through regulations. Until recently, all humans had no choice but to eat a healthy diet with modest portions of food that were low in sugar, saturated fat, and salt, but high in fiber. They also had no choice but to walk and sometimes run an average of five to ten miles a day. Mr. Bloomberg's paternalistic plan is not an aberrant form of coercion but a very small step toward restoring a natural part of our environment.

Though his big-soda ban would apply to all 10 New Yorkers, I think we should focus paternalistic laws on children. Youngsters can't make rational, informed decisions about their bodies, and our society agrees that parents don't have the right to make disastrous decisions on their behalf. Accordingly, we require parents to enroll their children in school, have them immunized, and make them wear seat belts. We require physical education in school, and we don't let children buy alcohol or cigarettes. If these are acceptable forms of coercion, how is restricting unhealthy doses of sugary drinks that slowly contribute to disease any different?

Along these lines, we should ban all unhealthy food in school — soda, pizza, French fries — and insist that schools provide adequate daily physical education, which many fail to do.

Adults need help, too, and we should do more to regulate companies that exploit our deeply rooted appetites for sugar and other unhealthy foods. The mayor was right to ban trans fats, but we should also make the food industry honest about portion sizes. Like cigarettes, mass-marketed junk food should come with prominent health warning labels. It should be illegal to advertise highly fattening food as "fat free." People have the right to be unhealthy, but we should make that choice more onerous and expensive by imposing taxes on soda and junk food.

We humans did not evolve to eat healthily and go to the gym; until recently, we didn't have to make such choices. But we did evolve to cooperate to help one another survive and thrive. Circumstances have changed, but we still need one another's help as much as we ever did. For this reason, we need government on our side, not on the side of those who wish to make money by stoking our cravings and profiting from them. We have evolved to need coercion.

Topics for Critical Thinking and Writing

1. On May 30, 2012, the *New York Times* quoted Stefan Friedman, a spokesman for the New York City Beverage Association, as saying — with implicit reference to the Bloomberg proposal:

   The New York City Health Department's unhealthy obsession with attacking soft drinks is again pushing them over the top. . . . It's time for serious health professionals to move on and seek solutions that are going to actually curb obesity.

These zealous proposals just distract from the hard work that needs to be done on this front.

You have just read an essay by a professor of biology. Do you think he would agree with Friedman? Why, or why not?

2. Perhaps the chief argument in favor of limiting the food we can buy and consume, particularly when it harms us, comes down to this: "Your right to harm yourself stops when I have to pay for it." What responses, if any, can you offer to this view?

3. Evaluate Daniel Lieberman's opening paragraph. Do you think it is an effective piece of argument? Why, or why not?

4. Lieberman's essay ends, "We have evolved to need coercion." Is he in effect saying, "Yes, we need a nanny," that is, the very view that the political ad on page 521 ridicules?

DONALD MARRON

Donald Marron is the Director of Economic Policy Initiatives and an Institute Fellow at the Urban Institute in Washington, D.C. He served in a number of senior posts in the White House and Congress from 2002 to 2009, including as a member of the President's Council of Economic Advisers (CEA), as acting director of the Congressional Budget Office (CBO), and as executive director of Congress's Joint Economic Committee (JEC). The following selection originally appeared in Forbes *in 2015 and summarizes the Urban Institute's most recent findings on taxing unhealthy foods and drinks.*

Should Governments Tax Unhealthy Foods and Drinks?

With obesity and diabetes at record levels, many public health experts believe governments should tax soda, sweets, junk food, and other unhealthy foods and drinks. Denmark, Finland, France, Hungary, and Mexico have such taxes. So do Berkeley, California, and the Navajo Nation. Celebrity chef Jamie Oliver is waging a high-profile campaign to get Britain to tax sugar, and the *Washington Post* has endorsed the same for the United States.

Do such taxes make sense? My Urban Institute colleagues Maeve Gearing and John Iselin and I explore that question in a new report, *Should We Tax Unhealthy Foods and Drinks?*

Many nutrients and ingredients have been suggested as possible targets for taxes, including fat, saturated fat, salt, artificial sweeteners, and caffeine. Our sense, though, is that only sugar might be a plausible candidate.

Sugar in foods and drinks contributes to obesity, diabetes, and other conditions. By increasing the price of products that contain sugar, taxes can get people to consume less of them and thus improve nutrition and health. Health care costs would be lower, and people would live healthier, longer lives. Governments could put the resulting revenue to good use, perhaps by helping low-income families or cutting other taxes.

That's the pro case for a sugar tax, and it's 5 a good one. But policymakers need to consider the downsides too. Taxes impose real costs on consumers who pay the tax or switch to other options that may be more expensive, less enjoyable, or less convenient.

That burden would be particularly large for lower-income families. We find that a U.S. tax on sugar-sweetened beverages would be highly regressive, imposing more than four times as much burden, relative to income, on people in the bottom fifth of the income distribution as on those in the top fifth.

Another issue is how well sugar consumption tracks potential health costs and risks. If you are trying to discourage something harmful, taxes work best when there is a tight relationship between the "dose" that gets taxed and the "response" of concern. Taxes on cigarettes and carbon are well-targeted given tight links to lung cancer and climate change, respectively. The dose-response relationship for sugar, however, varies across individuals depending on their metabolisms, lifestyle, and health. Taxes cannot capture that variation; someone facing grave risks pays the same sugar tax rate as someone facing minute ones. That limits what taxes alone can accomplish.

In addition, people may switch to foods and drinks that are also unhealthy. If governments tax only sugary soda, for example, some people will switch to juice, which sounds healthier but packs a lot of sugar. It's vital to understand how potential taxes affect entire diets, not just consumption of targeted products.

A final concern, beyond the scope of our report, is whether taxing sugar is an appropriate role for government. Some people strongly object to an expanding "nanny state" using taxes to influence personal choices. Others view taxes as acceptable only if individual choices impose costs on others. Eating and drinking sugar causes such "externalities" when insurance spreads resulting health care costs across other people. Others go further and view taxes as an acceptable way to reduce "internalities" as well, the overlooked harms consumers impose on themselves.

Policymakers must weigh all those concerns when considering whether to tax sugar. 10 If they decide to do so, they should focus on content, not proxies like drink volume or sales value. Mexico, for example, taxes sweetened drinks based on their volume, a peso per liter. That encourages consumers to reduce how much they drink but does nothing to encourage less sugary alternatives. That's a big deal because sugar content ranges enormously. Some drinks have less than 10 grams of sugar (2 1/2 teaspoons) per serving, while others have 30 grams (7 1/2 teaspoons) or more. Far better would be a content-based tax that encourages switching from the 30-gram drinks to the 10-gram ones.

Focusing on sugar content would bring another benefit. Most sugar tax discussions focus on changing consumer choices. But consumers aren't in this alone. Food and beverage companies and retailers determine what products they make, market, and sell. Taxing drink volumes or the sales value of sugary food gives these companies no incentive to develop and market lower-sugar alternatives. Taxing sugar content, however, would encourage them to explore all avenues for reducing the sugar in what we eat and drink.

Topics for Critical Thinking and Writing

1. Marron builds his essay around the question in paragraph 2: "Do [sugary food] taxes make sense?" Do you think that Marron answers that question satisfactorily? Why, or why not?

2. Marron mentions early in his essay that nutrients and ingredients other than sugar — such as fat, saturated fat, artificial sweeteners, caffeine, and sodium — have been considered as targets for taxes. However, in his estimation, "only sugar might be a plausible candidate" (para. 3). What evidence do you think Marron intends to support this claim?

3. Marron lists the pros of a sugar tax in paragraph 4, but he then lists the cons of a sugar tax in paragraphs 5–9, going into much greater detail for every con he raises. After reading these pros and cons, toward which side of the argument do you find yourself leaning? Do you think that would still be the case if the pros and cons were given more equal weight within Marron's essay?

4. What does Marron mean when he cites a sugary beverage tax as "regressive" (para. 6)?

5. Explain in your own words what Marron means by considering the "dose-response relationship" in relation to taxes (para. 7). Do you find the argument that sugar has a loose dose-response relationship persuasive? Why or why not?

6. Marron argues that it is "vital to understand how potential taxes affect entire diets" (para. 8), citing the concern that a tax on one type of sugary food or drink (such as soda) might drive people toward alternatives that are also unhealthy (such as juice). Do you think that this point bolsters or weakens the rest of Marron's arguments about a sugar tax? How so?

7. In paragraph 9, Marron wonders whether it is even the government's place to impose taxes designed to influence individual choices while noting arguments that taxes may be appropriate when individual choices impose costs on others or when they can help to reduce harm people may bring onto themselves without realizing it. As a taxpayer, where do you stand on the notion of using taxes to influence individual behavior? What possible pros and cons exist to such an approach?

8. Throughout his essay, Marron refers to "policymakers" who must consider the questions he raises in determining whether or not to tax sugary foods and drinks. If you were a policymaker, which question or set of questions would be most important to you, and why?

9. In 2016, Philadelphia Mayor Jim Kenney proposed a sugary drink tax in the city that would add three cents per ounce to artificially sweetened beverages — or thirty-six cents per 12-ounce drink. Citing the soda industry's tendency to market to low-income people, Kenney said, "What we're looking to do is take some of [their] profit, to put it back into the neighborhoods that have been their biggest customers." Tax revenues would be used to fund pre-kindergarten education and improve city parks and recreational facilities. Is this a good or bad idea? What questions or concerns would a policymaker responsibly raise as a counterargument to the proposed measure?

Letters of Response by Fizer et al.

George Orwell must be very pleased with himself. A sugar tax brings us one step closer to having a screen in every kitchen where Big Brother can watch us to make sure we finish our vegetables and only have one slice of cake at dinner.

The government has no right to try to tell me how I should be spending the money I earn to buy the food that I want to eat. If I want to buy a Milky Way bar and eat it, I can and I will, even if I have to pay a few cents extra for it.

Andrew Fizer, Berkeley

By arguing that sugar alone should be the ingredient we tax in unhealthy foods, policymakers are sending a dangerous message that sugar is the only thing that people should be thinking about when they make decisions about what to eat.

Sure, sugar isn't great for you. There's a well-documented link between sugar and diseases such as diabetes and obesity. But focusing on sugar as a target for taxes de-emphasizes the importance of regulating other ingredients, such as saturated fats and sodium, which are equally damaging to people's health, especially where obesity is concerned. What good does it do to tax a soda when it comes as part of a value meal with a greasy, fatty double-bacon cheeseburger? (For the record, bacon, beef, and cheese are all fairly low-sugar foods. Does that make them any less worthy of an additional tax if the goal is to try to improve the public's health?)

The idea of a sugar tax is simply too narrow to effectively improve public health on a large scale.

Annalisa Brown, Chattanooga

I think a sugar tax is a good step toward alleviating the stress that other people's poor choices put on the rest of the country.

When someone eats so much sugar that he winds up diabetic, he is obviously going to wind up with more medical expenses. But the added cost does not stop there: the more people who let themselves become unhealthy, the more the cost of healthcare goes up for everyone else. I exercise regularly, I eat healthy, and I generally just try to take good care of myself. People like me, who make good personal decisions, should not bear the burden of paying for other people's bad habits by having their health insurance costs increase by hundreds of dollars every year.

As for the added cost of the tax itself: A sugar tax targets people who tend to buy junk food anyway, so the cost increase from the taxes themselves would be minimal for people who make good choices. Moreover, the taxes might help to keep those people from continuing to make bad choices by getting them to buy different foods.

As long as the taxes are being put toward helping to cancel out other additional costs to individuals, I think the soda tax is a step in a better direction for all of us.

Erica Beaudoin, Portland

Suppose that you've had a long day, and all you want at the end of it is an ice-cold bottle of Mountain Dew. Last week, that 20-ounce Mountain Dew would have cost you $1.19. But you live in California, which just instituted a "health impact fee" of 2 cents per ounce on sodas that are sweetened with sugar. Now, that ice-cold Mountain Dew will cost you $1.59.

I could point out that the cost of the soda has increased by over a third of its original price. I could tell you that drinking sugar-sweetened soda contributes, as Donald Marron reminds readers, to obesity, diabetes, and other unpleasant health conditions. But I would still bet good money that you would buy that ice-cold Mountain Dew and guzzle every drop of it, extra forty cents be damned.

The idea behind taxing sugar-sweetened foods and drinks is well-intentioned, but the reality is that the tax is highly unlikely to inspire any fundamental changes in consumer behavior. Branding and habits are both strong forces, and charging two extra cents to the ounce (which would come to $1.35 for a two-liter bottle of soda) is not going to be enough to get through to people who are bound and determined to have their Coke, Sunkist, or whatever brand they want.

Donald Marron also mentions that taxes could potentially focus on sugar content, which is a terrific point that manufacturers should see as an opportunity. For instance, if Mountain Dew suddenly cut the amount of sugar in its drinks in half, most consumers would scan the little note on the label championing this new, healthier Dew (which would of course have the same great taste as before), then proceed to buy it as planned. By spending money on finding healthier options for sweeteners

and rebranding themselves as companies that are committed to health-consciousness, companies could potentially avoid higher taxes on their products and prevent themselves from winding up the subject of unflattering headlines about how sugar is making Americans fat and unhealthy.

Bottom line: Governments might be well-intentioned in imposing sugar taxes, but that intervention alone is not enough to get consumers to change their ways or to help make America healthier as a country. Companies need to take the lead.

JENNIFER RANDALL, BOSTON

Donald Marron's essay raises a number of good questions about whether or not taxing sugary drinks would result in a net public health benefit, but the most important question is not raised: How would cities and states *use* these new tax revenues? Marron recognizes that such taxes disproportionately affect poor people. If revenues from these new sugary drink taxes are simply placed in general funds, isn't this just another way of raising taxes on the poor, and letting the rich off the hook? Sugary drink tax revenues should be devoted to poverty issues and public health initiatives for the poor. After all, the poor are the ones paying for it.

JEFF SIMPSON, CLEVELAND

Topics for Critical Thinking and Writing

1. The first letter, by Andrew Fizer, claims, "A sugar tax brings us one step closer to having a screen in every kitchen where Big Brother can watch us to make sure we finish our vegetables and only have one slice of cake at dinner." Is this statement an example of the slippery slope fallacy (see page 356), and, if so, can the letter therefore be dismissed?

2. Draft a letter of response either to Erica Beaudoin or to Annalisa Brown, agreeing or disagreeing, in whole or in part.

3. Jennifer Randall responds to Marron's suggestion about taxes corresponding to sugar content by arguing that this kind of system could be beneficial to companies willing to make their products healthier. Do you think Randall's argument is sound? Can you provide a counterargument?

4. Jeff Simpson's letter suggests that sugary drink tax revenues should be used for the poor. Is this solution an adequate response to solving issues related to poverty and health? Why or why not?

22

Online versus IRL: How Has Social Networking Changed How We Relate to One Another?

JULES EVANS

Jules Evans is the author of Philosophy of Life and Other Dangerous Situations *(2013), and he hosts a Web site by the same name. He also runs the Well-Being Project at Queen Mary, University of London. In this article, published on June 10, 2013, in the* Huffington Post United Kingdom, *Evans notes that our desire for online approval and popularity might be coming at the cost of real-life happiness.*

Are We Slaves to Our Online Selves?

The public rage over revelations that governments snoop on our online activity comes partly from a sense that our online selves are not entirely in our control. The more networked we are, the more our selves are "out there," online, made public and transparent to a million eyes.

On the one hand the global interconnectedness of the internet gives us a feeling of euphoria — we are joined to humanity! We are Liked! On the other hand, we get sudden pangs of paranoia — what if all these online strangers don't wish us well, what if they are stalkers or con-men or bullies or spies? How are we coming across? Are we over-exposed? Does our bum look big in this?

Growing up in today's online world must be difficult, because every adolescent experiment, every awkward mistake, is out there online, perhaps forever. This makes me glad that I was a teenager in the 1990s, before the internet could capture my adolescent fuck-wittery for posterity. Depressingly often these days, we read about a teenager who has taken their own life because someone posted an unflattering photo or video of them online. They feel publicly shamed, desecrated, permanently damaged.

There is a word for what the internet and social media have done to us: alienation. It means, literally, selling yourself into slavery, from the Latin for slave, *alienus*. The word has its roots in ancient Greek philosophy, particularly in Plato and the Stoics, who warned that if you place too much value on your reputation or image, you enslave yourself to the fickle opinion of the public. You raise the public above you, turn it into a god, then cower before it and beg for its approval. You become dispossessed, your self-esteem soaring or crashing depending on how the public views you. This is a recipe for emotional sickness.

You can end up caring more about your image or reflection than your actual self. You replace actual loving human relations with the fickle adoration of the public. How many times do we see people sitting with friends or family at a pub or a restaurant, ignoring them while they anxiously check on their online selves? Our actual selves end up shriveled and unwell, while our unreal mirror selves suck up more and more of our attention. We can even turn our loved ones into props for public approval. Your fiance proposed? Share it! Everything is done for the public, for strangers, for people who don't really care about you at all.

I remember seeing a family at the beach, in Venezuela last year. The mother was a rather curvaceous lady in a bikini, and she insisted the father take endless photos of her, standing by the sea in various outlandish poses. Literally hundreds of photos. They completely ignored their little daughter, who gazed on her mother in confusion. Occasionally the daughter would come up to get the mother's attention, and she would be given a little shove to get out of the shot. It was like some grotesque fairy-tale. The mother was so obsessed with her online self, yet so palpably ugly inside.

The internet has become a vast pool, into which we gaze like Narcissus, bewitched by our own reflection. Our smart-phones are little pocket-mirrors, with which we're constantly snapping "selfies," trying to manage how the public perceives us. It's like we have a profound fear of insignificance and nothingness, so we check the pocket-mirror every few minutes to re-assure ourselves that we exist, that we are loved. We mistake Likes for love. We look to celebrities with a million followers, and beg them to follow us. Because then we'd be real! Celebrities do this too, tweeting about the other celebrities they hang out with, to create a sort of Hello! magazine existence for the public to gape at. Everything becomes a pose, a selfie.

I'm probably worse than the lot of you. I worry that extensive use of social media over the last decade has re-wired the way I think, so that I now have "share" buttons installed in my hypothalamus. No sooner do I have a thought than I want to share it. In the old days, perhaps individuals quietly spoke to God in their hearts. Now I find my thoughts instantly forming themselves into 140-character epigrams. Sublime sunset? Share it. New baby? Share it. Terminal cancer? Share it. Let's live-blog death, find eternity in re-tweets.

How much of our selves we offer up to the god of Public Opinion. How devotedly we serve it. How utterly we make ourselves transparent to its thousand-eyed stare, until we suddenly feel over-exposed and try to cover ourselves up.

What is the antidote to alienation? The Greeks thought the cure was simple: don't put too much value on your reputation or image. Recognise that it is out of your control. Remind yourself that there is not a direct correlation between a person's image and their actual value, that the public is not a perfect mirror, that it distorts like a circus mirror. And try not to gaze into the mirror too often. Tend to the garden within, to your deeper and better self, even if it doesn't get a hundred Likes on Facebook.

This is not an easy thing to do. No sooner did I think of this, than I immediately thought, good idea: share it! Pin it! Reddit! My over-networked self needs to be reminded of the value of disconnection, of silence and contemplation, to let deeper thoughts rise up. With that in mind, I'm off on a retreat this week in the Welsh countryside (not a re-tweet, a retreat), in search of a deeper way to connect, a better Cloud to sit on. I hope they don't have Wi-Fi.

Topics for Critical Thinking and Writing

1. Jules Evans starts his article with a basic paradox of online existence: we don't control our online identities, yet so much of our sense of self these days seems tied up with that identity. We resent those who snoop into our online activity, yet we get a "feeling of euphoria" (para. 2) when something happens online that confirms our existence (e.g., we get a Like!). What is the basis of this dynamic? Can something, if anything, be done to change it? Explain your response.

2. In paragraph 4, Evans cites the wisdom of the ancient Greeks: We shouldn't put too much stock in what others think of us. He calls this a "recipe for emotional sickness." Why is that? In your opinion, is it realistic not to care about what others think of us? Can good things result from an awareness of the opinion of others? Why, or why not? Be specific.

3. In paragraph 5, Evans calls out the problem of "caring more about your image or reflection than your actual self." What is meant by the term "actual self"? How disparate or different are public and private senses of self likely to be? Provide specific examples.

4. Evans gives the example of a beautiful woman posing for pictures at the beach, all the while ignoring her little daughter (para. 6). Did this example surprise you? To what extent does the concept of the "selfie" take over the interpretation of this anecdote? (Consider that young men have been taking photographs of young women at the beach long before the invention of the smartphone.) In this sense, is Evans's example deliberately misleading? Support your answer.

5. What is the point of the story of Narcissus? Why does Evans include a reference to it in this essay? In your opinion, is its use effective? Why, or why not?

6. Evans states in paragraph 8 that he's worried that the extensive use of social media has "re-wired the way I think." Research current findings on how the use of electronic media, the Internet, and social media specifically are or are not changing the way we think. Are our brains physically adapting to these changes? If so, how? What does this mean for the future?

7. Evans states that we offer ourselves up "to the god of Public Opinion" (para. 9). Later in the same paragraph, the god appears more like a monster with its "thousand-eyed stare." According to Evans, our relationship with this god is contradictory: We seek its approval sometimes; at other times we cover ourselves to hide from it. In your opinion, is this assessment correct? Why, or why not? Cite specific examples.

8. Evans ends his article by stating that he's going on vacation, hoping to "be reminded of the value of disconnection, of silence and contemplation, to let deeper thoughts rise up" (para. 11). Is he right to be worried that being overconnected somehow causes us to be separated from ourselves? Why, or why not?

NAVNEET ALANG

Navneet Alang is freelance writer, journalist, and blogger who's interested in the intersection of technology and popular culture. He has contributed to Hazlitt, The Globe and Mail, Canadian Business *magazine, and the* Toronto Standard, *among others. This article appeared in the* New Republic *on August 5, 2015. Alang examines what types of videos go viral and, in particular, how viral videos reveal the Westernization of the world.*

Eat, Pray, Post

"This is the cause for obesity in America!" exclaims an Indian subject after eating a Pop Tart in a charming bit of viral fluff called "Indians Taste Test American Sweets." It's one of an endless video series produced by Buzzfeed, in which people from one country are filmed tasting the foods from another. They're simple, relatable, occasionally controversial, and basically engineered to go viral. I say charming, however, because this clip in particular gives us a perspective we so rarely see: young, urban people from outside the West, gently critiquing American excess. It feels, briefly, like a viral video done right — ephemeral and shareable, to be sure, but still refreshingly challenging.

More importantly, posting a video to one's social media accounts is a performative act of self-definition. *Look,* it says, *this is who I am* — at least in the terms chosen by Buzzfeed's crack viral teams who, sitting in airy, open-concept offices in California and New York, dole out content that spills out from America to fill the world's screens.

It's true that most viral stuff works this way. Yet, while perusing Buzzfeed's various international sites, I noticed a discomfiting uniformity. The listicles and the slickly edited videos center around the same ideas: relationship quirks, patriotic celebrations, food, or the usual highly specific ephemera of "only people from this city will get this." An optimist might look at this sameness as revealing a fundamental humanity, that glibly utopian notion that, underneath it all, we are the same. But perhaps viral culture is more sinister. Perhaps it isn't about universalism and it isn't just harmless fun; perhaps it is part and parcel of an inevitable Westernization.

The video that criticizes America's oddness is, after all, a bit of an anomaly. Most of the Taste Test series is about Americans testing snacks from all over — India, Singapore, Indonesia, and so on — and expressing their bewilderment and disgust at what are, to billions around the world, ordinary things. It's often uncomfortable to watch, almost the quintessence of punching down, disturbingly mimicking the disregard for non-Western cultures that underpinned colonialism (The British, for example, made it a point to denigrate Indian culture in order to replace it with their own). Even clips about Russian or European food include the word "bizarre" in the title. One is forced to ask: Bizarre to whom, exactly?

The tone and content of these videos are also remarkably Western. The language is that of Tumblr, Twitter, or even early Gawker: clipped, ironic, disaffected. Posts about Snapchats that only Indians will understand are peppered with American idioms — "this could be us but u playing," many mentions of "bae." GIFs of Bollywood star Aishwarya Rai are used just like GIFs of Rihanna, as aspirational symbols meant to reassure and entertain. In the video in which those same young, hip Indians criticize American excess and Kellogg's Pop Tarts, they do so in American terms: There's even a guy who says, based solely on watching *Breaking Bad,* that candy Pop Rocks "seriously look like meth."

At the same time, though, the production of these potentially viral posts is intended to appeal to differing demographics. As someone of Indian descent, Buzzfeed India's posts have been most clearly appealing to — and targeted at — me, and the content pushed there is often distinctly, uniquely Indian. From collections of photos that show how beautiful India is to a Tumblr that uses GIFs to describe life in Delhi, the content is breezy, fun, and (when compared to the too-white nature of most pop culture) refreshingly relatable.

There's something deeply gratifying about seeing one's culture as of the moment. When so much of what is defined as contemporary explicitly caters to a Western audience, seeing something as specific (and silly) as "19 Indian foods that taste better when it's raining" — something that plays off the uniquely celebratory attitude toward rain in India — makes one feel vital, hip, and modern. To see yourself represented is to be more alive, more real.

What does it mean, however, that so much of this representation is not only so American in style, but that the nature of online virality makes its dissemination so self-reinforcing? On one hand, there is undoubtedly a case to be made that this kind of viral grammar marks a particular style as a *global* contemporary, as opposed to a Western one. Our bloggy way of speaking is a kind of international connective tissue, making people in Jakarta and Paris and Mumbai part of an emerging, connected, privileged international demographic.

On the other hand, when that global culture flows in mostly one direction — the fact that it is in English and borrows its style from Brooklyn- and L.A.-based blogs — we have a larger problem: virality starts to look like soft cultural imperialism. It's an assertion of Western values, neatly packaged as 7 GIFs You Won't Believe.

When virality becomes the dominant mode 10 of spreading culture, the content shifts depending on location — "23 Incomparable Joys of Growing Up in Chennai" and so forth — but the form remains the same. The ideology is carried along. A post about a Bollywood power couple giving us #relationshipgoals is fun, but it also implies a specific perspective.

What this means, of course, is that virality has a kind of circular function. Many of Buzzfeed India's most popular posts draw from the popularity of the *Harry Potter* series — something that, last time I checked, wasn't exactly part of the ancient Hindu texts, the Vedas. Virality predominantly functions by reproducing what is already popular, while only occasionally propelling something to popularity itself. It's rarely inventive.

The fact that Buzzfeed India's style is indistinguishable from Brooklyn blog-speak is evidence of the circular relation of capital and culture, and the non-coincidence that centers of global finance are also centers of global culture. The nature of Buzzfeed's global operations is to produce local content in its own image: replicating a business model around the world as it also replicates a cultural one.

There is some resistance, though, elements that refuse to translate. A post on Buzzfeed India of bilingual English-Hindi puns may be groan-worthy, but its very indecipherability to a Western audience is important: It marks the cultural specificity of Northern India as unable to be neatly subsumed into a binary model of Eastern and Western.

All that said: It's hard not to wonder about power, and where it fits into the global nature of virality. As theorist Homi Bhabha argued in his book *Location of Culture*, the first world is always considered the present and future on a timeline on which the third world is perpetually the past. And perhaps online virality — in the way that it tightens itself into ever smaller circles of self-referentiality — is a sign that Bhabha was correct: That someone ten thousand miles away is talking about American obesity at all is indicative of not only how things work, but a sign that perhaps it is already too late to stop the march into a Westernized, viral future.

Topics for Critical Thinking and Writing

1. Navneet Alang states in paragraph 2 that "posting a video to one's social media accounts is a performative act of self-definition." What does he mean by this? What qualities does Alang attribute to the typical video that goes viral? Why is this important in terms of self-definition? Be specific.

2. In paragraph 3, Alang proposes that the culture of the viral video may not be promoting a "utopian" future but something "more sinister." His thesis is that the viral video is "part and parcel of an inevitable Westernization." (You may wish to watch the video "Indians Taste Test American Sweets" to better understand what Alang is referring to.) What is it about the viral video that seems created to Westernize its audience? Explain.

3. Many countries around the world were at one time colonies of European powers (or the United States), which is why language is such an important marker of culture and history. For example, the British colonized India; thus, many Indians today still speak English. How is language connected today with Westernization in the twenty-first century?

4. When discussing virality, Alang states, "To see yourself represented is to be more alive, more real" (para. 7). Why? How does this sentiment tap right into the very idea of the viral video itself: to be gently amused by something familiar? Explain your response.

5. In paragraph 8, Alang presents a new idea: Perhaps what is being shown is a new style he terms "*global* contemporary" [author's italics]. Do you agree with this idea? Why, or why not? Be specific.

6. Alang also uses the expression "soft cultural imperialism" (para. 9) in which Western values are asserted. Examine the concept of cultural imperialism in general. What would "hard" cultural imperialism be as compared to "soft"? In your opinion, is there anything wrong with this? Support your answer with specific details.

7. In paragraph 11, Alang states, "Virality predominantly functions by reproducing what is already popular." Later he says that virality is "rarely inventive." What does he mean? Do you agree? Why, or why not?

8. In his conclusion, Alang cites the argument of Homi Bhabha that "the first world is always considered the present and future on a timeline on which the third world is perpetually the past" (para. 14). Consider the economic rise of India and China in today's world as well as the continued domination of Western cultural values. Are Bhabha's words still true? Why, or why not?

TIM KREIDER

Tim Kreider is an essayist and cartoonist whose work has appeared in the New York Times, *the* Men's Journal, The New Yorker's *Page-Turner blog, and* Film Quarterly, *among others. His most recent book is* We Learn Nothing *(2013), a collection of essays and cartoons. In this essay, which appeared in the* New York Times *on June 15, 2013, Kreider points out how recognizing the disparity between the way we view ourselves and the way others see us can be an unpleasant experience.*

I Know What You Think of Me

Recently I received an e-mail that wasn't meant for me, but was about me. I'd been cc'd by accident. This is one of the darker hazards of electronic communication, Reason No. 697 Why the Internet Is Bad — the dreadful consequence of hitting "reply all" instead of "reply" or "forward." The context is that I had rented a herd of goats for reasons that aren't relevant here and had sent out a mass e-mail with photographs of the goats attached to illustrate that a) I had goats, and b) it was good. Most of the responses I received expressed appropriate admiration and envy of my goats, but the message in question was intended not as a response to me but as an aside to some of the recipient's co-workers, sighing over the kinds of expenditures on which I was frittering away my uncomfortable income. The word "oof" was used.

I've often thought that the single most devastating cyberattack a diabolical and anarchic mind could design would not be on the military or financial sector but simply to simultaneously make every e-mail and text ever sent universally public. It would be like suddenly subtracting the strong nuclear force from the universe; the fabric of society would instantly evaporate, every marriage, friendship and business partnership dissolved. Civilization, which is held together by a fragile web of tactful phrasing, polite omissions and white lies, would collapse in an apocalypse of bitter recriminations and weeping, breakups and fistfights, divorces and bankruptcies, scandals and resignations, blood feuds, litigation, wholesale slaughter in the streets and lingering ill will.

This particular e-mail was, in itself, no big deal. Tone is notoriously easy to misinterpret over e-mail, and my friend's message could have easily been read as affectionate head shaking rather than a contemptuous eye roll. It's frankly hard to parse the word "oof" in this context. And let's be honest — I am terrible with money, but I've always liked to think of this as an endearing foible. What was surprisingly wounding wasn't that the e-mail was insulting but simply that it was unsympathetic. Hearing other people's uncensored opinions of you is an unpleasant reminder that you're just another person in the world, and everyone else does not always view you in the forgiving light that you hope they do, making all allowances, always on your side. There's something existentially alarming about finding out how little room we occupy, and how little allegiance we command, in other people's heads.

This experience is not a novelty of the information age; it's always been available to us by the accident of overhearing a conversation at the wrong moment. I've written essays about friends that I felt were generous and empathetic, which they experienced as devastating. I've also been written about, in ways I could find no fault with but that were nonetheless excruciating for me to read. It is simply not pleasant to be objectively observed — it's like seeing a candid photo of yourself online, not smiling or posing, but simply looking the way you apparently always do, oblivious and mush-faced with your mouth open. It's proof that we are visible to others, that we are seen, in all our naked silliness and stupidity.

Needless to say, this makes us embarrassed 5 and angry and damn our betrayers as vicious two-faced hypocrites. Which, in fact, we all are. We all make fun of one another behind one another's backs, even the people we love. Of course we do — they're ridiculous. Anyone worth knowing is inevitably also going to be exasperating: making the same obvious mistakes over and over, dating imbeciles, end-lessly relapsing into their dumb addictions and self-defeating habits, blind to their own hilarious flaws and blatant contradictions and fiercely devoted to whatever keeps them mis-erable. (And those few people about whom there is nothing ridiculous are by far the most preposterous of all.)

Although sometimes, let's just admit, we're simply being mean. A friend of mine described the time in high school when someone walked up behind her while she was saying something clever at that person's expense as the worst feel-ing she had ever had — and not just because of the hurt she'd inflicted on someone else but because of what it forced her to see about her-self. That she made fun of people all the time, people who didn't deserve it, who were beneath her in the social hierarchy, just to ingratiate herself or make herself seem funny or cool.

Another friend once shared with me one of the aphorisms of 12-step recovery programs: "What other people think of you is none of your business." Like a lot of wisdom, this sounds at first suspiciously similar to idiotic nonsense; obviously what other people think of you is

your business, it's your main job in life to try to control it, to do tireless P.R. and spin control for yourself. Every woman who ever went out with you must pine for you forever. Those who rejected you must regret it. You must be loved, respected — above all, taken seriously! They who mocked you will rue the day! The problem is that this is insane — the psychology of dicta-tors who regard all dissent as treason, and peri-odically order purges to ensure unquestioning loyalty. It's no way to run a country.

THE operative fallacy here is that we believe that unconditional love means not seeing any-thing negative about someone, when it really means pretty much the opposite: loving some-one despite their infuriating flaws and essential absurdity. "Do I want to be loved *in spite of*?" Donald Barthelme writes in his story "Rebecca" about a woman with green skin. "Do you? Does anyone? But aren't we all, to some degree?"

We don't give other people credit for the same interior complexity we take for granted in ourselves, the same capacity for holding contradictory feelings in balance, for com-plexly alloyed affections, for bottomless gener-osity of heart and petty, capricious malice. We can't believe that anyone could be unkind to us and still be genuinely fond of us, although we do it all the time.

Years ago a friend of mine had a dream 10 about a strange invention; a staircase you could descend deep underground, in which you heard recordings of all the things anyone had ever said about you, both good and bad. The catch was, you had to pass through all the worst things people had said before you could get to the highest compliments at the very bottom. There is no way I would ever make it more than two and a half steps down such a staircase, but I understand its terrible logic: if we want the rewards of being loved we have to submit to the mortifying ordeal of being known.

Topics for Critical Thinking and Writing

1. Tim Kreider begins his essay with a story about receiving an e-mail not meant for him, but about him. Consider different forms of communication in the digital world: social media, texting, messaging, e-mails. How does technology make such mistakes more likely to occur?

2. In paragraph 3, Kreider states, "Civilization, which is held together by a fragile web of tactful phrasing, polite omissions, and white lies, would collapse in an apocalypse." Aside from the humorous exaggeration about the results, to what extent is Kreider right? Support your answer with specific details.

3. Kreider states, "Hearing other people's uncensored opinions of you is an unpleasant reminder that you're just another person in this world" (para. 3). What does he mean by this? Consider how we form perceptions of ourselves. To what extent do our personal interactions with friends, family, coworkers, neighbors, and others shape perceptions of ourselves?

4. Kreider says that being "objectively observed" is like "seeing a candid photo of yourself online" (para. 4). Is a photograph a good metaphor for being objectively observed, or are there problems with the metaphor? Why, or why not?

5. Examine paragraph 5, in which Kreider writes that teasing is an act of affection. Do you agree with this interpretation, or do you regard teasing as a form of bullying? Is there a way to tell the difference? Support your response with specific details.

6. In paragraph 7, Kreider argues that only a dictator would think that everyone must like him (or her) at all times. What does he mean by this as it applies to everyday life? Include specific examples in your response.

7. Look at paragraph 8 for Kreider's definition of unconditional love. Do you agree with what he's saying? Why, or why not?

8. Kreider says, "We don't give other people credit for the same interior complexity we take for granted in ourselves" (para. 9). In your experience, is this true? Why, or why not?

9. In his final paragraph, Kreider recounts a dream that his friend had about a staircase you could walk down, hearing everything bad anyone had ever said about you before then hearing everything good anyone had said about you. Would you go all the way to the bottom of the staircase and hear everything, both good and bad? Why, or why not?

CHARLES SEIFE

Charles Seife is a professor of journalism at New York University, holding degrees from Princeton, Yale, and Columbia. He has been writing about math and science for over two decades; his most recent book is Virtual Unreality: Just Because the Internet Told You So, How Do You Know It's True? *(2014), from which this excerpt is taken. In this passage, Seife argues that Internet games often encourage behavior that doesn't even bring users enjoyment, but provides game makers with crucial information that can be sold to others.*

This Is Your Brain . . .

In November 2012, legendary game designer Peter Molyneux released *Curiosity.* The game involved a giant box made up of tiny cubes. Players clicked on those tiny cubes to remove them, one at a time, layer by layer. Each time someone removed a cube, he earned a coin. Enough coins and he could buy a tool to remove those cubes more efficiently. Within a few weeks of its launch, several million people had played *Curiosity,* and about 300,000 visited daily, slowly chipping away at the monstrous virtual box. Four months after the game started, players had clicked away more than 200 layers, meaning that people had clicked tens of millions of times per day. Even with all these players clicking again and again, it took more than six months of work before the very last cube was clicked, revealing what was inside the box. It was an amazing and baffling waste of manpower — the spiritual antithesis of building the pyramids — for a single purpose: to get to the center of an imaginary object.

What's at the center? While the game was under way, Molyneux was coy, promising only that the secret at the center would be "amazing" and "life changing." But there was a catch. Only one player would find out. Yes, after millions of people click-click-click to chip away at an enormous virtual box for month after month, a single person got a glimpse of what was inside.[1] You can almost hear the ghost of B. F. Skinner cackling in appreciation.

Curiosity is the *reductio ad absurdum* of a kind of experiment pioneered by B. F. Skinner, one of the most influential psychologists of the twentieth century. Skinner's scientific work mostly involved operant conditioning — the use of punishments and rewards to modify an organism's behavior. A pigeon or a rat might get a pellet of food or an electrical shock after acting in a certain way — hitting a lever, for example — and, over time, the animal would change its behavior to gain the most rewards and to avoid the punishments. To understand the process of conditioning, Skinner tweaked the experiments in various ways. For example, he might suddenly cut off the reward for hitting a lever and watch how long the rat would continue to press the lever in hopes of receiving a food pellet. (The behavior would gradually disappear, a process known as "extinction.") Or he might decide to give pigeons birdseed on a completely random basis and watch what happened. (The pigeons would pick up weird behaviors — spinning counterclockwise three times or "tossing" their heads as if they were lifting an invisible bar — in hopes of getting seeds to drop. In other words, the pigeons had become superstitious.)

The only fundamental difference between *Curiosity* and a Skinnerian experiment is the level of reward. No self-respecting rat or pigeon would click a lever all day with the vague hope that several months from now, he'd be the lucky one out of millions of rats who got a reward for all that effort. We humans, though, are supreme in the animal kingdom in deferring our immediate gratification in hopes of a larger reward to come. As a result, in many ways we're easier to manipulate than rats or pigeons. We're happy to change our behavior

---

[1] The lucky fellow was treated to a video explaining his prize: he was to become a digital god in Molyneux's upcoming game, *Godus.* (And he apparently gets to keep some portion of the income from the game.) We know this only because the lucky winner chose to share the video. It would have been even more amusing had he kept it secret. [Seife's note.]

in hopes of getting more abstract, more insubstantial, more infrequent rewards than any other creature under the sun.

Skinner manipulated his rats and pigeons [5] for a definite end: he wanted to learn about how changing an organism's environment directly affected its behavior. So, too, are the designers of *Curiosity* manipulating us for a definite end. Precisely what end that is, we don't know. But if you listen to what Molyneux has been saying, it's clear that *Curiosity* is not a game but an experiment. It's an attempt not to amuse people, but to look at their interactions with the cube and to draw inferences about their behavior. Molyneux made this plain on the *Pocket Gamer* website: "We're capturing all the analytical data, and we'll share what people are doing with the coins and what they're saving up for and the analysis of how the cube decayed. All of that is just fascinating stuff," he said. This data, Molyneux added, will help him make more games. It's hard to be more explicit. As *Curiosity* players clicked away toward the center of the box, their every move was being observed.[2] They were subjects in a three-million-person experiment, test animals who were performing a mindless task in a virtual fishbowl so that the experimenters can extract some knowledge that will allow them to manipulate people better.

Skinnerian methods existed long before the internet. Slot machines and instant-win lotteries, for example, are attractive — for some, addictive — because they dole out little rewards at intervals that urge us to keep playing. Other mind-control mechanisms were well known before the dawn of the digital era. In the 1950s, Solomon Asch did a series of experiments in which he showed that people asked to perform a very simple task — comparing the lengths of various lines — could be induced by others in the room not just to give the wrong answers, but also to believe that the wrong answers were correct. There are a number of other studies that demonstrate how social pressure can cause people to act against their better judgment, discard their morals, and even misperceive facts. Phil Zimbardo's Stanford Prison Experiment used social pressure to get students to abuse others. Stanley Milgram's experiments used social pressure to get subjects to give peers "dangerous" electric shocks. Social pressure, like Skinnerian conditioning, is a potent mind-control technique.

But what *Curiosity* and *FarmVille*[3] make plain is that the internet makes it trivial to combine the raw power of individual Skinnerian conditioning with the mind-bending force of mass social pressure. *Curiosity* probably wouldn't survive a week if the players were unaware of the other people chipping away at the box — the very fact that there are so many others working at the same task as you reinforces the seeming importance of the goal that everyone collectively is working toward. Similarly, the never-ending barrage of messages telling you how well your friends are doing at *FarmVille* and the constant requests to have you help tend their crops go a long way toward defusing the feeling that the whole pursuit is an idiotic waste of time. Skinnerian conditioning, crossed with social pressure, is now an ever-present invisible hand that tries to manipulate all of your actions on the internet. This is the hand that is making you act against your own self-interest. Once you recognize

---

[2]It's unclear exactly what Molyneux's team was measuring. One might imagine that he's figuring out when and where people around the world log in, how long they play before they get bored and log off, how susceptible they are to the vague and hyperbolic promises of a serial letdown artist — that kind of thing. [Seife's note.]

[3]A social network game that simulates various farming situations, developed by Zynga in 2009. [Editors' note.]

it, you see it everywhere, hovering over you, trying to make you click your mouse or press buttons on your smartphone, giving up your valuable time, money, or information in return for little or nothing at all.

Foursquare is a social networking application that allows people to use their mobile devices to "check in" to various locations they visit. Each check-in earns points (which don't seem to have any function other than putting your name on a leaderboard) and has the potential to earn a badge. If you're the most frequent Foursquare visitor to a certain location, you can become the "mayor" of that site. Sometimes, checking in, earning a badge, or becoming the mayor of a site can earn a person a minor reward (the mayor of a Pizza Hut, for example, gets free breadsticks with every large pizza), but most of the time there's no palpable reason for whipping out one's cell phone and telling the Foursquare team where you are. Checking in becomes an end in itself, a meaningless scavenger hunt to collect badges and points in an attempt to beat out your friends who are also trying to collect those same badges and points. (And plenty of people take the game seriously enough to cheat at it—enough of them that the Foursquare team had to crack down on phony mayors.)

Other than the very rare reward and the pride of becoming the mayor of your local Burger King, there isn't much value to checking in on Foursquare. In fact, there are some very real dangers in giving up your location to a company—and publishing it so that the whole world can see it. In 2010, three computer scientists set up PleaseRobMe.com, a website that used Foursquare and Twitter information to determine when a user was far away from his home—and then to broadcast that the person's domicile was empty and ripe for burglary. The website made very clear something that

people often overlook: information is valuable, and to give it up thoughtlessly is to act against your own interest. If you were required by a court order to check in to a website every time you entered a new location, you'd consider it an oppressive action of a police state. Yet, thanks to the abstract Skinnerian rewards provided by the Foursquare team, combined with the gentle social pressure of competing with friends and strangers in a never-ending scavenger hunt for badges, fascist oppression becomes a fun pastime. People don't think twice about reflexively transmitting their whereabouts to a company that's trying to bend your mind and make you a frequent visitor to your local Pizza Hut, Hess gas station, or RadioShack.[4] Foursquare is not just attempting to gather information about your behavior, but subtly trying to modify it for the benefit of its sponsors—and for its own bottom line.

It's no coincidence that the mechanics [10] of Foursquare resemble those of a game like *FarmVille*; both are attempting to use the same mechanisms to make us do their bidding. *FarmVille* advertises itself as a game, but Foursquare is not even that. It's a computer program that's supposed to "[help] you and your friends make the most of where you are." It's not technically a game—it's a social service—but in very many ways, its structure is familiar. Points, coins, badges, and rewards tickle the parts of our brains that respond to Skinnerian conditioning, while the social elements keep us entangled in a web of commitment—and of competitive drive not to fall behind our peers. In short, by creating artificial rewards and engineering social pressures, Foursquare controls your behavior by superimposing a

---

[4]Companies have long used rewards—usually cash, free items, or discounts—to get you to give up information or alter your behavior. But your CVS card doesn't try to keep you playing the game, or get you to try to recruit your family. [Seife's note.]

video-game structure on your everyday life. This is "gamification."

Gamification is common on the internet. Media websites like *The Huffington Post* encourage you to comment on (and spread) stories by giving you badges ("level 2 networker") or titles ("superuser") for accomplishing achievements. Social networking websites like Klout give you scores for how many followers you have and how much influence you exert upon them. Job networking sites like LinkedIn reward you for having a lot of data on your profile page. Khan Academy, an educational site, gives students "energy points" and badges for completing lessons. But gamification extends well beyond the virtual world and, assisted by digital technology, is creeping into the outdoors. Nike has introduced a set of bracelets that track your motion and give you "fuel" points for your physical activity, grant you badges for achieving goals, and allow you to challenge your friends to various physical tasks. Coca-Cola created a "Happiness Quest" scavenger hunt, which encouraged people to use their cell phones to scan soda-vending machines in various locations.

It's a brilliant strategy. Running around town taking photos of vending machines can never be considered fun in its own right. By superimposing a gamelike structure on top of that activity — a structure that uses operant conditioning and social pressure to give it heft — Coca-Cola functionally twisted our brains to redefine fun for us. And not so coincidentally, its definition of fun means buying things from vending machines.

There's nothing inherently wrong with the idea of gamification. It's a tool that can be used for good — when we need to modify our behavior, Skinnerian techniques, combined with social pressures, can be a powerful way

to bring us back in line. Look beneath the surface of Alcoholics Anonymous and you see proto-gamification: the sobriety coins are trinkets to give palpable Skinnerian reinforcement, and the group sessions provide the social network to keep you embedded in the "game." It's a technique that's potent enough to wean us from alcohol, help us lose weight, make us exercise more.

In the days before the internet, such powerful techniques were limited by the sheer difficulty of creating and hooking in to the social networks needed to sustain the game. You already had to be somewhat committed to a cause to get your butt out of bed to visit your local AA or Weight Watchers meeting each week.

That's no longer the case. Our social networks are now no further than our computer keyboards — or our mobile phones. We're in constant touch with other people playing the game. Because of the near-universal interconnectedness that the internet provides, we no longer have to exercise our will to expose ourselves to a peer group; the peer group is always right there in our pockets, staring back at us every time we pull out our smartphones. The barrier to entering a peer-pressure group is so reduced that we don't do it consciously anymore. We used to have to make an active decision to try to enter a behavior-modification program. Now we're signing up for powerful mind-control pressures without an active decision to do so, without even understanding that this is what we're doing when we sign up for the latest social fad.

At the same time, the volume and precision of data flowing back and forth between players and game masters allow for a complexity and frequency of rewards — badges, ribbons, achievements, points, coins — that would have been unimaginable prior to the advent of digital information. "Players" in one of these behavior-modification schemes are subject to a nearly unending and endlessly varied — yet personalized — flood of positive reinforcement so long as they continue playing the game. Computer algorithms dole out virtual treats to push you along, while the social networks keep you embedded. Pretty soon you lose perspective — you don't realize how much you've given up to keep playing this game seven days a week.

That's one common denominator in all of these Skinnerian social games: you're forced to give something up in order to belong. Sometimes you're giving up something as obvious as money; by paying a few dollars to the *Farm-Ville* team, you boost your efficiency and social status so that you're ahead of other, more casual players. But more often, you're giving up something more abstract. Sometimes you're merely giving up your time. Other times you're giving up information — your location, your spending habits, even your weight — that allows companies to understand (and control) you better. Outside of the context of a social application, you wouldn't casually give out this information to a stranger; you'd only reveal it for a good reason — say, to a doctor or a credit counselor. But nowadays we are willing to share almost everything reflexively, even to the point that it could be considered *anti*social.

A decade ago, if a corporation asked for the e-mail addresses of all of your friends and family members, you'd almost certainly have refused. From the advent of the internet, everyone knew that e-mail addresses needed to be protected, to some extent, from outsiders who were constantly on the lookout for new people to spam. If you gave out people's e-mail addresses willy-nilly, you'd probably piss off quite a few of them. But

nowadays, people are happy to hand their entire e-mail contact list over to LinkedIn or Facebook or Google or Pinterest or any other site that convinces people to sell out their closest acquaintances in hopes of increasing their own social status. Our social norms are changing as a result of these commercial enterprises.

There's no telling how far this trend will go. As powerful as Skinnerian conditioning with social pressure might be, we humans have a fairly potent defense against such manipulation: boredom. It may be that our short attention spans — our constant need for novelty — will limit the effect that these gamified behavior-modifying programs can have upon us. Perhaps with overuse of the technique we will become less susceptible. Zynga, the maker of *FarmVille,* is already seeing its revenue flatten out after its initial booming growth. Foursquare is even beginning to drop in popularity. Even so, there's no question that, right now, the behavior-modification business, which uses digital technology to try to put us all in socially connected Skinner boxes, is a multi-billion-dollar enterprise. And this is because it works.

Seldom do we really question why we're [20] taking a particular action. We, as autonomous, intelligent beings, find it hard to imagine that our minds are being manipulated by unseen forces. Yet if you take a step back and look carefully at how you spend your time on the internet, on your computer, or on your smartphone, you might well discover that you might have been sacrificing your own self-interest — in almost imperceptible ways — to benefit a commercial enterprise. And it is through self-awareness that we can once again take control of our own brains, despite the parasites that are trying to use us for their own purposes.

Topics for Critical Thinking and Writing

1. Early in his essay, Charles Seife discusses the famous behaviorist psychologist B. F. Skinner, who used "punishments and rewards to modify an organism's behavior" (para. 3). Yet in recounting some of Skinner's experiments, Seife states, "we're easier to manipulate than rats or pigeons" (para. 4). Do you agree with Seife's statement? Support your stance with specific details.

2. In paragraph 6, Seife argues that people have exhibited responses like Skinner's rats and pigeons in ways long before the Internet gave them opportunities to do so. He cites slot machines and lottery tickets as two examples. Research and argue how people are influenced to engage in behavior that is not in their best interests, such as gambling. How does that reflect Skinner's ideas about behaviorism?

3. The presence of applications on smartphones often works against the best interests of the user, by providing virtual benefits at real-life cost — in terms of either time, money, or information. Given this rather unequal relationship, why do such applications continue to be popular? Cite examples beyond those mentioned in the excerpt, and analyze how they work to modify a user's behavior for the good of someone else.

4. In paragraph 9, Seife recounts how three scientists set up a site called PleaseRobMe.com. The purpose was to show how much information people were giving away on their phones, to the point that someone could rob their home, safe in the knowledge that the inhabitants were away. Why are people so willing to divulge information that in other circumstances they would not — such as telling strangers when they'll be away from home? How does this connect to Seife's theory about the behavioral patterns of people who play games like *Curiosity*?

5. Social media sites come at a price — not of money, but of information. Why are people willing to give out information about themselves, their family, and their friends for an opportunity to be part of the site? Do research on the psychological value of feeling part of a community. Is this a fair tradeoff, in your opinion? Support your response with specific details.

6. In paragraph 19, Seife says that "the behavior-modification business, which uses digital technology to try to put us all in socially connected Skinner boxes, is a multi-billion-dollar enterprise. And this is because it works." Therefore, should there be regulation or oversight of the use of such technologies that invade our privacy and change our behavior? Why, or why not?

STEPHEN MARCHE

Stephen Marche (b. 1976) has written essays, stories, and a novel. We reprint an essay that was originally published in The Atlantic *in May 2012. You can friend Marche on Facebook or follow him on Twitter.*

Is Facebook Making Us Lonely?

Yvette Vickers, a former *Playboy* playmate and B-movie star, best known for her role in *Attack of the 50 Foot Woman*, would have been eighty-three last August, but nobody knows exactly how old she was when she died. According to the Los Angeles coroner's report, she lay dead for the better part of a year before a neighbor and fellow actress, a woman named Susan Savage, noticed cobwebs and yellowing letters in her mailbox, reached through a broken window to unlock the door, and pushed her way through the piles of junk mail and mounds of clothing that barricaded the house. Upstairs, she found Vickers's body, mummified, near a heater that was still running. Her computer was on too, its glow permeating the empty space.

The *Los Angeles Times* posted a story headlined "Mummified Body of Former Playboy Playmate Yvette Vickers Found in Her Benedict Canyon Home," which quickly went viral. Within two weeks, by Technorati's count, Vickers's lonesome death was already the subject of 16,057 Facebook posts and 881 tweets. She had long been a horror-movie icon, a symbol of Hollywood's capacity to exploit our most basic fears in the silliest ways; now she was an icon of a new and different kind of horror: our growing fear of loneliness. Certainly she received much more attention in death than she did in the final years of her life. With no children, no religious group, and no immediate social circle of any kind, she had begun, as an elderly woman, to look elsewhere for companionship. Savage later told *Los Angeles* magazine that she had searched Vickers's phone bills for clues about the life that led to such an end. In the months before her grotesque death, Vickers had made calls not to friends or family but to distant fans who had found her through fan conventions and Internet sites.

Vickers's web of connections had grown broader but shallower, as has happened for many of us. We are living in an isolation that would have been unimaginable to our ancestors, and yet we have never been more accessible. Over the past three decades, technology has delivered to us a world in which we need not be out of contact for a fraction of a moment. In 2010, at a cost of $300 million, 800 miles of fiber-optic cable was laid between the Chicago Mercantile Exchange and the New York Stock Exchange to shave three milliseconds off trading times. Yet within this world of instant and absolute communication, unbounded by limits of time or space, we suffer from unprecedented alienation. We have never been more detached from one another, or lonelier. In a world consumed by ever more novel modes of socializing, we have less and less actual society. We live in an accelerating contradiction: the more connected we become, the lonelier we are. We were promised a global village; instead we inhabit the drab cul-de-sacs and endless freeways of a vast suburb of information.

At the forefront of all this unexpectedly lonely interactivity is Facebook, with 845 million users and $3.7 billion in revenue last year. The company hopes to raise $5 billion in an initial public offering later this spring, which will make it by far the largest Internet IPO in history. Some recent estimates put the company's potential value at $100 billion, which would make it larger than the global coffee industry — one addiction preparing to surpass the other. Facebook's scale and reach are hard to comprehend: last summer, Facebook became, by some counts, the first Web site to receive 1 trillion page views in a month. In the last three months of 2011, users generated an average of 2.7 billion "likes" and comments every day. On whatever scale you care to judge Facebook — as a company, as a culture, as a country — it is vast beyond imagination.

Despite its immense popularity, or more likely because of it, Facebook has, from the beginning, been under something of a cloud of suspicion. The depiction of Mark Zuckerberg, in *The Social Network*, as a bastard with symptoms of Asperger's syndrome, was nonsense. But it felt true. It felt true to Facebook, if not to Zuckerberg. The film's most indelible scene, the one that may well have earned it an Oscar, was the final, silent shot of an anomic Zuckerberg sending out a friend request to his ex-girlfriend, then waiting and clicking and waiting and clicking — a moment of superconnected loneliness preserved in amber. We have all been in that scene: transfixed by the glare of a screen, hungering for response.

When you sign up for Google+ and set up your Friends circle, the program specifies that you should include only "your real friends, the ones you feel comfortable sharing private details with." That one little phrase, *Your real friends* — so quaint, so charmingly mothering — perfectly encapsulates the anxieties that social media have produced: the fears that Facebook is interfering with our real friendships, distancing us from each other, making us lonelier; and that social networking might be spreading the very isolation it seemed designed to conquer.

Facebook arrived in the middle of a dramatic increase in the quantity and intensity of human loneliness, a rise that initially made the site's promise of greater connection seem deeply attractive. Americans are more solitary than ever before. In 1950, less than 10 percent of American households contained only one person. By 2010, nearly 27 percent of households had just one person. Solitary living does not guarantee a life of unhappiness, of course.

In his recent book about the trend toward living alone, Eric Klinenberg, a sociologist at NYU, writes: "Reams of published research show that it's the quality, not the quantity of social interaction, that best predicts loneliness." True. But before we begin the fantasies of happily eccentric singledom, of divorcées dropping by their knitting circles after work for glasses of Drew Barrymore pinot grigio, or recent college graduates with perfectly articulated, Steampunk-themed, 300-square-foot apartments organizing croquet matches with their book clubs, we should recognize that it is not just isolation that is rising sharply. It's loneliness, too. And loneliness makes us miserable.

We know intuitively that loneliness and being alone are not the same thing. Solitude can be lovely. Crowded parties can be agony. We also know, thanks to a growing body of research on the topic, that loneliness is not a matter of external conditions; it is a psychological state. A 2005 analysis of data from a longitudinal study of Dutch twins showed that the tendency toward loneliness has roughly the same genetic component as other psychological problems such as neuroticism or anxiety.

Still, loneliness is slippery, a difficult state to define or diagnose. The best tool yet developed for measuring the condition is the UCLA Loneliness Scale, a series of twenty questions that all begin with this formulation: "How often do you feel...?" As in: "How often do you feel that you are 'in tune' with the people around you?" And: "How often do you feel that you lack companionship?" Measuring the condition in these terms, various studies have shown loneliness rising drastically over a very short period of recent history. A 2010 AARP survey found that 35 percent of adults older than forty-five were chronically lonely, as opposed to 20 percent of a similar group only a decade earlier. According to a major study by a leading scholar of the subject, roughly 20 percent of Americans — about 60 million people — are unhappy with their lives because of loneliness. Across the Western world, physicians and nurses have begun to speak openly of an epidemic of loneliness.

The new studies on loneliness are beginning to yield some surprising preliminary findings about its mechanisms. Almost every factor that one might assume affects loneliness does so only some of the time, and only under certain circumstances. People who are married are less lonely than single people, one journal article suggests, but only if their spouses are confidants. If one's spouse is not a confidant, marriage may not decrease loneliness. A belief in God might help, or it might not, as a 1990 German study comparing levels of religious feeling and levels of loneliness discovered. Active believers who saw God as abstract and helpful rather than as a wrathful, immediate presence were less lonely. "The mere belief in God," the researchers concluded, "was relatively independent of loneliness."

But it is clear that social interaction matters. Loneliness and being alone are not the same thing, but both are on the rise. We meet fewer people. We gather less. And when we gather, our bonds are less meaningful and less easy. The decrease in confidants — that is, in quality social connections — has been dramatic over the past twenty-five years. In one survey, the mean size of networks of personal confidants decreased from 2.94 people in 1985 to 2.08 in 2004. Similarly, in 1985, only 10 percent of Americans said they had no one with whom to discuss important matters, and 15 percent said they had only one such good friend. By 2004, 25 percent had nobody to talk to, and 20 percent had only one confidant.

In the face of this social disintegration, we have essentially hired an army of replacement confidants, an entire class of professional carers. As Ronald Dworkin pointed out in a 2010 paper for the Hoover Institution, in the late 1940s, the United States was home to 2,500 clinical psychologists, 30,000 social workers, and fewer than 500 marriage and family therapists. As of 2010, the country had 77,000 clinical psychologists, 192,000 clinical social workers, 400,000 nonclinical social workers, 50,000 marriage and family therapists, 105,000 mental-health counselors, 220,000 substance-abuse counselors, 17,000 nurse psychotherapists, and 30,000 life coaches. The majority of patients in therapy do not warrant a psychiatric diagnosis. This raft of psychic servants is helping us through what used to be called regular problems. We have outsourced the work of everyday caring.

We need professional carers more and more, because the threat of societal breakdown, once principally a matter of nostalgic lament, has morphed into an issue of public health. Being lonely is extremely bad for your health. If you're lonely, you're more likely to be put in a geriatric home at an earlier age than a similar person who isn't lonely. You're less likely to exercise. You're more likely to be obese. You're less likely to survive a serious operation and more likely to have hormonal imbalances. You are at greater risk of inflammation. Your memory may be worse. You are more likely to be depressed, to sleep badly, and to suffer dementia and general cognitive decline. Loneliness may not have killed Yvette Vickers, but it has been linked to a greater probability of having the kind of heart condition that did kill her.

And yet, despite its deleterious effect on health, loneliness is one of the first things ordinary Americans spend their money achieving. With money, you flee the cramped city to a house in the suburbs or, if you can afford it, a McMansion in the exurbs, inevitably spending more time in your car. Loneliness is at the American core, a by-product of a long-standing national appetite for independence: The Pilgrims who left Europe willingly abandoned the bonds and strictures of a society that could not accept their right to be different. They did not seek out loneliness, but they accepted it as the price of their autonomy. The cowboys who set off to explore a seemingly endless frontier likewise traded away personal ties in favor of pride and self-respect. The ultimate American icon is the astronaut: Who is more heroic, or more alone? The price of self-determination and self-reliance has often been loneliness. But Americans have always been willing to pay that price.

Today, the one common feature in American secular culture is its celebration of the self that breaks away from the constrictions of the family and the state, and, in its greatest expressions, from all limits entirely. The great American poem is Whitman's "Song of Myself." The great American essay is Emerson's "Self-Reliance." The great American novel is Melville's *Moby-Dick*, the tale of a man on a quest so lonely that it is incomprehensible to those around him. American culture, high and low, is about self-expression and personal authenticity. Franklin Delano Roosevelt called individualism "the great watchword of American life."

Self-invention is only half of the American story, however. The drive for isolation has always been in tension with the impulse to cluster in communities that cling and suffocate. The Pilgrims, while fomenting spiritual rebellion, also enforced ferocious cohesion. The Salem witch trials, in hindsight, read like attempts to impose solidarity — as do the McCarthy hearings. The history of the United States is like the famous parable of the porcupines in the cold, from Schopenhauer's *Studies*

in Pessimism — the ones who huddle together for warmth and shuffle away in pain, always separating and congregating.

We are now in the middle of a long period of shuffling away. In his 2000 book *Bowling Alone*, Robert D. Putnam attributed the dramatic post-war decline of social capital — the strength and value of interpersonal networks — to numerous interconnected trends in American life: suburban sprawl, television's dominance over culture, the self-absorption of the Baby Boomers, the disintegration of the traditional family. The trends he observed continued through the prosperity of the aughts, and have only become more pronounced with time: the rate of union membership declined in 2011, again; screen time rose; the Masons and the Elks continued their slide into irrelevance. We are lonely because we want to be lonely. We have made ourselves lonely.

The question of the future is this: Is Facebook part of the separating or part of the congregating; is it a huddling-together for warmth or a shuffling-away in pain?

Well before Facebook, digital technology was enabling our tendency for isolation, to an unprecedented degree. Back in the 1990s, scholars started calling the contradiction between an increased opportunity to connect and a lack of human contact the "Internet paradox." A prominent 1998 article on the phenomenon by a team of researchers at Carnegie Mellon showed that increased Internet usage was already coinciding with increased loneliness. Critics of the study pointed out that the two groups that participated in the study — high-school journalism students who were heading to university and socially active members of community-development boards — were statistically likely to become lonelier over time. Which brings us to a more fundamental question: Does the Internet make people lonely, or are lonely people more attracted to the Internet?

The question has intensified in the Facebook era. A recent study out of Australia (where close to half the population is active on Facebook), titled "Who Uses Facebook?" found a complex and sometimes confounding relationship between loneliness and social networking. Facebook users had slightly lower levels of "social loneliness" — the sense of not feeling bonded with friends — but "significantly higher levels of family loneliness" — the sense of not feeling bonded with family. It may be that Facebook encourages more contact with people outside of our household, at the expense of our family relationships — or it may be that people who have unhappy family relationships in the first place seek companionship through other means, including Facebook. The researchers also found that lonely people are inclined to spend more time on Facebook: "One of the most noteworthy findings," they wrote, "was the tendency for neurotic and lonely individuals to spend greater amounts of time on Facebook per day than non-lonely individuals." And they found that neurotics are more likely to prefer to use the wall, while extroverts tend to use chat features in addition to the wall.

Moira Burke, until recently a graduate student at the Human-Computer Institute at Carnegie Mellon, used to run a longitudinal study of 1,200 Facebook users. That study, which is ongoing, is one of the first to step outside the realm of self-selected college students and examine the effects of Facebook on a broader population, over time. She concludes that the effect of Facebook depends on what you bring to it. Just as your mother said: you get out only what you put in. If you use Facebook to communicate directly with other individuals — by using the "like" button,

commenting on friends' posts, and so on — it can increase your social capital. Personalized messages, or what Burke calls "composed communication," are more satisfying than "one-click communication" — the lazy click of a like. "People who received composed communication became less lonely, while people who received one-click communication experienced no change in loneliness," Burke tells me. So, you should inform your friend in writing how charming her son looks with Harry Potter cake smeared all over his face, and how interesting her sepia-toned photograph of that tree-framed bit of skyline is, and how cool it is that she's at whatever concert she happens to be at. That's what we all want to hear. Even better than sending a private Facebook message is the semi-public conversation, the kind of back-and-forth in which you half ignore the other people who may be listening in. "People whose friends write to them semi-publicly on Facebook experience decreases in loneliness," Burke says.

On the other hand, nonpersonalized use of Facebook — scanning your friends' status updates and updating the world on your own activities via your wall, or what Burke calls "passive consumption" and "broadcasting" — correlates to feelings of disconnectedness. It's a lonely business, wandering the labyrinths of our friends' and pseudo-friends' projected identities, trying to figure out what part of ourselves we ought to project, who will listen, and what they will hear. According to Burke, passive consumption of Facebook also correlates to a marginal increase in depression. "If two women each talk to their friends the same amount of time, but one of them spends more time reading about friends on Facebook as well, the one reading tends to grow slightly more depressed," Burke says. Her conclusion suggests that my sometimes unhappy reactions to Facebook may be

20

more universal than I had realized. When I scroll through page after page of my friends' descriptions of how accidentally eloquent their kids are, and how their husbands are endearingly bumbling, and how they're all about to eat a home-cooked meal prepared with fresh local organic produce bought at the farmers' market and then go for a jog and maybe check in at the office because they're so busy getting ready to hop on a plane for a week of luxury dogsledding in Lapland, I do grow slightly more miserable. A lot of other people doing the same thing feel a little bit worse, too.

Still, Burke's research does not support the assertion that Facebook creates loneliness. The people who experience loneliness on Facebook are lonely away from Facebook, too, she points out; on Facebook, as everywhere else, correlation is not causation. The popular kids are popular, and the lonely skulkers skulk alone. Perhaps it says something about me that I think Facebook is primarily a platform for lonely skulking. I mention to Burke the widely reported study, conducted by a Stanford graduate student, that showed how believing that others have strong social networks can lead to feelings of depression. What does Facebook communicate, if not the impression of social bounty? Everybody else looks so happy on Facebook, with so many friends, that our own social networks feel emptier than ever in comparison. Doesn't that *make* people feel lonely? "If people are reading about lives that are much better than theirs, two things can happen," Burke tells me. "They can feel worse about themselves, or they can feel motivated."

Burke will start working at Facebook as a data scientist this year.

John Cacioppo, the director of the Center for Cognitive and Social Neuroscience at the University of Chicago, is the world's leading expert on loneliness. In his landmark book, *Loneliness*, released in 2008, he revealed just how profoundly the epidemic of loneliness is affecting the basic functions of human physiology. He found higher levels of epinephrine, the stress hormone, in the morning urine of lonely people. Loneliness burrows deep: "When we drew blood from our older adults and analyzed their white cells," he writes, "we found that loneliness somehow penetrated the deepest recesses of the cell to alter the way genes were being expressed." Loneliness affects not only the brain, then, but the basic process of DNA transcription. When you are lonely, your whole body is lonely.

To Cacioppo, Internet communication allows only ersatz intimacy. "Forming connections with pets or online friends or even God is a noble attempt by an obligatorily gregarious creature to satisfy a compelling need," he writes. "But surrogates can never make up completely for the absence of the real thing." The "real thing" being actual people, in the flesh. When I speak to Cacioppo, he is refreshingly clear on what he sees as Facebook's effect on society. Yes, he allows, some research has suggested that the greater the number of Facebook friends a person has, the less lonely she is. But he argues that the impression this creates can be misleading. "For the most part," he says, "people are bringing their old friends, and feelings of loneliness or connectedness, to Facebook." The idea that a Web site could deliver a more friendly, interconnected world is bogus. The depth of one's social network outside Facebook is what determines the depth of one's social network within Facebook, not the other way around. Using social media doesn't create new social networks; it just transfers established networks from one platform to another. For the most part, Facebook doesn't destroy friendships—but it doesn't create them, either.

In one experiment, Cacioppo looked for a connection between the loneliness of subjects and the relative frequency of their interactions via Facebook, chat rooms, online games, dating sites, and face-to-face contact. The results were unequivocal. "The greater the proportion of face-to-face interactions, the less lonely you are," he says. "The greater the proportion of online interactions, the lonelier you are." Surely, I suggest to Cacioppo, this means that Facebook and the like inevitably make people lonelier. He disagrees. Facebook is merely a tool, he says, and like any tool, its effectiveness will depend on its user. "If you use Facebook to increase face-to-face contact," he says, "it increases social capital." So if social media let you organize a game of football among your friends, that's healthy. If you turn to social media instead of playing football, however, that's unhealthy.

"Facebook can be terrific, if we use it properly," Cacioppo continues. "It's like a car. You can drive it to pick up your friends. Or you can drive alone." But hasn't the car increased loneliness? If cars created the suburbs, surely they also created isolation. "That's because of how we use cars," Cacioppo replies. "How we use these technologies can lead to more integration, rather than more isolation."

The problem, then, is that we invite loneliness, even though it makes us miserable. The history of our use of technology is a history of isolation desired and achieved. When the Great Atlantic and Pacific Tea Company opened its A&P stores, giving Americans self-service access to groceries, customers stopped having relationships with their grocers. When the telephone arrived, people stopped knocking on their neighbors' doors. Social media bring this process to a much wider set of relationships. Researchers at the HP Social Computing Lab who studied the nature of people's

connections on Twitter came to a depressing, if not surprising, conclusion: "Most of the links declared within Twitter were meaningless from an interaction point of view." I have to wonder: What other point of view is meaningful?

Loneliness is certainly not something that 30 Facebook or Twitter or any of the lesser forms of social media is doing to us. We are doing it to ourselves. Casting technology as some vague, impersonal spirit of history forcing our actions is a weak excuse. We make decisions about how we use our machines, not the other way around. Every time I shop at my local grocery store, I am faced with a choice. I can buy my groceries from a human being or from a machine. I always, without exception, choose the machine. It's faster and more efficient, I tell myself, but the truth is that I prefer not having to wait with the other customers who are lined up alongside the conveyor belt: the hipster mom who disapproves of my high-carbon-footprint pineapple; the lady who tenses to the point of tears while she waits to see if the gods of the credit-card machine will accept or decline; the old man whose clumsy feebleness requires a patience that I don't possess. Much better to bypass the whole circus and just ring up the groceries myself.

Our omnipresent new technologies lure us toward increasingly superficial connections at exactly the same moment that they make avoiding the mess of human interaction easy. The beauty of Facebook, the source of its power, is that it enables us to be social while sparing us the embarrassing reality of society — the accidental revelations we make at parties, the awkward pauses, the farting and the spilled drinks and the general gaucherie of face-to-face contact. Instead, we have the lovely smoothness of a seemingly social machine. Everything's so simple: status updates, pictures, your wall.

But the price of this smooth sociability is a constant compulsion to assert one's own happiness, one's own fulfillment. Not only must we contend with the social bounty of others; we must foster the appearance of our own social bounty. Being happy all the time, pretending to be happy, actually attempting to be happy — it's exhausting. Last year a team of researchers led by Iris Mauss at the University of Denver published a study looking into "the paradoxical effects of valuing happiness." Most goals in life show a direct correlation between valuation and achievement. Studies have found, for example, that students who value good grades tend to have higher grades than those who don't value them. Happiness is an exception. The study came to a disturbing conclusion:

> Valuing happiness is not necessarily linked to greater happiness. In fact, under certain conditions, the opposite is true. Under conditions of low (but not high) life stress, the more people valued happiness, the lower were their hedonic balance, psychological well-being, and life satisfaction, and the higher their depression symptoms.

The more you try to be happy, the less happy you are. Sophocles made roughly the same point.

Facebook, of course, puts the pursuit of happiness front and center in our digital life. Its capacity to redefine our very concepts of identity and personal fulfillment is much more worrisome than the data-mining and privacy practices that have aroused anxieties about the company. Two of the most compelling critics of Facebook — neither of them a Luddite — concentrate on exactly this point. Jaron Lanier, the author of *You Are Not a Gadget*, was one of the inventors of virtual-reality technology. His view of where social media are taking us reads like dystopian science fiction: "I fear that we are beginning to design ourselves to suit digital models of us, and I worry about a leaching of empathy and humanity in that process." Lanier argues that Facebook imprisons us in the business of self-presenting, and this, to his mind, is the site's crucial and fatally unacceptable downside.

Sherry Turkle, a professor of computer culture at MIT who in 1995 published the digital-positive analysis *Life on the Screen*, is much more skeptical about the effects of online society in her 2011 book, *Alone Together*: "These days, insecure in our relationships and anxious about intimacy, we look to technology for ways to be in relationships and protect ourselves from them at the same time." The problem with digital intimacy is that it is ultimately incomplete: "The ties we form through the Internet are not, in the end, the ties that bind. But they are the ties that preoccupy," she writes. "We don't want to intrude on each other, so instead we constantly intrude on each other, but not in 'real time.'"

Lanier and Turkle are right, at least in 35 their diagnoses. Self-presentation on Facebook is continuous, intensely mediated, and possessed of a phony nonchalance that eliminates even the potential for spontaneity. ("Look how casually I threw up these three photos from the party at which I took 300 photos!") Curating the exhibition of the self has become a 24/7 occupation. Perhaps not surprisingly, then, the Australian study "Who Uses Facebook?" found a significant correlation between Facebook use and narcissism: "Facebook users have higher levels of total narcissism, exhibitionism, and leadership than Facebook nonusers," the study's authors wrote. "In fact, it could be argued that

Facebook specifically gratifies the narcissistic individual's need to engage in self-promoting and superficial behavior."

Rising narcissism isn't so much a trend as the trend behind all other trends. In preparation for the 2013 edition of its diagnostic manual, the psychiatric profession is currently struggling to update its definition of narcissistic personality disorder. Still, generally speaking, practitioners agree that narcissism manifests in patterns of fantastic grandiosity, craving for attention, and lack of empathy. In a 2008 survey, 35,000 American respondents were asked if they had ever had certain symptoms of narcissistic personality disorder. Among people older than sixty-five, 3 percent reported symptoms. Among people in their twenties, the proportion was nearly 10 percent. Across all age groups, one in sixteen Americans has experienced some symptoms of NPD. And loneliness and narcissism are intimately connected: a longitudinal study of Swedish women demonstrated a strong link between levels of narcissism in youth and levels of loneliness in old age. The connection is fundamental. Narcissism is the flip side of loneliness, and either condition is a fighting retreat from the messy reality of other people.

A considerable part of Facebook's appeal stems from its miraculous fusion of distance with intimacy, or the illusion of distance with the illusion of intimacy. Our online communities become engines of self-image, and self-image becomes the engine of community. The real danger with Facebook is not that it allows us to isolate ourselves, but that by mixing our appetite for isolation with our vanity, it threatens to alter the very nature of solitude. The new isolation is not of the kind that Americans once idealized, the lonesomeness of the proudly nonconformist, independent-minded, solitary stoic, or that of the astronaut who blasts into new worlds.

Facebook's isolation is a grind. What's truly staggering about Facebook usage is not its volume — 750 million photographs uploaded over a single weekend — but the constancy of the performance it demands. More than half its users — and one of every thirteen people on Earth is a Facebook user — log on every day. Among eighteen-to-thirty-four-year-olds, nearly half check Facebook minutes after waking up, and 28 percent do so before getting out of bed. The relentlessness is what is so new, so potentially transformative. Facebook never takes a break. We never take a break. Human beings have always created elaborate acts of self-presentation. But not all the time, not every morning, before we even pour a cup of coffee. Yvette Vickers's computer was on when she died.

Nostalgia for the good old days of disconnection would not just be pointless, it would be hypocritical and ungrateful. But the very magic of the new machines, the efficiency and elegance with which they serve us, obscures what isn't being served: everything that matters. What Facebook has revealed about human nature — and this is not a minor revelation — is that a connection is not the same thing as a bond, and that instant and total connection is no salvation, no ticket to a happier, better world or a more liberated version of humanity. Solitude used to be good for self-reflection and self-reinvention. But now we are left thinking about who we are all the time, without ever really thinking about who we are. Facebook denies us a pleasure whose profundity we had underestimated: the chance to forget about ourselves for a while, the chance to disconnect.

1. In his first three paragraphs, Stephen Marche argues that despite modern technology, "We have never been more detached from one another, or lonelier." What methods does he go on to use, in his effort to persuade? Did his essay convince you? Please explain.

2. In paragraph 6, Marche states that "social networking might be spreading the very isolation it seemed designed to conquer." Does your own experience confirm or refute this assertion? Explain your response.

3. In paragraph 17, Marche speaks of "social capital." What does this term mean? How do you know?

4. In paragraph 20, Marche discusses the findings of an Australian study of Facebook users. How do you interpret their finding of "significantly higher levels of family loneliness" among Facebook users?

5. Evaluate Marche's final paragraph as a conclusion.

JOSH ROSE

Josh Rose is the chief creative officer at Weber Shandwick, an internationally recognized public relations firm. We reprint this article that was published on Mashable.com, an online source that reports on digital innovation, on February 23, 2011.

How Social Media Is Having a Positive Impact on Our Culture

Two events today, although worlds apart, seem inextricably tied together. And the bond between them is as human as it is electronic.

First, on my way to go sit down and read the newspaper at my coffee shop, I got a message from my ten-year-old son, just saying good morning and letting me know he was going to a birthday party today. I don't get to see him all the time. He's growing up in two houses, as I did. But recently I handed down my old iPhone 3G to him to use basically as an iPod touch. We both installed an app called Yak, so we could communicate with each other when we're apart.

The amount of calming satisfaction it gives me to be able to communicate with him through technology is undeniably palpable and human. It's the other side of the "I don't care what you ate for breakfast this morning" argument against the mundane broadcasting of social media. In this case, I absolutely care about this. I'd listen to him describe a piece of bacon, and hang on every word. Is it better than a conversation with "real words"? No. But is it better than waiting two more days, when the mundane moment that I long to hear about so much is gone? Yes.

I guess one man's TMI is another man's treasure.

Moments later, I sat down and opened 5 the paper. A headline immediately stood out: "In China, microblogs finding abducted kids" with the subhead, "A 6-year-old who was snatched when he was 3 is discovered with a family 800 miles away." Apparently, the occurrence of reclaimed children through the use of China's version of Twitter — and other online forums — has become triumphant news over there. I'm reading about the father's tears, the boy's own confusing set of emotions, the rapt attention of the town and country, and I'm again marveling at the human side of the Internet.

THE PARADOX OF ONLINE CLOSENESS

I recently asked the question to my Facebook friends: "Twitter, Facebook, Foursquare...is all this making you feel closer to people or farther away?" It sparked a lot of responses and seemed to touch one of our generation's exposed nerves. What is the effect of the Internet and social media on our humanity?

From the outside view, digital interactions appear to be cold and inhuman. There's no denying that. And without doubt, given the choice between hugging someone and "poking" someone, I think we can all agree which one feels better. The theme of the responses to my Facebook question seemed to be summed up by my friend Jason, who wrote: "Closer to people I'm far away from." Then, a minute later, wrote, "but maybe farther from the people I'm close enough to." And then added, "I just got confused."

It is confusing. We live in this paradox now, where two seemingly conflicting realities exist side-by-side. Social media simultaneously draws us nearer and distances us. But I think very often, we lament what we miss and forget to admire what we've become. And it's human nature to want to reject the machine at the moment we feel it becoming ubiquitous. We've seen it with the printing press, moving pictures, television, video games, and just about any other advanced technology that captures our attention. What romantic rituals of relationship and social interaction will die in the process? Our hearts want to know.

In the *New Yorker* this week [February 14, 2011] Adam Gopnik's article "How the Internet Gets Inside Us" explores this cultural truism in depth. It's a fantastic read and should be mandatory for anyone in an online industry. He breaks down a whole slew of new books on the subject and categorizes it all into three viewpoints: "the Never-Betters, the Better-Nevers, and the Ever-Wasers." In short, those who see the current movement as good, bad, or normal. I think we all know people from each camp. But ultimately, the last group is the one best equipped to handle it all.

FILLING IN THE SPACE WITH CONNECTIONS

Another observation from the coffee shop: 10 In my immediate vicinity, four people are looking at screens and four people are reading something on paper. And I'm doing both. I see Facebook open on two screens, but I'm sure at some point, it's been open on all of them. The dynamic in this coffee shop is quite a bit more revealing than any article or book. Think about the varied juxtapositions of physical and digital going on. People aren't giving up long-form reading, considered thinking, or social interactions. They are just filling all the space between. And even that's not entirely true as I watch the occasional stare out the window or long glance around the room.

The way people engage with the Internet and social media isn't like any kind of interaction we've ever seen before. It's like an intertwining sine wave that touches in and out continuously. And the Internet itself is more complex and interesting than we often give it credit for. Consider peer-to-peer networking as just one example, where the tasks are distributed among the group to form a whole. It's practically a metaphor for the human mind. Or a township. Or a government. Or a family.

The Internet doesn't steal our humanity, it reflects it. The Internet doesn't get inside us, it shows what's inside us. And social media isn't cold, it's just complex and hard to define. I've always thought that you really see something's value when you try to destroy it. As we have now laid witness to in recent news, the Internet has quickly become the atom of cultural media; intertwined with our familial and cultural bonds, and destroyed only at great risk. I think if we search our own souls and consider our own personal way of navigating, we know this is as true personally as it is globally. The machine does not control us. It is a tool. As advanced today as a sharpened stick was a couple million years ago. Looked at through this lens, perhaps we should reframe our discussions about technology from how it is changing us to how we are using it.

Topics for Critical Thinking and Writing

1. In paragraph 8, Josh Rose says, "Social media simultaneously draws us nearer and distances us." If you agree, write a short essay (350–500 words) citing examples that may help to convince a reader of the truth of this assertion.

2. Rose begins his final paragraph with these three sentences:

   > The Internet doesn't steal our humanity, it reflects it. The Internet doesn't get inside us, it shows what's inside us. And social media isn't cold, it's just complex and hard to define.

   Assume for the moment that he is right. Go on to continue his paragraph, offering details that support these sentences.

23

Immigration: What Is to Be Done?

DAVID COLE

David Cole (b. 1958), a professor at Georgetown University Law Center, is a volunteer staff attorney for the Center for Constitutional Rights. This essay originally appeared in The Nation *on October 17, 1994.*

Five Myths about Immigration

For a brief period in the mid-nineteenth century, a new political movement captured the passions of the American public. Fittingly labeled the "Know-Nothings," their unifying theme was nativism. They liked to call themselves "Native Americans," although they had no sympathy for people we call Native Americans today. And they pinned every problem in American society on immigrants. As one Know-Nothing wrote in 1856: "Four-fifths of the beggary and three-fifths of the crime spring from our foreign population; more than half the public charities, more than half the prisons and almshouses, more than half the police and the cost of administering criminal justice are for foreigners."

At the time, the greatest influx of immigrants was from Ireland, where the potato famine had struck, and Germany, which was in political and economic turmoil. Anti-alien and anti-Catholic sentiments were the order of the day, especially in New York and Massachusetts, which received the brunt of the wave of immigrants, many of whom were dirt-poor and uneducated. Politicians were quick to exploit the sentiment: There's nothing like a scapegoat to forge an alliance.

I am especially sensitive to this history: My forebears were among those dirt-poor Irish Catholics who arrived in the 1860s. Fortunately for them, and me, the Know-Nothing movement fizzled within fifteen years. But its pilot light kept burning, and is turned up whenever the American public begins to feel vulnerable and in need of an enemy.

Although they go by different names today, the Know-Nothings have returned. As in the 1850s, the movement is strongest where immigrants are most concentrated: California and Florida. The objects of prejudice are of course no longer Irish Catholics and Germans; 140 years later, "they" have become "us." The new "they" — because it seems "we" must always have a "they" — are Latin Americans (most recently, Cubans), Haitians, and Arab Americans, among others.

But just as in the 1850s, passion, misinfor- 5 mation, and shortsighted fear often substitute for reason, fairness, and human dignity in today's immigration debates. In the interest of advancing beyond know-nothingism, let's look at five current myths that distort public debate and government policy relating to immigrants.

① *America is being overrun with immigrants.* In one sense, of course, this is true, but in that sense it has been true since Christopher Columbus arrived. Except for the real Native Americans, we are a nation of immigrants.

It is not true, however, that the first-generation immigrant share of our population is growing. As of 1990, foreign-born people made up only 8 percent of the population, as compared with a figure of about 15 percent from 1870 to 1920. Between 70 and 80 percent of those who immigrate every year are refugees or immediate relatives of U.S. citizens.

Much of the anti-immigrant fervor is directed against the undocumented, but they make up only 13 percent of all immigrants residing in the United States, and only 1 percent of the American population. Contrary to popular belief, most such aliens do not cross the border illegally but enter legally and remain after their student or visitor visa expires. Thus, building a wall at the border, no matter how high, will not solve the problem.

② *Immigrants take jobs from U.S. citizens.* There is virtually no evidence to support this view, probably the most widespread misunderstanding about immigrants. As documented by a 1994 A.C.L.U. Immigrants' Rights Project report, numerous studies have found that immigrants actually *create* more jobs than they fill. The jobs immigrants take are of course easier to see, but immigrants are often highly productive, run their own businesses, and employ both immigrants and citizens. One study found that Mexican immigration to Los Angeles County between 1970 and 1980 was responsible for 78,000 new jobs. Governor Mario Cuomo reports that immigrants own more than 40,000 companies in New York, which provide thousands of jobs and $3.5 billion to the state's economy every year.

③ *Immigrants are a drain on society's resources.* 10 This claim fuels many of the recent efforts to cut off government benefits to immigrants. However, most studies have found that immigrants are a net benefit to the economy because, as a 1994 Urban Institute report concludes, "immigrants generate significantly more in taxes paid than they cost in services received." The Council of Economic Advisers similarly found in 1986 that "immigrants have a favorable effect on the overall standard of living."

Anti-immigrant advocates often cite studies purportedly showing the contrary, but these generally focus only on taxes and services at the local or state level. What they fail to explain is that because most taxes go to the federal government, such studies would also show a net loss when applied to U.S. citizens. At most, such figures suggest that some redistribution of federal and state monies may be appropriate; they say nothing unique about the costs of immigrants.

Some subgroups of immigrants plainly impose a net cost in the short run, principally those who have most recently arrived and have not yet "made it." California, for example, bears substantial costs for its disproportionately large undocumented population, largely because it has on average the poorest and least educated immigrants. But that has been true of every wave of immigrants that has ever reached our shores; it was as true of the Irish in the 1850s, for example, as it is of Salvadorans today. From a long-term perspective, the economic advantages of immigration are undeniable.

Some have suggested that we might save money and diminish incentives to immigrate illegally if we denied undocumented aliens public services. In fact, undocumented immigrants are already ineligible for most social programs, with the exception of education for schoolchildren, which is constitutionally required, and benefits directly related to health and safety, such as emergency medical care and nutritional assistance to poor women, infants, and children. To deny such basic care to people in need, apart from being inhumanly callous, would probably cost us more in the long run by exacerbating health problems that we would eventually have to address.

Aliens refuse to assimilate, and are depriving us of our cultural and political unity. This claim has been made about every new group of immigrants to arrive on U.S. shores. Supreme Court Justice Stephen Field wrote in 1884 that the Chinese "have remained among us a separate people, retaining their original peculiarities of dress, manners, habits, and modes of living, which are as marked as their complexion and language." Five years later, he upheld the racially based exclusion of Chinese immigrants. Similar claims have been made over different periods of our history about Catholics, Jews, Italians, Eastern Europeans, and Latin Americans.

In most instances, such claims are simply not true; "American culture" has been created, defined, and revised by persons who for the most part are descended from immigrants once seen as anti-assimilationist. Descendants of the Irish Catholics, for example, a group once decried as separatist and alien, have become presidents, senators, and representatives (and all of these in one family, in the case of the Kennedys). Our society exerts tremendous pressure to conform, and cultural separatism rarely survives a generation. But more important, even if this claim were true, is this a legitimate rationale for limiting immigration in a society built on the values of pluralism and tolerance?

Noncitizen immigrants are not entitled to constitutional rights. Our government has long declined to treat immigrants as full human beings, and nowhere is that more clear than in the realm of constitutional rights. Although the Constitution literally extends the fundamental protections in the Bill of Rights to all people, limiting to citizens only the right to vote and run for federal office, the federal government acts as if this were not the case.

In 1893 the executive branch successfully defended a statute that required Chinese laborers to establish their prior residence here by the testimony of "at least one credible white witness." The Supreme Court ruled that this law was constitutional because it was reasonable for Congress to presume that nonwhite witnesses could not be trusted.

The federal government is not much more enlightened today. In a pending case I'm handling in the Court of Appeals for the Ninth Circuit, the Clinton Administration has argued that permanent resident aliens lawfully living here should be extended no more First Amendment rights than aliens applying for first-time admission from abroad — that is, none. Under this view, students at a public university who are citizens may express themselves freely, but students who are not citizens can be deported for saying exactly what their classmates are constitutionally entitled to say.

Growing up, I was always taught that we will be judged by how we treat others. If we are collectively judged by how we have treated immigrants — those who would appear today to be "other" but will in a generation be "us" — we are not in very good shape.

Topics for Critical Thinking and Writing

1. What are the "five current myths" (para. 5) about immigration that David Cole identifies? Why does he describe them as "myths" (rather than errors, mistakes, or falsehoods)?

2. In an encyclopedia or other reference work in your college library, look up the "Know-Nothings" (para. 1). What, if anything, of interest do you learn about this movement that is not mentioned by Cole in his opening paragraphs (1–4)?

3. Cole attempts to show how insignificant the immigrant population really is (in paras. 7 and 13) because it involves such a small fraction (8 percent in 1990) of the total population. Suppose someone said to him, "That's all very well, but 8 percent of the population is still 20 million people — far more than the 15 percent of the population during the years from 1870 to 1920." How might he reply?

4. Suppose Cole is right that most illegal immigration results from overstaying visitor and student visas (para. 8). Why not pass laws prohibiting foreign students from studying here, since so many abuse the privilege? Why not pass other laws forbidding foreign visitors?

5. Cole cites a study (para. 9) showing that "Mexican immigration to Los Angeles County between 1970 and 1980 was responsible for 78,000 new jobs." Suppose it were also true that this immigration was responsible for 78,000 other Mexican immigrants who joined criminal gangs or were otherwise not legally employed. How might Cole respond?

6. Cole admits (para. 12) that in California, the large population of undocumented immigrants imposes "substantial costs" on taxpayers. Does Cole offer any remedy for this problem? Should the federal government bear some or all of these extra costs that fall on California? Explain your response.

7. Cole thinks that "cultural separatism" among immigrants "rarely survives a generation" (para. 15). His evidence? Look at the Irish Catholics. But suppose someone argued that this is weak evidence: Because today's immigrants are not Europeans, but are Asian and Hispanic, they will never assimilate to the degree that European immigrants did — their race, culture, religion, and language and the trend toward "multiculturalism" all block the way. How might Cole reply?

8. Do you think that immigrants who are not citizens and not applying for citizenship ought to be allowed to vote in state and local elections? (The Constitution forbids them to vote in federal elections, as Cole points out in para. 16.) Why, or why not? How about illegal immigrants?

BARRY R. CHISWICK

*Barry R. Chiswick (b. 1942) holds a Ph.D. in economics from Columbia University. A special-
ist in the labor market, Chiswick is head of the economics department at George Washington
University. We reprint an essay that originally appeared in the* New York Times *in June 2006.*

The Worker Next Door

It is often said that the American economy needs low-skilled foreign workers to do
the jobs that American workers will not do.
These foreign workers might be new immigrants, illegal aliens, or, in the current debate,
temporary or guest workers. But if low-skilled
foreign workers were not here, would lettuce
not be picked, groceries not bagged, hotel
sheets not changed, and lawns not mowed?
Would restaurants use disposable plates and
utensils?

On the face of it, this assertion seems
implausible. Immigrants and low-skilled foreign workers in general are highly concentrated
in a few states. The "big six" are California,
Florida, Illinois, New Jersey, New York, and
Texas. Even within those states, immigrants
and low-skilled foreign workers are concentrated in a few metropolitan areas — while
there are many in New York City and Chicago, relatively few are in upstate New York or
downstate Illinois.

Yet even in areas with few immigrants,
grass is cut, groceries are bagged, and hotel
sheets are changed. Indeed, a large majority
of low-skilled workers are native to the United
States. A look at the 2000 census is instructive:
among males age twenty-five to sixty-four
years employed that year, of those with less
than a high school diploma, 64 percent were
born in the United States and 36 percent were
foreign born.

Other Americans nominally graduated
from high school but did not learn a trade or
acquire the literacy, numeracy, or decision-
making skills needed for higher earnings. Still
others suffer from a physical or emotional ail-
ment that limits their labor productivity. And
some low-skilled jobs are performed by high
school or college students, housewives, or the
retired who wish to work part time. Put simply,
there are no low-skilled jobs that American
workers would not and do not do.

Over the past two decades the number of
low-skilled workers in the United States has
increased because of immigration, both legal
and illegal. This increase in low-skilled workers
has contributed to the stagnation of wages for all
such workers. The proposed "earned legalization"
(amnesty) and guest worker programs would
allow still more low-skilled workers into the
country, further lowering their collective wages.

True, the prices of the goods and services that these new immigrants produce are
reduced for the rich and poor alike. But the
net effect of this dynamic is a decline in the
purchasing power of low-skilled families and
a rise in the purchasing power of high-income
families — a significant factor behind the
increase in income inequality that has been of
considerable public concern over the past two
decades.

In short, the continued increase in the flow
of unskilled workers into the United States is

the economic and moral equivalent of a regressive tax.

If the number of low-skilled foreign workers were to fall, wages would increase. Low-skilled American workers and their families would benefit, and society as a whole would gain from a reduction in income inequality.

Employers facing higher labor costs for low-skilled workers would raise their prices, and to some extent they would change the way they operate their businesses. A farmer who grows winter iceberg lettuce in Yuma County, Arizona, was asked on the ABC program *Nightline* in April what he would do if it were more difficult to find the low-skilled hand harvesters who work on his farm, many of whom are undocumented workers. He replied that he would mechanize the harvest. Such technology exists, but it is not used because of the abundance of low-wage laborers. In their absence, mechanical harvesters—and the higher-skilled (and higher-wage) workers to operate them—would replace low-skilled, low-wage workers.

But, you might ask, who would mow the lawns in suburbia? The higher wages would attract more lower-skilled American workers (including teenagers) to these jobs. Facing higher costs, some homeowners would switch to grass species that grow more slowly, to alternative ground cover, or to flagstones. Others would simply mow every other week, or every ten days, instead of weekly. And some would combine one or more of these strategies to offset rising labor costs.

Few of us change our sheets and towels at home every day. Hotels and motels could reduce the frequency of changing sheets and towels from every day to, say, every third day for continuing guests, perhaps offering a price discount to guests who accept this arrangement.

Less frequent lawn mowing and washing of hotel sheets and towels would reduce air, noise, and water pollution in the bargain.

With the higher cost of low-skilled labor, we would import more of some goods, in particular table-quality fruits and vegetables for home consumption (as distinct from industrial use) and lower-priced off-the-rack clothing. But it makes no sense to import people to produce goods in the United States for which we lack a comparative advantage—that is, goods that other countries can produce more efficiently.

The point is that with a decline in low-skilled foreign workers, life would go on. The genius of the American people is their ingenuity, and the genius of the American economy is its flexibility. And throughout our nation's history, this flexibility, the finding of alternative ways of doing things, has been a prime engine of economic growth and change.

Topics for Critical Thinking and Writing

1. Reread Barry Chiswick's first paragraph, and try to remember the effect it had on you when you first read it. Did you think, "Hey, he's right; of course the lettuce would get picked, the groceries would be bagged, and the hotel sheets would be changed"? Or did you think, "Where is this guy going?" Or something else? Evaluate Chiswick's first paragraph as the opening of an argument.

2. What is the program known as "earned legalization" (para. 5)?

3. In paragraph 6, Chiswick says that although cheap labor reduces the price of goods and services for the poor as well as for the rich, "the net effect . . . is a decline in the purchasing power of low-skilled families." Are you convinced? Why, or why not?

4. What is a "regressive tax" (para. 7)?

5. Why does Chiswick think (para. 8) wages would increase if the number of low-skilled foreign workers declined? Are you convinced by his argument? Why, or why not?

6. Analyze and evaluate Chiswick's essay as an example of persuasive writing. What devices does he use, and how effectively does he use them?

JOHN TIERNEY

John Tierney (b. 1953), has written for the New York Times *since 1990, where he is now a regular columnist. He is the coauthor of a comic novel,* God Is My Broker *(1998), and the author of* The Best-Case Scenario Handbook *(2002), which tells readers how to cope with such unlikely things as an ATM that keeps disgorging money. We reprint one of his columns written for the* New York Times *in April 2006.*

Ángels in America

Ángel Espinoza doesn't understand why Republicans on Capitol Hill are determined to deport Mexicans like him. I don't get it, either. He makes me think of my Irish grandfather.

They both left farms and went to the South Side of Chicago, arriving with relatively little education. My grandfather took a job in the stockyards and lived in an Irish boarding house nearby. Espinoza started as a dishwasher and lived with his brother in a Mexican neighborhood.

Like my grandfather, who became a streetcar motorman and then a police officer, Espinoza moved on to better-paying jobs and a better home of his own. Like my grandfather, Espinoza married an American-born descendant of immigrants from his native country.

But whereas my grandfather became a citizen, Espinoza couldn't even become a legal resident. Once he married an American, he applied, but was rejected because he'd once been caught at the border and sent home with an order to stay out. Violating that order made him ineligible for a green card and eligible for deportation.

"I had to tell my four-year-old daughter that one day I might not come home," he said. "I work hard and pay taxes and don't want any welfare. Why deport me?"

The official answer, of course, is that he violated the law. My grandfather didn't. But my grandfather didn't have to. There weren't quotas on Europeans or most other immigrants in 1911, even though, relative to the population, there were more immigrants arriving and living here than there are today. If America could absorb my grandfather, why keep out Espinoza?

It's been argued that Mexicans are different from past immigrants because they're closer to home and less likely to assimilate. Compared with other immigrants today, they're less educated, and their children are more likely to get poor grades and drop out of school. Therefore, the argument goes, Mexicans are in danger of becoming an underclass living in linguistically isolated ghettos.

Those concerns sound reasonable in theory. But if you look at studies of immigrants, you find that the typical story is much more like Espinoza's. He dropped out of school at age sixteen in southern Mexico, when his family needed money for medical bills. He paid a coyote to sneak him across the border and went to the Mexican neighborhood of Pilsen in Chicago, a metropolitan area that is now home to the second-largest Mexican population in the nation.

Espinoza started off making less than $4 an hour as a dishwasher in a restaurant that flouted the minimum-wage law. But he became a cook and worked up to $15 an hour. He switched to driving a street-cleaning truck, a job that now pays him $17 an hour, minus taxes and Social Security.

By age twenty-four, he and his wife, Anita, [10] had saved enough to buy a house for about $200,000 in Villa Park, a suburb where most people don't speak Spanish. Now twenty-seven, Espinoza's still working on his English (we spoke in Spanish), but his daughter is already speaking English at her preschool.

There's nothing unusual about his progress. More than half of the Mexican immigrants in Chicago own their own homes, and many are moving to the suburbs. No matter where they live, their children learn English.

You can hear this on the sidewalks and school corridors in Mexican neighborhoods like Pilsen, where most teenagers speak to one another in English. A national survey by the Pew Hispanic Center found that nearly all second-generation Latinos are either bilingual or English-dominant, and by the next generation 80 percent are English-dominant and virtually none speak just Spanish.

Yesterday, the Senate seemed close to a deal letting most immigrants become legal residents. But it fell apart when Republicans fought to add restrictions, including some that could prevent an immigrant with Espinoza's history from qualifying.

Bobby Rush, a Democratic representative from Chicago, is trying to pass protections for the Espinozas and other families in danger of being separated. The issue has galvanized other Chicago public officials and immigrant advocates, who are planning to take the families to Washington to press their case.

I'd like to see Republicans on Capitol Hill [15] explain to Espinoza why he's less deserving than their immigrant ancestors, but that's probably too much to expect. Espinoza has a simpler wish: "I would like them to tell my American daughter why her father can't stay with her."

Topics for Critical Thinking and Writing

1. Evaluate the effectiveness of John Tierney's use of Ángel Espinoza in this essay. What does Tierney gain by introducing us to Espinoza?

2. In paragraph 4, Tierney explains why Espinoza is not eligible for a green card. If you could change the system, would you change the provision that makes him ineligible? Why, or why not?

3. Tierney ends his sixth paragraph with a question. What answer would you give to this question?

4. Who or what is a "coyote" (para. 8)?

5. In paragraph 8, Tierney refers to "studies of immigrants," but he does not cite any. Do you assume that there are such studies? Do you also assume, perhaps, that other studies may come to different conclusions? Do you believe that "studies" of this sort are highly relevant to the issue of whether immigration laws concerning Mexicans should or should not be revised? Explain your response.

6. Tierney ends his essay by saying that he would like to hear Republicans on Capitol Hill explain why Espinoza is less deserving than their own ancestors. What do you think a Republican on Capitol Hill might say? What would *you* say?

7. Tierney implies that there are only bad reasons for excluding Latino immigrants from citizenship. Do you agree? Why, or why not?

VICTOR DAVIS HANSON

Victor Davis Hanson, born in 1953 in Fowler, California, did his undergraduate work at the University of California–Santa Cruz and his Ph.D. work at Stanford University. A specialist in military history, he has taught classics at California State University–Fresno. A noted conservative, Hanson is a senior fellow at the Hoover Institution. This piece first appeared at realclearpolitics .com on May 25, 2006.

Our Brave New World of Immigration

In the dark of these rural spring mornings, I see full vans of Mexican laborers speeding by my farmhouse on their way to the western side of California's San Joaquin Valley to do the backbreaking work of weeding cotton, thinning tree fruit, and picking strawberries.

In the other direction, even earlier morning crews drive into town — industrious roofers, cement layers, and framers heading to a nearby new housing tract. While most of us are still asleep, thousands of these hardworking young men and women in the American Southwest rise with the sun to provide the sort of unmatched labor at the sort of wages that their eager employers insist they cannot find among citizens.

But just when one thinks that illegal immigration is an efficient win-win way of providing excellent workers to needy businesses, there are also daily warnings that there is something terribly wrong with a system predicated on a cynical violation of the law.

Three days ago, as I watched the daily early-morning caravan go by, I heard a horrendous explosion. Not far from my home, one of these vans had crossed the white line down the middle of the road and hit a pickup truck head-on. Perhaps the van had blown a bald tire. Perhaps the driver was intoxicated. Or perhaps he had no experience driving an overloaded minivan at high speed in the dark of early morning.

We will probably never know — since the driver ran away from the carnage of the accident. That often happens when an illegal alien who survives an accident has no insurance or driver's license. But he did leave in his wake his three dead passengers. Eight more people were injured. Both cars were totaled. Traffic was rerouted around the wreckage for hours.

Ambulances, fire trucks, and patrol cars lined the nearby intersection. That accident alone must have imparted untold suffering for dozens of family members, as well as cost the state thousands of dollars.

Such mayhem is no longer an uncommon occurrence here. I have had four cars slam into our roadside property, with the drivers running off, leaving behind damaged vines and trees, and wrecked cars with phony licenses and no record of insurance. I have been broadsided by an undocumented driver, who ran a stop sign and then tried to run from our collision.

These are the inevitable but usually unmentioned symptoms of illegal immigration. After all, the unexpected can often happen when tens of thousands of young males from Mexico arrive in a strange country, mostly alone, without English or legality — an estimated 60 percent of them without a high-school degree and most obligated to send nearly half of their hard-won checks back to kin in Mexico.

Many Americans — perhaps out of understandable and well-meant empathy for the dispossessed who toil so hard for so little — support this present open system of non-borders. But I find nothing liberal about it.

Zealots may chant *¡Sí, se puede!* all they want. And the libertarian right may dress up the need for cheap labor as a desire to remain globally competitive. But neither can disguise a cynicism about illegal immigration, one that serves to prop up a venal Mexican government, undercut the wages of our own poor, and create a new apartheid of millions of aliens in our shadows.

We have entered a new world of immigration without precedent. This current crisis is unlike the great waves of nineteenth-century immigration that brought thousands of Irish, Eastern Europeans, and Asians to the United States. Most immigrants in the past came legally. Few could return easily across an ocean to home. Arrivals from, say, Ireland or China could not embrace the myth that our borders had crossed them rather than vice versa.

Today, almost a third of all foreign-born persons in the United States are here illegally, making up 3 to 4 percent of the American population. It is estimated that the United States is home to 11 or 12 million illegal aliens, whose constantly refreshed numbers ensure there is always a perpetual class of unassimilated recent illegal arrivals. Indeed almost one-tenth of Mexico's population currently lives here illegally!

But the real problem is that we, the hosts, are also different from our predecessors. Today we ask too little of too many of our immigrants. We apparently don't care whether they come legally or learn English — or how they fare when they're not at work. Nor do we ask all of them to accept the brutal bargain of an American melting pot that rapidly absorbs the culture of an immigrant in exchange for the benefits of citizenship.

Instead, we are happy enough that most labor vans of hardworking helots stay on the road in the early-morning hours, out of sight and out of mind. Sometimes, though, they tragically do not.

Topics for Critical Thinking and Writing

1. Speakers and writers who take care to present themselves as decent, trustworthy people are concerned with what the Greeks called *ethos,* character. What impression do you get of Victor Davis Hanson's character from the first two paragraphs? If you had to guess — basing your guess only on the first two paragraphs — where Hanson stood on immigration, what would you say? Why?

2. Hanson's title alludes to Aldous Huxley's 1931 dystopian novel, *Brave New World.* In that story, a World State has established a global caste system in which the lower castes are systematically bred to work for the hedonistic enjoyments of the upper castes. Habituated to conformity, all citizens are discouraged from thinking critically about the status quo. What is the purpose of Hanson's analogy between our own and Huxley's "brave new world"?

3. Paragraph 3 begins with "But," a clear transition indicating that the essay will be going in a different direction. What other words in the third paragraph indicate what the writer's position will be?

4. What does Hanson mean in paragraph 3 when he calls the labor market in the San Joaquin Valley "a system predicated on a cynical violation of the law"? Do you agree with that description? Why, or why not?

5. In paragraph 11, Hanson speaks of "the myth that our borders had crossed [the immigrants from Mexico]" rather than vice versa. What does he mean by this? Do you agree that it is a myth? Explain your response.

6. What are the differences between current immigration from Mexico and historic immigration from Europe a century ago (see para. 11)?

7. How does Hanson know that "almost a third of all foreign-born persons in the United States are here illegally" (para. 12)? Could it be that from a sample of arrested immigrants, 30 percent or so turn out to be illegal? Is such a method of calculation persuasive? Explain your response.

8. In his next-to-last paragraph, Hanson says, "We apparently don't care whether [immigrants] come legally or learn English." Do you agree with this assertion? On what evidence do you base your response?

9. Evaluate Hanson's final paragraph. Given his earlier paragraphs, does the paragraph make an effective ending? Why, or why not?

Analyzing Visuals: Immigration Then and Now

From the mid-1800s through the early twentieth century, the average number of immigrants to America was around 600,000 per year. This large-scale movement came to be known as the first "Great Wave" of immigration. The majority of these immigrants came from Europe and intended their journey to be temporary, staying only long enough to work and save enough money to improve their prospects upon their return home. America was undergoing massive industrialization at the time, so there was an ever-increasing demand for factory workers. Moreover, studies have shown that the average immigrant during this time made wages comparable to people who were already in the United States, and immigrants tended to advance within their jobs at a commensurate rate.

That's a far cry from the modern immigration landscape, wherein people looking to settle elsewhere sometimes have to take drastic and even dangerous measures to do so. What's more, those who make it face other difficulties and challenges when they reach their destinations, especially if they have entered a new country without proper documentation. In addition to social stigmas that some people thrust upon nonnative residents, many immigrants earn much lower wages than native workers, especially if they have come from less developed countries. Yet as of 2015, an estimated 244 million people—roughly 3.3 percent of the world's population—lived outside their country of origin.

Immigrants on the deck of the S. S. *Patricia*, an Atlantic liner. The *Patricia* came from Hamburg to New York in late 1900.

Christophe Archambault/AFP/Getty Images

Rohingya migrants swimming to collect food supplies dropped by a Thai army helicopter in the Andaman Sea in 2015. The boat was found adrift, and passengers reported that several people, including children, had died in the days before the boat was found.

John Moore/Getty Images

Border Patrol agents detaining undocumented immigrants in McAllen, Texas, after they crossed the border from Mexico into the United States in 2015.

The Immigrant Building at Ellis Island, New York, circa 1904. Ellis Island opened in upper New York harbor near the Statue of Liberty in 1892 and closed in 1954, during which time it served as the main gateway for the new immigrants coming to America.

Library of Congress, Prints & Photographs Division, Reproduction number LC-USZ62-15539

Topics for Critical Thinking and Writing

1. Even if you knew nothing about the history of immigration, what kinds of differences would stand out to you between the early-twentieth-century photos versus the pictures from 2015?

2. Compare the two images that depict immigrants making journeys via boat. What kinds of figurative meanings, if any, do you read from each image?

3. Examine the two photos of immigrants who have just arrived at their destinations. How do these images contrast? Do they imply that people immigrating in 1900 faced similar challenges to people immigrating now? Why, or why not?

The Carceral State: Why Are So Many Americans in Jail?

ADAM GOPNIK

Adam Gopnik (b. 1956) was educated at McGill University in Montreal, Canada, where his parents were professors. Gopnik has been a staff writer for The New Yorker *since 1986, and he has written fiction, nonfiction, memoirs, and criticism. In this essay, which appeared in* The New Yorker *on January 30, 2012, Gopnik examines the phenomenon of mass incarceration in the United States; he argues that both the left and the right are wrong in their analysis of why crime rates have gone down in recent years.*

The Caging of America

A prison is a trap for catching time. Good reporting appears often about the inner life of the American prison, but the catch is that American prison life is mostly undramatic — the reported stories fail to grab us, because, for the most part, nothing *happens*. One day in the life of Ivan Denisovich[1] is all you need to know about Ivan Denisovich, because the idea that anyone could live for a minute in such circumstances seems impossible; one day in the life of an American prison means much less, because the force of it is that one day typically stretches out for decades. It isn't the horror of the time at hand but the unimaginable sameness of the time ahead that makes prisons unendurable for their inmates. The inmates on death row in Texas are called men in "timeless time," because they alone aren't serving time: they aren't waiting out five years or a decade or a lifetime. The basic reality of American prisons is not that of the lock and key but that of the lock and clock.

That's why no one who has been inside a prison, if only for a day, can ever forget the feeling. Time stops. A note of attenuated panic, of watchful paranoia — anxiety and boredom and fear mixed into a kind of enveloping fog,

---

[1]Ivan Denisovich is the protagonist in Aleksandr Solzhenitsyn's 1962 novel *One Day in the Life of Ivan Denisovich*. The action of the book follows the dire conditions that Ivan Denisovich, a prisoner, experiences over the course of a single day in a gulag (a Soviet labor camp) in the 1950s. [Editor's note.]

covering the guards as much as the guarded. "Sometimes I think this whole world is one big prison yard, / Some of us are prisoners, some of us are guards," Dylan sings, and while it isn't strictly true — just ask the prisoners — it contains a truth: the guards are doing time, too. As a smart man once wrote after being locked up, the thing about jail is that there are bars on the windows and they won't let you out. This simple truth governs all the others. What prisoners try to convey to the free is how the presence of time as something being done to you, instead of something you do things with, alters the mind at every moment. For American prisoners, huge numbers of whom are serving sentences much longer than those given for similar crimes anywhere else in the civilized world — Texas alone has sentenced more than four hundred teen-agers to life imprisonment — time becomes in every sense this thing you serve.

For most privileged, professional people, the experience of confinement is a mere brush, encountered after a kid's arrest, say. For a great many poor people in America, particularly poor black men, prison is a destination that braids through an ordinary life, much as high school and college do for rich white ones. More than half of all black men without a high-school diploma go to prison at some time in their lives. Mass incarceration on a scale almost unexampled in human history is a fundamental fact of our country today — perhaps *the* fundamental fact, as slavery was the fundamental fact of 1850. In truth, there are more black men in the grip of the criminal-justice system — in prison, on probation, or on parole — than were in slavery then. Over all, there are now more people under "correctional supervision" in America — more than six million — than were in the Gulag Archipelago under Stalin at its height. That city of the confined and the controlled, Lockuptown, is now the second largest in the United States.

The accelerating rate of incarceration over the past few decades is just as startling as the number of people jailed: in 1980, there were about two hundred and twenty people incarcerated for every hundred thousand Americans; by 2010, the number had more than tripled, to seven hundred and thirty-one. No other country even approaches that. In the past two decades, the money that states spend on prisons has risen at six times the rate of spending on higher education. Ours is, bottom to top, a "carceral state," in the flat verdict of Conrad Black, the former conservative press lord and newly minted reformer, who right now finds himself imprisoned in Florida, thereby adding a new twist to an old joke: A conservative is a liberal who's been mugged; a liberal is a conservative who's been indicted; and a passionate prison reformer is a conservative who's in one.

The scale and the brutality of our prisons are the moral scandal of American life. Every day, at least fifty thousand men — a full house at Yankee Stadium — wake in solitary confinement, often in "supermax" prisons or prison wings, in which men are locked in small cells, where they see no one, cannot freely read and write, and are allowed out just once a day for an hour's solo "exercise." (Lock yourself in your bathroom and then imagine you have to stay there for the next ten years, and you will have some sense of the experience.) Prison rape is so endemic — more than seventy thousand prisoners are raped each year — that it is routinely held out as a threat, part of the punishment to be expected. The subject is standard fodder for comedy, and an uncoöperative suspect being threatened with rape in prison is now represented, every night on television, as an ordinary and rather lovable bit of policing. The normalization of prison rape — like eighteenth-century japery about watching men struggle as they die on the gallows — will surely strike our descendants as chillingly sadistic, incomprehensible on the part of people who thought themselves civilized. Though we avoid looking directly at prisons, they seep obliquely into our fashions and manners. Wealthy white teen-agers in baggy jeans and laceless shoes and multiple tattoos show, unconsciously, the reality of incarceration that acts as a hidden foundation for the country.

How did we get here? How is it that our civilization, which rejects hanging and flogging and disemboweling, came to believe that caging vast numbers of people for decades is an acceptably humane sanction? There's a fairly large recent scholarly literature on the history and sociology of crime and punishment, and it tends to trace the American zeal for punishment back to the nineteenth century, apportioning blame in two directions. There's an essentially Northern explanation, focusing on the inheritance of the notorious Eastern State Penitentiary, in Philadelphia, and its "reformist" tradition; and a Southern explanation, which sees the prison system as essentially a slave plantation continued by other means. Robert Perkinson, the author of the Southern revisionist tract "Texas Tough: The Rise of America's Prison Empire," traces two ancestral lines, "from the North, the birthplace of rehabilitative penology, to the South, the fountainhead of subjugationist discipline." In other words, there's the scientific taste for reducing men to numbers and the slave owners' urge to reduce blacks to brutes.

William J. Stuntz, a professor at Harvard Law School who died shortly before his masterwork, "The Collapse of American Criminal Justice," was published, last fall, is the most forceful advocate for the view that the scandal of our prisons derives from the Enlightenment-era, "procedural" nature of American justice. He runs through the immediate causes of the incarceration epidemic: the growth of post-Rockefeller drug laws, which punished minor drug offenses with major prison time; "zero tolerance" policing, which added to the group; mandatory-sentencing laws, which prevented judges from exercising judgment. But his search for the ultimate cause leads deeper, all the way to the Bill of Rights. In a society where Constitution worship is still a requisite on right and left alike, Stuntz startlingly suggests that the Bill of Rights is a terrible document with which to start a justice system — much inferior to the exactly contemporary French Declaration of the Rights of Man, which Jefferson, he points out, may have helped shape while his protégé Madison was writing ours.

The trouble with the Bill of Rights, he argues, is that it emphasizes process and procedure rather than principles. The Declaration of the Rights of Man says, Be just! The Bill of Rights says, Be fair! Instead of announcing general principles — no one should be accused of something that wasn't a crime when he did it; cruel punishments are always wrong; the goal of justice is, above all, that justice be done — it talks procedurally. You can't search someone without a reason; you can't accuse him without allowing him to see the evidence; and so on. This emphasis, Stuntz thinks, has led to the current mess, where accused criminals get laboriously articulated protection against procedural errors and no protection at all against outrageous and obvious violations of simple justice. You can get off if the cops looked in the wrong car with the wrong warrant when they found your joint, but you have no recourse if owning the joint gets you locked up for life. You may be spared the death penalty if you can show a problem with your appointed defender, but it is much harder if there is merely enormous accumulated evidence that you weren't guilty in the first place and the jury got it wrong. Even clauses that Americans are taught to revere are, Stuntz maintains, unworthy of reverence: the ban on "cruel and unusual punishment" was designed to *protect* cruel punishments — flogging and branding — that were not at that time unusual.

The obsession with due process and the cult of brutal prisons, the argument goes, share an essential impersonality. The more professionalized and procedural a system is, the more insulated we become from its real effects on real people. That's why America is famous both for its process-driven judicial system ("The bastard got off on a technicality," the cop-show detective fumes) and for the harshness and inhumanity of its prisons. Though all industrialized societies started sending more people to prison and fewer to the gallows in the eighteenth century, it was in Enlightenment-inspired America that the taste for long-term, profoundly depersonalized punishment became most aggravated. The inhumanity of American prisons was as much a theme for Dickens, visiting America in 1842, as the cynicism of American lawyers. His shock when he saw the Eastern State Penitentiary, in Philadelphia — a "model" prison, at the time the most expensive public building ever constructed in the country, where every prisoner was kept in silent, separate confinement — still resonates:

> I believe that very few men are capable of estimating the immense amount of torture and agony which this dreadful punishment, prolonged for years, inflicts upon the sufferers. . . . I hold this slow and daily tampering with the mysteries of the brain, to be

immeasurably worse than any torture of the body: and because its ghastly signs and tokens are not so palpable to the eye and sense of touch as scars upon the flesh; because its wounds are not upon the surface, and it extorts few cries that human ears can hear; therefore I the more denounce it, as a secret punishment which slumbering humanity is not roused up to stay.

Not roused up to stay — that was the point. Once the procedure ends, the penalty begins, and, as long as the cruelty is routine, our civil responsibility toward the punished is over. We lock men up and forget about their existence. For Dickens, even the corrupt but communal debtors' prisons of old London were better than *this*. "Don't take it personally!" — that remains the slogan above the gate to the American prison Inferno. Nor is this merely a historian's vision. Conrad Black, at the high end, has a scary and persuasive picture of how his counsel, the judge, and the prosecutors all merrily congratulated each other on their combined professional excellence just before sending him off to the hoosegow for several years. If a millionaire feels that way, imagine how the ordinary culprit must feel.

In place of abstraction, Stuntz argues for the saving grace of humane discretion. Basically, he thinks, we should go into court with an understanding of what a crime is and what justice is like, and then let common sense and compassion and specific circumstance take over. There's a lovely scene in "The Castle," the Australian movie about a family fighting eminent-domain eviction, where its hapless lawyer, asked in court to point to the specific part of the Australian constitution that the eviction violates, says desperately, "It's . . . just the *vibe* of the thing." For Stuntz, justice ought to be just the vibe of the thing — not one procedural error caught or one fact worked around. The criminal law should once again be more like the common law, with judges and juries not merely finding fact but making law on the basis of universal principles of fairness, circumstance, and seriousness, and crafting penalties to the exigencies of the crime.

The other argument — the Southern argument — is that this story puts too bright a face on the truth. The reality of American prisons, this argument runs, has nothing to do with the knots of procedural justice or the perversions of Enlightenment-era ideals. Prisons today operate less in the rehabilitative mode of the Northern reformers "than in a retributive mode that has long been practiced and promoted in the South," Perkinson, an American Studies professor, writes. "American prisons trace their lineage not only back to Pennsylvania penitentiaries but to Texas slave plantations." White supremacy is the real principle, this thesis holds, and racial domination the real end. In response to the apparent triumphs of the sixties, mass imprisonment became a way of reimposing Jim Crow. Blacks are now incarcerated seven times as often as whites. "The system of mass incarceration works to trap African Americans in a virtual (and literal) cage," the legal scholar Michelle Alexander writes. Young black men pass quickly from a period of police harassment into a period of "formal control" (i.e., actual imprisonment) and then are doomed for life to a system of "invisible control." Prevented from voting, legally discriminated against for the rest of their lives, most will cycle back through the prison system. The system, in this view, is not really broken; it is doing what it was designed to do. Alexander's grim conclusion: "If mass incarceration is considered as a system of social control — specifically, racial control — then the system is a fantastic success."

Northern impersonality and Southern revenge converge on a common American theme: a growing number of American prisons are now contracted out as for-profit businesses to for-profit companies. The companies are paid by the state, and their profit depends on spending as little as possible on the prisoners and the prisons. It's hard to imagine any greater disconnect between public good and private profit: the interest of private prisons lies not in the obvious social good of having the minimum necessary number of inmates but in having as many as possible, housed as cheaply as possible. No more chilling document exists in recent American life than the 2005 annual report of the biggest of these firms, the Corrections Corporation of America. Here the company (which spends millions lobbying legislators) is obliged to caution its investors about the risk that somehow, somewhere, someone might turn off the spigot of convicted men:

> Our growth is generally dependent upon our ability to obtain new contracts to develop and manage new correctional and detention facilities. . . . The demand for our facilities and services could be adversely affected by the relaxation of enforcement efforts, leniency in conviction and sentencing practices or through the decriminalization of certain activities that are currently proscribed by our criminal laws. For instance, any changes with respect to drugs and controlled substances or illegal immigration could affect the number of persons arrested, convicted, and sentenced, thereby potentially reducing demand for correctional facilities to house them.

Brecht could hardly have imagined such a document: a capitalist enterprise that feeds on the misery of man trying as hard as it can to be sure that nothing is done to decrease that misery.

Yet a spectre haunts all these accounts, [15] North and South, whether process gone mad or penal colony writ large. It is that the epidemic of imprisonment seems to track the dramatic decline in crime over the same period. The more bad guys there are in prison, it appears, the less crime there has been in the streets. The real background to the prison boom, which shows up only sporadically in the prison literature, is the crime wave that preceded and overlapped it.

For those too young to recall the big-city crime wave of the sixties and seventies, it may seem like mere bogeyman history. For those whose entire childhood and adolescence were set against it, it is the crucial trauma in recent American life and explains much else that happened in the same period. It was the condition of the Upper West Side of Manhattan under liberal rule, far more than what had happened to Eastern Europe under socialism, that made neo-con polemics look persuasive. There really was, as Stuntz himself says, a liberal consensus on crime ("Wherever the line is between a merciful justice system and one that abandons all serious effort at crime control, the nation had crossed it"), and it really did have bad effects.

Yet if, in 1980, someone had predicted that by 2012 New York City would have a crime rate so low that violent crime would have largely disappeared as a subject of conversation, he would have seemed not so much hopeful as crazy. Thirty years ago, crime was supposed to be a permanent feature of the city, produced by an alienated underclass of super-predators; now it isn't. Something good happened to change it, and you might have supposed that the change would be an opportunity for celebration and optimism. Instead, we mostly content ourselves with grudging and sardonic references to the silly side of gentrification, along with a few all-purpose explanations, like broken-window policing. This is a general human truth: things that work interest us less than things that don't.

So what *is* the relation between mass incarceration and the decrease in crime? Certainly, in the 1970s and 1980s, many experts became persuaded that there was no way to make bad people better; all you could do was warehouse them, for longer or shorter periods. The best research seemed to show, depressingly, that nothing works — that rehabilitation was a ruse. Then, in 1983, inmates at the maximum-security federal prison in Marion, Illinois, murdered two guards. Inmates had been (very occasionally) killing guards for a long time, but the timing of the murders, and the fact that they took place in a climate already prepared to believe that even ordinary humanity was wasted on the criminal classes, meant that the entire prison was put on permanent lockdown. A century and a half after absolute solitary first appeared in American prisons, it was reintroduced. Those terrible numbers began to grow.

And then, a decade later, crime started falling: across the country by a standard measure of about forty per cent; in New York City by as much as eighty per cent. By 2010, the crime rate in New York had seen its greatest decline since the Second World War; in 2002, there were fewer murders in Manhattan than there had been in any year since 1900. In social science, a cause sought is usually a muddle found; in life as we experience it, a crisis resolved is causality established. If a pill cures a headache, we do not ask too often if the headache might have gone away by itself.

All this ought to make the publication of [20] Franklin E. Zimring's new book, "The City

That Became Safe," a very big event. Zimring, a criminologist at Berkeley Law, has spent years crunching the numbers of what happened in New York in the context of what happened in the rest of America. One thing he teaches us is how little we know. The forty per cent drop across the continent — indeed, there was a decline throughout the Western world — took place for reasons that are as mysterious in suburban Ottawa as they are in the South Bronx. Zimring shows that the usual explanations — including demographic shifts — simply can't account for what must be accounted for. This makes the international decline look slightly eerie: blackbirds drop from the sky, plagues slacken and end, and there seems no absolute reason that societies leap from one state to another over time. Trends and fashions and fads and pure contingencies happen in other parts of our social existence; it may be that there are fashions and cycles in criminal behavior, too, for reasons that are just as arbitrary.

But the additional forty per cent drop in crime that seems peculiar to New York finally succumbs to Zimring's analysis. The change didn't come from resolving the deep pathologies that the right fixated on — from jailing super-predators, driving down the number of unwed mothers, altering welfare culture. Nor were there cures for the underlying causes pointed to by the left: injustice, discrimination, poverty. Nor were there any "Presto!" effects arising from secret patterns of increased abortions or the like. The city didn't get much richer; it didn't get much poorer. There was no significant change in the ethnic makeup or the average wealth or educational levels of New Yorkers as violent crime more or less vanished. "Broken windows" or "turnstile jumping" policing, that is, cracking down on small visible offenses in order to create an atmosphere that refused to license crime, seems to

have had a negligible effect; there was, Zimring writes, a great difference between the slogans and the substance of the time. (Arrests for "visible" nonviolent crime — e.g., street prostitution and public gambling — mostly went *down* through the period.)

Instead, small acts of social engineering, designed simply to stop crimes from happening, helped stop crime. In the nineties, the N.Y.P.D. began to control crime not by fighting minor crimes in safe places but by putting lots of cops in places where lots of crimes happened — "hot-spot policing." The cops also began an aggressive, controversial program of "stop and frisk" — "designed to catch the sharks, not the dolphins," as Jack Maple, one of its originators, described it — that involved what's called pejoratively "profiling." This was not so much racial, since in any given neighborhood all the suspects were likely to be of the same race or color, as social, involving the thousand small clues that policemen recognized already. Minority communities, Zimring emphasizes, paid a disproportionate price in kids stopped and frisked, and detained, but they also earned a disproportionate gain in crime reduced. "The poor pay more and get more" is Zimring's way of putting it. He believes that a "light" program of stop-and-frisk could be less alienating and just as effective, and that by bringing down urban crime stop-and-frisk had the net effect of greatly reducing the number of poor minority kids in prison for long stretches.

Zimring insists, plausibly, that he is offering a radical and optimistic rewriting of theories of what crime is and where criminals are, not least because it disconnects crime and minorities. "In 1961, twenty six percent of New York City's population was minority African American or Hispanic. Now, half of New York's population is — and what that does in an enormously hopeful way is to destroy the rude assumptions of supply side criminology," he says. By "supply side criminology," he means the conservative theory of crime that claimed that social circumstances produced a certain net amount of crime waiting to be expressed; if you stopped it here, it broke out there. The only way to stop crime was to lock up all the potential criminals. In truth, criminal activity seems like most other human choices—a question of contingent occasions and opportunity. Crime is not the consequence of a set number of criminals; criminals are the consequence of a set number of opportunities to commit crimes. Close down the open drug market in Washington Square, and it does not automatically migrate to Tompkins Square Park. It just stops, or the dealers go indoors, where dealing goes on but violent crime does not.

And, in a virtuous cycle, the decreased prevalence of crime fuels a decrease in the prevalence of crime. When your friends are no longer doing street robberies, you're less likely to do them. Zimring said, in a recent interview, "Remember, nobody ever made a living mugging. There's no minimum wage in violent crime." In a sense, he argues, it's recreational, part of a life style: "Crime is a routine behavior; it's a thing people do when they get used to doing it." And therein lies its essential fragility. Crime ends as a result of "cyclical forces operating on situational and contingent things rather than from finding deeply motivated essential linkages." Conservatives don't like this view because it shows that being tough doesn't help; liberals don't like it because apparently being nice doesn't help, either. Curbing crime does not depend on reversing social pathologies or alleviating social grievances; it depends on erecting small, annoying barriers to entry.

One fact stands out. While the rest of the country, over the same twenty-year period, saw the growth in incarceration that led to

our current astonishing numbers, New York, despite the Rockefeller drug laws, saw a marked decrease in its number of inmates. "New York City, in the midst of a dramatic reduction in crime, is locking up a much smaller number of people, and particularly of young people, than it was at the height of the crime wave," Zimring observes. Whatever happened to make street crime fall, it had nothing to do with putting more men in prison. The logic is self-evident if we just transfer it to the realm of white-collar crime: we easily accept that there is no net sum of white-collar crime waiting to happen, no inscrutable generation of super-predators produced by Dewar's- guzzling dads and scaly M.B.A. profs; if you stop an embezzlement scheme here on Third Avenue, another doesn't naturally start in the next office building. White-collar crime happens through an intersection of pathology and opportunity; getting the S.E.C. busy ending the opportunity is a good way to limit the range of the pathology.

Social trends deeper and less visible to us may appear as future historians analyze what went on. Something other than policing may explain things—just as the coming of cheap credit cards and state lotteries probably did as much to weaken the Mafia's Five Families in New York, who had depended on loan sharking and numbers running, as the F.B.I. could. It is at least possible, for instance, that the coming of the mobile phone helped drive drug dealing indoors, in ways that helped drive down crime. It may be that the real value of hot spot and stop-and-frisk was that it provided a single game plan that the police believed in; as military history reveals, a bad plan is often better than no plan, especially if the people on the other side think it's a good plan. But one thing is sure: social epidemics, of crime or of punishment, can be cured more quickly than we might hope with simpler and more superficial mechanisms than we imagine. Throwing a Band-Aid over a bad wound is actually a decent strategy, if the Band-Aid helps the wound to heal itself.

Which leads, further, to one piece of radical common sense: since prison plays at best a small role in stopping even violent crime, very few people, rich or poor, should be in prison for a nonviolent crime. Neither the streets nor the society is made safer by having marijuana users or peddlers locked up, let alone with the horrific sentences now dispensed so easily. For that matter, no social good is served by having the embezzler or the Ponzi schemer locked in a cage for the rest of his life, rather than having him bankrupt and doing community service in the South Bronx for the next decade or two. Would we actually have more fraud and looting of shareholder value if the perpetrators knew that they would lose their bank accounts and their reputation, and have to do community service seven days a week for five years? It seems likely that anyone for whom those sanctions aren't sufficient is someone for whom no sanctions are ever going to be sufficient. Zimring's research shows clearly that if crime drops on the street, criminals coming out of prison stop committing crimes. What matters is the incidence of crime in the world, and the continuity of a culture of crime, not some "lesson learned" in prison.

At the same time, the ugly side of stop-and-frisk can be alleviated. To catch sharks and not dolphins, Zimring's work suggests, we need to adjust the size of the holes in the nets — to make crimes that are the occasion for stop-and-frisks *real* crimes, not crimes like marijuana possession. When the New York City police stopped and frisked kids, the main goal was not to jail them for having pot but to get their fingerprints, so that they could be identified if they committed a more serious crime. But all over America the opposite happens: marijuana possession becomes the serious crime. The cost is so enormous, though, in lives ruined and money spent, that the obvious thing to do is not to enforce the law less but to change it now. Dr. Johnson said once that manners make law, and that when manners alter, the law must, too. It's obvious that marijuana is now an almost universally accepted drug in America: it is not only used casually (which has been true for decades) but also talked about casually on television and in the movies (which has not). One need only watch any stoner movie to see that the perceived risks of smoking dope are not that you'll get arrested but that you'll get in trouble with a rival frat or look like an idiot to women. The decriminalization of marijuana would help end the epidemic of imprisonment.

The rate of incarceration in most other rich, free countries, whatever the differences in their histories, is remarkably steady. In countries with Napoleonic justice or common law or some mixture of the two, in countries with adversarial systems and in those with magisterial ones, whether the country once had brutal plantation-style penal colonies, as France did, or was once itself a brutal plantation-style penal colony, like Australia, the natural rate of incarceration seems to hover right around a hundred men per hundred thousand people. (That doesn't mean it doesn't get lower in rich, homogeneous countries — just that it never gets much higher in countries otherwise like our own.) It seems that one man in every thousand once in a while does a truly bad thing. All other things being equal, the point of a justice system should be to identify that thousandth guy, find a way to keep him from harming other people, and give everyone else a break.

Epidemics seldom end with miracle cures. 30 Most of the time in the history of medicine, the best way to end disease was to build a better sewer and get people to wash their hands. "Merely chipping away at the problem around the edges" is usually the very best thing to do with a problem; keep chipping away patiently and, eventually, you get to its heart. To read the literature on crime before it dropped is to see the same kind of dystopian despair we find in the new literature of punishment: we'd have to end poverty, or eradicate the ghettos, or declare war on the broken family, or the like, in order to end the crime wave. The truth is, a series of small actions and events ended up eliminating a problem that seemed to hang over everything. There was no miracle cure, just the intercession of a thousand smaller sanities. Ending sentencing for drug misdemeanors, decriminalizing marijuana, leaving judges free to use common sense (and, where possible, getting judges who are judges rather than politicians) — many small acts are possible that will help end the epidemic of imprisonment as they helped end the plague of crime.

"Oh, I have taken too little care of this!" King Lear cries out on the heath in his moment of vision. "Take physic, pomp; expose thyself to feel what wretches feel." "This" changes; in Shakespeare's time, it was flat-out peasant poverty that starved some and drove others as mad as poor Tom. In Dickens's and Hugo's time, it was the industrial revolution that drove kids to mines. But every society has a poor storm that wretches suffer in, and the attitude is always the same: either that the wretches, already dehumanized by their suffering, deserve no pity or that the oppressed, overwhelmed by injustice, will have to wait for a better world. At every moment, the injustice seems inseparable from the community's life, and in every case the arguments for keeping the system in place were that you would have to revolutionize the entire social order to change it — which then became the argument for revolutionizing the entire social order. In every case, humanity and common sense made the insoluble problem just get up and go away. Prisons are our this. We need take more care.

Topics for Critical Thinking and Writing

1. In the opening paragraphs of the article, Adam Gopnik makes much of the absence of anything going on in prison. Indeed, he states, "time becomes in every sense this thing you serve" (para. 2). What is his point? How does it connect to the arguments that he develops later in the article?

2. In paragraph 4, Gopnik points out that the rate of "spend[ing] on prisons has risen at six times the rate of spending on higher education." What is the point of this observation? Did this statistic surprise or anger you? Why, or why not?

3. In paragraph 5, Gopnik begins with a claim: "The scale and the brutality of our prisons are the moral scandal of American life." Do you agree? Why, or why not?

4. How does Gopnik's division of the approach to prisons into northern and southern attitudes reflect divisions of the nation during the Civil War? How do the old Civil War differences affect the prison system to this day? Why does Gopnik believe neither approach is just?

5. Why does William J. Stuntz argue that the problems with the justice system in America can be traced directly back to the United States Constitution? Argue for or against Stuntz's logic, including specific references to the Constitution and other texts, such as France's "The Declaration of the Rights of Man."

6. In paragraph 9, Gopnik states, "The more professionalized and procedural a system is, the more insulated we become from its real effects on real people." What does Gopnik mean by this? Is the advent of the modern system of mass incarceration more just than earlier justice systems, which often used capital punishment for crimes far less serious than murder? Research different justice systems, both past and present, from around the world. Argue which system (or systems) seems most just.

7. Do you agree or disagree with Gopnik in his arguments against for-profit companies running prisons and other detention centers? Defend your answer.

8. Gopnik recalls the rise of inner-city crime in the 1960s and 1970s and the psychic trauma they caused. Yet now, crime rates in major cities are significantly lower than they were in those decades. To what does Gopnik attribute the drop in crime? What does that mean for approaches to fighting crime in the future?

9. One police technique that Gopnik argues has been highly successful is "profiling" — a controversial practice that many civil rights activists claim unfairly focuses on minority men. Research the issue of profiling as a police tactic, and argue either for or against its validity in safeguarding public safety.

HEATHER ANN THOMPSON

Heather Ann Thompson is a Princeton-educated associate professor of African American studies and history at Temple University. She is the author of several books on race, activism, and politics, including Blood in the Water: The Attica Uprising of 1971 and Its Legacy *(2016). In this article, which appeared in the* Atlantic *on October 7, 2013, Thompson examines how the Fourteenth Amendment and the War on Crime unintentionally worked to disenfranchise African American voters.*

How Prisons Change the Balance of Power in America

What has it really cost the United States to build the world's most massive prison system?

To answer this question, some point to the nearly two million people who are now locked up in an American prison — overwhelmingly this nation's poorest, most mentally ill, and least-educated citizens — and ponder the moral costs. Others have pointed to the enormous expense of having more than seven million Americans under some form of correctional supervision and argued that the system is not economically sustainable. Still others highlight the high price that our nation's already most-fragile communities, in particular, have paid for the rise of such an enormous carceral state. A few have also asked Americans to consider what it means for the future of our society that our system of punishment is so deeply racialized.

With so many powerful arguments being made against our current criminal justice system, why then does it persist? Why haven't the American people, particularly those who are most negatively affected by this most unsettling and unsavory state of affairs, undone the policies that have led us here? The answer, in part, stems from the fact that locking up unprecedented numbers of citizens over the last forty years has *itself* made the prison system highly resistant to reform through the democratic process. To an extent that few Americans have yet appreciated, record rates of incarceration have, in fact, undermined our American democracy, both by impacting who gets to vote and how votes are counted.

The unsettling story of how this came to be actually begins in 1865, when the abolition of slavery led to bitter constitutional battles over who would and would not be included in our polity. To fully understand it, though, we must look more closely than we yet have at the year 1965, a century later — a moment when, on the one hand, politicians were pressured into opening the franchise by passing the most comprehensive Voting Rights Act to date, but on the other hand, were also beginning a devastatingly ambitious War on Crime.

FROM VOTING RIGHTS TO THE WAR ON CRIME

The Voting Rights Act of 1965 gave the federal government a number of meaningful tools with which it could monitor state elections and make sure that states with a particularly grim history of discriminatory voting practices would make no voting policy without its approval. The act had been intended to combat the intimidation and legal maneuvers — such as passage of poll taxes, literacy requirements, and so-called "Grandfather clauses" — that had left only 5 percent of black Americans, by the 1940s, able to vote, despite passage of the 14th and 15th amendments after the Civil War.

But the very same year that Lyndon Johnson signed the Voting Rights Act of 1965, he also signed another Act into law: the Law Enforcement Administration Act (LEAA), a piece of legislation that, well before crime rates across America hit record highs, created the bureaucracy and provided the funding that would enable a historically and internationally unparalleled war on crime.

So, at the *very same moment* that the American Civil Rights Movement had succeeded in newly empowering African Americans in the political sphere by securing passage of the Voting Rights Act of 1965, America's white politicians decided to begin a massive new war on crime that would eventually undercut myriad gains of the Civil Rights Movement — *particularly* those promised by the Voting Rights Act itself.

FROM THE WAR ON CRIME TO MASS INCARCERATION

Thanks to LEAA and America's post-1965 commitment to the War on Crime, and more specifically, thanks to the dramatic escalation of policing in cities across the nation as well as the legal changes wrought by an ever-intensifying War on Drugs, between 1970 and 2010 more people ended up in prison in this country than anywhere else in the world. At no other point in this nation's recorded past had the economic, social, and political institutions of a country become so bound up with the practice of punishment.

By the year 2007, 1 in every 31 U.S. residents lived under some form of correctional supervision. By 2010, more than 7.3 million Americans had become entangled in the criminal justice system and 2 million of them were actually locked up in state and federal prisons. By 2011, 39,709 people in Louisiana alone were living behind bars and 71,579 were either in jail, on probation, or on parole. And this was by no means a "southern" phenomenon. In Pennsylvania, 51,638 people were actually locked behind bars in 2011 and a full 346,268 lived under some form of correctional control by that year.

The nation's decision to embark on a massive War on Crime in the mid-1960s has had a profound impact on the way that American history evolved over the course of the later 20th and into the 21st centuries. As we now know from countless studies, such staggering rates of incarceration have proven both socially devastating and economically destructive for wide swaths of this country—particularly those areas of America inhabited by people of color. This nation's incarceration rate was hardly color blind. Eventually one in nine young black men were locked up in America and, by 2010, black women and girls too were being locked up at a record rate.

DILUTING OUR DEMOCRACY

So how did this overwhelmingly racialized mass incarceration end up mattering to our very democracy? How is it that this act of locking up so many Americans, particularly Americans of color, itself distorted our political process and made it almost impossible for those most affected by mass incarceration to eliminate the policies that have undergirded it at the ballot box? The answer lies back in the 1870s and in a little-known caveat to the 14th Amendment.

Ratifying the 14th Amendment was one of Congress's first efforts to broaden the franchise after the Civil War. A key worry among northern politicians, however, was that since white southerners could no longer rely on the notorious "three-fifths" rule to pad their own political power, they would now try to inflate their census population for the purposes of representation by counting African Americans as citizens while denying them to access the ballot.

So, to prevent any power grab on the part of ex-Confederates, Congress decided to add so-called Section 2 to the 14th Amendment. Firstly it stipulated that any state that "denied" the vote "to any of the male inhabitants of such state, being twenty-one years of age, and citizens of the United States" would have its representation downsized in proportion to the number of individuals being disenfranchised. Secondly, Section 2 allowed for the disenfranchisement of otherwise eligible citizens—without affecting representation—if they had participated "in rebellion, or other crime." The idea here was to keep those who had committed crimes against the Union and those who might still be in rebellion against the Union from wielding political power in the wake of the Civil War.

This latter provision of Section 2, however, proved damaging to black freedom—political and otherwise. Almost overnight, white southerners began policing African Americans with new zeal and charging them with "crimes" that had never before been on the books. Within a decade of the Civil War, thousands of African Americans found themselves leased

10

out and locked up on prison plantations and in penitentiaries.

Southern whites, of course, profited from these new laws politically as well as economically. By making so many blacks into convicts, whites could deny them the right to vote under Section 2 without undermining their state's census population for the purposes of political representation. And, because of another clause of another Amendment, the 13th, which allowed the continuation of slavery for those who had committed a crime, these same white southerners were able to force thousands of newly imprisoned black southerners to work for free under the convict lease system.

Fast-forward 100 years when, in the wake of the Civil Rights movement, another War on Crime began that also, almost overnight, led to the mass imprisonment of this nation's African American citizens.

In 1974, as the numbers of imprisoned Americans was rising precipitously and when states once again began to disfranchise individuals with criminal convictions, the U.S. Supreme Court was asked in a landmark case, *Richardson v. Ramirez*, to rule explicitly on the issue of whether it was constitutional under the 14th Amendment to disfranchise those serving, or who have served, time in prison. The court did the same thing that many southern states did after the Civil War — it interpreted Section A of the 14th Amendment very, very differently than it was intended to be interpreted. It, too, decided that disenfranchisement would be permitted when a citizen was convicted of *any* crime, without regard to whether such crimes might be thought of as ideologically analogous to rebellion or were more likely to affect African Americans than others.

Notably, Justice Thurgood Marshall dissented vigorously in this case. The purpose of Section 2, he argued, was clearly to enfranchise,

not disenfranchise, former slaves and their descendants. Marshall's fellow members of the bench, though, felt that their decision would not have any discriminatory effect because the nation already had the Voting Rights Act of 1965 to handle this issue.

And yet, the negative impact of *Richardson v. Ramirez* on African American voting was vast and immediate. By the year 2000, 1.8 million African Americans had been barred from the polls because so many felon disfranchisement laws had been passed in states across the country after 1974. Not only were their votes not counted in that year's hotly contested presidential election, but by the next presidential election a full ten states, according to The Sentencing Project, had "African American disenfranchisement rates above 15%," which clearly affected the outcome of that contest as well.

By 2006, 48 out of 50 states had passed disfranchisement laws and, with more than 47 million Americans (one-fourth of the adult population) having criminal records by that year, the nation's political process had been fundamentally altered. By 2011, 23.3% of African Americans in Florida, 18.3 % of the black population of Wyoming, and 20.4% of African Americans in Virginia were barred from the ballot.

According to sociologists Jeff Manza and Christopher Uggen, not only did African Americans pay a high price for the disfranchisement policies that accompanied the nation's War on Crime, but so did liberal voters in general. According to their research, such policies "affected the outcome of seven U.S. Senate races from 1970 to 1998 . . . [and] in each case the Democratic candidate would have won rather than the Republican victor" and these outcomes likely "prevented Democratic control of the Senate from 1986 to 2000" as well.

DISTORTING OUR DEMOCRACY

Disfranchising thousands of voters is only part of the story of how mass incarceration has distorted American democracy. Today, just as it did more than a hundred years earlier, the way the Census calculates resident population also plays a subtle but significant role. As ex-Confederates knew well, prisoners would be counted as residents of a given county, even if they could not themselves vote: High numbers of prisoners could easily translate to greater political power for those who put them behind bars.

With the advent of mass incarceration, and as the number of people imprisoned not only rose dramatically, but also began moving urbanites of color into overwhelmingly white rural counties that housed prisons, the political process was again distorted. In short, thanks to this process that we now call "prison-gerrymandering," overwhelmingly white and Republican areas of the United States that built prisons as the War on Crime escalated got more political power, whereas areas of country where policing was particularly concentrated and aggressive, areas in which levels of incarceration were, as a result, staggering, lost political power.

Consider research by the Prison Policy Initiative showing how voters across the country gain political power from housing a penal facility. In Powhatan County, Virginia, 41% of the 5th Board of Supervisors District that was drawn after the 2000 Census were actually people in prison and in both the First and Third Supervisory Districts of Nottoway County, approximately one-fourth of their population comes from large prisons within the county. In the case of Southampton County, such prison-based gerrymandering means that votes of those citizens who live there are worth almost more than twice as much as votes cast in other districts that have the required number of actual residents.

In Michigan as well, mass incarceration has meant distorted democracy. A full four state senate districts drawn after the 2000 Census (17, 19, 33 and 37), and a full five house districts (65, 70, 92, 107 and 110) meet federal minimum population requirements only because they claim prisoners as constituents. Similarly in Pennsylvania, no fewer than eight state legislative districts would comply with the federal "one person, one vote" civil rights standard if non-voting state and federal prisoners in those districts were not counted as district residents.

WHY WE SHOULD CARE

As Americans go to the polls this November to vote on criminal justice issues that directly affect our lives—ranging from proposals to decriminalize marijuana, to roll back three strikes laws, to fund more prison construction—the massive carceral state that we are trying to shape at the ballot box has already distorted our democracy. Americans' power to even rethink, let alone undo, the policies and practices that have led to mass incarceration via the franchise has been severely compromised—in no small part due to the fact that the parties that benefited the most from the rise of this enormous carceral state are now empowered, seemingly in perpetuity, by its sheer size and scope.

There are, of course, other ways to dismantle the carceral state. Indeed, history shows us that we ended the brutal convict leasing system of the post–Civil War era not by going to the polls but by grassroots and legal activism. Nevertheless, we should all be concerned about the ways mass incarceration has eroded our democracy. Even if we don't care about the record rate of imprisonment in this country — despite its myriad ugly consequences, its unsustainable cost, and its particularly devastating fallout on communities of color — when the principle of "one person, one vote" no longer has real meaning in a society, and when political power is no longer attained via its people but rather through a manipulation of their laws, we must all question the future of our nation.

Topics for Critical Thinking and Writing

1. In paragraph 2, Heather Thompson notes that the mass incarceration of "this nation's poorest, most mentally ill, and least-educated citizens" has had costs beyond financial. What does she mean by this? Research the "costs" mass incarceration has had on the minority communities, the mentally ill, and the poor. Argue whether these costs outweigh the benefits of mass incarceration, or not.

2. Research the history of how the black vote, particularly in the southern states, was suppressed by such means as poll taxes and literacy requirements, as noted in paragraph 5. Compare those efforts to today's push for voter identification. In your opinion, are voter identification laws another way to suppress the votes of blacks? Why, or why not? Be specific in your response.

3. At times, Thompson uses language that opens up some avenues of investigation by a critical reader. For instance, in paragraph 4 she states, "politicians were pressured into opening the franchise by passing the most comprehensive Voting Rights Act to date." By using the term "pressured," Thompson insinuates that many politicians in 1965 were not sincere in their vote to pass the Voting Rights Act (although she doesn't say if the pressure came from American voters, President Lyndon Johnson, or some other source). Are there other examples of this sort of language in Thompson's article, and what might it suggest about her own assumptions and biases?

4. Thompson reads the intent of the writers of the Fourteenth Amendment, Section 2, as being directed toward white southerners of the time who might still wish to rebel against the Union. If Thompson is right, why then did that section get reinterpreted in *Richardson v. Ramirez* in 1974? Research the history of the Fourteenth Amendment and the *Richardson v. Ramirez* case, and write either a defense or a criticism of the Supreme Court's decision.

5. One problem Thompson identifies is that because so many African Americans have had their right to vote taken away, election results have been affected. In paragraph 21, she argues that the outcome of at least seven U.S. Senate races were affected, and that in turn affected which party held the majority. Research the numbers of convicted felons of all races who have had their right to vote removed. Is there a racial bias — which might translate into an unfair advantage for one political party — in the disenfranchisement of convicted felons? Explain your response.

6. Another consequence of mass incarceration is that prisoners are counted as citizens within whatever district their prison is located, not their original home district. Thompson argues that this has given many rural, largely white districts a higher population count, leading to greater political power — what she refers to in paragraph 23 as "prison-gerrymandering." In your opinion, is this simply a necessary evil that cannot be readdressed, or are there realistic alternatives to the practice? Defend your stance.

7. Behind the current practice of the disenfranchisement of felons lies the history of post–Civil War voter suppression. In paragraph 27, Thompson warns, "when political power is no longer attained via its people but rather through a manipulation of their laws, we must all question the future of our nation." In your opinion, is Thompson correct or is she being overly alarmist? Defend your answer.

MARIAN WRIGHT EDELMAN

Marian Wright Edelman (b. 1939), educated at Spelman College and Yale University, is the founder of the Children's Defense Fund, a group, according to its Web site, that is dedicated to "the needs of poor children, children of color and those with disabilities." She has received numerous awards, including a MacArthur Fellowship (1985), the Albert Schweitzer Prize for Humanitarianism (1988), and the Presidential Medal of Freedom (2000). In this article, which appeared as an editorial in Preventing Chronic Disease: Public Health Research, Practice, and Policy *in July 2007, she argues that large numbers of children of color are susceptible to winding up in the prison system, a scourge that she likens to an infectious disease overtaking children across the nation.*

The Cradle to Prison Pipeline

Suppose that during the next decade, a quarter of all the children born in New York, North Carolina, Texas, Colorado, Ohio, and Pennsylvania were infected by a virulent new strain of polio or tuberculosis sometime during their youth. Clearly, our response to a health crisis affecting that many children would be to mobilize the nation's vast public health resources. Medical laboratories would operate around the clock to develop new vaccines.

Unfortunately, an infection akin to this hypothetical tragedy is actually coursing through African American and Latino communities across the nation. I'm not referring to a virus such as HIV/AIDS or a hazardous bacterium. I'm talking about the criminalization of poor children and children from minority races who enter what the Children's Defense Fund (CDF) identified as America's Cradle to Prison Pipeline. Together, African Americans and Latinos comprise a segment of the U.S. population equal to that of the six states I mentioned earlier. Like the victims of a crippling or wasting disease, once drawn into the prison pipeline, massive numbers of young people lose their opportunity to live happy, productive lives, not because of festering microbes but because of years spent behind bars.

Through its Cradle to Prison Pipeline initiative, the Children's Defense Fund has studied the grim effects of being trapped in a criminalizing environment from which the obstacles to escape are formidable. The Cradle to Prison Pipeline consists of a complex array of social and economic factors as well as political choices that converge to reduce the odds that poor children — especially poor black and Latino children — will grow up to become productive adults. These factors include limited access to health care (including mental health care), underperforming schools, broken child welfare and juvenile justice systems, and a toxic youth culture that praises pimps and glorifies violence.

Hardened by long terms of incarceration, released criminalized youngsters return to communities that are ill equipped to reintegrate them positively. Outcast and unemployed, they become the teachers and role models for a new crop of youngsters pushed onto the streets of America's most depressed neighborhoods. This cycle of infection makes the Cradle to Prison Pipeline one of the most damaging health problems in America today.

A major factor in determining whether 5 a child enters the prison pipeline is access to health care. Currently, nine million children in America are without health insurance (1). Among low-income communities, there is a high incidence of teen pregnancy and low-birthweight babies (1). Physical and mental developmental delays among young children are commonly left undiagnosed and often go untreated (2,3). Unlike the children from affluent families, children from low-income families rarely have access to institutions that can intervene and address their health problems (2,3).

Few public schools in economically depressed neighborhoods have the resources to recognize health issues such as dyslexia, attention deficit disorder, hyperactivity disorder, or post-traumatic stress disorder and then to provide counseling and therapy for children with these disorders (1). Instead, their behavior is more often perceived as insubordinate or disruptive than it is recognized as symptomatic of a disorder or of the environment in which these children live (1,4). In these cases, zero-tolerance disciplinary standards are frequently applied, and thousands of students are expelled and even arrested for subjectively defined behaviors such as "disorderly conduct" and "malicious mischief" (5).

We must dismantle the Cradle to Prison Pipeline now because all children are sacred. What is required are collaborative efforts at the community, municipal, and state levels. To start with, we should demand the passage of legislation that would guarantee health care, including mental health care, to all children.

We need new investment to support proven community health delivery programs such as the National Campaign to Prevent Teen Pregnancy, which promotes community and school programs focused on delaying sexual activity (6), and the Nurse-Family Partnership, which supplies nurses for home visits to low-income, first-time mothers through their pregnancies and for two years after they give birth (7). Other valuable programs provide early intervention in cases of family violence (8). A healthy child is an empowered child. Communities should strive to replicate model umbrella programs that mentor and empower children such as the Harlem Children's Zone (9), the Boston Ten-Point Coalition (10), and the CDF Freedom Schools program (11).

The effects of the Cradle to Prison Pipeline constitute a scourge of epidemic proportions. We must act to dismantle the prison pipeline now. We fail at our peril. The future of our nation is at stake.

REFERENCES

1. The state of America's children 2005. Washington (DC): Children's Defense Fund; 2005. Available from: http://www.childrensdefense.org/site/DocServer/Greenbook_2005.pdf?docID=1741

2. Manderscheid RW, Berry JT. Mental health, United States, 2004. Rockville (MD): U.S. Department of Health and Human Services, Substance Abuse and Mental Health Services Administration; 2004. Available from: http://download.ncadi.samhsa.gov/ken/pdf/SMA06-4195/CMHS_MHUS_2004.pdf

3. Burns BJ, Phillips SD, Wagner HR, Barth RP, Kolko DJ, Campbell Y, et al. Mental health need and access to mental health services by youths involved with child welfare: a national survey. *J Am Acad Child Adolesc Psychiatry* 2004;43(8):960-70.

4. Cocozza JJ, Skowyra KR. Youth with mental health disorders: issues and emerging responses. *Juvenile Justice* 2000;7(1):3-13.

5. Advancement Project, Civil Rights Project of Harvard University. Opportunities suspended: the devastating consequences of zero tolerance and school discipline. Proceeding from the National Summit on Zero Tolerance. 2000 Jun 15-16; Washington, D.C. Available from: http://www.civilrightsproject.harvard.edu/research/discipline/cover_tableofcontents.pdf

6. Kirby D. No easy answers: research findings on programs to reduce teen pregnancy (summary). Washington (DC): The National Campaign to Prevent Teen Pregnancy; 1997.

7. Nurse-Family Partnership overview. Denver (CO): NFP National Service Office; [cited 2007 Feb 15]. Available from: http://www.nursefamilypartnership.org/resources/files/PDF/Fact_Sheets/NFPOverview.pdf

8. Fisher BS, editor. Violence against women and family violence: developments in research, practice, and policy. Rockville (MD): National Criminal Justice Reference Service; 2004. Available from: http://www.ncjrs.gov/pdffiles1/nij/199701.pdf

9. Harlem children's zone [homepage]. New York (NY): Harlem Children's Zone; [cited 2007 Feb 15]. Available from: http://www.hcz.org/index.html

10. Boston TenPoint Coalition [homepage]. Boston (MA): Boston TenPoint Coalition; [cited 2007 Feb 15]. Available from: http://www.bostontenpoint.org/index.html

11. Children's Defense Fund freedom schools. Washington (DC): Children's Defense Fund; [cited 2007 Feb 15]. Available from: http://www.childrensdefense.org/site/PageServer?pagename=Freedom_Schools

Topics for Critical Thinking and Writing

1. In your opinion, how effective is the opening to Marian Edelman's article? Did drawing a comparison between physical diseases like tuberculous and polio to the "criminalization of poor children" (para. 2) strike you as appropriate or exaggerated? Why, or why not?

2. In paragraph 3, Edelman states that many children grow up in a "criminalizing environment." Is it clear what she means? Support your answer.

3. Edelman also speaks of a "toxic youth culture that praises pimps and glorifies violence" (para. 3). Argue whether you agree or disagree that youth culture contributes to the prison pipeline. Be specific.

4. Edelman argues that lack of access to health care is part of what contributes to the prison pipeline. How are health care and crime connected? Be specific.

5. In paragraph 6, Edelman discusses the problems with "zero-tolerance disciplinary standards." Research the zero-tolerance standards, particularly in schools. Investigate why they were created and what effects they have had. Then argue either for or against the use of zero-tolerance standards.

6. Research some of the programs Edelman mentions in paragraph 8 that she thinks should receive greater financial support. Have these programs have been as effective as Edelman claims? Why, or why not?

7. The overarching idea of the "Cradle to Prison Pipeline" slogan suggests that some children in our society are virtually doomed from birth to wind up in prison. Opponents might argue that individual choices and responsibilities are at the root of crime, not environment. Do you agree with Edelman or her opponents? Support your answer.

JED S. RAKOFF

Jed S. Rakoff (b. 1943) is a U.S. district judge in New York who was educated at Swarthmore, Oxford, and Harvard. He has written extensively about the law, publishing four books, most recently Federal Corporate Sentencing: Compliance and Mitigation *(2007), as well as hundreds of articles and judicial decisions. In this article, which first appeared on May 21, 2015, in the* New York Review of Books, *Rakoff argues that there is no proof that mass incarceration is the main reason for the recent decline in crime rates.*

Mass Incarceration: The Silence of the Judges

For too long, too many judges have been too quiet about an evil of which we are a part: the mass incarceration of people in the United States today. It is time that more of us spoke out.

The basic facts are not in dispute. More than 2.2 million people are currently incarcerated in US jails and prisons, a 500 percent increase over the past forty years. Although the United States accounts for about 5 percent of the world's population, it houses nearly 25 percent of the world's prison population. The per capita incarceration rate in the United States is about one and a half times that of second-place Rwanda and third-place Russia, and more than six times the rate of neighboring Canada. Another 4.75 million Americans are subject to the state supervision imposed by probation or parole.

Most of the increase in imprisonment has been for nonviolent offenses, such as drug possession. And even though crime rates in the United States have declined consistently for twenty-four years, the number of incarcerated persons has continued to rise over most of that period, both because more people are being sent to prison for offenses that once were punished with other measures and because the sentences are longer. For example, even though the number of violent crimes has steadily decreased over the past two decades, the number of prisoners serving life sentences has steadily increased, so that one in nine persons in prison is now serving a life sentence.

And whom are we locking up? Mostly young men of color. Over 840,000, or nearly 40 percent, of the 2.2 million US prisoners are African-American males. Put another way, about one in nine African-American males between the ages of twenty and thirty-four is now in prison, and if current rates hold, one third of all black men will be imprisoned at some point in their lifetimes. Approximately 440,000, or 20 percent, of the 2.2 million US prisoners are Hispanic males.

This mass incarceration—which also 5 includes about 800,000 white and Asian males, as well as over 100,000 women (most of whom committed nonviolent offenses)—is the product of statutes that were enacted, beginning in the 1970s, with the twin purposes of lowering crime rates in general and deterring the drug trade in particular. These laws imposed mandatory minimum terms of imprisonment on many first offenders. They propounded sentencing guidelines that initially mandated, and still recommend, substantial prison terms for many other offenders. And they required lifetime imprisonment for many recidivists. These laws also substantially deprived judges of sentencing discretion and effectively guaranteed imprisonment for many offenders who would have previously received probation or deferred prosecution, or who would have been sent to drug treatment or mental health programs rather than prison.

The unavoidable question is whether these laws have succeeded in reducing crime. Certainly crime rates have come down substantially from the very high levels of the 1970s and 1980s that gave rise to them. Overall, crime rates have been cut nearly in half since they reached their peak in 1991, and they are now at levels not seen in many decades. A simple but powerful argument can be made that by locking up for extended periods the people who are most likely to commit crimes, we have both incapacitated those who would otherwise be recidivists and deterred still others from committing crimes in the first place.

But is this true? The honest answer is that we don't know. And it is this uncertainty that makes changing the status quo so difficult: for, the argument goes, why tamper with what seems to be working unless we know that it isn't working?

There are some who claim that they do know whether our increased rate of incarceration is the primary cause of the decline in crime. These are the sociologists, the economists, the statisticians, and others who assert that they have "scientifically" determined the answer. But their answers are all over the place. Thus, for example, a 2002 study by the sociologist Thomas Arvanites and the economist Robert DeFina claimed that while increased incarceration accounted for 21 percent of the large decline in property crime during the 1990s, it had no effect on the similarly large decline in violent crime. But two years later, in 2004, the economist Steven Levitt—of *Freakonomics* fame—claimed that incarceration accounted for no less than 32 percent of the decline in crime during that period.[1]

Levitt's conclusions, in turn, were questioned in 2006, when the sociologist Bruce Western reexamined the data and claimed that only about 10 percent of the crime drop in the

1990s could be attributed to increased incarceration. But two years after that, in 2008, the criminologist Eric Baumer took still another look at the same data and found that it could support claims that increased incarceration accounted for anywhere between 10 percent and 35 percent of the decrease in crime in the 1990s.

As these examples illustrate, there is nothing close to an academic consensus on the proportion of the decrease in crime attributable to increased incarceration. Last year, a distinguished committee of the National Research Council, after reviewing the studies I have mentioned as well as a great many more, was able to conclude only that while most of the studies "support the conclusion that the growth in incarceration rates reduced crime . . . the magnitude of the crime reduction remains highly uncertain."[2]

Most recently, in February 2015, the Brennan Center for Justice at NYU Law School published a study entitled "What Caused the Crime Decline?" that purports to show that increased incarceration has been responsible for only a negligible decrease in crime. One cannot help but be impressed by the sheer scope of the study. The authors identify the fourteen most popular theories for the decline in crime in the last few decades and attempt to test each of them against the available data.

Five of the theories involve criminal justice policies: increased incarceration, increased police numbers, increased use of statistics in devising police strategies to combat crime, threat of the death penalty, and enactment of right-to-carry gun laws (which theoretically deter violent criminals from attacking victims who they now have to fear might be armed). Another four of the theories are economic in nature, involving changes in unemployment, income, inflation, and consumer confidence. The final five theories involve environmental and social factors: aging population, decreased alcohol consumption, decreased crack use, legalized abortion, and decreased lead in gasoline (which theoretically reduces the supposed tendency of lead fumes to cause overaggressive behavior).

The primary findings of the Brennan study are that "increased incarceration has had little effect on the drop in violent crime in the past 24 years" and has "accounted for less than 1 percent of the decline in property crime this century." To reach these striking results, the authors rely (as did most of the earlier studies cited above) on the social scientist's favorite method, a multivariable regression analysis that "controls for the effects of each variable on crime, and each variable on other variables." But as anyone familiar with regression analysis knows, it rarely speaks to causality, as opposed to correlation; and even to show correlation, the analysis involves a lot of educated guesswork. The authors admit as much, but seek to downplay the level of uncertainty, stating: "There is always some uncertainty and statistical error involved in any empirical analysis." But when you are dealing with matters as difficult to measure as how much of the decrease in crime can be attributed to everything from decreased alcohol consumption to increased consumer confidence, your so-called "estimates" may be little more than speculations.

In an attempt to adjust to this difficulty, the authors state the percentage of crime decrease attributable to each given factor as a range, e.g., increased police numbers accounted, according to the study, for between 0 percent and 5 percent of the decline in crime between 1990 and 2013. But if you take the low end of each of the ranges, the fourteen factors analyzed in the Brennan study collectively accounted for as little as 10 percent of the decline in crime over that period; and even if you take the high end of each of the ranges, the various factors still accounted for only 40 percent of the decline in crime. Under any analysis, therefore, either the decline in crime in the last twenty years or so was chiefly the product of forces that none of the leading theorists has identified, or (as seems more likely) the regression analysis used by the authors of the Brennan study is too imperfect a tool to be of much use in this kind of situation.

My point is not to criticize the Brennan study. It is in many respects the most ambitious and comprehensive study of its kind undertaken to date. But as the National Research Council report points out in discussing the many similar studies that, as noted, led to a wide range of results, there are simply too many variables, uncertainties, estimates, and challenges involved in the question to rely on a regression analysis that is little more than speculation dressed up as statistics. The result is that one cannot fairly claim to know with any degree of confidence or precision the relative role of increased incarceration in decreasing crime.

Put another way, the supposition on which our mass incarceration is premised — namely, that it materially reduces crime — is, at best, a hunch. Yet the price we pay for acting on this hunch is enormous. This is true in the literal sense: it costs more than $80 billion a year to run our jails and prisons. It is also true in the social sense: by locking up so many young men, most of them men of color, we contribute to the erosion of family and community life in ways that harm generations of children, while creating a future cadre of unemployable ex-cons many of whom have learned in prison how better to commit future crimes. And it is even true in the symbolic sense: by locking up, sooner or later, one out of every three African-American males, we send a message that our

society has no better cure for racial disparities than brute force.

So why do we have mass incarceration? As mentioned, it is the product of laws that were passed in response to the substantial rise in crime rates that began in the 1960s and continued through the 1980s. These laws varied widely in their specifics, but they had two common characteristics: they imposed higher penalties and they removed much of judicial discretion in sentencing.

The most pernicious of these laws were the statutes imposing mandatory minimum terms of imprisonment. Although there were a few such laws prior to 1970 — for example, criminal contempt of Congress carried a mandatory minimum sentence of six months in prison — beginning in the 1970s Congress passed laws dictating much harsher mandatory minimum terms of imprisonment for a very wide variety of criminal violations. Most notably these laws imposed mandatory minimums of five, ten, and twenty years for various drug offenses, and as much as twenty-five additional years for possession of guns during drug trafficking. But they also imposed mandatory minimum terms of imprisonment for such widely varying offenses as possession of child pornography, aggravated identity theft, transportation of aliens into the United States for commercial advantage, hostage taking, unlawful possession of antiaircraft missiles, assault on US servicemen, stalking other persons in violation of a restraining order, fraudulent use of food stamp access devices — and much more besides. The dictate common to all these laws was that no matter how minor the offender's participation in the offense may have been, and no matter what mitigating circumstances might be present, the judge was required to send him to prison, often for a substantial number of years.

Throughout the 1970s and 1980s, many of the fifty states — with the full support of the federal government, which hugely increased its funding for state prisons during these years — passed similar mandatory minimum laws, and some went a step further and imposed mandatory minimum sentences of life imprisonment for recidivists (California's "three strikes" law being a noteworthy case). Not to be outdone, Congress not only passed "career offender" laws similar to the "three strikes" statute, but also, in 1984, enacted, with bipartisan support, the Federal Sentencing Guidelines. These guidelines, although initially intended to minimize disparities in sentencing, quickly became a vehicle for greatly increased sentences for virtually every federal crime, chiefly because Congress repeatedly instructed the Sentencing Commission to raise their levels.

Moreover, these so-called "guidelines" were, for their first twenty-one years, mandatory and binding. And while, in 2005, the Supreme Court declared that they were unconstitutional unless discretionary, federal judges were still required to treat them as the starting point for determining any sentence, with the result that they continued to be followed in most cases. More generally, both state and federal judges became accustomed to imposing prison terms as the "norm"; and with the passage of time, there were fewer and fewer judges on the bench who had even experienced a gentler approach.

But why, given the great decline in crime in the last quarter-century, have most of the draconian laws that created these harsh norms not been repealed, or at least moderated? Some observers, like Michelle Alexander in her influential book *The New Jim Crow* (2010),[3] assert that it is a case of thinly disguised racism. Others, mostly of an economic determinist persuasion, claim that it is the result of the rise of a powerful private prison industry that has an economic stake in continuing mass incarceration. Still others blame everything from a continuing reaction to the "excesses" of the 1960s to the never-ending nature of the "war on drugs."

While there may be something to each of these theories, a simpler explanation is that most Americans, having noticed that the crime-ridden environment of the 1970s and 1980s was only replaced by the much safer environment of today after tough sentencing laws went into force, are reluctant to tamper with the laws they believe made them safer. They are not impressed with academic studies that question this belief, suspecting that the authors have their own axes to grind; and they are repelled by those who question their good faith, since they perceive nothing "racist" in wanting a crime-free environment. Ironically, the one thing that might convince them that mass incarceration is not the solution to their safety would be if crime rates continued to decrease when incarceration rates were reduced. But although this has in fact happened in a few places (most notably New York City), in most communities people are not willing to take the chance of such an "experiment."

This, then, is a classic case of members of the public relying on what they believe is "common sense" and being resentful of those who question their motives and dispute their intelligence. What is called for in such circumstances is leadership: those whom the public does respect should point out why statutes prescribing mandatory minimums, draconian guidelines, and the like are not the solution to controlling crime, and why, in any case, the long-term price of mass incarceration is too high to pay, not just in economic terms, but also in terms of shared social values.

Until quite recently, that leadership appeared to be missing in both the legislative and executive branches, since being labeled "soft on crime" was politically dangerous. Recently, however, there have been some small signs of progress. For example, in 2013, Attorney General Eric Holder finally did away with the decades-old requirement that federal prosecutors must charge offenders with those offenses carrying the highest prison terms. And in the last Congress, a bill to eliminate mandatory minimum sentences for nonviolent drug offenders was endorsed not only by the Department of Justice, but also by such prominent right-wing Republican senators as Ted Cruz and Rand Paul. On the other hand, prosecutors still have discretion to charge offenders with the most serious offenses available, and they usually do. And the aforementioned bill to modify the applicability of mandatory minimum sentences never reached a vote.

So where in all this stands the judiciary? In some ways, this should be our issue, not just because sentencing has historically been the prerogative of judges, but also because it is we judges who are forced to impose sentences that many of us feel are unjust and counterproductive. It is probably too much to ask state judges in the thirty-seven states where judges are elected to adopt a position that could be characterized as "soft on crime." But what about the federal judiciary, which is protected by lifetime tenure from political retaliation and, according to most polls, is generally well regarded by the public as a whole?

On one issue — opposition to mandatory minimum laws — the federal judiciary has been consistent in its opposition and clear in its message. As stated in a September 2013 letter to Congress submitted by the Judicial Conference of the United States (the governing board of federal judges), "For sixty years, the Judicial Conference has consistently and vigorously opposed mandatory minimum sentences and has supported measures for their repeal or to ameliorate their effects." But nowhere in the nine single-spaced pages that follow is any reference made to the evils of mass incarceration; and, indeed, most federal judges continue to be supportive of the federal sentencing guidelines. As for Congress, while occasionally approving reductions in the guidelines recommended by the Sentencing Commission, it has much more often required the Sentencing Commission to increase the prison time reflected in those guidelines, thereby further supporting mass incarceration.

Yet even within the judiciary there is some modest cause for hope. Several brave federal district judges — such as Lynn Adelman of Wisconsin, Mark Bennett of Iowa, Paul Friedman of the District of Columbia, and Michael Ponsor of Massachusetts, as well as former federal judges Paul Cassell and Nancy Gertner — have for some time openly denounced the policy of mass incarceration. More recently, a federal appellate judge, Gerard Lynch of New York, expressed his agreement (albeit in an academic article):

> The United States has a vastly overinflated system of incarceration that is excessively punitive, disproportionate in its impact on the poor and minorities, exceedingly expensive, and largely irrelevant to reducing predatory crime.[4]

Perhaps the most encouraging judicial statement was made just a few weeks ago, on March 23, 2015, when Justice Anthony Kennedy — the acknowledged centrist of the Supreme Court — told a House subcommittee considering the Court's annual budget that "this idea of total incarceration just isn't working," adding that in many instances it would be wiser to assign offenders to probation or other supervised release programs. To be sure, Justice Kennedy was quick to tie these views to cost reductions, avoidance of prison overcrowding, and reduced recidivism rates — all, as he said, "without reference to the human factor." Nor did he say one word about the racially disparate impact of mass incarceration. Yet his willingness to confront publicly even some of the evils of mass incarceration should be an inspiration to all other judges so inclined.

In many respects, the people of the United States can be proud of the progress we have made over the past half-century in promoting racial equality. More haltingly, we have also made some progress in our treatment of the poor and disadvantaged. But the big, glaring exception to both these improvements is how we treat those guilty of crimes. Basically, we treat them like dirt. And while this treatment is mandated by the legislature, it is we judges who mete it out. Unless we judges make more effort to speak out against this inhumanity, how can we call ourselves instruments of justice?

NOTES

[1] In the Brennan study discussed below, the authors recalibrate Levitt's study and find that, if his assumptions are indulged, incarceration accounted for no less than 58 percent of the violent crime drop and 41 percent of the property crime drop during the 1990s. [All notes are the author's.]

[2] National Research Council, *The Growth of Incarceration in the United States: Exploring Causes and Consequences*, edited by Jeremy Travis, Bruce Western, and Steve Redburn (National Academies Press, 2014); reviewed by Christopher Jencks, October 9, 2014.

[3] See the review by Darryl Pinckney, "Invisible Black America," March 10, 2011.

[4] Gerard E. Lynch, "Ending Mass Incarceration: Some Observations and Responses to Professor Tonry," *Criminology and Public Policy*, Vol. 13, No. 4 (November 2014).

Topics for Critical Thinking and Writing

1. Jed Rakoff opens the article with the use of strong language: "For too long, too many judges have been too quiet about an evil of which we are a part" (para. 1). What is he referring to? In your opinion, is the use of the word "evil" an overstatement? Why, or why not?

2. In paragraph 4, Rakoff cites statistics that reveal how much the burden of mass incarceration is borne by young men of color. Research the effects of mass incarceration on communities of color. Do these communities suffer more because of the absence of these individuals (mostly men), or do they benefit from safer neighborhoods because criminals are behind bars? Defend your answer.

3. A key part of the war on crime that began in the 1960s was increased punishments for drug offenses. A key argument by many detractors is that the imprisonment of drug offenders is wrong and that both the drug user and society would benefit more from other approaches, such as treatment and rehabilitation. Research the relationship between crime and drug use. Argue whether being tough on drug offenders pays off by lowering other types of crime as well, or whether that approach is ineffective or, worse, harmful.

4. Rakoff argues in paragraph 10 that "there is nothing close to an academic consensus on the proportion of the decrease in crime attributable to increased incarceration." What makes determining that relationship so difficult? If a cause-and-effect relationship cannot be firmly defined, would it be reasonable for the criminal justice system to seek ways to decrease the number of people incarcerated? Why, or why not?

5. In paragraph 11, Rakoff refers to a study published by the Brennan Center for Justice at New York University. Researchers examined fourteen possible causes for the decline of crime. Each potential cause was assigned an element of probability (i.e., the likelihood that that cause lessened crime), yet in the end, the probability of all fourteen causes amounted to only about 40 percent of the total contributing factors to the decline in crime, not 100. What does this suggest about the nature of our ability to understand crime? How might this have an impact on public policy related to fighting crime?

6. A core problem, as Rakoff sees it, comprises mandatory minimum sentencing laws that take away much of a judge's discretion in sentencing. What are the key problems with mandatory minimums? How has that created mass incarceration? Before answering these questions, you may wish to research some of the history behind the motivations for passing harsher sentencing laws and the types of crimes that became subject to them.

7. In paragraph 21, Rakoff notes that some people argue that mass incarceration is actually just a new form of racism, a way of maintaining state control over people of color. Research this issue, and argue whether you find the argument credible. Defend your answer.

8. Rakoff's use of the first person plural (i.e., "we" or "us" or "our") shows that he has a primary audience in mind that is not the general public. Who is his primary audience? How does that affect the way he has written this article? Yet because the article was published in a general interest publication, the *New York Review of Books*, he knew he would also have a broader readership. Examine Rakoff's writing. How does he use a sense of audience to determine what and how he writes? Does this sense of audience change at times in the article? How?

9. In the final paragraph, Rakoff notes that in the United States we treat the guilty "like dirt." In your opinion, is this true? Is it fair? Why, or why not? Use research to support your answer.

PETER WAGNER AND BERNADETTE RABUY

Peter Wagner is the cofounder and executive director of the Prison Policy Initiative, an organization promoting criminal justice reform. Bernadette Rabuy is the senior policy analyst at the Prison Policy Initiative and has conducted extensive research on prison and jail visitation and increasing public accessibility to key criminal justice data. In this report, first published at prisonpolicy.org on March 12, 2014, the authors point out the difficulty in determining exactly how many people are behind bars in the United States because of the many different layers of government and types of facilities. Only after those numbers are determined can we understand the full extent of mass incarceration.

Mass Incarceration: The Whole Pie

Wait, does the United States have 1.4 million or more than 2 million people in prison? Are most people in state and federal prisons locked up for drug offenses? Frustrating questions like these abound because our systems of confinement are so fragmented and controlled by various entities. There is a lot of interesting and valuable research out there, but varying definitions **make it hard** — for both people new to criminal justice and for experienced policy wonks — **to get the big picture**.

This report offers some much needed clarity by piecing together this country's disparate systems of confinement. The American criminal justice system holds more than 2.3 million people in 1,719 state prisons, 102 federal prisons, 942 juvenile correctional facilities, 3,283 local jails, and 79 Indian Country jails as well as in military prisons, immigration detention facilities, civil commitment centers, and prisons in the U.S. territories.[1] And we go deeper to provide further detail on *why* convicted and not convicted people are locked up in local jails.

---

[1] The number of state and federal facilities is from Census of State and Federal Correctional Facilities, 2005; the number of youth facilities is from Juvenile Residential Facility Census, 2012: Selected Findings (we included only detention centers, reception/diagnostic centers, and training schools/long-term secure facilities but not shelters, group homes, ranch/wilderness camps, and residential treatment centers); the number of jails is from Census of Jail Facilities, 2006; and the number of Indian Country jails is from Jails in Indian Country, 2014. We aren't currently aware of a good source of data on the number of the facilities of the other types. [All notes are the authors'.]

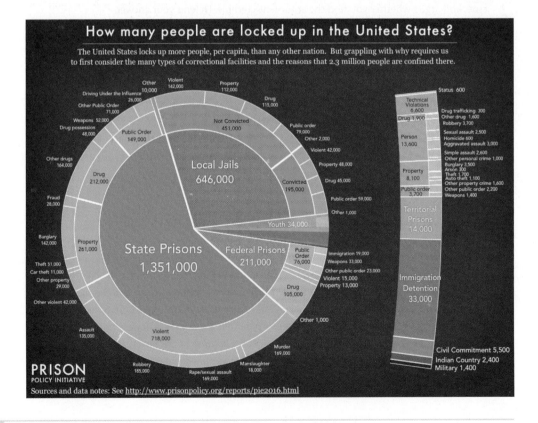

How many people are locked up in the United States?

The United States locks up more people, per capita, than any other nation. But grappling with why requires us to first consider the many types of correctional facilities and the reasons that 2.3 million people are confined there.

PRISON
POLICY INITIATIVE

Sources and data notes: See http://www.prisonpolicy.org/reports/pie2016.html

CHAPTER 24 | THE CARCERAL STATE: WHY ARE SO MANY AMERICANS IN JAIL?

While this pie chart provides a comprehensive snapshot of our correctional system, the graphic does not capture the **enormous churn** in and out of our correctional facilities and the far larger universe of people whose lives are affected by the criminal justice system. Every year, 636,000 people walk out of *prison* gates, but people go to *jail* over 11 million times each year.[2] Jail churn is particularly high because most people in jails[3] have not been convicted. Some have just been arrested and will make bail in the next few hours or days, and others are too poor to make bail and must remain behind bars until their trial. Only a small number (195,000) have been convicted, generally serving misdemeanors sentences under a year.

With a sense of the big picture, a common follow-up question might be: how many people are locked up for a drug offense? We know that almost half a million people are locked up because of a **drug offense**.[4] The data confirms that nonviolent drug convictions are a defining characteristic of the *federal* prison system, but play only a supporting role at the *state* and local levels. While most people in state and local facilities are not locked up for drug offenses, most states' continued practice of arresting people for drug possession[5] destabilizes individual lives and communities. Drug arrests give residents of over-policed communities criminal records, which then reduce employment prospects and increase the likelihood of longer sentences for any future offenses.

All of the offense data presented comes 5 with an important set of caveats. A person in prison for multiple offenses is reported only for the most serious offense[6] so, for example, there are people in prison for **"violent" offenses** who might have also been convicted of a drug offense. Further, almost all convictions are the result of **plea bargains**, where people plead guilty to a lesser offense, perhaps of a different category or one that they may not have actually committed.

And many of these categories group together people convicted of a wide range of offenses. For example, "murder" is generally considered to be an extremely serious offense, but "murder" groups together the rare group of serial killers, with people who committed acts that are unlikely for reasons of circumstance or advanced age to ever happen again, with offenses that the average American may not consider to be murder at all. For example, the felony murder rule says that if someone dies during the commission of a felony, everyone involved is as guilty of murder as the person who pulled the trigger. Driving a getaway car during a bank robbery where someone was

---

[2] Eleven million jail admissions probably amounts to less than 11 million unique individuals cycling through jails in a year. According to a presentation, *The Importance of Successful Reentry to Jail Population Growth* [Powerpoint] given at the Jail Reentry Roundtable, Bureau of Justice Statistics, statistician Allen Beck estimates that of the 12 to 12.6 million jail admissions in 2004–2005, 9 million were unique individuals.

[3] The local jail population in the pie chart excludes the people being held in jails for other agencies so the population physically in jails (744,592) is larger than the population under jail jurisdiction reflected in the pie chart (646,000). See Table 1 of *Jail Inmates at Midyear 2014.* The "not convicted" population is driving jail growth.

[4] The data doesn't show how many people are convicted of drug law violations and are held in territorial prisons or Indian Country jails. The military prison system holds less than 100 people for drug law violations.

[5] In 2012, there were 1,552,432 drug arrests in the U.S., the far majority of which were for drug possession or use rather than for sale or manufacturing. See Arrest Data Analysis Tool.

[6] The federal government defines the hierarchy of offenses with felonies higher than misdemeanors. And "[w]ithin these levels, . . . the hierarchy from most to least serious is as follows: homicide, rape/other sexual assault, robbery, aggravated assault, burglary, larceny/motor vehicle theft, fraud, drug trafficking, drug possession, weapons offense, driving under the influence, other public-order, and other." See page 13 of *Recidivism of Prisoners Released* (1994).

accidentally killed is indeed a serious offense, but few people would really consider that to be murder.[7]

This "whole pie" methodology also exposes some disturbing facts about the youth entrapped in our **juvenile justice system**: Too many are there for a "most serious offense" that is **not even a crime**. For example, there are almost 7,000 youth behind bars for "technical violations" of the requirements of their probation, rather than for a new offense. Further, 600 youth are behind bars for "status" offenses, which are "behaviors that are not law violations for adults, such as running away, truancy, and incorrigibility."[8]

Turning finally to the people who are locked up criminally and civilly for **immigration-related issues**, we find that 19,000 people are in federal prison for criminal convictions of violating federal immigration laws. A separate 33,000 are civilly detained by U.S. Immigration and Customs Enforcement (ICE) separate from any criminal proceedings and are physically confined in special immigration detention facilities or in local jails under contract with ICE. (Notably, these categories do not include immigrants represented in other pie slices because of non-immigration related criminal convictions.)

Now, armed with the big picture of how many people are locked up in the United States, where, and why, we have a better foundation for the long overdue conversation about criminal justice reform. For example, the data makes it clear that ending the War on Drugs will not alone end mass incarceration, but that the federal government and some states have effectively reduced their incarcerated populations by turning to drug policy reform. Looking at the "whole pie" also opens up other conversations about where we should focus our energies:

- What is the role of the federal government in ending mass incarceration? The federal prison system is just a small slice of the total pie, but the federal government can certainly use its financial and ideological power to incentivize and illuminate better paths forward. At the same time, how can elected sheriffs, district attorneys, and judges slow the flow of people into the criminal justice system?

- Are state officials and prosecutors willing to rethink both the War on Drugs and the reflexive policies that have served to increase both the odds of incarceration and length of stay for "violent" offenses?

- Do policymakers and the public have the focus to confront the second largest slice of the pie: the thousands of locally administered jails? And does it even make sense to arrest millions of poor[9] people each year[10] for minor offenses,

---

[7]The felony murder rule has also been applied when the person who died was a participant in the crime. For example, if one of the bank robbers is killed by the police during a chase, the surviving bank robbers can be convicted of felony murder of their colleague. For example, see *People v. Hudson*, 222 Ill. 2d 392 (Ill. 2006) and *People v. Klebanowski*, 221 Ill. 2d 538 (Ill. 2006).

[8]In 2013, more than half of juvenile status offense cases were for truancy. See page 66 of *Juvenile Court Statistics 2013*.

[9]Our report on the pre-incarceration incomes of those imprisoned in state prisons, Prisons of Poverty: Uncovering the Pre-incarceration Incomes of the Imprisoned, found that, in 2014 dollars, incarcerated people had a median annual income that is 41% less than non-incarcerated people of similar ages. Our preliminary analysis of jail data shows that people in jails may have even lower incomes. For pre-incarceration incomes of those in jails in 2002, see page 9 of *Profile of Jail Inmates 2002*.

[10]Recall from above that people go to jail over 11 million times each year.

make them post cash bail, and then lock them up when they can't afford to pay it? Will our leaders be brave enough to redirect corrections spending to smarter investments like community-based drug treatment and job training?

- Can we implement reforms that both reduce the number of people incarcerated in the U.S. *and* the well-known racial and ethnic disparities in the criminal justice system?

And once we have wrapped our minds around the "whole pie" of mass incarceration, we should zoom out and note that being locked up is just one piece of the larger pie of correctional control. There are another 820,000 people on **parole** (a type of conditional release from prison) and a staggering 3.8 million people on **probation** (what is typically an alternative sentence). Particularly given the often onerous conditions of probation, policymakers should be cautious of "alternatives to incarceration" that sometimes widen the net of criminalization to people who are not a threat to public safety.

Now that we can see the big picture of how many people are locked up in the United States in the various types of facilities, we can see that **something needs to change**. Looking at the big picture requires us to ask if it really makes sense to lock up 2.3 million people on any given day, giving this nation the dubious distinction of having the highest incarceration rate in the world. Both policymakers and the public have the responsibility to carefully consider each individual slice in turn to ask whether legitimate social goals are served by putting each category behind bars, and whether any benefit really outweighs the social and fiscal costs.

We're optimistic that this "whole pie" approach can give Americans, who are ready for a fresh look at the criminal justice system, some of the tools they need to demand meaningful changes to how we do justice.

Topics for Critical Thinking and Writing

1. The authors begin with a series of questions about the numbers of people who are incarcerated. What is the purpose of posing those questions? What other sorts of questions might they prompt? What is the importance of this data — the numbers of people incarcerated — in arguments about prisons, their purpose, their problems, and possible reforms? What story does it tell about the types of crimes, types of people, and types of incarceration in America?

2. In paragraph 3, the authors argue that "the **enormous churn** [the authors' emphasis] in and out of our confinement facilities underscores how naïve it is to conceive of prisons as separate from the rest of our society." Why? In what ways are prison systems and the larger society interconnected? Why is that important in discussions about the criminal justice system?

3. In paragraph 4, the authors focus on the numbers of those locked away for drug offenses. Why do they focus on this population? What unstated assumption do the authors make when they look specifically for those statistics? In your opinion, should the criminal justice

system treat drug offenders differently from those charged for other offenses? Why, or why not?

4. The authors also examine the numbers of children in the juvenile justice system, which holds thousands of children in custody for offenses that wouldn't be considered a crime for adults. Investigate the problems of the juvenile justice system. Argue if reforms are needed to better serve the juveniles themselves and the general public at large, and if so, what those reforms would be. If you feel that reforms are not needed, argue why the current system of juvenile justice should be kept as is.

5. In paragraph 8, the authors address immigration law and the thousands of people who are in prisons or otherwise detained for immigration offenses. Research the process of what happens to a person accused of violating immigration law who otherwise has not committed a criminal offense. In your opinion, is this nation's approach to prosecuting immigration law offenses right or wrong? Defend your position.

6. In paragraph 11, in regard to the levels of mass incarceration across the United States, the authors state, "we can see that **something needs to change**" [the authors' emphasis]. Do you agree? Why, or why not?

25

American Exceptionalism: How Should the United States Teach about Its Past?

CONOR FRIEDERSDORF

Conor Friedersdorf is a graduate of Pomona College and New York University and a regular contributor to the Atlantic. *Friedersdorf is a self-described conservative, but he refuses to be bound by doctrine. In this article, originally published in the* Atlantic *in October 2013, Friedersdorf uses the popular television series* Breaking Bad *as an allegory for how America has compromised its principles since the events of September 11, 2001.*

Breaking Bad: America Has Used Walter White Logic since 9/11

In *Breaking Bad*, Walter White starts off as the most sympathetic of all possible meth cooks. A brilliant chemist, he is stuck teaching bored students at an Albuquerque high school. He does his best to support his pregnant wife and their partially disabled son, but earns so little that he must work night shifts at an area car wash just to make ends meet. Despite it all, he soldiers on dutifully until he is unexpectedly diagnosed with lung cancer. That trauma changes him. Suddenly he confronts the prospect of dying penniless. He doesn't want an impoverished widow or two kids without a college fund or even a small savings account. So he resolves to cook (and later sell) just enough meth to give his family a middle-class existence.

Of course, his plan from the start is to manufacture a dangerous narcotic. His profits will come from addicts whose lives are being ruined by his product. But we still begin in his corner. We see White as an unlucky man playing the hand he's dealt in a fallen world, where drug addicts will get high with or without his blue meth. Isn't it better, in a way, for him to manufacture Albuquerque's choice high? At least he isn't going to accidentally blow up his lab during a cook, or put out an impure product. Surely it's better for a dying, middle-class family man to be enriched than Tuko Salamanca, the cartel-backed sociopath who White and his product displace.

That's what we told ourselves.

America sometimes reminds me of Walter White.

Not in every way, of course. There isn't any-[5]thing like a perfect parallel between the plot of *Breaking Bad* and the course that the U.S. has taken since the September 11 terrorist attacks, the unexpected trauma that made us look at our place in the world anew. I certainly don't think *Breaking Bad*'s writers were attempting an allegory. But I submit that the show's arc (especially Walter White's character arc) imparts lessons about moral logic and its consequences that the U.S. ought to heed.

White starts off with everyone's sympathy. But as soon as the writers have us rooting for him to get rich (and get out) before he gets caught, they produce five seasons that amount to a slowly unfolding rebuke to everyone who felt any investment in his success.

The source of our moral discomfort?

White "has cooked crystal meth in bulk, hooking addicts from his native Albuquerque all the way to Prague," Ross Douthat explains. "He has personally killed at least seven people and is implicated in the deaths of hundreds more. He has poisoned an innocent child, taken out a contract on his longtime partner, and stood by and watched a young woman choke." Every season is more riveting than the last, in part because having bought into the logic that prompted White to start cooking, we are implicated in the predictable consequences, and they just keep getting more gruesome. *Of course* he wouldn't be satisfied with the initial, relatively modest sum of money that he sought. *Of course* he would become implicated in the violence of the black market. *Of course* lying

to his wife and son would be corrosive, and *of course* exempting himself from core mores and norms would put him on a slippery slope, where the prospect of being caught or killed keeps helping him to rationalize "one last" horrific moral compromise, even when there are alternatives.

At some point, White crosses a line. *Breaking Bad* fans may not agree on the particular moment, but he eventually does something that causes a given viewer to think, "That's unforgivable."

But as abhorrent as we find his worst trans-[10]gressions, as much as we tell ourselves that we could never condone them, we can't help but see how they flowed logically, if not quite inevitably, from the initial course of moral compromise he chose. It causes us to reflect on the earliest episodes and to reconsider our initial judgement. Is the lesson that it was always wrong to grant White any license to break bad? Or is there an alternative trajectory in which White could have cooked for a while without becoming a moral monster or doing much harm?

Either way, viewers can't escape the fact that White rationalizes even his worst atrocities with logic not unlike what viewers condoned when he first cooked. *I'm not a bad person. I'm just trying to fulfill my responsibility to provide for my family. Bad circumstances forced me into these compromising positions — when I do bad things, it isn't the same as when other drug dealers do them. After all, I am not a criminal.* Implicit all along is an unspoken rationalization. Walter White is a man who believes in his own exceptionalism. That's how he manages to think of himself as a good person, even as he orchestrates the death of an innocent man and poisons a child. As chilling as most viewers found that self-justifying quality, how many forgave him lesser sins early on in part because they saw him as an exceptional case?

Americans are, like Walter White, a self-justifying sort.

We see ourselves as exceptional. Oftentimes we behave as if the rules that apply to the rest of the world, rules we want constraining them, don't and needn't really apply to us. *We're not a regular nation, not like the Chinese or the Brazilians or even the French.* Take it from the *New York Times*, our paper of record. Other nations forcing water into a prisoner's lungs is torture.

When we do it? Enhanced interrogation.

America doesn't torture. We're the good guys! 15

After 9/11 we wanted national-security officials to provide for our safety. Understandably so. They felt tremendous pressure to fulfill that responsibility. Couldn't they have done so without transgressing against basic laws, mores, and norms? Many in the Bush Administration didn't think so, but they didn't fully share that with us. They decided on what they thought was best for us, but thought telling us would be a bad idea: We might not go along with their plans for torture, indefinite detention, or warrantless spying. To be honest, many of us didn't really want to know the details of policy, or to follow the ideas of those making it to their logical conclusions.

What scary implications!

Over time, the consequences of the moral license that national-security officials granted themselves after 9/11 became impossible to ignore. Different Americans awakened to reality at different times. Some became apologists for the people in charge. A word or statute could always be twisted to launder their actions into what passed as legal, and it was easy enough to conflate "legal" with morally defensible.

Yet many others grew morally uncomfortable. Why?

Over 12 years, the United States has 20 rounded up an unknown number of innocents and held them alongside terrorists at an island prison, without evidence, charges, or trial, *keeping some for years even after deeming them no threat*. The U.S. tortured an unknown number of prisoners in an official torture program, then destroyed evidence of it. Americans ran a prison at Abu Ghraib where many others were tortured and abused in the most disgusting ways imaginable. The Iraq War implicates us in the deaths of tens of thousands of innocents. Successive presidents set precedents such that American citizens can now be put on a secret kill list *on one man's orders* and killed without any due process. A 16-year-old American was killed in a drone strike with no explanation given to this day; scarcely no one in power demanded one. With the blessings of the White House, the New York Police Department has ethnically profiled and spied on innocent Muslim Americans who were deemed suspicious for no reason besides their religion.

The NYPD failed to apologize, even after that destructive surveillance program sowed anxiety and mistrust in the community *and produced zero counterterrorism leads*.

America's drone program has resulted in the deaths of hundreds of innocents and nightmarish living conditions for Yemenis and Pakistanis under regular flight paths. What's more, the U.S. doesn't apologize, explain itself, and compensate the families of the dead when it inadvertently kills innocent people with drones. Instead, we do our best to pretend that we had no role in the killing, leaving impoverished survivors to bury their own dead, to repair their own homes, and to wonder if seemingly arbitrary death from the sky will take them next.

As well, we've built a global surveillance apparatus unprecedented in human history, one so unaccountable that Americans only found out about violations of the Fourth Amendment and data collection on tens of millions of Americans because a contractor gave up his comfortable life in Hawaii and risked his freedom to tell us about it. If not for Edward Snowden, even the blatant legal violations of the NSA would still remain completely unknown to us. The United States is also violating the privacy of hundreds of millions of innocent foreigners, including leaders of close allies; intentionally undermining the security of global IT systems to facilitate spying; and doing great harm to American companies whose security we've breached.

Looking back, this shouldn't surprise us.

On 9/11, innocents of all races and religions were murdered en masse. Additional attacks seemed imminent, and it wasn't long before anthrax was sent through the mail and snipers terrorized the Capitol. The shock changed our national-security officials.

In secret memos and rushed legislation, they resolved to transgress against moral and legal norms just enough "to keep us safe," and the public started off in their corner. Of course, almost from the start they were plotting torture, spying on innocents, exploiting the terrorist attack to push an invasion of Iraq and detaining the not guilty. But the U.S. public was still sympathetic. They saw America as a target of terrorism playing the hand it was dealt in a fallen world, where innocents were hurt and killed regardless. Wasn't it better, in a way, for America to maintain its role as benevolent global hegemon? We weren't going to start a nuclear war, as North Korea or Pakistan might in our absence. Better for America to assert itself overseas than to cede the Middle East to al-Qaeda, Saddaam Hussein, and Hezbollah.

It was a self-justifying kind of illogic with conclusions that seldom followed from the premises.

Even today, national-security officials tell themselves that everything they've done has flowed naturally enough from that initial recalibration of their moral decision-making, their repudiation of a "pre-9/11 mindset," which Americans happily endorsed as the cancer of al-Qaeda filled the lungs of New Yorkers with black smoke.

That is exactly right: We got it wrong from the moment we declared that "everything changed," and it has stayed wrong. Lots of old rules did still apply, or should have.

Flouting them has proved corrosive.

Of course this is what happens when a traumatized nation gives its leaders license to hastily rewrite laws, reinterpret others in secret, and wield unaccountable power across the globe. *Of course* we invaded a country unnecessarily. *Of course* we've found self-justifying ways to torture illegally and kill innocents without taking responsibility for doing so. *Of course* we're still holding some innocents at Gitmo. Of course our civil liberties are being shredded and Muslim Americans are hit hardest. The world dealt us an unfair blow, and we used it as an excuse to break bad.

We permitted who knows what to be done in secret. What did we expect?

We became inured to the selfishness of our actions.

We slid predictably down the slope upon which we stepped, and the farther we go the uglier it gets.

We haven't hit bottom yet or anything close to it.

National-security officials still insist all their actions are taken for the sake of their country. Dissenters can't help but suspect that, at least *sometimes,* that's just something they tell themselves as they enjoy wielding extraordinary power and making their own rules as they go. In any case, their actions have done more to harm than help the United States, just as Walter White did more to harm than to help his family. That's what happens when people decide they need no longer abide by civilizational norms.

Core values are there for a reason.

What Americans have seen more clearly with every year are the consequences of granting ourselves extraordinary moral license, as if American exceptionalism means that anything we do is justified so long as there's a chance defensible ends will be advanced. It's Walter White logic we embraced—and it enabled morally monstrous behavior. Many legal and moral constraints serve as vital checks on human nature, and that doesn't change when you hire Saul Goodman or John Yoo to get around them.

The elaborate legal apologia for U.S. behavior obscures beneath jargon certain hard truths:

America is not justified in torturing because someone might have intelligence that may prove useful.

America is not justified in invading any country because *it may one day* pose a threat.

America is not justified in holding anyone on earth prisoner for as long as it likes, without presenting any evidence or issuing any charges or holding any trial, due to a chance he's dangerous.

America is not justified in killing innocents with drones and fleeing the scene like a hit-and-run driver because it would be inconvenient for us to bear the consequences of our actions.

America is not justified in spying on anyone and everyone on earth, just because it's possible that invading the privacy of hundreds of millions might make us infinitesimally safer.

Yet we've done all that, and felt justified in 40 doing so.

The trauma of 9/11 is not an excuse. That we have a history of behaving more morally than some countries, that the world is better off with an American rather than a Russian or Chinese hegemon, is not an excuse. That national-security officials are often motivated by keeping their families and yours safe is not an excuse.

The real, ongoing threat of terrorism is not an excuse.

For so many of our actions, there is no excuse. And so we should reject the moral code that has enabled us to behave inexcusably. We should abide by older laws and norms whose value are now more apparent. To tweak and repurpose a great line from Skyler White, this country needs someone to protect us from the people who are protecting this country. We need it fast. And we're the only someones around to do it.

Topics for Critical Thinking and Writing

1. How does Conor Friedersdorf argue that our sympathy for Walter White, the main character in *Breaking Bad*, serves as a symbol of America's willingness to compromise its values in the post-9/11 world?

2. Friedersdorf argues that the moral compromises that White makes in the series, including poisoning an innocent child, manipulate viewers from feeling sympathy for White to "a slowly unfolding rebuke to everyone who felt any investment in his success" (para. 6).

How does this slippery slope relate to the actions the United States has taken to protect American lives and interests since 9/11?

3. In paragraph 8, Friedersdorf points out, by repeating the phrase "of course" in italics, that the logic of moral compromise would necessarily lead to undesirable results. What are the results of moral compromise for America since 9/11? Were those results, in your opinion, inevitable or avoidable? Why?

4. In paragraph 11, Friedersdorf points out that Walter White thinks of himself as an exception, that he is a good person in spite of the horrific things that he has done. In judging one's character, what is the difference between one's actions and one's self-image? How, then, does this relate to nations and the actions they take versus the values they claim to uphold?

5. Friedersdorf states, with sarcasm, "America doesn't torture. We're the good guys" (para. 15). Research the use of torture by the United States against its enemies, especially at Abu Ghraib. In your opinion, was the use of torture — or "enhanced interrogation" (para. 14) — justified? Why, or why not?

6. Research the internment of prisoners at Guantanamo Bay (or "Gitmo" for short). Argue whether the U.S. policy of indefinite imprisonment — in some cases without trial — is justified.

7. In paragraph 23, Friedersdorf refers to Edward Snowden, an American who leaked evidence about violations of privacy rights being committed by the National Security Administration. Research the Snowden case, and argue whether Snowden was right or wrong in leaking this classified information.

8. Friedersdorf argues that national security officials have turned their back on what they call a "pre-9/11 mindset" (para. 28). What does this mean? What dangers to democracy have resulted from this movement?

9. A key aspect of American exceptionalism is the idea that America is better than other nations because its formation is based on values more than on physical location. Does this mean that American exceptionalism is compromised when, as Friedersdorf argues in paragraph 38, that "anything we do is justified as long as there's a chance defensible ends will be advanced"? Defend your answer.

10. In paragraph 39, Friedersdorf makes a series of arguments that "America is not justified . . ." when speaking of a series of actions. Then in paragraph 41, he shifts to a series of arguments with the phrase " . . . is not an excuse." Do you agree or disagree with the author? Defend your answer.

STEPHEN M. WALT

Stephen M. Walt (b. 1955) is a professor of international affairs at Harvard's John F. Kennedy School of Government. He has published numerous articles and three books, including Taming American Power *(2005). This article, which appeared on the Web site* Foreignpolicy.com *on October 11, 2011, argues that the idea of American exceptionalism rests upon myths about America, not reality, which in turn distorts our understanding of America's place in the world.*

The Myth of American Exceptionalism

Over the last two centuries, prominent Americans have described the United States as an "empire of liberty," a "shining city on a hill," the "last best hope of Earth," the "leader of the free world," and the "indispensable nation." These enduring tropes explain why all presidential candidates feel compelled to offer ritualistic paeans to America's greatness and why President Barack Obama landed in hot water — most recently, from Mitt Romney — for saying that while he believed in "American exceptionalism," it was no different from "British exceptionalism," "Greek exceptionalism," or any other country's brand of patriotic chest-thumping.

Most statements of "American exceptionalism" presume that America's values, political system, and history are unique and worthy of universal admiration. They also imply that the United States is both destined and entitled to play a distinct and positive role on the world stage.

The only thing wrong with this self-congratulatory portrait of America's global role is that it is mostly a myth. Although the United States possesses certain unique qualities — from high levels of religiosity to a political culture that privileges individual freedom — the conduct of U.S. foreign policy has been determined primarily by its relative power and by the inherently competitive nature of international politics. By focusing on their supposedly exceptional qualities, Americans blind themselves to the ways that they are a lot like everyone else.

This unchallenged faith in American exceptionalism makes it harder for Americans to understand why others are less enthusiastic about U.S. dominance, often alarmed by U.S. policies, and frequently irritated by what they see as U.S. hypocrisy, whether the subject is possession of nuclear weapons, conformity with international law, or America's tendency to condemn the conduct of others while ignoring its own failings. Ironically, U.S. foreign policy would probably be more effective if Americans were less convinced of their own unique virtues and less eager to proclaim them.

What we need, in short, is a more realis- 5 tic and critical assessment of America's true character and contributions. In that spirit, I offer here the Top 5 Myths about American Exceptionalism.

Myth 1
There Is Something Exceptional about American Exceptionalism.

Whenever American leaders refer to the "unique" responsibilities of the United States, they are saying that it is different from other powers and that these differences require them to take on special burdens.

Yet there is nothing unusual about such lofty declarations; indeed, those who make them are treading a well-worn path. Most great powers have considered themselves superior to their rivals and have believed that they were advancing some greater good when they imposed their preferences on others. The British thought they were bearing the "white man's burden," while French colonialists invoked *la mission civilisatrice* to justify their empire. Portugal, whose imperial activities were hardly distinguished, believed it was promoting a certain *missão civilizadora*. Even many of the officials of the former Soviet Union genuinely believed they were leading the world toward a socialist utopia despite the many cruelties that communist rule inflicted. Of course, the United States has by far the better claim to virtue than Stalin or his successors, but Obama was right to remind us that all countries prize their own particular qualities.

So when Americans proclaim they are exceptional and indispensable, they are simply the latest nation to sing a familiar old song. Among great powers, thinking you're special is the norm, not the exception.

Myth 2
The United States Behaves Better Than Other Nations Do.

Declarations of American exceptionalism rest on the belief that the United States is a uniquely virtuous nation, one that loves peace, nurtures liberty, respects human rights, and embraces the rule of law. Americans like to think their country behaves much better than other states do, and certainly better than other great powers.

If only it were true. The United States may [10] not have been as brutal as the worst states in world history, but a dispassionate look at the historical record belies most claims about America's moral superiority.

For starters, the United States has been one of the most expansionist powers in modern history. It began as 13 small colonies clinging to the Eastern Seaboard, but eventually expanded across North America, seizing Texas, Arizona, New Mexico, and California from Mexico in 1846. Along the way, it eliminated most of the native population and confined the survivors to impoverished reservations. By the mid-19th century, it had pushed Britain out of the Pacific Northwest and consolidated its hegemony over the Western Hemisphere.

The United States has fought numerous wars since then — starting several of them — and its wartime conduct has hardly been a model of restraint. The 1899–1902 conquest of the Philippines killed some 200,000 to 400,000 Filipinos, most of them civilians, and the United States and its allies did not hesitate to dispatch some 305,000 German and 330,000 Japanese civilians through aerial bombing during World War II, mostly through deliberate campaigns against enemy cities. No wonder Gen. Curtis LeMay, who directed the bombing campaign against Japan, told an aide, "If the U.S. lost the war, we would be prosecuted as war criminals." The United States dropped more than 6 million tons of bombs during the Indochina war, including tons of napalm and lethal defoliants like Agent Orange, and it is directly responsible for the deaths of many of the roughly 1 million civilians who died in that war.

More recently, the U.S.-backed Contra war in Nicaragua killed some 30,000 Nicaraguans, a percentage of their population equivalent to 2 million dead Americans. U.S. military action has led directly or indirectly to the deaths of 250,000 Muslims over the past three decades (and that's a low-end estimate, not counting the deaths resulting from the sanctions against Iraq in the 1990s), including the more than 100,000 people who died following the invasion and occupation of Iraq in 2003. U.S. drones and Special Forces are going after suspected terrorists in at least five countries at present and have killed an unknown number of innocent civilians in the process. Some of these actions may have been necessary to make Americans more prosperous and secure. But while Americans would undoubtedly regard such acts as indefensible if some foreign country were doing them to us, hardly any U.S. politicians have questioned these policies. Instead, Americans still wonder, "Why do they hate us?"

The United States talks a good game on human rights and international law, but it has refused to sign most human rights treaties, is not a party to the International Criminal Court, and has been all too willing to cozy up to dictators — remember our friend Hosni Mubarak? — with abysmal human rights records. If that were not enough, the abuses at Abu Ghraib and the George W. Bush administration's reliance on waterboarding, extraordinary rendition, and preventive detention should shake America's belief that it consistently acts in a morally superior fashion. Obama's decision to retain many of these policies suggests they were not a temporary aberration.

The United States never conquered a vast [15] overseas empire or caused millions to die through tyrannical blunders like China's Great Leap Forward or Stalin's forced collectivization. And given the vast power at its disposal for much of the past century, Washington could certainly have done much worse. But the record is clear: U.S. leaders have done what they thought they had to do when confronted by external dangers, and they paid scant attention to moral principles along the way. The idea that the United States is uniquely virtuous may be comforting to Americans; too bad it's not true.

Myth 3
America's Success Is Due to Its Special Genius.

The United States has enjoyed remarkable success, and Americans tend to portray their rise to world power as a direct result of the political foresight of the Founding Fathers, the virtues of the U.S. Constitution, the priority placed on individual liberty, and the creativity and hard work of the American people. In this narrative, the United States enjoys an exceptional global position today because it is, well, exceptional.

There is more than a grain of truth to this version of American history. It's not an accident that immigrants came to America in droves in search of economic opportunity, and the "melting pot" myth facilitated the assimilation of each wave of new Americans. America's scientific and technological achievements are fully deserving of praise and owe something to the openness and vitality of the American political order.

But America's past success is due as much to good luck as to any uniquely American virtues. The new nation was lucky that the continent was lavishly endowed with natural resources and traversed by navigable rivers. It was lucky to have been founded far from the other great powers and even luckier that the native population was less advanced and highly susceptible to European diseases. Americans were fortunate that the European great powers were at war for much of the republic's early history, which greatly facilitated its expansion across the continent, and its global primacy was ensured after the other great powers fought two devastating world wars. This account of America's rise does not deny that the United States did many things right, but it also acknowledges that America's present position owes as much to good fortune as to any special genius or "manifest destiny."

Myth 4
The United States Is Responsible for Most of the Good in the World.

Americans are fond of giving themselves credit for positive international developments. President Bill Clinton believed the

United States was "indispensable to the forging of stable political relations," and the late Harvard University political scientist Samuel P. Huntington thought U.S. primacy was central "to the future of freedom, democracy, open economies, and international order in the world." Journalist Michael Hirsh has gone even further, writing in his book *At War with Ourselves* that America's global role is "the greatest gift the world has received in many, many centuries, possibly all of recorded history." Scholarly works such as Tony Smith's *America's Mission* and G. John Ikenberry's *Liberal Leviathan* emphasize America's contribution to the spread of democracy and its promotion of a supposedly liberal world order. Given all the high-fives American leaders have given themselves, it is hardly surprising that most Americans see their country as an overwhelmingly positive force in world affairs.

Once again, there is something to this 20 line of argument, just not enough to make it entirely accurate. The United States has made undeniable contributions to peace and stability in the world over the past century, including the Marshall Plan, the creation and management of the Bretton Woods system, its rhetorical support for the core principles of democracy and human rights, and its mostly stabilizing military presence in Europe and the Far East. But the belief that all good things flow from Washington's wisdom overstates the U.S. contribution by a wide margin.

For starters, though Americans watching *Saving Private Ryan* or *Patton* may conclude that the United States played the central role in vanquishing Nazi Germany, most of the fighting was in Eastern Europe and the main burden of defeating Hitler's war machine was borne by the Soviet Union. Similarly, though the Marshall Plan and NATO played important roles in Europe's post–World War II success, Europeans deserve at least as much credit for rebuilding their economies, constructing a novel economic and political union, and moving beyond four centuries of sometimes bitter rivalry. Americans also tend to think they won the Cold War all by themselves, a view that ignores the contributions of other anti-Soviet adversaries and the courageous dissidents whose resistance to communist rule produced the "velvet revolutions" of 1989.

Moreover, as Godfrey Hodgson recently noted in his sympathetic but clear-eyed book, *The Myth of American Exceptionalism,* the spread of liberal ideals is a global phenomenon with roots in the Enlightenment, and European philosophers and political leaders did much to advance the democratic ideal. Similarly, the abolition of slavery and the long effort to improve the status of women owe more to Britain and other democracies than to the United States, where progress in both areas trailed many other countries. Nor can the United States claim a global leadership role today on gay rights, criminal justice, or economic equality — Europe's got those areas covered.

Finally, any honest accounting of the past half-century must acknowledge the downside of American primacy. The United States has been the major producer of greenhouse gases for most of the last hundred years and thus a principal cause of the adverse changes that are altering the global environment. The United States stood on the wrong side of the long struggle against apartheid in South Africa and backed plenty of unsavory dictatorships — including Saddam Hussein's —

when short-term strategic interests dictated. Americans may be justly proud of their role in creating and defending Israel and in combating global anti-Semitism, but its one-sided policies have also prolonged Palestinian statelessness and sustained Israel's brutal occupation.

Bottom line: Americans take too much credit for global progress and accept too little blame for areas where U.S. policy has in fact been counterproductive. Americans are blind to their weak spots, and in ways that have real-world consequences. Remember when Pentagon planners thought U.S. troops would be greeted in Baghdad with flowers and parades? They mostly got RPGs and IEDs instead.

Myth 5
God Is on Our Side.

A crucial component of American excep-[25] tionalism is the belief that the United States has a divinely ordained mission to lead the rest of the world. Ronald Reagan told audiences that there was "some divine plan" that had placed America here, and once quoted Pope Pius XII saying, "Into the hands of America God has placed the destinies of an afflicted mankind." Bush offered a similar view in 2004, saying, "We have a calling from beyond the stars to stand for freedom." The same idea was expressed, albeit less nobly, in Otto von Bismarck's alleged quip that "God has a special providence for fools, drunks, and the United States."

Confidence is a valuable commodity for any country. But when a nation starts to think it enjoys the mandate of heaven and becomes convinced that it cannot fail or be led astray by scoundrels or incompetents, then reality is likely to deliver a swift rebuke. Ancient Athens, Napoleonic France, imperial Japan,

and countless other countries have succumbed to this sort of hubris, and nearly always with catastrophic results.

Despite America's many successes, the country is hardly immune from setbacks, follies, and boneheaded blunders. If you have any doubts about that, just reflect on how a decade of ill-advised tax cuts, two costly and unsuccessful wars, and a financial meltdown driven mostly by greed and corruption have managed to squander the privileged position the United States enjoyed at the end of the 20th century. Instead of assuming that God is on their side, perhaps Americans should heed Abraham Lincoln's admonition that our greatest concern should be "whether we are on God's side."

Given the many challenges Americans now face, from persistent unemployment to the burden of winding down two deadly wars, it's unsurprising that they find the idea of their own exceptionalism comforting—and that their aspiring political leaders have been proclaiming it with increasing fervor. Such patriotism has its benefits, but not when it leads to a basic misunderstanding of America's role in the world. This is exactly how bad decisions get made.

America has its own special qualities, as all countries do, but it is still a state embedded in a competitive global system. It is far stronger and richer than most, and its geopolitical position is remarkably favorable. These advantages give the United States a wider range of choice in its conduct of foreign affairs, but they don't ensure that its choices will be good ones. Far from being a unique state whose behavior is radically different from that of other great powers, the United States has behaved like all the rest, pursuing its own self-interest first and foremost, seeking to improve its relative position over time, and devoting relatively little blood or treasure to purely idealistic pursuits. Yet, just like past great powers, it has convinced itself that it is different, and better, than everyone else.

International politics is a contact sport, ₃₀ and even powerful states must compromise their political principles for the sake of security and prosperity. Nationalism is also a powerful force, and it inevitably highlights the country's virtues and sugarcoats its less savory aspects. But if Americans want to be truly exceptional, they might start by viewing the whole idea of "American exceptionalism" with a much more skeptical eye.

Topics for Critical Thinking and Writing

1. In paragraph 1, Stephen Walt quotes a number of phrases that have been used to describe the United States. Research the origins of these phrases and the history of their use. Argue whether their use (typically by politicians) is more based on propaganda — and a desire to influence opinion or to get votes — or a fair and accurate description of the United States. Defend your answer.

2. In paragraph 3, Walt states that by embracing exceptionalism, "Americans blind themselves to the ways that they are a lot like everyone else." What does he mean by this? Provide specific examples from history or current events that demonstrate how the United States does indeed act like other nations.

3. Walt addresses what he terms Myth 1: "There is Something Exceptional about American Exceptionalism." It's the myth that President Barack Obama was referring to when he referenced examples of British and Greek exceptionalism. The core idea is that all great powers have thought of themselves as exceptional. Do you find Walt's critique of this myth convincing? Why, or why not?

4. Beginning with Myth 2 ("The United States Behaves Better Than Other Countries Do"), Walt offers a list of historical examples of ways in which the United States has acted aggressively to expand its territory, international influence, and military power. Review his accounts, and do additional research if necessary to learn more about the events he mentions. In your opinion, do these events prevent us from considering America as exceptional? Why, or why not?

5. Walt's third myth is that "America's Success Is Due to Its Special Genius." Why does he say that this is a product of good luck (para. 18)? Is that an overly simple rejection of the myth? Explain your response.

6. The fourth myth is that "America Is Responsible for Most of the Good in the World." This myth rests upon the premise that Americans tend to overlook the contributions toward good made by other countries. In your opinion, is this a valid statement? Use specific examples to support your answer.

7. Myth 5 states that "God Is on Our Side." This myth is a core aspect of American exceptionalism, and the success of America — economically, politically, militarily, socially, culturally — is

often cited as proof that God favors America. What are the dangers inherent in citing God as favoring one nation over all others? Cite examples from history and the current events of nations and other groups that claim the favor of a deity. Or, argue how Walt may be wrong about this myth.

8. Walt's article is particularly focused on American exceptionalism and foreign policy, not domestic issues. In what ways is American exceptionalism present — or not present — in our domestic sphere? Support your answer with specific examples.

HERMAN CAIN

Herman Cain (b. 1945) is an American businessman who briefly led the race to win the 2012 Republican nomination for president. Well known as a conservative and Tea Party activist, Cain continues to be an active presence online, on television, on the radio, and in the print media. In this article, published in the March 2011 edition of the American Spectator, *Cain defends the concept of American exceptionalism in the face of what he sees as President Barack Obama's rejection of the concept.*

In Defense of American Exceptionalism

There is no denying it: America is the greatest country in the world. We are blessed with unparalleled freedoms and boundless prosperity that for generations have inspired an innovative and industrious people. America is exceptional.

American Exceptionalism is the standard that our laws reflect the understanding that we are afforded certain God-given rights that can never be taken away. We know that God, not government, bestows upon us these inalienable rights, and because of that, they must not be compromised by the whims of man. This makes us a unique nation, a nation that remains, as President Ronald Reagan once said, "a model and hope to the world."

Unfortunately, some politicians have either forgotten or chosen to ignore the glory of our founding. In April 2009, President Obama told a reporter in Strasbourg, France: "I believe in American exceptionalism, just as I suspect that the Brits believe in British exceptionalism and the Greeks believe in Greek exceptionalism." In saying this, the president implied that American Exceptionalism is nothing terribly special and instead simply chalked it up to the romanticism of patriotism.

Americans know better. We see American Exceptionalism not as an empty cry for nationalism, but instead, the blessings of God that keep our nation strong, independent, and free. We see the American story as one of tenacity and triumph, not as one inherently flawed and in need of rewriting. We recognize the times we have stumbled but are assured that it is not due to weakness of our foundation, but instead, the imperfection of mankind.

Most importantly, conservatives see America 5 as exceptional because of our shared belief in the dignity and creativity of the individual. We know that it is innately human to work, to risk, and to dream. We understand that these virtues, coupled with the conditions American Exceptionalism provides, allow us to enjoy the economic and social mobility that other countries envy. Liberals lament that such success wasn't guaranteed.

At its very core, progressivism rejects American Exceptionalism. Progressives view the Constitution as a roadblock, as they seek an unlimited federal government with more authority than the states and more power than the people. Because they strive for a limitless federal government, they are willing to sacrifice the rugged individualism that has made this nation exceptional in exchange for the collective salvation they believe a vast government provides. And the darling of the progressive movement is, of course, President Obama.

"Let me be clear," President Obama: America is the greatest nation on Earth. We are not just any other nation, and we are certainly not analogous to our friends in Europe and elsewhere. Our exceptionalism is forever ingrained in our founding documents that spell out exactly the roles of the federal government in relation to individual rights and states' rights.

Truth is eternal, and simply ignoring the truths of the Declaration of Independence and the Constitution won't make them go away. And frankly, there are enough Americans, including me, who love it and our country far too much to allow our exceptionalism to be bartered for further expansion of an already out-of-control federal government.

Topics for Critical Thinking and Writing

1. In paragraph 2, Herman Cain argues that American exceptionalism is a result of God-given rights. Why does that make the United States a "unique nation," as he states? What is the basis of rights in other countries? Do research to support your answer.

2. Cain refers to an interview that President Barack Obama had given two years earlier in which he appears to give only a back-handed acceptance of the concept of American exceptionalism by stating how other nations may also feel exceptional — more rooted in national pride than anything especially different or remarkable (para. 3). What are the dangers of nationalism, and does belief in American exceptionalism feed into that? Why, or why not?

3. In paragraph 4, Cain rejects American exceptionalism as simply an expression of nationalism. What is the basis of this rejection? Do you find his argument convincing? Why, or why not?

4. In paragraph 6, Cain takes on the opposition, which he believes "rejects American Exceptionalism." What is the basis of his argument? Do you find this to be a fair characterization? Why, or why not?

5. Cain begins his conclusion with the statement, "Truth is eternal" (para. 8). To what particular truth is he referring? What is the basis of his support?

6. Considering that this article was published during a time when Cain was running for the nomination for president, how do the rhetoric and language of this article resemble a campaign speech? How might it have helped to advance his own political goals?

CLIFFORD D. MAY

Clifford D. May (b. 1951) is president of the Foundation for the Defense of Democracies, a think tank, according to its Web site, dedicated to "fighting terrorism and promoting freedom." May has been a journalist, editor, and political activist, particularly in support of conservative causes and the Republican Party. In this article, published on June 2, 2011, in the National Review, *May defends the concept of American exceptionalism in the face of criticism that such a concept is smug and narcissistic.*

In Defense of American Exceptionalism

Some years ago, John Podhoretz, a right-of-center writer, now the editor of *Commentary,* admonished his colleagues on the left: "We speak liberal as well as our own tongue. Why don't you speak conservative?"

I was put in mind of this quip while reading a recent column by the *Washington Post's* Richard Cohen. In "The Myth of American Exceptionalism," he boldly posits that the "problem of the 21st century" is "the culture of smugness. The emblem of this culture is 'American exceptionalism.' It has been adopted by the right to mean that America, alone among the nations, is beloved of God."

Cohen provides no evidence that anyone on the right defines exceptionalism as he does. What do those of us who use, defend and advocate exceptionalism mean instead?

Among other things, that America is simply different from other nations. It is a nation of immigrants from every corner of the Earth, a nation bound not by ancestral blood but by revolutionary ideas and beliefs brilliantly articulated more than two centuries ago in the Declaration of Independence and the Constitution.

The founding of the United States ushered in the modern democratic experiment, along with new concepts of freedom and human rights. In the 20th century, the Greatest Generation fought for the survival of that experiment against its totalitarian enemies, Nazi, Fascist and communist alike. Today, the challenges posed by Islamic totalitarianism test a new generation.

America has been a uniquely productive nation: a font of invention, creativity and economic dynamism. In America, tens of millions of people have risen from poverty. The United States has been a singularly generous, if not always effective, provider of assistance to other countries including those where Americans are not popular.

But, most of all, exceptionalism implies that the responsibility for global leadership rests on America's shoulders. Not because Americans hunger for power but because there is no good alternative.

At the conclusion of World War II, the British rejected Winston Churchill — without whose vision and determination Hitler might well have triumphed — and turned inward to focus on building a welfare state. That meant relinquishing global leadership. They could do that because they could pass the torch to America.

If that torch has now become too heavy for Americans, or if it is seen as unfair for America to continue to lead, who is prepared to take America's place? Those who rule Iran, China and Russia are no doubt eager. But they are despots as Cohen ought to appreciate.

There are those on the left known as "transnational progressives." They believe the United Nations and similar organizations should be recognized as a world government to which

America will increasingly cede power and sovereignty. To favor that option requires willfully ignoring the corruption, financial and moral, that infects the U.N. and the extent to which it is manipulated by dictators and such anti-democratic and supremacist blocs as the Organization of the Islamic Conference.

In other words: At present, there is no substitute for American leadership. America is the indispensible nation. That is what makes it exceptional.

Cohen goes on to link exceptionalism to such maladies as America's high murder rate, execution rate and dysfunctional education system — rather a stretch, it seems to me. But he is most peeved by what he sees as the theological implications of exceptionalism, what he calls the "huge role of religion in American politics." He contends that those who invoke exceptionalism — he specifically cites "Mitt Romney, Mike Pence, Newt Gingrich, Rick Santorum, Mike Huckabee and, of course, Sarah Palin" — claim to know what God wants and therefore insist: "What God prefers should not be monkeyed with."

To bolster his case, Cohen sets off on a historical digression, writing that "in the years preceding the Civil War, both sides of the slavery issue claimed the endorsement of God. . . . Within five years, Americans were slaughtering one another on the battlefield. . . . Therein lies the danger of American exceptionalism. It discourages compromise, for what God has made exceptional, man must not alter."

Is it really Cohen's view that the abolitionists were wrong to oppose slavery on moral grounds? Does he actually think Lincoln should have compromised on slavery in the hope of settling the conflict between the North and South non-violently?

What's more, Cohen conspicuously ignores 15 the view Lincoln himself expressed on precisely this matter. In the midst of the Civil War, the first Republican president was asked by a clergyman if God was on his side. Lincoln's reply: "Sir, my concern is not whether God is on our side. My great concern is to be on God's side."

Such humility is implicit in the idea of American exceptionalism. Americans value freedom not least because we don't think anyone has a monopoly on truth or the private email address of the Almighty. This is the polar opposite of Cohen's interpretation of exceptionalism as a word "that reeks of arrogance and discourages compromise. American exceptionalism ought to be called American narcissism. We look perfect only to ourselves."

No, we exceptionalists do not think that. What we think instead: Americans will never perfect themselves or "form a more perfect union" by letting transnational bureaucrats, politicians and professors run our lives.

Exceptionalists do not deny that America has many faults and that Americans have made many mistakes in the past and are likely to do so in the future. But that doesn't make the United States the equivalent of Norway, Uruguay, Burkina Faso and New Guinea. That doesn't lead us to the Lake Woebegone-all-children-are-above-average view of the world expressed by President Obama two years ago in Europe: "I believe in American exceptionalism, just as I suspect that the Brits believe in British exceptionalism and the Greeks believe in Greek exceptionalism."

We exceptionalists look instead to President Reagan, for whom exceptionalism meant that America remained "the last best hope for a mankind plagued by tyranny and deprivation." To keep that hope alive will require efforts — one might say exceptional efforts — on the part of Americans. It also will require that pundits such as Richard Cohen try harder to understand what his friends on the right are saying.

Topics for Critical Thinking and Writing

1. The article begins with a joke about people speaking "conservative" or speaking "liberal" (para. 1). What does the writer mean by this? Why do you suppose Clifford D. May chose to begin his article with this quotation? How does it reflect the theme of the rest of the article?

2. May rejects Cohen's definition of American exceptionalism and introduces his own in paragraph 4. Consider what other authors have said in defining American exceptionalism. Is May's definition a fair and complete one? If not, cite other writers whose definitions have differed, or who have emphasized different aspects of the concept.

3. In paragraph 8, May recounts how the British voted Winston Churchill out of office even as World War II was coming to a victorious conclusion. Why does May use that example, and how does it relate to the concept of American exceptionalism? Might this not play into the idea that American exceptionalism exists because Great Britain was no longer the dominant world power? In other words, do the most powerful nations always feel themselves to be exceptional? Why, or why not?

4. What is a "transnational progressive," according to May (para. 10)? Who is the anonymous "they" that May mentions? Research transnational progressivism, both arguments in favor of it as well as those against. Is the concept of a transnational progressive a straw man fallacy (i.e., the creation of an opposition that is easily disposed of), or is it real? Defend your answer.

5. In paragraph 13, May quotes Cohen as recalling how both sides in the Civil War felt that God was on their side, and he argues that attitude "discourages compromise." What is May's response to this criticism, and do you think it is effective? Why, or why not?

6. Not surprisingly, considering that the author has been actively involved in national security and foreign policy issues, much of the focus of the article is on America's strength and ability to influence world events — as opposed to discussion of religious liberty at home or social mobility. In your opinion, how is the concept of American exceptionalism connected to the conduct of foreign policy? How have events since the attacks of 9/11 influenced that? Be specific in your response.

DAVID BROMWICH

David Bromwich (b. 1951) teaches at Yale University, where he is the Sterling Professor of English. He has numerous publications to his credit, including The Intellectual Life of Edmund Burke *(2014), a book about the noted Irish-born member of the British Parliament who supported the American Revolution but opposed the French Revolution. In this article, which appeared in* The Nation *on October 24, 2014, Bromwich argues that belief in American exceptionalism requires historical ignorance as well as a large dose of arrogance.*

It's Time to Rethink American Exceptionalism

The origins of the phrase "American exceptionalism" are not especially obscure. The French sociologist Alexis de Tocqueville, observing this country in the 1830s, said that Americans seemed exceptional in valuing practical attainments almost to the exclusion of the arts and sciences. The Soviet dictator Joseph Stalin, on hearing a report by the American Communist Party that workers in the United States in 1929 were not ready for revolution, denounced "the heresy of American exceptionalism." In 1996, the political scientist Seymour Martin Lipset took those hints from Tocqueville and Stalin and added some of his own to produce his book *American Exceptionalism: A Double-Edged Sword*. The virtues of American society, for Lipset — our individualism, hostility to state action, and propensity for *ad hoc* problem-solving — themselves stood in the way of a lasting and prudent consensus in the conduct of American politics.

In recent years, the phrase "American exceptionalism," at once resonant and ambiguous, has stolen into popular usage in electoral politics, in the mainstream media, and in academic writing with a profligacy that is hard to account for. It sometimes seems that exceptionalism for Americans means everything from generosity to selfishness, localism to imperialism, indifference to "the opinions of mankind" to a readiness to incorporate the folkways of every culture. When President Obama told West Point graduates last May that "I believe in American exceptionalism with every fiber of my being," the context made it clear that he meant the United States was the greatest country in the world: our stature was demonstrated by our possession of "the finest fighting force that the world has ever known," uniquely tasked with defending liberty and peace globally; and yet we could not allow ourselves to "flout international norms" or be a law unto ourselves. The contradictory nature of these statements would have satisfied even Tocqueville's taste for paradox.

On the whole, is American exceptionalism a force for good? The question shouldn't be hard to answer. To make an exception of yourself is as immoral a proceeding for a nation as it is for an individual. When we say of a person (usually someone who has gone off the rails), "He thinks the rules don't apply to him," we mean that he is a danger to others and perhaps to himself. People who act on such a belief don't as a rule examine themselves deeply or write a history of the self to justify their understanding that they are unique. Very little effort is involved in their willfulness. Such exceptionalism, indeed, comes from an excess of will unaccompanied by awareness of the necessity for self-restraint.

Such people are monsters. Many land in asylums, more in prisons. But the category also encompasses a large number of high-functioning autistics: governors, generals, corporate heads, owners of professional sports teams. When you think about it, some of these people do write histories of themselves and in that pursuit, a few of them have kept up the vitality of an ancient genre: criminal autobiography.

All nations, by contrast, write their own 5 histories as a matter of course. They preserve and exhibit a record of their doings; normally, of justified conduct, actions worthy of celebration. "Exceptional" nations, therefore, are compelled to engage in some fancy bookkeeping which exceptional individuals can avoid — at least until they are put on trial or subjected to interrogation under oath. The exceptional nation will claim that it is not responsible for its exceptional character. Its nature was given by God, or History, or Destiny.

An external and semi-miraculous instrumentality is invoked to explain the prodigy whose essence defies mere scientific understanding. To support the belief in the nation's exceptional character, synonyms and variants of the word "providence" often get slotted in. That word gained its utility at the end of the seventeenth century—the start of the epoch of nations formed in Europe by a supposed covenant or compact. Providence splits the difference between the accidents of fortune and purposeful design; it says that God is on your side without having the bad manners to pronounce His name.

Why is it immoral for a person to treat himself as an exception? The reason is plain: because morality, by definition, means a standard of right and wrong that applies to all persons without exception. Yet to answer so briefly may be to oversimplify. For at least three separate meanings are in play when it comes to exceptionalism, with a different apology backing each. The glamour that surrounds the idea owes something to confusion among these possible senses.

First, a nation is thought to be exceptional by its very nature. It is so consistently worthy that a unique goodness shines through all its works. Who would hesitate to admire the acts of such a country? What foreigner would not wish to belong to it? Once we are held captive by this picture, "my country right or wrong" becomes a proper sentiment and not a wild effusion of prejudice, because we cannot conceive of the nation being wrong.

A second meaning of exceptional may seem more open to rational scrutiny. Here, the nation is supposed to be admirable by reason of history and circumstance. It has demonstrated its exceptional quality by adherence to ideals which are peculiar to its original character and honorable as part of a greater human inheritance. Not "my country right or wrong" but "my country, good and getting better" seems to be the standard here. The promise of what the country could turn out to be supports this faith. Its moral and political virtue is perceived as a historical deposit with a rich residue in the present.

A third version of exceptionalism derives 10 from our usual affectionate feelings about living in a community on the scale of a neighborhood or township, an ethnic group or religious sect. Communitarian nationalism takes the innocent-seeming step of generalizing that sentiment to the nation at large. My country is exceptional *to me* (according to this view) just because it is mine. Its familiar habits and customs have shaped the way I think and feel; nor do I have the slightest wish to extricate myself from its demands. The nation, then, is like a gigantic family, and we owe it what we owe to the members of our family: "unconditional love." This sounds like the common sense of ordinary feelings. How can our nation help being exceptional to us?

TEACHER OF THE WORLD

Athens was just such an exceptional nation, or city-state, as Pericles described it in his celebrated oration for the first fallen soldiers in the Peloponnesian War. He meant his description of Athens to carry both normative force and hortatory urgency. It is, he says, the greatest of Greek cities, and this quality is shown by its works, shining deeds, the structure of its government, and the character of its citizens, who are themselves creations of the city. At the same time, Pericles was saying to the widows and children of the war dead: Resemble them! Seek to deserve the name of Athenian as they have deserved it!

The oration, recounted by Thucydides in the *History of the Peloponnesian War,* begins by praising the ancestors of Athenian democracy who by their exertions have made the city exceptional. "They dwelt in the country without break in the succession from generation to generation, and handed it down free to the present time by their valor." Yet we who are alive today, Pericles says, have added to that inheritance; and he goes on to praise the constitution of the city, which "does not copy the laws of neighboring states; we are rather a pattern to others than imitators ourselves."

The foreshadowing here of American exceptionalism is uncanny and the anticipation of our own predicament continues as the speech proceeds. "In our enterprises we present the singular spectacle of daring and deliberation, each carried to its highest point, and both united in the same persons. . . . As a city we are the school of Hellas"—by which Pericles means that no representative citizen or soldier of another city could possibly be as resourceful as an Athenian. This city, alone among all the others, is greater than her reputation.

We Athenians, he adds, choose to risk our lives by perpetually carrying a difficult burden, rather than submitting to the will of another state. Our readiness to die for the city is the proof of our greatness. Turning to the surviving families of the dead, he admonishes and exalts them: "You must yourselves realize the power of Athens," he tells the widows and children, "and feed your eyes upon her from day to day, till love of her fills your hearts; and then when all her greatness shall break upon you, you must reflect that it was by courage, sense of duty, and a keen feeling of honor in action that men were enabled to win all this." So stirring are their deeds that the memory of their greatness is written in the hearts of men

in faraway lands: "For heroes have the whole earth for their tomb."

Athenian exceptionalism at its height, as the words of Pericles indicate, took deeds of war as proof of the worthiness of all that the city achieved apart from war. In this way, Athens was placed beyond comparison: nobody who knew it and knew other cities could fail to recognize its exceptional nature. This was not only a judgment inferred from evidence but an overwhelming sensation that carried conviction with it. The greatness of the city ought to be experienced, Pericles imagines, as a vision that "shall break upon you."

GUILTY PAST, INNOCENT FUTURE

To come closer to twenty-first-century America, consider how, in the Gettysburg Address, Abraham Lincoln gave an exceptional turn to an ambiguous past. Unlike Pericles, he was speaking in the midst of a civil war, not a war between rival states, and this partly explains the note of self-doubt that we may detect in Lincoln when we compare the two speeches. At Gettysburg, Lincoln said that a pledge by the country as a whole had been embodied in a single document, the Declaration of Independence. He took the Declaration as his touchstone, rather than the Constitution, for a reason he spoke of elsewhere: the latter document had been freighted with compromise. The Declaration of Independence uniquely laid down principles that might over time allow the idealism of the founders to be realized.

Athens, for Pericles, was what Athens always had been. The Union, for Lincoln, was what it had yet to become. He associated the greatness of past intentions—"We hold these truths to be self-evident" — with the resolve he hoped his listeners would carry out in the present moment: "It is [not for the noble dead but] rather for us to be here dedicated to the great task remaining before us — that from these honored dead we take increased devotion to that cause for which they gave the last full measure of devotion — that we here highly resolve that these dead shall not have died in vain — that this nation, under God, shall have a new birth of freedom."

This allegorical language needs translation. In the future, Lincoln is saying, there will be a popular government and a political society based on the principle of free labor. Before that can happen, however, slavery must be brought to an end by carrying the country's resolution into practice. So Lincoln asks his listeners to love their country for what it may become, not what it is. Their self-sacrifice on behalf of a possible future will serve as proof of national greatness. He does not hide the stain of slavery that marred the Constitution; the imperfection of the founders is confessed between the lines. But the logic of the speech implies, by a trick of grammar and perspective, that the Union was always pointed in the direction of the Civil War that would make it free.

Notice that Pericles's argument for the exceptional city has here been reversed. The future is not guaranteed by the greatness of the past; rather, the tarnished virtue of the past will be scoured clean by the purity of the future. Exceptional in its reliance on slavery, the state established by the first American Revolution is thus to be redeemed by the second. Through the sacrifice of nameless thousands, the nation will defeat slavery and justify its fame as the truly exceptional country its founders wished it to be.

Most Americans are moved (without [20] quite knowing why) by the opening words of the Gettysburg Address: "Four score and seven years ago our fathers. . . ." Four score and seven is a biblical marker of the life of one person, and the words ask us to wonder whether our nation, a radical experiment based on a radical "proposition," can last longer than a single life-span. The effect is provocative. Yet the backbone of Lincoln's argument would have stood out more clearly if the speech had instead begun: "Two years from now, perhaps three, our country will see a great transformation." The truth is that the year of the birth of the nation had no logical relationship to the year of the "new birth of freedom." An exceptional character, however, whether in history or story, demands an exceptional plot; so the speech commences with deliberately archaic language to ask its implicit question: Can we Americans survive today and become the school of modern democracy, much as Athens was the school of Hellas?

THE TIES THAT BIND AND ABSOLVE

To believe that our nation has always been exceptional, as Pericles said Athens was, or that it will soon justify such a claim, as Lincoln suggested America would do, requires a suppression of ordinary skepticism. The belief itself calls for extraordinary arrogance or extraordinary hope in the believer. In our time, exceptionalism has been made less exacting by an appeal to national feeling based on the smallest and most vivid community that most people know: the family. Governor Mario Cuomo of New York, in his keynote address at the 1984 Democratic convention, put this straightforwardly. America, said Cuomo, was like a family, and a good family never loses its concern for the least fortunate of its members. In 2011, President Obama, acceding to Republican calls for austerity that led to the sequestration of government funds, told us that the national economy was just like a household budget and every family knows that it must pay its bills.

To take seriously the metaphor of the nation-as-family may lead to a sense of sentimental obligation or prudential worry on behalf of our fellow citizens. But many people think we should pursue the analogy further. If our nation does wrong, they say, we must treat it as an error and not a crime because, after all, we owe our nation unconditional love. Yet here the metaphor betrays our thinking into a false equation. A family has nested us, cradled us, nursed us from infancy, as we have perhaps done for later generations of the same family; and it has done so in a sense that is far more intimate than the sense in which a nation has fostered or nurtured us. We know our family with an individuated depth and authority that can't be brought to our idea of a nation. This may be a difference of kind, or a difference of degree, but the difference is certainly great.

A subtle deception is involved in the analogy between nation and family; and an illicit transfer of feelings comes with the appeal to "unconditional love." What do we mean by unconditional love, even at the level of the family? Suppose my delinquent child robs and beats an old man on a city street, and I learn of it by his own confession or by accident. What exactly do I owe him?

Unconditional love, in this setting, surely means that I can't stop caring about my child; that I will regard his terrible action as an aberration. I will be bound to think about the act and actor quite differently from the way I would think about anyone else who committed such a crime. But does unconditional love also require that I make excuses for him? Shall I pay a lawyer to get him off the hook and back on the streets as soon as possible? Is it my duty to conceal what he has done, if there is a chance of keeping it secret? Must I never say what he did in the company of strangers or outside the family circle?

At a national level, the doctrine of exceptionalism as unconditional love encourages habits of suppression and euphemism that sink deep roots in the common culture. We have seen the result in America in the years since 2001. In the grip of this doctrine, torture has become "enhanced interrogation"; wars of aggression have become wars for democracy; a distant likely enemy has become an "imminent threat" whose very existence justifies an executive order to kill. These are permitted and officially sanctioned forms of collective dishonesty. They begin in quasi-familial piety, they pass through the systematic distortion of language, and they end in the corruption of consciousness.

The commandment to "keep it in the family" is a symptom of that corruption. It follows that one must never speak critically of one's country in the hearing of other nations or write against its policies in foreign newspapers. No matter how vicious and wrong the conduct of a member of the family may be, one must assume his good intentions. This ideology abets raw self-interest in justifying many actions by which the United States has revealingly made an exception of itself—for example, our refusal to participate in the International Criminal Court. The community of nations, we declared, was not situated to understand the true extent of our constabulary responsibilities. American actions come under a different standard and we are the only qualified judges of our own cause.

The doctrine of the national family may be a less fertile source of belligerent pride than "my country right or wrong." It may be less grandiose, too, than the exceptionalism that asks us to love our country for ideals that have never properly been translated into practice. And yet, in this appeal to the family, one finds the same renunciation of moral knowledge — a renunciation that, if followed, would render inconceivable any social order beyond that of the family and its extension, the tribe.

Unconditional love of our country is the counterpart of unconditional detachment and even hostility toward other countries. None of us is an exception, and no nation is. The sooner we come to live with this truth as a mundane reality without exceptions, the more grateful other nations will be to live in a world that includes us, among others.

Topics for Critical Thinking and Writing

1. What is the importance of David Bromwich's recounting of the origin of the phrase "American exceptionalism" (para. 1). Does this serve to oppose an innate concept of American exceptionalism? If so, how? If not, explain why not.

2. In paragraph 1, Bromwich cites Lipset's ideas of American exceptionalism as preventing "a lasting and prudent consensus in the conduct of American politics." What does he mean by this? Do you agree or disagree? Support your answer.

3. In paragraph 2, Bromwich seems to suggest that American exceptionalism encompasses so many ideas that in itself it means nothing. He remarks about the nature of President Barack Obama's speech at West Point, saying that it ultimately represented a "paradox." What does he mean by this? Do you agree or disagree? Support your answer.

4. Bromwich notes that people who support the notion of exceptionalism are "monsters" (para. 4). What does he mean by this? Do you agree or disagree? Support your answer.

5. Bromwich compares the actions of individuals to the actions of nations in paragraph 5 when he states that the nation's actions are not to be taken as "fancy bookkeeping" but as a nature derived from "God, or History, or Destiny." If American exceptionalism is an idea taken from God, how is that so? Be specific in your answer.

6. In paragraph 7, Bromwich writes that morality is "a standard of right and wrong that applies to all persons without exception." How is that problematic with the concept of American exceptionalism? What specifically makes the two ideas difficult to resolve?

7. Bromwich makes an implied criticism of American history in paragraph 9 when he states that a nation "is supposed to be admirable by reason of history and circumstance." In what specific ways has the United States not been admirable? Do those shortcomings lessen its claim to exceptionalism? Why, or why not?

8. Bromwich cites the example of ancient Greece, particularly Athens under the rule of Pericles, as an example of another nation that saw itself as exceptional. In what ways does the example of Athens undermine the concept of American exceptionalism? In what ways does that example support the concept of American exceptionalism?

9. How does Lincoln's Gettysburg Address anticipate the concept of American exceptionalism? Why is the difference between past and the future important in this discussion?

10. In paragraph 19, Bromwich states, "The future is not guaranteed by the greatness of the past; rather, the tarnished virtue of the past will be scoured clean by the purity of the future." How does this relate to the present situation in the United States, if at all? Defend your answer.

11. What is the weakness of the nation as family metaphor? What is its strength?

12. In paragraph 26, Bromwich speaks of the temptation to "keep it in the family" as a corruption. Why is that? What is the danger of keeping America's sins to itself?

ELLEN BRESLER ROCKMORE

Ellen Bresler Rockmore (b. 1967) is a lecturer at the Institute of Writing and Rhetoric at Dartmouth College, having received her B.A. at Yale. She also has a law degree from New York University. In this article, published in the New York Times *on October 22, 2015, she argues that conservative revisionist readings of history distort what actually occurred, often for the purpose of making the past abuses more palatable to present audiences.*

How Texas Teaches History

A Texas high school student and his mother recently called attention to a curious line in a geography textbook: a description of the Atlantic slave trade as bringing "millions of workers" to plantations in the American South. McGraw-Hill Education, the publisher of the textbook, has since acknowledged that the term "workers" was a misnomer.

The company's chief executive also promised to revise the textbook so that its digital version as well as its next edition would more accurately describe the forced migration and enslavement of Africans. In the meantime, the company is also offering to send stickers to cover the passage.

But it will take more than that to fix the way slavery is taught in Texas textbooks. In 2010, the Texas Board of Education approved a social studies curriculum that promotes capitalism and Republican political philosophies.

The curriculum guidelines prompted many concerns, including that new textbooks would downplay slavery as the cause of the Civil War.

This fall, five million public school students in Texas began using the textbooks based on the new guidelines. And some of these books distort history not through word choices but through a tool we often think of as apolitical: grammar.

In September, Bobby Finger of the website 5 Jezebel obtained and published some excerpts from the new books, showing much of what is objectionable about their content. The books play down the horror of slavery and even seem to claim that it had an upside. This upside took the form of a distinctive African-American culture, in which family was central, Christianity provided "hope," folk tales expressed "joy" and community dances were important social events.

But it is not only the substance of the passages that is a problem. It is also their form. The writers' decisions about how to construct sentences, about what the subject of the sentence will be, about whether the verb will be active or passive, shape the message that slavery was not all that bad.

I teach freshman writing at Dartmouth College. My colleagues and I consistently try to convey to our students the importance of clear writing. Among the guiding principles of clear writing are these: Whenever possible, use human subjects, not abstract nouns; use active verbs, not passive. We don't want our students to write, "Torture was used," because that sentence obscures who was torturing whom.

In the excerpts published by Jezebel, the Texas textbooks employ all the principles of good, strong, clear writing when talking about the "upside" of slavery. But when writing about the brutality of slavery, the writers use all the tricks of obfuscation. You can see all this at play in the following passage from a textbook, published by Houghton Mifflin Harcourt, called *Texas United States History*:

> *Some slaves reported that their masters treated them kindly. To protect their investment, some slaveholders provided adequate food and clothing for their slaves. However, severe treatment was very common. Whippings, brandings, and even worse torture were all part of American slavery.*

Notice how in the first two sentences, the "slavery wasn't that bad" sentences, the main subject of each clause is a person: slaves, masters, slaveholders. What those people, especially the slave owners, are doing is clear: They are treating their slaves kindly; they are

providing adequate food and clothing. But after those two sentences there is a change, not just in the writers' outlook on slavery but also in their sentence construction. There are no people in the last two sentences, only nouns. Yes, there is severe treatment, whippings, brandings and torture. And yes, those are all bad things. But where are the slave owners who were actually doing the whipping and branding and torturing? And where are the slaves who were whipped, branded and tortured? They are nowhere to be found in the sentence.

In another passage, slave owners and their [10] institutionalized cruelty are similarly absent: "Families were often broken apart when a family member was sold to another owner."

Note the use of the passive voice in the verbs "were broken apart" and "was sold." If the sentence had been written according to the principles of good draftsmanship, it would have looked like this: Slave owners often broke slave families apart by selling a family member to another owner. A bit more powerful, no? Through grammatical manipulation, the textbook authors obscure the role of slave owners in the institution of slavery.

It may appear at first glance that the authors do a better job of focusing on the actions of slaves. After all, there are many sentences in which "slaves" are the subjects, the main characters in their own narrative. But what are the verbs in those sentences? Are the slaves suffering? No, in the sentences that feature slaves as the subject, as the main actors in the sentence, the slaves are contributing their agricultural knowledge to the growing Southern economy; they are singing songs and telling folk tales; they are expressing themselves through art and dance.

There are no sentences, in these excerpts, anyway, in which slaves are doing what slaves actually did: toiling relentlessly, without remuneration or reprieve, constantly subject to confinement, corporal punishment and death.

The textbook publishers were put in a difficult position. They had to teach history to Texas's children without challenging conservative political views that are at odds with history. In doing so, they made many grammatical choices. Though we don't always recognize it, grammatical choices can be moral choices, and these publishers made the wrong ones.

Topics for Critical Thinking and Writing

1. Ellen Rockmore begins by citing an example from a Texas schoolbook that refers to the slave trade as bringing "workers" (para. 1) to the American South. What is the difference between calling someone a "worker" and calling someone a "slave"? Why did the textbook use the term "worker," and in your opinion, what harm might the use of that word cause?

2. Look up in a dictionary the word "misnomer," cited in paragraph 1 by the publisher. Is that word used appropriately in this context? Why, or why not?

3. In paragraph 3, Rockmore notes that the new textbooks "downplay slavery as the cause of the Civil War." What might be the other causes of the Civil War? In your opinion, was slavery the principal cause of the war? Support your answer with specific details.

4. Rockmore observes that the Texas history books use two voices — active and passive — in different ways. The active voice, which requires a noun or pronoun to do an action, is used when writing positive statements about slavery. The passive voice, which does not need to show who did an action, is used when describing unpleasant facts about slavery. Why is the shift in voice important? What does it show about the writers' attitudes about the negative issues associated with slavery?

5. In paragraph 13, Rockmore states that the authors avoid mention of what slaves actually did: "toiling relentlessly, without remuneration or reprieve, constantly subject to confinement, corporal punishment, and death." In your opinion, why has this been omitted?

6. Consider the issue of audience: Who is the audience for these textbooks? Students? Teachers? Parents? Administrators? The general public? How does the issue of audience affect the way in which a text is written?

7. The adoption of a textbook by the Texas Board of Education can have an influence far beyond the borders of Texas. Research the influence that the Texas board has on the textbook adoption policies of other states, and argue how what Texas decides matters in classrooms around the country. Be specific.

PART SIX

Enduring Questions

Essays, a Story, Poems, and a Play

26

What Is the Ideal Society?

THOMAS MORE

The son of a prominent London lawyer, More (1478–1535) served as a page in the household of the Archbishop of Canterbury, went to Oxford University, and then studied law in London. More's charm, brilliance, and gentle manner caused Erasmus, the great Dutch humanist who became his friend during a visit to London, to write to a friend: "Did nature ever create anything kinder, sweeter, or more harmonious than the character of Thomas More?"

More served in Parliament, became a diplomat, and after holding several important positions in the government of Henry VIII, rose to become lord chancellor. But when Henry married Anne Boleyn, broke from the Church of Rome, and established himself as head of the Church of England, More refused to subscribe to the Act of Succession and Supremacy. Condemned to death as a traitor, he was executed in 1535, nominally for treason but really because he would not recognize the king rather than the pope as the head of his church. A moment before the ax fell, More displayed a bit of the whimsy for which he was known: When he put his head on the block, he brushed his beard aside, commenting that his beard had done no offense to the king. In 1886 the Roman Catholic Church beatified More, and in 1935, the four-hundredth anniversary of his death, it canonized him as St. Thomas More.

More wrote Utopia *(1514–1515) in Latin, the international language of the day. The book's name, however, is Greek for "no place" (ou topos), with a pun on "good place" (eu topos).* Utopia *owes something to Plato's* Republic *and something to then-popular accounts of voyagers such as Amerigo Vespucci.* Utopia *purports to record an account given by a traveler named Hytholodaeus (Greek for "learned in nonsense"), who allegedly visited Utopia. The work is playful, but it is also serious. In truth, it is hard to know exactly where it is serious and how serious it is. One inevitably wonders, for example, if More the devoted Roman Catholic could really have advocated euthanasia. And could More the persecutor of heretics really have approved of the religious tolerance practiced in Utopia? Is he perhaps in effect saying, "Let's see what reason, unaided by Christian revelation, can tell us about an ideal society"? But if so, is he nevertheless also saying, very strongly, that Christian countries, though blessed with the revelation of Christ's teachings, are far behind these unenlightened pagans? Utopia has been widely praised by all sorts of readers — from Roman Catholics to communists — but for all sorts of reasons. The selection presented here is about one-twelfth of the book (in a translation by Paul Turner).*

From *Utopia*

[A DAY IN UTOPIA]

And now for their working conditions. Well, there's one job they all do, irrespective of sex, and that's farming. It's part of every child's education. They learn the principles of agriculture at school, and they're taken for regular outings into the fields near the town, where they not only watch farm work being done, but also do some themselves, as a form of exercise.

Besides farming which, as I say, is everybody's job, each person is taught a special trade of his own. He may be trained to process wool or flax, or he may become a stonemason, a blacksmith, or a carpenter. Those are the only trades that employ any considerable quantity of labor. They have no tailors or dressmakers, since everyone on the island wears the same sort of clothes — except that they vary slightly according to sex and marital status — and the fashion never changes. These clothes are quite pleasant to look at, they allow free movement of the limbs, they're equally suitable for hot and cold weather — and the great thing is, they're all home-made. So everybody learns one of the other trades I mentioned, and by everybody I mean the women as well as the men — though the weaker sex are given the lighter jobs, like spinning and weaving, while the men do the heavier ones.

Most children are brought up to do the same work as their parents, since they tend to have a natural feeling for it. But if a child fancies some other trade, he's adopted into a family that practices it. Of course, great care is taken, not only by the father, but also by the local authorities, to see that the foster father is a decent, respectable type. When you've learned one trade properly, you can, if you like, get permission to learn another — and when you're an expert in both, you can practice whichever you prefer, unless the other one is more essential to the public.

The chief business of the Stywards[1] — in fact, practically their only business — is to see that nobody sits around doing nothing, but that everyone gets on with his job. They don't wear people out, though, by keeping them hard at work from early morning till late at night, like cart horses. That's just slavery — and yet that's what life is like for the working classes nearly everywhere else in the world. In Utopia they have a six-hour working day — three hours in the morning, then lunch — then a two-hour break — then three more hours in the afternoon, followed by supper. They go to bed at 8 P.M., and sleep for eight hours. All the rest of the twenty-four they're free to do what they like — not to waste their time in idleness or self-indulgence, but to make good use of it in some congenial

---

[1]**Stywards** In Utopia, each group of thirty households elects a styward; each town has two hundred stywards, who elect the mayor. [All notes are the editors'.]

activity. Most people spend these free periods on further education, for there are public lectures first thing every morning. Attendance is quite voluntary, except for those picked out for academic training, but men and women of all classes go crowding in to hear them — I mean, different people go to different lectures, just as the spirit moves them. However, there's nothing to stop you from spending this extra time on your trade, if you want to. Lots of people do, if they haven't the capacity for intellectual work, and are much admired for such public-spirited behavior.

After supper they have an hour's recreation, either in the gardens or in the communal dining-halls, according to the time of year. Some people practice music, others just talk. They've never heard of anything so silly and demoralizing as dice, but they have two games rather like chess. The first is a sort of arithmetical contest, in which certain numbers "take" others. The second is a pitched battle between virtues and vices, which illustrates most ingeniously how vices tend to conflict with one another, but to combine against virtues. It also shows which vices are opposed to which virtues, how much strength vices can muster for a direct assault, what indirect tactics they employ, what help virtues need to overcome vices, what are the best methods of evading their attacks, and what ultimately determines the victory of one side or the other.

But here's a point that requires special attention, or you're liable to get the wrong idea. Since they only work a six-hour day, you may think there must be a shortage of essential goods. On the contrary, those six hours are enough, and more than enough to produce plenty of everything that's needed for a comfortable life. And you'll understand why it is, if you reckon up how large a proportion of the population in other countries is totally unemployed. First you have practically all the women — that gives you nearly 50 percent for a start. And in countries where the women *do* work, the men tend to lounge about instead. Then there are all the priests, and members of so-called religious orders — how much work do they do? Add all the rich, especially the landowners, popularly known as nobles and gentlemen. Include their domestic staffs — I mean those gangs of armed ruffians that I mentioned before. Finally, throw in all the beggars who are perfectly hale and hearty, but pretend to be ill as an excuse for being lazy. When you've counted them up, you'll be surprised to find how few people actually produce what the human race consumes.

And now just think how few of these few people are doing essential work — for where money is the only standard of value, there are bound to be dozens of unnecessary trades carried on, which merely supply luxury goods or entertainment. Why, even if the existing labor force were distributed among the few trades really needed to make life reasonably comfortable, there'd be so much overproduction that prices would fall too low for the workers to earn a living. Whereas, if you took all those engaged in nonessential trades, and all who are too lazy to work — each of whom consumes twice as much of the products of other people's labor as any of the producers themselves — if you put the whole lot of them on to something useful, you'd soon see how few hours' work a day would be amply sufficient to supply all the necessities and comforts of life — to which you might add all real and natural forms of pleasure.

[THE HOUSEHOLD]

But let's get back to their social organization. Each household, as I said, comes under the authority of the oldest male. Wives are subordinate to their husbands, children to their parents, and younger people generally to their elders. Every town is divided into four districts of equal size, each with its own shopping center in the middle of it. There the products of every household are collected in warehouses, and then distributed according to type among various shops. When the head of a household needs anything for himself or his family, he just goes to one of these shops and asks for it. And whatever he asks for, he's allowed to take away without any sort of payment, either in money or in kind. After all, why shouldn't he? There's more than enough of everything to go round, so there's no risk of his asking for more than he needs — for why should anyone want to start hoarding, when he knows he'll never have to go short of anything? No living creature is naturally greedy, except from fear of want — or in the case of human beings, from vanity, the notion that you're better than people if you can display more superfluous property than they can. But there's no scope for that sort of thing in Utopia.

[UTOPIAN BELIEFS]

The Utopians fail to understand why anyone should be so fascinated by the dull gleam of a tiny bit of stone, when he has all the stars in the sky to look at — or how anyone can be silly enough to think himself better than other people, because his clothes are made of finer woollen thread than theirs. After all, those fine clothes were once worn by a sheep, and they never turned it into anything better than a sheep.

Nor can they understand why a totally 10 useless substance like gold should now, all over the world, be considered far more important than human beings, who gave it such value as it has, purely for their own convenience. The result is that a man with about as much mental agility as a lump of lead or a block of wood, a man whose utter stupidity is paralleled only by his immorality, can have lots of good, intelligent people at his beck and call, just because he happens to possess a large pile of gold coins. And if by some freak of fortune or trick of the law — two equally effective methods of turning things upside down — the said coins were suddenly transferred to the most worthless member of his domestic staff, you'd soon see the present owner trotting after his money, like an extra piece of currency, and becoming his own servant's servant. But what puzzles and disgusts the Utopians even more is the idiotic way some people have of practically worshipping a rich man, not because they owe him money or are otherwise in his power, but simply because he's rich — although they know perfectly well that he's far too mean to let a single penny come their way, so long as he's alive to stop it.

They get these ideas partly from being brought up under a social system which is directly opposed to that type of nonsense, and partly from their reading and education. Admittedly, no one's allowed to become a full-time student, except for the very few in each town who appear as children to possess unusual gifts, outstanding intelligence, and a special aptitude for academic research. But every child receives a primary education, and most men and women go on educating themselves all their lives during those free periods that I told you about. . . .

In ethics they discuss the same problems as we do. Having distinguished between three types of "good," psychological, physiological, and environmental, they proceed to ask whether the term is strictly applicable to all of them, or only to the first. They also argue about such things as virtue and pleasure. But their chief subject of dispute is the nature of human happiness—on what factor or factors does it depend? Here they seem rather too much inclined to take a hedonistic view, for according to them human happiness consists largely or wholly in pleasure. Surprisingly enough, they defend this self-indulgent doctrine by arguments drawn from religion—a thing normally associated with a more serious view of life, if not with gloomy asceticism. You see, in all their discussions of happiness they invoke certain religious principles to supplement the operations of reason, which they think otherwise ill-equipped to identify true happiness.

The first principle is that every soul is immortal, and was created by a kind God, Who meant it to be happy. The second is that we shall be rewarded or punished in the next world for our good or bad behavior in this one. Although these are religious principles, the Utopians find rational grounds for accepting them. For suppose you didn't accept them? In that case, they say, any fool could tell you what you ought to do. You should go all out for your own pleasure, irrespective of right and wrong. You'd merely have to make sure that minor pleasures didn't interfere with major ones, and avoid the type of pleasure that has painful aftereffects. For what's the sense of struggling to be virtuous, denying yourself the pleasant things of life, and deliberately making yourself uncomfortable, if there's nothing you hope to gain by it? And what *can* you hope to gain by it, if you receive no compensation after death for a thoroughly unpleasant, that is, a thoroughly miserable life?

Not that they identify happiness with every type of pleasure—only with the higher ones. Nor do they identify it with virtue—unless they belong to a quite different school of thought. According to the normal view, happiness is the *summum bonum*[2] toward which we're naturally impelled by virtue—which in their definition means following one's natural impulses, as God meant us to do. But this includes obeying the instinct to be reasonable in our likes and dislikes. And reason also teaches us, first to love and reverence Almighty God, to Whom we owe our existence and our potentiality for happiness, and secondly to get through life as comfortably and cheerfully as we can, and help all other members of our species to do so too.

The fact is, even the sternest ascetic tends 15 to be slightly inconsistent in his condemnation of pleasure. He may sentence *you* to a life of hard labor, inadequate sleep, and general discomfort, but he'll also tell you to do your best to ease the pains and privations of others. He'll regard all such attempts to improve the human situation as laudable acts of humanity—for obviously nothing could be more humane, or more natural for a human being, than to relieve other people's sufferings, put an end to their miseries, and restore their *joie de vivre*, that is, their capacity for pleasure. So why shouldn't it be equally natural to do the same thing for oneself?

Either it's a bad thing to enjoy life, in other words, to experience pleasure—in which case you shouldn't help anyone to do it, but should try to save the whole human race from such a frightful fate—or else, if it's good for other people, and you're not only allowed, but positively obliged to make it possible for them, why shouldn't charity begin at home?

---

[2]*summum bonum* Latin for "the highest good."

After all, you've a duty to yourself as well as to your neighbor, and, if Nature says you must be kind to others, she can't turn round the next moment and say you must be cruel to yourself. The Utopians therefore regard the enjoyment of life — that is, pleasure — as the natural object of all human efforts, and natural, as they define it, is synonymous with virtuous. However, Nature also wants us to help one another to enjoy life, for the very good reason that no human being has a monopoly of her affections. She's equally anxious for the welfare of every member of the species. So of course she tells us to make quite sure that we don't pursue our own interests at the expense of other people's.

On this principle they think it right to keep one's promises in private life, and also to obey public laws for regulating the distribution of "goods" — by which I mean the raw materials of pleasure — provided such laws have been properly made by a wise ruler, or passed by common consent of a whole population, which has not been subjected to any form of violence or deception. Within these limits they say it's sensible to consult one's own interests, and a moral duty to consult those of the community as well. It's wrong to deprive someone else of a pleasure so that you can enjoy one yourself, but to deprive yourself of a pleasure so that you can add to someone else's enjoyment is an act of humanity by which you always gain more than you lose. For one thing, such benefits are usually repaid in kind. For another, the mere sense of having done somebody a kindness, and so earned his affection and goodwill, produces a spiritual satisfaction which far outweighs the loss of a physical one. And lastly — a belief that comes easily to a religious mind — God will reward us for such small sacrifices of momentary pleasure, by giving us an eternity of perfect joy. Thus they

argue that, in the final analysis, pleasure is the ultimate happiness which all human beings have in view, even when they're acting most virtuously.

Pleasure they define as any state or activity, physical or mental, which is naturally enjoyable. The operative word is *naturally*. According to them, we're impelled by reason as well as an instinct to enjoy ourselves in any natural way which doesn't hurt other people, interfere with greater pleasures, or cause unpleasant after-effects. But human beings have entered into an idiotic conspiracy to call some things enjoyable which are naturally nothing of the kind — as though facts were as easily changed as definitions. Now the Utopians believe that, so far from contributing to happiness, this type of thing makes happiness impossible — because, once you get used to it, you lose all capacity for real pleasure, and are merely obsessed by illusory forms of it. Very often these have nothing pleasant about them at all — in fact, most of them are thoroughly disagreeable. But they appeal so strongly to perverted tastes that they come to be reckoned not only among the major pleasures of life, but even among the chief reasons for living.

In the category of illusory pleasure addicts they include the kind of person I mentioned before, who thinks himself better than other people because he's better dressed than they are. Actually he's just as wrong about his clothes as he is about himself. From a practical point of view, why is it better to be dressed in fine woollen thread than in coarse? But he's got it into his head that fine thread is naturally superior, and that wearing it somehow increases his own value. So he feels entitled to far more respect than he'd ever dare to hope for, if he were less expensively dressed, and is most indignant if he fails to get it.

Talking of respect, isn't it equally idiotic to [20] attach such importance to a lot of empty gestures which do nobody any good? For what real pleasure can you get out of the sight of a bared head or a bent knee? Will it cure the rheumatism in your own knee, or make you any less weak in the head? Of course, the great believers in this type of artificial pleasure are those who pride themselves on their "nobility." Nowadays that merely means that they happen to belong to a family which has been rich for several generations, preferably in landed property. And yet they feel every bit as "noble" even if they've failed to inherit any of the said property, or if they have inherited it and then frittered it all away.

Then there's another type of person I mentioned before, who has a passion for jewels, and feels practically superhuman if he manages to get hold of a rare one, especially if it's a kind that's considered particularly precious in his country and period — for the value of such things varies according to where and when you live. But he's so terrified of being taken in by appearances that he refuses to buy any jewel until he's stripped off all the gold and inspected it in the nude. And even then he won't buy it without a solemn assurance and a written guarantee from the jeweler that the stone is genuine. But my dear sir, why shouldn't a fake give you just as much pleasure, if you can't, with your own eyes, distinguish it from a real one? It makes no difference to you whether it's genuine or not — any more than it would to a blind man!

And now, what about those people who accumulate superfluous wealth, for no better purpose than to enjoy looking at it? Is their pleasure a real one, or merely a form of delusion? The opposite type of psychopath buries his gold, so that he'll never be able to use it, and may never even see it again. In fact, he deliberately loses it in his anxiety not to lose it — for what can you call it but lost, when it's put back into the earth, where it's no good to him, or probably to anyone else? And yet he's tremendously happy when he's got it stowed away. Now, apparently, he can stop worrying. But suppose the money is stolen, and ten years later he dies without ever knowing it has gone. Then for a whole ten years he has managed to survive his loss, and during that period what difference has it made to him whether the money was there or not? It was just as little use to him either way.

Among stupid pleasures they include not only gambling — a form of idiocy that they've heard about but never practiced — but also hunting and hawking. What on earth is the fun, they ask, of throwing dice onto a table? Besides, you've done it so often that, even if there was some fun in it at first, you must surely be sick of it by now. How can you possibly enjoy listening to anything so disagreeable as the barking and howling of dogs? And why is it more amusing to watch a dog chasing a hare than to watch one dog chasing another? In each case the essential activity is running — if running is what amuses you. But if it's really the thought of being in at the death, and seeing an animal torn to pieces before your eyes, wouldn't pity be a more appropriate reaction to the sight of a weak, timid, harmless little creature like a hare being devoured by something so much stronger and fiercer?

So the Utopians consider hunting below the dignity of free men, and leave it entirely to butchers, who are, as I told you, slaves. In their view hunting is the vilest department of butchery, compared with which all the others are relatively useful and honorable. An ordinary butcher slaughters livestock far more sparingly, and only because he has to, whereas a hunter kills and mutilates poor little creatures purely for his own amusement. They say you won't find that type of blood lust even among animals, unless they're particularly savage by nature, or have become so by constantly being used for this cruel sport.

There are hundreds of things like that, which are generally regarded as pleasures, but everyone in Utopia is quite convinced that they've got nothing to do with real pleasure, because there's nothing naturally enjoyable about them. Nor is this conviction at all shaken by the argument that most people do actually enjoy them, which would seem to indicate an appreciable pleasure content. They say this is a purely subjective reaction caused by bad habits, which can make a person prefer unpleasant things to pleasant ones, just as pregnant women sometimes lose their sense of taste, and find suet or turpentine more delicious than honey. But however much one's judgment may be impaired by habit or ill health, the nature of pleasure, as of everything else, remains unchanged.

Real pleasures they divide into two categories, mental and physical. Mental pleasures include the satisfaction that one gets from understanding something, or from contemplating truth. They also include the memory of a well-spent life, and the confident expectation of good things to come. Physical pleasures are subdivided into two types. First there are those which fill the whole organism with a conscious sense of enjoyment. This may be the result of replacing physical substances which have been burnt up by the natural heat of the body, as when we eat or drink. Or else it may be caused by the discharge of some excess, as in excretion, sexual intercourse, or any relief of irritation by rubbing or scratching. However, there are also pleasures which satisfy no organic need, and relieve no previous discomfort. They merely act, in a mysterious but quite unmistakable way, directly on our senses, and monopolize their reactions. Such is the pleasure of music.

Their second type of physical pleasure arises from the calm and regular functioning of the body — that is, from a state of health undisturbed by any minor ailments. In the absence of mental discomfort, this gives one a good feeling, even without the help of external pleasures. Of course, it's less ostentatious, and forces itself less violently on one's attention than the cruder delights of eating and drinking, but even so it's often considered the greatest pleasure in life. Practically everyone in Utopia would agree that it's a very important one, because it's the basis of all the others. It's enough by itself to make you enjoy life, and unless you have it, no other pleasure is possible. However, mere freedom from pain, without positive health, they would call not pleasure but anesthesia.

Some thinkers used to maintain that a uniformly tranquil state of health couldn't properly be termed a pleasure since its presence could only be detected by contrast with its opposite — oh yes, they went very thoroughly into the whole question. But that theory was exploded long ago, and nowadays nearly everybody subscribes to the view that health is most definitely a pleasure. The argument goes like this — illness involves pain, which is the direct opposite of pleasure, and illness is the direct opposite of health, therefore health involves pleasure. They don't think it matters whether you say that illness *is* or merely *involves* pain. Either way it comes to the same thing. Similarly, whether health *is* a pleasure, or merely *produces* pleasure as inevitably as fire produces heat, it's equally logical to assume that where you have an uninterrupted state of health you cannot fail to have pleasure.

Besides, they say, when we eat something, what really happens is this. Our failing health starts fighting off the attacks of hunger, using the food as an ally. Gradually it begins to prevail, and, in this very process of winning back its normal strength, experiences the sense of enjoyment which we find so refreshing. Now, if health enjoys the actual battle, why shouldn't it also enjoy the victory? Or are we to suppose that when it has finally managed to regain its former vigor — the one thing that it has been fighting for all this time — it promptly falls into a coma, and fails to notice or take advantage of its success? As for the idea that one isn't conscious of health except through its opposite, they say that's quite untrue. Everyone's perfectly aware of feeling well, unless he's asleep or actually feeling ill. Even the most insensitive and apathetic sort of person will admit that it's delightful to be healthy — and what is delight, but a synonym for pleasure?

They're particularly fond of mental plea- 30 sures, which they consider of primary importance, and attribute mostly to good behavior and a clear conscience. Their favorite physical pleasure is health. Of course, they believe in enjoying food, drink, and so forth, but purely in the interests of health, for they don't regard such things as very pleasant in themselves — only as methods of resisting the stealthy onset of disease. A sensible person, they say, prefers keeping well to taking medicine, and would rather feel cheerful than have people trying to comfort him. On the same principle it's better not to need this type of pleasure than to become addicted to it. For, if you think that sort of thing will make you happy, you'll have to admit that your idea of perfect felicity would be a life consisting entirely of hunger, thirst, itching, eating, drinking, rubbing, and scratching — which would obviously be most unpleasant as well as quite disgusting.

Undoubtedly these pleasures should come right at the bottom of the list, because they're so impure. For instance, the pleasure of eating is invariably diluted with the pain of hunger, and not in equal proportions either — for the pain is both more intense and more prolonged. It starts before the pleasure, and doesn't stop until the pleasure has stopped too.

So they don't think much of pleasures like that, except insofar as they're necessary. But they enjoy them all the same, and feel most grateful to Mother Nature for encouraging her children to do things that have to be done so often, by making them so attractive. For just think how dreary life would be, if those chronic ailments, hunger and thirst, could only be cured by foul-tasting medicines, like the rarer types of disease!

They attach great value to special natural gifts such as beauty, strength, and agility. They're also keen on the pleasures of sight, hearing, and smell, which are peculiar to human beings — for no other species admires the beauty of the world, enjoys any sort of scent, except as a method of locating food, or can tell the difference between a harmony and a discord. They say these things give a sort of relish to life.

However, in all such matters they observe the rule that minor pleasures mustn't interfere with major ones, and that pleasure mustn't cause pain — which they think is bound to happen, if the pleasure is immoral. But they'd never dream of despising their own beauty, overtaxing their strength, converting their agility into inertia, ruining their physique by going without food, damaging their health, or spurning any other of Nature's gifts, unless they were doing it for the benefit of other people or of society, in the hope of receiving some greater pleasure from God in return. For they think it's quite absurd to torment oneself in the name of an unreal virtue, which does nobody any good, or in order to steel oneself against disasters which may never occur. They say such behavior is merely self-destructive, and shows a most ungrateful attitude toward Nature — as if one refused all her favors, because one couldn't bear the thought of being indebted to her for anything.

Well, that's their ethical theory, and short of some divine revelation, they doubt if the human mind is capable of devising a better one. We've no time to discuss whether it's right or wrong — nor is it really necessary, for all I undertook was to describe their way of life, not to defend it.

[TREATMENT OF THE DYING]

As I told you, when people are ill, they're 35 looked after most sympathetically, and given everything in the way of medicine or special food that could possibly assist their recovery. In the case of permanent invalids, the nurses try to make them feel better by sitting and talking to them, and do all they can to relieve their symptoms. But if, besides being incurable, the disease also causes constant excruciating pain, some priests and government officials visit the person concerned, and say something like this:

"Let's face it, you'll never be able to live a normal life. You're just a nuisance to other people and a burden to yourself — in fact you're really leading a sort of posthumous existence. So why go on feeding germs? Since your life's a misery to you, why hesitate to die? You're imprisoned in a torture chamber — why don't you break out and escape to a better world? Or say the word, and we'll arrange for your release. It's only common sense to cut your losses. It's also an act of piety to take the advice of a priest, because he speaks for God."

If the patient finds these arguments convincing, he either starves himself to death, or is given a soporific and put painlessly out of his misery. But this is strictly voluntary, and, if he prefers to stay alive, everyone will go on treating him as kindly as ever.

[THE SUMMING UP]

Well, that's the most accurate account I can give you of the Utopian Republic. To my mind, it's not only the best country in the world, but the only one that has any right to call itself a republic. Elsewhere, people are always talking about the public interest, but all they really care about is private property. In Utopia, where's there's no private property, people take their duty to the public seriously. And both attitudes are perfectly reasonable. In other "republics" practically everyone knows that, if he doesn't look out for himself, he'll starve to death, however prosperous his country may be. He's therefore compelled to give his own interests priority over those of the public; that is, of other people. But in Utopia, where everything's under public ownership, no one has any fear of going short, as long as the public storehouses are full. Everyone gets a fair share, so there are never any poor men or beggars. Nobody owns anything, but everyone is rich — for what greater wealth can there be than cheerfulness, peace of mind, and freedom from anxiety? Instead of being worried about his food supply, upset by the plaintive demands of his wife, afraid of poverty for his son, and baffled by the problem of finding a dowry for his daughter, the Utopian can feel absolutely sure that he, his wife, his children, his grandchildren, his great-grandchildren, his great-great-grandchildren, and as long a line of descendants as the proudest peer could wish to look forward to, will always have enough to eat and enough to make them happy. There's also the further point that those who are too old to work are just as well provided for as those who are still working.

Now, will anyone venture to compare these fair arrangements in Utopia with the so-called justice of other countries? — in which I'm damned if I can see the slightest trace of justice or fairness. For what sort of justice do you call this? People like aristocrats, goldsmiths, or moneylenders, who either do no work at all, or do work that's really not essential, are rewarded for their laziness or their unnecessary activities by a splendid life of luxury. But laborers, coachmen, carpenters, and farmhands, who never stop working like cart horses, at jobs so essential that, if they *did* stop working, they'd bring any country to a standstill within twelve months — what happens to them? They get so little to eat, and have such a wretched time, that they'd be almost better off if they *were* cart horses. Then at least, they wouldn't work quite such long hours, their food wouldn't be very much worse, they'd enjoy it more, and they'd have no fears for the future. As it is, they're not only ground down by unrewarding toil in the present, but also worried to death by the prospect of a poverty-stricken old age — since their daily wages aren't enough to support them for one day, let alone leave anything over to be saved up when they're old.

Can you see any fairness or gratitude in ⁴⁰ a social system which lavishes such great rewards on so-called noblemen, goldsmiths, and people like that, who are either totally unproductive or merely employed in producing luxury goods or entertainment, but makes no such kind provision for farmhands, coal heavers, laborers, carters, or carpenters, without whom society couldn't exist at all? And the climax of ingratitude comes when

they're old and ill and completely destitute. Having taken advantage of them throughout the best years of their lives, society now forgets all the sleepless hours they've spent in its service, and repays them for all the vital work they've done, by letting them die in misery. What's more, the wretched earnings of the poor are daily whittled away by the rich, not only through private dishonesty, but through public legislation. As if it weren't unjust enough already that the man who contributes most to society should get the least in return, they make it even worse, and then arrange for injustice to be legally described as justice.

In fact, when I consider any social system that prevails in the modern world, I can't, so help me God, see it as anything but a conspiracy of the rich to advance their own interests under the pretext of organizing society. They think up all sorts of tricks and dodges, first for keeping safe their ill-gotten gains, and then for exploiting the poor by buying their labor as cheaply as possible. Once the rich have decided that these tricks and dodges shall be officially recognized by society — which includes the poor as well as the rich — they acquire the force of law. Thus an unscrupulous minority is led by its insatiable greed to monopolize what would have been enough to supply the needs of the whole population. And yet how much happier even these people would be in Utopia! There, with the simultaneous abolition of money and the passion for money, how many other social problems have been solved, how many crimes eradicated! For obviously the end of money means the end of all those types of criminal behavior which daily punishments are powerless to check: fraud, theft, burglary, brawls, riots, disputes, rebellion, murder, treason, and black magic. And the moment money goes, you can also say goodbye to fear, tension, anxiety, over-work, and sleepless nights. Why, even poverty itself, the one problem that has always seemed to need money for its solution, would promptly disappear if money ceased to exist.

Let me try to make this point clearer. Just think back to one of the years when the harvest was bad, and thousands of people died of starvation. Well, I bet if you'd inspected every rich man's barn at the end of that lean period you'd have found enough corn to have saved all the lives that were lost through malnutrition and disease, and prevented anyone from suffering any ill effects whatever from the meanness of the weather and the soil. Everyone could so easily get enough to eat, if it weren't for that blessed nuisance, money. There you have a brilliant invention which was designed to make food more readily available. Actually it's the only thing that makes it unobtainable.

I'm sure that even the rich are well aware of all this, and realize how much better it would be to have everything one needed, than lots of things one didn't need — to be evacuated altogether from the danger area, than to dig oneself in behind a barricade of enormous wealth. And I've no doubt that either self-interest, or the authority of our Savior Christ — Who was far too wise not to know what was best for us, and far too kind to recommend anything else — would have led the whole world to adopt the Utopian system long ago, if it weren't for that beastly root of all evils, pride. For pride's criterion of prosperity is not what you've got yourself, but what other people haven't got. Pride would refuse to set foot in paradise, if she thought there'd be no underprivileged classes there to gloat over and order about — nobody whose misery could serve as a foil to her own happiness, or whose poverty she could make harder to bear, by flaunting her own riches. Pride, like a hellish serpent gliding through human hearts — or shall we say, like a sucking-fish that clings to the ship of state? — is always dragging us back, and obstructing our progress toward a better way of life.

But as this fault is too deeply ingrained in human nature to be easily eradicated, I'm glad that at least one country has managed to develop a system which I'd like to see universally adopted. The Utopian way of life provides not only the happiest basis for a civilized community, but also one which, in all human probability, will last forever. They've eliminated the root causes of ambition, political conflict, and everything like that. There's therefore no danger of internal dissension, the one thing that has destroyed so many impregnable towns. And as long as there's unity and sound administration at home, no matter how envious neighboring kings may feel, they'll never be able to shake, let alone to shatter, the power of Utopia. They've tried to do so often enough in the past, but have always been beaten back.

Topics for Critical Thinking and Writing

1. Thomas More, writing early in the sixteenth century, was living in a primarily agricultural society. Laborers were needed on farms, but might More have had any other reason for insisting (para. 1) that all people should do some farming and that farming should be "part of every child's education"? Do you think everyone should put in some time as a farmer? Why, or why not?

2. More indicates that in the England of his day many people loafed or engaged in unnecessary work (producing luxury goods, for one thing), putting an enormous burden on those who engaged in useful work. Is this condition, or any part of it, true of our society? Explain.

3. The Utopians cannot understand why the people of other nations value gems, gold, and fine clothes. If you value any of these, can you offer an explanation?

4. What arguments can you offer against the Utopians' treatment of persons who are incurably ill and in pain?

5. Take three or four paragraphs to summarize More's report of the Utopians' idea of pleasure.

6. More's Utopians cannot understand why anyone takes pleasure in gambling or in hunting. If either activity gives you pleasure, in an essay of 500 words explain why, and offer an argument on behalf of your view.

7. As More makes clear in the part we entitle "The Summing Up," in Utopia there is no private property. In a sentence or two summarize the reasons he gives for this principle, and then in a paragraph evaluate them.

NICCOLÒ MACHIAVELLI

Niccolò Machiavelli (1469–1527) was born in Florence at a time when Italy was divided into five major states: Venice, Milan, Florence, the Papal States, and Naples. Although these states often had belligerent relations with one another as well as with lesser Italian states, under the Medici family in Florence they achieved a precarious balance of power. In 1494, however, Lorenzo de' Medici, who had ruled from 1469 to 1492, died, and two years later Lorenzo's successor was exiled when the French army arrived in Florence. Italy became a field where Spain, France, and Germany competed for power. From 1498 to 1512 Machiavelli held a high post in the diplomatic service of the Florentine Republic, but when the French army reappeared and the Florentines in desperation recalled the Medici, Machiavelli lost his post, was imprisoned, tortured, and then exiled. Banished from Florence, he nevertheless lived in comfort on a small estate nearby, writing his major works and hoping to obtain an office from the Medici. In later years he was employed in a few minor diplomatic missions, but even after the collapse and expulsion of the Medici in 1527 and the restoration of the republic, he did not regain his old position of importance. He died shortly after the restoration.

Our selection comes from The Prince, *which Machiavelli wrote in 1513 during his banishment, hoping that it would interest the Medici and thus restore him to favor; but the book was not published until 1532, five years after his death. In this book of twenty-six short chapters, Machiavelli begins by examining different kinds of states, but the work's enduring power resides in the discussions (in Chapters 15–18, reprinted here) of qualities necessary to a prince — that is, a head of state. Any such examination obviously is based in part on assumptions about the nature of the citizens of the realm.*

This selection was taken from a translation by W. K. Marriott.

From *The Prince*

CONCERNING THINGS FOR WHICH MEN, AND ESPECIALLY PRINCES, ARE PRAISED OR BLAMED

It remains now to see what ought to be the rules of conduct for a prince towards subject and friends. And as I know that many have written on this point, I expect I shall be considered presumptuous in mentioning it again, especially as in discussing it I shall depart from the methods of other people. But, it being my intention to write a thing which shall be useful to him who apprehends it, it appears to me more appropriate to follow up the real truth of the matter than the imagination of it; for many have pictured republics and principalities which in fact have never been known or seen, because how one lives is so far distant from how one ought to live, that he who neglects what is done for what ought to be done, sooner effects his ruin than his preservation; for a man who wishes to act entirely up to his professions of virtue soon meets with what destroys him among so much that is evil.

Hence it is necessary for a prince wishing to hold his own to know how to do wrong, and to make use of it or not according to necessity. Therefore, putting on one side imaginary things concerning a prince, and discussing those which are real, I say that all men when they are spoken of, and chiefly princes for being more highly placed, are remarkable for some of those qualities which bring them either blame or praise; and thus it is that one is reputed liberal, another miserly, using a Tuscan term (because an avaricious person in our language is still he who desires to possess by robbery, whilst we call one miserly who deprives himself too much of the use of his own); one is reputed generous, one rapacious; one cruel, one compassionate; one faithless, another faithful; one effeminate and cowardly, another bold and brave; one affable, another haughty; one lascivious, another chaste; one sincere, another cunning; one hard, another easy; one grave, another frivolous; one religious, another unbelieving, and the like. And I know that everyone will confess that it would be most praiseworthy in a prince to exhibit all the above qualities that are considered good; but because they can neither be entirely possessed nor observed, for human conditions do not permit it, it is necessary for him to be sufficiently prudent that he may know how to avoid the reproach of those vices which would lose him his state; and also to keep himself, if it be possible, from those which would not lose him it; but this not being possible, he may with less hesitation abandon himself to them. And again, he need not make himself uneasy at incurring a reproach for those vices without which the state can only be saved with difficulty, for if everything is considered carefully, it will be found that something which looks like virtue, if followed, would be his ruin; whilst something else, which looks like vice, yet followed brings him security and prosperity.

CONCERNING LIBERALITY AND MEANNESS

Commencing then with the first of the above-named characteristics, I say that it would be well to be reputed liberal.

Like Obama?. how so?. too.

Nevertheless, liberality exercised in a way that does not bring you the reputation for it, injures you; for if one exercises it honestly and as it should be exercised, it may not become known, and you will not avoid the reproach of its opposite. Therefore, anyone wishing to maintain among men the name of liberal is obliged to avoid no attribute of magnificence; so that a prince thus inclined will consume in such acts all his property, and will be compelled in the end, if he wish to maintain the name of liberal, to unduly weigh down his people, and tax them, and do everything he can to get money. This will soon make him odious to his subjects, and becoming poor he will be little valued by anyone; thus, with his liberality, having offended many and rewarded few, he is affected by the very first trouble and imperiled by whatever may be the first danger; recognizing this himself, and wishing to draw back from it, he runs at once into the reproach of being miserly.

Therefore, a prince, not being able to exercise this virtue of liberality in such a way that it is recognized, except to his cost, if he is wise he ought not to fear the reputation of being mean, for in time he will come to be more considered than if liberal, seeing that with his economy his revenues are enough, that he can defend himself against all attacks, and is able to engage in enterprises without burdening his people; thus it comes to pass that he exercises liberality towards all from whom he does not take, who are numberless, and meanness towards those to whom he does not give, who are few.

Do this matter for the area?

We have not seen great things done in our 5 time except by those who have been considered mean; the rest have failed. Pope Julius the Second was assisted in reaching the papacy by a reputation for liberality, yet he did not strive afterwards to keep it up, when he made war on the King of France; and he made many wars without imposing any extraordinary tax on his subjects, for he supplied his additional expenses out of his long thriftiness. The present King of Spain would not have undertaken or conquered in so many enterprises if he had been reputed liberal. A prince, therefore, provided that he has not to rob his subjects, that he can defend himself, that he does not become poor and abject, that he is not forced to become rapacious, ought to hold of little account a reputation for being mean, for it is one of those vices which will enable him to govern.

And if anyone should say: Caesar obtained empire by liberality, and many others have reached the highest positions by having been liberal, and by being considered so, I answer: Either you are a prince in fact, or in a way to become one. In the first case this liberality is dangerous, in the second it is very necessary to be considered liberal; and Caesar was one of those who wished to become pre-eminent in Rome; but if he had survived after becoming so, and had not moderated his expenses, he would have destroyed his government. And if anyone should reply: Many have been princes, and have done great things with armies, who have been considered very liberal, I reply: Either a prince spends that which is his own or his subjects' or else that of others. In the first case he ought to be sparing, in the second he ought not to neglect any opportunity for liberality. And to the prince who goes forth with his army, supporting it by pillage, sack, and extortion, handling that which belongs to others, this liberality is necessary, otherwise he would not be followed by soldiers. And of that which is neither yours nor your subjects' you can be a ready giver, as were Cyrus, Caesar, and Alexander; because it does not take away your

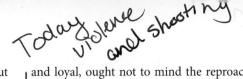

reputation if you squander that of others, but adds to it; it is only squandering your own that injures you.

And there is nothing wastes so rapidly as liberality, for even whilst you exercise it you lose the power to do so, and so become either poor or despised, or else, in avoiding poverty, rapacious and hated. And a prince should guard himself, above all things, against being despised and hated; and liberality leads you to both. Therefore it is wiser to have a reputation for meanness which brings reproach without hatred, than to be compelled through seeking a reputation for liberality to incur a name for rapacity which begets reproach with hatred.

CONCERNING CRUELTY AND CLEMENCY, AND WHETHER IT IS BETTER TO BE LOVED THAN FEARED

Coming now to the other qualities mentioned above, I say that every prince ought to desire to be considered clement and not cruel. Nevertheless he ought to take care not to misuse this clemency. Cesare Borgia[1] was considered cruel; notwithstanding, his cruelty reconciled the Romagna, unified it, and restored it to peace and loyalty. And if this be rightly considered, he will be seen to have been much more merciful than the Florentine people, who, to avoid a reputation for cruelty, permitted Pistoia[2] to be destroyed. Therefore a prince, so long as he keeps his subjects united

Dictator?

and loyal, ought not to mind the reproach of cruelty; because with a few examples he will be more merciful than those who, through too much mercy, allow disorders to arise, from which follow murders or robberies; for these are wont to injure the whole people, whilst those executions which originate with a prince offend the individual only.

And of all princes, it is impossible for the new prince to avoid the imputation of cruelty, owing to new states being full of dangers. Hence Virgil, through the mouth of Dido, excuses the inhumanity of her reign owing to its being new, saying, "against my will, my fate / A throne unsettled, and an infant state, / Bid me defend my realms with all my pow'rs, / And guard with these severities my shores."[3] Nevertheless, he ought to be slow to believe and to act, nor should he himself show fear, but proceed in a temperate manner with prudence and humanity, so that too much confidence may not make him incautious and too much distrust render him intolerable.

Upon this a question arises: whether it be better to be loved than feared or feared than loved? It may be answered that one should wish to be both, but, because it is difficult to unite them in one person, it is much safer to be feared than loved, when, of the two, either must be dispensed with. Because this is to be asserted in general of men, that they are ungrateful, fickle, false, cowardly, covetous, and as long as you succeed they are yours entirely; they will offer you their blood, property, life, and children, as is said above, when the need is far distant; but when it approaches they turn against you. And that prince who, relying entirely on their promises, has neglected other precautions, is ruined; because friendships that are obtained by

---

[1] **Cesare Borgia** The son of Pope Alexander VI, Cesare Borgia (1476–1507) was ruthlessly opportunistic. Encouraged by his father, in 1499 and 1500 he subdued the cities of Romagna, the region including Ferrara and Ravenna. [All notes are the editors'.]

[2] **Pistoia** A town near Florence; Machiavelli suggests that the Florentines failed to treat dissenting leaders with sufficient severity.

[3] In *Aeneid* I, 563–64, **Virgil** (70–19 B.C.) puts this line into the mouth of **Dido**, the queen of Carthage.

payments, and not by greatness or nobility of mind, may indeed be earned, but they are not secured, and in time of need cannot be relied upon; and men have less scruple in offending one who is beloved than one who is feared, for love is preserved by the link of obligation which, owing to the baseness of men, is broken at every opportunity for their advantage; but fear preserves you by a dread of punishment which never fails.

Nevertheless, a prince ought to inspire fear in such a way that, if he does not win love, he avoids hatred; because he can endure very well being feared whilst he is not hated, which will always be as long as he abstains from the property of his citizens and subjects and from their women. But when it is necessary for him to proceed against the life of someone, he must do it on proper justification and for manifest cause, but above all things he must keep his hands off the property of others, because men more quickly forget the death of their father than the loss of their patrimony. Besides, pretexts for taking away the property are never wanting; for he who has once begun to live by robbery will always find pretexts for seizing what belongs to others; but reasons for taking life, on the contrary, are more difficult to find and sooner lapse. But when a prince is with his army, and has under control a multitude of soldiers, then it is quite necessary for him to disregard the reputation of cruelty, for without it he would never hold his army united or disposed to its duties.

Among the wonderful deeds of Hannibal[4] this one is enumerated: that having led an enormous army, composed of many various races of men, to fight in foreign lands, no dissensions arose either among them or against

the prince, whether in his bad or in his good fortune. This arose from nothing else than his inhuman cruelty, which, with his boundless valor, made him revered and terrible in the sight of his soldiers, but without that cruelty, his other virtues were not sufficient to produce this effect. And short-sighted writers admire his deeds from one point of view and from another condemn the principal cause of them. That it is true his other virtues would not have been sufficient for him may be proved by the case of Scipio,[5] that most excellent man, not only of his own times but within the memory of man, against whom, nevertheless, his army rebelled in Spain; this arose from nothing but his too great forbearance, which gave his soldiers more license than is consistent with military discipline. For this he was upbraided in the Senate by Fabius Maximus, and called the corrupter of the Roman soldiery. The Locrians were laid waste by a legate of Scipio, yet they were not avenged by him, nor was the insolence of the legate punished, owing entirely to his easy nature. Insomuch that someone in the Senate, wishing to excuse him, said there were many men who knew much better how not to err than to correct the errors of others. This disposition, if he had been continued in the command, would have destroyed in time the fame and glory of Scipio; but, he being under the control of the Senate, this injurious characteristic not only concealed itself, but contributed to his glory.

Returning to the question of being feared or loved, I come to the conclusion that, men loving according to their own will and fearing according to that of the prince, a wise prince should establish himself on that which is in

---

[4]**Hannibal** The Carthaginian general (247–183 B.C.) whose crossing of the Alps with elephants and full baggage train is one of the great feats of military history.

[5]**Scipio** Publius Cornelius Scipio Africanus the Elder (235–183 B.C.), the conqueror of Hannibal in the Punic Wars. The mutiny of which Machiavelli speaks took place in 206 B.C.

his own control and not in that of others; he must endeavor only to avoid hatred, as is noted.

CONCERNING THE WAY IN WHICH PRINCES SHOULD KEEP FAITH

Everyone admits how praiseworthy it is in a prince to keep faith, and to live with integrity and not with craft. Nevertheless our experience has been that those princes who have done great things have held good faith of little account, and have known how to circumvent the intellect of men by craft, and in the end have overcome those who have relied on their word. You must know there are two ways of contesting, the one by the law, the other by force; the first method is proper to men, the second to beasts; but because the first is frequently not sufficient, it is necessary to have recourse to the second. Therefore it is necessary for a prince to understand how to avail himself of the beast and the man. This has been figuratively taught to princes by ancient writers, who describe how Achilles and many other princes of old were given to the Centaur Chiron[6] to nurse, who brought them up in his discipline; which means solely that, as they had for a teacher one who was half beast and half man, so it is necessary for a prince to know how to make use of both natures, and that one without the other is not durable. A prince, therefore, being compelled knowingly to adopt the beast, ought to choose the fox and the lion; because the lion cannot defend himself against snares and the fox cannot defend himself against wolves. Therefore, it is necessary to be a fox to discover the snares and a lion to terrify the wolves. Those who rely simply on the lion do not understand what they are about. Therefore a wise lord cannot, nor ought he to, keep faith when such observance may be turned against him, and when the reasons that caused him to pledge it exist no longer. If men were entirely good this precept would not hold, but because they are bad, and will not keep faith with you, you too are not bound to observe it with them. Nor will there ever be wanting to a prince legitimate reasons to excuse this non-observance. Of this endless modern examples could be given, showing how many treaties and engagements have been made void and of no effect through the faithlessness of princes; and he who has known best how to employ the fox has succeeded best.

But it is necessary to know well how to disguise this characteristic, and to be a great pretender and dissembler; and men are so simple, and so subject to present necessities, that he who seeks to deceive will always find someone who will allow himself to be deceived. One recent example I cannot pass over in silence. Alexander the Sixth[7] did nothing else but deceive men, nor ever thought of doing otherwise, and he always found victims; for there never was a man who had greater power in asserting, or who with greater oaths would affirm a thing, yet would observe it less; nevertheless his deceits always succeeded according to his wishes, because he well understood this side of mankind.

Therefore it is unnecessary for a prince to have all the good qualities I have enumerated,

---

[6]**Chiron** (Kĭ'ron) A centaur (half man, half horse) who was said in classical mythology to have been the teacher not only of Achilles but also of Theseus, Jason, Hercules, and other heroes.

[7]**Alexander the Sixth** Pope from 1492 to 1503; father of Cesare Borgia.

but it is very necessary to appear to have them. And I shall dare to say this also, that to have them and always to observe them is injurious, and that to appear to have them is useful; to appear merciful, faithful, humane, religious, upright, and to be so, but with a mind so framed that should you require not to be so, you may be able and know how to change to the opposite. And you have to understand this, that a prince, especially a new one, cannot observe all those things for which men are esteemed, being often forced, in order to maintain the state, to act contrary to fidelity, friendship, humanity, and religion. Therefore it is necessary for him to have a mind ready to turn itself accordingly as the winds and variations of fortune force it, yet, as I have said above, not to diverge from the good if he can avoid doing so, but, if compelled, then to know how to set about it.

For this reason a prince ought to take care that he never lets anything slip from his lips that is not replete with the above-named five qualities, that he may appear to him who sees and hears him altogether merciful, faithful, humane, upright, and religious. There is nothing more necessary to appear to have than this last quality, inasmuch as men judge generally more by the eye than by the hand, because it belongs to everybody to see you, to few to come in touch with you. Everyone sees what you appear to be, few really know what you are, and those few dare not oppose themselves to the opinion of the many, who have the majesty of the state to defend them; and in the actions of all men, and especially of princes, which it is not prudent to challenge, one judges by the result.[8]

For that reason, let a prince have the credit of conquering and holding his state, the means will always be considered honest, and he will be praised by everybody; because the vulgar are always taken by what a thing seems to be and by what comes of it; and in the world there are only the vulgar, for the few find a place there only when the many have no ground to rest on. One prince of the present time, whom it is not well to name, never preaches anything else but peace and good faith, and to both he is most hostile, and either, if he had kept it, would have deprived him of reputation and kingdom many a time.

---

[8] **one judges by the result** The original Italian, *si guarda al fine*, has often been translated erroneously as "the ends justify the means." Though this saying is often attributed to Machiavelli, he never actually wrote it.

Topics for Critical Thinking and Writing

1. In the opening paragraph, Niccolò Machiavelli claims that a ruler who wishes to keep in power must "know how to do wrong" — that is, must know where and when to ignore the demands of conventional morality. In the rest of the excerpt, does he give any convincing evidence to support this claim? Can you think of any recent political event in which a political leader violated the requirements of morality, as Machiavelli advises? Explain your response.

2. Machiavelli says in paragraph 2 that "a man who wishes to act entirely up to his professions of virtue soon meets with what destroys him among so much that is evil." (By the way, the passage is ambiguous. "Entirely" is, in the original, a squinting modifier. It may look

backward to a man acting on his "professions of virtue" or forward to "destroys him," but Machiavelli probably means that a man who at all times wishes to make a profession of being good will come to ruin among so many who are not good.) Is this view realistic or cynical? (What is the difference between these two?) Assume for the moment that the view is realistic. Does it follow that society requires a ruler who must act according to the principles Machiavelli sets forth? Explain your response.

3. In paragraph 2, Machiavelli claims that it is impossible for a ruler to exhibit *all* the conventional virtues (trustworthiness, liberality, and so on). Why does he make this claim? Do you agree with it? Why, or why not?

4. In paragraph 5, Machiavelli cites as examples Pope Julius the Second, the king of France, the king of Spain, and other rulers. Is he using these examples to illustrate his generalizations or to provide evidence for them? If you think he is using them to provide evidence, how convincing do you find the evidence? (Consider: Could Machiavelli be arguing from a biased sample?)

5. In paragraphs 8 to 13, Machiavelli argues that it is sometimes necessary for a ruler to be cruel, and so he praises Cesare Borgia and Hannibal. What in human nature, according to Machiavelli, explains this need to have recourse to cruelty? (By the way, how do you think *cruelty* should be defined here?)

6. Machiavelli says that Cesare Borgia's cruelty brought peace to Romagna and that, in contrast, the Florentines who sought to avoid being cruel in fact brought pain to Pistoia. Can you think of recent episodes supporting the view that cruelty can be beneficial to society? If so, restate Machiavelli's position, using these examples from recent history. Then go on to write two paragraphs, arguing on behalf of your two examples. Or if you believe that Machiavelli's point here is fundamentally wrong, explain why, again using current examples.

7. In *The Prince,* Machiavelli is writing about how to be a successful ruler. He explicitly says he is dealing with things as they are, not things as they should be. Do you think that in fact one can write usefully about statecraft without considering ethics? Explain. Or you may want to think about it in this way: The study of politics is often called *political science.* Machiavelli can be seen as a sort of scientist, objectively analyzing the nature of governing — without offering any moral judgments. In an essay of 500 words, argue for or against the view that the study of politics is rightly called *political science.*

8. In the final paragraph, Machiavelli declares that "in the actions of all men . . . one judges by the result." Taking account of the context, do you think the meaning is that (a) any end, goal, or purpose of anyone justifies using any means to reach it or (b) the end of governing the state, nation, or country justifies using any means to achieve it? Or do you think Machiavelli means both? Something else entirely?

9. In 500 words, argue that an important contemporary political figure does or does not act according to Machiavelli's principles.

10. If you have read the selection from Thomas More's *Utopia*, write an essay of 500 words on one of these two topics: (a) why More's book is or is not wiser than Machiavelli's or (b) why one of the books is more interesting than the other.

11. More and Machiavelli wrote their books at almost exactly the same time. Write a dialogue of two or three double-spaced typed pages in which the two men argue about the nature of the state. (During the argument, they will have to reveal their assumptions about the nature of human beings and the role of government.)

THOMAS JEFFERSON

Thomas Jefferson (1743–1826) was a congressman, the governor of Virginia, the first secretary of state, and the president of the United States, but he said he wished to be remembered for only three things: drafting the Declaration of Independence, writing the Virginia Statute for Religious Freedom, and founding the University of Virginia. All three were efforts to promote freedom.

Jefferson was born in Virginia and educated at William and Mary College in Williamsburg, Virginia. After graduating he studied law, was admitted to the bar, and in 1769 was elected to the Virginia House of Burgesses, his first political office. In 1776 he went to Philadelphia as a delegate to the second Continental Congress, where he was elected to a committee of five to write the Declaration of Independence. Jefferson drafted the document, which was then subjected to some changes by the other members of the committee and by the Congress. Although he was unhappy with the changes (especially with the deletion of a passage against slavery), his claim to have written the Declaration is just.

The Declaration of Independence

When in the course of human events, it becomes necessary for one people to dissolve the political bands which have connected them with another, and to assume among the Powers of the earth, the separate and equal station to which the Laws of Nature and of Nature's God entitle them, a decent respect to the opinions of mankind requires that they should declare the causes which impel them to the separation.

We hold these truths to be self-evident, that all men are created equal, that they are endowed by their Creator with certain unalienable Rights, that among these are Life, Liberty and the pursuit of Happiness.

That to secure these rights, Governments are instituted among Men, deriving their just powers from the consent of the governed.

That whenever any Form of Government becomes destructive of these ends, it is the Right of the People to alter or to abolish it, and to institute a new Government, laying its foundation on such principles and organizing its powers in such form, as to them shall seem most likely to effect their Safety and Happiness. Prudence, indeed, will dictate that

Governments long established should not be changed for light and transient causes; and accordingly all experience hath shown that mankind are more disposed to suffer, while evils are sufferable, than to right themselves by abolishing the forms to which they are accustomed. But when a long train of abuses and usurpations pursuing invariably the same Object evinces a design to reduce them under absolute Despotism, it is their right, it is their duty, to throw off such government, and to provide new Guards for their future security.

Such has been the patient sufferance of these Colonies; and such is now the necessity which constrains them to alter their former Systems of Government. The history of the present King of Great Britain is a history of repeated injuries and usurpations, all having in direct object the establishment of an absolute Tyranny over these States. To prove this, let Facts be submitted to a candid world. 5

He has refused his Assent to Laws, the most wholesome and necessary for the public good.

He has forbidden his Governors to pass Laws of immediate and pressing importance, unless suspended in their operation till his Assent should be obtained; and when so suspended, he has utterly neglected to attend to them.

He has refused to pass over Laws for the accommodation of large districts of people, unless those people would relinquish the right of Representation in the Legislature, a right inestimable to them and formidable to tyrants only.

He has called together legislative bodies at places unusual, uncomfortable, and distant from the depository of their Public Records, for the sole purpose of fatiguing them into compliance with his measures.

He has dissolved Representative Houses 10 repeatedly, for opposing with manly firmness his invasions on the rights of the people.

He has refused for a long time, after such dissolutions, to cause others to be elected; whereby the Legislative Powers, incapable of Annihilation, have returned to the People at large for their exercise; the State remaining in the mean time exposed to all the dangers of invasion from without, and convulsions within.

He has endeavored to prevent the population of these States, for that purpose obstructing the Laws of Naturalization of Foreigners; refusing to pass others to encourage their migration hither, and raising the conditions of new Appropriations of Lands.

He has obstructed the Administration of Justice, by refusing his Assent to Laws for establishing Judiciary Powers.

He has made Judges dependent on his Will alone, for the tenure of their offices, and the amount and payment of their salaries.

He has erected a multitude of New Offices, 15 and sent hither swarms of Officers to harass our People, and eat out their substance.

He has kept among us, in time of peace, Standing Armies without the consent of our Legislature.

He has affected to render the Military independent of and superior to the Civil Power.

He has combined with others to subject us to jurisdictions foreign to our constitution, and unacknowledged by our laws; giving his Assent to their acts of pretended Legislation:

For quartering large bodies of armed troops among us:

For protecting them, by a mock Trial, from 20 Punishment for any Murders which they should commit on the Inhabitants of these States:

For cutting off our Trade with all parts of the world:

For imposing Taxes on us without our Consent:

For depriving us in many cases, of the benefits of Trial by Jury:

For transporting us beyond Seas to be tried for pretended offenses:

For abolishing the free System of English Laws in a Neighbouring Province, establishing therein an Arbitrary government, and enlarging its boundaries so as to render it at once an example and fit instrument for introducing the same absolute rule into these Colonies:

For taking away our Charters, abolishing our most valuable Laws, and altering fundamentally the Forms of our Governments.

For suspending our own Legislatures, and declaring themselves invested with Power to legislate for us in all cases whatsoever.

He has abdicated Government here, by declaring us out of his Protection and waging War against us.

He has plundered our seas, ravaged our Coasts, burnt our towns and destroyed the Lives of our people.

He is at this time transporting large Armies of foreign Mercenaries to compleat the works of death, desolation and tyranny, already begun with circumstances of Cruelty & perfidy scarcely paralleled in the most barbarous ages, and totally unworthy the Head of a civilized nation.

He has constrained our fellow Citizens taken Captive on the high Seas to bear Arms against their Country, to become the executioners of their friends and Brethren, or to fall themselves by their Hands.

He has excited domestic insurrections amongst us, and has endeavored to bring on the inhabitants of our frontiers, the merciless Indian Savages, whose known rule of warfare is an undistinguished destruction of all ages, sexes and conditions.

In every stage of these Oppressions We Have Petitioned for Redress in the most humble terms: Our repeated petitions have been answered only by repeated injury. A Prince, whose character is thus marked by every act which may define a Tyrant, is unfit to be the ruler of a free People.

Nor have We been wanting in attention to our British brethren. We have warned them from time to time of attempts by their legislature to extend an unwarrantable jurisdiction over us. We have reminded them of the circumstances of our emigration and settlement here. We have appealed to their native justice and magnanimity and we have conjured them by the ties of our common kindred to disavow these usurpations, which would inevitably interrupt our connections and correspondence. They too have been deaf to the voice of justice and of consanguinity. We must, therefore, acquiesce in the necessity, which denounces our Separation, and hold them, as we hold the rest of mankind, Enemies in War, in Peace Friends.

We, therefore, the Representatives of the United States of America, in General Congress, Assembled, appealing to the Supreme Judge of the world of the rectitude of our intentions, do, in the Name, and by Authority of the good People of these Colonies, solemnly publish and declare, That these United Colonies are, and of Right ought to be, Free and Independent States; that they are Absolved from all Allegiance to the British Crown, and that all political connection between them and the State of Great Britain, is and ought to be totally dissolved; and that as Free and Independent States, they have full power to levy War, conclude Peace, contract Alliances, establish Commerce, and to do all other Acts and Things which Independent States may of right do. And for the support of this Declaration, with a firm reliance on the protection of Divine Providence, we mutually pledge to each other our lives, our Fortunes and our sacred Honor.

Topics for Critical Thinking and Writing

1. According to the first paragraph, for what audience was the Declaration written? To what other audiences do you think the document was (in one way or another) addressed?

2. The Declaration states that it is intended to "prove" that the acts of the government of George III had as their "direct object the establishment of an absolute Tyranny" in the American colonies (para. 5). Write an essay of 500 to 750 words showing whether the evidence offered in the Declaration "proves" this claim to your satisfaction. (You will, of course, want to define *absolute tyranny*.) If you think further evidence is needed to "prove" the colonists' point, indicate what this evidence might be.

3. Paying special attention to the paragraphs beginning "That whenever any Form of Government" (para. 4), "In every stage" (para. 33), and "Nor have We been wanting" (para. 34), in a sentence or two set forth the image of themselves that the colonists seek to convey.

4. In the Declaration of Independence it is argued that the colonists are entitled to certain things and that under certain conditions they may behave in a certain way. Make explicit the syllogism that Jefferson is arguing.

5. What evidence does Thomas Jefferson offer to support his major premise? His minor premise?

6. In paragraph 2, the Declaration cites "certain unalienable Rights" and mentions three: "Life, Liberty and the pursuit of Happiness." What is an unalienable right? If someone has an unalienable (or inalienable) right, does that imply that he or she also has certain duties? If so, what are these duties? John Locke, a century earlier (1690), asserted that all men have a natural right to "life, liberty, and property." Do you think the decision to drop "property" and substitute "pursuit of Happiness" improved Locke's claim? Explain.

7. The Declaration ends thus: "We mutually pledge to each other our lives, our Fortunes and our sacred Honor." Is it surprising that honor is put in the final, climactic position? Is this a better ending than "our Fortunes, our sacred Honor, and our lives," or than "our sacred Honor, our lives, and our Fortunes?" Why, or why not?

8. King George III has asked you to reply, on his behalf, to the colonists, in 500 to 750 words. Write his reply. (Caution: A good reply will probably require you to do some reading about the period.)

9. Write a declaration of your own, setting forth in 500 to 750 words why some group is entitled to independence. You may want to argue that adolescents should not be compelled to attend school, that animals should not be confined in zoos, or that persons who use drugs should be able to buy them legally. Begin with a premise, then set forth facts illustrating the unfairness of the present condition, and conclude by stating what the new condition will mean to society.

ELIZABETH CADY STANTON

Elizabeth Cady Stanton (1815–1902), a lawyer's daughter and journalist's wife, proposed in 1848 a convention to address the "social, civil, and religious condition and rights of women." Responding to Stanton's call, women and men from all over the Northeast traveled to the Woman's Rights Convention held in the village of Seneca Falls, New York. Her Declaration, adopted by the Convention — but only after vigorous debate and some amendments by others — became the platform for the women's rights movement in this country.

Declaration of Sentiments and Resolutions

When, in the course of human events, it becomes necessary for one portion of the family of man to assume among the people of the earth a position different from that which they have hitherto occupied, but one to which the laws of nature and of nature's God entitle them, a decent respect to the opinions of mankind requires that they should declare the causes that impel them to such a course.

We hold these truths to be self-evident: that all men and women are created equal; that they are endowed by their Creator with certain inalienable rights; that among these are life, liberty and the pursuit of happiness; that to secure these rights governments are instituted, deriving their just powers from the consent of the governed. Whenever any form of government becomes destructive of these ends, it is the right of those who suffer from it to refuse allegiance to it, and to insist upon the institution of a new government, laying its foundation on such principles, and organizing its powers in such form, as to them shall seem most likely to effect their safety and happiness. Prudence, indeed, will dictate that governments long established should not be changed for light and transient causes; and accordingly all experience hath shown that mankind are more disposed to suffer, while evils are sufferable, than to right themselves by abolishing the forms to which they were accustomed. But when a long train of abuses and usurpations, pursuing invariably the same object, evinces a design to reduce them under absolute despotism, it is their duty to throw off such government, and to provide new guards for their future security. Such has been the patient sufferance of the women under this government, and such is now the necessity which constrains them to demand the equal station to which they are entitled.

The history of mankind is a history of repeated injuries and usurpations on the part of man toward woman, having in direct object the establishment of an absolute tyranny over her. To prove this, let facts be submitted to a candid world.

He has never permitted her to exercise her inalienable right to the elective franchise.

He has compelled her to submit to laws, in 5 the formation of which she had no voice.

He has withheld from her rights which are given to the most ignorant and degraded men — both natives and foreigners.

Having deprived her of this first right of a citizen, the elective franchise, thereby leaving her without representation in the halls of legislation, he has oppressed her on all sides.

He has made her, if married, in the eye of the law, civilly dead.

He has taken from her all right in property, even to the wages she earns.

He has made her, morally, an irresponsible being, as she can commit many crimes with impunity, provided they be done in the presence of her husband. In the covenant of marriage, she is compelled to promise obedience to her husband, he becoming to all intents and purposes, her master — the law giving him power to deprive her of her liberty, and to administer chastisement.

He has so framed the laws of divorce, as to what shall be the proper causes, and in case of separation, to whom the guardianship of the children shall be given, as to be wholly regardless of the happiness of women — the law, in all cases, going upon a false supposition of the supremacy of man, and giving all power into his hands.

After depriving her of all rights as a married woman, if single, and the owner of property, he has taxed her to support a government which recognizes her only when her property can be made profitable to it.

He has monopolized nearly all the profitable employments, and from those she is permitted to follow, she receives but a scanty remuneration. He closes against her all the avenues to wealth and distinction which he considers most honorable to himself. As a teacher of theology, medicine, or law, she is not known.

He has denied her the facilities for obtaining a thorough education, all colleges being closed against her.

He allows her in Church, as well as State, but a subordinate position, claiming Apostolic authority for her exclusion from the ministry, and, with some exceptions, from any public participation in the affairs of the Church.

He has created a false public sentiment by giving to the world a different code of morals for men and women, by which moral delinquencies which exclude women from society, are not only tolerated, but deemed of little account in man.

He has usurped the prerogative of Jehovah himself, claiming it as his right to assign for her a sphere of action, when that belongs to her conscience and to her God.

He has endeavored, in every way that he could, to destroy her confidence in her own powers, to lessen her self-respect, and to make her willing to lead a dependent and abject life.

Now, in view of this entire disfranchisement of one-half the people of this country, their social and religious degradation — in view of the unjust laws above mentioned, and because women do feel themselves aggrieved, oppressed, and fraudulently deprived of their most sacred rights, we insist that they have immediate admission to all the rights and privileges which belong to them as citizens of the United States.

In entering upon the great work before us, we anticipate no small amount of misconception, misrepresentation, and ridicule; but we shall use every instrumentality within our power to effect our object. We shall employ agents, circulate tracts, petition the State and National legislatures, and endeavor to enlist the pulpit and the press in our behalf. We hope this Convention will be followed by a series of Conventions embracing every part of the country.

[The following resolutions were discussed by Lucretia Mott, Thomas and Mary Ann McClintock, Amy Post, Catharine A. F. Stebbins, and others, and were adopted:]

Whereas, The great precept of nature is conceded to be, that "man shall pursue his own true and substantial happiness." Blackstone in his Commentaries remarks, that this law of Nature being coeval with mankind, and dictated by God himself, is of course superior in obligation to any other. It is binding over all the globe, in all countries, and at all times; no human laws are of any validity if contrary to this, and such of them as are valid, derive all their force, and all their validity, and all their authority, mediately and immediately, from this original; therefore,

Resolved, That such laws as conflict, in any way, with the true and substantial happiness of woman, are contrary to the great precept of nature and of no validity, for this is "superior in obligation to any other."

Resolved, That all laws which prevent woman from occupying such a station in society as her conscience shall dictate, or which place her in a position inferior to that of man, are contrary to the great precept of nature, and therefore of no force or authority.

Resolved, That woman is man's equal — was intended to be so by the Creator, and the highest good of the race demands that she should be recognized as such.

Resolved, That the women of this country 25 ought to be enlightened in regard to the laws under which they live, that they may no longer publish their degradation by declaring themselves satisfied with their present position, nor their ignorance, by asserting that they have all the rights they want.

Resolved, That inasmuch as man, while claiming for himself intellectual superiority, does accord to woman moral superiority, it is preeminently his duty to encourage her to speak and teach, as she has an opportunity, in all religious assemblies.

Resolved, That the same amount of virtue, delicacy, and refinement of behavior that is required of woman in the social state, should also be required of man, and the same transgressions should be visited with equal severity on both man and woman.

Resolved, That the objection of indelicacy and impropriety, which is so often brought against woman when she addresses a public audience, comes with a very ill-grace from those who encourage, by their attendance, her appearance on the stage, in the concert, or in feats of the circus.

Resolved, That woman has too long rested satisfied in the circumscribed limits which corrupt customs and a perverted application of the Scriptures have marked out for her, and that it is time she should move in the enlarged sphere which her great Creator has assigned her.

Resolved, That it is the duty of the women 30 of this country to secure to themselves their sacred right to the elective franchise.

Resolved, That the equality of human rights results necessarily from the fact of the identity of the race in capabilities and responsibilities.

Resolved, therefore, That, being invested by the Creator with the same capabilities, and the same consciousness of responsibility for their exercise, it is demonstrably the right and duty of woman, equally with man, to promote every righteous cause by every righteous means; and especially in regard to the great subjects of morals and religion, it is self-evidently her right to participate with her brother in teaching them, both in private and in public, by writing and by speaking, by any instrumentalities proper to be used, and in any assemblies proper to be held; and this being a self-evident truth growing out of the divinely implanted principles of human nature, any custom or authority adverse to it, whether modern or wearing the hoary sanction of antiquity, is to be regarded as a self-evident falsehood, and at war with mankind.

[At the last session Lucretia Mott offered and spoke to the following resolution:]

Resolved, That the speedy success of our cause depends upon the zealous and untiring efforts of both men and women, for the overthrow of the monopoly of the pulpit, and for the securing to woman an equal participation with men in the various trades, professions, and commerce.

Topics for Critical Thinking and Writing

1. Elizabeth Cady Stanton echoes the Declaration of Independence because she wishes to associate her ideas and the movement she supports with a document and a movement that her readers esteem. And she must have believed that if readers esteem the Declaration of Independence, they must grant the justice of her goals. Does her strategy work, or does it backfire by making her essay seem strained? Explain your response.

2. When Stanton insists that women have an "inalienable right to the elective franchise" (para. 4), what does she mean by "inalienable"?

3. Stanton complains that men have made married women, "in the eye of the law, civilly dead" (para. 8). What does she mean by "civilly dead"? How is it possible for a person to be biologically alive and yet civilly dead?

4. Stanton objects that women are "not known" as teachers of "theology, medicine, or law" (para. 13). Is this still true today? Do some research in your library, and then write three 100-word biographical sketches, one each on well-known woman professors of theology, medicine, and law.

5. How might you go about proving (rather than merely asserting) that, as paragraph 24 says, "woman is man's equal — was intended to be so by the Creator"?

6. The Declaration claims that women have "the same capabilities" as men (para. 32). Yet in 1848 Stanton and the others at Seneca Falls knew, or should have known, that history recorded no example of a woman philosopher comparable to Plato or Kant, a composer comparable to Beethoven or Chopin, a scientist comparable to Galileo or Newton, or a mathematician comparable to Euclid or Descartes. Do these facts contradict the Declaration's claim? If not, why not? How else but by different intellectual capabilities do you think such facts can be explained?

7. Stanton's Declaration is over 165 years old. Have all of the issues she raised been satisfactorily resolved? If not, which ones remain?

8. In our society, children have very few rights. For instance, a child cannot decide to drop out of elementary school or high school, and a child cannot decide to leave his or her parents to reside with some other family that he or she finds more compatible. Whatever your view of children's rights, compose the best Declaration of the Rights of Children that you can.

MARTIN LUTHER KING JR.

Martin Luther King Jr. (1929–1968) was born in Atlanta and educated at Morehouse College, Crozer Theological Seminary, and Boston University. In 1954 he was called to serve as a Baptist minister in Montgomery, Alabama. During the next two years he achieved national fame when, using a policy of nonviolent resistance, he successfully led the boycott against segregated bus lines in Montgomery. He then organized the Southern Christian Leadership Conference, which furthered civil rights, first in the South and then nationwide. In 1964 he was awarded the Nobel Peace Prize. Four years later he was assassinated in Memphis, Tennessee, while supporting striking garbage workers.

The speech presented here was delivered from the steps of the Lincoln Memorial, in Washington, D.C., in 1963, the hundredth anniversary of the Emancipation Proclamation. King's immediate audience consisted of more than two hundred thousand people who had come to demonstrate for civil rights.

I Have a Dream

I am happy to join with you today in what will go down in history as the greatest demonstration for freedom in the history of our nation.

Five score years ago, a great American, in whose symbolic shadow we stand today, signed the Emancipation Proclamation. This momentous decree came as a great beacon light of hope to millions of Negro slaves who had been seared in the flames of withering injustice. It came as a joyous daybreak to end the long night of their captivity. But one hundred years later, the Negro still is not free. One hundred years later, the life of the Negro is still sadly crippled by the manacles of segregation and the chains of discrimination. One hundred years later, the Negro lives on a lonely island of poverty in the midst of a vast ocean of material prosperity. One hundred years later, the Negro is still anguished in the corners of American society and finds himself in exile in his own land. And so we have come here today to dramatize a shameful condition.

In a sense we have come to our nation's capital to cash a check. When the architects of our republic wrote the magnificent words of the Constitution and the Declaration of Independence, they were signing a promissory note to which every American was to fall heir. This note was the promise that all men — yes, black men as well as white men — would be guaranteed the inalienable rights of life, liberty, and the pursuit of happiness.

It is obvious today that America has defaulted on this promissory note insofar as her citizens of color are concerned. Instead of honoring this sacred obligation, America has given the Negro people a bad check, a check which has come back marked "insufficient funds." But we refuse to believe that the bank of justice is bankrupt. We refuse to believe that there are insufficient funds in the great vaults of opportunity of this nation; and so we have come to cash this check, a check that will give us upon demand the riches of freedom and the security of justice.

We have also come to this hallowed spot 5 to remind America of the fierce urgency of *now.* This is no time to engage in the luxury of cooling off or to take the tranquilizing drug of gradualism. *Now* is the time to make real promises of democracy. *Now* is the time to rise from the dark and desolate valley of segregation to the sunlit path of racial justice. *Now* is the time to lift our nation from the quicksands of racial injustice to the solid rock of brotherhood. *Now* is the time to make justice a reality for all of God's children.

It would be fatal for the nation to overlook the urgency of the moment. This sweltering summer of the Negro's legitimate discontent will not pass until there is an invigorating autumn of freedom and equality. Nineteen sixty-three is not an end, but a beginning. And those who hope that the Negro needed to blow off steam and will now be content will have a rude awakening if the nation returns to business as usual. There will be neither rest nor tranquility in America until the Negro is granted his citizenship rights. The whirlwinds of revolt will continue to shake the foundations of our nation until the bright day of justice emerges.

But there is something that I must say to my people who stand on the warm threshold which leads into the palace of justice. In the process of gaining our rightful place, we must not be guilty of wrongful deeds. Let us not seek to satisfy our thirst for freedom by drinking from the cup of bitterness and hatred. We must forever conduct our struggle on the high plane of dignity and discipline. We must not allow our creative protest to degenerate into physical violence. Again and again we must rise to the majestic heights of meeting physical force with soul force. And the marvelous new militancy which has engulfed the Negro community must not lead us to a distrust of all white people; for many of our white brothers, as evidenced by their presence here today, have come to realize that their destiny is tied up with our destiny, and they have come to realize that their freedom is inextricably bound to our freedom.

We cannot walk alone. And as we walk we must make the pledge that we shall always march ahead. We cannot turn back. There are those who are asking the devotees of civil rights, "When will you be satisfied?" We can never be satisfied as long as the Negro is the victim of the unspeakable horrors of police brutality. We can never be satisfied as long as our bodies, heavy with the fatigue of travel, cannot gain lodging in the motels of the highways and the hotels of the cities. We cannot be satisfied as long as the Negro's basic mobility is from a smaller ghetto to a larger one. We can never be satisfied as long as our children are stripped of their selfhood and robbed of their dignity by signs stating "For Whites Only." We cannot be satisfied as long as the Negro in Mississippi cannot vote and a Negro in New York believes he has nothing for which to vote. No, no, we are not satisfied, and we will not be satisfied until justice rolls down like waters and righteousness like a mighty stream.[1]

I am not unmindful that some of you have come here out of great trials and tribulations. Some of you have come fresh from narrow jail cells. Some of you have come from areas where your quest for freedom left you battered by the storms of persecution and staggered by the winds of police brutality. You have been the veterans of creative suffering. Continue to work with the faith that unearned suffering is redemptive.

Go back to Mississippi, and go back to Alabama. Go back to South Carolina. Go back to Georgia. Go back to Louisiana. Go back to the slums and ghettos of our Northern cities, knowing that somehow this situation can and will be changed. Let us not wallow in the valley of despair.

I say to you today, my friends, even though we face the difficulties of today and tomorrow, I still have a dream. It is a dream deeply rooted in the American dream. I have a dream that one day this nation will rise up and live

---

[1] **justice . . . stream** A quotation from the Hebrew Bible: Amos 5:24. [All notes are the editors'.]

out the true meaning of its creed: "We hold these truths to be self-evident, that all men are created equal." I have a dream that one day, on the red hills of Georgia, sons of former slaves and the sons of former slave owners will be able to sit down together at the table of brotherhood. I have a dream that one day even the state of Mississippi, a state sweltering with the heat of injustice, sweltering with the heat of oppression, will be transformed into an oasis of freedom and justice. I have a dream that my four little children will one day live in a nation where they will not be judged by the color of their skin, but by the content of their character.

I have a dream today. I have a dream that one day down in Alabama — with its vicious racists, with its governor's lips dripping with the words of interposition and nullification — one day right there in Alabama, little black boys and black girls will be able to join hands with little white boys and white girls as sisters and brothers.

I have a dream today. I have a dream that one day every valley shall be exalted and every hill and mountain shall be made low, the rough places will be made plain and the crooked places will be made straight, and the glory of the Lord shall be revealed, and all flesh shall see it together.[2]

This is our hope. This is the faith that I go back to the South with. And with this faith we will be able to hew out of the mountain of despair a stone of hope. With this faith we will be able to transform the jangling discords of our nation into a beautiful symphony of brotherhood. With this faith we will be able to work together, to play together, to struggle together, to go to jail together, to stand up for freedom together, knowing that we will be free one day.

And this will be the day — this will be the day when all of God's children will be able to sing with new meaning:

My country, 'tis of thee,
Sweet land of liberty,
   Of thee I sing;
Land where my fathers died,
Land of the Pilgrim's pride,
From every mountainside
   Let freedom ring.

And if America is to be a great nation, this must become true.

And so let freedom ring from the prodigious hilltops of New Hampshire. Let freedom ring from the mighty mountains of New York. Let freedom ring from the heightening Alleghenies of Pennsylvania. Let freedom ring from the snow-capped Rockies of Colorado. Let freedom ring from the curvaceous slopes of California.

But not only that. Let freedom ring from Stone Mountain of Georgia. Let freedom ring from Lookout Mountain of Tennessee. Let freedom ring from every hill and molehill of Mississippi. "From every mountainside let freedom ring."

And when this happens — when we allow freedom to ring, when we let it ring from every village and every hamlet, from every state and every city — we will be able to speed up that day when all of God's children, Black men and white men, Jews and Gentiles, Protestants and Catholics, will be able to join hands and sing in the words of the old Negro spiritual: "Free at last! Free at last! Thank God Almighty. We are free at last!"

---

[2]**every valley . . . see it together** Another quotation from the Hebrew Bible: Isaiah 40:4–5.

Topics for Critical Thinking and Writing

1. Analyze the rhetoric — the oratorical art — of the second paragraph. What, for instance, is gained by saying "five score years ago" instead of "a hundred years ago"? By metaphorically calling the Emancipation Proclamation "a great beacon light of hope"? By saying that "Negro slaves . . . had been seared in the flames of withering injustice"? And what of the metaphors "daybreak" and "the long night of . . . captivity"?

2. Do the first two paragraphs make an effective opening? Why?

3. In paragraphs 3 and 4, Martin Luther King uses the metaphor of a bad check. Rewrite the third paragraph *without* using any of King's metaphors, and then in a paragraph evaluate the differences between King's version and yours.

4. King's highly metaphoric speech appeals to emotions. But it also offers *reasons*. What reasons, for instance, does King give to support his belief that African Americans should not resort to physical violence in their struggle against segregation and discrimination?

5. When King delivered the speech, his audience at the Lincoln Memorial was primarily African American. Do you think that the speech is also addressed to other Americans? Explain.

6. The speech can be divided into three parts: paragraphs 1 through 6; paragraphs 7 ("But there is") through 10; and paragraph 11 ("I say to you today, my friends") to the end. Summarize each of these three parts in a sentence or two so that the basic organization is evident.

7. King says (para. 11) that his dream is "deeply rooted in the American dream." First, what is the American dream, as King seems to understand it? Second, how does King establish his point — that is, what evidence does he use to convince us — that his dream is the American dream? (On this second issue, one might start by pointing out that in the second paragraph King refers to the Emancipation Proclamation. What other relevant documents does he refer to?)

8. King delivered his speech in 1963, more than fifty years ago. In an essay of 500 words, argue that the speech still is — or is not — relevant. Or write an essay of 500 words in which you state what you take to be the "American dream," and argue that it now is or is not readily available to African Americans.

W. H. AUDEN

Wystan Hugh Auden (1907–1973) was born in York, England, and educated at Oxford University. In the 1930s his witty left-wing poetry earned him wide acclaim as the leading poet of his generation. In 1939 he came to the United States, becoming a citizen in 1946 but returning to England for his last years. Much of Auden's poetry is characterized by a combination of colloquial diction and technical dexterity. The poem reprinted here was originally published in 1940.

The Unknown Citizen

(To JS/07/M/378
This Marble Monument
Is Erected by the State)

He was found by the Bureau of Statistics to be
One against whom there was no official
    complaint,
And all the reports on his conduct agree
That, in the modern sense of an old-fashioned
    word, he was a saint,
For in everything he did he served the Greater 5
    Community.
Except for the War till the day he retired
He worked in a factory and never got fired,
But satisfied his employers, Fudge Motors Inc.
Yet he wasn't a scab or odd in his views,
For his Union reports that he paid his dues, 10
(Our report on his Union shows it was sound)
And our Social Psychology workers found
That he was popular with his mates and liked
    a drink.
The Press are convinced that he bought a
    paper every day
And that his reactions to advertisements were 15
    normal in every way.
Policies taken out in his name prove that he
    was fully insured,

And his Health-card shows he was once in
    hospital but left it cured.
Both Producers Research and High-Grade
    Living declare
He was fully sensible to the advantages of the
    Installment Plan
And had everything necessary to the Modern 20
    Man,
A phonograph, radio, a car and a frigidaire.
Our researches into Public Opinion are
    content
That he held the proper opinions for the time
    of year;
When there was peace, he was for peace;
    when there was war, he went.
He was married and added five children to the 25
    population,
Which our Eugenist says was the right
    number for a parent of his generation,
And our teachers report that he never
    interfered with their education.
Was he free? Was he happy? The question is
    absurd:
Had anything been wrong, we should
    certainly have heard.

Topics for Critical Thinking and Writing

1. Who is the narrator in W. H. Auden's poem, and on what sort of occasion is he speaking? How do you know?

2. France, Great Britain, and the United States all have monuments to "The Unknown" (formerly "The Unknown Soldier"). How is Auden's proposed monument like and unlike these war memorials?

3. The poem ends by asking "Was he free? Was he happy?" and the questions are dismissed summarily. Is that because the answers are so obvious? What answers (obvious or subtle) do you think the poem offers to these questions?

4. Evaluate the poem, making clear the reasons behind your evaluation.

5. If you have read the selection from Thomas More's *Utopia*, write an essay of 500 to 750 words — in More's voice — setting forth More's response to Auden's poem.

EMMA LAZARUS

Emma Lazarus (1849–1887) was born in New York City as the fourth of seven children in a well-established family. Her parents provided her with a private education, and her father supported her writing: When Lazarus was just seventeen, her father had a collection of Lazarus's poetry, called Poems and Translations: Written between the Ages of Fourteen and Sixteen, *printed for private circulation. In addition to poetry, Lazarus wrote essays, plays, several highly respected translations, and a novel, going on to become part of the literary elite in late-nineteenth-century New York. Lazarus is probably known best for the poem that follows, "The New Colossus." She wrote this sonnet in 1883 as a donation to an auction held to raise money to build the pedestal for the Statue of Liberty. The poem was installed on the base of the statue in 1903, nearly two decades after Lazarus's death in 1887.*

The New Colossus

Not like the brazen giant of Greek fame,
With conquering limbs astride from land to land;
Here at our sea-washed, sunset gates shall stand
A mighty woman with a torch, whose flame
Is the imprisoned lightning, and her name   5
Mother of Exiles. From her beacon-hand
Glows world-wide welcome; her mild eyes command
The air-bridged harbor that twin cities frame.
"Keep, ancient lands, your storied pomp!" cries she
With silent lips. "Give me your tired, your poor,   10
Your huddled masses yearning to breathe free,
The wretched refuse of your teeming shore.
Send these, the homeless, tempest-tost to me,
I lift my lamp beside the golden door!"

Topics for Critical Thinking and Writing

1. In the opening line of the poem, Lazarus alludes to the Colossus of Rhodes — a statue of the Greek titan-god of the sun Helios that was erected in the city of Rhodes in 280 B.C. The Colossus was 98 feet tall, making it one of the tallest statues of the ancient world. Compare the language that Lazarus uses to describe this "brazen giant of Greek fame" (l. 1) to the language she uses to describe the Statue of Liberty, the "Mother of Exiles" (l. 6). If both statues are symbols for nations, then what kind of argument does Lazarus make by describing the two statues as she does?

2. Lazarus refers to the Statue of Liberty as the "Mother of Exiles." Do you think this description still holds up today in light of current debates about immigration laws? Write a brief essay of about 500 words using both historical evidence and current events to support your argument.

3. Note the description of the Statue of Liberty's eyes as "mild" in line 7. Do you think this is an accurate depiction of how "the homeless, tempest-tost" are generally seen in the United States today? Why, or why not?

WALT WHITMAN

Walt Whitman (1819–1892) is one of the most renowned poets in the American canon. He was born in Huntington, Long Island, as the second of nine children to Walter and Louisa Van Velsor Whitman. He attended public school until age eleven, at which time he concluded his formal schooling and took a job as a printer's assistant. He quickly learned the printing trade, and at age seventeen, he became a teacher. He continued to teach until 1841, when he became a full-time journalist. Whitman founded and served as editor of the Long-Islander, *a weekly Huntington newspaper, and went on to edit several other newspapers in the New York area as well as the New Orleans* Crescent *before leaving the newspaper business in 1848. He moved back in with his parents at that point, working as a part-time carpenter and beginning work on* Leaves of Grass, *his most enduring and famous collection of poems. He first published* Leaves *at his own expense in 1855, though he continued to revise it several times throughout the rest of his life. "One Song, America, Before I Go" first appeared in the 1900 edition of* Leaves of Grass.

One Song, America, Before I Go

One song, America, before I go,
I'd sing, o'er all the rest, with trumpet sound,
For thee — the Future.

I'd sow a seed for thee of endless Nationality;
I'd fashion thy Ensemble, including Body and   5
    Soul;
I'd show, away ahead, thy real Union, and how
    it may be accomplish'd.

(The paths to the House I seek to make,
But leave to those to come, the House itself.)

Belief I sing — and Preparation;
As Life and Nature are not great with refer-   10
    ence to the Present only,
But greater still from what is yet to come,
Out of that formula for Thee I sing.

Topics for Critical Thinking and Writing

1. Whitman identifies his poem as a song for America. What kinds of songs do you usually think of when you think about America? What kind of song of America does Whitman sing here (and to what other songs does he allude)? How do you think Whitman's tone compares to other songs about the country?

2. Why is the future important in this poem? What argument is Whitman making about the present and past of America?

3. "One Song, America, Before I Go" was originally published in 1900. If Whitman were alive today, how do you think he would assess the state of America? Do you think he would think that the "Belief" and "Preparation" (l. 9) he advised had been heeded? Why, or why not?

URSULA K. LE GUIN

Ursula K. Le Guin was born in 1929 in Berkeley, California, the daughter of a distinguished mother (Theodora Kroeber, a folklorist) and father (Alfred L. Kroeber, an anthropologist). After graduating from Radcliffe College, she earned a master's degree at Columbia University; in 1952 she held a Fulbright Fellowship for study in Paris, where she met and married Charles Le Guin, a historian. She began writing in earnest while bringing up three children. Although her work is most widely known to buffs of science fiction, because it usually has larger moral or political dimensions, it interests many other readers who normally do not care for sci-fi.

Le Guin has said that she was prompted to write the following story by a remark she encountered in William James's "The Moral Philosopher and the Moral Life." James suggests there that if millions of people could be "kept permanently happy on the one simple condition that a certain lost soul on the far-off edge of things should lead a life of lonely torment," our moral sense "would make us immediately feel" it would be "hideous" to accept such a bargain. This story first appeared in New Dimensions 3 *(1973).*

The Ones Who Walk Away from Omelas

With a clamor of bells that set the swallows soaring, the Festival of Summer came to the city Omelas, bright-towered by the sea. The rigging of the boats in harbor sparkled with flags. In the streets between houses with red roofs and painted walls, between old moss-grown gardens and under avenues of trees, past great parks and public buildings, processions moved. Some were decorous: old people in long stiff robes of mauve and gray, grave master workmen, quiet, merry women carrying their babies and chatting as they walked. In other streets the music beat faster, a shimmering of gong and tambourine, and the people went dancing, the procession was a dance. Children dodged in and out, their high calls rising like the swallows' crossing flights over the music and the singing. All the processions wound towards the north side of the city, where on the great water-meadow called the Green Fields boys and girls, naked in the bright air, with mudstained feet and ankles and long, lithe arms, exercised their restive horses before the race. The horses wore no gear at all but a halter without bit. Their manes were braided with streamers of silver, gold, and green. They flared their nostrils and pranced and boasted to one another; they were vastly excited, the horse being the only animal who has adopted our ceremonies as his own. Far off to the north and west the mountains stood up half encircling Omelas on her bay. The air of morning was so clear that the snow still crowning the Eighteen Peaks burned with white-gold fire across the miles of sunlit air, under the dark blue of the sky. There was just enough wind to make the banners that marked the racecourse snap and flutter now and then. In the silence of the broad green meadows one could hear the music winding through the city streets, farther and nearer and ever approaching, a cheerful faint sweetness of the air that from time to time trembled and gathered together and broke out into the great joyous clanging of the bells.

Joyous! How is one to tell about joy? How describe the citizens of Omelas?

They were not simple folk, you see, though they were happy. But we do not say the words of cheer much any more. All smiles have become archaic. Given a description such as this one tends to make certain assumptions. Given a description such as this one tends to look next for the King, mounted on a splendid stallion and surrounded by his noble knights, or perhaps in a golden litter borne by great-muscled slaves. But there was no king. They did not use swords, or keep slaves. They were not barbarians. I do not know the rules and laws of their society, but I suspect that they were singularly few. As they did without monarchy and slavery, so they also got on without the stock exchange, the advertisement, the secret police, and the bomb. Yet I repeat that these were not simple folk, not dulcet shepherds, noble savages, bland utopians. They were not less complex than us. The trouble is that we have a bad habit, encouraged by pedants and sophisticates, of considering happiness as something rather stupid. Only pain is intellectual, only evil interesting. This is the treason of the artist: a refusal to admit the banality of evil and the terrible boredom of pain. If you can't lick 'em, join 'em. If it hurts, repeat it. But to praise despair is to condemn delight, to embrace violence is to lose hold of everything else. We have almost lost hold, we can no longer describe a happy man, nor make any celebration of joy. How can I tell you about the people of Omelas? They were not naïve and happy children — though their children were, in fact, happy. They were mature, intelligent, passionate adults whose lives were not wretched. O miracle! But I wish I could describe it better. I wish I could convince you. Omelas sounds in my words like a city in a fairy tale, long ago and far away, once upon a time. Perhaps it would be best if you imagined it as your own fancy bids, assuming it will rise to the occasion, for certainly I cannot suit you all. For instance, how about technology? I think that there would be no cars or helicopters in and above the streets;

this follows from the fact that the people of Omelas are happy people. Happiness is based on a just discrimination of what is necessary, what is neither necessary nor destructive, and what is destructive. In the middle category, however — that of the unnecessary but undestructive, that of comfort, luxury, exuberance, etc. — they could perfectly well have central heating, subway trains, washing machines, and all kinds of marvelous devices not yet invented here, floating light-sources, fuelless power, a cure for the common cold. Or they could have none of that: it doesn't matter. As you like it. I incline to think that people from towns up and down the coast have been coming in to Omelas during the last days before the Festival on very fast little trains and double-decked trams, and that the train station of Omelas is actually the handsomest building in town, though plainer than the magnificent Farmers' Market. But even granted trains, I fear that Omelas so far strikes some of you as goody-goody. Smiles, bells, parades, horses, bleh. If so, please add an orgy. If an orgy would help, don't hesitate. Let us not, however, have temples from which issue beautiful nude priests and priestesses already half in ecstasy and ready to copulate with any man or woman, lover or stranger, who desires union with the deep godhead of the blood, although that was my first idea. But really it would be better not to have any temples in Omelas — at least, not manned temples. Religion yes, clergy no. Surely the beautiful nudes can just wander about, offering themselves like divine soufflés to the hunger of the needy and the rapture of the flesh. Let them join the processions. Let tambourines be struck above the copulations, and the glory of desire be proclaimed upon the gongs, and (a not unimportant point) let the offspring of these delightful rituals be beloved and looked after by all. One thing I know there is none of in Omelas is guilt.

But what else should there be? I thought that first there were no drugs, but that is puritanical. For those who like it, the faint insistent sweetness of *drooz* may perfume the ways of the city, *drooz* which first brings a great lightness and brilliance to the mind and limbs, and then after some hours a dreamy languor, and wonderful visions at last of the very arcana and inmost secrets of the Universe, as well as exciting the pleasure of sex beyond all belief; and it is not habit-forming. For more modest tastes I think there ought to be beer. What else, what else belongs in the joyous city? The sense of victory, surely, the celebration of courage. But as we did without clergy, let us do without soldiers. The joy built upon successful slaughter is not the right kind of joy; it will not do; it is fearful and it is trivial. A boundless and generous contentment, a magnanimous triumph felt not against some outer enemy but in communion with the finest and fairest in the souls of all men everywhere and the splendor of the world's summer: this is what swells the hearts of the people of Omelas, and the victory they celebrate is that of life. I really don't think many of them need to take *drooz*.

Most of the processions have reached the Green Fields by now. A marvelous smell of cooking goes forth from the red and blue tents of the provisioners. The faces of small children are amiably sticky; in the benign grey beard of a man a couple of crumbs of rich pastry are entangled. The youths and girls have mounted their horses and are beginning to group around the starting line of the course. An old woman, small, fat, and laughing, is passing out flowers from a basket, and tall young men wear her flowers in their shining hair. A child of nine or ten sits at the edge of the crowd, alone, playing on a wooden flute. People pause to listen, and they smile, but they do not speak to him, for he never ceases playing and never sees them, his dark eyes wholly rapt in the sweet, thin magic of the tune.

He finishes, and slowly lowers his hands 5 holding the wooden flute.

As if that little private silence were the signal, all at once a trumpet sounds from the pavilion near the starting line: imperious, melancholy, piercing. The horses rear on their slender legs, and some of them neigh in answer. Sober-faced, the young riders stroke the horses' necks and soothe them, whispering, "Quiet, quiet, there my beauty, my hope. . . ." They begin to form in rank along the starting line. The crowds along the racecourse are like a field of grass and flowers in the wind. The Festival of Summer has begun.

Do you believe? Do you accept the festival, the city, the joy? No? Then let me describe one more thing.

In a basement under one of the beautiful public buildings of Omelas, or perhaps in the cellar of one of its spacious private homes, there is a room. It has one locked door, and no window. A little light seeps in dustily between cracks in the boards, secondhand from a cobwebbed window somewhere across the cellar. In one corner of the little room a couple of mops, with stiff, clotted, foul-smelling heads, stand near a rusty bucket. The floor is dirt, a little damp to the touch, as cellar dirt usually is. The room is about three paces long and two wide: a mere broom closet or disused tool room. In the room a child is sitting. It could be a boy or a girl. It looks about six, but actually is nearly ten. It is feeble-minded. Perhaps it was born defective, or perhaps it has become imbecile through fear, malnutrition, and neglect. It picks its nose and occasionally fumbles vaguely with its toes or genitals, as it sits hunched in the corner farthest from the bucket and the two mops. It is afraid of the mops. It finds them horrible. It shuts its eyes, but it knows the mops are still standing there; and the door is locked; and nobody will come. The door is always locked; and nobody ever comes, except that sometimes—the child has no understanding of time or interval—sometimes the door rattles terribly and opens, and a person, or several people, are there. One of them may come in and kick the child to make it stand up. The others never come close, but peer in at it with frightened, disgusted eyes. The food bowl and the water jug are hastily filled, the door is locked, the eyes disappear. The people at the door never say anything, but the child, who has not always lived in the tool room, and can remember sunlight and its mother's voice, sometimes speaks. "I will be good," it says. "Please let me out. I will be good!" They never answer. The child used to scream for help at night, and cry a good deal, but now it only makes a kind of whining, "eh-haa, eh-haa," and it speaks less and less often. It is so thin there are no calves to its legs; its belly protrudes; it lives on a half-bowl of corn meal and grease a day. It is naked. Its buttocks and thighs are a mass of festered sores, as it sits in its own excrement continually.

They all know it is there, all the people of Omelas. Some of them have come to see it, others are content merely to know it is there. They all know that it has to be there. Some of them understand why, and some do not, but they all understand that their happiness, the beauty of their city, the tenderness of their friendships, the health of their children, the wisdom of their scholars, the skill of their makers, even the abundance of their harvest and the kindly weathers of their skies, depend wholly on this child's abominable misery.

This is usually explained to children when 10 they are between eight and twelve, whenever they seem capable of understanding; and most of those who come to see the child are young people, though often enough an adult comes, or comes back, to see the child. No matter how well the matter has been explained to them, these young spectators are always shocked and sickened at the sight. They feel disgust, which they had thought themselves superior to. They feel anger, outrage, impotence, despite all the explanations. They would like to do something for the child. But there is nothing they can do. If the child were brought up into the sunlight out of that vile place, if it were cleaned and fed and comforted, that would be a good thing, indeed; but if it were done, in that day and hour all the prosperity and beauty and delight of Omelas would wither and be destroyed. Those are the terms. To exchange all the goodness and grace of every life in Omelas for that single, small improvement: to throw away the happiness of thousands for the chance of the happiness of one: that would be to let guilt within the walls indeed.

The terms are strict and absolute; there may not even be a kind word spoken to the child.

Often the young people go home in tears, or in a tearless rage, when they have seen the child and faced this terrible paradox. They may brood over it for weeks or years. But as time goes on they begin to realize that even if the child could be released, it would not get much good of its freedom: a little vague pleasure of warmth and food, no doubt, but little more. It is too degraded and imbecile to know any real joy. It has been afraid too long ever to be free of fear. Its habits are too uncouth for it to respond to humane treatment. Indeed, after so long it would probably be wretched without walls about it to protect it, and darkness for its eyes, and its own excrement to sit in. Their tears at the bitter injustice dry when they begin to perceive the terrible justice of reality, and to accept it. Yet it is their tears and anger, the trying of their generosity and the acceptance of their helplessness, which are perhaps the true source of the splendor of their lives. Theirs is no vapid, irresponsible happiness. They know that they, like the child, are not free. They know compassion. It is the existence of the child, and their knowledge of its existence, that makes possible the nobility of their architecture, the poignancy of their music, the profundity of their science. It is because of the child that they are so gentle with children. They know that if the wretched one were not there snivelling in the dark, the other one, the flute-player, could make no joyful music as the young riders line up in their beauty for the race in the sunlight of the first morning of summer.

Now do you believe in them? Are they not more credible? But there is one more thing to tell, and this is quite incredible.

At times one of the adolescent girls or boys who go to see the child does not go home to weep or rage, does not, in fact, go home at all. Sometimes also a man or woman much older falls silent for a day or two, and then leaves home. These people go out into the street, and walk down the street alone. They keep walking, and walk straight out of the city of Omelas, through the beautiful gates. They keep walking across the farmlands of Omelas. Each one goes alone, youth or girl, man or woman. Night falls; the traveler must pass down village streets, between the houses with yellow-lit windows, and on out into the darkness of the fields. Each alone, they go west or north, towards the mountains. They go on. They leave Omelas, they walk ahead into the darkness, and they do not come back. The place they go towards is a place even less imaginable to most of us than the city of happiness. I cannot describe it at all. It is possible that it does not exist. But they seem to know where they are going, the ones who walk away from Omelas.

Topics for Critical Thinking and Writing

1. Summarize the point of the story — not the plot but what the story adds up to, what the author is getting at. Next, set forth what you would probably do (and why) if you were born in Omelas.

2. Consider the narrator's assertion that happiness "is based on a just discrimination of what is necessary" (para. 3). Do you agree? Why, or why not?

3. Do you think the story implies a criticism of contemporary American society? Explain.

27

How Free Is the Will of the Individual within Society?

Thoughts about Free Will

All theory is against the freedom of the will; all experience for it.　　—SAMUEL JOHNSON

Free will is doing gladly and freely that which one must do.　　—CARL G. JUNG

The will is never free—it is always attached to an object, a purpose. It is simply the engine in the car—it can't steer.　　—JOYCE CARY

A man may be a pessimistic determinist before lunch and an optimistic believer in the will's freedom after it.　　—ALDOUS HUXLEY

Fatalism, whose solving word in all crises of behavior is all striving is vain, will never reign supreme, for the impulse to take life strivingly is indestructible in the race. Moral creeds which speak to that impulse will be widely successful in spite of inconsistency, vagueness, and shadowy determination of expectancy. Man needs a rule for his will, and will invent one if one be not given him.　　—WILLIAM JAMES

Man is a masterpiece of creation if for no other reason than that, all the weight of evidence for determinism notwithstanding, he believes he has free will.　　—GEORG C. LICHTENBERG

We human beings do have some genuine freedom of choice and therefore some effective control over our own destinies. I am not a determinist. But I also believe that the decisive choice is seldom the latest choice in the series. More often than not, it will turn out to be some choice made relatively far back in the past.　　—ARNOLD TOYNBEE

We are responsible human beings, not blind automatons; persons, not puppets. By endowing us with freedom, God relinquished a measure of his own sovereignty and imposed certain limitations upon himself. If his children are free, they must do his will by a voluntary choice.

— MARTIN LUTHER KING JR.

Life is a card game. You play the hand that is dealt to you.

— PROVERBIAL

We must believe in free will. We have no choice.

— ISAAC BASHEVIS SINGER

Topics for Critical Thinking and Writing

1. If any one of these passages especially appeals to you, make it the thesis of an essay of about 500 words.

2. Take two of these passages — perhaps one that you especially like and one that you think is wrong-headed — and write a dialogue of about 500 words in which the two authors converse. They may each try to convince the other, or they may find that to some degree they share views and they may then work out a statement that both can accept. If you do take the position that one writer is on the correct track but the other is utterly mistaken, try to be fair to the view that you think is mistaken. (As an experiment in critical thinking, imagine that you accept it, and make the best case for it that you possibly can.)

PLATO

Plato (427–347 B.C.), an Athenian aristocrat by birth, was the student of one great philosopher (Socrates) and the teacher of another (Aristotle). His legacy of more than two dozen dialogues — imaginary discussions between Socrates and one or more other speakers, usually young Athenians — has been of such influence that the whole of Western philosophy can be characterized, A. N. Whitehead wrote, as "a series of footnotes to Plato." Plato's interests encompassed the full range of topics in philosophy: ethics, politics, logic, metaphysics, epistemology, aesthetics, psychology, and education.

The selection reprinted here, Crito, *is the third of four dialogues telling the story of the final days of Socrates (469–399 B.C.). The first in the sequence,* Euthyphro, *portrays Socrates in his typical role, questioning someone about his beliefs (in this case, the young aristocrat Euthyphro). The discussion is focused on the nature of piety, but the conversation breaks off before a final answer is reached — perhaps none is possible — because Socrates is on his way to stand trial before the Athenian assembly. He has been charged with "preaching false gods" (heresy) and "corrupting the youth" by causing them to doubt or disregard the wisdom of their elders. (How faithful to any actual event or discussion* Euthyphro *and Plato's other Socratic dialogues really are, scholars cannot say with assurance.)*

In Apology, *the second dialogue in the sequence, Plato (who remains entirely in the background, as he does in all the dialogues) recounts Socrates's public reply to the charges against him. During the speech, Socrates explains his life, reminding his fellow citizens that if he is (as* the oracle had pronounced) "the wisest of men," then it is only because he knows that he doesn't know what others believe or pretend they do know. The dialogue ends with Socrates being found guilty and duly sentenced to death.

The third in the series is Crito, but we will postpone comment on it for a moment and glance at the fourth dialogue, Phaedo, in which Plato portrays Socrates's final philosophical discussion. The topic, appropriately, is whether the soul is immortal. It ends with Socrates, in the company of his closest friends, bidding them a last farewell and drinking the fatal cup of hemlock.

Crito, the whole text of which is reprinted here, is the debate provoked by Crito, an old friend and admirer of Socrates. He visits Socrates in prison and urges him to escape while he still has the chance. After all, Crito argues, the guilty verdict was wrong and unfair, few Athenians really want to have Socrates put to death, his family and friends will be distraught, and so forth. Socrates will not have it. He patiently but firmly examines each of Crito's arguments and explains why it would be wrong to follow his advice.

Plato's Crito thus ranks with Sophocles's tragedy Antigone as one of the first explorations in Western literature of the perennial theme of our responsibility for obeying laws that challenge our conscientious moral convictions. Antigone concludes that she must disobey the law of Creon, tyrant of Thebes; Socrates concludes that he must obey the law of democratic Athens. In Crito, we have not only a superb illustration of Socratic dialogue and argument but also a portrait of a virtuous thinker at the end of a long life, reflecting on its course and on the moral principles that have guided him. We see Socrates living an "examined life," the only life he thought was worth living.

This translation is by Hugh Tredennick.

Crito

(SCENE: *A room in the State prison at Athens in the year 399 B.C. The time is half an hour before dawn, and the room would be almost dark but for the light of a little oil lamp. There is a pallet bed against the back wall. At the head of it a small table supports the lamp; near the foot of it Crito is sitting patiently on a stool. He is an old man, kindly, practical, simple-minded; at present he is suffering from acute emotional strain. On the bed lies Socrates asleep. He stirs, yawns, opens his eyes, and sees Crito.)*

SOCRATES: Here already, Crito? Surely it is still early?

CRITO: Indeed it is.

SOCRATES: About what time?

CRITO: Just before dawn.

SOCRATES: I wonder that the warder paid any attention to you. 5

CRITO: He is used to me now, Socrates, because I come here so often; besides, he is under some small obligation to me.

SOCRATES: Have you only just come, or have you been here for long?

CRITO: Fairly long.

SOCRATES: Then why didn't you wake me at once, instead of sitting by my bed so quietly?

CRITO: I wouldn't dream of such a thing, Socrates. I only wish I were not so sleepless and depressed myself. I have been wondering at you, because I saw how comfortably you were sleeping; and I deliberately didn't wake you because 10

I wanted you to go on being as comfortable as you could. I have often felt before in the course of my life how fortunate you are in your disposition, but I feel it more than ever now in your present misfortune when I see how easily and placidly you put up with it.

SOCRATES: Well, really, Crito, it would be hardly suitable for a man of my age to resent having to die.

CRITO: Other people just as old as you are get involved in these misfortunes, Socrates, but their age doesn't keep them from resenting it when they find themselves in your position.

SOCRATES: Quite true. But tell me, why have you come so early?

CRITO: Because I bring bad news, Socrates; not so bad from your point of view, I suppose, but it will be very hard to bear for me and your other friends, and I think that I shall find it hardest of all.

SOCRATES: Why, what is this news? Has the boat come in from Delos — the boat which ends my reprieve when it arrives?[1]

CRITO: It hasn't actually come in yet, but I expect that it will be here today, judging from the report of some people who have just arrived from Sunium and left it there. It's quite clear from their account that it will be here today; and so by tomorrow, Socrates, you will have to — to end your life.

SOCRATES: Well, Crito, I hope that it may be for the best; if the gods will it so, so be it. All the same, I don't think it will arrive today.

CRITO: What makes you think that?

SOCRATES: I will try to explain. I think I am right in saying that I have to die on the day after the boat arrives?

CRITO: That's what the authorities say, at any rate.

SOCRATES: Then I don't think it will arrive on this day that is just beginning, but on the day after. I am going by a dream that I had in the night, only a little while ago. It looks as though you were right not to wake me up.

CRITO: Why, what was the dream about?

SOCRATES: I thought I saw a gloriously beautiful woman dressed in white robes, who came up to me and addressed me in these words: "Socrates, to the pleasant land of Phthia on the third day thou shalt come."

CRITO: Your dream makes no sense, Socrates.

SOCRATES: To my mind, Crito, it is perfectly clear.

CRITO: Too clear, apparently. But look here, Socrates, it is still not too late to take my advice and escape. Your death means a double calamity for me. I shall not only lose a friend whom I can never possibly replace, but besides a great many people who don't know you and me very well will be sure to think that I let you down, because I could have saved you if I had been willing to spend the money; and what could be more contemptible than to get a name for thinking more of money than of your friends? Most people will never believe that it was you who refused to leave this place although we tried our hardest to persuade you.

SOCRATES: But my dear Crito, why should we pay so much attention to what "most people" think? The really reasonable people, who have more claim to be considered, will believe that the facts are exactly as they are.

---

[1] **Delos . . . arrives** Ordinarily execution was carried out immediately after sentencing, but the day before Socrates's trial was the first day of an annual ceremony that involved sending a ship to Delos. When the ship was absent — in this case for about a month — executions could not be performed. As Crito goes on to say, Socrates could easily escape, and indeed he could have left the country before being tried. [All notes are the editors'.]

CRITO: You can see for yourself, Socrates, that one has to think of popular opinion as well. Your present position is quite enough to show that the capacity of ordinary people for causing trouble is not confined to petty annoyances, but has hardly any limits if you once get a bad name with them.

SOCRATES: I only wish that ordinary people *had* unlimited capacity for doing harm; then they might have an unlimited power for doing good; which would be a splendid thing, if it were so. Actually they have neither. They cannot make a man wise or stupid; they simply act at random.

CRITO: Have it that way if you like; but tell me this, Socrates. I hope that you aren't worrying about the possible effects on me and the rest of your friends, and thinking that if you escape we shall have trouble with informers for having helped you to get away, and have to forfeit all our property or pay an enormous fine, or even incur some further punishment? If any idea like that is troubling you, you can dismiss it altogether. We are quite entitled to run that risk in saving you, and even worse, if necessary. Take my advice, and be reasonable.

SOCRATES: All that you say is very much in my mind, Crito, and a great deal more besides.

CRITO: Very well, then, don't let it distress you. I know some people who are willing to rescue you from here and get you out of the country for quite a moderate sum. And then surely you realize how cheap these informers are to buy off; we shan't need much money to settle them; and I think you've got enough of my money for yourself already. And then even supposing that in your anxiety for my safety you feel that you oughtn't to spend my money, there are these foreign gentlemen staying in Athens who are quite willing to spend theirs. One

30

of them, Simmias of Thebes, has actually brought the money with him for this very purpose; and Cebes and a number of others are quite ready to do the same. So as I say, you mustn't let any fears on these grounds make you slacken your efforts to escape; and you mustn't feel any misgivings about what you said at your trial, that you wouldn't know what to do with yourself if you left this country. Wherever you go, there are plenty of places where you will find a welcome; and if you choose to go to Thessaly, I have friends there who will make much of you and give you complete protection, so that no one in Thessaly can interfere with you.

Besides, Socrates, I don't even feel that it is right for you to try to do what you are doing, throwing away your life when you might save it. You are doing your best to treat yourself in exactly the same way as your enemies would, or rather did, when they wanted to ruin you. What is more, it seems to me that you are letting your sons down too. You have it in your power to finish their bringing up and education, and instead of that you are proposing to go off and desert them, and so far as you are concerned they will have to take their chance. And what sort of chance are they likely to get? The sort of thing that usually happens to orphans when they lose their parents. Either one ought not to have children at all, or one ought to see their upbringing and education through to the end. It strikes me that you are taking the line of least resistance, whereas you ought to make the choice of a good man and a brave one, considering that you profess to have made goodness your object all through life. Really, I am ashamed, both on your account and on ours your friends'; it will look as though we had played something like a coward's part all through this affair of yours. First, there was the way you came into court when it was quite unnecessary — that was the first act; then there was the conduct of the defense — that was the second; and finally, to complete the farce, we get this situation, which makes it appear that we have let you slip out of our hands through some lack of courage and enterprise on our part, because we didn't save you, and you didn't save yourself, when it would have been quite possible and practicable, if we had been any use at all.

There, Socrates; if you aren't careful, besides the suffering there will be all this disgrace for you and us to bear. Come, make up your mind. Really it's too late for that now; you ought to have it made up already. There is no alternative; the whole thing must be carried through during this coming night. If we lose any more time, it can't be done, it will be too late. I appeal to you, Socrates, on every ground; take my advice and please don't be unreasonable!

SOCRATES: My dear Crito, I appreciate your warm feelings very much — that is, assuming that they have some justification; if not, the stronger they are, the harder they will be to deal with. Very well, then; we must consider whether we ought to follow your advice or not. You know that this is not a new idea of mine; it has always been my nature never to accept advice from any of my friends unless reflection shows that it is the best course that reason offers. I cannot abandon the principles which I used to hold in the past simply because this accident has happened to me; they seem to me to be much as they were, and I respect and regard the same principles now as before.

So unless we can find better principles on this occasion, you can be quite sure that I shall not agree with you; not even if the power of the people conjures up fresh hordes of bogies to terrify our childish minds, by subjecting us to chains and executions and confiscations of our property.

Well, then, how can we consider the question most reasonably? Suppose that we begin by reverting to this view which you hold about people's opinions. Was it always right to argue that some opinions should be taken seriously but not others? Or was it always wrong? Perhaps it was right before the question of my death arose, but now we can see clearly that it was a mistaken persistence in a point of view which was really irresponsible nonsense. I should like very much to inquire into this problem, Crito, with your help, and to see whether the argument will appear in any different light to me now that I am in this position, or whether it will remain the same; and whether we shall dismiss it or accept it.

Serious thinkers, I believe, have always held some such view as the one which I mentioned just now: that some of the opinions which people entertain should be respected, and others should not. Now I ask you, Crito, don't you think that this is a sound principle? — You are safe from the prospect of dying tomorrow, in all human probability; and you are not likely to have your judgment upset by this impending calamity. Consider, then; don't you think that this is a sound enough principle, that one should not regard all the opinions that people hold, but only some and not others? What do you say? Isn't that a fair statement?

CRITO: Yes, it is.

SOCRATES: In other words, one should regard the good ones and not the bad?

CRITO: Yes.

SOCRATES: The opinions of the wise being good, and the opinions of the foolish bad?

CRITO: Naturally.

SOCRATES: To pass on, then: What do you think of the sort of illustration that I used to employ? When a man is in training, and taking it seriously, does he pay attention to all praise and criticism and opinion indiscriminately, or only when it comes from the one qualified person, the actual doctor or trainer?

CRITO: Only when it comes from the one qualified person.

SOCRATES: Then he should be afraid of the criticism and welcome the praise of the one qualified person, but not those of the general public.

CRITO: Obviously.

SOCRATES: So he ought to regulate his actions and exercises and eating and drinking by the judgment of his instructor, who has expert knowledge, rather than by the opinions of the rest of the public.

CRITO: Yes, that is so.

SOCRATES: Very well. Now if he disobeys the one man and disregards his opinion and commendations, and pays attention to the advice of the many who have no expert knowledge, surely he will suffer some bad effect?

CRITO: Certainly.

SOCRATES: And what is this bad effect? Where is it produced? — I mean, in what part of the disobedient person?

CRITO: His body, obviously; that is what suffers.

SOCRATES: Very good. Well now, tell me, Crito — we don't want to go through all the examples one by one — does this apply as a general rule, and above all to the sort of actions which we are trying to decide about: just and unjust, honorable and dishonorable, good and bad? Ought we to be guided and intimidated by the opinion of the many or by that of the one — assuming that there is someone with expert knowledge? Is it true that we ought to respect and fear this person more than all the rest put together; and that if we do not follow his guidance we shall spoil and mutilate that part of us which, as we used to say, is improved by right conduct and destroyed by wrong? Or is this all nonsense?

CRITO: No, I think it is true, Socrates.

SOCRATES: Then consider the next step. There is a part of us which is improved by healthy actions and ruined by unhealthy ones. If we spoil it by taking the advice of nonexperts, will life be worth living when this part is once ruined? The part I mean is the body; do you accept this?

CRITO: Yes.

SOCRATES: Well, is life worth living with a body which is worn out and ruined by health?

CRITO: Certainly not.

SOCRATES: What about the part of us which is mutilated by wrong actions and benefited by right ones? Is life worth living with this part ruined? Or do we believe that this part of us, whatever it may be, in which right and wrong operate, is of less importance than the body?

CRITO: Certainly not.

SOCRATES: It is really more precious?

CRITO: Much more.

SOCRATES: In that case, my dear fellow, what we ought to consider is not so much what people in general will say about us but how we stand with the expert in right and wrong, the one authority, who represents the actual truth. So in the first place your proposition is not correct when you say that we should consider popular opinion in questions of what is right and honorable and good, or the opposite. Of course one might object "All the same, the people have the power to put us to death."

CRITO: No doubt about that! Quite true, Socrates; it is a possible objection.

SOCRATES: But so far as I can see, my dear fellow, the argument which we have just been through is quite unaffected by it. At the same time I should like you to consider whether we are still satisfied on this point: that the really important thing is not to live, but to live well.

CRITO: Why, yes.

SOCRATES: And that to live well means the same thing as to live honorably or rightly?

CRITO: Yes.

SOCRATES: Then in the light of this agreement we must consider whether or not it is right for me to try to get away without an official discharge. If it turns out to be right, we must make the attempt; if not, we must let it drop. As for the considerations you raise about expense and reputation and bringing up children, I am afraid, Crito, that they represent the reflections of the ordinary public, who put people to death, and would bring them back to life if they could, with equal indifference to reason. Our real duty, I fancy, since the argument leads that way, is to consider one question only, the one which we raised just now: Shall we be acting rightly in paying money and showing gratitude to these people who are going to rescue me, and in escaping or arranging the escape ourselves, or shall we really be acting wrongly in doing all this? If it becomes clear that such conduct is wrong, I cannot help thinking that the question whether we are sure to die, or to suffer any other ill effect for that matter, if we stand our ground and take no action, ought not to weigh with us at all in comparison with the risk of doing what is wrong.

CRITO: I agree with what you say, Socrates; but I wish you would consider what we ought to *do*.

SOCRATES: Let us look at it together, my dear fellow; and if you can challenge any of my arguments, do so and I will listen to you; but if you can't, be a good fellow and stop telling me over and over again that I ought to leave this place without official permission. I am very anxious to obtain your approval before I adopt the course which I have in mind; I don't want to act against your convictions. Now give your attention to the starting point of this inquiry — I hope that you will be satisfied with my way of stating it — and try to answer my questions to the best of your judgment.

CRITO: Well, I will try.

SOCRATES: Do we say that one must never willingly do wrong, or does it depend upon circumstance? Is it true, as we have often agreed before, that there is no sense in which wrongdoing is good or honorable? Or have we jettisoned all our former convictions in these last few days? Can you and I at our age, Crito, have spent all these years in serious discussions without realizing that we were no better than a pair of children? Surely the truth is just what we have always said. Whatever the popular view is, and whether the alternative is pleasanter than the present one or even harder to bear, the fact remains that to do wrong is in every sense bad and dishonorable for the person who does it. Is that our view, or not?

CRITO: Yes, it is.

SOCRATES: Then in no circumstances must one do wrong.

CRITO: No.

SOCRATES: In that case one must not even do wrong when one is wronged, which most people regard as the natural course.

CRITO: Apparently not.

SOCRATES: Tell me another thing, Crito: Ought one to do injuries or not?

CRITO: Surely not, Socrates.

SOCRATES: And tell me: Is it right to do an injury in retaliation, as most people believe, or not?

CRITO: No, never.

SOCRATES: Because, I suppose, there is no difference between injuring people and wronging them.

CRITO: Exactly.

SOCRATES: So one ought not to return a wrong or an injury to any person, whatever the provocation is. Now be careful, Crito, that in making these single admissions you do not end by admitting something contrary to your real beliefs. I know that there are and always will be few people who think like this; and consequently between those who do think so and those who do not there can be no agreement on principle; they must always feel contempt when they observe one another's decisions. I want even you to consider very carefully whether you share my views and agree with me, and whether we can proceed with our discussion from the established hypothesis that it is never right to do a wrong or return a wrong or defend one's self against injury by retaliation; or whether you dissociate yourself from any share in this view as a basis for discussion. I have held it for a long time, and still hold it; but if you have formed any other opinion, say so and tell me what it is. If, on the other hand, you stand by what we have said, listen to my next point.

CRITO: Yes, I stand by it and agree with you. Go on.

SOCRATES: Well, here is my next point, or rather question. Ought one to fulfill all one's agreements, provided that they are right, or break them?

CRITO: One ought to fulfill them.

SOCRATES: Then consider the logical consequence. If we leave this place without first persuading the State to let us go, are we or are we not doing an injury, and doing it in a quarter where it is least justifiable? Are we or are we not abiding by our just agreements?

CRITO: I can't answer your question, Socrates; I am not clear in my mind.

SOCRATES: Look at it in this way. Suppose that while we were preparing to run away from here (or however one should describe it) the Laws and Constitution of Athens were to come and confront us and ask this question: "Now, Socrates, what are you proposing to do? Can you deny that by this act which you are contemplating you intend, so far as you have the power, to destroy us, the Laws, and the whole State as well? Do you imagine that a city can continue to exist and not be turned upside down, if the legal judgments which are pronounced in it have no force but are nullified and destroyed by private persons?" — how shall we answer this question, Crito, and others of the same kind? There is much that could be said, especially by a professional advocate, to protest against the invalidation of this law which enacts that judgments once pronounced shall be binding. Shall we say "Yes, I do intend to destroy the laws, because the State wronged me by passing a faulty judgment at my trial"? Is this to be our answer, or what?

CRITO: What you have just said, by all means, Socrates.

SOCRATES: Then what supposing the Laws say, "Was there provision for this in the agreement between you and us, Socrates? Or did you undertake to abide by whatever judgments the State pronounced?" If we expressed surprise at such language, they would probably say: "Never mind our language, Socrates, but answer our questions; after all, you are accustomed to the method of question and answer. Come now, what charge do you bring against us and the State, that you are trying to destroy us? Did we not give you life in the first place? Was it not through us that your father married your mother and begot you? Tell us, have you any complaint against those of us Laws that deal with marriage?" "No, none," I should say. "Well, have you any against the laws which deal with children's upbringing and education, such as you had yourself? Are you not grateful to those of us Laws which were instituted for this end, for requiring your father to give you a cultural and physical education?" "Yes," I should say. "Very good. Then since you have been born and brought up and educated, can you deny, in the first place, that you were our child and servant, both you and your ancestors? And if this is so, do you imagine that what is right for us is equally right for you, and that whatever we try to do to you, you are justified in retaliating? You did not have equality of rights with your father, or your employer (supposing that you had had one), to enable you to retaliate; you were not allowed to answer back when you were scolded or to hit back when you were beaten, or to do a great

many other things of the same kind. Do you expect to have such license against your country and its laws that if we try to put you to death in the belief that it is right to do so, you on your part will try your hardest to destroy your country and us its Laws in return? And will you, the true devotee of goodness, claim that you are justified in doing so? Are you so wise as to have forgotten that compared with your mother and father and all the rest of your ancestors your country is something far more precious, more venerable, more sacred, and held in greater honor both among gods and among all reasonable men? Do you not realize that you are even more bound to respect and placate the anger of your country than your father's anger? That if you cannot persuade your country you must do whatever it orders, and patiently submit to any punishment that it imposes, whether it be flogging or imprisonment? And if it leads you out to war, to be wounded or killed, you must comply, and it is right that you should do so; you must not give way or retreat or abandon your position. Both in war and in the law courts and everywhere else you must do whatever your city and your country commands, or else persuade it in accordance with universal justice; but violence is a sin even against your parents, and it is a far greater sin against your country" — What shall we say to this, Crito? — that what the Laws say is true, or not?

CRITO: Yes, I think so.

SOCRATES: "Consider, then, Socrates," the Laws would probably continue, "whether it is also true for us to say that what you are now trying to do to us is not right. Although we have brought you into

95

the world and reared you and educated you, and given you and all your fellow citizens a share in all the good things at our disposal, nevertheless by the very fact of granting our permission we openly proclaim this principle: that any Athenian, on attaining to manhood and seeing for himself the political organization of the State and us its Laws, is permitted, if he is not satisfied with us, to take his property and go away wherever he likes. If any of you chooses to go to one of our colonies, supposing that he should not be satisfied with us and the State, or to emigrate to any other country, not one of us Laws hinders or prevents him from going away wherever he likes, without any loss of property. On the other hand, if any one of you stands his ground when he can see how we administer justice and the rest of our public organization, we hold that by so doing he has in fact undertaken to do anything that we tell him; and we maintain that anyone who disobeys is guilty of doing wrong on three separate counts: first because we are his parents, and secondly because we are his guardians; and thirdly because, after promising obedience, he is neither obeying us nor persuading us to change our decision if we are at fault in any way; and although all our orders are in the form of proposals, not of savage commands, and we give him the choice of either persuading us or doing what we say, he is actually doing neither. These are the charges, Socrates, to which we say that you will be liable if you do what you are contemplating; and you will not be the least culpable of your fellow countrymen, but one of the most guilty." If I said "Why do you say that?" they would no doubt pounce upon me with perfect justice and point out that there are very few people in Athens who have entered into this agreement with them as explicitly as I have. They would say "Socrates, we have substantial evidence that you are satisfied with us and with the State. You would not have been so exceptionally reluctant to cross the borders of your country if you had not been exceptionally attached to it. You have never left the city to attend a festival or for any other purpose, except on some military expedition; you have never traveled abroad as other people do, and you have never felt the impulse to acquaint yourself with another country or constitution; you have been content with us and with our city. You have definitely chosen us, and undertaken to observe us in all your activities as a citizen; and as the crowning proof that you are satisfied with our city, you have begotten children in it. Furthermore, even at the time of your trial you could have proposed the penalty of banishment, if you had chosen to do so; that is, you could have done then with the sanction of the State what you are now trying to do without it. But whereas at that time you made a noble show of indifference if you had to die, and in fact preferred death, as you said, to banishment, now you show no respect for your earlier professions, and no regard for us, the Laws, whom you are trying to destroy; you are behaving like the lowest type of menial, trying to run away in spite of the contracts and undertakings by which you agreed to live as a member of our State. Now first answer this question: Are we or are we not speaking the truth when we say that you have undertaken, in deed if not in word, to live your life as a citizen in obedience to us?" What are we to say to that, Crito? Are we not bound to admit it?

CRITO: We cannot help it, Socrates.

SOCRATES: "It is a fact, then," they would say, "that you are breaking covenants and undertakings made with us, although you made them under no compulsion or misunderstanding, and were not compelled to decide in a limited time; you had seventy years in which you could have left the country, if you were not satisfied with us or felt that the agreements were unfair. You did not choose Sparta or Crete — your favorite models of good government — or any other Greek or foreign state; you could not have absented yourself from the city less if you had been lame or blind or decrepit in some other way. It is quite obvious that you stand by yourself above all other Athenians in your affection for this city and for us its Laws; — who would care for a city without laws? And now, after all this, are you not going to stand by your agreement? Yes, you are, Socrates, if you will take our advice; and then you will at least escape being laughed at for leaving the city.

"We invite you to consider what good you will do to yourself or your friends if you commit this breach of faith and stain your conscience. It is fairly obvious that the risk of being banished and either losing their citizenship or having their property confiscated will extend to your friends as well. As for yourself, if you go to one of the neighboring states, such as Thebes or Megara, which are both well governed, you will enter them as an enemy to their constitution[2] and all good patriots will eye you with suspicion as a destroyer of law

and order. Incidentally you will confirm the opinion of the jurors who tried you that they gave a correct verdict; a destroyer of laws might very well be supposed to have a destructive influence upon young and foolish human beings. Do you intend, then, to avoid well governed states and the higher forms of human society? And if you do, will life be worth living? Or will you approach these people and have the impudence to converse with them? What arguments will you use, Socrates? The same which you used here, that goodness and integrity, institutions and laws, are the most precious possessions of mankind? Do you not think that Socrates and everything about him will appear in a disreputable light? You certainly ought to think so. But perhaps you will retire from this part of the world and go to Crito's friends in Thessaly? That is the home of indiscipline and laxity, and no doubt they would enjoy hearing the amusing story of how you managed to run away from prison by arraying yourself in some costume or putting on a shepherd's smock or some other conventional runaway's disguise, and altering your personal appearance. And will no one comment on the fact that an old man of your age, probably with only a short time left to live, should dare to cling so greedily to life, at the price of violating the most stringent laws? Perhaps not, if you avoid irritating anyone. Otherwise, Socrates, you will hear a good many humiliating comments. So you will live as the toady and slave of all the populace, literally 'roistering in Thessaly,' as though you had left this country for Thessaly to attend a banquet there; and where will your discussions about goodness and uprightness be then, we should like to

---

[2] **as an enemy to their constitution** As a lawbreaker.

know? But of course you want to live for your children's sake, so that you may be able to bring them up and educate them. Indeed! by first taking them off to Thessaly and making foreigners of them, so that they may have that additional enjoyment? Or if that is not your intention, supposing that they are brought up here with you still alive, will they be better cared for and educated without you, because of course your friends will look after them? Will they look after your children if you go away to Thessaly, and not if you go away to the next world? Surely if those who profess to be your friends are worth anything, you must believe that they would care for them.

"No, Socrates; be advised by us your guardians, and do not think more of your children or of your life or of anything else than you think of what is right; so that when you enter the next world you may have all this to plead in your defense before the authorities there. It seems clear that if you do this thing, neither you nor any of your friends will be the better for it or be more upright or have a cleaner conscience here in this world, nor will it be better for you when you reach the next. As it is, you will leave this place, when you do, as the victim of a wrong done not by us, the Laws, but by your fellow men. But if you leave in that dishonorable way, returning wrong for wrong and evil for evil, breaking your agreements and covenants with us, and injuring those whom you least ought to injure—yourself, your friends, your country, and us—then you will have to face our anger in your lifetime, and in that place beyond when the laws of the other world know that you have tried, so far as you could, to destroy even us their brothers, they will not receive you with a kindly welcome. Do not take Crito's advice, but follow ours."

That, my dear friend Crito, I do assure you, is what I seem to hear them saying, just as a mystic seems to hear the strains of music; and the sound of their arguments rings so loudly in my head that I cannot hear the other side. I warn you that, as my opinion stands at present, it will be useless to urge a different view. However, if you think that you will do any good by it, say what you like.

CRITO: No, Socrates, I have nothing to say.

SOCRATES: Then give it up, Crito, and let us follow this course, since God points out the way.

Topics for Critical Thinking and Writing

1. State as precisely as you can all the arguments Crito uses to try to convince Socrates that he ought to escape. Which of these arguments seems to you to be the best? The worst? Why?

2. Socrates says to Crito, "I cannot abandon the principles which I used to hold in the past simply because this accident [the misfortune of being convicted by the Athenian assembly and then sentenced to death] has happened to me" (para. 35). Does this remark strike you as self-righteous? Stubborn? Smug? Stupid? Explain.

3. Socrates declares that "serious thinkers" have always held the view that "some of the opinions which people entertain should be respected, and others should not" (para. 37). There are two main alternatives to this principle: (a) One should respect *all* the opinions that others hold, and (b) one should respect *none* of the opinions of others. Socrates attacks

(a), but he ignores (b). What are his objections to (a)? Do you find them convincing? Why, or why not? Can you think of any convincing arguments against (b)?

4. As Socrates shows in his reply to Crito, he seems ready to believe (para. 63) that there are "expert[s] in right and wrong" — that is, persons with expert opinion or even authoritative knowledge on matters of right and wrong conduct — and that their advice should be sought and followed. Do you agree? Consider the thesis that there are no such experts, and write a 500-word essay defending or attacking it.

5. Socrates, as he comments to Crito, believes that "it is never right to do a wrong or return a wrong or defend one's self against injury by retaliation" (para. 85). He does not offer any argument for this thesis in the dialogue (although he does elsewhere). It was a very strange doctrine in his day, and even now it is not generally accepted. Write a 1,000-word essay defending or attacking this thesis.

6. Socrates seems to argue that (a) no one ought to do wrong, (b) it would injure the state for someone in Socrates's position to escape, and (c) this act would break a "just agreement" between the citizen and his state; therefore, (d) no one in Socrates's position should escape. Do you think this argument is valid? If not, what further assumptions would be needed to make it valid? Do you think the argument is sound (i.e., both valid and true in all its premises)? If not, explain. If you had to attack premise (b) or (c), which do you think is the more vulnerable, and why?

7. In the imaginary speech by the Laws of Athens to Socrates, especially in paragraph 93, the Laws convey a picture of the supremacy of the state over the individual — and Socrates seems to assent to this picture. Do you? Why, or why not?

8. The Laws (para. 95) claim that if Socrates were to escape, he would be "guilty of doing wrong on three separate counts." What are they? Do you agree with all or any? Why, or why not? Read the essay by Martin Luther King Jr., "Letter from Birmingham Jail" (p. 699), and decide how King would have responded to the judgment of the Laws of Athens.

9. At the end of their peroration (para. 99), the Laws of Athens say to Socrates: Take your punishment as prescribed, and at your death "you will leave this place . . . as the victim of a wrong done not by us, the Laws, but by your fellow men." To what wrong do the Laws allude? Do you agree that it is men and not laws who perpetrated this wrong? If you were in Socrates's position, would it matter to you if you were being wronged not by laws but only by men? Explain your response.

10. Compose a letter from Socrates to Martin Luther King Jr. in which Socrates responds to King's "Letter from Birmingham Jail" (p. 699).

GEORGE ORWELL

George Orwell was the pen name adopted by Eric Blair (1903–1950), an Englishman born in India. Orwell was educated at Eton, in England, but in 1921 he went back to the East and served for five years as a police officer in Burma (now Myanmar). Disillusioned with colonial imperialism, he returned to Europe, doing odd jobs while writing novels and stories. In 1936 he fought in the Spanish Civil War on the side of the Republicans, an experience he reported in Homage to Catalonia *(1938). His last years were spent writing in England. His best-known work probably is the satiric allegory* 1984 *(1949), showing a totalitarian state in which the citizens are perpetually under the eye of Big Brother. The following essay is from* Shooting an Elephant and Other Essays *(1950).*

Shooting an Elephant

In Moulmein, in Lower Burma, I was hated by large numbers of people—the only time in my life that I have been important enough for this to happen to me. I was subdivisional police officer of the town, and in an aimless, petty kind of way anti-European feeling was very bitter. No one had the guts to raise a riot, but if a European woman went through the bazaars alone somebody would probably spit betel juice over her dress. As a police officer I was an obvious target and was baited whenever it seemed safe to do so. When a nimble Burman tripped me up on the football field and the referee (another Burman) looked the other way, the crowd yelled with hideous laughter. This happened more than once. In the end the sneering yellow faces of young men that met me everywhere, the insults hooted after me when I was at a safe distance, got badly on my nerves. The young Buddhist priests were the worst of all. There were several thousands of them in the town and none of them seemed to have anything to do except stand on street corners and jeer at Europeans.

All this was perplexing and upsetting. For at that time I had already made up my mind that imperialism was an evil thing and the sooner I chucked up my job and got out of it the better. Theoretically—and secretly, of course—I was all for the Burmese and all against their oppressors, the British. As for the job I was doing, I hated it more bitterly than I can perhaps make clear. In a job like that you see the dirty work of Empire at close quarters. The wretched prisoners huddling in the stinking cages of the lock-ups, the grey, cowed faces of the long-term convicts, the scarred buttocks of the men who had been flogged with bamboos—all these oppressed me with an intolerable sense of guilt. But I could get nothing into perspective. I was young and ill-educated and I had had to think out my problems in the utter silence that is imposed on every Englishman in the East. I did not even know that the British Empire is dying, still less did I know that it is a great deal better than the younger empires that are going to supplant it. All I knew was that I was stuck between my hatred of the empire I served and my rage against the evil-spirited little beasts who tried to make my job impossible. With one part of my mind I thought of the British Raj[1] as an unbreakable tyranny, as something clamped down, *in saecula saeculorum*,[2] upon the will of prostrate peoples; with another part I thought that the greatest joy in the world would be to drive a bayonet into a Buddhist priest's guts. Feelings like these are the normal

---

[1]**British Raj** British imperial government in India and Burma. [All notes are the editors'.]
[2]*in saecula saeculorum* Forever (Latin). A term used in Christian liturgy.

by-products of imperialism; ask any Anglo-Indian official, if you can catch him off duty.

One day something happened which in a roundabout way was enlightening. It was a tiny incident in itself, but it gave me a better glimpse than I had had before of the real nature of imperialism — the real motives for which despotic governments act. Early one morning the sub-inspector at a police station the other end of the town rang me up on the 'phone and said that an elephant was ravaging the bazaar. Would I please come and do something about it? I did not know what I could do, but I wanted to see what was happening and I got on to a pony and started out. I took my rifle, an old .44 Winchester and much too small to kill an elephant, but I thought the noise might be useful *in terrorem*.[3] Various Burmans stopped me on the way and told me about the elephant's doings. It was not, of course, a wild elephant, but a tame one which had gone "must."[4] It had been chained up, as tame elephants always are when their attack of "must" is due, but on the previous night it had broken its chain and escaped. Its mahout, the only person who could manage it when it was in that state, had set out in pursuit, but had taken the wrong direction and was now twelve hours' journey away, and in the morning the elephant had suddenly reappeared in the town. The Burmese population had no weapons and were quite helpless against it. It had already destroyed somebody's bamboo hut, killed a cow and raided some fruit-stalls and devoured the stock; also it had met the municipal rubbish van and, when the driver jumped out and took to his heels, had turned the van over and inflicted violences upon it.

The Burmese sub-inspector and some Indian constables were waiting for me in the quarter where the elephant had been seen. It was a very poor quarter, a labyrinth of squalid bamboo huts, thatched with palm-leaf, winding all over a steep hillside. I remember that it was a cloudy, stuffy morning at the beginning of the rains. We began questioning the people as to where the elephant had gone and, as usual, failed to get any definite information. That is invariably the case in the East; a story always sounds clear enough at a distance, but the nearer you get to the scene of events the vaguer it becomes. Some of the people said that the elephant had gone in one direction, some said that he had gone in another, some professed not even to have heard of any elephant. I had almost made up my mind that the whole story was a pack of lies, when we heard yells a little distance away. There was a loud, scandalized cry of "Go away, child! Go away this instant!" and an old woman with a switch in her hand came round the corner of a hut, violently shooing away a crowd of naked children. Some more women followed, clicking their tongues and exclaiming; evidently there was something that the children ought not to have seen. I rounded the hut and saw a man's dead body sprawling in the mud. He was an Indian, a black Dravidian coolie, almost naked, and he could not have been dead many minutes. The people said that the elephant had come suddenly upon him round the corner of the hut, caught him with its trunk, put its foot on his back and ground him into the earth. This was the rainy season and the ground was soft, and his face had scored a trench a foot deep and a couple of yards long. He was lying on his belly with arms crucified and head sharply twisted to one side. His face was coated with mud, the eyes wide open, the teeth bared and grinning

---

[3] *in terrorem* As a warning.
[4] **"must"** Into sexual heat.

with an expression of unendurable agony. (Never tell me, by the way, that the dead look peaceful. Most of the corpses I have seen looked devilish.) The friction of the great beast's foot had stripped the skin from his back as neatly as one skins a rabbit. As soon as I saw the dead man I sent an orderly to a friend's house nearby to borrow an elephant rifle. I had already sent back the pony, not wanting it to go mad with fright and throw me if it smelt the elephant.

The orderly came back in a few minutes with a rifle and five cartridges, and meanwhile some Burmans had arrived and told us that the elephant was in the paddy fields below, only a few hundred yards away. As I started forward practically the whole population of the quarter flocked out of the houses and followed me. They had seen the rifle and were all shouting excitedly that I was going to shoot the elephant. They had not shown much interest in the elephant when he was merely ravaging their homes, but it was different now that he was going to be shot. It was a bit of fun to them, as it would be to an English crowd; besides they wanted the meat. It made me vaguely uneasy. I had no intention of shooting the elephant — I had merely sent for the rifle to defend myself if necessary — and it is always unnerving to have a crowd following you. I marched down the hill, looking and feeling a fool, with the rifle over my shoulder and an ever-growing army of people jostling at my heels. At the bottom, when you got away from the huts, there was a metalled road and beyond that a miry waste of paddy fields a thousand yards across, not yet ploughed but soggy from the first rains and dotted with coarse grass. The elephant was standing eight yards from the road, his left side towards us. He took not the slightest notice of the crowd's approach. He was tearing up bunches of grass, beating them against his

knees to clean them and stuffing them into his mouth.

I had halted on the road. As soon as I saw the elephant I knew with perfect certainty that I ought not to shoot him. It is a serious matter to shoot a working elephant — it is comparable to destroying a huge and costly piece of machinery — and obviously one ought not to do it if it can possibly be avoided. And at that distance, peacefully eating, the elephant looked no more dangerous than a cow. I thought then and I think now that his attack of "must" was already passing off; in which case he would merely wander harmlessly about until the mahout came back and caught him. Moreover, I did not in the least want to shoot him. I decided that I would watch him for a little while to make sure that he did not turn savage again, and then go home.

But at that moment I glanced round at the crowd that had followed me. It was an immense crowd, two thousand at the least and growing every minute. It blocked the road for a long distance on either side. I looked at the sea of yellow faces above the garish clothes — faces all happy and excited over this bit of fun, all certain that the elephant was going to be shot. They were watching me as they would watch a conjurer about to perform a trick. They did not like me, but with the magical rifle in my hands I was momentarily worth watching. And suddenly I realized that I should have to shoot the elephant after all. The people expected it of me and I had got to do it; I could feel their two thousand wills pressing me forward, irresistibly. And it was at this moment, as I stood there with the rifle in my hands, that I first grasped the hollowness, the futility of the white man's dominion in the East. Here was I, the white man with his gun, standing in front of the unarmed native crowd — seemingly the leading actor of the piece; but in reality I was only an absurd puppet pushed to and fro by the will of those yellow faces behind. I perceived in this moment that when the white man turns tyrant it is his own freedom that he destroys. He becomes a sort of hollow, posing dummy, the conventionalized figure of a sahib. For it is the condition of his rule that he shall spend his life in trying to impress the "natives," and so in every crisis he has got to do what the "natives" expect of him. He wears a mask, and his face grows to fit it. I had got to shoot the elephant. I had committed myself to doing it when I sent for the rifle. A sahib has got to act like a sahib; he has got to appear resolute, to know his own mind and do definite things. To come all that way, rifle in hand, with two thousand people marching at my heels, and then to trail feebly away, having done nothing — no, that was impossible. The crowd would laugh at me. And my whole life, every white man's life in the East, was one long struggle not to be laughed at.

But I did not want to shoot the elephant. I watched him beating his bunch of grass against his knees, with that preoccupied grandmotherly air that elephants have. It seemed to me that it would be murder to shoot him. At that age I was not squeamish about killing animals, but I had never shot an elephant and never wanted to. (Somehow it always seems worse to kill a *large* animal.) Besides, there was the beast's owner to be considered. Alive, the elephant was worth at least a hundred pounds; dead, he would only be worth the value of his tusks, five pounds, possibly. But I had got to act quickly. I turned to some experienced-looking Burmans who had been there when we arrived, and asked them how the elephant had been behaving. They all said the same thing; he took no notice of you if you left him alone, but he might charge if you went too close to him.

It was perfectly clear to me what I ought to do. I ought to walk up to within, say, twenty-five yards of the elephant and test his behavior. If he charged, I could shoot; if he took no notice of me, it would be safe to leave him until the mahout came back. But also I knew that I was going to do no such thing. I was a poor shot with a rifle and the ground was soft mud into which one would sink at every step. If the elephant charged and I missed him, I should have about as much chance as a toad under a steamroller. But even then I was not thinking particularly of my own skin, only of the watchful yellow faces behind. For at that moment, with the crowd watching me, I was not afraid in the ordinary sense, as I would have been if I had been alone. A white man mustn't be frightened in front of "natives"; and so, in general, he isn't frightened. The sole thought in my mind was that if anything went wrong those two thousand Burmans would see me pursued, caught, trampled on and reduced to a grinning corpse like that Indian up the hill. And if that happened it was quite probable that some of them would laugh. That would never do. There was only one alternative. I shoved the cartridges into the magazine and lay down on the road to get a better aim.

The crowd grew very still, and a deep, low, [10] happy sigh, as of people who see the theatre curtain go up at last, breathed from innumerable throats. They were going to have their bit of fun after all. The rifle was a beautiful German thing with cross-hair sights. I did not then know that in shooting an elephant one would shoot to cut an imaginary bar running from ear-hole to ear-hole. I ought, therefore, as the elephant was sideways on, to have aimed straight at his ear-hole; actually I aimed several inches in front of this, thinking the brain would be further forward.

When I pulled the trigger I did not hear the bang or feel the kick — one never does when a shot goes home — but I heard the devilish roar of glee that went up from the crowd. In that instant, in too short a time, one would have thought, even for the bullet to get there, a mysterious, terrible change had come over the elephant. He neither stirred nor fell, but every line of his body had altered. He looked suddenly stricken, shrunken, immensely old, as though the frightful impact of the bullet had paralyzed him without knocking him down. At last, after what seemed a long time — it might have been five seconds, I dare say — he sagged flabbily to his knees. His mouth slobbered. An enormous senility seemed to have settled upon him. One could have imagined him thousands of years old. I fired again into the same spot. At the second shot he did not collapse but climbed with desperate slowness to his feet and stood weakly upright, with legs sagging and head dropping. I fired a third time. That was the shot that did for him. You could see the agony of it jolt his whole body and knock the last remnant of strength from his legs. But in falling he seemed for a moment to rise, for as his hind legs collapsed beneath him he seemed to tower upward like a huge rock toppling, his trunk reaching skywards like a tree. He trumpeted, for the first and only time. And then down he came, his belly towards me, with a crash that seemed to shake the ground even where I lay.

I got up. The Burmans were already racing past me across the mud. It was obvious that the elephant would never rise again, but he was not dead. He was breathing very rhythmically with long rattling gasps, his great mound of a side painfully rising and falling. His mouth was wide open — I could see far down into caverns of pale pink throat. I waited a long time for him to die, but his breathing did not weaken. Finally I fired my two remaining shots into the spot where I thought his heart must be. The thick blood welled out of him like red velvet, but still he did not die. His body did not even jerk when the shots hit him, the tortured breathing continued without a pause. He was dying, very slowly and in great agony, but in some world remote from me where not even a bullet could damage him further. I felt that I had got to put an end to that dreadful noise. It seemed dreadful to see the great beast lying there, powerless to move and yet powerless to die, and not even to be able to finish him. I sent back for my small rifle and poured shot after shot into his heart and down his throat. They seemed to make no impression. The tortured gasps continued as steadily as the ticking of a clock.

In the end I could not stand it any longer and went away. I heard later that it took him half an hour to die. Burmans were bringing dahs[5] and baskets even before I left, and I was told they had stripped his body almost to the bones by the afternoon.

Afterwards, of course, there were endless discussions about the shooting of the elephant. The owner was furious, but he was only an Indian and could do nothing. Besides, legally I had done the right thing, for a mad elephant has to be killed, like a mad dog, if its owner fails to control it. Among the Europeans opinion was divided. The older men said I was right, the younger men said it was a damn shame to shoot an elephant for killing a coolie, because an elephant was worth more than any damn Coringhee coolie. And afterwards I was very glad that the coolie had been killed; it put me legally in the right and it gave me a sufficient pretext for shooting the elephant. I often wondered whether any of the others grasped that I had done it solely to avoid looking a fool.

---

[5]**dahs** Large knives.

Topics for Critical Thinking and Writing

1. Did George Orwell shoot the elephant of his own free will? Or did he shoot the elephant because he *had* to shoot it? What does he say about this? Do you find his judgment convincing or not? Write a 500-word essay explaining your answer.

2. Was Orwell justified in shooting the elephant? Did he do the right thing in killing it? In the aftermath, did he think he did the right thing? Do you? Write a 500-word essay explaining your answers.

3. Orwell says, "As soon as I saw the elephant I knew with perfect certainty that I ought not to shoot him" (para. 6). How could he claim to "know" this, when moments later he did shoot the elephant?

4. Orwell says in passing, "Somehow it always seems worse to kill a *large* animal" (para. 8). Explain why you think Orwell says this and whether you agree.

5. A biographer who did research on Orwell in Burma reported that he could find no supporting documentation, either in the local newspapers or in the files of the police, that this episode ever occurred. Suppose that Orwell made it up. If so, is your response different? Explain.

6. If, pressured by circumstances, you have ever acted against what you might think is your reason or your nature, report the experience, and give your present evaluation of your behavior.

WALTER T. STACE

Walter T. Stace (1886–1967), a professor of philosophy at Princeton University for many years, was the author of several books, including Religion and the Modern Mind *(1952), from which this selection is taken. The title is the editors'.*

Is Determinism Inconsistent with Free Will?

The second great problem which the rise of scientific naturalism has created for the modern mind concerns the foundations of morality. The old religious foundations have largely crumbled away, and it may well be thought that the edifice built upon them by generations of men is in danger of collapse. A total collapse of moral behavior is, as I pointed out before, very unlikely. For a society in which this occurred could not survive. Nevertheless the danger to moral standards inherent in the virtual disappearance of their old religious foundations is not illusory.

I shall first discuss the problem of free will, for it is certain that if there is no free will there can be no morality. Morality is concerned with what men ought and ought not to do. But if a man has no freedom to choose what he will do, if whatever he does is done under compulsion, then it does not make sense to tell him that he ought not to have done what he did and that he ought to do something different. All moral precepts would in such case be meaningless. Also if he acts always under compulsion, how can he be held morally responsible for his actions? How can he, for example, be punished for what he could not help doing?

It is to be observed that those learned professors of philosophy or psychology who deny the existence of free will do so only in their professional moments and in their studies and lecture rooms. For when it comes to doing anything practical, even of the most trivial kind, they invariably behave as if they and others were free. They inquire from you at dinner whether you will choose this dish or that dish. They will ask a child why he told a lie, and will punish him for not having chosen the way of truthfulness. All of which is inconsistent with a disbelief in free will. This should cause us to suspect that the problem is not a real one; and this, I believe, is the case. The dispute is merely verbal, and is due to nothing but a confusion about the meanings of words. It is what is now fashionably called a semantic problem.

How does a verbal dispute arise? Let us consider a case which, although it is absurd in the sense that no one would ever make the mistake which is involved in it, yet illustrates the principle which we shall have to use in the solution of the problem. Suppose that someone believed that the word "man" means a certain sort of five-legged animal; in short that "five-legged animal" is the correct *definition* of man. He might then look around the world, and rightly observing that there are no five-legged animals in it, he might proceed to deny the existence of men. This preposterous conclusion would have been reached because he was using an incorrect definition of "man." All you would have to do to show him his mistake would be to give him the correct definition; or at least to

show him that his definition was wrong. Both the problem and its solution would, of course, be entirely verbal. The problem of free will, and its solution, I shall maintain, is verbal in exactly the same way. The problem has been created by the fact that learned men, especially philosophers, have assumed an incorrect definition of *free will,* and then finding that there is nothing in the world which answers to their definition, have denied its existence. As far as logic is concerned, their conclusion is just as absurd as that of the man who denies the existence of men. The only difference is that the mistake in the latter case is obvious and crude, while the mistake which the deniers of free will have made is rather subtle and difficult to detect.

Throughout the modern period, until quite recently, it was assumed, both by the philosophers who denied free will and by those who defended it, that *determinism is inconsistent with free will.* If a man's actions were wholly determined by chains of causes stretching back into the remote past, so that they could be predicted beforehand by a mind which knew all the causes, it was assumed that they could not in that case be free. This implies that a certain definition of actions done from free will was assumed, namely that they are actions *not* wholly determined by causes or predictable beforehand. Let us shorten this by saying that free will was defined as meaning indeterminism. This is the incorrect definition which has led to the denial of free will. As soon as we see what the true definition is we shall find that the question whether the world is deterministic, as Newtonian science implied, or in a measure indeterministic, as current physics teaches, is wholly irrelevant to the problem.

Of course there is a sense in which one can define a word arbitrarily in any way one pleases. But a definition may nevertheless be called correct or incorrect. It is correct if it accords with a *common usage* of the word defined. It is incorrect if it does not. And if you give an incorrect definition, absurd and untrue results are likely to follow. For instance, there is nothing to prevent you from arbitrarily defining a man as a five-legged animal, but this is incorrect in the sense that it does not accord with the ordinary meaning of the word. Also it has the absurd result of leading to a denial of the existence of men. This shows that *common usage is the criterion for deciding whether a definition is correct or not.* And this is the principle which I shall apply to free will. I shall show that indeterminism is not what is meant by the phrase "free will" *as it is commonly used.* And I shall attempt to discover the correct definition by inquiring how the phrase is used in ordinary conversation.

Here are a few samples of how the phrase might be used in ordinary conversation. It will be noticed that they include cases in which the question whether a man acted with free will is asked in order to determine whether he was morally and legally responsible for his acts.

JONES: I once went without food for a week.
SMITH: Did you do that of your own free will?
JONES: No. I did it because I was lost in a desert and could find no food.

But suppose that the man who had fasted was Mahatma Gandhi. The conversation might then have gone:

GANDHI: I once fasted for a week.
SMITH: Did you do that of your own free will?
GANDHI: Yes. I did it because I wanted to compel the British Government to give India its independence.

Take another case. Suppose that I had stolen some bread, but that I was as truthful as George Washington. Then, if I were charged with the crime in court, some exchange of the following sort might take place:

JUDGE: Did you steal the bread of your own free will?
STACE: Yes. I stole it because I was hungry.

Or in different circumstances the conversation might run: [10]

JUDGE: Did you steal of your own free will?
STACE: No. I stole because my employer threatened to beat me if I did not.

At a recent murder trial in Trenton some of the accused had signed confessions, but afterwards asserted that they had done so under police duress. The following exchange might have occurred:

JUDGE: Did you sign this confession of your own free will?
PRISONER: No. I signed it because the police beat me up.

Now suppose that a philosopher had been a member of the jury. We could imagine this conversation taking place in the jury room.

FOREMAN OF THE JURY: The prisoner says he signed the confession because he was beaten, and not of his own free will.
PHILOSOPHER: This is quite irrelevant to the case. There is no such thing as free will.
FOREMAN: Do you mean to say that it makes no difference whether he signed because his conscience made him want to tell the truth or because he was beaten?
PHILOSOPHER: None at all. Whether he was caused to sign by a beating or by some

desire of his own — the desire to tell the truth, for example — in either case his signing was causally determined, and therefore in neither case did he act of his own free will. Since there is no such thing as free will, the question whether he signed of his own free will ought not to be discussed by us.

The foreman and the rest of the jury would rightly conclude that the philosopher must be making some mistake. What sort of a mistake could it be? There is only one possible answer. The philosopher must be using the phrase "free will" in some peculiar way of his own which is not the way in which men usually use it when they wish to determine a question of moral responsibility. That is, he must be using an incorrect definition of it as implying action not determined by causes.

Suppose a man left his office at noon, and were questioned about it. Then we might hear this:

JONES: Did you go out of your own free will?
SMITH: Yes. I went out to get my lunch.

But we might hear:

JONES: Did you leave your office of your own free will?
SMITH: No. I was forcibly removed by the police.

We have now collected a number of cases of actions which, in the ordinary usage of the English language, would be called cases in which people have acted of their own free will. We should also say in all these cases that they *chose* to act as they did. We should also say that they could have acted otherwise, if they had chosen. For instance, Mahatma Gandhi was not compelled to fast; he chose to do so. He could have eaten if he had wanted

to. When Smith went out to get his lunch, he chose to do so. He could have stayed and done some more work, if he had wanted to. We have also collected a number of cases of the opposite kind. They are cases in which men were not able to exercise their free will. They had no choice. They were compelled to do as they did. The man in the desert did not fast of his own free will. He had no choice in the matter. He was compelled to fast because there was nothing for him to eat. And so with the other cases. It ought to be quite easy, by an inspection of these cases, to tell what we ordinarily mean when we say that a man did or did not exercise free will. We ought therefore to be able to extract from them the proper definition of the term. Let us put the cases in a table:

Free Acts	Unfree Acts
Gandhi fasting because he wanted to free India.	The man fasting in the desert because there was no food.
Stealing bread because one is hungry.	Stealing because one's employer threatened to beat one.
Signing a confession because one wanted to tell the truth.	Signing because the police beat one.
Leaving the office because one wanted one's lunch.	Leaving because forcibly removed.

It is obvious that to find the correct definition of free acts we must discover what characteristic is common to all the acts in the left-hand column, and is, at the same time, absent from all the acts in the right-hand column. This characteristic which all free acts have, and which no unfree acts have, will be the defining characteristic of free will.

Is being uncaused, or not being determined by causes, the characteristic of which we are in search? It cannot be, because although it is true that all the acts in the right-hand column have causes, such as the beating by the police or the absence of food in the desert, so also do the acts in the left-hand column. Mr. Gandhi's fasting was caused by his desire to free India, the man leaving his office by his hunger, and so on. Moreover there is no reason to doubt that these causes of the free acts were in turn caused by prior conditions, and that these were again the results of causes, and so on back indefinitely into the past. Any physiologist can tell us the causes of hunger. What caused Mr. Gandhi's tremendously powerful desire to free India is no doubt more difficult to discover. But it must have had causes. Some of them may have lain in peculiarities of his glands or brain, others in his past experiences, others in his heredity, others in his education. Defenders of free will have usually tended to deny such facts. But to do so is plainly a case of special pleading, which is unsupported by any scrap of evidence. The only reasonable view is that all human actions, both those which are freely done and those which are not, are either wholly determined by causes, or at least as much determined as other events in nature. It may be true, as the physicists tell us, that nature is not as deterministic as was once thought. But whatever degree of determinism prevails in the world, human actions appear to be as much determined as anything else. And if this is so, it cannot be the case that what distinguishes actions freely chosen from those which are not free is that the latter are determined by causes while the former

are not. Therefore, being uncaused or being undetermined by causes must be an incorrect definition of free will.

What, then, is the difference between acts which are freely done and those which are not? What is the characteristic which is present to all the acts in the left-hand column and absent from all those in the right-hand column? Is it not obvious that, although both sets of actions have causes, the causes of those in the left-hand column are *of a different kind* from the causes of those in the right-hand column? The free acts are all caused by desires, or motives, or by some sort of internal psychological states of the agent's mind. The unfree acts, on the other hand, are all caused by physical forces or physical conditions, outside the agent. Police arrest means physical force exerted from the outside; the absence of food in the desert is a physical condition of the outside world. We may therefore frame the following rough definitions. *Acts freely done are those whose immediate causes are psychological states in the agent. Acts not freely done are those whose immediate causes are states of affairs external to the agent.*

It is plain that if we define free will in this [20] way, then free will certainly exists, and the philosopher's denial of its existence is seen to be what it is — nonsense. For it is obvious that all those actions of men which we should ordinarily attribute to the exercise of their free will, or of which we should say that they freely chose to do them, are in fact actions which have been caused by their own desires, wishes, thoughts, emotions, impulses, or other psychological states.

In applying our definition we shall find that it usually works well, but that there are some puzzling cases which it does not seem exactly to fit. These puzzles can always be solved by paying careful attention to the ways in which words are used, and remembering that they are not always used consistently. I have space for only one example. Suppose that a thug threatens to shoot you unless you give him your wallet, and suppose that you do so. Do you, in giving him your wallet, do so of your own free will or not? If we apply our definition, we find that you acted freely, since the immediate cause of the action was not an actual outside force but the fear of death, which is a psychological cause. Most people, however, would say that you did not act of your own free will but under compulsion. Does this show that our definition is wrong? I do not think so. Aristotle, who gave a solution of the problem of free will substantially the same as ours (though he did not use the term "free will"), admitted that there are what he called "mixed" or borderline cases in which it is difficult to know whether we ought to call the acts free or compelled. In the case under discussion, though no actual force was used, the gun at your forehead so nearly approximated to actual force that we tend to say the case was one of compulsion. It is a borderline case.

Here is what may seem like another kind of puzzle. According to our view an action may be free though it could have been predicted beforehand with certainty. But suppose you told a lie, and it was certain beforehand that you would tell it. How could one then say, "You could have told the truth"? The answer is that it is perfectly true that you could have told the truth *if* you had wanted to. In fact you would have done so, for in that case the causes producing your action, namely your desires, would have been different, and would therefore have produced different effects. It is a delusion that predictability and free will are incompatible. This agrees with common sense. For if, knowing your character, I predict that you will act honorably, no one would say when you do act honorably, that this shows you did not do so of your own free will.

Since free will is a condition of moral responsibility, we must be sure that our theory of free will gives a sufficient basis for it. To be held morally responsible for one's actions means that one may be justly punished or rewarded, blamed or praised, for them. But it is not just to punish a man for what he cannot help doing. How can it be just to punish him for an action which it was certain beforehand that he would do? We have not attempted to decide whether, as a matter of fact, all events, including human actions, are completely determined. For that question is irrelevant to the problem of free will. But if we assume for the purposes of argument that complete determinism is true, but that we are nevertheless free, it may then be asked whether such a deterministic free will is compatible with moral responsibility. For it may seem unjust to punish a man for an action which it could have been predicted with certainty beforehand that he would do.

But that determinism is incompatible with moral responsibility is as much a delusion as that it is incompatible with free will. You do not excuse a man for doing a wrong act because, knowing his character, you felt certain beforehand that he would do it. Nor do you deprive a man of a reward or prize because, knowing his goodness or his capabilities, you felt certain beforehand that he would win it.

Volumes have been written on the justification of punishment. But so far as it affects the question of free will, the essential principles involved are quite simple. The punishment of a man for doing a wrong act is justified, either on the ground that it will correct his own character, or that it will deter other people from doing similar acts. The instrument of punishment has been in the past, and no doubt still is, often unwisely used; so that it may often have done more harm than good. But that is not relevant to our present problem. Punishment, if and when it is justified, is justified only on one or both of the grounds just mentioned. The question then is how, if we assume determinism, punishment can correct character or deter people from evil actions.

Suppose that your child develops a habit of telling lies. You give him a mild beating. Why? Because you believe that his personality is such that the usual motives for telling the truth do not cause him to do so. You therefore supply the missing cause, or motive, in the shape of pain and the fear of future pain if he repeats his untruthful behavior. And you hope that a few treatments of this kind will condition him to the habit of truth-telling, so that he will come to tell the truth without the infliction of pain. You assume that his actions are determined by causes, but that the usual causes of truth-telling do not in him produce their usual effects. You therefore supply him with an artificially injected motive, pain and fear, which you think will in the future cause him to speak truthfully.

The principle is exactly the same where you hope, by punishing one man, to deter others from wrong actions. You believe that the fear of punishment will cause those who might otherwise do evil to do well.

We act on the same principle with nonhuman, and even with inanimate, things, if they do not behave in the way we think they ought to behave. The rose bushes in the garden produce only small and poor blooms, whereas we want large and rich ones. We supply a cause which will produce large blooms, namely fertilizer. Our automobile does not go properly. We supply a cause which will make it go better, namely oil in the works. The punishment for the man, the fertilizer for the plant, and the oil for the car are all justified by the same principle and in the same way. The only difference is that different kinds of things require different kinds of causes to make them do what they should. Pain may be the appropriate remedy to apply, in certain cases, to human beings, and oil to the machine. It is, of course, of no use to inject motor oil into the boy or to beat the machine.

Thus we see that moral responsibility is not only consistent with determinism, but requires it. The assumption on which punishment is based is that human behavior is causally determined. If pain could not be a cause of truth-telling there would be no justification at all for punishing lies. If human actions and volitions were uncaused, it would be useless either to punish or reward, or indeed to do anything else to correct people's bad behavior. For nothing that you could do would in any way influence them. Thus moral responsibility would entirely disappear. If there were no determinism of human beings at all, their actions would be completely unpredictable and capricious, and therefore irresponsible. And this is in itself a strong argument against the common view of philosophers that free will means being undetermined by causes.

Topics for Critical Thinking and Writing

1. Walter Stace asserts that "if there is no free will there can be no morality" (para. 2). What is his reasoning (see para. 23)? Do you agree? Why, or why not?

2. "The dispute is merely verbal," Stace proclaims in paragraph 3. What "dispute"? Why "merely verbal"? What would Stace say to someone who insists that the existence or nonexistence of free will is a question of *fact*?

3. What is *determinism* (para. 5)? Why does Stace seem to think that philosophers are strongly inclined to believe in it?

4. Stace claims that he will show that "indeterminism is not what is meant by . . . 'free will' *as it is commonly used*" (para. 6). What is his argument? What does he think *free will* means as the term is "commonly used"? Are you convinced? Why, or why not? Write a 500-word essay answering these questions.

5. Stace insists that "all human actions . . . are . . . at least as much determined as other events in nature" (para. 18). How might one argue against this?

6. Complete the following definition so that it captures Stace's view: "When Smith did *X*, he acted freely if and only if . . ."

7. Stace mentions some "puzzling cases" (para. 21) that do not quite fit, he admits, his analysis of free will. Give an example of such a case, and explain why it is puzzling.

8. Why does Stace conclude in paragraph 22 that "it is a delusion that predictability and free will are incompatible"? Do you agree? Why, or why not?

9. It seems paradoxical to assert, as Stace does in his last paragraph, that "moral responsibility is not only consistent with determinism, but requires it." Explain Stace's view here in no more than 250 words.

MARTIN LUTHER KING JR.

Martin Luther King Jr. (1929–1968) was born in Atlanta and educated at Morehouse College, Crozer Theological Seminary, and Boston University. In 1954 he was called to serve as a Baptist minister in Montgomery, Alabama. During the next two years he achieved national fame when, using a policy of nonviolent resistance, he successfully led the boycott against segregated bus lines in Montgomery. He then organized the Southern Christian Leadership Conference, which furthered civil rights, first in the South and then nationwide. In 1964 he was awarded the Nobel Peace Prize. Four years later he was assassinated in Memphis, Tennessee, while supporting striking garbage workers.

In 1963 King was arrested in Birmingham, Alabama, for participating in a march for which no parade permit had been issued by city officials. In jail he wrote a response to a letter that eight local clergymen had published in a newspaper.

Note: Their letter, titled "A Call for Unity," is printed here, followed by King's response.

A CALL FOR UNITY

April 12, 1963

We the undersigned clergymen are among those who, in January, issued "An Appeal for Law and Order and Common Sense," in dealing with racial problems in Alabama. We expressed understanding that honest convictions in racial matters could properly be pursued in the courts, but urged that decisions of those courts should in the meantime be peacefully obeyed.

Since that time there had been some evidence of increased forebearance and a willingness to face facts. Responsible citizens have undertaken to work on various problems which cause racial friction and unrest. In Birmingham, recent public events have given indication that we all have opportunity for a new constructive and realistic approach to racial problems.

However, we are now confronted by a series of demonstrations by some of our Negro citizens, directed and led in part by outsiders. We recognize the natural impatience of people who feel that their hopes are slow in being realized. But we are convinced that these demonstrations are unwise and untimely.

We agree rather with certain local Negro leadership which has called for honest and open negotiation of racial issues in our area. And we believe this kind of facing of issues can best be accomplished by citizens of our own metropolitan area, white and Negro, meeting with their knowledge and experience of the local situation. All of us need to face that responsibility and find proper channels for its accomplishment.

Just as we formerly pointed out that "hatred and violence have no sanction in our religious and political traditions," we also point out that such actions as incite to hatred and violence, however technically peaceful those actions may be, have not contributed to the resolution of our local problems. We do not believe that these days of new hope are days when extreme measures are justified in Birmingham.

We commend the community as a whole, and the local news media and law enforcement officials in particular, on the calm manner in which these demonstrations have been handled. We urge the public to continue to show restraint should the demonstrations continue, and the law enforcement officials to remain calm and continue to protect our city from violence.

We further strongly urge our own Negro community to withdraw support from these demonstrations, and to unite locally in working peacefully for a better Birmingham. When rights are consistently denied, a cause should be pressed in the courts and in negotiations among local leaders, and not in the streets. We appeal to both our white and Negro citizenry to observe the principles of law and order and common sense.

— C.C.J. Carpenter, D.D., L.L.D., Bishop of Alabama; Joseph A. Durick, D.D., Auxiliary Bishop, Diocese of Mobile-Birmingham; Rabbi Milton L. Grafman, Temple Emanu-El, Birmingham, Alabama; Bishop Paul Hardin, Bishop of the Alabama-West Florida Conference of the Methodist Church; Bishop Nolan B. Harmon, Bishop of the North Alabama Conference of the Methodist Church; George M. Murray, D.D., L.L.D., Bishop Coadjutor, Episcopal Diocese of Alabama; Edward V. Ramage, Moderator, Synod of the Alabama Presbyterian Church in the United States; Earl Stallings, Pastor, First Baptist Church, Birmingham, Alabama.

Letter from Birmingham Jail

April 16, 1963

My Dear Fellow Clergymen:

While confined here in the Birmingham city jail, I came across your recent statement calling my present activities "unwise and untimely."[1] Seldom do I pause to answer criticism of my work and ideas. If I sought to answer all the criticisms that cross my desk, my secretaries would have little time for anything other than such correspondence in the course of the day, and I would have no time for constructive work. But since I feel that you are men of genuine good will and that your criticisms are sincerely set forth, I want to try to answer your statement in what I hope will be patient and reasonable terms.

I think I should indicate why I am here in Birmingham, since you have been influenced by the view which argues against "outsiders coming in." I have the honor of serving as president of the Southern Christian Leadership Conference, an organization operating in every southern state, with headquarters in Atlanta, Georgia. We have some eighty-five affiliated organizations across the South, and one of them is the Alabama Christian Movement for Human Rights. Frequently we share staff, educational, and financial resources with our affiliates. Several months ago the affiliate here in Birmingham asked us to be on call to engage in a nonviolent direct-action program if such were deemed necessary. We readily consented, and when the hour came we lived up to our promise. So I, along with several members of my staff, am here because I was invited here. I am here because I have organizational ties here.

But more basically, I am in Birmingham because injustice is here. Just as the prophets of the eighth century B.C. left their villages and carried their "thus saith the Lord" far beyond the boundaries of their home towns, and just as the Apostle Paul left his village of Tarsus and carried the gospel of Jesus Christ to the far corners of the Greco-Roman world, so am I compelled to carry the gospel of freedom beyond my own home town. Like Paul, I must constantly respond to the Macedonian call for aid.

Moreover, I am cognizant of the interrelatedness of all communities and states. I cannot sit idly by in Atlanta and not be concerned about what happens in Birmingham. Injustice anywhere is a threat to justice everywhere. We are caught in an inescapable network of mutuality; tied in a single garment of destiny. Whatever affects one directly, affects all indirectly. Never again can we afford to live with the narrow, provincial "outside agitator" idea. Anyone who lives inside the United States can never be considered an outsider anywhere within its bounds.

You deplore the demonstrations taking place in Birmingham. But your statement, I am sorry to say, fails to express a similar concern for the conditions that brought about the demonstrations. I am sure that none of you would want to rest content with the superficial kind of social analysis that deals merely with

[1] This response to a published statement by eight fellow clergymen from Alabama (Bishop C.C.J. Carpenter, Bishop Joseph A. Durick, Rabbi Milton L. Grafman, Bishop Paul Hardin, Bishop Nolan B. Harmon, the Reverend George M. Murray, the Reverend Edward V. Ramage, and the Reverend Earl Stallings) was composed under somewhat constricting circumstances. Begun on the margins of the newspaper in which the statement appeared while I was in jail, the letter was continued on scraps of writing paper supplied by a friendly Negro trusty, and concluded on a pad my attorneys were eventually permitted to leave me. Although the text remains in substance unaltered, I have indulged in the author's prerogative of polishing it for publication. [King's note.]

effects and does not grapple with underlying causes. It is unfortunate that demonstrations are taking place in Birmingham, but it is even more unfortunate that the city's white power structure left the Negro community with no alternative.

In any nonviolent campaign there are four basic steps: collection of the facts to determine whether injustices exist; negotiation; self-purification; and direct action. We have gone through all these steps in Birmingham. There can be no gainsaying the fact that racial injustice engulfs this community. Birmingham is probably the most thoroughly segregated city in the United States. Its ugly record of brutality is widely known. Negroes have experienced grossly unjust treatment in the courts. There have been more unsolved bombings of Negro homes and churches in Birmingham than in any other city in the nation. These are the hard, brutal facts of the case. On the basis of these conditions, Negro leaders sought to negotiate with the city fathers. But the latter consistently refused to engage in good-faith negotiation.

Then, last September, came the opportunity to talk with leaders of Birmingham's economic community. In the course of the negotiations, certain promises were made by the merchants — for example, to remove the stores' humiliating racial signs. On the basis of these promises, the Reverend Fred Shuttlesworth and the leaders of the Alabama Christian Movement for Human Rights agreed to a moratorium on all demonstrations. As the weeks and months went by, we realized that we were the victims of a broken promise. A few signs, briefly removed, returned; the others remained.

As in so many past experiences, our hopes had been blasted, and the shadow of deep disappointment settled upon us. We had no alternative except to prepare for direct action, whereby we would present our very bodies as a means of laying our case before the conscience of the local and the national community. Mindful of the difficulties involved, we decided to undertake a process of self-purification. We began a series of workshops on nonviolence, and we repeatedly asked ourselves: "Are you able to accept blows without retaliating?" "Are you able to endure the ordeal of jail?" We decided to schedule our direct-action program for the Easter season, realizing that except for Christmas, this is the main shopping period of the year. Knowing that a strong economic-withdrawal program would be the by-product of direct action, we felt that this would be the best time to bring pressure to bear on the merchants for the needed change.

Then it occurred to us that Birmingham's mayoralty election was coming up in March, and we speedily decided to postpone action until after election day. When we discovered that the Commissioner of Public Safety, Eugene "Bull" Connor, had piled up enough votes to be in the run-off, we decided again to postpone action until the day after the run-off so that the demonstrations could not be used to cloud the issues. Like many others, we waited to see Mr. Connor defeated, and to this end we endured postponement after postponement. Having aided in this community need, we felt that our direct-action program could be delayed no longer.

You may well ask: "Why direct action? 10 Why sit-ins, marches, and so forth? Isn't negotiation a better path?" You are quite right in calling for negotiation. Indeed, this is the very purpose of direct action. Nonviolent direct action seeks to create such a crisis and foster such a tension that a community which has constantly refused to negotiate is forced to confront the issue. It seeks so to dramatize the issue that it can no longer be ignored. My citing the creation of tension as part of the work of the nonviolent-resister may sound rather shocking. But I must confess that I am not afraid of the word "tension." I have earnestly opposed violent tension, but there is a type of constructive, nonviolent tension which is necessary for growth. Just as Socrates felt that it was necessary to create a tension in the mind so that individuals could rise from the bondage of myths and half-truths to the unfettered realm of creative analysis and objective appraisal, so must we see the need for nonviolent gadflies to create the kind of tension in society that will help men rise from the dark depths of prejudice and racism to the majestic heights of understanding and brotherhood.

The purpose of our direct-action program is to create a situation so crisis-packed that it will inevitably open the door to negotiation. I therefore concur with you in your call for negotiation. Too long has our beloved Southland been bogged down in a tragic effort to live in monologue rather than dialogue.

One of the basic points in your statement is that the action that I and my associates have taken in Birmingham is untimely. Some have asked: "Why didn't you give the new city administration time to act?" The only answer that I can give to this query is that the new Birmingham administration must be prodded about as much as the outgoing one, before it will act. We are sadly mistaken if we feel that the election of Albert Boutwell as mayor will bring the millennium to Birmingham. While Mr. Boutwell is a much more gentle person than Mr. Connor, they are both segregationists, dedicated to maintenance of the status quo. I have hope that Mr. Boutwell will be reasonable enough to see the futility of massive resistance to desegregation. But he will not see this without pressure from devotees of civil rights. My friends, I must say to you that we have not made a single gain in civil rights without determined legal and nonviolent pressure. Lamentably, it is an historical fact that privileged groups seldom give up their privileges voluntarily. Individuals may see the moral light and voluntarily give up their unjust posture; but as Reinhold Niebuhr[2] has reminded us, groups tend to be more immoral than individuals.

We know through painful experience that freedom is never voluntarily given by the oppressor; it must be demanded by the oppressed. Frankly, I have yet to engage in a direct-action campaign that was "well timed" in the view of those who have not suffered unduly from the disease of segregation. For years now I have heard the word "Wait!" It rings in the ear of every Negro with piercing familiarity. This "Wait" has almost always meant "Never." We must come to see, with one of our distinguished jurists, that "justice too long delayed is justice denied."[3]

We have waited for more than 340 years for our constitutional and God-given rights. The nations of Asia and Africa are moving with jetlike speed toward gaining political independence, but we still creep at horse-and-buggy pace toward gaining a cup of coffee at a lunch counter. Perhaps it is easy for those who have never felt the stinging darts of segregation to say, "Wait." But when you have seen vicious mobs lynch your mothers and fathers at will and drown your sisters and brothers at whim; when you have seen hate-filled policemen curse, kick, and even kill your black brothers and sisters; when you see the vast majority of your twenty million Negro brothers smothering in an airtight cage of poverty in the midst of an

<hr>

[2]**Reinhold Niebuhr** Niebuhr (1892–1971) was a minister, political activist, author, and professor of applied Christianity at Union Theological Seminary. [All notes are the editors' unless otherwise specified.]

[3]**Justice . . . denied** A quotation attributed to William E. Gladstone (1809–1898), British statesman and prime minister.

affluent society; when you suddenly find your tongue twisted and your speech stammering as you seek to explain to your six-year-old daughter why she can't go to the public amusement park that has just been advertised on television, and see tears welling up in her eyes when she is told that Funtown is closed to colored children, and see ominous clouds of inferiority beginning to form in her little mental sky, and see her beginning to distort her personality by developing an unconscious bitterness toward white people; when you have to concoct an answer for a five-year-old son who is asking: "Daddy, why do white people treat colored people so mean?"; when you take a cross-country drive and find it necessary to sleep night after night in the uncomfortable corners of your automobile because no motel will accept you; when you are humiliated day in and day out by nagging signs reading "white" and "colored"; when your first name becomes "nigger," your middle name becomes "boy" (however old you are) and your last name becomes "John," and your wife and mother are never given the respected title "Mrs."; when you are harried by day and haunted by night by the fact that you are a Negro, living constantly at tiptoe stance, never quite knowing what to expect next, and are plagued with inner fears and outer resentments; when you are forever fighting a degenerating sense of "nobodiness" — then you will understand why we find it difficult to wait. There comes a time when the cup of endurance runs over, and men are no longer willing to be plunged into the abyss of despair. I hope, sirs, you can understand our legitimate and unavoidable impatience.

You express a great deal of anxiety over our 15 willingness to break laws. This is certainly a legitimate concern. Since we so diligently urge people to obey the Supreme Court's decision of 1954 outlawing segregation in the public schools, at first glance it may seem rather paradoxical for us consciously to break laws. One may well ask: "How can you advocate breaking some laws and obeying others?" The answer lies in the fact that there are two types of laws: just and unjust. I would be the first to advocate obeying just laws. One has not only a legal but a moral responsibility to obey just laws. Conversely, one has a moral responsibility to disobey unjust laws. I would agree with St. Augustine[4] that "an unjust law is no law at all."

Now, what is the difference between the two? How does one determine whether a law is just or unjust? A just law is a man-made code that squares with the moral law or the law of God. An unjust law is a code that is out of harmony with the moral law. To put it in the terms of St. Thomas Aquinas:[5] An unjust law is a human law that is not rooted in eternal law and natural law. Any law that uplifts human personality is just. Any law that degrades human personality is unjust. All segregation statutes are unjust because segregation distorts the soul and damages the personality. It gives the segregator a false sense of superiority and the segregated a false sense of inferiority. Segregation, to use the terminology of the Jewish philosopher Martin Buber, substitutes an "I-it" relationship for an "I-thou" relationship and ends up relegating persons to the status of things. Hence segregation is not only politically, economically, and sociologically unsound, it is morally wrong and sinful. Paul Tillich[6] has said that sin is separation. Is not segregation an

[4]**St. Augustine** Augustine of Hippo (354–430), an early Christian philosopher.
[5]**St. Thomas Aquinas** Aquinas (1225–1274) was a Catholic priest and an important medieval philosopher and theologian.
[6]**Paul Tillich** Tillich (1886–1965), born in Germany, taught theology at several German universities, but in 1933 he was dismissed from his post at the University of Frankfurt because of his opposition to the Nazi regime. At the invitation of Reinhold Niebuhr, he came to the United States and taught at Union Theological Seminary.

existential expression of man's tragic separation, his awful estrangement, his terrible sinfulness? Thus it is that I can urge men to obey the 1954 decision of the Supreme Court, for it is morally right; and I can urge them to disobey segregation ordinances, for they are morally wrong.

Let us consider a more concrete example of just and unjust laws. An unjust law is a code that a numerical or power majority group compels a minority group to obey but does not make binding on itself. This is *difference* made legal. By the same token, a just law is a code that a majority compels a minority to follow and that it is willing to follow itself. This is *sameness* made legal.

Let me give another explanation. A law is unjust if it is inflicted on a minority that, as a result of being denied the right to vote, had no part in enacting or devising the law. Who can say that the legislature of Alabama which set up that state's segregation laws was democratically elected? Throughout Alabama all sorts of devious methods are used to prevent Negroes from becoming registered voters, and there are some counties in which, even though Negroes constitute a majority of the population, not a single Negro is registered. Can any law enacted under such circumstances be considered democratically structured?

Sometimes a law is just on its face and unjust in its application. For instance, I have been arrested on a charge of parading without a permit. Now, there is nothing wrong in having an ordinance which requires a permit for a parade. But such an ordinance becomes unjust when it is used to maintain segregation and to deny citizens the First Amendment privilege of peaceful assembly and protest.

I hope you are able to see the distinction I am trying to point out. In no sense do I advocate evading or defying the law, as would the rabid segregationist. That would lead to anarchy. One who breaks an unjust law must do so openly, lovingly, and with a willingness to accept the penalty. I submit that an individual who breaks a law that conscience tells him is unjust, and who willingly accepts the penalty of imprisonment in order to arouse the conscience of the community over its injustice, is in reality expressing the highest respect for law.

Of course, there is nothing new about this kind of civil disobedience. It was evidenced sublimely in the refusal of Shadrach, Meshach, and Abednego to obey the laws of Nebuchadnezzar, on the ground that a higher moral law was at stake. It was practiced superbly by the early Christians, who were willing to face hungry lions and the excruciating pain of chopping blocks rather than submit to certain unjust laws of the Roman Empire. To a degree, academic freedom is a reality today because Socrates practiced civil disobedience. In our own nation, the Boston Tea Party represented a massive act of civil disobedience.

We should never forget that everything Adolf Hitler did in Germany was "legal" and everything the Hungarian freedom fighters did in Hungary was "illegal." It was "illegal" to aid and comfort a Jew in Hitler's Germany. Even so, I am sure that, had I lived in Germany at the time, I would have aided and comforted my Jewish brothers. If today I lived in a Communist country where certain principles dear to the Christian faith are suppressed, I would openly advocate disobeying that country's antireligious laws.

I must make two honest confessions to you, my Christian and Jewish brothers. First, I must confess that over the past few years I have been gravely disappointed with the white moderate. I have almost reached the regrettable conclusion that the Negro's great stumbling block in his stride toward freedom is not the White Citizen's Counciler or the Ku Klux

Klanner, but the white moderate, who is more devoted to "order" than to justice; who prefers a negative peace which is the absence of tension to a positive peace which is the presence of justice; who constantly says: "I agree with you in the goal you seek, but I cannot agree with your methods or direct action"; who paternalistically believes he can set the timetable for another man's freedom; who lives by a mythical concept of time and who constantly advises the Negro to wait for a "more convenient season." Shallow understanding from people of good will is more frustrating than absolute misunderstanding from people of ill will. Lukewarm acceptance is much more bewildering than outright rejection.

I had hoped that the white moderate would understand that law and order exist for the purpose of establishing justice and that when they fail in this purpose they become the dangerously structured dams that block the flow of social progress. I had hoped that the white moderate would understand that the present tension in the South is a necessary phase of the transition from an obnoxious negative peace, in which the Negro passively accepted his unjust plight, to a substantive and positive peace, in which all men will respect the dignity and worth of human personality. Actually, we who engage in nonviolent direct action are not the creators of tension. We merely bring to the surface the hidden tension that is already alive. We bring it out in the open, where it can be seen and dealt with. Like a boil that can never be cured so long as it is covered up but must be opened with all its ugliness to the natural medicines of air and light, injustice must be exposed, with all the tension its exposure creates, to the light of human conscience and the air of national opinion before it can be cured.

In your statement you assert that our actions, even though peaceful, must be condemned because they precipitate violence. But is this a logical assertion? Isn't this like condemning a robbed man because his possession of money precipitated the evil act of robbery? Isn't this like condemning Socrates because his unswerving commitment to truth and his philosophical inquiries precipitated the act by the misguided populace in which they made him drink hemlock? Isn't this like condemning Jesus because his unique God-consciousness and never-ceasing devotion to God's will precipitated the evil act of crucifixion? We must come to see that, as the federal courts have consistently affirmed, it is wrong to urge an individual to cease his efforts to gain his basic constitutional rights because the quest may precipitate violence. Society must protect the robbed and punish the robber.

I had also hoped that the white moderate would reject the myth concerning time in relation to the struggle for freedom. I have just received a letter from a white brother in Texas. He writes: "All Christians know that the colored people will receive equal rights eventually, but it is possible that you are in too great a religious hurry. It has taken Christianity almost two thousand years to accomplish what it has. The teachings of Christ take time to come to earth." Such an attitude stems from a tragic misconception of time, from the strangely irrational notion that there is something in the very flow of time that will inevitably cure all ills. Actually, time itself is neutral; it can be used either destructively or constructively. More and more I feel that the people of ill will have used time much more effectively than have the people of good will. We will have to repent in this generation not merely for the hateful words and actions of the bad people but for the appalling silence of the good people. Human progress never rolls in on wheels of inevitability; it comes through the tireless efforts of men willing to be co-workers with God, and without this hard work, time itself becomes an ally of the forces of social stagnation. We must use time creatively, in the knowledge that the time is always ripe to do right. Now is the time to make real the promise of democracy and transform our pending national elegy into a creative psalm of brotherhood. Now is the time to lift our national policy from the quicksand of racial injustice to the solid rock of human dignity.

You speak of our activity in Birmingham as extreme. At first I was rather disappointed that fellow clergymen would see my nonviolent efforts as those of an extremist. I began thinking about the fact that I stand in the middle of two opposing forces in the Negro community. One is a force of complacency, made up in part of Negroes who, as a result of long years of oppression, are so drained of self-respect and a sense of "somebodiness" that they have adjusted to segregation; and in part of a few middle-class Negroes who, because of a degree of academic and economic security and because in some ways they profit by segregation, have become insensitive to the problems of the masses. The other force is one of bitterness and hatred, and it comes perilously close to advocating violence. It is expressed in the various black nationalist groups that are springing up across the nation, the largest and best-known being Elijah Muhammad's Muslim movement. Nourished by the Negro's frustration over the continued existence of racial discrimination, this movement is made up of people who have lost faith in America, who have absolutely repudiated Christianity, and who have concluded that the white man is an incorrigible "devil."

I have tried to stand between these two forces, saying that we need emulate neither the "do-nothingism" of the complacent nor the hatred and despair of the black nationalist. For there is the more excellent way of love and nonviolent protest. I am grateful to God that, through the influence of the Negro church, the way of nonviolence became an integral part of our struggle.

If this philosophy had not emerged, by now many streets of the South should, I am convinced, be flowing with blood. And I am further convinced that if our white brothers dismiss as "rabble-rousers" and "outside agitators" those of us who employ nonviolent direct action, and if they refuse to support our nonviolent efforts, millions of Negroes will, out of frustration and despair, seek solace and security in black-nationalist ideologies — a development that would inevitably lead to a frightening racial nightmare.

Oppressed people cannot remain oppressed 30 forever. The yearning for freedom eventually manifests itself, and that is what has happened to the American Negro. Something within has reminded him of his birthright of freedom, and something without has reminded him that it can be gained. Consciously or unconsciously, he has been caught up by the *Zeitgeist*,[7] and with his black brothers of Africa and his brown and yellow brothers of Asia, South America, and the Caribbean, the United States Negro is moving with a sense of great urgency toward the promised land of racial justice. If one recognizes this vital urge that has engulfed the Negro community, one should readily understand why public demonstrations are taking place. The Negro has many pent-up resentments and latent frustrations, and he must release them. So let him march; let him make prayer pilgrimages to the city hall; let him go on freedom rides — and try to understand why he must do so. If his repressed emotions are not released in nonviolent ways, they will seek expression through violence; this is not a threat but a fact

---

[7]***Zeitgeist*** Spirit of the age (German).

of history. So I have not said to my people: "Get rid of your discontent." Rather, I have tried to say that this normal and healthy discontent can be channeled into the creative outlet of nonviolent direct action. And now this approach is being termed extremist.

But though I was initially disappointed at being categorized as an extremist, as I continued to think about the matter I gradually gained a measure of satisfaction from the label. Was not Jesus an extremist for love: "Love your enemies, bless them that curse you, do good to them that hate you, and pray for them which despitefully use you, and persecute you." Was not Amos an extremist for justice: "Let justice roll down like waters and righteousness like an ever-flowing stream." Was not Paul an extremist for the Christian gospel: "I bear in my body the marks of the Lord Jesus." Was not Martin Luther an extremist: "Here I stand; I cannot do otherwise, so help me God." And John Bunyan: "I will stay in jail to the end of my days before I make a butchery of my conscience." And Abraham Lincoln: "This nation cannot survive half slave and half free." And Thomas Jefferson: "We hold these truths to be self-evident, that all men are created equal. . . ." So the question is not whether we will be extremists, but what kind of extremists we will be. Will we be extremists for hate or for love? Will we be extremists for the preservation of injustice or for the extension of justice? In that dramatic scene on Calvary's hill three men were crucified. We must never forget that all three were crucified for the same crime — the crime of extremism. Two were extremists for immorality, and thus fell below their environment. The other, Jesus Christ, was an extremist for love, truth, and goodness, and thereby rose above his environment. Perhaps the South, the nation, and the world are in dire need of creative extremists.

I had hoped that the white moderate would see this need. Perhaps I was too optimistic; perhaps I expected too much. I suppose I should have realized that few members of the oppressor race can understand the deep groans and passionate yearnings of the oppressed race, and still fewer have the vision to see that injustice must be rooted out by strong, persistent, and determined action. I am thankful, however, that some of our white brothers in the South have grasped the meaning of this social revolution and committed themselves to it. They are still all too few in quantity, but they are big in quality. Some — such as Ralph McGill, Lillian Smith, Harry Golden, James McBride Dabbs, Ann Braden, and Sarah Patton Boyle — have written about our struggle in eloquent and prophetic terms. Others have marched with us down nameless streets of the South. They have languished in filthy, roach-infested jails, suffering the abuse and brutality of policemen who view them as "dirty nigger-lovers." Unlike so many of their moderate brothers and sisters, they have recognized the urgency of the moment and sensed the need for powerful "action" antidotes to combat the disease of segregation.

Let me take note of my other major disappointment. I have been so greatly disappointed with the white church and its leadership. Of course, there are some notable exceptions. I am not unmindful of the fact that each of you has taken some significant stands on this issue. I commend you, Reverend Stallings, for your Christian stand on this past Sunday, in welcoming Negroes to your worship service on a nonsegregated basis. I commend the Catholic leaders of this state for integrating Spring Hill College several years ago.

But despite these notable exceptions, I must honestly reiterate that I have been disappointed with the church. I do not say this as one of those negative critics who can always find something wrong with the church. I say this as a minister of the gospel, who loves the church; who was nurtured in its bosom; who has been sustained by its spiritual blessings and who will remain true to it as long as the cord of life shall lengthen.

When I was suddenly catapulted into the [35] leadership of the bus protest in Montgomery, Alabama, a few years ago, I felt we would be supported by the white church. I felt that the white ministers, priests, and rabbis of the South would be among our strongest allies. Instead, some have been outright opponents, refusing to understand the freedom movement and misrepresenting its leaders; all too many others have been more cautious than courageous and have remained silent behind the anesthetizing security of stained-glass windows.

In spite of my shattered dreams, I came to Birmingham with the hope that the white religious leadership of this community would see the justice of our cause and, with deep moral concern, would serve as the channel through which our just grievances could reach the power structure. I had hoped that each of you would understand. But again I have been disappointed.

I have heard numerous southern religious leaders admonish their worshipers to comply with a desegregation decision because it is the law, but I have longed to hear white ministers declare: "Follow this decree because integration is morally right and because the Negro is your brother." In the midst of blatant injustices inflicted upon the Negro, I have watched white churchmen stand on the sideline and mouth pious irrelevancies and sanctimonious trivialities. In the midst of a mighty struggle to rid our nation of racial and economic injustice, I have heard many ministers say: "Those are social issues, with which the gospel has no real concern." And I have watched many churches commit themselves to a completely otherworldly religion which makes a strange, unbiblical distinction between body and soul, between the sacred and the secular.

I have traveled the length and breadth of Alabama, Mississippi, and all the other southern states. On sweltering summer days and crisp autumn mornings I have looked at the South's beautiful churches with their lofty spires pointing heavenward. I have beheld the impressive outlines of her massive religious-education buildings. Over and over I have found myself saying: "What kind of people worship here? Who is their God? Where were their voices when the lips of Governor Barnett dripped with words of interposition and nullification? Where were they when Governor Wallace gave a clarion call for defiance and hatred? Where were their voices of support when bruised and weary Negro men and women decided to rise from the dark dungeons of complacency to the bright hills of creative protest?"

Yes, these questions are still in my mind. In deep disappointment I have wept over the laxity of the church. But be assured that my tears have been tears of love. There can be no deep disappointment where there is not deep love. Yes, I love the church. How could I do otherwise? I am in the rather unique position of being the son, the grandson, and the great-grandson of preachers. Yes, I see the church as the body of Christ. But, Oh! How we have blemished and scarred that body through social neglect and through fear of being nonconformists.

There was a time when the church was [40] very powerful—in the time when the early Christians rejoiced at being deemed worthy to suffer for what they believed. In those days the church was not merely a thermometer that recorded the ideas and principles of popular opinion; it was a thermostat that transformed the mores of society. Whenever the early Christians entered a town, the people in power became disturbed and immediately sought to convict the Christians for being "disturbers of the peace" and "outside agitators." But the Christians pressed on, in the conviction that they were "a colony of heaven," called to obey God rather than man. Small in number, they were big in commitment. They were too God-intoxicated to be "astronomically intimidated." By their effort and example they brought an end to such ancient evils as infanticide and gladiatorial contests.

Things are different now. So often the contemporary church is a weak, ineffectual voice with an uncertain sound. So often it is an arch-defender of the status quo. Far from being disturbed by the presence of the church, the power structure of the average community is consoled by the church's silent—and often even vocal—sanction of things as they are.

But the judgment of God is upon the church as never before. If today's church does not recapture the sacrificial spirit of the early church, it will lose its authenticity, forfeit the loyalty of millions, and be dismissed as an irrelevant social club with no meaning for the twentieth century. Every day I meet young people whose disappointment with the church has turned into outright disgust.

Perhaps I have once again been too optimistic. Is organized religion too inextricably bound to the status quo to save our nation and the world? Perhaps I must turn my faith to the inner spiritual church, the church within the church, as the true *ekklesia*[8] and the hope of the world. But again I am thankful to God that some noble souls from the ranks of organized religion have broken loose from the paralyzing chains of conformity and joined us as active partners in the struggle for freedom. They have left their secure congregations and walked the streets of Albany, Georgia, with us. They have gone down the highways of the South on tortuous rides for freedom. Yes, they have gone to jail with us. Some have been dismissed from their churches, have lost the support of their bishops and fellow ministers. But they have acted in the faith that right defeated is stronger than evil triumphant. Their witness has been the spiritual salt that has preserved the true meaning of the gospel in these troubled times. They have carved a tunnel of hope through the dark mountain of disappointment.

I hope the church as a whole will meet the challenge of this decisive hour. But even if the church does not come to the aid of justice, I have no despair about the future. I have no fear about the outcome of our struggle in Birmingham, even if our motives are at present misunderstood. We will reach the goal of freedom in Birmingham and all over the nation, because the goal of America is freedom. Abused and scorned though we may be, our destiny is tied up with America's destiny. Before the pilgrims landed at Plymouth, we were here. Before the pen of Jefferson etched the majestic words of the Declaration of Independence across the pages of history, we were here. For more than two centuries our forebears labored in this country without wages; they made cotton king; they built the homes of their masters while suffering gross injustice and shameful humiliation — and yet out of a bottomless vitality they continue to thrive and develop. If the inexpressible cruelties of slavery could not stop us, the opposition we now face will surely fail. We will win our freedom because the sacred heritage of our nation and the eternal will of God are embodied in our echoing demands.

---

[8]*ekklesia* A gathering or assembly of citizens (Greek).

Before closing I feel impelled to mention one other point in your statement that has troubled me profoundly. You warmly commended the Birmingham police force for keeping "order" and "preventing violence." I doubt that you would have so warmly commended the police force if you had seen its dogs sinking their teeth into unarmed, nonviolent Negroes. I doubt that you would so quickly commend the policemen if you were to observe their ugly and inhumane treatment of Negroes here in the city jail; if you were to watch them push and curse old Negro women and young Negro girls; if you were to see them slap and kick old Negro men and young boys; if you were to observe them, as they did on two occasions, refuse to give us food because we wanted to sing our grace together. I cannot join you in your praise of the Birmingham police department.

It is true that the police have exercised a degree of discipline in handling the demonstrators. In this sense they have conducted themselves rather "nonviolently" in public. But for what purpose? To preserve the evil system of segregation. Over the past few years I have consistently preached that nonviolence demands that the means we use must be as pure as the ends we seek. I have tried to make clear that it is wrong to use immoral means to attain moral ends. But now I must affirm that it is just as wrong, or perhaps even more so, to use moral means to preserve immoral ends. Perhaps Mr. Connor and his policemen have been rather nonviolent in public, as was Chief Pritchett in Albany, Georgia, but they used the moral means of nonviolence to maintain the immoral end of racial injustice. As T. S. Eliot has said: "The last temptation is the greatest treason: To do the right deed for the wrong reason."

I wish you had commended the Negro sit-inners and demonstrators of Birmingham for their sublime courage, their willingness to suffer, and their amazing discipline in the midst of great provocation. One day the South will recognize its real heroes. They will be the James Merediths, with the noble sense of purpose that enables them to face jeering and hostile mobs, and with the agonizing loneliness that characterizes the life of the pioneer. They will be old, oppressed, battered Negro women, symbolized in a seventy-two-year-old woman in Montgomery, Alabama, who rose up with a sense of dignity and with her people decided not to ride segregated buses, and who responded with ungrammatical profundity to one who inquired about her weariness: "My feets is tired, but my soul is at rest." They will be the young high school and college students, the young ministers of the gospel and a host of their elders, courageously and nonviolently sitting in at lunch counters and willingly going to jail for conscience's sake. One day the South will know that when these disinherited children of God sat down at lunch counters, they were in reality standing up for what is best in the American dream and for the most sacred values in our Judaeo-Christian heritage, thereby bringing our nation back to those great wells of democracy which were dug deep by the founding fathers in their formulation of the Constitution and the Declaration of Independence.

Never before have I written so long a letter. I'm afraid it is much too long to take your precious time. I can assure you that it would have been much shorter if I had been writing from a comfortable desk, but what else can one do when he is alone in a narrow jail cell, other than write long letters, think long thoughts, and pray long prayers?

If I have said anything in this letter that overstates the truth and indicates an unreasonable impatience, I beg you to forgive me. If I have said anything that understates the truth and indicates my having a patience that allows me to settle for anything less than brotherhood, I beg God to forgive me.

I hope this letter finds you strong in the faith. I also hope that circumstances will soon make it possible for me to meet each of you, not as an integrationist or a civil-rights leader but as a fellow clergyman and a Christian brother. Let us all hope that the dark clouds of racial prejudice will soon pass away and the deep fog of misunderstanding will be lifted from our fear-drenched communities, and in some not too distant tomorrow the radiant stars of love and brotherhood will shine over our great nation with all their scintillating beauty.

Yours for the cause of Peace and Brotherhood,
Martin Luther King Jr.

Topics for Critical Thinking and Writing

1. In his first five paragraphs of the "Letter," how does Martin Luther King assure his audience that he is not a meddlesome intruder but a man of goodwill?

2. In paragraph 3, King refers to Hebrew prophets and to the Apostle Paul, and later (para. 10) he refers to Socrates. What is the point of these references?

3. In paragraph 11, what does King mean when he says that "our beloved Southland" has long tried to "live in monologue rather than dialogue"?

4. King begins paragraph 23 with "I must make two honest confessions to you, my Christian and Jewish brothers." What would have been gained or lost if he had used this paragraph as his opening?

5. King's last three paragraphs do not advance his argument. What do they do?

6. Why does King advocate breaking unjust laws "openly, lovingly" (para. 20)? What does he mean by these words? What other motives or attitudes do these words rule out?

7. Construct two definitions of *civil disobedience*, and explain whether and to what extent it is easier (or harder) to justify civil disobedience, depending on how you have defined the expression.

8. If you feel that you wish to respond to King's letter on some point, write a letter nominally addressed to King. You may, if you like, adopt the persona of one of the eight clergymen whom King initially addressed.

9. King writes (para. 46) that "nonviolence demands that the means we use must be as pure as the ends we seek." How do you think King would evaluate the following acts: (a) occupying a college administration building to protest the administration's unsatisfactory response to a racial incident on campus or its failure to hire minority persons as staff and faculty; (b) occupying an abortion clinic to protest abortion? Set down your answer in an essay of 500 words.

10. Compose a letter from King in which he responds to Plato's "Crito" (p. 672).

PETER CAVE

Peter Cave (b. 1952) teaches philosophy at the Open University and City University of London. He is the author of Can a Robot Be Human? 33 Perplexing Philosophy Puzzles *(2007) and* What's Wrong with Eating People? 33 More Perplexing Philosophy Puzzles *(2008). We reprint an essay from the second book.*

Man or Sheep?

Thomas Hobbes, a key political philosopher of the seventeenth century, wrote that man's life was "solitary, poor, nasty, brutish, and short." The obvious reply is, "It could have been worse, Thomas; it could have been solitary, poor, nasty, brutish — and long."

Hobbes was describing life before the existence of a state, government, and law. Humans are competitive. They lack reason to trust each other, unless there is a powerful authority that sets laws and punishes law-breakers. In a state of nature, individuals would be in constant conflict or, at least, always on their guard, insecure, and ready for battle. The state of nature, of life pre-government, is a state of war. With the state of nature so horrible, human beings would obviously want to get out, into something better. According to Hobbes, they would come together and agree on a sovereign, an absolute authority, to represent and rule over them, giving them security and opportunity to lead reasonable lives.

There are many puzzles, not least why individuals in the state of nature would risk trusting each other to keep to any agreement. Let us, though, not worry about how government arises. Here we are, living within a state. Let us assume we have a government democratically elected. However, whatever the degree of democracy, laws are imposed that restrict what we may do. We may disapprove of some laws because of some moral or religious principles;

we may disapprove of other laws simply because they prevent us from getting what we want. The general concern becomes: By what authority does any government rightfully rule over us?

WHY SHOULD WE OBEY THE STATE AND ITS LAWS?

We may answer in practical terms. We obey the law because we are scared of the consequences of disobedience, not wanting to risk fines and imprisonment. The rational thing to do, given the aim of getting on with our lives as best we can, is to obey. When asked whether man or mouse, some of us tend to squeak and take the cheese. Even more so may most of us squeak, when the tentacles of the law and the long arm of the police take hold. We mice may, indeed, be more akin to sheep, sheepishly following each other in our general obedience. Our puzzle though is what, if anything, makes obeying the law the *right* thing to do — even if we could get away with disobeying.

Many of us benefit because of the state's existence: We are defended from others, receive state education, health services, in return for paying taxes. We are better off with law than without. So, we are obligated, in return, to obey the laws that confer those benefits. One immediate objection is that this justification for lawful obedience fails to work for those who

5

overall do not benefit. A significant number do very badly, sleeping rough, being denied state benefits, and being avoided by those better off. Why should they obey? Also, some at society's top may argue that they contribute more than they receive — probably forgetting that they secured the more because of society's stability and protection of gross inequalities often inherited.

Even when overall we do benefit from the state's existence, it does not follow that we are under any obligation to the benefactor. Did we ever sign up, agreeing that we would accept benefits in return for obeying the law? If someone buys us a drink, without our asking, are we under an obligation to buy one in return?

Reference to "signing up" casts us along another line, a line orientated toward the "social contract." What justifies the state and our obedience is that we consented to the set-up. Some philosophers, John Locke and arguably Hobbes, believed that historically some individuals made contracts to be governed by an authority acting in their interests, leading to our societies. Of course, there is no reason to believe in such historical events; but, even if they occurred, whatever relevance do they have for us today? We were not around hundreds of years ago, engaged in any contractual deals.

The response to that last thought is to spot features of our current lives that may indicate consent. We make use of the state's services; we travel freely on the King's highway, notes Locke — well, today the Queen's highway. This shows that we tacitly consent to the state — or does it? Just because we remain in this country, using its facilities, it does not follow that we consent: After all, what other options are available? Can most people afford to go elsewhere? Would other countries, with acceptable laws, permit entry? It is as if we find ourselves on a ship in the middle of the ocean, with the captain making the point that we are free to leave.

Rationality is often wheeled out, to come to the rescue. True, we were not involved in any original social contract; true, our remaining within our society fails to establish consent. But suppose we were rational, not yet in a society, and needing to create society's laws. Suppose, too, we were ignorant of our sex, race, abilities, and the position we probably would reach in society, be it through chance or talent. In such an original position, behind a veil of ignorance, where everything is fair between us, our thinking, even though we remain as individuals, would not be distorted by a distinctive self-interest differing from the self-interest of others. Rather, our common rationality and interests should lead us to see and accept what would be fair laws, benefits, and rights for all. Behind the veil of ignorance, it would seem rational to consent to a society that permitted basic freedoms, did not discriminate between individuals on irrelevant grounds, and provided welfare benefits for when things go badly. After all, behind the veil of ignorance, we have no idea whether we may end up belonging to minority groups or hitting on hard times. If our current society possesses the features it would be rational to consent to behind the veil, then our obedience today is justified by this hypothetical consent, by what is seen as a hypothetical contract.

The response, by way of jibe, is that hypo- [10] thetical contracts are not worth the paper they are not written upon. Hypothetical consent is not consent. The jibe, though, misses the point. Justifications can rightly involve hypotheticals. Why did you battle with the man, yanking him from the cliff's path, despite his protests? "Because, had he been sober, he would have consented to the yanking, to save him from risking a fatal fall."

The resort to the veil of ignorance, to rationality, and the hypothetical, though, raises its own puzzles. Quite what does rationality involve behind such a veil? Is it rational, for example, to place liberty higher than greater welfare benefits requiring higher levels of taxation?

Whatever justifications are offered for general obedience to the state, sometimes we morally ought to disobey. Had only many, many consulted their conscience instead of the law, various atrocities, instituted by governments, could have been avoided. Had only many, many been aware of their humanity rather than going along with the mice and the sheep . . .

Mind you, that is so easy for me to say and you to read as, in all likelihood, we sit reasonably well off, looking at this book, not having to stand up and be counted—and also not scraping a living in desperate circumstances. We are cocooned, indeed, from millions of dispossessed in the world for whom life is certainly nasty, brutish, and short.

Topics for Critical Thinking and Writing

1. Name five things or services (e.g., paved sidewalks, the police) that you did not create or establish but from which you benefit (para. 6).

2. Why is the "social contract" so called (paras. 6–8)?

3. Did the voyagers on the *Mayflower* (1620) create a social contract among themselves? How can you tell?

4. Is the following proposition — "We are not morally obligated by the deeds of our predecessors" — true? Why, or why not? Explain your answer.

5. What counts as a free, voluntary compact to obey some laws? What would you have to do to show that you (no longer) consent to be governed by the government under which you live?

THOMAS HARDY

Thomas Hardy (1840–1928) was born in Dorset, England, the son of a stonemason. Despite great obstacles, he studied the classics and architecture, and in 1862 he moved to London to study and practice as an architect. Ill health forced him to return to Dorset, where he continued to work as an architect and to write. Best known for his novels, Hardy ceased writing fiction after the hostile reception of Jude the Obscure *in 1896 and turned to writing lyric poetry. We print a poem of 1902.*

The Man He Killed

"Had he and I but met
By some old ancient inn,
We should have sat us down to wet
Right many a nipperkin°!

"But ranged an infantry,   5
And staring face to face,
I shot at him as he at me,
And killed him in his place.

---

4 nipperkin Cup.

"I shot him dead because —
Because he was my foe,   10
Just so: my foe of course he was;
That's clear enough; although

"He thought he'd 'list, perhaps,
Off-hand like — just as I —

Was out of work — had sold his traps° —   15
No other reason why.

"Yes; quaint and curious war is!
You shoot a fellow down
You'd treat if met where any bar is,
Or help to half-a-crown."   20

---

15 traps Personal belongings. [Both notes are the editors'.]

Topics for Critical Thinking and Writing

1. Thomas Hardy published this poem in 1902, at the conclusion of the Boer War (1899–1902, also called the South African War), a war between the Boers (Dutch) and the British for possession of part of Africa. The speaker of the poem is an English veteran of the war. Do you think such a poem might just as well have been written by an English (or American) soldier in World War II? Explain your response.

2. Characterize the speaker. What sort of man does he seem to be? Pay special attention to the punctuation in the third and fourth stanzas — what do the pauses indicated by the dashes, the colons, and the semicolons tell us about him? — and pay special attention to the final stanza, in which he speaks of war as "quaint and curious" (line 17). Do you think that Hardy too would speak of war this way? Why, or why not? Can you imagine an American soldier in the Vietnam War speaking of the war as "quaint and curious"? Explain.

3. Do you think we can reasonably say that the speaker of Hardy's poem possesses free will? Explain your position.

T. S. ELIOT

Thomas Stearns Eliot (1888–1965) was born into a New England family that had moved to St. Louis. He attended a preparatory school in Massachusetts, graduated from Harvard University, and then continued his studies in literature in France, Germany, and England. In 1914 he began working for Lloyds Bank in London, and three years later he published his first book of poems, which included "Prufrock." In 1925 he joined a publishing firm, and in 1927 he became a British citizen and a member of the Church of England. In 1948 he received the Nobel Prize for Literature.

The Love Song of J. Alfred Prufrock

S'io credesse che mia risposta fosse
A persona che mai tornasse al mondo,
Questa fiamma staria senza più scosse.
Ma perciocchè giammai di questo fondo
Non torno vivo alcun, s' i' odo il vero,
Senza tema d'infamia ti rispondo.°

Let us go then, you and I,
When the evening is spread out against the
   sky
Like a patient etherised upon a table;
Let us go, through certain half-deserted
   streets,
The muttering retreats   5
Of restless nights in one-night cheap hotels
And sawdust restaurants with oyster-shells:
Streets that follow like a tedious argument
Of insidious intent
To lead you to an overwhelming question . . .   10
Oh, do not ask, "What is it?"
Let us go and make our visit.

In the room the women come and go
Talking of Michelangelo.

The yellow fog that rubs its back upon the   15
   window-panes,
The yellow smoke that rubs its muzzle on the
   window-panes
Licked its tongue into the corners of the
   evening,
Lingered upon the pools that stand in drains,

Let fall upon its back the soot that falls from
   chimneys,
Slipped by the terrace, made a sudden leap,   20
And seeing that it was a soft October night,
Curled once about the house, and fell asleep.

And indeed there will be time
For the yellow smoke that slides along the
   street,
Rubbing its back upon the window-panes;   25
There will be time, there will be time
To prepare a face to meet the faces that you
   meet;
There will be time to murder and create,
And time for all the works and days° of hands
That lift and drop a question on your plate;   30
Time for you and time for me,
And time yet for a hundred indecisions,
And for a hundred visions and revisions,
Before the taking of a toast and tea.

In the room the women come and go   35
Talking of Michelangelo

And indeed there will be time
To wonder, "Do I dare?" and, "Do I dare?"
Time to turn back and descend the stair,
With a bald spot in the middle of my hair —   40
[They will say: "How his hair is growing
   thin!"]
My morning coat, my collar mounting firmly
   to the chin,
My necktie rich and modest, but asserted by a
   simple pin —
[They will say: "But how his arms and legs are
   thin!"]
Do I dare   45
Disturb the universe?

S'io . . . rispondo The Italian epigraph that begins the poem is a quotation from Dante's *Divine Comedy* (1321). In this passage, a damned soul in hell who had sought absolution before committing a crime addresses Dante, thinking that his words will never reach the earth. He says: "If I thought that my answer were to someone who could ever return to the world, this flame would be still, without further motion. But because no one has ever returned alive from this depth, if what I hear is true, without fear of shame I answer you." [All notes are the editors'.]

---

29 works and days The title of a poem on farm life by Hesiod (Greek, eighth century B.C.).

In a minute there is time
For decisions and revisions which a minute
	will reverse.

For I have known them all already, known
	them all:—
Have known the evenings, mornings,		50
	afternoons,
I have measured out my life with coffee spoons;
I know the voices dying with a dying fall°
Beneath the music from a farther room.
	So how should I presume?

And I have known the eyes already, known		55
	them all—
The eyes that fix you in a formulated phrase,
And when I am formulated, sprawling on a pin,
When I am pinned and wriggling on the wall,
Then how should I begin
To spit out all the butt-ends of my days and		60
	ways? And how should I presume?

And I have known the arms already, known
	them all—
Arms that are braceleted and white and bare
[But in the lamplight, downed with light
	brown hair!]
Is it perfume from a dress		65
That makes me so digress?
Arms that lie along a table, or wrap about a
	shawl.
	And should I then presume?
	And how should I begin?
		. . . . .

Shall I say, I have gone at dusk through		70
	narrow streets
And watched the smoke that rises from the
	pipes
Of lonely men in shirt-sleeves, leaning out of
	windows? . . .

---

52 **dying fall** Echoes Shakespeare's *Twelfth Night* 1.1.4.

I should have been a pair of ragged claws
Scuttling across the floors of silent seas.

		. . . . .

And the afternoon, the evening, sleeps so		75
	peacefully!
Smoothed by long fingers,
Asleep . . . tired . . . or it malingers,
Stretched on the floor, here beside you
	and me.
Should I, after tea and cakes and ices,
Have the strength to force the moment to its		80
	crisis?
But though I have wept and fasted, wept and
	prayed,
Though I have seen my head [grown slightly
	bald] brought in upon a platter,°
I am no prophet—and here's no great
	matter;
I have seen the moment of my greatness
	flicker,
And I have seen the eternal Footman hold my
	coat, and snicker,		85
And in short, I was afraid.

And would it have been worth it, after all,
After the cups, the marmalade, the tea,
Among the porcelain, among some talk of you
	and me,
Would it have been worth while,		90
To have bitten off the matter with a smile,
To have squeezed the universe into a ball
To roll° it toward some overwhelming
	question,
To say: "I am Lazarus,° come from the dead,
Come back to tell you all, I shall tell you		95
	all"—

---

82 **head . . . platter** Alludes to John the Baptist, whose head
was delivered on a platter to Salome.
92–93 **ball / To roll** Echoes Andrew Marvell's "To His Coy
Mistress," lines 41–42 (see p. 398).
94 **Lazarus** Mentioned in the New Testament: John 11; Lazarus
rises from the dead at the command of Jesus.

If one, settling a pillow by her head,
	Should say: "That is not what I meant
at all.
	That is not it, at all."

And would it have been worth it, after all,
Would it have been worth while,
After the sunsets and the dooryards and the
	sprinkled streets,
After the novels, after the teacups, after the
	skirts that trail along the floor —
And this, and so much more? —
It is impossible to say just what I mean!
But as if a magic lantern threw the nerves in
	patterns on a screen:
Would it have been worth while
If one, settling a pillow or throwing off a
	shawl,
And turning toward the window, should say:
	"That is not it at all,
	That is not what I meant, at all." 110

	. . . . .

No! I am not Prince Hamlet,° nor was meant
	to be;
Am an attendant lord, one that will do
To swell a progress, start a scene or two,
Advise the prince; no doubt, an easy tool.
Deferential, glad to be of use, 115

Politic, cautious, and meticulous;
Full of high sentence,° but a bit obtuse;
At times, indeed, almost ridiculous —
Almost, at times, the Fool.

I grow old . . . I grow old . . . 120
I shall wear the bottoms of my trousers
	rolled.

Shall I part my hair behind? Do I dare to eat
	a peach?
I shall wear white flannel trousers, and walk
	upon the beach.
I have heard the mermaids singing, each to 105
	each.
I do not think that they will sing to me. 125

I have seen them riding seaward on the
	waves
Combing the white hair of the waves blown
	back
When the wind blows the water white and
	black.

We have lingered in the chambers of the sea
By sea-girls wreathed with seaweed red and 130
	brown
Till human voices wake us, and we drown.

100

111 **Prince Hamlet** The next few lines allude to lesser figures in Shakespeare's tragedy, specifically to Polonius, a self-satisfied fatuous courtier.

117 **Full of high sentence** Full of thoughtful sayings; comes from Chaucer's description of the Oxford student in *The Canterbury Tales.*

Topics for Critical Thinking and Writing

1. One of the most famous images of the poem compares the evening to "a patient ether-ised upon a table" (line 3). Does the image also suggest that individuals — for instance, Prufrock — may not be fully conscious and therefore are not responsible for their actions or their inactions? Explain your response.

2. Are lines 57 to 60 meant to evoke the reader's pity for the speaker? If not, what (if any) response are these lines intended to evoke?

3. The speaker admits he is "At times, indeed, . . . / Almost . . . the Fool" (lines 118–19). Where, if at all, in the poem do we see him not at all as a fool?

4. Do you take the poem to be a criticism of an individual, a society, neither, or both? Why?

5. Evaluate this critical judgment, offering evidence to support your view: "The poem is obscure: It begins in Italian, and it includes references that most readers can't know. It is not at all uplifting. In fact, in so far as it is comprehensible, it is depressing. These are not the characteristics of a great poem."

6. The poem is chiefly concerned with the thoughts of a man, J. Alfred Prufrock. Do you think it therefore is of more interest to men than to women? Explain your response.

7. The speaker describes the streets he walks as "follow[ing] like a tedious argument" (line 8). Is the simile apt? When do you think an argument becomes tedious?

SUSAN GLASPELL

Susan Glaspell (1882–1948) was born in Davenport, Iowa, and educated at Drake University in Des Moines. In 1903 she married George Cram Cook and, with Cook and other writers, actors, and artists, in 1915 founded the Provincetown Players, a group that remained vital until 1929. Glaspell wrote Trifles *(1916) for the Provincetown Players, but she also wrote stories, novels, and a biography of her husband. In 1931 she won the Pulitzer Prize for* Alison's House, *a play about the family of a deceased poet who in some ways resembles Emily Dickinson.*

Trifles

(SCENE: *The kitchen in the now abandoned farmhouse of John Wright, a gloomy kitchen, and left without having been put in order — unwashed pans under the sink, a loaf of bread outside the breadbox, a dish towel on the table — other signs of incompleted work. At the rear the outer door opens, and the Sheriff comes in, followed by the County Attorney and Hale. The Sheriff and Hale are men in middle life, the County Attorney is a young man; all are much bundled up and go at once to the stove. They are followed by the two women — the Sheriff's Wife first; she is a slight wiry woman, a thin nervous face. Mrs. Hale is larger and would ordinarily be called more comfortable looking, but she is disturbed now and looks fearfully about as she enters. The women have come in slowly and stand close together near the door.*)

COUNTY ATTORNEY (*rubbing his hands*). This feels good. Come up to the fire, ladies.

MRS. PETERS (*after taking a step forward*). I'm not — cold.

SHERIFF (*unbuttoning his overcoat and stepping away from the stove as if to the beginning of official business*). Now, Mr. Hale, before we move things about, you explain to Mr. Henderson just what you saw when you came here yesterday morning.

COUNTY ATTORNEY. By the way, has anything been moved? Are things just as you left them yesterday?

SHERIFF (*looking about*). It's just the same. When it dropped below zero last night, 5

I thought I'd better send Frank out this morning to make a fire for us — no use getting pneumonia with a big case on; but I told him not to touch anything except the stove — and you know Frank.

COUNTY ATTORNEY. Somebody should have been left here yesterday.

SHERIFF. Oh — yesterday. When I had to send Frank to Morris Center for that man who went crazy — I want you to know I had my hands full yesterday. I knew you could get back from Omaha by today, and as long as I went over everything here myself —

COUNTY ATTORNEY. Well, Mr. Hale, tell just what happened when you came here yesterday morning.

HALE. Harry and I had started to town with a load of potatoes. We came along the road from my place; and as I got here, I said, "I'm going to see if I can't get John Wright to go in with me on a party telephone." I spoke to Wright about it once before, and he put me off, saying folks talked too much anyway, and all he asked was peace and quiet — I guess you know about how much he talked himself; but I thought maybe if I went to the house and talked about it before his wife, though I said to Harry that I didn't know as what his wife wanted made much difference to John —

COUNTY ATTORNEY. Let's talk about that later, 10 Mr. Hale. I do want to talk about that, but tell now just what happened when you got to the house.

HALE. I didn't hear or see anything; I knocked at the door, and still it was all quiet inside. I knew they must be up, it was past eight o'clock. So I knocked again, and I thought I heard somebody say, "Come in." I wasn't sure, I'm not sure yet, but I opened the door — this door (*indicating the door by which the two women are still standing*),

and there in that rocker — (*pointing to it*) sat Mrs. Wright. (*They all look at the rocker.*)

COUNTY ATTORNEY. What — was she doing?

HALE. She was rockin' back and forth. She had her apron in her hand and was kind of — pleating it.

COUNTY ATTORNEY. And how did she — look?

HALE. Well, she looked queer.   15

COUNTY ATTORNEY. How do you mean — queer?

HALE. Well, as if she didn't know what she was going to do next. And kind of done up.

COUNTY ATTORNEY. How did she seem to feel about your coming?

HALE. Why, I don't think she minded — one way or other. She didn't pay much attention. I said, "How do, Mrs. Wright, it's cold, ain't it?" And she said, "Is it?" — and went on kind of pleating at her apron. Well, I was surprised; she didn't ask me to come up to the stove, or to set down, but just sat there, not even looking at me, so I said, "I want to see John." And then she — laughed. I guess you would call it a laugh. I thought of Harry and the team outside, so I said a little sharp: "Can't I see John?" "No," she says, kind o' dull like. "Ain't he home?" says I. "Yes," says she, "he's home." "Then why can't I see him?" I asked her, out of patience. "'Cause he's dead," says she. *"Dead?"* says I. She just nodded her head, not getting a bit excited, but rockin' back and forth. "Why — where is he?" says I, not knowing what to say. She just pointed upstairs — like that (*himself pointing to the room above*). I got up, with the idea of going up there. I walked from there to here — then I says, "Why, what did he die of?" "He died of a rope around his neck," says she, and just went on pleatin' at her apron. Well, I went out and called Harry. I thought I might — need help. We went upstairs, and there he was lyin' —

COUNTY ATTORNEY. I think I'd rather have you go 20 into that upstairs, where you can point it all out. Just go on now with the rest of the story.

HALE. Well, my first thought was to get that rope off. I looked . . . *(Stops, his face twitches.)* . . . but Harry, he went up to him, and he said, "No, he's dead all right, and we'd better not touch anything." So we went back downstairs. She was still sitting that same way. "Has anybody been notified?" I asked. "No," says she, unconcerned. "Who did this, Mrs. Wright?" said Harry. He said it businesslike — and she stopped pleatin' of her apron. "I don't know," she says. "You don't *know*?" says Harry. "No," says she. "Weren't you sleepin' in the bed with him?" says Harry. "Yes," says she, "but I was on the inside." "Somebody slipped a rope round his neck and strangled him, and you didn't wake up?" says Harry. "I didn't wake up," she said after him. We must 'a looked as if we didn't see how that could be, for after a minute she said, "I sleep sound." Harry was going to ask her more questions, but I said maybe we ought to let her tell her story first to the coroner, or the sheriff, so Harry went fast as he could to Rivers' place, where there's a telephone.

COUNTY ATTORNEY. And what did Mrs. Wright do when she knew that you had gone for the coroner?

HALE. She moved from that chair to this over here . . . *(Pointing to a small chair in the corner.)* . . . and just sat there with her hands held together and looking down. I got a feeling that I ought to make some conversation, so I said I had come in to see if John wanted to put in a telephone, and at that she started to laugh, and then she stopped and looked at me — scared. *(The County Attorney, who has had his notebook out, makes a note.)* I dunno, maybe it wasn't scared. I wouldn't like to say it was. Soon Harry got back, and then Dr. Lloyd came, and you, Mr. Peters, and so I guess that's all I know that you don't.

COUNTY ATTORNEY *(looking around)*. I guess we'll go upstairs first — and then out to the barn and around there. *(To the Sheriff.)* You're convinced that there was nothing important here — nothing that would point to any motive?

SHERIFF. Nothing here but kitchen things. *(The* 25 *County Attorney, after again looking around the kitchen, opens the door of a cupboard closet. He gets up on a chair and looks on a shelf. Pulls his hand away, sticky.)*

COUNTY ATTORNEY. Here's a nice mess. *(The women draw nearer.)*

MRS. PETERS *(to the other woman)*. Oh, her fruit; it did freeze. *(To the Lawyer.)* She worried about that when it turned so cold. She said the fire'd go out and her jars would break.

SHERIFF. Well, can you beat the woman! Held for murder and worryin' about her preserves.

COUNTY ATTORNEY. I guess before we're through she may have something more serious than preserves to worry about.

HALE. Well, women are used to worrying over 30 trifles. *(The two women move a little closer together.)*

COUNTY ATTORNEY. *(with the gallantry of a young politician)*. And yet, for all their worries, what would we do without the ladies? *(The women do not unbend. He goes to the sink, takes a dipperful of water from the pail and, pouring it into a basin, washes his hands. Starts to wipe them on the roller towel, turns it for a cleaner place.)* Dirty towels!

(*Kicks his foot against the pans under the sink.*) Not much of a housekeeper, would you say, ladies?

MRS. HALE (*stiffly*). There's a great deal of work to be done on a farm.

COUNTY ATTORNEY. To be sure. And yet . . . (*With a little bow to her.*) . . . I know there are some Dickson county farmhouses which do not have such roller towels. (*He gives it a pull to expose its full length again.*)

MRS. HALE. Those towels get dirty awful quick. Men's hands aren't always as clean as they might be.

COUNTY ATTORNEY. Ah, loyal to your sex. I see. 35 But you and Mrs. Wright were neighbors. I suppose you were friends, too.

MRS. HALE (*shaking her head*). I've not seen much of her of late years. I've not been in this house — it's more than a year.

COUNTY ATTORNEY. And why was that? You didn't like her?

MRS. HALE. I liked her all well enough. Farmers' wives have their hands full, Mr. Henderson. And then —

COUNTY ATTORNEY. Yes — ?

MRS. HALE (*looking about*). It never seemed a 40 very cheerful place.

COUNTY ATTORNEY. No — it's not cheerful. I shouldn't say she had the homemaking instinct.

MRS. HALE. Well, I don't know as Wright had, either.

COUNTY ATTORNEY. You mean they didn't get on very well?

MRS. HALE. No, I don't mean anything. But I don't think a place'd be any cheerfuller for John Wright's being in it.

COUNTY ATTORNEY. I'd like to talk more of that 45 a little later. I want to get the lay of things upstairs now. (*He goes to the left, where three steps lead to a stair door.*)

SHERIFF. I suppose anything Mrs. Peters does'll be all right. She was to take in some clothes for her, you know, and a few little things. We left in such a hurry yesterday.

COUNTY ATTORNEY. Yes, but I would like to see what you take, Mrs. Peters, and keep an eye out for anything that might be of use to us.

MRS. PETERS. Yes, Mr. Henderson. (*The women listen to the men's steps on the stairs, then look about the kitchen.*)

MRS. HALE. I'd hate to have men coming into my kitchen, snooping around and criticizing. (*She arranges the pans under the sink which the Lawyer had shoved out of place.*)

MRS. PETERS. Of course it's no more than their 50 duty.

MRS. HALE. Duty's all right, but I guess that deputy sheriff that came out to make the fire might have got a little of this on. (*Gives the roller towel a pull.*) Wish I'd thought of that sooner. Seems mean to talk about her for not having things slicked up when she had to come away in such a hurry.

MRS. PETERS (*who has gone to a small table in the left rear corner of the room, and lifted one end of a towel that covers a pan*). She had bread set. (*Stands still.*)

MRS. HALE (*eyes fixed on a loaf of bread beside the breadbox, which is on a low shelf at the other side of the room. Moves slowly toward it*). She was going to put this in there. (*Picks up loaf, then abruptly drops it. In a manner of returning to familiar things.*) It's a shame about her fruit. I wonder if it's all gone. (*Gets up on the chair and looks.*) I think there's some here that's all right, Mrs. Peters. Yes — here; (*Holding it toward the window.*) this is cherries, too. (*Looking again.*) I declare I believe that's the only one. (*Gets down, bottle in her hand. Goes* to the sink and wipes it off on the outside.) She'll feel awful bad after all her hard work in the hot weather. I remember the afternoon I put up my cherries last summer. *(She puts the bottle on the big kitchen table, center of the room. With a sigh, is about to sit down in the rocking chair. Before she is seated realizes what chair it is; with a slow look at it, steps back. The chair, which she has touched, rocks back and forth.)*

MRS. PETERS. Well, I must get those things from the front room closet. *(She goes to the door at the right, but after looking into the other room steps back.)* You coming with me, Mrs. Hale? You could help me carry them. *(They go into the other room; reappear, Mrs. Peters carrying a dress and skirt, Mrs. Hale following with a pair of shoes.)*

MRS. PETERS. My, it's cold in there. *(She puts the* 55 *cloth on the big table, and hurries to the stove.)*

MRS. HALE *(examining the skirt).* Wright was close. I think maybe that's why she kept so much to herself. She didn't even belong to the Ladies' Aid. I suppose she felt she couldn't do her part, and then you don't enjoy things when you feel shabby. She used to wear pretty clothes and be lively, when she was Minnie Foster, one of the town girls singing in the choir. But that — oh, that was thirty years ago. This all you was to take in?

MRS. PETERS. She said she wanted an apron. Funny thing to want, for there isn't much to get you dirty in jail, goodness knows. But I suppose just to make her feel more natural. She said they was in the top drawer in this cupboard. Yes, here. And then her little shawl that always hung behind the door. *(Opens stair door and looks.)* Yes, here it is. *(Quickly shuts door leading upstairs.)*

MRS. HALE *(abruptly moving toward her).* Mrs. Peters?

MRS. PETERS. Yes, Mrs. Hale?

MRS. HALE. Do you think she did it? 60

MRS. PETERS *(in a frightened voice).* Oh, I don't know.

MRS. HALE. Well, I don't think she did. Asking for an apron and her little shawl. Worrying about her fruit.

MRS. PETERS *(starts to speak, glances up, where footsteps are heard in the room above. In a low voice).* Mr. Peters says it looks bad for her. Mr. Henderson is awful sarcastic in speech, and he'll make fun of her sayin' she didn't wake up.

MRS. HALE. Well, I guess John Wright didn't wake when they was slipping that rope under his neck.

MRS. PETERS. No, it's strange. It must have been 65 done awful crafty and still. They say it was such a — funny way to kill a man, rigging it all up like that.

MRS. HALE. That's just what Mr. Hale said. There was a gun in the house. He says that's what he can't understand.

MRS. PETERS. Mr. Henderson said coming out that what was needed for the case was a motive; something to show anger or — sudden feeling.

MRS. HALE *(who is standing by the table).* Well, I don't see any signs of anger around here. *(She puts her hand on the dish towel which lies on the table, stands looking down at the table, one half of which is clean, the other half messy.)* It's wiped here. *(Makes a move as if to finish work, then turns and looks at loaf of bread outside the breadbox. Drops towel. In that voice of coming back to familiar things.)* Wonder how they are finding things upstairs? I hope she had it a little more red-up there. You know, it seems kind of *sneaking.* Locking her up in town and then coming out here and trying to get her own house to turn against her!

MRS. PETERS. But, Mrs. Hale, the law is the law.

MRS. HALE. I s'pose 'tis. (Unbuttoning her coat.) Better loosen up your things, Mrs. Peters. You won't feel them when you go out. (Mrs. Peters takes off her fur tippet, goes to hang it on hook at the back of room, stands looking at the under part of the small corner table.)

MRS. PETERS. She was piecing a quilt. (She brings the large sewing basket, and they look at the bright pieces.)

MRS. HALE. It's log cabin pattern. Pretty, isn't it? I wonder if she was goin' to quilt or just knot it? (Footsteps have been heard coming down the stairs. The Sheriff enters, followed by Hale and the County Attorney.)

SHERIFF. They wonder if she was going to quilt it or just knot it. (The men laugh, the women look abashed.)

COUNTY ATTORNEY (rubbing his hands over the stove). Frank's fire didn't do much up there, did it? Well, let's go out to the barn and get that cleared up. (The men go outside.)

MRS. HALE (resentfully). I don't know as there's anything so strange, our takin' up our time with little things while we're waiting for them to get the evidence. (She sits down at the big table, smoothing out a block with decision.) I don't see as it's anything to laugh about.

MRS. PETERS (apologetically). Of course they've got awful important things on their minds. (Pulls up a chair and joins Mrs. Hale at the table.)

MRS. HALE (examining another block). Mrs. Peters, look at this one. Here, this is the one she was working on, and look at the sewing! All the rest of it has been so nice and even. And look at this! It's all over the place! Why, it looks as if she didn't know what she was about! (After she has said

this, they look at each other, then start to glance back at the door. After an instant Mrs. Hale has pulled at a knot and ripped the sewing.)

MRS. PETERS. Oh, what are you doing, Mrs. Hale?

MRS. HALE (mildly). Just pulling out a stitch or two that's not sewed very good. (Threading a needle.) Bad sewing always made me fidgety.

MRS. PETERS (nervously). I don't think we ought to touch things.

MRS. HALE. I'll just finish up this end. (Suddenly stopping and leaning forward.) Mrs. Peters?

MRS. PETERS. Yes, Mrs. Hale?

MRS. HALE. What do you suppose she was so nervous about?

MRS. PETERS. Oh — I don't know. I don't know as she was nervous. I sometimes sew awful queer when I'm just tired. (Mrs. Hale starts to say something, looks at Mrs. Peters, then goes on sewing.) Well, I must get these things wrapped up. They may be through sooner than we think. (Putting apron and other things together.) I wonder where I can find a piece of paper, and string.

MRS. HALE. In that cupboard, maybe.

MRS. PETERS (looking in cupboard). Why, here's a birdcage. (Holds it up.) Did she have a bird, Mrs. Hale?

MRS. HALE. Why, I don't know whether she did or not — I've not been here for so long. There was a man around last year selling canaries cheap, but I don't know as she took one; maybe she did. She used to sing real pretty herself.

MRS. PETERS (glancing around). Seems funny to think of a bird here. But she must have had one, or why should she have a cage? I wonder what happened to it?

MRS. HALE. I s'pose maybe the cat got it.

MRS. PETERS. No, she didn't have a cat. She's got that feeling some people have about cats — being afraid of them. My cat got in her room, and she was real upset and asked me to take it out.

MRS. HALE. My sister Bessie was like that. Queer, ain't it?

MRS. PETERS (*examining the cage*). Why, look at this door. It's broke. One hinge is pulled apart.

MRS. HALE (*looking, too*). Looks as if someone must have been rough with it.

MRS. PETERS. Why, yes. (*She brings the cage forward and puts it on the table.*)

MRS. HALE. I wish if they're going to find any evidence they'd be about it. I don't like this place.

MRS. PETERS. But I'm awful glad you came with me, Mrs. Hale. It would be lonesome for me sitting here alone.

MRS. HALE. It would, wouldn't it? (*Dropping her sewing.*) But I tell you what I do wish, Mrs. Peters. I wish I had come over sometimes when *she* was here. I — (*Looking around the room.*) — wish I had.

MRS. PETERS. But of course you were awful busy, Mrs. Hale — your house and your children.

MRS. HALE. I could've come. I stayed away because it weren't cheerful — and that's why I ought to have come. I — I've never liked this place. Maybe because it's down in a hollow, and you don't see the road. I dunno what it is, but it's a lonesome place and always was. I wish I had come over to see Minnie Foster sometimes. I can see now — (*Shakes her head.*)

MRS. PETERS. Well, you mustn't reproach yourself, Mrs. Hale. Somehow we just don't see how it is with other folks until — something comes up.

MRS. HALE. Not having children makes less work — but it makes a quiet house, and Wright out to work all day, and no company when he did come in. Did you know John Wright, Mrs. Peters?

95

MRS. PETERS. Not to know him; I've seen him in town. They say he was a good man.

MRS. HALE. Yes — good; he didn't drink, and kept his word as well as most, I guess, and paid his debts. But he was a hard man, Mrs. Peters. Just to pass the time of day with him. (*Shivers.*) Like a raw wind that gets to the bone. (*Pauses, her eye falling on the cage.*) I should think she would 'a' wanted a bird. But what do you suppose went with it?

MRS. PETERS. I don't know, unless it got sick and died. (*She reaches over and swings the broken door, swings it again; both women watch it.*)

MRS. HALE. You weren't raised around here, were you? (*Mrs. Peters shakes her head.*) You didn't know — her?

105

MRS. PETERS. Not till they brought her yesterday.

MRS. HALE. She — come to think of it, she was kind of like a bird herself — real sweet and pretty, but kind of timid and — fluttery. How — she — did — change. (*Silence; then as if struck by a happy thought and relieved to get back to everyday things.*) Tell you what, Mrs. Peters, why don't you take the quilt in with you? It might take up her mind.

MRS. PETERS. Why, I think that's a real nice idea, Mrs. Hale. There couldn't possible be any objection to it, could there? Now, just what would I take? I wonder if her patches are in here — and her things. (*They look in the sewing basket.*)

100

MRS. HALE. Here's some red. I expect this has got sewing things in it. (*Brings out a fancy box.*) What a pretty box. Looks like something somebody would give you. Maybe her scissors are in here. (*Opens box. Suddenly puts her hand to her nose.*) Why — (*Mrs. Peters bends nearer, then turns her face away.*) There's something wrapped up in this piece of silk.

MRS. PETERS. Why, this isn't her scissors.

MRS. HALE (lifting the silk). Oh, Mrs. Peters — it's — (Mrs. Peters bends closer.)

MRS. PETERS. It's the bird.

MRS. HALE (jumping up). But, Mrs. Peters — look at it. Its neck! Look at its neck! It's all — other side to.

MRS. PETERS. Somebody — wrung — its neck. (Their eyes meet. A look of growing comprehension of horror. Steps are heard outside. Mrs. Hale slips box under quilt pieces, and sinks into her chair. Enter Sheriff and County Attorney, Mrs. Peters rises.)

COUNTY ATTORNEY (as one turning from serious things to little pleasantries). Well, ladies, have you decided whether she was going to quilt it or knot it?

MRS. PETERS. We think she was going to — knot it.

COUNTY ATTORNEY. Well, that's interesting, I'm sure. (Seeing the birdcage.) Has the bird flown?

MRS. HALE. (putting more quilt pieces over the box). We think the — cat got it.

COUNTY ATTORNEY (preoccupied). Is there a cat? (Mrs. Hale glances in a quick covert way at Mrs. Peters.)

MRS. PETERS. Well, not now. They're super- stitious, you know. They leave.

COUNTY ATTORNEY (to Sheriff Peters, continu- ing an interrupted conversation). No sign at all of anyone having come from the outside. Their own rope. Now let's go up again and go over it piece by piece. (They start upstairs.) It would have to have been someone who knew just the — (Mrs. Peters sits down. The two women sit there not looking at one another, but as if peering into something and at the same time holding back. When they talk now, it is the manner of feeling their way over strange ground, as

if afraid of what they are saying, but as if they cannot help saying it.)

MRS. HALE. She liked the bird. She was going to bury it in that pretty box.

MRS. PETERS (in a whisper). When I was a girl — my kitten — there was a boy took a hatchet, and before my eyes — and before I could get there — (Covers her face an instant.) If they hadn't held me back, I would have — (Catches herself, looks upstairs where steps are heard, falters weakly.) — hurt him.

MRS. HALE (with a slow look around her). I won- der how it would seem never to have had any children around. (Pause.) No, Wright wouldn't like the bird — a thing that sang. She used to sing. He killed that, too.

MRS. PETERS (moving uneasily). We don't know who killed the bird.

MRS. HALE. I knew John Wright.

MRS. PETERS. It was an awful thing was done in this house that night, Mrs. Hale. Killing a man while he slept, slipping a rope around his neck that choked the life out of him.

MRS. HALE. His neck. Choked the life out of him. (Her hand goes out and rests on the birdcage.)

MRS. PETERS (with a rising voice). We don't know who killed him. We don't know.

MRS. HALE (her own feeling not interrupted). If there'd been years and years of nothing, then a bird to sing to you, it would be awful — still, after the bird was still.

MRS. PETERS (something within her speaking). I know what stillness is. When we home- steaded in Dakota, and my first baby died — after he was two years old, and me with no other then —

MRS. HALE (moving). How soon do you suppose they'll be through, looking for evidence?

MRS. PETERS. I know what stillness is. (*Pulling herself back.*) The law has got to punish crime, Mrs. Hale.

MRS. HALE (*not as if answering that*). I wish you'd seen Minnie Foster when she wore a white dress with blue ribbons and stood up there in the choir and sang. (*A look around the room.*) Oh, I *wish* I'd come over here once in a while! That was a crime! That was a crime! Who's going to punish that?

MRS. PETERS (*looking upstairs*). We mustn't — take on. 135

MRS. HALE. I might have known she needed help! I know how things can be — for women. I tell you, it's queer, Mrs. Peters. We live close together and we live far apart. We all go through the same things — it's all just a different kind of the same thing. (*Brushes her eyes, noticing the bottle of fruit, reaches out for it.*) If I was you, I wouldn't tell her her fruit was gone. Tell her it *ain't*. Tell her it's all right. Take this in to prove it to her. She — she may never know whether it was broke or not.

MRS. PETERS (*takes the bottle, looks about for something to wrap it in; takes petticoat from the clothes brought from the other room, very nervously begins winding this around the bottle. In a false voice*). My, it's a good thing the men couldn't hear us. Wouldn't they just laugh! Getting all stirred up over a little thing like a — dead canary. As if that could have anything to do with — with — wouldn't they *laugh*! (*The men are heard coming downstairs.*)

MRS. HALE (*under her breath*). Maybe they would — maybe they wouldn't.

COUNTY ATTORNEY. No, Peters, it's all perfectly clear except a reason for doing it. But you know juries when it comes to women. If there was some definite thing. Something to show — something to make a story about — a thing that would connect up with this strange way of doing it. (*The women's eyes meet for an instant. Enter Hale from outer door.*)

HALE. Well, I've got the team around. Pretty cold out there. 140

COUNTY ATTORNEY. I'm going to stay here a while by myself. (*To the Sheriff.*) You can send Frank out for me, can't you? I want to go over everything. I'm not satisfied that we can't do better.

SHERIFF. Do you want to see what Mrs. Peters is going to take in? (*The Lawyer goes to the table, picks up the apron, laughs.*)

COUNTY ATTORNEY. Oh, I guess they're not very dangerous things the ladies have picked up. (*Moves a few things about, disturbing the quilt pieces which cover the box. Steps back.*) No, Mrs. Peters doesn't need supervising. For that matter, a sheriff's wife is married to the law. Ever think of it that way, Mrs. Peters?

MRS. PETERS. Not — just that way.

SHERIFF (*chuckling*). Married to the law. (*Moves toward the other room.*) I just want you to come in here a minute, George. We ought to take a look at these windows. 145

COUNTY ATTORNEY (*scoffingly*). Oh, windows!

SHERIFF. We'll be right out, Mr. Hale. (*Hale goes outside. The Sheriff follows the County Attorney into the other room. Then Mrs. Hale rises, hands tight together, looking intensely at Mrs. Peters, whose eyes take a slow turn, finally meeting Mrs. Hale's. A moment Mrs. Hale holds her, then her own eyes point the way to where the box is concealed. Suddenly Mrs. Peters throws back quilt pieces and tries to put the box in the bag she is carrying. It is too big. She opens box, starts to take the bird out, cannot touch it, goes to pieces, stands there helpless.*)

Sound of a knob turning in the other room. Mrs. Hale snatches the box and puts it in the pocket of her big coat. Enter County Attorney and Sheriff.)

COUNTY ATTORNEY *(facetiously).* Well, Henry, at least we found out that she was not going to quilt it. She was going to — what is it you call it, ladies?

MRS. HALE *(her hand against her pocket).* We call it — knot it, Mr. Henderson.

Topics for Critical Thinking and Writing

1. The dead canary in the box isn't evidence that Mrs. Wright has killed her husband. So what is the point of the dead canary in the play?

2. Do you think the play is immoral? Explain your response.

3. Assume that Minnie is indicted for murder and that you are asked to serve as her defense lawyer. If you somehow know that the evidence of the canary has been suppressed, would you accept the case? Why, or why not? (It is unlawful for *prosecutors* to suppress evidence, but it is not unlawful for defense lawyers to withhold incriminating evidence.)

4. Assume that you have accepted Minnie's case. In 500 words, set forth the defense you will offer for her. (Take any position that you wish. You may, for example, argue that she committed justifiable homicide or that — on the basis of her behavior as reported by Mr. Hale — she is innocent by reason of insanity.)

5. Assume that Minnie has been found guilty. Compose the speech she might give before being sentenced.

6. "*Trifles* is badly dated. It cannot speak to today's audience." In an essay of 500 words, evaluate this view: Offer an argument supporting or rejecting it, or take a middle position.

MITSUYE YAMADA

Mitsuye Yamada, the daughter of Japanese immigrants to the United States, was born in Japan in 1923, during her mother's return visit to her native land. Yamada was raised in Seattle, but in 1942 she and her family were incarcerated and then relocated to a camp in Idaho, when Executive Order 9066 (signed by President Franklin D. Roosevelt that year) gave military authorities the right to remove any and all persons from "military areas." In 1954 she became an American citizen. A professor of English at Cypress Junior College in San Luis Obispo, California, until she retired in 1989, Yamada is the author of poems and stories.

Yamada's poem concerns the compliant response to Executive Order 9066, which brought about the incarceration and relocation of the entire Japanese and Japanese American population on the Pacific coast — about 120,000 people. More than two-thirds of the people moved were native-born citizens of the United States. (The 158,000 Japanese residents of the Territory of Hawaii were not affected.) There was virtually no protest at the time, but in recent years the order has been widely regarded as an outrageous infringement on liberty, and some younger Japanese Americans cannot fathom why their parents and grandparents complied with it. This poem first appeared in Camp Notes and Other Poems *in 1976.*

To the Lady

The one in San Francisco who asked:
Why did the Japanese Americans let
the government put them in
those camps without protest?

Come to think of it I   5
    should've run off to Canada
    should've hijacked a plane to
       Algeria
    should've pulled myself up from my
    bra straps
    and kicked'm in the groin   10
    should've bombed a bank
    should've tried self-immolation
    should've holed myself up in a
    woodframe house
    and let you watch me   15
    burn up on the six o'clock news
    should've run howling down the street
    naked and assaulted you at breakfast
    by AP wirephoto

    should've screamed bloody murder   20
    like Kitty Genovese°

Then
YOU would've
    come to my aid in shining armor
    laid yourself across the railroad track   25
    marched on Washington
    tattooed a Star of David on your arm
    written six million enraged
    letters to Congress
But we didn't draw the line   30
anywhere
law and order Executive Order 9066
social order moral order internal order
YOU let'm
I let'm   35
All are punished.

---

21 Kitty Genovese In 1964 Kitty Genovese of Kew Gardens, New York, was stabbed to death when she left her car and walked toward her home. Thirty-eight persons heard her screams, but no one came to her assistance. [Editors' note.]

Topics for Critical Thinking and Writing

1. Has the lady's question (lines 2–4) ever crossed your mind? If so, what answers did you think of?

2. What, in effect, is the speaker really saying in lines 5–21? And in lines 22–29?

3. What possible arguments can you offer for and against the removal of Japanese Americans in 1942?

4. Do you think the survivors of the relocation are entitled to some sort of redress? Why, or why not? If you think they merit compensation, what should the compensation be?

28

What Is Happiness?

Thoughts about Happiness, Ancient and Modern

Here are some brief comments about happiness, from ancient times to the present. Read them, think about them, and then write on one of the two topics that appear after the last quotation.

> *Happiness is prosperity combined with virtue.*
> — ARISTOTLE (384–322 B.C.)

> *Pleasure is the beginning and the end of living happily. . . . It is impossible to live pleasurably without living wisely, well, and justly, and impossible to live wisely, well, and justly without living pleasurably.*
> — EPICURUS (341–270 B.C.)

> *Very little is needed to make a happy life.*
> — MARCUS AURELIUS (121–180)

> *Society can only be happy and free in proportion as it is virtuous.*
> — MARY WOLLSTONECRAFT SHELLEY (1759–1797)

> *The supreme happiness of life is the conviction that we are loved.*
> — VICTOR HUGO (1802–1885)

> *Ask yourself whether you are happy, and you cease to be so.*
> — JOHN STUART MILL (1806–1873)

> *A lifetime of happiness! No man alive could bear it: it would be hell on earth.*
> — GEORGE BERNARD SHAW (1856–1950)

> *We have no more right to consume happiness without producing it than to consume wealth without producing it.*
> — GEORGE BERNARD SHAW (1856–1950)

> *If only we'd stop trying to be happy, we could have a pretty good time.*
> — EDITH WHARTON (1862–1937)

Happiness makes up in height for what it lacks in length. — ROBERT FROST (1874–1963)

Point me out the happy man and I will point you out either egotism, selfishness,
evil — or else an absolute ignorance. — GRAHAM GREENE (1904–1991)

Those who are unhappy have no need for anything in this world but people capable
of giving them their attention. — SIMONE WEIL (1909–1943)

Happiness is always a by-product. It is probably a matter of temperament, and
for anything I know it may be glandular. But it is not something that can be
demanded from life, and if you are not happy you had better stop worrying
about it and see what treasures you can pluck from your own brand of
unhappiness. — ROBERTSON DAVIES (1913–1995)

Topics for Critical Thinking and Writing

1. If any one of these passages especially appeals to you, make it the thesis of an essay of about 500 words.

2. Take two of these passages — perhaps one that you especially like and one that you think is wrong-headed — and write a dialogue of about 500 words in which the two authors converse. They may each try to convince the other, or they may find that to some degree they share views and they may then work out a statement that both can accept. If you do take the position that one writer is on the correct track but the other is utterly mistaken, try to be fair to the view that you think is mistaken. (As an experiment in critical thinking, imagine that you accept it, and make the best case for it that you possibly can.)

DANIEL GILBERT

Daniel Gilbert (b. 1957), a professor of psychology at Harvard, is the author of Stumbling on Happiness *(2006) — a best seller that won the Royal Society Prize ($20,000) for Science Books. Hearing of the award, Gilbert said, "There are very few countries, including my own, the United States, where a somewhat cheeky book about happiness could win a science prize — but the British invented intellectual humor and have always understood that enlightenment and enter-tainment are natural friends."*

A high school dropout, Gilbert was nineteen when he visited a community college, intending to take a writing course but enrolling instead in the only course still open — a psychology course.

We reprint here an essay that appeared in Time *a few days before Father's Day in June 2006.*

Does Fatherhood Make You Happy?

Sonora Smart Dodd was listening to a sermon on self-sacrifice when she decided that her father, a widower who had raised six children, deserved his very own national holiday. Almost a century later, people all over the world spend the third Sunday in June honoring their fathers with ritual offerings of aftershave and neckties, which leads millions of fathers to have precisely the same thought at precisely the same moment: "My children," they think in unison, "make me happy."

Could all those dads be wrong?

Studies reveal that most married couples start out happy and then become progressively less satisfied over the course of their lives, becoming especially disconsolate when their children are in diapers and in adolescence, and returning to their initial levels of happiness only after their children have had the decency to grow up and go away. When the popular press invented a malady called "empty-nest syndrome," it failed to mention that its primary symptom is a marked increase in smiling.

Psychologists have measured how people feel as they go about their daily activities, and have found that people are less happy when they are interacting with their children than when they are eating, exercising, shopping, or watching television. Indeed, an act of parenting makes most people about as happy as an act of housework. Economists have modeled the impact of many variables on people's overall happiness and have consistently found that children have only a small impact. A small negative impact.

Those findings are hard to swallow because 5 they fly in the face of our most compelling intuitions. We love our children! We talk about them to anyone who will listen, show their photographs to anyone who will look, and hide our refrigerators behind vast collages of their drawings, notes, pictures, and report cards. We feel confident that we are happy with our kids, about our kids, for our kids, and because of our kids — so why is our personal experience at odds with the scientific data?

Three reasons.

First, when something makes us happy we are willing to pay a lot for it, which is why the worst Belgian chocolate is more expensive than the best Belgian tofu. But that process can work in reverse: When we pay a lot for something, we assume it makes us happy, which is why we swear to the wonders of bottled water and Armani socks. The compulsion to care for our children was long ago written into our DNA, so we toil and sweat, lose sleep and hair, play nurse, housekeeper, chauffeur, and cook, and we do all that because nature just won't have it any other way. Given the high price we pay, it isn't surprising that we rationalize those costs and conclude that our children must be repaying us with happiness.

Second, if the Red Sox and the Yankees were scoreless until Manny Ramirez hit a grand slam in the bottom of the ninth, you can be sure that Boston fans would remember it as the best game of the season. Memories are dominated by their most powerful — and not their most typical — instances. Just as a glorious game-winning homer can erase our memory of eight and a half dull innings, the sublime moment when our three-year-old looks up from the mess she is making with her mashed potatoes and says, "I wub you, Daddy," can erase eight hours of no, not yet, not now, and stop asking. Children may not make us happy very often, but when they do, that happiness is both transcendent and amnesic.

Third, although most of us think of heroin as a source of human misery, shooting heroin doesn't actually make people feel miserable. It makes them feel really, really good — so good, in fact, that it crowds out every other source of pleasure. Family, friends, work, play, food, sex — none can compete with the narcotic experience; hence all fall by the wayside. The analogy to children is all too clear. Even if their company were an unremitting pleasure, the fact that they require so much company means that other sources of pleasure will all but disappear. Movies, theater, parties, travel — those are just a few of the English nouns that parents of young children quickly forget how to pronounce. We believe our children are our greatest joy, and we're absolutely right. When you have one joy, it's bound to be the greatest.

Our children give us many things, but an increase in our average daily happiness is probably not among them. Rather than deny that fact, we should celebrate it. Our ability to love beyond all measure those who try our patience and weary our bones is at once our most noble and most human quality. The fact that children don't always make us happy — and that we're happy to have them nonetheless — is the fact for which Sonora Smart Dodd was so grateful. She thought we would all do well to remember it, every third Sunday in June.

Topics for Critical Thinking and Writing

1. How would you define the "empty-nest syndrome" (para. 3)?

2. Do you believe the "studies" that Daniel Gilbert mentions in paragraph 3? Why, or why not? Similarly, do you believe the "psychologists" of paragraph 4? Explain your response.

3. What does Gilbert mean when he describes the happiness that children cause their parents as "transcendent" (para. 8)? Are there other, nontranscendent kinds of happiness that parents experience? Explain your response.

4. Let's assume that even if you don't fully accept Gilbert's view about fatherhood and happiness, you're willing to grant that it is just possible that there may be something to what he says. Are you willing to take the next step and say that what he says of fatherhood — he was writing in time for Father's Day — may also be true of motherhood? Why, or why not?

5. What do you think Gilbert's chief purpose is in this essay? To inform? To persuade? To entertain? Something else? Support your answer with evidence.

6. You may have been told not to write paragraphs consisting of only a sentence or two, but Gilbert's essay includes two such paragraphs, 2 and 6. Should Gilbert have revised these paragraphs? Or does their brevity serve a purpose? Explain your response.

HENRY DAVID THOREAU

Henry David Thoreau (1817–1862) was born in Concord, Massachusetts, where he spent most of his life ("I have travelled a good deal in Concord"). He taught and lectured, but chiefly he observed, thought, and wrote. From July 5, 1847, to September 6, 1847, he lived near Concord in a cabin at Walden Pond, an experience recorded in Walden *(1854).*

"As for Clothing" (editors' title) comes from Walden, *Chapter 1. "We do not Ride on the Railroad; It Rides upon Us" (also the editors' title) is from Chapter 2.*

Selections from *Walden*

[AS FOR CLOTHING]

As for Clothing, to come at once to the practical part of the question, perhaps we are led oftener by the love of novelty and a regard for the opinions of men, in procuring it, than by a true utility. Let him who has work to do recollect that the object of clothing is, first, to retain the vital heat, and secondly, in this state of society, to cover nakedness, and he may judge how much of any necessary or important work may be accomplished without adding to his wardrobe. Kings and queens who wear a suit but once, though made by some tailor or dressmaker to their majesties, cannot know the comfort of wearing a suit that fits. They are no better than wooden horses to hang the clean clothes on. Every day our garments become more assimilated to ourselves, receiving the impress of the wearer's character, until we hesitate to lay them aside, without such delay and medical appliances and some such solemnity even as our bodies. No man ever stood the lower in my estimation for having a patch in his clothes; yet I am sure that there is greater anxiety, commonly, to have fashionable, or at least clean and unpatched clothes, than to have a sound conscience. But even if the rent is not mended, perhaps the worst vice betrayed is improvidence. I sometimes try my acquaintances by such tests as these, — Who could wear a patch, or two extra seams only, over the knee? Most have as if they believed that their prospects for life would be ruined if they should do it. It would be easier for them to hobble to town with a broken leg than with a broken pantaloon. Often if an accident happens to a gentleman's legs, they can be mended; but if a similar accident happens to the legs of his pantaloons, there is no help for it; for he considers, not what is truly respectable, but what is respected. We know but few men, a great many coats and breeches. Dress a scarecrow in your last shift, you standing shiftless by, who would not soonest salute the scarecrow? Passing a cornfield the other day, close by a hat and coat on a stake, I recognized the owner of the farm. He was only a little more weather-beaten than when I saw him last. I have heard of a dog that barked at every stranger who approached his master's premises with clothes on, but was easily quieted by a naked thief. It is an interesting question how far men would retain their relative rank if they were divested of their clothes. Could you, in such a case, tell surely of any company of civilized men which belonged to the most respected class? When Madam Pfeiffer,[1] in her adventurous travels round the world, from east to west, had got so near home as Asiatic Russia, she says that she felt the necessity of wearing other than a traveling dress, when she went to meet the authorities, for she "was now in a civilized country, where . . . people are judged of by their clothes." Even in our democratic New England towns the accidental possession of wealth, and its manifestation in dress and equipage alone, obtain for the possessor almost universal respect. But they who yield such respect, numerous as they are, are so far heathen, and need to have a missionary sent to them. Beside, clothes introduced sewing, a kind of work which you may call endless; a woman's dress, at least, is never done.

---

[1]**Madame Pfeiffer** Ida Pfeiffer (1797–1858), author of travel books. [All notes are the editors'.]

A man who has at length found something to do will not need to get a new suit to do it in; for him the old will do, that has lain dusty in the garret for an indeterminate period. Old shoes will serve a hero longer than they have served his valet — if a hero even has a valet — bare feet are older than shoes, and he can make them do. Only they who go to soirées and legislative halls must have new coats, coats to change as often as the man changes in them. But if my jacket and trousers, my hat and shoes, are fit to worship God in, they will do; will they not? Who ever saw his old clothes — his old coat, actually worn out, resolved into its primitive elements, so that it was not a deed of charity to bestow it on some poor boy, by him perchance to be bestowed on some poorer still, or shall we say richer, who could do with less? I say, beware of all enterprises that require new clothes, and not rather a new wearer of clothes. If there is not a new man, how can the new clothes be made to fit? If you have any enterprise before you, try it in your old clothes. All men want, not something to *do with,* but something to *do,* or rather something to *be.* Perhaps we should never procure a new suit, however ragged or dirty the old, until we have so conducted, so enterprised or sailed in some way, that we feel like new men in the old, and that to retain it would be like keeping new wine in old bottles. Our moulting season, like that of the fowls must be a crisis in our lives. The loon retires to solitary ponds to spend it. Thus also the snake casts its slough, and the caterpillar its wormy coat, by an internal industry and expansion; for clothes are but our outmost cuticle and mortal coil. Otherwise we shall be found sailing under false colors, and be inevitably cashiered at last by our own opinion, as well as that of mankind.

We don garment after garment, as if we grew like exogenous plants by addition without. Our outside and often thin and fanciful clothes are our epidermis, or false skin, which partakes not of our life, and may be stripped off here and there without fatal injury; our thicker garments, constantly worn, are our cellular integument, or cortex; but our shirts are our liber,[2] or true bark, which cannot be removed without girdling and so destroying the man. I believe that all races at some seasons wear something equivalent to the shirt. It is desirable that a man be clad so simply that he can lay his hands on himself in the dark, and that he live in all respects so compactly and preparedly, that, if an enemy take the town, he can, like the old philosopher, walk out the gate empty-handed without anxiety. While one thick garment is, for most purposes, as good as three thin ones, and cheap clothing can be obtained at prices really to suit customers; while a thick coat can be bought for five dollars, which will last as many years, thick pantaloons for two dollars, cowhide boots for a dollar and a half a pair, a summer hat for a quarter of a dollar, and a winter cap for sixty-two and a half cents, or a better be made at home at a nominal cost, where is he so poor that, clad in such a suit, *of his own earning*, there will not be found wise men to do him reverence?

When I ask for a garment of a particular form, my tailoress tells me gravely, "They do not make them so now," not emphasizing the "They" at all, as if she quoted an authority as impersonal as the Fates, and I find it difficult to get made what I want, simply because she cannot believe that I mean what I say, that I am so rash. When I hear this oracular sentence, I am for a moment absorbed in thought, emphasizing to myself each word separately that I may come at the meaning of it, that I may find out by what degree of consanguinity *They* are related to *me*, and what authority they may have in an affair which affects me so nearly; and finally, I am inclined to answer her with equal mystery, and without any

---

[2]**liber** Inner bark of a tree.

more emphasis of the "they" — "It is true, they did not make them so recently, but they do now." Of what use this measuring of me if she does not measure my character, but only the breadth of my shoulders, as it were a peg to hang the coat on? We worship not the Graces,[3] nor the Parcæ,[4] but Fashion. She spins and weaves and cuts with full authority. The head monkey at Paris puts on a traveller's cap, and all the monkeys in America do the same. I sometimes despair of getting anything quite simple and honest done in this world by the help of men. They would have to be passed through a powerful press first, to squeeze their old notions out of them, so that they would not soon get upon their legs again; and then there would be some one in the company with a maggot in his head, hatched from an egg deposited there nobody knows when, for not even fire kills these things, and you would have lost your labor. Nevertheless, we will not forget that some Egyptian wheat was handed down to us by a mummy.

On the whole, I think that it cannot be [5] maintained that dressing has in this or any country risen to the dignity of an art. At present men make shift to wear what they can get. Like shipwrecked sailors, they put on what they can find on the beach, and at a little distance, whether of space or time, laugh at each other's masquerade. Every generation laughs at the old fashions, but follows religiously the new. We are amused at beholding the costume of Henry VIII, or Queen Elizabeth, as much as if it was that of the King and Queen of the Cannibal Islands. All costume off a man is pitiful or grotesque. It is only the serious eye peering from and the sincere life passed within it which restrain laughter and consecrate the costume of any people. Let Harlequin be taken with a fit

of the colic and his trappings will have to serve that mood too. When the soldier is hit by a cannon ball rags are as becoming as purple.

The childish and savage taste of men and women for new patterns keeps how many shaking and squinting through kaleidoscopes that they may discover the particular figure which this generation requires today. The manufacturers have learned that this taste is merely whimsical. Of two patterns which differ only by a few threads more or less of a particular color, the one will be sold readily, the other lie on the shelf, though it frequently happens that after the lapse of a season the latter becomes the most fashionable. Comparatively, tattooing is not the hideous custom which it is called. It is not barbarous merely because the printing is skin-deep and unalterable.

I cannot believe that our factory system is the best mode by which men may get clothing. The condition of the operatives is becoming every day more like that of the English; and it cannot be wondered at, since, as far as I have heard or observed, the principal object is, not that mankind may be well and honestly clad, but, unquestionably, that the corporations may be enriched. In the long run men hit only what they aim at. Therefore, though they should fail immediately, they had better aim at something high.

[WE DO NOT RIDE ON THE RAILROAD; IT RIDES UPON US]

Still we live meanly, like ants; though the fable tells us that we were long ago changed into men; like pygmies we fight with cranes; it is error upon error, and clout upon clout, and our best virtue has for its occasion a superfluous and evitable wretchedness. Our life is frittered away by detail. An honest man has hardly need to count more than his ten fingers, or in

---

[3]**Graces** In Greek mythology, the Graces were three minor goddesses who were patrons of earthly pleasures such as happiness, creativity, beauty, and fertility.
[4]**Parcæ** Goddesses of fate in Roman mythology.

extreme cases he may add his ten toes, and lump the rest. Simplicity, simplicity, simplicity! I say, let your affairs be as two or three, and not a hundred or a thousand; instead of a million count half a dozen, and keep your accounts on your thumb nail. In the midst of this chopping sea of civilized life, such are the clouds and storms and quicksands and thousand-and-one items to be allowed for, that a man has to live, if he would not founder and go to the bottom and not make his port at all, by dead reckoning, and he must be a great calculator indeed who succeeds. Simplify, simplify. Instead of three meals a day, if it be necessary eat but one; instead of a hundred dishes, five; and reduce other things in proportion. Our life is like a German Confederacy, made up of petty states, with its boundary forever fluctuating, so that even a German cannot tell you how it is bounded at any moment. The nation itself, with all its so-called internal improvements, which, by the way are all external and superficial, is just such an unwieldy and overgrown establishment, cluttered with furniture and tripped up by its own traps, ruined by luxury and heedless expense, by want of calculation and a worthy aim, as the million households in the land; and the only cure for it as for them is in a rigid economy, a stern and more than Spartan simplicity of life and elevation of purpose. It lives too fast. Men think that it is essential that the *Nation* have commerce, and export ice, and talk through a telegraph, and ride thirty miles an hour, without a doubt, whether *they* do or not; but whether we should live like baboons or like men, is a little uncertain. If we do not get out sleepers,[5] and forge rails, and devote days and nights to the work, but go to tinkering upon our *lives* to improve *them*, who will build railroads? And if railroads are not built, how shall we get to heaven in season? But if we stay at home and mind our business, who will want railroads? We do not ride on the railroad; it rides upon us. Did you ever think what those sleepers are that underlie the railroad? Each one is a man, an Irishman, or a Yankee man. The rails are laid on them, and they are covered with sand, and the cars run smoothly over them. They are sound sleepers, I assure you. And every few years a new lot is laid down and run over; so that, if some have the pleasure of riding on a rail, others have the misfortune to be ridden upon. And when they run over a man that is walking in his sleep, a supernumerary sleeper in the wrong position, and wake him up, they suddenly stop the cars, and make a hue and cry about it, as if this were an exception. I am glad to know that it takes a gang of men for every five miles to keep the sleepers down and level in their beds as it is, for this is a sign that they may sometime get up again.

---

[5]**sleepers** The woody ties beneath railroad rails.

Topics for Critical Thinking and Writing

1. What, according to Henry David Thoreau, are the legitimate functions of clothing? What other functions does he reject, or fail to consider?

2. Many of Thoreau's sentences mean both what they say literally and something more; often, like proverbs, they express abstract or general truths in concrete, homely language. How might these sentences be interpreted?

a. We know but few men, a great many coats and breeches.
b. Dress a scarecrow in your last shift, you standing shiftless by, who would not soonest salute the scarecrow?
c. If you have any enterprise before you, try it in your old clothes.
d. Every generation laughs at the old fashions, but follows religiously the new.
e. When the soldier is hit by a cannon ball rags are as becoming as purple.

3. We have just quoted some of Thoreau's epigrammatic sentences. Is this style effective or not? Explain your response.

4. Notice that Thoreau writes in long paragraphs. (The first of them runs to more than 450 words — the length of many respectable essays.) Can such long paragraphs do their job effectively? What is the job of a paragraph? Or is there no one such job? Explain your response.

5. Toward the end of paragraph 2, we meet the cliché "new wine in old bottles." Do you think this sentence is effective? Why, or why not? Was this expression a cliché already in Thoreau's day? Complete the following definition: "A word or phrase is a cliché if and only if . . ."

6. In paragraph 7, Thoreau criticizes the factory system. Is the criticism mild or severe? Explain. Point out some of the earlier passages in which he touches on the relation of clothes to a faulty economic system.

7. In paragraph 8, Thoreau asserts that "Our life is frittered away by detail." Is it possible to argue that "Yes, our life is frittered away by detail, but, perhaps oddly, attention to detail — studying for examinations, grading papers, walking the dog — is largely responsible for human happiness"? Explain your response.

DARRIN M. McMAHON

Darrin M. McMahon was educated at the University of California–Berkeley, where he received his Ph.D. in 1997. The author of Happiness: A History *(2006), he has taught at Columbia University, Yale University, and New York University. We reprint an essay first published in the* New York Times *on December 29, 2005.*

In Pursuit of Unhappiness

"Happy New Year!" We seldom think of those words as an order. But in some respects that is what they are.

Doesn't every American want to be happy? And don't most Americans yearn, deep down, to be happy all of the time? The right laid out in our nation's Declaration of Independence — to pursue happiness to our hearts' content — is nowhere on better display than in the rites of the holiday season. With glad tidings and good cheer, we seek to bring one year to its natural happy conclusion, while preparing to usher in a happy new year and many happy returns.

Like the cycle of the seasons, our emphasis on mirth may seem timeless, as though human beings have always made merry from beginning to end. But in fact this preoccupation with perpetual happiness is relatively recent. As Thomas Carlyle observed in 1843, "'Happiness our being's end and aim' is at bottom, if we will count well, not yet two centuries old in the world."

Carlyle's arithmetic was essentially sound, for changes in both religious and secular culture since the seventeenth century made "happiness," in the form of pleasure or good feeling, not only morally acceptable but commendable in and of itself. While many discounted religious notions that consigned life in this world to misery and sin, others discovered signs of God's providence in earthly satisfaction. The result was at once to weaken and transpose the ideal of heavenly felicity, in effect bringing it to earth. Suffering was not our natural state. Happy was the way we were meant to be.

That shift was monumental, and its implications far reaching. Among other things, it was behind the transformation of the holiday season from a time of pious remembrance into one of unadulterated bliss. Yet the effects were greater than that. As Carlyle complained, "Every pitifulest whipster that walks within a skin has had his head filled with the notion that he is, shall be, or by all human and divine laws ought to be, 'happy.'"

Carlyle was notoriously cranky, but his central insight — that the new doctrine of happiness tended to raise expectations that could never possibly be fulfilled — remains as relevant today as it was in 1843. Despite enjoying far better living standards and more avenues for pleasure than before, human beings are arguably no happier now than they've ever been.

Sociologists like to point out that the percentage of those describing themselves as "happy" or "very happy" has remained virtually unchanged in Europe and the United States since such surveys were first conducted in the 1950s. And yet, this January, like last year and next, the self-help industry will pour forth books promising to make us happier than we are today. The very demand for such books is a strong indication that they aren't working.

Should that be a cause for concern? Some critics say it is. For example, economists like Lord Richard Layard and Daniel Kahneman have argued that the apparent stagnancy of happiness in modern societies should prompt policymakers to shift their priorities from the creation of wealth to the creation of good feelings, from boosting gross national product to increasing gross national happiness.

But before we take such steps, we might do well to reflect on the darker side of holiday cheer: those mysterious blues that are apt to set in while the streamers stream and the corks pop; the little voice that even in the best of souls is sometimes moved to say, "Bah, humbug." As Carlyle put it, "The prophets preach to us, 'Thou shalt be happy; thou shalt love pleasant things.'" But as he well knew, the very commandment tended to undermine its fulfillment, even to make us sad.

Carlyle's sometime friend and long-time rival, the philosopher John Stuart Mill, came to a similar conclusion. His words are all the more worth heeding in that Mill himself was a determined proponent of the greatest happiness for the greatest number. "Ask yourself whether you are happy, and you cease to be so," Mill concluded after recovering from a serious bout of depression. Rather than resign himself to gloom, however, Mill vowed instead to look for happiness in another way.

"Those only are happy," he came to believe, "who have their minds fixed on some object other than their own happiness; on the happiness of others; on the improvement of mankind, even on some art or pursuit, followed not as a means, but as itself an ideal end. Aiming thus at something else, they find happiness by the way." For our own culture, steeped as it is in the relentless pursuit of personal pleasure and endless cheer, that message is worth heeding.

So in these last days of 2005 I say to you, "Don't have a happy new year!" Have dinner with your family or walk in the park with friends. If you're so inclined, put in some good hours at the office or at your favorite charity, temple, or church. Work on your jump shot or your child's model trains. With luck, you'll find happiness by the by. If not, your time won't be wasted. You may even bring a little joy to the world.

Topics for Critical Thinking and Writing

1. Who or what gives us the "order" to be happy — or is the whole idea silly? (See paras. 1 and 9.) Explain your response.

2. What's the difference between happiness and pleasure, or are these two different ways of saying the same thing? Explain your response.

3. Has Darrin McMahon persuaded you to think of happiness in a fresh way? Why, or why not?

4. McMahon's article was originally published on December 29, so it's not surprising that in paragraph 2 he says his readers are preparing "to usher in a happy new year." Try to recall how you spent the most recent New Year's Eve. Was it a happy evening? Or was it tinged with melancholy, perhaps even with sorrow as you remembered sad things and hoped that the next year would be happier? If you can't remember New Year's Eve, think of the last year as a whole: Was it predominantly happy or unhappy? Or can't you judge it in such terms? Explain your response.

5. McMahon says (para. 4) that since the seventeenth century a shift in thinking has occurred: "Suffering [is] not our natural state. Happy was the way we were meant to be." Assume you are speaking to someone who has not read McMahon's essay. How would you explain this point?

6. John Stuart Mill (para. 10) is often described as a hedonist. What do you have to do or believe to be a hedonist? Are you a hedonist? Explain why or why not in 250 words.

7. Are you likely to take the advice McMahon offers in his final paragraph? Why, or why not?

8. Suppose you believed that we (say, American citizens) are happier today than we were three centuries ago. How would you go about arguing for your belief?

EPICTETUS

Epictetus (pronounced Epic-TEE-tus) was born in Phrygia (now southwestern Turkey) some sixty years after Jesus and died about 135 C.E. His mother was a slave, and he was brought to Rome as a slave. At an uncertain date he was given his freedom, and he went to Nicopolis in northwestern Greece, where he taught philosophy. One of his students, a Roman named Flavius Arrian, recorded the teachings of Epictetus in two books written in Greek, the Discourses *(or*

Lectures) *and the* Handbook *(or* Manual, *often known by its Greek title,* Enchiridion). *Our selection is from a translation by Helena Orozco.*

The doctrine that Epictetus taught is stoicism, which can be briefly characterized thus: The goal of life (as other philosophers of the period would agree) is "happiness" or "a flourishing life" (eudaimonia). The way to achieve this condition is to understand the nature of the good. Such things as health, wealth, and rank are not good because they do not always benefit those who possess them. True, such things are "preferred," and sickness, poverty, and low social status are "not preferred," but all of these are "indifferent" when it comes to being good or evil. The only true good is virtue. Yes, wealth can be useful, but it is not good or bad. What is good or bad is the way in which one makes use of what one has. The life that is happy or fruitful (eudaimôn) is the virtuous life. Of course, some things are beyond our power, but we are able to judge whatever comes to us, to see that what is "not preferred"—for instance, poverty—is not bad but is morally indifferent (just as wealth is morally indifferent). And we also have the power to adapt ourselves to whatever comes our way. A slightly later contemporary reported that Epictetus said that if one wanted to be free from wrongdoing and wanted to live a peaceful life, then one should endure *and* abstain.

The stoic doctrine of enduring was put in its most uncompromising way by the Victorian poet William Ernest Henley (1849–1903), in a poem called "Invictus" (i.e., "unconquered"). The first stanza runs thus:

Out of the night that covers me,
Black as the Pit from pole to pole,
I thank whatever gods may be
For my unconquerable soul.

And here is the final stanza:

It matters not how strait the gate,
How charged with punishment the scroll,
I am the captain of my fate;
I am the master of my soul.

From *The Handbook*

1. Some things are in our control, and some are not. Our opinions are within our control, and our choices, our likes and dislikes. In a word, whatever is our own doing. Beyond our control are our bodies, our possessions, reputation, position; in a word, things not our own doings.

Now, the things that are within our control are by nature free, unhindered, unimpeded, but those beyond our control are weak, slavish, hindered, up to others. Keep in mind, then, that if you think things are free that by nature are slavish, and if you think that things that are up to others are yours, you will be hindered,

you will suffer, you will complain, you will blame the gods and your fellows. But, on the other hand, if you take as yours only what in fact is yours, and if you see that what belongs to others belongs to others, nobody will compel you, nobody will restrict you; you will blame nobody, and you will do nothing against your will. No one will harm you, you will have no enemies.

5. People are not disturbed by what happens but by the view they take of what happens. For instance, death is not to be feared; if it were to be feared, Socrates would have

feared it. The fear consists in our wrong idea of death, our idea that it is to be feared. When, therefore, we are disturbed or feel grief, we should not blame someone else, but our [false] opinion. An uneducated person blames others for his misfortunes; a person just starting his education blames himself; an educated person blames neither others nor himself.

6. Do not take pride in any excellence that is not your own. If a horse could be proud, it might say, "I am handsome," and such a statement might be acceptable. But when you proudly say, "I have a handsome horse," you should understand that you are taking pride in a horse's good. What has the horse's good to do with you? What is yours? Only your reaction to things. When you behave in accordance with nature, you will take pride only in some good that is your own.

7. As when on a voyage, when the ship is at anchor, if you go ashore to get fresh water, you may amuse yourself by picking up a seashell or a vegetable, but keep the ship in mind. Be attentive to the captain's call, and when you hear the call, give up the trifles, or you will be thrown back into the ship like a bound sheep. So it is in life: If instead of a seashell or a vegetable, you are given a wife or child, fine, but when the captain calls, you must abandon these things without a second thought. And if you are old, keep close to the ship lest you are missing when you are called.

9. Sickness impedes the body but not the ability to make choices, unless you choose so. Lameness impedes the leg, but not the ability to make choices, unless the mind chooses so. Remember this with regard to everything that happens: Happenings are impediments to something else, but not to you.

15. Remember, behave in life as though you are attending a banquet. Is a dish brought to you? Put out your hand and take a moderate share. Does the dish pass you by? Do not grab for it. Has it not yet reached you? Don't yearn for it, but wait until it reaches you. Do this with regard to children, a spouse, position, wealth, and eventually you will be worthy to banquet with the gods. And if you can forgo even the things that are set before you, you are worthy not only to feast with the gods but to rule with them.

17. Remember: You are an actor in a play that you did not write. If the play is short, then it is short; if long, then it is long. If the author has assigned you the part of a poor man, act it well. Do the same if your part is that of a lame man or a ruler or an ordinary citizen. This is yours to do: Act your part well (but picking the part belongs to someone else).

21. Keep in mind death and exile and all other things that appear terrible — especially death — and you will never harbor a low thought nor too eagerly covet anything.

36. At a feast, to choose the largest portion might satisfy your body but would be detrimental to the social nature of the affair. When you dine with another, then, keep in mind not only the value to the body of the dishes set before you, but the value of your behavior to your host and fellow diners.

43. Everything has two handles, one by which it can be carried and one by which it cannot. If your brother acts unjustly, do not take up the affair by the handle of his injustice, for it cannot be carried that way. Rather, take the other handle: He is your brother, he was brought up with you. Taken this way, it can be carried.

Topics for Critical Thinking and Writing

1. Does Epictetus exaggerate the degree to which events in our lives are under our control? Write a 250-word essay explaining your answer.

2. Epictetus advises us not to fear death. What is his argument?

3. Would you agree with Epictetus that sickness "impedes the body but not the ability to make choices" (excerpt 9)? Is he wrong because there is such a thing as mental illness? Explain your response.

4. Choose one from among the eleven paragraphs by Epictetus that best expresses your own view of life — or are you entirely at odds with what Epictetus believes? Explain your response.

"If I won the lottery, I would go on living as I always did."

Mischa Richter The New Yorker Collection/The Cartoon Bank

BERTRAND RUSSELL

Bertrand Russell (1872–1970), British mathematician and philosopher, was born in Wales and educated at Trinity College, Cambridge, where he later taught. His pacifist opposition to World War I cost him this teaching appointment and earned him a prison sentence of six months. In 1940 an appointment to teach at the College of the City of New York was withdrawn because of his unorthodox moral views. But he was not always treated shabbily. He won numerous prizes, including a Nobel Prize for Literature in 1950. Much of his work is highly technical, but he also wrote frequently for the general public. We reprint a passage from one of his most widely read books, The Conquest of Happiness *(1930).*

The Happy Life

The happy life is to an extraordinary extent the same as the good life. Professional moralists have made too much of self-denial, and in so doing have put the emphasis in the wrong place. Conscious self-denial leaves a man self-absorbed and vividly aware of what he has sacrificed; in consequence it fails often of its immediate object and almost always of its ultimate purpose. What is needed is not self-denial, but that kind of direction of interest outward which will lead spontaneously and naturally to the same acts that a person absorbed in the pursuit of his own virtue could only perform by means of conscious self-denial. I have written in this book as a hedonist, that is to say, as one who regards happiness as the good, but the acts to be recommended from the point of view of the hedonist are on the whole the same as those to be recommended by the sane moralist. The moralist, however, is too apt, though this is not, of course, universally true, to stress the act rather than the state of mind. The effects of an act upon the agent will be widely different, according to his state of mind at the moment. If you see a child drowning and save it as the result of a direct impulse to bring help, you will emerge none the worse morally. If, on the other hand, you say to yourself, "It is the part of virtue to succor the helpless, and I wish to be a virtuous man, therefore I must save this child," you will be an even worse man afterwards than you were before. What applies in this extreme case, applies in many other instances that are less obvious.

There is another difference, somewhat more subtle, between the attitude toward life that I have been recommending and that which is recommended by the traditional moralists. The traditional moralist, for example, will say that love should be unselfish. In a certain sense he is right, that is to say, it should not be selfish beyond a point, but it should undoubtedly be of such a nature that one's own happiness is bound up in its success. If a man were to invite a lady to marry him on the ground that he ardently desired her happiness and at the same time considered that she would afford him ideal opportunities of self-abnegation, I think it may be doubted whether she would be altogether pleased. Undoubtedly we should desire the happiness of those whom we love, but not as an alternative to our own. In fact the whole antithesis between self and the rest of the world, which is implied in the doctrine of self-denial, disappears as soon as we have any genuine interest in persons or things outside ourselves. Through such interests a man comes to feel himself part of the stream of life, not a hard separate entity like a billiard ball, which can have no relation with other such entities except that of collision. All unhappiness depends upon some kind of disintegration or lack of integration; there is disintegration within the self through lack of coördination between the conscious and the unconscious mind; there is lack of integration between the self and society, where the two are not knit together by the force of objective interests and affections. The happy man is the man who does not suffer from either of these failures of unity, whose personality is neither divided against itself nor pitted against the world. Such a man feels himself a citizen of the universe, enjoying freely the spectacle that it offers and the joys that it affords, untroubled by the thought of death because he feels himself not really separate from those who will come after him. It is in such profound instinctive union with the stream of life that the greatest joy is to be found.

Topics for Critical Thinking and Writing

1. In paragraph 1, Bertrand Russell says, "The happy life is to an extraordinary extent the same as the good life." First, how do you suppose Russell knows this? How might one confirm or refute the statement? Second, do you agree with Russell? Explain in detail.

2. In his final paragraph, Russell says that it is through their interests that people come to feel they are "part of the stream of life, not a hard separate entity like a billiard ball, which can have no relation with other such entities except that of collision." Does this sentence strike you as (a) effective and (b) probably true? Why, or why not?

3. In the final paragraph, Russell says that happy people feel connected to themselves (do not feel internally divided) and connected to society (do not feel pitted against the world). Describe in some detail a person who seems to you connected to the self and to society. Do you think that person is happy? Explain. Describe two people, one of whom seems to you internally divided, and one of whom seems to you separated from society. Now think about yourself. Do you feel connected to yourself and to the world? If so, are you happy? Why, or why not?

THE DALAI LAMA AND HOWARD C. CUTLER

The fourteenth Dalai ("ocean-wide") Lama ("superior person"), Tenzin Gyatso, is the spiritual leader of the Tibetan people but has lived in exile in Dharamsala, India, since 1959, when China invaded Tibet. In 1989 he was awarded the Nobel Peace Prize. In 1982 Howard C. Cutler, a psychiatrist who practices in Phoenix, Arizona, met the Dalai Lama while visiting India to study Tibetan medicine. Cutler and the Dalai Lama had frequent conversations, which Cutler later summarized and submitted to the Dalai Lama for approval. The material was then published in a book they entitled The Art of Happiness *(1998). We give one selection.*

Inner Contentment

Crossing the hotel parking lot on my way to meet with the Dalai Lama one afternoon, I stopped to admire a brand-new Toyota Land Cruiser, the type of car I had been wanting for a long time. Still thinking of that car as I began my session, I asked, "Sometimes it seems that our whole culture, Western culture, is based on material acquisition; we're surrounded, bombarded, with ads for the latest things to buy, the latest car and so on. It's difficult not to be influenced by that. There are so many things we want, things we desire. It never seems to stop. Can you speak a bit about desire?"

"I think there are two kinds of desire," the Dalai Lama replied. "Certain desires are positive. A desire for happiness. It's absolutely right. The desire for peace. The desire for a more harmonious world, a friendlier world. Certain desires are very useful.

"But at some point, desires can become unreasonable. That usually leads to trouble. Now, for example, sometimes I visit supermarkets. I really love to see supermarkets, because I can see so many beautiful things. So, when I look at all these different articles, I develop a feeling of desire, and my initial impulse might be, 'Oh, I want this; I want that.' Then, the second thought that arises, I ask myself, 'Oh, do I really need this?' The answer is usually no. If you follow after that first desire, that initial impulse, then very soon your pockets will empty. However, the other level of desire, based on one's essential needs of food, clothing, and shelter, is something more reasonable.

"Sometimes, whether a desire is excessive or negative depends on the circumstances or society in which you live. For example, if you live in a prosperous society where a car is required to help you manage in your daily life, then of course there's nothing wrong in desiring a car. But if you live in a poor village in India where you can manage quite well without a car but you still desire one, even if you have the money to buy it, it can ultimately bring trouble. It can create an uncomfortable feeling among your neighbors and so on. Or, if you're living in a more prosperous society and have a car but keep wanting more expensive cars, that leads to the same kind of problems."

"But," I argued, "I can't see how wanting or buying a more expensive car leads to problems for an individual, as long as he or she can afford it. Having a more expensive car than your neighbors might be a problem for them — they might be jealous and so on — but having a new car would give you, yourself, a feeling of satisfaction and enjoyment."

The Dalai Lama shook his head and replied firmly, "No. . . . Self-satisfaction alone cannot determine if a desire or action is positive or negative. A murderer may have a feeling of satisfaction at the time he is committing the murder, but that doesn't justify the act. All the nonvirtuous actions — lying, stealing, sexual misconduct, and so on — are committed by people who may be feeling a sense of satisfaction at the time. The demarcation between a positive and a negative desire or action is not whether it gives you an immediate feeling of satisfaction but whether it ultimately results in positive or negative consequences. For example, in the case of wanting more expensive possessions, if that is based on a mental attitude that just wants more and more, then eventually you'll reach a limit of what you can get; you'll come up against reality. And when you reach that limit, then you'll lose all hope, sink down into depression, and so on. That's one danger inherent in that type of desire.

"So I think that this kind of excessive desire leads to greed — an exaggerated form of desire, based on overexpectation. And when you reflect upon the excesses of greed, you'll find that it leads an individual to a feeling of frustration, disappointment, a lot of confusion, and a lot of problems. When it comes to dealing with greed, one thing that is quite characteristic is that although it arrives by the desire to obtain something, it is not satisfied by obtaining. Therefore, it becomes sort of limitless, sort of bottomless, and that leads to trouble. One interesting thing about greed is that although the underlying motive is to seek satisfaction, the irony is that even after obtaining the object of your desire, you are still not satisfied. *The true antidote of greed is contentment.* If you have a strong sense of contentment, it doesn't matter whether you obtain the object or not; either way, you are still content."

So, how can we achieve inner contentment? There are two methods. One method is to obtain everything that we want and desire — all the money, houses, and cars; the perfect mate; and the perfect body. The Dalai Lama has already pointed out the disadvantage of this approach; if our wants and desires remain unchecked, sooner or later we will run up against something that we want but can't have. The second, and more reliable, method is not to have what we want but rather to want and appreciate what we have.

The other night, I was watching a television interview with Christopher Reeve, the actor who was thrown from a horse in 1994 and suffered a spinal cord injury that left him completely paralyzed from the neck down, requiring a mechanical ventilator even to breathe. When questioned by the interviewer about how he dealt with the depression resulting from his disability, Reeve revealed that he had experienced a brief period of complete despair while in the intensive care unit of the hospital. He went on to say, however, that these feelings of despair passed relatively quickly, and he now sincerely considered himself to be a "lucky guy." He cited the blessings of a loving wife and children but also spoke gratefully about the rapid advances of modern medicine (which he estimates will find a cure for spinal cord injury within the next decade), stating that if he had been hurt just a few years earlier, he probably would have died from his injuries. While describing the process of adjusting to his paralysis, Reeve said that while his feelings of despair resolved rather quickly, at first he was still troubled by intermittent pangs of jealousy that could be triggered by another's innocent passing remark such as, "I'm just gonna run upstairs and get something." In learning to deal with these feelings, he said, "I realized that the only way to go through life is to look at your assets, to see what you can still do; in my case, fortunately I didn't have any brain injury, so I still have a mind I can use." Focusing on his resources in this manner, Reeve has elected to use his mind to increase awareness and educate the public about spinal cord injury, to help others, and has plans to continue speaking as well as to write and direct films.[1]

---

[1]Christopher Reeve died on October 10, 2004. [Editors' note.]

Topics for Critical Thinking and Writing

1. In paragraph 1, Howard Cutler says that he had long wanted a Toyota Land Cruiser. Exactly why might a person want such a vehicle? Do you want a Toyota Land Cruiser or some other new car? Why, or why not? (By the way, a friend of ours — a professor of philosophy — says,

"The key to happiness is the key to the ignition." In your opinion, how much truth is there in this philosophic view?)

2. At the end of paragraph 8, Cutler reports that the Dalai Lama suggests that the best way to achieve inner contentment "is not to have what we want but rather to want and appreciate what we have." In the next (final) paragraph, Cutler cites the example of Christopher Reeve. Drawing on your own experiences — which include your experience of persons whom you know or have heard about — can you offer confirming evidence? Explain your response.

3. Compare the Dalai Lama's views with those of Epictetus (p. 739). Would you say they are virtually the same? Why, or why not?

C. S. LEWIS

Clive Staples Lewis (1898–1963) taught medieval and Renaissance literature at Oxford, his alma mater, and later at Cambridge. He wrote about literature; he wrote fiction and poetry. Lewis became an atheist at age thirteen. He held that view until he was about thirty-one years old. He wrote numerous essays and books on Christianity from the point of view of a believer.

We Have No "Right to Happiness"

"After all," said Clare, "they had a right to happiness."

We were discussing something that once happened in our own neighborhood. Mr. A. had deserted Mrs. A. and got his divorce in order to marry Mrs. B., who had likewise got her divorce in order to marry Mr. A. And there was certainly no doubt that Mr. A. and Mrs. B. were very much in love with one another. If they continued to be in love, and if nothing went wrong with their health or their income, they might reasonably expect to be very happy.

It was equally clear that they were not happy with their old partners. Mrs. B. had adored her husband at the outset. But then he got smashed up in the war. It was thought he had lost his virility, and it was known that he had lost his job. Life with him was no longer what Mrs. B. had bargained for. Poor Mrs. A., too. She had lost her looks — and all her liveliness. It might be true, as some said, that she consumed herself by bearing his children and nursing him through the long illness that overshadowed their earlier married life.

You mustn't, by the way, imagine that A. was the sort of man who nonchalantly threw a wife away like the peel of an orange he'd sucked dry. Her suicide was a terrible shock to him. We all knew this, for he told us so himself. "But what could I do?" he said. "A man has a right to happiness. I had to take my one chance when it came."

I went away thinking about the concept of 5 a "right to happiness."

At first this sounds to me as odd as a right to good luck. For I believe — whatever one school of moralists may say — that we depend for a very great deal of our happiness or misery on circumstances outside all human control. A right to happiness doesn't, for me, make much more sense than a right to be six feet tall, or to have a millionaire for your father, or to get good weather whenever you want to have a picnic.

I can understand a right as a freedom guaranteed me by the laws of the society I live in. Thus, I have a right to travel along the public roads because society gives me that freedom; that's what we mean by calling the roads "public." I can also understand a right as a claim guaranteed me by the laws, and correlative to an obligation on someone else's part. If I have a right to receive £100 from you, this is another way of saying that you have a duty to pay me £100. If the laws allow Mr. A. to desert his wife and seduce his neighbor's wife, then, by definition, Mr. A. has a legal right to do so, and we need bring in no talk about "happiness."

But of course that was not what Clare meant. She meant that he had not only a legal but a moral right to act as he did. In other words, Clare is — or would be if she thought it out — a classical moralist after the style of Thomas Aquinas, Grotius, Hooker, and Locke. She believes that behind the laws of the state there is a Natural Law.

I agree with her. I hold this conception to be basic to all civilization. Without it, the actual laws of the state become an absolute, as in Hegel. They cannot be criticized because there is no norm against which they should be judged.

The ancestry of Clare's maxim, "They have a right to happiness," is august. In words that are cherished by all civilized men, but especially by Americans, it has been laid down that one of the rights of man is a right to "the pursuit of happiness." And now we get to the real point.

What did the writers of that august declaration mean?

It is quite certain what they did not mean. They did not mean that man was entitled to pursue happiness by any and every means — including, say, murder, rape, robbery, treason, and fraud. No society could be built on such a basis.

They meant "to pursue happiness by all lawful means"; that is, by all means which the Law of Nature eternally sanctions and which the laws of the nation shall sanction.

Admittedly this seems at first to reduce their maxim to the tautology that men (in pursuit of happiness) have a right to do whatever they have a right to do. But tautologies, seen against their proper historical context, are not always barren tautologies. The declaration is primarily a denial of the political principles which long governed Europe: a challenge flung down to the Austrian and Russian empires, to England before the Reform Bills, to Bourbon France. It demands that whatever means of pursuing happiness are lawful for any should be lawful for all; that "man," not men of some particular caste, class, status, or religion, should be free to use them. In a century when this is being unsaid by nation after nation and party after party, let us not call it a barren tautology.

But the question as to what means are "lawful" — what methods of pursuing happiness are either morally permissible by the Law of Nature or should be declared legally permissible by the legislature of a particular nation — remains exactly where it did. And on that question I disagree with Clare. I don't think it is obvious that people have the unlimited "right to happiness" which she suggests.

For one thing, I believe that Clare, when she says "happiness," means simply and solely "sexual happiness." Partly because women like Clare never use the word "happiness" in any other sense. But also because I never heard Clare talk about the "right" to any other kind. She was rather leftist in her politics, and would have been scandalized if anyone had defended the actions of a ruthless man-eating tycoon on the ground that his happiness consisted in making money and he was pursuing his happiness. She was also a rabid teetotaler; I never heard her excuse an alcoholic because he was happy when he was drunk.

A good many of Clare's friends, and especially her female friends, often felt — I've heard them say so — that their own happiness would be perceptibly increased by boxing her ears. I very much doubt if this would have brought her theory of a right to happiness into play.

Clare, in fact, is doing what the whole western world seems to me to have been doing for the last forty-odd years. When I was a youngster, all the progressive people were saying, "Why all this prudery? Let us treat sex just as we treat all our other impulses." I was simple-minded enough to believe they meant what they said. I have since discovered that they meant exactly the opposite. They meant that sex was to be treated as no other impulse in our nature has ever been treated by civilized people. All the others, we admit, have to be bridled. Absolute obedience to your instinct for self-preservation is what we call cowardice; to your acquisitive impulse, avarice. Even sleep must be resisted if you're a sentry. But every unkindness and breach of faith seems to be condoned provided that the object aimed at is "four bare legs in a bed."

It is like having a morality in which stealing fruit is considered wrong — unless you steal nectarines.

And if you protest against this view you are usually met with chatter about the legitimacy and beauty and sanctity of "sex" and accused of harboring some Puritan prejudice against it as something disreputable or shameful. I deny the charge. Foam-born Venus . . . golden Aphrodite . . . Our Lady of Cyprus . . . I never breathed a word against you. If I object to boys who steal my nectarines, must I be supposed to disapprove of nectarines in general? Or even of boys in general? It might, you know, be stealing that I disapproved of.

The real situation is skillfully concealed by saying that the question of Mr. A.'s "right" to desert his wife is one of "sexual morality." Robbing an orchard is not an offense against some special morality called "fruit morality." It is an offense against honesty. Mr. A.'s action is an offense against good faith (to solemn promises), against gratitude (toward one to whom he was deeply indebted) and against common humanity.

Our sexual impulses are thus being put in a position of preposterous privilege. The sexual motive is taken to condone all sorts of behavior which, if it had any other end in view, would be condemned as merciless, treacherous, and unjust.

Now though I see no good reason for giving sex this privilege, I think I see a strong cause. It is this.

It is part of the nature of a strong erotic passion — as distinct from a transient fit of appetite — that it makes more towering promises than any other emotion. No doubt all our desires make promises, but not so impressively. To be in love involves the almost irresistible conviction that one will go on being in love until one dies, and that possession of the beloved will confer, not merely frequent ecstasies, but settled, fruitful, deep-rooted, lifelong happiness. Hence *all* seems to be at stake. If we miss this chance we shall have lived in vain. At the very thought of such a doom we sink into fathomless depths of self-pity.

Unfortunately these promises are found often to be quite untrue. Every experienced adult knows this to be so as regards all erotic passions (except the one he himself is feeling at the moment). We discount the world-without-end pretensions of our friends' amours easily enough. We know that such things sometimes last—and sometimes don't. And when they do last, this is not because they promised at the outset to do so. When two people achieve lasting happiness, this is not solely because they are great lovers but because they are also—I must put it crudely—good people; controlled, loyal, fairminded, mutually adaptable people.

If we establish a "right to (sexual) happiness" which supersedes all the ordinary rules of behavior, we do so not because of what our passion shows itself to be in experience but because of what it professes to be while we are in the grip of it. Hence, while the bad behavior is real and works miseries and degradations, the happiness which was the object of the behavior turns out again and again to be illusory. Everyone (except Mr. A. and Mrs. B.) knows that Mr. A. in a year or so may have the same reason for deserting his new wife as for deserting his old. He will feel again that all is at stake. He will see himself again as the great lover, and his pity for himself will exclude all pity for the woman.

Two further points remain.

One is this. A society in which conjugal infidelity is tolerated must always be in the long run a society adverse to women. Women, whatever a few male songs and satires may say to the contrary, are more naturally monogamous than men; it is a biological necessity. Where promiscuity prevails, they will therefore always be more often the victims than the culprits. Also, domestic happiness is more necessary to them than to us. And the quality by which they most easily hold a man, their beauty, decreases every year after they have come to maturity, but this does not happen to those qualities of personality—women don't really care twopence about our *looks*—by which we hold women. Thus in the ruthless war of promiscuity women are at a double disadvantage. They play for higher stakes and are also more likely to lose. I have no sympathy with moralists who frown at the increasing crudity of female provocativeness. These signs of desperate competition fill me with pity.

Secondly, though the "right to happiness" is chiefly claimed for the sexual impulse, it seems to me impossible that the matter should stay there. The fatal principle, once allowed in that department, must sooner or later seep through our whole lives. We thus advance toward a state of society in which not only each man but every impulse in each man claims *carte blanche*. And then, though our technological skill may help us survive a little longer, our civilization will have died at heart, and will—one dare not even add "unfortunately"—be swept away.

Topics for Critical Thinking and Writing

1. Having read the entire essay, look back at C. S. Lewis's first five paragraphs and point out the ways in which he is not merely recounting an episode but is already conveying his attitude and seeking to persuade his readers.

2. Do you want to argue: If I have a right to happiness, you or someone has a duty to see to it that I'm happy (see para. 7)? Or do you want to argue: No one has a right to happiness because no one has a duty to make anyone happy? Argue one of these positions in 250 words.

3. What's the difference between being happy in a marriage and being content in a marriage? Explain the difference in an essay of 250 words.

4. What is absurd about the idea (para. 6) of having "a right to be six feet tall"? Explain in 100 words or fewer.

5. What, if anything, do the absurd candidates for rights (para. 6) have in common?

6. What's the difference between having a legal right to something and having a moral right to that thing (see paras. 8–9)? Give an example of each.

7. Do you agree with Lewis (paras. 26, 29) that "a right to happiness" really means "a right to sexual happiness"? Why, or why not?

8. Do you agree with Lewis (para. 28) that monogamy is "a biological necessity" for women? Explain, in an essay of 250 words.

DANIELLE CRITTENDEN

Danielle Crittenden (b. 1963), the founder of The Woman's Quarterly, *has written for numerous publications, including the* New York Times *and the* Wall Street Journal. *We reprint a selection from her book,* What Our Mothers Didn't Tell Us: Why Happiness Eludes the Modern Woman *(1999). Do you agree or disagree with her argument that women can be happy only if they put aside what she describes as misleading feminist ideas about independence?*

About Love

From a feminist view, it would be nice, I suppose—or at the very least handy—if we were able to derive total satisfaction from our solitude, to be entirely self-contained organisms, like earthworms or amoebas, having relations with the opposite sex whenever we felt a need for it but otherwise being entirely contented with our own company. Every woman's apartment could be her Walden Pond. She'd be free of the romantic fuss and interaction that has defined, and given meaning to, human existence since its creation. She could spend her evenings happily ensconced with a book or a rented video, not having to deal with some bozo's desire to watch football or play mindless video games. How children would fit into this vision of autonomy, I'm not sure, but surely they would infringe upon it; perhaps she could simply farm them out. If this seems a rather chilling outcome to the quest for independence, well, it is. If no man is an island, then no woman can be, either. And it's why most human beings fall in love, and continue to take on all the commitments and responsibilities of family life. We *want* the warm body next to us on the sofa in the evenings; we *want* the noise and embrace of family around us; we *want*, at the end of our lives, to look back and see that what we have done amounts to more than a pile of pay stubs, that we have loved and been loved, and brought into this world life that will outlast us.

The quest for autonomy—the need "to be oneself" or, as Wurtzel declares, the intention "to answer only to myself"—is in fact not a brave or noble one; nor is it an indication of strong character. Too often, autonomy is merely the excuse of someone who is so fearful, so weak, that he or she can't bear to take on any of the responsibilities that used to be shouldered by much younger but more robust and mature souls. I'm struck by the number of my single contemporaries—men and women in their early to mid-thirties—who speak of themselves as if they were still twenty years old, just embarking upon their lives and not, as they actually are, already halfway through them. In another era, a thirty-three-year-old man or woman might have already lived through a depression and a world war and had several children. Yet at the suggestion of marriage—or of buying a house or of having a baby—these modern thirtysomethings will exclaim, "But I'm so young!" their crinkled eyes widening at the thought. In the relationships they do have—even "serious" ones—they will take pains to avoid the appearance of anything that smacks of permanent commitment. The strange result is couples who are willing to share *everything* with each other—leases, furniture, cars, weekends, body fluids, holidays with their relatives—just as long as it comes with the right to cancel the relationship *at any moment*.

Unfortunately, postponing marriage and all the responsibilities that go with it does not prolong youth. It only prolongs the illusion of it, and then again only in one's own eyes. The traits that are forgivable in a twenty-year-old—the constant wondering about who you are and what you will be; the readiness to chuck one thing, or person, for another and move on—are less attractive in a thirty-two-year-old. More often what results is a middle-aged person who retains all the irritating self-absorption of an adolescent without gaining any

of the redeeming qualities of maturity. Those qualities—wisdom, a sense of duty, the willingness to make sacrifices for others, an acceptance of aging and death—are qualities that spring directly from our relationships and commitments to others.

A woman will not understand what true dependency is until she is cradling her own infant in her arms; nor will she likely achieve the self-confidence she craves until she has withstood, and transcended, the weight of responsibility a family places upon her—a weight that makes all the paperwork and assignments of her in-basket seem feather-light. The same goes for men. We strengthen a muscle by using it, and that is true of the heart and mind, too. By waiting and waiting and waiting to commit to someone, our capacity for love shrinks and withers. This doesn't mean that women or men should marry the first reasonable person to come along, or someone with whom they are not in love. But we should, at a much earlier age than we do now, take a serious attitude toward dating and begin preparing ourselves to settle down. For it's in the act of taking up the roles we've been taught to avoid or postpone—wife, husband, mother, father—that we build our identities, expand our lives, and achieve the fullness of character we desire.

Still, critics may argue that the old way was 5 no better; that the risk of loss women assume by delaying marriage and motherhood overbalances the certain loss we'd suffer by marrying too early. The habit of viewing marriage as a raw deal for women is now so entrenched, even among women who don't call themselves feminists, that I've seen brides who otherwise appear completely happy apologize to their wedding guests for their surrender to convention, as if a part of them still feels there is something embarrassing and weak about an intelligent and ambitious woman consenting to marry. But is this true? Or is it just an alibi we've been handed by the previous generation of women in order to justify the sad, lonely outcomes of so many lives?

What we rarely hear — or perhaps are too fearful to admit — is how *liberating* marriage can actually be. As nerve-racking as making the decision can be, it is also an enormous relief once it is made. The moment we say, "I do," we have answered one of the great, crucial questions of our lives: We now know with whom we'll be spending the rest of our years, who will be the father of our children, who will be our family. That our marriages may not work, that we will have to accommodate ourselves to the habits and personality of someone else — these are, and always have been, the risks of commitment, of love itself. What is important is that our lives have been thrust forward. The negative — that we are no longer able to live entirely for ourselves — is also the positive: *We no longer have to live entirely for ourselves!* We may go on to do any number of interesting things, but we are free of the gnawing wonder of *with whom* we will do them. We have ceased to look down the tunnel, waiting for a train.

The pull between the desire to love and be loved and the desire to be free is an old, fierce one. If the error our grandmothers made was to have surrendered too much of themselves for others, this was perhaps better than not being prepared to surrender anything at all. The fear of losing oneself can, in the end, simply become an excuse for not giving any of oneself away. Generations of women may have had no choice but to commit themselves to marriage early and then to feel imprisoned by their lifelong domesticity. So many of our generation have decided to put it off until it is too late, not foreseeing that lifelong independence can be its own kind of prison, too.

Topics for Critical Thinking and Writing

1. In paragraph 2, Danielle Crittenden quotes a writer who speaks of "the need 'to be oneself.'" What does "to be oneself" mean? Perhaps begin at the beginning: What is "oneself"? In *Hamlet*, Polonius says to his son,

   > This above all, to thine own self be true,
   > And it must follow, as the night the day,
   > Thou canst not then be false to any man.

   What is the "self" to which one should be true? Notice that in paragraph 4, Crittenden says that "it's in the act of taking up [certain] roles . . . that we build our identities, expand our lives, and achieve the fullness of character we desire." Does this make sense to you? Explain your response.

2. In paragraph 3, Crittenden talks about "postponing marriage and all the responsibilities that go with it." What responsibilities go with marriage? Might these responsibilities *add* to one's happiness? Explain your response.

3. In paragraph 6, Crittenden says, "What we rarely hear . . . is how *liberating* marriage can actually be." Consider the married people whom you know best. Does Crittenden's statement apply to some? To most? Does your experience — your familiarity with some married people — tend to offer evidence that confirms or refutes her assertion? Why, or why not?

JUDY BRADY

Born in San Francisco in 1937, Judy Brady married in 1960 and two years later earned a bachelor's degree in painting at the University of Iowa. Active in the women's movement and in other political causes, she has worked as an author, an editor, and a secretary. The essay reprinted here, written before she and her husband separated, appeared originally in the first issue of Ms. magazine in 1971.

I Want a Wife

I belong to that classification of people known as wives. I am A Wife. And, not altogether incidentally, I am a mother.

Not too long ago a male friend of mine appeared on the scene fresh from a recent divorce. He had one child, who is, of course, with his ex-wife. He is looking for another wife. As I thought about him while I was ironing one evening, it suddenly occurred to me that I, too, would like to have a wife. Why do I want a wife?

I would like to go back to school so that I can become economically independent, support myself, and, if need be, support those dependent upon me. I want a wife who will work and send me to school. And while I am going to school I want a wife to take care of my children. I want a wife to keep track of the children's doctor and dentist appointments. And to keep track of mine, too. I want a wife to make sure my children eat properly and are kept clean. I want a wife who will wash the children's clothes and keep them mended. I want a wife who is a good nurturant attendant to my children, who arranges for their schooling, makes sure that they have an adequate social life with their peers, takes them to the park, the zoo, etc. I want a wife who takes care of the children when they are sick, a wife who arranges to be around when the children need special care, because, of course, I cannot miss classes at school. My wife must arrange to lose time at work and not lose the job. It may mean a small cut in my wife's income from time to time, but I guess I can tolerate that. Needless to say, my wife will arrange and pay for the care of the children while my wife is working.

I want a wife who will take care of *my* physical needs. I want a wife who will keep my house clean. A wife who will pick up after my children, a wife who will pick up after me. I want a wife who will keep my clothes clean, ironed, mended, replaced when need be, and who will see to it that my personal things are kept in their proper place so that I can find what I need the minute I need it. I want a wife who cooks the meals, a wife who is a *good* cook. I want a wife who will plan the menus, do the necessary grocery shopping, prepare the meals, serve them pleasantly, and then do the cleaning up while I do my studying. I want a wife who will care for me when I am sick and sympathize with my pain and loss of time from school. I want a wife to go along when our family takes a vacation so that someone can continue to care for me and my children when I need a rest and change of scene.

I want a wife who will not bother me with 5 rambling complaints about a wife's duties. But I want a wife who will listen to me when I feel the need to explain a rather difficult point I have come across in my course of studies. And I want a wife who will type my papers for me when I have written them.

I want a wife who will take care of the details of my social life. When my wife and I are invited out by my friends, I want a wife who will take care of the babysitting arrangements. When I meet people at school that I like and want to entertain, I want a wife who will have the house clean, will prepare a special meal, serve it to me and my friends, and not interrupt when I talk about things that interest me and my friends. I want a wife who will have arranged that the children are fed and ready for bed before my guests arrive so that the children do not bother us. I want a wife who takes care of the needs of my guests so that they feel comfortable, who makes sure that they have an ashtray, that they are passed the hors d'oeuvres, that they are offered a second helping of the food, that their wine glasses are replenished when necessary, that their coffee is served to them as they like it. And I want a wife who knows that sometimes I need a night out by myself.

I want a wife who is sensitive to my sexual needs, a wife who makes love passionately and eagerly when I feel like it, a wife who makes sure that I am satisfied. And, of course, I want a wife who will not demand sexual attention when I am not in the mood for it. I want a wife who assumes the complete responsibility for birth control, because I do not want more children. I want a wife who will remain sexually faithful to me so that I do not have to clutter up my intellectual life with jealousies. And I want a wife who understands that *my* sexual needs may entail more than strict adherence to monogamy. I must, after all, be able to relate to people as fully as possible.

If, by chance, I find another person more suitable as a wife than the wife I already have, I want the liberty to replace my present wife with another one. Naturally, I will expect a fresh, new life; my wife will take the children and be solely responsible for them so that I am left free.

When I am through with school and have a job, I want my wife to quit working and remain at home so that my wife can more fully and completely take care of a wife's duties.

My God, who *wouldn't* want a wife? 10

Topics for Critical Thinking and Writing

1. If one were to summarize Judy Brady's first paragraph, one might say it adds up to "I am a wife and a mother." But analyze it closely. Exactly what does the second sentence add to the first? And what does "not altogether incidentally" add to the third sentence?

2. Brady uses the word *wife* in sentences where one ordinarily would use *she* or *her*. Why? And why does she begin paragraphs 4, 5, 6, and 7 with the same words, "I want a wife"?

3. In paragraph 2, Brady says that the child of her divorced male friend "is, of course, with his ex-wife." In the context of the entire essay, what does this sentence mean?

4. Complete the following sentence by offering a definition: "According to Judy Brady, a wife is . . ."

5. Try to state the essential argument of Brady's essay in a simple syllogism. (*Hint:* Start by identifying the thesis or conclusion you think she is trying to establish, and then try to formulate two premises, based on what she has written, that would establish the conclusion.)

6. Drawing on your experience as observer of the world around you (and perhaps as husband, wife, or former spouse), do you think Brady's picture of a wife's role is grossly exaggerated?

Or is it (allowing for some serious playfulness) fairly accurate, even though it was written in 1971? If grossly exaggerated, is the essay therefore meaningless? If fairly accurate, what attitudes and practices does it encourage you to support? Explain your response.

7. Whether or not you agree with Brady's vision of marriage in our society, write an essay (500 words) titled "I Want a Husband," imitating her style and approach. Write the best possible essay, and then decide which of the two essays — yours or hers — makes a fairer comment on current society. Or if you believe Brady is utterly misleading, write an essay titled "I Want a Wife," casting the matter in a different light.

8. If you feel that you have been pressed into an unappreciated, unreasonable role — built-in babysitter, listening post, or girl (or boy or man or woman) Friday — write an essay of 500 words that will help the reader to see both your plight and the injustice of the system. (*Hint:* A little humor will help to keep your essay from seeming to be a prolonged whine.)

TEXT CREDITS

Navneet Alang, "Eat, Pray, Post," *The New Republic*, August 5, 2015. Copyright © 2015 Navneet Alang. Used with permission.

Robert Applebaum, "Debate on Student Loan Debt Doesn't Go Far Enough," from *The Hill*, May 8, 2012, is reprinted by permission of the publisher.

W. H. Auden "The Unknown Citizen," copyright 1940 and renewed 1968 by W. H. Auden, from *Collected Poems of W. H. Auden*. Used by permission of Random House, Inc. Any third party use of this material, outside of this publication, is prohibited. Interested parties must apply directly to Random House, Inc. for permission. Electronic use by permission of Curtis Brown, Ltd.

Baltimore Sun Editorial Board, "No 'Ferguson Effect,'" *Baltimore Sun*, October 26, 2015. Copyright © 2015 *Baltimore Sun*. All rights reserved. Used by permission and protected by the copyright laws of the United States. The printing, copying, redistribution, or retransmission of this content without express written permission is prohibited.

Sig Behrens, "The Education-Technology Revolution is Coming," *U.S. News*, March 1, 2013.

Derek Bok, "Protecting Freedom of Expression on the Campus," originally published as "Protecting Freedom of Expression at Harvard." From *The Boston Globe*, May 21, 1991. Copyright © 1991 by Derek Bok. Reprinted by permission of the author.

Judy Brady, "I Want a Wife." Reprinted by permission of the author.

David Bromwich, "It's Time to Rethink American Exceptionalism," *The Nation*, October 24, 2014. Copyright © 2014 The Nation. All rights reserved. Used by permission and protected by the copyright laws of the United States. The printing, copying, redistribution, or retransmission of this content without express written permission is prohibited.

Susan Brownmiller, "Let's Put Pornography Back in the Closet," originally published in *Newsday*, 1979. Copyright © 1979 by Susan Brownmiller. Reprinted by permission of the author.

Stephen Budiansky, "Math Lessons for Locavores," from *The New York Times*, Aug. 20, 2010, copyright © 2010 by *The New York Times*. All rights reserved. Used by permission and protected by the copyright laws of the United States. The printing, copying, redistribution, or retransmission of this content without express written permission is prohibited.

Herman Cain, "In Defense of American Exceptionalism," *National Review*. Copyright © 2016 National Review. Used with permission.

Peter Cave, "Man or Sheep?" from *What's Wrong with Eating People?* is reprinted by permission of Oneworld Publications.

Steve Chapman, "Are Blacks to Blame for Police Actions?" *Chicago Tribune*, December 5, 2014. Copyright © 2014 *Chicago Tribune*. All rights reserved. Used by permission and protected by the copyright laws of the United States. The printing, copying, redistribution, or retransmission of this content without express written permission is prohibited.

Barry R. Chiswick, "The Worker Next Door," from *The New York Times*, June 3, 2006, copyright © 2006 by *The New York Times*. All rights reserved. Used by permission and protected by the copyright laws of the United States. The printing, copying, redistribution, or retransmission of this content without express written permission is prohibited.

David Cole, "Five Myths about Immigration," *The Nation*, October 17, 1994. Copyright © 1994 The Nation. All rights reserved. Used by permission and protected by the copyright laws of the United States. The printing, copying, redistribution, or retransmission of this content without express written permission is prohibited.

Ed Conard, "We Don't Need More Humanities Majors," from *The Washington Post*, July 30, 2013 issue. Copyright © 2013 Ed Conard. Used with permission.

Charles R. Lawrence III, "On Racist Speech," from *The Chronicle of Higher Education*, October 25, 1989. Copyright © 1989. Reprinted by permission of the author, professor of law at Centennial University, professor at University of Hawaii, Manoa.

Ursula K. Le Guin, "The Ones Who Walk Away from Omelas," copyright © 1973 by Ursula K. Le Guin, first appeared in "New Dimension 3" in 1973, and then in *The Wind's Twelve Quarters*, published by HarperCollins in 1975. Reprinted by permission of Curtis Brown, Ltd.

C. S. Lewis, "We Have No Right to Happiness," from *God in the Dock* by C. S. Lewis, copyright © C. S. Lewis Pte. Ltd. 1967. Extract reprinted by permission.

Daniel E. Lieberman, "Evolution's Sweet Tooth," from *The New York Times*, June 6, 2012. Copyright © 2012 *The New York Times*. All rights reserved. Used by permission and protected by the copyright laws of the United States. The printing, copying, redistribution or retransmission of this content without express written permission is prohibited.

Heather Mac Donald, "The New Nationwide Crime Wave," *Wall Street Journal*, May 29, 2015. Copyright © 2015 by Dow Jones. Republished with permission of Dow Jones; permission conveyed through Copyright Clearance Center, Inc.

Christian Madsbjerg and Mikkel B. Rasmussen, "We Need More Humanities Majors," from *The Washington Post*, July 30, 2013 issue. Copyright © 2013 by Christian Madsbjerg. Used by permission.

Stephen Marche, "Is Facebook Making Us Lonely?" from *The Atlantic Monthly*, May 2012. Copyright © 2012 The Atlantic Media Co., as first published in *The Atlantic Magazine*. Distributed by Tribune Media Services.

Donald Marron, "Should Governments Tax Unhealthy Foods and Drinks?" from *Forbes*, December 14, 2015. Copyright © 2015 Forbes. Used with permission.

Clifford D. May, "In Defense of American Exceptionalism," *American Spectator*, June 2, 2011. Used with permission.

Jena McGregor, "Military Women in Combat: Why Making It Official Matters," from *The Washington Post*, May 25, 2012 issue. Copyright © 2012 *The Washington Post*. All rights reserved. Used by permission and protected by the copyright laws of the United States. The printing, copying, redistribution, or retransmission of the material without express written permission is prohibited.

Darrin M. McMahon, "In Pursuit of Unhappiness," from *The New York Times*, Dec. 29, 2005, copyright © 2005 by *The New York Times*. All rights reserved. Used by permission and protected by the copyright laws of the United States. The printing, copying, redistribution, or retransmission of this content without express written permission is prohibited.

James E. McWilliams, "The Locavore Myth," from *Forbes*, Aug. 3, 2009. Copyright © 2009 by *Forbes*. All rights reserved. Used by permission and protected by the copyright laws of the United States. The printing, copying, redistribution, or retransmission of this content without express written permission is prohibited.

George Orwell, "Shooting an Elephant," from *Shooting an Elephant and Other Essays* by George Orwell, copyright 1946 by Sonia Brownell Orwell and renewed 1974 by Sonia Orwell. Reprinted by permission of Houghton Mifflin Harcourt Publishing Company. All rights reserved.

Plato, "Crito," from *The Last Days of Socrates* by Plato, trans. by Hugh Tredennick (Penguin Classics 1954, Third edition 1969). Copyright © 1954, 1959, 1969 by Hugh Tredennick. Reproduced by permission of Penguin Books Ltd.

Plato, from *The Republic*, trans. with an introduction by Desmond Lee (Penguin Classics 1955, Fourth Rev. Edition 2002). Copyright © 1953, 1974, 1987, 2002 by H. D. P. Lee. Reproduced by permission of Penguin Books Ltd.

Jed S. Rakoff, "Mass Incarceration: The Silence of the Judges," from *The New York Review of Books*. Copyright © 2016 by Jed S. Rakoff. Used with permission.

Index of Authors and Titles

Index of Terms

Enthymeme, 91
Equal probabilities, 349–50
Equivocation, fallacy of, 354
Ethical appeal, 147, 184, 247
Ethos, 81, 185, 247, 262, 412
Evaluation, 12, 162, 386–88
Evidence, 23, 96–105, 148, 184. 229, 346, 349
Example, 55, 84–85, 97–101, 250
Experimentation, 96–97
Explicit assumptions, 29

Facial expressions, of speaker, 413
Fact, matters of, 348, 409
Factual claims, 345
Factual distortion, 355
Fallacies, 352–65
    of ambiguity, 353–54
    of presumption, 355–59
    of relevance, 359–63
False analogy, fallacy of, 357
False dichotomy, 358
False premises, 94
Fear, appeal to, 141, 361
Final draft, 282
Final paragraph, 36, 260, 282
First draft, 280
First-person pronouns, 251–52
Footnotes, 288–89
Forensic argument, 409
Formal debates, 414–16
Formal outline, 246
Forum, 409
Freewriting, 222–23

Gender-neutral words, 253
Generalization, 95, 277–78, 329, 346–47
    fallacies of, 356, 358–59
Genetic fallacy, 359–60
Gestures of speaker, 413
Graphs, 102, 165, 166, 167–69, 170
Grounds, 326–27, 334

Hasty generalization, 356
Headings and subheadings, 36
Heuristics, 17, 43
Highlight, 42

Humor, 106, 141, 146
Hypothesis, 347
    confirmation of, 352
    protecting, 362–63
Hypothetical cases, 98–99

Ignorance, appeal to, 360
Images, as arguments, 139, 142, 148–60
    See also Visual rhetoric
Implicit assumptions, 29
Induction, 83, 95–96, 325, 327, 345–52
Inference, 346–47
Infographic, 424, 425
Intended audience. *See* Audience
Internet search engines, 264. *See also* Web sites
Interpretation, 385
Interviews, 269–70, 292–93, 300
Invalid syllogisms, 94–95
Invented instances, 98–99
Invention, 18, 222, 225
Irony, 106

Journal, 230, 299
Judging, in literary criticism, 386–88

Key terms, 182, 223–24

Language, 253, 412–13
Lead-ins and lead-outs, 287–88
Library databases, 264, 267–68
Linear thinking, 24
Listing, 223–24
List of References, 304–6, 308, 322
Literal *vs.* figurative meaning, 144
Literary criticism, 384–408
Literature, argument about, 402–4
Loaded words, 250
Logos, 80, 412
Long quotations, 285
Looking *vs.* seeing, 143–44, 149

Main idea, 36. *See also* Thesis
Many questions, fallacy of, 355
Maps, 165, 166
Mean, 103